THE CONFESSIONAL PRINCIPLE

AND THE CONFESSIONS OF THE LUTHERAN CHURCH

Theodore E. Schmauk
and C. Theodore Benze

with translations from the introductions
and writings of Theodor Kolde

CONCORDIA PUBLISHING HOUSE • SAINT LOUIS

This edition published 2005 by Concordia Publishing House
3558 S. Jefferson Ave., St. Louis, MO 63118-3968
1-800-325-3040 • www.cph.org

Originally published under the title *The Confessional Principle and the Confessions of the Lutheran Church as Embodying the Evangelical Confession of the Christian Church* by the Board of Publication of the General Council of the Evangelical Lutheran Church in North America.

Manufactured in the United States of America

ISBN 0-7586-0991-4

1 2 3 4 5 6 7 8 9 10   14 13 12 11 10 09 08 07 06 05

INTRODUCTION.

THIS book is written in the belief that the one ultimate authority among men is Truth; and that all derivative authority—whether confessional, as in the Faith; or institutional, as in the joint exercise and application of the Faith in the Church; or historical, as in tradition of Teaching or Worship, which is to be respected highly in ordinary relations for various reasons,[1]—stands or falls as it harmonizes or fails to harmonize with the Truth.

It, further, is written in the belief that the one great torch of the Truth is genuine and original Witness—a witness which arises not simply from the intellect, but which grows out of the whole heart—mind, soul and spirit.

Witness, as distinct from tradition or acceptance by imitation, as differing from argument and logical conclusion, is the result of an original contact in experience with the Truth; not perhaps with the mere bare principle, which is often an elusive abstraction, but with the Truth as clothed and revealed in historical fact.

This book is founded on the assurance that God Himself, Who is the Truth, has not left Himself without Witness; that this Witness is genuine, and has produced conviction in times past by original contact; that God's Witness has been of Word and in Person; and that we possess this Witness in Christ and in the Scriptures; that therefore the Word of God, the Scriptures, is a self-legitimating authority, the testimony of a true and faithful Higher Life brought

[1] The historical in teaching and worship claims our respect, because individualism leads to anarchy ; because the test of time weeds out the unworthy ; because truth itself is a seed or leaven needing generations to unfold and develop ; and, because God's Spirit is active in the historical unfolding and growth of the Church

(iii)

down and borne into our lower life; that this Testimony of the Higher is to be accepted on faith, and is grasped by faith (as is always the case also with our hold on the realities of our common every-day life) even where its grounds, nature and scope cannot be technically discerned, or where our lower penetration is in contradiction to it; that the Church of Christ on earth is not the Source of divine and authoritative Testimony, but that God alone, in His Prophets and in Christ, is the Source; that the Church is the uninspired Witness of those who have come into contact with the Scripture in their experience; and that the genuine collective witness of the Church, coming forth in the Confessions, is Testimony of the highest value—of higher value presumptively than any individual Witness; and that such collective Witness is not to be set aside, unless it can be shown from Scripture or from undoubted fact that God's people together have made a mistake in their faith—that their Confession is erroneous.

This work is written in the belief that the one native, real, unassailable, as well as effective, attitude of the believer with reference to Christ, Christianity and the Church, to-day, no less than in the Apostolic Age, is that of a Witness. Not mere belief, still less legalized or traditional authority,[2] on the one hand; nor open-minded doubt or critical investigation, on the other, will make us teachers in the Church of Christ; but the power of its truth will shine and testify only as we bear witness.[3] If we cannot bear witness to Christ and the Church, we cannot, in any other way, teach His doctrine.

The weakness of Protestantism to-day is its failure to

---

[2] Conformity to authority, which is unaccompanied by inner intellectual conviction and whole-souled sympathy, is as harmful as critical complaint and constant exception to or wholesale defiance of authority. We agree with v. C. P. Huizinga (*The Function of Authority in Life*) that " if codified standards become rules for individual life, appearances come to play a large part in life. Legalism has a bad flavor, especially because of those consistent, law-abiding moralists and religionists, the pharisees."—*Vid.* Schürer, *Gesch. d. Jüdischen Volkes im Zeitalter Jesu Christi* (" Life under the Law ").

[3] In this attitude, the breath of life, the voice of freedom, and the hand of authority, are all conserved.

recognize the necessity and the value of a common witness by the connected from generation to generation Church, and, consequently, also the necessity of using and maintaining a common Testimonial authority, or Confessional Doctrine. Religion is thought, even by many ministers, to be a matter of private and personal conviction, in its inner aspect (*Privatsache*); and the fact that it has been planted, watered, increased and ordered in a Church [*] which Christ Himself established, and in which the Holy Spirit works through the Word, is overlooked and neglected. Wherever there are a number of personal wills united in one organism or body, as in the Church, there must be one fundamental Authority— the Conviction—the *Faith*.

The underlying Conviction that animates, holds together and directs the wills in their Communion with each other— the Faith, and its Confession,—must be a common one. And this general principle of a common life of the many members in one body is all the more true in the case of the Church, because the union of persons in the Church is not primarily a union of wills, as between each other; but it is first a rooting of each will in Christ, and thus only a realization of inner union with one another.

The fundamental attitude of much scholarship, to-day, toward religion forgets that authority—whether external or internal, or both—is always essential in human thought and life. Goethe has declared that "every liberation of intellect without a correlate growth in control, is fatal." Authority is the co-ordinate, and the complement of liberty. Neither are to be suppressed; both are to be maintained—in balance.

Without authority—for direction, appeal, and decision,— no step of intellectual, spiritual or social activity is possible. The question is not really as to authority, but as to its proper seat and location. The motto of the ancient pre-

---

[*] " The right of the Church as an organized society to have a mind regarding the great truths contained in the Scriptures, to express that mind and exhibit that mind, can hardly be disputed. A statement so produced is a church creed. It is one of the most legitimate and important functions to which the Church can address itself.—Bauslin, *Freedom of Teaching*.

Christian, of the mediæval, and of modern Roman, civilization, is "Society above the individual." This ancient tyranny repeats itself to-day in scientific form in the motto,
"The race above the individual"; in sociological form,
when the State assumes to encroach upon the rights of the
individual, and passes laws which propose to regulate the
personal life, health, education, acts, interests, and happiness
of the individual; and in political form, when the axiom of
authority, "The majority rules", is pressed ruthlessly against
the minority. The same tyranny is found or imported
into nature as the seat of authority, when its laws are interpreted as reducible to the axiom that "Might makes right",
or " The strongest survive."

The reaction against this tyranny over the individual,
so characteristic of the ancient world, and manifesting itself in modern sociology and science, is the extreme Roman-
tic, or revolutionary, position, well expressed in the motto of
Rousseau: "The individual above society." If the absolute
enforcement of authority upon the individual is Romanism,
this elevation of the individual to the supreme seat is Protestantism gone to seed. It was already inherent in the
humanism of the Reformation, and occasioned the controversies with Fanaticism in theology, and the Peasants' War
in sociology, in Luther's day.

Hence, while the tyranny of Rome is the supreme authority of the Church over conscience, the tyranny of liberal
Protestantism is the supreme authority of every man's conscience over the Scripture and the Church. Both positions
are extreme and sceptical. That of Rome distrusts the
Truth in its power over the individual conscience, while that
of liberal Protestantism suspects the Truth of Scripture
and the Church, and does not believe that there is one objective and stable centre of truth revealed from above in
which the consciences of all perfect men can believe and unite.
As against the scepticism of the isolated, thinking Protestant, Rome is almost sure to win in the end, for having tried

every position of solitary speculation, the mind, exhausted and unwilling to abide all alone, will yield to the fundamental craving for authority, and fall back helplessly into the strong arms that seem to offer it certainty in a guaranteed and absolute sense. The end of Protestantism without the Word of God as the one common and absolute authority is either skepticism or Romanism.

For the result of the elevation of the individual as a law unto himself in defiance of any established order—whether it be in theology, philosophy, ethics, politics, sociology, or the state itself,—is always anarchy. "Anarchism", it has been said, " is the acute outbreak of individualism." It is "The permanent liberty of change," the elevation of the right of individual change into law. It is self-destructive in theology, as elsewhere. It does possess one value, in an effete system, or society, or state, viz., it is a purgative. It loosens up all the various elements and principles, tearing them out of their old relations, and puts each to the test of vindicating its own strength, and renders new combinations of relation possible. But this property of violent revolution may destroy the good with the evil—the wheat with the tares; and even when ultimate good is attained by it, it is at a fearful expense—and only because *ultimately a new order, and a new authority is re-established.* So that the very highest value that can be assigned to supreme individualism is a temporary one, which always issues in a new form of authority.

Since one of the essential elements of religion, as of all truth, is unchangeableness; and since in religion there must be both unchangeableness and finality, even this Twentieth Century should see that, if it is to keep any religion at all, it must not be a religion of individualism, of poetic values, of speculative outlook, of temperamental trust, but a religion of authority. However, this authority must have the freedom of an unrestrained and living faith and a voluntary trust, as its corollary. Neither Romanism, nor the axiom,

"Religion ist Privatsache" (*i. e.,* Religion is a private matter), will meet the case.

Sabatier,[a] in his great discussion, admits the necessity of authority; but, after the manner of the positivist school, he seeks to ground it in humanity. How feebly such an authority gains the assent of reason, and how inadequately it answers the requirements of the religious, the moral, and the social life, would soon be concretely demonstrated, if the Ritschlian doctrine of judgments of value were to actually become the sole rule of faith and life, and modern pragmatism were to prevail.

Sabatier does not see that the life-roots of the immanent everywhere penetrate into the transcendent; and that, if you cut away the transcendent, the two paradisical trees of Liberty and Authority will both die. Without faith in Truth above the grasp of reason, it is impossible to ground authority. While Sabatier is right in declaring that " an established authority, however great its antiquity or its power (the Church is such an authority), never carries its justification in itself "; yet the something outside of " the established authority ", which does " carry its justification in itself ", is not the Truth which the human reason is able to discover and formulate; for that is relative, conditioned, and lacks finality. The only Truth which carries its justification in itself is the Truth which is stretched out after and gratefully grasped by faith—the Truth of God, whose apprehensibility or inapprehensibility by our reason, does not condition its validity. Final authority comes from God, through His Word; and not from humanity, through its reason.

But such final authority does not bind or oppress the reason. It is actual and effectual, but not compulsory. The reason is free to pass upon and reject it. And yet reason is simply a subjective and private scales whose tests may help or harm its owner, tests that are private and *post-eventu*

---

[a] *Religions of Authority.*

experiments, which, whether successful or unsuccessful, in no wise affect the order of God.[6] The reason does not ordain, establish, determine, or even accept, religious authority. The final authority, if grasped at all, is grasped by faith. Authority is a power of fact that, like a star, exists and shines and rules, even though a blind world is unable to discern its existence. For those who do discern that the seat of all authority is above, in God, and in God's Word; and that it is not mediated through reason, but taken hold of by faith, as final, immutable, and adequate,—God's Word carries its own justification in itself. It testifies to man's faith and conscience in such way as to produce certainty, a deep inner conviction, which then, in turn, rises into Witness on behalf of such authority.

It is this Witness, the Witness of God to man, in the Scripture ("Thy Word is Truth"), and the Witness of man to the Truth of God, in the communion of Him Who is the Personal Truth of God, of which this book treats. This Witness of the Church of Christ is her Confession. Though authority accepted 'by faith', and not 'by sight', is the foundation of this book, and of its witness, we are confident that the book cannot justly be termed reactionary. Change in itself is not progress; and the right of every individual to think as he pleases is not, in itself, the attainment of liberty—least of all, the glorious liberty of the children of God, whose thought is qualified by the deep knowledge they have gained by their fear, love and trust in their Heavenly Father.

The spirit of this work is that of progress, but progress in a development whose line is already foreordained and fixed in the eternal and unchangeable principle of Christ,

---

[6] Nature is not the whole of God's world, neither is history. Nature is not a whole, nor is history, apart from God's greater world. "Nature and history do not exist in isolation; for they are caught up into a moral and spiritual system with which they are throughout in vital relations. It is not for anyone to say offhand what is or is not naturally or historically conceivable in such a system. . . . If anything is certain, it is that the world is not made to the measure of any science or philosophy, but on a scale which perpetually summons philosophy and science to construct themselves anew."—Denney, *Jesus and the Gospel.*

given us in the Word. As new lights begin to glow, and new thoughts and points of view begin to be occupied, and the right of an age to its own developing thought and feeling is maintained, there will be, we admit, a change in the established intellectual construction of the faith; but this change will not concern any particle of the Scriptural substance, only the human form of its apprehension in the Confession. The distinction cannot be drawn between soundness in faith and soundness in doctrine,[7] except in so far as doctrine is not clearly the unchangeable revelation of the unchangeable Word of God.

When then the thought of a new age and the life of a new movement in the Church seeks to come to its own, we say: Yes, so long as the principle of the new age does not assume to set aside, but finds its proper historical place in *the one principle of all the ages,* let there be progress. As a believing witness, we are ready to stand and to suffer for the Confession that abides through all the ages, because it corresponds to the Truth that forms, rules, and judges, all the ages.

We realize the cost of this position. The currents of knowledge are flowing away from a fixed faith, and are beating against a fixed Confession. The Church is told plainly that she will be left high and dry—a mere fossilized sea-shell on a desert beach,—if she does not come down from her confessional rocks, and join the living forces battling in the waves.

We realize to the full that the new order has revolutionized historical, spiritual and social values, even for those whose life and love are found within the Church. Modernism does not stand without, and is not knocking as a suppliant at the doors of the Church. It is rising in the hearts of the children, whose fathers' blood has always been loyal to the great Mother. The enemies of the Church's doctrine and Confession are often her own most brilliant and thoughtful sons. The Mother sees her own offspring repudiate their

[7] As Denney attempts to do.—*Jesus and the Gospel,* p. 340.

material birthright, even when—at times—they are proud
to bear her face and name.

The Church is, in part, but only in part, to blame. Her
own children disciplined in an atmosphere of experimental
science, rather than of mighty faith, know no final authority,
save in modernly established truth.   Our poor organ of
reason has been exalted in their eyes.   To them each new
achievement in knowledge is a new revelation of God.
" The doctrines of the Christian faith are not inflexible, but
are to be accommodated to every new measure of intellectual
truth."   They have come to believe that the evangelical
Church is keeping herself preoccupied with the spiritual
teachings of a bygone age and is thus living apart from the
actual life of to-day.

They tell us plainly that " The Church cannot expect to
reproduce the conditions of thought of the long past period
out of which came the sacred symbols of its faith.   The new
age is ready to break away from familiar channels of expression.   There is a change of intellectual attitude, and a
temper of investigation towards all authority, so deep and
far-reaching that even the most conservative observer is
startled." " Between a world which exalts intellectual integrity, and an institution which demands of its disciples
limitation of thought, there can be no abiding union," they
declare.

Accredited liberal theologians tell us that " the official
ministry of the Church grows less and less attractive to the
generous-minded youth of to-day."   " No loving parent can
ever again accept the monstrous doctrine that the child of
their love is ' conceived and born in sin '.   Against the authority of the Church (and of Scripture), *human consciousness has raised up a higher authority,* and *dictates the voice
of a diviner truth* to the souls of men."   " The Church is
blindly bent on upholding obsolete doctrine, and remains
strangely detached from the vital interests of the rising
giant of industrial democracy, with its new social standards,

and its new estimate of the worth of the individual in this world; as well as from the controlling spirit of the moral and intellectual world. The questions of historic, liturgical and doctrinal phrase, and ecclesiastical propagation of missions with which the Church is so largely occupied, imply a different condition of life and thought. The Church lives amid lingering memories of a world that has passed away. The divisions of Protestantism have become temperamental rather than doctrinal, and we look for the Protestant chrysalis soon to emerge from the cocoon (or carcass) of outworn doctrine." Even when the Church tries to stoop and take hold of the problems of life and social change, its way of approach is grotesque to the modern mind. "The Church is concerned with its heritage of rights, and its protection of past glories, with its traditions and forms, which it holds to be essential elements of its life and authority. It has something to preserve which is alien to to-day's thought, and completely fails to meet modern conditions with a modern mind."

This is the situation with which Protestantism in general, and the Lutheran Confession in particular, is confronted, in the educational and sociological world of to-day. Men who are filled with noble ardor and enthusiasm to do things, and men who are not deeply rooted, or who live in the moment, or who are time-servers, would yield up, some more, some less, the Confession of the Evangelical Church, with its doctrines of justification, faith, the Word, and the Sacraments. In their view, the Church has no excuse for 'winding the garments of Mediævalism around the neck and limbs of generations yet unborn.' The very mention of Confessional fidelity throws a dark and gloomy shadow athwart the stream of Twentieth-Century Life to such as these. If this Twentieth-Century Spirit be a part of the *Divine progress upward,* Lutheranism should immediately abandon her labors in the Faith.

But if the Truth—the Truth that will save the race—has come down from above, and is not rising up from beneath; if God did speak to men in the fulness of time; if there is a fixed and immutable principle amid the changing; if this present age is not the only one to be considered, but there is a sum of all the ages; if God has given us not only the truth discovered to-day, but the Gospel revealed many days ago,—then Lutheranism, which has cast off the clumsy armor of Mediæval Rome, and yet has retained the staff, and the wallet, and the stone of the olden day, is here,—unpretentious, unheralded, and uncostumed, but also unterrified and strong· in the fear and love of God,—to fight the battle against the giant, whether he be the boaster of an aggressive Pelagian social order, or the cultured humanistic theologian. Lutheranism does not fight negatively by criticism; by the raising of doubt; by amalgamation with more powerful forces; or by conciliation of the philosophies that threaten her position. Nor does she attempt to uphold and introduce her principle of truth into the world by law, by legislation, by social influence, or by plausible reasoning. The one weapon in her sling is quick and powerful, piercing even to the dividing asunder of soul and spirit; and is a discerner of the thought and intents of the heart. She is the Church who stakes all on bearing Witness. Her office is one of Public Proclamation and Confession of the Truth as it is in Christ Jesus. The Preaching of God's Word, pure and as given in Scripture, is her central activity. She is not here, primarily, to regulate, reconstruct or reform society. She is not here as a visible and hierarchical embodiment of the kingdom of God on earth; but she is here to proclaim and apply God's Word, in Scripture, sermon and sacrament. She is the Church of faithful, regular and continuous Witness to the Truth. Hence the source of her Witness, the Word; and the standard of her Witness,. the Confessions, are central; and she is willing,—as indeed she must be, if she wishes to live,—to abide by and uphold her Confessional Principle.

Preface

CHRISTIANITY exerting itself for twenty centuries upon the life and history of God's fallen world, has not crystallized into one universally accepted principle, or clad itself in one all-embracing seamless garment. Neither its Faith, nor its Church, have emerged and appear as a perfect reflection, in a flawless human unity, of the heavenly entity. Its Faith has issued in a four-branched Confession. The secret of this divergent effect of the One Truth is to be sought in the relation which man has accepted for his mind to the Word and institution of Christ. Absolute dependence on the Church visualized has resulted in the Graeco-Roman Confession. Absolute dependence on the Word, that is, on the Holy Spirit in the Word, in the Church, has resulted in the Evangelical Lutheran Confession. Relative dependence on the Book and on the Spirit in the heart, and relative independence of the Word in the Church has resulted in modern Evangelical Protestantism. Complete independence of Christ's Word and Church, and some dependence on Christ's Spirit in the heart has resulted in a rational Protestantism.

Thus we reach four fundamentally diverse answers as to the nature, means and effect of Christianity. Does Christ come to man at all? The Christian says, He does. Does Christ touch man *sola* through the Church? The Romanist says, He does. Does Christ touch man *sola* through His Word in the Church? The Lutheran says, He does. Does Christ touch man *partly* through the Book, *partly* through the Holy Spirit direct? The modern Evangelical Protestant says, He does. Does Christ touch the heart *sola* through the natural influence of His words and life, without a supernatural power in Word or institution? The rational Protestant says, He does. The four divergent branchings of the Christian Principle, thus acknowledged and held by men, may be summed up as follows: absolute dependence on the Church, absolute dependence on the Word, relative dependence on the Book, and mental independence of Book, Word and Church.

Christianity, to the Lutheran Church, is dependence on Christ. The dependence is absolute, invisible, and real. Its sole means is Christ's own Word. That Word is brought to us, as a matter of fact, in an institution, which, though it is not a source of authority, is nevertheless a divine and objective reality, Christ's invisible communion or body in which the power of God unto salvation is found and in which it works. This is the Lutheran Confession.

The Holy Spirit has been applying the mighty Word of Christ and building the Church from the day of Pentecost down. Of the eighteen centuries of Christian history, the first four and the last four have been epochal. The ancient centuries were catholic, and the modern are Protestant. Lutheranism accepts the Catholic unfolding, and stood, herself, at the head of the Protestant development. In 1917 it will be four hundred years since the sound of Luther's hammer awoke the Christian world to the Gospel and to the evils of Romanism, and one hundred years since Claus Harms' clarion call stirred the Church from Rationalism to a realization of her Gospel treasures, and to a resistance of the enfeebling meshes of Latitudinarianism and Unionism.

For Lutheranism, though not ascetic, but accepting heartily a full-orbed human life, including the virility and the efflorescence of the humanities, the virtues of the heart, the value of the deed, the gracious strength and helpfulness of human brotherhood, in their own sphere in the relation of man to fellow man, is the one persistent protest on this earth against humanism as a religion; and against the adulteration of the divine salvation with human values, and the incorporation of elements of character, love, brotherhood, knowledge, speculation or science into the texture of the Christian Faith. On the one hand, the seamless garment of Christ is not His Church as the ecclesiastics tell us; on the other hand, it is not a big heart, a sympathetic view, a fraternal grasp, and a helping hand as the humanist would have us believe. Its one thread in warp and woof is simply and solely the Word of Christ. The difference between this teaching and the current religious consciousness of the day is as the difference between heaven and earth.

The true Lutheran will not gloss over this difference but will recognize the seriousness of the struggle which the Lutheran Confession at times asphyxiated in the house of its friends, has to make in order to effectively proclaim its message.

Religion no longer hovers on the mountain cliffs of the invisible world, and the Church faces distaste for a salvation not visibly effective here on earth. Protestantism is inclined to find salvation in the green lowlands of social brotherhood. Christ walked in these lovely lowlands, and His walk rather than His work, in Scripture, are held before the eye. The one really essential fact in the Church is made to be that it teach and represent the great brotherhood of our common life, a brotherhood of fellow-sympathy, a brotherhood of work, of altruistic action, and social aim, on which the community is to build its higher hope. The one unessential fact, apparently, is that the Church represent the brotherhood revealed in the Gospel, the brotherhood of faith.

This raises the question in the Church, for those who hold the Word of God as the only power and judge of spiritual, that is, eternal life, whether the determining principle of 'brotherhood' is to be the sentiment and exercise of charity;[1] or whether Christ's principle of brotherhood in His Church is the Gospel offer of a brotherhood of faith. Are we brethren because we are of one blood, or are we brethren in Christ because we are blood-bought and justified by faith in His blood, through and in Him alone doing the will of His Father which is in Heaven? Has Christ a peculiar people, or do all good Americans, let us say, belong to Him and His flock? Are we saved by faith *sola,* or are we entitled to fellowship without saving faith?

---

[1]The determining principle toward our fellowmen, according to the law of God and the command of Christ, is Charity. "Thou shalt love thy neighbor as thyself" is the second law of the decalogue. But there is a difference between 'neighbor' and 'brother.' Christ did not select the Good Samaritan, or those who gave a cup of cold water to His little ones, but those who gave it for His name's sake, who confessed *Him* in a wicked generation, as His friends and brethren. "Who are my brethren? And he stretched forth his hand *toward his disciples,* and said, Behold my mother and my brethren! For whosoever shall *do the will of my Father* which is in heaven, the same is my brother, and sister, and mother."—Matt. 12:48-50. "There is no man that hath *left....brethren....for the kingdom of God's sake,* who shall not receive manifold more."—Luke 18:29-30. "*Conformed to the image* of his Son, that he might be *the first-born among many brethren....whom he called, them he also justified.*"—Rom. 8:29-30. "For it became him....in bringing *many sons unto glory,* to make the captain of their salvation perfect through sufferings. For both *he that sanctifieth,* and they *who are sanctified* are all of one: for which cause he is not ashamed *to call them brethren,* saying, I will declare thy name unto my brethren: in the midst of the church will I sing praise unto thee," etc.—Heb. 2:10-17. "Inasmuch as ye have done it unto one of the least of these *my brethren* (*i. e.,* children of the Father, who by faith inherit the kingdom, v. 34), ye have done it unto me."—Matt. 25:40.

B

Are Christians, who regard themselves as saved[2] by character, in the unity of the Church of Christ? Or, if faith is the principle, shall *its minimum* be taken as the normal condition of fellowship? Shall apprehension of some fundamentals be sufficient for the Church, or shall the unity be determined by the full truth of God's Word? Have God's representatives on earth the option to offer a discount on the terms set by God, in order to meet a given situation? May we overlook the *sola fide* in order that our churches on earth be filled with guests, and that Heaven itself be not too utterly empty?

The Church of the Lutheran Reformation has wrought in America for well-nigh three centuries, and will in a few years be adding one more century to its history. Her value in this land depends upon her fidelity to her Confession. If her Confession is out of date, she herself is but an obsolete barrier in the pathway to a common development, and deserves to disappear into the common and indeterminate Protestantism of her American environment.

Few will realize that' it has been almost forty years since *The Conservative Reformation,* that mighty protagonist of confessional English Lutheranism, lifting up its stature and spear, head and shoulders above all the host of Israel, establishing the Church in her old faith, and defending her against all assault, made its powerful presence felt in the Church in this land. Since that day there has not appeared in our language any complete work devoted to Confessional Lutheranism,[3] save only the small book on *Distinctive Doctrines of the Lutheran Church.*

But since that day a new generation has arisen whose eyes never beheld the formative conflicts. Old issues have taken on new forms. The substance of *The Conservative Reformation* has been absorbed and become an element of strength in the leaders of the Church now in their maturity. The important occasion of the old polemic has disappeared. Progress has been made in sound Confession. Ecclesiastical efforts have aimed to reach a position on which the Lutheran Church as a whole could be planted. Now that this ac-

---

[2]This is the practical teaching of many American Protestants.

[3]Of Dogmatic Treatises there have been a rich array: Schmid, *Doctrinal Theology,* Jacobs, *Elements of Religion,* Köstlin, *Theology of Luther,* Seeberg, *History of Doctrines,* Valentine, *Christian Theology,* and Jacobs, *Summary of the Christian Faith.* In addition there appeared in 1882 the monumental *Book of Concord,* edited and translated for the English reader by Jacobs.

tivity apparently has given way to the tendency to emphasize an external Confessionalism, or, on the other hand, to over-estimate the external fact of denominational fellowship, the time is here for a more ample setting forth of the Church's full and inner Confessional Principle, in a just and adequate manner, with no partisan intent, but in the majestic light of the original Catholic and the real Evangelical testimony, and in such form that the power of the old Witness will appeal to the thought and the soul of the generation of this day; and may bring to the service of Christ's unchangeable Word, and to the preservation of the one Evangelical Catholic Church, the will, the words, and the works of those who are moved to abide in the Word and institution of Christ and in its Confession.

After *The Conservative Reformation* had appeared, Philip Schaff issued his great work describing *The Creeds of Christendom*. and remarked that in a country like ours, where we daily meet people of all possible beliefs, men should devote more attention to the study of the Christian Confession, that they may give those with whom they discuss the subject a convincing reason for the faith that is in them. The intelligent study and appropriation of the symbols of one's faith, from whose principles the varied medley of religious teachings that cry aloud in our time, or come under our observation, may be examined and tested, is as important, at least, as the study of the underlying principles and causes of our ethical or social structure and its problems.

A new, and strictly historical, examination of the Confessional structure of the Lutheran Faith, from the solid view-point of the introductions to the new German edition of the Book of Concord, cannot be postponed without injury to the Church. The researches of the last two decades in Germany, and alleged recent discoveries, by such scholars as Brieger on the one hand, and Kolde on the other, have rendered this examination necessary, as well to those who confess the specific and vital, as to those who rest in the mere generic, Faith of the Church.

The history of the Lutheran Confession has been written often. The first print of the oldest narration of the Diet at Augsburg, in 1530, from the arrival of his Majesty to the delivery of the Confes-

sion, bears the title, *Ain kurtze Anzaygung.*[4] The history of the
Augsburg Confession which the Roman Catholics printed in 1530
with imperial privilege bears the title, *Pro Religione Christiana
res gestae.*[5] This Roman Catholic history of the Augsburg Confession was refuted by a Saxon minister shortly after the Diet, under
the title, *Folgen verzeichent alle Stück so im Druck dem Handel
müssen inferirt und eingeleibt werden.* Though ready for print,
the work was left lie at Weimar. Müller in his *History of the
Protestation* has taken many remarkable things from this manuscript, while Seckendorf, in his *History of Lutheranism,* p. 202,
believes that neither Cölestin nor Chyträus knew of the work.[6]

To these original rills must be added Brück, *Geschichte der Re-
ligionsverhandlungen auf dem Reichstag zu Augsburg im J. 1530,*[7]
and the always indispensable and abounding *Corpus Reformatorum;* but the real historical stream gathered itself in the works of
Chyträus, Cölestin, Müller, Salig, Cyprian and Weber. All these
men used the Reformation documents stored in the German archives, and tried to draw their material from the original acts.
Chyträus, in his *Historia of the Augsburg Confession,* in 1576,
took pains to obviate all doubt as to his translations and writings,
and placed at the end of his German edition a list of the most
prominent documents that he incorporated in his history, together
with a clear statement of the places from which they were taken.
He says that he gathered from the official acts and trustworthy testimonies of those who themselves were participants in the Confessional proceedings, and "took particular pains not to include any
uncertain or suspicious writings." He says, therefore, "I pray that
others will allow this work to remain unaltered and unimproved."

As to Cölestin, Weber assails him bitterly, and tries to prove
that, despite his abundant access to historical materials, he was unscrupulous in his use of them. He admits that Cölestin journeyed
to the Archives of the holy Roman Empire at Maintz in 1556, and
that in 1576 he undertook a second journey. At all events, Cölestin
has given the world a notable gathering of historical papers.

Cyprian rests entirely upon original documentary foundations.
He says, "If the necessary aptitude and health had been mine, this

---

[4] Printed in *Cyprian, Beilagen,* p. 60.
[5] *Ib.* p. 85.
[6] The beginning of the work is printed in *Cyprian, Beilagen,* p. 108.
[7] In Förstemann, *Archiv,* Vol. I.

history of the Augsburg Confession would hardly have had its like. But the lack of these qualities and a journey that could not be postponed in the midst of all my labors, cause me to be able to assure only this, that my book has been composed honestly and diligently and without any attempt to twist matters in the works and writings, and with an effort to preserve the mode of speech of the original documents."

Salig is the most voluminous of these early writers on our Confessional history, and is full of details, some of more, and some of less value; but he drew from reliable historical sources, and his work is of permanent value.

Chyträus was of the manner and heart of Melanchthon, with the doctrine of Luther. Cölestin, Wigand, and Cyprian were men who defended the full Lutheran Confession. Salig likewise did so, but his sentiment and leanings were pietistic, and softened toward the Melanchthonian tendencies. Weber was a determined and bitter Melanchthonian, thoroughly rationalistic. "If I have been so fortunate," he says, "as to have made progress in research, it is not to be ascribed to me, but to the spirit of the age. . . . In thus far my work can be regarded as a contribution to the history of the human understanding (des menschlichen Verstandes)."

Weber's works, therefore, on the Confessional principle, invaluable as they are, relate to the periphery. The weakness of his general position and feeling are as evident as are the values of the specific critical results of his documentary investigations. His conclusions are based on the readings of texts, rather than on the truth and teachings that well up within the texts.

It was the Confessional activity leading to the Formula of Concord that gave us Chyträus and Cölestin. The second centennial of the Augsburg Confession gave us Cyprian and Salig, and Weber came half a century later.

The Nineteenth Century has again opened to us the investigation of originals in the researches of Förstemann (*Archiv*, 1831; *Urkundenbuch*, 1833) and Schirrmacher (*Briefe und Akten*, 1876), in the gathering of Luther's Letters by De Wette, 1825, and Enders, 1884, and in the constructive efforts of Calinich, Bindseil, Knaake, Köllner, Plitt, Zöckler, Brieger, Kolde, and Tschackert.

The massive literature of the Lutheran Church on the Book of Concord and on various doctrinal aspects of the Lutheran Confession is too extensive even to allude to, and will be found in part in the bibliographical lists connected with the Table of Contents.

Krauth's work, as an examination and an active force in the Confessional field, will never be superseded. To term it ecclesiastical in origin is an injustice. It was a long struggle, against earlier ecclesiastical limitations, for the truth. Though polemic in form and occasional in origin, it is so thoroughly grounded on the sources and so masterfully elaborated that it will remain the great Confessional classic in English Lutheran theology. The critical maze of historical facts had been threaded by Krauth years before he spoke.[8] Weber's conclusions and work had been digested in detail by him as early as the Fifties (1854).

In 1858 he published his *Select Analytical Bibliography* of the Augsburg Confession in twenty-two pages. In 1868 he published *The Augsburg Confession.*[9] His presentation of the correspondence of Luther and Melanchthon, and of the utterances of Luther on the Confession are unsurpassed to this day, and, for brevity, his statement of the fate of the German text of the Augsburg Confession is

---

[8] *V.* Krauth's article in *Ev. Rev.,* I. p. 234, Oct. 1849, on "The Relation of Our Confessions to the Reformation, and the Importance of Their Study, with an Outline of the Early History of the Augsburg Confession." This article was written on the basis of Walch's *Introduction to the Symbolical Books,* Carpzov's *Isagoge to the Symbolical Books,* Salig's *Historie* and Cyprian's *Historie* together with several other works such as Seckendorf's *Historia.*

[9] "Literal translation from the original Latin with the most important additions of the German text incorporated: together with the general creeds; and an introduction, notes, and analytical index, Philadelphia Tract and Book Society of St. John's Evangelical Lutheran Church, Lutheran Bookstore, 807 Vine Street, 1868." His introduction comprises questions on the nature and necessity of creeds; early creeds; Romanism and its creed; preliminaries and the preparation of the Augsburg Confession; Luther's works on the Augsburg Confession; absence of Luther from Augsburg; correspondence with Luther; Luther's opinion of the Augsburg Confession; object of the Augsburg Confession; the presentation of the Confession; Latin and German texts; the Augsburg Confession altered; the current editions of the Augsburg Confession: Latin and German; structure and divisions of the Augsburg Confession; the literature of the Augsburg Confession; what is involved in the right reception of the Augsburg Confession; the character and value of the Augsburg Confession.

unequaled.[10] The positions taken later in the Conservative Reformation with reference to the Augsburg Confession are already advanced here and fully argued. He was thus early a complete master
of the facts in the case so far as then known. His strong and
solid argument for the position that the Confession was practically
complete, as the conjoint work of Luther and Melanchthon, by May
22nd, 1530, when it was sent to Luther for final ratification, is
found here. The argument would be unanswerable were it not for
the following difficulties:

(1) It does not explain the negotiations of Melanchthon with
Valdés.

(2) It knows nothing of the recently discovered Nuremberg draft
of the Confession which seems to show the Confession's incompleteness at a very late date; and which throws an entirely new light on
Melanchthon's Exordium.

(3) It does not take account of the genetic growth of the Confession and of the changes made as the situation developed; but
assumes that Luther and Melanchthon possessed a full *a priori*
knowledge of what exactly was to be confessed at Augsburg, whereas the letters of Luther seem to show a lack of such knowledge,
and an omission of the mention of a previously-made Confession.
The activities of Eck, the movements of Melanchthon, and our
critical knowledge of the Nuremberg and other manuscripts seem
to corroborate the conclusions of Kolde, without however
invalidating the strength of the general position of the Conservative Reformation.

(4) The theory of the Conservative Reformation assumes a
trustworthiness and fidelity of Melanchthon toward Luther and a

---

[10] The latter is to be found on pp. 563-565 of this book, and concludes
as follows :

"While therefore the ordinary edition of the Augsburg Confession, the
one found in the Book of Concord, and from which the current translations
of the Confession have been made, does not differ in meaning at all from
the original edition of Melanchthon, it is, nevertheless, not so perfect in
style, and where they differ, not so clear. The highest critical authority,
then, both German and Latin, is that of Melanchthon's own original editions.

"The current edition of the German, and the earliest edition of Melanchthon, are verbally identical in the largest part of the articles, both of doctrine and of abuses. The only difference is, that Melanchthon's edition is
occasionally somewhat fuller, especially on the abuses, is more perfectly parallel with the Latin at a few points, and occasionally more finished in style.
When the question between them has a practical interest, it is simply because
Melanchthon's edition expresses in terms, or with greater clearness, what is
simply implied, or less explicitly stated in the other."

stability in political temptation which it is somewhat difficult to find corroborated in the subsequent life of Melanchthon.

(5) The position of the Conservative Reformation assumes a centrality at the Diet of Augsburg from the start for the Confession of the Evangelical doctrine, which Luther would indeed have liked to have seen, but which probably did not fully exist in advance, in either the mind of the Emperor, the Elector, or Melanchthon; but which the Providence of God forced upon the Diet.

Yet any modification in the position taken by the Conservative Reformation, it must be remembered, casts no further credit upon Melanchthonianism and takes no further credit from the ways and judgment of Luther. It upholds the Confession, not because it was the product of either Luther or Melanchthon, but because the hand of God clearly and actually made it what it was, and is, and will ever remain hereafter.

The most elaborate chapter in the work now under the reader's eye, on "The Hand of God in the Formation of the Augsburg Confession," was written and in type, before the author consulted, in fact, at that time recalled, Krauth's elaborate and accurate "Chronicle of the Augsburg Confession," 1878, which grew out of his controversy with Dr. Brown following on a discussion at the First Free Lutheran Diet. The annalistic or diary form in the chapter of the present writer was not suggested by the work of Dr. Krauth. The method and purpose of the two writings are different: Dr. Krauth's paper is an argument to prove a single point, while the chapter of the present work essays to be a general historical study of the situation at Augsburg, from its background, and in its larger range of activities as affairs developed from day to day.

The two studies are independent, and the agreement that they manifest on many points is a striking testimony of fact. The differences are to be explained first, by the fact that Dr. Krauth's object was documentary rather than historical; and, secondly, by the fact that he could not avail himself of discoveries which have been made since his death. His approach on certain lines of indirect evidence toward what is now known is remarkable. The only uses made of Dr. Krauth's Chronicle are references or quotations in several places for the reader's convenience, and the citation from Melanchthon's Latin Preface of 1560.

The present work is a broad attempt to do justice to the Confessional Principle of the Evangelical Church, in the midst of a feeling or spirit of our time which does it injustice. The work has been written unexpectedly and most reluctantly. It is devoted to the true Church wherever and under whatever form she may be found. It desires to set forth more fully this Church's comprehensive and vitalizing grasp of the Confessional Principle of Christianity, in the belief that our Confession comes direct from Christ in the Word of Scripture, as the answer and testimony of Faith unto its Lord, and unto all the world; and in the assurance that this Faith will ever enlarge its circles of contact, and that it holds in its embrace the strength of the past, the potency of the present, and the hope of the future.

The practical aim is an effort to make clear to the judgment and conscience of English Lutherans that the chief matter before the Lutheran Church today, as a Church of the living Faith, is not its relation to an outside Christianity, however timely or pressing—or even embarrassing—that may seem to be; but that the great and immediate duty of the Church is to learn to know, and to more fully develop her own highest principle and character, as the bearer of Word and Sacrament.

What she is in her own heart and to her own children—as a mother of faith, strength, life and character,—is her first and chief object of knowledge, and is not to be determined by any supposed ideas of what she ought be to her neighbor. On the contrary, what she is to the denominations around her, in her second commandment of love, "like unto the first," will follow from what she is in her own heart; as does the love of God in the first commandment determine the love to our neighbor in the second commandment. The more true her children are to her own self, the less false will they be to others round about her.

We shall one day see that our own faith's most secret conviction is nobler than what the world proclaims from the housetops; that "the most private is the most public energy"; that it is an inversion, as Thoreau says, to dig common silver ore in cartloads, while we neglect to work our mines of gold, known only to ourselves, far up in the Sierras, where we pulled up a bush in our mountain-walk with God, and saw the rare and glittering treasure. "Let us return thither. Let it be the price of our freedom to make that known."

The path traversed by this book, though it everywhere crosses familiar regions, and frequently takes advantage of well-trodden roads, has been difficult, and has required much pioneer work. It will be easy to discover faults in plan and detail, to criticise the compression of such a range of subject matter into one volume, or to point out the undue and repeated elaboration of certain points. It may be possible to say that the work contains nothing new. We have feared lest it be too original. At all events, it will bear comparison with its predecessors in the English field on this point.

The position taken is positive and the work is structural in purpose. It has nothing in common with any polemic press of the hour, and its authors—so far as we recall—have not spoken one word on current controversial issues discussed with much animation in ecclesiastical papers during the last year or two, but have been silent up to this moment. The volume does not deal with or mention any contemporary synodical or ecclesiastical complications. So far as we know, the name of any of the General Lutheran Bodies in America does not occur, except in titles. Our chief concern is for the Lutheran Faith and for its Confession, rather than for ecclesiastical situations arising out of the present moment, loyal as we may be, and are, to that specific part of the Lutheran Church to which our heart and energies have been devoted.

Inasmuch as the object of this work is constructive, we have endeavored not to use the polemic form, though the handling of materials liable at any moment to spontaneous combustion, renders it possible that we have struck flame without so intending. Should the Lord grant us the grace of silence under stricture, the sparks on our side ought not enkindle into conflagration.

This book is the first presentation to the English public of the ripe fruits of the studies of the great Luther scholar, Professor Kolde, a descendant of Chancellor Brück, on the Confessions, as found in his Introductions to the new German Book of Concord, together with his particular discoveries as to the Augsburg Confession. We also reproduce the first and only English translation of the oldest known Form of the Augsburg Confession. This is the document that has settled a great many things since Dr. Krauth wrote the Conservative Reformation. The work before the reader, further, contains a thorough and searching study of Melanchthon

and Melanchthonianism, showing in detail that the spirit of compromise issues, in history, in disaster to the Lutheran Church.

The volume contains the following essays of Kolde, translated
for the first time into English:—

(1) *The Introduction to the Augsburg Confession,* from the new
Müller edition of the Symbolical Books.   Chapter **XV.**

(2) *Melanchthon's Unsuccessful Attempts as a Diplomatist,*
from "Die älteste Redaktion der Augsburger Konfession." Chapter XVI.

(3) *Kolde's Discussion of the Oldest Known Redaction of the
Augsburg Confession,* from the same work (Kolde's discussion of
detailed phrases is omitted).   Chapter XVII.

(4) *The Oldest Known Redaction of the Augsburg Confession,*
as given in Kolde's work.   Chapter XVIII.

(5) *The Editions and Manuscripts of the Augsburg Confession*
(this is a continuation of Kolde's Introduction to the Augsburg
Confession), from the new Müller edition of the Symbolical
Books.   Chapter XXI.

(6) *The Origin of the Formula of Concord.* This chapter originally was a translation of Kolde's Introduction to the Formula in
the new Müller edition, but was subsequently enlarged and enriched
by us from other sources.   Chapter XXVI.

(7) *The Book of Concord.* This chapter is a translation from
Kolde's Introduction in Müller.   Chapter XXXVI.

Several of these Introductions of Kolde were published originally
in *The Lutheran Church Review.* To them there was to have been
added an Introduction pointing out the relevance of the essays to
the American Confession situation. Then came the suggestion of
two Philadelphia laymen to interweave Prof. Kolde's writings in
a logical treatment of the complete subject, resulting in this
volume.

In type for a year and a half, and, except a small portion, in
plate form for more than a year, this volume long lacked only the
reading of about a hundred pages of proof, and some processes of
verification, to bring it to the point of publication. The delay in
its issue has been due to several serious illnesses, dating from last
spring a year ago, and to the extraordinary pressure of official
duties and of affairs in the Seminary at Philadelphia.

Meantime, there has appeared an important work in the same field minutely discussing the Reformation Era from a historico-confessional point of view, and for a purpose almost the reverse of that of this work. The object of this work is to confirm the strength of the Church in her Confessions: the effect of the other work is to unsettle the Church in her Confessions and to free her from the inference of an abiding historical confessional principle. The new work on "The Confessional History of the Lutheran Church" is a monument to the pains-taking research of its author, and opens up a greater wealth of documentary detail, valuable for present-day investigation, than is probably to be found at this moment in any volume in the English language. And if the temper of the author were as broad and undogmatic and tolerant as is the position for which he is contending, and if his use of the documents were as scholarly as his knowledge of them, the work would take its place as a standard authority in the Church, to be respected, even on the position which it occupies. But in this age it is impossible to maintain uncritically the dogma of Biblical infallibility, in the same breath with a loose, critical and destructive dogma of confessional fallibility. The quill that bristles against the Confessions, cannot successfully spread its shelter over their Source.

We not only believe that the fundamental position held by this book will prove to have been a concession of historical Christianity to modernism, but we believe that the paradox manifest in its spirit, namely, that of a dogmatic polemic against polemic dogmatics, is a house divided against itself. Since the work is looked up to as bringing the new discoveries in historical research to bear upon the disputed points in Lutheran confessional writings, we should not be doing our duty to our readers if we failed to take some notice of the positions assumed by this latest investigation, inasmuch as the delay in our own work, which would normally have preceded the other in its issue, has rendered a brief discussion of this new material possible.

In our Church in America, it has, for the last three or four decades, been customary to assume either one of two confessional positions, namely, that the Book of Concord is the confessional treasure of the Church, or, if not, that the Augsburg Confession in itself is the Church's sufficient and generic confessional treasure. The new book we are criticising not only combats the former position with all intensity, but in view of more recent discoveries concerning the Augsburg Confession, and in a sense, as their herald, it assumes the startling attitude of combating the generic perfection of the Augsburg instrument as a Lutheran Confession. It goes so far as to term the Augsburg Confession inadequate, to characterize it as defective, as misrepresenting the Lutheran party at Augsburg, and as untruthful. This position, while it sacrifices the Augsburg Confession as the final and adequate basis of a generic Lutheranism, and adjudges it as Romanizing in outlook, nevertheless is of immeasurable help to its author in several respects. First of all, it provides a ground to stand upon in view of recent historical discoveries. Secondly, if the original Confession was so imperfect and untruthful, this fact surely frees Melanchthon from blame in his numerous attempts to "improve" it in the variata. It also establishes the presumption that a Confession framed in any emergency in the past is no longer binding on a higher and more Scripturally enlightened present. Hence it frees the Lutheran Church of the present from any inner historical adherence to the Confessions of the past. Lutheranism thus freed from the burdensome forms and substance of its own historical development, except in the one main doctrine of justification by faith, can connect directly with the real and infallible rule of Faith, the Scripture; and thus the Lutheran center, directly grounded in Scripture, can be co-ordinated with a modern apprehension of Christianity. Unfortunately for the author, in this position, his very doctrine of justification by faith, on which, in rejecting so much, he grounds himself, is vitiated by a synergism so obvious that a generation or two of progressive thinking along his lines will perhaps suffice to play the whole position into the hands of a radical Protestantism.

We hope to have placed before the English reader, especially in Chapter XIX, a more natural arrangement of historical materials, —the documentary and epistolary background of the Augsburg Confession,—for the first time appearing in the English language, than is to be found in any English work, for a study, at first hand, of the sources of the Reformation History. This refers especially to the translations of documents and of the Luther-Melanchthon correspondence, difficult to reproduce in its organic relationship.

Letters, written as they are on the inspiration of the moment, and without premeditation, reveal the mind and heart. It is on these records of the moment, as interpretative of the more formal documents, that we lay some stress in attempting to give an insight into the Confession made at Augsburg.

The value of Luther's letters was recognized early. A collection of four of them was printed in 1530. In 1546, the year of Luther's death, Cruciger issued eight letters, and this number was increased later. Then came Aurifaber, Chytraeus, Cölestin.

In the Eighteenth Century came the epochal labors of Walch, Stroebel (1780), and of Schütze (3 vols., 1784). In 1826 De Wette issued his first five volumes of Luther's Letters, with the bibliography of each of them.

In 1884 Enders issued the first volume of Luther's Briefwechsel running into the tenth volume in 1903. Köstlin and Kolde (1884), published letters and extracts; and Buchwald issued 91 letters in 1898.

While our volume was in preparation, or shortly before, Margaret Currie, of Glasgow, published an interesting volume, "The Letters of Martin Luther, Selected and Translated." The volume came too late, except in one or two instances, for use in this work. It does not contain Replies written to Luther, and the translator, in her history of the letters, has no proper conception of the inner history on which the Reformation pivoted itself. But the thought of Luther is reproduced in excellent and natural English. Currie[11] gives perhaps a score of the letters we have translated in this volume.

On controverted points, as a rule, we have preferred to state situations and arguments in the words of writers who might have weight with readers that differ from us. This is the reason for the frequent quotation of such a standard American Work as Schaff, *Creeds of Christendom,* and for an apparent preference given Melanchthonian rather than rigidly Lutheran authorities. Their words will probably be conceded as unbiased, or at least not biased in favor of the position of this book, in quarters where the citation from strict Lutheran authors might not be welcome. We

---

[11] Miss Currie's work contains 500 letters from 1507-1546, about one-fifth of the total number preserved.

believe it will be found that justice has been done to all authors, and that no language or spirit has been attributed to them which they themselves would not corroborate as genuine.

Chapter xxxvii is a slight sketch of the development of confessional thinking from the day of the Book of Concord to the present time; written under reaction from the widely prevalent unionistic view expressed by Schaff in his "Creeds of Christendom," and as a thread of connection between the Reformation and the present day. If it were to be re-written today, we might possibly be tempted to a full presentation of the confessional development of the nineteenth century in the light of the Book of Concord, including the movements from Harms to (Hase, Meyer, Köllner), Rudelbach, Guericke, Richter, Stahl, Harless, Sartorius, Twesten, Hengstenberg, Caspari, Kliefoth, Philippi, (Kahnis, v. Hoffmann), Löhe, to Luthard, Frank and Zöckler, on the one side, and to (Marheineke), Bretschneider, Johannsen, (Heppe), and Dorner on the other. However, such a treatment would not only diverge from the line of connection running through the present work; but would also have been an embarrassment to this book in the voluminousness of its substance.

Much credit is due to the Rev. George M. Scheidy for a general, vigilant and invaluable supervision of the details of this work, especially during the time of the writer's illness, for many suggested improvements in style, for translation of certain documents, for careful reading of manuscript and proofs, and for arduous and continued general assistance without which this work could not have been issued. Acknowledgment is also due to the Rev. J. D. M. Brown for the preparation of the Index, to the Rev. J. J. Cressman and the Rev. F. P. Mayser, D.D., for the loan of rare and valuable works, to the Rev. F. B. Clausen for work in the libraries of New York City, and for verification of citations; to the Rev. Luther D. Reed for the use of several important volumes from the Krauth Memorial Library; to the Rev. J. J. Cressman for verification; and to the Rev. Dr. W. L. Hunton, and Mr. C. B. Opp, for help afforded in many ways.

The book as a whole stands or falls as it agrees or disagrees with the Word of God. If it is based on the Word, and is a witness thereto, the Church cannot be dislodged from the position here taken. The faith which believes, and therefore saves; which believes, and therefore confesses; which believes, and therefore examines, which believes, and therefore testifies, and transmits and upholds the testimony dear to it; which believes, and acts because it lives in its belief: this faith in which heart and voice and work unite, because one and the same Spirit fills them all, is irresistible in the Church, and is the victory that overcometh the world.

Contents

By Books

———

C

xxxiii

Contents

By Chapters

xxxv

CHAPTER XIV.
THE LUTHERAN CONFESSION.

CHAPTER XV.
THE ORIGIN OF THE AUGSBURG CONFESSION.

CHAPTER XVI.
MELANCHTHON'S UNSUCCESSFUL ATTEMPTS AS A DIPLOMATIST.

CHAPTER XVII.
THE DISCOVERY OF THE FIRST KNOWN DRAFT OF THE AUGSBURG CONFESSION.

CHAPTER XVIII.
THE OLDEST KNOWN FORM OF THE AUGSBURG CONFESSION.

CHAPTER XIX.
THE HAND OF GOD IN THE FORMATION OF THE AUGSBURG CONFESSION.

CHAPTER XX.
THE AUGSBURG CONFESSION PRESERVED UN-ALTERED.

CHAPTER XXI.
HISTORY OF THE EDITIONS AND MANUSCRIPTS OF THE AUGSBURG CONFESSION.

Contents

With Analysis and Bibliography

xli

CHAPTER VI.

SHOULD CONFESSIONS CONDEMN AND EXCLUDE?

principles that militate against the Enforcement of confessional authority.

the church of the pure Word does not abrogate the use of Discipline

CHAPTER VII.

WHAT GIVES THE CONFESSION VALIDITY?

a confession is Testimony

neither Agreement, nor Contract

its aim is Instruction, not Obligation (Verpflichtung)

the agreement is the pre-existing one of Doctrine

cannot be put together by Negotiation

the result (not the cause) of the substantial Unities in Christ

not a Platform; nor a delineation for comparative Distinction

the stress of Providence

its validity is that of Testimony

evidence of the Lutheran Confession

analysis of the Legal situation

not based on Social Pact

the Binding clauses of our confessions

CHAPTER VIII.

DO CONFESSIONS BIND?

galling to Those who are Not At Home in them

joy and freedom to Those who Confide in their teaching

the Former should not remain in them

the Latter should accustom themselves to their restrictions

why we train Posterity in them

why we ask loyalty from our Teachers

why the church needs a settled Faith taught

how free Investigation is to be reconciled with confessional principle and obligation; Protestantism, with the abiding communion of saints

how and why the confessions must hold us Loyal

Eberhard, Ist die Augsb. Confess. eine Glaubensvorschr., etc. 1795-97.——(Negative) **Johannsen,** Untersuch. der Rechtmassigk. d. Verpfl. a S. B. Altona. 1833.——**Sartorius,** Ueber die Nothwendigk. u. Verbindlichk. d. Kirch. Glaubens-bekenntn. Stuttgart. 1845.——**Müller,** Die Symbolischen Bücher, 1848, Hist.-theol. Einl. I.——**Rietschel,** G., Luther und die Ordination. 1883.—— **Derselbe,** ThStKr. 1895. Heft I "Luthers Ordinationsformular usw."——**For Luther and the Condemnation of Heretics,** v.——**Köhler,** W., Reformation u. Ketzerprozess. 1901. But Köhler's statement on p. 38 that Luther changed his opinion concerning the heretics after 1528, and gave his consent to the "Opinion of the Theologians at Wittenberg" that demanded their punishment, so that he also, if he had lived to see it, would have justified the execution of Servetus, no less than Melanchthon, is combated by **Tschackert,** Entstehung..Kirchenlehre, p. 50. He, referring to the said opinion (C. R. 4, 737ff.), shows that it deals with Anabaptists who are to be punished as revolutioners. Melanchthon wrote the opinion and Luther placed under it the following: "Placet mihi Martino Luthero. Although it seems to be cruel to punish some with a sword, it is still more cruel that they condemn the ministerium verbi, and have no certain teaching, and suppress the true doctrine, and in addition **want to destroy** the **Regna mundi.**" (C. R. 4, 740.)

p. 78

CHAPTER IX.

THE RISE OF THE CONFESSIONAL PRINCIPLE IN THE CHURCH.

from Faith within to outer Witness

from Testimony to Confession

the first confessions in the New Testament

the Pentecostal and Baptismal confessions

the Fixed confessional Forms of the New Testament

the confessions of the Second Century

Caspari, Ungedruckte, Quellen z. Gesch. d. Taufsymbols, Christiania. 1866, 1869, 1875. Alte u. Neue Quellen z. Gesch. d. Taufsymbols, ib. 1879.—— **Zezschwitz,** v., Katechetik.——**Hahn,** Bibl. der Symbole u. Glaubensregeln, 1877.——**Zahn,** Glaubensregel u. Taufbek. in d. alt. K. in Ztschr. f. k. Wiss. 1881, p. 302ff.——**Zahn,** Das. ap. Symb. 1892.——**Kattenbusch,** Das. ap. Symb. i.iiff. 1894.——**Swete,** the Apostles' Creed. 1894.——**Kunze,** Glaubensregel, heil. Schrift u. Taufbekenntniss.——**Seeberg,** Der Katechismus der Urchristenheit. 1903.——**Harnack,** History of Dogma III. 209.——**Hort,** Dissertations II.

p. 93

CHAPTER X.

THE DEVELOPMENT OF THE CONFESSIONAL PRINCIPLE IN THE CHURCH.

the Apostles' Creed

the Nicene Creed

CHAPTER XI.

THE CONFESSIONAL PRINCIPLE IN THE AUGSBURG CONFESSION.

the confessional Authorship of the Augsburg Confession
the confessional Content of the Augsburg Confession
the confessional Progress of the Augsburg Confession
the general confessional Characteristics of the same
    the principle of stable Objectivity
    the principle of catholic Continuity
    the principle of personal salvation by personal Faith
    the principle of respectful maintenance of Freedom
    the principle of Simplicity
    the principle of measured Protest against previous error
the Fate of the Augsburg Confession as Variata,
its Essence as Invariata
the wide Difference between the theology of the Augsburg Confession and pure American Protestantism

CHAPTER XII.

THE HISTORY AND TENDENCY OF THE CONFESSIONAL PRINCIPLE IN THE CHURCH.

confession and faith Go Together
Faith reaches its most impressive power in Confession

Preaching is the most active and regular form of confession
the church's confessions are Dynamic, and the term 'symbol'
is inadequate
Christ the High Priest of our confession
the church Developing her confession
after the first cooling of confessional ardor and the fresh outburst of faith in the Reformation, the church rose to heroic
and complete confession
the two periods of the Dying Away of faith in the church
relaxing of confessional ardor led to the science of Symbolics.

Neander, Geschichte der Pflanzung und Leitung der christlichen Kirche
durch die Apostel. Hamburg, 1832.——**Lambert,** J. C., in Hasting's Dictionary of the Bible.——**Heinrich,** Versuch einer Geschichte der verschiedenen Lehrarten der christlichen Glaubenswahrheiten und der merkwürdigsten
Systeme und der Compendien derselben. Lpz. 1790.——**Gasz,** Geschichte der
protestant. Dogmatik in ihrem Zusammenhange mit der Theologie überhaupt.
——**Heppe,** Dogmatik des deutschen Protestantismus im 16. Jahrhundert. (cp.
the sections: Symbolik, Polemik.)——**Tholuck,** der Geist der lutherischen Theologen Wittenbergs. Hamburg, 1852.——**Chemnitii,** Examen concilii Tridentini.
Fref. 1588.——**Rechtenbach,** encyclopaedia symbolica, vel analysis Confessionis August., Art. Smalc. etc. Lips. 1612.——**Carpzovii,** Isagoge in libros
ecclesiarum luth. symbolicos. Lips. 1665.——**v. Sanden,** Theologia symbolica
lutherana, etc. Fref. et Lips. 1688.——**Walch,** Introductio in libros eccl. luth.
symbol. Jen. 1732.——**Baumgarten,** Erläuterungen der im chr. Concordienbuch
enthaltenen symb. Schriften. Halle, 1747.——The historico-theolog. Introductions to the Concordienbuch of Pipping (1703. 4.), Pfaff (1730),
Hase, Franke, and Müller.——**Semler,** Apparat, ad Libros Symb. Eccles.
Luth. Halle. 1775.——**Planck,** Gesch. der Entstehung, der Veränder-
ungen, und der Bildung des prot. Lehrbegriffs. Leips. 1781-1800.——
Planck, Abriss einer historischen und vergleichenden Darstellung der verschiedenen Dogmatischen Systeme. Götting. 1796, 3 ed., 1822.——**Marheineke,**
Christliche Symbolik. Heidelberg, 1810-1813.——**Marheineke,** Inst. Symbolicae
Doctrinarum. Berlin, 1812.——**Winer,** Comparative Darstellung des Lehrbegriffs der verschiedenen Christlichen Kirchenparteien. Leipsig, 1824. Later ed.
1866. Eng. trans. (not in full), Clarke, Edbg.——**Köllner,** Symbolik aller
Christlichen Confessionen. Hamburg, 1837. 1844, 2 vols. (Completed only for
the Lutheran and the Reformed Churches.)

Guericke, allgem. christl. Symbolik, eine vergleichende Darstellung..vom
luther.-kirchl. Standpunkte. Leipz. 1839-46.——**Schenkel,** das Wesen des
Protestantismus aus den Quellen des Reformationszeitalters. Schaffh. 1846.
——**Moehler,** J. A., Symbolik. 1832. 7 Ed. 1864. Symbolism, or Exposition of
the Doctrinal Differences between Catholics and Protestants. Lon. 1847.——
Baur, der Gegensatz des Katholicism. und Protestantismus. 1834.——**Nitzsch,**
protest. Beantwortung der Symbolik Möhler's. Hamburg, 1835.——**Matthes,**
Comparative Symbolik, 1854.——**Baier,** Symbolik, 1854.——**Hofmann,** Symbolik, 1857.——**Plitt,** Grundrisz der Symbolik, 1875.——**Reiff,** Glaube der Kirch-
en und Kirchenparteien, 1875.——**Oehler,** Lehrbuch der Symbolik, 1876.——
Scheele v., Teologisk Symbolik, 1877—translated into German, 1881. Also in
Zöcklers Handbuch der theologischen Wissensch., 1883.——**Philippi,** Vor-
lesung, 1883.——**Schaff,** Creeds of Christendom. 1884. 3 vols.——**Nösgen,** Symbolik.——**Kattenbusch,** (Ritschlian,) Lehrbuch der vergleichenden Confessions-
kunde, i. Freiburg, 1892.——**Walther,** W. Luthers Glaubensgewissheit. Halle,
1892.——**Walther,** W., Das Erbe der Reformation. Leipzig, 1893 u. 1894.——
Müller, Karl. Symbolik, 1896. (Reformed.)——**Orr,** Progress of Dogma. Lon-

CHAPTER XIII.

THE CONFESSIONAL USE OF THE WORD 'SYMBOL.'

the meaning of the Term
its use by the Church Fathers
its use in the Reformation and in the Book of Concord

CHAPTER XIV.

THE LUTHERAN CONFESSION.

was it born at Augsburg
the great Living confession of the church was Luther
the Reasons why he was the church's living confession
his relation to External confessional statements
the Weakness of a living witness

CHAPTER XV.

THE LUTHERAN CONFESSION.

THE ORIGIN OF THE AUGSBURG CONFESSION. KOLDE'S INTRODUCTION.

the Emperor
the Torgau Articles
the Elector at Coburg
the Beginning of the confession
what Luther saw on May 11th
the Saxon Draft
the Other Estates admitted
the negotiations of Melanchthon
the Delivery of the confession
the confession and Luther

CHAPTER XVI.

THE LUTHERAN CONFESSION.

MELANCHTHON'S UNSUCCESSFUL ATTEMPTS AS A
DIPLOMATIST. KOLDE'S ESSAY.

the activity of Melanchthon at Augsburg
characterized by Kolde
the Defense of Melanchthon by Brieger
why Brieger is Wrong
the Documentary evidence
the lack of sympathy in Melanchthon with Zwinglians
was the Final Work on confession begun before June 21st
the affirmative of Brieger
the reply of Kolde
the negotiations by Melanchthon with Rome rejected
the Consequences of their rejection
the Four Points of Melanchthon as formulated by Valdés.

D

CONTENTS

FOR LUTHER AT THE DIET OF WORMS, etc.

"**Acta D. Martini Lutheri** in Comitiis Principum Wormatiae" (1521), **E. A.**
v. a. 6, 13 f.
Köstlin, Luthers Rede in Worms. Halle, 1874.
Kolde, Luthers Stellung, u. s. w. (1876).
Kolde, Luther auf dem Reichstag zu Worms. Halle, 1883.
Köstlin, Martin Luther I. Elberfeld, 1883.
Lämmer, Hugo, Die vortridentinisch-katholische Theologie des Reformationszeitalters. Berlin, 1858.
Dieckhoff, Luthers Lehre in ihrer ersten Gestalt. Rostock, 1887.
Tschackert, Die Entstehung der lutherischen und der reformierten Kirchenlehre (The Theological Beginnings of Luther, 34) passim. 1910.

FOR THE RELATION OF THE REFORMERS TO THE STATE AND TO
THE PAPACY.
Brieger, Th., Die kirchl. Gewalt der Obrigkeit nach den Anschauungen
Luthers. ZThK. II, 513ff.
Jäger, G., Die politischen Ideen Luthers und ihr Einfluss auf die innere
Entwicklung Deutschlands. .Pr. Jahrb, 1903. Aug.-Heft, 210ff.
Schornbaum, K., Zur Politik des Markgrafen Georg von Brandenburg.
München, 1906.
Kolde, A. "Philipp der Grossmütige" RE. 15, 296ff.
Stähelin, R., Huldreich Zwingli, sein Leben u. Wirken. 2 Bde. Basel, 1895
u 1897.
Sleidanus, De Statu Religionis et Reipublicae Carole V. Caesare, 1555.
Francfort, 1785.
Sepulveda, Historia Caroli V. Leipzig, 1841-46.
Armstrong, The Emp. Charles V. Lon., 1902.
For Crowning of Charles V., v. **Baumgarten,** Gesch. Karls V. II 704.
Gachard, Correspondence de Ch. V. et d'Adrien vi., Brussels, 1862 (Eng.
trans., London, 1862).
Lämmer, Analecta Vaticana, 1521-46. Freiburg, 1863. (The Elector John.)
Ranke, Deutsche Geschichte, Book 5, Chap. 9 (Vol. III. 211 sqq.). (The
Elector John.)
Anton, Apologia Mspta., fol. 62b. (The Elector's Appeal for the Public
Reading of the Confession.)

FOR THE PROTEST AT THE DIET OF SPIRES, etc.

For Protestation, v. **Hauser,** Die Protestation von Speier, 1904.
For the Protest, v. **Sleidanus,** De Statu Religionis, 1557, 98 sq. (a condensation).
For the Decree and the Protest, v. **Cölestin,** Hist. II. 192 sqq.
For the Appellation, v. J. J. **Müller,** Historie von der Evangelischen Stände
Protestation, etc. 51 sqq.
For the Federation, v. **Kolde,** Beiträge zur Reformationsgeschichte (1896),
96.
For Confederations-Notel, v. J. J. **Müller,** Historie, 236 sqq.
For Rotach Conference, v. Strassburg Politische Correspondenz, 269 sqq.
For the History of Embassy from Diet of Spires to the Emperor, v. **Salig,**
Hist. d. Augsp. Con. II. 136-138.
Dolzig's Report in **Förstemann's** Urkundenbuch. I. 127 et seqq.

THE DIET AT AUGSBURG.
DOCUMENTARY.

Förstemann, K. E., Urkundenbuch zu der Geschichte des Reichstags zu
Augsburg im Jahre, 1830. Halle, 1833-35.
Schirrmacher, F. W., Briefe und Akten zu der Geschichte des Religions-
gespräches zu Marburg und des Reichstages zu Augsburg. 1530. Gotha, 1876.

Knaake, Luther's Anteil an d. A. C. Berlin, 1863.
Engelhardt in Niedner's Zeitschrift. 1865. 515-629.
Plitt, Einleitung in die Augustana. 1867-68.
Krauth, The Conservative Reformation. 1871.
Kolde, Der Kanzler Brück u. seine Bedeutung für die Entwicklung der Reformation. Halle, 1874.
Kolde, Analecta Lutherana, Briefe und Actenstücke. Gotha, 1883.
Brieger in Kirchengeschichtliche Studien. 1888. 268-320.
Brieger, Die Torgauer Artikel, in Kirchengeschichtliche Studien. Leipzig, 1888.
(For an English Translation of the So-called Torgau Articles in Förstemann, Urkundenbuch. I. 68 sqq. *v.* **Jacobs,** Book of Concord. II. 75-103.)
Kolde, Beitrage zur Reformationsgeschichte. 94 et seqq.
Kolde, Die Augsburgische Konfession lateinisch und deutsch kurz erläutert. Gotha, 1896.
Tschackert, Die unveränderte Augsb. Konf. Leipzig, 1901.
Brieger, Zur Geschichte des Augsburger Reichstages von 1530. Leipzig, 1903.
Kolde, Die aelteste Redaktion der Augsburger Konfession. Guetersloh, 1906.
Kolde, Neue Augustanastudien. Neue kirchl. Zeitschr. XVII. 1906. 729 seqq.
Hoennicke, Melanchthon's Stellung auf dem Reichstage zu Augsburg. 1530. Deutsch Ev. Blätter, Nov. 1908.
For the Literature of the more recent discussions and discoveries, see Literature to chapters XV, XVI, XVII, XVIII.   .   .   .   p. 283

CHAPTER XX.

THE LUTHERAN CONFESSION.

THE AUGSBURG CONFESSION REMAINED UNALTERED.

the tears of Melanchthon: their cause

the peace of Luther: its cause

ready to stand by the confession even to Martyrdom

was Melanchthon open-hearted to Luther

the correspondence from June 25th to July 1st

Luther's attempt to counteract Melanchthon's lack of faith

the course of Events from the diet to the confutation

the attempts at Compromise under Melanchthon

their Failure and the departure of the Elector

Corpus Reformatorum ed. Bretschneider. Halis Saxonum. 1839ff. II. 2. 372 sq.——**Seckendorf,** V. L. v., Commentarius historicus et apologeticus de Lutheranismo, etc. Francofurti et Lipsiae, 1692.——**Salig,** Vollstaendige Historie d. A. C., etc. Halle, 1730. II. 334 sq.——**Camerarius,** Vita Melanchthonis (1566) Stroebel. Noesselt, Halae, 1777.——**Meyers,** J. F., Dissert. de Lenitate Phil. Melanchthonis.——**Köllner,** Symbolik der Luth. Kirche. Hamburg, 1837.——**Plitt,** Die. Apol. 'd. August, 1873.——**Calinich,** Zeitschrift für wissenschaftliche Theologie. 1873. 541 et seqq.——**Jacobs,** Book of Concord, II. Philadelphia, 1883.——**Ficker,** Die Confut. d. Augsb. Bek. in ihrer ersten Gestalt. 1891.——**Kolde,** Die Augsb. Conf. 1896 (together with the Marburg, Schwabach, and Torgau Articles, the Confutation, and the Augustana variata).——**Sell, K.,** Melanchthon und die deutsche Reformation bis 1531. Halle, 1897.——**Kawerau, G.,** Die Versuche Melanchthon zur katholischen Kirche zurückzuführen. 1902.——*v.* also Literature of Chap. XIX and XXIV.

p. 436

CHAPTER XXI.

THE LUTHERAN CONFESSION.

THE AUGSBURG CONFESSION: THE FURTHER HIS-
TORY OF ITS EDITIONS AND MANUSCRIPTS.

*KOLDE'S ESSAY, WITH A SUMMARY OF THE ARGUMENT
AS IT BEARS ON THE CONFESSIONAL QUESTION,
BY T. E. S.*

For information on the **First Prints,** *v.* C. R. XXVI, 477, sq. **Weber, I,** 394, sqq., **Zöckler,** Die Augsburgische Konfession, 31.

For a clear summary as to whether the **Editio Princeps** may be termed the Invariata, *v.* **Neve,** in Luth. Ch. Rev. XXX, "Are we Justified in Distinguishing Between an Altered and an Unaltered Augustana?"

For an attempt to reconstruct the **Original Text,** from the 39 copies of it taken especially before its delivery, *v.* **Tschackert,** Die unverändert Augsburgische Konfession, deutsch und lateinisch, nach den besten Handschriften aus dem Besitze der Unterzeichner. Leipzig, 1901.

For a Bibliography of the **Latin and German Manuscripts** of the Augsburg Confession in the Archives *v.* **Krauth,** The Conservative Reformation, 1871, footnote on pp. 242, 243.

For the **Variata of 1540** and 1542, *v.* translation in full in **Jacobs'** Book of Concord, II. 103-158.

For the **Texts** and the **Texts of the Variata** of 1540 and 1542 *v.* **Bindsell,** C. R., XXVI. 343; **Weber,** Kritische Geschichte d. A. C., 1782; **Kolde, Die** Augsburg Konfession; in English, **Jacobs,** Book of Concord, II. 103 sq.

CHAPTER XXII.

THE LUTHERAN CONFESSION.

PROTESTANTISM UNDER THE AUGSBURG CONFES-
SION TO THE DEATH OF LUTHER.

the Apology and its confessional import
the Schmalkald League
the Princes and Estates
the faith taught in the Loci
the olive branch waved by Melanchthon to Bucer
the Wittenberg Concord
the Schmalkald Articles
the marriage of Philip of Hesse
the Variata
the Regensburg Interim
the Reformation of Cologne
the Death of Luther

CHAPTER XXIII.

THE LUTHERAN CONFESSION.

PROTESTANTISM FROM THE DEATH OF LUTHER TO
THE DEATH OF MELANCHTHON AND TO THE
DISINTEGRATION OF LUTHERANISM.

years of Reaction
the leadership of Melanchthon
political Events 1546-1555
the Augsburg and Leipzig Interims, Mauricé
the Papacy and the Empire in these events
the Controversies following Luther's death
Adiaphoristic
Osiandrian
the Two great Parties
Majoristic
Antinomistic
Crypto-Calvinism
Eucharistic
Synergistic
the synergism of Melanchthon
the Corpus Philippicum
partisan Warfare
dire Results

The Leipzig Interim. Jacobs, Book of Concord, II. 260-272.

Walch, Einleitung in d. Rels. Streitigktn. innerh. u. ausserh. der **Luth.** Kirche. 1730 ff.

Planck, Gesch. des prot. Lehrbegriffes. 1781 ff.

Wolf, Gesch. des deutsch. Protestanten. 1555-58, 1588.

Wolf, Ambrose, Historia von der Augsburgischen Confession.

Heppe, Gesch. des deutsch. Protestantism. 1555-81. 4 vols. 1852 ff.

Gieseler, Kirchengeschichte III, 2 1853. S. 115-351 mit sorgsam ausgewählten Excerpten aus Quellenschriften.

Frank, Theol. der Con. Form. 4 vols. 1858 ff.

Preger, W., Mathias Flacius Illyricus und seine Zeit. 2 vols. **1861.**

Frank, G., Gesch. d. prot. Theologie I. 1862.

Möller, Andreas Osiander. Leben und Ausgewählte Schriften.

Hergang, K. Th., Das Augsburger Interim.

Schmid, H., Der Kampf der luth. Kirche um Luthers Lehre vom Abendmahl im Reformationszeitalter. Leipzig, 1868.

Krauth, The Conservative Reformation. 1871.

Walther, Der Concordienformel Kern und Stern. 1877.

Vogt, O., Melanchthons u. Bugenhagens Stellung zum Interim. Jahrb. f. prot. Th. 1887. 1 ff.

Thomasius-Seeberg, Dogmengeschichte II. 1889.

Haussleiter, Joh., Aus der Schule Melanchthons. Theologische Disputationen und Promotionen zu Wittenberg in den Jahren, 1546-1560. Greifswald. 1897

lvi

CONTENTS

The Writings of Melanchthon: Corpus Doctrinae Christianae, das ist, Gantze Summa der rechten Christlichen Lehre, etc. Leipzig, 1560 fol.
Opera Omnia, Peucer, Wittenb., 1562-64. 4 vols. fol. (Preceded by the Basle edition of 1541.)
Opera quae supersunt omnia. Bretschneider and Bindseil. Halle, 1834-1860. 28 vols. 4to. In Corpus Reformatorum I-XXIV. (The Letters of M. are found in I-IX, with a subsequent Vol. added 1879 by Bindseil.) (The Classic edition.)
Bibliotheca Melancthoniana. Bindseil. Halle, 1868. (A 28-page c-talogue of the editions of Melanchthon's writings.)
Loci. The Corpus Reformatorum, XXI. Contains three main editions Latin and German, with introductions, Bretschneider and Bindseil.
Loci. Plitt-Kolde, 1890.——Loci...in ihrer Urgestalt—herausgegeb. und erläutert. Kolde, 1900.
Annales Vitae. XXVIII. in C. R.
Camerarius, 1566; **Strobel,** 1777; **Schmidt,** 1861. (*v. infra.*)
Galle, Fr., Versuch einer Charakteristik Melanchthons als Theologen. Halle, 1840.
Henke, Das Verhältniss Luthers und Melanchthons zu einender. Marburg, 1860.
Schmidt, K., Ph. Melanchthon, Leben und ausgewählte Schriften. Elberf., 1860-1861. (Still the best Biography for Scientific purposes.)
Herrlinger, Th., Die Theologie Melanchthons in ihrer geschichtl. Entwicklung, Gotha. F. A. Perthes, 1870.
Bindseil, Ph. Melanchthonis epistolae, etc. Halle, 1874.

CHAPTER XXV.

THE LUTHERAN CONFESSION.

THE NEED OF A CONCORDIA REALIZED, AND ITS ORIGIN ATTEMPTED.

four periods of Development
the Variata insufficient
the Situation, 1560-1576
the Statements of Andreae in 1569
the Six Sermons sent to Chemnitz in 1573
the commission of Augustus
the Torgau Book
the Bergen Book
the Calvinistic Protests

For the official documents connected with the **Lichtenberg Convention, v. Hutter,** Cap. IX., pp. 75 et seqq.

For historical details, v. **Anton,** pp. 156 et seqq.——**Planck,** VI., 437 et seqq.——**Walch,** Introductio, pp. 715 et seqq.——**Heppe,** III., 84 et seqq.—— **Pressel** in Jahrbücher für Deutsche Theologie, 1877, pp. 10 et seqq.—— **Müller's** Die Symbolischen Bücher, Einleitung, IX. edition, p. lxxi.——**Fritschel,** Quellen aus der Zeit der Conc. Formel. Dubuque. 1910.

v. also **Thomasius,** Dogmengeschichte.——**Seeberg,** Hist. of Doctrines. II. 347-390.——**Schaff,** Creeds of Christendom.——**Krauth,** Conservative Reformation.——v. Literature under Chap. XX.   .   .   .   .   p. 637

CONTENTS

CHAPTER XXVI.

THE LUTHERAN CONFESSION.

THE FORMULA OF CONCORD: ITS ORIGIN, BASED ON KOLDE'S INTRODUCTION, ETC.

the six Controversies and the Points at issue
the pliant and scholastic nature of Melanchthon
the rise of Calvinism
the disruption of the Schmalkald League and
the helplessness of the Protestants
the Corpora doctrinae
the efforts of Andreae
the effort of Chemnitz and Duke Julius
the effort of Augustus
the Schwabian Concordia sent to Augustus by Julius, and
the Maulbronn Formula sent by the South Germans
recast into the Torgian Formula and the Bergen Book
the Subscription to the Formula

Andreae, J., Fuenff predigen von dem wercke der concordien und endlicher vergleichung der vorgefallenen streitigen religionsartickeln etc. Dressden 1580. ——**Fuegers,** Caspar, Kurtzer, wahrhafftiger und einfelt. bericht von dem buch, Formula Concordiae. Dressden 1580.——**Selnecceri,** Nic., Recitationes aliquot 1. de Consilio scripti libri Concordiae, et modo agendi, qui in subscriptionibus servatus est. 2. de Persona Christi et Coena Dom. 3. de auctoritate et sententia Conf. Aug. 4. de auctoritate Lutheri et Philippi. 5. de controversis nonnullis articulis. Lips. 1581.——Nunc denuo editae cum notationibus brevibus ad cuiusdam Calyiniani, qui fingit sibi nomen Jo. Balaei, Neapoli Nemetum publicatas calumnias. Lips. 1582. (1583.)——Aus der Christlichen Concordia erklerung etlicher streitiger Artickel: Deutsch und Lateinisch. gegeneinander ueber. Ex forma Christianae Concordiae Declaratio Articulorum qui post D. Lutheri obitum in controuersiam in Ecclesiis et Academiis A. C. addictis uenerunt. Opera et priuato studio **Selnecceri, Nic.** Lipsiae 1582. **Chemnitii,** Chr., Collegium theol. super Form. Conc. Jen. 1659. vermehrt mit Zusaetzen aus der Apologie und anderen Schriften. 1761.——**Rangonis,** Conr. Tiburt, Haereticorum et Syncretistarum Obex Formula Concordiae, d. i. Warhaffte Erzehlung des Ursprungs. Fortgangs und Ansehens der Concordien-Formul. Hamburg u. Frankf. 1683. 12.——**Musaei,** Jo., Praelect. in epitomen F. C. Jen. 1701.——Acta F. C. in **Bergensi Coenobio** tempore Praesidis Ulneri a. 1577. revisae ex Hutteri Conc. conc., Goebelii Progr. jubil., Arnoldi Haeret. hist. et Saccii concione funebri in Abb. Ulnerum, acc. Oratio Sim. Frid. Hahnii de ortu et fatis Coen. Bergensis a. 1706. habita. Franc. ad M. (s. a.) [1707.] fol.——**Acc. H. Meibomii** Chronicon Bergense contin. a. S. F. Hahnio, ibid. 1708 fol.——**Loescher,** Val., Historia motuum. Lipsiae 1723. (tom. III. lib. VI, c. 5 and 9)——**Balthasar,** Jac. H., Historie des Torg. Buchs. als des naehesten Entwurfs des Berg. Concordienbuchs—nebst andern zur Geschichte des Concordienbuchs gehoerigen und bisher unbekannten Nachr, etc. Greifswald und Leipzig. St. 1-6. 1741-44. 4. St. 7. 1-4 & St. 5, 8. 1756.——**Anton, Jo.**

CONTENTS lix

CHAPTER XXVII.

THE LUTHERAN CONFESSION.

THE INTRODUCTION OF THE CONCORDIA, AND THE AUGUSTANA PRESERVED.

not introduced by papal or imperial Mandate
but Sent Forth and Discussed throughout Germany
none other so fully Tested
the Quedlinburg Declaration
a good cause not accountable for the sins of Individuals
the Signatories not condemnable
the adverse judgment of Planck
more Unanimous than would be possible in America today
no creed really Oecumenical
no undue political Influence
the opinion of Kolde and of Müller
the extent of the Adoption
rejected by Calvinistic States
the Lutherans who failed to subscribe
the opinion of Planck, Köllner and Thomasius
the real confessional Validity

CHAPTER XXXI.

THE LUTHERAN CONFESSION.

THE ANSWER TO THE FORMULA'S OUTER FORM TO THE QUESTION, IS THE FORMULA A CONFESSION?

the Title of the Formula and its Language
no confessional claim for the Solida Declaratio
is the Formula a "Commentary"
in what sense it is a mere Repetition, and not a new confession
a comparison with the Form of the Augsburg Confession
why the Formula presents doctrine by Antagonism
in what sense the Formula is a Commentary
is the Formula a treatise on Dogmatics
does the Formula represent all types of Lutheranism
does sharpness of Logical Form condemn, with the Epitome
as a confession

Müller, Die Symbolischen Bücher.——**Krauth,** The Conservative Reformation.
p. 729

CHAPTER XXXII.

THE LUTHERAN CONFESSION.

THE ANSWER OF THE FORMULA'S SUBJECT MATTER TOUCHING THE QUESTION, IS THE FORMULA OF CONCORD A CONFESSION?

the Subjects Treated were subjects of the day
they were agitating the whole Christian World
the need of settling them was felt by the Melanchthonians
the Formula starts by planting itself firmly on Scripture
treats the vital doctrines of Christianity, centering all in Christ
the Formula treats of Christ—His Work, Presence, Person

CHAPTER XXXIII.

THE LUTHERAN CONFESSION.

THE PERSON OF CHRIST AND THE FORMULA OF
CONCORD.

the Person of Christ the Centre
the Consequences in Lutheran theology
the 'Person of Christ' in the Formula
not a new doctrine to bolster up the Real Presence
the divergence here between the two Branches of Protestantism
the doctrine of Christ is rooted in Luther
Luther on the Person of Christ in detail
Whence Luther derived this doctrine
Luther's rescue of the Sacrament
the Communicatio Idiomatum vs. the Zwinglian Alloesis
the Misrepresentation of the Lutheran Faith
the Personal Omnipresence a fundamental fact in the Person
the most potent Objection to the Personal Omnipresence
the critique of Schaff
the inconsistency of critics of the 'Ubiquity'
the scriptural origin of the Communicatio Idiomatum
the testimony of the Ancient Creeds
the testimony of the Church Fathers
the Formula and the Living Christ

CHAPTER XXXIV.

THE LUTHERAN CONFESSION.

CONCORDIA THE CHURCH'S CONFESSION OF CHRIST

the Material of Concordia
its Field is salvation
its Subject is Christ
the Church should stand upon the Concordia
it treats some other doctrines, but
it is the great confession of the Person and Work of Christ

CHAPTER XXXV.

THE LUTHERAN CONFESSION.

WHAT THE FORMULA OF CONCORD ACCOMPLISHED AS A CONFESSION OF THE CHURCH.

it is the substance of the Gospel
set together after Protestantism had been tested
it is the confession of Teachers and Congregations
it rescued the church from a petty doctrinal Territorialism
it recovered the church from the weaknesses of its Friends
the estimate of Seeberg
it preserved the existence of the Church
it made possible a substantial Catholic Evangelical Church
it guarded the relation of the Divine and the Human in all the great doctrines
it settled the question of Justification, of Synergism, and of the Sacraments
it is the white-winged standard of Peace
it is the first permanent synthesis of Luther and Melanchthon
it deserves to be accepted by the Lutheran Church

CONTENTS

CHAPTER XXXVI.

THE LUTHERAN CONFESSION.

THE BOOK OF CONCORD. THE FACTS OF ITS ORIGIN AND PUBLICATION. KOLDE'S ESSAY.

its Publication began in 1578.
the adoption of the Three General Creeds
the Earliest editions of the Book of Concord
the Title of the Book of Concord
the Arrangement of the Book of Concord
the Later editions

The Earliest and the Most Important Editions of the Book of Concord.

(a) German.

Concordia. Christliche, Widerholete, einmütige Bekenntnüs nachbenanter Churfürsten, Fürsten und Stende Augspurgischer Confession, und derselben zu ende des Buchs underschriebener Theologen Lere und Glaubens, Mit angeheffter, in Gottes wort, als der einigen Richtschnur, wolgegründter erklärung etlicher Artickel, bei welchen nach D. Martin Luthers seligen Absterben disputation und streit vorgefallen. Aus einheiliger vergleichung und beuehl obgedachter Churfürsten, Fürsten und Stende, derselben Landen, Kirchen, Schulen und Nachkommen, zum underricht und warnung in Druck vorfertiget. Mit Churf. G. zu Sachsen befreihung. Dressden. M. D. LXXX. fol.

[Concerning the variation in the first prints of this edition, v. the treatment in the chapter.]

Concordia.——Magdeburgk 1580. 4.

Tübingen 1580. fol. (without the Tauf- und Traubüchlein, with variations in the signatures).

Dressden 1581. 4. (without the Tauf- und Traubüchlein, with addition of the signatures of the Saxon theologians following the first edition).

Frankfurt a. d. O. 1581. fol.

Magdeburgk 1581. 4. (with the Preface of the Administr. Joachim Friedrich of Juli 10, 1580.)

Magdeburgk 1580. 4. (but later than the above.)

Heydelberg 1582. fol. (without Tauf- und Traubüchl. and Catalog. testimon. On the other hand there are found first,—and that ahead of the others—the signatures of the Palatine theologians, then those of Steier, Krain and Kärnthen.)

Heydelberg 1582. fol. (as the former.)

Dressden 1589. fol. (with Tauf- und Traubüchl.)

Tübingen 1599. 4. (with Tauf- und Traubüchl., without the signatures of the Austrian theologians, but with those of the Palatinate.)

Leipzig 1603. 4. (with the German Preface of the Elector Christian II, without signatures.)

Stuttgard 1611. 4. (with Preface of the Duke Joh. Friedrich.

Leipzig 1622. 4.

Stuttgarten 1660. 4. (with Preface of the Duke Eberhard.)

Stuttgart 1681. 4.'

Concordia.——With Heinr. Pippings (Int. to) Symbol. Schriften der Evangel.-Luther. Kirchen. Leipzig 1703. 4. (vid. Acta Erud. Lips. a. 1703, p. 238 f. Here first the Saechsischen Visitenartikel).—2. Ausgabe with **Christian Weissens** Conclusions. Leipzig 1739. 4.

Christliches Konkordienbuch together with different variants of previous publications, published by **Siegm. Jac. Baumgarten.** Halle 1747. 2 Tille. 8.

(vid. Kraffts Neue Theol. Bibl. Bd. XI. St.)——Christl. Konk.-Buch with the Leipz. Theol. Facultät introduction, etc. Wittenberg 1760. 8.—1766.—1789. (vid. J. Aug. Ernesti. Neue Theol. Bibl. Bd. 1. S. 752 ff.)——Die Symb. Bücher der evang.-luth. Kirche. with hist. Einl., Anmerkungen, Erörterungen, etc., published by J. W. Schöpff. Dresden. 1. Teil, 1826. 2. Teil, 1827. 8.——Concordia, Die Symb. Bücher der evang.-luth. Kirche, with Einleitung. published by F. A. Köthe. Leipzig 1830. 8.——Evang. Konkordienbuch oder saemt. in dem Konkordienbuche enthaltenen symbolische Glaubensschriften der evang.-luth. Kirche. With Erläuterungen und kurzen geschichtlichen Bemerkungen aufs Neue deutsch herausgegeben von Dr. J. A. Detzer. Nuernberg 1830. 1842. 1847.——Evangelisches Konkordienbuch oder die symbol. Bücher der evang. luth. Kirche. With geschichtl. Einleit. und Anmerk. herausgeg. von Fr. Wilh. Bodemann. Hannover 1843. (The Apology is not in the original German text but in an original translation from the Latin.) Concordienbuch, das ist, die symbolischen Bücher der ev. luth. Kirche. Neue, nach dem Urtext vom Jahre 1580 revidirte Ausgabe. Festgabe für das Jubeljahr 1880. St. Louis, Mo. 1880.

(b) Latin.

Concordia.—Pia et Vnanimi consensu repetita Confessio Fidei et doctrinae Electorum, Principum et Ordinum Imperii, atque eorundem Theologorum, qui Augustanam Confessionem amplectuntur et nomina sua huic libro subscripserunt. Cui ex sacra scriptura, vnica illa veritatis norma et regula, quorundam Articulorum, qui post Doctoris Martini Luther felicem ex hac vita exitum, in controuersiam vener.nt solida accessit Declaratio. Communi Consilio et Mandato eorundem Electorum, Principum ac Ordinum Imperii. et erudiendis et monendis subditis, Ecclesiis et Scholis suis, ad memoriam posteritatis typis vulgata Lipsiae. Anno MDLXXX. Cum gratia et privilegio Elect. Sax. 4.

[Concerning the peculiarities of this (private) edition of Selnecker, not recognized by him, v. the text of the chapter.]

Concordia. Pia — — denuo typis vulgata. Lipsiae 1584. 4.

[The first authentic edition of the Latin Text, bearing the same title as the edition above, yet as the signatures are wanting, the following words are also lacking in the title: et nomina subscripserunt.]

Concordia.—Lipsiae 1602. 8. (With the Praefatio Christian II., without the Tauf- und Traubuechlein, without signatures.)—Lipsiae 1606. 1612. 1618. 1626. 8.—Stetini 1654. 8a. E. Jenae 1654.—Lipsiae 1654. 8.—Stregnesiae 1669. 8.— Lipsiae 1669. 8.—1677.—Cum Appendice tripartita Dr. Adami Rechenbergii 1678. 8.—1698.—1712.—1725.—1742.

Concordia.—Cura et cum annotat. Phil. Muelleri. Jenae 1705. 4.

[The text of this edition is unusable because it follows the Selnecker edition of 1580 with all the errors of that edition. Otherwise it contains very valuable historical additions.]

Ecclesiae Evangelicae libri symbolici, tria Symb. Oecum, Aug. Conf. invariatae eiudem Apologia, Artic. Smalcald., uterque Catech. D. Lutheri. Form. Conc. Pfaffius, C. M., ex editionib. prim. et praest. recensuit. varias lectiones adiunxit, allegat. locorum penitiorem indicem supplevit, loca difficilia explanavit et vindicavit, introductionem histor. praemisit, atque in Appendice Articulos XVII. Torgenses, Confutationem A. C. a Theologis Pontificiis in Comitiis Aug. fatam, A. C. variatam, primam Apologiae A. C. delineationem etc. subiunxit. Tubingae 1730. 8. vid. Unschuld. Nachr. a. 1752. p. 263.—Libri symbolici Eccles. evang. lutheranae accuratius editi variique generis animadvers. ac disput. illustrati a Mich. Webero. Viteb. 1809-11. 8.

[Copies of this edition, but containing only the oecumenical creeds, both catechisms and the Augsburg Confession with the Confutation, are rare, as almost the whole edition was destroyed in a conflagration.]

Libri Symbolici ecclesiae evangelicae. Ad fidem optim. exemplorum recens. J. A. H. Tittmann. Lipsiae 1817. 8.—1827.—Libri Symbolici ecclesiae evangelicae sive Concordia. Recens. C. A. Hase. Lipsiae 1827. 8.—1837.—1845.—

E

CONTENTS

Libri Symbolici ecclesiae luther. ad editt. principes.—rec. praecipuam lectionum diversitatem notav., Christ. II. ordinumque evangelicor, praefationes, artic. Saxon. visitator et Confut. A. C. Pontific. adj. H. H. Guil. **Meyer,** Goetting. 1830. 8.—Libri Symbolici ecclesiae Lutheranae. Pars 1. Symb. oecum., Conf. Aug. et Apol. Confess. Pars II. Art. Smalcald. et Catech. uterque. Pars III. Form. Concordia. Ad editionem Lipsiensem A. 1584. Berolini. 1857.

(c) German-Latin.

Concordia. Germanico-Latina ad optima et antiquiss. exempla recognita, adjectis fideliter allegator. dictor. S. Scr. capitibus et vers. et testimonior. P. P. aliorumquqe Scriptorum locis—notisque aliis. nec non indicibus, c. approb. Facult. Theol. Lips. Witt. et Rostoch. Studio Ch. **Reineccii.** Lipsiae 1708. 4.—1735.

Christliches Konkordienbuch. Deutsch und Lateinisch mit historischen Einleitungen J. G. **Walchs.** Jena 1750. 8.

Die symbolischen Bücher der evangelisch-lutherischen Kirche, deutsch und lateinisch. Neue sorgfältig durch-gesehene Ausgabe, mit den sächsischen Visitations-Artikeln, einem Verzeichnis abweichender Lesarten, historischen Einleitungen und ausführlichen Registern. Besorgt von J. T. **Müller.** Stuttgart, 1848.

(d) Translations.

Dutch: Concordia of Lutherische Geloofs Belydenis in't licht gegeven door Zach. Dezius. Rotterdam, 1715, 8vo.——**Swedish:** Libri Concordiae Versio Suecic, Christeliga, och Uprepade och Läras, etc. Norköping, 1730, 4to.—— **English:** The Christian Book of Concord, or Symbolical Books of the Evangelical Lutheran Church, translated by Ambrose and Socrates Henkel, (two Lutheran clergymen of Virginia), with the assistance of several other Lutheran clergymen. Newmarket, Virginia, 1851; 2d ed. revised, 1854.——The Book of Concord; or, The Symbolical Books of the Evangelical Lutheran Church. Jacobs. Philadelphia, 1882.

THE CHIEF CONTROVERSIAL PUBLICATIONS.

Theologorum et Ministrorum Ecclesiarum in ditione Jo. Casimiri Palatini Admonitio Christiana de libro Concordiae, quem vocant, a quibusdam Theologis, nomine quorundam Ordinum Aug. Confessionum. edita Neustadii in Palatinatu. 1584. 4.——Warhaffte und christliche Verantwortung der Prediger zu Bremen—von der Person Christi, h. Tauff, h. Abendmahl, Wahl, Ceremonien. Bremen 1581. 4.——**Chr. Irenaei,** Examen des ersten Artickels und des Wirbelgeistes. im neuen Concordienbuche. 1581.——**Apologia** oder Verantw. des Christl. Concordien-Buchs. Gestellt durch etl. hierzu verord. Theol., a. 1583. Heydelberg 1583. Wahrhaffte Christl. und gegruendte Widerlegung der vermeynten Entschuld. der Prediger zu Bremen in den Art. von der Person Christi und H. Abendtmal. Heydelberg 1583. fol. 1. and 2. part of the Erfurt Apology of Tim. Kirchner. Nick. Selecker and Mart. Chemnitz, usually called the Erfurt Book. Part 3: **Refutatio Irenaei,** Gruendtl. Bericht auf das Examen M. Chr. Irenaei. Heydelberg 1583. fol.——The same 1593. 4.——Apologia oder Verantwort. des Christl. Concord.-Buchs etc. Dressden 1584. fol. (Editions Magdeburg 1584. Erfurt 1584 etc. Lat. Heidelberg 1583. f.) Part 4 (vid. Salig. Historie der Augsb. Konfession I, 744 f.): Gruendliche wahrhafftige Historie von der Augspurgischen Confession etc. Leipzig 1584. Magdeburg 1584, also called **Historie des Sakramentsstreits,** directed against Ambrosius Wolf (Christ. Herdesianus), Historie der Augsburgischen Confession, Wider die Patres Bergenses und anderen Vbiquitisten verfuehrerischen Betrug. Neustadt a. d. Hardt 1580. 4.——**Aeg. Hunnii,** Nothwend. Verantwort. des christl. Concordibuchs wider Dan. Hoffmanni Beschuld. I. als sollt des H. Christi nach s. Menschl. Natur. Gegenwaert. in Regierung aller Creat. im Buch der Concord. nicht begriffen sein; II. dass das Concordibuch nach allgem. Unterschreibung gefehrlicher Weiss mutirt sey. Frankfurt am Mayn 1597.—— Also. Dess. Widerleg. der ungegruendten Aufflagen, and Dan. Hoffmann ——

CONTENTS

OLDER PUBLICATIONS ON THE HISTORY.

CHAPTER XXXVII.
FROM THE BOOK OF CONCORD TO THE PRESENT DAY.

how Christian Union and the Formula have worked, according
summary of the early Lutheran Dogmatik   [to Schaff
the Reaction in Calixtus
the drop into modern Individualism in Europe
the modern situation in America
the comparative importance of Dogmatic System

CONTENTS

Chapter XXXVIII.

THE BOOK OF CONCORD AND HISTORICAL LUTHER-ANISM IN AMERICA.

Luther and the Discovery of America Contemporary
was this Providential
the Lutheran Church Coming to America
it came on the basis of the Unaltered Augsburg Confession
and the Book of Concord
the Lutheran Church in New York
the Swedes on the Delaware
Justus Falckner, the first minister to be ordained
the Palatine Immigration, with the Savoy Constitution
John Caspar Stoever and his churches in Pennsylvania
Henry Melchior Muhlenberg in Pennsylvania
the Book of Concord the foundation of all his churches
the Ministerium of Pennsylvania
the words of Melanchthon as applicable to the Book of Concord

I. WORKS

Hallesche Nachrichten von den vereinigten Deutschen Evangelisch-Lutherischen Gemeinen in Nord America. Mann-Schmucker-Germann, Allentown, 1886.——**Documentary History** of the Evangelical Lutheran Ministerium of Pennsylvania and Adjacent States. 1748 to 1821. Board of Publication of the General Council of the Evangelical Lutheran Church in North America. Philadelphia, 1898.——**Nicum,** Geschichte des New York's Ministerium. Reading, Pa., 1888.——**Schmauk,** History of the Lutheran Church in Pennsylvania. General Council Board of Publication. Philadelphia. I, 1903.——**Bernheim,** History of the German Settlements and of the Lutheran Church in North and South Carolina. Philadelphia, the Lutheran Book Store, 1872.——**Mann,** Life and Times of Henry Melchior Mühlenberg, Philadelphia, 1887.——**Schmucker,** B. M., The Organization of the Congregation in the Early Lutheran Churches in America. Luth. Ch. Rev. 1887. VI. 188.——**Wolf,** The Lutherans in America. New York, 1889.——**Nicum,** Die Lutheraner in America. New York, 1891.——**Nicum,** Confessional History of the Lutheran Church in the United States in Pro. of Amer. Soc. of Ch. Hist., Dec., 1891. New York, 1892.——**Gräbner,** Geschichte der Lutherischen Kirche in America. I. St. Louis, 1892.——**Jacobs,** History of the Lutheran Church in the United States. Christian Literature Co., 1893.——**Loy-Valentine-Fritschel-Jacobs-Pieper-Horn,** Distinctive Doctrines, 1893.——**Morris,** Sources of Information on the History of the Lutheran Church in America. 1895.——**Fritschel,** G. J., Geschichte der Lutherischen Kirche in Amerika. Gütersloh, 1896.——**Ochsenford, Krotel, Spaeth, Jacobs,** In Commemoration of the 150th Anniversary of the Ministerium of Pennsylvania, 1748-1898. [Reprint from Lutheran Church Review, January and April, 1898.]——**Jacobs-Haas,** The Lutheran Cyclopedia, New York, 1899.——**Spaeth,** in Herzog-Hauck Realencyklopädie: Die lutherische Kirche, in article Nordamerika, 1903. Also New Schaff-Herzog, 1910. VII.——**Neve-Stump,** Brief History of the Lutheran Church in America. Burlington, 1904.——**Spaeth,** Charles Porterfield Krauth, 1898-1909. I 330-413. II. 1-246.——**Richard,** J. W., The Confessional History of the Lutheran Church. Philadelphia, 1909.

II. ARTICLES IN PERIODICALS AND SPECIAL WORKS

1833.

Kurtz   The Lutheran Observer.

1842.

Greenwald }
Loy 1864 } The Lutheran Standard.

1843.

Walther   Der Lutheraner.
"   Lehre und Wehre.

1847.

Brobst   Der Jugend-Freund.

1849.

The Evangelical Review. I-XXI. Gettysburg, 1849-1870.

Krauth, C. P., Schmid's Dogmatik. I. 119.——**Thomasius,** trans. by C. P. Krauth, Sr., The Principle of Protestantism. I. 199; II. 215-236.——**Krauth,** C. P., The Relation of Our Confessions to the Ref., with An Outline of the Early His. of the Augs. Confession. I. 234.

1834-1870.

Schmucker, S. S. Elements of Popular Theology, Andover, 1834, 9th ed. 1860; Fraternal Appeal to the American Churches on Christian Union, New York, 1838; The American Lutheran Church, historically, doctrinally and practically delineated, Phila., 1851; The Lutheran Manual on Scriptural Principles, or The Augsburg Confession illustrated and sustained by Scripture and Lutheran Theologians, Phila., 1855; The Lutheran Symbols, or Vindication of American Lutheranism, Baltimore, 1856; The Church of the Redeemer as developed within the General Synod of the Evangelical Lutheran Church, Baltimore, 1867; True Unity of Christ's Church, New York, 1870.

1850.

May 27, 1850. T h e **Pennsylvania Ministerium** renews its adherence to the Symbolical Books. v. **Proceedings** of Ministerium in Pottsville, p. 12: "The Conference desired that the Synod should give an expression of opinion in regard to the Symbolical Books, and especially with reference to the Unaltered Augsburg Confession. This opened a wide field for discussion. A number of the brethren embraced this opportunity of expressing their opinions upon this subject. All spoke freely, and after the matter had been discussed for some time in a kind and harmonious spirit, the following resolution was unanimously adopted:

"**Resolved,** That, like our fathers, we regard ourselves as a part of the one and only Evangelical Lutheran Church, that we too acknowledge the Word of God as contained in the Holy Scriptures as the only ground of our faith, and that we too have never renounced the Confessions of our Church, but continue to regard them as a faithful exposition of the Divine Word."

Schaeffer, C. F., Symbolic Theology. Ev. Rev. I. 457-483.——**Krauth, C. P.,** Sr., The Lutheran Church in the United States. II. 1-16.——**Schaeffer, C. F.,** Symbolic Theology. II. 36-57.——**Krauth,** C. P., Translation of The Articles of Torgau. II. 78-84.——**Hoffman,** J. N, The Ev. Lutheran Church. Her Wrongs and Difficulties. Designed to Meet the Antagonistic Tendency of Our Age and Country. II. 265-281.

CONTENTS

CONTENTS

CONTENTS

CONTENTS

CONTENTS

CONTENTS

III. OTHER PERIODICALS

CHAPTER **XXXIX.**

THE CONFESSIONAL PRINCIPLE OF THE BOOK OF CONCORD AND AMERICAN PROTESTANTISM.

the sources of spiritual Authority—Scripture, Reason, Church.
the relation of Spiritual Forces
the Confessional principle a Balance
the Confessional principle and Liberality
is the Confessional principle accepted in all parts of the Lutheran Church
is the confessional principle of the Unaltered Augsburg Confession that of the Book of Concord
what an ex animo confession of the Unaltered Augsburg Confession Involves
v. Literature under Chapter V., I. . . . . p. 874

CHAPTER **XL.**

THE CONFESSIONAL PRINCIPLE OF THE BOOK OF CONCORD AND CHRISTIAN CO-OPERATION.

co-operation in the view of the Lutheran Reformers
co-operation today
the Sphere of the Church in Civil Reform
the Dangers in co-operation
the True Confessional principle in co-operation
The confessional principle and Those Outside the Lutheran Church
the confessional principle and Christian Fellowship
the confessional principle of Concordia and Christian Union

Chapter XLI.

THE CONFESSIONAL PRINCIPLE OF THE BOOK OF CONCORD AND THE BROTHERHOOD OF THE CHRISTIAN CHURCH.

Conscience, Principle and Charity in the Church
tolerance in the Church
the question of the Majority in Protestantism
the question of a Visible Unity in Protestantism
confessional attitude of Lutherans revealed by Attitude toward Denominational Protestantism

Chapter XLII.

THE CONFESSIONAL PRINCIPLE OF THE BOOK OF CONCORD AND THE FUTURE OF THE CHURCH IN AMERICA.

the Field of the Confessional Principle in America. Its sub-stance is to penetrate and control every department of life.
the three separate spheres of Faith, Love and Law; and the three separate institutions of Church, Home, and State, not properly distinguished by Radical and Reformed Protest-antism
the Lutheran solution of Religious Problems in America
some Reformed results
some Lutheran results
the confessional principle no hindrance to the Future Church
it will Broaden the Church
a Recapitulation of the Argument of this Book
the Conclusion

CONTENTS

Historical Introduction

With Some Reference to Several Recent Works

THE Augsburg Confession is the Answer, at the dawn of modern history, of the Church's Faith to the world's Might. In form it is a secular instrument written by laymen, in consultation with the clergy, and offered by Princes, to the highest court of the realm. In essence it is the carrier and conservator of the convictions and conscience, under the direct touch of God's Word, of the unwillingly Protestant Church as to the True Faith and the True Ecclesiastical Practice of Christianity.

In response to the demand of the sovereign of Germany, the Netherlands, Austria, Italy, Spain, and the new world of America, at the moment when this sovereign,[1] in league with and under the direction of the head of the Church of Rome, was attempting to crush liberty of conscience and of worship, the Augsburg Confession became, by reason of its presentation in a due and legal manner at a specially called Diet of the Empire, the great historic appeal, declaration, and confession of the Evangelical Church, on behalf of conscience, truth, and religious liberty.

This answer, though occasional in origin, became a fixed point in history and permanently definitive of principle. It belongs to the family of charter-documents which, when they once receive the stamp of authority, as representing

---

[1] The Augsburg Confession begins as follows: "Most Invincible Emperor, Caesar Augustus, most Clement Lord: Inasmuch as Your Imperial Majesty has summoned a Diet of the Empire here at Augsburg. . . . And inasmuch as we, the undersigned Electors and Princes, with others joined with us, have been called to the aforesaid Diet, the same as the other Electors, Princes and Estates, in obedient compliance with the Imperial mandate we have come to Augsburg." . . .

Weber had the original Call of Charles V., written at Bologna, Jan. 26th, 1530, in his hands, when writing his book in 1783.

the activities of a movement, definitely define, and form the basis of the principles of that movement. It pertains to the essence of their validity that they are unalterable, except at rare intervals and upon occasions at least as representative and formal as those which gave birth to the instrument. In becoming an unalterable basal instrument, their character is not always immediately perceived by those who originated them. This was the case with the Scriptures themselves, and it has been so with many other historical documents. So long as the Living Witness to the principles is present, so long the written testimony may appear to be secondary, and its all-time value may not be discernible. But after the Living Voice has disappeared, and new generations arise, it becomes the one authoritative and unalterable basis of future interpretation. This is a fundamental fact, and it is particularly important in the case of the Augsburg Confession in view of many statements to the contrary by a recent writer on the confessional history of the Lutheran Church, e. g.:

Some Recent Utterances

"Melanchthon changed the Augsburg Confession. Luther approved the changes."—*The Confessional History of the Lutheran Church*, p. 306.

"This formula . . . was not meant to make the impression on the subscriber that he must regard the Confession as an unchangeable norm of doctrine."—*Ib*. p. 284.

"Even the Princes who had subscribed the Augsburg Confession . . . gave their theologians instruction to examine the Confession again in the light of the Scriptures, and to change it. . . . The occasional obligation of men to the Confession and to the Apology arose from diverse considerations and from accident—not from a deliberate and united purpose to bind men to those documents as symbols of the Lutheran faith."—*Ib*. p. 289.

"In all these Church Orders, which appeared before the Religious Peace (of Augsburg, 1555), there is nowhere an unconditioned binding to the Augsburg Confession or to any other symbolical book, but only the requirement that the preachers shall preach the pure Gospel of Christ according to its pure intent, and free from human opinions."—*Ib*. p. 287.

"They hold that it is *defective*."—*Ib*. p. 97.

"There is misrepresentation [in the Confession] if we take into consideration the *compass* of the teaching."—*Ib*. p. 98.

"We cannot hold that the statement made at the close of Article XXI, viz., that the doctrinal articles constitute about the sum of the doctrine taught . . . is correct."—*Ib.* p. 98.

"Melanchthon did not regard the Confession as the Protestant *ultimatum*" (p. 199).

Taken in connection with the following on Luther:

"The evidence is conclusive that he did not regard it as a law for the conscience, and that he did not think that it had spoken the last word on any article of the Christian faith, and that he did not think of binding himself to the letter or to the form of the Confession. Otherwise he would not have accepted Melanchthon's printed editions of the Confession—all of them *variatae*—and would not have counselled the revision of 1540 and would not have approved it and called it 'the dear Confession.' "— *Ib.* p. 207.[2]

"There is no such document in use, nor even known to exist, as the *original and unaltered* Augsburg Confession."—*Ib.* p. 210.

"Any . . . application of them [the words 'original' and 'unaltered'] to any *printed edition* of the Confession, is a *falsification of fact and of history*, since every known printed edition of the Augsburg Confession is known to be, and can be shown to be, MATERIALLY different from the Augsburg Confession as it was officially read and delivered, June 25, 1530." [The italics, etc., are those of the author of "*The Confessional History of the Lutheran Church.*"]—*Ib.* p. 210.

"There is no such document in ecclesiastical use today, and never has been as '*that first and unaltered Augsburg Confession,*' . . . hence it is not only invidious, but it is untrue, as a matter of fact, when any ecclesiastical body says: 'We accept the Unaltered Augsburg Confession.' "— *Ib.* p. 211.[3]

In many of these statements there is a truth. They may state a fact, but err in the inference which they desire the reader to draw from it. Or they may state a fact without regard to the real significance of its inner bearing. Or they confuse the relations of letter and spirit, form and substance, external legal pledge and hearty voluntary attestation.

---

[2] But comp. Luther, 1533 in his letter of warning to the Franckfurters: "Es ist nun für alle Welt kommen die herrliche Confession und Apologia, so für Käys. Majt. zu Augspurg von vielen der höhesten Stände des R. Reichs frey bekant und erhalten, darinn auch die Papisten, ob sie uns wol über alle massen gefährliche Sünden, dennoch keinen Schwermer-Articul uns können Schuldgeben. Wir haben nicht Mum Mum gesagt, und unter den Hütlein gespielet, sondern da stehet unser helle, dürr, frey Wort ohn alles tunckeln und mausen."—Luther in Warnungs-Schrift an die zu Franckfurt am Mayn, 1533. Tom VI. Jen. Germ. p. 113. Carpzov. *Isag.* p. 99.

[3] *Cp.* Statement in *The Lutheran*, March 12, 1908, p. 419, "The specification of the word 'Unaltered' or 'Invariata' is a mere quibble."

1

The believer who is neither a literalist on the one hand, nor open to constant changes in the supposed interests of progress on the other, finds little consideration in this volume. The test applied to confessions, confessors, and synodical bodies, is in accord with the spirit of the Melanchthonian doctrine, and after the manner of Weber. It respects the precise external obligation, rather than the living spirit and fountain of faith within, which confesses voluntarily and heartily, and not under compulsion. The charge of deficiency, incompleteness, and misrepresentation, urged against the Augsburg Confession as a whole might perhaps not be inapplicable, in such aspect, to this book itself, in its total outcome.

Confessions Unalterable

"Each symbol," says Philip Schaff,[4] "bears the impress of its age, and the historical situation out of which it arose." In truly reflecting that situation, it cannot always also fully explicate the absolute and unrelated force of its principles. It is true absolutely in its own situation, just as its principle is true absolutely in every other situation to which it is legitimately applied. Every true Confession, like every genuine book of Scripture, rises in its principle beyond the local situation in which it took its first origin, though it also reflects the particular horizon of its own time period. It responds in the form of its immediate environment to the inquirings that have compelled it to speak, and its response is a true note struck, no less on the relative scale of time, than on the timeless scale of unchangeable value.

Every true Confession is an answer. It is neither a manifesto nor an ordinance. It is the public and common answer of the flock of Christ to the inquiries which have been put to it and pressed upon it by the spirit of a particular age. The answer is the truth of Scripture living in the witness, and applied, not under a Divine Inspiration, but under the ordinary laws of Providence to the particular questions it is intended to meet. The framework of the answer is that of the age which has asked the question, and of the history in which the witness lives, and some of it will pass away; but the truth of the answer, in all its clear-cut sharpness, and without one iota of deviation or

---

[4] *Creeds of Christendom,* p. 4.

compromise, will abide forever. For the framework in the answer is under the ordinary laws of Providence, but the truth in the answer, that is the Confessional Principle itself, is none other than the inspired word of God.

To claim that the earthly framework, which fits it in as the answer of an earthly query put by a passing age of history to the Church, is inspired, or is binding, is contrary to Scripture, and to the laws of Providence. But to claim that the declaratory doctrine, or truth, or teaching of the Confession, which is a hearty and well-established reflection in the confessor, of the pure truth of God's Word, is open to interpretation or to individual judgment, or to ambiguous explanation, or is only substantially correct, or is a *quatenus* rather than a *quia* declaration of the confessor, is to render the Confession valueless for the purpose for which it exists.[5]

The sound Confessional Principle, like every other principle, is a golden and substantial mean, which has to contend with two extravagant extremes. The one extreme is *the evaluation* of its confessional content by the use of private judgment and mental reservation. The other extreme is *the externalization* of the Confession into a mechanical literalism which then becomes chiefly a law and a pledge for subscription. Each of the two extremes is destructive of the true intent of a Confession. Where a Confession ceases to be a conviction chiefly, and becomes a law chiefly, it is a failure. The principle of the Confession is always the principle of the Gospel, namely Testimony, and the object of Testimony is neither Enforcement nor Evasion, but is Teaching and Conviction. To these the external Law of Testimony, where it is necessary, is subsidiary.

This presupposition as to the true nature of the Confessional Principle is fundamental, and lies back of any proper interpretation of the Scripture and the Confessions. It commits the confessor to the whole Confes-

---

[5] "It is an astonishing phenomenon in a Church calling itself Evangelical Lutheran, that there should be so much liberty allowed where the New Testament allows none,—we mean in Articles of Faith, and so little where the New Testament allows all liberty, we mean in things indifferent."—C. P. Krauth, Spaeth's *Life of Krauth*, II, p. 19.

sion, words, history, and truth, and to the acceptation of every statement,[6] whether of doctrine or fact, "in its own true, native, original and only sense, so that those who confess must not only agree to use the same words, but use and understand those words in one and the same sense"; but it places that which is local, earthly, and historical, and pertains to the generation from which the Confession emanated, under the ordinary laws of Providence, Who is always guiding the affairs of the Church and world, and who permits men and churches to remain fallible; and not under the extraordinary laws of Inspiration of the Holy Ghost, Who spake His Word in times long past unto the fathers by the prophets and the apostles.[7]

---

[6] *Cp.* "The Confessional Subscription," *The Lutheran*, March 5, 1908, p. 403; and Feb. 20, 1908, p. 391, and "Confessional Subscription," *Lutheran World*, March 24, 1908.

[7] The distinction between "Articles of Faith" and ordinary statements of fact, in a Confession, is historical in our Church, and was elaborated in America, in an article on "Symbolic Theology" by C. F. Schaeffer (*Evangelical Review*, April, 1850, pp. 457-483). Among other things Prof. Schaeffer says:
"If our symbolical books were set forth in the form of the three ancient symbols, presenting barely a rigid doctrinal text, *and nothing else,* we would, on assuming the whole as our creed, assume also all the details. But they present a wide range of subjects, communicate doctrinal truth, interpret Scripture passages, quote ancient authors, introduce controversial discussions, relate historical events, refer largely to persons and things whose importance diminishes in the course of time, until it fades entirely away, and are as miscellaneous in their character as various books of the Bible. The latter, Paul's Epistles for instance, by no means intend to be simply creeds, in the technical sense of the word, but also design to notice passing events as well as to teach eternal truth, and we interpret the symb. books precisely as we interpret the Bible itself. It is a canon universally recognized by all sound interpreters, that the principles of interpretation are common to the Scriptures and to uninspired compositions, and hence the same general rules are applicable to the symb. books which guide the expounder of the Bible. We regard the Scriptures as our sole rule of faith and practice, but not as a textbook for scientific lectures, nor as a volume of the 'Universal History.' Thus, too, we regard the symb. books as the expression of our faith, but not as our Commentary on the Scriptures. If Paul quotes a harsh but well-deserved description of the Cretians by the poet Epimenides, whom he calls a 'prophet,' (Titus 1:12), and if Peter (2 Peter 2:22) is equally plain in his strictures on the unfaithful, the *force* of their language does not detract from its truth. The 'cloak, books and parchments' of St. Paul, and 'Alexander the coppersmith,' (2 Tim. 4:13, 14) may be mentioned in an apostolic letter as really existing, without assuming the rank of articles of faith. The oration of Tertullus is introduced into a canonical book (Acts ch. 24) without securing our approbation of its denunciations of St. Paul; the discourse even of Gamaliel, a 'doctor of the law had in reputation,' (Acts, ch. 5) is characterized only by good sense but not by inspiration; and, in this manner, large portions of the contents of the Scriptures are separated from the creed of every sincere Christian, *as they were not intended by the sacred writers to constitute articles of faith*, but were necessarily introduced in writings, which, besides conveying doctrinal truth, and precepts of morality, were designed to refer to persons and things of a local and temporary character.
"The interpretation of the Scriptures is materially influenced by the interpreter's theory of inspiration; the strictest views and most orthodox senti-

Adherence to Confessions

The day for party adherence to a Church's Confessional Answer is gone; but the day for precise expression of intelligent and common conviction of faith, and for loyal adherence to it, will never go. The Church must be prepared to answer as to her Faith. Like the Word of God, her Answer may contain that on which the believer is not competent to use his judgment, but what he does apprehend will enable him not to stumble at historical, or critical difficulties in which the spiritual treasures of all ages may have been enveloped by past generations. And the victories of a historical Answer, whose fruits are being enjoyed today, will awaken in us the love and the loyalty which the Answer deserves.

If Christianity is to make a *fixed* and *steady* Answer to God's Word, and if the Christian Church is to teach the unchanging truth of that Word, Creeds are a necessity. Creeds are the Faith in fixed form, and go back as far as the Scripture.

"In fact," says Prof. Schodde, "there was a creed before there were New Testament writings, in the Baptismal Formula of Christ Himself (Matt. 28:19), which formed the historical and doctrinal basis of the Apostles' and later formulas of faith. That the existence of such faith is presup-

ments, however, on this subject, are perfectly consistent with the following passage: 'In I Cor. 7 :6, 10, 12, 25, 40,' says Olshausen on I Corinth. 7. p. 563, 'we find that the apostle distinguishes between *his own* and the *Lord's* declarations, between a positive command of Christ, and his own subjective opinion or judgment. . . . Although it is clear from verse 40, that this is not designed to be placed in opposition to inspiration, since it truly proceeded from the Holy Ghost, ... still it is plain that Paul makes this distinction for the purpose of intimating, that Christ's command indeed, but not his own judgment, must be unconditionally fulfilled ; even when his counsels are not followed, (according to verse 36) sin is not necessarily thereby committed . . . . . Where doctrines or positive commands are concerned, Paul insists on his apostolic authority, his judgment is precisely on this account decisive, because it is enlightened by the Divine Spirit. But in adiaphora or things indifferent, it is true wisdom to refrain from positive commands.' etc. This view of the orthodox commentator is established on the principle, that, while the declarations of the apostles are to be regarded as obligatory in matters of faith and practice, their private opinions, however worthy of respect, possess no absolute authority. In truth, this principle is practically adopted by all classes of Christians, for they have long ceased to observe several usages described in the Acts as established or sanctioned by the apostles, ('they had all things common,' Acts 2 :44 : 4 :32 : 'look ye out among you seven men,' etc. 6 :3) and yet subsequently abandoned without sin."

posed by such writings, is apparent from II Tim. 13 : 14 ; II Tim. 6 : 20 ;
Heb. 6 : 1 sq."

A Confession is an acknowledgment by the Church of what the Scripture has brought to her. A fixed Confessional Principle, drawn from Scripture, as the essence of the Church's Testimony, whether it proceed[8] from
the general life of the Church, without an individual authorship, as the
Apostles' Creed, or be promulgated by the Councils of the Church such as
the Nicene Creed, or be the work of one or several writers acting under
the sanction of the Church, as were the Lutheran Confessions, is a necessity.

The Confession of Christianity, the Confession of the
Christian Faith, the Confession of the Evangelical Lutheran Faith, is not an idea in the mind of man. It is a fixed
fact. It is a recognition of God's reality as revealed in His
Word. Its principle never varies, no matter in how many
different confessional writings it may be embodied. It
continues as the steady line of truth through all generations. The Lutheran Confession is unchangeable. "The
Church may add a fuller expression of its doctrines, but
she cannot change them."[9]

Our Confession is our well-known and long-published
conviction of the entire Teaching of the Word of God. It
is not an assemblage of doctrines, but an unchanging entity. Hence we cannot adjust it in order to unite with
other Christians. Nor can we assume a common religious
experience for all evangelical Christians, from which we
are merely differentiated by peculiarities.

"We cannot begin where other denominations leave off. We have to
grow our experience from the beginning, and the root of all progress . . .
is the sense of necessity."[10] An anonymous writer in a remarkable article
on Justification by Faith, in the *Evangelical Review* in the year 1859,[11]
explains this point as follows :

"The Reformed theology . . . not only diverges from the Lutheran in
single points, which are commonly termed the distinctive doctrines of the
Lutheran Church, but it is an essentially different system from beginning
to end. Doctrines which are apparently identical with our own, if viewed
simply by themselves, are found to assume quite another shape, when
looked upon from the Reformed standpoint. . . . In the Calvinistic, as

---

[8] Prof. Schodde.
[9] Spaeth, *Life of Krauth,* p. 101.
[10] *Ib.* p. 43.
[11] pp. 225-256. *Extract* on pp. 231-237.

well as all Calvinizing theologians, the doctrine of justification by faith
is stripped of its practical, paramount import. It is a mere accessory. . . .

"Redemption is made to be a plan or device over which God presides
precisely as the mind of man may be said to rule a machine, and Christ
comes in simply in the way of outward instrumental help to carry 'out
the scheme. . . .

"Throughout the Protestant world, we have only two *radically* different
theories—the Lutheran, which places itself on Divine grace in the form
of Christian life; and the Reformed, which is also based *confessedly* on
grace, but in the *form of thought*. . . .

"The sacramental doctrines and christology of Luther were no outward
fungus upon his system. They lie imbedded in its inmost life. To part
with them is to surrender the cause of the Reformation itself, as Luther
had it in his mind, and to rob his creed of its original physiognomy, life
and heart."

As to the inner constraint which a confession of the
Confessions may exercise upon the thinking mind, it is
sufficient to quote the words of W. J. Mann:

"No one should receive the Lutheran confession on the
authority of another, but find it again and again, as a result of his own investigations, in the sacred Scriptures.
He will then not be in danger of lifeless orthodoxy, but
heartily rejoice at the enlightened understanding with
which his Church has been favored, and gladly proclaim
her doctrines."[12]

Subscription to Confession

As to the *binding subscription* of a minister or Church,
this is not a matter of Confession, but of Church Order.
The first Verpflichtungsformel was drawn up *before the
Lutheran Church possessed its Confession.*

In December, 1529, by Henry Winckel, a quiet and faithful minister,
who expressed the feelings of all north Germany in desiring to protect the
Church against the teachings of Zwingli. It contained a vow of ordination pledging those ordained to the Bible and Luther's writings. The
Wittenberg Verpflichtung of Melanchthon of 1533 came into general use.
Osiander combated it vigorously in 1552 in language similar to what is
heard today: "Not a word is said of the Holy Scripture, given by God.
. . . What other result can such an oath have than to tear away from
the Holy Scripture those who swear to it, and bind them to the Symbols
and the doctrine of Philip!" A graduate of Wittenberg is represented

---

[12] Mann, *Lutheranism in America*, 1857. p. 76.

by Osiander as "a poor fellow tied up with obligations to an oath that strangles and confuses his conscience, for he has sworn away God's Word, and sworn himself to Philip's doctrine."[13]

In defense, Melanchthon speaks of fanatics then arising and who *in all ages* will be spreading false doctrine. The obligation is honorable in purpose, and not at all a "tyranny"; for the promise is of no further import than a repeating of the Augsburg Confession. This is necessary in order that the true Church may be distinguished. The Symbols are the boundary-line markers, beyond which one dare not go without danger, to which Tschackert remarks that this is "a theological judgment, worthy of being respected for all ages." The obligation of a candidate not to go ahead in theological controversy on his own accord, but first to consult some of the older teachers, Melanchthon explains as follows: "Unus vir non videt omnia"; and "Nolumus audacia et authadeiâ juniorum deleri ecclesiae judicia." Tschackert remarks, "That was reason enough. The whole address is a standing proof of Melanchthon's genuine churchly thoughtfulness." (p. 380.)[14]

But the real substance of the Church's objection to individual freedom of teaching goes deeper. The Lutheran Church has the Word and the Sacrament, and the Office for their administration. The thing taught is not truths and opinions of scholars, but the well-established and universally confessed Word. The person teaching is not of importance in himself, but his personal mind and view are submerged in the Office. The person holds the Office only as he proclaims and applies that which the Church confesses as the Word. He is bound to this, not chiefly by a subscription, but in the nature of the case. To maintain the doctrine of personal freedom of teaching in Church and school, really denies the Lutheran doctrine of the Office, the Word, and the Church.

Luther himself speaks strongly against concession to individual opinions, e. g.: "He who holds his teaching, faith and confession to be true, cannot stand in the same stall with those who teach false doctrine or are inclined thereto. A teacher who is silent against error and still professes to be a true teacher, is worse than an open fanatic, doing more harm.

---

[13] *V. Tschackert,* pp. 378, 379.

[14] Compare G. Rietschel, *Luther und die Ordination.* 2 Aufl. 1889.—W. Köhler, *Reformation und Ketzerprozess* 1901.—P. Drews, *Die Ordination, Prüfung und Lehrverpflichtung der Ordinanden in Wittenberg* 1535. Giessen 1904.

. . . He would not offend anybody—not proclaim the Word for Christ, nor pain the devil and the world."[15]

"It is an awful thing to me to hear that both parties approach and receive the sacrament in one and the same church and at one and the same altar, and that the one party is to believe that it receives nothing but bread and wine, and the other is to believe that it receives the true body and blood of Christ. I often doubt if it is to be believed that a pastor could be so hardened and malicious as to keep silent and permit both parties to go, each according to its opinion that they all receive the same sacrament, but each party according to its faith."[16]

Evolution of the Augsburg Confession

In the Augsburg Confession, *the Renewed Church of Christ* in the German Reformation *confessed the real Gospel*, when formally called to account by the old world-order. The old world-order was the supreme authority in Church and State.

Luther as an individual had made bold answer to this authority as early as 1521. For one decade the question in Europe was whether and how the liberty-answer of Luther should become the answer of an Evangelical Church, or whether and how the old world-order could throttle the new spirit in the Church. In 1526 the Evangelical or Luther-confession of Christianity in the Churches gained legal standing. At the Diet in 1529 the Emperor and the Roman Church succeeded by a majority vote in removing that legal standing, and in ordering all churches to return to the faith and practices of Rome.

On April 17th, 19th, 25th, 1529, the Evangelical minority protested, in legal form, against the decision at Spires, and appealed to the Emperor, to the next free General Council of Christendom, or to an Assembly of the German Nation. The Diet at Augsburg was the result of that appeal, and the Augsburg Confession proved to be the final and historical answer of Lutheranism, as to its own existence, and in contrast with a more radical Protestantism, and with heresies with which it was unwilling to be confused, to the Emperor and Rome.

The Evangelical Princes left the Diet of Spires with the threat of extermination hanging over their heads. No one knew what would happen

---

[15] *Walch,* XVII, p. 1477.
[16] *Ib.* p. 2446.

after the Emperor had received, read, and determined his action on the protest and appeal of the Protestants.

The Protestants were united among themselves only as to protest. It is true that the Elector of Saxony and the Landgrave of Hesse had made an alliance on the basis of Torgau 1526, and Magdeburg, at the Diet of Spires, together with the cities of Nuremberg, Ulm, and Strasburg, for defense against attack, or against interference in the spiritual supervision of the Churches; but this alliance was made hurriedly, and the Elector and Melanchthon returned from the Diet greatly worried concerning it. No details had been considered, but delegates were to meet at Rotach in June and adopt terms of agreement. Yet how could a Protestantism agree in action, when its only ultimate source of unity was the negative one of protest?

From the fountainhead, Protestantism was *divided*. There was an irresponsible revolutionary wing, which already had grasped the sword, and which the Elector and Luther had disclaimed. There was a radical wing, with Zwingli at its head, which was rationalistic and looked to reason as much as to the Gospel for authority, and was eager to carry the religious difficulty into politics. And there was the conservative or Lutheran wing which desired to remain obedient in all things, (but with freedom and a good conscience as to the Gospel,) to the existing civil constitution.

It was the life aim of one lay Lutheran leader of magnificent executive ability, but of defective fundamental principle, Philip of Hesse, to unite these wings and make them parties in a common cause which he foresaw would soon come to a clash with the Pope and the Emperor. He therefore, already in the spring of 1529, attempted to get the spiritual leaders of the Protestant cause to his castle at Marburg in order that they might settle their religious differences and enter into a Protestant Federation against the forces of the Pope and Emperor; but by this time the Elector's leaders had discovered that the Protestant agreement entered into hurriedly at Spires also contemplated a political alliance against the Emperor.

Melanchthon, who had borne the brunt of the protest at Spires, was very much opposed to such a colloquy at Marburg, and during the month of May both he (11th) and Luther (22d) warned the Elector against it. The Elector in his anxiety did not go to Rotach, but sent Hans von Minkwitz with instructions to agree only to an alliance in defence of Articles of Faith to be decided on at a future meeting. Nuremberg, and the Margrave, took the same position. On June 28th Luther again expressed himself against the Federation.

One day later, on the 29th of June, the peace of Barcelona was concluded between the Emperor and the Pope, who hitherto had not been at one for political reasons, and among the items of agreement was one in which the Emperor promised *to root out the Lutheran doctrine.*

During the month of July (12th), Charles accordingly sent out a warning to the Estates, and on the 9th of August he landed at Genoa from Spain, for the purpose of being crowned by the Pope, of entering into a further understanding with him, of stamping differences out of the Church, and of firmly uniting both the Empire and the Church.

Meantime the convention met at Rotach and issued such an unsatisfactory Confederation-Notel, that Philip of Hesse came all the way to Wittenberg on July 1st to arrange for the colloquy at Marburg. On July 8th a meeting of the representatives of the Elector, the Margrave, and Philip, was held at Saalfeld, but as neither the Elector nor the Margrave were willing to include the radical Protestants of Strasburg and the Swiss cities in the alliance, no result was attained.

It recently has been supposed that from the middle of July to the middle of September articles for the alliance of the Princes were being gradually formulated in order to be ready for the coming convention at Schleiz, and that these articles, completed before the Marburg Colloquy, are the articles carried to Schwabach and presented there on the 18th of October (von Schubert in *Zeitschrift für Kirchengeschichte,* XXIX. Band, 3. Heft, p. 377. See also J. J. Müller, *Historie,* pp. 280 et seqq.;)[17] but we have

---

[17] *The Confessional History* says (p. 22), •The Schwabach Articles are utterly incompatible with the frame of mind which both Luther and Melanchthon brought with them from Marburg, unless we are willing to conclude that both are doublefaced." Yet on October 4th' Luther wrote to his wife, "We do not want the 'brethren and members' business;'" and on October 12th he wrote to Agricola, "They requested that we should at least regard them as brethren; but it was not possible to consent to it. Nevertheless we did extend to them the hand of peace and love, that now bitter writings and words may cease, and every one may hold his faith without hostile assaults, yet not without defence and confutation. Thus we parted." Melanchthon in a postscript to the same letter calls the whole matter a farce.

There was nothing in the psychological temper of these men in those October days to prevent them from honestly composing the Schwabach Articles.

not found the reasons urged for this transfer of the composition of the Schwabach Articles to the early date conclusive.[18]

During the month of September the deputies, sent earlier by those protesting at the Diet of Spires, found the Emperor, and were received ungraciously, and on the 12th of October the Emperor replied to them that the minority must submit to the Decree of Spires, and that means would be found to compel the Elector of Saxony and the others to bow to the inevitable. Hence, on October 14th, came the appeal of the Protestant Estates to a Christian Council.

Meantime Philip had succeeded in getting the two wings of Protestantism together at Marburg on the first four days of October, but without an agreement, and the Marburg Articles had been drawn up (4th). Luther went from Marburg to Schleiz, whither the Elector had summoned him as well as Melanchthon and Jonas, in order to deliberate on the organizing of an alliance embracing those Protestants alone who were in the full unity of the Lutheran faith. On October 16th the Estates met again, and the Elector proposed to them the Schwabach Articles that probably had been written by Luther,[19] at the request of the Elector, perhaps at Schleiz; and the imperial cities Strasburg and Ulm declined to sign them.

---

[18] V. T. E. Schmauk in *Lutheran Church Review*, XXVIII, p. 278, *Is There Any New Light Concerning the Schwabach Articles?*

[19] The "Articles of the Elector of Saxony touching the faith," prepared by Luther at the Elector's request, and laid before the Assembly of the States at *Schwabach.*"—Krauth, *Chronicle of the Augsburg Confession*, p. 12. "*The Confessional History*," p. 29, quotes Luther's Preface written against the Hans Bern edition, as follows: "It is true that I helped to compose such articles, for they were not composed by me alone." "*The Confessional History*" quotes from the declaration at Schmalkald, Dec. 1529, that "the articles of faith were very carefully considered, and were composed with the wise counsel of learned and unlearned counsellors," and concludes from this, "Hence there can be no doubt that the hand of Melanchthon was quite as active in composing those articles as was the hand of Luther." Vid. also "*The Confessional History*," pp. 9, 21, 61-62, 68; but "*The Confessional History's*" conclusions as to these Articles are overdrawn. The Elector himself had part in them. Vid. also Kolde, *Augsburg Konfession*, p. 119 ff., and v. Schubert, *Beiträge zur Geschichte der evang. Bekenntnis- u. Bündnisbildung,* 1529-30: Zeit. Kirch. Gesch. XXIX, 3 (1908), and f.; Tschackert, *Die Entstehung der luth. u. d. reformierten Kirchenlehre*, 1910, p. 281, simply says, "The 17 Schwabach Articles contain the chief articles of Lutheran doctrine cut clear and sharp."

For Luther's copy of the Schwabach Articles *v. Erl.* 24. 334 sq. For Ulm **Ms. *v.* Weber I, Appendix. For Strasburg copy *v. Kolde, Augsb. Konf.* II. Beilage.**

On the 5th of November the Emperor entered Bologna and met the Pope. The Pope insisted on his stamping out the Protestants, but the imperial chancellor Mercurinus pled for a Christian Council. The Emperor was thus inclined, but the Pope would not hear to it.

By the end of November, word reached Germany that the Spires' deputies had been arrested and imprisoned. A convention of the Protestants was held at Schmalkald, and the three deputies, escaped from the Emperor, were present. The Lutherans still held to their two great principles, that there could be no agreement between contrary faiths, and no alliance between politics and religion; and decided that only those who signed the Schwabach Articles should meet at Nuremberg on the 6th of January.

On the 21st of January, the Emperor issued a Call, which summoned all the Estates to Augsburg, in words that seemed full of hope.

He desired to put an end to discord, to hear both sides of the case, and to decide according to that which was right. However, his entrance to Germany, where, during the early spring he held court at Innsbruck, gave the Catholic south German Estates, especially through the appearance of the theses of John Eck, an opportunity, eagerly fostered by the papal representatives, to prejudice the Emperor's mind against the Protestants, and to attempt to abort the holding of the Diet of Augsburg.

In March (11th), the Elector received the Emperor's Call.[20] He consulted with his Chancellor, Brück who suggested that a Confession be drawn, and that it be presented at the Diet.[21] The Elector determined to bring forward his

---

[20] "At the court of the Elector much was expected of this Diet, for it was considered to be a substitute for the Council hitherto wished for in vain. Therefore the Elector ordered the Wittenberg theologians to consult regarding all articles of controversy. . . . At the close of the Torgau Articles, it is referred to the Elector, that if any one still desires to know what is taught in his land, there are also articles of doctrine which he could deliver. As such articles of doctrine the Schwabach articles were extant. So the Elector already had two valuable prefatory labors that could be wrought out further according to need."—Tschackert, *Die Entstehung der lutherischen und der reformierten Kirchenlehre*, p. 282.

[21] *V. Brück's Letter to the Elector*, on this important subject. Brück said, "Inasmuch as the Imperial Rescript provides that the opinion and view of each one is to be heard, it would be a good thing for us to bring together systematically, in writing, the views maintained by our party, and to fortify them out of Holy Writ, so as to present them in writing, in case the preachers should not be admitted to participation in the transactions. This will facilitate business, and it will serve to remove misunderstanding to have such views and opinions presented."—*Förstemann*, I. p. 39.

side of the case at the Diet without alliance with any of the other Protestants.[22]

On March 14th he commanded his four theologians to prepare a paper on the Articles of Faith in dispute. On March 26, "The articles 'not to be yielded' are determined on."—Krauth, *Chronicle*, p. 13.

In the beginning of April (3d), his theologians left Wittenberg for the Electoral court at Torgau.[23] A fortnight later (15th), the Elector and his procession arrived at Coburg, after some days' stay at Weimar.

Easter (17th) was spent there, and a few days later (23d), in as much as the Elector could not secure a safe-conduct for Luther from the city of Augsburg, and not even from Nuremberg, Luther was taken to the castle at Coburg.[24] On the 30th the Elector received his safe-conduct into Augsburg.[25]

Early in May (2d), the Elector reached Augsburg,[26] and hearing of the great change of sentiment at the imperial court, due to the publication of Eck's theses, he sent[27] a

[22] *"The Confessional History"* is not correct in emphasizing, above all, the fact that "the Saxon Court at Torgau was fully possessed by the thought, desire and purpose of reconciliation with the Church," and that this "explains the conduct and the concessions of the entire electoral party in the negotiations subsequently made at Augsburg for the complete restoration of concord and unity." All this was only true of the period *before* the month of June, and true only upon the basal condition laid down by the Emperor himself that *both sides* would be *fairly heard,* and a right and just result would be arrived at. The theory of *"The Confessional History"* is disproved by the Elector's sturdy and continued refusal, at the very start, to give up preaching in Augsburg, and by all his action prior to the opening of and during the Diet.

[23] April 3. "Melanchthon begins to write the heads of doctrine to be presented at the Diet."—Krauth, *Chronicle of the Augsburg Confession,* p. 14.

[24] For reasons why Luther was left at Coburg, *cp.* *"The Confessional History"* pp. 37-39, in which the facts are well given, although the conclusion may not be entirely justifiable.

[25] The Safe-conduct says, "But we make an exception, if His Electoral Grace should have with him and bring hither any one who has broken the peace of His Imperial Majesty and of the Holy Empire, and become liable to penalty and punishment; to such an one we have no power to grant a safe-conduct." *Müller,* p. 454. *Förstemann,* I, pp. 160, 161, No. 61.

[26] "Here it was immediately learned that the Bavarian Dukes had commissioned the theological faculty at Ingolstadt to gather together all the heresies of Luther and to show how they might be refuted most effectively. Then came Eck's theses dedicated to the Emperor and the realm."—*Tschackert,* p. 283.

[27] On May 12th already, Campeggius sent a Despatch from Innsbruck to Rome, still preserved, which is translated by the author of *"The Confessional History"* as follows: "The Elector of Saxony has sent to the Emperor at Innsbruck a Declaration of his Faith, which, so far as I can learn, is entirely catholic at the beginning, but full of poison at the end." *v.* Brieger, *Kirchengeschichtliche Studien für Reuter,* 1887, p. 312. For an English translation of the Confession Sent to the Emperor, made from a copy secured by the author of *"The Confessional History,"* in 1900, from the secret archives of the Pope, and the copy itself, *v.* *Lutheran Quarterly,* July, 1901.

translation of the Schwabach Articles to the Emperor as his confession of faith, while Hans Bern created a sensation by printing these Articles as the coming Augsburg Confession.

A few days later (May 4th), Melanchthon informed Luther that he had made the Exordium[28] of the electoral Apology more elaborate, and, a few days later still, because of the slanders of Eck, he transformed the Apology into a Confession embracing nearly all the Articles of Faith. On the 11th this Confession was sent to Luther.[29] On the 12th Philip of Hesse arrived at Augsburg, soon to agitate for a Common Confession to include also the Zwinglians.

On the 15th the Nuremberg delegates came,[30] having a confession written by their preachers, with which Melanchthon was pleased. The next day they learned from the Elector that his Confession was ready, and had been sent to Luther.[31]

---

[28] Förstemann, *Urkundenbuch*, I, 68-84. Krauth, writing long prior to the discovery of the earliest known draft of the Confession by Kolde, maintains strenuously, in the interest of a completed confession sent to Luther on May 11th, that the exordium was not a mere preface, but probably a summary of doctrine. *Chronology of the Augsburg Confession*, pp. 17-19, 21. *The Conservative Reformation*, pp. 222, 223. See also the 'Preface' itself in this volume, pp. 251-259. See *"The Confessional History,"* pp. 50-53. *The Confessional History*, p. 73, says: "The discovery of the 'long and rhetorical Preface' has put to flight forever the figment that the 'Articles of Faith' constitute the Preface of which Melanchthon writes to Luther on the fourth of May," to which we may add that the discovery has also 'put to flight forever the figment' that the chief credit for the success of the Augsburg Confession as a statesmanlike document inheres in Melanchthon. It has shown *why* Melanchthon's long and elaborate effort had to be altogether discarded.

[29] Tschackert expresses his views as follows: "Melanchthon would indeed have wished that Luther had made a more thorough examination of the articles of faith (Vellem percurrisses, *Tschackert*, p. 283). What Luther sent to Melanchthon was doubtless the whole Augsburg Confession, as far as it was then complete, and probably both texts, the German and the Latin."

[30] *Strobel Miscellan.*, II. p. 22.

[31] On the following day, May 17th, Kress was told by Brück that the Elector "though he had been *first of all* ready with *his Counsel* concerning this Article" (of the faith), "and that consequently the same (Counsel) had been put into writing in German and Latin, yet that it had not yet been finally closed, and had been sent to Doctor Luther to examine, and that it was expected that it would be back from him tomorrow or the day after (May 17 or 18), and he (the Chancellor) did not doubt that when the aforesaid proposition (the Counsel) came, a copy of it would be given to us if we requested it." *Corp. Ref.*, II, No. 690.

The same day the Nuremberg delegates wrote again to Nuremberg, "His Electoral Grace would abide by the answer of the Chancellor of the previous

On the 22d Melanchthon was ready to send Luther the Confession a second time, with the changes.[32] On the 24th the Margrave George arrived, while Brück was working "vornen und hinten" on the Confession, which, it was then

evening, to wit: that as soon as the Counsel (Rathschlag) came back from Luther it should be furnished to us." In the same letter they mention that at the mandate of the Elector they then entered in the Counsel of the Nuremberg preachers.

By May 20th Melanchthon had examined it, and told the Nurembergers that it was almost the same in meaning as the electoral confession, but that the latter was milder.

[32] The position taken by Krauth, viz., that there were three separate sendings of the Augsburg Confession by Melanchthon to Luther, the first on May 11th, the second on May 22nd, and the third before it was delivered (between June 8th and 25th), has become historic in America. (*Conservative Reformation*, pp. 227-241). This position was taken in 1871. Unfortunately in *"The Conservative Reformation,"* on p. 234, Luther's letter of July 3rd to Melanchthon in which he says, "I yesterday re-read your Apology entire, with care, and it pleases me exceedingly," is printed as being of date of June 3rd, through a slip of the pen or a typographical error.

In 1877, Dr. Conrad (*"First Diet,"* p. 209) in an essay at the First Free Lutheran Diet in America, said that the Confession was sent to Luther "between the 25d of May and the 2d of June". This statement was based on the typographical error in the Conservative Reformation, and its correctness was called into question on the floor of the Diet. Dr. J. A. Brown (*"First Diet,"* p. 237) challenged proof of the fact. Dr. Krauth, in a note, added in answer to Dr. Brown's challenge, in the printed discussions of the Diet, defends the essential statement of the Conservative Reformation, namely, that the Augsburg Confession "was sent as nearly as possible in its complete shape to Luther for a third time, before it was delivered, and was approved by him in what may probably be called its final form." (*"First Diet,"* pp. 238-242).

The next year (August 1878), Dr. Krauth published *"A Chronicle of the Augsburg Confession"* (Philadelphia, J. Frederick Smith, Publisher, 1878), which he designed to be "supplementary, in some sense, to the 'Conservative Reformation', and to the Essays and Debates of the 'First Lutheran Diet', Philadelphia, 1877." Both in the *Conservative Reformation,* and in this *Chronicle* (pp. 26-31, 73-76), Dr. Krauth presents an exhaustive argument to show that Luther received Melanchthon's letter of May 22d, and that all contemporary and later historians regard this fact as proof that Luther received the Confession a second time on May 22d.

In support of Melanchthon's third sending of the Confession to Luther, prior to its delivery, Dr. Krauth quotes and analyzes Melanchthon's own description of the writing of the Augsburg Confession, made just prior to Melanchthon's death (*Chronicle of the Augsburg Confession,* pp. 54-61, 83-92); while Dr. Jacobs, in a separate essay entitled *"A Question of Latinity",* analyzes the meaning of the disputed phrases in Melanchthon's letter. This work reveals the intimate and minute acquaintance of Dr. Krauth with the formative stages of the Augsburg Confession. He thoroughly appreciated the fact that up to the second week in June, the Confession was a Saxon document, and he has examined every scrap of available evidence, in a masterly manner. But he never saw the draft of the Confession discovered by Kolde, which throws so much light on the nature of the "exordium" and on other important points.

said, was to be issued in German, Latin and French. On
the same day the Emperor sent an embassy commanding
the Elector to silence the preaching, but the Elector (31st)
replied that he cannot do without the Gospel. On the 28th
Brück and his lay counsellors were making changes in the
Confession so as to put it in such a form as would conform
with the Emperor's Call and other legal conditions so that
the Emperor and the Diet would not be able to ignore it.[33]
On the 29th the Landgrave made efforts to participate in
the Confession. On the 31st the Estates request the Emperor to hasten to Augsburg; and the Confession is communicated without Preface or Conclusion to the delegates
of Nuremberg.[34]

Early in June (3d), Duke George and Cochläus make
overtures to Melanchthon. On the next day (4th),
Melanchthon writes to the Archbishop of Maintz to see to
it that war does not arise. On the same day the imperial
chancellor dies, and two days later (6th), the Emperor
leaves Innsbruck for Augsburg.[35] On the next day (7th).
Luther's admonition to the clergy reaches Augsburg. A
day later Vogler points out that the Saxon Apology is only
in the name of the Elector,[36] and three days later the Landgrave opposes submitting the religious question to the
Diet, and again tries to secure confederation with the
Zwinglians. Three days later still (13th), Melanchthon
opposes the Landgrave's views and is willing to harmonize

---

[33] The Nuremberg Legates write, "The Chancellor of the Elector of Saxony
told us that the Counsellors and the learned men were holding daily sittings
on their Counsel in matters of faith, to make changes in it, and improve it,
to the intent that they might put it and present it in such form, that it could
not well be passed by ; so that a hearing of the matter must be accorded,
when they shall be ready with the Counsel. We shall apply again, that we
may send it to you."

[34] On June 3d the Nuremberg delegates received the Preface and sent the
Confession home with the remark, "An article or two are lacking at the end,
together with the Conclusion, at which the Saxon theologians are still
working."

[35] About this time Luther had received intelligence from Nuremberg "that
the Emperor is not coming to the Diet at all, and that the whole thing will
prove a failure." On the 5th he wrote to Linke, "I am sorry to hear that
there are doubts about the Diet," and gives as the reason why he does not
want so many visitors at Coburg that "it would offend the Prince."

[36] See also letter of the Nuremberg delegates to the Nuremberg Senate.
C. R. II, p. 715.

2

with Rome if five practical points are conceded. He writes
to Luther that the Emperor would make peace with the
Elector if the Elector kept free from alliances.

On the 15th the Emperor arrives in Augsburg, and interviews *the Protestants together* at night, after the ceremonies. On the same day the Elector *admits the other
Lutheran Estates* to the Confession. Next morning the
Protestants fail to participate in the procession of Corpus
Christi, while Melanchthon comes into touch with Schepper, the Emperor's Secretary. On the next day (17th) the
Elector and Princes give reasons to the Emperor why they
cannot stop the Protestant preaching. This creates a tur-
moil among the Princes, but on the 18th the Protestants
agree to stop preaching temporarily, if the Romanists do
likewise. On the 17th Valdés, the Spanish Secretary, who
has been interviewed by Melanchthon, brings Melanchthon's proposal to the Emperor, and on the next day Valdés, authorized by the Emperor and Campeggius, asked
Melanchthon to present the points of controversy in briefest form for private settlement.

On Sunday (19th), there is no preaching. The Nurembergers write that Melanchthon reports that the controversy may be narrowed down to a few points. On the 20th,
the Diet opens with the Elector bearing the sword before
the Emperor, and the Landgrave standing in the gallery.
On the 21st, Melanchthon's plan for settlement[37] is
broached to the Elector and is rejected, and the work of
revising and completing the Confession is hurriedly begun.
The next day (22d), the Emperor orders the Elector to
have his Confession ready by Friday. On the day following (23d), the Confession is finally read, the text fixed, and

---

[37] Krauth knew of the interview between Melanchthon and Valdés, but
clearly regards the initiative as having been taken by the Roman Secretary,
and obviously does not regard the proposition as a substitute for the Confession. After quoting what the Nuremberg legates wrote home on June 21st,
he says, "It is evident that the point involved in the conference between
Valdésius and Melanchthon was that of the abuses to be corrected, and not
the question of doctrine." *Chronicle of the Augsburg Confession*, pp. 44, 45.
Krauth's high estimate of Melanchthon and his loyalty to Philip are shown
here. But comp. Kolde, Tschackert and other recent writers. *"The Confessional History"* leaves this point an open question.

it is signed. On Friday (24th), the Protestants are
put off, and the Emperor attempts to suppress the Confession. On Saturday (25th), the Confession is presented
and read.

After the Delivery of the Confession

It is quite true that the Reformers at Augsburg strongly
desired peace, and not war, and that all the theologians
from Luther down considered it necessary to use every effort to avoid a breach with the Emperor. But a breach
with the Papacy or with the Church, for conscience' sake,
is not the same thing in their mind as a breach with the
Emperor. The desire of the reformers was to continue
in the old ecclesiastical order if possible, so long as the
pure preaching of the Word of God was permitted in their
dominions, and so long as their conscience was not injured
as to ecclesiastical abuses. It was a very difficult matter to
find and locate this exact point practically as a modus
vivendi, but, we believe that, if Melanchthon be an exception, at no time were there any of the leading reformers who were willing to give up the Word of God or to
wound their consciences in order that they might remain
within the pale of the Roman Church.

We cannot therefore help regarding, as a serious misrepresentation,
the statement that is made in "The Confessional History of the Lutheran
Church" (p. 140) in describing "the efforts at reconciliation" at Augsburg after the delivery of the Confession, as follows: "The Protestants
could not brook the idea of leaving the Catholic Church, nor the thought
of being thrust out of it. The Catholics knew full well what it meant to
the Catholic Church to have the Protestant Princes and their people
separated from that Church. There is no doubt that both parties felt
the awful power of the old dogma 'that there is no salvation out of the
Church.'"

We cannot believe that the Elector, so well grounded in the Word, was
troubled by the dogma, "There is no salvation outside of the Church."
The facts do not at all show that Melanchthon received instruction from
the Elector to make new advances to Campeggius and to beg for harmony.
Yet from this point of view, of a yielding Electoral party, the whole issue
at Augsburg is treated by the author in question.

On the contrary, the Elector was standing, now, as before, on the
original terms of the Call, which proposed reconciliation, but after a fair
hearing of both sides of the case, that the truth might prevail. This is

a different position from any willingness on his part to give up the truth. The letters written by Melanchthon to Cardinal Campeggius simply show how far *Melanchthon* was willing to go in his diplomatic statements and representations of the Protestant position. It was Melanchthon who was trying to force the Protestant party into compromise. And when, on the 6th of July, he wrote a letter under instruction from the Protestant Princes to Campeggius, we may be sure that he placed the position of the Protestant Princes in as favorable and conciliatory a light toward Rome as possible. The letter is characteristically Melanchthonian, but even in it the Protestant Princes promise to "accept such conditions as will promote peace and concord, and as will tend to retain the ecclesiastical order" only "*in so far as it can be done without wounding their consciences.*" And they declare "that they by no means wish the ecclesiastical order and the *lawful* authority of the bishops to collapse."[38] If this letter be interpreted in the light of Melanchthon's other letter to the Cardinal,[39] in which he declares that he will show fidelity to the Roman Church "to the last breath," it is clear how such evidence confirms the unreliability of such a delineation of the Protestant powers, not the confessional collapse of the powers themselves.

There is no doubt that the Elector stood throughout for the Word of God, and not, as we are told by a recent writer, for the Church.

The fundamental theory of *The Confessional History*, namely that the entire Electoral party's chief concern at Augsburg was to be permitted to remain in the bosom of the Roman Church, at almost any sacrifice, is wholly untenable. The author of *The Confessional History* seems to have overlooked, from first to last, the heroic *acts and utterances* of the Elector and of the Margrave. Consider the Elector's reply of May 31st to the Emperor; the Elector's letter to Luther on June 4th; the Elector's refusal to kneel on June 15th, at the bridge of the Lech, or in the Cathedral that evening; the Elector's and Margrave's persistent refusal that night to celebrate Corpus Christi next day; the Margrave's exclamation, "Before I would deny my God and His Gospel, I would have my head struck off"; the answer of the Elector on June 17th; the Elector's insistence on signing the Confession, instead of Melanchthon and the theologians; Melanchthon's letter to Luther on July 27th in which he declares that "Those who are here help me little," and his letter to Luther of August 6th, in which he severely blames the Princes for their *apathy toward his proposed peace negotiations.*

As to Luther's position on this point, we may cite his unwillingness to accept the Emperor as judge in his letter of July 1st and 6th; his letter to the Archbishop of Mentz, July 6th, "They would rather endure hell

---

[38] *C. R.* II, p. 171.
[39] *Ib.* II, p. 168.

itself than yield to us"; his letter to Melanchthon of July 9th, "They have a sad finale to look to, we a joyous one. Not indeed that unison in doctrine will ever be restored, for how can any one hope that Belial will come into concord with Christ." We cite also the strong later letters of Luther. In this connection additional facts should be taken into account, viz.: the Explanation of the Protesting Estates that no More Articles will be Handed in, of July 10th, in which they demand that the Emperor live up to his Call; the refusal of the Protestants to accept the Emperor's decision that they do not confute the Confutation; also Melanchthon's letter to Luther of July 27th, and the one of August 6th.[40]

At this particular time the Elector was looking, by reason of the great change and the kindly conduct in the Emperor, for a fair treatment of the Protestant case on the basis of the Call. This would naturally dispose him and his side toward conciliation, and if they already had on any point temporarily gone further, in yielding the evangelical principle, than they were conscious of, the yielding was temporary, and when they became conscious of the issues involved, the reaction was all the sharper. And this, in spite of the fact that Melanchthon already had done all in his power, both in handling the case with the Emperor and the Cardinal and, also in his attitude toward the Elector and the Protestant party to bring about a return to Rome even at a sacrifice of the essential principle of the Reformation.

We point, further, to the reply of the Elector to the Emperor on July 21st, in which he personally recognized the difference between the teaching in God's Word and that of Rome, and re-confessed, here and now, all the articles of the Confession. We also point to the scene *prior* to the selection of the so-called "Committee of Sixteen," which scene is not brought out properly in *"The Confessional History."* The Protestants' side of what took place on the afternoon of August 7th is not sketched in real proportion,[41] although the Catholic reply is given in large outline.

"The Confessional History" lays much stress on the "Explanation," under the lead of Melanchthon, of August 18th, and raises the question whether this was the true and intended meaning of the Augsburg Confession. It says, "There is the Declaration. It speaks for itself. It shows conclusively that the Protestant seven were willing to make peace on terms that must prove humiliating to themselves and disastrous to their cause." It devotes about seven pages to this "Explanation," and says at

---

[40] v. *The Confessional Principle,* footnote on p. 488.
[41] *C. R.* II, p. 266.

the close, "The fact is, the Protestants, as we shall hereafter learn, had almost completely lost their courage, and seemed willing—that is the Saxons and Margravians—to purchase peace at almost any price." But it fails to speak of the storm of dissent which arose *outside the committee* against Melanchthon's program of concession.

One cannot but feel surprise at the inclusion of the Elector and the whole Saxon party, as the responsible movers, in Melanchthon's treacherous compromise, when, in *The Confessional History*, on p. 167, a vital admission as to the Elector's position, as over against Melanchthon, is made respecting the authorship of the report of Melanchthon of August 21st, as follows, "There can scarcely be a doubt that this Opinion *was written by command of the Elector.*"

In conclusion, as throwing light on the idea, plan and course of Melanchthon, we point back to his "Rhetorical Preface" framed as far back as April and found in "The First Draft." As differing from Brück and the Elector, and also the Landgrave, Melanchthon then already proposed to make, and declared *the Emperor* to be, *the sole arbiter in religion.* This Preface (according to *"The Confessional History"*) evaded the question of doctrine and laid all stress on Church Uniformity. This is the hand of Melanchthon at that early day, rather than that of the Elector or Brück. *"The Confessional History"* would involve even Luther in the plan of the "Rhetorical Preface," but Luther himself is our witness in his emphatic testimony that he had no heart for such a Confession.

The Confessional History explains Melanchthon's yielding in various statements, among others, as follows:

"He hated the democratic principles of the Swiss with a perfect hatred. . . .

"Success on the part of Philip, and of the Swiss, would utterly defeat the purpose and the desire of his party to obtain and to enjoy their rights within the Church. . . .

"He stood almost with the devotion of a martyr, by the Empire and by the Church. . . .

"Hence Melanchthon's concessions at Augsburg—in the Confession, in his correspondence with Campeggius, in the peace negotiations—did not proceed from personal weakness, but from an honest desire to serve his party, to carry out their determination to remain in the Church, to vindicate the Lutherans from identification with the Zwinglians and the Anabaptists, and to maintain the integrity of the Holy Roman Empire of the German Nation."

The author of *"The Confessional History"* does not seem to see that he has here set down the case against Melanchthon in a nutshell. The motives which he attributes to Melanchthon are partly personal, largely political, in part ecclesiastical, and in every instance partisan. To maintain, to uphold, to vindicate, to confess, the pure Word of God, though the heavens fall, was not part of his plan.

The author's quotation from Baumgarten's *Geschichte Karls V.*, 3, p. 28, is a condemnation of the main position of *The Confessional History* respecting Melanchthon: "War die Konfession, welche der Kurfürst von Sachsen in seinem und seiner lutherischen Glaubensgenossen Namen am 25. Juni vor Kaiser und Reich verlesen liess, im Sinne äusserster Annährung an die alte Kirche und schroffster Absonderung von den Zwinglischen gehalten, so ging Melanchthon in den später geführten Verhandlungen noch sehr weit über diese Linie hinaus."

Tschackert's Latest Work

In the most recent work treating the subject, Tschackert upholds the distinction we draw between the method and views of Melanchthon and the position of the Electoral party. Tschackert says:[42]

"Today it is almost a part of that which is incomprehensible in Melanchthon's character, that he regarded the Confession, which his judgment, at best, must have looked at as an official state document of the Evangelical Estates, which had been read and delivered in solemn session, which was an important part of German civil and church history, as his private writing.[43]

"It was thus regarded by him immediately after the Diet and during his long life, and changed it as often as he issued it in print. Attempts are made to excuse this: it is said that Melanchthon acted in the interest of a scientific teaching, in order to render the expressions more clear or more exact. Further it is said that the Evangelical Estates and the theologians took no offense at Melanchthon's changes, for decades.

"Both of these facts may be correct, but they do not alter the fact, that the editor-in-chief of the Confession had no understanding of the historical importance of this official state document of the Evangelical Estates. That, on the other hand, the Elector John Frederick regarded the Confession as *his* and that of the other signatories, is shown by his remonstrance to Brück of May 5th, 1537."

The Old Question of Authorship

As to the much-discussed question, treated in several different places in this volume also, of the authorship of the Augsburg Confession, we have no exception to take to the main estimate of *"The Confessional History."*

---

[42] *Die Entstehung der luth. u. der Ref. Kirchenlehre*, 1910, p. 288.
[43] Kolde, *v. Footnote* 21, p. 529, of the present volume, takes a less strict view —T. E. S.

It affirms that Melanchthon's "confessional restatement of the chief doctrines of Christianity was something . . . distinctly new in the life and history of the German people. . . . . It cannot be denied that the Augsburg Confession, taken as a whole, and as a conception, is vastly different from the Schwabach Articles, vastly different from any creed or confession of faith that had previously existed or that has since come into existence, vastly different from anything that had been written by Luther, or previously by Melanchthon."[44] "As Luther's classic monument is the Small Catechism, so Melanchthon's classic monument is the Augsburg Confession. In the erection of that monument he was not an editor, a translator, a compiler, but an author." (p. 69.)[45]

After endorsing *The Confessional History* on this point, it however is still pertinent to inquire in how far *the substance* of the Testimony in the Augsburg Confession, and especially all that which has made the Confession the bulwark of our Faith today, emanates from Melanchthon. Can we say, from what we know of Melanchthon's ideas in the First Draft of the Confession, and at Augsburg during the months of June, July and August, and in later years, that what Luther testified to in private form in the nailing of the Theses, at the Diet of Worms, and what the Electors stood for in later Diets, including the one at Spires, and what came to final expression at Augsburg, was the work of Melanchthon?

Tschackert, writing later than *The Confessional History*,

---

[44] p. 69.

[45] But there is abundant room for varying opinions, on such a subject, depending on the point of view from which a writer approaches the problem, and we do not believe that the cause of objective historical truth is furthered by allusions to "some dogmaticians, or those who have reflected the dogmatic temper, or those who have borrowed the Flacianist calumniations, or those who have superficially examined the facts"; nor by the endorsement of Weber's sarcastic disparagement of "the illustrious man of God, Herr Luther," and of "the Bergic Form of Concord"; nor by the endorsement of Planck's "independence of judgment" and authoritativeness in opinion; nor by the one-sided rhetoric of *The Confessional History's* own summation: "It became the fashion in places to disparage Melanchthon in the Church which he had helped to create, and to name Luther the author of the matter and the doctrine of the Augsburg Confession, and to call Melanchthon the author of its form, of its *rhetoric*, of its *style*. That is, the profound scholar, the accomplished writer, the learned theologian, the trusted counsellor of Princes did the work of an amanuensis at Augsburg! The Prōtón Pseûdos once started, it suited the taste and temper of a dogmatic age to keep it moving, though there have always been those who had the manly courage to protest against the great injustice."—*The Confessional History*, pp. 69-73.

and citing it in his work, has given the right estimate, as follows:

"The day after the delivery of the Confession a copy of it was sent by Melanchthon to Luther, who only now learned to know its final form. But in content it was built out of his thought material, so that he on occasion could even describe it as *his* confession. Luther testified to Melanchthon his agreement to the confession, but was of the opinion that one dare not yield any further to the opponent. On the 6th of July he expressed his joy that he has lived to this hour. It is true that when new negotiations for reconciliation were entered into with the opposite side in Augsburg, he, on the 25th of July, said of the soft-stepping Apology that it had kept silent concerning certain articles, concerning purgatory, worship of the saints, and most of all 'the antichrist, the pope.' But at the close of the Diet he nevertheless gave Melanchthon and his co-workers, on the 16th of September, the praise: 'Christum confessi estis, pacem obtulistis, Caesari oboedistis, injurias tolerastis, blasphemiis saturati estis nec malum pro malo reddidistis; summa, opus sanctum Dei, ut sanctos decet, digne tractastis.' "[46]

In another place, Tschackert, declaring that the circumstance that the Augsburg Confession and its Apology were composed by Melanchthon, does not interfere with the fact that the development of the Confession of our Church was Lutheran, gives as the reason for this that "in both writings Melanchthon works with Luther's thought-material."[47] This is a fundamental conclusion with Tschackert.

He speaks of it again on p. 275, and once again on p. 304. He says: "The Augsburg Confession arose out of Luther's thoughts. Freely speaking, the real period of the formation of the Symbols of Lutheran Protestantism lies between 1529 and 1537; for in this time the original Luther confessional writings arose, both catechisms out of Luther's pen, the Augsburg Confession out of Luther's thoughts, but composed by Melanchthon, to which Melanchthon in his Apology to the same added a theological treatise (Lehrschrift); at last the Schmalkald Articles, also composed by Luther."[48]

"An investigation of the doctrinal content of the Lutheran confessions furnishes the result that as to the main matter it has flowed forth from the fundamental thought of Luther. . . . The Lutheran Church doctrine has flowed from the spirit of Luther, as he indeed has also composed both catechisms and the Schmalkald Articles, but likewise has termed the Augustana 'his,' while Melanchthon furnished the theological

---

[46] *Die Entstehung der lutherischen und der reformierten Kirchenlehre.* p. 286.
[47] p. 274.
[48] p. 275.

defense of the same in the Apology with Luther's thought-material. In content therefore the Lutheran Church doctrine remains Luther's creation."[49]

The estimate well combines and covers Melanchthon's own statements as given partially at different times.

On June 27th, Melanchthon wrote to Luther, "Res sunt antea deliberatae ut scis, sed semper aliter in acie se dant quam antae sunt deliberatae."[50]

On August 27th, he wrote to Camerarius, "Nihil adhuc concessimus adversariis praeter ea, quae Lutherus censuit esse reddenda, re bene ac diligenter deliberata ante conventum."[51] And his final statement as to his work is as follows: "Nil sumpsi mihi; praesentibus principibus et aliis gubernatoribus et concionatoribus disputatum est ordine de singulis sententiis."

The Development of the Lutheran Confession

Technically, the Apology was a controversion of the Confutation of the Augustana. Substantially, it was the Augustana's confirmation. Made known to the laity in the devotional German of Jonas, it was set alongside the Augsburg Confession by the Evangelical Estates at Schweinfurt in 1532, as "a Protection and Explanation of the Confession."[52] Thenceforward, these two works were counted as the official confessions of the Evangelical Church and their recognition was made a condition for membership in the Schmalkald League. Both were confessed in the Wittenberg Concord of 1536 and at Schmalkald in 1537.[53]

Melanchthon worked continuously at the improvement of the text of the Augustana. His enlargements of 1533, especially in Articles IV, V, VI, XII, XV, and XX, in which he adopted explanatory thoughts out of the Apology in parenetic interests, and even the changes in Article XVIII on Free Will, which is not to be interpreted synergistically so much in itself as in its comparison with the

---

[49] p. 304.
[50] *C. R.* II. p. 146.
[51] *Ib.* II. p. 334.
[52] *Cp.* O. Winkelmann, *Der Schmalkaldische Bund,* etc., Strassburg, 1892, p. 197, p. 304 ff.
[53] The changes in the later editions of the Apology are not of the character of a change in the teaching to the same extent as they are in the Augustana. *Cp. Tschackert,* p. 296.

changed mode of treatment in the Latin editions of the
Loci (1535 and later), do not deflect the Confession so
seriously, as the change in the tenth Article on the Lord's
Supper. The omission of the vere et substantialiter adesse
and the reprobatio, just at the time when Melanchthon was
drawing closer to Bucer, and in conjunction with the Wittenberg Concord of 1536, and the censures of the Elector
John Frederick of 1537, justify us, as Kolde says, in coming to the conclusion that in view of his gradually differing
interpretation of the Lord's Supper, Melanchthon made the
change in the Confession in order to leave the way open for
union with the Highlanders.

Luther's peculiar situation was such that he could not
bring himself to a public disagreement with Melanchthon,
and it was only after Luther's death, under the influence of
the doctrinal controversies, when, under the attacks of the
Gnesio-Lutherans, the edition of 1540 became a fortunate
symbol for the Melanchthonians, and later became such
even to the Crypto-Calvinists, that the Variata fell into
disrepute in the eyes of good Lutherans. It was this disrepute that awakened in the confessors of the Book of Concord the intense desire to go back to the original text.

The question has been raised by Kolde and others as to whether the instructions given to the theologians at Schmalkald in 1537, with respect to
revising the Augustana, may not have been a precedent which Melanchthon followed three years later in his publishing the Variata. We doubt
whether it is possible to give an affirmative answer to this view. In the
first place the question arises as to how far *Melanchthon himself* may
not have been the source of the idea to revise, at Schmalkald already in
1535, and, later, in 1537. In the second place the question presents itself
as to whether such a revision would have been made by actual change
in the text of the document itself, and not by way of appendix or additional confession. The difficulty in the way of fairly revising such an historical and official document may have been itself the strongest reason
why it was not actually undertaken. In the third place, if such a revision had occurred, on order of the estates, and in this public way, it
would, by express command, not have touched the substance of the Confession, and it would have been made publicly and officially by the representative of the powers who originally signed the Confession. In both
these respects, it would have differed from Melanchthon's revision of
1540, and probably would have constituted no precedent for the appearance of the Variata.

That the Elector of Saxony was opposed at this very time to the changes, can be seen from the instructions that he gave to Brück in asking that Luther's Articles should be discussed by the other Wittenberg theologians, and that they should state their view frankly, and not merely seem to agree, without opening their heart fully at this time, and then afterwards at another time, teach something different, "as had already happened on the part of several of them in several instances before this." On this Köstlin remarks[54] that it produces the impression that the Elector had already had his attention drawn to the peculiar attitude of Melanchthon in the question of the Lord's Supper. Tschackert's account of the affair is as follows:

"At the convention at Schmalkald in February, 1537, the proceedings ran counter to the intentions of the Saxon Elector. The Evangelical Princes and Estates accompanied by numerous theologians had arrived. But before they had reached a conclusion concerning the question as to the preparation for the Council, the theologians received the commission to reach an understanding concerning the doctrine, so that in case of a possible attendance of the Council they would know what they had to stand for. Of a conclusive acceptance of the articles of Luther there was no thought on the part of the Estates; *Melanchthon who had been advised*[55] *on this point by the Landgrave Philip of Hesse, prevented it, because the article concerning the Lord's Supper did not suit him.* Hence the theologians now received the commission, 'die Augsb. Konfession zu übersehen, nichts wider deren Inhalt und Substanz, auch der Konkordie (der Wittenberger von 1536) zu ändern, allein das Papsttum herauszustreichen, das vormals auf dem Reichstage der Kais. Maj. zu untertänigem Gefallen und aus Ursachen unterlassen,' etc.[56] (Kolde, *Analecta Lutherana* 1883, p. 297.) Accordingly the theologians were first of all to go through the Augustana, second, to furnish an additional article, lacking there, on the papacy. The Augustana and the Apology again met approval and were signed by them. Luther did not participate because he was ill in bed."[57]

Luther was not thus ill from the start, at Schmalkald. On February 9th he wrote to Justus Jonas that the princes were in secret deliberations, and that he had nothing to do. He could neither know nor guess what was being transacted nor what would happen. On the 14th he wrote to Justus Jonas, "It is now the eighth day on which we are being de-

---

[54] II, p. 387.

[55] However *Cp. Footnote 17, p.* 527, and *Footnote 20, p.* 528, for Kolde's opinion on this point. (The italics in the text are ours.)

[56] "Nichts wider deren Inhalt und substanz auch der concordy endern, allein das babstum heruss zu strichen, des vormals uff dem richsdog der key. Mt. zu underthenigem gefallen und uss ursachen underlossen."—Report of the Strassburg Theologians, *Analecta Lutherana,* p. 293.

[57] *Tschackert,* p. 300.

tained here, or are being kept in suspense. We are nothing but an idle gathering. The princes and estates are deliberating concerning other matters than we thought of, and without us. Christ give their deliberations and their undertakings success." So that, at Schmalkald, Melanchthon was active, but Luther was inactive. He always remained in ignorance of the fact that his articles were not officially adopted by the convention. The amplification he made later on in these articles constitutes the strongest formal justification for similar amplification on the part of Melanchthon. But there is a great difference, as to revision, between these Schmalkald Articles and the Augsburg Confession. Luther did not change the substance of them; and, in the second place, the Articles themselves were never actually brought before a Diet or General Council for adoption.[58]

Up to this point at least, the testimony of Tschackert is confirmatory of the position maintained in this book. Tschackert goes so far as to declare, "One may say a hundred times, in scientific circles, that the Symbols must be understood in a purely historical sense—and this we also are trying to do here—nevertheless the fact remains, that the Symbols in Lutheran Protestantism have gained an entirely unique significance: *they represent the genuine Lutheran Church doctrine.* . . . We therefore treat the fixation of the Lutheran fundamental thoughts in the genuine Lutheran confessional writings."[59]

But Tschackert differs from us in this, that he confines the genuine Confessions of the Lutheran Church to the writings accepted in the life-time of Luther. There is something to be said for this position, yet on the whole it is not well grounded. As a matter of historical fact one cannot circumscribe the crystallization of the principle of a new movement to the life-time of its founder. Time is needed to settle the process. As a matter of precedent, not one of the oecumenical creeds could abide such a test. Christ was raised from the grave and ascended into heaven

---

[58] "He has prefixed a long preface to the manuscript and has enlarged the text itself at various places, but without altering the real content and tenor of the whole. He did the same in the edition of 1543."—*Tschackert*, p. 302.

"The Book of Concord, when it took the Schmalkald Articles into the line of Lutheran confessional writings, only witnessed to a situation of fact that was already existing."—*Ib.* p. 302.

[59] p. 275.

long before the Apostles' Creed came into being. Finally, as a matter of principle, the right of the Christian Church, not to alter the old, but to confirm the old by the addition of new Confessional testimony, at any time in the future when this might become necessary, though the right be rarely exercised, must be kept open. Neither the Formula of Concord, nor a Twentieth Century Confession could legitimately be shut out from a genuine Confessional standing in the Church on the ground advanced by Tschackert.

This is the point, says Seeberg, whether there is a continuity in the teachings of all our Confessions; and whether we become conscious of an inner connection of the religious tendencies of the Formula with our own faith. "If this is the case, the verdict of the abiding value of the Bekenntnisnorm will be apparent even for our day. The Lutheran . . must not conceal his positive attitude toward the last Confession of his Church."[60]

The Variations of the Augsburg Confession

There remains, in connection with the Augsburg Confession, one further topic to be touched. We cannot, without danger of being misunderstood, pass over the confessional bearing of the changes introduced by Melanchthon into the various editions of the Augsburg Confession. The statements of *"The Confessional History,"* with their lack of the historic sense, and their subtlety in dogmatic statement, would, if they were correct, undermine the stability of the Augsburg, and every other Christian Confession. Against these statements are Kolde, Tschackert, and even Weber, so far as the Latin *Editio Princeps* is concerned.

Among the statements made by *"The Confessional History,"* we select the following:

"The *editio princeps* . . . is the private work of Melanchthon."— *The Confessional History of the Lutheran Church*, p. 214.

"If one compares the *editio princeps* with Prof. Tschackert's Critical Edition, he cannot resist the conclusion that he has here an *altered* Augsburg Confession."—*Ib*. p. 216.

---

[60] *Herzog-Hauck Real Encyclopaedie*

"Melanchthon's German *editio princeps* is very much varied."—*Ib.* p. 217.

"In all the qualities named above, it cannot be denied that these German *Variatae* greatly surpass the *editio princeps.*"—*Ib.* p. 224.

" 'That first and unaltered Augsburg Confession' is not known to exist anywhere in the world."—*Ib.* p. 230.

"The Lutheran doctrine has not been corrupted in the *Variatae*, but it has been clarified, amplified in statement, fortified by argument, rendered more decidedly Protestant, and more distinctively Lutheran."—*Ib.* p. 231.

"Such a confession [the *editio princeps*] could not have formed the *fundamentum* of a Protestant Church, but rather a convenient bridge for crossing to the right bank of the Tiber. Thanks to Melanchthon! The deficiencies and ambiguities that every theologian encounters in the *editio princeps*, to say nothing of the '*Invariata*,' are removed by the later *Variatae*, which, for almost fifty years, supplanted the *editio princeps*, and helped to determine the meaning of the Augsburg Confession, and to distinguish the Lutheran doctrine."—*Ib.* p. 231.

"The thanks of the entire Church are due to Melanchthon for his *Variatae*. He represents progress and adaptation in the Lutheran Church; and in the fact that Luther and his co-reformers approved and endorsed his changes and adaptations, and made them their own, we have the positive proof that the authority of the Confession in their estimation, was not to be sought in the letter, or in any particular form of words, but in the content and in the conception of the doctrine.

"In this form [*editio princeps*] the Augsburg Confession has had its widest recognition, but in this form it is not the *Confessio Augustana Invariata*, and no intelligent theologian, not blinded by prejudice, would claim for it any such distinction,   ."—*Ib.* p. 232.

"He [Luther] knew of and *approved the changes* made by Melanchthon in the Augsburg Confession." [The italics are ours.]—*Ib.* p. 312.

As against the theory of a Melanchthonian private authorship, it will be sufficient to quote Kolde's remark:[61] "The fact that Melanchthon does not style himself the author, as he does in the case of the Apology, shows that he regarded the Augustana as an official document."[62]

---

[61] *Kolde*, p. 524 in this volume.

[62] Even Weber upholds the priority of the Latin quarto of 1530, and calls it the "Melanchthonische Haupt-Ausgabe." His investigation maintains its authenticity, and he declares that it remains 'the most precious treasure of the Evangelical Church'. Weber says, further (II. p. 5) : "If the editions are to be distinguished from one another without falling into confusion, it is necessary to single out the first one, which, according to Melanchthon's admissions, was printed critically and after a good and trustworthy copy from the others, which contain his further elaborations and elucidations." Weber in II, p. 230 says, "In my opinion, it is not an easy thing to exhibit Melanch-

Weber rightly emphasizes the point that Melanchthon
was filled with the desire to present the truths of the Evangelical doctrine in an ever more clear and determinate
way and to preserve them from all misunderstandings; but
he fails to perceive two facts in this connection: first, that
Melanchthon was not doing this but the opposite, when he
introduced such variations as approximate to the Roman doctrine (Synergism), and to the Reformed doctrine
(Sacramentarianism). Here Melanchthon was repudiating his own position taken at Augsburg, and thus was
contributing to confusion instead of to clearness in the
Evangelical doctrine. In the second place, the constant
varying of the terms of Evangelical doctrine, as pursued
continuously by Melanchthon, thwarted the very object he
had in mind according to Weber, viz., "To present the
truths of the Evangelical doctrine more and more deutlich
and bestimmt."

Weber admits that it is a question whether it would perhaps not have
been better if Melanchthon had allowed the Confession to stand simply
according to the letter and had incorporated his additions in the Apology.

Weber I p. 59 rightly says that the question of the original manuscript
of the Augsburg Confession was never raised in earlier Reformation days,
partly because it was believed, and could also rightly be believed, that Melanchthon in his quarto edition of the years 1530-31 had seen to a good
and correct copy of the Latin and German Confession; and in part because the Confession was not at that time looked upon as an obligating
symbol for the Protestant Church.

For the critical value of the first Quarto Latin edition of
Melanchthon Weber gives the reasons: (1) That Melanchthon himself should be believed. (2) That we would not
know what archive copies to trust, without the first edition
of Melanchthon... (3) Lindan had the Latin original in his
hands and collated with the Quarto of 1531 and does not
speak of any variations, which as a bitter enemy of the
Protestants he would surely have done if he had found
them. (4) It is highly probable that the variations which

thon's changes and improvements. I do not mean the variations in respect
to the different editions, but I mean the history of the variations as to the
mode of origin and content,—further, whether Melanchthon can be excused
on this account by thoughtful people."

the Melanchthon edition manifests as over against the other two were also found in the original writing.

Weber says further that Melanchthon's improved editions of the Augsburg Confession are nothing more than paraphrases, or, if one will, commentaries on the first Print.

In addition to the judgment expressed more fully in the body of our book, we quote the two most recent writers on the variations, viz., Tschackert and Neve. Tschackert[63] says: "The attempt is made to excuse this: Melanchthon is said to have acted in the interests of a better teaching, in order to make clearer or more exactly to explain the expressions. Again it is said that the Evangelical Estates and the theologians took no offense at Melanchthon's changes for a whole decade. Both of these statements may be correct, but that does not change the fact that the editor in chief of the Confession had no comprehension of the world-historical importance of these public documents of the Evangelical Estates. That on the other hand the Elector John Frederick regarded the Confession as *his* and as belonging to the other subscribers of the Confession, is proved by his admonition to Brück of May 5, 1537."

To this may be added the judgment of Neve:[64]

"We can, strictly speaking, not call the Editio Princeps an Invariata, because the edition also contains changes from the original. Yet inasmuch as these changes are of no doctrinal importance, *we will be justified in using that term in contrast to an edition which does contain very significant changes.* And this distinction will never disappear from the terminology of the historians on this subject, nor will the Lutheran Church ever cease to make that distinction."

And again: "In the Variata we have the unconscious, embryonic beginnings of a theology which in the soon following Crypto-Calvinistic troubles became the fermenting element, and which in a following age received a temporary expression in Syncretism, and finally became permanently embodied in the Prussian Union established in 1817. And

---

[63] *Die Entstehung der luth. und der reformierten Kirchenlehre*, p. 286.
[64] "Are we Justified in Distinguishing Between an Altered and an Unaltered Augustana as the Conf. of the Luth. Ch.?"—*Luth. Ch. Rev.*, Jan., 1911.

3

insignificant as the changes may have appeared at first, in connection with the soon following aggressive advances of Crypto-Calvinism, with the Variata as its shibboleth, this altered edition of Melanchthon was bound to become discredited in the Lutheran Church."

It is a peculiarity of any generation not to observe the gradual development, in its midst, of the seeds of evil from day to day, until the evil has come to full bloom, and thus it was with the theologians of the early Evangelical church and Melanchthon's Variata.

"The Confessional History," with dramatic effect, sets a Critical Text put together in 1901 by Tschackert from the best official manuscripts in the hands of the original signers, against the *Editio Princeps,* as the real Invariata, but in this seems to have overlooked the verdict of Kolde against the certitude of Tschackert's text.

"The Confessional History" exalts this *"unveraenderte Augsburgische Konfession . . . Kritische Ausgabe* (1901), constructed by Professor Tschackert, and accepted by all Augsburg Confession scholars as reproducing 'the original and unaltered Augsburg Confession' with a high degree of accuracy; and consequently as discrediting utterly the *Textus Receptus,* German and Latin, of the Book of Concord, and all the Melanchthon, and all other printed editions. . . . It shows, if not verbally and literally, yet certainly, to a high degree of accuracy, the Augsburg Confession as it was read and delivered, June 25, 1530; and it enables us to settle forever, in its essential aspects, the hitherto hazy and uncertain contention over the *Confessio Invariata.* It shows, further, that no edition of the Augsburg Confession in official use in the Lutheran Church today can be claimed by its subscribers as *'that first and unaltered Augsburg Confession,'* not even in a technical sense as over against the Latin *Variata* of 1540," etc.— (pp. 210-211).

As against this we set Kolde's statement:[65] *"We do not really know the text actually presented,* notwithstanding all the valuable attempts to determine it, by means of critical methods, from the extant oldest copies."

On the principles of the work to which we have taken exception, it is difficult to discover great harm in Variata texts of the Confession.

If the text is variant as to form, we are not bound by the form; if it is variant as to substance, the substance may be an improvement. Yet the work, (perhaps recalling Weber), terms, (p. 212), a German text

---

[65] p. 524 in this volume.

taken by mistake into the Book of Concord, a text with many minor changes of no textual value, but also of no injury to the substance, "a *vicious* copy of a German manuscript"; and Tschackert's judgment of 1901, "*without authentic value*," "*through and through inaccurate*" is several times (p. 224, 233) repeated; whereas Tschackert's own statement, in 1910, as to this text, is:

"The Saxon theologians acted in good faith, and the *Mainz copy is even better* indeed than *Melanchthon's German Original Druck;* but compared with the complete and trustworthy, that is with the original that was delivered over with the contemporary signatures of the signers, the Mainz text nevertheless shows itself faulty in many places." (p. 621) . . .

"Since the greatest emphasis was laid on taking the Unaltered Augsburg Confession into the Book of Concord, they would surely have been as glad to use a copy of the 'Original' for the Latin text, as they were to secure one for the German text out of the archives at Mainz; but the imperial archives contained no Latin manuscript of the Confession, and Latin original copies in the possession of those who signed were not known at that time. Therefore there was nothing else to do but to take Melanchthon's Editio princeps, the quarto edition, which had been printed in 1530 and had been issued in 1531 at the same time that the Latin Apology was. This text, then, was accepted since no better one was known." [66]

As to the Latin text, we have not found, in the work we are discussing, any statement of the *real reason* why the *Octavo* edition of 1531 was used by Selnecker.

On the contrary its use is expressly attributed to *ignorance*, "Proof this," says the author, "that the theologians of that period knew very little about the different editions of the Confession and Apology."[67]

The Culmination of the Lutheran Confession

The Augsburg Confession was but a beginning. Though in it all other Protestants had been excluded from participation, and the Evangelical Church of Luther had given its final answer to the old world-order and to Rome, the Church of the Augsburg Confession had not yet given any answer to the antithesis in Protestantism itself.

The spirit of protest in and for itself, to be exercised as the rule, and not as the great exception; the desire to cast away the authority of the fixed and the old, even where this authority was not abnormal; the introduction of a rational

---

[66] p. 624.
[67] p 526.

spirit, as the arbiter of faith, into religion; and of restless reform into society, was farther away, if possible, from the aim of the Lutherans, than was Rome herself. What to do as to the remaining parts of Protestantism—the Swiss and Strasburgers, the humanists, the sectarians, the English—now became the Confessional problem, from 1530 on. Unless conservative Protestantism, midway between two extremes, could give a sufficient and final answer to its own extreme in its own wing, even as it had given answer to the Roman extreme in the other wing, it would be ground to powder between the two, and disappear.

It was here that Melanchthon, unable to satisfy his humanistic mind in the deeper mysteries of the faith, and turned by the success of Protestantism, and by Bucer, farther away from Rome, sought to bridge the chasm between Luther's religion of faith alone, and the Highlander's religion of faith and reason. Tschackert, in his recent work,[63] presents a fine picture of the inner thought of Melanchthon, in which he says:

"Melanchthon was a born Greek and came as such to Wittenberg; but carried away by the fascinating power of the mighty preacher of the Word of God, he became interested along theological lines. From Luther he absorbed the Pauline understanding of the Gospel and in his Loci he brought the anti-Roman propositions of Luther into teachable form . . . But more and more clearly, as time went on, did Melanchthon's own peculiar nature separate itself alongside of and in distinction from Luther.

"Luther's fundamental religious trait was that of the boldest religious supranaturalism; he had experienced faith as a deed of God's grace done to him, and in his religious heroism he did not concern himself with any reflections as to how this fact was possible or by what means it had been accomplished. But Melanchthon needed an ethical mediation of the life of faith, and he did not perceive this fully until after Luther's conflict with Erasmus. . . . The Classics of the Greeks had represented the highest pure human wisdom of life in a knowledge of nature and in the culture of morals to Melanchthon.

" . . . But after the conflict of Luther with Erasmus, Melanchthon would have been most glad to withdraw himself from theological lectures. Through the instrumentality of Luther he was nevertheless entrusted with the theological professorate by the Elector John of Saxony

---

[63] *Die Entstehung der lutherischen und reformierten Kirchenlehre*, Göttingen, 1910, pp. 502-504.

in the year 1526, although he was neither a licentiate nor a doctor of theology. After that he also belonged to the Theological Faculty and labored untiringly in this his position for theology and the Church, and particularly after the death of Luther he accomplished wonderful things for the theological development of the students at Wittenberg by means of his touching fidelity to the duty of a teacher.

"But despite his holding fast to Luther, he went his own way in scientific theology after the second half of the second decade. First of all he retired the doctrine of predestination because it appeared to him as an 'unentwirrbares Labyrinth der Gewissen.' . . . Further he was ruled by a strongly ethical method of viewing thought. . . . This fundamental view led him to synergism in the doctrine of conversion . . . it also led him to the emphasis of the necessity of good works in the Christian life. Then finally he desired a simplification of the doctrine in matters of the Lord's Supper, and a reduction of the same to that which was necessary for personal faith in salvation with the exclusion of metaphysical propositions. If these peculiarities of teaching were to be emphasized in a one-sided way, they could easily become the foundation of theological differences. To this was added the fact that Melanchthon himself after the death of Luther, in the confusions subsequent to the Schmalkald War, had more and more to assume the role of a public leader, not only in theology, but much more in affairs of the Church.

. . . "In spite of all the personal weaknesses of Melanchthon, it remains his merit that he led the stream of humanism into the bed of Protestantism, and united science and faith in salvation in innermost unity. . . . He proved in his own person that religious faith could exist alongside of the most brilliant culture, while in Italy humanism deteriorated into skepticism and atheism.

"Nevertheless Melanchthon dare not be set up as a parallel alongside of Luther. . . . So long as Luther lived, Melanchthon strengthened the Protestant backbone; but after Luther's death Melanchthon lost all hold cn the public guidance of the Church. In an unfortunate private letter of the 28th of April, 1548, to Carlowitz, the counsel of the Elector Maurice of Saxony, the intimidated man confessed that under Luther he had suffered an 'almost ignominious captivity' and gives to understand that he was obliged to 'conceal' his own views. 'Tuli etiam antea servitutem paene deformem, cum saepe Lutherus magis suae naturae, in qua φιλονεικία erat non exigua, quam vel personae suae vel utilitati communi serviret. Et scio, omnibus aetatibus, ut tempestatum incommoda, ita aliqua in gubernatione vitia modestis arte ferenda et dissimulanda esse.. . . . Fortassis natura sum ingenio servili.' [69] From that time on the cunning receiver of the letter knew that Melanchthon was wax in his hands."[70]

---

[69] *C. R.* 9, 879ff.
[70] pp. 502-504.

Thus it was that the concealed antithesis between Luther and Melanchthon, on doctrine now often regarded as not fundamental, led to violent and extreme disruption in the Church after the death of the principals, and that the conflict should concentrate in the central and typical mystery of the Christian Faith, the Sacrament of the Lord's Supper. "There is not a day nor a night for the last ten years," declares Melanchthon, "that I did not meditate upon the doctrine of the Lord's Supper." But the meditation of Melanchthon was upon a truth that might be held in reason,[71] while the meditation of Luther was upon a reality [72] embraced by faith. To Luther the Sacrament is God's unchangeable fact.

"Can you think," he says, "that God is so concerned about what we do and believe, as on that account to change his institutions?" [73] "The chief point," says he, "is the Word and institution of God." Hence he presents the Sacrament (Small Catechism, Part V) not as a mode of truth, nor as a result gained by argument, but as the great fact of Christianity, to be used as such. It is this dependence on the fact, which was the strength of Luther and Lutheranism. "The doctrines of the Lutheran Church cannot be changed," says Krauth.[74] Is it any wonder that Melanchthon's changes could not voice these doctrines?

Tender, conciliatory, peace-loving, hoping to the last, even after the Convention of Worms in 1557, for a reconciliation of the various branches of the Christian Church, Melanchthon's principle centred in the human side of Christianity, the unity of the Church, while Luther's principle centred in the divine side of Christianity, the reality, even into all mystery, of Christ.

"The Confessional History of the Lutheran Church" treats the years and the movements between the death of Luther and the adoption of the Formula of Concord, with fulness. Of the period between the Augsburg and the Leip-

---

[71] *Cp.* The admission in *The Confessional History*, p. 113, "With Luther, sacrament was *res sacra*, with Melanchthon it was *ritus.* See *Apology, De Numero et Usu Sacramentorum.*"

[72] *Cp. Large Cat.*: "The entire Gospel is by the Word embodied in this Sacrament."—*B. of C. Jacobs*, p. 479.

[73] *Large Catechism, Ib.* pp. 476-477.

[74] *C. P. Krauth* by Spaeth, p. 101.

zig Interims, the author writes of Melanchthon, "His conduct was *all that could be reasonably expected of him in these perilous times.*"[75]

He quotes v. Ranke with approval as follows: "And so much is certain, that though they yielded and followed, still they did not violate the Evangelical system in its essence" (p. 321). The endorsement of the Augsburg interim was *unfortunate chiefly,* in the eyes of "The Confessional History" *because it introduced the spirit of schism* into the Lutheran Church, which has haunted it to this day" (p. 323). Flacius "*outLuthered Luther*" (p. 324), and appears as the author of the strife with Major and Osiander (p. 325). In the Crypto-Calvinistic controversy "*neither side maintained the Luther-Melanchthon doctrine* of the Lord's Supper" (p. 329).

Nearly forty pages are devoted by the author to the doctrine of Predestination and Free Will.

Luther's position in the *De Servo Arbitrio* is characterized as *fatalistic* or *necessitarian* (p. 366), and it is declared (p. 370) that "The Philippists maintained the true Lutheran doctrine of sin, both original and actual; maintained the Lutheran doctrine of the universality of the Call, and taught that when the Will (Voluntas) is *excited* and *assisted* by the Holy Spirit through the Word, it is not absolutely inactive, but assents to or rejects the divine promise and offer of salvation."

In discussing the later Christological controversy, Luther's position is properly presented—

"And yet Luther . . . shows a preference, or at least a great fondness for the human nature of Christ" (p. 373). Melanchthon (p. 374) "regarded the *communicatio idiomatum* as a figure of speech"[76] Melanchthon's teaching "does not differ in its Christological aspects from the doctrine of Luther, except that it has no speculative element, such as Luther introduced in connection with his doctrine of the Lord's Supper, and no mystical element, such as Luther often introduced in his *The Freedom of a Christian Man,* and in his *House Postils,* though as Luther grew older his sense of the Christ *for* us more and more took precedence of his sense of the Christ *in* us." (p. 376.)

In coming to a comparison between the teaching of the two recent works on the Formula of Concord, which have appeared since our own volume was written, we find that Tschackert defends the Formula, as the crystallization of a certain consensus, which had gradually formed

---

[75] p. 321. (The italics are ours.)
[76] *C. R.* XXI, p. 363.

itself during and after the doctrinal conflicts, and which expressed the genuine Lutheran doctrine, in the way of the day, it is true, but in a manner that clarified and gave a decisive directive to Lutheran theology.[77]

The other volume before us finds, after careful and prolonged examination, that the Formula of Concord is a partisan writing which was *forced* upon the churches, whose "unreconciled antitheses and spirit of controversy" has done no good to the Church, but has been productive of a great amount of injury.

Tschackert does not regard the Formula as a Symbol of the Church, because it arose after the death of Luther, and because it is of a theological rather than of a popular religious character. The other author does not regard it as a Symbol since it was born in a bad way, was acknowledged chiefly by coercion, and has been the cause of pretty nearly all the trouble and harm that has come to the Lutheran Church in Germany and in America since its own day.

Tschackert concludes that the content and scope of the Formula was determined entirely by the circumstances of the times. Each article is an independent little monograph, corresponding to its own independent doctrinal controversy. "Yet they are not altogether neutral toward each other; they all arise out of a common soil, the Lutheran scriptural doctrine of justification with its presuppositions and consequences; on this their inner connection rests." "Thus the Formula of Concord wrought in clarifying and further developing the relation of human freedom to divine grace, in conversion, in justification, in good works, in the Lord's Supper, in Christology and Predestination."

The other author finds in the Formula a useless reviving of controversies that already had died down of their own accord, an internal weakening and external dividing of the Church, and the introduction of doctrinal confusion, rather than the "reestablishment of continuity with genuine Lutheran doctrine."

As to the dialectic method of the Formula, Tschackert

---

[77] pp. 571, 572.

explains it as that of "dogmatic *loci,* to whose form everyone was accustomed through the school of Melanchthon."
In this, namely that the hardening of form was not due to
an extreme Lutheranism, he is in agreement with Seeberg,
and takes issue with Kawerau and Loofs. Tschackert
says,

"The criticism that the Formula of Concord has changed Luther's doctrine of the faith is not applicable. Doubtless it has emphasized the intellectual element in Luther's conception of faith in a one-sided way, and
also has, on occasion, called the Gospel a 'doctrine, which teaches what
man shall believe.' But at the same time and in the same connection
the Formula of Concord has expressly declared that faith consists 'only
in *trust in the Lord Jesus.'* (This is in answer to Moeller-Kawerau,
Kirchengeschichte III, 268: 'This sentence shows most clearly the
change that had come over Luther's doctrine of faith.' Loofs goes still
further, *Dogmengeschichte* 927: that through the Formula of Concord
and the Book of Concord the 'doctrinal torpidness [Erstarrung] of the
Reformation thought had come to its climax.') Neither is the ethical
motive in Luther's conception of faith at all wanting in the Formula of
Concord. We can surely point to the fact that the Augsburg Confession
itself in its seventh article says that the unity of the Church is conditioned by the '*doctrina evangelii*' together with the scriptural administration of the sacraments."

As to the *doctrinal effect* of the Formula, Tschackert
says,

"The Formula of Concord restored a unity of doctrine in the majority of
Lutheran countries; it pushed Philippism to a side and distinguished itself
from Calvinism. The extremes of the Gnesio-Lutherans were decidedly
rejected, but on the whole none of the opponents was mentioned by name
in order that no personalities might creep into the work of union. That
the composers over-valued the importance of their work and gave to it
the significance of a *rule of doctrine for the future* is to be regretted:
but this view of their own work exercised no influence upon the formation
of the Formula of Concord. Therefore this judgment as to itself, which
at any rate comes to light only incidentally, can be left out of consideration when we are dealing with a valuation of the content. Thus the
whole presents itself as a carefully thought out and sharply distinct
thought-structure which has given decisive directives to the Lutheran
theology." [78]

As to the ecclesiastical effect Tschackert says:

"The authoritative character of the Book of Concord brought it about
that the churches of those countries that governed themselves by it, felt

---

[78] pp. 571-572.

themselves as the 'Lutheran Church' . . . In the Formula of Concord the churches of the Augsburg Confession are still called 'ecclesiae reformatae.' But since in foreign lands, in France, Holland and England the evangelicals there called themselves 'Reformed,' and since the Philippists, who in Germany annexed themselves to Calvinism after the introduction of the Book of Concord, took the characterization 'Reformiert' for their Particular Church, the adherents of the Book of Concord at the same time distinguished themselves from these as the 'Lutheran Church.' " [79]

The manner of introducing the Formula, Tschackert explains as follows:

"The introduction of the Book of Concord as the rule of doctrine, was on act of the ecclesiastical authority in each of the estates which since Luther's appeal 'to the Christian Nobility' had gradually developed itself of its own accord in the realm of Protestantism." [80]

As to *the range* of the acceptance of the Formula, Tschackert says,

"All the Corpora doctrinae mentioned up to this point possessed a significance only for the local state churches, but almost all of them lost even this of themselves, when a confessional book of almost universal acceptance came into being in the sphere of Lutheranism (in Bereich des Luthertums ein nahezu allgemein giltiges Bekenntnisbuch), the Book of Concord of the year 1580. After the Formula of Concord had been completed and recognized by numerous evangelical estates, the plan is resolved on in Electoral Saxony now to set up a unifying Corpus doctrinae for all adherents to the same." [81]

As to the Churches that failed to sign the Formula, Tschackert expresses the following judgment:

"Those who did not sign the Formula by no means refused for dogmatic reasons. On the other hand their reasons were chiefly political or local or personal, and if King Frederick by his decree of July 24th, 1580 forbade the publication of the Formula of Concord in the Lutheran churches of Sweden and Denmark on penalty of death, this was purely for political reasons. Although later still some dissenting state churches accepted the Formula of Concord, it has nevertheless never formally been the confession of the whole of Lutheranism (Kolde, *Introduction*, LXXIII." [82]

There are two points in which Tschackert does not agree with us in his estimate of the Formula of Concord. In the first place he sets it down as "only an Order of Doctrine"

---

[79] p. 625.
[80] p. 625.
[81] p. 620.
[82] p. 569.

but admits, in this connection, that according to the thinking of the second half of the sixteenth century, it was the
"pure doctrine" which conditioned "the existence of the
churches themselves."

He says, "It is this pure doctrine which establishes the whole and
stable existence of the religion, worship, and thought of the Church;
faith, worship, good works, the relation to the state, everything receives
its direction through the pure doctrine." But for our modern day he
accepts the canon, "The more theology a confession contains, the less
proper is it for a confession of the congregation," and cites the Apostles'
Creed as an incomparable confession for the congregation because it contains no theology at all, but only faith in the divine plan of salvation.
He admits that his modern canon "was not yet needed for the second
generation of the Reformation theologians and their Christian state
authorities."[83]

The second point of difference in Tschackert is his view
that the Formula of Concord develops the doctrine of the
two natures of Christ on the teaching of the Council of
Chalcedon, and that the Formula of Concord has based its
teaching on the philosophical doctrine of the ubiquity of
the Person of Christ. Thus he says,[84] "Luther's theory of
the Ubiquitas corporis Christi has not been carried over
into our Symbols; it was only taken up later by the Formula of Concord under the stimulus of the renewed controversies concerning the Lord's Supper."

Yet in making these two criticisms of the Formula,
Tschackert at the same time offers most substantial concessions to the strength of the teaching of the Formula.
As differentiating the teaching of the Formula from the
doctrine of the two natures of the Council of Chalcedon,

---

[83] We do not believe that Tschackert's modern confessional canon has any
sound basis in the necessities of this age. If it had, and if a confession is
to be limited to that which can readily be used by the congregation in its
worship, not only the Formula of Concord, but the Augsburg Confession, the
Apology and the Schmalkald Articles, all of which Tschackert numbers among
the confessions of the Church, would likewise be ruled out. The fact is that
an "unreflective lay Christianity" as over against a "theologico-scientific"
apprehension of the Gospel is less characteristic of our condition today than
ever, for this is a day when theology, with all its doctrines, is being discussed
by clergy and laymen in nearly all the papers and popular magazines of the
and. There never has been a time when the educated layman has been so
"reflective" on the matter of the substantial content of creeds, notwithstanding his aversion to their fixed form.

[84] p. 323.

Tschackert declares that the Formula "continues to develop it to a definite doctrine of the Unio personalis and the real and total Communicatio idiomatum." He says definitely, "The unity of both natures dare not be thought of in the manner of the Nestorian and the Antiochian theologians as purely external.. . . . On the other hand both natures enter into such a unity with each other that they constitute a single and unique person. Thus both natures enter into the innermost conceivable communion with each other."[85] Again he says, "The Formula of Concord describes the transfer of the divine attributes to the human nature of the Godman in incomparable terms."[86]

The true fact is that Luther drew his doctrine of the Person of Christ directly from the Scripture. It was *the reality in Scripture* which became the *reality in his teaching*. It was *Christ Himself* in His Word, Whom the reformers knew thoroughly. Out of their experience of Christ, they taught the doctrine of the Person of Christ. Tschackert himself tells us that it is wrong to suppose that the Lutheran Christology was developed for the purpose of supporting the Lutheran theory of the Lord's Supper. From the beginning, the doctrine of the Person of Christ, according to Tschackert, was purely religious[87] and not theological. It was a religious experience, effected by God's Word. The theological explanation of the doctrine came after the experience of the reality, and did not precede it. Whatever was used from the old church doctrine was not creative of the nature and personality of Christ as an idea, but was the building out of an already well known fact of experience, and whatever was added from the still wider periphery of philosophy, was regarded as illustrative and not as the foundation of the reality.

It is for this reason, among others, that we object so strenuously to characterizing the teaching of Luther and the Formula on the Person of Christ in the doctrine of the Lord's Supper as a philosophical doctrine, rather than as

---

[85] p. 553.
[86] p. 555.
[87] p. 320.

a revealed fact in the Word of God. And for this reason too the philosophic term "ubiquity" does not describe the real content and essence of the Formula's teaching.[88] Tschackert himself feels this, and therefore says (p. 557), "In the ultimate analysis we find it to be a religious interest which causes the theory of ubiquity to be set up; this is true of the Formula of Concord the same as of Luther." And then, by way of apology and defense he goes on to say that "a formula free from objections has not been found either for this theory or for the whole communicatio idiomata." It is therefore so true that the doctrine of Christ, drawn directly from the Scripture, is the fundamental teaching in the Formula. The Godman is the Mediator of salvation according to His whole person, not only in the history of salvation, so far as it pertains to the past, but also for the present and for the whole future.

Although Luther knew Biel and Peter D'Ailly almost by heart and the nominalistic point of view made it easy for him to regard Christianity as a historical fact rather than a philosophical system, and although D'Ailly's doubt as to the doctrine of transubstantiation was the starting point of Luther's own doubt, yet it cannot be said that philosophy or anything else than Scripture controlled Luther's thinking. Melanchthon had studied the Nominalists just as thoroughly as Luther, yet Luther's development, in spite of the similarity of the Nominalist influence upon both, is different from Melanchthon's.[89]

Turning to *"The Confessional History,"*[90] we find the following formal statement on the Book of Concord:

"After careful and prolonged examination of by far the larger part of the official and other trustworthy literature in connection with the composition, subscription and introduction of the Formula of Concord"

---

[88] Möller-Kawerau (*The Confessional History*, p. 485) has admitted that "undoubtedly, ubiquity was not expressed [in the Formula of Concord] in the absolute sense of the Würtembergers."

[89] The passage in which Luther refers to this matter is found in the Babylonian Captivity. Erl., op. lat. var. arg. V., 29, and as quoted by Tschackert runs as follows: "Dedit mihi quondam, quum theologiam scholasticam haurirem, occasionem cogitandi D. Cardinalis Camerarensis [*i. e.*, Ailli], libro Sententiarum IV acutissime disputans, multo probabilius esse et minus superfluorum miraculorum poni, si in altari verus panis verumque vinum, non autem sola accidentia esse astruerentur, nisi ecclesia determinasset contrarium. Postea videns, quae esset ecclesia, quae hoc determinasset, nempe Thomistica, hoc est Aristotelica, audacior factus sum."

[90] pp. 515, 516.

the author of "The Confessional History" holds "the following propositions to be historically incontrovertible:

"1. The Formula of Concord was *forced* upon the churches," [91] etc.

"2. The *chief* objections raised against the Formula of Concord were the hypothesis of ubiquity, and the uses made of that hypothesis as a basis of the doctrine of the real bodily presence," [92] etc.

"3. The great majority of the Lutheran churches which rejected the Formula of Concord vindicated their Lutheran character by appealing to the older Lutheran confessions." [93]

"4. The Formula of Concord was the cause of the most bitter controversies, dissensions and alienations." [94]

"And now, in the presence of these propositions, which can be established, and must be established, by every historian who searches and writes in the interest of historical science, and not for the purpose of supporting a prepossession, the question naturally arises, Did the Formula of Concord do more harm than good? . . . The question is one for historical solution by the use of all the facts involved. . . . The history itself[95] must constitute the basis of judgment. . . ." (pp. 515, 516.)

"Taking all those things into account, we believe that the impartial verdict of history will be that the Formula of Concord has done more harm than it has done good. . . . At no time has it been an instrument of concord for the entire Lutheran Church. Its unreconciled antitheses . . . and the spirit of controversy and condemnation which it breathes . . . and which it has communicated to so many of its adherents, has helped to make the Lutheran Church the most controversial of all the Protestant communions."

---

[91] "It was not some theological party that had forced its views upon the Lutheran Church, but a germ of a consensus which had been at hand, had attained to its unfolding in the Formula of Concord. It represented a Melanchthonian Lutheranism."—*Seeberg* in *Herzog-Hauck Realencyclopedia.*

[92] Against this see our argument in chapter XXXIII.

[93] Their objections were not, as a rule, of a confessional character.

[94] Against this see the argument in chapter XXXV.

It was able to pacify the Lutheran Church.—*Seeberg* in *Herzog-Hauck Realencyclopedia.*

[95] A new confession was a historical necessity.—*Seeberg* in *Herzog-Hauck Realencyclopedia.*

The Melanchthonian conception of the Church itself demanded such a decisive judgment of doctrinal differences.—*Ib.*

The Formula of Concord arose from a necessity of history, and within its sphere it solved the problem in a prudent and far-sighted way.—*Ib.*

Nothing is better fitted to show the historical necessity of a final Lutheran confession than the temporary dominion of Philippism in Electral-Saxony which broke to pieces the moment that the dishonorable guise in which it had hitherto maintained itself, was torn away.—*Ib.*

Since *"The Confessional History"* rises far above the field of polemics into an atmosphere of equanimity and concord, and is purified from all tinge of the controversial temper, and since its aim is the grand work of pacification in the Church, we must give it the credit of this attainment without having been influenced thereunto by the Book of Concord. It cannot be accused of devotion either to the *positiva* or the *negativa* in the Formula. It sacrifices no section of its space to the praises of the Formula, although there is a chapter on its censures (The Censures of the Torgau Book); and the Sources for these censures are, among others [96] such admirers of our Church as Hospinian and Heppe.

"The Confessional History" opens its discussion of modern confessional issues with a eulogy of Schleiermacher, and of Claus Harms; with a defence of the Prussian Union; with a brief description of the confessional movement in Germany.

Under Rudelbach, Guericke, Köllner, Sartorius, Richter and Harless. The description is good except that the contention of the anti-symbolists that "the Symbolical Books go beyond the doctrine of the Scripture and in many points pass it by," is quoted, and unquestioned.[97] "It does not appear that any one wished to abolish the Symbolical Books entirely, for even a Paulus of Jena had subscribed the Symbolical Books," etc.[98] The activity of Stahl, Kliefoth, Philippi, Thomasius, Kahnis, von Hofmann, Schmid, Luthard, Frank and Zöckler is suggested as being the Romanticising of Lutheranism. In the discussion of the modern German formulae of subscription, it quotes approvingly the essay of Braun (1875), in which the following occurs: "The Formula of Concord is scarcely any longer to be named a Confession, yea, it itself expressly declares that it is not intended to be a Confession"; and the following: "The narrow-hearted letter-slaves of the Symbols think that they advance the interest of the Church by their conduct. They do not see that in that way they only split the Church into fragments. . . . But there will be symbol-slaves so long as there is a Church and a Confession, for the tendency in that direction lies deep in human nature. Hence we must bear this evil as we have to bear a thousand others," etc.

In describing the confessional subscription of Denmark, the act of

---

[96] p. 452.
[97] p. 579.
[98] p. 579.

Frederick II is quoted with apparent approval, but hardly the formula of subscription of 1870 which speaks of "the Symbolical Books of our Danish Evangelical Lutheran Church." As to present-day Norway, the author seems to commend the clergymen who in 1908 "advocated the shelving of the Nicene and Athanasian Symbols," and says, "A country where such an advocation is respectfully listened to, will of course hold its own against any possible, but improbable, attempt to foist the Book of Concord upon it." [99]

As for the attitude of Sweden to the Book of Concord we refer to Prof. Forsander's discussion of the adoption of the Book of Concord in Sweden. [100]

We are nonplussed by the chapter in *The Confessional History* on the Confessions in America. Many facts are given, intermingled with statements that are true in a sense as statements, but not true in the impression which they convey. We wonder whether the author understood, or whether he consciously minimized the significance of the "Amsterdam Church Order"? Muhlenberg is declared not to be a "confessionalist," a charge which the Patriarch refuted in his own life time. The Ministerium of Pennsyl-

---

[99] p. 598.

[100] *The Adoption of the Augsburg Confession and the Book of Concord in Sweden.* [N. Forsander, *The Council of Upsala*, pp. 8, 9.]

"During both sessions of the following day the remaining part of our glorious Lutheran confession was earnestly discussed and unanimously adopted. At the discussion of the tenth article, that of the Lord's Supper, the president severely admonished the clergy carefully to guard themselves against Calvinistic errors, whereupon bishop Petrus Jonae arose and freed himself from suspicions for such views. When the reading and discussion of the whole confession was finished, bishop Petrus Jonae stepped forth and solemnly asked the senators and all members present : 'Do ye sanction this confession, as it is now read and approved?' All standing up unanimously declared, that they would never forsake it, but willingly sacrifice life and blood for the same. The president then exclaimed loudly : 'Now Sweden has become one man, and we all have one Lord and one God !'

"Such a question as this might be raised by some of us : 'Why did the men of the Council in 1593 then not adopt the whole Book of Concord, which was published already in 1580?' Nicolaus Olavi and several of the leading men at Upsala in 1593 had studied theology at Rostock under Dr. David Chytraeus, one of the chief editors of the Formula of Concord, and by their actions and writings these members present at the Council have clearly shown that they were in full and hearty accord with their esteemed teacher and with all the Symbolical books contained in the Book of Concord. But these Symbolical books were at that time not known enough in Sweden to be all treated and adopted intelligently in some few days allotted to the Council. It was also pedagogical wisdom to delay the adoption of the whole Book of Concord by the Swedish Church until the appropriate time would come. This adoption was asked for by the clergy in 1647, and was authorized by the government in 1663."

vania is termed "a Philadelphia organization," and it is
said of it "neither did it formally declare its relations to
the confessions of the Lutheran Church." But the most
glaring misrepresentation is to be found[101] in this
text-book's interpretation of the Fundamental Principles of the general body of which the Ministerium is
a part. The author says that this body is bound

"to the very words of the Symbols, and makes no distinction between
their form and their substance, and virtually it places them on a level
of authority with the Holy Scriptures, since it declares 'that the Unaltered Augsburg Confession, in its original sense, is throughout in conformity with the pure truth of which God's Word is the only rule'; for if
it be throughout in conformity with the pure truth of God's Word, then
it must have the same authority as God's Word, for things that are
throughout in conformity with each other must have the same value
and authority."

This is a rigid enforcement of the letter of scholastic
logic, the like of which we do not recall in the Formula of
Concord, or even in the decrees of the Council of Trent.

Its fallacy is as apparent as its rigidity. That which conforms to an
original, by this very fact is secondary, and not primary. It does not
usually possess either the creative vitality or the authority of the original,
to which it conforms. If the original were not of a higher type than it is,
there would be no virtue in its conforming to the original as a standard.
If we suppose that the will of a spiritual man conforms itself throughout
to the will of the Lord, we do not therefore say, that the human will,
which conforms, "must have the same value and authority," as the
Divine will, to which it conforms.

Moreover, the premises quoted are falsified. They are correctly quoted
a little earlier[102] thus, "We accept and acknowledge *the doctrines* of the
Unaltered Augsburg Confession in its original sense as throughout in
conformity with the pure truth." But this author, after stating that
these words point to the very letter of the Symbol and make no distinction
between form and substance, in his proof of his assertion, omits the
vital word *doctrines*, and conveys the impression that not only the *doctrines* but 'the very words,' and the outer historical form of the Augsburg
Confession, are binding on this general body to the full extent to which
those who hold to the doctrine of the verbal inspiration of Scripture find
the latter binding upon themselves.

---

[101] pp. 610, 611.
[102] p. 610.

4

Are not students to be pitied who must form their conception of the conservative Lutheran Church on the basis of a history which omits or alters the crucial word in a symbolical statement of an adversary? Can it be that young men are being seriously taught that a large body of Lutherans in this land is pledged and bound down, not only to the infallibility of the confessions,—that it is *impossible* for them to err; but also to *their verbal inspiration?*

Perhaps, on the whole, the most remarkable fact in The Confessional History is its laying the responsibility of doctrinal controversy, dissension and difference in the Lutheran Church of America at the door of the Formula of Concord.

This statement is found in the chapter on Subscription to the Formula of Concord on p. 507. It runs as follows: "Certain it is that the doctrinal controversies that have distracted and separated the Lutherans in America have sprung out of the Formula of Concord. . . ." So that the Augsburg Confession, the Definite Platform, the influence of Presbyterianism, Methodism, and of the Reformed Church, the writings of Dr. S. S. Schmucker, the doctrine of Predestination, the doctrine of the Ministry as held by Walther, Grabau, and Löhe, and other theological questions outside the Formula, have had nothing to do with the controversies in American Lutheranism; but rather all differences have sprung out of the Formula of Concord.

The conclusion of "The Confessional History," without any general outlook, or any suggestion of hope, or any proposal for the future, is dispiriting. We are not told whether "the Augsburg Confession (Altered)," or any document substituted for it in the days of the nineteenth century, has been "an instrument of concord in the Lutheran Church in America," but we are informed that the Book of Concord has not been such an instrument,[103] although one of the general bodies that accepts it "has been very pacific, and tries to act as a peacemaker between other Lutheran Synods that have not yet come to see eye to eye" (p. 623). Beyond the critical picture of harm and ruin, and this single synodical attempt to stay the same, no constructive ideal has been set up toward which the Church of the future may hopefully look forward.

---

[103] p. 617.

And how can there ever be any hope for Lutheranism, with its doctrine of the Word, if its Confessions are but a clog about its neck? He is not a Lutheran who regards the innermost mystery of God's Word as a clog. We subordinate the light of reason and the law of science to God's Word. God's Word is the only law of Christian truth.[104] He who abides completely within God's Word, "shall know the truth, and the truth shall make him free."[105] Confessions of Faith and Love are a clog only to him who doubts, or who does not heartily love. Men are incapable of joyous Confession who do not unreservedly love and believe.

There is hope for the Lutheran Church in the future in this land, not because of any present outlook, or because the Lutheran Church seems to have a peculiar mission in this country, or because other denominations have much to learn from her, but because the principle within and beneath her, is the principle of the Person and Redemption of Christ her Lord, revealed in the Scripture and witnessed unto in her Confession, before all the world, in contrast to errors ancient and modern, in every age.

---

[104]John 17 : 17.
[105]John 8 ; 31-32.

THE CONFESSIONAL PRINCIPLE

AND

THE CONFESSIONS

OF

THE LUTHERAN CHURCH

CHAPTER I.

WHAT IS THE QUESTION?

The Question Concerning Confessions—The Union Question—The Lutheran Question—The Twentieth Century Atmosphere—Incidental Questions.

SHOULD the Evangelical Lutheran Church be loyal to her Confessional Principle and abide by her Confessions? This is not a new question, but the grave and eventful problem of three and a quarter centuries ago which has sprung up in this new land and in this new century, destined by Providence as the seat of the greatest unfolding of the true Evangelical Faith of the living Gospel, in the midst of the impressive external strength of a false catholicism and the mighty moral emphasis of a federation of Reformed protestantism, on the one hand; and, on the other, the looseness of a fitful evangelism and the broadness of a sheer rationalism.

Though the Confessional question now upon us is the old one, it is also always new. It was raised, but not settled, in the Sixteenth Century. It was accentuated to a formal and logical close in the Seventeenth Century. It decayed,

1

by way of reaction, in the Eighteenth Century. It sprang up again under a new synthesis in the Nineteenth Century. And it is here once more as a reaction of the old faith against the spirit of unionism, which has taken on a wider form than ever, in the Twentieth Century. Whatever this book may or may not establish, its material will probably convince its readers that the question of unionism and confederation to-day, is the question that arose in the fountain-head of Protestantism, the question of Marburg,—hidden partially in Augsburg,—the question of the Wittenberg Concord, of the Leipzig Interim, and of the acceptance or rejection of the Formula of Concord.

The widest form of unionism, which may be defined as a desire for amalgamation into one earthly communion, or for alliance or federation, of religious organizations of different faiths, at the compromise[1] of custom, government or principle, in order to secure solidarity of life and action, has been seriously proposed by Friedrich Delitzsch, who originally was set into the foreground of favor by the German Emperor. Delitzsch's proposal is the uniting, on the basis of the Scriptures, of the three great occidental faiths, viz., Judaism, Christianity and Mohammedanism. The only thing that need be sacrificed, according to Delitzsch, in this scheme of union is the divinity of Christ,[2] and the advantage to be gained is an equality or a preponderance of our western racial faith as over against all oriental religions. The Parliament of Religions, held some years ago at Chicago, was suggestive of the possibility of a similar, but wider-principled union, which included even oriental faiths.

Several other proposals of union, almost equally chimerical, but emanating from responsible ecclesiastical sources, such as the Lambeth Conference, or the Pope at Rome, or the now defunct Evangelical Alliance, and the far more prac-

---

[1] This is often not admitted, but it occurs practically at every union service, in every union religious effort, and in a majority of union moral movements.

[2] Compare Luther: "Und steur des Papsts und Türken Mord, Die Jesum Christum, deinen Sohn, Wollen stürtzen von deinem Thron."

tical and often quite evangelical Federation of Protestant Churches, have limited themselves to a reunion of parts of Christendom alone.

Within the Protestant world itself, the questions of confessionalism and union, which are co-respondents in this aspect, have come up ceaselessly within the life of the last generation. Not only have Presbyterians, and Presbyterianism and Congregationalism, and Congregationalism in connection with various other smaller denominations, and the several branches of the Reformed Church, been agitated by it; but a growing sentiment and great organizations for interdenominational confession and work, and for common work on undenominational ground, in such fields as the Young Men's Christian Association, Foreign Missionary enterprises, and the work of spiritual salvation and physical rescue among the fallen, the foreigner, and other elements that form the material of "settlement work," have made tremendous progress.

Within the Lutheran Church the same—quite laudable and noble—spirit and desire to hold, cherish, maintain and express a common faith and a common worship, to live within common forms of communion and congregational fellowship, and to progress in a common spirit by means of a common activity, have manifested themselves in many ways.

The most universal of these movements in our communion is the International Lutheran Conference, which originated in the land of the Reformation, and which in the midst of many difficulties has maintained at least a precarious existence. The attempts to furnish the American Church a common Lutheran service, a common translation of the Catechism, to recognize common limitations in Home and Foreign Mission work, and to be helpful rather than harmful to each other in these fields; the calling into being of a common organization, national in scope, of the young people of the Church; the attempt to provide common courses of instruction in the schools of the Church, and to unite and combine publications within the Church; the holding of General Conferences between the three older general bodies of the Church; and of Inter-synodical Conferences between the three younger and more Germanic bodies of the Church, all indicate how deeply the spirit of union and the desire for unification dwell within the heart.

Union and unification *are* desirable things, to be sought ceaselessly, and, like peace, are Scripturally enjoined, so far as they are possible; and they become the antithesis and antagonist of confessionalism only when the means through which they intend to attain their object lie in the compromise of a principle of faith. Any union or unification which can be harmoniously accomplished without sacrifice of the faith, in any of its principles, should be commended and carried out.

In this general atmosphere of our land and century, and during the attempt of Church bodies to approach each other, the question of The Confessions of the Lutheran Church, and of their relation to a true Lutheranism, has arisen.

It is a question which will never be settled until it is settled right, on the basis of the real character of the original foundation, and in recognition of the light thrown upon it by four centuries of history,—unless it be settled, as Schaff intimates,[8] by the absorption of the Lutherans of this land in and under the Reformed principle.

---

[8] *Creeds of Christendom,* I, p. 213.

CHAPTER II.

HOW IS THE QUESTION TO BE DISCUSSED?

From Centre or simply from Periphery?—Not a Question of Subscription, Name, Party, or Technical Acceptance—A Question of Loyal Maintenance of the Complete Principle of the Faith—There is such a Faith, not merely Documentary, but Actual.

THE discussion of the relation of true Lutheranism to the Symbolical Books will drift into externals, and go down in confusion, unless it be begun and maintained from the right point of view. To us the fundamental, and not any incidental point of view, is the right one. Therefore it is necessary for us to keep clear in mind *what the question in point is* and *what it is not.*

The controversy is not at bottom a controversy covering the quality or duty of confessional subscription, nor concerning adherence to certain historical documents, nor an investigation as to compatibility of temperament between Melanchthon and Luther, nor a strife as to who legitimately may lay claim to the name Lutheran, or as to who may honorably term themselves the followers of Luther; nor a question as to how best to deal with those Christians that are non-Lutherans.

But at bottom this controversy is one as to the nature and constitution of the Church's true religion and Faith, and as to her willingness to stand for this, where need be, in its complete expression. The controversy is not one of narrowness or broadness; of parts or parties or partizanship; of

5

the correct ascription of names or the proper weight of numbers; but it is a controversy as to the principle itself.[1] The other questions which seem to be connected with the fundamental question of principle, viz.: Who is entitled to bear the name? What kinds of Lutherans are in the majority? How many, if any, Confessions must be subscribed by a good Lutheran? Should the minimum or the maximum historical Confessional position be required? Is it possible for the Church to demand a subscription to some one of the Confessions as a public and official necessity, and to encourage or permit subscription to others privately? Is any one Confession sufficient as the basis of the Church? Should this one Confession be the first or the last, the shortest or the longest, the most generic or the most specific? Which edition of which Confession should be the one to be insisted on, or may various editions be disregarded?—these questions, though they be important, and may indeed be decisive in their time and place, are really incidental to the great issue which is now before the Church; and, by being placed in the foreground as the leading matter, often tend to obscure it.

The real question before the Church to-day, as in the days of Christ, as in the days of Augsburg and a half century later, and every century since, is as to our thorough adherence, our open acceptance, and our loyal defence of the great Principle in all its integrity, and against all coun-

---

[1] The great error of Schaff in his *Creeds of Christendom*, and of many liberal Lutherans, is the assumption that Lutheranism is a form of Protestantism colored by the personal opinions of two reformers, Luther and Melanchthon. Lutheranism is the old faith of the Church, catholic and evangelical, protestant only as to Roman errors, founded on the teaching of Scripture, without the admixture of human reason. Luther and Melanchthon as the authors of " personal opinions," have no more to do with Lutheranism than the crack of the Liberty Bell has to do with our national liberty itself.

Compare Jacobs: " The unity of the Church does not consist in subscription to the same Confessions, but in the acceptance and teaching of the same doctrines. Where the doctrines of the Confessions are not believed, it is the solemn duty of the person who questions them to testify on all occasions against them, instead of seeking to hide his dissent under an ambiguous or indefinite formula." Also, " It is not subscription to Confessions of faith that is desired so much as to the faith of the Confessions."—*Distinctive Doctrines of the Lutheran Church in the United States*, p. 94.

terfeits, resemblances and approximations coming up from a temporary or divergent basis.

The question is this: "Are we ready to accept, adhere to, defend and carry out completely the teaching, on the Word and Sacraments, of our Church as found in any or all of her Confessions?" If so, *any one* Confession will be sufficient *for us* (that is, in our informal relations to each other, and not considering questions that come to us from a legal insistence without); if not, even a quasi or a complete formal acceptance of *all* the Confessions will not suffice.

In the latter case, discussion, instead of bringing forth, promulgating and defending inner conviction, will degenerate into skirmishes for position and advantage, and into quibbling over points, technical, historical and practical, which do not touch the heart of the issue.

Ecclesiastically, the great question at the present moment in the English Lutheran Church in America is as to the need, the legitimacy and the authority of the Symbolical Books of our Church. But underlying this is the great question of all ages as to the willingness of the Church, or of any parts of it in question, to accept, to proclaim and maintain, and to loyally defend the complete Principle of which the Symbolical Books, any one of them singly, or all together, are but a documentary exposition.

It is a question as to the living faith itself, and not as to any circumstantialities of its external record, or of any of the various modes in which it became crystallized into history.

There is a real, living, whole and full-orbed Lutheran Faith—the reflex of the living divine Word,—which appears in the visible Church only in historical, and therefore temporal, and incomplete forms, and which is more than and above the forms, but of which the forms are the only original expression; and the question is concerning our possession of this full Faith. As in the Lord's Supper it is not a question of this or that as to bread or wine, but it is the question of what we receive in, with and under the bread and the wine; so is the Confessional question fundamentally a question of the real Faith; *i. e.,* it is a germinal question, and not one of the outer historical investiture in which it has been handed down to us.

As the main question concerning the Scripture is always and in every age a question of the living Word of God, and not any of the subordinate matters of criticism or history in which it has manifested itself in the successive layers of recorded revelation, but of the complete Word itself, and our full acceptance and defence of it by faith, so is the Confessional question one of our real Faith itself, and not of attendant documents or of selection of single historical moments, or men, or phraseologies, to which our adherence is to be pinned as to a mere external touchstone in place of a spiritual fact.

CHAPTER III.

WHAT ARE CONFESSIONS?

Scripture Assimilated and Pulsating in the Church—Scripture Condensed Into Public Standards—The Common Principle of the Church's Faith—The Common Framework of the Church's Doctrine—The Common Mark of the Church's Truth—The Common Flag of the Church's Loyalty.

CONFESSIONS are Scripture digested, assimilated, and beating in the life pulses of the Church.

Pulse-beats of Scripture are they, come up out of the believing Church's heart into free, public, courageous, joyous and solemn utterance. As thus born out of the heart of a believing Church, they incarnate the faith of man in visible form, even as God incarnated His own Son in the visible form of our own flesh, and His own Word in the visible form of written Scripture.

They differ from Scripture in origin—they are human;[1] in native strength—they are not original, but reflex; in order—they are not historical, but doctrinal; and in compass—they are comparatively brief, as a summary. They agree with Scripture in substance and in intent; and spread its truth by echo, by reflection, refraction and transmission. Confessions are *" a witness and a declaration of the Faith* as to how at any time the Holy Scriptures have been understood and explained in the Church of God."[2]

Confessions are the answer of earth to the revelation from

---

[1] Like all things in the Church, except Word and Sacrament, very human.
[2] *Formula of Concord*, Intro., 8. Cp. also Walch, *Int. in Libros Symbolicos*, p. 16, section 4. Cp. Luther, 1533: " Wir haben nicht Mum Mum gesagt, und unter den Hütlein gespielet, sondern da stehet unser helle, dürr, frei Wort ohn alles tunckeln und mausen."

9

Heaven. They are the response of faith to the testing questions of the Lord, Who is still present as of old, not visibly,
but in Word and Sacrament; and is still guiding the word and
deed of His Church through a multitude of dangers. They
are not the word of the populace or the cry of the moment;
but in form, matter and purpose they are weighty, thoughtful
and representative or common declarations, embodying the
faith of multitudes and generations, and bearing forward the
best and greatest witness of an age come to climax into
the teachings and faith of all following ages.

They are " Witnesses, in what manner' and at what places
the purer doctrine of the apostles and prophets was preserved." [3]   They thus constitute the public standards of
the Church's faith; or, as the Formula of Concord declares,
they are best defined as " brief, plain confessions, regarded
as the unanimous, universal Christian Faith and Confession
of the orthodox and true Church." [4]

They are not the source of light—the sun is Scripture
itself; but they are great and public lamps of life, lit from
the sun, that illumine our pathway through the intricate
forestland of faith and life.

Confessions are the one common and abiding inner unity
left to the Protestant Church. " For thorough, permanent
unity in the Church it is before all things necessary that we
have a comprehensive, unanimously approved summary and
form, wherein are brought together from God's Word the
common doctrines, reduced to a brief compass, which the
Churches that are of the true Christian religion acknowledge
as confessional." [5]

They spring from conscience, not from custom; yet they
come from the past, and reach into the future. Though only
a fixed declaration of a common faith, they are neverthe-

---

[3] *Formula of Concord,* 2.
[4] *Ib.,* 3. (" Sunt Confessiones publicæ Ecclesiæ . . . , non ut principium
fidei generandæ sint, sed ut ex Scripturâ explicent credenda."—Carpzov, *Isag.
in Lib. Eccl. Luth. Symb.* Lip. 1675, p. 2.)
[5] *Ib.,* Sol. Decl., 1.

less the one common embodiment and sum of the principle which holds together the Church and the men in it. " We have a unanimously received, common form of doctrine, which our Evangelical Churches together and in common confess; from and according to which, because it has been derived from God's Word, all other writings should be judged." [6]

This unanimous and common confessional form of the Lutheran Church is not composed of the Augsburg Confession alone,[7] but " we have embodied the Augsburg Confession, Apology, Smalcald Articles, Luther's Large and Small Catechisms, *as the sum of our Christian doctrine,* for the reason that *these have been always and everywhere regarded* as containing the common, unanimously received understanding of the Churches." [7] The Formula of Concord further says: " Since the chief and most enlightened theologians of that time subscribed them, and all evangelical Churches and schools have cordially received them. As they also, as before mentioned, were all written and sent forth before the divisions among the theologians of the Augsburg Confession arose, and then because they were held as impartial, and neither can nor should be rejected by any part of those who have entered into controversy, *and no one who is true to the Augsburg Confession will complain of these writings, but will cheerfully accept and tolerate them as witnesses."* [8]

Confessions are, therefore, the sum of Scripture, its very pulse-beat or accent, in time, as the true Church, in her Witness, divinely commanded, best knows how to utter it. Confessions are the Scripture itself worked up by the believing Church's convictions amid the tests of human life and experience, and under the same guidance of the Holy Spirit that inheres in the office of the preacher in bearing witness to Christ in the pulpit,—into Common **Principles**

---

[6] *Formula of Concord,* 10. [7] *Book of Concord,* p. **537.**

[8] *Formula of Concord,* Sol. Decl., 11.

of Faith, on which the Churches can rest, and in which the Church of the future can find anchorage.

Confessions are the under-framework of the Church—the spars and the ribs of the ship, resting upon and extending from a centre of strength, the Word, to give protection to any point in the circumference, the Church, where there may be weakness and consequent possibility of wreck. Confessions are the rails; and, let us understand well, not the roadbed or the solid rock, on which the ecclesiastical trains run. The bed is Scripture and the rock is Christ, and they determine the direction; but the rails are of human workmanship, condensing the roadbed to an effective point, and giving guidance, protection and impetus to the moving trains above.

Common Principles of Faith in a Church, within and beneath, correspond to and are the presupposition of a common expression in a common worship and in common work, or in a common name, above and without. The Common Faith and the Common Service [9] are both elaborated in the Church on the basis of Scripture: the one is for the establishment and strengthening of the mind and soul within; the other, for the expression of the lips without. Scripture itself will not serve either as a form of public Confession or as a form of public worship, for the simple reason that Scripture has been given to us in historical and not in doctrinal or liturgical form.

This, among other things, means that the Word of God in Scripture is so connected with local incident and detail, and extends over so many lifetimes, that its very bulk would prevent it from being used, without selection, either to confess or to worship. But the selective use of Scripture in Confession or in worship brings about a systematic form of both, a form that has been moulded into a unity in passing through the Christian mind and consciousness.

---

[9] The Common Faith is an essential; the Common Service is a common result of Christian liberty.

It is true that there are some Christians, such as the old-line Presbyterians, who try to exclude the selective process in worship, and who will sing, for instance, only the Psalms of David, and not the hymns in which Christian truth has been remoulded by passing through hearts that have been inspired by the Gospel; but these people are few in our day, and we do not believe that there are many who will insist that either a common Confession or a common Worship may not pass through Christian experience in receiving its final form, but that it must be plucked crudely and mechanically from the external phraseology of Scripture. No; under the guidance of the Holy Spirit in the Word it is not only our right, but it becomes our duty, in developing the Church of Christ, to bring system and order into both our faith and worship, and not to leave these lie simply in the foundation as they are given to us in Scripture.

Both the Confession and the Order of Service are, therefore, historically and genetically a stage higher in the building of the Church than the Scripture itself. They are not more valuable than Scripture, and their construction, unlike the Scripture, is human in its combining elements; but so far as they are Scriptural, the power of the Scripture in them gives them a more pointed and useful form for the purpose for which they are intended, than that of the Scripture itself, which, like nature, is a great undistributed mine or quarry from which the materials are to be taken for the construction of all forms of truth through all ages. Systematically, though not intrinsically, the Confessions rise— like the house described by the Apostle as being built humanly of silver and gold, with some hay and straw and stubble—above the foundation itself. The foundation of the Confession, *i. e.,* Scripture, determines every line and measurement and angle in the house. But the house is an elaboration, not useless, but necessary, of the foundation.

The Common Principles which brace, uphold and protect the Church, and the Common Worship and activities in which
5

the Principles are manifested, consequently rise in proper order, and in God's own intended historical development, upon the foundation. The religion of our age is not a sudden and independent result effected by an abrupt break with the past; but it is connected stone by stone with all that has gone before, from the first day of God's revelation, and especially from the fulness of time in Christ, up to the present moment. Both the Faith and the Worship have a historical aspect. Genetically they must both spring out of the history of the past. If we would be true to ourselves and true to the future, we must be real and vital links [10] connecting the past with the future. We can no more turn our backs upon the one than upon the other; and the best of what the past furnishes us both in faith and in worship is to be apprehended by us and passed on, if it have reached its more final form, for the help of the future.

Thus we see how Common Principles of Faith and a common expression of Faith in a common Order of Worship are the finished product and express the reaction of the preceding Christian generations of the Church at any particular stage in its work upon the present and successive generations.[11]

The reactions of Scripture upon men, in the course of history, constantly bring about four results. The first and, from a personal view, the most important of these results is the reaction on the individual, viz., the salvation of souls. The second result is the expressing of this individual salvation within a common social organization, itself divine in origin, which is the Church. The third result is the expression of this salvation in a common organization of worship; and the fourth of these results of the reaction of

---

[10] The tendency is to consider the single link that glows with the fire and vitality of the present moment as of more import and value than all that has gone before and all that will follow.

[11] After writing the foregoing, we find the following confirmation of this view from Plitt: " It is as impossible for the Church to be without a Confession as without preaching and divine service, and sooner or later the summons must come to the entire Church or an individual part of it to give to its confession not only a clear, but also an established and definite expression." —Trans. in Jacobs *Book of Concord*, p. 312.

Scripture upon the hearts and minds of men is the expression of the salvation in an articulate organism of Principles. This organization of common principles is our Confession; and our Confession, as coming forth in the providential development of history, is found in the form of our Confessions.

The Confessional principle springs forth *in variety* to meet the historical, just as the principle of worship springs forth in variety to meet the liturgical occasion (Matins, Vespers, Orders for Baptism, the Holy Communion, etc.). This variety of Common Services and common Confessions is not a complication. Our various Confessions are useful treasures of priceless value, and not impediments to us in our ecclesiastical life. The more powerful a railway becomes the larger is likely to be the number of rails and tracks, and the more numerous are the switchboards to meet local conditions. Though the more extensive equipment seems more complicated, yet it does not complicate; but it greatly simplifies and facilitates the general traffic. Thus, also, the more amply a Church is furnished with Confessions, the more fully will it be able to advance and protect itself, from every doctrinal point of view, and the more simple and progressive will be its future course through the many intricate labyrinths of theory and falsehood and truth.

We must always remember that the truth in God's world does not ordinarily lie upon the surface of things, but deep beneath it. Many experiences of investigators and great efforts at combination on the part of human art and science are necessary before natural truth can be freed from the many counterfeits and clinging shades of error and stated purely; and still further effort is needed before it can be reduced to an actual working principle.

Very commonly, indeed, isolated principles and rules of practice are easily picked up, and are used for many ages; but the proper combination into God's own intended system of principle and practice is not found until the ultimate principles of the science itself are discovered. Mere dislocated truth itself, then, before it is worked out into principles, and before these principles are differentiated from error, and are properly related to each other in a unity, does not correspond to the Divine reality, and is not satisfactory to the mind; nor does it afford a practicable basis for effective action.

The saving truth in religion has been revealed by God in Scripture, and it is the only active and efficient potency which the Church possesses. It gives the Church life, light and power. But, as given, it deals with concretes. It is not organized nor connected. It is the province of the Confession to arrange, to organize [12] the whole counsel of God, the whole Word of God, as found in the Scripture, into such relationships as will enable us to apply it effectively against the errors of any or every age. The Confession, then, is not the truth revealed by God, but God's Word apprehended and comprehended by us, which we have assimilated and know how to utilize, and which we have tagged and stamped as being in our possession and our own property.

The Confession is not the truth unstamped, but bears the *mark* of the truth, by which we can recognize the truth amid a thousand other things, at once.

The Confession is not itself the great cause of God around which we rally, but it is the signal, the standard, the flag, the symbol, which condenses and gathers into itself the various elements of the cause, and gives us a clear and distinctive token by which, incidentally, we know ourselves from others and others know us from themselves.

The Confession thus is not the source [13] of God's cause, which is God's gracious Will expressed in God's Word, nor the essence of the cause, which is the fact of salvation work-

---

[12] Some later Lutheran theologians in America deny this.

[13] Libros Symb. non esse principium sed principiatum, et fidem non exinde generari, sed praesupponi. Quod enim quis profitetur ac testatur, id jam jam in corde suo habet.—Carp. *Isag.*, p. 3.

ing itself out in the complications of history, but it is the *sign* of the cause.

The merchant's trade-mark[14] is not his business nor its creative source; but if the trade-mark is a good one, he will stand by it as standing for his business, as symbolizing that which is most valuable and precious to him in his public activities, as making known and giving character and definiteness to the nature and quality of his business.

The more, then, we prize and love the truth, the more we will repair to and stand by and show honor to its sign, not for the sign's sake, but for the sake of that for which it stands, and which could not be so clearly understood, identified, prized, defended and propagated without it.

It is only the extreme individualist who objects to associate action under a sign, or who finds the defining limitations of the sign too restrictive. Those who really believe in the cause and principle of the associative action with all their heart, hail the appearance and prominence of the sign with greatest joy. To them it is the banner of the Lord, which they bravely follow to the top of the hill.

---

[14] The Confession is a less personal, wider and truer sign-mark of the Church than the signet-emblem of Luther, its greatest modern Confessor.

CHAPTER IV.

DOES THE CHURCH NEED CONFESSIONS?

Value and Use of Creeds—The Great Reality for which the Church Confession Stands—Apostolic Confession—Use of Confessions—They come in Historical Form—This is not a Barrier—Spring Forth Under Pressure—Are Born, not Made—Do not Hem the Church In—The More Creeds the Better—Do not Crush Independent Thought—Are Fitted to Specific Needs.

THERE are some Christians,[1] and among them there may be some Lutherans, who maintain that the Church needs no creed, and that the mind and heart of her members should be bound by no Confession of Faith.[2]

But these Lutherans are very few. A personal creed is the mature and settled expression of a man's most serious thought and the response of his deepest conviction on any subject of grave importance which comes before him for action, and in which he has had real experience. It is the reaction of his personality on special problems of life, worked out into permanency; as a flag, to easily show the world on what ground he stands, as a common rallying point for all who live under the same power of his own convictions, as a sure guide for him in critical moments of hesitation and uncertainty, and in the more ordinary walks of his life; as a testimony willingly given to the value of the truths

---

[1] Many of the sects of Protestantism reject all creeds. Some of them have condemned symbolical books as a yoke of human authority and a new kind of popery. Others go so far as to reject the authority of Scripture itself, and to subordinate it to reason or to the inner light.

[2] " But the creeds, as such, are no more responsible for abuses than the Scriptures themselves, of which they profess to be merely a summary or an exposition. Experience teaches that those sects which reject all creeds are as much under the authority of a traditional system or of certain favorite writers, and as much exposed to controversy, division, and change, as churches with formal creeds."—Schaff *Creeds of Christendom*, I, p. 9.

18

under and for which he has lived, and as the most precious legacy of his thought and heart which he would like to see transmitted and used by his children even to the remotest generation. The more he is convinced of the value of any particular article, truth, or principle in his creed, the more important will it become to him, the less easily can he brook its slight or neglect in his presence, and the more intense are his activities on its behalf.

There is not a business house whose experience has not crystallized into more or less of a creed or principle of faith and rule of action on the more grave problems that recur in its activities. It may be nothing but a series of sententious mottoes, or the unwritten habits of mind, deeply graven by experience, that are at once the test and the guide for all new propositions that are submitted to it; or there may be a more formal charter and rules of action laid down.

Such a creed may be a pure statement of our apprehension of truth, by way of making things clear and decisive in time of danger, as was the Declaration of Independence; or it may take the shape of a more or less complete plan of action for the future, as was the Constitution of the United States.

In all cases it is rooted more or less deeply in the historical experience of the past; it is marked with the issues of the present; and it bears a fruitage more or less enduring in the proportion of its vitality, largeness and intrinsic summing up of valuable truth, for the future.

We have to do with a greater reality than the largest business or greatest government on earth. " I believe that there is upon earth a holy assembly and congregation of pure saints, under one head, even Christ, collected together by the Holy Ghost in one faith, one mind and understanding, with manifold gifts, yet one in love, without sects or schisms. And I also am part and member of the same, a participant and joint owner of all the good it possesses, brought to it and incorporated into it by the Holy Ghost, in that I have heard and continue to hear the Word of God, which is the means of entrance."[3]

This holy Christian Church in which the Gospel is rightly taught is to continue forever,[4] and "is principally a fellowship of faith and the Holy Ghost in hearts; which fellowship has outward marks, the pure doctrine of the Gospel and the administration of the sacraments. And this Church alone is called the body of Christ. The Church signifies the congregation of saints which have with each other the fellowship of the same Gospel or doctrine.

" We see the infinite dangers which threaten the destruction of the Church. And this Church is properly the pillar of the truth. For it retains the pure Gospel, and, as Paul says (1 Cor. 3: 11), the ' foundation,' *i. e.,* the true knowledge of Christ and faith. And the writings of the holy Fathers testify that sometimes even they ' built stubble ' upon the foundation. Most of those errors which our adversaries defend overthrow faith. Although wicked teachers go about in the Church, yet they are not properly the kingdom of Christ.

"As Lyra testifies, 'The Church consists of those persons in whom there is a true knowledge and confession of faith and truth.' " [5]

This " true knowledge and confession " is crystallized in our creeds. The creeds of the Church of Christ are the mature reactions of her heart and thought on Scripture in reference to questions of faith arising in the course of her conflict and growth, in fighting for the conquest of every soul for Christ, and thus, also, for the consequent realization of the kingdom of God.

The whole spirit of the Word of Christ, one chief work of the Holy Ghost, and the gravest responsibility and deepest joy of those who confess Christ, is to *bear witness* to the truth as it is in Christ Jesus.

---

[3] *Large Catechism,* II, 51.   [4] *Aug. Conf.,* VII.   [5] *Apol.,* 4: 5.

In the primitive Apostolic Church this expression of conviction was more spontaneous, more off-hand and occasional
in its character, as befitted a new-born and youthful Church;
but as the personal experiences and memories of fellowship
with Jesus waned, and time flowed on; as the truths apprehended, won, defended and preserved in one age needed to
be passed on as a precious heritage to the next generation;
as the Church passed forever out of the provincial and entered the continental and cosmopolitan sphere; as it was
obliged to compete for supremacy with the large problems of
barbarism and civilization, with the errors and half-truths
of other religions, with the insidious treachery within its own
self (where pride is always raising the flag of rationalism,
and sin the flag of rebellion and anarchy), it became more
than ever necessary to fix and fasten the measures of truth
on which it had already maturely reacted, and which it rejoiced to confess, as a standard for present use [*] and as a
guide for future faith and action.

The use of Confessions, then, is clear: first, They summarize Scripture for us; secondly, They interpret it for the
Church; thirdly, They bring us into agreement in the one
true interpretation, and thus set up a public standard, which
becomes a guard against false doctrine and practice; fourthly,
and this is their most important use, They become the medium of instruction, or education, of one generation to the
next, in their preservation, transmission and communication
through all future ages of the one true faith of the Church.

We have now reached a general idea of the growth of
Confessions in answer to a need. Their specific nature is
conditioned by several points in their use and growth.

In the first place, Confessions do not come to us in
ideal form, but they clearly reflect the particular angle
and view-point of the period within which they originated

---

[*] "That a symbol originates is no matter of chance or option, but of
necessity. It is owing to the nature of the Church as a communion, which
has also a historical visible side to its existence, and unfolds its being and
fulfills its office in historical life."—*Plitt.*

and developed. The clumsy and out-of-date historical environment in which they are clothed, and which seems to us
like an archaic and unnecessary residuum, is what the ancient towns and cities in ruins are to the life of our Lord;
namely, the most weighty testimony to their genuineness,
enabling us to guage more precisely the extent and value of
their intention. This local setting is the brand showing that
they have actually passed through the fiery flame of history
and have survived it.

We should also bear in mind, secondly, that the historical element[1] in creeds, according to one of the great methods of God in unfolding law and life, is not any more of a
barrier to their acceptance than is the historical element in
the Scriptures. God chose that both the Scripture and our
Church Confession of it should come into being at various
times and in various places, and that they should appear
subject to the historical order under which the human race
is obliged to develop, mature and fulfill His will.

A third fact to be noted of Confessions is that those which
abide spring forth in periods of most intense and searching
spiritual life; and those which disappear are the product of
a calmer, and more rationalistic, era.

The Apostles' Creed, the Athanasian Creed, the Nicene
Creed, and the Sixteenth Century Confessions of our Church
are each and every one of them the product of the greatest
upheavals and the most intense crises in the Church of
Christ. Creeds are born, not made. They are wrung in
the agony and anxiety of a confession at an epoch fraught
with the possibility of perilous consequences to the confessors.

Such creeds, the mighty foundations of our Fathers, do
not bind us, but they plant us on solid ground. They do not
throttle, but they protect us. They specialize, differentiate
and qualify our Church's activity, render it more effective,

---

[1] Including the unworthy motives of formulators, and the unseemly elements of conflict in assemblies in which they were discussed.

and save much experimental waste. They no more hem us in and bind us down than noble old trees, planted by our fathers, hem in, destroy and narrow down the landscape.

It is true that the landmarks are set for us, and we have not the liberty of an endless prairie or a barren plain; but we are advanced far beyond this low order of liberty, merely formal, to the possession of a richly furnished park, in which various generations are called to do their share in its preservation and perfection, that those who come after us will have greater abundance of living values, though they find less loose and unorganized material about them than their fathers. The succeeding generation builds upon the foundation constructed and left as a legacy by its predecessor.

From this point of view a whole clump, a copse of stately tree-growths, is more valuable than only a single trunk. Of genuine Creeds, confessing the whole truth in Christ, we say, not the less, but *the more,* the better.

He who regards them negatively as an impediment to his own personal liberties, either cherishes a very lofty estimate of his own powers of mind and soul, else he would not stand up against the accumulated wisdom of the Church for many centuries; or he fails perhaps to realize the greatness and momentousness of the problems before him, else he were willing to bow in the reverence of faith, and work out the great things of God according to the scale and plan provided.

Even Luther clung desperately, and so long as he could, to the scale historically provided; and for every theological fledgling to-day to go forth into the Church and the world, and demand, on the plea of personal liberty, that he may work things out on the scale and plan he approves for the moment—perhaps he may reject his present scale and take a totally different one a year or two hence (again on the plea of personal liberty)—is simply a fearful waste to the Church, is the one great extravagance of Protestantism, and would not be tolerated, no, not for a moment, in any sound and established business plant in the country.

As a rule, the more radical and unrestricted and liberty-loving the theologian, the more highly he is exalting the importance of his own opinions and personality as an individual, and the less seriously does he take himself as the servant of the Lord in the work of the Church. Lutherans should never forget that it was not an intellectual issue in the Professor's chair, but the deadly working of common gross falsehood in the congregation, under his pastoral care, that made Luther a Protestant. Luther was to the end of his days the true servant of the Church, and the mere possession of an unfettered liberty to think what he pleased, as a private personal right, had little attraction for him.

"Wherefore the Church can never be governed and preserved better than if we all live under one head, Christ, and all the bishops, equal in office, be diligently joined in unity of doctrine, faith, sacraments, prayer and works of love." [8]

Some claim against creeds that they deprive of intellectual liberty and crush out independent thought. Others, on the contrary, claim that they are too conducive to a mere religion of the intellect, and that they oppress spiritual fervor and vitality.

Both charges may be true when the man or the Church is out of joint with the living Word of God, but when the Word is truly operative, creeds are no more an obstruction to the Church or the man than are the guns and armor of a battleship an obstruction to the engines or the mariners who have the battle to fight. It is a question of adjustment, proportion and proper use, and of understanding and co-operating with the plan of the vessel as a whole. The man who says, "Luther's Catechism is confession enough for me," is the man who would use his personal revolver in an attempt to batter down the defences of Gibralter; and the man who would make his catechumens commit the Formula of Concord to memory is the man who would use the great sixteen-inch gun in the tower to fire on a tiny steam launch. As there

___

[8] *Schmalkald Articles,* II, 9.

is a place for every true man, so there is a place for every true creed in the kingdom of God.

Neither the Augsburg Confession,[*] nor the Formula of Concord, should be idolized. Nor, on the other hand, should either of them be rejected by the Lutheran Church. The Augsburg Confession is a foundation without a roof. Solidly as it was laid, the storms and frosts of time were playing havoc with its upper and outer stones, and the destruction might have been entire, if the work had not been so laboriously completed by the perilous but finally successful raising of a covering in the Formula of Concord. The foundation is always more simple than the roof and easier to stand on, but not less necessary. There are many children of nature who do not like to come in under a roof, or see its need—until it rains.

The Augsburg Confession was the first seed that must develop under the test of wind and storm into a full-grown tree. It was the first great confessional reservoir of truth since the Athanasian Creed, built to check the flood of ecclesiastical degeneracy; but the waters it contained and saved must now still be clarified and spread healthfully over the fields of the Church, as by proper irrigation we transform our western barren plateaus into fertile plains. The later Confessions were the sluices that gave to every part of our symbolical system its due portion and proportion of truth.

What the Augsburg Confession proclaimed, had to be worked out into the life-blood of the Church. It was written by a few and expressed the feeling of the many, but the painful process had now to begin, viz., the transmuting of that feeling into solid conviction, and the conversion of that conviction into the real but changing facts of history. This must be done apart from the *lives* of the two Reformers, for they must die some time.

With the lives of the Reformers left out of it, the history

---

[*] Perhaps for that reason Providence has involved the original edition in obscurity

sinks from the mountain to the valley; but it is the valley, and not the mountain that gives direction to the final current and determines in what direction the waters shall emerge into the plain. ·

CHAPTER V.

DO CONFESSIONS CONSTRICT, OR DO THEY CONSERVE?

IT has been intimated that the Lutherans who object to a creed are few. Yet there are many who feel that the matter of confessing may be overdone. The sum total of the Symbolical Books is oppressive, they feel, by their quantity. The confessional spirit itself, if given full sway, tends to too great sharpness of edge and narrowness of blade. There is such a thing as over-emphasizing the confessional side. Our Confession is fundamental and necessary, but it should be characterized by more simplicity, larger elasticity, greater moderateness and wider liberality.

The Apostolic and not the Mediæval Church should be its model. The simplicity as it is in Christ, and not the complexity as it is in the dogmaticians, should be its characteristic. Let us have the Lutheran Confession, but let us boil it down and reduce it to its lowest terms. In fact, let us get back to the early and purer days before dogma was formulated thetically. Why not greet the spirit of the age and join in the cry, "Back to Christ!" Let us breathe the pure air of Scripture itself, and not the confining and gloomy atmosphere of a historic monastery. Christ's own words and the Scripture itself, are a better confession than any technical and long-drawn-out formulary that we can substitute for it; and in them we feel that we can breathe free and open.

These words are strenuous, and frequently very honest. They accord with the modern determination to be free and shake off every encumbrance. We hesitate to suggest that they spring up so easily, from the surface of religious thought, since they are rooted in so shallow ground.

Is the plan of abrupt return to the simple fountain-head of faith really desirable? Is it possible? Can the Twentieth Century go back with a leap, to the First? 'Can the adult go back to the ideal days of childhood? Is our model the un-developed child? *As* little children, we are to become, but not little children. Has God been at work in His world, and in all these ages, for nothing? Can and should the stream re-fuse its wider channels, its newer filtration beds, and flow backwards to its higher and purer source?

Because Christ spoke in the First Century, are there no further words for Luther to speak in the Sixteenth Century, and no words for me to speak in mine? Am I not to make the Bible *my own,* for myself and for to-day, and to testify and confess it against the errors that have been growing for a thousand years in Rome, and that are springing up prolific-ally in the superficial Christianity around me?

All Christendom says the Bible is its creed, but do I thereby know what Christendom believes? One and the same Bible Dictionary contains within its covers no less than a half-dozen conflicting faiths. If any one of them is the true faith, the others are partially or totally false faiths. Which one of them is my faith?

Do I know what I believe without a creed? Can I give every man a reason for the faith that is in me? Will the world know what I believe, if I say the Bible is my creed? The Bible says, "There is no remembrance of the wise more

---

[1] Compare *Conservative Reformation,* p. 83, which characterizes them as " sophistical to the core."

than of the fool forever." Is that my creed? The Bible says, "I praised the dead which are already dead, more than the living which are yet alive. Yea, better is he than both they, which hath not yet been, who hath not seen the evil work that is done under the sun." Is that my creed? The Bible says, "We are justified by faith without the works of the law." It also says, "Faith without works is dead." Which of these is my creed? The Bible says, Jesus is the Son of man, and also says that He is the Son of God; is it right in both cases, or in only one? and why?

The Bible raises ten thousand questions. If you answer any one of them in your own way only, and without looking farther, and say, "This is what I believe," you are setting up a personal creed of your own. If you simply content yourself with the assertion, "The Bible is my creed," you are leaving unanswered many of the most important and vital questions of faith and life. And a Church's answer, more than your own, must be ample to meet all questions. When you refuse to take a definite stand on vital issues in the Christian Faith, but say, "The Bible is my creed," are you really confessing Christ, or are you taking the problems of religious life easy, and evading the unpleasant but important doctrines which the Spirit of God has brought to an issue in the development of the Faith and His Church in history?

The religious fanatics, the narrow-minded legalists, as well as the most liberal and the most loose communions, have claimed to make the Bible their creed. If there be no testing of these claims, and no framing of the true doctrine after the test in a way in which I can bravely confess it before all the world, am I witnessing to the truth as it is in Christ Jesus?

It is not the truth in the printed and dead page of the Bible, but the truth that drops like a living seed[2] into my willing heart, and which is applied there by the Holy Ghost,

---

[2] " The seed is the Word of God."

and which springs up into living faith that freely testifies of itself, and which makes me a believer.

Dr. C. P. Krauth was right when he said, "Faith makes men Christians; but Confession alone marks them as Christians." He was right when he said, "The Scripture is God's voice to us, and the Confession, our reply of assent to it." He was right when he said, "The Bible can no more be any man's creed than the stars can be any man's astronomy."

Even the Quaker Friend will believe that the words of the Bible are true—the Bible is his Creed—yet he does not believe that any of the words of the Bible are more inspired than his own inner light. Even the Unitarian says he believes all the statements in the Bible concerning Jesus, yet he also believes that there is no Trinity, and that our Lord is a mere man.

Unless you carefully put the meaning of the Bible, on any particular point, into such definite language as cannot be used by a man who has a different faith than yours, you are not really bearing witness to your faith. But such a clear and unambiguous statement of your faith is a creed.

A Creed is the exact substance, or teaching, of the Bible, as you believe it, with all the outer shells of vague language removed. A Creed is what the particular "Statement of the Case" is as compared with the common law of the land. A Creed is what a filtering and distributing reservoir is as compared with the original springs, pure at the source, but quickly polluted in their flow down the mountain side. A Creed is that which gathers, which selects, which holds and which distributes and applies the waters of life.

God's system of evaporation and condensation, of rainfall and percolation, of gravity and syphonage in the provision for waters is good; but God also intended that we, as civilization progresses, should guard the sources, preserve the waters and effectively distribute them through artificial mains and pipes, as an improvement, yea, a necessity under present conditions, in addition to His natural system, of original sources.

Creeds are just such a necessity in the gathering, selection and application of the true and saving doctrine found in the sources of the Bible. And any man who says, "The whole matter is too cumbersome: let us abandon the Creeds, and go back to the original wells of salvation, back to the old oaken bucket and the pitcher that the Samaritan woman carried on her head and rested on the brim of Jacob's well," is a man who is taking a step backward and not a step forward.

The world, and the best men in it, the truest Christians that have ever lived, the heroes and the martyrs of past ages, have thought long and painfully of the problems of salvation and faith, and of the truth as it is in Christ Jesus, and have given us the results of their rich but dearly-bought experience in the Creeds of the Church; and now after the Lord has thus enriched His children in the present generation, shall we say, "No. No progress has been made by the truth. Let us go back to the original simplicity and the first beginning?"

The fallacy of all such reasoning lies here, viz., in presuming that the Scripture contains the very word of God, and that the Creed does not. The fact is that the Scripture is *the word of God extended;* and the Creed is *the word of God condensed;* but condensed in the one way in which we can do it, viz., by a universal, churchly, scholarly and providential human effort. It is not true that Scripture is more simple (*vide* the Epistles to the Romans, the Ephesians, the Colossians, the Hebrews), less abstract and formal (*vide* the argumentation in Paul, the deep things in John, and the Jewish apprehension and application of Old Testament passages in Matthew), or less extended, than our Lutheran Confessions.

Not only is the creed the Word of God condensed, but it is the Word of God pointed to defense, confession and judgment. Scripture is a whole world of life, and has many uses, public and private, besides the important one of Confession;

but the Creed takes the word of God in Scripture, *as confessional,* and applies it to the problems of truth that are confronting our mind, our thought, our efforts for Christ and our Church.

The Confession is God's Word pointed—it may be very clumsily; but it is needed for this purpose and there is nothing to take its place, not even, as we have seen, the Scriptures.

The words of the Confession "are not in themselves as clear and as good as the Scripture terms; but as those who use them can absolutely fix the sense of their own phraseology by a direct and infallible testimony, the human words may more perfectly exclude heresy than the divine words do. The term 'Trinity,' for example, does not, in itself, as clearly and as well express the doctrine of Scripture as the terms of the Word of God do; but it correctly and compendiously states that doctrine, and the trifler who pretends to receive the Bible, and yet rejects its doctrine of the Trinity, cannot pretend that he receives what the Church means by the word ' Trinity.'

" While the Apostles lived, the Word was both a rule of faith and, in a certain sense, a confession of it; but when the Canon was complete, when its inspired authors were gone, when the living teacher was no longer at hand to correct the errorist who distorted his word, the Church entered on her normal and abiding relation to the Word and the Creed, which is involved in these words: the Bible is the rule of faith, but not the confession of it; the Creed is not the rule of faith, but is the confession of it." [1]

It is the mode of a loose and superficial Christianity to-day to turn its back on the grand old symbols of the Church, that rise like a range of Alpine mountain peaks out of the valleys of time, hoary with the frost of many a morning, but mighty in the granite of many ages, and green with the perennial verdure that springs about their sheltered base. They

---

[1] *The Conservative Reformation.*

are dismissed with the sneer that they are only "human explanations of divine doctrine." But they are no more human, because they have come in the heat of contest and passion, than the everlasting hills are less divine, because they were raised from the level by the power of earthquake and volcano.

" In exact proportion as the Word of God, opened to the soul by the illumination of the Holy Spirit, is truly and correctly apprehended, just in that proportion is the 'human explanation' coincident with the divine truth. I explain God's truth, and if I explain it correctly, my explanation is God's truth."[*]

God's truth in the Scripture, like God's gold in the hills, was given to be applied by men to the wants of man. Whether it be a coin in the purse, or a watch in the pocket, or a filling in the tooth, or a frame for the lens, or a pen with iridium points for the flow of thought, it is, in all these shapes and forms and degrees of fineness, God's own gold. And if its fashioning into a stamp, or standard, for testing metals, or resistance to acids, be done by human hands, it is not on that account any the less divine. Our Confessions are God's truth fashioned into a standard. They have been set together by hearts and minds of experience, in such graduated and fitting form, as that God's Word can be applied as a standard to the opinions and principles of men. They are human in their form, in their combination, and in their application; but they are divine in their quality. The standard they exhibit is not human. The doctrines they set forth are not human. The faith they express, and the teaching they convey, is the very Word of God itself.

But why must we be confined to a *credal* Confession that is *historical,* composed of *various documents* (six or nine short ones instead of the sixty-six long ones of Scripture), and that covers all the ground? Why do we not leave it as wide

---

[*] *Con. Ref.,* pp. 185 sq.

in spirit as it is in compass? Why should it be narrowed down to anything less than a general Christianity itself? Why should it be exclusive? Dare we use it to exclude other human beings who are members of the Lord's Church and whom we expect to meet in Heaven? Is not this the very mark of a narrow sectarian orthodoxy, to deem one's own peculiar teachings so important that we will not associate with other followers of Christ who are as good Christians as we are?

This very widespread feeling among Christians of our day can only be dealt with when we are discussing it with people who will admit that religion is not chiefly a social sentiment—" sweetness and light," as Matthew Arnold puts it— but the most serious and thorough-going business of life. In serious business, distinctions, classification, grades of value, the separation of the genuine from the specious, and of first quality from that a little more inferior, are of prime importance.

In separating a man not of our faith from ourselves or our communion, we are simply taking religion seriously, as the most practical business of life. We are not attempting to exclude such a man from the Christian Church, nor passing judgment on his eternal welfare; but we are marking him as a non-Lutheran in belief and practice and as not properly belonging to its particular communion and faith. We are asking him to go to his own spiritual people, where his kind of faith is promulgated and used as a basis of hope and life, where he will not be a disturbing element to other people's principles, and where he can be cared for on his own principles. Is it charitable to encourage him to be faithless toward his own principles? Even though his personal tastes, or his earthly fellowships, should draw him into our communion, can we, from any justifiable motive, ask him, even once, to testify against his own principles, which should be more precious to him than life; and to participate in the most sacred and crowning act of faith (*e. g.,* the Sacrament), of which we are capable, but in which he is at variance with us? The bride does not ask even her most intimate and honored friends and guests at the wedding to participate with her in her act of marriage with the groom. We must draw the line in all sacred relationships. The more important the relationship, the more careful our action.

We are doing nothing more nor less, in fact, than what everybody believes to be right in the case of the United States, when it allows only naturalized citizens to vote; and when it excludes from its voting membership those who either do not go to the trouble, or are, for any more serious reason, unwilling to take the oath of allegiance and subscribe to our national Confession, the Constitution. This is not illiberal, but just and, in the long run, charitable to all.

A real reason why people justify this care and strictness in the State and criticise it in the Church is that they estimate the importance of citizenship as above that of Church membership, and allow matters of convenience, sentiment as to family relationship and general friendship, and other secondary considerations, to operate in religion, but not in politics. A man will go five hundred miles to vote, and will not walk five squares to church. That tells the whole story of his estimate of the comparative importance of this world's rule and order, and rule and order in the kingdom of God.

Confessional fidelity is a matter of conscience as it works itself out into order; for order is Heaven's first law, not only in business but also in religion. Good order is not the antagonist of sweet charity; but sweet charity appreciates the value of order, and is willing to take the other car rather than stand on the platform or cling to a footboard outside, when there are good public reasons for keeping people either entirely inside or entirely outside.

After the above was written, the author was called away from his study, and the following conversation was repeated to him as having just taken place at a public table: "Are you a member of any Church?" "No; but my wife is a Lutheran." "And is she a good Lutheran?" "What do you mean by 'good Lutheran'?" "I mean one who attends her Church regularly." "I cannot say that she is, at least we are now going to the Presbyterian Church, because we have met some very fine people in that church, with whom we are quite social." That is the " exclusive " question in a nutshell. In our daily walk and confession, religion is to be regarded as secondary to sociability and social considerations.

But is our discussion, up to this point, completely fair? Does it exhaust the subject? How shall we recognize the unity that embraces in itself all true Christians of every land, many of whom are *entirely outside the Lutheran Church?* Or is there no such unity?

Yes, there is such a unity—the only really universal and eternal unity of believers. But *it is invisible.* No one but God knows who are its members. No Church or denomination upon earth composes it as such. And the Churches upon earth can not presume to be identical with the communion of saints, or to assert the relations of their visible membership to it. They each claim to have its principles, or if they do not, they are greatly injuring the Kingdom of the Lord by maintaining separate organizations; and they each must act conscientiously, just as men do in private and business life, being faithful to that which they believe and know, and leaving that which they see through a glass darkly to the Day of the Lord.

With many Christians to-day, the importance of unity is not its real inner existence, but its outer demonstration. It is not to *be one,* but to impress outsiders properly with the fact that we are one, and are mighty as one. It is not the unity for its own sake, but the unity for the sake of what it will do and show in this world. This is the difference between union and unity. Both are legitimate, but both are not equally important. Unionism, which is union by compromise is not legitimate, nor abidingly important.

The Church is not designed chiefly to bring men into outward earthly associations, or to make them acquainted with each other as preparatory to an acquaintanceship in Heaven; but it is designed to implant the saving Word of truth within them, and to relate them organically through the Spirit to the Head of the Church and, *through Him only,* to each other. The Church is thus the body of Christ, the pillar and ground of His saving truth; and the Confession is our deepest conviction of that saving truth.

CHAPTER VI.

SHOULD CONFESSIONS CONDEMN AND EXCLUDE?

Against the enforcement of Confessional Authority are Toleration, Church Rivalries, Individualism and Democracy, Historical Persecution—But Abuse does not abrogate Use—The Responsibility of Lutheranism—Discipline and Minatory Elements in Scripture and the Confessions.

MANY complicated causes contribute to the modern feeling that the Church should be sufficiently broad and liberal, not to raise its voice in condemnation of error, nor its hand in excluding even the unworthy and the reprobate from its membership.

The spirit of universal toleration, which is indifferent to doctrine, and regards it rather as a dead heirloom from a historical past, and more or less of an incubus to the Church of the present, than as the dynamic of faith and life; and which substitutes the common sense and personal judgment of each Christian individual, for the collective judgment of the Church as recorded in its Confessions, is a prime cause for this feeling. But there are others.

One of these is the existence of many rival Protestant organizations, each claiming by the fact of their separate existence (and many of them repudiating their own claim by laxity of word and act), that they are the true Church, and that their confession and discipline are decisive. This spectacle does not in itself disprove that there really is some one Church which possesses the true doctrine, for the truth is nearly always surrounded by approximations and counter-

38

feits of itself; but, in view of the fact that human nature is prone to regard *itself* as right, and to set up an exclusive claim of right *for its own party,* and to condemn all who are outside of its party—which the pages of history illustrate abundantly—the world to-day feels that even the true Church should be modest and slow to condemn others' errors and sins, since, very likely, at least a part of the condemnatory act is to be attributed to the ordinary frailty of human nature, found even in the true Church, and not to the purity of doctrine which it rightly claims to emphasize.

Still another prejudice against Confessions that condemn is to be found in the emphasis which our modern life places upon the individual, as being of more importance than the institution, and upon the low views of the congregation of Christ which are current in our country. This is a serious thing. The general public has almost ceased to regard the Protestant Church as a divine institution, but looks on it as a voluntary human association into which individuals enter when they desire, in which they remain as long as they please, and from which they are privileged to withdraw, as they would from any other mere society, as a matter of course and of right, whenever they wish to do so, for any or no cause whatsoever. Each individual brings to the congregational society his sensitive personality, together with his " doctrinal views and opinions," which must be respected not only in discipline, but also in preaching, and which will resent any rebuke or allusion to them as error, even though the admonition be of the mildest kind.

The doctrine of the Church as the Communion of Saints has fallen so low, that the Church is no longer regarded as a real brotherhood subject to the teaching and the discipline of a common Scriptural life. Not the doctrine of the Confessions, but the "sentiments", "opinions" and "views" of pastor and members, which are influenced rather by contemporary philosophical discussion than by a searching of the Scriptures or an assimilation of the Confessions, prevail in the congregation. There is a disposition to allow the pulpit, and the mind of the hearer, to be open and untrammeled on all sides, and to accept such ideas as seem to each individual to be most helpful to his own spiritual life. Hence each member is to be left to regulate his faith and life by ideas that appeal to him, rather than by the strict doctrine that is revealed in Scripture.

We reach one deep root of the matter when we say that the Church of this age, with all our other institutions, is affected by a reaction which the spirit of democracy is awakening against all authority. Whether the authority is good and lawful or not makes no difference. There is, especially in our nation, something in the nature of a universal protest against constraint or discipline of any kind. The disinclination to admit and to use authority, and the difficulty in which officials find themselves in administering their authority justly, without making a far-reaching mistake, or involving the cause which they represent in destructive consequences, have become exceedingly great. The feeling exists that "truth is mighty and will prevail." Give it a fair opportunity to fight its own battles, and stand back far enough, and it will win. What a pity it did not win in the Garden of Eden! Calvary and the Cross would then have been unnecessary. It will prevail indeed—in the end, when God shall be all in all. Meanwhile members of the Church are growing up with the idea that saving faith consists in subjective individual sentiment, and in the acceptance of the privileges of religion, without the acceptance of the duties and burdens and responsibilities which the Church must, if she is true to her Lord and to her members, impose upon all.

There is little willingness in the modern spirit to accept rebuke either for sin or for error. The Protestant idea of the individual right of conscience is carried so far that the Church, in its collective capacity, as representing God, cannot speak out against a torpid conscience without being regarded as narrow and as attempting to exceed her authority.

For ourselves, we freely confess both our faith and our sympathy with the positive method of quietly and continuously sowing good seed over and over again, rather than in the continuous attempt and effort to pursue and destroy error by the use of ecclesiastical authority. While it will not do to allow error to spring up unchecked,[1] since it is so much more prolific and overshadowing than truth; yet, nevertheless, the chief aim of the Church should be the planting of truth, and not the rooting out of error. The two go together, but there is constant danger that the zealot will turn his Christian devotion into a military fervor for destruction, and will "breathe out threatenings and slaughter " against error; and there is equally constant danger that the latitudinarian is neglecting the extirpation of error, because it is no eyesore to him and because he is not devoted, heart and soul, to the implantation of the sound doctrine.

The road to truth [2] is not a straight one, but, as the world is constituted, has been reached through controversy with the extremes of error. "Honest and earnest controversy," says Dr. Philip Schaff, " conducted in a Christian and catholic spirit, promotes true and lasting union. Polemics looks to Irenics. The aim of war is peace." To this we heartily subscribe; and while it is not possible in this age to beat the sword into ploughshares, nor to turn the spears into pruning hooks,[3] yet the right thing to do is to use the ploughshare regularly and faithfully, and to hang up the sword in reserve for those occasions in which the ploughshare will not suffice. The point here is that the presence of the sword (of the Spirit) is wholesome, and that the Confessions have the right to hold it in reserve and to wield it as actual necessity may require.

---

[1] The parable of the wheat and the tares is not applicable in this connection to the Church's testing, and condemnation, and exclusion of heresy and error.

[2] The line to truth is a straight one, as the bird flies, but not the actual road on earth. There are high mountains and winding valleys to be traversed.

[3] In which capacity they would often be useless, since the liberal modern Church neither desires nor tolerates " pruning."

In addition to the objections mentioned above as lying in the public mind against the enforcement of Confessional authority, there is still another. The history of the Christian congregation in its efforts to uphold pure doctrine and sound spiritual life among its membership, especially during the many centuries of the rule of Rome, and even under the dominion of the sterner kinds of Protestantism, has been so sad, and is so permeated by the sinfulness of human nature, that the very principle of ecclesiastical authority itself, in spiritual things, which is as legitimate in its right use as it is illegitimate in its abuse, is now being·denied as valid.

It is true that the tyranny of much of the earlier Protestantism, as exemplified in this country particularly by the laws of Puritanism, is not to be found in the Lutheran Church, whose heart is foreign to a rule of legalism of any sort. Krauth has plead the conspicuous innocence of the Lutheran Church as follows:

"The glorious words of Luther were, 'The pen, not the fire, is to put down heretics. The hangmen are not doctors of theology. This is not the place for force. Not the sword, but the Word, fits for this battle. If the Word does not put down error, error would stand, though the world were drenched with blood.' By these just views, the Lutheran Church has stood,[*] and will stand forever. But she is none the less earnest in just modes of shielding herself and her children from the teachings of error which takes cover under the pretence of private judgment. She would not burn Servetus, nor, for opinion's sake, touch a hair of his head; neither, however, would she permit him to bear her name, to 'preach another Jesus' in her pulpits, to teach error in her universities, or to approach with her children the table of their Lord, Whom he denied. Her name, her confessions, her history, her very being protest against the supposition of such

---

[*] Notwithstanding the bitterness and the exceptional cases of persecution which occurred after Luther's death in the midst of the Protestant internal controversies, by civil rulers, at the instigation of the extremists of all parties.

'fellowship with the works of darkness,' such sympathy with heresy, such levity in regard to the faith. She never practiced thus. She never can do it. Those who imagine . . . the right of men, within the Lutheran Church, to teach what they please in the face of her testimony, know not the nature of the right they claim, nor of the Church, whose very life involves her refusal to have fellowship with them in their error. It is not the right of private judgment which makes or marks a man Lutheran. . . . It and the right of Church discipline are co-ordinate and harmonious rights, essential to the prevention, each of the abuse of the other. To uphold either intelligently, is to uphold both. In maintaining, therefore, as Protestants, the right and duty of men to form their own convictions, unfettered by civil penalties or inquisitorial powers, we maintain, also, the right and duty of the Church to shield herself from corruption in doctrine by setting forth the truth in her Confession, by faithfully controverting heresy, by personal warning to those that err, and, finally, with the contumacious, by rejecting them from her communion, till, through grace, they are led to see and renounce the falsehood for which they claimed the name of truth." [5]

" No church, apart from the fundamentals of the gospel in which her unity and very life are involved, is so mild, so mediating, so thoroughly tolerant as our own. Over against the unity of Rome under a universal Head, the unity of High-Churchism under the rule of Bishops, the unities which turn upon like rites or usages as in themselves necessary, or which build up the mere subtleties of human speculation into articles of faith, over against these the Lutheran Church was the first to stand forth, declaring that the unity of the Church turns upon nothing that is of man. Where the one pure Gospel of Christ is preached, where the one foundation of doctrine is laid, where the ' one faith ' is confessed, and the alone divine Sacraments administered aright, there is the one Church; this is her unity.

---

[5] *Con. Ref.*, pp. 174 sq. For the following, *Vid. ib.*, pp. 181 sq.

"Our fathers clearly saw and sharply drew the distinction between God's foundation and man's superstructure, between faith and opinion, between religion and speculative theology, and, with all these distinctions before them, declared, that consent in the doctrine of the Gospel and the right administration of the Sacraments is the only basis of the unity of the Church. This basis, the Lutheran Church has defined and rests on it, to abide there, we trust, by God's grace, to the end of time."

If the Lutheran Church is true to Scripture and true to herself, as the Church of the pure Word and Sacraments she cannot avoid the responsibility of condemnation and exclusion. Her ministers and congregations, after making all due allowance for the fact that they differ from the Church in Apostolic days in that they have not the Saviour or the inspired Apostles to guide them, that we are ignorant of the inner life, motives and principles of other men, and are not acquainted with either the conditions that determine their action, or the possibilities of amendment that their future may contain, and with due reference to the fact that others are not to be judged by us, that is, to receive a sweeping and final verdict on general principles at our hands; and, further, remembering that it is necessary to exercise the greatest patience and forbearance, and at times to refrain from judging even where the outward evidence seems to convince (John 8: 11; 1 Cor. 4: 5), must, nevertheless, both warn and exclude error from the Church.

The Lutheran doctrine of Absolution is not complete and is never really exercised, unless the "binding" accompanies the "loosing," unless the Word is applied not only for release, but also for condemnation. The witness of the Church is to be two-edged (Matt. 16: 19; 18: 18; John 20: 23). Exclusion, as exercised by the Christian Church, was instituted by our Lord (Matt. 18: 15, 18), and commanded and practiced by St. Paul (1 Tim. 1: 20; 1 Cor. 5: 7; Titus 3: 10).

The three-fold admonition, first privately, then in the presence of two or three witnesses, and finally before the Church, leads to a recognized and appointed way in which a church member must at last become to his brethren as a heathen man and publican. This exclusion is to follow on the member's unrepentant rejection of the censure of the church passed on him for a trespass which he has committed.

St. Paul not only gives directions to "admonish the disorderly" (1 Thess. 5: 14ff; 1 Tim. 5: 20), and to hold aloof from members who are openly wicked (1 Cor. 5: 11), or who refuse to obey his word in his letters (2 Cor. 3: 14ff; Rom. 16: 17), but also claims the right to exercise discipline (compare 2 Cor. 1: 23; 13: 10). His letters refer to the exercise of this authority in the case of two offenders cut off from the Church (1 Cor. 5; 1 Tim. 1: 19, 20). Persons were disciplined not only for moral offences, but for a schismatic spirit (Titus 3: 10, " A man that is heretical, after a first and second admonition refuse"). In 2 John 5, 10, false doctrine is made the ground for absolute breach of intercourse.

Moreover, the Apostle Paul writes positively that we are to cut ourselves off, or withdraw, from those who do not obey sound doctrine (2 Thess. 3: 14; Rom. 16: 17; Gal. 5: 2; 1 Tim. 6: 3). The rulers of some of the seven Churches in Revelation are rebuked for their latitudinarian spirit and teaching; and St. Paul emphatically declares, " Though we or an angel from Heaven preach any other Gospel unto you than that we have preached unto you, let him be accursed" (Gal. 1: 8, 9); *i. e.,* "disclaim and renounce all communion with him."

The fact that the exercise of this duty of condemnation or exclusion often was abused (compare Luke 6: 22; John 9: 22; 12: 42; 16: 2; 3 John 9, 10), was not regarded in the New Testament as a reason for retiring the exercise of this function of the Word into the background.

Our own Confessions, in accordance with Scripture, recognize excommunication. Melanchthon does so in the Apology, chap. IV, 3. Speaking of Confession, in the Apology

7

(chapter IV, 61), Melanchthon[6] says, " Excommunication is also pronounced against the openly wicked and the despisers of the Sacraments. These things are thus done, both according to the Gospel and according to the old canons."

The Schmalkald Articles carefully distinguish between the civil and the spiritual excommunication, in Part III, 9. They say, "The greater excommunication, as the Pope calls it, we regard only as a civil penalty, and not pertaining to us ministers of the Church. But the less is true Christian excommunication, which prohibits manifest and obstinate sinners from the sacrament and other communion of the Church until they are reformed and avoid sin." This power inheres in the ministry. "Therefore the bishop has the power of the order, *i. e.,* the ministry of the Word and Sacraments; he has also the power of jurisdiction, *i. e.,* the authority to excommunicate those guilty of open crimes, and again to absolve them if they are converted and seek absolution."[7] " It is right to restore this jurisdiction to godly pastors, and to see to it that it be legitimately exercised for the reformation of life and the glory of God." [8]

Compare also " The Office of the Keys as the Head of the Family should Teach it in all Simplicity to his Household," in Luther's Small Catechism: " I believe that when the called ministers of Christ deal with us by His divine command, especially when they exclude manifest and impenitent sinners from the Christian congregation, and, again, when they absolve those who repent, . . . this is as valid and certain, in heaven also, as if Christ, our dear Lord, dealt with us Himself."

The Augsburg Confession itself (article XXVIII) declares

---

[6] That Melanchthon could condemn we see in the Apology where, in speaking of the Trinity, he says: " We constantly affirm that those thinking otherwise are outside of the Church of Christ, and are idolatrous, and insult God."—*Apol.* Art. I.

[7] *Ibid.,* p. 288.

[8] The *Schmalkald Articles,* Power and Primacy of the Pope, 343.

that the power of the "Keys" is "a power of preaching the Gospel, of remitting or retaining sins and of administering the Sacraments." Thus our earlier Confessions, in manner as mild as possible, reject errors and heresies, ancient and modern, that are contrary to the Word of God.

In terms not any less measured than these, but with the keen experience of half a century behind them, the confessors in the Preface to the Book of Concord declare: "It seemed exceedingly necessary that, amidst so many errors that had arisen in our times, as well as causes of offence, variances and these long-continued dissensions, a godly explanation and agreement concerning all these controversies, derived from God's Word, should exist, according to which the pure doctrine might be discriminated and separated from the false. Besides, this matter is of importance also in this respect, viz., that troublesome and contentious men, who do not suffer themselves to be bound to any formula of the purer doctrine, may not have the liberty, according to their good pleasure, to excite controversies which furnish ground for offence, and to publish and contend for extravagant opinions. For the result of these things, at length, is that the purer doctrine is obscured and lost, and nothing is transmitted to posterity except academical opinions and suspensions of judgment."

That, however, this condemnation of unsound doctrine is exceedingly mild in our Confessional writings is to be seen from another statement in the Preface to the Book of Concord:

" Thus as it is in no way our design and purpose to condemn those men who err from a certain simplicity of mind, and, nevertheless, are not blasphemers against the truth of the heavenly doctrine, much less indeed entire churches, which are either under the Roman Empire of the German nation or elsewhere; nay, rather it has been our intention and disposition, in this manner, to openly censure and condemn only the fanatical opinions and their obstinate and blasphemous teachers (which we judge should in no way be tolerated in our dominions,[*] churches and schools), because these errors conflict with the express Word of God, and that too in such a way that they cannot be reconciled with it. We have also undertaken this for this reason, viz., that all godly persons might be warned concerning diligently avoiding them. . . .

"Wherefore, by this writing of ours, we testify in the sight of Almighty God, and before the entire Church, that it has never been our purpose, by means of this godly formula for union, to occasion trouble or danger to the godly who today are suffering persecution. For as, moved by Christian love, we have already entered into the fellowship of grief with them, so we are shocked at the persecution and most grievous tyranny which with such severity is exercised against these poor men, and sincerely detest it. For in no way do we consent to the shedding of that innocent blood, for which undoubtedly a reckoning will be demanded with great severity from the persecutors at the awful judgment of the Lord, and before the tribunal of Christ, and they will then certainly render a most strict account and suffer fearful punishment."

When we come to examine the condemnatory elements to be found in the Confessions of the Lutheran Church, we shall perhaps be surprised to see how much more mild they are, comparatively, than is the Scripture itself. We may also be surprised to find that the Augsburg Confession is not any stronger in its condemnations than is the Athanasian Creed, and that the Formula of Concord is probably as mild in its condemnation as is the Augsburg Confession.

It is strange that it does not occur to the Lutheran who condemns the Confessions for their minatory passages that they

---

[*] The separation of Church and State, possible in America, enables the Lutheran Church to develop her confessional principle of Law and Gospel, entirely apart from the aid of the State, more fully than she could in Germany in the Reformation era. As a Church she will not even pass the customary resolutions that ask the State not to tolerate the secularization of the Lord's day ("Sabbath desecration").

are far less minatory than the Scriptures themselves. Will we be consistent and *condemn Scripture* because *Scripture* condemns error, heresy and wickedness?

The fact is that the whole Scripture is terribly negative in dealing with error and sin. Every one, except the third, of the Ten Commandments is a negative. A large part of our Saviour's utterances are negative and condemnatory in form, and *all* of them are in view of the existence of evil, to be witnessed against, struck down, suffered for and overcome.

The sharp condemnation of the Christian Church in her old theology is usually attributed to the influence of the Apostle Paul and his more narrow and rabbinic outlook; but if any more terrible denunciations have ever come from human lips than those that came so freely from the mild and gentle Son of Man in the Sermon on the Mount, in the picture of the children of the kingdom cast into outer darkness, in upbraiding Chorazin and Bethsaida, in comparing the men of Nineveh with His own generation, in condemning those who have ears to hear and hear not, in ruling out the tradition of the elders (Matt. 15), in rebuking His own disciples, and the unbelief of those who listened to Him, and the wickedness of the unjust debtor, and rich men who trust in their riches, and the useless fig tree, and those who reject the Cornerstone, and the bidden who would not come, and the man without a wedding garment, and the unprofitable servant to be cast into outer darkness, and, above all, the Pharisees who shall receive the greater damnation, in woes and denunciations most terrible (see also the whole Gospel of St. John, including even the stern words in the tender parable of the Good Shepherd)—if any condemnation more stern and terrible than this has come from the mouth of man, we know not where to find it.

The Old Testament, it will be admitted, is full of condemnation and exclusion, but we doubt whether the fulness of its volume is appreciated.

The first scene in the Bible closes with a curse on man and

his exclusion from the Garden of Eden. The next scene shows us Cain being branded by the Lord as a murderer. Then comes the condemnation of the whole earth and its punishment in the flood. The punishments of Jacob and his sons, the warnings, condemnations, ceremonial exclusions and severe visitations on rebellious Israel in the wanderings, the punishments of the inhabitants of Canaan, of Israel under the judges and kings, are notable. Can you pick up a passage from Isaiah or any one of the prophets and find it unmingled with commination? We shall not speak of the imprecatory Psalms; but we direct attention to the fact that with all the change of attitude from the Old Testament to the New, in the coming of *Grace* and *Truth,* while love takes the place of hate toward our enemies, there is no intimation that toleration has taken the place of condemnation in our relation to error and falsehood.

"Think not that I am come to destroy the law or the prophets: I am not come to destroy, but to fulfil. For verily I say unto you, Till heaven and earth pass, one jot or one tittle shall in no wise pass from the law till all be fulfilled. Whosoever therefore shall break one of these least commandments, *and shall teach men so,* he shall be called the least in the kingdom of heaven: but whosoever shall do, and teach them, the same shall be called great in the kingdom of heaven. Beware of false prophets, which come to you in sheep's clothing, but inwardly they are ravening wolves. Ye shall know them by their fruits."—Matt. Chapts. 5-7.

"But in vain do they worship me, teaching for doctrines the commandments of men. Every plant, which my heavenly Father hath not planted, shall be rooted up."—Matt. 15: 9, 13.

"For I know this, that after my departing shall grievous wolves enter in among you, not sparing the flock."—Acts 20: 29.

" Now I beseech you, brethren, mark them which cause divisions and offences, contrary to the doctrine which ye have learned; and avoid them. For they that are such serve not our Lord Jesus Christ, but their own belly, and by good words and fair speeches deceive the hearts of the simple."—Rom. 16: 17, 18.

"For we are not as many which corrupt the word of God: but as of sincerity, but as of God, in the sight of God, speak we in Christ."—2 Cor. 2: 17.

"For such are false apostles, deceitful workers, transforming themselves into the apostles of Christ. And no marvel; for Satan himself is transformed into an angel of light. Therefore it is no great thing if his ministers also be transformed as the ministers of righteousness, whose end shall be according to their works."—2 Cor. 11: 13-15.

"And this I say, lest any man should beguile you with enticing words. Beware lest any man spoil you through philosophy and vain deceit, after the tradition of men, after the rudiments of the world, and not after Christ."—Col. 2: 4, 8.

"But there were false prophets also among the people, even as there shall be false teachers among you, who privily shall bring in damnable heresies, even denying the Lord that bought them, and bring upon themselves swift destruction." —2 Peter 2: 1.

We have brought these passages to remembrance to make it evident that the elements of condemnation in the Symbolical Books of the Lutheran Church are not as severe as the condemnation of false teaching and living to be found in Scripture.

Analyzing the condemnatory elements in the Augsburg Confession, we find that Article i condemns those who set up two eternal principles of good and evil, and those who contend that there is only one person in the Trinity. Article ii condemns the Pelagians, who argue that a man may by the strength of his own reason be justified before God. Article v condemns the Anabaptists and others who imagine that the Holy Spirit is given to men without the outward Word. Article viii condemns the Donatists. Article ix condemns those who condemn Infant Baptism. Article x "disapproves" of those that teach non-Lutheran doctrine on the Lord's Supper. Article xii condemns those who maintain the doctrine of sinless perfection. Article xiii condemns an *opus operatum* use of the Sacraments. Article xvii condemns those who believe in a limited state of torment and in a millenium. Article xviii condemns the Pelagians, who believe that we are able to love God without His Spirit.

Neither the Apology[10] nor the Schmalkald Articles (except with reference to the Papists), nor the Small nor the Large Catechisms contain formal condemnatory matter. The Formula of Concord, which was composed to deal with and settle controversies, and which is written in most moderate tone, rejects and condemns thirteen false doctrines concerning original sin, without, however, mentioning any contemporaries. It rejects eight false doctrines concerning the free-will, without mentioning contemporaries. It rejects and condemns eleven errors respecting the righteousness of faith, without mentioning any names at all. It rejects and condemns three false doctrines concerning good works, without mentioning any names. It rejects and condemns the wrong teaching concerning the Law and the Gospel, without mentioning any names.

It also condemns twenty-one doctrines of the Sacramentarians concerning the Lord's Supper. It rejects twenty false doctrines concerning the Person of Christ, without mentioning contemporaries; four false doctrines concerning church rites, and four false doctrines concerning predestination, without mentioning any names. It also "simply enumerates the mere articles wherein the heretics of our time err and teach what is contrary to our Christian faith and Confession." Among these are seventeen errors of the Anabaptists, eight of the Schwenkfeldians, one of the new Arians and one of the anti-Trinitarians.

---

[10] But v. p. 46.

In other words, it covers the whole field of error as it presented itself to the Lutheran Church at that time, and clearly presents the errors, without a trace of personality or any bitterness of discussion. It says, "We cannot forbear testifying against them publicly, before all Christendom, that we have neither part nor fellowship with these errors, but reject and condemn them one and all as wrong and heretical, contrary to the Scriptures of the Prophets and Apostles, as well as to our well-grounded Augsburg Confession."

To our mind there can be no more useful service performed by a public standard of the Church, than to point out the dangers and pitfalls of doctrine which have come up in the course of actual experience and which threaten the true faith in Christ. As Frederic Meyrick says, "If Christianity is merely a philosophical idea thrown into the world to do battle with other theories, and to be valued according as it maintains its ground or not in the conflict of opinions, excommunication and ecclesiastical discipline are unreasonable. If a society has been instituted for maintaining any body of doctrine and any code of morals, they are necessary to the existence of that society. That the Christian Church is a spiritual kingdom of God on earth is the declaration of the Bible."

CHAPTER VII.

WHAT GIVES THE CONFESSION VALIDITY?

A Confession is Testimony, not Agreement, nor Contract—Its Aim is Instruction, not Obligation—The Agreement is the Pre-existing one of Doctrine—Cannot be put together by Negotiation—The Result (Not the Cause) of the Substantial Unities in Christ—Not a Platform, nor a Delineation for Comparative Distinction —Born, not Made—The Stress of Providence—Its Validity is that of Testimony —Evidence of the Lutheran Confession—Analysis of the Legal Situation—Not Based on Social Pact—Lacks the Essence of Contract, viz.: An Interchange of Legal Rights Whose Transfer the Law Will Compel—The Binding Clauses of our Confessions.

THE Church's Confession is testimony, and its validity lies in its witness. The form in which this witness is cast is unessential, if the substance be complete and perfect and the form do no injustice to the substance. The strength of the Confession is the strength of God's truth, which, in Christ, builds and holds the Church; and which, besides the bodily utterance, is the chief thing in the Confession. The strength of the Church's Confessions is her Confession.

The agreement of men in this Confessional testimony, is that of a common conviction in which they find themselves, not that of a common understanding at which they have arrived. The number of those sharing the conviction and confessing it does not add validity, though it may add credibility, under the regular conditions of number in evidence, to the witness. The value of a witness depends on conscience as it is intelligently enlightened through revealed truth, and not on any attempt to make our witness agree with that of others. When the witness of two or three agrees, the added force arises because we see the truth to be strong enough to simultaneously affect a number of consciences. It shows that the Confession is that of a communion in which every conscience testifies to the same effect.

Four different classes of agreement centre in a Confession: 1, the agreement of the Confession with Scripture; 2, the agreement of the Confession with the confession and with itself; 3, the agreement of the confessors with the Confession, and 4, the agreement of the confessors with each other as to the Confession. The validity of the Confession depends upon the first kind of agreement: "The value of creeds depends upon the measure of their agreement with the Scriptures. The Bible is the *norma normans;* the Confession the *norma normata.* The Bible is the rule of faith (*regula fidei*); the Confession the rule of doctrine (*regula doctrinae*)."[1]

The chief permanent use of a Confession is based on its power as genuine and valid testimony. Its chief purpose in the Church is to illuminate, to clarify and to convince. Its chief binding power is the binding power of the truth. Its chief hold is its hold on the conscience of those whose mind has been illuminated and convinced by it.

This, in modern terms, is but another way of saying that the chief value of a Church Confession is educational, rather than restrictive. In itself, the whole restrictive strength of the Confession lies in its moral force. An additional act, exterior to itself, is required to turn its validity into the validity of ecclesiastical law. And it is important to separate this additional act, as an inferior function, from the Confession's main office of testimony. The first duty of the Church is to instruct its members in its testimony so thoroughly that they will come to voluntary agreement with it under the influence of its truth. If, in addition, the Church feel it to be salutary to make her members promise, in vow or by subscription, to remain faithful to such Confession, this act is in itself an important incidental application of

---

[1] *Creeds of Christendom,* I, p. 7.

the Confession as a part of a precautionary ecclesiastical administration. But as the main use of Scripture is not its normative use, so the main use of the Confession is not *Verpflichtung.*[2]

That the Lutheran Confessions take this view of their validity[3] and regard their chief purpose to be instruction, is to be seen from the manner in which they characterize themselves. The Augsburg Confession terms itself "Summary of the Doctrine of our Teachers." The Large Catechism terms itself "A Course of Instruction"[4] and "A Treatment of the Five Articles of the Entire Christian Doctrinae."[5] The Formula of Concord declares itself to be "A Summary Exhibition of Doctrine."[6] And while the Confessors state their mutual agreement in the doctrines and declare "to stand on them, if God so will, even to death;"[7] and agree, in the Formula of Concord, to "neither speak nor write anything contrary to this declaration, but intend to abide thereby," yet the chief matter is the *"wish to testify* that the above declaration and no other, is our faith, doctrine and confession."

Any agreement in confession, which has not had a pre-existence as a fact, perhaps not explicit, yet actually wrought, in the hearts and minds of those who are under the power of the pure Gospel, does not add to the strength of the Confession. Any agreement which is not in itself the spontaneous originating cause of uniting men in their testimony, but which is the result of a concerted attempt to agree and which locates and places the agreement in the formulation and does not regard the latter as an explication and expression of a fact already existent, weakens the validity of the Confession.

---

[2] In Europe, where Church and State have always been united, and where the Confessional obligation has ultimately been to the State, the matter of *Verpflichtung* early assumed a serious, if not overshadowing, importance. For such *Verpflichtungs formeln,* see *Köllner,* I. 121 sqq.

[3] Schaff declares that the Lutheran Confessions were "originally intended merely as testimonies or confessions of faith."—*Creeds of Christendom,* p. 222.

[4] Second Preface.   [5] *Ibid.*   [6] *F. C.,* p. 537.   [7] *Schmalkald Articles.*

It is a misinterpretation of the origin of a true Confession to say that various wings of a Church came together and agreed on a sum of doctrine which they put forth to be confessed. If the Confession is a true one, as we believe those of our Church to be, they came together to *find* or to *express* the agreement *already existing* in their doctrine, and not to make a doctrine or consensus of doctrine in which they would agree to agree. In the case of the Augsburg Confession, Melanchthon's wish to thwart the full and open confession of the faith, his attempts to conciliate the opposite party and to subordinate the real end of confession to a conciliation of the Emperor came to naught through the Providential course of events, and he was obliged to give form to the full Lutheran truth in spite of himself. In the Formula of Concord, where the discovery was of confessional truth which two internal extremes would recognize and confess as their own, the difficulties were overcome by a thorough study of Scripture and a constant reference and adherence to it step by step.

The existence of a contract to agree, or even of an intention to come to agreement at all events, prior to the sufficient discovery of agreement, is, in so far, a presumption against the validity of a Confession.

The fundamental fact is that Confessions in their real nature, their real purpose and their main usefulness are of the order of testimony and not of the order of contract.

So far from Confessions being of the nature of a contract between men, by means of which they may agree in their religious thoughts and organizations and activities,[8] and to attain which, they may add here a little and subtract there

---

[8] It is true that the Preface of the Electors and Princes to the Book of Concord calls the Formula " a formula of agreement," *"haec pacificationis formula,"* " *diese jetzige Vergleichung ; "* but this phrase does not mean *an agreement as to what the truth of the confession shall be,* but *an agreement that will follow from the discovery of what the truth is.* The parties do not come together, and by a selection of some points, and a compromise of others make the truth on which they agree to agree ; but the parties search out the various partial statements, and statements with light and shadow in them, as presented from the different sides, until they discover the real and fundamental objective fact as it is, which fact convinces them all and brings them into agreement.

a little, Confessions are only real and valuable in so far as they embody and reflect God's own Word. It is from their objective substance, that they derive their value. This object is uniformly the grace of God, as revealed in Scripture, and offered in Word and sacrament.

This objective and intrinsically valuable content of the Confession never varies; and it is not composed of the assemblage of propositions in which the Faith is attempted to be expressed, but is the reality of the facts in the Divine will, revealed in Scripture, accepted by faith, and witnessed to by Confession; and on which facts we rely for our life and salvation, and which we attempt to fix in human language. Confessions, as the soul's and the Church's apprehension and expression of the divine reality, are matters of conscience.

So little is the idea of confession, in God's Word, merely a conviction of the understanding, that we find it, in Scripture, to be an acknowledgment of man's going out of himself, and resting in the grace of God in confident trust. It is a movement of the whole inner man that seizes the heart and moves the mouth to utterance (Rom. 10: 9-11).

A Common Confession in a Church is not mediated by the intellect, or by the thoughtful arrival at a form of words that will cover contraries and bridge chasms, but it becomes common and united because the members of the Church themselves are united in one Head, one Faith, one Baptism, one God and Father of all.

We cannot emphasize too strongly that confession and the Confessions, in so far as they are delineative, and in so far as they possess combining power, are the result of other and more substantial unities in Christ, and not the cause of them.

Christ, the Faith, the Church, the Truth, the Principles, the Doctrine—all existed before they were apprehended and set forth by our faith, or formulated by our thought, or expressed by our mouth; and therefore they cannot legitimately be touched, modified, softened down, or toned up and heightened by any human agreement.

That was the fatal mistake of Melanchthon,[*] and is the undercurrent of weakness in the attempt of men to "get together" on "a common platform of faith," in every age. Such a confession is a " platform," a human thing; built up by man's thought and skill, and according to his ideas, which change from age to age; and cannot be the source of that strength and certainty, that comes from submissive and total reliance on revelation, and that courses through the channels of the objective unity already existent between the Head of the Church and its members.

If to the above it be objected that no particular Church can claim to have the objective and final confession, and to have as its unity that objective oneness that holds together Christ and His members, we reply that to the degree in which the particular Church is true in faith and life, it is within the compass of the pure faith and the real bonds of union in Christ. What holds true of the accuracy and faithfulness of the old orthodox Lutheran Confessions as a true reflex of the objective content in Scripture is emphasized by the rationalistic but keen-sighted Carl Hase in the following language:

"Jene alte Orthodoxie,—welche Lessing, ihr ehrwürdigster Gegner, wegen ihres starken und Kühnen Geistes bewunderte, während vor der neuen Rechtgläubigkeit ihm zuweilen eben so übel wurde, als vor der neuen Aufklärung,—sie ist dargestellt worden *in ihrer ganzen Kraft* und *Consequenz;* und eine solche Darstellung, *ohne irgend eine äussre Rücksicht,* schien allerdings der Wissenschaft in mancher Hinsicht förderlicher [the true Lutheran would say, "schien allerdings dem Zeugnisse des Wortes Gottes mehr gemäsz"], als *die neuern Concordate* zwischen dem alten Kirchenglauben und der Philosophie oder Unphilosophie des Tages, welche nicht selten *in scheinbarem Vereine von beiden Seiten Widerstrebendes ver-*

---

[*] The Confession, as being under the laws of testimony (not of contract), is susceptible of adjustment to the perspective, proper for the time in which it is uttered; and therefore Melanchthon was justified in changing the adjustment (but not in concealing or weakening the truth) of the Confession, on learning more and more of the nature of the Diet, until the moment of its utterance.

mischen und Eigenthümliches aufopfern. . . . Eine Wissenschaft von dem Glauben, für welchen unsre Vorfahren Gut und Blut eingesetzt haben, verdient wenigstens von ihren Nachkommen genau gekannt zu werden. . . .

"Nicht als wenn die Formeln der Vorzeit gelten sollten, *weil* sie gegolten haben: aber davon ziemt Jünglingen, den künftigen Lehrern und Hirten der Kirche, auszugehn, wovon die Geschichte unsrer Kirche selbst ausgegangen ist, damit sie die Zeit, die vor ihnen gewesen ist, und aus der die Gegenwart geworden ist, daher aus ihr auch verstanden wird, in der wissenschaftlichen Erinnerung durchleben, und fest gewurzelt in der Vergangenheit vorwärts streben und aufwärts." [10]

The *written* or *formulated* Confessions of the Church are an expression, in careful language, of the objective substance of the Confession. They were not framed to show the differences of the writers as a church party, or to distinguish one church party from another, though they are thus used by theologians and comparative historians. But they were framed to enable us to acknowledge, indicate and defend our objective Scriptural teaching of God's Word, especially on loci that have been represented as different from what they are, by other denominations. The *occasion* of the framing is not necessarily the purpose of Providence, or even the deepest purpose of the confessors in bringing them into being.

They were framed to protect and preserve the truth and the Church; and other beliefs and denominations are, at best, the occasion, or the foil, furnishing the material for contrast, and not the real ground for the existence of these formularies. Thus it was not to distinguish between Lutheranism and Romanism, not to designate comparatively the differences between what Rome taught and what Lutheranism taught, that the Augsburg Confession was framed; but it was to enable Lutheranism to confess the one faith of the Scripture on such

---

[10] Karl Hase, *Hutter Redivivus*, Oct., 1828.

points as had been obscured or perverted by Rome. The true faith, "the sum of the doctrine," and not the distinctions between the parties, is the object.

The agreement consequently is not between the confessing members, but is between the Confession and the Scripture. The agreement reached between the members, is not as to what they will agree to, but as to what Scripture obliges them to confess and binds them to hold. If there be a contract in the confessional formulary, it is between the Lord and men, and not between men and men. The strength, the sanction, the validity lies in the relation of the confessors to the One Whom they confess, and not in the relation to each other as signatories.

The latter relation, so far as it exists, is secondary, and is mediated between them only through the Head of the Church. Neither does the number of signatories affect the validity, the truthfulness and the strength of the Formulary as a religious document or a marker of faith. Otherwise the validity of a Confession would often be determined by the political dexterity and the adaptation to governmental expediency with which it was framed and introduced. Two or three gathered in Jesus' name may confess the good and valid Confession, and a whole Council purporting to represent all Christendom might formulate an invalid Confession."

It is on this account that the *stress of Providence,* the

" The same fact is true with respect to the validity of a broken or changed Confession. Jacobs says of a Church that tries to change her creed: "When she teaches otherwise than they taught who were her historical ancestors, she has broken her unity with them, and is no longer the same Church, no difference though the name be retained, or however preponderant on her side may be numerical majorities. If every member would agree to a change in her Creed, this would not change the testimony of the communion which was fixed at its organization. It would only show that the historical successor was a different Church. The Roman Catholic Church cannot amend the decrees of the Council of Trent so as to remove elements on which the Tridentine fathers insisted, or to include Protestant conceptions of doctrine, without thereby ceasing to be the same Church as that which for three centuries and a half has recognized those decrees as the standard of teaching, and excluded from the hope of salvation all who disputed their authority."—*Distinctive Doctrines and Usages,* p. 92.

objective necessity of a situation, is essential to bring forth a valid confession. This is the reason why a number of able scholars cannot get together on their own initiative and restate the old truths in the terms of the age, and have the Church adopt the result as her Confession. A Church Confession is that which has been forced out of the Church by Providence, Who has put a strain and a necessity on the confessors that compels them to speak, and that enables them to come to speak as with one mind and one soul, in the unity of the Spirit. The minor adjustment of phrase, style and outer expression, on which agreement may be secured by vote or by predominant weight of scholarship, only clothes and does not constitute the Confession. All matters of degree, and quality, and relative importance, and form, which are matters of judgment, and which need agreement between confessors, are not the ground of the validity of the Confession.

The validity of the Formulary is the validity of testimony, and not of contract. The official Confession, formulated and accepted, is testimony as it stands *finally, after* thorough cross-examination and testing, in which all the error is eliminated, and in which, in the best conviction, all the truth remains. The agreement of many or all men as fellow-confessors in this one conviction is evidential and not contractual; neither is it essential to " a good confession " on the part of the Church.

A strong light is thrown on the real, that is, the confessional, meaning and purpose of a symbol in the Formula of Concord itself,[12] by the manner in which the Formula acknowledges the preceding symbols of the Church. Of the three œcumenical creeds it says: " Because, of old, the true Christian doctrine, in a pure, sound sense, was collected from God's Word into brief articles, or sections, against the corruption of heretics, we accept as Confessional the three Œcumenical Creeds as *glorious Confessions* of the *faith, brief, devout* and *founded upon God's Word.*

---

[12] Part II, 569.

"Because God, out of special grace, has brought His truth again to light, and has collected the same doctrine, from and according to God's Word, into the articles and sections of the Augsburg Confession; we confessionally accept also the first Unaltered Augsburg Confession (*not because it was composed by our theologians,* but because it has been *derived from God's Word*) as the symbol of our time whereby [13] our Reformed Churches are distinguished from the Papists, after the custom of the early Church.

"We unanimously accept this also [the Apology] as Confessional, because in it the said Augsburg Confession . . . is confirmed by clear, irrefutable testimonies of Holy Scripture.

" The articles composed, approved and received at Schmalkald in the large assembly of theologians in the year 1537, we confessionally accept.

"Because these highly important matters belong also to the common people and laity, who, *for their salvation,* must *distinguish between pure* and *false doctrines,* we accept as Confessional also the Large and the Small Catechisms of Dr. Luther . . . because they have been unanimously approved and received . . . and publicly used . . . and because also in them, *the Christian doctrine from God's Word is comprised* in the most correct and simple way, and, in like manner, is sufficiently explained for simple laymen.

"These *public common writings* have been always *regarded* in the pure churches and schools *as the sum* and *type* of the *doctrine* [14] which the late Dr. Luther has admirably deduced against the Papacy and other sects from God's Word.

"By what has thus far been said concerning the summary of our Christian doctrine we have only meant that we have a unanimously received *definite, common form of doctrine,* which our Evangelical Churches together *and in common confess.*

---

[13] As one of the effects, not as the controlling purpose, in which case the language would have been " are to be distinguished."

[14] " Die Summa und Vorbild der Lehre," " compendaria hypotyposi seu forma sanæ doctrinæ."

"For that we have embodied the above-mentioned writings, viz., the Augsburg Confession, the Apology, the Schmalkald Articles, Luther's Large and Small Catechisms, *as the sum of our Christian doctrine,* has occurred for the reason that these have been always and everywhere regarded as containing the *common,*[15] *unanimously received understanding*[16] of our Churches, since the chief and most enlightened theologians of that time subscribed them, and all Evangelical Churches and schools have cordially received them. . . No one who is true to the Augsburg Confession will complain of these writings, but will cheerfully accept and tolerate them *as witnesses;* no one, therefore, can blame us that we derive from them an explanation and decision of the articles in controversy, and that, as we lay God's Word, the eternal truth, as the foundation, so also we introduce and quote these writings *as a witness of the truth,* and a presentation of the *unanimously received correct understanding*[17] of our predecessors who have steadfastly held fast to the pure doctrine."

In 573, 3, "Of the Antithesis," the Formula declares, "Because some divisions arose among some theologians of the Augsburg Confession, we have wished plainly, distinctly and clearly to state and declare our faith and confession concerning each and every one of these taken in thesis and antithesis, . . . for *the purpose of rendering the foundation of divine truth manifest*[18] and censuring all unlawful, doubtful, suspicious and condemned doctrines; so that everyone may be faithfully warned to avoid errors diffused on all sides.

---

[15] "Dasz solche für den gemeinen einhelligen Verstand unserer Kirchen je und allwege gehalten worden."

[16] In the sense of "perception of meaning," not in the sense of "a tacit agreement to construe things in a certain way." See same word at end of paragraph.

[17] "Wie wir Gottes Wort, als die ewige Wahrheit, zum Grunde legen, also auch diese Schriften *zum Zeugnis der Wahrheit,* und *für den einhelligen rechten Verstand unserer Vorfahren,* so *bei der reinen Lehre standhaftig* gehalten, einführen und anziehen."

[18] "Haben wir unsern Glauben und Bekenntnis rund, lauter und klar in *thesi et antithesi,* das ist die rechte Lehr und Gegenlehr, setzen und erklären wollen, *damit der Grund göttlicher Wahrheit in allen Artikeln offenbar* (sei)."

. . . If the Christian reader will carefully examine this declaration and compare it with the writings enumerated above, he will find that *what was in the beginning confessed,* and what was *afterward restated, and is repeated* by us in this document, is in no way contradictory, but *the simple, immutable, permanent truth."*

In its highest, or *religious* sense, a Symbol is the Church's Confession of Faith springing forth from her accurate and whole-souled appropriation of the content of the Word of God. It is the Church's witness and testimony of *her faith within* to *the Faith without.* As such the Symbol need not be authenticated nor officially adopted or decreed. Its common use speaks sufficiently for it.

In the *theological* sense, a Symbol is an acknowledged and recognized delineation or summary, generally official, of the Church's faith as drawn from the standard of God's Word, in view of a public necessity to present or defend it. Except where it, in its own inner material, refers, by way of contrast or rejection, to other faiths, or where it is within the scope of its own purpose to distinguish between its own and other faiths, such distinguishing is not an essential, but an accident, in its definition.

A Symbol in an *ecclesiastical* sense is an officially recognized and accepted document which lays down the Faith of the Church, and to which all teachers and ministrants within the Church are expected to conform. As such, it may become the basis of an implied or expressed contract between the Church and those in her positions.

We have seen that the Symbol, in its highest essence, is the Church's Witness and Testimony of the faith within to the Faith without.[19] As such, it implies and involves, as

---

[19] It is fair to define a Confession by its highest and main purpose. The spiritual portion generally comprises nearly the whole of the document; and the agreement clause is insignificant, and often omitted.

It is possible to define man as a biped or as an animal with business capacity; or to define a congregation as a corporation composed of those who have voluntarily united and properly organized, under a charter, for religious worship; but these definitions are not the ones to be accepted in the Church.

does all expression of action in which more than a single unity is engaged, agreement of various kinds. It is an agreement of the truth it professes, with the Source from which the truth is drawn. It is an agreement of the various doctrines composing this truth, with each other. To become recognized as a Symbol it involves an agreement "with heart and mouth," of its confessors. To become officially recognized, it involves a concurrence of those duly authorized to accept or reject it on behalf of the Church. As an ecclesiastical instrument, and as inserted into the charter of a religious corporation, for the purpose of fixing the faith for which that corporation exists, it may become the spiritual basis of a legal contract between the Church and those who hold her positions.

We have enlarged upon the subject of this chapter because we are impressed with the serious enfeeblement of the confessing spirit and the confessional principle in the Church, if she allow the great Confessions of her Faith to drop to the level of a contract. It must be admitted that a long and honorable usage, to be traced back to the etymology and the historical usage of one of the chief terms used in designating the Christian Confessions, viz., the word Symbol (for the discussion see chap. XIII), justifies a weight of traditional authority that may be urged against our position. We therefore desire to make some analysis of the underlying formal relations that are embodied in the several terms whose usage in custom, language, and law will determine the propriety of their application to our Confessions.

Let us turn first of all to the most general and inclusive formal term, viz., the word "agreement." In its widest sense, agreement is the concurrence of two or more persons in expressing a common intention, with the view of altering their rights and duties (See 3 Savigny Syst. 309; Poll. Cont. 2). It is "aggregatio mentium, or the union of two or more minds in a thing done or to be done" (I Com. Dig. 311; 5 East 10; 2 Sm. Lead. Cas., 241).

An agreement in this sense is without legal effect when existing by itself, but is an essential preliminary to every true contract, gift, payment, conveyance and compromise, and of every voluntary variation or discharge of a contract or other obligation.[20]

When analyzed, the essential marks of an agreement are these: "There must be at least two persons; they must definitely intend the same thing; they must communicate this intention to one another; and the object of their intention must be such as will, when carried out, alter their legal positions, *e. g.*, by producing the transfer of property, or the creation or extinction of a right."[21]

Such an agreement or common intention involves a set of promises[22] made in consideration of each other. If not enforcible by law, an agreement is said to be void. If enforcible by law, it is a contract.[23] It is in that case a writing showing the terms and conditions of the agreement between the two parties involved.

The narrowest definition of a contract is that of Kant, who describes it as "the united will of two persons for the transfer of property."[24] He takes property in a wide sense. Hegel also limits the term contract to the transfer of property, though more generally. Windscheid, one of the most reliable of German writers on fundamental law, defines a contract as consisting in the union of two declarations of intentions. The one party declares to the effect that he will be a debtor to the other party, subjecting his will to the will of the other party; the declaration of the other party is that he accepts this subjection. Koch[25] defines a

---

[20] " Thus in a formal deed of conveyance the introductory recital always refers to the agreement in pursuance of which the conveyance is executed." This agreement is " the mutual assent of the parties at the time the deed is executed."

[21] Rapalje and Lawrence *Am. and Eng. Law,* Art. " Agreement."

[22] A promise is the declaration of a person or persons, without consideration, to do a thing.

[23] *Contract Act of 1872.*

[24] *Metaphysische Anfangsgründe der Rechtslehre,* pp. 98-103.

[25] Koch *Forderungen,* §69.

contract to be a reciprocal express agreement of two or more persons in a common expression of will, by which their legal relations are determined. Blackstone defines a contract to be an agreement, on sufficient consideration, to do or not to do a particular thing. The German code[26] declares a contract to be a reciprocal assent to the acquisition or alienation of a right. Savigny defines a contract as the union of two or more persons in a common expression of will, by which their legal relations are determined. This broadens the field somewhat and includes some forms of agreement which are not obligatory engagements, though even Kant defined such relationships as that of marriage, as obligatory contracts. A contract must have *defined legal rights* as its object; anything less is held to be a moral obligation or a mere engagement of honor. Wharton defines a contract as *an interchange by agreement of legal rights.* To be a contract, it must concern a right whose transfer the law will compel. It must consist of *a business proposal and acceptance bearing on a specific act.* A contract is resolvable into proposal and acceptance.

" ' Contract,' therefore, differs from ' agreement ' in the primary sense of that word, in including, in addition to the unity of intention and the juridical nature of the subject-matter constituting a simple agreement, the incident of one of the parties being bound to a future performance or forbearance, and of the other party doing or agreeing to do something in return. On the side of the party so bound to a future performance or forbearance, the expression of his willingness or intention to do it is called a 'promise', and the performance or forbearance done or promised by the other party is called the ' consideration for his promise.' " [27]

The Confessions of the Lutheran Church, or the particular Confessions of any church, are not in themselves, or by virtue of any mutual agreement between the confessors to

---

[26] *Allg. Landrecht*, 1, 5, ?1.
[27] R. and L., *Am. and Eng. Law.*

abide by them, or of any implied agreement between the Church and its ministry to remain faithful to them, in any wise a contract in the above sense.

Would it not be stretching language very far to say that a declaration of truth or of rights, though joined in and agreed to by many persons, is of the essence of contract? Neither the ultimate basis of the State, nor that of the Family, nor that of the Church, rests on contract. The Constitution of the United States is not even an instrument of agreement, but one of ordination and establishment, and rests on the authority and power that reside in the community, which are expressed and defined in the Constitution, but do not originate in its features as an agreement.

The general theory of Social Contract, originated in antiquity by Epicurus, and in modern days by the rationalism of the Eighteenth Century, is a vicious thing in the State; and is still more vicious in the Church. It is not by any choice or act of volition on our part that the State exists. We did not make it. No agreement of ours can either continue or destroy it. "It is not a physical but a spiritual fact." [28] And this elevation above human choice is more true of the Church. No denomination lives,—either as to its particular order, which is its faith, or as to its ecclesiastical order, which is its historical form,—by contract. Men cannot contract with each other to testify to the truth. The truth itself is the high obligating motive and power which compels them both in their agreement and in their testimony.

Hence, Symbols, in our opinion, are not even a sacred compact or covenant, although they may be thrown into the quasi form of a covenant or agreement, in order more conveniently to gain universal assent. Such a form, however, is not determinative either of the validity, or the accuracy, or the substance, or the durability of a Symbol. A most striking proof of all this is to be found in the Confession to which the term "Symbol" was originally applied, and which

---

[28] Robert Ellis Thompson.

is not in the form of an agreement between two or more persons, but in the form of an individual declaration. The Apostles' Creed says not "I agree to believe," but "I believe."

But contract is more than simple agreement or even covenant. It is *a bargain,* and one that can be legally enforced. A Symbol is not a contract because there are, as such, *no legal rights in it.* It may, where State and Church are united, or in a state religion, become the basis of legal rights, and it may in itself become determinative of legal rights. But as such, and without the addition of that which makes it a legal instrument, it bears no legal authority. The Unaltered Augsburg Confession does not convey or preserve ownership in any church in eastern Pennsylvania; although if the deed makes certain specifications, leading up to this Confession, or if there are certain facts and decisions in the history of the local or larger Church that lead up to this Confession, the Confession may be the basis on which ownership will be decided, just as it might be decided on the basis of any natural relationship. A Symbol may become the basis of contract between churches, but only as the churches are incorporated, or are in possession of a legal instrument covering property, and as the Symbol is recognized in the incorporation or in the instrument.

Legally, there is something further to be considered. The fundamental fact in a contract, namely, that of an *interchange,* is lacking in a Symbol. There is no relation of Promissor or Promisee in a Symbol. It is of the nature of a contract that one party has something to give, which the other party receives, and *vice versa.* There are always two parties on opposite sides. In a Confession all parties give and agree on the one and same thing. There is no opposite side.

In the next place, a Symbol is not a contract because it *does not concern a right whose transfer the law will compel.* A Lutheran cannot sell his property in the Augsburg Confesfession as a Symbol and make it effective at law. Moreover, the joint liability of the parties in agreement in a Symbol, such as, for instance, that of the signers of the Augsburg Confession or of the Formula of Concord, unless extended by legal statute, or unless there be some special personal obligation assumed by the members individually, will not extend beyond the range and the life of the corporate estate. The Symbol would cease to be such at the end of the lives of the signers, and outside of the regions they control, unless it were formally held in continuance and extended, wherever it is extended, by a legal renewal of the original formalities.

If the Symbol is to be regarded as belonging to the Church in a general corporate sense, we must remember that, to be valid even as a moral obligation, there would have to be no confusion between the corporation and individuals in it. For the corporation and the persons composing it are in no sense convertible. Neither does a corporation receive into its membership the legal representatives of its deceased members, and there is a limit of a certain number of years on the ordinary contractural relations into which it enters.

The very idea, then, of a contract is not suitable for the characterization of a Confession. As a frame of definition, it does not sum up the higher confessional relations. A Confession is the Church's united avowal of its faith.

The Church's existence and its right to exist, to teach, to judge truth, to affirm and condemn, are bound up in the rightness and sureness of its Faith; and therefore it may be and is exceedingly important for the Confession to compare, to discriminate and to mark any or all the facts of its Faith, but only for the ultimate purpose of avowal. The primary purpose of a Confession or Creed is not, as is often stated, to distinguish one Faith, or one religious communion from another; but it is to distinguish in order to teach, and to teach in order to bring about a united avowal. Any creed or confession or teaching which rests in the terms of a mutual contract, or stops short of active testimony and avowal of the truth as it is in Christ Jesus, fails in the one main function in which it is of value to Christ and the Church. For, confession is the *necessary* utterance of faith (Rom. 10: 10; Matt. 12: 34[b]).

The Confessions of the Church, especially the œcumenical creeds, are termed Symbols;[29] and the common name for the Book of Concord is " The Symbolical Books of the Evangelical Lutheran Church."

The word "symbol" draws attention to the external and the human side of a Confession, and neither to that inner substance of it which is the Word of God, nor to that inner apprehension of it which causes it to be a witness of living and saving faith. Its fundamental idea is the human operation of comparing different truths for the purpose of reaching a decision as to them, and finally of so marking the conclusion reached that it can be distinguished and recognized.

It is, therefore, a term of society, indicating a discriminative process, such as we find, for instance, in men of a political party coming together to construct a platform; or a scientific process, such as we find in the comparative delineation and estimate of various creeds in the science of "symbolics." But it does not in the faintest way allude to either the life or the power of God's Word which springs up out of the heart of a believing Church in the utterance of weighty and united testimony, which is, indeed, the main and substantial thing in the Confessions of the Church. The Confessions of the Church are the Testimony of its Faith to all the world.

It is in this sense also that the Formula of Concord is a true Confession. The word " Symbol " is not used by the authors in designating it in its title, but they call it, " Wiederholung und Erklärung etlichen Artikel Augsburgischen Confession," "Repetitio et Declaratio. . . . Augustanæ Confessionis."[30]

The " Christliche, Widerholete, einmütige Bekenntnüs, Confessio Fidei," in its title; and the air of conviction and

---

[29] See chap. XIII. Cp. *Book of Concord*, II, 535, 1 ; 537, **9.**
[30] The comparative idea appears in the title of the Formula in its own subordinate place. "nach Anleitung Gottes Worts und summarischem Inhalt unser christlichen Lehr beigelegt und verglichen."

piety that breathes in its pages, show how truly it, in essence, is a book of soul and conviction, and not of comparative religious science. It is only in a later time, especially in those editions issued in the rationalistic period of the Eighteenth Century, that the term "Symbol" begins to occur in the title of the Book of Concord. (*Cp.* Hutter *Comp.* Wittb. 1610, p. 10.) There is, in fact, no Confession of our Church which terms itself a Symbol; or which, indeed, is termed a Symbol, when alluded to in its vital and essential, as apart from its historical and ecclesiastical, relations.

The Confessions, or Symbols, are valuable because they contain the *articles of faith,* and the articles of faith are the substance of the divine Word on each of the various points of revelation, to be trustingly received by the sinner for his salvation. It is found that "their connection is so intimate that, when one is removed, the rest cannot continue sound and whole." [31]

The articles of faith embody the things that are to be believed as such. They treat of the mysteries of faith that transcend the comprehension of unaided human reason,[32] and that are revealed in the Word of God.

The Symbols embrace these articles as they have been called forth from time to time, as, in various periods, particular parts and teachings of the Word of God were put under stress, and tested, and purified, and preserved for us in permanent form. Together the articles constitute *the Confession of the Church's faith.* Since the articles are found in their original and permanent form in the Symbols, the latter are summaries of true religion, from various points of view, embracing the Christian faith.

"They are public Confessions, drawn up after much deliberation and consultation, in the name of the Church, by orthodox men, with reference to certain articles of faith, *so that the members of the orthodox church might be removed*

---

[31] Hollazius *Exam. Theol. Acroam.,* p. **44.**
[32] *Ib.,* p. 45.

from the ignorance and heretical wickedness of infidels and be preserved in the proper profession of the faith." [33] "They are called Symbols because they were the tests of the ancient Church by which the orthodox could be distinguished from the heterodox." [34]

The term " Symbolical Books," so far as we know, was not used on the title-page of the Concordia, or "Widerholete, einmütige Bekenntniss," before the Eighteenth Century. In the earlier day the confessional idea was the prominent one; and by Hollazius, the last of the old dogmaticians, in the middle of the Eighteenth Century, their necessity was still defined as "to establish solid, permanent and firm concord in the Church of God, so that there may be a certain compendious form, or type, approved by universal consent, in which the common doctrine, which the churches of the purer doctrine profess, collected from the Word of God, may be contained; to furnish an account of the Christian religion if it be demanded by the civil authority, and to distinguish the true members of the Church from her enemies, the heretics and schismatics." [35]

If now we come to examine the Confessions for their own definition of their actual character, and for any clauses that may be regarded as the binding clauses of the agreement, we shall find none in the œcumenical creeds. The Augsburg Confession speaks of itself as the "Articles in which is our Confession and in which is seen a summary of the doctrine of those who teach among us."

The Apology terms itself, "A Reply to the Confutation;" and Melanchthon says as to signing it: "I give my name so that no one may complain that the book has been published anonymously." The Schmalkald Articles terms itself "A Declaration to stand on them, if God so will, even to death." The Articles on the Power and Primacy of the Pope are

---

[33] Hollazius *Exam. Theol. Acroam.*, p. 54.

[34] Calovius, *Syst. Loc. Theol.*, I. p. 101.

[35] Schmidt *Dogmatik*, Trans. by Jacobs, p. 121.

called "A harmonious Declaration of Approval;" and by John Brentz, a Testimony that "I thus hold, confess and constantly will teach." The Small Catechism denominates itself a "Statement of the Christian doctrine" in very brief and simple terms (Preface). The Large Catechism declares itself to be "A Course of Instruction" (Second Preface); and again, "A Treatment of the Five Articles of the Entire Christian Doctrine" (Second Preface).

The Epitome of the Formula of Concord declares "that this is *the doctrine, faith* and *confession* of us all, for which we will answer at the last day before the just Judge, our Lord Jesus Christ, and that against this we will neither secretly nor publicly speak or write, but that we intend, by the grace of God, to persevere therein, we have, after mature deliberation, testified in the true fear of God and invocation of His name by signing with our own hands this Epitome."

In analyzing this declaration, promise and testimony, we find nothing of the essence of contract. There is a testimony as to their *"doctrine, faith* and *confession"* (and a promise not to *"speak or write"* contrarily), made solemnly ("answer before the just Judge"), "after mature deliberation," "in the true fear of God and invocation of His name," "signing with our own hands"; but that is all.

The corresponding clause in the "Comprehensive Summary" is emphasized as a *Testimony* and *Declaration.* It reads as follows:

"In the sight of God and of all Christendom, to those . . . who shall come after us, we wish to testify that the above Declaration . . . is our faith, doctrine and confession, in which we will appear before the judgment seat. We will neither speak nor write anything contrary to this Declaration, but . . . intend to abide thereby."

We find here no contract or article of agreement but, first, a Testimony in the sight of God and all Christendom; second, a Declaration to those who come after us (and who cannot therefore be the party of the second part); third, an Acknowledgment of the substance as "faith, doctrine and confession;" and fourth, a Promise, general, but impliedly, to each other, and a Declaration of intention " to abide thereby."

On the whole, then, we may conclude that the confessional element of our Confessions, and not any agreement in them, is their essential part and gives them their validity. They are not—except secondarily—a solemn contract to regulate officials in the church, nor a convenient mark by which people outside the Lutheran Church may recognize us, nor a bond of union by which we recognize each other. They are a witness and testimony—uniting their confessors in the cogency of the truth—to the Church's Faith.

They arose not to mark distinctions between denominations, but from the inner necessity of bearing witness to the truth and against error. Their most important use is not to mark religious distinctions in Protestantism, but to testify and to teach within the Church.

The main purpose of the Confession is to teach the Church. Their testimony is to become part of the Church's blood and sinew. As the Catechism is already the standard teaching book in every congregation, so the Symbolical Books should be the great fountain whence should flow into the very life and character of every theological seminary the Confessional principle.

Our object in training young men in theology is not to give them a knowledge of comparative, historical, apologetic, or even systematic divinity, but to make them confessors of the Faith well-grounded and able to render every man a reason for it, living witnesses, and faithful administrators of the Word and Sacraments. This Confessional conception of a seminary differentiates it from the scientific institution in which theology as a science, rather than the true faith, is taught; and our Church, both in Germany and in our own country, howsoever liberal her academic, collegiate and university training may, and, in truth, should be, can not possibly be made to shine like a city set upon a hill until her seminaries' chief aim is to send forth witnesses of God's Word and confessors of the Church's Faith as the future pastors of our congregations.

The Apostolic injunctions to individuals on this point apply with still greater force to congregations, synods and institutions, and to the Church as the total of believers.

The Formula of Concord implies that presenting "pure, wholesome doctrine" aright, and reproving those "who teach otherwise," is the main function of both the preacher and teacher. The great thing in the Church is that faith be awakened and the Faith be witnessed to and preserved in its purity, and the ways of error be pointed out. "The Church must direct the teachers to her Symbols and make it their duty faithfully and uprightly to impress their doctrine." [36]

Confessions stimulate and preserve the unity of the Faith and the oneness of the Church, not because they create it, or form its bonds, but because they point to the deeper unities in the body of Christ. " The God of our Lord Jesus Christ, the Father of glory," [37] "hath put all things under his feet, and gave him to be the head over all things to the Church, which is his body, the fulness of him that filleth all in all;" [38] that we "may grow up into him in all things, which is the head, even Christ: from whom the whole body fitly joined together and compacted by that which every joint supplieth, according to the effectual working in the measure of every part, maketh increase of the body unto the edifying of itself in love;" [39] for of this body "Christ is the head," [40] "from which all the body by joints and bands having nourishment ministered, and knit together, increaseth with the increase of God." [41]

---

[36] Mueller, *Einleit.*
[39] 4 :15,16.
[37] Eph. 1 :17.
[40] 5 :23.
[38] 1 : 22, 23.
[41] Col. 2 : 19.

9

CHAPTER VIII.

DO CONFESSIONS BIND?

Intellectual Liberty and the Official Christian Confessor—Why the Church Asks
Loyalty from those in Office—Why the Church needs Settled Teaching—Free
Investigation and Confessional Obligation.

THE eagle chafes, behind golden bars, in a foreign land.
It was made to soar. It cheerfully accepts the
limitations of bare cliffs, and narrow crags, and snow-capped
summits, and clouds whirling in tremendous storm; but it
pines in confinement.

If our conscience, heart and convictions are not at home
in a Confession that has not been made, approved or chosen
by us, but in which we find ourselves, we shall chafe under
its limitations. We shall continually be seeing the fence
instead of enjoying the farm; we shall be peering between
the bars, and climbing the pickets, and making ourselves
miserable, in the effort to convince the men within, and the
world without, that we are *prisoners.*

Yet the sagacious dog, more noble and more civilized than
the eagle, faithful to his master, enters eagerly into the law
and confines of a domestic and common life, and languishes,
or even dies, apart from the presence of his master. One of
the most forlorn objects on the earth is a lost dog—a dog
that has become "free," that is, exiled from its home and the
companionship and voice of its master.

The man who sleeps within the four limiting walls of his
house *locks the doors* and lies down to rest in peace, *a free
soul,* because he is *at home;* while the ill and fevered spirit
rising from its bed and seeking every avenue to escape is a

78

prisoner, who knows not why, and knows not where to find repose.

To some men Confessions are not only binding, but galling. They fret beneath the yoke. Their hearts are not at home in the limitations, and the result is inevitable. A sentimental desire for freedom impels them, eagle-like, to soar above and beyond the vineyard rather than to work within it. Yet limitations are necessary, and are a condition not only of life, and thought, and truth, but of country and achievement, and age, and position, and also of faith.

Whether the accountability for rebellion against the limitations of a Confession resides in the individual; or in his early training and uncongenial environment, or in the Confession itself, is not always easy to decide.

The secret of the whole matter is sometimes to be found in the man himself. Saul was an ambitious, an ardent and a vengeful man. Jesus told him that the dissatisfaction of his nature was his own fault: "It is hard for thee to kick against the pricks;" and when he was converted this self-same man actually joyed in living within these distressing limitations, in being a "slave" and a "yoke-fellow" under Christ. Although, when Peter tried to throw the net of Pharisaic realism around him, he yielded not—no, not for an instant—yet the thorn in his flesh was accepted with thanks.

The galling power of truth itself is great to those who do not desire to abide in and by it. They feel they must escape. They cannot breathe in the same khan with Jesus of Nazareth. They must escape to the Bedouin of the desert; or if the Bedouin are in possession of the khan, there will be "no room for the young child in the inn."

A trustful, confiding and converted spirit desires to keep well within the law and will of the object of its confidence, and finds its joys in the fulfilment of any given prescriptions. For such as these there is always the widest freedom. For them there is no law. Love has become the fulfiling of the law, and is unhappy beyond the forbidden bounds.

There is a service *in* the law, which is result and satisfaction; a service *above* the law, which is joy and freedom; and a service *under* the law, which is tyranny and bondage. It may be the selfsame service in all three cases. It is a galling service in bondage, to the weak man, the critic, the dissatisfied man, and the thinker of untamed instincts. It is a service in law, to the man of serious conscience. It is a service above law, to the man of ardent loyalty and generous affection.

We may conclude, then, that where there is confidence, faith and trust, the Confession will not need to bind, and cannot gall. But where there is doubt, mistrust, or any trace of the undevoted and critical mind, the Confession holds an eagle behind the bars.

Has it the right to do so? Can it bind intellectually, morally, legally? If the bird of freedom has been trapped on his upper crag, and has been brought unwillingly as a captive into the confines of the Church, there is no intellectual or moral right to hold him; but, if he has come down as a freebooter in search of prey or as an independent soarer of spreading wing, who wishes to abide with us and yet will not say, "liberty *and union,* one and inseparable," it is well that he be bound.

The trouble, however, may not be in the eagle, but in the confining domain. There are necessary and proper limits to the binding power of Confessions. "The Church has no power to bind the conscience, except as she truly teaches what her Lord teaches, and faithfully commands what He has charged her to command".[1]

The trouble very often is in the man's environment. He has not been brought up to see the need of certain truths, not to understand the importance of an honest and clear-cut Confession. He may not realize the bearings of doctrines that to him seem far away. He is in the Confession, but not thoroughly of it, having failed to appropriate it; and he

---

[1] *Cf. "Fundamental Principles of Faith and Church Polity."*

is unwilling to give up his right, at least abstractly, to overstep it.

The Confirmation Confession, most solemn, and made on the basis of the Smaller Catechism—which is the Larger Catechism, the Augsburg Confession, the Formula of Concord, yea, Scripture itself, condensed into manual form—is, like the marriage avowal, or any other solemn promise or covenant with the Lord, binding in this case for life. The Ordination or Installation Confession, which is a similar condensation, but shows more explicit apprehension of the doctrine, is similarly binding. Yet the confessional bond is not as inflexible as the marriage bond. To any and all classes of men whatsoever, we say that the Church has no desire to keep them in the confessional cage; no right to keep them, as it were, in captivity, when they wish to be at liberty—as they say—to worship according to the dictates of their own conscience. The door is open, let them spread their wings and fly to that happier clime where the limitations accord with their conscience and more enlightened conviction. "Go in peace," we say.

A faith, a love, a conviction, an enlightenment, an atmosphere, such as the old Church, with her heavy foundations and honest walls and bare brown rafters, offers, does not suit you. You are restless here; and even if we "modernize" the old home, and introduce the elegancies and conveniences, and consign the antiques to the flames, and give you an up-to-date twenty-four-hour alarm clock in place of the old precious timepiece of grandfather, on the stairs, and a veneered mahogany table in place of the solid old family heirloom, you will not be satisfied. The Scriptural doctrine is too heavy for you. You require a modern newspaper treatment. We cannot help you.

But to those men who, with the door standing open before them, nevertheless do not fly, but desire to remain with us within the limitations, we say: "You should observe the order of this old home. You are not by yourself, alone up on the rocks; nor journeying, without responsibility to fixed relations, in 'a far country.' You are here in what we believe to be a God-framed order, and if you elect to stay with us, you cannot in good conscience do so, with the feeling of a rebel against us; but we must presume that your presence among us is from a noble motive, and not merely the result of self-interest and personal convenience, that you appreciate our protective bulwark and believe in the power of our principles, and that therefore you are ready to train yourself in accordance with our restrictions.

" If you go, you are free. But if you stay in our house, you are bound by the law of our house, which is our Confession, or, rather, by the Scripture, which is our only rule, but of which our Confession is the faithful, trusty, convenient, tested, proven and accurate witness."

The Church desires this: that the harmonies of the doctrinal teaching of her symbols with the pure Scripture doctrine be recognized by those that belong to her and wish to enjoy the benefits of her membership.

The Church asks no one to give assent to her doctrine without inner conviction, but she also regards no one as belonging to her, who is not able to make her Confession his own. She cannot interpret her symbols so broadly and unfaithfully as to leave room for every opinion that has been reduced to a minimum of Christian faith.

The Church must speak out decidedly what she believes; which doctrine she accepts in God's Word, and which doctrine she rejects as being against it. If it were otherwise, she would open herself as an arena for all kinds of heresies, and would deserve her own destruction.[2] Sartorius goes to the root of the whole matter when he says that "In giving up her Confessions, the Protestant Church gives up herself. But in adhering faithfully to them, her lasting continuance as well as her living development is guaranteed."

----

[2] Mueller, *Einleitung.*

On account of this necessity, the Formula of Concord is impelled to state: "As some divergencies have arisen between theologians of the Augsburg Confessions, because of the Interim and other matters, we have desired to set up and declare our faith and Confession, *'rund, lauter und klar'*, *'in thesi et antithesi'*, *i. e.,* in the true doctrine and its opposite, concerning *each and every one* of these matters, that the *foundation of divine truth may be clear* in all the articles, and *all wrong,* doubtful suspicious and condemned *doctrines,* whoever may be disposed to defend them, *may be exposed,* and every person be faithfully warned."

The supporting beams of our household of faith must be kept *' rund, lauter und klar;'* and if your heart no longer values them, but has cast them aside, if your love no longer holds to the principle of our home, and you have cast that principle aside, you may not use our roof and our shelter, to attack the thing we cherish. If we have not the same faith, and you cannot join our glad and open adherence to it, you ought not be of our household. For our household is a household of faith. Its communion and its union consists of persons who are animated by a common faith.

Our fellowship has been instituted to conserve the faith. "You have the civil and the moral right to form your impressions in regard to truth. But there the right stops. You have not the right to remain in our Christian union, except as our terms of membership give you that right. So easy is this distinction, and so clearly a part of practical morals, that the law of the land recognizes it. You have not the right to call yourself what you are not, and to keep what does not belong to you."

Lutheranism is the exercise of the inalienable right of judging according to one's own conscience. But it does not stop there. That is only the formal side of it. Its substance is a positive result, a well-defined system of faith, which is no less precious than the form. Rationalism has never been able to clear itself from the dishonor of its evasion, when it pretended to bear the Lutheran name, in exercise of the *formal* right of freedom, and yet rejected the Lutheran *result* of that exercise of freedom, viz., the glorious principle of justification by faith.

The very life of Lutheranism involves her refusal to have fellowship with rationalism, whether it comes to her from without, or whether it arises within the precincts of her own home. The Augsburg Confession lays the foundations of that home in the confession of the one Faith and the administration of the sacraments of that Faith. The marks of the Church are the pure and sound Doctrine of the Gospel and the right use of the sacraments; and it is sufficient for the true unity of the Church to agree upon these two things. This basis the Lutheran Church has declared as fundamental, and upon it, it is obliged to abide.

These considerations apply with manifold force to those whom we have chosen as the pastors and teachers of our household and the pillars in our home. In meekness and in faith should they implant the ingrafted Word, which is able to save our souls. We look to them to hold fast the form of sound words, to take heed unto themselves and the doctrine, and to continue in them. We look to them to stand fast in one spirit, with one mind striving together for the faith of the Gospel. We look to them to be of like mind, one toward another, to speak the same thing, to have no divisions among themselves, but to be perfectly joined together, in the same mind and the same judgment. It is only thus that they can really teach our doctrines. For where confidence and unity in the faith are lacking among teachers, there doubt immediately arises among hearers and scholars. But faith is the one thing needful, and doubt is the one thing destructive, to the future of our household.

We are so sure that we are right in our confidence in Christ, in His Scripture, in our Church, in her Faith, as confessed in her Confessions, that we are ready to act and to take the responsibility for those who come after us; as every serious-minded parent and institution feel it their duty to do. We therefore train our children in that which we have found to be of such saving power ourselves, and when they are sufficiently mature we desire them to confess it in a lifelong, gladsome vow. This we do not simply to perpetuate the institution, the Church; not simply from the instinct of self-preservation—that is the base insinuation which the world casts up into our face; and while there is legitimate motive in taking this position, it is not our highest and deepest motive. It is the *preciousness* of our treasure, which moves us to transmit it; it is our *calling and vocation* from the Lord to bring up our children in the Faith and to hold on to it ourselves, that moves us; it is the *service* which the Faith renders in the work of salvation, that moves us to extend it to others.

This binding extension to others we do not make apart from their conviction, but with their free consent. Only thus does the Church bind her own, whether catechumen or public teacher, to her Confessions.

If there is any one in this world of whom the Church can expect loyalty, it is her own teachers. They have offered themselves for her service. They have come up out of her life-blood and her faith. They have been trained in her principles and her hopes and her institutions. They have not been taken unawares. At every successive step in the preliminary years, their intellect, their feeling, their conscience and conviction have had opportunity to enter into honorable freedom. They know what the Church expects of them, before they assume the vows of fidelity and service, viz.: that they will make "a good confession before many witnesses." They have had a long time to deliberate, to investigate. As a rule, they are graduates of colleges and bear the degree of M. A., and are perhaps as old as Martin Luther was when he nailed the ninety-five Theses on the church door at Wittenburg, sufficiently mature to know their own faith and their own mind. If anyone in this life ever had sufficient time to consider an obligation, the coming pastors of the Church certainly are among them. The Church can therefore justly expect them to be faithful, and to enter her work with a convinced and loyal, and not with a critical spirit.

The faithful and single-minded fulfilment of such an obligation is not only not a tyrannical expectation, but it is fair and equitable to all parties. It is fair to the pastor, and protects him in many ways; it is fair to the flock, and is a most important protection to them and their children; it is fair to the Church, and protects her in her most essential principles and work.

"From the conception of the symbol as a common or congregational testimony to the truth, proceeds, *eo ipso,* its obligation upon ministers, whose calling it is to be witnesses of the truth for the Christian community. The symbols are public confessions, and the preacher is a public confessor; but only then an official confessor in the Church, when he confesses himself in harmony with the confession of the church by whose servants he is ordained a fellow-servant. And where the preacher does not consent to the confessions of the church, by whose servants he has been ordained, he is no fellow-confessor, and certainly cannot be a preacher of a confession which he does not acknowledge. In no event is the preacher individually any more a witness to the truth than the common testimony of the church in the symbols. He is not *above* the symbols, nor *under* the symbols, but *a joint witness* with them.

"Hence he does not submit in his ordination to some law of faith, forced upon him by some higher or extrinsic authority; but the purport of his obligation, in giving his consent to the forms of doctrine contained in the symbols, is essentially this: that the minister, being called to the service of a public confession of the truths of the Gospel, first acknowledges these truths as his own personal faith. The ceremony of his consecration, the laying on of the hands of the ordaining minister and of the assisting brethren, indicates the fellowship of the ministerial and witnessing *office* to which he is dedicated." [3]

It is *the Confession* through which the minister publicly testifies his union with Christ the Head, and with the members who are the Church. And if there is no confidence to be placed in his confession, or if he makes it with secret reservations, it is hardly possible to see how his preaching is to be confided in. Upon the ground of his confession Peter received his apostolic commission. Paul also, in his first Epistle to Timothy, which may be rightly called an Epistle on ordination, reminds that young minister very impressively of his good profession which he had professed before many witnesses. And in the second letter in which he brings to mind his unfeigned faith, and urges him to stir up the gift of God which was in him by the laying on of hands, he further says, "Be not thou therefore, ashamed of the testimony of our Lord as a faithful fellow-confessor of the Gospel." It is not upon the person of Peter and his successors that the Church is founded—this is a Romish error—but upon his faith and confession, and upon his successors in the same faith and the same confession. As a co-confessor of the confession of the Apostles and the Church, the minister plants himself upon that same foundation-rock, upon which the congregation is as free from his personal mutability as he himself is from the fluctuation of his members. For as the minister is no lord of the congregation's faith, so the congregation dare not lord it over his faith by the changing opinions of the majority. [4]

Those who object to the binding authority of the Confessions in the teaching and witnessing office of the Church, do not seem to realize that the office in its nature and purpose is for service toward the flock and not for a convenience for the

---

[3] Sartorius. *Über die Nothwendigkeit u. Verbindlichkeit d. kirch. Glaubensbekenntnisses.*

[4] Seiss, *Ev. Rev.,* IV, pp. 16-17.

utterance of the individual. The individual becomes, by free will indeed, and yet really, an organ, a representative.

The binding character of the principles or instructions of a house or firm, in ordinary business relations, is regarded as unquestioned, and its breach would not be tolerated for a moment. For a representative of any house to represent it with reservations, to mingle doubt and suspicion in his statements, is treachery and sufficient reason for immediate discharge. The same principle is operative in the binding character of the Church Confessions upon its representatives. They are bound, not in contract, but in the nature of the case. In both cases the representatives do not lose their freedom in entering the service; they are free to be true to the principles in whose interests they serve, and they are free to quit the service. They are not free to be untrue to the principles and to continue the service.

It is clear that the Church, which claims to be a faithful and reliable witness of the Word of God, and to whom has been committed the office of the Word, cannot agree that everyone within her should teach according to his own thought of what is well, or what he desires; but if she is to fulfil her calling, and is not herself to disintegrate, she must declare that only that teaching be accorded authority, and be proclaimed, which accords with the existing, historically-founded and publicly-recognized faith.[5]

Those who demur against this proposition, which seems to be almost self-evident, do so from another point of view, viz. : on the ground of the fundamental right of Protestantism, a right without which it itself could not have come into existence, namely, the right of free investigation, which dare not

---

[5] The teaching oath was in use in the Roman Church before the Reformation. In 1533, Luther, Jonas and others enacted a statute requiring candidates for the degree of Doctor of Theology to swear to the incorrupt doctrine of the Gospel as taught in the symbols. After the Interims and the hardening of the lines in the states, in the middle of the century, subscription began to be enforced at times under pain of deposition and exile.—Köllner *Symbolik* I, pp. 106 sqq.

Modern forms of subscription, as of ordination and worship, vary greatly in the European States, and also in the American Church.

be bound or limited by any human formularies, but which acknowledges the Scripture alone (sometimes not even Scripture) as its judge.

They overlook the fact, however, that the right of free investigation is not abridged in the least by Confessional obligation. For, as v. Burger points out, the Lutheran Church is full of the good assurance that her Confessions will stand the test of every investigation according to the Scripture; and she does not ask for faithfulness toward her Confession as antithesis to free investigation, but upon the ground that such an investigation, most ample and searching and thorough, most free and yet duly and properly appointed, has been made in time past, and shall have been made as a sufficient and thorough preliminary in each individual case.

The investigation should be so broad indeed as to include in its field not only the Confession, but also the conscience of the investigator, so that he may be sure in advance that he is willing to bring every thought and imagination of his own into captivity to Christ; and that he is free from a constitutional instinct which leans toward other Confessions, and toward giving battle to the Confession of his Church to weaken or destroy it; and that his chief concern in the office about to be assumed is not the philosophical one, which is the exaltation of pure reason, nor the scientific one, which is the exaltation of pure natural law and fact, but the real confessing motive, which is the exaltation of pure faith, and which works to the strengthening and establishing of the Church as the institution of faith.

It is quite true that the teacher's intellect may see things in a different light in different stages of life, and that there may be a development of the mind, or of science to which the mind is drawn, which may shake the faith of the man in his Confessions, and, if he be of good conscience, will put him out of touch with them. For conscience is and ever should be supreme; and where a man is convinced that his salvation, intellectual and spiritual, is outside of the Confession, it becomes his duty to inform the Church. The right of protest, properly guarded as to weight of substance and motive, still remains unshattered in the mother of Protestantism. But "protest" as an intellectual and ecclesiastical convenience is an abuse of the most sacred and most exceptional right of the Christian. When the exception becomes the rule, and the protesting habit becomes chronic, we may safely conclude that it is evaluated: that its source is an over-exaggerated estimate by an individual of the importance of his own reasoning powers in contrast with the combined judgment and wisdom of the Church; and that he conceives of his ecclesiastical position much in the same way in which a mule regards his stall, as a sphere in which he may give vent to his critical faculties by continuous reaction, without restraining interference on the part of the owners of the stable. Nature has endowed such a "protestant" with extraordinary gifts of pedal reaction, and he must be free to exercise them against whatever may come within the range of contact.

We must never forget that the Truth, as a general principle, is the quality, but not the essence, of the Confession; and that quality is only formally and not actually, superior to essence. In real life, essence with quality is of more service and less hindrance than quality without essence. In the life of the Church the use of the substance of the Confession is of more ordinary and regular importance than the critical devotion to quality which, itself, without the essence, can scarcely be kept free from a foreign essence.

Those clerical scholars who exalt intellectual freedom above spiritual freedom, and who seek it *before* they seek the things of the kingdom, do not normally, nor usually, come to the Confessions with a really impartial mind. They come unconsciously swollen with prejudice of quality, with philosophic theory, and thus they propose to test the essence. They are no more free than is the devout and loyal mind, in approaching the Confession.

A critical attitude, one in which unverified doubt is richly suggestive and springing, does not bring an uninfluenced state of mind to the investigation of the truth. He who is in a critical attitude, or who already believes that the Confession is not correct, is in a position which prevents him from being a devoted teacher of the Church.

He who, in advance, is a party against or suspicious of the Church, should not desire to be commissioned as her servant. He who is a faithful teacher of the Church confesses and teaches the Confession, not because the Confession forces him to do it as a law laid upon him, but because he recognizes and acknowledges the Scriptural truth in the Confession. Therefore he also assumes the obligation, not in *so far* as the symbol agrees with the Scripture, but *because* it does so. Without this conviction, he should not desire membership, much less public service in the Church.

But is there no freedom in the Church; is there no consideration for the various growing and maturing convictions of students; are there no rights for those who have faithfully accepted the Church's Faith, and approved themselves as its pastors and public teachers? Is there no room to be left for the development, progress and adjustment of the Faith under the new light, new scholarship, and the new conditions which each successive generation brings with it? Yes, there is large room—the Church must welcome all new light, new research, and new progress; but its confessional principle and its safety —as the only protection of Protestantism against individualism—require that such new teaching be not private, or experimental, or a prerogative of one or a few; but that it first be tested by the Church, and be officially formulated and accepted before it be taught.

The binding power of the Confessions is with reference to all the facts of principle or doctrine, and not to the human side of their statement as such. Here they differ from Scripture, the only rule.[*] We are not bound to assert and confess

---

[*] Not being inspired.

the absolute correctness of their method of applying every Scripture passage cited, or every historical allusion introduced, or of every form of logical proof they employ; but we are bound in conscience to that which the Confessional writings declare to be the faith and doctrine of the Church. Some of the Confessions are very free and occasional, others are very well considered and balanced in their form, just as is the case with their Rule, the Scriptures. Our obligation is not on these points, but on the content and sum; in the spirit, and not in the letter, of their teaching.

The obligation assumed is not a contract in the strict or legal sense of the term, unless there is a property consideration or a salary involved, in which case the obligation, if used as a basis for legally binding rights and property to principle, becomes amenable to the law of the land. But as a religious obligation, it is not a contract which requires a consideration of value to make it valid, nor a promissory oath; but, as a general ecclesiastical act, it is in the form of a vow to hold and to teach the Confession with the help of the Holy Spirit. In this light, the obligation to the Confessions is unassailable. The Church, if she is true to her Lord, herself and her members, has the right and duty of demanding it.

After a thorough understanding of the general relations between Faith and Truth, between Freedom and Loyalty, between Liberty and Standing Order, between Criticism and Service, between a Call and an Acceptance, only those could dispute the propriety of such an obligation who find themselves outside the Confession, but who desire to remain in the service from other than the highest motives; or by those who, influenced by a false ideal of the abstract rights of truth, desire to be unfettered in making their own confession effective. But, as v. Burger observes, to ask freedom from the Church itself to do this, is not any longer a right of her servants, but a violation of the same.

CHAPTER IX.

THE RISE OF THE CONFESSIONAL PRINCIPLE IN THE CHURCH.

Faith Within Manifests Itself in Outer Witness—Testimony Develops into the Confession—The First Confessions in the New Testament—The Pentecostal and Baptismal Confessions—The Fixed Confessional Forms of the New Testament—The Confessions of the Second Century.

FAITH is the divinely wrought and spontaneous confidence and devotion of the soul to that to which it clings. It may be a devotion to principles, or to principles incarnate, *i. e.,* to a person.

As soon as it becomes a part of the soul's experience, it rushes to all possible pathways of utterance. It testifies by the eye, by the lingering thought, by the lip, and by the act. But this new-born confidence and devotion affects and often changes the most important relations of life; and because of the supreme character of its trust, it willingly makes new adjustments in experience, and testifies to their existence.

It thus enters the realm of history, primarily as an informal and spontaneous modifier of all that it touches, but finally as a witness to great, final and formal changes in the historical order. Thus the devotion of personal love, first expressing itself spontaneously and on occasion, gradually becomes a regular confessional manifestation, and finally issues in a solemn covenant, involving change of relationship to all

10

the world and transplanting the potencies of a long historical development.

It is in this way that faith in Jesus, the Lord of grace and glory, first rising in the hearts of a few, and then in an ever-widening circle of followers, has developed gradually from spontaneous and single confessions of devotion to a complete change of relationship, and finally into *a solemn and formal testimony,* covering the whole field of principles involved in the change of historical relationships, and summed up, from time to time, and especially under the arraignment of doubt and aspersion from without, into a deliberate and documentary Declaration of the Church, respecting its various relations to its Lord and Head; and from which, in turn, its subordinate relations to the other issues of life are determined and, as may become necessary, are formulated.

Thus the Confession of the Christian Church is a confession springing from faith in Christ. The more true its Confessional principle is, the less will it start with abstract dogmatic relations, and the more will it centre in Him in Whom is all the Church's trust.[1] The Church confesses her Head, and the Head in turn confesses its members (Matt. 10: 32). There is nothing in the true Church's Confession which is not at least an inference from its Lord's person or doctrine or work.

The first spontaneous utterances of the Church's Confession are very interesting. We hear Andrew, hastening out and seeking his own brother, saying to him, "We have found the Messiah." We see Nathanael coming to Jesus and confessing, "Rabbi, thou art the Son of God, thou art the King of Israel." We discover Nicodemus and the Samaritan woman moved spontaneously to at least a temporary and incomplete confession. We find Matthew, the man of acts, confessing the Lord completely by his sudden severance of existing earthly relations. We hear Peter, in a time when many

---

[1] This is true of the Lutheran as over against the Reformed Confession.

deserted the Lord, declaring, "Thou hast the words of eternal life, and we believe and are sure that thou art that Christ, the Son of the living God." We behold the man born blind brought by the act and word of Jesus to say, "Lord, I believe on the Son of God." We hear Martha from beneath the dark cloud exclaim, "Yea, Lord; I believe that thou art the Christ, the Son of God, which should come into the world." Every one of these spontaneous confessions contains the germ of a more formal credal statement.

But the high point of spontaneous apostolic Confession was reached by Peter on the Mount of Transfiguration long before the Resurrection, and by Thomas thereafter. These two confessions deserve to be contrasted. The first one is based on more imperfect perception and less scientific material, but on more glowing faith. The second one is based on experimental evidence of the most definite and conclusive character. The one is by the most ardent and the other by the most pessimistic of the apostles. Yet, strange to say, the first one, the one of ardent impulse, is most objective; and the second one, the one of cold-blooded scientific examination of testimony, is the most subjective one. Which of the two the Lord preferred need not be stated. For Peter's Confession He had nothing but pure praise; for Thomas' Confession He had a comparison that implied rebuke: "Blessed are they that have not seen, and yet have believed."

To our Lord, then, the confession of a living Church is more than that of a dead historico-critical dogmatic. So much emphasis did Christ place upon the inner conviction and the outer confession of faith in Himself, that He declared to Peter, what was the actual fact, as we shall see, that it was on this rock of inner conviction and outer confession that His Church would be built. In the light of these words, His declaration of Luke 12: 8, which makes the public acknowledgment of Himself in His person and work the great test of true membership in Him, takes on a new meaning; and in the light of Peter's Confession in Matthew 16:16, the same disciple's later three-fold denial, followed by a three-fold searching question to Peter after the Resurrection, shows what pre-eminence the Lord attributed to a Confession flowing out from the deep conviction of faith, and loyally maintained in the hour of greatest crisis.

The pre-eminent importance of the duty of faithful confession was also shown by Christ Himself in His own hour of trial, when He stood before Pontius Pilate and made Confession as to Himself, declaring that He was born and had come into the world for the purpose of bearing testimony to the truth.

Thus from the very start of Christianity, faith has risen into confession, and confession has taken the external form of a Confession. "In a certain sense," claims Schaff,[2] "it may be said that the Christian Church has never been without a creed (*Ecclesia sine symbolis nulla*). The baptismal formula and the words of institution of the Lord's Supper are creeds. These and the Confession of Peter antedate even the birth of the Christian Church on the day of Pentecost. The Church is, indeed, not founded on symbols, but on Christ; not on any words of man, but on the Word of God; yet it is founded on Christ as *confessed* by men; and a creed is man's answer to Christ's question, man's acceptance and interpretation of God's Word. Hence it is after the memorable confession of Peter that Christ said, 'Thou art Rock, and upon this rock I shall build my Church,' as if to say, 'Thou art the Confessor of Christ, and on this Confession, as an immovable rock, I shall build my Church.' Where there is faith, there is also profession of faith. As 'faith without works is dead,' so it may be said also that faith without confession is dead."

On the day of Pentecost, when the Church was established, and immediately thereafter, there was only one Article of Faith. All those who confessed Jesus as the Messiah, were

---

[2] *Creeds of Christendom*, I, p. 5.

baptized at once, without the more explicit instruction that preceded baptism in later days. This first rudiment of Confessionalism in the new-born Christian Church, which consisted of faith in Christ as its one objective content, and which became recognized as the standard of a good Christian Confession, developed under the working of the Holy Ghost through the Word, into a gradual consciousness of the whole content of Christian faith.

"Out of this one 'Article of Faith,' viz., of 'Jesus the Messiah,' it followed, in the nature of the case, that the whole conception of that which the Messiah should be in the rightly understood letter and spirit of the Old Testament promises, was transferred to Him, so that He was recognized as the Redeemer from sin, the Ruler of the kingdom of God, to Whom one's whole life was to be consecrated, Whose laws were to be followed in every respect, Who revealed Himself by the impartation of a new divine power of life, which conferred upon those redeemed and ruled by Him, the certainty of the forgiveness of sin received from Him, and which was to be the pledge of all the gifts that were to be granted them in His kingdom.

"He who acknowledged Jesus as the Messiah also thereby acknowledged Him as the infallible Prophet of God, Whose instruction, as He Himself had imparted it upon earth, and as He further imparted it through the Apostles, into whom He had put new souls, would also further be appropriated by Himself.

"Therefore baptism was at this time characterized as to its peculiar Christian import according to this one Article of Faith, which constituted the essence of Christianity, as a Baptism upon Jesus, upon the name of Jesus as Messiah.

"It is true that one cannot positively conclude from this characterization of baptism that the *Formula* of Baptism was not something else. Yet it is probable that in the original Apostolic Formula of Baptism only this one point was emphasized. This shorter Baptismal Formula contains in itself all that is to be found in the words which Christ used at the institution of Baptism. It includes the whole of Christian doctrine in itself; but the consciousness of this content was not yet developed in the baptismal subject." [3]

This Baptism in the name of Jesus for the remission of sins, with the reception of the Holy Ghost (Acts 2: 38), undoubtedly implied also a Confession, in a more explicit form, of the exaltation of the crucified Jesus, "that same Jesus whom God hath made," that same Jesus " whom ye have crucified, both Lord and Christ" (Acts 2: 36). Such may have been the earliest actual form of Christian Creed.

It is very clear from the baptism of the Eunuch that some simple Confession was connected with the administration of Baptism from the beginning. The Eunuch said, "What doth hinder me to be baptized?" Philip said, "If thou believest with all thine heart, thou mayest." The Eunuch answered and said, "I believe that Jesus Christ is the Son of God." Then Philip baptized the Eunuch (Acts 8: 37, 38). The baptisms recorded in the Acts of the Apostles all involve a brief Confession. [4]

The words of our Lord, "Into the name of the Father and of the Son and of the Holy Spirit," in instituting baptism as the means of grace, and membership in the Church, were probably used as a Formula by candidates for baptism in confessing their faith at a very early date, and developed in the West into the Apostolic, and in the East into the Nicene Creed.

Whether the summaries of the Apostle Paul, *e. g.*, Romans

---

[3] Neander, *Geschichte der Pflanzung und Leitung der Christlichen Kirche durch die Apostel,* I, pp. 26-28.

[4] " It has been pointed out that where baptism is mentioned historically in the New Testament, it is into the name of the Lord Jesus (Acts 19: 5; etc.), and not into the triune name (Matt. 28: 19) ; but the surprise of Paul in Acts 19: 3, that any one could have been baptized without hearing of the Holy Spirit is fair evidence that the Holy Spirit was mentioned, whenever Christian baptism was dispensed (Observe the force of the illative in Acts 19; 3)."—Denney.

For the treatment of this problem as it affected the early centuries of Church History and the development of the Apostles' Creed, see pp. 101 sqq.

1: 3, "Jesus Christ our Lord, which was made of the seed of David according to the flesh; and declared to be the Son of God with power, according to the Spirit of holiness, by the resurection from the dead;" and 1 Cor. 15: 3, 4, "How that Christ died for our sins according to the scriptures; and that he was buried, and that he rose again the third day according to the scriptures;" and 2 Thess. 2: 13, "God hath from the beginning chosen you to salvation, through sanctification of the Spirit, and belief of the truth: whereunto he called you by our gospel, to the obtaining of the glory of our Lord Jesus Christ. Therefore, brethren, stand fast, and hold the traditions which ye have been taught, whether by word, or our epistle;" and 1 Tim. 3: 16, "God was manifest in the flesh, justified in the Spirit, seen of angels, preached unto the Gentiles, believed on in the world, received up into glory;" and Titus 3: 4-8, "The kindness and love of God our Saviour toward man appeared, not by works of righteousness which we have done, but according to his mercy he saved us, by the washing of regeneration, and renewing of the Holy Ghost; which he shed on us abundantly, through Jesus Christ our Saviour; that being justified by his grace, we should be made heirs according to the hope of eternal life. This is a faithful saying, and these things I will that thou affirm constantly:"—whether these summaries are connected with the sacrament of baptism or not, they all aided to put the substance of Christian fact and doctrine into fixed form, and perhaps influenced the formulation of Christian truth for Catechetical purposes.

One of these fixed confessional forms may be referred to by Paul when he bids Timothy to "hold fast the form of sound words, which thou hast heard of me, in faith and love which is in Christ Jesus" (2 Tim. 1: 13). A fixed form of dogma, whether Confessional or not, is evidently alluded to in Rom. 6: 17, "Ye have obeyed from the heart that form of doctrine which was delivered you;" and in Heb. 6: 1, 2, there is the implication of a certain round or system of doctrines well-known and confessed: "Therefore leaving the principles of the doctrine of Christ, let us go on unto perfection; not laying again the foundation of repentance from dead works, and of faith toward God, of the doctrine of baptisms, and of laying on of hands, and of resurrection of the dead, and of eternal judgment."

We have thus seen that, in connection with the sacrament of baptism, the Apostles insisted on the confession of Jesus as the outer token of faith. This Confession contained an avowal of Jesus as Lord (Rom. 10: 9; 1 Cor. 12: 3), and, as we have noted, probably contained a confession of the resurrection. Almost all the elements, yes, the very clauses of the Apostles' Creed, are to be found, in the above quoted passages, already under consideration. They were combined on the basis of the baptismal formula, "The Father, the Son and the Holy Spirit;" but were confessed, *first of all,* as the truth that is in Christ Jesus, since the approach to the unconverted comes through Christ, and then naturally *develops* (as we see in 1 Cor. 12: 4-6; 2 Cor. 13: 14; Eph. 2: 8; Jude 20, 21; John 14: 16) into the faith and Confession of the Father and the Spirit.

It is possible that the contents of the Church Confessions, insisted on at Baptism, varied with the circumstances and experience of the convert, and only gradually came to include certain constant elements. Though always connected with Christ, the Confession apparently was not always a definite formulation. In Heb. 4: 14, for instance, the Confession to be made by the Christian, and held fast to, is evidently the substance of doctrine and not its form: "Seeing then that we have a great High Priest, that is passed into the heavens, Jesus the Son of God, *let us hold fast our profession."*

It was the almost immediate appearance of false teaching that undoubtedly caused the elements of the truth in Christ Jesus to be drawn together into a *fixed Confessional Form.* In the Epistles to John, for instance, the fuller Confession of the Church as to the Fatherhood of God and the true Sonship

in Jesus, sets itself in antithesis to the errors of gnosticism;
and in Paul's teaching in such churches as Ephesus, the Confession had doubtless rapidly crystallized into a "form of
sound words."

We thus come to the point where early formulated Confessions of the Church arose out of that confession of personal faith which was required of the candidate for Baptism,
especially during the struggles of the Church with diverse
forms of heresy.

Seeberg believes that the original oral traditions included a Formula of Belief, of which 1 Cor. 15: 3ff is a preserved fragment, and that this Formula had a Confessional
character and was used at the administration of Baptism.
He concludes that there was therefore a formulated basis of
instruction, that is, a Baptismal Confession for those who
desired to receive the sacrament (Rom. 6: 3ff; cf. 4: 14;
Eph. 4: 5ff; 1 Pet. 3: 21ff; 1 Tim. 6: 20; 1 John 2: 20).
From 1 Cor. 15: 3, he concludes that this Formula was
already known and used at the time of the baptism of Paul;
and from the many trinitarian passages in Scripture, some of
which have already been quoted, he believes that the Formula
of Confession was arranged in a triad, and thus became the basis from which at a later day our Apostles' Creed was derived.[5]

While baptism originally was administered in the name of
Christ, the instruction and Confession recognized the Father,
the Son and the Spirit; for the baptized person looked forward at once to the reception of the Spirit. And, so, the
more elementary and primitive form of Christ gave way,
finally, to the triune and more complete form of Matthew.

We have thus, in the period of the Apostolic Fathers, a
Church Confession in use as the Baptismal Formula.[6] Irenæus and Tertullian maintained that the "Canon of the

---

[5] Seeberg, *History of Doctrines,* tr. by Hay, I, p. 37.

[6] *Didache* 7: 1; Justin, *Apol.,* 183; and Tertullian, *de Praescr.,* 9, 13, 37,
44, goes so far as to credit it to Christ Himself.

Truth" was identical with the Baptismal Formula, and everywhere employed in the Church since the time of the Apostles.[7]

All scholars agree that this "Canon of the Truth" of the Apostolic Fathers includes the baptismal Confession.[8]

"And he who thus holds inflexible for himself the 'Canon of Truth,' which he received by his baptism"—here follows a short summary of the creed, which must accordingly be the content of the baptismal confession.[9] This short statement of the great realities of the Christian faith, which Irenæus (i, 9: iv) calls "the brief embodiment (somátion) of truth," is the first received confession of the Church. Seeberg feels that the historic significance of this brief summary of saving truth was very great: "it preserved intact the consciousness that salvation is dependent upon the deeds of Christ. It taught the Church to construct Christian doctrine as the doctrine of the deeds of God; and finally taught men to view the deeds of God under the three-fold conception of Father, Son and Holy Spirit."[10]

Irenæus and Tertullian declare that the Rule of Faith was handed down from the time of the Apostles. Ignatius and Justin bear testimony to Formulas of Confession in the middle of the Second Century.[11]

The Roman form may be traced to the middle of the Third Century (cf. Novatian *de Trinitate*), and the most ancient text of the Roman Creed that has been found dates from the middle of the Fourth Century (Marcellus *in Epiph. haer.* 52 al. 72, A. D. 337 or 338).

---

[7] Iren. *adv. haer.* i. 10. 1, 2 ; iii. 4. 1, 2. Tertul. *de praescr. haeret.* 37, 44, 42, 14, 26, 36 ; *de virg.* l.

[8] Kunze, in his *Glaubensregel, Heilige Schrift und Taufbekenntniss,* holds that the "Canon of the Truth" includes the Holy Scripture also, and not solely the baptismal confession.

[9] Iren. i. 9. 4, cf. 10. 1. Tert. *de spectac.* 4 ; *de coron.* 3 ; *de bapt.* 11 ; *praescr.* 14. See also Justin *Apol.* i. 61 *extr.* *Clem. Al. Strom.* viii. 15, p. 887. Potter. vi. 18, p. 826. *Paed.* i. 6, p. 116. Cf. Caspari : *Hat die Alex. Kirche zur Zeit des Clem. ein Taufbek. besessen oder nicht,* in *Ztschr. f. k. Wiss.,* 1886, p. 352ff. Also esp. Cyprian *Ep.* 69. 1 ; 70. 2 ; 75. 10 fin.

[10] I, 86.

[11] Ign. *Magn.* 11. *Eph.* 7. *Trall.* 9. *Smyrn.* 1. *Just. Apol.* 1. 13, 31, 46. *Dial.* 85.

In spite of the fact that Irenæus and Tertullian regarded this Church Confession as thoroughly œcumenical, and that its origin was located by them in the Apostolic age, Harnack, as is well known, came to the conclusion that this Confessional Formula appeared at Rome about A. D., 150, and spread from thence through all the churches of the West; and that this baptismal Confession, with the Canon of the New Testament, was created by the Roman Church as an infallible rule of faith in order to crush out heresy; and that it became the cause of leading Christianity away from the historical Christ into historical Catholicism.

But Kunze [12] has shown that apostolic origin and not ecclesiastical sanction gave the Creed and the Canon their authority before the heretical conflicts arose. From the Fathers, Kunze concludes that the Rule of Faith in the Old Catholic Church is the Confession at Baptism, in so far as it was used against heresy, and is completed and illustrated from Holy Scripture, Holy Scripture itself being always included.

Kattenbusch,[13] in the most exhaustive treatise on the Apostles' Creed extant, re-discusses the old Roman "Apostolic" form with great detail, and reviews the studies of Harnack and Kunze. He argues for the existence of the Roman form as early as A. D., 100; and that the evidence shows it to have been circulated in Gallia, Africa and parts of Asia Minor in the Second Century.

---

[12] *Glaubensregel, Heilige Schrift und Taufbekenntniss.* Untersuchungen über die dogmatische Autorität, ihr Werden, und ihre Geschichte, vornehmlich in der alten Kirche.

[13] *Das Apostolische Symbol,* seine Entstehung, sein geschichtlicher Sinn, seine ursprüngliche Stellung in Kultus und in der Theologie der Kirche. Ein Beitrag zur Symbolik und Dogmengeschichte.

CHAPTER X.

THE DEVELOPMENT OF THE CONFESSIONAL PRINCIPLE IN THE CHURCH.

The Apostles' Creed—The Nicene Creed—The Athanasian Creed—The Mediæval Interval—The Ninety-Five Theses—The Marburg and Schwabach Articles—The Augsburg Confession as a Confessional Development—The Confessional Connection of the Augsburg Confession.

WE now have traced the rise of the Confessional Principle, the answer of the soul and the Church to the Word, as it sprang from the lips of Christ and the first disciples, as it accompanied the use of the Sacraments in the Apostolic Church, and as it developed into the Apostles' Creed in the days of the Church Fathers.

In the Apostles' Creed we possess the first rich and full jewel of confessionalism, viz., a personal declaration of the baptized member's faith in the one true and living God, Who made us, redeemed us, and sanctified us in His Church. This Apostolic Confession grew naturally out of the baptismal formula; and it summed up in three short articles of faith the facts of the Christian religion, in the order of God's own revelation, beginning with God and creation, continuing on a larger and central scale through the person and work of Christ, and concluding with the work of the Holy Spirit in the Church, culminating in the resurrection of the body and the life everlasting.

This Apostles' Creed is the very spinal column of our faith, in fact and doctrine, and rightly takes its place in our order of service as the fit liturgical medium for the regular, ordinary and united confession, or testimony, of faith of the worshiping congregation.

As the Apostles' Creed arose in its Roman form in the churches of the West, so the Nicene Creed arose out of the baptismal formula used as a confession of faith at the baptismal service in the churches of the East. Just as the Apostles' Creed bears the marks of the simple, practical and stable Roman temperament; so the Nicene Creed bears the more metaphysical, dogmatic and polemic form of the thought of the East.

Like the Apostles' Creed, it was a growth of time, and was the result of many changes, not in doctrine or substance, but in form and statement.

It was the first creed to obtain universal authority, having gradually arisen in the East, in the Fourth and Fifth Centuries; and having been adopted in the West, with the addition of "filioque" in Spain, at the end of the Sixth Century; in England and France in the Eighth Century, and in Italy and elsewhere in the Ninth Century.

This gradual growth of the œcumenical Nicene Confession, extending through centuries, and the lack of œcumenical character of the Apostles' Creed, has an instructive parallel on a smaller scale in the gradual growth of the Lutheran Confession in the Sixteenth Century, and in the lack of the Formula of Concord to gain an entirely universal assent in the Lutheran Church. As the validity of the Apostles' Creed and of the Formula of Concord are both rooted in Scripture, and not in the universal assent of the Church (in which at least two out of the so-called three[1] œcumenical Creeds would fail in the test to-day, and all of them would have failed in the earlier ages of the Church), we need feel no concern as to the real confessional value of either of them.

---

[1] Even the Nicene Creed is used very little in the Reformed Churches of Protestantism. Calvin depreciated it.

The Nicene Creed,[2] the only universal Creed, has come down to us out of a warfare and struggle, compared with which that in the Sixteenth Century was small indeed; and one small word in it, which, however, in our form of Christianity, ultimately triumphed, was the source of more confessional strife than has ever arisen from the attempts to uphold the Augustana Invariata as over against the changes of substance introduced by Melanchthon. So influential was this one word *filioque* that it, as Schaff puts it, "next to the authority of the Pope, is the chief source of the greatest schism in Christendom."

After all, then, history teaches that a single phrase can stand for a great deal in a confessional movement, and must be respected for the background it brings with it. As has been pointed out by historians, the controversies concerning the double procession of the Holy Spirit were rooted in a more general and deeper underlying cause, *i. e.,* in a difference of *spirit* of which this one point happened to be a single illustration.

The glorious waves of Confession in the Nicene Creed enlarge on the Apostles' Creed in their more explicit declarations of the divinity of Christ and of the Holy Ghost. "The terms 'co-essential' or 'co-equal,' 'begotten before all worlds,' 'very God of very God,' 'begotten, not made,' are so many trophies of orthodoxy," says Schaff, "in its mighty struggle with the Arian heresy which agitated the Church for more than half a century." They remind us, in their

---

[2] Tulloch, with the prejudice of his position, goes so far as to say: "The two others associated with it in the services of the Western Church have not only never had acceptance beyond the range of that church, but are very gradual *growths* within it, without any definite parentage or deliberate and consultative authority. They emerge gradually during many centuries from the confusions and variations of Christian opinion, slowly crystallizing into definite shape: and such authority as belongs to them is neither primitive nor patristic. It is the reflected assent of the later church in the West, and the uncritical patronage of a comparatively ignorant age, which have alone elevated them to the same position as the faith defined at Nicæa, which is the only truly Catholic or universal symbol of the universal church." The tone of these British words condemnatory of the Apostles' Creed as a Confession, rings with almost identical quality among us in the condemnation of the Formula of Concord as a real Confession.

fulness and their repeated recurrence, of the incoming tide of the sea, which joyfully and steadily rises over every rock of opposition in its pathway.

The Athanasian Creed is a further advance of one step in doctrinal development over the Apostles' and the Nicene Creeds. It formulates the absolute unity of the divine being or essence, and the trinity of the Father, the Son, and the Holy Spirit. Its strength depends on its meaning of the term *persona,* by which it avoids Sabellianism on the one hand and Tri-theism on the other. "If the mystery of the Trinity can be logically defined, it is done here", says Schaff; and we might add, there is nothing more metaphysical in basis and method in the whole Formula of Concord than what we find on this point in this œcumenical Creed. Its second part declares the doctrine of the person of Christ, in opposition to the Apollinarian, the Nestorian and the Eutychian heresies.

Of this symbol Luther says, "Es ist also gefasset, dass ich nicht weiss, ob seit der Apostel Zeit in der Kirche des Neuen Testamentes etwas Wichtigeres und Herrlicheres geschrieben sei." [3] Of it Schaff says, It "is a remarkably clear and precise summary of the doctrinal decisions of the first four œcumenical Councils (from A. D. 325 to A. D. 451), and of the Augustinian speculations on the Trinity and the Incarnation. Its brief sentences are artistically arranged and rhythmically expressed. It is a musical creed or dogmatic psalm. Dean Stanley calls it 'a triumphant pæan' of the orthodox faith. It resembles, in this respect, the older *Te Deum;* but it is much more metaphysical and abstruse, and its harmony is disturbed by a threefold anathema."

This œcumenical symbol with its threefold anathema and the declaration that its faith in the Trinity and the Incarnation is the indispensable condition of salvation, and that all who reject it will be lost forever, stronger than the condem-

---

[3] *Walch.* VI, 2315.

natory clauses of the Augsburg Confession and the Formula of Concord, is, nevertheless, adopted by the Lutheran and the Reformed and other Protestant Churches,[4] though it has never become an official symbol in the Greek Church and is there used only for private devotion.

The strangest peculiarity of the Athanasian Creed is that it is a *pseudonym;* and that, if its validity depended upon its authorship and the circumstances connected with its adoption into the Church, it could not remain a symbol of the Church. It does not date back earlier, in fact, than toward the close of the Eighth or the beginning of the Ninth Century.

Those who are inclined to find fault with the controversies, the situation and the authors—in short, the historical source whence originated the Lutheran Confessions; and to therefrom attempt to invalidate one or the other of them, might profitably consider this earlier course of confessional development in the Christian Church in its instructive parallels.

The Lutheran and the Anglican Churches have recognized and embodied these three Creeds in their doctrinal and liturgical standards. Luther clearly connected Protestantism with them, and the Formula of Concord calls them 'catholica et generalia summæ auctoritatis symbola.'

With the Athanasian Creed, the development of the Confessional Principle, which had been at work for eight hundred years, came to a stop for an almost equally long period. And no wonder! Confessions are the answer of the soul and the Church to Scripture. But the Scripture had disappeared as the rule of Faith, and the Church itself took the soul in charge, apart from the Scripture, and did its thinking, furnishing it with its doctrine ready-made and complete, and allowing only the scholastic comment of the schoolmen

---

[4] The Protestant Episcopal Church in the United States eliminated both the Nicene and the Athanasian Creeds, together with the clause, "He descended into hell," of the Apostles' Creed, from their prayerbook, in 1785; but it was compelled to restore everything but the Athanasian Creed before the Church of England would grant it the right of ordination.

thereon. In these ages, the soul of the Confessor did not answer to the Word, for the face of the Word was hid.

"There are no further symbols, though theology was greatly cultivated. Scholasticism is nothing else than the vast expression of the intellectual labor bestowed on these subjects during these ages. But it worked on the basis of the doctrinal data already adopted and authorized by the Church. Developing these data in endless sentences and commentaries,"[5] heresy was extirpated by force, and there was no room for the witness and testimony of the individual conscience. The individual no longer apprehended the truth as it is in Christ Jesus in a vital manner, but accepted it mechanically.

As confessional needs arose, such as they were, it was not additional Confession of the Scriptures, but edicts of the Pope, that became both authority and testimony for Christianity: not truth reflected from Christ in the Word of God, but rules formulated by the head of the Church, which were to be received without question.

With the awakening in the Reformation it was inevitable that the Confessional principle should rise even more quickly than it had subsided. A purified Church would find the neglected and inactive fountains of testimony to faith and teaching, gushing forth anew their clear and salutary waters to quench the universal thirst of mankind. The foundation, laid in the old symbols, long covered with dust, was swept clean once more, and the confessional building was carried upward toward completion, each new stone laid in it "bearing the impress of the time and the historical relations out of which it grew."[6]

We present a summary of this period of re-awakening in the words of Principal Tulloch, of the University of St. Andrews: "A new era of creed-formations or confessions of faith set in. The process of exposition, out of which the

---

[5] Mueller, *Einleitung.*
[6] *Ib.,* p. 23.

11

'Athanasian' symbol gradually rose, became once more urgent, not only in the disrupted branches of the Church but also in the Roman Church from which the Confessions were broken off. The Confessions of the Lutheran Church claim the first attention in chronological order. The first of these is the Confessio Augustana. Secondly, immediately following was numbered the Apologia, nearly five times larger than the Confession itself. To these two primary documents were afterwards added, thirdly, the Articles of Schmalkald, signed at Schmalkald by an assembly of Evangelical theologians; and fourthly, the Formula Concordiæ composed in 1576, after considerable doctrinal divisions had broken out in Lutheranism.

"This latter document was not so universally accepted as the others by the Lutheran Churches, *but it has always been reckoned along with them as of confessional authority.* To these remain to be added Luther's two Catechisms, which have also a Confessional position among the Lutherans. The collective documents are issued as a Concordia or Liber Concordiæ, printed with the three older creeds, and together they sum up the confessional theology of Lutheranism."

The very first act of the Reformation, the nailing up of the Ninety-Five Theses, was a confessional one. And these Theses of 1517 already contained the germs of the Confession at Augsburg in 1530. The doctrines of original sin, baptism, the merits of Christ, good works, repentance, faith, forgiveness, absolution and the power of the Church, all of them important in the Augsburg Confession, are central here.

In 1518, Luther took the first step toward a common form of doctrine for teaching the people, and in 1520, he published his "Short Form of the Ten Commandments, the Creed and the Lord's Prayer." Meantime, in 1518, Melanchthon had reached Wittenberg and become his co-laborer. "So constant and unreserved was the intimacy between them," says Jacobs,[1] beautifully, "that, from this time on, it becomes im-

---

[1] *Life of Luther*, p. 106.

possible to absolutely separate their labors, since in the preparation of most books and papers, and in their decisions on all important questions, they acted with mutual consultation and revision of each other's work. It was the work of Luther to draw from the Holy Scriptures, under the pressure of severe conflict, the testimony which the particular emergency required. These testimonies came forth like sparks from the anvil without regard to any rigid system. Melanchthon gathered them together, reduced them to scientific statement and methodical order, enriched them by his more varied reading, and carried to completion much that Luther had only suggested."

Luther went to meet the papal legate at Augsburg and disputed with Eck at Leipzig in 1519, burned the papal Bull in 1520, confessed at the Diet of Worms in 1521; translated the New Testament in 1522-3; published the "Deutsches Taufbüchlein " in 1523; the first hymn book in 1524; the " Deutsche Messe und Ordnung des Gottesdienstes " in 1526; wrote his " Large Catechism " in 1528; and his "Small Catechism" in 1529, the year of the Diet of Spires.[*]

Thus we come to the earliest of the Lutheran Confessions,

---

[*] We find the following historical summary in Johnson's *Cyclopedia*, V, on " *The Lutheran Church*," signed by Jacobs : " Luther's internal conflicts, his theses, the meetings with Cajetan, Miltitz, the Leipzig disputation, the attraction of Melanchthon into his mighty orbit, his era of storm and pressure (1520-21), the bull, the efforts of Charles V. at repression, the Diet of Worms, the hiding at the Wartburg, the outbreak of radicalism at Wittenberg under Karlstadt (1522-25), the Peasant war and Anabaptist sedition (1529), the controversies with Henry VIII. and Erasmus (1523-26)—all had within them potencies for the future of the Church, on which Luther's name, in the face of his protest, was to be fixed. The Lutheran Reformation showed its unfolding strength in the empire at the Diet of Nuremberg (1522-23) ; in the extension of the evangelical doctrine (1522-24) at the second Diet of Nuremberg (Jan. 14, 1524) ; at the convention of Ratisbon (1524), called to resist it; in the growing decision of the evangelical states (1524) ; in the Torgau confederacy (1526). With the year 1526 the estates began to use the right, successfully claimed at the Diet of Spires, to regulate ecclesiastical matters in their own territories. In the years following (1526-29) a number of the Lutheran state churches began to be established and organized. Electoral Saxony, by Luther's advice, began with a thorough visitation of the churches. The church constitution and Luther's two catechisms (1529), which grew out of this visitation, became guides in the organization and training of other state churches. The first martyrs were two young Augustinian monks of Antwerp (1523), whose memory is kept green by Luther's hymn."

the Large and the Small Catechisms of Dr. Martin Luther, published in 1529, for the use, respectively, of all faithful and godly pastors and teachers, in instructing their congregations. In his preface to the Small Catechism Luther calls the little book a "statement of the Christian doctrine," which he has prepared in "very brief and simple terms," and which he desired to have introduced among the young. He refers to the custom of the Church before him in teaching *the Lord's Prayer, the Creed* and *the Ten Commandments;* and shows how "our office has now assumed a very different character from that which it bore under the Pope; it is now of a very grave nature and is very salutary in its influence."

This earliest Confession of the Lutheran Church is a wonderful exponent of true Evangelical doctrine. It sums up the whole Christian Faith as Law and Gospel in its first two parts, the Christian life under the influence of the Word and in communion with the Father in the third part, and the Sacraments in the fourth and fifth parts.

We believe that this great symbol of the Church may be most briefly and effectively characterized as The Confession of the Word and the Sacraments, and as the fulness of the teaching of Article VII of the Augsburg Confession: "The Church is the congregation of saints in which the Gospel is rightly taught and the Sacraments rightly administered."

While this earliest Confession begins with Law, it is the Law of the Gospel, and the central position of the Confession, *i. e.,* the second article of the Creed, dominates the whole Catechism.

This little pioneer book really organizes the Lutheran conception of the doctrine of the Church and of the Christian life under the influence of the Word and the Sacraments.

In it, the old Apostles' Creed, in the explanation to the second and third articles, receives a wealth and fulness of doctrinal content, such as is contained by no other Confession of the Church in so few words. The whole full round of Evangelical Protestant teaching lies therein as in a germ;

and what is said in the later Confessions of the Church is but building upon this foundation, and from a more enlarged and different point of view.

Luther gives the purpose as follows: "Thus there are in all five parts of the entire doctrine which should be constantly practiced and heard recited word for word. For you must not depend upon that which the young people may learn and retain from the sermon alone. The reason that we exercise such diligence in preaching so often upon the Catechism is in order that its truths may be inculcated on our youth, not in an ambitious and acute manner, but briefly and with the greatest simplicity, so as to enter the mind readily and be fixed in the memory."

When he comes to speak of the fourth part, he says, "We have now finished the three chief parts of common Christian doctrine. Besides these we have as yet to speak of our two Sacraments instituted by Christ, of which also every Christian should have at least some short elementary instruction; because without them there can be no salvation, although hitherto no instruction has been given. But in the first place we take up baptism, by which we are first received into the Christian Church. That it may be readily understood, we will carefully treat of it, keeping only to that which it is necessary to know. For how it is to be maintained and defended against heretics and saints we will commend to the learned."

The confessional development in Luther's mind between the Catechisms and the Marburg Articles is not difficult to see. The Marburg Articles proceed upon the basis of the Apostles' Creed, including the additions of the Nicene and the Athanasian, and expand upon Luther's explanation of the third article of the Apostles' Creed, giving particular attention to Justification and the Word, and then proceed to the Sacraments.

The two earliest symbols of the Lutheran Church were works of testimony and confession intended for the upbuilding of the Church within. The same year, on October 3rd, 1529, came the fifteen Marburg Articles, drawn up by Luther, and which were intended to conserve and strengthen the Evangelical faith as it looked outward. The Augsburg Confession is rooted in these articles; and the seventeen articles of Luther at Schwabach, October 15th, 1529, elaborate the Marburg Articles. These two sets of articles, the teaching of Luther (and without any condemnatory clauses), *within six months* of the preparation of the Augsburg Confession and *nine months* of its delivery, form the foundation of the doctrinal articles of the Augsburg Confession.

The first article of Marburg and the first of Schwabach is the substance of the *first* article of the Augsburg Confession. The fourth article of Marburg, and of Schwabach, is the substance of the *second* article of the Augsburg Confession. The second and third articles of both Marburg and Schwabach are the substance of the *third* article of the Augsburg Confession. Article V of Marburg and of Schwabach is the substance of the *fourth* article of the Augsburg Confession. Articles VI, VII and VIII of Marburg and VI and VII of Schwabach are the basis of the *fifth* article of the Augsburg Confession. Article X of Marburg is the basis of the *sixth* article of the Augsburg Confession. Article XII of Schwabach is the basis of the *seventh* article of the Augsburg Confession. Articles IX of Marburg and VIII and IX of Schwabach are the basis of the *ninth* article of the Augsburg Confession. Article X of Schwabach is the basis of the *tenth* article of the Augsburg Confession. Article XI of Marburg and of Schwabach is the basis of the *eleventh* article of the Augsburg Confession. Article XV of Marburg is the basis of the *thirteenth* article of the Augsburg Confession. Article XVII of Schwabach is the basis of the *fifteenth* article of the Augsburg Confession. Article XII of Marburg is the basis of the *sixteenth* article of the Augsburg Confession. Articles XIII and XIV of Schwabach are the basis of the *seventeenth* article of the Augsburg Confession. Articles

XVIII and XIX, the two philosophical and metaphysical articles of the Augsburg Confession, touching subjects such as those treated in the Formula of Concord, have no basis in the Luther articles of Marburg and Schwabach.

If the foundation of the first seventeen articles of the Augsburg Confession are to be found in the Marburg and Schwabach articles, the foundation of the remaining articles of the Augsburg Confession from twenty to twenty-eight are to be found in the Torgau articles, written, it is supposed, by Luther, certainly by Melanchthon, Jonas and Bugenhagen, March 14-20th, 1530, within about *three months* prior to the reading of the Augsburg Confession. Article XX of the Augsburg Confession closely follows "B. Of Faith and Works" of Torgau. Article XXI of the Augsburg Confession, "Worship of Saints," is found in substance in the same article of Torgau. Article XXII, "Of Both Kinds in the Sacraments," is found essentially in the article, "Of Both Forms," in Torgau. Article XXIII, "Of the Marriage of Priests," is found in short compass under the same article in Torgau; and Article XXIV, "Of the Mass," and Article XXV, "Of Confession," are similarily found under said article. Article XXVI, "Of Traditions of Men," is found under the head of "The Doctrines and Ordinances of Men" in Torgau. Article XXVII, "Of Monastic Vows," is found under the same heading in Torgau. Article XXVIII, "Of the Power of the Bishops," is found under the heading of "Ordination" in Torgau, and also in "C. Of the Power of the Keys."

It thus will be seen that the substantial form of Lutheran doctrine, both in its connection with the old œcumenical symbols, in its special teachings as to Justification by Faith and not by works, in its doctrine of the Word, the Sacraments and the Church, and in every other positive point, except the doctrine of Free Will, as well as in every other negative point as contrasted with the Roman Church, was developed by or well known to Luther, after passing through his Cate-

chisms in 1528-9, in the articles of Marburg, Schwabach and
Torgau in 1529-30, *shortly prior* to the issuance of the Augsburg Confession by Melanchthon. Though Luther had never
written a line of the Augsburg Confession, nor ever even seen
a sentence of it until after it was delivered to the emperor, it
was, nevertheless, in substance, *his* teaching and the work of
his mind, with the adjustments, to the occasion, made by
Melanchthon, under the direction and supervision of the
Elector and his chancellor.

CHAPTER XI.

THE CONFESSIONAL PRINCIPLE IN THE AUGS-
BURG CONFESSION.

The Confessional Authorship of the Augsburg Confession—The Confessional Content of the Augsburg Confession—The Confessional Progress of the Augsburg Confession—The General Confessional Characteristics of the Augsburg Confession—The Fate of the Augsburg Confession as Variata and its Essence as Invariata—The Wide Difference between the Theology of the Augsburg Confession and Pure American Protestantism.

THE question as to the credit of the authorship of the Augsburg Confession, as a Confession, is, to an unbiased mind, and in view of all the light now shed upon the situation, an idle one.[1] The Augsburg Confession is a true confessional writing, in which the Providence of God, as over against the will and hand of man, was the determining and decisive factor.

When the Elector of Saxony learned that the Emperor would come to Germany and hold a diet at Augsburg, and started with his group of theologians to meet him, the doctrine of the Evangelical Churches was already developed and known. Luther, the great living Witness, was as near at hand as God, through the Emperor, had designed and allowed. The clear statements of doctrine from which the Confession was to be drawn, and which had come largely from Luther himself, with much consultation as to the same, were in the hand

---

[1] Weber, Köllner, Rückert, Heppe (Reformed), and Zöckler (as to spirit), emphasize Melanchthon's authorship. Gieseler is influenced by his rationalistic training at Halle; and he was a member of the Masonic Fraternity.

117

and mind of Melanchthon. The responsibility and the balance of power which would finally determine the quantity of substance and the quality of form, lay with the wise and steadfast elector (a layman) and his sturdy and clear-sighted chancellor (also a layman). The modifying elements, providentially permitted to enter, at the last moment, and serving, with other factors, to give that golden poise on all sides to the firmness of the Confession, were the awakened and friendly Estates that joined in it. The inexorable demands of circumstance, changing from day to day in the development of the situation in the Emperor's mind—demands that threw Master Philip's mind out of its original channel and, finally, almost frightened him out of his wits—were beyond human control; and each and all these factors were directly contributory to the substance, and to the formal content of the Augsburg Confession. Then came Melanchthon, the adaptable and gifted servant of the cause and of the Lord, in himself not a prophet, but a moulder of the prophetic voice, who combined a multitude of indispensable elements, and gave to the result a ripe inner compactness, a beautiful outer dress, and an abiding form of strength. To quote one of those who love Melanchthon much, Kahnis [2] says:-

"Luther war der Meister des Inhalts, Melanchthon der Meister der Form. . . . Melanchthon war der Mann, welcher mit Objektivität, Feinheit, Klarheit, Milde zu schreiben verstand. Und wie nie hat er diese Gabe in diesem Falle verwerthet." And Schaff declares that while the spirit and the literary composition are that of Melanchthon, "as to the doctrines, Luther had a right to say, 'The Catechism, the Exposition of the Ten Commandments, and the *Augsburg Confession,* are mine.' " [3]

If Melanchthon had been permitted to have his own way in the framing and presentation of the Augsburg Confession, and to exercise his own judgment as to material, purpose

---

[2] *Luth. Dogmatik,* II, p. 424.

[3] *Creeds of Christendom,* I, p. 229.

and style, it would have been an instrument different in substance and form from what we now happily find it. Owing to Melanchthon's want of stability, when diverse shades of doctrine appealed to his judgment, and his willingness to compromise with what appeared to be the most promising hope at the moment, the Augsburg Confession would proba- bly have been a dissimilar and diverse presentation each time, at any one of several critical moments, had it been handed in then, between the beginning of May and the end of June.

The same desire for union with those without, and the willingness to adapt and change, that kept Melanchthon busy with the document, after it had once become the public prop- erty of the Lutheran Church, inspired him to work inces- santly at it, in order to fit it to the kaleidoscopic changes of the political situation prior to the meeting of the diet. He started, first of all, with the idea of healing the breach with Rome.

To achieve this more effectively, it had been determined to abandon *all the doctrinal articles;* and, in place thereof, to substitute a lengthy Preface in which the elector was eulo- gized. The changes of faith and custom introduced into the Protestant churches by the reformers were to be minimized as much as possible, so as to cause them to look comparatively unimportant, and to convey the impression that the Evan- gelical Church was still, barring certain abuses, in complete harmony with Rome.

In thus modifying the language to conciliate Rome, which was the great threatening power in the horizon at that mo- ment, prior to the Diet at Augsburg, Melanchthon neces- sarily broke with the more radical elements of Protestantism, including the Zwinglians; and it was in his interest to show, at this time, the Emperor and the Pope how little the Evan- gelical Church, which he represented, had in common with

---

* In other words, the *Variata* would have been begun prior rather than subsequent to its historical delivery.

the Reformed churches, and thus widen the breach between them as much as possible.[5]

Hence, had Melanchthon remained in control, there might never have been an Augsburg Confession; for the document, if handed in to the Diet, would have been constituted of a Preface defending the Elector and declaring how near the churches in the electorate of Saxony approached the practice of Rome, and a statement of the abuses that the Protestants had justly been attempting to correct.

It was the attack on Lutheran doctrine as such by the Romanists, and the apparent impression of this attack on the Emperor before he arrived at Augsburg, and the wisdom and insistence of the Chancellor Brück,[6] that put a complete quietus on Melanchthon's plan, and compelled the introduction of the twenty-one doctrinal articles at the head of the Confession, and that finally cut off negotiations with Rome.

It was only at a late day that Philipp of Hesse, the friend of the Reformed Churches, was admitted into the counsels of the Elector of Saxony, and that the balance of the Confession was swung back to its true golden centre between Rome and the Reformed, and that thus the real objective treatment of Lutheran doctrine toward both its antitheses, viz., Rome on the one side, and the Reformed on the other, was really assured.

Had it been possible for Melanchthon to procure peace at Augsburg by a compromise of the confessional principle, we believe that he would, in accordance with the natural bent

---

[5] Comp. even Kahnis: "The desire for an understanding with the Papists made Melanchthon a very decided opponent of the Swiss, and even of the Strasburgers."—*Luth. Dogm.*, II, p. 436.

[6] How far it is possible for historians to get away from history, by the use of a fact interpreted wrongly, is to be seen in Schaff's condemnation of the present Preface to the Augsburg Confession, he not knowing how far Melanchthon leaned toward Rome and against Zwingli in the original Preface.

Schaff says: "The diplomatic Preface to the Emperor is not from his (Melanchthon's) pen, but from that of the Saxon Chancellor Brück. It is clumsy, tortuous, dragging, extremely obsequious, and has no other merit than to introduce the reader into the historical situation."—*Creeds of Christendom*, I, p. 233. If Schaff were to see Melanchthon's first Augsburg Confession, and knew how Brück's hand was *in restraint* of these very traits, would he apply the epithets of this estimate to Melanchthon?

of his mind, have embraced that situation rather than have prepared, as he finally was compelled and directed to do, the full and objective confessional statement of the doctrine of the Evangelical churches. But, in the Providence of God, owing to the concurrence of various historical elements, and with the over-shadowing power of sound Confessional Lutheranism as the key to the situation, the Confession came to embody the teaching of the Evangelical churches.

When we come to note the *progress of the Confessional principle,* as found in the Augsburg Confession, in comparison with the three œcumenical symbols, we find, first of all, in Article I of the Confession, a building on the old symbols, especially on the Nicene Creed, in the doctrine of the Trinity.

We find, in addition, a new confessional article, not in the œcumenical creeds, in the second article of the Augsburg Confession, namely, the one devoted to Anthropology and the Doctrine of Original Sin, which is the negative basis of redemption. We find in the third article a reiteration of the œcumenical creeds as to the Person of Christ. We find in the fourth the new but old and apostolic Doctrine of Justification by faith, in line with Luther's explanation of the third part of the creed, in the clause, " I believe in the forgiveness of sins." In Article V we find the new doctrine of the Word and the Sacraments. In Article VI we have the corollary of Article IV on Justification.

In Article VII we find the abridged doctrine of the Church on the basis of "I believe in the Holy Christian Church, the communion of Saints." In the eighth article we find a delineation of the relation of the communion of saints and the Word and Sacraments to the world. In Articles IX, X and XI we have the fourth and fifth parts of Luther's Catechism. In Article XII we have a part of the teaching of the Ninety-Five Theses, together with a condemnation of old and current errors. In Article XIII we find the teaching that the two Sacraments of the Church were not ordained chiefly to be "marks of profession among men" (on which rests the modern theory of open communion), "but rather to be signs and testimonies of the will of God toward us, instituted to awaken and confirm faith in those who use them." Articles XIV and XV relate to the internal ministry of the Church, and are intended to hold the Evangelical truth as over against both Roman and extreme Protestant error. Article XVI, on civil affairs, is intended to hold the true faith as against extreme Protestant error. Article XVII, an expansion of the final article in the Apostles' Creed, is also against extreme Protestant error. Articles XVIII and XIX, on the freedom of the will and on the cause of good works, revert back to Article II on the original nature of man. The remainder of the Confession, from Article XX on, is a defence of the Protestant doctrine as it has worked itself out into practice.

The great distinctive features of the Augsburg Confession, as going beyond the œcumenical creeds and the Catechisms of Luther, in the order of historical development, are its positive presentation of the doctrine of Luther's Ninety-Five Theses, the material principle of the Reformation, Justification by faith; its presentation of the one and great doctrine of the Word and Sacraments, as constituting the office of the Church; its teaching of the Church, in all its various aspects, in contrast with the wrong teaching of the Roman Church; and, particularly, its emphasis on the Church as invisible, and its larger teaching on the Sacraments.

It is in these points that it marks a Confessional advance over the Œcumenical Creeds, and sets fast forever a new and larger sum of confessional truth. But several things were still to follow.

In the Augsburg Confession the Evangelical Protestant development had not yet reached a confession of the formal principle of the Reformation, namely, that the Holy Scriptures are the only rule of faith and life; nor of the fundamental Lutheran truth of Law and Gospel; nor any full explanation of the Person of Christ, particularly in its relation to the Lord's Supper; nor any confession on the Scriptural teaching of predestination and election. These leading doctrines of revelation were reserved, in the Providence of God, to be wrought out and eventually were confessed in the Formula of Concord.

But let us now consider the Augsburg Confession as an entity in itself, from its own standpoint:—

The Confession divides itself into two parts: the one, dealing with dogma; the other, with ecclesiastical customs and institutions. The twenty-one doctrinal articles, begining with the Trinity and ending with the worship of saints, confess the truth of God held by the Evangelical faith, in common with Rome, in common with Augustinian theology (II, XVIII, XIX, VIII), in opposition to the semi-Pelagianism of Rome, and in distinction from the Zwinglians and the Anabaptists.

Linking itself to the old Catholic symbols in the doctrine of God and Christ, it, for the first time in the history of the Christian Church, adds to the Confessional principle the true doctrine of man, in his sinful nature (II) and enslaved will (XIX); and the true doctrine of the salvation of man, justification by faith (IV), repentance (XII), new obedience (VI), good works (XIX), daily life (XVI), and Christ the only mediator (XX); as well as the true doctrine of the Word and the ministry (V), ordination (XIV), the Church (VII, VIII), confession and absolution (XI), the Sacraments (IX, X [real bodily presence and distribution of Christ], XIII), and ecclesiastical rites (XV).

In common with the Church Catholic, the Confession records itself as in opposition to Unitarians, Arians, Pelagians, Donatists, Sacramentarians and Anabaptists (who are in error on the doctrines of infant baptism, the church, civil offices and the millennium); and opposes the following abuses of Rome: withdrawal of cup from the laity (I), celibacy of the clergy (II), sacrifice of the mass (III), detailed and obligatory auricular confession (IV), obligatory celebration of ceremonies and feasts and fasts (V), monastic vows (VI), and secular power of the bishop where it interferes with the purity of the holy office (VII).

The greatness of the Augsburg Confession lay not only in its confessional substance, in which it added the whole doctrine of man, salvation, faith, the church and the ministry of the Word and Sacraments, to the old œcumenical creeds; but also in its historical occasion, and in its general tone.

As to the *occasion,* it was presented, at the command of the German Emperor,[1] by Lutheran princes as an explicit statement of their faith, ostensibly that Catholics and Protestants might be united once again as one undivided Christian Church, in a war against the common enemy, the Turk, but, in reality, as an apology for the protesting attitude of the evangelical faith. In view of its ostensible purpose, so deeply cherished by Melanchthon, it treads very softly, as Luther says,[1a] and does not even mention the Papacy in many of its worst abuses; and declares itself in harmony, not only with Scripture, but also with the genuine tradition of the Roman Church. The historic heresies it condemns are those already punishable according to the laws of the German empire. It would come back to Rome, if Rome would leave its faith and praxis undisturbed. But we are not to conclude, from this irenic tone, that it conceals any truth. Its attitude is genuine, churchly, devout, Scriptural, and without compromise.

In reviewing the *general character* of the Augsburg Confession, we find in it, first, a wonderful tone of objective universality in which all its truths abide—and reach stability and rest. Who would suppose that these confessors were "protestants" or men of a perturbed past or unsettled future! The strength of the everlasting hills is in them, and that quiet confidence which usually comes only with the sta-

---

[1] The A. C. bases its right to exist upon the Emperor's Call, on which it builds, and which its Preface quotes freely, bringing Charles within its authorship.

[1a] "Ich hab M. Philippsen Apologiam überlesen: die gefället mir fast wohl, und weiss nichts daran zu bessern noch ändern, würde sich auch nicht schicken; denn ich so sanft und leise nicht treten kann."—Erl. 54. 145.

bility of ages. With common consent, and as an established and universal fact, the confessors declare, " our Churches do teach." They speak as part of "the one holy Church that continues forever." They calmly exhibit the summary of their doctrine, "so that it might be understood that in doctrine and ceremonies nothing has been received on our part against Scripture or the Church Catholic; " and in every sentence they utter, they impress upon the attentive reader the fact that they are true representatives of an abiding inner harmony, namely, "the churches," "our churches," against which the gates of hell cannot prevail.

The next striking feature in the Confession is the spirit of Catholic continuity, in which the Confession ranges itself in line with the whole development of historical Christianity, and with the Christian Church, as the abiding institution amidst all changes, as is clearly demonstrated by the internal evidence contained in the following statements : "That these matters may be settled and brought back to one perfect truth and Christian concord—that we may be able to live in unity and concord in the one Christian Church—that the dissension may be done away and brought back to the one true accordant religion; for as we all serve and do battle under one Christ, we ought to confess the one Christ—to the true unity of the Church, it is enough to agree concerning the doctrine of the Gospel and the administration of the sacraments—no one should publicly teach in the Church unless he be regularly called—in our doctrine there is nothing that varies from the Scripture, or from the Church Catholic, or from the Church of Rome as known from its writers—our churches dissent in no article of the Faith from the Church Catholic— our teachers must not be looked upon as having taken up this matter rashly or from hatred of the bishops—very many traditions are kept on our part which conduce to good order in the Church, as the Order of Lessons in the Mass, and the chief holy days—liberty in human rites was not unknown to our Fathers—our teachers, for the comforting of men's con-

12

sciences, were constrained to show the difference between the power of the Church and the power of the sword—since the power of the Church grants eternal things, it does not interfere with civil government—nothing has been received on our part against Scripture or the Church Catholic." We find in this flowing current of testimony a consciousness of connection with the Church of all ages; and in its broadest and deepest life; a consciousness that is very rare indeed in any declaration of principle, and which is truly œcumenical.

"The Confession exhibited the one undivided faith of the entire Lutheran Church in the Empire. It was not the work of men without authority to represent the Church, but was the voice of all the Churches. Its groundwork was laid by Luther; materials were brought together by the great theologians of the whole Lutheran Church—by Brentius, Jonas, Spalatin and others—who carefully examined and tested each other's work. The matchless hand of Melanchthon was employed in giving the most perfect form, the most absolutely finished statement of the faith; the Confession was subjected to the careful examination of Luther, by whom it was heartily approved. Melanchthon's own account is: ' I brought together the heads of the Confession, embracing almost the *sum of the doctrine of our Churches.* I took nothing on myself. In the presence of the Princes and the officials every topic was discussed by our preachers, *sentence by sentence.* A copy of the entire Confession* was then sent to Luther, who wrote to the Princes that he had read and that he approved the Confession.' [8]

"The very name of AUGSBURG, which tells us WHERE our Confession was uttered, reminds us of the nature of the obligations of those who profess to receive it. Two other Confessions were brought to that city: the Confession of Zwingle, and the Tetrapolitan Confession—the former openly opposed to the faith of our Church, especially in regard to the Sacraments; the latter, ambiguous and evasive on some of the vital

---

[8] See Chapter XV for Kolde's reasoning and position on this point.

points of the same doctrine. These two Confessions are now remembered . . . only because of the historical glory shed by ours over everything which came into any relation to it. But can it be . . . that what was not Lutheranism there is Lutheranism here; that what was Lutheranism then is not Lutheranism now; that Zwingli or Hedio, of Strasburg, could, without a change of views, honestly subscribe the Confession against which they had arrayed themselves, that very Confession the main drift of some of whose most important Articles was to teach the truth these men denied, and to condemn the errors these men fostered!

"The Confessors say that in the Confession: 'There is NOTHING which departs from the *Church Catholic, the Universal Christian Church.*'[9] They declare, moreover, that it is their grand design in the Confession to avoid the 'transmission as a *heritage to their children and to the descendants of another doctrine,* a doctrine not in conformity with the pure Divine word and Christian truth.' The witness of a true faith is a witness to the end of time. When, therefore, Brück, the Chancellor of Saxony, presented the Confession, he said: 'By the help of God and our Lord Jesus Christ, this Confession shall remain invincible against the gates of hell, to eternity.' "[10]

The third characteristic of the Augsburg Confession, that rises like an earnest strain in all its voices, is the note of personal salvation, through justification and remission of sins by faith; and in this it joins with Luther's second article of the Creed and the fourth and fifth parts of his Catechism. It is *the Gospel* idea made prominent in the Church Confession:-" Christ a sacrifice, not only for original guilt, but for all actual sins of men, when they believe that they are received into favor and that their sins are forgiven for Christ's sake—God, not for our own merits, but for Christ's sake, justifieth those who believe—remission of sins and jus-

---

[9] Ab Ecclesia Catholica—gemeiner Christlichen Kirchen.
[10] From *Con. Ref.*, pp. 261-267.

tification are apprehended by faith—through baptism is offered the grace of God—for those who have fallen after baptism there is remission of sins whenever they are converted—faith, born of the Gospel, or of absolution, believes that for Christ's sake sins are forgiven—the Sacraments were instituted to awaken and confirm faith in those who use them—observances are not necessary to salvation—the natural man receiveth not the things of the spirit—our works cannot reconcile God or merit forgiveness of sins, grace and Justification—Christ the only Mediator, Propitiation, High Priest and Intercessor—the doctrine of grace and of the righteousness of faith is the chief part of the Gospel and ought to stand out as the most prominent in the Church—the monks have taught that by their vows and observances they merited forgiveness of sins—the power of the keys is a power to preach the Gospel, to remit and retain sins, and to administer sacraments—that the bishops allow the Gospel to be purely taught, and that they relax some few observances which cannot be kept without sin." Where in all the literature of the Church is the Gospel of remission of sins unto salvation, by faith alone, preached in so personal and yet so sacramental a manner! This is the Gospel Confession confessing Christ crucified, believed on, and distributed in Word and Sacrament to every member of the Communion of Saints.

Still another majestic and most remarkable feature of the Augsburg Confession is that of respectful freedom, in which reverence and obedience for authority are combined in the true golden mean with perfect liberty of conscience:-" In obedience to Your Imperial Majesty's wishes, we offer our Confession—abundantly prepared to join issue and to defend the cause in a general, free Christian Council—to this General Council we have made appeal in this gravest of matters in due manner and form of law—to this appeal we still adhere—neither do we intend to relinquish it by this or any other document, of which this also is our solemn and public testimony—all men are born with sin; and cannot be justi-

fied before God by their own strength, but are freely justified for Christ's sake—concerning rites let men be admonished that consciences are not to be burdened—lawful civil
ordinances are good works of God—the Gospel does not
destroy the State or the family—man's will has some liberty
for the attainment of civil righteousness—faith is the mother
of a good will and right doing—insomuch as abuses could
not be approved with a good conscience, they have been to
some extent corrected—no law of man can annul the commandment of God—we condemn the traditions which prescribe certain days and certain meats, with peril of conscience—liberty in human rites was not unknown to the
Fathers—Christian perfection is to fear God from the
heart—some have awkwardly confounded the power of the
Church and the power of the sword—the power of the Church
and the civil power must not be confounded—let not the
Church prescribe laws to civil rulers concerning the form
of the Commonwealth—if bishops have the right to burden
churches with infinite traditions, and to ensnare consciences,
why does Scripture so often prohibit to make and to listen
to traditions?—it is necessary that the doctrine of Christian
liberty be preserved in the churches—the righteousness of
faith and Christian liberty must not be disregarded—bishops might retain obedience, if they would not insist upon
the observance of what cannot be kept with a good conscience—it is not our design to wrest the government from
the bishops, *but if they make no concession,* it is for them
to see how they shall give account to God for having, *by
their obstinacy, caused a schism"* (the last word of the
Confession).

Thus the Augsburg Confession calmly introduces the
modern doctrine of the complete separation of Church and
State, into the dawn of modern life; and does so, from a
purely spiritual point of view, for the sake of the souls of
men and the freedom of the Church, and without any ulterior design of usurping, as Rome attempted to do, the

reins of civil government; but, nevertheless, the spiritual liberty thus implanted in the souls, did lead to great and unexpected results within the sphere of the State. On this point, we quote the eloquent words of Krauth:—

"The Augsburg Confession had, and has, great value, in view of the sound political principles it asserted and guaranteed. Signed by the princes and free cities, it was a sovereign ratification and guarantee of the rights of the Church and of the individual Christian in the State. It asserted the independence on the State of the Church, as a Church; the distinctness of the spheres of the Church and State, the rights of the State over the Christian, as a subject; the Christian's duty to the State, as a subject; and the supremacy of God's law and of the demands of conscience, over all unrighteous enactments of man. It defined in brief, yet ample statements, the entire relation of ecclesiastical and civil power.[11] It overthrew the conception of the Church as a great world-dominating power—taught the obligation of legitimate civil ordinances, the lawfulness of Christians bearing civil office, the right of the State to demand oaths, to enact penalties, and to wage 'just wars,' and the obligation of the Christian citizen to bear part in them. It asserts that 'God's command is to be more regarded than all usage—that custom introduced contrary to God's command is not to be approved.' 'Christians should render obedience to magistrates and their laws in all things,' 'save only those when they command any sin, for then they must rather obey God than men.' It overthrew monasticism and enforced celibacy, those weaknesses of the State; curbed the insolence of Pope, Bishop and Clergy, and restored the normal and divine relations of man to man, of subject to ruler, of Church to State, of God's law to human law, of loyalty to the rights of conscience. The Lutheran Church gives to every State into which she enters, her great voucher of fidelity to the principles on which alone free governments can stand.

[11] Arts. VII., XVI., XXVIII.

"The Augsburg Confession was exquisitely adapted to all its objects, as a confession of faith, and a defence of it. In it the very heart of the Gospel beats again. It gave organic being to what had hitherto been but a tendency, and knit together great nationalities in the holiest bond by which men can be held in association. It enabled the Evangelical princes, as a body, to throw their moral weight for truth into the empire. These were the starting-points of its great work and glory among men. To it, under God, more than to any other cause, the whole Protestant world owes civil and religious freedom. Under it, as a banner, the pride of Rome was broken, and her armies destroyed. It is the symbol of pure Protestantism, as the three General Creeds are symbols of that developing Catholicity to which genuine Protestantism is related, as the maturing fruit is related to the blossom. To it the eyes of all deep thinkers have been turned, as to a star of hope amid the internal strifes of nominal Protestantism. Gieseler, the great Reformed Church historian, says:[12] ' If the question be, Which, among all Protestant Confessions, is best adapted for forming the foundation of a union among Protestant Churches? we declare ourselves unreservedly for the Augsburg Confession.' But no genuine union can ever be formed upon the basis of the Augsburg Confession, except by a hearty consent in its whole faith, an honest reception of all its statements of doctrine in the sense which the statements bear in the Confession itself. If there be those who would forgive Rome her unrepented sins, they must do it in the face of the Augsburg Confession. If there be those who would consent to a truce at least with Rationalism or Fanaticism, they must begin their work by making men forget the great Confession, which refused its covert to them from the beginning.

"With the Augsburg Confession begins the clearly recognized life of the Evangelical Protestant Church, the purified

---

[12] *Theolog. Stud. u. Kritik*, 1833, ii, 1142. Schenkel takes the same view.

Church of the West, on which her enemies fixed the name Lutheran. With this Confession her most self-sacrificing struggles and greatest achievements are connected." [13]

Up to this point we have seen dominant in the Augsburg Confession, as a General Creed of the true Church, the notes of Catholicism, of conservatism, of Gospel salvation through faith, of freedom from sin and law binding the conscience, which resulted also in civil freedom; and now we turn to the remarkable simplicity and the equally remarkable positiveness and objectiveness found in its teaching.

The great mysteries of the Trinity, the Fall, the Incarnation and Atonement, the doctrine of Justification, the Means of Grace, the Word and the Sacraments, the One holy Church, Religious Rites, and Civil Affairs, are gathered together in all their essentials, and without complications, and stated with the greatest force and simplicity, so that nowhere else can such comprehensive and exact delineation of the great mysteries of Christianity be found in space so small and in phrase so crystal. As an expansion of the dogmatic content of the Confessional principle, advancing upon the three older Creeds and the two newer Catechisms, in an utterance at once sufficient, concise, complete and confessional, the Augsburg Confession is without a peer.

As, finally, the Confession showed itself in sympathy with the great Church Catholic, even as it came through Rome, and condemned the independent sects that arose apart from it, so it does not hesitate to rebuke the errors which it knew and found in Rome. We shall let Krauth speak also on this point :-[14]

"The Augsburg Confession has incalculable value as an abiding witness against the Errors of the Roman Catholic Church. The old true Catholic Church was almost lost in pride, avarice, and superstition. The great labor of the body

---

[13] *Con. Ref.*, pp. 257-9.
[14] *Con. Ref.*, p. 255.

of the clergy was to defend the errors by which they were enriched. Two false doctrines were of especial value to this end: the first, that the Church tradition is part of the Rule of Faith; the second, that good works can merit of God. With both the formal and material principles of the Church corrupted, what could result but the wreck of much that is most precious in Christianity? The protest needed then is needed still. The Roman Church has indeed formally abrogated some of the worst abuses which found their justification in her false doctrines; the pressure of Protestant thinking forces, or the light of Protestant science, wins her children to a Christianity better than her theories; but the root of the old evil remains—the old errors are not given up, and cannot be. Rome once committed, is committed beyond redemption. It needs but propitious circumstances to bring up any of her errors in all their ancient force. The fundamental principle of infallibility, the pride of consistency, the power which these doctrines give her, make it certain that they will not be abandoned. Against all of Rome's many errors, and pre-eminently against those doctrines which are in some way related to them all, the Augsburg Confession must continue to hold up the pure light of the sole Rule of Faith, and of its great central doctrine of justification by faith." [15]

In the eyes of the Lutheran Church, the Augsburg Confession is its chief historic jewel, because, as Zöckler says, "It forms the foundation laid in common by Luther and Melanchthon for the whole Confessional literature of the Lutheran Church." Or, to put the matter differently, it unfolds the common Lutheran faith at that point of development, in which the later maturity of an inner dividedness had not yet revealed itself. It is the fair blossom upon which all can look back with joy, and not the final fruitage of the Reformation. The Protestant principle was begin-

---

[15] Fikenscher. *Gesch. d. R. z. Augsb.*, 208 ; Köllner, ii, 395.

ning to unfold in its completeness, and was just in the act of rising to its larger stage.

That Zöckler sets down as the first glory of the Augsburg Confession its worldly side, namely, its universal, historic importance, as the instrument that opened the way for the political recognition which it has secured for German Protestantism as well as that beyond Germany, has no interest for us here, where we are treating of the Confessions of the Church; and particularly not in this land of America, where the Church and the State are forever to remain separate, and where confessions of faith are neither to seek nor to receive any political influence. This political influence of the Augsburg Confession has often been a detriment to it as a confession, and to the sound Confessional principle of the Lutheran Church.

Melanchthon originally hoped to make the Augsburg Confession a common standing ground between the Lutheran and the Roman Church, by excluding the Reformed; and then, through long years, by changing the language of the instrument, and by his actions in the Interims, to make it a common standing ground with the Reformed churches. Before Melanchthon's death it was accepted by the Reformed leaders as the common Protestant political symbol;[16] but the worst political use to which it was put came in the following century, with the close of the Thirty Years' War, the Peace of Westphalia (already at Peace of Augsburg in 1555), when large numbers of Reformed theologians and princes, who by no means adhered to its doctrines, signed the Augsburg Confession in order to gain the rights allowed to Lutherans. Says Jacobs:[17]

"The Confession thus lost its place as a doctrinal test

---

[16] The Augsburg Confession was signed by John Calvin while ministering to the Church at Strasburg, and as delegate to the Conference of Ratisbon, 1541; by Farel and Beza at the Conference in Worms, 1557; by the Calvinists at Bremen, 1562; by Frederick III., (the Reformed) Elector of the Palatinate, at the Convent of princes in Naumburg, 1561, and again at the Diet of Augsburg, 1566; by John Sigismund, of Brandenburg, in 1614.

[17] *Distinctive Doctrines*, p. 105.

among Lutherans. The signatures to the Confession of many who did not accept all its doctrine rendered every signature doubtful. It was for such reason that Arndt in his dying testimony most solemnly confessed 'the true religion of the Formula of Concord,' and Spener wrote an especial treatise in defence of the same Formula, and the Halle Faculty declared that they held with absolute firmness to all the Symbolical Books, and Muhlenberg challenged his accusers to find anything that he had said or written in conflict with them."

The dream that a union of all Protestantism may some day be brought about on the basis of the Augsburg Confession is shattered even by such a unionist as Dr. Schaff, who, after referring to the subscription of the German Evangelical Diet of 1853 in Berlin, when over fourteen hundred clergymen— Lutheran, German-Reformed, Evangelical Unionists and Moravians—acknowledged the Augsburg Confession, with a saving clause as to the interpretation of the Tenth article, which compromise was *repudiated by the sound Lutheran university professors at Erlangen, Leipzig and Rostock " as a frivolous depreciation of the most precious symbol of German Evangelical Christendom," goes on to say:—

"On this fact and the whole history of the Augsburg Confession, some German writers of the evangelical Unionist school have based the hope that the Augsburg Confession may one day become the united Confession or œcumenical Creed of all the evangelical churches of Germany. This scheme stands and falls with the dream of a united and national Protestant Church of the German Empire. Aside from other difficulties, the Reformed and the majority of Unionists, together with a considerable body of Lutherans, can never conscientiously subscribe to the Tenth article as it stands in the proper historical Confession of 1530; while orthodox Lutherans, on the other hand, will repudiate the Altered edition of 1540. The *Invariata* is, after all, a purely Lutheran, that is, a denominational symbol; and the *Variata* is a friendly approach of Lutheranism towards the Reformed communion, which had no share in its original production and subsequent modification, although it responded to it. Neither the one nor the other edition can be the expression of a union, or confederation of two distinct denominations, of which each has its own genius, history and symbols of faith. Such an expression must proceed from the theological and religious life of both, and meet the wants of the present age. Great as the Augsburg Confession is, the Church will produce something greater still whenever the Spirit of God moves it to a new act of faith in opposition to the unbelief and misbelief of modern times. Every age must do its own work in its own way." [18]

This rejection of the Augsburg Confession as a basis for the union of Protestantism by the greatest Reformed symbolist in America is not due to the belief that there is any serious doctrinal difference between Lutheranism and the other evangelical Protestant bodies, but to these three prevalent and yet erroneous ideas: that in the opinion of modern theology, the Augsburg Confession, noble as it was for its day, is after all an outworn instrument; that historical continuity in confession is not vitally important; and that no Confession of a single historical denomination can meet up-to-date issues in an up-to-date way.

So far from considering that the teachings of the Augsburg Confession separate Lutherans from other Protestants, it is usually understood and declared by Reformed theologians, and by Lutheran Melanchthonians, that the great body of fundamental Protestant doctrines is held in common by all Protestant denominations, and that the difference between the Lutheran and the Reformed Confession is very small; that, in fact, they are identical, on the main points, and differ only as to one or two articles. Thus Schaff [19] himself says, "The doctrinal difference between Lutheranism and

[18] Schaff *Creed of Christendom*, I, p. 237.
[19] *Ib.* I, p. 212.

Reform, was originally confined to two articles, namely, the nature of Christ's presence in the Sacrament of the Eucharist, and the extent of God's sovereignty in the ante-historic and pre-mundane act of predestination." And, again, on the following page, he says, "The two great families of Protestantism are *united in all essential articles of faith."*

But this is a superficial view of the case. The difference between the various Protestant systems of faith lies not merely in some difference of their component elements, but also in the way in which those elements are set in their relation to each other; and the larger and more sweeping difference, which counts on the whole, is to be found in the latter fact. There is very little difference, so far as the elements are concerned, between H_2O and H_2O_2, but the small additional quantity of " O " in the combination creates the great difference between harmless water and the painful bleaching agent binoxide of hydrogen. There is absolutely no difference between the characters that make up the lovely word "star" and those that constitute the low word "rats," but the method of combination induces a difference almost as great as that between heaven and earth. The order of combination in the ' set ' of spiritual entities creates divergencies very great, between elements that seem at first glance to be almost or entirely identical.

The Roman Confession writes the doctrine of *the Church* large, and makes it the visible centre on which all else revolves. The original Reformed Confession writes the doctrine of *God,* our Sovereign and Creator, large, and makes it the centre and goal of the faith. Many of the older sects exalted the doctrine of *the individual* and his freedom, as the large and controlling element in their faith; and many of the newer Reformed and the churches of the New Theology write the doctrine of *Society,* of *the Kingdom of God as it is to develop in this world,* as the large central thing in religion. Our modern religious thought, especially that part which considers the old Confessions to be antiquated, instead of making the doctrine of God, or the doctrine of the Church the centre of their faith, makes *man himself* the central and most important figure in religion, and, in this connection, permits the introduction of all kinds of Pelagian and rationalistic error.

The Lutheran Confession is the one Confession that writes the doctrine of *Christ* large. "Of the Attributes of God and the Holy Trinity it has nothing to say, except as they are viewed in and through Christ. The doctrine of sin it learns in its full significance only as seen in the light of the incarnation, and as estimated from the standpoint of redemption. The facts of predestination, Luther taught, were to be considered only after the entire plan of salvation presented in the Gospel was learned. It discriminates between those books of the Bible that with greater and less fulness treat of the doctrine of Christ. If Christology is thus the centre, the centre of Christology is Christ's office as Priest, and particularly that of completed redemption through his vicarious satisfaction. In Word and Sacraments it recognizes the means whereby the fruits of this satisfaction are applied. The distinction between Law and Gospel, drawn with a clearness and fulness that may be searched for elsewhere in vain, has the same explanation. The doctrine of Christ is to it the solution of all the other doctrines. The union of the divine and human, unchanged and unconfused, and yet the one penetrating and energizing the other, pervades the entire system. This belongs to the doctrines of Inspiration, Providential Concurrence, Faith, the Mystical Union, the Word, the Sacraments, Prayer, as well as Christology." [20]

So far as the ordinary American Protestantism is concerned, much of whose leaven is infused into parts of the Lutheran Church; and many of whose leaders assume or declare that Lutheranism is only one of the many varieties of a common evangelical Christianity, with a peculiar doc-

---

[20] *Jacobs.*

trine of the Lord's Supper, we must say that Lutheranism differs from this Protestantism totally in the principle of the Church; and in larger or less part in the principle of salvation.

Let us take the principle of the Church, which, to the ordinary American Protestant, is either an institution of religious convenience; or is a visible body composed of the *aggregate* of the Protestant religious bodies in the land, able in their opinion to make it the one fold of the one Shepherd by their coming closer together, and by their recognizing each other in a common fellowship; and which springs up or dies away, as people have more or less contact with the Bible. The Bible is an *individual* thing, and salvation is an individual thing; and there is no particular fixed relation between the Bible and the Church, or the individual and the Church. The Bible is here, and the individual is here, and salvation is here, and, to spread the Bible and save the race, men join together and organize a Church.

To this conception we reply, that the Lutheran Church, though it, with all its heart, rejects the *Roman* doctrine of the Church, cannot agree to rob the Church of its own objective strength, with which it was clothed by Christ Himself.

Our faith holds that the Word of God, in its work in the world, has not returned unto Him void; but has brought forth rich results, which no individual can exhaust, and which no generation can neglect, and which are organically inherent in the Church of Christ, which is itself the continuous *living witness,* in the preaching of the Word and the administration of the Sacraments, of Christ and His truth.

Not that the Church is the Source of the Truth, or its Norm. It must itself be constantly tested, pruned and corrected by the Word; but with all its fallibility, it is Christ's true and trusty Witness, more valuable and more to be heeded, than the most brilliant self-commissioned individual or age, which goes to the Word on its own charges, and offers us that which it in itself and by itself has discovered to be true.

Extreme Protestantism ignores this continuous living Witness, the historical Church, as a negligible factor, and throws the congregation, the pastor and even the individual soul back, as an isolated unit, upon the rock of Scripture. It isolates Scripture from the help of its own results in contact with the greatest and most sanctified saints of the Church, and bids every raw mind draw not only faith and salvation, but the whole content of truth from Scripture, by its own unaided faculties.

In pure Protestantism, Scripture apprehended by me alone is the exclusive source of doctrine, worship, and organization; in our evangelical faith, Scripture, apprehended by the Church, summarized by the Confession, and approved by my judgment and conscience, is the norm and test of doctrine, worship and organization, that has grown under the constant application of the pure Word to the life of the Communion of Saints.

Pure Protestantism, if it be Augustinian, sets every element of revelation and faith under the centralizing influence of Divine Law. Pure Protestantism, if it be Pelagian, groups every element of revelation and faith around the centre of Human Freedom. But Evangelical and Catholic Protestantism groups every element of revelation and faith around Christ, the sacrificial source [21] of divine justification and the substance of human faith. Our faith does not centre its gravity either in the distant divine, or in the helpless human; but in the concrete, yet perfect divine-human Person of Christ. We hold to the Divine, both Law and Love, yet through Christ. We hold to the human, created in the Divine image and corrupted by sin, yet restored by Christ.

---

[21] *i. e.,* ground.

Freedom, salvation, gospel, grace, Christ, are elements in some Protestant systems; faith, freedom, works, are elements in other Protestant systems; but the BALANCE between God and man, as real in Christ, in Predestination, in Redemption, in the Person of Christ, in Scripture, in the Word of God, in Justification, Regeneration, Sanctification, in the Sacraments, in the Church, in Confession and Absolution, in the State, in History, and in the spiritual life of the Christian, is complete in the Lutheran Faith alone.

Pure Pelagian Protestantism comes to God through man, without the Gospel. Pure Semi-Pelagian Protestantism, in which are practically found the bulk of American Protestants to-day, comes to God through the Gospel *and* through man. Pure Augustinian Protestantism, rare in American Protestantism to-day, comes through God to the Gospel; but Pure Evangelical Faith comes to God through *the Gospel alone—sola.*

The resultant difference between denominational Protestantism—whether Augustinian or Semi-Pelagian, or merely sentimental, or Protestantism poised completely on a human centre—and Lutheranism, is fundamental; and runs into every channel of Confession, Worship, Organization, Spirit and Life. It is not a difference in degree, but in quality; yet not in all cases a difference in elements, for some Protestant faiths have the full evangelical elements, but a difference in the great organizing principle that is in control of the elements.

"Calvinism is the proper Protestant counterpart of Romanism. The whole system of the dependence of the individual on a power which absolutely determines him in his willing and doing, the system which is set up by Catholicism in its doctrine of the Church, is bound up by Calvinism in its absolute decree. In Calvinism, everything saving and salutary lies in the decree; in Romanism, it lies in the Church. The Lutheran system, with its faith reposing on the historical fact of the redemption, holds the mean be-

13

tween Calvinism and Romanism—between the transcendant idealism of the one, the external realism of the other."[22]

" The essential difference between Calvin and Trent consists not in the definition of the Church, but in the historic answer to the question, Is the Roman Church the true Church? For Calvin, the Church was a sacramental organization with an authoritative ministry of the Word, watching over the State in spiritual things, while the State did its behests in material things." [23]

For Zwingli, and for all humanists, the Church is the Kingdom of God upon earth, which watches over the State in spiritual things, and sees in the moral fruits of earthly citizenship the attainment of its goal and the realization of its ideals.[24]

But for us, the Church is the congregation of believing saints in which the Gospel, the saving Word and Sacraments of Christ, are faithfully used, and which has neither national goal, visible aim, nor earthly ideal, but embraces in its invisible fellowship of the body of Christ, true believers of every nation from the rising of the sun to the going down thereof.

Exceedingly superficial do the attempts appear that classify Lutheranism as a simple variation of the common Protestant

---

[22] *F. C. Baur.*

[23] Thos. Hall of Union Theological Seminary in *Hibbert Journal.*

[24] " In his practical operations in the church, Zwingli betrays his dependence upon the mediæval ideals. But the theocratic ideal which he pursued allows to neither church nor state its proper position. . . . The laws of the state are, after all, valid only in so far as they conform to the law of the church, or the Bible. This is a mediæval idea. The carrying out of his reformatory work embraced both a new system of doctrine and a new order of social and practical life, which must be enforced by the agency of the state. Christianity is an affair of the state, but the state is the organ of the church. Like Savonarola, Zwingli sought to reform his city according to the divine law of the Bible, with the help of the secular power. It was also in accord with the example of Savonarola that Zwingli's political ambition was not satisfied with the direction of his native city, but associated his direct reformatory labors with political combinations of the widest and most daring character. Thus, in every sphere of his doctrinal and practical activity, we are impressed with the mediæval and humanistic limitations of Zwingli, and that, too, in such forms as to emphasize the contrast between his ideas and those of Luther."—Seeberg, *Hist. of Doct.,* II, p. 317, 318.

doctrine. Luther was thoroughly in the right; and felt what he was unable briefly to express, with respect to the new shoot of rationalized Protestantism that was arising before him, when he said, "Ihr habt einen andern Geist als wir."

CHAPTER XII.

THE HISTORY AND TENDENCY OF THE CON-
FESSIONAL PRINCIPLE IN THE CHURCH.

Faith the Source of Confession—By Personal Confession the Word of the Lord
Multiplied and the Church Prevailed—The Confession of Peter—The Official
Testimony of the Church, as its Public Witness to the Word, is Dynamic—The
Confession is More than a Symbol—Christ the High Priest of our Confession—
The Church Developing her Confessions—The Cooling of Confessional Ardor—
Orthodoxy—Indifferentism in Both the Post-Nicene and the Post-Reformation
Periods—Calixtus above the Confessions—The Historical and Comparative
Standpoint—Walch—Planck—Marheinecke—Winer—Confessional Indifferent-
ism is the Body without the Breath of Life—The Later Eighteenth-Century
Rationalism—The Standpoint of True Lutheranism.

IT has already been pointed out that the New Testament intimately connects Confession and Faith. The two go together naturally and necessarily. Confession is the counterpart of faith—it is faith come to utterance. The Word
works faith, and faith brings forth Confession. Or, as St.
Paul says, "The word of faith is in heart and mouth,"
Romans 10: 8. "I have believed," says he, "and, *therefore,*
have I spoken."

In Confession, then, it is faith that is active. It testifies
in loyalty to conviction within, and in order to beget, reproduce and quicken faith in others. Incidentally, it strengthens its own conviction through the act of Confession.

Public Confession, which adds personal conviction to
proclamation, is the great builder and strengthener of the
Church. Nothing so transforms the "pale belief" of a congregation into "strong, full-blooded conviction," as public confession in its midst. The man who confesses has committed

144

himself in weighty matters of principle and life before his fellows. Sparks rising forth from the glowing truth within him kindle a flame in soul after soul. The Confession fills the assembled congregation with the inner and living power of the Word, so that it has become "of one mind and one soul."

Thus in public confession, faith in Christ reaches its most impressive power; and the "belief unto righteousness" in the heart, becomes the "confession unto salvation" with the mouth (Romans 10: 10). Thus the "full assurance of faith," in the heart, becomes the outer "holding fast to the confession of our hope," in the act (Heb. 10: 22, 23).

Thus we see it to be one of the main purposes of confession to give evidence of the faith that is within, "confessing the good confession before many witnesses" (1 Timothy 6: 12), and "not being ashamed of the testimony of our Lord" (2 Timothy 1: 8).

Thus confession is the living personal fountain located in the time and space of this outer world, whose source is faith, and whose utterance is the Faith.

Thus also the Confession is the Faith, uttered as suiting time and place, unfolded, and, when necessary, defined, distinguished, amplified; but always by a power within itself, *i. e.,* the Word of God. It is by means of such Public Confession, of which preaching is the one most active, most constant and most prominent form,[1] that the Faith is confirmed and spread, and that the Church itself, with its blessings, is extended.

On the occasion of the great Confession of Peter (Matt. 16: 15, 16), Christ, for the first time, spake of His Church; and declared that this Church was to be built on the rock of the Confession of Christ (Matt. 16: 18). "So it proved to be in after days. It was by St. Peter's powerful testimony

---

[1] The Confession of Sins is diverse from the Confession of Faith. In The Order of Public Service, the Office of the Word closely connects the Creed, the Confession of Faith by the Congregation, with the Sermon, the Confession of Faith by the one who administers, *i. e.,* preaches the Word.

to Jesus, as the risen Lord and Christ (Acts 2: 32-36), that, on the day of Pentecost, three thousand souls were led gladly to receive the Word, and, in Baptism, to confess for themselves, Christ (vv. 37-41). Paul knew the mighty power that inheres in Confession; and both in his preaching and writing confessed (Acts 22: 6 ff; 26: 12 ff; Gal. 1: 15 ff) Jesus afresh as his Saviour and Lord. It was above all else by the personal confessions of humble individuals—a testimony often sealed with blood (Rev. 2: 13; 12: 11)— that the pagan empire of Rome was cast down and the Church of Christ built upon its ruins. And it is still by personal confession, in one form or another, that the Word of the Lord grows and multiplies, and His Church prevails against 'the gates of Hell.' "

What is true of the living Confession of the preacher is true just as directly, even if more abstractly, but in a wider and, in certain respects, more weighty sense, of the official utterance and testimony of the Church, which is not, as we ministers are too apt to assume, a map showing the demarcations of the denominational field of Christianity for the convenience and guidance of its theologians, but which is a public witness and testimony of the Church's Faith before all the world.

The Church's Confessions, then, in their chief strength and purpose, and in their highest and dynamic sense, are not completely described in the traditional term, "Symbols," employed to designate them. A Symbol is the accepted and marked material resulting from a critical examination of the Faith in Scripture. The Symbol embraces two ideas: that of comparison, definition and identification, and that of the actual use of what has been thus compared, defined and identified in Confession. The first element is preliminary to the second, and is not complete, without the second, in itself. Even as the Word is more than the Scripture, so is the confession in the Confession more than the distinguishing and identifying element of the Symbol.

The supreme position of Confession is seen in the life and work of the Lord Jesus Christ, Who in "witnessing a good confession before Pontius Pilate " (1 Tim. 6: 13) testified that "to this end was I born, and for this cause came I into the world" (John 18: 37); and Whose deepest teachings were, not indeed a Confession in the sense of an avowal of saving faith, but a confession in the sense of requiring of such great faith an avowal of such supreme knowledge (Cp. His discourses, John, chapters 6-16).

Still further did He show the pre-eminent place that He gave to Confession, by His own most solemn teachings and warnings as to it, and the apostles reflect His words. "Whosoever shall confess me before men, him will I confess also before my Father which is in heaven." The Confession here asked is not a verbal subscription.[2] It is confessing Christ out of a state of inner oneness with Him. The confessor confesses out of his life in Christ, out of the identity between Christ and himself brought about by faith. It is the confession of those who have been "perfected into one" with Christ, " that the world may know that thou hast sent me." " Every spirit that confesseth that Jesus Christ is come in the flesh is of God " (1 John 4: 2). " If thou shalt confess with thy mouth the Lord Jesus, and shalt believe in thine heart that God hath raised him from the dead, thou shalt be saved." Thus Christ becomes the High Priest and Apostle of our Confession (Heb. 3: 1).

The Confession of Faith in the Christian Church gathers, as we saw at length in the last two chapters, around the name, person and work of Christ. The Gospels .and the Epistles are filled with the material for the elaboration of a full confession of Christ; and the Church, under the developing influence of the Holy Ghost, and in the refining hand of Providence, gave herself with great ardor to the creation, the maintenance and the defense of her great

---

[2] The " 'o Legŏn, Ky'rie, Ky'rie " of Matt. 7:21, in contradistinction to the " 'o Poiŏn," is a verbal subscriber.

Confession,—first in the embryonic elements of public Confession in the New Testament, as they were associated with the reception of new members in Holy Baptism; then in the Formula of the Baptismal Confession, as it grew earlier into the Apostles' Creed, and afterwards into the Nicene Creed; and still later, as it developed against error, into the Athanasian Creed.

With the fresh outburst of Faith at the beginning and during the Reformation, and amid new and mighty trials first from without, and then from within, the Church again became great and supreme in her Witness and Confession. Again, with the rise of Lutheranism, which is the synthesis of individual freedom in the conscience and of the authority of the divine Word within the communion of saints,[3] the Church rose to heroic and complete Confession, until at last the adjustment to Protestantism, so far as the Word was concerned, was completed.

In these two great cycles of Confession in the Christian Church we see a tendency and learn a lesson that is most instructive to the Church that now is and that is to come. When primeval confessional ardor begins to cool, and, like molten metal, to harden into fixed external form, as it will do with the lapse of time, there are two dangers to be feared. The one is that of a cast-iron rigidity in adherence, which becomes mechanical, superficial and oppressive. The other is a dead coldness of indifferentism which chills the vital touch between the confessing Church and its Confession.

In the first instance we have an insistence and severity of outer orthodoxy in rule and form that becomes almost absolute in its assertion of power. In the other case we have a dying away of the vitality of the inner substance, so that only the outer form is left, but as a mere historical remnant. The spirit has fled, and left an interesting shell be-

---

[3] Freedom of conscience, the first element of the synthesis, without the second element, is sectarianism; and the authority of the Church without the first element, freedom of conscience, is Romanism.

hind it, to be picked up and handled and made the object of research like other facts in the field of knowledge, but not to serve the purpose originally intended.

It is easy to see that both these dangers have been twice encountered by the Church of Christ in its historical development. After the mighty confessional life of the New Testament, and after the original glow and fervor of the Apostolic age had died away, and the Faith was now coming, and came, into heroic contact with the world powers, we find the Confessional Baptismal Formula and other forms of instruction hardening into the κανών τῆς ἀληθείας,[4] the *regula ecclesiae,* the *regula fidei,* the *gramma,* the *graphe*— " *Symbolum est regula fidei brevis et grandis* " (Augustine) —which attained, in the minds of the orthodox, almost to the strength of inspiration.

Again, in a similar period in the Seventeenth Century, we find the Confessions acting as an ecclesiastical *regula fidei,* mediately illuminated, and the confessional spirit hardening into extreme rigidity.[5]

On the other hand, in the post-Nicene period of the Ancient Church, when the world had entered into her counsels, we find the original orthodoxy of Apostolic confession on the wane. Pelagianism arose, A. D., 411-31, with Semi-Pelagianism, A. D., 427-29; and then there came the controversy and split between the East and the West on ceremonies and government, and the broadening out and filtering down of theology in Boethius, Cassiodorus, Isidore, Gregory of Tours, and the venerable Bede.

In the same way, after the Second Awakening of the

---

[4] " Apart from the Scriptures," says Harnack; " in connection with the Scriptures," says Kunze.

[5] " The dispute with Calixtus led the Lutheran theologians to postulate a mediate inspiration (illumination), and consequently, also, a divine authority for the Symbolical Books; but the distinction between the canon of Scripture and such standards is, nevertheless, constantly preserved in word, if not always in fact. In reality the Symbolical Books were regarded as a Kañon tōs Pisteōs throughout the Seventeenth Century side by side with the Scriptures, inasmuch as the faith was directly grounded on the symbol rather than on the Bible."

Church, and after the confessional ardor of the Reformation had first chilled into hard and superficial orthodoxy, it gave way in the Eighteenth Century to the confessional indifferentism of the periods of illumination and rationalism.

The Confessions now died away except as documentary material for historical examination. It is unfortunate, but natural, that the critical examination of the Confessions as pure history, and the comparative study of the Confessional Principle takes its first rise and receives its point of view and its terminology in this age of confessional indifferentism; and that the usual mode of approach and estimation of a symbol by us is based on the presupposition that it is a document of historical testimony, an exhibit of a past age, rather than a ripe fruit of the Christian Church, a living possession, for active confessional use in the present day. Much of the prejudice against Catechisms and a sound confessional spirit is a heritage to us from the latitudinarian rationalism of the Eighteenth Century.

It was the syncretistic controversy that marked the turning-point in the relation of theology to the Confessions, and that led to that change in the form of theological science that caused the Confessions to be regarded more as historical than as living testimonies. Calixtus claimed a theological viewpoint that lay above the Confessions, in his *consensus quinquesecularis ecclesiæ primævæ,* from which he sought to judge, on a comparative basis,. the doctrinal differences of the various Churches. It was no longer the confessional doctrines that were regarded as objective, but it was the confessional differences that were reviewed from this higher and supposedly objective standpoint.

The point of view was no longer that of the loyal confessor, but that of an objective **student** who regarded all these positions of the past with impartial equanimity. The antagonistic doctrines of conflicting confessions were treated historically, and not *confessionally.* The pioneer works of Walch, Semler, Planck and others, from whom we draw many conceptions to-day, were thus infected, as was also the extreme orthodox school, represented by Valentine Loescher in his *Reformations-Akta* and his *Historia motuum.* This was also the case with Chr. M. Pfaff, Buddeus, Baumgarten, J. S. Feuerlin, W. F. Walch, and others.

The old ardor of active testimony was extinguished; and we are thus burdened to-day yet with the historical and external atmosphere of comparative theology, in attempting to come into touch and to proper estimate of the Symbolical Books, through the isagogical work done on them at the ebb of the tide of the confessional principle.

The new science of historical Confessional study—Symbolics, as it came to be termed, later on—began with G. F. Planck, Winer, and Planck's disciple, Marheinecke. Planck provided a genetic, pragmatic exposition of the chief ecclesiastical systems in his known large works, *The History of the Protestant Lehrbegriff* and *The History of the Catholic Gesellschafts-Verfassung.* In his small volume, " *A Sketch of Historical and Comparative Delineation* of the Dogmatic Systems of our Leading Christian Parties according to their Fundamental Conceptions, and the Doctrinal Distinctions drawn therefrom and their Practical Consequences, Göttingen, 1796," he arranged the idea and the plan of a comparative Confessional Science.

Planck was the prince of pragmatic historians, springing up in the heart of the age of rationalism, and influenced, as he himself tells us, by the three great principles that separated his time, as by a chasm, from the old orthodoxy. The first of these was a *deeper critical foundation* for historical and dogmatic knowledge. The second was *freedom of investigation.* The third was *tolerance and justice* toward those thinking otherwise.

His own personal convictions did not seem so important to him as the fascinating wealth of historical investigation, and his tolerance was extended more liberally toward those of other beliefs than toward those of his own faith. He sought the explanation of history in subjective passions and motives, and in the strength and weaknesses of its leading figures; and thus he was led not only to overestimate the importance of personalities, but also to underestimate the weight and might of that general and unconscious progress of principle which is due to the purpose of God. Ambition, love of authority, eagerness for strife and agitation, lack of mildness, want of toleration and absence of humility, were the qualities he loved to find in the chief actors in any scene, and by which he interpreted the current of events. Thus, with all his learning, judgment and insight, he became an exponent of pragmatism in its lowest and most unworthy sense. He expected and sought for the meaner motives in analyzing movements with which his own mental structure was out of sympathy.

He is so important to us in this discussion because, in his mastery of the original sources of the confessional history of the Lutheran Church, he constantly applied these principles and motives, and has thus left an impression not only unsympathetic but unjust to the great confessional characters and activities of the Sixteenth Century—results that are inwoven to-day yet with our common historical conceptions, and from whose trammels it is difficult to be freed.

He wrote the great history of the Rise, the Variations, and the Forming of our Protestant Conception of Doctrine *from* the beginning of *the Reformation to* the Introduction of *the Formula of Concord,* in six volumes. This epoch-making study of Protestant Confessionalism in the development of its history and doctrine as seen by a pragmatic, unpartisan, tolerant and enthusiastic indifferentism, pictures the foundation and development of Reformation doctrine less as an unfolding of principle than as an attempt of the representative men of the age to influence the direction of doctrine.

In all the controversies, where conflict waxed hot, it is,

in Planck's delineation, rather Lessing's rationalistic and comparative search after truth than the desire to find and establish some truth that is felt. Even Schaff says of Planck's *Gesch. d. Prot. Lehrbegriffs* that it was "without proper appreciation of the doctrinal differences."[6] The fair comparative presentation of both sides of doctrine is more to him than any conclusion as to either, as we particularly see in his pioneer work on Symbolics, *"Historical and Comparative Delineation* of the Dogmatic Systems of our Leading Christian Parties" ("unserer verschiedenen christlichen Hauptparteien"), in which he sought to do away with all prepossession for any doctrinal system and to increase the respect for all alike.

This is the essence of the impartial historico-comparative idea, which haunts our religious teachings both elementary or catechetical, and advanced or technical, to this day; and which degenerates faith to opinion, and counts the open mind as more important than the certain heart. If faith be less than knowledge, if confession be an intellectual subscription, with or without mental reservation; if the Christian Church is not contending for treasures, but for logical terms; if witness bearing be of less account than weighing witness—in short, if principle lives chiefly to be pitted against principle, and conscience is to be evaporated into definition, then Planck's point of view is right; but even then his exaltation of unworthy personal motive ultimately invites to skepticism and contempt.[7]

Planck's great disciple was Marheinecke, who lectured upon the basis of Planck's sketch of this new science, and who gave it the name "Symbolics."

---

[6] *Creeds of Christendom,* I, p. 258.

[7] The value of the critical, the historical, the purely comparative principle, and of the results of the development through which the Church has passed under their influence is to be written large. Impartial and fearless search for the exact facts, bold and objective comparison, constant test and criticism, are methods to be prized as invaluable and as having been bought with a price. But their value is in their formal strength, and not in their substance. As means, and where they do not set themselves up as the end, their services are to be heartily welcomed.

Marheinecke attempted to eliminate the polemic element from the various confessional principles, which now manifested their main strength in antagonistic clashings, and "fought themselves to death;" and, in calmness, to produce a historico-dogmatic development of the peculiar *Lehrbegriff* (doctrinal concept) of each of the "Parties" in the Christian Church, on the basis of their respective symbols. The work was never completed, but he carried out the idea, less extensively, in his Latin compendium, *"Institutiones symbolicæ, doctrinarum Cathol., Protest., Socin., Eccl. Græcæ,"* etc., summam et discrimina exhibentes, in usum scholarum scr. Ph. M., Berlin, 1812. Thus Marheinecke sought to exhibit the internal unit of each separate denominational confession.

It remained for Winer to bring the comparative method, in its application to the science of Symbolics, to perfection. With his usual analytic and synthetic strength, and his objective method, he presented to view, side by side, in tabular form, the differences existing in the various Confessions, under the dissection of a skilful comparative analysis.

And here lies the secret of Confessional indifferentism. The breath of life had departed from the symbols, and the indefinable inner reserve of strength had disappeared. No longer devoted to any Confessional cause with heart and soul, the theologians no longer sought to exhibit and judge everything in the light of a believing witness; but they attempted, from a standpoint above the various Confessions, to present and estimate them henceforth as historically conditioned and, in this respect, equally justified, though not equally valuable, developments of the Christian idea. They described them as step-like approximations to a still higher ideal, to be reached comparatively, and by the process of elimination of the peculiarities of Christian Teaching.

Meantime doubts as to whether symbols were necessary at all arose even as early as Spener. A century later the obligation to adhere to the symbol was interpreted as referring only to "the essentials;" and most scholars viewed the essential matter in the Confessions as very small, compared with that which was "merely theological and not directly religious," and, therefore, unessential. Rationalism caused the subscription to degenerate to a hypocritical form, in which the obligation was assumed, but. nòt regarded as binding. Thus the faith once delivered to the saints gave way to subjective and scientific "approximations to the Christian idea," and the Protestant Confessions, in Nine-teenth-Century language, were to be "regarded simply as essays toward formulating the body of Christian doctrine, which may be tested by criticism and revised," and none of them as a doctrinally perfect attest of a "faith which belongs equally to our fathers and to us."

As we of a living Faith have learned to penetrate through and beyond the superficial illumination of the Eighteenth Century, by virtue of our hold on the Word and the Faith; so we of a living Confession should abandon the lower and comparative point of view of the Eighteenth Century, which not only throws the outer shell aside, but leads to a subjective approximation toward the "perfect Christian idea," instead of an objective salvation and a real justification by faith in Christ Jesus.

The standpoint of true Lutheranism lies not in the field of historical investigation, though that is "a good and useful outward discipline," nor in the field of comparative distinc-tion and estimate, nor in the discrimination of denomina-tional or sectarian peculiarities; but in the apprehension, assimilation, affirmation, and application, of our own sym-bols, as the historical channels of the Word, to the spiritual life and the upbuilding of our own people and our own Church.

CHAPTER XIII.

THE CONFESSIONAL USE OF THE WORD "SYMBOL."

The Meaning of the Term—Its Use by the Church Fathers—Its Use in the Reformation and in the Book of Concord.

THE word "Symbol," to denote the Church's formulated Confession of Faith, comes to us with an ancient history. Though Carpzov will not admit its use to antedate the Council of Nice, and while it is true that the term is but rarely found in the Church Fathers, the word nevertheless occurs in Cyprian[1] about the middle of the Third Century, and thenceforward it seems to have been used, at least occasionally, as a title given to the Apostles' Creed.

Ruffinus, in the middle of the Fourth Century, employed it as the title of his work, *Expositio in symbolum apostolorum;*[2] and Bossius justly argues from this and from the fact that Ruffinus says in his work, "symbolum autem hoc multis et justissimis ex causis appellare voluerunt," that the earlier use of the word must have been general.

Unlike the word "Confession," whose origin and lineage roots itself so thoroughly in Scripture, as we have seen in a former chapter, the word "symbol" is not Biblical, but came to the Church from the classical Greek and Latin.[3]

---

[1] Ep. 75 *ad Magnum.*

[2] Cp. Augustine, *De Fide et Symbolo;* Hilary, *De Symbolo.*

[3] For the meaning of *symbolum*, in classical and ecclesiastical Latin and Greek, see the Lexicons of Stephanus, Passow-Rost, Forcellini, and Suicer; and *Thesaurus eccl.*, II, 1084.

The ecclesiastical origin of the term is disputed, but etymologically the word is derived from the Greek *sumbállein,* which means, to throw one thing alongside of another, to compare, to talk over matters together and come to a united conclusion, an agreement. From this meaning there is but a step to the further signification, denoting a sign or mark agreed upon before, by which to infer or recognize anything. Thus has the word come to signify a badge of recognition. It further bore the meaning "watchword," "formula in the mysteries," and "a contract between two parties." [4]

Finally, the term came to designate the mark or sign by which the connection of individuals to a whole, *e. g.,* a corporation, or association, might be indicated. Such were the badges which secured admission to a banquet, *"the tessera militaris,"* the flag, and the password. As applied to religion it would be the *"formula credendorum, tanquam signum, quo inter se credentes distinguuntur."*

Cyprian employed this term to designate the Baptismal Formula. Ruffinus and the writers of the Middle Ages confine it to the Apostles' Creed; but in the Thirteenth Century it was applied to the additional œcumenical creeds by Alexander of Hales (A. D. 1230).

The term was not used in the early days of the Reformation; neither was it applied to Luther's Catechisms, nor to the Augsburg Confession; but its earliest appearance seems to have been in Wittenberg, in 1533, in the prescribed doctor's oath in the new statutes of the University of Wittenberg. Luther, five years later, in his older days (1538), applied it to the Apostles' and the Athanasian Creeds, and also to the Te Deum: "Die drey Symbola oder Bekentnis des Glaubens Christi inn der Kirchen eintrechtiglich gebraucht, Wittem., 1538."

Melanchthon uses the term in his "Corpus doctrinæ." In 1576, the Preface to the "Corpus Julium" characterized the

---

[4] Müller, *Symbol. Bücher, Einleitung, p. XX.*

14

Augsburg Confession as a "well-grounded *Symbol* of the Reformed Churches."[*]

A fine and, for us, regulative use of the term "symbol" occurs in the opening paragraph (the second) of the Preface of the Book of Concord, where the Augsburg Confession itself is termed a symbol; not primarily, indeed, but after calling it a "Confession" twice, we are told that it is confessed as the "Symbol," or watchword, "of our time in the contest with Papacy."

That the chief meaning and purpose of a symbol, as it is here applied to the Augsburg Confession, is not that of contract, but that of an approved witness to the faith, more spiritual in purpose, and wider in scope, than a binding agreement to certain doctrines, is to be seen in the language and spirit of those who put forth the Book of Concord, and who say in their "Preface to the Readers, One and All, to whom they Announce and Declare their Devotion and Friendship, combined with Willing Service:—

"A brief and succinct Confession was prepared from the Word of God, which was offered to the Emperor, and was presented to the deputies, and finally being circulated among all men professing Christian doctrine, and thus in the entire world was diffused everywhere, and began to be current in the mouth and speech of all.

"Afterwards many churches and schools embraced and defended this Confession, *as a symbol of the present time* in regard to the chief articles of faith, . . . and with perpetual agreement have appealed to it without any controversy and doubt. The doctrine comprised in it which they knew both to be supported by firm testimonies of Scripture,

---

[*] "Welcher Confession Artikel sind jetziger Zeit als ein rechtes, schönes, reines, wolgegründtes Symbolum der reformirten Kirchen."

Julius was duke of Brunswick and founder of the University of Helmstedt. He took offense at Chemnitz's criticism of him when he permitted his son to become a member of the Roman Church, and excluded the Formula of Concord from his Corpus doctrinæ. The Julian Corpus contains the three œcumenical symbols, the Augsburg Confession printed in 1531, the Apology, the Schmalkald Articles, and the two Catechisms of Luther—everything but the Formula.

and to be approved by the ancient and received symbols, they have also constantly judged to be the only and perpetual *consensus* of the truly believing Church, which was formerly defended against manifold heresies and errors."

The Augsburg Confession is here declared to be a confession which has become the symbol, or confessional standard, of the hour, to which all parties have agreed to appeal (not an appeal which all parties have agreed to make), and which contains the very doctrine found in the old tried symbols, which are the acknowledged *consensus* of all the Churches in their conflict with all kinds of sects; and have appealed to it with Christian unanimity, and without any controversy and doubt. Moreover, they have steadily held fast to the doctrine apprehended in it, which is well grounded in the divine Scripture, and is presented in brief compass in the old, tried symbols as the one old *consensus* accredited by the churches unanimously teaching the true doctrine, and acknowledged in repeated conflicts against heresy.

The *"consensus"* here is their agreement in doctrine, rather than an agreement to agree in doctrine. The Church, when using the word "symbol," used it in the sense not of a contract agreed upon, but of a Confession duly accredited as in agreement with Scripture.

The same conclusion is reached in considering the usage of the Formula of Concord, which defines symbols as "kurtze runde Bekenntnisse" (*"brief, plain Confessions"*). The definition occurs in the second part of the introduction to the Epitome: "And since immediately after the time of the Apostles, and even during their lives, inroads were made by false teachers and heretics; and *symbols, i. e., brief, plain confessions,* were set up against them in the early Church, and were held to be the one common Christian Faith and the Confession of the true and orthodox Churches, namely, the Apostles' Creed, the Nicene Creed. and the Athanasian Creed; we confess them as binding upon us, and herewith reject all heresies and dogmas, which were introduced into the Church of God contrary to their teachings."

Here, indeed, matters are clearly defined. Symbols are brief, plain *Confessions set up* (the setting up is a subordinate idea, and its mode and forms are not expressed) against the heresies of false teachers, and held to by the true Churches as the *one common Christian Faith,* and as *their Confession* of it.

,Finally, the whole, true, spiritual, churchly and confessional sense of a symbol as conceived by our fathers and held to in the Confessions is characterized most amply in the Preface to the Solid Declaration of the Formula, where they tell us:—

"From *our inmost hearts* we herewith once again *confess* this *Christian Augsburg Confession,* which is *so thoroughly grounded in God's Word.* We abide by the simple, clear and plain meaning that its words convey, and regard it in all respects as *a Christian symbol,* which at the present time *Christians should receive next to God's Word,* just as in former times, when great controversies arose in the Church of God, *symbols and confessions* were composed, which *pure teachers and hearers confessed with heart* and mouth. We intend also, by the grace of the Almighty, to faithfully abide until our end by this Christian Confession."

And in the part of the Preface on the "comprehensive summary, foundation, rule and standard," they tell us: "Since it is necessary, for thorough and permanent unity, above all to have a completely approved compendium in which *the concise and common doctrines confessed by the Churches* of the true Christian religion are brought together out of God's Word, just as the ancient Church always had its fixed symbols for this use; and as this authority should not be attached to private writings, but to such books as have been composed, approved and received in the name of the Churches who acknowledge one doctrine and religion; we have declared to one another with heart and mouth that we will neither make nor receive any separate or new

confession of our faith, but acknowledge as confessional the
public common writings which always and everywhere were
received in all the Churches of the Augsburg Confession,
as such *symbols or public confessions,* before the dissensions
arose among those who accept the Augsburg Confession,"
etc.

The word "symbol," then, as used in the Symbolical Books
of the Lutheran Church, is equivalent to *A Public Confession of the Faith,* made with heart and mouth, and which,
in the course of events, and after passing through the tests
of history and time, has received the stamp of churchly
approval and adoption as in harmony with the one old *consensus* of the true and faithful doctrine, and has become
an external sign and bond of their fellowship.

Symbols are old,[6] tested and approved confessions of the
faith, in shortest form, used as a confessional formulary,
while Symbolical Writings are public, common writings,
"publica et approbata scripta," not private writings ("Pri-
vatschriften"), but books that have been approved and accepted " in the name of the Churches which confess one doctrine and religion," and which " publicly delineate, ground
and defend the doctrine of the Church." [7]

As far as the Church is necessary, declares Sartorius, so
far does there exist a necessity for the Symbol as the concentrated expression of its common faith, and for the Confession as a manifestation of its general religious consciousness.

"The Symbol," says Sartorius, " is no law—no prescription
of the faith—but a confession—a testimony of it—as indicated in its form. It does not come in the imperative *crede,*
but in the indicative *credo.* '*Credo* ' begins the first, the
Apostles' Creed; and the last, the Formula of Concord, has
only translated the singular into the plural, and shows its
interior connection with the Apostles' doctrine, and follows

---

[6] " Bewährten, alten Symbolis."

[7] Müller, *Einleit.,* p. XXII.

in the oft-recurring form, '*Credimus, confitemur et doce-mus.*'"

"Every preacher," continues Sartorius, "is already a con-fessor; and as no preacher is a self-constituted confessor, the very nature of the office implies that there must be a common Confession—to which he declares himself as a *fellow*-confes-sor, both when he is invested with his office, and in the ful-filment of its duties. The ministry of the Church pre-supposes *the fellowship of a Confession or a Symbol.*"

CHAPTER XIV.

THE LUTHERAN CONFESSION.

Was It Born at Augsburg?—Luther the Great Living Confession of His Church—The Reasons Why He was the Church's Living Confession—His Relation to External Confessional Statements—The Weakness of a Living Witness.

L UTHER was himself the great Living Confession of his Church and day. Before the political necessity of a formal touch with the empire and the outer world had come to a focus at Augsburg, and, also afterwards, Luther was, in his own personality, the greatest promulgator, definer and defender of the Church's Faith. It was he who determined and decided and upheld the doctrine. He not only broke the path, but he built the road, while others followed, smoothing the surface and adjusting the side approaches. It was his discoveries, his utterances, his constructions, in university lectures to students, in numerous sermons, and still more numerous letters, in colloquies and disputations, with friends within and foes without, in advice and directions, in books and treatises, in the publication of catechisms and Scriptures, that made him the great rediscoverer and recoverer of and, next after Paul, the greatest Living Witness to the Faith.

And the cause for this is not hidden. Luther's daily, direct and lifelong contact with the Scriptures, from which he drew all his strength, and which furnished him with all the doctrine, and which, through his agency, reacted with instant and prevailing force among the Lutheran Churches, made him the one Living Witness, the one Living Confes-

163

sion of the Church of the day. He lived in the Scriptures, and in nothing else. He translated them, he applied them to every sphere. They were to him, in his days and his nights the only rule of faith and life. They were sufficient; and he cut off every human and civilizing source of power. To him the wisdom of the ancients, the classics, the philosophy of Aristotle, the logic of the scholastics, the councils and decisions of the Church, the ambitions in ecclesiastical politics, the teachings of other great scholars of his age, the adjustments of scholarship to the times—these were almost absolutely nothing. But the saving doctrine of Scripture in Christ, which ever came promptly to the surface in bold confession,—it, to him, was everything.

This explains Luther's low estimate of the mere external confessional statement, elaborated in complete and cautious phrase. To him, the doctrinal reality itself was more than the phrase. And he had little appreciation for that outer adjustment in the forms of language and in the terms of mutual avowal, which did not spring up spontaneously from the inner doctrinal reality. Therefore, also, he had little patience—though he often showed much patience— with any program of external mediation and conciliation. The inner spirit of the Word, which crystallized into clear and definite doctrine, was everything. For him no externally elaborated Confessions of the Church were sufficient. The Scripture itself was the rule—not in the sense in which modern theologians who dislike confessionalism, appeal from the Confessions to the Scriptures. With these it is often the desire to get rid of doctrine, and of its definite and emphatic confession. To him, Confessions were insufficient, because no Confession was sufficiently full of doctrine, nor could be made to express the sharp and clear distinctiveness of the doctrine, and the complete sum of doctrine with sufficient fulness. Confessions to him are inadequate, not because they go too far, but because they cannot and do not go far enough :—

"There is no Council or Father," he says, "in whom we can find or from which we can learn the entire Christian doctrine. That of Nice treats only of the fact that Christ is true God; that of Constantinople, that the Holy Ghost is God; that of Ephesus, that Christ is not two persons, but one; that of Chalcedon, that Christ has not one, but two natures. These are the four chief councils, and yet they have only these four doctrines. Nevertheless, this is not the Christian Faith. . . . In short, put all the Councils and all the Fathers together, and even then you cannot derive from them the entire doctrine of the Christian Faith. If the Holy Scriptures were not retained, the Church would not long abide by the Councils or the Fathers."[1]

But Luther does not allow sufficiently for God's gradual unfolding of His plan in history, through which each age is allotted some portion of the problem to conquer and some sheaf of the fruit to reap. The "doctrine of the Church does not," says Plitt, "in its entire extent, originate all at once. The Church is immediately certain of her salvation, which is decided in the person of Jesus Christ, her living Head. But Jesus Christ is an historical person, the goal of a series of facts of salvation tending towards Himself, and the beginning of another series arising within Himself. It is this rich diversity included in that living unity which should become the subject of the Church's knowledge, and which she should clothe in expressions designating its true nature.

"The knowledge of these manifold facts is only very gradually attained. No so-called accident, but inner necessity, determines the succession in which the treatment of the separate parts has been undertaken by the Church. Neither has the Church been impelled and led by any inner arbitrariness or the natural desire for knowledge. On the contrary, she has waited, until through her history, which is guided

---

[1] *Erlangen,* 25. 261.

by God, *a definite call* has reached her; she has constantly fulfilled the task which God Himself points out to her, through her development, which is controlled by His Spirit."[2]

Though Luther was the Living Confession of the Faith, Luther himself, who was more powerful in promulgating and determining, if not in actually defining and fixing the nature of the Faith, than even the Augsburg Confession itself (which was not formative, but a statement *ex eventu*); and who declared the insufficiency of all the œcumenical Confessions, because of their incompleteness—this Living Confession could not forever remain in the Church. With his personal removal, the Church would lose its Living Confession; and would be obliged to fall back and lean upon leaders who were unlike him in spirit and in his simple dependency on Scripture, but who drew strength also from humanistic sources and from the written statements which, like those in every great age of the Church, are left for the guidance of the future. Would the Church be able to confess, after its Living Confession was gone?

The strength of a Living Witness is also always his weakness. Life is growth. It implies development. Development cannot take place without change, and change introduces uncertainty. But the necessities of a Confession require that it state the doctrine in such a way that changes will not affect it. Otherwise its usefulness as a foundation and an anchor for the Church are gone. If the Confession be always changing, as is the individual mind, or as is history itself, it is of little service. At best, it is but an intermediary between the Scripture and the Church, fixing for the Church, amid the shifting waves and sands of time, a clear sight of the Scripture. If it itself be no better than the moving waves around it, its one regulative and healthful function largely disappears.

Therefore the utterances of Luther, since his experience

---

[2] Trans. in Jacobs, *Book of Concord,* II, pp. 312, 313.

of Scripture was constantly changing and developing, are not of final confessional value, except where they have been confirmed by the judgment of the Church, as in the case of the Catechisms and the Schmalkald Articles. Luther writes from the very centre of the Scripture, but throws the force of the doctrine into the temper of a single situation and into the time of a single moment. He speaks without qualification, and his growth, like that of every other great student, is a record of change, and at times of inconsistency. Yet, with all this change, he so powerfully and closely reflected Scripture that he was practically recognized as the personal confessional centre of the Church until his death.

CHAPTER XV.

THE LUTHERAN CONFESSION.

THE ORIGIN OF THE AUGSBURG CONFESSION. KOLDE'S INTRODUCTION.

The Emperor—The Torgau Articles—The Elector at Coburg—The Beginnings of the Confession—What Luther said on May 11th—The Saxon Draft—The Other Estates Admitted—Melanchthon's Negotiation—Delivery of the Confession—Luther and the Confession.

THE Diet of Spires, in the Spring of 1529, the attempt of the Roman party to overthrow the Evangelical side by a majority vote, and the Evangelical protest against this procedure, constituted an important landmark in the history of the Evangelical Church as it sprang into being. A closer union was more than ever imperative. The consciousness of the magnitude of the threatening danger led even in Spires to the attempt to bridge over the internal differences in the sacramentarian question, and to pave the way to a protective federation of the leading Evangelical estates. Of necessity this care had to increase, when, notwithstanding the Marburg Colloquium in the first days of October and the divers diplomatic negotiations between the Evangelical estates, neither the one nor the other was attained, and the rumor gained currency as early as the Fall of 1529, that the Emperor would come to Germany to hold a diet in person.

And Charles V. was really on the way to Germany! Without the presence of the German princes he had himself crowned as emperor in Bologna, February 24th, 1530, by Pope Clement VII. The information received concerning the relations between the two supreme powers gave little reason to expect any good for the Evangelical cause. Indeed, not a few among the opponents looked forward to the Emperor's coming with rejoicing, and hailed him as the longed-for deliverer and "avenger."[1]

But the official document in which the Emperor from Bologna on January 21st gave invitations to another diet that was to convene April 8th in Augsburg, had an unexpectedly peaceful setting. Besides the repulsing of the Turkish peril, the principal reason was stated thus:—" How the error and schism in the holy faith and the Christian religion might be discussed and settled." The Emperor promised and admonished "to allay controversy, to abandon dislikes, to commit to the Saviour all error, and to use all diligence in hearing, understanding and weighing the opinion, thought and belief of every one in love and clemency, bring all to one harmonious Christian truth, and to settle all things which are not right on either side, when thus presented and discussed, and dispose of them."[2]

It is true, not all dared to believe in the peaceful intentions of the Emperor. Landgrave Philip of Hessen, had small inclination to attend the Diet, and still less did the south German cities trust the matter. Nuremberg, certainly, which always strove to maintain friendly relations to the Emperor, hoped for the best, and so did Elector John of Saxony, at whose court in Torgau the document had been received on March 11th. His counsellors advised him to attend the Diet in person, for the sake of being invested with the electorate, and because the matter of religion was to be discussed, and, therefore, this Diet would take the place of a council or national council. His chancellor, Dr. Gregorius Brück (Pontanus), recommended, since, according to the summons, "the opinion and thought of every one was

---

[1] Cf. The Dithyrambus of the Dom. Joh. Dietenberger in W e d e w e r , Joh. Dietenberger, Freiburg, 1888, p. 120 sq., and Luther in E n d e r s , Luthers Briefwechsel, VII, 216.

[2] F ö r s t e m a n n . Urkundenbuch, I, 7 sq.

to be heard," "that such opinion upon which our side has heretofore stood and insisted, be properly drawn up in a document with thorough proof from the divine Scriptures, so that it may be presented to the estates in writings in case the· estates would not be permitted to let the preachers present these matters in the discussions."[3]

Thereupon, on March 14th, a call was sent to Luther, Justus Jonas, John Bugenhagen and Melanchthon, since the Diet might take the place of a council or national assembly, to take prompt counsel on all articles " concerning which there is a reported dissension, both in doctrine and in external ecclesiastical usages and ceremonies," and to render a personal report on the same by March 20th. But, although the matter was hurried as much as possible, and Luther in the night of the same 14th of March, recalled Jonas, who was absent on visitations, it required a second call, on March 21st,[4] and the result of the Wittenberg discussions was probably not presented to the Elector in Torgau until March 27th.[5]

Among the many extant writings and opinions of the Wittenberg theologians of that time, which directly or indirectly refer to what was to be treated at the approaching Diet, there is none entitled " Torgau Articles," or " Opinion presented at Torgau," but all indications point to the fact that we must look for the much-sought " *Torgau Articles*" in an opinion composed by Melanchthon, which the Elector took to Augsburg as an important document, and which plainly forms the basis of the second part of the Augsburg Confession.

---

[3] F ö r s t e m a n n , Urkundenbuch, II, 39 sq.

[4] E n d e r s V I I , 253. C. R. II, 33.

[5] At least we know from Melanchthon's letters to Myconius, C. R. II, 33, that the former was in Torgau on Mch. 27th, while Luther's presence, since he knows only by hearsay of the errors of John Companus, concerning which the discussion was then waged (E n d e r s VII, 288 sq.), is very unlikely.

[6] While E d . E n g e l h a r d t , Die innere Genesis u. d. Zusammenhang der Marburger, Schwabacher u. Torgauer Artikel, sowie der Augsburg. Conf. in Ztschr. für histor. Theol. 1865, pp. 515-629, was on the right road, T h . B r i e g e r in " Kirchengesch. Studien " (Leipzig, 1888), p. 269 sqq., where the former discoveries are appreciated, has made it highly probable that the

The fact that, contrary to the Elector's demands to report on *doctrine* and ceremonies, it treats only of the latter, is explained by the introductory statements, according to which, as the opponents themselves admitted, the doctrine preached in the electoral territory "was Christian and comforting, and right in itself," and the "controversy had arisen principally on account of several abuses that had arisen through human doctrine and teaching." Hence it was confined to presenting the reasons for abolishing those abuses, but at the close it was stated in case "it is desired to know what else my most clement lord has preached, articles may be presented in which the whole Christian doctrine is properly arranged, so that it may be seen that my most clement lord has suffered no heretical doctrine; but has had the holy gospel of our Lord Christ preached in its utmost purity." At the same time a further recasting of this opinion, which was originally intended only for the Elector for official copy in Augsburg, and quickly jotted down, was planned from the outset, for after the first paragraph we find the remark: " In hanc sententiam prodest proponere præfacionem longam ac rhetoricam."

On April 3rd Luther, Melanchthon and Jonas left Wittenberg, for, as it was stated in the first call on March 14th, they were to accompany the Elector at least as far as Coburg, where they should learn "what should be done at the Diet at Augsburg concerning the presentation of every one's opinion and thought," and whether the preachers were to be admitted.[7] On the way George Spalatin, from Altenburg, John Agricola, from Eisleben, and Kaspar Aquila, from Saalfeld, joined the retinue of the Elector. On April 15th, Good Friday, they reached the boundary of the electoral ter-

---

essay published by F ö r s t e m a n n , I, 68-84, is the document which (according to F ö r s t e m a n n , I, 138) was taken to Augsburg under the title: " Der gelerten zu Wittemberg bedenken," etc., and must be regarded as the sought-for " Torgau Articles." Under this caption, with the articles numbered, see Th. K o l d e , D. Augsburgische Konfess. p. 128 sqq.

[7] F ö r s t e m a n n , I, 44.

ritory in Coburg, and the Elector determined to remain here until after the Easter holidays, awaiting further tidings concerning the coming of the Emperor. Since the original plan, so much desired abroad, to take Luther along to Augsburg,[8] had to be abandoned on account of the imperial ban resting on him, the Elector desired to leave the Reformer in Nuremberg during the Diet, so as to have him at least in a safe place and as near as possible. But the negotiations in regard to this matter failed, since the Nuremberg Council, in its timidity and its anxious care to retain the favor of the Emperor, would not even venture to assure Luther of a free passage.[9] Hence, on April 23rd, he was brought to the fortress of Coburg, while the Elector journeyed onward with his retinue, and reached Augsburg on May 2nd.

While still in Coburg, Melanchthon had begun to put in good style the Torgau Articles, the "Apology" to be presented at the Diet, and to write an introduction[10] to the same, all with the idea that nothing more would need to be done than to defend the abolition of the Roman abuses. But he had hardly arrived in Augsburg when he became convinced that he could not thus limit himself. Before they had received the summons to the Diet, and on the mere information that the Emperor would have the religious controversy discussed at a diet, the Bavarian dukes, in a call dated February 10th, had bidden the theological faculty at Ingolstadt to arrange in an extract all articles that had been preached by Luther for the last twelve years, and to show their discrepancy with the true Christian faith, together with the way in which they could most successfully be

---

[8] Brück in F ö r s t e m a n n , Archiv., p. 17: " Several parties who were interested in the matter solicited the Elector of Saxony to have his electoral highness bring Dr. Luther along to Augsb. on account of the great importance of the matter, as the one whom God had given understanding before all others," etc.

[9] Concerning the transactions with reference to Luther's stay in Nuremberg, cf. T h . K o l d e , Beiträge zur Ref. Gesch. in " Kirchengesch. Studien," dedicated to Reuter, Leipzig, 1888, p. 251 sqq.

[10] Melanchthon to Luther, May 4th, C. R. II, 39 :—" I made the introduction of our apology somewhat more rhetorical, quam Coburgi scripseram.

refuted, so that the dukes might have this document to hand in case of need.[11]

This must have been the external occasion for John Eck of Ingolstadt, to issue a writing dedicated to the Emperor, in which he collected 404 articles of "those who disturb the peace of the Church." In these he first repeats the theses of Luther condemned in the papal bull, also Eck's theses for the disputations at Leipzig, Baden and Bern, and then passages from the writings of Luther, Melanchthon, Zwingli and Carlstadt, wrenched from their context and placed under certain rubrics and put in line with statements of Anabaptists, such as John Denk, Hubmeyer and others. At the same time the author offered to prove in open disputation before the Emperor and the Diet that the theses quoted were unchristian.[12]

Now, there could be no doubt that the writing of defence must also contain articles of *doctrine,* and for this reason, and because the Emperor would have no time to listen to long dissertations, Melanchthon determined to incorporate articles of doctrine, and thus to give the whole more of the character of a *confession.*[13] Thus the apology became a confession of faith, and at least externally the defence of the abolition of abuses was moved to the second place.

The " Marburg Articles " agreed to on October 4th, 1529, at the close of the colloquium, and the articles afterward called "Schwabach Articles,"[14] which were mainly composed by Luther, and which were intended for a common

---

[11] V. A. W i n t e r , Gesch. d. Schicksale d. ev. Lehre in und durch Bayern bewirkt, Munich, 1809, I, 269.

[12] Sub dom. Jhesu et Mariae patrocinio. Articulos 404. partim ad disputationes, Lips., Bad., et Bern. attinentes, etc. Ingolstadii impressum, 1530. quarto.

[13] Melanchthon to Luther, May 11th: " I send you our apology, which is more properly a confession. The Emperor does not care to listen to prolonged discussions, but still I said what I thought would either profit most or be most becoming. With this purpose in mind I composed nearly all the articles of faith. As Eck composed the most diabolical slanders against us I wished to oppose a remedy to them."—C. R. II, 45.

[14] The Marburg and Schwabach Articles in T h . K o l d e , D. Augs. Konf., p. 119 sq. and 123 sq. Cf. in the same. Der Tag von Schleiz u. d. Entstehung d. Schwab. Art. in Beiträge zur Ref. Gesch. Gotha, 1896, p. 94, sqq.

15

basis of faith for the political federation of the evangelical
estates, but which on account of their specifically Wittenberg
coloring were not adopted by the Highland theologians at
the Schwabach convention on October 16th, 1529, could do
service as a pattern for the doctrinal articles. But one cannot fail to observe that the reference to Eck's articles has
also partially determined the selection of the material, and
we may conclude from the apparently surprising rejection of
heresies of the early and mediæval church that Melanchthon
knew how much Eck, in an irritating letter to the Emperor
on March 14th, and in the manuscript copy of his pamphlet
intended for the latter, had heightened his attack by placing
evangelical theses on a par with former heretical positions.[15]

The Exordium written at Coburg was now recast, and, as
Melanchthon reported to Luther, "set more rhetorically."
In a few days the work had progressed so far that as early
as May 11th the Elector was able to send it to Luther with
the wish to have him look it over, and if he desired "to add
to it or omit from it," to make a marginal note of the fact.
And Luther returned it on May 15th and wrote to the Elector:
*"I have read M. Philipp's Apologia: I like it very well, in-
deed, and do not know how I could improve or alter it, and
it would not be proper to do so, for I myself cannot tread so
gently and softly. May Christ our Lord help that it may bear
much and great fruit, as I hope and pray. Amen."*[16] In
spite of his ironical allusion to Melanchthon's well-known
endeavor to give no offence anywhere, he must have intended
to express his full assent to the document; but this does not
exclude the possibility of his having made some marginal
notes.[17] There cannot have been many, of course, since

---

[15] Cf. G. L. P l i t t , Einleit. in d. Augustana, I, 527, sqq.

[16] Melanchthon to Luther, C. R. II, 391. The Elector to Luther E n d e r s
VII, 328. Luther's answer, D e W e t t e , IV, 17.

[17] This would be certain if the "Concepta ermelter Confession durch Dr.
Martin Luther und Philippum Melanchthon seligen gedechtnus mit eigen han-
den corrigirt u. dareingeschrieben," which were claimed to exist in Dresden in
1577 were the same as the concept sent to Luther (Cf. K o l d e Zeitschr. für
K. G. IV, 624 sq.). According to J o h . M a r b a c h , Christtl. u. wahrhaftiger

Melanchthon complains that Luther had not thoroughly examined the articles.[18]

But what was it that Luther saw at the time? The oft-repeated view that the Confession sent him contained only the first 17 articles, the doctrinal ones,[19] is erroneous, for the Elector sends the articles, put into a statement by Luther and the other theologians at Wittenberg, "that are in controversy in religion," and which Melanchthon has " revised and formally expressed," *i. e.,* the whole, and probably in German and in Latin,[20]—as far as it was then formulated. How much that was, can be only partly determined, since the manuscript sent Luther, or a copy of it, has not been preserved. It surely contained Melanchthon's Introduction, for the author of it considered it so important that he would have liked to present it to Luther in person.[21] Of the doctrinal articles, Art. 20 (Of Faith and Good Works) was entirely lacking, and so was Art. 21 (Of Invocation of the Saints); but it is still more important to know that Luther saw hardly one article in the form in which the Confession was afterward presented. For before the articles had come back from Luther Melanchthon had continued to work on them, as he writes to Luther on May 22nd; nay more, he found something to alter every day. We learn at the same time, that he replaced Art.

Unterricht, etc., Strassburg (1565), p. 149, Luther is said to have added to the 10th article the words " et improbant secus docentes." This cannot be proven : but is slightly supported by a remark of Melanchthon on the signature of the Landgrave : " He subscribed the Confession for us in which is also the article concerning the Lord's Supper, near Luther's sentence."—C. R. II, 142. As Melanchthon at that time was as strenuously opposed to the Zwinglians as Luther, the remark is at least striking.

[18] " I wish you had read through the articles of faith, and if you thought there is no mistake in them, we shall treat of the rest at some time." To Luther on May 22nd, C. R. II, 60, K n a a k e ' s assertion that then these articles had not come back, is erroneous, since Melanchthon's letter is the reply to Luther's of May 15th (E n d e r s VII, 334), and reached Augsburg on the same day as that of the Elector. Only so much is conceivable, that Melanchthon had not yet examined the articles as they came back from Luther since the messenger arrived between writings.

[19] K n a a k e 75. E n d e r s VII, 331.

[20] T h . K o l d e , Die älteste Redaktion, p. 73 sq.

[21] " I shall bring the Introduction in a short time, or, if the Prince does not permit it, will send it." To Luther, May 4th, C. R. II, 39 sq.

27 (Of Vows), which seemed too scant, by a fuller one, and was busy also working over the 28th article.[22] This article, which then treated De Potestate Clavium, and also of the Power of the Pope, is preserved to us in the original form in which Luther saw it;[23] but through the influence of Chancellor Brück, who, as the Nuremberg delegates report, took a vivid interest in the alterations,[24] it received an essentially different form. It turned into an article De Potestate Ecclesiastica. There was nothing more said of the power of the Pope,[25] and it was no longer found necessary *"to submissively please his imperial majesty, and for certain reasons to praise the papacy,"* [26] for—and Melanchthon expressed this principle quite harmlessly to Luther—the articles ought to be adapted to circumstances (or the prevailing condition), and the Saxon counsellors desired to have the document *"formulated in such a way that there was no getting out of hearing the argument."* [27]

As soon as they had arrived in Augsburg, they had learned that they had overestimated the Emperor's peaceful intentions, which were seemingly guaranteed by the summons to the Diet, and that the papal legate, Lorenzo Campeggi, George of Saxony, and other princes of Roman propensities, who had journeyed to meet the Emperor at Innsbrück, had made their influence felt against the Protestants. In order to weaken the influence of the Eckian calumnies, and to testify to his own orthodoxy and his opposition to the "Sacramentarians," the Elector had under the utmost secrecy in the first days of his stay in Augsburg sent a poor transla-

---

[22] We change much of the Apology daily, etc., C. R. II, 60.   Cf. p. 71.

[23] F ö r s t e m a n n I, 87 sqq.

[24] On May 24th the Nuremberg delegates write (C. R. II, 62) : " The Saxon Counsel has been returned by Dr. Luther ; but Dr. Brück, the old chancellor, has to recast it from beginning to end."

[25] T h . K o l d e , Älteste Redaktion, p. 63 sq.

[26] Thus the Strassburg delegates reported 1537 from the Diet of Schmalkald. T h . K o l d e , Analecta Lutherana. Gotha. 1883, p. 297.

[27] C. R. II, 71.

tion of the Schwabach articles to the Emperor.[28] But he had small success with it, for Charles V. demanded that Evangelical preaching be prohibited in Augsburg.

Under these conditions the *oldest* draft of the Confession (so far known to us) was produced. It was received by the Nuremberg delegates May 31st, and, after they had also received the preface or introduction, was sent home by them on June 3rd, with the remark: *"It still lacks an article or two at the end, besides the resolution still being worked upon by the Saxon theologians."* The text in question was in Latin, but is known to us only through a German version prepared for the Nuremberg Council by Jerome Baumgartner. At any rate, we learn from it how far the Confession had progressed in scope and contents by the end of May.[29]

Following Melanchthon's Introduction, which was supposed to have been lost, and of which special mention will be made, comes the Confession itself, with its two chief divisions: *"the articles of faith"* and the *"disputed articles."* Hence the main outline and the subjects treated are (aside from the fact that the articles on "faith and good works" and on the "invocation of saints" are still wanting) the same as every one knows them from the completed confession. But in the framing of the separate parts there is at times quite a considerable difference, and the arrangement of the separate articles of faith then extant is altogether different.

Following the first article of God, the second of original sin, the third of the Son of God, *who justifies and sanctifies through the Holy Ghost,* comes a fourth, corresponding to the later fifth article (the office of teaching the Gospel), on *obtaining the Holy Ghost* through the Word and the Sacraments. The article on Justification does not come until the

---

[28] Th. Brieger, in Kirchengesch. Studien, p. 392. C. Stange, Kurf. Johanns Glaubensbekenntniss vom Mai 1530. Theol. Stud. u. Kritiken. 1903, p. 459 sqq. Ehses, Röm. Quartalschrift. XVII (1903), p. 385.

[29] Kolde, Älteste Redaktion, p. 4, sqq.

fifth place, and, in comparison with the later form in a frame somewhat less dogmatical in which the doctrine of the imputatio (Hanc fidem imputat Deus pro justitia coram Deo) is not yet clearly expressed. In article 6 at that time more stress was laid on the "through grace," later more on the "faith." The later articles 7 and 8, which stand in essentially the same form, are there still put together in *one* article, and clearly show that Melanchthon's endeavor was to treat not of the Church, but of the " unity of the Church."[30] The article on baptism was then an article on the necessity of *infant baptism,* while the one on the Lord's Supper had its present form. The later article 11, de confessione, was intended to treat of private absolution. This was followed with slight variations and changes of order by the articles on repentance and the use of the sacraments, and then (in an order which was changed soon after) the 13th article of human ordinances, of the ordo ecclesiasticus (evidently omitted from the manuscript) and (15) of civil affairs. The following, 16th, which was later changed to the 17th, "of the second coming of Christ," originally treated in by no means biblical fashion of the resurrection of the dead ("that all deceased persons shall be awakened with that same body of theirs in which they had died"), turned against the doctrine of the "followers of Origen and the Anabaptists" of the ultimate redemption of the damned and the devils, and rejects, besides Chiliasm, specially those who, ("in Jewish manner teach that the promise of the possession of the Promised Land is to be considered in a corporeal sense").[31] This is followed by the articles on the Freedom of the Will and the Summary, with their wording only slightly different from the final form.

The second part is opened in somewhat different form and with a renewed emphasis on the assertion that no article of faith has been departed from, by the same thoughts that

[30] T h . K o l d e , D. Augsb. Konfession, p. 32.
[31] T h . K o l d e , D. älteste Redaktion, p. 54 sq.

Melanchthon in the last revision placed partly in the Summary. The *material* differences in the " disputed articles " are not so great in comparison with the later form (even the Nuremberg text shows the previously mentioned recasting of the (28th) article on "The Power of the Keys" to the "Power of the Church"), but they are more numerous, a thing into which we need not enter here.[32] It is characteristic, that Melanchthon has the greatest trust in the Emperor even yet, and yields to the temptation in the article on the Marriage of Priests [33] to address an apostrophe to him. Another characteristic thing is the great severity against the Sacramentarians. Thus we read at the close of the then very short article on the Mass, which, however, contained a very caustic objection to Masses for the Dead, which was afterward suppressed, the following remark: "In this connection we also condemn the unchristian teaching which denies that the body and blood of Christ are truly present." [34]

But this earliest redaction only assumes full significance in connection with Melanchthon's Introduction. If Eck's attacks had moved him to convert the "Apology" into a confession, he all the more readily seized upon the opportunity to give the detailed Introduction, which must be considered an integral part of the whole Saxon Counsel, the character of a *defense of his Elector.*

Next to God, the latter places his full trust in the ever manifest goodness and grace of the Emperor, who had ever sought only the peace of Europe, and had shown nothing but clemency in the religious controversies, so that he is unjustly accused of cruelty, and had even now declared his readiness to inquire into the matter. And, as can be learned from Ps. 2: 10, there is nothing more well pleasing to God than if the Emperor would use all his power toward a unifi-

---

[32] T h . K o l d e , D. älteste Redaktion, p. 57 sq.

[33] *Ib.,* p. 18.

[34] *Ib.,* pp. 19 and 59.

[35] *Ib.,* p. 20.

cation of Christendom, just as formerly Theodoric, Charlemagne and Henry II., to whom Charles V. is in no wise inferior in virtues and piety, and whom he far surpasses in power and glory.

Before, then, discussing the doctrine preached in the electorate, it must be shown that the Elector did not foster this new doctrine from malign purpose. He and his brother Frederick have through all their lives been inclined to the Christian religion and faith, and have built and adorned churches and institutions partly at their own expense. They have always preserved allegiance to the Roman emperors, and in all affairs of the empire have rendered considerable help in money and armature. They have never entered into treaties with foreign nations or the enemies of the Empire, nor given any occasion for discord, but rather have shown patience in the interest of peace, and more than once "by their diligence and pains have brought others who were always armed, to peace and quiet." No one could believe that the Elector, without great reason, would have gotten himself and his family into such great danger; but the matter had proceeded from the many pious souls, who were hindered by the many human ordinances and the daily increasing abuses, and the fact that nothing more was said about repentance and the free grace offered, not for the sake of our own merit, but the faith in Christ.

Then it is told how the preaching of indulgences had induced Luther to contradict "scholastically" and not before the people, and without abusing the papacy, in "several pamphlets;" but that his opponents, whom he was obliged to answer, had created a great controversy. Since then many had found great delight in his salutary and comforting doctrine of repentance, it would have been contrary to conscience to do anything against the adherents of this doctrine, inasmuch as if the learned preachers had been removed, the perversion of doctrine would have become much worse. For even before Luther had written anything, obnoxious and erroneous doctrine had originated, and would have caused dangerous innovation and revolt, had not Luther interposed. Thus many heresies against the holy sacrament had been suppressed; also the doctrine of the Anabaptists ("which had started before Luther") against possession of temporal property, judgment and power of the authorities, and against all civil order, would have spread much further had not the hearts of men been strengthened by evangelical teaching. But the matter had been made obnoxious by the common rumor that the evangelical people had done away with all ceremonies and had overthrown all spiritual order. But it could be truthfully said that in all Germany the mass (during which, beside the Latin singing, there were also German hymns) was observed according to the usual custom, with no greater fear of God than in the Electorate of Saxony. And in order to prove the unfoundedness of assertions to the contrary, Melanchthon seeks to draw a picture of the ecclesiastical order in Saxony. He points to the frequent participation in the Lord's Supper by the people, the retention of confession, the praise of the power of the Keys in preaching, the maintenance of schools, etc., and above all to the very useful observance once diligently maintained and then dropped through laziness of pastors and people, and by which an effort was now made in Saxony to lead the children to a Christian understanding of faith and doctrine, namely, the Catechism and Christian instruction.

Hence the order of the Church was "for the most part in accordance with ancient custom and usage of the Roman Church according to the instruction of the holy teachers." And if the Bishops who persecuted the Evangelical people on account of the marriage of priests, etc., were a little inclined to suffer such matters no one would have any occasion to lament that the order of the Church is broken. They maintained without reason that the Evangelical people aimed at suppressing spiritual power. If the bishops gave up a few improper and oppressive innovations, they would suffer no

loss of power and glory, and would not need to worry about
their possessions, "although some others before our time repeatedly undertook under the semblance of a reformation to
deprive the clerics of their possessions." The poverty of the
bishops in itself was of no advantage to the Church. The
advantage lay in their preaching the gospel purely and without error. "Thus we teach," says the close, "to consider all
civil commands and orders under secular and spiritual power
as an order of God, for the sake of peace and unity. There has
never been a reformation undertaken so utterly without violence as this one, as it is manifest that others have been
brought to peace through ours, though they were already in
arms."

Hence the *Saxon Counsel,* which nowhere paid attention to
the general condition of Evangelical believers, and never
said a word about the question of a council, was a private
confession in the full sense of the word. What the Elector
and his theologians strive for, is to put into the most favorable light the ecclesiastical conditions in their own country (though it be at the expense of others) and their own
loyalty, and also, above all things, to maintain peace in their
own land. We must, of course, remember that Melanchthon
and all the Wittenbergians were from the beginning opposed
to the efforts for confederation.

But the Emperor, according to the official invitation, desired
to hear the opinion of *everybody* and other estates had also
made preparations to this effect, notably Strasburg, Reutlingen, Ulm, Constance, Heilbronn.[36] On the mere tidings of
the impending Diet, Margrave George, of Brandenburg, had
as early as 1530 demanded of his principal pastors to deliver
an opinion in "untwisted" words on the true doctrine and

---

[36] S t r a s s b u r g : T h . K e i m , Schwäb. Ref. Gesch. Tübingen 1855, p.
149.—R e u t l i n g e n : G a y l e r , Hist. Denkwürdigkeiten der ehem. freien
Reichsstadt Reutlingen. Reutlingen, 1840, p. 350 sq.—U l m : G . E n g e l-
h a a f , Deutsche Geschichte im 16. Jahrh. Vol. II. Leipzig, 1892, p. 142 sq.,
und T h . K o l d e , Älteste Redak., p. 183.—C o n s t a n c e : J o h n F i c k e r ,
Das Konst. Bekennt. für d. Reichstag zu Augsb., 1530 (Theo. Abhandl. für H.
J. Holtzmann) Tübingen, 1902.—H e i l b r o n n : D u n c k e r , Analekten zur
Ref. Gesch. Heilbronns ZKG. XXV, p. 311 sqq.

the justification for abolishing abuses. But we do not learn
that any attempt was made upon the basis of the individual
opinions received to elaborate a confession in the name of
the princes; on the contrary, the Margrave intended from the
start to confer with Nuremberg, Saxony, and those who were
in harmony with him concerning the sacrament. This probably from the beginning was the standpoint of Nuremberg,
for, although an opinion had been there elaborated, the
Nuremberg delegates to the Diet, Christopher v. Kress and
Clement Volkamer, had received orders to remain in
close touch with the Saxons.[37] The Landgrave of Hessen,
who was utterly opposed to having the question of religion
decided at the Diet, does not seem to have prepared any confession. Nevertheless, he was probably the first, who perhaps unofficially in conversation with the Saxon theologians
had uttered the desire to unite with the Saxon Confession.
The same was done perhaps soon after the arrival of the
Margrave, on May 29th, by the Ansbach councillors and the
delegates of Reutlingen and Nuremberg.[38]

But the old Elector was hard to deal with. He did not
care for a confederation. He wished to maintain his isolation, and above all things would brook no interference. To
the Nuremberg delegates he sent word through the Chancellor
Brück: " His electoral Grace did not like many councillors
in such an affair, for the devil," these were his words, "was
fond of too much counsel." [39] But finally they at least on their
request obtained the copy previously mentioned. But the negotiations did not advance. As late as June 8th the Brandenburg Chancellor Vogler and Kress complain that the Confession was made only in the name of the Elector, for, as
Melanchthon had done in the name of the Elector, "the introduction might separately specify where it could not be done

---

[37] T h . K o l d e , Andreas Althamer, Erlangen, 1895, pp. 45, 65. C.
S c h o r n b a u m , Zur Politik des Markgrafen Georg von Brandenburg,
München, 1906, pp. 118 sq. and 426 sqq.

[38] T h . K o l d e , Älteste Redaktion. p. 40 sq.

[39] C. R., II, 53.

in common, what every one had done for H. I. M." [40]   It is in
this sense that the Nurembergians and the Margrave desired
to have Melanchthon's Introduction altered. The Landgrave's
views were different. As appears from his correspondence [41]
carried on with Melanchthon, May 11th-13th, he believed that
a prerequisite for a confederation was fraternalism (with the
Highland theologians) and the invitation to a council, *i. e.,*
he persisted in the early demands of the Evangelical party,
and declined to leave the decision with the Emperor and the
Diet as Melanchthon and the Elector desired to do.

In the meantime Melanchthon had continued to work on
the Confession. This is borne out by the German text, [42] preserved in Spalatin's hand, and which has been produced gradually. This for the greater part must be assigned to the
first half of June, and approaches the one finally adopted,
and in its alterations here and there plainly shows the influence of the negotiations with the Landgrave. [43]

By June 15th the Saxon court had determined upon the
principle of admitting other estates to the confession; for the
German text, which on this day was sent to Nuremberg, and
in which appears for the first time the twentieth article "On
Faith and Good Works," which was not yet completed in the
Latin, contained at the place where the Latin said that in the
Electorate of Saxony this or that was preached, "a common
word which can be applied to all estates;" but neither the Nurembergians nor the Margrave had received a definite answer
up to this time. [44]   The decision followed soon after.

---

[40] C. R., II, 88 sq.   [41] *Ib.*, 92 sqq.

[42] F ö r s t e m a n n, Urkundenbuch I, 310, and K o l d e, Älteste Red. p. 71.

[43] Thus the very caustic passage against the Sacramentarians (Älteste Red.
p. 20 etc.) is omitted and replaced by a milder but not final form. On the
other hand, Melanchthon still puts his greatest trust in the Emperor, and in
the article on the marriage of priests praises him as a special lover of chastity
(F ö r s t e m a n n p. 329 sq.).

[44] C. R. II, p. 105. (In Spalatin's copy the article on " Faith and Good
Works " is inserted later.) The article on the " Invocation of Saints " was
still wanting.   This non-extant Nuremberg German text must have had the
same form of the "Articles of Faith " as the so-called I Ansbach Manuscript in
F ö r s t e m a n n, Urkundenbuch I, 341 sq. (And the I Hannoverian. Cf.
T s c h a c k e r t in Archiv f. Ref. Gesch. II, 69 sqq.) only that the Ansbacher
manuscript, which is several days older, does not yet contain the 20th article.

On June 15th the Emperor had entered Augsburg. He at once demanded that the princes should take part in the Corpus Christi procession and renewed his demand to desist from preaching the Gospel. The magnitude of the danger in which they found themselves, especially after the death at Innsbrück, on June 4th, of the High Chancellor Mercurinus Gattinara, who was considered a lover of peace, had been the first thing to bring the evangelical princes together. The Elector, the Margrave, Duke Ernest of Lüneburg, and the Landgrave, who had been commanded by the Emperor upon his arrival in Augsburg to meet him in a separate apartment, had in common maintained their evangelical standpoint in the matter of preaching and the procession,[45] and in the opinion delivered on June 16th by the Brandenburg Chancellor Vogler, who favors the plan of delivering the Articles of Faith at once to the Emperor in order to convince him of the orthodoxy of the Protestants, the *princes,* including Duke Francis of Lüneburg, already appear as a closed party.[46]

The first one who was accepted as a fellow-confessor was undoubtedly the Margrave, for from him and the Elector together the Nurembergians, on June 18th, received the promise to "receive them together with their graces in this matter." [47] At the same time, although nothing direct is recorded on this point, Duke Ernest of Lüneburg, Duke Wolf of Anhalt and the city of Reutlingen must also have been admitted, while the negotiations with the Landgrave were not yet concluded. A Latin text of the Articles of Faith, which was probably sent him during this time, and which must have been of prime importance to him on account of his position in reference to the Zwinglians, shows the final form with but few variations, and contains the newly added article (probably first written in Latin) on the "Invocation of the Saints."[48]

[45] *Ib.,* 106. T h . K o l d e , Martin Luther II, 342.

[46] F ö r s t e m a n n , Urkundenbuch I, 215.

[47] C. R. II, 112.

[48] See the French text based on the Latin Cassel, (now Marburg) manuscript in F ö r s t e m a n n 1, 357. Älteste Red., p. 69.

But now a memorable episode occurred. The unexpectedly harsh conduct of the Emperor in the matter of the Corpus Christi procession and of preaching had made an overwhelming impression on the faint-hearted Melanchthon. Even before, he had been busy to impress upon influential personalities of the opposite party, his own love of peace, the insignificance of the departure from the Roman church in doctrine and usages, and not the least the fact that he had nothing in common with the hated Zwinglians. Now, after the arrival of the Emperor, in his consuming anxiety and urgent desire to settle the matter as soon as possible, he at once sought to get in touch with two imperial secretaries.[49]

One of them, Cornelius Schepper, a Netherlander, who was very reticent, only confirmed his fear that the Emperor was determined to proceed against the Lutherans. As for the other, Lorenzo Valdés, a Spaniard, he succeeded in convincing him of the thing which at the time appeared most important to Melanchthon, that the matter was not by far so difficult, and that the main issues were the twofold form of the sacrament, the marriage of priests and the abolishment of private masses. This man made a report to the Emperor, who was long desirous of effecting harmony without an extended examination and discussion, and now transmitted Melanchthon's presentations to Cardinal Campeggi. Since the latter did not pronounce himself unfavorably, Melanchthon, on June 18th, received from Valdés the Emperor's command to present the controversial points in briefest and least diffuse form, "in order to be able to consider the matter, if possible, in all privacy and quiet." Melanchthon thereupon, as he informed the Nuremberg delegates on June 19th, believed momentarily that they would be able to desist from

---

[49] Th. Kolde, Anal. Lutherana 136, 140, C. R. II, 118 sq. 122. For the initiative of Melanchthon and the details of the transactions and their appreciation (against Brieger's contrary conception, Zur Gesch. d. Augsb. Reichstags von 1530, Leipzig, 1903, Progr.) see Kolde, Älteste Red., 76 sqq.

presenting the Confession and delayed finishing it. But before he continued his negotiations, he considered it advisable to confer with Chancellor Brück and with other theologians concerning the matters to present to the Emperor. This was on June 21st, on the day following the official opening of the Diet. The result was the rejection of Melanchthon's independent negotiations, which would have given up the legal foundation of the invitation, and a resolution was adopted the same day now to draw into the deliberation the councillors and theologians of the separate estates and complete a common Confession.

Now, in connection with the transactions concerning the final accession of the Landgrave, the matter of the Introduction and the final "presentation" must have been decided. The Landgrave himself had in the meantime reached the conclusion that it would not be possible to effect a union with the Swiss theologians.[50] On the other hand, it had become evident, how dangerous it would be to leave the decision to the Emperor and the Diet as Melanchthon and the Saxons desired, and that only the simultaneous falling back upon the demand for a council, as Hessen emphasized, could guarantee safe protection. Besides the original desire of the Margrave and the Nurembergians to see their services to the Emperor and the country brought forward in the Introduction as Melanchthon had done for Saxony, proved to be impracticable even for formal reasons. Thus a compromise was effected. *Melanchthon's Introduction was completely laid aside.* In its place was put a preface edited in German by the Chancellor Brück, and translated into Latin by Justus Jonas.[51] At the same time this preface omitted (as the

---

[50] This "fraternalism" he had given up by signing the explanation of the Ev. princes in the preaching question, June 17th (F ö r s t e m a n n I, 288. Cf. T h . K o l d e , Älteste Red., p. 45).

[51] That the German preface derives from Brück and was translated into Latin by Justus Jonas, is proven by a marginal note of the latter (?) in a copy of the first edition of the Augustana, 1531, in the Wittenberg -Theol. Seminary: "Translated from Brück's German text by Justus Jonas." Cf. F ö r s t e m a n n I, p. 460.

Landgrave, in the midst of his political relations to the Swiss and Highlanders, could hardly do otherwise than demand) all the more or less open attacks of Melanchthon's Introduction, upon the Sacramentarians and the declarations upon the jurisdiction of the bishops, which could hardly be harmonized with the positions assumed at the last Diet of Spires. Referring in a businesslike way to the invitation to a diet, the explanation is given that the Evangelical estates hereby " deliver their opinion and judgment on account of errors, schisms and abuses," and are ready, if the other estates did the same (of which Melanchthon's Introduction made no mention), to discuss with them "in proper and legitimate manner." And quite in accordance with the view of the Landgrave, mention was made of the Diet transactions of later years, and the Emperor's declaration not to permit the Diet to legislate in matters of religion, but to demand a council of the Pope. For this reason the Evangelical estates " superfluously " offer to come to a free Christian council, by renewing their former appeal to one. Thereby this offer, the summing up of their demands and standpoints, for which the Nurembergians had always waited, and which originally was to have been put at the close, was put in the introduction where it belonged.[52]

But we do not know exactly when the introduction was finished, though it probably was in the final consultation on Thursday, June 23rd. This was participated in by the Elector of Saxony, the Landgrave of Hessen, the Margrave of Brandenburg, the Dukes of Lüneburg, the representatives of Nuremberg and Reutlingen, as well as their counsellors and no less than twelve theologians.[53] As for the Confession, Melanchthon altered and filed it up to the last, and put things more mildly, because he had learned to his anxiety that the before-mentioned imperial secretary, Valdés, whom he had

---

[52] See K o l d e , Älteste Red., pp. 45 sq.

[53] Cf. the Report of the Nuremberg delegates, C. R. II, 127 sq. where Prince Wolfg. of Anhalt is not mentioned, nor during the presentation.

permitted to look at it, had found it much too caustic. It was once more discussed and reviewed, during which process several individual points received special consideration. Melanchthon desired very much to grant full jurisdiction to the bishops, as he had done in his introduction; but he could not accomplish his purpose.[54] That was probably the time when, if not earlier, in the article on the sacrament in either kind (22nd) the paragraph against processions with the host must have been added. The statements against the sacramentarians, as already stated, were partly omitted and partly softened down. The attempt (which was probably made) in the interest of the Highland theologians, who were willing to join only if Article 10 were omitted, to make a change in the statements about the Lord's Supper, was futile. The 10th article kept its form to the sorrow of the Landgrave. But he yielded.[55] The following finally signed: Elector John, of Saxony; Margrave Georg, of Brandenburg; Duke Ernest, of Brunswick-Lunenburg; Landgrave Philipp, of Hessen; Prince Wolfgang, of Anhalt; the representatives of the cities Nuremberg and Reutlingen, and probably also Elector John Frederick and Duke Francis, of Lüneburg.[56]

Thus the Confession was at last completed June 23rd. As early as the 24th, after a postponement[57] had in vain been asked through the Cardinal of Mayence, for the purpose of gaining time to produce a clean copy, it was to have been presented in the Diet. But negotiations with the papal legate

---

[54] Mel. to Camerarius on June 19th (?), C. R. II, 119: " I yield the whole jurisdiction, etc., to the bishops, etc." To the same (June 26, C. R. II, 140): " I changed and recast daily " etc. Jonas to Luther, June 30th (E n d e r s VIII, 67): " Our Master Philipp is marching with the best disposition cautiously and carefully. . . . And we have also had some strife about the power and jurisdiction of the bishops, which I shall whisper about to you."

[55] K o l d e , Älteste Red., p. 66: The Argentinenses solicited rather often to be received without the article of the sacrament; but the princes were unwilling. V i r c k , Polit. Korresp. d. Stadt Strassburg (Strassburg, 1882), I, 458. Also K o l d e , Anal. Luth., 125 and C. R. II, 97 sqq.

[56] K ö l l n e r , Symbolik I, 201. B r ü c k , p. 28. J. T. M ü l l e r , p. 585,

[57] K o l d e , Neue Augustanastudien. Neue Kirchl. Zeitschr. XVII (1906), p. 737 sqq.
16

and a long presentation of the representatives of Karinthia and Krain on the Turkish danger had taken up so much time that the Emperor and his counsellors declared it would not be necessary to read the Confession, and desired to have it merely presented. But the Evangelical Estates,[58] who were anxious to confess their faith publicly in view of the public accusations of their opponents, insisted on the privilege of reading it, which had been previously granted them, and the eloquence of their spokesman, Chancellor Brück, finally prevailed, and the privilege was granted, the time for the reading being fixed for the next day.

Not in the council room (the "House"), where the proceedings of the Diet usually took place, but in the " Palace in the lower large apartment" (these are the words of the imperial herald, Kaspar Sturm), *i. e.,* in the chapter-room of the episcopal palace, where the Emperor sojourned, was the meeting held, on Saturday, June 25th, at 3 P. M. The two Saxon chancellors, Dr. Greg. Brück and Dr. Chr. Beyer, one with the Latin, the other with the German copy of the Confession, entered the middle space, while the Evangelical Estates, as many as had the courage to make an open confession of the evangelical cause, arose from their seats. The Emperor desired to hear the Latin copy read. But after Elector John had reminded him that the Diet was held on German soil, and expressed his hope to have the Emperor permit the reading in German, the permission was granted.[59]

Thereupon Dr. Beyer read the Confession. It took about two hours, but he read so clearly and distinctly that the many who had not gained admittance, and stood in the outside court, understood every word.[60] Then the two copies were presented. The Latin one was taken by the Emperor him-

---

[58] Jonas to Luther, in E n d e r s , VIII, 26. B r ü c k , p. 52. C. R. II, 128.

[59] C o e l e s t i n, Hist. Comitiorum, in S e c k e n d o r f II, 170.

[60] The impression on the opponents, C. R. II, 143, 145, 150, 154. E n d e r s , VIII, 66 sqq. D o b e l , Memmingen IV, 40. B i n t e r i m , Der Reichstag zu Augsb., etc., Düsseldorf, 1844.

self; the German he gave to the imperial Chancellor, the Elector of Mayence,[61] and at the same time prohibited the publication of the Confession.

Immediately after the presentation a complete copy was sent to Luther.[62] Although he would surely have expressed many things otherwise, and probably more sharply, and found too great concessions in it (Pro mea persona, plus satis, cessum est in ista Apologia, see Enders, viii, 42), and missed clear statements on purgatory, worship of saints, and especially on "the Pope as the Antichrist," he nevertheless gave the same full approval to the work as a whole, as he had done to the section he had seen before, and saw in it a fulfilment of Ps. 119: 46, the word of Scripture, which the first copies printed in Augsburg and then regularly all printed copies bore as a motto. And once, later on, he actually said: Catechismus, tabulæ, Confessio Augustana mea,[63] which, of course, must be looked upon only as a most emphatic assent to the contents of the Confession. He had taken part in the elaboration of the Torgau articles, and it is not to be doubted that Melanchthon had discussed with him before the Diet, all other matters that might yet enter into consideration.[64] Neither is there any doubt that in the last redaction of the Articles of Faith he reached back to the Marburg and Schwabach articles of Luther; but Luther's direct participation in the framing of the Confession was very slight. Nevertheless, we cannot say, as has been said repeatedly and without proof, that un-Lutheran or Melanchthonian ideas in the stricter sense have come into it.

---

[61] S p a l a t i n , Annalen ed. Cyprian p. 139. S e c k e n d o r f II, 170. J. T. M ü l l e r, 587. K o l d e , Neue Aug. Studien, N. K. Z. S., XVII, p. 738.

[62] C. R. II, 140. E n d e r s , VIII, 33.

[63] This is the original form of the Tabletalk in K r o k e r , Leipzig, 1903.

[64] Melanchthon to Luther, June 27th, 1530, *C. R.* II, 146. E n d e r s VIII, 39: "The things were deliberated before, as you know, but they always turn out otherwise in battle-line." To Camerarius Aug. 27th (*C. R.* II, 334) : "We have so far granted nothing to the adversaries, besides those things which Luther thought ought to be rendered, the matter being well and carefully deliberated before the meeting." *Cp.* T h . K o l d e . *Älteste Red.,* p. 74 sq.

CHAPTER XVI.

THE LUTHERAN CONFESSION.

MELANCHTHON'S UNSUCCESSFUL ATTEMPTS AS A DIPLOMATIST. KOLDE'S ESSAY.

Melanchthon at Augsburg—Characterized by Kolde—Brieger's Defense of Melanchthon—Why Brieger is Wrong—The Documentary Evidence—Melanchthon's Lack of Sympathy with the Hated Zwinglians—Was the final Completion of the Confession begun before June 21st?—Brieger says it was—Kolde's
Reply—Melanchthon's Negotiations with Rome Rejected—The Consequences
of their Rejection—Melanchthon's Four Points as Formulated by Valdés.

AMONG the unpleasant episodes in the life of Melanchthon that have been rocks of offence for many, must
be mentioned his peculiar conduct in the transactions with
the imperial secretary, Alphonso Valdés, and the papal
legate, Lorenzo Campeggi, during the Diet of Augsburg.
Even in more recent times caustic judgment has been passed
upon the episode, and I, too, on the basis of renewed investigations and with all endeavor to be just to him, or rather
(to speak correctly) to understand him, could not refrain
from concluding that Melanchthon (to confine ourselves first
to his relations with Valdés) lost heart completely in the face
of the menacing condition into which the Evangelical party
was thrown unexpectedly right after the arrival of the Emperor; that he, for his own person, entered into private negotiations with the imperial secretaries, and during the course
of these negotiations persuaded himself that perhaps it would

not become necessary to present a confession, and that, there-fore, he dallied with its completion.[1]

While a number of distinguished investigators assented to these conclusions, or independently reached the same re-sults,[2] Th. Brieger more recently opposed them. In a mono-graph entitled "Zur Geschichte des Augsburger Reichstages von, 1530,"[3] he critically reviewed in his well-known, ex-tremely careful manner the negotiations with Valdés (and Campeggi), and reached results, which, if they were conclu-sive, would be of no mean importance to the history of the formation of the Confession, and which at any rate compel a new investigation of the matter.

His opinion, to preface the most important points, is this: 1. The negotiations of Melanchthon with the imperial secre-taries were opened by them and not by Melanchthon. (On this point Brieger returns to the view formerly defended by Maurenbrecher.[4]) 2. The negotiations were carried on by Melanchthon, not upon his own authority, but with the con-sent of the Elector's counsellors. 3. If Melanchthon replies to the Nuremberg delegates who were urging the presenta-tion of the complete confession, "the matter will probably not come to such a far-reaching action, but will be withdrawn and settled more briefly," it must not be understood that he intended in accordance with the Emperor's wishes to accom-plish a compromise on the quiet, and if possible, without "verbose public hearing and discussion," but that it has refer-ence to the proposal made by the Margrave's chancellor, Vog-ler (who, in order to change the Emperor's intention in re-

---

[1] Cf. T h . K o l d e , M. Luther II, 343. Also K o l d e , Die Augsb. Conf., p. 7. Prot. Realencykl. II, 245. Sharper and not always just, V i r c k , Melanchthon's polit. Stellung auf. d. Reichstage zu Augsb. Z. K. G. IX (1888), pp. 92 seq.

[2] Cf. F r . v . B e z o l d , Gesch. d. deutsch. Ref. Berlin, 1890, p. 621. K a w - e r a u , Lehrbuch d. Kirchengesch. III (Reform. u. Gengenref. 2 A.) 1899, p. 97. K a r l M ü l l e r , Kirchengesch. II, 2. Freiburg 1902, p. 372 seq. G e o r g E l l i n g e r , Phil. Melanchthon. Berlin, 1902, pp. 268 seq.

[3] Leipzig, 1903. Programm.

[4] W i l h . M a u r e n b r e c h e r , Gesch. d. Kath. Ref. I, Nördlingen, 1880, pp. 287 seq.

gard to the matter of preaching, advised, on June 16th, "to present to him as an intermediate action the *Articles of Faith*"), and that the briefest possible confession which he had in mind was in reality this confession which was composed of only 19 articles, and is still extant in the Ansbach manuscript and other copies from the same period. Hence the completion of the manuscript was not delayed even for a day, and Melanchthon is to be exonerated from every charge of indecision.

Brieger's acute presentation, from which, as always in his works, much can be learned, at first sight looks very convincing on account of its logical form of statement; but a careful investigation of his argument must lead to the opposite view, as is to be shown in the following:[5]

Immediately upon the Emperor's entrance into Augsburg we find Melanchthon, according to authentic reports, in negotiation[6] with the imperial secretary, Alphonso Valdés.[7]

How did he come to do so?

Brieger, as is elsewhere stated,[8] considers it indubitable that these negotiations were begun not by Melanchthon, but by the followers of the Emperor: whether Valdés, the ardent admirer of Erasmus, independently entered into correspondence with the Wittenberg Humanist, and the Emperor then made use of the naturally resulting opportunity to question Melanchthon, and through him to influence the treatment of the religious matter; or whether, as is more probable, the imperial secretary from the beginning acted under orders from his lord, who by all means wished to settle the religious question "in private and in quiet," rather than to have it treated at the Diet in the manner offered in his call to a diet, viz., to

---

[5] I would note the following was ready in first draft, before I received new material in the "First Draft of the Augustana."

[6] Will be treated below.

[7] Compare on him and related literature the article of E d . B ö h m e r , Prot. Realencykl. 2 A. Vol. 16, 276 seq. The article lacks clearness and overestimates Valdés' love of peace.

[8] See Chap. XVII of this work.

hear the "opinion and judgment" of both sides, and then to effect a compromise (p. 5).

Let us look at the situation. We know that under Campeggi's influence and that of Duke George of Saxony, and other Catholic princes, and perhaps also under the impression caused by John Eck's challenge, the disposition of the Emperor toward the Evangelical party had become quite different from what it appeared to be in the call to the Diet. We know further that the secret presentation of his personal Confession of Faith (which was only a poor Latin paraphrase of the Schwabach Articles) had met with no success at the imperial court, and that the Emperor, while still at Innsbrück, demanded that evangelical preaching be stopped.

When Luther's sharp pamphlet, "Vermahnung an die Geistlichen versammelt auf dem Reichstag zu Augsburg,"[9] appeared, it only added oil to the fuel. It had hardly reached Augsburg, June 7th, when Jacob Sturm sent it to Strassburg; it was at once made known at the Emperor's court, and the Emperor commanded that it be prohibited in Augsburg.[10] Now came the Emperor himself. With him came the demand that the Protestants should take part in the Corpus Christi processions, and the renewal of the prohibition to preach, and all that, in the evident interest not only to do justice to the wishes of Campeggi, but also to intimidate the Protestants and to give them to understand for the present that the Emperor did not purpose to brook any alteration of the traditional forms of worship. And at this moment, he claims, Valdés, only because he was an Erasmian, approached Melanchthon, though in a tricky manner, to sound him and use him as a tool to carry out the plans of the Emperor. But who can prove that the things which the imperial secretary announced during the negotiations as the Emperor's purpose, to settle the religious questions in "quiet and secrecy," were

---

[9] E. A.² 24, 356 seqq. Cf. Th. Kolde, M. Luther II, 330.

[10] Cf. Strassburg's Polit. Korrespondenz I, 451 and 455.

originally his plan and not developed as such during the discussions with Melanchthon?

Brieger appeals for his view, that the initiative was made by Valdés, to the report of the Nuremberg delegates, *i. e.,* to what they learned of the matter. This may be so interpreted; but when they write: "We are informed that Alphonsus Waldesius, one of the principal secretaries of H. Imp. Maj., several times invited Philip Melanchthon to his house,"[11] it does not mean that the instigation cannot have been made by Melanchthon.

Then, too, the reference to Brück's histôry of the Diet,[12] in which he points to the fact that several of "the most prominent (wegernsten) of the papal party" repeatedly approached the theologians of the Christian estates, invited them to their quarters, and pretended that they would by no means hinder the gospel, and spoke to them of the controversial articles, etc., does not affect the question, for Brieger overlooks the fact that Brück states: *"Especially before his imperial majesty came to Augsburg,"* and nothing speaks for the fact that Brück also had in mind the imperial secretary, since we have knowledge of others who proceeded in the manner described by Brück, *e. g.,* Cochlæus, Usingen, Marius.[13]

Melanchthon's own statement must decide. On June 19th he writes to Myconius: *"Ego pertentavi unius atque alterius ex Hispanicis scribis animum; quantum proficiam videro."* The same day he writes to Camerarius: *"Nactus sum Hispanum secretarium, qui benigne pollicetur, et jam de mea sententia cum Cesare et Campegio collocutus est."*[14] Could Melanchthon say at all more clearly that he was the one who sought relations with the influential personalities, to insinuate to them his sententia concerning the prevailing condi-

---

[11] C. R. II, 122.

[12] F ö r s t e m a n n , Archiv. für Gesch. d. kirchl. Ref., Vol. I, Halle, 1831, p. 19.   B r i e g e r, p. 5.

[13] C. R. II, 86.   A d . W e i s z in Uffenheimer Nebenstunden, p. 686.   Cf. also A. S p a h n , Joh. Cochlæus. Berlin 1898, p. 154 seq.

[14] C. R. II, 118 seqq.

tions? I ask further: "What interest could Melanchthon have, if he did not take the initiative, to create this impression with Myconius and Camerarius, contrary to the truth?"

And what we see Melanchthon do here is entirely in line with what we can ascertain concerning his conduct otherwise in Augsburg. It was a peculiarity of his, which has proven fatal more than once, that the great theologian tried to act the diplomat now and then, and with the best of intentions entered into negotiations that were none of his business. We know now (a thing which Brieger, of course, could not know so fully) in what great measure he put his trust in the Emperor's clemency and love of peace. The imperial call to a diet had so completely captivated him that he at first entertained no fears of the influence of the papal legate, Campeggi, whom in contrast to Cajetanus, whose call was for a while rumored, he styled a virum peritum rerum civilium.[15] What concerned him most was to prove that his elector had the pure doctrine preached in this country, had abolished but few abuses which were recognized as such by the prudent ones among the opponents, pursued no warlike policies, but always opposed such, aimed only at peace and concord, and had absolutely no sympathy with the hated Zwinglians, who were always plotting war and revolution.

Cochlæus afterwards, in his hateful, exaggerating manner, accused Melanchthon of pretending to the utmost love of peace and thus forcing an entrance in Augsburg into the residences of private individuals, and also of cardinals, and even to the court of the Emperor;[16] but his assertions are not

---

[15] C. R. II, 40 and 42.

[16] J o a n n i s C o c h l e i, Philippicæ quatuor in Apologiam Philippi Melanchthonis. Lips. 1534, A iij ᵇ : (Translated)—" In the first place indeed Philippus ignores his own rudeness and tactlessness, for at Augsburg he did not only publicly pretend that he was a lover of peace and concord and zealous for the same ; but he also on his own initiative kept running here and there, bursting into and entering not only the homes and entertainment places of private individuals, but also the palaces of cardinals and other princes and even the M. T. court seeking by an altogether too insidious circuit whom he might devour by his hypocrisy. And indeed, by his wiles and simulated blandishments he deceived not a few, while he affirmed here and there in conferences and meetings that he could easily restore the peace of the church if only these three things were granted to his friends, the sacrament to the

pure inventions, for Melanchthon did certainly carry on private transactions with a great number of people. As early as the first days of June, *i. e.*, during the time when danger appeared more clearly, he carried on a most secretly-kept (and now evidently lost) correspondence with the cardinal of Mayence, as we learn from a hitherto unprinted letter " of John Rurer to And. Althamer, dated June 4th. In this he prayed the cardinal to use his influence that the matter might not lead to war.

His friendly intercourse with Catholic theologians, such as Cochlæus, Usingen and Marius, of course, was started by them. The cardinal of Salzburg, with whom Melanchthon had a long conversation but a few days before the presentation of the Confession, also seems to have invited him.[18]

It is not quite so sure to me that it was also without his initiative that he had the very remarkable conversation on June 13th with Henry of Brunswick. At any rate, he took advantage of it—it was in the very days in which he was negotiating with the Landgrave—to give very tactless expression in the presence of the Duke of Brunswick to his revulsion against the intentions and plans of Philip and his and Jacob Sturm's efforts at confederation. He rejoiced to receive the promise from the Duke that the two-fold form of the sacrament, the marriage of priests, monastic liberty, the abolishment of paid masses (missæ quæstuariæ) and freedom of foods were those points that could not rightly be condemned, and that harmony could be reached, if they were

---

laity sub utraque, marriage for the priests, and the use and communication of the mass. That in all other things his friends would be subject to the bishops and prelates throughout and obedient to their word," etc. C o c h - l a e u s tells the same as early as 1531 in his Petitio Philippi Melanchthonis. Ad R. D. Card. Campegium Augustæ scripta, etc., MDXXXI. In the letter of dedication we find the following story: "Besides I heard the R. D. Dr. John Fabri say there to a certain nobleman from Meissen, in my presence, that he would say to Philipp, unless he ceased frequenting the hotels of the Spaniards and excusing and proving his and Luther's writings to them, he himself would publicly hang up his most absurd and hateful errors on the church doors."

[17] K o l d e , Ält. Red., Beilage I, p. 108.

[18] Melanchthon reports to Luther June 25th (C. R. II, 126). According to the report of Jonas (K o l d e , Anal. Lutherana 140): The Salzburg Cardinal called Mr. Phil. Melanchthon through Wolffgang Stromer, the Nurembergian.

adopted, at least with the pre-supposition that the Zwinglians who wished to abolish the sacrament completely, were not to be included. [19]

This clearly shows the unvarying point in the private negotiations of Melanchthon. It is essentially the same that he presented a few days later to the imperial secretary. And it may be presumed also (we state it merely as a presumption) what moved him especially to convince the entourage of the Emperor of the innocuousness of the Protestants. As he himself was averse to confederation (and the cunning insinuation of the Duke of Brunswick concerning the plots of the Landgrave had only confirmed him in this), he had gained the conviction from the elector's epistolary negotiations with the Emperor, that Charles V. did, indeed, wish to make peace with his lord sed hac conditione, ἵνα μηδεμίαν ἔχοι συμμαχίαν. Thus he wrote to Luther on June 13th.[20] And just now the elector was on the point of giving up his long-maintained isolated position in the religious question and to unite with the other evangelical estates. And as matters stood, Melanchthon himself must desire to win the Landgrave, for otherwise he would be irretrievably driven into the arms of the Zwinglians. But he must have learned so much from the negotiations with Philip that took place in these days, that in this event the antithesis to the Zwinglian conception in the confession must be softened to the utmost. This increased the danger of being confused with the Zwinglians. But even the more tolerant Romans, and he had provided amply for that, were not inclined to tolerate these. Henry, of Brunswick, had confirmed this to him with clear words.[21] In this consuming anxiety (pæne consumor miserimis curis, he wrote to

---

[19] Report of Jonas to Luther, Anal. Luth., p. 133; E n d e r s VII, 380. Melanchthon presents an essentially different report to Luther, concerning the same conversation. E n d e r s VII, 383. Luther claimed to know that he had been invited to table by the Duke; but there is nothing about it in the letters written to him. E n d e r s VIII, 82.

[20] Mel. to Luther, E n d e r s VIII, 383.

[21] Cf. First Draft, etc.

Luther)[22] it might appear to him to be his duty to act as intermediary on his own responsibility and enter into negotiations with the followers of the Emperor.

We can even recognize the method which he pursued to attain his end. First he renewed the relations with the Flemish secretary, *Kornelius Schepper,* known to the Wittenbergers previously, and whom Brieger wrongly sets aside as having nothing to do with the matter.[23] According to the report of Jonas to Luther on June 18th, we may assume that the first conversation in which Jonas also took part, probably took place on Corpus Christi day, June 16th.[24] On a second occasion Jonas reports a meeting with Schepper on June 25th; but it is not quite certain whether this really has reference to a second conversation. But that it was not Schepper who sought the conversation may be concluded from Melanchthon's remark: "Videtur singulari diligentia cavere, ne veniat in suspicionem nostræ amicitiæ."[25] The things which Melanchthon on this occasion learned concerning the threat-

---

[22] Jonas to Luther, T h . K o l d e , Anal. Luth., 133. E n d e r s VII, 381. But that they would never subscribe with those who take away the sacrament of the Eucharist, as the Zwinglians do.

[23] B r i e g e r , p. 3, note 1: " Melanchthon's conversation with the Flemish secretary Cornel von Schepper is of no importance to our subject." But though Schepper was only the Dutch secretary and had no direct connection with the imperial government, yet he was well informed on the state of the matter. We know that he stood in close relations with Valdés, who entrusted to him the revision of the writing (Pro religione Christiana res gestæ in Comitiis Augusta Vindel. habitis, A. D. 1530), which above all was the cause of Brück's report on the Diet (F ö r s t e m a n n , Archiv. I, 1831), since he wrote to Dantiscus: "I am sending a report of the things done in this city with the Lutherans which I pray you to read in company with Dr. Cornelius if he is present and to add or omit whatever is to be added or omitted (E d . B ö h m e r in Art. Valdés in Prot. Real Encykl. 2 ed. Vol. XVI, p. 279, note).

[24] E n d e r s VII, 387. To this Mel. on June 19th, E n d e r s VIII, 2: " Cornelius says that he had some hope for peace while Mercurinus was living. He says that since M. is dead, there is nobody at court who has any authority to be the author of peace. Cornelius plays in his own way and seems to take extraordinary care not to be suspected of friendship with us. He is of no use to us at all. There is another Spanish secretary here, who blandly promises and has already conferred in regard to my sententia with the emperor and Campegius." The. same day he wrote to Camerarius, C. R. II, 119. "Cornelius Schepper affirms that he had good hope of peace so long as Mercurinus lived. That since his death there is no author of peace at court who is worthy in authority. I got hold of the Spanish secretary who promised faithfully and has already spoken concerning my view to the emperor and Campegius." To Myconius, ibid, June 19th: " I have tested the opinion of one and the other of the Spanish delegates."

[25] E n d e r s VIII, 24.

ening disposition at the imperial court had a crushing effect upon him. Jonas adds directly to his report to Luther: "D. Philippus, ut nosti virum misere discruciatur illis tantæ caussæ curis et solicitudinibus." [26]

The hope of negotiating with Campeggi is now completely destroyed. He is the very one, as M. now learned, who is stirring to war against the Protestants. But although nothing can be found in the reports to indicate that he has been given hope in this direction, he clings to his old confidence in the Emperor and his clemency: Nihil in aula Cæsaris ipso mitius Cæsare.[27] Yes, he even claims to have heard from kindly disposed courtiers nihil spei se habere *de cognitione,* *i. e.,* only upon investigation of the matter after examining the evangelical "opinion and view," the evangelical confession.

There is only one recourse left, and that is to endeavor to maintain the Emperor in his benevolent disposition. Hence he determines, and he must have done so at once, since on the 19th he reports concerning the negotiations with the Emperor and the legates, to apply to the much more influential personality, the imperial secretary, Alfonso Valdés, in order to learn more from him, and above all, to acquaint him of his sententia, and, if possible, to influence the Emperor through him. And he succeeded in getting hold of the secretary: *Nactus sum Hispanum.* In view of this statement the remark in the letter of the Nurembergians, which was written only after the negotiations had progressed further (that "Waldesius . . . invited Melanchthon *several times"*), can occupy only a secondary importance.

I must also maintain that at least his first visit to Valdés was kept relatively secret, though Melanchthon mentions the matter, in very general terms, it is true, almost unintelligibly, in letters to Luther and Camerarius, *i. e.,* to those outside, for Jonas, who was accustomed to gossip in his letters about everything he found out, does not seem to have learned about

---

[26] E n d e r s VII, 387.

[27] C. R. 117. Also M e n i u s. See B i n d s e i l, Supplem., p. 61.

it, and only mentions the conversation with Schepper. [28]   I also consider it altogether out of the question that Melanchthon should have acted in harmony with the counsellors of the elector.   Brück, the chancellor, whom we know to have his hand in the game everywhere, knew him well enough at that time, to be sure that this timid theologian, who could be startled by a mere threat, was not the proper person to undertake such a momentous political negotiation.

But what was Melanchthon's sententia on the state of affairs, and what came of the negotiations?   This we learn in the first place from the report of the Nuremberg delegates, dated Sunday, June 21st.   We must have it before us to judge it properly.   It reads thus:[29]

---

[28] It must be observed that the vigilant Strassburgian, who had also ferreted out the secret undertaking of the Schwabach Articles to Innsbrück (Z w i n g l i , opp. VIII, 458 ; V i r c k , Politische Korrespondenz, I, 446), did not learn anything of the matter.

[29] C. R. II, 122.   The items here given are confirmed by an oft-printed paper, " Schrift Aus Augsburg." It is first found in the Wittenberg ed. IX, 409, then in the remaining Luther editions to Walch (XVI, 873 seq. 912, 936), then in perhaps more early form in Bretschneider, C. R., X, 125 seq.   The passage on the relations with Valdés has been worked up by Aurifaber in his report with few changes.   If we look at the contents of this report (which since the Leipzig Luther edition XX, 202, is ascribed to Spalatin, whether correctly or not, cannot be determined), we find that it was written on different days.   The beginning to " God may send His Holy Spirit " Wttbg. IX, 410.   C. R. X, 128, was written Sat., June 18, Cf.   "Now Maj. is on Sat." and " On Mon. the Diet will be opened."   The following, to which Bretschneider wrongly adds the note :   Haec omnia quae jam sequuntur in opp. Lutheri non leguntur," was not written until Mon. or Tues. Cf.   "On said Saturday."   " On Saturday, Alfonsus."   " On Sunday H. Imp. Maj." " On Mon. they will hear the mass."   " So much has been done till now." The Nuremberg report and this paper therefore were written, so far as they refer to Valdés, at exactly the same time.   The paper reports the following (C. R. X, 129) :   "*Alfonsus* the Chancellor of H. Imp. Maj. in Spain and Cornelius have had several pleasant conversations with *Philipp* and told him that the Spaniards had been informed that they did not believe in God nor the Holy Trinity nor Christ nor Mary, so that they thought that if they killed a Lutheran they did God a greater service than by killing a Turk.   He says that though he conversed much with them, he persuaded few.   The rest remained in their own belief.

On Saturday *Alfonsus* sent for *Philippus* and informed him that in the morning he had visited H. Imp. Maj. and for a long time had no more suitable time or place to speak with H. Maj. and that he had informed H. Maj. concerning all the Lutheran articles and that they do not believe contrary to the church.   Then the emperor said " Quid volunt de Monachis," etc., and commanded *Alfonso* to tell *Philipp* to send in brief and without long discourses the articles upon which they insisted.   Then that *Philip* did so and also asked *Alfonso* to go to the legate.   This was also done, and now the greatest objection is in regard to the mass.   God be praised !   It appears now as if the emperor were willing to help.   God has used His means on him also."   An essential difference lies in this, that the paper says that Melanchthon *really wrote* the articles and that Valdés after the Saturday meeting delivered these written articles to the legate.

"We are informed that *Alfonsus Waldesius,* one of the
"most prominent secretaries of H. I. Maj., several times in-
"vited *Philips Melanchthon* to his house, treated with him
"concerning the Lutheran matter, and finally asked him to
"report what was the desire of the Lutherans and how the
"matter might be helped. And then *Melanchthon* reported to
"him about the matter as much as had been considered orally
"and in set speeches about in this manner: The Lutheran
"matter is by no means so extensive and out of the way as
"H. I. Maj. was perhaps informed, and the controversy prin-
"cipally concerned the two-fold form of the sacrament, the
"marriage of priests and monks, and the mass, namely, that
"the Lutherans could not approve of the special private
"masses. If an agreement were reached in regard to these ar-
"ticles, it was his opinion that ways and means could be
"found concerning all the others. Above mentioned *Alfon-*
"*sus Waldesius* had undertaken to present this report to H.
"Imp. Maj., and on Saturday had again sent for *Philippus*
"and announced to him that H. Imp. Maj. had been glad to
"hear it and was well pleased with it, and had asked him,
"*Alfonso,* to inform the papal legate, and he had done so.
"The legate also was well pleased with the report, and did
"not specially object to the articles on the two-fold form of
"the sacrament or the marriage of priests and monks, but
"was opposed to the abolition of private masses, and *A'fonsus,*
"after such information, said finally to *Philippus*: It was
"the desire of H. Imp. Maj. that *Philippus* should make a
"brief statement of the articles which the Lutherans desired
"and hand them to *Alfonsus,* and he would present them to
"H. Maj. for further consideration. But it was H. Maj.
"desire that he should not state such matter profusely, but
"very briefly, so that H. Maj. might have more reason to
"take action toward settling and ending this error. H. Maj.
"also thought it was best to consider this matter privately and
"not in open argument and discussion, for such arguments and
"discussions merely caused further dissension and no unity.

"Upon said request *Philippus* offered to consider the mat-
"ter and write the statement; but he desired to-day to con-
"verse regarding it with Dr. Brück and other theologians,
"then to write a draft for the elector, and if he approved, and
"considered it, to give it to *Alfonso.*" Here follows in the
original [30] following passage which was omitted by *Bretschneider,* but is not unimportant, and describes the secrecy with
which the transaction was carried on: "This we desired to
report to your worthies and did not wish it to be undiscov-
ered, though they, for the present, wish to keep it a secret."

To this we must add a remark of Melanchthon's reported
by the Nuremberg delegates on June 19th, and which could
not have been made until after his meeting with Valdés on
June 18th: "For as Philippus Melanchthon reports, the
matter will perhaps not be carried so far, but will be drawn
much closer, and written and treated more briefly. But whatever action shall be taken, whether the former [scil. confes-
sion] be completed or a new one drawn up, shall be reported
by us to your worthies."[31]

When I connected this remark, as I could not possibly help
doing, with the negotiations with Valdés, I came to the
conclusion that Melanchthon, after having been instructed
by the Emperor on June 18th to hasten to present a list of
the points in controversy, for this very reason delayed the
completion of the confession, and actually believed for a
while that its delivery would not be insisted upon; that he
afterwards deemed it quite proper to consult with Brück and
other theologians on June 21st, and that they did not approve of his secret agreements, as they imperilled the legal
status of the call to the Diet.[32] This *Brieger* contradicted
in all principal details.

First let us dispose of a chronological question. Accord-

---

[30] The letters of the Nuremberg delegates to the council are now preserved in the Nuremberg City Archives.

[31] C. R. II, 112, seq.

[32] Th. Kolde, M. Luth. II, 343; Augsb. Conf. p. 7; Pr. Realencykl., II,
245.

ing to Brieger (p. 8 sq.) the "work on the confession was not delayed a single day by the negotiations with Valdés." "Since the last three days of the week were entirely consumed with the negotiations caused by the prohibition to preach," they did not wait till after the opening (on Monday, June 20th) till June 21st, but immediately, "Sunday morning, June 19th, began the completion of the document of defence and the Nurembergians were immediately consulted." That the resumption of the work in the confession contrary to the accepted view took place, not on the 21st, but on the 19th, is splendidly argued by *Brieger* by endeavoring to prove that the postscript of the letter of the Nurembergians, which informs us on this point, and is printed in the Corp. Ref. II, 124, as an addition to the letter of June 21st, in reality belongs to the letter of June 19th. He correctly observes that the council, in an answer on June 23rd, does not refer to the sending of Osiander desired in said postscript, but does so on June 25th, where, as *Brieger* thinks, the remark "from your *former* writing", in contrast with "your *most recent* writing", (thus the answer on 23rd describes that of 21st) means the one of 19th. In fact, we must be grateful to this acute critic for touching upon this point, but his surmise is erroneous, though he cannot be made responsible for that. The postscript[33] in question actually belongs to the letter of the delegates of June 21st (though as a separate piece in the documentary find it might just as well belong to any other letter). On examining the correspondence books of the council in the Nuremberg Archive we discover that the publisher, *Vogt,* who displayed very little care, *actually did not print* the passage in which the council in its answer speaks of the call of Osiander (just as in other letters he omitted much that is of value to the investigator).

---

[33] This contains a section in the original through which the reply of 25th, (Vogt, p. 19) becomes intelligible. " This I offered to report fully to your worthies and if your worthies will order me up, as I regard needful and useful, y. w. will please write to me whom you appointed and how many there will be, so that we may provide lodging near by, since we can place nobody else in our lodging place."

17

We read at the close of the letter of June 23rd (after the part published by Vogt, p. 18 seq.): "If time should permit we will not withhold our intention, and will reply to your writing regarding the sending of Osiander in our next message. The sixth hour of the day." This explains why the question is not discussed by the council until June 25th, after being in the meantime deliberated upon by the council.[34] And since this establishes the fact that the postscript in question belongs to the letter of June 21st, we also know definitely that the *"final completion of the confession was not begun until after the opening of the Diet, Tuesday, June 21st."*

This would allow ample *time* for the delay maintained by me and others, but the important question is whether this delay was caused by Melanchthon's negotiations with Valdés and Campeggi, or from the standpoint of the criticism of sources, the answer to the question, *"Of what did Melanchthon think when he informed the Nuremberg delegates that the matter would perhaps not reach such a full discussion, but would be drawn closer and framed more briefly."*

Brieger admits that the Nuremberg *delegates* drew the conclusion that possibly a new concept (*i. e.,* article of defence) would be elaborated, but he overlooks the fact that the Nuremberg *council* (and I, too) from what it learned of the transactions, drew the conclusion that eventually, contrary to the call to the Diet, the delivery of a written apology in Latin and German would be given up.[35] At any rate, *Brieger* considers this view to be erroneous, and thinks rather that Melanchthon, and not he alone, thought of a *much abbreviated form of the confession.* In a very skilful

---

[34] On June 25th the council resolution was passed: "That Mr. Osiander should ride to Augsburg, to send him at once and to receive him in the lodging of our gentlemen, and to write this up more fully.

That in 8 days Mr. Krystoff Koller and Jo. Baumgartner should ride to Augsb. and that this be hereby indicated and that they be received in the lodging of our gentlemen." On Sunday, June 26th, Osiander was accordingly sent: " and. onssiander (!) preacher is to ride on."

[35] V o g t, p. 18.

investigation he connects the matter with a peculiarly formed recension of the Augustana, embracing only 19 articles of faith, the so-called first Ansbach manuscript (mentioned in another connection), and further with the fact ascertained by *Förstemann,* and also known to us before, that Chancellor Vogler, in an opinion dated June 16th, in the transactions on the preaching question, recommends to inform the Emperor as to the Christian character of evangelical preaching:[36] "And in order that your Imp. Maj. may *in brief* be thoroughly informed about the teaching and preaching of our preachers, which we consider a pure gospel and the Word of God, we hereby deliver to your Imp. Maj. a clear statement of the same, in haste briefly stated."

This recension may gain weight for the question before us, since in Spalatin's manuscript of the Augustana, and in a Latin one (the Hessian and French translation)[37] we have a confession of equal limitation (and as Brieger seeks to prove) with a conclusion (the summa) which gave no occasion to the view that it was only a transition to a second part which formulated the reasons for abolishing certain ceremonies. It was rather to be an epilogue closing the confession. Brieger, also, while pointing out that Spalatin's text (which is evidently older than the Ansbach text) does not have the later summa, but a quite different transition to the second part, is of the opinion that these above-mentioned documents, which were in existence (before the arrival of the Emperor) in the middle of June, must actually be considered independent forms of the confession (p. 24). He also thinks it may be proven that in view of the impending danger the evangelical princes more and more became of the opinion that it would be proper to confess their faith in brief and concise form, and by confirming their doctrine and preaching with the clear truth of the word of God to silence the accu-

[36] B r i e g e r , p. 13, twice writes wrongly July 16th. The opinion in F ö r s - t e m a n n I, 274 seq.

[37] F ö r s t e m a n n , I, 355. Here already the article on invocation of saints.

sation of heresy; and, on the other hand, to reserve the defence of their alterations of church ceremonies for the discussion, which, according to the call to the Diet, had to follow the mutual declaration of opinions.

Brieger sums up his opinion, which I will repeat verbatim, in the following theses (p. 29):

I. In the time of which we speak (shortly before the arrival of the Emperor) we find the German confession, and possibly about the same time, also the Latin (and this also in a French version) in much briefer form, *i. e.,* limited to the articles of faith, and provided with an addition not in existence a week before, which in its Latin version gives the impression of a concluding passage, and in the German can be so understood so that we can hardly conceive that this briefer form owes its existence to chance.

II. At that very time, before the arrival of the Emperor, a pause was made in the final revision of the preface and conclusion belonging to the great confession.

III. A proposition made June 16th by the Margrave-Brandenburg side to employ the (German) abbreviated confession as the basis of an apology to be delivered to the Emperor the next day was declined by Saxony. This short form of the confession, giving information only on the faith and preaching of the Protestants, was not prepared for such a purpose as the private instruction of the Emperor.

IV. When two days later the Nuremberg delegates, immediately after being officially admitted to the confession of the princes, requested to be told the preface and conclusion of the comprehensive document previously delivered to them, they learn that the "conclusion is not yet composed," and Melanchthon does not explain this by that reason of which he had spoken a few days before to the Nurembergians, who then were not yet formal allies, nor the circumstance that during the last few days which were entirely taken up with the care about the preservation of evangelical preaching, there was no time left for composing the conclusion; but he refers to the uncertainty of the elector as to the compass of his apology.

V. Immediately the next morning (June 19th) a session of the councils of Saxony, Brandenburg, Hessen and Lüneburg takes place for the purpose of examining and editing the "instructions in faith," as ordered by the elector, and the same of which the Nurembergians had "received copei." A Nuremberg delegate is called to the session and informed that this work has been resumed. We can hardly be mistaken if we assume that at this session the hesitation in regard to the extent of the document is ended and the resolution adopted to complete the *large* apology.

According to this, Melanchthon, when he made said remark to the Nurembergians, thought of the intention of proceeding eventually to the articles of faith, and, therefore, the uncertainty about this question had lasted until June 21st.

To this of Brieger I have the following reply to make:

I. The existence of Augustana manuscripts that contain only the articles of faith is no proof that they were written only to form documents complete in themselves **and to** serve special purposes.[38] And if Brieger repeatedly emphasizes the fact that so often the contemporaneous documents speak of *what is preached and taught,* and infers that the doctrinal articles were pushed to the front and tries to prove that the intention was to *deliver only the doctrinal articles,* I would like to state that the entire *Augustana* after its delivery was considered to be a summary of all that the preachers taught. This, *e. g.,* was the opinion of the Strassburg delegates upon the basis of what they heard and a copy received from the landgrave: *"which contains nothing more than their preachers teach."* [39]

II. It is correct that the Summa received its later form no earlier than in June, but it owes its origin not to "chance," as a comparison of Na with the later revision proves, but to

---

[38] See report of Nuremberg delegates.

[39] Pol. Korrespondenz I, 463.

the proper consideration that the statements already made in Na, but divided between the close of the first and the beginning of the second part, would be more effective, if they were all placed at the close of the first part.

III. It is correct that the Latin Summa does sound as if one did not need to expect a second part,[40] but that does not justify the view that it was to be an *epilogue,* actually closing the confession, for, as Brieger must also have seen, it is found unchanged in the confession as afterward delivered.

IV. It is *not* correct that Melanchthon, as Brieger states in his fourth point, gives it as a reason why the apology is not yet completed that the elector is in doubt as to the extent of the apology. There is no mention made of it in the report of June 19th, and that is very important; *Melanchthon* is in doubt whether the matter could not be drawn more closely and treated in terser form.

V. It is correct that Chancellor Vogler, in discussing the preaching question, made the proposition to deliver to the Emperor only the articles of faith, to prove the Christianity of evangelical preaching; but this thought of the chancellor or his margrave was only ephemeral, and that in the full sense of the word. On June 16th the opinion was stated on the same evening the matter was discussed,[41] and upon voting down Chancelor Vogler's motion, the document composed by Chancellor Brück was adopted and then sent on the 17th.[42] This document was signed not only by the elector,

---

[40] B r i e g e r admitted p. 22 that this was not the case in the German Summa.

[41] Report of the Nurembergians June 16th: "Jorg Vogler reports that said princes have determined not to omit the preaching and that on the morrow they are willing to deliver a written explanation to H. Imp. Maj." C. R. II, 108.

[42] F ö r s t e m a n n, I, 283. B r i e g e r, p. 30, says that Vogler's proposition was declined by Saxony and adds: "Possibly also by Hessen and Lunenburg, in case they as is probable had already allied themselves to the elector in matters of faith. This can be proven no earlier than June 19th". The only document reporting this declining is the writing to the emperor of June 17th, since the evangelical princes there first appear in writing as allies in the

but also by *Margrave George,* Duke Ernst, of Lüneburg, Landgrave Philip, of Hessen, and Prince Wolf, of Anhalt. And if the thought had ever come to one prince or another, to subscribe *only to the articles of faith,* it was thereby repudiated. For if in that document they demand that they be not condemned prematurely by the abolition of evangelical preaching, but according to the call everyone's opinion and view was here heard, and then everything that *was wrongly undertaken on either side was to be abolished and brought to Christian unity* (p. 285), and if further they point to the "terrible innovations" on the other side, both in doctrines, customs and walk (p. 286), I deem the view excluded that the princes could think of delivering only articles of faith." It is equally impossible that Melanchthon, in his reply to the Nurembergians (say on June 18th), thought only of a confession limited to the articles of faith.

The same result is reached by an analysis of the reports concerning Melanchthon's negotiations with Valdés. (See above.)

Even according to Brieger the negotiations with the imperial secretary began soon after the arrival of the Emperor,

matter of confession. It is to be noticed that Brück there used Vogler's Opinion. Cf. the statements that the Word must not be bound, the Word of God is the food of the soul and the reference to Matth. 4, " Man does not live by bread alone." F ö r s t e m a n n , I, 275 and 284.

"⁴³ B r i e g e r certainly, who, so far as I can see, has not used this document, remarks on the declining of Vogler's proposition : " This form of the confession, brief as it was and giving informaton only on the faith and preaching of the Protestants, was not prepared for such a purpose as the instruction of the emperor." But it can not be proven that the first part was " made over " for the purpose of presenting it alone. If Brieger attaches importance (p. 13) to the fact that Vogler proposes to write: " Thus we deliver to your Imp. Maj. a pure statement *in haste briefly framed"* (F ö r s t e m a n n p. 280) the expression is easily explained from the fact that he well knew that the articles of faith would not receive their final form for a long time. And further, if we can easily understand Vogler's intention to deliver the articles of faith to the emperor temporarily on account of the preaching question, I can not understand what occasion there could be without this special reason to be silent at first about the abolition of abuses, the dogmatic relation of which certainly would have to be treated at the Diet, and to postpone them for an oral discussion which could not be avoided.

and Melanchthon in the course of the conversation, after Valdés (according to the "message") had informed him of the Spanish views of the Lutheran heresy, had tried to prove to him that the Lutheran cause was not so terribly out of the way as H. Imp. Maj. was perhaps informed, and that the controversy concerned principally these articles, viz.: the two-fold form of the sacrament, the marriage of priests and monks and of masses, that, namely, the Lutherans could not approve of special private masses. "If these points were agreed upon," he thought, "order and ways and means might be devised for the rest." [44]

These remarks must have been made before Saturday, June 18th, for the Nurembergians further write: "Above-mentioned Alfonsus undertook to deliver said report, and on *Saturday* invited Philippus again." From this it is clear that when Melanchthon (according to the report of June 19th) no later than June 18th, remarked to the delegates "that the matter perhaps would not reach such a lengthy discussion, but would be drawn closer and treated more briefly," he had the same thing in mind. If both statements, which are so very nearly contemporaneous, are placed side by side without prejudice, there really can be no doubt that Melanchthon thought here as there and as at the delivery of the Torgau Articles of this point, that the *discussion of those practical points was the principal thing,* and that therefore the apology, at least in its present extent, would perhaps be unnecessary.

At any rate I cannot conceive that the same Melanchthon, who according to Brieger even negotiates with Valdés with the knowledge of the elector's counsellors, explained this to

---

[44] Notice the agreement with what Melanchthon according to Jonas' report had treated June 13th with Henry of Brunswick. Enders VII, 381: "The Duke of Brunswick talked for a while with Philipp some very good things concerning the public cause. He said that he formerly and now every now and then, ever since his return from Italy, read the New Testament and had derived much profit from this reading, and that he saw that the sacrament sub utraque, the marriage of priests, monastic liberty and the abolition of private masses, and liberty in meats, were articles that could not rightly be condemned, and that there with the help of God means of concord could be discovered."

him and at the same time (as we must assume with Brieger's hypothesis) thought of giving the apology a form which from principle refrains from the ceremonies and practical questions and of delivering the articles of faith to the Emperor as the *principal matter,* even though only for the present.

And Valdés and the Emperor look upon the matter similarly with the Nurembergians. Melanchthon's remarks are transmitted by Valdés to the Emperor, who receives them with approval, as does also the papal legate whom the Emperor has informed. All this takes place from June 16th to 18th. And as late as the 18th Valdés invites Melanchthon and reports to him what has been done in the meantime. We learn that the Emperor, from what he has heard, has gained the impression that it might be possible to avoid the public hearing, the announcement of which he regretted for some time. He has Melanchthon informed of his conviction that "it would be the most profitable thing to undertake the matter in quiet and privacy and not in an extended public argument and discussion," *i. e.,* as it had been specified in the Call. The Emperor and Valdés evidently infer from Melanchthon's remark that "the Lutheran cause was not so terribly out of the way" that this is *his* intention also. How could they do otherwise? How is it, therefore, possible, I ask again, to think that Melanchthon, when he at the same time said to the Nurembergians that the Confession might be drawn more closely and stated more briefly, thought of delivering to the Emperor a Confession embracing merely the articles of faith?

I must, therefore, maintain what *Brieger* opposes quite determinedly, that Melanchthon hesitated to complete the Confession and momentarily believed the delivery of it might even be dispensed with. For he agrees to the desire to state most briefly the articles which the Lutherans especially demanded (those questions on ceremonies) and to present them to Alfonso. The Nuremberg delegates report expressly:

"Upon such request, Philippus offered to consider the case and furnish a list."

And yet, before he went further, he determined to get the consent of Chancellor Brück and the elector,—toward which he first proceeded three days later (surely no argument for the view that he has been acting up to this point in harmony with the elector's counsellors). And the result was the rejection of his private negotiations and the resolution to finish the Confession at last and proceed to it at once.[45] And this was not the case, as *Brieger* assumes, on Sunday, the 19th, but, as was ascertained before, on Tuesday, June 21st.

This ended Melanchthon's negotiations officially at least; but how much had they attained?

At this point we observe a difference between the two reports that have come down to us from evangelical circles, namely, the letter of the Nurembergians and the message from Augsburg, that the latter adds to the statement that the Emperor had commanded Valdés " to tell Philippus to send H. Maj. a short statement without profuseness:" *"That Philippus did so,* and therefore also commanded Alphonso to go to the legate and negotiate with him. This was done and the shock was greatest everywhere in the mass. This entitles to good hope, thanks be to God, that the Emperor is willing to help the matter and God has helped it along."* This statement would be worth even more if it could be proven that Spalatin is the reporter; but that seems to be merely a later supposition. Since the Augsburg report is not clear as to its chronology, we cannot conclude from it that Melanchthon

---

[45] That is not directly reported anywhere, but since the Nuremberg delegate Christoph. Kress in the postscript to the letter in which he reports that Melanchthon would " to-day converse " with Brück, makes the statement that he was just called into the hotel of the elector, where in the presence of the counsellors of Saxony, Brandenburg, Hessen and Lüneburg, he was informed that they were on the point of " revising, writing and completing the articles," the conclusion is justified that Melanchthon's statements to Brück and the consultation, and the resolution of the assembled evangelical counsellors are connected with each other.

delivered anything in writing either before or after the consultation with Brück, and it is extremely improbable. In the Augsburg message there might possibly be a confusion of the points verbally fixed.

After all, the negotiations with Valdés and mediately with Campeggi had further consequences. What importance was attached to them is seen from the fact that foreign embassadors, who heard about them, hastened to report the impending change at home. The Mantuan ambassador, Antonio Bogarotto, wrote to the Duke of Mantua, that the Lutheran *princes* had made "supplication" to have four points granted them: 1. The confirming of the confiscated church properties to the possession of the laity. 2. The sacrament sub utraque. 3. The changes made in the mass. 4. The marriage of priests. The Emperor was said to have replied that he would act according to duty and reason, and to have sent Granvella at once to the legate to confer with him on the basis of these demands, quid agendum.[46]

This report, which does not even mention Melanchthon, and relates the demands of the " princes " immediately after the negotiations of the evangelical estates with the Emperor concerning the question of preaching, was written no later than June 20th.[47] Hence it can apply only to what was related in connection with Melanchthon's verbal statements and not to points fixed in writing. If the question concerning church properties here appears as a new point, it can not be due to mere invention. At least it is quite probable that Valdés also touched upon this point and that Melanchthon then had no other choice than to remark that it was a self-evident demand of the Protestants to grant the bestowal of church properties.[48]

[46] First in (T h o m a s) M. Luther u. d. Ref. Bewegung in Deutschl. vom J. 1520-1532 in Auszügen aus Marino Sanutos Diarien. Ansbach 1883, p. 169. Complete in the Diarii di Marino Sanuto. Vol. 53, Venice 1899, p. 326.

[47] To my knowledge first ascertained by Brieger, p. 36.

[48] Note that the Protestants in those days feared to be attacked upon this very point. According to a council resolution June 25, the Nuremberg Council resolved " to deliberate concerning monasteries, in case of controversy." (Kreisarchiv in Nuremberg.)

To the same time evidently belongs also the related report of the Venetian embassador, Tiepolo, which unfortunately is not dated.[49] While the Mantuan (at least this is the most probable) had his news from Valdés or Campeggi, much speaks for the assumption that the Venetian received the wishes of the " preachers " as it is here stated, through direct intercourse with Melanchthon, which relation can be definitely proven. Of course the notorious letter of Melanchthon to Campeggi, which in several manuscripts is ascribed to Oratori Thepulo (Tiepolo)[50] is not addressed to him, but really to Campeggi. An epistle to Tiepolo, not extant, which in the middle of the fifties was circulated by the enemies of Melanchthon, must have been a forgery. We can believe Melanchthon when, September 5th, 1556, he writes that he never wrote to Tiepolo; but in the same letter to Flacius in which he states this he tells us of a *conversation* which he had with Tiepolo during the Augsburg Diet.[51] According to it the Venetian embassador had been instructed to offer his services to the Saxon elector. Melanchthon had been sent to Tiepolo with Chancellor Brück, avowedly to thank the Venetian senate, evidently because the speech had to be made in Latin. After his address, in which, according to his statement, he had not mentioned the religious controversies, the embassador had protested against receiving his remarks as an assent to the doctrine accepted in the Saxon country. " I replied," says Melanchthon, " that we had not thus regarded the matter. Thereupon, as was befitting, I spoke of the virtue of the prince, his true piety and that he confessed (amplecti) the doctrine of the Catholic Church, but rejected

---

[49] S a n u t o , p. 312 [Kolde's original prints the quotation, which states the above-mentioned four points].

[50] July 6th. C. R. II, 169 seq. Cf. the Letters of R o s e l l u s , Venice, C. R. II, 226 and 243. B e n r a t h , Jahrb. für Prot. Theol. 1882, p. 179. There can be no doubt of the authenticity of Melanchthon's Letter to Campeggi, B r i e g e r (p. 37 note) to the contrary notwithstanding, as he does not enter upon M.'s relations to Tiepolo. It agrees perfectly with M.'s original view of Campeggi and with all that has been discovered about his position in the introduction to the Augustana, etc.

[51] C. R. VIII, 939. Cf. S a l i g , Vollständ. Historie der Augsb. Konfession. III, (Halle 1735) p. 329.

the abuses, and desired to have the controversial questions which had arisen, decided and provision made for the welfare of the entire church." In this sense he had spoken to this man who was hostile to the evangelical people, and perhaps had said a few general things to defend them, but could not definitely remember his words. *Afterwards his words had been committed to writing, and* [52] that may have been the origin of said letter.

It does not concern us what was the nature of this letter; but what Melanchthon reports about the conversation gives rise to the supposition that at this occasion he also referred to those points which according to his view were essential, and that the embassador fixed upon them as the demand of the *preachers* and reported home accordingly. That Tiepolo gives them first place in his report, even before mentioning the opening of the Diet (June 20th), only proves the importance which the zealous representative of the Catholic Church attached to these remarks, and is no proof that this conversation with which I hypothetically connect his report took place before the 20th, although that is quite possible. Neither can it be concluded from the fact that Brück was present during these discussions that Melanchthon negotiated with Valdés in agreement with Brück. According to Melanchthon's own description of the situation, his remarks about the religious question, the abolition of abuses, etc., were only made incidentally with the view to exonerate his prince and Protestants in general, but not, as in the negotiations with Valdés, to attach definite propositions to them. The whole episode only serves to show how much Melanchthon was inclined to awaken the thought among opponents that the issue was essentially about doing away with certain abuses, or about certain concessions on the part of those of the old faith.

According to the information given by the imperial secretary, Cardinal Campeggi had also received the impression that this would be the chief point in the " opinion and inten-

---

[52] " Afterwards my words were annotated in some manner."

tion" prepared by the protesting estates.[53]   He writes, as
Brieger proves probably (p. 39), on the 23rd, that he had
learned in various ways that the Protestants in the "opinion" which they were to present the next day would confine
themselves to four points: the sacrament sub utraque, the
celibacy of priests, the canon of the mass, and *what appears
here for the first time* and is very important for the whole
investigation, a General Council.[54]   "They also desire, as is
said, to confiscate the possessions of the clergy."[55]   The way
in which this point is here added, confirms the supposition I
expressed above, that this question was touched upon only
incidentally in the negotiations.   In this general form Campeggi made his report to the cardinal secretary of state, Salviati, in his message, written in intervals and sent June 26th.

At the same time, as *Brieger* has proven in a masterly
investigation, he must have sent officially to Rome, directly
to the Pope (perhaps by private messenger),[56] four definite
points as the demands of the Lutherans.   The question then
arises, "Whence come these four points?"   Did Melanchthon perhaps, after all, as the message from Augsburg sug-
gests, fix the demand of the Protestants for Valdés, *i. e.* (we
must assume this), since he wanted to confer with Brück,
officially with the sanction of Brück and the elector?   I consider that impossible in view of the preparation made for the
immediate delivery of the confession.

But how did they arise then?   Probably in the same way
as those sent to Venice by Tiepolo.   "Their formulation,"

---

[53] For diverse reasons I intend that they should restrict themselves to
the four points. L ä m m e r , Monum. Vaticana. Freiburg 1861, p. 43.   This
incompletely transmitted message is well examined in B r i e g e r , p. 39.

[54] The fourth that there should by all means be a General Council in which
I know the mind of N. S. (L ä m m e r , p. 44).

[55] They also speak of confiscating the ecclesiastical possessions, which would
be a robbery upon the whole eccl. state. *Ibid.*

[56] It is sufficient to refer to B r i e g e r , p. 41, and the sources there mentioned.
I would like to add that to this message to the Pope must have been joined
the Diet proposition which Campeggi originally wished to join with his message to Salviati. (L ä m m e r , p. 42), but which must have been sent sooner
than the writing of the 26th to Salviati, as according to the report of Andreas
del Burgo of July 12th (B r i e g e r , p. 49) was read in the consistory on
the 6th.

says Brieger correctly (p. 43), "may be traced to Valdés, since he fixed the demands of the Protestants upon the basis of Melanchthon's verbal statements." But if Brieger thinks he can safely gather their contents from the report of the Nurembergians, although the fourth article probably refers to the demands for a General Council, and sees the occasion of fixing them in the negotiations carried on until *June 19th,* I can not consider this to be correct, since the addition of the demand for a *Council* speaks against it.

I would rather venture another combination—and in the scantiness of sources we all are dependent upon combinations and surmises.

For Melanchthon, after the conversation with Brück on June 21st, the negotiations with Valdés were not yet closed. If he did not dare to conduct them in the name of the Evangelical estates, he did consider himself justified in continuing them personally. We learn that from him directly, for as he writes to Camerarius (June 26th) he has permitted Valdés to examine the confession before its delivery. To his terror he learned that Valdés, notwithstanding the author's endeavor to state everything as mildly as possible, had found it sharper (πικρότερον) than the opponents could stand.[57] After the earlier negotiations it is probable that Melanchthon showed him the second part specially, for the πικρότερον in the opinion of Valdés can refer only to it. We can readily assume that the three points were again mentioned, for that they remained the principal thing to Melanchthon even after all that had been treated in the last deliberations of the Evangelical estates can be seen from the fact that on the same day, without special occasion on the part of the opponents, he wrote to Luther: Nunc mihi constituendum, priusquam respondeant adversarii, quid velimus concedere ipsis; *de utraque specie, de conjugio, de privata Missa; omnis erat deliberatio.*[58]

---

[57] C. R. II, 140.
[58] *Ib.,* 141.

But during this conversation with Valdés, which, according to the letter to Camerarius, could not have taken place earlier than June 22d or 23d, Melanchthon, after Brück's preface was completed, must also have acquainted him with the renewed demand of a *Council*. This explains the circumstances to me that after the previous negotiations, as far as I see, this question was not again broached by the Protestants. Campeggi in his report to Salviati now mentions the demand for a Council as the fourth point. For we must almost surely conclude that Campeggi, when he wrote this, had again been acquainted by Valdés of the progress of affairs, since he, as *an argument of the opponents for the abolition of the celibacy* introduces a very *special statement from the confession.* This he could scarcely have learned from anyone but Valdés, who has seen the confession. "Allegano nostri Canonisti, quali dicono che cosi come la Chiesa ex magna causa ordino il Celibato, cosi adesso majori ex causa si doveria levari." [59]

We need no further declaration that Valdés also informed Granvella or the Pope of those things which he had heard of Melanchthon in renewed conversation. Though Melanchthon had spoken only as a private man, he was still the best known among the evangelical theologians, and his remarks could pass as an authoritative statement of the sentiment. Thereupon, Valdés must have received the commission to fix them in writing, and, so as to know for all cases, how Rome would act in regard to them, to send them to Rome directly through Campeggi. Before he sent his message to Salviati they must have gone to Rome, as articles of Melanchthon,[60] since the consistory debated them July 6th.

Thus on the foundation of fragmentary sources we must imagine things to have taken place, until new discoveries teach us something else.

---

[59] L ä m m e r, p. 44.

[60] J . F i c k e r, D. Konfutation d. Augsb. Bekennt. Leipzig 1891, p. XVII. The demand of a council was not a demand of Melanchthon's, who in this point was willing to defer to the emperor. C. R. II, 94.

CHAPTER XVII.

THE LUTHERAN CONFESSION.

KOLDE ON THE FIRST KNOWN DRAFT, OR OLDEST REDACTION, OF THE AUGS- BURG CONFESSION AND ITS DISCOVERY.

The Discovery of the Document—Its Significance—A Brief Analysis of Its Contents, Including Especially Melanchthon's Introduction—Fate of this Redaction.

DIE ÄLTESTE REDAKTION

DER AUGSBURGER KONFESSION [1]

MIT MELANCHTHONS EINLEITUNG

zum erstenmal herausgegeben und geschichtlich gewürdigt

VON

D. THEODOR KOLDE,

o. Prof. der Kirchengeschichte in Erlangen.

Gütersloh:
Druck und Verlag von C. Bertelsmann.
1906.

---

[1] *The Oldest Redaction of the Augsburg Confession, with Melanchthon's
Introduction,* for the first time published and historically rated, by D r .
T h e o d o r K o l d e, regular Professor of Church History in Erlangen, etc.

PREFACE.

HABENT sua fata libelli. The publisher's desire that I should write an entirely new introduction to the Symbolical Books (which would be proportionate to the present status of science, and which, the Lord willing, is to appear during the next year) for "J. T. Müller's Die symbolischen Bücher der evangelisch-lutherischen Kirche," led me first of all to resume my Augustana researches, and especially to reach clear conclusions as to Th. Brieger's newest work, "Zur Geschichte des Augsburger Reichstags von 1530." Out of this work grew the dissertation* published in the second part of the present book "On Melanchthon's Negotiations with Alphonso Valdés and Lor. Campeggi." It was almost completed in the first draft when the discovery of the earliest redaction, which is here printed** for the first time, claimed my entire attention. It was a matter of course that the historical appreciation of this document should now come to the fore, for, as I believe to have proven, it has brought us a great deal further in our knowledge of the origin of the principal evangelical confession. At the same time we have caught important new glimpses of the political and ecclesi-

---

[* Constitutes Chap. XVI of this Book.]

[** Constitutes Chap. XVIII of this Book.]

astical history of the Augsburg Diet. As this also throws new light on Melanchthon's private negotiations, which are so closely connected with the history of the Augustana text, I deemed it my duty to append my investigations as a second part, although the rather long title of my book does not make special references to it.

D. TH. KOLDE.

Erlangen, Dec. 5th, 1905.

I.

THE OLDEST REDACTION OF THE AUGSBURG CONFESSION.

Next to the question about the genuine text of the Augsburg Confession as it was read and presented June 25th, 1530, to the Emperor and the land, the problem concerning its gradual formation has from the start abundantly occupied scientific investigators. Since the fundamental works of G. G. Weber,[2] Förstemann[3] and Bindseil,[4] a large and ever increasing literature on the subject, has come into being, and we owe it many an important result even in later years. We know now, among other things, and it is one of the merits of Th. Brieger[5] to have determined it, what is meant by the "Torgau Articles," that opin-

---

[2] G. G. Weber, *Kritische Geschichte der Augspurgischen Confession.* Frankfurt a. M. 1783 and 1784. 2 vols.

[3] K. Ed. Förstemann, *Urkundenbuch zu der Geschichte des Reichstags zu Augsburg* im Jahre 1530. Halle 1830 f. 2 vols.

[4] H. E. Bindseil in the *Corpus Ref.,* vol. xxvi (Brunswick 1858), pp. 97 seqq.

[5] Th. Brieger, *The Torgau Articles,* in Kirchengeschichtliche Studien, Leipzig. 1888 pp. 265 seqq.

ion of the Wittenberg theologians that was delivered to the Prince Elector at Torgau toward the end of April. With this first draft of that which gradually grew into the Augsburg Confession, we have gained a secure foundation for further research. The more thorough examination of the material in letters and official documents has given us information about many details, and the origin and value of various manuscript recensions of the Augustana as it grew into shape, have been discussed in many instances. But notwithstanding the acumen devoted to these problems, we are still far from having a clear understanding of the history of the gradual formation of the Confession, much less can we determine with any degree of certainty the single phases through which its text passed under the ever-amending hand of Melanchthon and the influence of circumstances. The fact is, that all the copies extant from the time before the presentation of the Confession, including even Spalatin's which is deserving of special consideration, take us back not much further than about the time of the arrival of the Emperor, that is, the middle of June.

For this very reason the question which justly was treated again and again, concerning the extent and contents of the "Apology" sent May 11th to Luther and approved by him, could be answered only in the most imperfect manner. It was surmised that it contained a rather rhetorically written introduction, which Melanchthon, as soon as he arrived in Augsburg, substituted* for a simpler one written in Koburg, and which afterward, before the presentation of the Confession, had to give way to a preface written by the diplomat Brück. Then it was determined, with considerable certainty, that the "Apology" did not contain the (XX.) article "Of Faith and Good Works," that the (XXVII.) article "Of Monastic Vows" was given in shorter form than as we know it now,

---

* Melanchthon to Luther, May 2nd (*Corp. Ref.* II, 39 seq.). Ego exordium nostrae apologiae feci aliquanto ῥητορικότερον quam Coburgae scripseram.

and that the (XXVIII.), "De Potestate Ecclesiastica," which perhaps was not even written, most certainly was not known to Luther in the form presented June 25th.[7]

A document of importance to the question as to what Luther had really seen, could be expected to be found in the *Latin* version which the Nuremberg delegates received May 31st and sent to Nuremberg on June 3rd.[8] For even if the text probably was no longer the same that Luther had seen, since, as we know, many changes were made in it directly after it returned from Koburg,[9] it was still to be assumed that the version sent to Nuremberg was after all nearer the original one than it was to the final revision. And, in any event, it must be an important stage in the history of the Augustana text. But all searching for that "incomplete" Latin version was in vain up to the present.

Then Dr. Karl Schornbaum, to whom the investigation of the history of the Frankish-Brandenburgian Reformation is so much indebted, in a letter dated July 11th, called my attention to a document without date or title, found by him in the Nuremberg district archives. He stated, "It agrees to a remarkable degree with the Editio Princeps of the Augustana, although it makes mention of none but Saxons." When on July 20th, I investigated the matter at the place of discovery, I discovered that it was an error to assume any agreement with the Editio Princeps, but that here was discovered a link hitherto completely unknown in the history of the growing Confession, and which, since we can determine its origin, can give us some entirely unexpected information.

---

[7] Cf. B r i e g e r , as above, p. 278.

[8] *C. R.* II, 78 and 83.

[9] Luther to Melanchthon May 22nd (C. R. II, 60) : " In Apologia quotidie mutamus ; locum de votis, quia erat exilior iniusto, exemi, supposita alia disputatione eadem de re paulo uberiore. Nunc de potestate clavium etiam disputo. Vellem percurrisses articulos fidei, in quibus si nihil putaveris esse vitii reliqua utcunque tractabimus. Subinde enim mutandi sunt atque ad occassiones accomodandi."

[N. B.—In place of Kolde's lapsus above, read, "Mel. to Luther."—T. E. S.]

The following is the version of the document:[10]

[Here follows, in Kolde's German volume, the text of the newly discovered manuscript. In this work, it constitutes chapter XVIII.]

What, then, is the nature of this manuscript? It needs no argument to prove that we have an early redaction of the Augustana before us. If the reader is observant he will at once receive the impression that he is perusing a *translation,* and that one which was made while in course of writing. The many passages that are crossed out and corrected (and which are carefully reproduced in the reprint), with few exceptions, constitute no corrections of mistakes in writing, but, as is clearly discernible, of errors in translation. And the "German," too, which in some cases evidently clings slavishly to the literal rendering of terms not entirely familiar to the layman, and in others employs specifically German idioms to facilitate the understanding while preserving the peculiarities of the foreign pattern, clearly shows that we are dealing with a translation of a *Latin* original, and not with an earlier emendation of the German text. The time and origin are easily determined by documentary proof.

We know from a letter sent by the Nuremberg delegates (to Augsburg), Christoph Kress and Clemens Volkamer, to the council on May 31st, that on said day they had obtained the "Articles like those previously composed in Latin," but without preface or conclusion, and that they intended to have

---

[10] The manuscript, which has no title of any kind, and is preserved in the Nuremberg District Archive in a bundle of documents bearing the signature S. I. L. 68. No. 6 (recently reported by Schornbaum, Z. K.-G. xxvi, p. 146), consists of 16 folio leaves in two layers of four sheets each, fastened together. The first leaf and the last are blank. At the foot in the margin are found signatures in part, but not continued A ij., etc. Dr. Schornbaum had the kindness to copy the document for me, which is hereby most gratefully acknowledged. Apart from the fact that double consonants were omitted and the initial v's were changed to u, the spelling of the manuscript is accurately reproduced. It was necessary also to mark in the annotations the words crossed out or corrected in the text, which prove that we have a translation before us. (See below on this point.) *The punctuation, which is almost entirely lacking in the manuscript, has been inserted by me.*

them copied by "Mr. Jerome Ebner's sons" and sent to the Council of Nuremberg."

This was done on June 3rd, on which day they wrote home: "Herewith we send your worships a copy of the Saxon resolution in Latin, accompanied by the preface or preamble. But it lacks an article or two at the end and the conclusion, since the Saxon *Theologi* are still at work on these parts." [12] According to this, the delegates upon their instance had also obtained the preface, and it is easy to understand from its contents that Melanchthon did not like to publish it too soon. As early as June 4th (which shows how quickly messages were carried in those days from Augsburg to Nuremberg) the resolution was in the hands of the council, [13] and on the same day it was resolved to present a copy to the theologians, but to provide that no further copy be made, nor that it be put into other hands. [14]

The subsequent history of the document is related in a letter of the council dated June 15th (resp. 17) to the delegates, in which we read: "We . . . have meanwhile, since your writing, had the Latin defence of the Prince Elector of Saxony *translated into intelligible German.*" [15] A resolution of the council, dated June 10th, also informs us that a no less personage than the illustrious Jerome Baumgartner was entrusted with this task and excused from attendance at the sessions of the council during the course of his work. And this industrious man had finished his translation in three days, for as early as June 14th the council had examined the contents and determined to have its delegates in-

---

[11] *Corpus Reformatorum* II, 78.

[12] *Ib.,* 83.

[13] V o g t , *Die Korrespondenz des Nürnberger Rats,* etc. Mitt. d. Ver. f. d. Gesch. Nürnbergs, IV. Heft. (1882), p. 13.

[14] "That the Latin resolution of the Saxons be presented to our theologians and previously be copied ; but that provision be made that it be not copied nor put into the hands of any one." Resolution of the council, June 4, 1530. (*District Archive* at Nuremberg.)

[15] V o g t , p. 13.

quire of the Elector whether it would be agreeable to him to have the signatures of the councillors.[16]

Since a comparison of this manuscript with other writings definitely known to have been produced by Baumgartner, prove him to have been the real writer, there can be no doubt that the Augustana text before us—I shall henceforth designate it with Na—is the *translation of the Latin resolution* produced in Nuremberg for the information of the council and made from the copy sent home June 3rd by the delegates.

The regrettable circumstance that the Latin original was not preserved is easily understood from the fact that the council did not preserve it in its archives, but sent back the Latin articles June 15th (resp. 17) to the delegates "to have at hand if needed." [17]   At any rate, the discovery of this document presents us (though it be only in a German translation) the Augustana according to the stage at the end of May, 1530, and along with it the *oldest extant redaction of the Confession,* together with *Melanchthon's preface,* which was hitherto considered lost—a circumstance which gives peculiar value to the document.

––––––––––––

The document is divided into the preface, the articles of doctrine, 18 resp. 17 (see below), and the "controversial articles in which are recounted the altered and abolished abuses."

Let us first look at the long preface, which ought more correctly to be styled an introduction.   Up to the present we knew only the first short draft which Melanchthon prefixed

––––––––––––

[16] Resolution, Tuesday, June 14th :—" That the delegates at Augsburg be written that the Saxon resolution pleased a certain council and that they ascertain from the Elector whether his grace would permit that a council affix its signatures, and that they also send the decree of the Elector." To this was added " or whether discriminations were to be made." Concerning the above negotiations of the Nuremberg theologians in the matter of joining the Elector, Dr. C. Schornbaum will soon present more information in a book entitled " The Politics of George the Pious."

[17] V o g t , as above p. 15, before the last Alinea omitted the following sentence from the original (correspondence of the Nuremberg Council 101, p. 118) :—" We return to you your copy of said apology sent us by you, that you might have it at hand in case of necessity." The delegates in sending it had requested to have it returned. (*C. R.* II, 84.)

to the Torgau Articles with the remark: "In hanc sententiam prodest proponere prefacionem longam et rhetoricam." We also knew (if we may repeat the statement) that on his journey to Augsburg, while in Koburg, he prepared that introduction of which, as I am inclined to assume, there is preserved to us a fragment in a writing from his own hand and preserved in the archive at Weimar,[18] and which he immediately after his arrival in Augsburg elaborated more rhetorically.[19] There can be no doubt that in Na we possess Melanchthon's introduction as then prepared, although we cannot be sure whether it underwent further changes until May 31st or not.

And it is characteristic enough. The original plan of the Torgau Articles is still recognizable; but it has received other contents. In order to obtain a historical appreciation of this circumstance we must remember that it was written under the impression caused by John Eck's well-known writing and the preface of the Ingolstadt disputator,[20] which stirred the Emperor to the greatest extremes. If Melanchthon, as he himself recounts, found himself induced to transform the original apology into a Confessio, he considered it all the more stringent to give his introduction a strongly apologetical character.

He begins with a very evident *captatio benevolentiæ.* In the face of his calumniators the Elector next to God puts all his hope upon the constantly proven goodness and clemency of the Emperor. As he had always sought the peace of Europe without pride, insolence or lust of blood, thus in the religious controversies he had constantly shown clemency

---

[18] F ö r s t e m a n n I, 109. *C. R.* II, 63.

[19] Melanchthon to Luther, *C. R.* II. 39 seq. It is no longer believed that the document printed by F ö r s t e m a n n I, 639 seqq. in *C. R.* IV, 999 seq., which in its whole tenor could hardly originate with Melanchthon, is a draft of the exordium prepared in Augsburg, as Bretschneider presumed and P l i t t I, 524, found highly creditable   Brieger's view (*Torgau Art.,* p. 296) that it is probably an instruction for Dolzig on one of his embassies to the imperial court, is probably nearer the truth.

[20] See K o l d e, as above. Preface by P l i t t, *Einleit. in d. Aug.,* I (Erlangen 1867), pp. 527 seq.

alone, and was falsely accused of lust of blood, which was evident from his declared readiness to hear the case. And as the Elector desired nothing more than thus to further the glory of God and establish universal peace, so nothing would be better pleasing to God, than if the Emperor would use his power to unite Christendom, just as formerly Theodoric, Charlemagne and Henry II. had done, for the Holy Ghost actually admonished princes to protect the faith. And since the present Emperor was endowed with no fewer virtues and fear of God than said princes, and even far surpassed them in power and splendor, it would not be beneath him to hear the cause of Christendom and to unite it.

But before the doctrine preached in the Electorate is discussed, the attempt is made to prove that the Elector did not further the new doctrine with an evil purpose.[21] Never before did the two brothers, Dukes Frederick and Hans, fall under any suspicion or evil report, for they were kind to every one, no matter what his condition, and they have built or adorned churches and institutions to a large degree with their own means. They have always kept their allegiance to the Roman emperors, and in all affairs of the government they supplied noteworthy aid in money and armature. They never entered into alliances with foreign nations or the opponents of the government, and for the sake of the peace and unity of Germany they never gave occasion for discord to anyone, but in the face of great provocation they were patient in the interest of peace, and more than once "by their pains and exertions they brought to peace and quiet others who were only too ready in arms." How could it be thought that the Elector, without any great cause, would involve his honor, property, children and grandchildren in such danger? What advantage could accrue to him from such dissension? It was hidden from him what troubles he would assume along with this matter. It did not originate with him, but with the many pious souls, who were aggrieved because Christian

---

[21] Compare the Introduction of the Torgau Art., T h . K o l d e , p. 128.

doctrine was oppressed and obscured with human opinions, useless talk and daily increasing abuses, while no one was able to speak concerning repentance and the grace offered us not for the sake of our satisfaction, but through faith in Christ.

Furthermore, it was the preaching of indulgences in Saxony, which were unduly exalted, that induced Luther to offer objections in several pamphlets, academically as it were, and not before the people, and without any slander of the Pope. But his opponents at once stirred up strife and secured his banishment before the case was even tried. Luther was compelled to give answer and many were pleased therewith, not because he rejected indulgences, but because of the salutary and comforting doctrine of repentance and justification by faith.

Hence it seemed a grievous and sinful thing to the Elector to undertake anything against the originators of this doctrine, especially since those who were concerned in it would not venture to do anything in the matter, and the changes in religion would have been much worse if the learned preachers had been removed. For before Luther wrote anything, offensive and erroneous doctrine had arisen, and would have caused dangerous innovations and rebellion, if Luther had not prevented it. The opponents themselves, who now speak much more guardedly of their own inventions, must admit that there is much that is wholesome and useful in this doctrine.

It is evident that through it many heresies against the holy sacrament have been suppressed. Then, too, the doctrine of the Anabaptists against the holding of earthly possessions, against the courts, the power of the civil authorities and all civil order would have been spread much more widely had not the hearts of men been strengthened by this (evangelical) doctrine. It is even unfounded to say that the Anabaptists and their ilk were sprung from Luther's doctrine. "For such things have started before Luther and abounded most in those places where there was a dearth of true pastors that might have strengthened and guarded the conscience of men against false doctrine."

The matter had been made odious chiefly through the common talk that the Evangelicals had done away with all ceremonies and destroyed all spiritual order. On the contrary, their constant endeavor was to retain them with all godly fear, so that it could be said that the mass was not celebrated with greater devoutness anywhere else in Germany. They followed the ordinary custom, too, except that along with the Latin singing they also used the German. The people received the sacrament with greater reverence and oftener than formerly, and every one was examined beforehand, a thing which formerly could hardly be done, as people sometimes came to it in crowds. Confession is also observed, the power of the keys is lauded in public preaching, and the sermons are pure and intelligible, and this surely is the most acceptable offering before God.

At times psalms and the litany are sung, not for the sake of lucre or money, but by the pupils and the assembled people, whereby the ignorant receive practice and are earnestly admonished to prayer through God's Word, and that is the purpose of the ceremonies.

The holy days are also observed with the exception of a few newer ones, with which more enlightened men have long been displeased. To this is added a very useful ceremony, which in former times was very diligently observed and later on was completely lost sight of, owing to the sloth of the pastors and the people, namely, the catechising or instruction of the young. For this the boys and girls are gathered in the churches and the principles and foundations of the Christian faith are explained to them, and they are then examined as to what they have remembered. All this is of great advantage in spreading Christian knowledge. The churches, too, are maintained at great expense to the government.

This is the ordering of the churches in the Electorate of Saxony, and the Evangelicals wished nothing better than that it were pleasing to the bishops also, but these persecuted it on account of the marriage of the priests and such reasons. "If they," writes Melanchthon, "were a little better disposed, no one would need to complain that the order of the Church is broken. It is unfounded to say that the object of this doctrine is to suppress spiritual power." If the bishops would give up some new causes of complaint, their power and glory would in no wise be diminished, and they would not need to worry about their possessions. To this Melanchthon adds very characteristically, "However, some others more than once have attempted under the guise of a reformation to deprive the ecclesiastics of their possessions." Also the Bohemians had said at the Council of Basle that ecclesiastics ought not to have any possessions, but the evangelical doctrine was that every Christian, also bishops and other ecclesiastics, ought to be permitted to own property. The poverty of bishops does not help the Church. The essential thing is that the gospel be preached in its truth and purity.

Once again the statement is emphasized that the seditious attempts to rob the clergy of their possessions have nothing whatever to do with the doctrine of the Evangelicals, who desire only that Christians be instructed in pure doctrine and consciences remain undisturbed by unchristian precepts. In conclusion it is stated: "Thus we teach that all civil ordinances and laws under spiritual and temporal power be considered the order of God for the sake of peace and unity. Never has a reformation been undertaken so utterly without violence as this one, and it is well known that our friends have brought others to peace who were already prepared for an uprising."

This is Melanchthon's significant introduction. How diplomatically stated it must have appeared to its author, and how little it was so in reality! There is not the slightest reference to the political situation, and the question of a council, which was so prominent in the minds of the leading men, is not even touched upon. Melanchthon expects everything from the Emperor. Hence his purpose is, above all, to gain him and to reduce the contrasts to the lowest degree.

It is easy to see how much he was concerned to gain Luther's consent to this introduction, which is almost an integral part of the whole, and that he purposed to get it personally by traveling to Koburg.[22] And Luther's remark in his letter to the Elector, of May 15th,[23] that he could not step so softly will now be seen to apply by no means in the least degree to this introduction. And surely it would hardly be possible to step more softly than was done here!

It is also evident that this introduction, aside from its special pointing toward Saxony, was by no means framed in such a way as to be a common confession, and could not even be made the foundation of one. The appeal to the Emperor as the founder of religious peace and the divinely appointed protector of pure doctrine,[24] even if it was agreeable to the gentle Nurembergers, could hardly have been acceptable to the Landgrave. And the manner in which the merits of the Elector were brought to light at the expense of others, and with almost unmistakable allusion to Philipp's procedure in the Pack Conspiracy and his propensity for entering into alliances, even outside the Empire, was dwelt upon, must actually have proven offensive to other Evangelical Estates.

---

[22] Letter to Luther, May 4th: "I made the introduction to our apology somewhat more rhetorical than I had written it at Koburg. But I shall bring it to you myself, or if the Prince will not permit it, shall send it." *C. R.* II, 39 seq.

[23] De Wette IV, 17.

[24] The document mentioned before, which most probably came from the Saxon chancery, and which must have contained instructions for Dolzig, shows that the entourage of the Elector very soon gave up this view. For in this the Emperor is to be admonished as follows: "That your Majesty would condescend to be content with the obedience of the temporal sword since your Majesty has no command of God over the spiritual sword to rule over souls and therefore owe it to God not to usurp it nor to rule or constrain the souls to believe thus or so." Förstemann I, 64.

This must have sealed the fate of this introduction in the days in which confederate action was proposed.

We can trace this even now, and many statements in the documents referring to this matter are only now becoming intelligible in connection with Melanchthon's document.

The first one who uttered the desire to subscribe to the Saxon Confession must have been the Landgrave.[25] But this could have been mentioned only in conversation with the theologians with whom he was treating concerning an alliance with the Zwinglians[26] without any knowledge of the Apology,[27] and by no means officially. At least Christopher Kress, the Nuremberg delegate (whom he immediately, upon his arrival, sought to win for the thought of urging a council as such, and by no means to permit the estates of the Empire to judge the matters of faith), understood the Landgrave to have said "that his Grace had not specially conversed with the Elector about it, and also thought that they were not on the best of terms with each other."[28]

Also the Nuremberg delegates who, like those from Reut-

---

[25] Melanchthon writes as early as May 22nd: "Nunc Macedo agit ut orationi nostrorum subscribat" (*C. R.* II, 60.) This must refer to the Confessio, although the term oratio is surprising.

[26] I am inclined to think that Melanchthon s information came from Urban Rhegius, who writes to Luther on May 21st about a recent conversation with the Landgrave Philipp and sums up his opinion thus (K o l d e , *Analecta Lutherana*, p. 124; E n d e r s VII, 341): "In short I formed the hope concerning the Hessian that he would by no means reject the sane counsels of Philipp and others." Compare with this Melanchthon's report (*C. R.* II, 60): "Now Macedo is treating about subscribing to our oration and seems able to be won over to our side; but we need your letters. (Both documents may have been sent to Luther simultaneously.) The only question is, whether the immediately preceding sentence of Melanchthon, "All at once the articles must be changed and accommodated to circumstances" must be referred to the Landgrave's wish also to subscribe to the Apology. At any rate there is in Na no trace of deference to his conception.

[27] This conclusion must be drawn from the fact that the Nurembergians, although Chancellor Brück had promised to send them a copy of the document upon his return from Luther (*C. R.* II, 51), even though they had presented their *own* counsel, did not at once receive it.

[28] *C. R.* II, 52.

lingen,[29] had received only the general instructions to side with the Elector in matters of faith, did not begin definite negotiations until they had Na in hands.[30] *Above all things, the Elector himself in the beginning, so far as can be seen, did not care at all about joining forces.* When Chancellor Brück informed him of the desire of the Nurembergians to see the counsel, he sent them the very plain answer: "His electoral highness does not care to have many counsellors in such an affair, for the devil (and the reporter adds these were his very words), was fond of mixing in counsel." [31] It is easily seen that he wished to act alone, and especially to brook no interference. He had independently and secretly, without consulting his theologians, in the first days after his arrival in Augsburg, sent a translation of the Schwabach Articles to Innsbrück to convince the Emperor of his orthodoxy.[32]

Neither did the Ansbach counsellors advance any farther. As their partisanship up to date made natural, they sought to get into contact with the Elector probably soon after the Margrave's arrival on May 24th.[33]

As late as June 8th Chancellor Vogler conversed with Kress on the "Defect that the Saxon document was offered only in the name of the Elector," while his lord thought best to "have it offered in the name of all the princes and cities that are in unity in the articles of faith." He thought, and now only can we understand this demand, since we have discovered Melanchthon's recounting of the merits of the Elector

---

[29] *C. R.,* II, 57. Ad. Weiss' Diarium in G e o r g i i , *Uffenheimer Nebenstunden.* Schwabach 1743, p. 683, May 5: " The Reutlingians in these days are assuring the princes, the Elector of Saxony and ours (i. e., George of Brandenburg), that they will persevere with them throughout, in common risk and doctrine."

[30] K o l d e , p. 33 note 4.

[31] *C. R.* II, p. 53.

[32] B r i e g e r , p. 392.   C . S t r a n g e , Kurfürst Johanns Glaubensbekenntniss vom Mai 1530.   *Theol. Studien u. Kritiken,* 1903, pp. 459 seq.

[33] *C. R.* 69.   That the Margrave from the beginning intended to go with the Elector and Nuremberg (" as we are in unity with them in the articles of our holy faith and the order of visitation ") is proven by the instruction to his councillors on March 24th.   Cf. F ö r s t e m a n n I, 119 seqq.   (Additional information may be expected from S c h o r n b a u m , *Die Politik Georgs des Frommen,* which is to appear soon.)

—that *"In the introduction whatever any one had done for his imperial majesty and the empire, might be specified and mentioned in particular, where it could not be done in general, for the sake of every prince and estate."* This shows in what manner the Margrave and the Nuremberg delegates wished to remodel Melanchthon's introduction.

This was not the case with the Landgrave, who, a few days later, seems to have made earnest endeavors to effect a union with the Elector. We have no direct proof for this, but it is borne out by the Landgrave's correspondence of the period from June 11th-13th with Melanchthon and Brenz [34] concerning the "Counsel regarding the division of the sacrament," which had been sent him from Strassburg. Neither can we affirm with certainty whether Philipp already knew the wording of the Saxon "counsel" with Melanchthon's introduction; [35] but he did know that Melanchthon intended to exclude the Zwinglians, and to grant the Emperor the right of decision in the religious question (a thing which can refer only to the "counsel"), and to substitute the Diet mediately for the Council.

He protests against both. "If this here is to be a council, it will undoubtedly be a council such as there has never been before. And if all of us who confess Christ were to wait for the resolution to be adopted here, I must be mistaken in my reading of the Scripture." [36] And it really appears as if he meant to repudiate Melanchthon's statement in the introduction, when he refers to Luther's teaching that "the authority of the government does not extend so far; but that the gov-

---

[34] The correspondence *C. R.* II, 92 seqq. As to the origin of the " counsel " —Melanchthon says only : " The writer of said document " in loc. p. 94— V i r c k , *Strassburg's Politische Korrespondenz* I, 447—Brenz, who, with Adam Weiss, was invited to dinner at the Landgrave's, June 13, had a verbal discussion with him de re sacramentaria. Cf. Weiss' Diarium in G e o r g i i , *Uffenkeimer Nebenstunden*, p. 689.

[35] One remark is even against it, namely p. 99, where he says : " And I hope by no means that you intend to compel the Zwinglians by force to accept your faith or that you will pass them by on account of their faith ; . . . I do not think you are capable of that, *although much is told me.*"

[36] *C. R.* II, 98.
19

ernment must rule only over the body and property, and not over souls and consciences." Or again, in answering the attack upon the Zwinglians (in Melanchthon's letter: "whatever foreign following they may have") just as if to minimize to the utmost Melanchthon's assertion in the introduction that the Elector never allied himself with foreign nations or the enemies of the empire,[37] he very strikingly remarks that the "Elector has also made alliances with princes and cities, and daily seeks such."[38] At any rate, "the confederation and the invitation to a council[39] were the two points which Landgrave Philipp originally established as the conditions for his going with those of Wittenberg."[40]

It is upon this point that negotiations must have been entered the next few days following, after the question of preaching clearly showed the menacing danger, and made the Saxons more ready to include their former allies in their confession; but unfortunately we are not informed as to particulars in this matter. On June 15th the question of going together was settled in principle. At least Melanchthon, in the "German" text which the Nurembergians then sent home, had put "a common word that could be applied to all estates"[41] in place of the statement "of the Latin text that in the Electorate of Saxony this or that was preached or observed;" but the work on the introduction and conclusion had been postponed. Evidently they were delaying the decision on Melanchthon's introduction, which the Elector must have been very loathe to give up, and much to their discourage-

---

[37] *Vid.* Chap. XVIII.

[38] *C. R.* II, 99.

[39] *Ib.*, II, 92 seq.

[40] A third question, but one in which the Landgrave did not stand alone, was the one concerning the jurisdiction of the bishops. What Melanchthon wrote in regard to it to Camerarius, June 19th: " Jurisdictionem totam καὶ τὸ ἀξίωμα reddo Episcopis. Hoc fortasse urit quosdam qui aegre patiuntur sibi libertatem suam adimi " (C. R. II, 119), does not agree with his statements in Na nor in A, but with the introduction. How far he was ready to go in this matter—perhaps even then—is best seen in his letter to Camerarius, Aug. 31st. *Ib.*, 334.

[41] *Ib.*, 105. This German text, which would be an important document for the history of the text, has not yet been discovered.

ment neither the Margrave nor the Nuremberg delegates received any information on the condition of the question."[42]

But on the very day on which Kress wrote this, the common danger had brought the princes closer together. Together the Elector, the Margrave, the Duke of Lüneburg and the Landgrave, being invited to a "particular apartment" by the Emperor, had maintained their evangelical position in the question about preaching and the processions.[43] They must now stand together. And in the remarkable opinion of Chancellor Vogler, delivered June 16th, on the preaching question, and in which he advises to deliver to the Emperor the doctrinal articles of the confession so as to convince him of the orthodoxy of the Protestants, the evangelical *princes* at least are denoted as a fixed confessional group. It bears the title "Certain considerations why my most clement lord, the Elector of Saxony; Margrave George, of Brandenburg; Duke Ernest and Duke Francis, of Brunswick and Lüneberg; Philipp Landgrave, of Hessen, and Wolfgang, Prince of Anhalt, cannot consent to postpone or set aside the preaching of his electoral and princely grace."[44] Not until June 18th did the Nuremberg delegates receive the promise from the Elector and the Margrave "to receive them in this matter along with his grace."[45] Besides, if the observation of the delegates was correct, that "the Margrave in this promise was more frank and friendly with the Saxons," we may conclude that the Elector had consented against his will. Now, however, the question concerning the introduction and the invitation, which was not yet forthcoming, had to become a more burning one.

The Landgrave must have convinced himself that the Swiss

---

[42] " Since there is such a delay with the introduction and conclusion and no reference is made either to Margrave George or to us, we think that there might be a way to negotiate with Margrave George and then in the name of his princely grace and your grace, a start be made with the Elector."—*C. R.*, II, 105.

[43] *Ib.*, 106. Th. Kolde, *Martin Luther*, II, 342.

[44] Förstemann, I, 275. The paper sent to the Emperor in this matter the next day bears the same signatures, except that of Duke Francis of Lüneburg.—*C. R.* II, 106.

[45] *Ib.*, 112.

and Highlanders were not to be included in the confession, and in matters of the "brotherhood" he had already yielded very much, when in his writing to the Emperor concerning the postponement of the preaching he subscribed the sentence: "Thus they make a true report concerning several doctrines, which (presented to the people for the sake of the sacrament and, therefore, difficult, and for the sake of bettering them as we trust in God) it would prove detrimental, if our preacher were to cease preaching, though we might agree to such postponement, and we would judge our own conscience before God, if we were guilty of such evil." [46]

On the other hand, it must be seen from the latter occurrences, what great danger it involved to leave the decision to the Emperor and the Diet as Melanchthon desired in his great reliance upon the clemency and goodness of the Emperor. Secondly, it must be observed that only a dependence upon the expected council, which was the Landgrave's chief demand, promised sure defence. Besides the desire of the Margrave and the Nurembergians as first expressed, to exalt their services to the Emperor and the Empire in the same manner as Melanchthon had done for the Elector, proved unfeasible for formal reasons. Thus the compromise was effected, which we possess in Brück's masterly address.

Melanchthon's introduction was entirely set aside. With it were dropped all of its more or less open attacks upon the Sacramentarians and the declarations upon the jurisdiction of the bishops which could hardly be harmonized with the sentiment expressed at the last Diet of Spires. Even, as may here be remarked, the attack upon the Sacramentarians, which may be found in Na in the article on the Mass,[47] was [48]

---

[46] Förstemann I, 288.

[47] *Vid.* Art. on the Mass in Chapt. XVIII.

[48] In a weakened form there is a recollection of it in the later German text at the close of the first paragraph: " At the same time instruction is given against erroneous teaching of the sacrament." This formula, which is so general that the Landgrave and even a Zwinglian could accept it, must surely be due to a compromise, for shortly before, Spalatin's text had it " At the same time instruction is given against the wrong and erroneous

omitted, although, much to the Landgrave's sorrow, the Tenth Article retained the original phraseology.

But he was much more successful in regard to the other point. In an entirely businesslike way it is mentioned in reference to the call to a Diet, that the Evangelical Estates present their "Opinion and View on account of errors, schisms and abuses," and offer, if the other Estates did as much (of which Melanchthon's introduction says nothing), to confer with them "in an amicable, harmonious manner." At the same time, quite in agreement with the Landgrave, and referring to the Diet transactions of recent years, they recall the declaration of the Emperor that he did not purpose to let the Diet render a decision in matters of faith, but repeatedly stated that he would request a council from the Pope.

For this reason the Evangelical Estates "superfluously" offer to take part in such a common, free Christian council, and renew their former appeal to one. Thus the "offer" which summarized their demands and positions, and for which the Nurembergians continued to wait,[49] and which originally was to have been placed in the conclusion, was put in the introduction where it belonged, and they contented themselves with a short epilog, which perhaps was not added until the final recension on June 23rd. It cannot as yet be fully determined from the documents extant when the introduction was written, but it might be certain that the distinct repudiation of the thought to let the Diet decide on a matter of religion was occasioned[50] in part by the imperial proposition on the opening of the Diet on June 20th, and agreed

teaching of the sacrament," which could refer only to the Zwinglians. (F ö r s t e m a n n , I, 331.)

[49] "To write the delegates from Augsburg to send down as quickly as possible the beginning and ending of the Saxon Council. Friday, June 17th". (Council resolution).

[50] "And therefore his majesty is graciously disposed to consider and *dispose* of the matter in this manner," etc. (F ö r s t e m a n n I, 308. Cf. also the remark of the Strassburg delegates. V i r c k , *Politische Korrespondenz* I, 458 : " And thus they are silent concerning their oft promised council ").

upon in the common deliberations of the Evangelical Estates on June 21st.[51]

[From the foregoing results as well as from a detailed comparison of the texts in Na and A, it becomes evident that the production of the text which was read to the Emperor at the Augsburg Diet, was a matter of painstaking labor involving many alterations in the original manuscripts. We are now in a position to state with much ground for confidence by what process certain expressions found their way into A and to whom certain statements were due. If we were presenting the original text as Kolde did in regard to Na, it would be possible to build up the argument critically. But as these texts are not here at hand such an investigation would prove almost useless. We therefore confine ourselves to the summarized statement of the results of the investigation as presented by Kolde, being convinced that the facts in the case will bear out his conclusions, as he has stated them in the following] :—

After these detailed investigations it will not be necessary to point out again the importance of the Augustana text newly acquired in Na. The only thing now is to combine the old and the new and to state concisely the conclusions which we now reach as to the gradual development of the text of the Augustana.

An earlier shorter introduction developing the introductory remarks in the Torgau Articles and which is not extant, was written by Melanchthon in Koburg and a later and much

---

[51] *C. R.* II, 124. That the Landgrave did not definitely join until the end, may be inferred not only from a remark of Melanchthon *C. R.* II, 125 (155), but also from the fact that, *e. g.*, the manuscripts Dresden 2 and Koburg which date from the time before the final revision, do not name Philip of Hessen among the Confessors, which (as *T s c h a c k e r t* says, *Archiv für Ref. Gesch.* II, p. 62) can not be caused by inexactness or from the fact that some one subsequently added the subscriptions from memory. (This is assumed for Dresden 2.) This is disproven from the fact that the Elector Francis of Lüneburg and Albrecht of Mansfield are wanting, although in their case it might be and was a question as to whether, according to their position, they were *eligible* to appearance with the real Estates of the empire.

fuller one during the first days of the stay at Augsburg.
We possess it, though perhaps with a few modifications, in
Na. As a result of the transactions carried on concerning a
confederation of the Evangelical Estates and probably not
before the 21st [52] it was supplanted by the Praefatio written
by Brück in German and translated into Latin by Justus
Jonas.

The *Latin* edition of the Confession in its so far earliest
form as presented to us in Na comprised XIX articles in the
first part (resp. XVIII as Melanchthon had contracted VII
and VIII into one) but in such a way that Articles IV and V
and XIV-XVI were transposed. Hence Article XX, concerning "Faith and Good Works" was lacking, as we knew before,
and beside this to our surprise, Article XXI, provided for
in the Torgau Articles concerning "The Invocation of
Saints." The XX. Article is first mentioned in the German
version, not extant, which the Nuremberg delegates sent
home on June 15th. From the letter which they sent with it,
we learn that "it was not yet done into Latin" [53] hence its
Latin form was given shape after the 15th. The first German one which was finally after very many but stylistic
changes,[54] adopted in the Augustana, is extant in Spalatin's
text. The XXI. Article concerning the "Invocation of
Saints," which was written in Latin originally, just as the
later inserted version in Spalatin's text is only a translation
of the *Latin* one and was afterward expunged,[55] appears
first in the I. Marburg version and the French translation
which was made with it as a basis.[56] The German version

[52] In connection with the very late addition of the Praefatio it must also be
observed that it was added only as a supplement to the *Latin* Ansbach text.
Cf. T s c h a c k e r t , p. 41.

[53] C. R. II, 115.

[54] To this was added (Cf. F ö r s t e m a n n I, 326) the passage in A:
" For it is taught concerning faith in Hebrews 11,—as also the devils know."
In T s c h a c k e r t , p. 110, 9-19. The quotation in F ö r s t e m a n n I, 326
is omitted : " Since the Holy Ghost is given through faith, as St. Paul says
in the first chapter of the Epistle to the Hebrews."

[55] F ö r s t e m a n n I, 322.

[56] *Ib.,* 367.

sent June 15th to Nuremberg did not contain it, since only the article on "Faith and Good Works" is mentioned as being added to Na. Hence in its *German* setting (A) it must have gotten into the Confession as the last article.

The Summa at the close of the first part in its Latin version is found in its original form in Na. The second and final form (aside from some unimportant variants) we possess in Marburg I (and the French text).

For since these manuscripts in the order and contents of the articles of faith which they alone contain, show an essentially different form, preparing the text of A and almost identical with it, their text originated after Na and most certainly not before June 8th, for at this date the Nuremberg delegates and the Ansbach counsellors know nothing else than that the Confession is presented in the name of the Elector alone.[57] The *copy* itself (resp. the French translation) must have been made about June 15th, *i. e.,* at the time when the Evangelical Estates were beginning to draw together. And the fact that it contains only the Articles of Faith is easily explained by the circumstance that the Landgrave in view of his relations to the Zwinglians must have desired above all things to learn to know the Articles of Faith, and also that the "Articles in Dispute" were still undergoing the most numerous alterations.

The two oldest *German* texts of the Articles of Faith, are (as has been recently emphasized with justice)[58] the one of Spalatin and the first Ansbach.[59] These too did not receive their final form before June, since they both approach the type of A, and it cannot be assumed that Melanchthon presented his Latin text to the Nuremberg delegates on May 31st while he had already undertaken such important alterations extending even to the arrangement of the articles in his German version, and because in them the Elector no

[57] C. R. II, 88.

[58] Cf. Th. Brieger, Zur Geschichte des Augsburger Reichstages, p. 17.

[59] Förstemann I, 310 seqq. and 343 seqq.

longer appears in them as the sole confessor. As a matter of fact it is now proven that the *Anspach* text was already then in existence and must have served as an enclosure with Chancellor Vogler's Opinion [60] composed June 16th in the form preserved in the manuscript at Nuremberg as Förstemann was the first to conjecture.[61]

Since, further, Spalatin's text is considerably closer to Na, as shown above, though much of Na is already omitted or altered, the view stated first by G. G. Weber,[62] will prevail, according to which Sp. is older than Ansbach I, but of no earlier origin than the first week in June. Thus we would possess two different versions of the German text of the Articles of Faith from the first half of June; but the Summary in only one version, since it is not given in Spalatin's manuscript,[63] and that version with the exception of slight variations in the same form in which it afterwards entered into the Confession.

For the "Articles in Dispute " or the second part, we know the Latin version only in the form recognizable in Na and the final one in A. The former *German* version which corresponds to Na is lacking completely both for the Articles of Faith and the second part. But for Article XXVIII we have the earliest form in Förstemann, I. 87. While then all the other unfinished German and Latin manuscripts that originated before the final determination, show no new type even though they differ in particulars, Spalatin's text undoubtedly assumes the mean between the text to be determined for the time of Na and the later ones presenting in the main the form of A.

---

[60] F ö r s t e m a n n I, 274. Ad rem below.

[61] The same type is found in Hannover I. Cf. P. T s c h a c k e r t , Neue Untersuchungen über Augustanahandschriften. Archiv für Ref. Gesch. II (1904) 69 seqq.

[62] Krit. Gesch. der Augsb. Konf. I, 310.

[63] The fact that Spalatin's text does not reproduce the Summary, is no proof that it did not then exist, as B r i e g e r , Zur Gesch. des Augsb. Reichstags p. 18 seems to assume We know from Na that it existed in Latin. Spalatin must have omitted the passage, because he knew that there was something missing after Art. XIX and later when Art. XX (and XXI) came to him, forgot to insert it, or did not do so, for want of space.

But Spalatin's manuscript is noteworthy from still another relation. In the first place it is clearly a real private undertaking, instigated by that collector's zeal to which we owe so many valuable notes from the hand of Spalatin. It takes a peep at Melanchthon's work at a time when the latter himself did not consider it finished or at all right for inspection by a third party. And this is what makes it especially valuable. Besides, as was mentioned before, it arose gradually and Articles XXI and XX were clearly not inserted until later. And not only that. A new investigation of the manuscript[64] has convinced me that the rest was not written consecutively either. Right in the second layer (fol. 46) begins the second part: " Of the Articles in Dispute," and over this, as over the title of " Articles of Faith and Doctrine," Spalatin made a cross, just as he was accustomed to do over the beginning of most of the documents and letters coming from him. From this I infer that he wrote the two parts which were not combined until later, apart from each other, according as they were accessible to him.

If my remarks above concerning the federation of the Evangelical estates are correct, then *e. g.* the Article on the Mass, which probably also in the German text originally contained the severe condemnation of the Zwinglians, later omitted [*Vid.* Art. XVI, p. 264], can only have originated when the negotiations with the Landgrave were already in progress, but not yet ended, for Spalatin does not contain said passage, but an indirect and much more severe reservation against their doctrine than the final version.[65] Why Spalatin suddenly broke off his copy in the Article on "Vows" and unfortunately did not preserve for us the article so important to the history of the Confession, on the Authority of the Bishops we do not know. I should like to state my surmise that he stopped when he learned that the whole

---

[64] I examined it there Sept. 27th, 1905.

[65] See note 26, p. 235.

document had in the meantime received an essentially different form which made his copy superfluous.

But Spalatin's text also permits of a thing which is closely connected with the origin of the Confession, namely important observations for the determination of the question as to the *languages* in which the individual articles were first written.

In the first place we must emphasize over against errors[66] that continue to be repeated, that the Latin and the German text arose independently beside each other, and that both possess equal authenticity. In detail it cannot be proven everywhere, but at least for some articles, that one was written first in German, the other in Latin and that a certain dependence can be observed even in the received text. That Article XX as noted repeatedly[67] was written first in German, has been handed down direct, and that the German text is virtually a translation from the Latin, is unmistakable. Also the Article on the " Invocation of Saints," is, as shown before, in the German version preserved in Spalatin, only a translation of the Latin. At the same time I consider it possible that Spalatin's text is only a translation of his own and for his own purposes, of the Article so far extant only in Latin and that the later German version must be regarded as an independent one and not a revision of the text found in Spalatin. Also the XXIII. Article on the " Marriage of Priests " was written first in Latin as indicated elsewhere[68] and as can also be seen from a comparison with Spalatin's text. The same may be observed in Article XXVII " On Monastic Vows," since its German text, at least in the final version seems to be only a recasting of the

---

[66] Thus T s c h a c k e r t p. 7, who refers to several passages in the report of the Nuremberg delegates C. R. II, 80, 83, 105 ; but these are disproven by other sources and the critical investigation, that the *Latin* text of the Augsb. Conf. was prepared first.

[67] C. R. II, 106.

[68] B r i e g e r observed this. Torg. Art. p. 300, note 2.

original Latin text.[69] We would have to conclude therefore that Melanchthon first wrote the detailed elaboration of this article, of which he wrote to Luther on May 22nd, in Latin, for the fragment of this article preserved in Spalatin has so many points of resemblance to Na, that one is justified in thinking of the same Latin original for both.

This leads to a further question. Did Luther see the German or the Latin text of the Apology, as far as it was done up to May 10th, or both? So far no absolutely reliable reply can be given to this question. It has indeed been considered proven that Luther saw the Apology in both versions, from the fact that the "Protocoll" of the Nuremberg delegates for May 16th states that the "Counsel written in German and Latin, but not finally determined upon, was sent to Dr. Luther to look over."[70] But this so-called protocoll is no independent source contemporaneous with the events recorded, but a subsequent narration based upon the correspondence of the Nuremberg city council.

As Melanchthon rather wrote Latin than German, and as the Latin version was completed relatively sooner than the German, as can be inferred from various indications, it would be quite natural to infer that Luther saw only the Latin. But this is contrary to the consideration that it was the Elector who sent him the Apology and that the latter must first have read and approved it. Hence, until proof is brought to the contrary it must be assumed as *probable* that Luther saw *both* versions so far as they were finished.

But what *was* finished till then? As for the number of articles seen by him, my investigations have brought out only

---

[69] To mention one example. Quod ei obligatio votorum nullas haberet causas, ut mutari possit. (Tschackert p. 175, 6), is rendered quite awkwardly in German, "wo die Pflich der Gelubde kein *ander* ursach hette, dass sie möcht aufgehoben werden," while Baumgarten renders the sense much better: "Sollten den diese Gelubd nit mogen aufgelost werden," etc.

[70] Thus J . T . M ü l l e r in his Einleitung of his edition of the Symbolical Books. 4. Aufl. Gütersloh 1876, p. LVII and after him K n a a k e et al. Luthers Anteil an der Augsb. Konf. Berlin 1863, p. 75.

this new fact that beside Art. XX, Art. XXI was lacking.[71] The question as to the contents and form of the articles seen by him, is far more important. Even on this point nothing absolutely certain can be stated; but we are justified in stating this very fact as a result of our investigations.

The comparison of Na with A, shows conclusively what great changes the Articles suffered in the last two or three weeks before the presentation. As we can not state positively that Luther saw even the version in Na, but rather all things seem to indicate that the text sent him was considerably altered up to the time when Na was completed, and since the correspondence between Augsburg and Koburg does not offer the slightest indication that he had any part in the altera-tions made, or that any of the later versions was sent him, Luther's direct part in the framing of the Confession, which was defended during the last forty or fifty years more from a confessional than scientific and historical interest, is rela-tively small.[72] Luther helped to frame the Torgau Articles and as can be proven, discussed with Melanchthon before the Diet[73] all other points that might come up and offered no objection to what he saw in the days of May. But that is all.

On the other hand it is also indubitable and must ever be repeated, that nothing un-Lutheran in doctrine, or even Melanchthonian, as has been asserted, has gotten into the Confession by means of the many changes made by Melanch-thon and which Luther would have disliked if he could have

---

[71] As is known from a letter of Luther's dated July 21st (D e W e t t e IV. 110 ; E n d e r s VIII, 133) he missed an article de sanctorum cultu, although it was in the completed Augustana.   This may be explained by the fact that he missed it in the original draft and had not noticed the short article in the finished copy.

[72] I think of the works of L . J . R ü c k e r t , Luthers Verhältnis zum Augsb. Bek. Jena 1854.   C a l i n i c h , Luther und d. Aug. Konf. Leipzig 1861. J . K . F . K n a a k e , Luthers Anteil an d. Augsb. Konf. Berlin, 1863, etc.

[73] Cf. Melanchthon to Luther, June 27th (C . R . II , 146) :   Res sunt antea deliberatæ ut scis, sed semper aliter in acie se dant quam antea sunt de-liberatæ.   To Camerarius, Aug. 27th (C . R . II, 334) :   Nihil adhuc conces-simus adversariis præter ea, quæ Lutherus censuit esse reddenda, re bene ac diligenter deliberata ante conventum.

seen them in detail, merely because such changes were always unpleasant to him and they frequently veiled the antithesis and he would have expressed many things more incisively. We know what great praise the Reformer bestowed upon the work when done and how he rejoiced to have lived to the hour " of this beautiful confession of Christ before such an assembly " [74] and saw Ps. 119, 46 fulfilled in it. " I will speak of thy testimonies also before kings and will not be ashamed "—that word which the first copies prepared in Augsburg and after that all printed editions of the Confession bore as a motto.

[74] To Konrad Cordatus, July 6th : " Mihi vehementer placet, vixisse in hanc horam, quia Christus per suos tantos confessores in tanto consessu publice est prædicatus confessione plane pulcherrima." D e W e t t e IV, 71; E n d e r s VIII, 83.

CHAPTER XVIII.

THE OLDEST REDACTION[1] OF THE AUGSBURG CONFESSION.

Preface of Melanchthon—The Eighteen Articles of Faith—The Articles in Dispute.

SINCE there has been much and all kinds of talk about the Elector of Saxony because his grace has permitted and suffered the change of some few abuses in the order of the Church, his Elec. Gr. has placed his highest hope and trust next to God in the clemency and goodness of Y. Imp. Maj., which is as famous and glorious with every one as the powerful conquest of your enemies. And although in former ages no emperor achieved as much against his enemies, there is nothing more glorious and laudable than that Y. Maj. has done in this nothing else than seek the peace of all Europe. Besides, no pride, insolence or cruelty has been noticeable in this conduct. Also that Y. Maj. in the odious actions, which arose from a difference in common religion and faith, has shown your clemency so manifestly, that you have been willing to consent to graciously hear such dissension. Hence no cruelty may be ascribed to Y. Imp. Maj., since you have so graciously permitted us to come to such a hearing of the case, contrary to the opinion of some.

Hence it is the submissive request of the Elector of Saxony that Y. Imp. Maj. would, in the first place, not suffer your-

---

[1] Kolde, in printing the manuscript, indicates in a series of footnotes the textual readings of many words in this document as they were originally written, but afterward stricken out and supplanted by the readings of the final text. The MS. contains scarcely any punctuation.—*Vid.* Kolde, *Die älteste Redaktion*, p. 3, note 1, and p. 4, note 1.

self to be moved to any disfavor or suspicion against him, and secondly, to hear and consider the case in such a way that thereby the glory of God may be furthered and common peace be preserved and maintained, which the Elector of Saxony desires, not only in view of his age; but also on account of the danger which every one may expect in it. May God help Y. Imp. Maj. to further the unity of Christendom with the same grace as has been done in other matters, since Y. Maj. could perform nothing more well-pleasing to God, nor more glorious or honorable to yourself forever, than to use your power and might for the inquiry into this case and the unification of Christendom.

Therefore, Y. Maj. should also endeavor to follow the example of the most famous emperors, Theodosius, Charlemagne and Henry the Second, who rightly considered it to be a duty of their office to weigh the dissensions of faith and to bring about the preaching of pure doctrine in Christendom, as the Holy Ghost specially admonishes princes to defend the faith, when he says in the second Psalm, "Now, therefore, be wise, oh ye kings; be instructed, ye judges of the earth," and elsewhere: "The princes of the peoples gather themselves together unto the God of Abraham." When the princes of the land gather unto God, God is praised gloriously. With such words the prophet would indicate that God's honor is furthered when the people are induced by the piety of the princes, and the princes maintain God-fearing preachers. Therefore, He also calls the princes the protectors of the land, since they are to protect and defend the righteous and the God-fearing with their power.

Since Y. Imp. Maj. is endowed with no fewer virtues and fear of God than above-mentioned Theodosius, Charlemagne and Henry, yea, far transcends several of them in power and glory, it would not ill become Y. Maj. to examine into the affairs of Christendom and bring about a union. The Apostles have prophesied that Christendom in these last times would have much adversity, wherefore it would be quite necessary to mark the present evils in such a manner that things may not become worse and more dangerous.

But, later on, we will indicate what the doctrine is that is taught in the Electorate of Saxony. At present we will briefly show of what mind the Elector of Saxony is in this matter, so that it might not be thought that he would further and abet this new doctrine out of evil purpose.

The honorable Electors of Saxony, Duke Frederick and Duke Hans, brothers, have always been of such an honorable and brave nature that they have never been known or suspected of any evil. It is also manifest how kind and gracious they have always been toward everyone, no matter of what estate; moreover how much they have always inclined to the Christian religion and faith, is attested publicly, not only by their whole life, but also the institutions and churches which they have in part, at their own expense, built from the foundation, and in part adorned and endowed. Thus they have also shown their faith and allegiance to the Roman Emperors in such a manner as became honorable electors. In all affairs of the empire they have never fallen short in furnishing money or sending stately well-armed auxiliaries. With foreign nations or enemies of the empire they have never had any understanding or treaty. For the peace and unity of a common Germany they have been so inclined that they neither ever gave any one occasion for disturbance; but, though they were highly tempted, they have shown patience for the sake of common peace, so that the disturbance did not become greater. They have also more than once, when others were already arrayed in arms, by their diligence and care brought them to peace and quiet.

And though such things as told above are more than suffi-- cient, more and more praiseworthy things may yet be shown from which the faith and good-will of above-mentioned Electors of Saxony may be seen to greater evidence.

Who would imagine that the Elector of Saxony, without notable and honorable reason, would imperil his honor, chil-

20

dren and grandchildren to such an extent? Or what advantage might accrue to him from this miserable discord and dissension, that could be compared with this danger which he undergoes and sees before his eyes daily? From this it may well be concluded that if his conscience had not driven him, he would not have undertaken to represent these matters, for it was not hidden from him what a burden he would thus load upon himself, although the matter did not originate with the Elector, but with others.

In the first place, many pious and learned people took pleasure in this doctrine, since all upright men were desirous of a pure doctrine, and bore it grievously that the Christian doctrine was oppressed and darkened with the teachings of men and with useless talk. Every one complained of the abuses that increased daily; all teaching in the schools was corrupted; some showed and praised their philosophy; some exalted human teachings. But the things that were given us through Christ, of repentance, of forgiveness of sins that is given us not for the sake of our merit, but through faith in Christ,—of all this no one could speak, although among Christians, above all things, the righteousness ought to be preached that comes from faith, the forgiveness of sins from faith, etc. Every day new forms of worship were invented in the Church that brought revenue, new ways of selling the mass, new saints, new ceremonies, indulgences without number, new monkery, and the consciences of the simple were daily burdened with new commandments.

But there was no one who informed or comforted the consciences with the gospel. This was the complaint, not only of the common man, but also of the bishops, though in secret, for nobody could speak against these things publicly, since the monks ruled so powerfully in Christendom, even over the bishops. But it happened that the indulgence and letters of remission were preached in Saxon lands and exalted unduly. This *Martinus Luther* contradicted by means of several smaller treatises, scholastically and not before the people, and also without abusing or maligning the Pope. But his adversaries quickly kindled a great controversy and published many malicious books in both languages, and soon, before the case was heard, brought up the ban and condemnation of the doctrine. Through such unjust action its respect was somewhat dimmed, and a change took place in many locations.

Nevertheless, *Luther* was importuned to answer, and many pious and learned people took pleasure in his answer, not because he rejected the indulgence, but on account of the salutary and comforting doctrine of repentance and the righteousness that follows from faith. Thus this doctrine was adopted by many pious people, so that it would have been difficult for the Elector of Saxony to proceed in any wise against the originator of this doctrine on account of so many brave and learned people that clung to it, and on account of his own conscience. This was especially the case, since those whose duty it was did not wish to undertake the matter and the change of religion was already at hand, and would only have become greater and worse, if the learned preachers had been put away. For before *Luther* had written anything, all sorts of erroneous and scandalous doctrine had already arisen, which would have caused much grievous change and oppression in Christendom if Luther had not prevented it.

And the adversaries, if they have any sense at all, cannot deny that much that is salutary and useful to the salvation of the soul is contained in this doctrine, which they themselves accept and allow. For it has brought this about that the preachers now teach much more thoughtfully of the power of the keys, of forgiveness of sins, of work-righteousness, of the use of the sacraments, of evangelical counsels, of worldly statutes, of the merit of monastic life and such like human doctrine, of the worship of saints, after such things have been brought to light by us. They also dispute more sharply with us, and even endeavor to slay us with our own sword.

And, as can be proven, more than one heresy has thereby been allayed, which had arisen with new and unchristian writings against the holy sacraments. The Anabaptists had spread a seductive and seditious doctrine against the possession of temporal property, against the courts, against the power of the magistrates, against all civil order, against preaching, against the holy sacrament, all of which would have been spread much further had not the hearts of men been warned and strengthened by this teaching, whereby authority and civil order are well maintained, and the righteousness of faith is so bravely defended against the hypocrisy of the Anabaptists and their imagined angelic holiness. Hence it is not denied by any upright, honest man, that in these schisms much has been brought to light that is absolutely essential to know. It is also entirely unfounded to say that the Anabaptists or their ilk have originated from Luther's doctrine, for such things have occurred before Luther, and most of all in such places where there was a lack of skilful pastors who ought to have strengthened and warned the consciences of men against false doctrine.

This cause was made specially odious on account of the general rumor spread by our adversaries that we had done away with all ceremonies, and were destroying all spiritual order and rule. With how much reason such things are attributed to us the facts will show. For this doctrine is not directed to the end that ceremonies be done away with but rather that they should be preserved with true fear of God, and we can say with truth, that in all Germany the mass is not celebrated with greater fear of God and greater participation of the people than with us. It is also celebrated according to common custom, except that along with the Latin singing we also use German, so that the people may have something which they can understand and learn.

The sacrament is received by the people with greater reverence and oftener than before, and every one is previously examined and instructed, a thing which formerly could not easily be done, as at such a time a whole crowd was accustomed to go together.

Confession is likewise still observed, and the power of the keys is ofttimes praised in preaching and the people admonished what a great power there is in absolution.

The sermons are pure and sensible, which beyond doubt is the most acceptable sacrifice unto God.

Psalms and the litany are also chanted at the proper time, not for lucre or money, but by the pupils and the congregation of people. Thereby the unskilled are practiced and earnestly urged through the Word of God to pray. For this reason the ceremonies must be observed in the churches.

The holy days are still observed, with the exception of a few more recent ones, which have long been displeasing to well-informed men, for which reason the bishops and princes have often counselled how they might abolish some.

Besides all this a very useful ceremony is also observed, which formerly was used with great diligence in Christendom, but afterward fell into desuetude owing to negligence of the pastors and the people, namely, the catechism and and instruction of the young. For this the boys and girls are asked to come together to the churches, where one of the preachers delivers to them the beginning and foundation of Christian doctrine, as the Creed, the Ten Commandments, the Lord's Prayer, several portions of the Gospel on the remission of sins, of repentance, of faith in Christ, of good works, of the cross, of Baptism and the Sacrament of the Altar. Afterward every one is examined as to what it has retained. Thus the children advance exceedingly in Christian knowledge, which formerly was lacking even to the older ones on account of much useless disputation and talk.

The schools are maintained with great diligence and at great expense to the authorities.

This is the order of the churches in the Electorate of Saxony, mostly in accordance with ancient custom and usage of the Roman Church, according to the instruction of holy teachers, and we desire nothing more than that such should also be acceptable to the bishops; but they are a little too hard on us, because they persecute us on account of the marriage of priests and such like things.

But if they were inclined toward us with somewhat more grace, no one would need to complain that the order of the Church is being broken. For the matter of which many accuse us, as if this doctrine had the sole tendency to break up the power of the clergy, is altogether without foundation. For they would lose nothing of their power and magnificence if they would only let up on some new and improper abuses. They would also not need entertain any fear for their possessions, although many others more than once before us have endeavored, under the semblance of a reformation, to take away the possessions of the clergy.

The Bohemians at the Council of Basel, among other things, have also postulated that the servants of the Church should have no private property; but our teaching is entirely different, namely, that as it is permissible to every Christian to use other external things, just so every Christian, whether he be a bishop or a pastor, may legally have and possess his own property. For even if bishops should become poor and lose their properties, that would not help other Christians. But it would help them, if the bishops would provide for the preaching of the pure and unadulterated Word. These seditious propositions to take from the clergy what belongs to it have nothing to do with our doctrine, which demands only that Christendom be instructed in the pure teaching, and the consciences be unburdened from unchristian commandments, for the Christian Church is born and maintained solely from the Word as it is written: He has begotten us through the Word of truth. Thus we teach that all civil laws and ordinances under spiritual and secular power are to be observed as an order of God for the sake of peace and unity. Never has a reformation been undertaken so entirely without violence as this one, as it is evident that through our adherents others have been brought to peace who were already arrayed in arms.

Up to this point we have shown that this controversy arose not without cause, and that it was not tolerated by the Elector of Saxony from a malicious purpose. Now we speak of the doctrine, and first of all enumerate the principal articles of faith from which Y. Imp. Maj. may learn that the Elector of Saxony does not tolerate any unchristian teaching in his territory, but has given all diligence to the universal Christian faith.

The Articles of Faith.

ARTICLE I.

In the Electorate of Saxony it is taught and preached with common consent that the decree of the Council of Nicæa concerning the Unity of the Divine Essence and Three Persons is to be held and believed without doubting; that is to say, that there is one Divine Essence, which is called and is God; one, without body, without parts, of inexpressible might, wisdom and goodness, the Preserver of all things visible and invisible; and yet that there are three Persons of one essence, might and eternity, namely, the Father, the Son and the Holy Ghost. And the term "person" is understood here as the Fathers have used it, to signify not a part or quality in another, but that which subsists of itself.

On the other hand, all heresies are condemned that have sprung up against this article, as the Manichæans, Valentinians, etc.

ARTICLE II.

Also it is taught that, since the Fall of Adam all men according to nature are born in sin, that is, without fear of and trust in God, full of concupiscence, etc., and that this disease

of origin is truly sin, which condemns and brings into
eternal death all those who are not born again through
baptism.

ARTICLE III.

Thirdly, it is taught that the Son of God did take man's
nature in the womb of the Holy Virgin Mary, so that the
Two Natures, the divine and the human, inseparably conjoined in the one Person are the one Christ, true God and
true man, truly born, suffered, crucified, dead and buried as
a sacrifice, not only for original sin, but' also for the actual
sin of all men. He also descended into Hell, and truly rose
again on the third day; afterward He ascended into Heaven,
that He might sit on the right hand of the Father, and
forever reign, justify, sanctify, quicken and defend all who
believe in Him by sending the Holy Ghost into their hearts.
He shall openly come again, and judge the quick and the
dead, as we confess in the Creed.

ARTICLE IV.

Fourthly, that the Holy Ghost is given by means of the
Word and the Sacraments, as Paul saith, "Faith cometh by
hearing." Here the Anabaptists and their ilk are rejected,
who despise the Word and the Sacraments, and think the
Holy Ghost is obtained through human preparation.

ARTICLE V.

Fifthly, that we cannot obtain remission of sins and justification before God by any work or satisfaction of ours;
but we receive it free, gratis and unbought, if we believe
that our sin is forgiven us through Christ and we are received
through grace. For Christ came into the world to this end,
that all who believe in Him should not perish. John 3.
Through such faith in the Gospel or promise of grace we

receive the Holy Ghost, as Paul says, Gal. 3, that we have received the promise of the Spirit through faith.

ARTICLE VI.

Sixthly, that this faith brings forth good works, or that it is necessary to do good works because of God's will, but that we do not thereby merit forgiveness of sins and justification before God, but these are freely given us if we believe that the Father has graciously received us for Christ's sake, and that we are justified, as the early teachers speak, *e. g.,* Ambrosius, the epistle to the Corinthians: "It is ordained of God that he who believes in Christ is saved, freely receiving remission of sins, without works, by faith alone."

ARTICLE VII.

Seventhly, that One Holy Church is to continue forever. The Church is the congregation of saints, in which the Gospel is preached and the sacraments administered. And to the unity of the Church it is enough to agree concerning the Gospel and the sacraments. But it is not necessary that the ceremonies or other human observances should be everywhere alike, as Christ says, "The Kingdom of God cometh not with observation." Although the Church is, properly speaking, a congregation of saints and true believers, nevertheless, since in this life many hypocrites and evil persons are mingled therewith, we may well and without danger use the sacraments that are administered by evil men, according to the saying of Christ: "The Scribes and the Pharisees sit in Moses' seat." Both the Sacraments and Word are effectual by reason of the institution and commandment of Christ, notwithstanding they be administered by evil men.

In this connection they condemn the Donatists and others who taught that the ministry of evil men should not be used in the Church, for what they do is of none effect.

Article VIII.

Eighthly, that children are to be baptized, and that through Baptism they are offered to God and are received into His grace.

Here again they reject the Anabaptists, who say that baptism is of no use to children, and that little children are saved without baptism.

Article IX.

Ninthly, that the Body and Blood of Christ are truly present and distributed in the Supper, and they reject those who teach otherwise.

Article X.

Tenthly, that private absolution ought to be retained in the Church, although in confession it is not necessary to enumerate all sins, for that is impossible.

Article XI.

Eleventh, that those who have sinned after baptism may at any time be renewed by repentance, and that the Church ought to impart absolution to such. But Repentance consists of two parts: firstly, contrition or terror of the conscience through the knowledge of sin; the other is faith, born of the Gospel or of absolution, which believes that for Christ's sake sins are forgiven, and thus comforts and strengthens the conscience. Then good works are bound to follow as fruits of repentance.

Here are rejected the Novatians, who would not permit any one who had sinned after baptism to come to repentance and absolution. They are also rejected who teach that remission of sins is obtained through our satisfaction, and not through Christ. Also the Anabaptists, who teach that one who has once been justified cannot again fall.

Article XII.

Twelfthly, that the sacraments are not only ordained as marks among men, but rather to a testimony of the divine will toward us, instituted to strengthen faith in those who use them. Wherefore we must so use the sacraments as to believe the promises that are added through the sacraments.

Article XIII.

Thirteenth, that all rites that are instituted by men among Christians to obtain grace and justification are unchristian, and offend the honor and merit of Christ; wherefore monastic vows, difference of days and meats and similar traditions of men are useless unto justification. But those usages that are profitable that all things in the church may be done decently and in order we teach ought to be observed for the sake of peace and unity, such as ordering of holidays, chanting and the like; but they must not be made a matter of necessity or of merit.

Article XIV.

[Not extant.]

Article XV.

Fifteenth, of civil matters, that lawful civil ordinances are a good work of God, that a Christian may bear a civil office, sit as judge, determine matters by the existing imperial laws, award just punishment, engage in just wars, buy and make other contracts, hold property, make oath when required by the magistrates, marry, etc.

Here again they reject the Anabaptists who forbid all these things to Christians, also those who do not place the perfection of the Gospel in the fear of God and in faith, but in forsaking civil offices; for the Gospel teaches an eternal righteousness of the heart. Meanwhile it does not destroy external order

and rule, but will have the same used as ordinances of God for
the exercise of charity. Therefore a Christian is bound to
obey the magistrates and their laws, save when they command something unchristian and against God, for then he
ought to obey God rather than men.

Article XVI.

Sixteenth, that all men who have died shall again be awakened with the same body of theirs wherein they died, for the
judgment of Christ, among whom the elect shall really be
saved; but the damned together with the devils shall never
in all eternity be saved from the torment of hell.

Here are rejected the followers of Origen and the Anabaptists, who teach that in the end also the damned and the devils
will be saved from torment, also those who according to
Jewish opinion say that the promise of the possession of the
Promised Land must be understood in a bodily sense, and
that before the resurrection and final judgment the ungodly
shall everywhere be suppressed by the saints, and these shall
obtain the civil power.

Article XVII.

Seventeenth, of the freedom of the will we teach that man's
will has some liberty for the attainment of civil righteousness
and for the choice of things subject to reason. Nevertheless
it has no power without the Holy Ghost to work the inner
spiritual righteousness that counts before God, since the
natural man receiveth not the things of the Spirit of God;
but this righteousness is wrought in the heart when the Holy
Ghost is received through the Word. As Augustine says:
" We grant that all men have a certain freedom of will according to the natural reason, whereby, however, they are
not capable either to begin or to complete aught spiritual or
divine, but only in works of this life, whether good or evil,

the good as to labor in the field, eat, drink, clothe, beget, etc., the evil, as to worship idols, commit murder, adultery, etc."

ARTICLE XVIII.

Of sin we teach that although God has created nature and preserves it, yet the cause of sin is nothing but the evil will of the devil and ungodly men, which will, unaided of God, turns itself from God, as the prophet Hosea says in the 13th chapter: "O Israel, thou hast destroyed thyself; but in me is thine help."

This is about the Sum of the Doctrine in the Electorate of Saxony, in which there is nothing that is contrary to the Holy Scriptures or the Church Catholic or the Church of Rome, in so far as it is founded on tried and accepted teachers. Hence we are unjustly decried as heretics. The whole disagreement is on certain abuses which have crept in without the consent of Christendom. And even in these, if there were some difference, there should be proper lenity on the part of bishops to bear with us by reason of the present confession of our faith, and not sever us from the Christian Church nor reject us, for their own canons are not so severe as to demand the same rites and ceremonies everywhere, nor has it ever been so.

Here follow the Articles in Dispute, in which are reviewed the Abuses which have been Corrected and Abolished.

Inasmuch as in the Electorate of Saxony there is no dissent in any article of the Faith from the holy Scriptures nor the Church Catholic; but only some abuses are omitted which without any reason have become rooted among Christians, we pray that your Imperial Majesty would graciously hear both what has been changed and also what were the reasons for such changes, since it may not be said of us with any truth that we abolish all ancient usages and ceremonies; but we desire to observe them as much as possible. But the common complaint about the abuses in the Church is not a new one of the present moment, wherefore it has been necessary to correct a few as follows:

Of Both Kinds in the Sacrament.

To the laity are given Both Kinds in the holy Sacrament, because Christ has thus commanded, Matt. 26: "Drink ye all of it;" where Christ has manifestly commanded concerning the cup, that all should drink, and lest any man should say that Christ hereby meant only the priests, we refer him to the tenth chapter of Paul's first Epistle to the Corinthians, from which it appears that the whole congregation did use both kinds, when He says, "We are all partakers of one bread and of one cup." This usage has long remained in the Church, nor is it known when or by whose authority it was changed. Cyprian indicates as much in many passages. Thus it was previously nowhere forbidden. Indeed Pope Gelasius commands that the sacrament be not divided. Only custom, not so ancient, has it otherwise. But it is evident that a custom introduced against the commandment of God is not to be allowed. Therefore both kinds are to be used, since Christ Himself commands it, and the canons do so also, and the Church has observed this for a long time. From which it follows that this correction has been made with propriety.

Of the Marriage of Priests.

There has been common complaint concerning the scandalous lives of priests who were not chaste. For this reason also Pope Pius the Second is reported to have said repeatedly, that there were certain reasons why marriage was taken away from priests, but that there were far weightier ones why it ought to be given back. Since therefore our priests were desirous to avoid these open scandals, they married wives and teach that it is lawful for them to do so, since Paul says: "To avoid fornication, let every man have his own wife," etc. Also: "It is better to marry than to burn." Secondly, Christ says: "All men cannot receive this saying," when He teaches that not all men are fit to lead a single life, for God created man for procreation, Gen. 1, nor is it in man's power, without a singular gift and work of God to alter this purpose. Therefore those who are not fit to lead a single life ought to contract marriage. For no man's law, no vow can annul the commandment and ordinance of God.

In the early ages this was the custom in the Church as Paul testifies: "A bishop shall be the husband of one wife." And in Germany, four hundred years ago for the first time, the priests were violently compelled to lead a single life, who indeed offered such resistance that the Archbishop of Mayence, when about to publish the Pope's decree concerning this matter, was almost killed by them. And so harsh was the dealing in the matter that not only were marriages forbidden for the time to come, but existing marriages also were torn asunder, contrary to divine and human law, contrary to their own canons and the laws of many Councils.

In this connection may your Imp. Maj., in order to preserve general morality and honesty, remember that as the world is aging man's nature is gradually growing weaker, and therefore it is quite necessary to guard that no more scandal and vice steal in. For God has ordained marriage to be a help against human infirmity. The Canons themselves say that rigor ought to be relaxed according to the weakness of men, which is devoutly to be wished were done also in this matter, for the marriage of priests, especially of pastors and preachers, is not to the disadvantage of the Church. But although

God has commanded such things and it was the custom from the beginning, and celibacy causes many scandals, adulteries and other abominable vices, yet it is evident that not even wrong-doing or crime is punished so horribly as the marriage of priests. Who has ever seen or heard that anyone should be punished on account of marriage which God has commanded to honor, and which in all well-ordered commonwealths is held in honor even among the heathen. But now the priests are tortured and put to death, contrary to the Canons and for no other cause. Paul calls that a doctrine of devils which forbids marriage. This may now be readily understood when such a prohibition must be maintained with killing and murder.

But as no law of man can annul any commandment of God, so also can no vow abrogate God's commandment. Accordingly also Cyprian advises that women who do not keep the chastity they have promised, should marry. And even the Canons show some leniency toward them who have taken vows before the proper age.

Of the Mass.

We are falsely accused of having abolished the mass, for it is celebrated by us with the highest reverence. But here again it has been a public complaint that they have been basely profaned and a regular fair has been made of them, that priests had no desire for it and yet use it for the sake of lucre. When therefore such abuse among us was reprimanded by the preachers, Private Masses were discontinued, since St. Paul severely threatens those who eat and drink this bread and cup unworthily. But this abuse had crept in so extensively that scarcely any Private Masses were celebrated, except for lucre's sake, which the bishops ought to have corrected.

Besides this it was also abused in another way, as if it could blot out another's sin and bring profit to the dead and the living, wherefore it increased and multiplied to such an extent. Our preachers have also reproved this, since the Scriptures teach in many passages that we are justified through faith alone and not through works, whether they be masses or other works, etc. Christ by His death has obtained for us the remission of sins, hence we must not look for it in the Mass. Christ also did not command it, but He said to us, to do it in remembrance of Him, that is to believe that He will keep His promise made to us, for even Jews and infidels remember Him in other ways. Wherefore the Mass is of use to strengthen faith only to him who holds it, as Ambrose says: "Because I sin daily, I must daily take medicine." Also Christ says: "This do in remembrance of me," from which it follows that the Mass is of no use to the dead, whose faith and memory can not be strengthened thereby. Likewise the Scriptures say that we should thereby proclaim the death of the Lord. What shall we proclaim to the dead?

Therefore in the Electorate of Saxony a single mass is celebrated by the pastor, very much according to the accustomed usage. He administers the Holy Sacrament to those who desire it; but they must first be proved and absolved, and thus it was formerly also held in the Roman Church, as we find recorded.

The people are also advised with the greatest diligence and instructed concerning the use and profit of the sacrament, how faith is strengthened thereby, in order that the people may learn to trust in God and to expect and ask of Him all that is good. This worship pleases God best.

Here we also reject the unchristian doctrine which denies that the body and blood of Christ are truly present, and the people are admonished to receive the sacrament frequently.

Of Confession.

Confession in our churches is not abolished; for the sacrament is administered to no one except he have been previously

21

examined and absolved. And the people are most carefully taught concerning the assurance of absolution about which aforetime not much was known. The power of the keys is commended and we show what great consolation it brings to anxious consciences, and that God requires of us that we should believe such absolution as a voice sounding from Heaven, from which faith follows the forgiveness of sins.

Aforetime much was said about our satisfaction alone, of faith and the merit of Christ little was said. Wherefore on this point we are unjustly accused. For this even our adversaries must concede that we have most diligently treated the doctrine concerning repentance.

But of Confession we teach that consciences be not burdened with enumeration of all sins. For that is impossible, as the psalm says, "Who can understand his errors?" Thus the ancient writers have held, as Chrysostomus: "I say not to thee that thou shouldest disclose thyself in public; nor that thou accuse thyself before others; but I would have thee obey the voice of the prophet who says, 'Disclose thy way before God.' Therefore confess thy sins before God, the true Judge, and recount thy trespass with prayer, not with the tongue, but with the memory of thy conscience." These words indicate that the enumeration of sins is not necessary although confession is not to be abolished on account of the great benefit of absolution.

OF THE DISTINCTION OF MEATS.

It has been thought that making Distinctions of Meats and like traditions are a satisfaction for sins and merit grace. Thus many have taught and daily thought out something new. Such error we did not wish to endure longer, since it is quite contrary to the merit of Christ and the righteousness of faith, which is constantly preached in the Church and ought to be preached. Wherefore also Paul in almost all his epistles opposes this point, in order that men may see that righteousness comes not from such works but from faith in Christ. Some say, although without reason, that we oppose this point, only because we would lessen spiritual authority, some that we are bringing heathen customs into the world, but we do not oppose and abolish all human ordinances in common. But we had to make plain to people what must be thought of it. Besides we are not the first who have taught about it in this manner. Augustine says that they should be considered a matter of liberty. Gerson forbids binding men's consciences with them and thus has given comfort to many pious people; for no one ever came to earth who has observed all these traditions. Many fell into despair and some even took their own lives because they did not have the comfort of the righteousness from faith. But those who kept some of these traditions thought to acquire forgiveness thereby; besides, such traditions were placed far above the commandments of God. If any one fasted at an appointed time or did anything else of the kind, he thought he was a Christian; but no one paid attention to his calling, yea, it was not worth while, that a Christian should concern himself with such matters as managing the household, governing wife, children and servants, and educating them, etc. Such works were accounted as belonging to the weak and imperfect, and only the works of hypocrisy had an honorable name in being accounted holy, Christian and well-pleasing to God.

The masters of canons and the theologians did not touch on the Scriptures, but were forever busy with these things and had no leisure to discourse about faith, hope, the cross and the like. In this matter the bishops ought to have interfered and put an end to such misery. Now even our adversaries are deriving profit on these points and are able to judge the traditions of men more clearly than heretofore.

Our teaching on this point is to this effect that the traditions and ordinances of men do not merit the remission of sins and are not to be exalted as necessary unto the salvation of souls. This we prove from the Scriptures. When the

Apostles were accused of having transgressed those command-ments, Christ said: "In vain do they worship me with the commandments of men." Likewise: "Whatsoever goeth into the mouth, defileth not the man." Likewise Paul: "Let no man therefore judge you in meat," etc. Also Acts 15: "Why tempt ye God, to put a yoke on the neck of the disciples, which neither our fathers nor we were able to bear; but we believe that through the grace of the Lord Jesus Christ, we shall be saved, even as they." Likewise Paul calls the prohibition of meats a doctrine of devils. Therefore such things should not be demanded of Christians as necessary.

Nevertheless many traditions are observed among us, such as holy days, chanting and other things which are serviceable to good order in the Church. At the same time the people are warned that such observances are kept, not of necessity, but for the sake of peace and that it should not be made sin, if they are omitted without scandal.

Such liberty was also used by the Fathers, as can be learned from many decrees and canons. In the East they kept Easter at another time than at Rome, this brought no discord into the Church.

On Monastic Vows.

This discussion does not concern the whole Church; but only a few special persons, for which reason the whole con-gregation can not justly be rejected, even if wrong should be found in this change. Nevertheless we will also recount here what we teach and observe in this matter.

It is generally known what has been the state of the mon-asteries and how many things were done in them contrary to the Canons. In Augustine's time, they were free associations. Afterward, when discipline was corrupted, vows were every-where added, for the purpose of strengthening discipline. Gradually many other observances were added besides vows. And these fetters were laid upon many before the lawful age, contrary to the Canons. Many also entered through ignorance, being unable to judge their strength, though they were of sufficient age. Being thus ensnared, they were compelled to remain, even though they could have been freed by the provision of the Canons. This was more the case in convents of women than of men, although more consideration should have been shown them on account of their weakness. This rigor displeased many good men before this time, who saw that young men and maidens were thrown into convents for a living and what unfortunate results came from this procedure, what scandals, what snares upon the consciences! It is a grievous thing to learn that the Canons were so utterly despised in this matter.

To this was added an all too great exaltation and praise of vows although this also was not pleasing to every one. They taught, namely, that monastic vows were equal to baptism and that they merited forgiveness of sins and justification before God, and even greater things, because they kept not only the commandments, but also the "counsels."

Thus they believed that the monastic life was much better than baptism and more meritorious than the life of magistrates and pastors who serve their calling according to God's commands.

But what came to pass in the monasteries? Aforetime they were schools in which the Holy Scriptures and other branches profitable to the Church were taught and thence pastors and bishops were obtained. In those days they came together for the sake of studying. Now they feign that it is a life instituted to merit grace and righteousness, yea, they preach that they are in a state of perfection and they put it far above other kinds of life ordained of God. These things we have rehearsed in the least odious manner, to the end that it might be the better understood what our teachers hold on this point.

First, concerning such as contract matrimony, they teach that it is lawful for all who are not fitted for the single life, to contract matrimony, because vows cannot annul the commandment and ordinance of God. But the commandment of

God is: "To avoid fornication, let every man have his own wife." Nor is it the commandment only, but also the creation and ordinance of God which forces those to marry who are not excepted by a singular work of God, according to the text: "It is not good that the man should be alone." Therefore they do not sin who obey this commandment and ordinance of God. What objection can be raised to this? Let men extol the vow as much as they list, yet it cannot annul the commandment of God. The Canons teach that the right of the superior is excepted in every vow; how then can these vows be of force against God's ordinance?

If then those vows could not be changed, the Popes could not have given dispensation so often, for what God binds, no man can loose. But the Popes have prudently judged in exercising leniency and not always exercising rigor.

In the second place, why do they exaggerate the obligation of a vow when at the same time they are silent about the kind and nature of the vow, that it ought to be possible, free and chosen spontaneously? But it is not known to what extent perpetual chastity is in the power of man. And how many are there who have taken the vow spontaneously and deliberately? Truly very few. Young men and maidens, before they are able to judge, are persuaded and sometimes even compelled to take the vow. Wherefore it is not fair to insist so rigorously on the obligation, since it must be acknowledged that there can be no vow unless that is vowed which is possible, free and chosen spontaneously.

Many Canons rescind vows made before the age of fifteen, for before that age there does not seem sufficient judgment in a person to decide concerning the whole future of one's life. Another Canon concedes three more years to human weakness that fixes the age at eighteen years. Which shall we follow? A great number of those who come from the monasteries have the excuse that they took the vow before that time.

Finally although the violation of a vow might be rebuked,

it does not follow that marriage between such persons should be invalid, as Augustine writes, whose authority herein is justly esteemed although other men afterwards thought otherwise.

And although God's command concerning marriage delivers many from the monastic vow, yet we introduce another argument why vows should be invalid and void. For every service of God, ordained without God's command, to merit justification and grace is unchristian and contrary to God, as Christ says: "In vain do they worship me with the commandments of men." And Paul teaches everywhere that righteousness is not to be sought by our own observances and merits, but through faith in Christ, etc.

Now the monks have taught unblushingly, that their monastic life works satisfaction for sin and merits grace and justification. What else is this than to detract from the glory of Christ and to deny the righteousness of faith? It follows therefore undeniably that these vows are an unchristian service and therefore void. No vow shall obligate to any evil, as if any one vows to commit a murder, he does wrong; but if he breaks this vow and does not keep it, he does right.

Also, Paul says: " Christ is become of no effect to you, whosoever of you are justified by the law: ye are fallen from grace." They, therefore, who want to be justified by their vows have fallen from grace and Christ.

Above all this, they have imparted their good works to others, and other such things of which they are now ashamed. It is truly no small offence to set forth to the people a service devised by men, without the commandment of God, and to teach that man is thereby justified. For the righteousness of faith which chiefly ought to be preached, as well as God's commandment and the true worship of God are thereby obscured, when the people are informed that only the monks live in a state of perfection, in which are all who fear God from the heart and have a sure trust that for Christ's sake He will be gracious to us and ask of God and assuredly expect His aid in all things.

But the people conceive many pernicious opinions from the false commendations of monastic life. They hear unmarried life praised beyond measure; therefore they lead their married life with offense to their consciences. They hear that only beggars are perfect, therefore they keep their possessions and do business with offence to their consciences. They hear that it is an evangelical counsel not to avenge; therefore some in private life are not afraid to take revenge, for they hear that it is but a counsel and not a commandment. It also follows from this that a Christian cannot properly hold a civil office or be a magistrate.

There are examples on record of men who forsaking marriage and the administration of the Commonwealth, have hid themselves in monasteries. This they call fleeing from the world and seeking a life which should be more pleasing to God. Neither did they see, that God ought to be served in those commandments which He Himself has given and not in commandments devised of men. Every estate that has a word and commandment of God is good and perfect. That which has no word and commandment of God is dangerous. It is necessary to admonish men of these things. And before these times Gerson rebuked the monks for calling their life one of perfection and says that in his day it was still a new and unusual thing to say so. So many erroneous, unchristian things are inherent in vows that they must justly be considered void.

Of the Power of the Church.

Aforetime there has been much controversy concerning the Power of the Bishops, in which some have awkwardly confounded the power of the Church and the power of the sword. And from this confusion great wars and tumults have resulted, while the bishops, emboldened by their power of the keys, not only have instituted new services, and burdened consciences with reservation of cases and the powerful ban, but have also undertaken to transfer the kingdoms of this world and to take the Empire from the Emperor. These wrongs have long since in the Church been rebuked by learned and pious men. Therefore for the comforting of men's consciences, we were constrained to show the difference between the power of the Church and the power of the sword. We teach on this point: that the power of the bishops or the power of the keys, is a power or commandment of God to preach the Gospel, to remit and retain sins, and to administer the sacraments. For with that commandment Christ sends out His Apostles: "As my Father hath sent me, even so send I you. Receive ye the Holy Ghost. Whosesoever sins ye remit," etc. Mark 16: "Go, preach the Gospel to every creature."

This power is exercised only by preaching the Gospel and administering the sacraments, to one or more as one is called. For thereby are granted, not bodily, but eternal things: as eternal righteousness, the Holy Ghost, eternal life. These things cannot come but by the ministry of the Word and the Sacraments. As Paul says: " The Gospel is the power of God unto salvation to every one that believeth." And Psalm 118: " Thy Word quickeneth me." Therefore since the power of the Church grants eternal things and is exercised only by the ministry of the Word, it does not interfere with civil government, no more than singing or arithmetic interferes with civil government. For civil government deals with other things than does the Gospel; the civil rulers defend not the souls, but the bodies and bodily things against manifold injuries and restrain men with the sword and bodily punishments in order to preserve civil justice and peace.

Therefore the power of the Church and civil power must not be confounded. The spiritual power has its own commandment, to teach the Gospel and to administer the sacraments. Let it not break into the office of another, let it not transfer the kingdoms of the world, let it not abrogate the laws of civil rulers; let it not abolish lawful obedience; let it not interfere with judgments concerning civil ordinances or contracts, let it not prescribe laws to civil rulers concerning the form of the Commonwealth. As Christ says: " My kingdom is not of this world." Also: " Who made me a judge or a divider over you ?" Paul also says: "Our citizenship is in heaven." Likewise: " The weapons of our warfare are not carnal; but mighty through God to the casting down of imaginations." Thus we discriminate between the duties, might and office of both these powers, and command that both be honored as gifts of God.

If the bishops have any worldly power besides, they have it not as bishops, by the commission of the Gospel, but by human law, having received it of kings and emperors for the civil administration of what is theirs. This, however, is another office than the ministry of the Gospel.

Our teachers[2] have always taught, for the avoidance of rebellion and riot, that temporal possessions and power, whether possessed by bishops or secular gentlemen, are of no hindrance to the conscience. An honest distribution of property and magistracies is not contrary to the Gospel. The Apostles were fishermen, Luke a physician, Paul a weaver. Their art and craft they retained with a clear conscience and practiced it, although that was different from the ministry of the Gospel and yet their conscience was not burdened thereby. Thus every pastor may own property, some less, some more, for the Gospel commands that an adequate support be given the pastors; but they are to use their temporal possessions in such a way as not to neglect their ministry. Thus bishops are to be mindful of the duties of their office and not only manage their secular government, although it is very difficult to do both at once.

When therefore a question arises concerning the juris-

---

[2] The following was already known to us from the Ansbach text (*Förstemann*, I, 542) and the pre-Melanchthonian print which had it for a source, namely, the so-called editio antiquior (*C. R.*, XXVI, 231).

diction of bishops, civil authority must be distinguished from ecclesiastical jurisdiction. For according to the Gospel or the commandment of God, to the bishops as bishops, no power belongs, except the ministry of the Word and the sacraments, to forgive sins, to discern between Christian and unchristian doctrine, and reject the unchristian, to exclude from the communion of the Church wicked men whose wickedness is known, and this without human force, simply by the Word. Herein the congregations are bound by the Divine Law to obey them, as it is written: " He that heareth you, heareth me."

But when they teach or ordain anything against the Gospel, we are prohibited from obeying them. Matth. 7: "Beware of false prophets." Gal. 1: " Though an angel from heaven preach another Gospel, let him be accursed." Likewise 1 Cor. 13: "We can do nothing against the truth, but for the truth." Also: " The power which the Lord hath given me to edification and not to destruction." Thus also the canonical laws say more elsewhere, and St. Augustine says: " Not even to Catholic bishops must we submit, if they chance to err or hold anything contrary to the Canonical Scriptures of God."

Moreover, it is disputed whether bishops or pastors have the right to introduce ceremonies in the Church, and to make laws concerning meats, holy days and orders of ministers, etc. They that claim this right for the bishops refer to this word of Christ: " I have yet many things to say unto you, but ye cannot bear them now. Howbeit, when he the Spirit of truth is come, he will guide you into all truth." They also refer to the example of the Apostles, who commanded to abstain from blood and from things strangled. They refer to the Sabbath day, as having been changed into the Lord's Day, contrary to an express commandment of God, upon which they insist most of all, that a bishop should have such power.

Concerning this question, it is taught on our part, that

no bishop has power to decree anything against the Gospel. Now it is plainly against the Scriptures to establish any observance, whereby we may come into grace or make satisfaction for sins. For thereby Christ is dishonored. From this reason, that men have thought to merit much thereby, such traditions as holy days, fasting and worship of saints have so much multiplied in the Church. It is manifestly against God to make a sin of meat and holy days, as though we were still under the Old Testament. Hence perhaps some bishops have been tempted to make such observances. Hence it is that they make it a mortal sin even without offence to others, to do manual labor on holy-days, or to omit the Canonical Hours.

Whence have the bishops the right to ensnare consciences with these traditions, when Peter forbids to put a yoke on the neck of disciples, and Paul says that the power given him was unto edification, not to destruction? " If ye be dead with Christ from the rudiments of the world, why, as though living in the world, are ye subject to ordinances, touch not, taste not, handle not, which all are to perish with the using, after the commandments and doctrines of men?" Also in Titus: " Not giving heed to Jewish fables and commandments of men, that turn from the truth." Likewise Christ says, of those who require traditions, Matth. 15: " Let them alone, they are blind leaders of the blind." Likewise: " Every plant which my Heavenly Father hath not planted, shall be plucked up."

Hence it follows that it is not lawful for any bishop to institute or exact such services, since the Holy Ghost did not warn us against this in vain, especially if they be considered necessary, or one thinks to obtain grace thereby. For Christian liberty must everywhere be preserved in the Church, so that all may know that we are justified not through the Law or works, but from grace through faith in Christ.

What, then, are we to think of the change of the Sabbath to Sunday? To this we answer, we confess that it is lawful for bishops to make ordinances that things be done orderly in the Church, not that thereby we should merit grace or make satisfaction for sins, or that consciences should be bound not to break them. So Paul ordains, that women should cover their head in the congregation and that interpreters should be heard in order in the Church.

It is proper that such ordinances should be kept for the sake of peace and tranquillity, that all things be done in the churches in order, and that no one be given offence and that no conscience be burdened.

Thus it is with Sunday, Easter, Pentecost and other holy days. For those who judge that they are ordered thus of necessity, do greatly err. The Gospel has utterly abrogated the Sabbath and other Jewish ceremonies, and yet it was necessary to appoint a certain day that the people might come together, for which purpose the Church elected the Sunday, perhaps, also, for the sake of Christian liberty, so that one might see that we are not bound to the Sabbath.

But the bishops might easily retain the lawful obedience of the people, if they would not insist upon the observance of such traditions as can not be kept with a good conscience. Now they command celibacy. They admit none, unless they swear that they will not teach the pure doctrine of the Gospel. We do not ask that the bishops should restore concord at the expense of their honor, which, nevertheless, it would be proper for good pastors to do. We only ask that they would release unjust burdens which are new and have been received contrary to the Church Catholic. It may be that there were plausible reasons for some of these ordinances; and yet they are not adapted to modern times. It is also evident that some were adopted through erroneous conceptions. Therefore it would be befitting the clemency of the bishops to mitigate them now; because such a modification does not shake the unity of the Church. For many human traditions have been changed, as the canons themselves show.

But if it be impossible to obtain a mitigation of such ob-

servances as cannot be kept without sin, we are bound to follow the Apostolic rule, which commands us to obey God
rather than men. Peter forbids bishops to be lords and to rule
over the churches. Now, it is not our design to wrest the
government from the bishops, but we ask that they allow the
Gospel to be purely taught and that they relax some few
observances which cannot be kept without sin. But if they
make no concession, it is for them to see how they shall give
account to God, for having, by their obstinacy, caused a
schism.

CHAPTER XIX.

THE HAND OF GOD IN THE FORMATION OF THE AUGSBURG CONFESSION, AS SHOWN BY THE COURSE OF EVENTS IN 1529 AND 1530, AND IN THE LETTERS OF LUTHER, AND OF MELANCHTHON.

The Real Question as to the Augsburg Confession—The Emperor's Call—The History of the Reformation up to Augsburg—The Elector takes the Beginnings of his Apology to Augsburg—The Emperor Delays and the Elector Awaits His Coming—The Saxon Apology Becomes a Confession—The Question of Preaching a Test—The Submission of the Confession to Luther—The Emperor's Entry into Augsburg—The Opening of the Diet—The First Ten Days of Suspense—The Confession Completed and Delivered—The Attitude of Melanchthon—Confessional History Subsequent to the Delivery of the Augsburg Confession—The Hand of Providence.

THIS chapter is a chronological study of events, and of the original sources,—aiming, among other things, to place the facts before the reader, in order that he may be in a position to investigate the evidence for himself, and to form his own judgment. With this chapter, Chapters XV and XI of this work, the former by Theodor Kolde, and Chapter VI of " The Conservative Reformation," should be constantly compared.

We have seen that it is a mistake, in discussing the history of the Augsburg Confession, to lay all stress on attempting to establish the claim of authorship in behalf of one or another person.

The real question is, how the Augsburg Confession, in all

its greatness, came into being as the resultant of the forces struggling for the mastery in this critical epoch of the Christian Church. How did the great principles of which the Confession is the great bearer, come to their maturity in the form in which they were—to the surprise of all— formally presented and confessed at Augsburg?

Investigators and historians have been looking on the Augsburg Confession as *a matter of form intended,* and as complete in the eye and mind and hand of Luther and Melanchthon, one or both; whereas, in fact, these men were not conscious of the standard character and the finality of what they would be obliged to evolve and present, in the situation which they were called to meet at Augsburg. The Augustana, as the *magna charta* of the Evangelical Church, was not premeditated by either the Elector, Luther, or Melanchthon, but was a growth resulting from many historical factors, solely under the Providence of God.

That the two leading personalities of the Reformation had no previous conception of the universal and immortal character of the Confession they were preparing; that many historical elements contributed, despite the unwillingness of each and all the principals on both the Lutheran and the Roman sides of the struggle, to the mighty result, attained in this Confession for all time—a result unforeseen by all, and in which the labors of each, beside the clear and marvelous guidance of Providence, sink into comparative insignificance: it is the object of this chapter to establish.

As for the authorship itself, notwithstanding the change of view-point and the modification of details brought about by modern discoveries, we find nothing that will set aside the substantiality of the old verdict that the Augsburg Confession is Luther's *Lehr* in Melanchthon's *mouth.*[1] Barring

---

[1] Melanchthon, *historia de vita Lutheri* lit. B. 3: Quam formam doctrinæ & administrationis sacramentorum probauerit Lutherus, liquet ex confessione, quam elector Johannes, & Philippus Landgrafius imp. Carolo V. anno 1530. exhibuerunt.—*Cyprian*, p. 58.

John's part, this is in line with other documents prepared in consultation by these two great Confessors of the Reformation, except that Luther's enforced absence from Augsburg gave Melanchthon a centrality and a standing in the work of public confession, which had been lacking hitherto, and which is seen still more fully developed in the authorship of the Apology to the Augsburg Confession. The real significance of the new light upon the Augsburg Confession is this: that in the course of events during the Spring of 1530, by the hand of God, the presentation at Augsburg became something very different from what it was originally intended to be, and that it bears its present broad, clear and permanent form, not by the conscious intention of Luther or Melanchthon, but as a result of unexpected pressure from foes, and under the constructive hand of the various Lutheran forces—undesignedly united—that signed it.

It should be borne in mind that the Emperor himself set the matter in motion, and in his Call to the Protestants to attend the Diet, unexpectedly promised great mildness and grace in dealing with them. This Imperial Call filled the Elector, Luther and Melanchthon with hope. For the Elector, this trust, with cautious distrust, in the Emperor probably continued to abide until the latter delayed his coming, and then issued the command to the Protestants to stop preaching at Augsburg. It continued much longer in Melanchthon, though broken temporarily by the sudden revelation, precipitating Melanchthon into great fright, of the Emperor's harshness at Corpus Christi; while in Luther it was not so enthusiastic, but is visible in his "Admonition" and in his private correspondence, and because of his meagre information at Coburg probably continued until after the delivery of the Confession.

22

THE EMPEROR'S CALL FOR THE DIET AT AUGSBURG.

———————

Original in the Archives at Weimar.
Printed in Förstemann, Urkundenbuch I, p. 2; Lünig's Reichs-Archiv, part. gen. cont. I, p. 496.

January 21st, 1530.

To the High-born John, Duke of Saxony,
Landgrave of Thüringen and Margrave of Meissen,
Chief Marshall of the Holy Roman Empire.

Our Dear Uncle and Elector:

Charles by God's grace the elected Roman Emperor, etc. . . . . We should like to abolish all injustice after hearing and diligently weighing every opinion and view in the honorable German nation, and to uphold what is right and honorable by the papal holiness and our imperial might, authority, and permission, and thus have the Holy Empire of the German nation once more brought into unity. . . .

Recently the arch-enemy of our holy faith, the Turk, has invaded the Christian Kingdom of Hungary and our Fatherland, the arch-duchy of Austria. . . .

We have found in the Pope a much greater desire than we hoped, to order all things in the German nation and in the Christian religion, in a right and honorable way. . . .

Therefore we, as Roman Emperor and Head of Christendom, have thought it good and useful to undertake a common Diet [Reichstag] and Assembly, and have resolved to hold it on the eighth day of the coming month of April in our and the holy city of Augsburg. . . .

Because of the duty you owe to us and to the empire, we command you to appear in person at Augsburg on that day, together with the other princes and estates, ... that we may take up the matter of deliverance from the Turk; further, how, because of error and division, it may be possible to deal and determine in respect to the Holy Faith and the Christian Religion.

And in order that this may occur in a more wholesome way, (we desire to) settle the differences, abandon obstinacy, give over past erroneousness into the hand of our Redeemer, and use diligence to listen to, understand and weigh every expression, opinion and view in love and graciousness among ourselves, to compare and to bring them to a single Christian Truth, and to do away with everything that has not been explained or transacted right on both sides, that we all may hold one single and true Religion, and, as we all are and do battle under one Christ, we may thus all live in one Commonwealth, one Church and one Unity. . . .

Given on the first and twentieth day of January.

CAROL.

Ad mandatum Cæsareæ et Catholica Majest. proprium.[1a]

——————

[1a] The document is lengthy, and for brevity's sake we have included only some of the more vital utterances, in condensed translation. We have also condensed many of the documents and letters which follow in this chapter. Otherwise it would have been impossible to reproduce them for the reader. In every instance, pains has been taken to convey the substance and render the exact sense.—*T. E. S.*

This summons, commanding the Electors, Princes, and all the Estates of the Empire to meet at Augsburg on the 8th of April, was issued at Bologna. No threats marred the invitation. The Emperor announced that he meant to leave all past errors to the judgment of the Redeemer; that he wished to give a charitable hearing to every man's opinions; and that his only desire was to secure to all the right to live under the one Christ, in one Commonwealth, one Church, and one Unity.

Thus there appeared in the Protestant world this Call for the purification of the Church and the reunion of a rended Christendom after every diverging judgment had been graciously and fairly weighed, and every difference honorably adjusted. Thus by the sweet, gracious and winning way of the thirty-year-old Emperor, who was coming to his German dominions at last, with a fair mind against errors and abuses, but a closed heart against protest, were the Elector, Luther, and Melanchthon deceived.

THE EMPEROR.

The sturdy German princes and rulers of the holy Roman empire, in electing Charles, were under the illusion that they would secure a German ruler, after the fashion of old Max, the beloved grandfather of Charles; but, too late, they found they had *a Spaniard!*

Not that the young Emperor lacked principles, convictions, conscientiousness, integrity and honor; but that his outlook, his ideas of unity, government and rule, were those of the Latin race; and his court and counsellors, with one or two notable exceptions, were under the spell of Rome. He was not on the side of the Pope in politics, and he was not committed to the Curial view of absolute papal supremacy; but he was a loyal son of the visible Church Catholic, and he felt it to be his highest duty to preserve the unity and continuity of the Mediaeval ecclesiasticism with its authority and its rites; though he clave to the idea of purification in doctrine and rites, and to the principle that the ultimate earthly seat of authority was not the Pope, but a General Council.

From his earliest days to his final hours of rule this one thing seemed to be the chief matter on his conscience, that he must not allow the " rending of the seamless mantle of the Church." [2]

This conviction, gradually working out into history, made Charles the real great and decisive political enemy of the Lutheran faith; and the course of Protestant events is affected at every point by his activity. In this one point he was, like Melanchthon, and like the unionist to-day, prepared to sacrifice inner issues to the restoration of visible unity.

Charles was born in 1500, and was a mere youth of twenty years when he first saw Luther at the Diet at Worms in 1521, where Luther was brought so close to him on that memorable afternoon, that the Reformer's[3] heart was moved to pity as he saw the thoughtful Emperor's face, and felt his youthful Majesty was " like some poor lamb surrounded by swine and hounds."[4]

Yet the address the Emperor read on that fateful occasion might have convinced the most skeptical that his one ultimate determination, to the achievement of which he would sacrifice success and empire, was to put down the Lutheran Reformation as a separate movement. Hear his words:

CHARLES V., AT WORMS, 1521.

"What my forefather established at Constance and other Councils, it is my privilege to uphold. A single monk led astray by private judgment has set him-

---

[2] Armstrong, *The Emp. Charles V.*, Lon. 1902. I. 71.

[3] Luther was facing death. He had said to Melanchthon in taking leave, " My dear brother, if I do not come back, if my enemies put me to death, you will go on teaching and standing fast in the truth. If you live, my death will matter little."

De Wette, *Br.* I. 589.

self against the faith held by all Christians for a thousand years and more, and impudently concludes that all Christians up to this time had erred. *I have there-fore resolved to stake upon this cause* all my dominions, my friends, my body and my blood, my life and soul." [5]

Had the Elector and the Reformers, when they read the Emperor's Call to Augsburg a decade later, forgotten the man they had to deal with, or thought that the imminent presence of the Turk disposed his heart differently toward Evangelical Germany? It was ten full years now since his attention had first been directed to the Reformation. On May 12th, 1520, Juan Manuel, his embassador at Rome, had written to Charles asking him to consider " a certain Martin Luther who belongs to the following of the Elector of Saxony,"[6] and whose preaching was not satisfactory to the Roman Curia. Manuel meant that Luther might be a serv-iceable foil for the Emperor's use in a diplomatic contest with the Curia.

One year after this, Charles, who owed his crown to the supporters of Luther in Germany and who needed the sup-port of Germany in the impending conflict with Francis I., nevertheless gravely declared, as we have seen, that he would put down Lutheranism though it cost him his dominions, his blood, and his soul.

THE SIGNIFICANCE OF THE DIETS PRIOR TO AUGSBURG.

But the German princes at Worms formed a cordon of safety around their precious Luther. They held stoutly to the political doctrine that their fellow-countryman should

---

[5] *Deutsche Reichstagsakten,* etc., ii, 595.

[6] *Calendar of State Papers—Spanish,* 1509-1525, Lon. 1866, p. 305.
In 1521, the King of England wrote that Luther's doctrine was already known at that time in the whole world. *Docum. reform.,* II, p. 223. In this year the wealthy King Emmanuel of Portugal sent an embassador to the Elector of Saxony begging him to punish Luther according to the magnitude of his deeds, and to rout out his doctrine.—*Docum. reformationis,* II, p. 213. The King of England, Henry VIII, also begged the Emperor in a writing that he would destroy Luther, as far as possible, with fire, force and the sword.—*Cyprian,* p. 28.

not be set under the ban before he were heard, with themselves (not the Pope) as his judges. It was April 19th,
1521, when the Emperor proposed the ban; and when the
Germans, forcing him to temporarily yield, drew forth from
him his innermost determination in the paper referred to
above. Later he warmly insisted that he would never alter
one iota of his declaration. There was to be no compromise
between him and Luther:[7] the edict was passed, and the ban[8]
was to be published; but Luther had disappeared.

The imperial edict was unheeded and never harmed
Luther.[9] The following Diet of 1522, and that of 1523,
reminded Hadrian VI., who was not versed in German affairs, that if the Pope had grievance against Luther, Germany had grievance against the Pope, for permitting abuses
which he was blaming Luther for pointing out. The Diet
in 1524[10] also did nothing to execute the edict of Worms
against Luther. It agreed to enforce the edict "as far as
possible," and agitated for a National Council—to the alarm
of the Pope, who thereupon succeeded in having the German
Catholic princes organize into a secret League, thus for the

---

[7] Charles, shortly before his death, regretted that Luther had not been
burned by him.

[8] The Emperor signed the edict with a smile. We meet *Valdés* already
at this time. A humanist, and a follower of Erasmus, Valdés blamed the
Pope for the ban. Lindsay says strikingly, " The humanist young sovereign
and the humanist pope, from whom so much had been expected, congratulated
each other on Luther's condemnation."

In the edict of Worms the Emperor expressly states that the Pope had
requested him to give over the bodily sword to him for the rescue of the
honor of Christ; and that, in accordance with this, *he now places this devil,*
transformed into human form and wearing the robe of a monk, *under the
ban.—Cyprian,* p. 27.

[9] Duke George complained that Luther's presence at Wittenberg was an
insult to the Empire.

[10] Hadrian had died, and Clement VII., who was under French influence,
took his place. It was at this diet that *Campeggio* first appeared on the
scene as the nuncio of Clement.

The exiled Queen of Denmark, the sister of Charles V., Isabella, at this
time became a confessor of the Evangelical religion. Carlstadt began his
fanaticism as to the doctrine of the Holy Supper in this year, from which the
lamentable division between the Evangelicals and the Reformed arose.—*Cyprian,* p. 32.

first time dividing Germany against itself, politically, into Protestant and Catholic.[11]

Up to this date the Elector of Saxony confidently expected a peaceful and unanimous settlement of the religious difficulties in Germany, but in 1525 the great storm of the Peasants' uprising swept across the country, for which Luther was blamed,[12] which solidified the South German anti-Protestant Federation, composed of Austria, Bavaria and ducal Saxony, and which for all subsequent time introduced a Roman and a Lutheran party into the religious politics of Germany.[13]

The Diet this year, 1525, was held at Augsburg; but was poorly attended and the crisis was delayed until 1526, when the Diet should be held at Spires. In 1526 at Spires the Lutherans were in the majority though Ferdinand presided,

---

[11] Chytræus in his *Historia Der Augspurgischen Confession* on pp. 3 and 4 sums up the imperial situation to this point, admirably, in the following paragraphs:—

"The Emperor Charles V. put Martin Luther under the ban at Worms in 1521; but Luther stood firm as a rock, immovable either to storm or the waves of the sea. Samson-like he overthrew the two most prominent pillars of the papacy, namely, the abomination of the masses, and the vows of the monks, and wrote refutations in his Patmos.

"Meanwhile the Emperor Charles was called away on account of the discord and disturbances among his subjects in Spain, and because of the war in Navarre, and again in Spain, and eight whole years hereafter was burdened with the Italian Wars. Although Italy has been greatly plagued by these wars, nevertheless, as God does not allow anything to happen without our getting some good out of it, so I believe that the Emperor Charles was detained through Providence by these wars so that in his absence the execution of the edict of Worms might be postponed, and the doctrine of the Gospel might be securely and early spread forever into Germany and other nations. But, meantime other Diets concerning religious affairs were held: the first at Nürnberg, where the estates, through fear of the growing restlessness and disturbances in the people themselves, delayed the execution of the edict of Worms and the Gospel was both to be preached according to the understanding and interpretation given it by the Church of God; and, then, in order that the conflict in worship might be settled and abuses in the Romish Churches might be done away with, the General Free Christian Council in Germany was asked for."

[12] This combination of democracy and fanaticism, in which Zwingli, as well as Müntzer had a hand, and which had been stimulated by Luther's powerful writings in behalf of individual liberty and the universal priesthood, still further impelled Luther, though he was a peasant's son, to side permanently with the established order of the princes, and to look ever afterward with distrust on democracy and "the common man." The Peasants' War must not be forgotten in Luther's general view of Zwingli's life and character.

[13] The Lutheran party called into being to offset the Catholic Federation (*i. e.*, "The Swabian League, which persecuted the Lutherans and their pastors in South Germany") was composed of the Elector of Saxony, the Landgrave of Hesse, the Margrave of Brandenburg, his brother Albert, Dukes Otto Ernest and Francis of Brunswick-Lüneberg, and the Counts of Mansfeld.

and they gained a great victory as follow : The Word of God was to be preached without disturbance, indemnity was to be granted for past offences against the edict of Worms, and until a General Council met in a German city, each State should so live as it hoped to answer for its conduct to God and the Emperor."[14] The Protestant princes and cities interpreted this resolution as conferring upon them the legal right to reorganize territorial churches, and to reform the worship to accord with their evangelical faith. Within the next three years all North Germany[15] became Protestant.

But when the Diet met again at Speyer in 1529, the Pack conspiracy and the mistakes of Philip of Hesse, together with the coming reunion of Pope and Emperor, placed the Romanists in a large majority. The clerical princes who up to this time had chimed in with the evangelical complaints, because of the pretensions of the Papal Chair, now, since they saw that the conflict had turned into one that involved their own existence, stood, with ranks closed, entirely on the side of the Pope, and had come to the Diet of Worms in great numbers, under capable leaders, to decide this matter. The political princes, even those who hitherto had not been enemies of the Reformation because of aversion to the clericals, now realized that the new teaching had made sufficient inroad into the repute and the power of the clericals, and since the matter was threatening to assume a political complexion, linked themselves closely with the clericals and zealous defenders of the old state of affairs. In addition to all this, the Emperor and the Pope were now reconciled to each other, and combined to gain the victory over their opponents.

The Lutheran minority stood weak and discredited, and the imperial commissioners were able to abolish the ordi-

---

[14] Thus was the territorial system given legitimacy.

[15] Except Ducal Saxony, Brandenburg, and Brunswick-Wolfenbüttel.
The Lutheran faith was introduced into Sweden in 1527. " But in Sweden, the religion, as Luther brought it forth out of God's Word, was introduced by King Gustave, and in Denmark by King Frederick I."—*Cyprian,* p. 35.

dance of 1526, which granted the Lutherans a right to found territorial churches, and to take measures to restore the Roman rule. Ferdinand was able to tell the Evangelicals, "All is over. Submission is the only thing that remains." At this fateful instant, upon which the existence of the Evangelical cause depended, the Evangelical Estates withdrew for consultation, praying a few moments' grace. But King Ferdinand and the Imperial Commissaries departed from the assembly. Shortly thereafter the Evangelicals returned and read their *protest* before the Estates still assembled. This was the celebrated Protest at Spires (April 19th, 1529). The Protesting Estates would abide by the recess of 1526, for that of 1529 was not binding because they were not consenting parties. If forced to choose between obedience to God and obedience to the Emperor, they would choose to obey God. They appealed from this Diet *to the Emperor,* to the next *free General Council of Christendom,* or to an *assembly of the German nation.*[16] The Protest was signed by the Elector John of Saxony, Margrave George of Brandenburg, Dukes Ernest and Francis of Brunswick-Lüneburg, Landgrave Philip of Hesse, Prince Wolfgang of Anhalt, and fourteen cities, a number of them Zwinglian.

SALIG ON THE PROTEST.

This Protestation conferred upon the Evangelical Estates the name of *Protestants*, which they hold to-day yet. This name is a historical monument whose memory the Lutheran Church will never allow to grow old. The Protest was a precursor of the Augsburg Confession, preparing the way to a fearless confession, and clearing the path of hindrances which otherwise would have sprung up in great numbers. It confirmed the name "Steadfast" for the dear Elector John, and cost the excellent Electoral-prince John Frederick many a sigh and care. It was he who encouraged his steadfast father in many hearty letters to confess the truth unabashed, and not to permit himself to be led away from it.—*Hist. d. Augsp. Conf.*, II, 134-135.

---

[16] Affected by the withdrawal of Ferdinand, and the injury thus done to their honor and their rights, they seized upon the legal measure of an Appellation, which, attested by a notary and witnesses, they addressed to the Emperor, to the promised free General Council, and to the whole German Nation. The impression created was a profound one.

These men, who thus protested and appealed, both on the seventeenth of April after the writing of the Decree, and also once again solemnly and formally on the twenty-fifth before the Diet and every Christian judge, to the majesty of the Emperor and a free Christian Council, did not believe that they were bound to give up the action of the last Diet of Spires, which had been brought about as with one mind and heart and which wrought stability, peace and unity. They did not believe that the majority which now thought otherwise and which now desired to destroy this action, should be permitted to put their faith and the common good in peril. Ferdinand refused to incorporate the Protest into the Decree. So each of the Princes regarded himself responsible for making it known, and it was resolved to send an announcement of it to the Emperor by a special embassy.

LUTHER'S OPINION CONCERNING THE DECREE OF THE DIET OF SPIRES AS TO WHAT REASONS THE ELECTOR SHOULD GIVE THE EMPEROR FOR REFUSING TO ACCEPT THE DECREE.

April, 1529.

1. Your electoral Grace would go against your own conscience, and condemn the doctrine which you recognize as Christian.

2. You would become a participant with all those who condemn such doctrine, and thus in addition to your own sin would load upon you numberless horrible strange sins.

3. Your electoral Grace has not the power to force anyone to re-establish the abuses that have been abolished, just as you were not the beginner or the cause of their disappearance, since this is a matter of the conscience of each one.

4. Your electoral Grace cannot assent that the abuses should again be established, for then you would be confirming the unbearable oppression of the clergy of which the complaint was at Worms, and would be strengthening the very abuses which his imperial Majesty himself promised to abolish.

5. That your electoral Grace has not dealt in an unchristian way can be seen by his imperial Majesty in the fact that the estates of the empire have not condemned this teaching, but have postponed it to a Council, which they would not have done if they had regarded it as downright unchristian.

6. And since all the estates of the empire are awaiting a Council, and his imperial Majesty has also encouraged them in this, may his imperial Majesty advise and help, that Christian peace may be brought about in a right and orderly way, and that the matter may come to a hearing, and may not be condemned in private, which would be a forced, and not hearty and willing peace.

The worst was to be feared. No wonder that three days after the reading of the Protest, the Elector of Saxony, Philip of Hesse, and the cities of Strasburg, Ulm and Nürnberg, concluded a secret treaty of mutual defence, in case they should be attacked by a party of the opposite faith or should be hindered in the discharge of their Christian duties.

In this Federation, divergency of Protestant doctrine had, for the moment, been overlooked. Cities such as Strasburg, Constance, Ulm, and the towns of the Swiss were received with the other Protestants. But the majority of the Lutheran theologians did not approve of the Federation. Melanchthon went home half dead with worriment concerning it. He told Luther, who especially was opposed to the position taken as to a Federation. To Luther's thoroughly religious disposition the Federation seemed a human business to help along the cause of God, which had arisen out of weak faith, human fear, and human anger. The pure work of the Gospel should have nothing in common with the calculating prudence of an anxious political diplomacy. In religion God should be left to rule and to care. How could the Elector make cause with those who did not believe God's Word as to the Sacraments! Though he had been moved by the sudden danger to enter into Federation, the Elector, on more sober thought, doubted the wisdom of what had been done.

The representations of Luther therefore made the greatest impression upon the Elector. Similar doubts arose in the hearts of others, and when the matter came up at Rotach, at the meeting agreed on already at Spires, to make more definite arrangements concerning the Federation, hesitant reserve on the part of Saxony, Nürnberg and other Lutherans caused the deliberations to be deferred to a later convention at Schwabach, which then was entirely given up by the Lutherans.

May 22nd, 1529.

Grace and peace in Christ ! Most gracious Lord. M. Philippus has brought me the news from the Diet that a new Federation is to be established particularly by the Landgrave of Hesse with certain cities. All of which moves me not a little. For I was severely burned last year, when God by his wondrous grace released us from the dangerous Federation. And, although I hope God will continue to preserve us, and will give your Grace His Spirit, and henceforth to keep you from such and similar Federations ; I have, nevertheless, because of the earnestness of my conscience, not been able to desist from writing to you, since one cannot be too diligent in circumventing the devil. The Lord grant that, although the Landgrave continues with his making of Federations, you be not bound and fettered in with them ; for we cannot even conceive of the trouble that would follow therefrom.

First of all, this is certain, that such a Federation does not come from God, or from trusting in God, but arises from human wit, and seeks human help alone, all of which is building without a good foundation. Then such a confederation is not necessary, for the multitude of papists has neither the courage nor the ability to accomplish anything which could not be withstood by the good men whom God has given us.

In the third place, our Federation will not accomplish any more than that the opposite party will be incited to also establish a Federation, and to do that which perhaps they would never otherwise have attempted.

In the fourth place, we must remember that the Landgrave, after establishing such a Federation, inasmuch as he is a restless young prince, might not keep the peace, but, as happened last year, might find causes not only for defense, but also for offensive attack ; and it certainly is not God-like to assume this attitude when no one is seeking to attack us.

In the next place, and this is the worst of all, such a Federation will consist of mostly those who strive against God and the Sacrament, and we all shall become participants of their blasphemy. I contend, indeed, that no more dangerous alliance could be undertaken. If there is no other way, may God help that your electoral Grace part from the Landgrave, as I hear the Margrave George says he will. Our Lord Jesus Christ Who has helped your electoral Grace, up to this time, against the Landgrave, will doubtless continue to do so.

In the last place God has always condemned such Federations of human help in the Old Testament, as Isaiah 30 : 15 says : " In quietness and in confidence shall be your strength ;" for we are to be children of faith toward God. The Landgrave, who already has made such a great mistake, is not to be trusted, especially because there does not seem to be any change in him, nor has he experienced any repentance or sorrow for his sin.

May the Lord preserve you from all attempts of the devil.

Your obedient

MARTIN LUTHER.

WITTENBERG, May 22nd, 1529.

The only one on the side of the Lutherans who was particularly pained by this failure of the Evangelicals to federate was the Landgrave Philip himself. He had set great hope upon the strength of the Federation, and upon the help of the Swiss. Great visions of future success arose in his mind, and now all this was to be shattered because of a mere unimportant doctrinal condition! A bold thought occurred to him. He would himself do away with the difficulty. He would invite both parties to a colloquy at Marburg. The Swiss theologians gladly accepted his invitation. The Saxons strove against it. They, especially Luther, did not see that it would bring any result.

MELANCHTHON AGAINST THE COLLOQUY AT MARBURG,

To the Elector.

C. R., I, 1066.

May 14th, 1529.

To deal with Zwingli is entirely useless. . . . If he has been summoned, it is not to be hoped that he would come. The others who dance to Zwingli's music would probably be timid. . . . I rest assured that I will have nothing to do with the Strasburgers as long as I live, and I know that Zwingli and his associates are mistaken on the Sacrament.

LUTHER (PROBABLY TO THE ELECTOR) ON THE COLLOQUY AT MARBURG.

June, 1529.

So far as my own person is concerned, I have no aversion to speaking with Oecolampadius of the sacrament, and have not declined to do so to the Landgrave ; and I wish to God it might be a serviceable thing. For this matter is not insignificant. They have a large following of such as are regarded as learned in all Germany, for reasons that I understand. Yet they are wanting in one thing, which they do not yet know, namely, how difficult it is to stand before God, without God's Word. Their way of dealing is that of mere earthly wit and brilliant frivolity.

To deal with Zwingli would be unfruitful. Therefore Oecolampadius is to be asked to come; and if he has been asked, it is nevertheless not to be hoped that he will come. . . . It is not well that the Landgrave mingles with those Zwinglians. I believe that he already has more pleasure in them than is good : for they are keen and shrewd people, such as the Landgrave likes.

But the Landgrave was not satisfied.   He insisted on his plan, and addressed a letter to Luther, to which Luther replied:

LUTHER TO THE LANDGRAVE OF HESSE.

June 15th, 1529.

Grace and peace in Christ.

Illustrious Prince ! I have obediently received your letter and gracious desire that I should go to Marburg, to have a discussion with Oecolampadius and his people concerning the dissension as to the Sacrament, so that God might give peace and unity.

Although I have poor hopes of such peace, yet your diligence and concern are praiseworthy, and I am willing, for my part, to undertake such a forlorn and perhaps dangerous service ; for I do not wish the other side to be able to say that they are more inclined to peace and unity than I.

If they really desired to seek peace, as they declare, they might have addressed us long ago in writing.   I know very well, that I shall not yield to them at all, and cannot do so.   I am positively sure that they are in error, and that, in addition, they are not certain concerning their own opinion ; for I have thoroughly investigated their whole ground in this affair.   They also, doubtless, have seen my ground.   Therefore it is my earnest prayer that you consider thoroughly whether the final result will do more good or more harm.   For this is sure that, if they do not yield, we shall part from one another fruitlessly, and shall have come together in vain ; your Grace's gifts and pains will have been lost ; and they will not be able to restrain themselves from boasting, as they have been accustomed to do hitherto, and from slandering us, so that we shall be pressed anew to defend ourselves.   Then matters will be worse than now.   This is what Satan wishes and seeks.

Willing,

Wittenberg, June 23rd, 1529.   MARTIN LUTHER.

The date of the Rotach convention, at which final arrangements were to be made concerning the Federation, was only a few days off, and Luther prepared a decisive Opinion for this convention.

LUTHER AGAINST FEDERATIONS.

OPINION FOR THE ROTACH CONVENTION.

June 28th, 1529.

First. Federation is impossible.   For it must ground itself on the conscience or faith of those who bind themselves to believe with one heart.   But we do not find such faith in the other party, and it certainly will be wrought in but few.   And if the Emperor should really make an attack at any spot, there would be very few to stand steadfast, and the rest would desert us. Too late we should learn that the cities, in themselves, are powerless, and the Federation would go to pieces in disgrace. Of this we have had examples enough in Muelhausen, Nordhausen, Erfurt, Augsburg, Nürnberg, Swabian Hall, etc. These at first really seemed to wish to eat the Gospel from very love, but now have fallen away from it. It is to be feared that the same would be the case with Ulm, Strasburg, etc. There are many in these cities who are hostile to the Gospel.

Federation is also hazardous on account of the Landgrave, because he is a restless man. He might, as he did the other time, become dangerous, and might storm monasteries without our consent. Yet afterward we would be bound by what he had done, or would be regarded as having co-operated with him. The same is the case with the cities of Basel and Strasburg, who have taken possession of the "Chapter" by their own power. In all this we would be regarded as participating, and would be obliged to defend it. This is contrary to God (Matt. 4 : 7).

In the third place, such a Federation will be a dubious and vexatious matter. For who can prevent so many people from seeking a brachium carnis, *i. e.,* more support in human help than in God, and although two of three should be pure, the rest would set up the Federation as their idol.

In the fourth place, it is unchristian, because of the heresy concerning the Sacraments ; for we should have to uphold and defend this heresy ; and if we would not defend it, they would probably become more angry than before. For as they are not changing their faith on this point, there is no hope that they will remain true and steadfast in the other points.

Suppose someone would say that the cities are in unity with us in all points but one, and that surely everything does not turn on this or that one thing. I would answer : He is no less an unchristian who denies one article, than Arius, or one of his kind. Moreover, the other party itself seems exceedingly concerned in respect to this one "small point;" for, though it is not necessary, they are stripping the Sacrament of all ceremonies, and making of it a simple collation, which we certainly cannot, forbearingly, be responsible for.

If another man should say, "This Federation does not concern the doctrine, but is a matter of external force," I would answer : Such a statement will not hold, for everyone knows that the opposite party desires to attack us for no other reason than because of the doctrine.

What is to be Written to the Emperor?

First of all, it would be well if our people would write, for themselves alone, without Zwingli. And that the valuable services of our Elector to the Church and the whole Empire be made clear, it should be said :—

1. That he has taught Christ and His Word most purely, as it has not been taught for a thousand years. That many abuses have been removed, such as have injured the Church and the common life, viz., traffic in the masses, misuses of indulgences and tyranny of the ban, which even the other party itself demanded at Worms that they be done away with.

2. That he has withstood the destroyers of pictures and Churches.

3. That the value of civil authority and of his Imperial Majesty has been brought out more clearly than has been the case for many hundreds of years.

4. That against the seditious Münzer-mobs, and in behalf of the common peace, we have done the most for the Emperor.

5. That no one has undertaken the defence of the Church against the Sacramentarians except us. The Papists were too weak.

6. The same is the case with the Anabaptists.

7. The same is the case with the deadly seed of other hurtful doctrines disseminated by these people concerning the Trinity, Faith in Christ and the like.

In this remarkable summary by Luther as to what was to be presented to the Emperor (perhaps by the embassy that bore the " Protest "), we see the germs of the Electoral Apology (compare the Preface of the Apology sent to Nürnberg on June 3rd, 1530), which gradually was transformed into the Augsburg Confession. The responsible figure and public representative of the whole Evangelical cause was a layman, the Elector of Saxony; and we shall interrupt the course of events at this point to gaze for a moment on this sober, steadfast and God-fearing prince, who confessed in deeds what Luther taught in words, and to whom, next to Luther, we owe the Evangelical Confession made at Augsburg.

The Elector of Saxony.

The responsibility in the nation for the existence of Lutheranism, and for the reconstruction of the German churches to the evangelical faith and life, and for the acceptance of a formal dividing line by the Protest in 1529, rested upon the Elector.[1] His brilliant, mercurial, and erratic anti-

---

[1] John, " the Constant," was born on the 30th of June, 1468, and reigned from 1525 to 1532. He was over fifty years of age when the battle of the Reformation began, but his earnest and receptive disposition caused him to attach himself to the Evangelical Confession. He prized Luther's sermons, and often made a copy of them for himself.

The seven years of his rule were years of growing intensity, and of reciprocal lack of confidence on the part of the different parties in Germany; in which, nevertheless, external union was preserved, and the Reformation progressed without hindrance, to which John's love of peace and his firmness contributed materially.

John's grasp of the Evangelical faith was independent and accurate, and he had the undaunted courage to defend it with property and life. His

thesis, Philip of Hesse, to whose youth he opposed the weight of age, to whose militant aggressiveness he opposed a settled peace; to whose human plans and restless activity, he opposed a trustful faith and a deep spirituality; and to whose desire for union, and for conquest, he opposed a plain and simple obedience to the Word of God,—offered a type of Protestantism, which, if it had triumphed at Rotach and Marburg and Schwabach and Augsburg, would have fought Rome with the weapons of Rome, and not *solely* with the Word; and attacked this world with the weapons of this world; and would have altered the whole history of our evangelical Protestantism. Under the stern and terrible necessity of giving answer for itself to those without, these crucial days of 1529 were deciding whether the Word alone, or also the world and its policies, should prevail within the Evangelical movement.

And here the Elector stood with Luther. Melanchthon and the other theologians also stood with Luther. And the Elector decided to be true to his faith, and to give answer to the Emperor without Federation with the Zwinglians. In all the efforts of Philip of Hesse, that Summer and Fall, the Elector's attitude seems to have been passive; and he went to Augsburg, as we shall see, on his own responsibility.

Up to this time, the Elector had accomplished great things for the Church and the faith. Not only had he, with his brother Frederick, shielded Luther from the ban of the Empire for ten long years, but by the action culminating in the Diet of 1526, which made reconstruction possible, and which had been carried into effect in his own and other

---

Chancellor, Brück, was the soul of his external and internal policies, and John gave his theologians a leading place in his decisions. He held Luther in particularly high esteem.

Luther honored him as " a pious, upright prince who has no bitterness at all," whose " trust in God was so earnest that he remained an uncorrupted man." Luther said of him that " Sincerity died with John, and Wisdom with his brother Frederick."

Schaff, *Creeds of Christendom,* I, 227, characterizes him thus: " The Elector John, justly styled the *Constant,* with all his loyalty to the Emperor and wish for the peace of Germany, refused to compromise his conscience, and, in full view of the possible ruin of his earthly interest, he resolved to stand by ' the imperishable Word of God.' "

23

domains for three years now, he had freed the Church and established it in the pure Word throughout Northern Germany.

The ecclesiastical question had ceased to be a matter of one poor monk, notably since 1526, when the princes formally assumed responsibility for the religion and the churches within their territory. The responsibility of Luther at Worms in 1521 was so evidently shifted upon the Elector and his estate that, in the Call to the Diet of Augsburg, the name of Luther was not even mentioned; and, so far as the purposes of the Diet were concerned, neither Luther, nor Melanchthon, nor any of the theologians, assumed a leading position, but were mere personal advisers to the Elector on such points of doctrine and ecclesiastical life concerning which he chose to consult them. As the official leader of the old Roman empire in Germany, and its chief marshal, the Call to Augsburg was sent to him.

Thus the Diet, even in its religious aspects, was a matter of the Princes and not of the theologians; and as the Elector was the central and deciding one among the Princes, the whole weight fell upon his shoulders.

Soon to be impressed with the apparently marvelous change in the manner of the Emperor, realizing the common danger at hand in the approach of the Turk, distrusting the aggressiveness of Philip of Hesse, and inferring from the Emperor's attitude that, if he would be dealt with favorably, it was necessary to eschew the radicalism of his more offensive associates and keep himself apart from their desires for alliance; hoping, doubtless, to show to the more favorable judgment of the Emperor that the Evangelical movement, despite the Protest, was a temporary and, until the convening of a General Council, not a real separation from the Church Catholic nor necessarily a final one from Rome; with the stirring events of only nine months ago in mind,—the appeal then made to a General Council or to a German Assembly of the nation to save the Evangelical

Church from ruin,—the Elector of Saxony received the Call of the Emperor, so sweetly and graciously written, to the new Diet which he himself would attend, and where all opinions were to be fairly heard and all divisions in the Church to be honorably settled, that there might be one Commonwealth and one Church of Christ, even as there was one Lord. Thus the Elector went to Augsburg.

What the Augsburg Confession finally became, it became through and by way of, and as representing the faith of the Elector, though his personality had, in the Providence of God, been eliminated in the document, and the other princes had been admitted as joint-confessors. " It is to John, Elector of Saxony, more than to any other prince, that the world is indebted for the Augsburg Confession. There is not a nobler prince than he commemorated on the pages of history (hardly one so eminently Christian). His exalted firmness conferred on him the title of the *Constant,* and never was it more admirably displayed than in connection with the Confession which was prepared under his auspices and by his command. The letter patent of the Emperor summoning a Diet at Augsburg reached him in Torgau."[18]

Having gained a clear conception of the personalities of the Emperor and the Elector, and of the course of history between the Diet of Worms in 1521 and the Diet of Spires in 1529, together with a knowledge of the Emperor's Call for a Diet at Augsburg in 1530, it will now be necessary to take the reader somewhat more in detail through the pregnant events of 1529 and 1530, where we come upon some surprising facts.

THE YEAR 1529.

April 19th, 1529.

King Ferdinand declares to the Princes: "All is over.

---

[18] C. P. Krauth in *Ev. Rev.,* I, p. 246.

Submission alone remains " ; and the Princes and Estates protest.

June 29th.

The Peace of Barcelona is established between the warring Emperor and Pope. The Emperor, on his part, promises to restore the Medici to Florence, and *to root out the Lutheran doctrine.*

July 12th.

THE EMPEROR'S WARNING TO THE ESTATES.

Mueller, Hist., p. 208 ; Lünig, Reichs-Archiv, part. gen. cont., II, p. 329.

July 12th, 1529.

We are reminded that you have not agreed to the Decree of the Diet at Spires on account of the Article concerning our holy Christian Faith. This displeases us with you not a little. You ought not have refused ; and since it is the old custom that in a general Assembly of the Empire the Majority rules, the minority should not withstand their decision, but obey it. If you remain in further disobedience to this gracious warning, we shall be obliged to punish you in earnest.

CHARLES.

August 9th.

Charles lands at Genoa, as a mighty Conqueror, with a court of Spanish grandees, and proceeds, as the restorer of peace in Italy, after full preparations, in state to Bologna to meet the Pope, from whom he expects to receive the imperial crown.

The Elector John in Saxony and his compeers received early tidings of the terms of the treaty at Barcelona, and the question was at once raised whether the Evangelical princes and estates should not immediately enter into a league with each other and "proceed against the Emperor with their military forces before he could debouch from the Welsh Mountains.

"But Dr. Luther, who was always given to peace, and who continuously advised against undertaking war under the guise of the Gospel, and had already several times persuaded those who were ready for battle to desist, then dissuaded the Evangelical Princes in a most earnest way from undertaking a league and war against the Emperor in this matter of religion. He commanded them to wait and pray God in firm faith for help and protection, since the matter belonged to God, and, in order to strengthen his faith and that of the Theologians and Princes, he gathered a number of comforting passages from the Scripture and published them.

"And at this time he put the 46th Psalm, ' God is our refuge and strength,' etc., into beautiful melody and words, that awaken a sad and troubled disposition and fill it with courage, and had them frequently sung in the churches."[19]

DR. MARTIN LUTHER'S LETTER TO THE ELECTOR OF SAXONY, IN WHICH HE ADVISES AGAINST WAR.

Grace and peace in Christ ! In our conscience we cannot justify nor advise such a League on which the shedding of blood might result. I would rather be dead ten times than have my conscience burdened by this, that our Gospel should be the cause of the shedding of blood or of injury.

There is no harm in your being obliged to be surrounded with danger. Our Lord Christ is mighty enough to ward it off, and we also believe that the Emperor's attitude is a pure threatening of the devil, that will be without power and will at last conduce to the destruction of the other side.

Therefore I admonish you to be comforted and unterrified in this danger, and I will pray and beseech God to accomplish more than they can do with all their violence, only so that we keep our hands free from blood ; and if it came to the worst (which I do not believe) and the Emperor insisted on demanding me or the others, I will appear with God's help on my own behalf, and will not place your Grace in danger. Everyone should defend his faith and not rely upon another. Christ our Lord comfort and strengthen you richly. Amen.

Meantime Protestant affairs were fairly blazing in Switzerland, with King Ferdinand unable to keep them in check ; and soon Charles was to be crowned as the head of the Holy Roman Empire, surrounded by the pageantry of the Spanish Court, and without any notification of the great event or any invitation to attend it being sent to the great German

---

[19] Chytræus, *Augsp. Conf.*, p. 11.

electors. Thus, for the last time in history, was the union of the spiritual and the civil hierarchy consummated.[20]

This coronation of Charles at the hand of the reluctant Roman Pontiff, and without the presence of the Elector of Saxony, had lifted him to the zenith of his power. "The sickly-looking youth of Worms," according to the brilliant picture painted of him by Lindsay,[21] had become a grave man of thirty, whose nine years of unbroken success had made him the most commanding figure in Europe. He had quelled the turbulent Spaniards; he had crushed his brilliant rival of France at the battle of Pavia; he had humbled the Pope, and had taught his Holiness in the sack of Rome the danger of defying the Head of the Holy Roman Empire. He had added to and consolidated the family possessions of the House of Hapsburg, and but lately his brother, Ferdinand, had won, in name at least, the crowns of Bohemia and Hungary.

October 1st.

THE MARBURG COLLOQUY.

Philip of Hesse would not hear to the policy of non-resistance, and bent his utmost efforts to uniting the Lutherans and Zwinglians into one Confederation. The Lutheran doctrine was the chief obstacle. It was the first of October before Philip succeeded in the difficult task of bringing the Lutheran and the Reformed theologians face to face to engage in a colloquy in his own castle at Marburg, in order to

---

[20] Seldom, if ever, in the history of the world has any one been born to such weighty responsibilities. Columbus had been discovering for Charles territories of unlimited extent. When he was fifteen years of age, the first European saw the Pacific Ocean, and ere he was twenty years on the throne of Spain, Pizarro had completed the conquest of Peru. It was the heroic period of Spain, when religious and military enthusiasm elevated the national character in an extraordinary manner, and the material wealth of great countries was available to an extent which has seldom been surpassed.— *Encyc. Britannica.*

[21] *History of the Reformation,* I, p. 359.

attempt to harmonize theological differences, in view of the supposed desperate political need of a united Protestantism.

October 4th.

LUTHER TO HIS WIFE.

From L. Chr. Mieg Monum. piet. et litter. Francof. 1671.
Walch XXI, 299 ; De Wette III, 512.

October 4th.

Grace and peace in Christ ! Dear Lord Kate. Our friendly conference at Marburg is at an end, and we are in unity in nearly all things, excepting that the other side wishes to retain simply bread in the Lord's Supper and to confess Christ as spiritually present therein. To-day the Landgrave is ascertaining whether we can become one, or at least, if we remain separate, nevertheless, regard ourselves as brethren and members of Christ among each other. To this end the Landgrave is strenuously active. But we do not want the "brethren and members' business" (Aber wir wollen des Brüderen und Glieders nicht). To be peaceful and well disposed we certainly desire. . . . Tell Herr Pommer that the best argument of Zwingli has been that the body cannot exist without locality ; therefore the body of Christ is not in the bread. The best argument of Oecolampadius is, that this sacrament is a sign of the body of Christ. I believe that God has blinded them so that they might not be able to advance anything. I have much to do and the messenger is in haste. Say Good-night to all and pray for us. We are all fresh and strong and live like princes. Kiss little Lena and little Hans for me. On the day of the present 1529.

Your willing servant,

MARTIN LUTHER.

John Brenz, Andreas Osiander, and Dr. Stephen, of Augsburg, have also come hither.

LETTER OF LUTHER TO AGRICOLA.

Original in Wolf., Extv. 84. 18. Bl. 3 ; MS. in Cod. Goth., B, 28, f. 40b.
Printed in De Wette, III, p. 513 ; in Erlangen, VII, p. 168 ; Buddeus, p. 71.

October 12th 1529.

Grace and peace in Christ ! . . . . They very humbly asked for peace. We spoke together for two days. I answered Oecolampadius as well as Zwingli, and held to the passage, "*This is my body.*" I disposed of every objection. These people are incompetent, and inexperienced in disputation. Although they saw that their arguments proved nothing, they nevertheless were unwilling to yield, especially on this one point, the presence of the body of Christ, and, I believe, more from fear and shame than from an evil disposition. But finally they yielded on all other points, as is to be seen on the printed report. Then at last they prayed, or requested, that we should at least regard them as brethren, and said that the princes would like to see this ; but it was not possible to consent to it. *Neverthe-*

less we did extend to them the hand of peace and love, that now bitter writings and words may cease, and everyone may hold his faith without hostile assaults, yet not without defence and confutation. Thus we parted. Pray for us. Amen !

MARTIN LUTHER.

JENA, October 12th, 1529.

Postscript by Melanchthon.

They prayed us from the heart that we would call them brethren, but see what folly ! While they are condemning us (verdammen), they still wish to be regarded by us as brethren ! We would not be able to grant them this. I surely believe that if the matter had not been as great, they would not now begin such a farce.

Luther has been severely blamed for refusing the proffer of Zwingli, but from his standpoint how could he do otherwise ? It has been cast up against him that such harshness was a result of his personal disposition. But in the letter translated above, Melanchthon appears to be even more harsh than Luther. Luther was neither vexed nor narrow-minded, but at this time was patient and in good temper.

It was a matter of *principle* to Luther. The sacrament was the central mystery of his faith; and, after it had been robbed of its power, and emptied of the divine presence, by those on the other side, he could not reach across the gulf thus created, and say, *"There is no important difference between us."* The hand "of peace and love" which he did really extend, and which is never mentioned in most modern accounts, shows either how ignorant or how unjust these latter are in attributing the position taken by Luther to his bitterness of feeling.

LUTHER TO LANDGRAVE PHILIPP.

Original in Zurich Archives in the Unsch. Nachr. 1756, p. 447.
DeWette, V, 87 ; Erl.Br. W., III, 84.

January 30th, 1535.

I have gladly perceived the great diligence you have used toward the uniting of us all in the article of the Lord's Supper. . . . I have come to the point of confidently believing that there are many among them who mean it with a true and earnest heart. On that account I am also more inclined to a union which shall be fundamental and stable. But since not everything has been investigated on both sides, in my opinion it is enough for this time to have come together so near, until God helps us more and grants it to us to conclude a certain union. Such a matter, which has grown so long and so deeply, cannot be accomplished suddenly and at once. For what I can ever do and suffer to the accomplishment of such a beginning, you may be certain, so far as God permits me, that I shall not be found failing. . . .

Your willing

D. MARTIN LUTHER.

Oct. 16th.

THE SEVENTEEN SCHWABACH ARTICLES OF LUTHER.

The object of the Landgrave failed, and now more than ever the Lutheran princes were resolved to withdraw from all political fellowship with the others. At a convention of the Lutherans at Schwabach [22] in October, it was demanded as a fundamental condition of being received into the Federation, that the so-called Schwabach Articles, framed so as to render it impossible for those who denied the true presence of the body of Christ in the sacrament to sign them, must be signed.

Thus the Lutherans stood alone when a new situation arose which entirely dissipated every idea of Federation. The Emperor had received the embassy (which had been sent to hand him the Protest and Appeal for a Council, after the Diet of Spires, and to represent to him the necessity of Protest, and at the same time to assure him of their fidelity and obedience) very ungraciously, and had had them imprisoned for a time. Hence the question would now arise, what was to be done if the Emperor himself should use force.

For, apparently, no one had considered this matter. The Emperor had been far away in Spain when at the Diet of

---

[22] The convention at Schwabach and the Colloquy at Marburg have the most intimate connection with the Augsburg Confession, and furnish a clue for guidance into the same.—Salig, *Hist. d. Augsp. Conf.,* II, 128.

Spires the hostile attitude of the German estates had caused the Evangelicals to federate against the hostile estates. As against equals, the right of defence was supposed to be possessed. But how would it be, if now the Emperor, their Lord, who meanwhile had come to Italy, and who next Spring would be expected in Germany, would range himself on the side of the enemies? Dare one resist him?

There was hesitation for a moment, but Luther saw nothing but rebellion and destruction in the attempt to oppose the Emperor. And most of the theologians agreed with him. One must suffer the Emperor's will, even if he acted un righteously. Country and people must remain bound to him as long as he is Emperor. Only in one case could obedience be denied. Should he wish to force princes and authorities to aid in the suppression of the Gospel, it would be right to obey God rather than man. This view prevailed. The princes and towns that were already resorting to arms for a defense, laid them down. They raised themselves to the high point of courage required to confess and to suffer what God should bring to pass. Luther's influence was supreme.

Thus Philip of Hesse's grand coalition with France and Switzerland against the Emperor had come to failure through the influence of Luther. The Elector was to stand before the Emperor by himself, and not to federate with one who differed in so much as a single article of faith.

The Fall of the year was full of thrilling minor incidents, each bearing on one of the two great problems. The theological fruit of this soul-searching period was Luther's precious Schwabach Articles, so clear, so short, so simple, so extraordinary a Confession of the full Evangelical Gospel; the political fruit was the impression made on the Emperor as to the necessity of holding either a Council or a National German Assembly, and the knowledge given him of the deep-rooted character of the religious question.

Oct. 14th.

APPEAL OF THE PROTESTANT ESTATES TO A CHRISTIAN COUNCIL.

The appeal for a Christian Council caused the Emperor to give most serious attention to the situation that would confront him when he should cross over into Germany. " In order to fit himself better for this important business he asked certain reliable, learned and prominent men for their opinions of the religious dissensions that had occurred.

"Some advised him not to allow any change in doctrine or in ceremonies, nor to permit any Council to assemble, but to suppress with force all preachers and estates who wilfully destroyed the common peace in the empire; for it is much more harmful to permit anything new to exist than to endure that which might perhaps be made better, because if the attempt be once made to change laws and customs, shallow and frivolous people would only be incited to still greater and more prolonged disputation and to further novel views.

"But others answered more mildly. Since the intention is to uphold God's honor, and not only peace in God's churches ; and since evidently many unrighteous and godless opinions have forced their way into the church through error, superstition, and avarice, God's honor demands that such errors shall be done away and practical doctrine and a right kind of worship shall be ordained, for where this does not occur, no permanent peace is to be had ; for as there will always be some who will attack errors and abuses, this will become all the more uncontrollable if it occurs without the pale of authority.

"Therefore it is proper not to exercise tyranny over the churches of God, but to wrestle with the difficulties gently. This gentleness to the churches of God is all the more proper since in them one is so often commanded to protect the weak. Last of all, as so many highly respected Princes appeal to a Council, what a tyranny it would be to exercise violence and cruelty prior to an investigation. To this the examples of many emperors were cited, who assembled Councils, such as Constantinus the Great, Theodosius, Arcadius, Marcianus, etc.

" The Emperor Charles, gracious by nature, opposed to all tyranny and devout, when he read both proposals, after long consideration and communication with prominent wise men, finally selected the right and the mild way and resolved to abide by it." [23]

---

[23] Chytræus, *Hist. Augsp. Conf.*, pp. 4b sq.

November 5th.

<hr>

CHARLES V. AND THE POPE AT BOLOGNE.

" When, then, in the year 1529, on the 5th of November, the Emperor came to Pope Clement toward Bononia, and when certain other matters had been attended to, the deliberation concerning the Lutheran affair and how again to establish peace and unity in the Christian churches was taken up.

" While now the Emperor and the Pope sat together in counsel, and while there stood around them on the one side, the old, wise cardinals Genutius, Farnesius and others; and on the other side, the Spanish and Italian Princes—the Emperor's Chancellor, Mercurinus, in a long, well-thought-out and earnest oration, indicated the Emperor's will, and desired a Council." [24]

THE PLEA OF THE CHANCELLOR MERCURINUS,

November 5th, 1529, [25]

In the Assembly of the Pope and Cardinals and in the Presence of the Emperor, in which he Begs the Pope, in the Name of the Emperor, to Call a General Council. [26]

1. Most Holy Father, Most Venerable Lord : Ever since the Invincible Emperor, at the beginning of his reign, became painfully conscious that a great dissension has arisen among the prominent teachers of the Church and is increasing from day to day, he cannot but notice how lamentable injury is being done, and many pious souls are scandalized ; yea, the heat of controversy has grown so intense that, if no one comes promptly to the aid of Christianity and the wretched Roman Empire, the church and all the estates in the Empire will be placed in the extremest peril : therefore his Imperial Majesty has from the beginning been thoughtfully striving to find some means to restore peace to the Church and the Empire, now swaying in danger, and to do away with all that seems to antagonize the common welfare.

2. Moreover, his Imperial Majesty well knows that the investigation of conflicts

<hr>

[24] Chyträus, *Hist. Augsp. Conf.*, pp. 5b sqq.

[25] The date is that given by Chytræus.—*Historia Augsp. Conf.*, p. 4b. Some place it at the end of February of the following year. *Vid.* § 3, " Coronation."

[26] Cölestin, *hist. comit.*, 1580, I, p. 10 ; Müller, *Hist. lib.*, III, Cap. 2, p. 402 ; Lünig, *orat. precer. Europ.*, XXVII.

in the doctrine and usage of the Church are the province of your Highness, and that as an old, pious and prudent man, you are concerned about the universal corruption. Therefore his Majesty, despite the Imperial business and the wars in which he has been involved, has often wished and prayed God that he might meet you and speak of these important matters and compass a proper conclusion.

3. Since now this wish has been realized, and, at this act of coronation and through his proposed journey to Germany, an opportunity has been given to personally honor your Reverend Holiness and to enter into consultation with you, his Majesty renders God the greatest thanks for the opportunity afforded ; since he firmly believes that Your Holiness will find a way in this venerable assembly to remedy the corruption of Christianity. For the Emperor is assured that you and he, the two highest heads of the Church and the State, will turn their care to the upbuilding of God's honor and the preservation of peace ; so that *the right and wholesome doctrine in the Church may be preserved pure and true ;* that where errors, false doctrines, and superstition have insinuated themselves, they shall be prevented ; that lapsed Church discipline shall be restored ; that bad morals in the clergy and among the people shall be improved; and *that the falsified doctrine of the Church shall be cleansed and purified.* In connection with which his Majesty sincerely believes that if we are not zealously in earnest to permit a book of instruction to be compiled from the Word of God, for healing the Church's injury and exercising a more strict discipline, still greater confusion, and more abhorrent barbarism than we have ever experienced will follow, not to speak of the fact that the most dreadful and righteous penalties will be visited upon those in authority and those who are under it.

4. When then his Majesty began to deliberate and asked the advice of honorable and intelligent men, they could find no more useful and appropriate remedy than the Diet already called, in which the conflicts belonging to the Church should be taken up in the fear of God, and *decided according to the rule and truth of the divine Word ;* and that pious and learned men should be called together out of all nations, and be given *the free assurance of safe conduct to speak openly,* to argue, to point out the truth, to discuss opinions in which they differ from each other in an upright way, and thus fully elucidate the sources of contention ; and finally that your Papal Holiness, or certain qualified and impartial judges, see to it that, after a thorough investigation, they *hold firm and fast to that which harmonizes with the evangelical teaching and with invincible truth ;* and, on the other hand, condemn harmful errors and abuses in teaching, *which are in conflict with the Word of God,* and either bring their originators into the right way, where possible, or give them over to the proper magistrate for punishment ; *but all is to be done in love, and not with force,* so that at last all teachers and hearers shall be brought to a true adoration and service of God, as well as to obedience to the Church, and to believe right according to the pattern laid down, to teach purely, to walk irreproachably and to glorify God in this way.

Your Imperial Majesty knows that your Papal Holiness has the right to call together councils, and that the conflicts that have originated in the Church are subject to you and your final judgment ; nevertheless his Majesty seeks all the less to abridge the rights of the Roman chair since he has just recently promised under oath to be and remain a friend and protector of the same ; but at the same time he realizes that pressing necessity is at hand, that the universal welfare of the Church demands it, that all right-minded people wish this one thing with great desire, and that there seems to be no other way which is right, customary, and praiseworthy, by which the respect and rights of your Holiness may be preserved, the declining Church may be set on its feet again, the anxious souls of the pious be converted, and *the truth of the evangelical doctrine of Christ be asserted,* than by the calling together of such an assembly: therefore his Imperial Majesty prays Your Holiness, for Christ's sake and for the general welfare, that you will, as early as possible, issue a call for a Council to be held at a suitable place, and believes that this method, which has already been in use for many hundreds of years, and is appointed by God and the Apostles themselves, is as necessary as useful, since such important controversies cannot possibly be decided by the verdict of one or another, or only a few, but that this must occur in a free assembly of the leaders and teachers.

5. Your Imperial Majesty confesses that love to the true religion and the example of the noblest emperors who have preceded him in rule, have impelled him to this step.   He remembers that when Arius scattered harmful and blasphemous errors, Constantine held a famous Synod at Nicaea to investigate and condemn the same, and brought matters so far that the proven errors were publicly condemned by the holy bishops and the holy Church fathers.   Also that the Emperor Theodosius and Valentinianus, not to speak of others, appointed similar great assemblies; and that after each one had a free opportunity of speaking, a common conclusion was resolved on, and the errors that had arisen *were condemned out of the Word of God,* and the originators thereof were visited with severe penalty.   It is certain that such conventions and deliberations have often been very useful to the Church of God and the whole world, and that one has never been able to investigate the truth to better advantage than through proper assemblies; and he does not see how in our times the peace that has been lost can be restored in a better manner, since the use of force in this affair is questionable.

7. Therefore his Majesty hopes that your Holiness will approve his prayer, and first of all by this mild means attempt a beginning of unification.

8. His Majesty also solemnly promises that he will ever stand by Your Holiness, and, in remembrance of his oath, will be a true and perfect defender of the apostolic chair, the evangelical truth, and all the subjects of the Roman Empire.

Thus closed what is perhaps the most remarkable plea for the pure Word of God, the unadulterated faith, the evangelical doctrine, and the cause of religious truth, that ever came before the Roman Curia from the lips of the representative of an imperial sovereign.

The eloquent man to whom the Pope and his Cardinal were obliged to give audience was the imperial Chancellor, Mercurinus Gattinara, the Emperor's chief adviser, known by the Wittenbergers as friendly to the Lutheran cause; and this fact may have contributed, especially with Melanchthon, to the hopes they had for Augsburg. But let the reader note that Mercurinus died on June 4th, 1530.

After Mercurinus had finished his plea to the Pope on that November day at Bologne, Pope Clement, " who was a wise and eloquent man, and who had bethought himself concerning this important matter, replied thus:—[27]

THE ANSWER OF POPE CLEMENT, IN WHICH HE DECLINES TO CALL A COUNCIL.

1. We do indeed believe, Emperor Charles, that you are pressing for a Synod in all sincerity, although in this matter, in which the Church is in great danger, the chief responsibility is with us ; for, in the Council of Nicaea it was decided that the divisions which arose in the Western Church should be brought before the Roman Bishop, and that our chair should call the assembly. We have therefore deliberated as to whether such matters should be dealt with in a Council, or whether the men should be seized by force who diverge from the decrees and usual opinions. Since we do not consider it advisable to call a Synod, we ask you here at the beginning that you do not think that we are in anxiety for the stability of our rule or that of the Roman Church. It is said of John XXIII. that he was sorry that he had held a Synod at Constance, since this caused his downfall. *And we also have recently been caught.*

We positively are not possessed with this foolish desire to hold an assembly. What has been decided in the past ought not to be robbed of its power by a new discussion. If such a discussion were truly useful to peace and our prosperity, we would not hinder it.

4. There are statements of doctrine which are not only false but also absurd, such as those of the Anabaptists, and those that all persons should hold their possessions in common ; that God has forbidden public law and punishment.

5. But just as everyone immediately runs to a fire to extinguish it, so should all the civil authorities have shown themselves eager to suppress these controversies in their very beginning ; and very bad consequences would follow if we should yet allow disputation over them. The Emperor Constantine was able to sit in the Council and hear blasphemy. Ought you be regarded as being as abandoned as Constantine that you would listen to such deceitful addresses with the deepest confidence ?

6. The other kind of error consists of confused teachings which it is not possible to solve. It is much better that these should never come up, since it is not possible to settle the conflicts. To this kind belong questions pertaining to the adoration of the Bread, of the Offering, and of the Mass.

"After the Pope had thus spoken, the Emperor, inasmuch as he determined to abide by his opinion and desire of

---

[27] Chytræus, *Hist. Augsp. Conf.*, pp. 6 sqq. ; Melanchthon, declamat., V, pp. 94 sqq. In Nov., says Chytr. ; but Mercurinus indicates Feb.

a Council, then commanded his Chancellor Mercurinus to answer the Pope; but when Mercurinus had begun, the Pope interrupted him while speaking, and said: 'How dare you thus rashly oppose me and stir up your Lord against me?'

" Then the Emperor himself stood up to answer the Pope. The Princes and the old Cardinals were filled with wonder to hear what the young Emperor wished to say, and listened breathlessly. And this[28] is the sum and substance of his speech:—

THE EMPEROR'S REPLY TO THE POPE.[29]

" I confess that I am young, and that I need the advice of this Mercurinus and other sensible and wise men, and I recognize that I ought properly to hear others who are of better understanding than I, but since I have conferred as to this important matter, which I know to be to the honor of God, and to the good of the whole race, with many wise and faithful people, I regard it as right and that it is highly necessary for the Christian churches that a Council be held, for you know yourself, Pope Clement, that all deserving people in the whole of Europe are requesting such a Council with continuous petition, one that will be ordered and ruled in a proper and Christian manner.

" Although I have faithfully weighed the arguments which you have just opposed to it, I have nevertheless come to the conclusion that a Council shall be called, and therefore you shall know that what was said by my Chancellor was said by my orders, and that I, so long as I live, will not deviate from this intention. Your opinion can indeed be maintained in an acceptable and respectable way by those who do not concern themselves much concerning God and the churches. But my opinion is more beneficial for the churches; and if you do not hinder me, I hope it shall be, with the help of God, wholesome for all Christendom.

" Neither am I moved to deviate from my opinion by your hard saying that one shall not allow any disputation as to false articles or those that are in conflict with all reason, or those that are confused, and not to be solved. For *not everything,* concerning which the battle now rages, *is in conflict with God's word and reason.* There are in the Church of God no such 'confused questions' concerning points necessary to salvation that cannot be decided.

" I have often quoted the saying of Plutarch, as one must permit some failings in our parents, so, in government and religion, one must be patient with failings and look at them through the fingers; but this has its limits.

" *The foundation of the true doctrine must indeed be preserved unfalsified.* But certain superstitious and blasphemous adorations have crept into the churches. Open disorder is before our eyes, and a Council is demanded not only for the doing away with this abuse, but *stern necessity demands that a well-*

---

[28] Chytræus, *Hist. Augsp. Conf.,* p. 8.

[29] *Ib.,* pp. 8 sqq.

grounded and rightly composed summa and corpus of the whole Christian doctrine be drawn up, which shall be preached and taught in all nations and in all churches with one voice, for you know, at this time there are great objections as to the teaching even among the Roman churches.

"And as certain evidently false doctrines have been circulated, the Council should oppose them by clear and sure arguments and by the testimony of Holy Scripture, by which the people should be strengthened, so that they will not be led astray any more.

"It does not comport with you as a Christian Bishop to say that no one can be brought into the clear concerning certain confused articles. For God has revealed Himself with especial grace, and if His doctrine were uncertain, it would not be divine.

"I am reminded of the advice of the Emperor Theodosius, who allowed the testimony of the old teachers to be brought to light in a Council, for I gladly listen to the Church as my Mother and Teacher. And how much more appropriate your decision will be if given in a Council ; for there will be much greater unity among all the nations, if they all receive this with unanimity. After a proper hearing, I shall also not be found wanting as to my office ; and that the hearing may occur in a proper way, after the example of the old Emperors, I will be present myself, and as much as is possible see to it that this honorable old law shall be maintained, that the decision shall not be given in caprice, but explained according to the Law, namely, according to the doctrine which has been given by God Himself.

"But what you now demand, namely, that I shall, without any previous hearing and investigation, extirpate both the good and the bad alike, I will in no wise do. For *I will not abolish the judgment of the churches and institute tyranny.* I have already shown my Christian humility and obedience toward the churches and toward the Roman chair, and toward you, with sufficient clearness, and will continue to do so."

"When the Pope and all the Princes present heard this address, they greatly marveled at the high understanding and the wonderful Christian courage of Charles; and on that account, that he might not be agitated more violently, the Pope answered quite gently: 'He would give more consideration to the matter, and take it into further deliberation with his Cardinals.'

" This transaction at Bononia is sufficient evidence that the Emperor Charles at that time proceeded with the great discretion and moderation in these affairs of religion, which he also subsequently showed at the Diet of Augsburg, in that he permitted the Confession containing the teaching of our Churches to be delivered to himself. All of which God the

24

Lord so ruled that the teaching of the Gospel might be manifested more clearly and spread more widely.

" But the Pope at the same time at once perceived, toward the last, there at Bononia, that the Emperor agreed that he would first of all proceed mildly with the Lutherans, that they might again be brought to the obedience of the Romish churches. But if they should be obstinate and abide in their determined disobedience, he would suppress them with force.

" When the Pope took his departure, his imperial Majesty, on the 21st of January, wrote a summons in very mild and gracious words for a Diet to convene in Augsburg on the 8th of April. In this he expressly said, with respect to the discord in religion, that he would hear, consider and weigh every deliverance, opinion, and thought of each estate in love, friendliness, and graciousness, and would reduce and compose them into a single Christian Truth. Everything that had not been rightly explained on either part, or that had been dealt with wrongly, would be abolished, that we might all accept and hold a single and true religion, as we are all under one Christ and also all battle in one communion of churches and live in one unity." [30]

THE YEAR 1530.

Jan. 21st.

Charles V. issues the Call convening the Diet at Augsburg. (This document appears earlier in the chapter.)

Early Spring.

The Emperor, leaving Bologna, crosses the Brenner Pass to pay the visit to Germany he had determined on, and by his personal presence to put an end to the Lutheran diffi-

---

[30] Thus far *Chytræus.*

culty in the Church, which was distracting the German portion of his empire; and to secure the imperial succession for Ferdinand by having him elected King of the Romans.

THE EMPEROR HOLDS COURT AT INNSBRÜCK.

Charles was welcomed most heartily on this side of the Alps. His court was a scene of brilliancy and power, and was visited by the Roman Catholic princes of Germany; but the Elector, the chief marshall of the Empire, was conspicuously absent.

Under this stimulating encouragement from part of Germany, Charles could afford to be less yielding and more constant to his real purpose in the matter of religion, than he had seemed to be, in the Call, a few months earlier; and the flatteries and persuasion of the Romanists, with the bluntness and the failures of the Evangelicals at Innsbrück, would not render the newly-crowned potentate less firm. The impression of his power made by the Emperor even upon Luther, is seen in a letter he wrote to the Elector.

End of February or Beginning of March.

LUTHER TO THE ELECTOR.

Printed by Hans Lufft, Wittb. IX, 543. De Wette, III, 555; Erl. Br. W., II, 134.

Grace and peace in Christ. The world is running so quickly to its end, that it strongly occurs to me as though the last day would break in before it is possible for me to completely translate the Holy Scripture into German. For this is certain that we have nothing of a more temporal character to await in the Holy Scripture. Everything is finished and fulfilled. The Roman Empire is at an end ; the Turk has come to his height ; the splendor of the Papacy is falling away, and the world is getting cracks at all its ends as though it would soon break and fall to pieces.

That this same Roman Empire has risen a little and become more powerful under our Emperor Charles than it has been for a long time past, it seems to me is the last act of God. As when a light or blade of straw, when burned out and about to be extinguished, suddenly gives out a large flame as if it were just beginning to burn right, and then, at the same instant, goes out ; such to-day is the case with Christendom and the bright Gospel.

No greater affliction has ever come upon earth and lasted longer than the abomination of Mohammed and the Pope.

March 11th.

The Elector receives the Emperor's Call in Torgau, and his Chancellor Brück advises that the points in Faith and Ceremonies on which they would have to take their stand be at once set together and grounded in Scripture.

March 14th.

Eck writes the Emperor, to stir him against the Protestants.

The Elector issues a command to his four theologians, to promptly prepare a paper on the Articles of Faith which were in dispute.

It was to be attended to immediately, for this was March 14th, and the Emperor had set April 8th as the date for the Diet at Augsburg.

COMMAND OF THE ELECTOR TO LUTHER, JONAS, POMERANUS AND MELANCHTHON.

Original in Archives at Weimar.
Printed in Cölestin, I, 134; Förstemann, I, 42.

Torgau, March 14th, 1530.

We have received a summons from the Roman Emperor to a Diet at Augsburg, with the other holy estates of the realm, on the 8th of April next, which the Emperor will attend in person. We enclose a copy of the substance of the imperial mandate.

Inasmuch as the division in our Christian religion will be one of the most weighty matters considered, and as it is important for the Estates themselves to hear, understand and test every opinion, in order to compare and bring to a single Christian truth, and to do away with everything that has not been properly explained or transacted right on both sides, that one true religion may be accepted and adhered to by us all, and as we all stand and contend under one Christ, and all live in one Commonwealth, Church and Unity, . . . in view of the pressing necessity, since it may be that said Diet is to be held in the place of a Council, or National Assembly (National-versammlung), in order that we may be rendered firm as to all the disputed Articles, both in the Faith and also in other external ecclesiastical customs and ceremonies ; so that we may before the beginning of such a Diet be thoroughly determined whether, and in what form, and in how far, we and other estates who have accepted and admitted the pure doctrine, may be able to do and suffer with a good conscience before God.

We ask you to break away from other affairs that you may finish this work between now and Oculi Sunday (March 20th), and come here to Torgau with your result.

The time between now and the Diet is very short, and we cannot delay.   And although the Call does not expressly give permission to every estate to come with preachers and theologians, yet we wish you, Dr. Martin, and Doctor Jonas, Provost, and also Magister Philip Melanchthon, to so regulate your affairs and those of the University at Wittenberg, that you may be with us at Torgau on the day mentioned, and with Magister Spalatin and Eisleben journey with us toward Coburg. Meantime we shall try to see whether it will be possible for the estates to command the preachers and theologians to come to them at Augsburg, that we may have you come to us from Coburg. If not, you are, and especially you, D. Martinus, to remain at Coburg until we come to a further decision.

In view of what these things mean to us all and to all Christendom, do not allow yourselves to be overcome with anxiety. You will thereby gain our earnest and gracious favor. Dated Torgau, Monday after Reminiscere, Anno Domini, 1530.

> To Doctor Martin
> Doctor Jonas
> Pommer
> Philip Melanchthon.

LUTHER WRITES TO JONAS.

Manuscript in Cod. Rostoch.
Printed in Cölest. I. 24 ; Er. Bf. W. VII, 253.

March 14th.

To Justus Jonas, Visitator in the Duchy of Saxony.

Grace and peace in Christ. The prince has written us, *i. e.*, you, Pomeranus, Philip, and myself, in a letter addressed to all in common, that we lay aside all other business, assemble, and complete, before next Sunday, what may be necessary for the coming Diet on April 8th. For Kaiser Carl will be present at Augsburg himself, in order to settle all differences, as he writes in his bull. On that account *we three, although you are absent, shall do as much as we can to-day and to-morrow.* Yet it will also be incumbent on you to give your work over to your associates, in order to fulfil the will of the Prince, and join us here tomorrow. For all is in haste. Christ grant that all occur to his honor. Amen.

About 12 o'clock on March 14th, 1530.

> MARTIN LUTHER.

A graphic picture indeed. It reveals many things as to the coming Confession—the centrality of the Elector and his serious sense of responsibility and sober zeal for the preservation of the pure doctrine, and the unity of the Faith; the leading position of Luther as the Elector's spiritual pillar, the lack of knowledge as to whether Augsburg would prove to be a Council of the Church which would unite and purify the whole Christian Church, or whether perhaps the stand taken against the Protestants at Spires would be modified; and contains a reflection of the Emperor's view.

March 21st.

Jonas had not been reached promptly by the call of the 14th, and a second summons is sent to him.[31]

March 27th.

Melanchthon is at the Elector's court at Torgau[32]—perhaps with the result of the labors of the theologians at Wittenberg; Luther was probably not yet there,[33] but he, with Melanchthon, arrived within a few days. Whether the work of the theologians had been finished in Wittenberg, and Melanchthon sent on with it in advance, or whether there was a Conference at Torgau after Luther arrived and before the Elector started, we do not know. At all events, the Torgau Articles, in the elaboration of which Luther had taken a principal part,[34] but which are in the writing of Melanchthon, were now presumably shown to the Elector as the answer of the Theologians.

What these Torgau Articles actually were, as a document, has been a matter of uncertainty, but historians have arrived at the conclusion that they are the document discovered by Förstemann in the "Beilagen" to Brück's *Geschichte d. Religions-Handlungen in 1530,* in the archives at Weimar (Bl. 311-323b), and printed in the *Urkunden Buch,* I, 68 sqq.

The Elector had definitely instructed them to prepare, first and foremost, the Articles of Faith in dispute, and as

---

[31] *C. R.* II. 33.

[32] *Ib.,* 23 sq.

[33] For Melanchthon was busy with the writings of the anti-Trinitarian Campanus, and Luther in a letter on April 1st (*C. R.,* III, 566) does not yet know what Campanus said.

[34] The Elector to Luther, May 11th, 1530: " As *you* and our other theologians at Wittenberg have brought into summary statement the articles of religion."

the Torgau Articles are in the form of single declarations concerning the abuses of the Roman Church which could not be yielded to, and from later events, we may perhaps infer that the Schwabach Articles of Luther, of five months before, were given to the Elector as the answer on Faith; and these Torgau Articles as the answer on Ecclesiastical Life and Ceremonies.

One week after the probable presentation of these Articles, we have a letter of Luther to his friend, Nicholas Hausmann.

April 2nd.

LUTHER TO HAUSMANN.

Original in the Archives at Anhalt.
Printed in Cölestin, I, 29; Erlangen Br.-W., VII, 290.

April 2nd.

To THE WONDERFULLY DEAR MAN, MR. NICOLAS HAUSMANN, THE ALTOGETHER PURE BISHOP OF THE CHURCH AT ZWICKAU, HIS SUPERIOR IN THE LORD.

Grace and Peace. . . . I am going with the Prince as far as Coburg, together with Philip and Jonas, until it becomes known what matters shall be taken up at Augsburg. You get your Church to pray diligently for this Diet, and keep yourself right truly in the grace of Christ, and also remember me in your prayer.

MARTIN LUTHER.

LUTHER TO CORDATUS.

Original Complete in Cod. Rostoch.
Printed in Er. Br.-W., VII, 292.

April 2nd.

Grace and peace in Christ. As I hear that you wish to hasten to the Diet, I positively advise you not to do so. First, since I have not been called thither, but for certain reasons shall only accompany the Elector within his territory. Second, because the matter of the Gospel will scarcely be taken up, or at least very late, since the Princes are not in such a hurry in the matter of godliness. Greet the companion of your sorrow, and also rejoice somewhat more in the living Christ, than grieve for your dead son.

MARTIN LUTHER, D.

April 3rd.

But the Emperor had delayed his journey to Germany, and had kept his plan from the Elector. Therefore the Elector did not wish to hasten his start for Augsburg. It was only on the 3rd of April, on Sunday, that Luther, Melanchthon and Jonas left Wittenberg in order to join the Elector in departing from Torgau. The following Saturday they were still staying at Weimar. From here Jonas reported that intelligence had now come in of the arrival of the Emperor in Trient, and that he would probably appear in Augsburg; if ever, it was now necessary to call upon the Lord in Heaven that He would steer His vessel through the stormy sea; Satan will surely attempt everything. Presumably the theological travelers were not idle on their leisurely journey of twelve days, but discussed the Confessional Articles to be used by the Elector.

April 15th.

After some days stay in Weimar, the princely procession arrived at Coburg on the 15th.

April 17th, Easter Day.

Luther preached two sermons, and another on second Easter. As always under similar circumstances he presented the great acts and truths of salvation simply, in his ordinary manner, without referring to present events in particular. Only in a general way did he furnish comfort and encouragement from the Gospel for the pressure caused by the Turk and the Pope, of which they were hearing now, as well as for other need, hunger, care, and the like.

Reports and rumors had come to Coburg concerning the Emperor and the approaching Diet. It was said that the former was still in Mantua, and would celebrate Easter there; that he would cross the Alps only in the beginning of

May, and then hold court in Innsbrück. It was said concerning the Papists, that they were laboring with all power to prevent the assembly of the Diet, since they feared unfavorable results from it. It was rumored that the Pope was angry at the Emperor because the latter had interfered in things ecclesiastical.

The one report, as we have seen, was true. Charles had come from Italy in the Springtime, and, being received magnificently by the Tyrolese, "eager to do all honor to the grandson of their beloved Kaiser Max," was holding court at Innsbrück. But the brilliancy of his reception had not blinded him to the purpose of his visit. His object was the pacification of Germany, and his thoughts were running on plans for that purpose. His letters to his brother Ferdinand, written during the stages of the journey, "reveal as fully as that reserved soul could unbosom itself" his intentions at Augsburg. "He meant to use every persuasion possible, to make what compromises his conscience permitted (for Catholicism was a faith with Charles), to effect a peaceful settlement. But if these failed, he was determined to crush the Reformation by force. He never seems to have doubted that he would succeed. Never a thought crossed his mind that he was about to encounter a great spiritual force whose depth and intensity he was unable to measure, and which was slowly creating a new world unknown to himself and to his contemporaries." [35]

At Innsbrück.

The Emperor delayed at Innsbrück in order to make every possible preparation for his success at Augsburg. With promises and presents, he sought to gain different members of the Diet for his policy. He did succeed here in reconverting the exiled King Christian of Denmark, his

---

[35] *Lindsay*, I, p. 360.

father-in-law, from Lutheranism to Catholicism—a victory that greatly pleased the Pope.

He even seems to have entertained hopes of bringing the Elector John himself over to his side, if he could succeed in inducing him to visit his court before the Diet. Duke George and other Catholic princes were to be there, and Campeggius, the Papal nuncio, was continually by his side. It would be exceedingly interesting to know more of the position taken by Mercurinus, his chancellor, in those days.

Into this brilliant assembly at Innsbrück there came a letter to the Emperor from the bitterest enemy of the Reformation, which was full of stirring lies, and with it a paper which set forth the Lutherans as heretics, not solely in one or two Articles, but in almost every point of the Christian faith, and which asserted that they were bringing back to life again all the worst heresies of the early ages. These were the Four Hundred and Four Theses of John Eck, which had been drawn from the writings of the Reformers and placed their teachings falsely side by side with those of the ancient heretical sects; and these were sent by Eck himself in a printed copy to the Emperor.

The change in the Emperor's mind—from his position in the Call—can be imagined. The Lutherans were now on trial as to the very fundamentals of their doctrine, and the fatuity of their appearing at Augsburg with a few points on ecclesiastical abuses is pathetic. No wonder the Counts of Nassau advised the Elector to prepare a thorough report in Latin or German on the matter of Religion.

No wonder, too, that the poor translation of the Schwabach Articles which the Elector sent to Innsbrück failed to make impression; that Luther's blunt Admonition to the Catholic Clerical Estates at Augsburg, which reached the Emperor's eye at Innsbrück, displeased him; and that he sent down a sharp demand that Evangelical preaching be stopped, and a request that the Elector come to meet him on the way. But we are anticipating, and must return back to the poor

Elector, and his guileless little company at Coburg, still sunning themselves in the imperial favor.

Luther was at Coburg, unconcerned. He asked the prayers of his friends, and spoke with calmness of the uncertain situation. His realm was that of the birds, and the sky, and the pure Word of God. He evidently did not believe that Augsburg was to be the great confessional Rubicon for the Church. It was to be the scene of another exhibition of diplomatic statesmanship. He did not care to write a Confession to suit such an occasion, and was of the opinion that the Princes at the Diet would not be very active in religious affairs.[36] Luther was really more concerned about the " Turk and Mohammed." It was Melanchthon who was filled with heavy cares concerning the inner situation of Germany.[37]

While the Elector and his train were waiting in Coburg, doubtless Melanchthon took the statements of abuses brought along from Torgau, and began to compose a connected writing on the foundation of the labors mentioned above, which should be delivered at Augsburg as the confession and justification of the Evangelical party. He did it in agreement with Luther;[38] and not only put the Articles themselves into good style, but began to write the Introduction[39] to this Saxon Confession, in praise of the Elector. According to A. Buchholzer, Melanchthon, many years after, in 1554, had exclaimed *valde irato animo:* " Etiam Lutherus ipse non voluit scribere talem aliquam confessionem," [40]—which he himself then was compelled to write.

---

[36] *Vid.* above letter to *Cordatus* of *April 2nd.* His experience in connection with the proposed " Bund " in Spring and Fall, and all the diplomacy he heard and saw doubtless convinced him of this. He had not calculated on a providential use of John Eck, as a blessing in disguise.

[37] Jonas from Weimar: *Pressel,* Jonas, 135; *Cod. Goth.,* 399; *Erlang.* XVII, 350 sqq.

[38] *C. R.,* II, 39 sq.

[39] To be inferred from the statement in *C. R.,* II, 39.

[40] *Libell. arcanorum,* etc., Msc. Dresd. B. 193. Seid. *K. u. S. Bl.,* 1877, p. 261.

April 17th.

The Elector arrived at Coburg on the 15th, and here awaited the results of an inquiry which he already had sent on to the magistrate of Nürnberg, which was evangelical, concerning a free safe conduct " for Luther's passing through. On April 17th, he received a reply of declination from Nürnberg, and since Luther was under the ban of the Empire, and there was no imperial safe-conduct to permit him to appear at Augsburg, it now finally seemed necessary to leave him back within the borders of the Electoral domain at Coburg, from where his advice could still be gained, in a few days, at Augsburg. In 1854, the rationalistic writer Rückert, in a work on " Luther's Relation to the Augsburg Confession," advanced the theory that Luther's detention at Coburg was part of a plan secretly arranged in advance by the Elector and the chancellor Brück, who proposed to compromise with Rome in a manner to which Luther would never consent, and decided to keep Luther here to prevent his spoiling their game. But the silence of Melanchthon (who reported so much—even in later years), the knowledge which Luther had of the Confession on which Melanchthon was working at Coburg, and especially the stand actually made by the Elector and by Brück at Augsburg with reference to preaching, and a consideration of the imperial and Papal tilt over a Free Council at Bologna, together with the fact that the Elector did not accept the invitation to go to the Emperor, and was not invested by the Emperor at Augsburg; and, above all, the express declaration of the messenger at Augsburg, in the letter of safe-conduct of the 30th of April, that, if the Elector had one in his train who stood under the ban of the Emperor, this safe-conduct should not be regarded as valid,[42] with the declination even

[41] For the negotiations with Nürnberg concerning the safe conduct see Kolde, *Analecta,* 119 sq. ; Förstemann, *Urkundenbuch,* 146 ; Kolde, *Theologische Literaturzeitung,* 1886, p. 445 ; Knaake, *Luthers Antheil an der Augsb. Conf.,* 36 sqq.

[42] Förstemann, *Urkundenbuch,* p. 161.

of Nürnberg, which was not a party to the Elector's original plans, to furnish a safe-conduct to Luther, show how unfounded this theory is. [43]

So Luther, the Confessor, summoned to Worms a decade earlier, was to remain in solitude, like a bird in its darkened cage, on the heights of Coburg, in the rooms of the mighty Castle. He should enjoy its protection: he did rejoice in its silence and loneliness.

When the pass through Nürnberg was denied, Luther wrote to his old friend, Coban Hess, then in Nürnberg, that he would send him four *living* letters in the shape of Melanchthon, Jonas, Spalatin and Agricola; and that he would gladly come as the fifth, but some one had said to him, " Keep silence: you have ' a bad voice ' " (*eine schlechte Stimme*); but that Hess would see him; *i. e.,* Luther, in Melanchthon. For he bestowed full confidence upon Melanchthon as his representative.

April 18th.

LUTHER TO N. HAUSMANN.

Original in Anhalt Gesammt-Archiv.
Cölestin, I, 29 ; Erlangen Br. W., VII, 296.

April 18th.

I have been ordered by the Prince to remain in Coburg, after the others have departed to the Diet. I do not know for what reason. So everything is uncertain from one day to another.

April 22nd.

LUTHER TO W. LINK.

Original in Wolfbüt., Cod. Helmst., 285, B.
Cölest., I, 30 ; Er. Br. W., VII, 299.

April 22nd.

As for the rest, we are lying here at Coburg, uncertain concerning the Diet and

---

[43] *Cp.* also *Knaake, in loco.*

the arrival of the Kaiser.   Although my colleagues go to Augsburg, the Prince desires that I remain here.   You will see them, viz., Philip, Jonas, Eisleben and Spalatin, when the Diet convenes.

On the Friday after Easter, the 22nd of April, the Elector, who up to this time had been awaiting reliable intelligence concerning the opening of the Diet, received an imperial rescript according to which he should appear, without fail, in Augsburg by the end of the month.   Immediately he fixed the next day for his departure from Coburg.

April 23rd.

Early in the morning, before four o'clock, while it is still dark, Luther was brought to the Castle."   His friends, Jonas, Melanchthon and Spalatin, started on the way to Augsburg with the Elector, while Agricola arrived at Augsburg as the companion of Count Albrecht of Mansfeld.   Luther's papers did not arrive promptly, and he spent the earlier part of the day in examining his new surroundings.   About three o'clock in the afternoon he wrote a letter to Melanchthon, whom he had left just that morning before dawn.

LUTHER TO MELANCHTHON.

MS. in Wolfenbüttel, Cod. Helmst. 108, f. 11.
Printed Cölestin I, 39; Erlang. Br. VII, 302.

April 23rd.

To his exceedingly dear brother, Master Philip, the faithful and prudent servant and disciple of Christ.

1. Grace and peace in the Lord Jesus.   At last we have reached our Sinai, dearest Philip, but we shall make a Zion out of it, and build three tabernacles : One for the Psalter, one for the Prophets, and one for Æsop.

The place is exceedingly pleasant and very well adapted to study, except that your absence makes me sad.   I am beginning to blaze up against the Turks and Mohammed in the bottom of my heart, for I see the raging of Satan against bodies and souls.   Therefore I shall pray without ceasing until I have the consciousness that my supplication is heard in Heaven.   You are troubled by the internal disorder

---

" Förstemann, *a. a. O.*, I, 143 sq. 152.   For Luther's getting to Coburg on the night of the 22nd, and morning of the 23rd, compare his letters written to Melanchthon, Jonas and Spalatin.

of our Empire. But we are the ones who are ordained to see and to suffer these last two woes. But this very violence is a testimony and a prophecy of Satan's end and our redemption.

2. I pray Christ that He will give you continuously good sleep, and that He will free your heart from cares, *i. e.*, from the fiery darts of Satan. Amen.

I am writing this because I am idle, for I have not yet received my chest with the papers and other things.

Everything here is in keeping with solitude ; the very large house that juts forth from the castle is entirely ours, and we hold the keys to all. It is said that over thirty people abide here, among them twelve night watchmen and two trumpeteers upon the towers. But why am I telling you this ? It is true there is nothing else that I can write. By evening I hope the "Kastner" will be here. Then, perhaps, we shall hear something new. The grace of God be with you. Amen.

3. Greet Doctor Caspar for me and M. Spalatin, for I will request Jonas to greet Agricola and Aquila. Out of the Kingdom of the Birds, at 3 o'clock this afternoon, 1530. Your

MARTIN LUTHER.

Luther then wrote to Jonas, who also had gone on with the Elector that morning.

LUTHER TO JONAS.

(*Out of the Kingdom of Birds.*)

MS. in Wolfenbüttel, Cod. Helmst., 108, fol. 9b.
Printed Cölestin, I, fol. 38b ; Erlang. Br., VII, 305.

April 23rd.

Grace and peace in Christ Jesus. At last we are sitting here beneath the clouds, and in truth in the Kingdom of the Birds. My dearest Jonas, not to speak of the other birds, whose mingled medley of sound rises clearly above the storm, the jack-daws have taken possession of a whole wood right before our eyes. They have been chattering from 4 o'clock this morning unwearily and unceasingly throughout the whole day, and perhaps they will keep it up all night. . . . Here I see before me the whole army of sophists and cochleits assembled out of all the world, so that I may become better acquainted with their wisdom and their sweet song. The nightingale has not yet appeared, but her forerunner, the cuckoo, praises itself in the glorious beauty of its voice. Likewise the robin and the lark are cheerfully prais-ing the Lord. You see that I have nothing to write to you. The Lord be with you, and we will pray for one another. This is necessary. Greet M. Agricola and Aquila for me. I will write them as early as possible. Farewell. Out of the Kingdom of Birds, especially of the "Dohlen," 1530. Your

MARTIN LUTHER.

We see that Luther was already at home amid his surroundings, and that, relieved from care, his imagination had
time to picture the Emperor and the coming Diet in the
feathered tribes outside his window with whom he had
already grown familiar. He knew the song was continuous,
when he wrote to Jonas, but did not yet know whether they
kept up their music in the early hours of the night.

In his first letter, to Melanchthon, Luther had sent greetings to Spalatin. About five o'clock, he determined to write
to Spalatin himself, and in this letter he refers to the two
missives he had finished, and repeats his fancies concerning
the birds to Spalatin also.

LUTHER TO SPALATIN.

MS. in Wolfenbüttel, Cod. Helmst., 108, fol. 13 (Dated, May 19th).
Printed in Cölestin, I, fol. 37b; Erlang. Br. W., VII, 307.

April 23rd.

To the dear man, Mr. George Spalatin, the faithful Servant of Christ in the
Gospel, his Superior.

Grace and peace in the Lord. You are not the only one, my dear Spalatin,
who are journeying to a Diet, for we also arrived at a Diet as soon as we parted
from you, and thus we have greatly anticipated you. And our journey to the Diet
was entirely without hindrance. It is true you are going to Augsburg, but you do
not know when you will see the beginning of your Diet. Here we have dropped
right into the midst of ours. Here you can see proud kings, dukes, and other
dignitaries of the realm, who are earnestly caring for all emergencies and for those
who belong to them, and who are making the air resonant with their resolutions
and their theses. They despise the folly of a raiment adorned with gold and silver,
and are all clothed in one color and with incredible similarity. They are all arrayed entirely in black. They all sing the same musical score in the same pitch,
except that there is a lovely difference between the voices of the old ones and the
young ones. I have not yet seen or heard their emperor. As much as I can understand from their interpreter they have unanimously resolved to undertake a year's
crusade against the barley fields. We very much enjoy the privilege of being
spectators at this Diet.

But enough of pleasantry, although it is necessary to drive away the earnest
thoughts that rise, if indeed it is possible to banish them. You will hear the rest
from Jonas and Philip. Out of the kingdom of the Winged Dohlen, about 5 o'clock,
1530.   Your

MARTIN LUTHER.

April 28th.

Five days later, Luther penned a beautiful little letter to the friends he had left in Wittenberg:—

LUTHER TO HIS TABLE COMPANIONS IN WITTENBERG.

MS. Cod. Goth. B. 28, fol. 72.
Printed Erlang. 54, p. 143.

April 28th.

Grace and peace in Christ. Dear Friends : We, namely, myself, Magister Veit and Cyriacus, are not going to the Diet at Augsburg, but we have come upon another kind of Diet. . . . To-day we have heard the first nightingale, for she did not quite trust April. Up to this time we had nothing but lovely weather. It has not rained at all, except yesterday a little. Perhaps it is otherwise with you. Herewith I commend you to God. Keep house well. From the Diet of the "Maltztürken," the 28th of April, 1530.

MARTINUS LUTHER. D.

April 29th.

Luther tells Melanchthon that his Admonition to the Clergy at Augsburg is well under way. Luther was in hope, calm and peace at Coburg, which contrasted greatly with the constant anxiety of Melanchthon.

LUTHER TO MELANCHTHON.

MS. in Wolfenbüttel, Cod. Helmst. 108, f , 10b.
Printed in Erlang. Br. VII, p. 313.

April 29th.

Grace and peace in Christ. The house of Jonas has been hallowed by the cry of a fifth child. . . . Find out what they of Strassburg are intending. But Carlstadt will make my prophecy true in that I said that he does not believe there is a God; yet they may go and do what they wish. Here there is no news except that we are wondering that no letters have come from you. I sent letters to you on the first day on which we separated. But now, because the messenger is in great haste, and I have been overwhelmed with a great multitude of letters, I have been unable to write several. We are living here like lords, and are treated too much as such. My shinbone does not want to heal yet. I judge that a sort of rheum will result, which I would like to prevent, and yet I do not know. I am writing about it to Dr. Caspar.

My admonition to the Clerical Estate is progressing. It is growing under my

25

hands, the material as well as the violence of attack, so that I am compelled to drive off a whole troop [*i. e.*, his thoughts] by force, since they do not cease to press in upon me unbidden. May the Lord, Who has blessed Jonas with a fifth little son, also bless you with a third, a second Georg. Amen. Amen. Out of the Diet of the Mäilander, April 29th, 1530.

MARTIN LUTHER.

Meantime the Elector and his train had spent the week in journeying on to Augsburg.

April 30th.

The Elector receives a safe-conduct for his train into Augsburg, but Luther is expressly excluded, though not mentioned by name.

May 2nd.

THE ELECTOR REACHES AUGSBURG.

To-day we see John the Constant entering the city of Augsburg. He is here, now, in response to the Call of his imperial lord, issued on January 21st, and received by him on March 22nd.[43]

The old Elector's coming all the way to Augsburg[44] had cost great effort, spiritual, confessional, diplomatic, and financial on his part, and to keep him there would be an even greater strain. He lived only a year or two longer.

But he was the first on the ground, to the surprise of everybody, especially the Papists, who had "supposed that the fear of so many mighty foes would hold him away. His steadfastness and unperturbed demeanor caught every eye, and the

---

[43] The first date for the Diet was April 8th. On the way, the Elector learned of a postponement to May 1st. Then the news came en route that the Emperor was celebrating Easter at Mantua. However, the Elector was on hand May 2nd, and the other princes came a week later. The Emperor did not arrive—in part to tire the Elector into submission—until June 15th, when the Roman Corpus Christi must first be celebrated, and the sessions did not open until the 20th. *Salig*, II, 156, says of the first postponement: "The business (after the crowning at Bologna) accumulated to such an extent that the Emperor had to postpone the opening of the Diet."

[44] For reasons why the Elector had decided to go to Augsburg, see *Cyprian*, p. 151.

majority wished that he had not come. He had sent a representative, Hans von Doltzig, to the counts of Nassau and Neuenar, asking them to look after his interests, especially in the matter of the electoral investiture, and the many religious charges preferred against him. Doltzig rode around through Germany and Italy unable to find the Emperor, until he at last reached Innsbrück five days in advance of Charles, and there gained a personal audience and a gracious reply from his Majesty."[45]

As soon as the Elector heard of the Emperor's arrival at Innsbrück, he sent congratulations through the hereditary marshalls, Sebastian and Joachim of Paffenheim, and despatched his counsel, Hans von Minqvitz, to Innsbrück, to notify the Emperor of his arrival at Augsburg, to congratulate his majesty on the coronation, and to aid Doltzig in his labors.[46]

The faithful Elector had been careful, in his arrangements, to adhere closely to the imperial instructions. After the Call had reached him on March 11th at home, his Chancellor Brück at once advised that the Saxon theologians prepare an Opinion "of that upon which our party has stood immovable up to now, mit gründlicher Bewahrung derselbigen aus göttlicher Schrift."[47] His theologians at the University, with Luther at the head, were bidden, on March 14th, to consult concerning the controversial articles "both in faith and also in other external ceremonies," and deliver a report at Torgau.[48] These "Torgau Articles" have never been found under this name, but Brieger[49] has shown that they are probably a document preserved by Förstemann,[50] which the Elector took with his party to Augsburg, and which was made the base of the earliest confession.

It contained propositions on Abuses, was discussed and

---

[45] Salig, *Hist. der Augsp. Conf.*, II, 161, 162.
[46] *Müller*, VIII, 466, 477.
[47] *Först.*, I, 39.
[48] *C. R.*, II, 25 sq.
[49] *K. Gesch. Studien*, 1888, 268 sqq.
[50] *Ur. B.*, II, 68-74.

given to the Elector at Torgau, and was doubtless further discussed and determined on by Luther and Melanchthon on the way to Coburg. It did not deal largely with doctrine, but took for granted that the doctrine preached by the Evangelicals was "Christian and comforting and not new," and recommended, if it were desired, "the delivery of Articles in which the whole doctrine was set forth in an orderly way."

This paper Melanchthon was commissioned to elaborate into a defensive delineation of the Saxon religious situation, referring not so much to the faith as to the changes in the rites in the churches; and not for the purpose of attacking abuses, but in order to defend the Elector's reform in Saxony as not being greatly at variance with Rome, except where, for self-evident reasons, this was absolutely necessary.

This was the Elector's "Apology," so-called because it was intended to defend the Elector and his reform before the outside world from the slanders that were constantly being uttered against it by the Romanists.[51]

A chief part of it consisted of a Preface in praise and defence of the Elector's loyalty to the Emperor and the church. At Coburg, Melanchthon had begun work on the Preface, continued at the same on the journey, and was still elaborating it when the Elector and his train reached Augsburg.[52]

LUTHER IS MISSING.

The Elector's central figure, Luther, was not among the Augsburg party. He had been left at Coburg because he was under the imperial ban, and the Apology went on to Augsburg in the hand of Melanchthon. There were a number of good reasons, from the Elector's point of view, why Luther should not be the bearer of the Electoral Apology in person. The Elector indeed had intended to take Luther along to Augsburg (Först., Archiv., p. 17), but he found it imprac-

---

[51] In Spain it was reported that the Lutherans did not even believe *in a God.*
[52] On this section, *cp.* Först., *Archiv.*, I, 17; Schirrmacher, *a. a. O.*, 25 sqq. ; Kolde, *Anal.*, 454 sqq.

ticable on account of the ban. Augsburg would not admit him. The Elector tried at least to have him close at hand in Nuremberg; but to keep terms with the Emperor, Nuremberg would not grant him even a safe conduct.

Moreover Luther *had not been summoned* to confess, this time. It was the Elector's own turn. This was not a Council of the Church, but a Diet of the State. The Emperor had exerted himself to secure a Council, but the Pope was obstinate,[52a] and the Emperor had then fallen back on the one recourse open to him, viz., another Diet. The Edict of 1526 and the Call of 1530 made the Elector the party responsible for the Faith in his territory. And if the Elector and the Estates, as Weber points out,[53] had attempted to deliver a Confession to the Emperor, of which it was known that the condemned Luther was the author, it would have awakened bitterness, and subverted the object of the Diet, which was an impartial presentation of differences, and a decision in unity.[54]

In the second place, as Melanchthon in later years himself reported to Camerarius, Luther did not care to write a Confession, or " Apology," for Augsburg—such as was at that time intended, namely, one that expressed differences in doctrine and practice as smoothly and gently as possible, and which was phrased in diplomacy; and which was to be offered to a political Diet, as the sum of what the Protestants might yield, and not to a religious Council. The Preface[55] already wrought out in praise of the Elector could not as a Confession have been to Luther's way of thinking, although Luther himself had suggested the leading points for another purpose. There is truth in Weber's statement[56] that it was not advisable

---

[52a] " The Emperor *experienced to satiety* at Bologna that a Council was not agreeable to the Pope."—*Cyprian*, p. 44 ; and to the Pope the Emperor was obliged to bend the knee—Ad pontificio pedes flexo genu provolutus.— *Masenius* d. 1. 171.

[53] *Gesch.*, I, 27.

[54] In deciding to keep Luther at Coburg, the Elector had no doubt also weighed the danger of an emphasis of Luther at Augsburg. Already at Worms the Elector's charge of Luther was accompanied with " schier etwas Mühe."

[55] *Cp.* the Oldest Redaction.

[56] *Gesch.*, I, 28.

to have Luther, who, when it came to speaking the truth, spared neither priest nor king, open his mouth before the Emperor and the kingdom in such a delicate situation as the religious situation that Spring. " For truth, if it is obliged to battle with prejudice, is more effective in its action upon the human heart, if it appear in an unassuming and pleasing garb, rather than in a rough prickly covering, which disgraces it, and which scratches the face and draws the blood of those who are filled with prejudice, but very seldom, if ever, improves the situation. . . . Melanchthon had a much quieter spirit, was gentle and modest, and knew how to tell the truth, in beautiful and pleasant style, in which he excelled the theologians of his time, without embittering the opposite party."

However, there was another fact—which documentary critics like Weber fail to catch—inwoven in the larger course of history, that bears upon this point. Melanchthon is to be credited with an independent point of view, which he had acquired at the Diet of Spires, which he had succeeded to some extent in impressing on Luther, which was, so far as the situation was a political one, responsible for the rejection of Zwingli and the Swiss at Marburg, and which harmonized very fully with the fundamental outlook of the imperial Call. It was this: that separation from Rome was not necessarily a finality, and that if the Lutherans on their part would renounce the more radical and irresponsible Sacramentarians (the Reformed), and Rome would purify herself of her worst errors, there would be a possibility, not merely of compromise, but of the restoration of unity with the old Church, on true Lutheran ground.[57]

---

[57] The delusiveness of this conviction, strong in both Melanchthon and the Emperor came to the surface first, when the Lutheran Faith was finally worked out into the Augsburg Confession, whose fundamental teachings, principles and tone, despite its soft tread, can never be brought into accord with Romanist doctrine ; and second, when all attempts at fair dealing and mutual understanding in the Diet were frustrated by the assumption, the claims and the secret machinations of Rome. The Diet of Augsburg, in its Confession and in its deliberations, is a graphic commentary, valuable for all time and for every country, on the irreconcilable conflict between Rome and the Protestant Christian conscience.

Still another fact that dare not be ignored is this: the call of Providence to confess at Augsburg was not a mere renewal of the primitive call to Luther at Worms. The Evangelical Faith had been planted in many localities and was growing to maturity. Melanchthon's Visitation Articles, or Saxon Confession, had already been written. Electoral Saxony and Evangelical Germany were themselves now *ripe* for confession. The Gospel found by Luther had been preached for more than a decade, and had been thoroughly tested by the Word, and by continuous battle, both with Rome, and with all kinds of radical divergencies and extravagances. What was now to be expected of the churches was not mere personal and heroic testimony of individual Reformers (such as Luther, *e. g.,* gives in his Admonition to the Augsburg Diet), but a maturity, an objectivity, and a calmness of utterance that befitted *the congregations,* the earthly representatives of the Communion of Saints.

In other words, the Confession at Augsburg was intended by Providence to be a *Church* Confession. It was to emphasize the common Christian doctrine, to bring the universal Christian foundations into light, and to put the unrighteous antithesis of the Romish teaching in as mild a form as the truth allowed.

Not that it was to be a complete and exhaustive summary of doctrinal principle. By its origin it had been limited to a statement of "Opinions and Grievances," and circumstances, divinely ordered, alone enlarged its scope. Its scale of truth was the *minimum* for which the Evangelical cause must stand; its temper was conciliation where possible; its method was adjustment, and an endeavor to meet the other party as far as possible. This in itself, while it aided the Confession as a mature statement of the Faith for the Diet, cut it off from being a complete, and still more from being the final Confession of the Faith.[58] The "Apology," in fact, was

---

[58] Its whole doctrinal part, as Kolde says, is intended to prove that Catholic and Lutheran doctrine are one. The Lutheran doctrines of. the Lord's Supper and of Baptism are treated most briefly. There is no rejection of the remain-

obliged to follow right on its heels, and to emphasize much that had been depressed in the Confession.

Luther, in truth, at this time, did not believe that there would be a very earnest attempt by the princes to make a real Confession, at a diet where political matters would probably claim precedence. He also may have felt that Philip of Hesse would be refractory.

In the third place, if Luther had been called to embody this Confession in its final form, his open honesty in stating conditions, his enthusiastic ardor for the truth, and his violent and personal aggressiveness against Rome, would have defeated the Elector's hope of gaining a fair hearing from the Emperor for the Lutheran party he represented. The Call to the Diet did not itself touch the heart of things. It gave each party a right to appear, but it made no promises of rooting out poisonous existing institutions. It looked to some possible compromise. No wonder that Luther lacked in enthusiasm in preparing a confession which should correspond in mildness to the terms set forth in the Call.

Although the Call promised that the error and division in the holy Christian faith were to be taken up and considered, and the opinion of each one should be heard in good will and love, and properly weighed, until true unity should be restored, "of the abolition of papal abuses, or of what was dangerous to the Evangelical truth, of the protection of those who were steadfast in the true faith, there was no word said." [59]

That Luther's "Stimme" was not "leise" will be seen at once when we come to examine his "Address to the Clergy" at the Diet. Luther did not think it right to keep silent, in any Confession, as to the false claims of the Pope, whom he regarded as Anti-Christ, to be testified against. But the subject

---

ing sacraments of Rome. Repentance is introduced in such a manner that it does not exclude the possibility of its being a sacrament. Transubstantiation is not rejected, and the emphasis of Scripture as the only rule of faith is not found. The *main emphasis* at that time was laid on the Second Part, "Of Abuses."

[59] *Salig*, II, 156.

is ignored in the Augsburg Confession. He also would have treated the ecclesiastical abuses more emphatically.

Yet there was a last and practical reason for taking the final form of the Confession out of Luther's hand, and it was insuperable. What was more pressing than all else was this: Luther could not be at the Elector's side, and could not meet the situation from day to day as it occurred. Though the principals felt they had settled the details pretty thoroughly before the Elector's train left Coburg, Providence was to bring about great changes in the situation, and consequently in the Confession.

THE PATHWAY BEHIND AND BEFORE THE ELECTOR.

While the Elector was passing on to Augsburg, history was being made and modified on the other side of the Alps. The Emperor, who had arrived at Bologna on the 5th of November, remained there four whole months, and lived in the same palace with the Pope. Separated only by a single partition, they were able to communicate with each other without observation at any time during the day or night.[60] The Pope finally succeeded in extorting a promise from Charles to suppress Luther's doctrine and bring the Lutherans to obedience to the Papal curia, first kindly, but if that did not avail, then by force of arms. To this Charles agreed at his coronation at Bologna, and it was but a renewal of the compact made at Barcelona, which was as follows: Charles and Ferdinand should lead the Lutherans back to their former religion, and if they would not do it, compel them by force of arms. Clement should also use all means to the same purpose, and should move the remaining princes to the accomplishment of such a godly work.[61]

---

[60] *Cyprian*, p. 61.

[61] *Spondanus.* Narrat *Belcarius,* episcopus Metensis, rerum Gallicarum commentariis anno 1529, p. m. 626. *Raynaldus* b. a. n. 62. verba foederis refert. *Cyprian,* 49, 50.

Except for Mercurinus, the Romanists felt secure. The Emperor had thrown the embassadors bearing the Spires protest into prison; he had on Matthias day at the coronation confirmed the original compact. The Pope's gold was at hand to stir up all rulers against the Lutherans. So sure were the Romanists of success that when the Emperor crossed into Germany, they cried out, *"Salvator venit!"* [62]

The Call had been framed with all this in view, and this was the real Roman object of the Diet. From now on every means was being used by the Romanists, and would soon be adopted by the Emperor himself, to evade that "fair, impartial hearing of every opinion," and "that acceptance of every doctrine that proved itself to be really Scriptural and true," which had been promised by the Emperor in the Call. The truth and import of all these events stretching back of him, the Elector could barely judge.

Still less did he foresee the pathway that stretched out before him into the future. First of all, during his lengthy stay at Augsburg, there were the six weeks of waiting, from May 2nd to June 15th, for the Emperor to appear, and the preliminary negotiations during that period which nerved the Elector to his final stand. Second, there would then begin that concentrated period of activity and suspense, during the ten days succeeding the Emperor's arrival and preceding the presentation of the Confession, from June 15th to June 25th. And third, the delivery of the Confession would be followed by that long and indeterminate Summer at Augsburg in which the Emperor attempted to force his counter-proposals upon the Protestants from June 25th to the day in September when the Elector and his fellow Princes and Confessors took their departure from the Diet. It was a pathway sufficiently rugged to test the bravery, the strength and the endurance of the great hero that the Elector proved himself to be.

---

[62] *Vid. Cyprian,* p. 54.

May 2nd-June 15th.

I. Period of Waiting and Preparation.

ECK'S "THESES," AND THE ELECTOR'S SECRET "CONFESSION."

Among the first tidings to fly to the Elector's ear on his reaching Augsburg, was that Four Hundred and Four Theses against "those who disturb the peace of the Church," *i. e.,* against the Lutheran party of whom the Elector was the head, with a flaming dedicatory preface, had been written on February 10th, and sent in manuscript to the Emperor on March 14th. John Eck, Professor at Ingolstadt, had responded to the request of the Bavarian Dukes, made in January, when they heard that the Emperor would deal with the matter of religion at the Diet, that the Ingolstadt Faculty should collect together "all Articles which had been published by Luther in the last twelve years in one paper, and show how they were out of harmony with the one Christian faith, together with the way in which they could be most profitably refuted." [63] Eck had also offered to dispute his positions before the Emperor at the Diet.

This was a new and startling situation. With it came the news that the Emperor would probably recede from the position of his Call. The Diet ahead was no longer to be a calm, free, open and unbiased deliberative assembly, at which every party would be cordially welcome to state its convictions and opinions, in order that, from a full consideration of them all, the truth might be arrived at impartially; but it now dawned on the Elector that the Emperor and the Pope would themselves together constitute the party of the one part, while the Lutherans would be practically, or perhaps actually, on trial as defendants. At the very least, the presumption was to be against them.

But if Eck's gross calumnies and misrepresentations had

---

[63] Winter, *Gesch. d. ev. Lehre in u. durch Baiern,* München, 1809, I, 270.

swerved the Emperor from his orbit, and had deceived him as to the real nature of the Evangelical Faith, which was not heretical, or revolutionary, but was to be depended upon for loyalty to the civil government, for fidelity to the one true church, and for opposition to the fanaticism of the Anabaptists and the Sacramentarians, it might still be possible to present to the Emperor a statement of the doctrines of the Lutheran party, which would convince him that the Evangelicals had been misrepresented. The Count of Nassau in his friendly letter advised the Elector to have a complete statement on Religion in Latin or German delivered to the Emperor before the beginning of the Diet.

If the Elector could only get his own real personal faith before the Emperor, as an antidote to the Theses of Eck, his most gracious Majesty might even yet come to see that the Lutheran doctrine was wholesome and true, and was a very different thing from the aggregation of old heresies in which Eck had painted it out. In any event Eck's Theses could not be ignored; and, besides, the Elector had some special personal rights in this case. He was his Majesty's uncle, the chief marshall of the realm, entitled to the investiture, and was the chief pillar of support for the empire in all northern Germany.[64]

If Eck could send in representations that defamed his faith, why should not the Elector personally do all he could to disabuse the mind of Charles before the meeting of the Diet?

But what should he send to Charles? The Apology in Melanchthon's hands would not meet the doctrinal situation created by Eck. Neither did he feel that Melanchthon or any of the theologians was the man with whom he could coun-

---

[64] So great was the prestige of the Saxon Electors that Frederick the Wise might have become the Emperor of the Holy Roman Empire. But he declined the honor, and used his influence in favor of Charles. *Cp. Masenius anima historia,* p. 55, quoted by *Cyprian,* p. 24: In 1519 the Emperor died, and the Elector of Saxony, pending the election of another, became the imperial Stadthalter. He could powerfully protect Luther, since he was the Prince most looked up to in the Empire, and since he also declined the imperial honor, and caused it to be conferred upon Charles V.

sel. Luther was at Coburg. What could he do? He had one paper that expressed his faith, viz.: Luther's Schwabach Articles. Without consulting his theologians, in secrecy, he sent the Emperor at Innsbrück a poor translation of the Schwabach Articles as his own personal[65] confession.

HANS BERN'S SENSATION.

Verily truth is stranger than fiction. For these same Schwabach Articles, sent with so much secrecy to the Emperor as the Elector's personal confession in religion, were now about to appear in print on the streets of Augsburg as the Confession of Luther himself, which he would hand in at the Diet. In response to the curiosity as to what statement the Protestants would make at Augsburg, an enterprising printer at Coburg had attached Luther's name to them, and put them forth as the coming Augsburg Confession. Both Luther and the Elector must have been startled when they saw what the printer Hans Bern had done. As they took up the little quarto leaf, they read the following title: "Die bekenntnus Martini Luthers auf den yetzigen angestelten Reichstag zu Augspurgk eynzulegen, In siebentzehen Artikel verfasset. Im XXX Jar"; and at the close, they saw, "Gedruckt zu Coburgk durch Hands Bern. 4. Ein Bogen"[66]

But other and more dangerous eyes soon caught this title, and, misled by the daring but gratuitous assumption of the

---

[65] *Vid.* Kürfurst Johannus Glaubens bekenntniss vom mai 1530. The original bears the endorsement, "Artickel vom Churfurst zu Sachssen des glaubens halb." But compare the statement of Salig, *Hist. Augsp. Conf.*, II, 143: "The pious Elector John did nothing in the matter of the confederation without Luther's advice, and since Luther had now advised . . . that the differences of opinions must show themselves in the accepting of certain prescribed articles, it is doubtless certain that the Elector John desired these Articles from Luther that they might be shown to the estates to be admitted to the League at the Schmalkald Convention. He who accepted these would become a part of the League. *In this way they also bear the title in the Archives of Ulm of Articul von Chürfursten von Sachsen des Glaubens halb,* because the Elector sent them to Schwabach through his representatives as a Symbol of the Confederated allies."

[66] Original found by Elias Frick in the Archives at Ulm, and printed by him in the German *Seckendorf*, p. 968.

Coburg printer, soon turned it to practical account. Among the Papist theologians were those of the Elector Joachim, with Wimpina at their head; and being very ungraciously disposed toward Luther,[67] they took advantage of this supposed early print of the coming Protestant Confession to prepare and issue a confutation of it in advance.

WIMPINA AND LUTHER CLASH.

Their brief Christian admonition against the Augsburg Confession of Martin Luther bears the following title: "Gegen die Bekenntnus Martini Luthers, auf den yetzigen angestelten Reichstag zu Augsspurg, auffs neue eingelegt, in siebenzehn Artickel verfasst. Kurtze und Christenlich underricht durch Conrad Wimpina Doctor, Johann Mensing Doctor, Wolffgang Redörffer Doctor, Rupert Elgersma Licenci zu Augspurg. 1530.4."[68]

In this confutation of the supposed Augsburg Confession, Wimpina tried to make it appear that Luther had omitted many parts and articles of his teaching, which, according to Wimpina, included revolution, idolatry, unchastity and the breaking of oaths.

It was really too bad. Here was the Elector's confidential Confession to the Emperor hawked about the streets of Augsburg, branded as the work of the arch-heretic Luther, accepted by the Romanist public as the coming Confession of the Protestant estates, and vilified by a Papist reply in print! Moreover these Articles, if their true history became known, would stand out as an attempt at agreement between the Lutherans and the Sacramentarians, with a view to a Protestant combination of estates to be engineered by Philip of Hesse. Yet one of Melanchthon's strongest points in the Apology he was amplifying, was that the Lutherans were

---

[67] *Cyprian*, p. 52.

[68] *Erl*. 2nd ed. 25. 344-355.

altogether different from the Sacramentarians, and had no sympathy with them.

The situation was serious; but Luther at Coburg was equal to it. He sat down and wrote a reply to the outcry and noise the Papists were making over these Articles. His broadside bears the following title: "Auf das schreyen etlicher Papisten über die sieben zehn Artickel, Antwort Martini Luthers. Wittemberg. Im M. D. XXX Jar. 4. Ein Bogen."[69] The Answer consisted simply of a reprint of the Articles themselves, since they were their own best witness, together with a Preface, in which Luther declares that he was not their sole author, that they were *not intended to be offered to the Augsburg Diet,* and that he had not desired or permitted their publication. After a dignified introductory paragraph, a sharp sally at the Papists, and a request to the printer not to make such a mistake again, he concludes by asking the Christian reader to pray for God's grace "upon the present Diet, and upon the pious, good Emperor Carol, who is sitting like an innocent little lamb between so many swine and dogs, yea between many devils." " *God Himself must* work the good at the Diet. Otherwise neither the counsel nor skill of Emperor, princes or estates will avail: so angry and bitter is the devil. . . . The devil has it in mind to introduce other articles, which are horrible to behold. God help us. Amen."

Thus were the flames of falsehood lit at both ends—at the Emperor's court en route and at Augsburg in prospect—against the Lutherans; and the conciliatory document, now being so industriously elaborated by Melanchthon, was already behind the actual march of events. The only consolation the Emperor had in store for the Elector in reply to the Confession secretly sent in, was a sharp command that he prohibit his ministers from preaching their Evangelical doctrine in the city of Augsburg.

---

[69] Cyprian, *Beil.,* p. 159; *Erl.* 2nd ed. 24. 337.

A GULF BEGINNING TO OPEN.

We now have reached the stage when it would soon dawn on all the little party at Augsburg (except Melanchthon) that the abyss between them and the Emperor was deep, and could not be crossed; and that the original intention to present only an Apology containing the Torgau statement on rites and abuses, and the rhetorical Preface in praise of the Emperor and the Elector would not meet the situation. The foundation of the Evangelical doctrine had been attacked in its main points. The Emperor had received information that the Lutherans were heretics throughout the whole range of faith, and they had been pointed to as men who had renewed the worst errors of the ancient heretics of Christianity, which was a far more serious thing than the changes in rites and ceremonies with which the Torgau Articles dealt. It became necessary to defend the Lutheran Teaching in every main doctrine, and to show that it was not heretical. The mere Apology would not suffice. A Confession of Faith must be prepared. It must furnish a summary of Evangelical doctrine; and by rejecting heresies, must put a stop to the numerous slanders which identified the Lutherans with old-time heretics.

Thus we see that in the Providence of God, the lying theses of John Eck were the occasion that brought about a readjustment of the Elector's intentions, and that introduced, so far as the Articles of Faith were concerned, a historical and a doctrinal character into the Augsburg Confession. As Eck had compared the supposed Lutheran heresies in parallel columns with ancient heresies of the Church, and with the teachings of Anabaptists and Evangelicals, it was necessary now to demonstrate, not merely that the Elector was not establishing a new Church, or simply desiring to restore the old one to a perfect condition; but it became imperative to show that the Lutherans held strictly and historically to the fundamental doctrines of the Ancient Church, and that they adhered to the great œcumenical Confessions of the past, and not to heretical tenets and to mere figments of doctrine as Eck represented.

May 3rd.

UNFURLS THE FLAG OF THE PURE GOSPEL.

The Elector took a bold and open stand in behalf of his religion as soon as he reached the city of Augsburg. It was not cowardice, or the hope of compromise that had caused him to leave Luther at Coburg. Scarcely had he arrived when he ordered one of his theologians to preach daily with open doors in the church of the Dominicans.[70]

This was his open and continuous Confession of his life and faith in God's Word. It was his natural testimony to the world, by simply putting into practice away from home that which was his most important concern at home. To the Elector this preaching was a very serious matter. It was the essence of his position.

May 4th.

Immediately after the first cares of his arrival had been settled, the Elector thought of the lonely man of God whom he had left behind in the castle, and who was praying for him with all his might. He could not refrain from writing him a brief personal letter:—

THE ELECTOR TO LUTHER.

Altenberger Ausgabe, V, 23.
Erl. Br. Wechs., VII, 327.

May 4th.

Dear Doctor! Take things easy. Do not let the time seem long to you. We are all very much concerned for your bodily health, and pray God that He

---

[70] *Seck.,* Latin, 193. *Salig,* II, 162, says "im *Franciscaner*-Closter," and "on the Sunday Jubilate held Evangelical service in the St. Catharine, the Virgin, Convent."

will long preserve you, for the sake of His dear Word; yea, and we admonish you yourself to take care of your health. *D.* Caspar, our physician, is sending you medicine with this messenger to strengthen head and heart; for he is your faithful friend, and we also remain desirous of every grace for you, etc.

For eleven days, Luther had remained in the castle before he heard these first tidings from the travelers in whom he was so deeply interested. Melanchthon also sends him an interesting letter on the same day, full of the news the party heard when they came to Augsburg. No prince is here, but some theologians have arrived; Duke George is on the way; the Emperor himself has probably reached Innsbrück; Cajetan will perhaps be with him; Eck has Theses; Nassau has sent a friendly letter; the Apology's Introduction is more elaborate, and is almost ready for Luther to examine.

MELANCHTHON TO LUTHER.

Original in Leipzig Stadt. Bibliothek.
C. R., II, 38; Erl., Br., VII, p. 323.

May 4th.

TO *D.* MARTIN LUTHER, HIS EXTRAORDINARILY DEAR FATHER.

May it be well with you! While I was wishing to write you through the messenger of Jonas, your unexpected, but welcome letter was delivered. Your friendliness makes us happy, and we pray you, despite your being so busy, to write often. I wrote you from Nuremberg, and have ordered this messenger to ask for the letter, if it have not already been sent off.

In Augsburg one of Count Albrecht's youths reports that the Emperor has left Trient; and if we are not deceived in our reckoning, he has already arrived at Innsbrück. Count Henry of Nassau has written a friendly letter to our Prince, admonishing him to come to the Diet early. Although various things are heard from the people, we nevertheless still have good hope in the will of the Emperor, yet the matter, as you know, is in God's hands; therefore you must pray, as I know you are doing.

There is no other Prince here but ours. It is said that Duke George will be here in three days, and will bring Cochläus with him, whose name needs to be altered only a letter or two to correspond to the kind of bird you wrote us about. And Eck, whose name resembles the cry of the jackdaw, has put together a great pile of theses.

In truth, there are going to be more jackdaws here than I can count. The Chancellor of the Hessians, Feige, arrived yesterday, and says his Prince is on the way. Schnepf, a very good man, and very friendly disposed toward you, came with him; so that we have some hope that his Prince will be kept in the right way, although he does not conceal the fact that the danger is great. He tells what a battle he had to endure with Philip [of Hesse] concerning the Lord's Supper. He says the latter is being continuously flooded with letters from the Swiss, and the Mayor Sturm stirs him up almost every month. This worries me very much. Perhaps it would do good if you would write him to establish the heart of Philip in the true doctrine. He often seems to take offense on slight occasion.

I have made the Introduction of our Apology a little more rhetorical than I wrote it at Coburg. In a short time, I shall either bring it myself, or if the Prince will not permit this, I will send it.

I have almost forgotten to number your Cajetan among the jackdaws, for it is said the Emperor will bring this fellow. In Nuremberg I heard it was Campeggius, but here they say it is Cajetan. I wish it would be Campeggius. He is an experienced man in civil affairs. The other is a rough and uncouth man with whom you can do nothing. Farewell, and write again. Wednesday after Philip and James, 1530.

PHILIPPUS.

Melanchthon has made some changes in the Apology which he does not write about, but concerning which he feels that he must explain to Luther personally:—

MELANCHTHON TO VEIT DIETRICH.

May 4th.

I will shortly run over to you, that I may bring to the Doctor [Luther] the Apology which is to be offered to the Emperor, that he [Luther] may examine it.

Melanchthon knew of the presentations of Eck, but it is doubtful whether he appreciated the seriousness of the change in the situation at the imperial court, until after the following Sunday. The Elector himself was doubtless hoping that the sending of his personal Confession, showing the true Lutheran teaching, would make all things right. The letters to Luther were written on Thursday. Friday and Saturday passed, and then came the first Sunday in Augsburg.

May 8th, Sunday.

The Elector had preaching in the Church of St. Catharine. "He has preaching every day here, and large numbers attend." [71]   To offset the effect of the Protestant preaching, the surprised Bishop of Augsburg appointed several of his priests to the same work in the pulpit, but they were unsuccessful.[72] In anger[73] they complained to Charles, and the result was Charles' sharp order to stop preaching. It was his first official word. The Romanists now told the Protestants that the Emperor would crush them—"*Evangelicas omnes obtriturum.*" [74]

MELANCHTHON WORKING ON THE APOLOGY.

Three more days passed, and the first week at Augsburg was gone. The tidings as to Eck's theses, and the Emperor's more unfavorable attitude, had compelled our party to change the plan of their religious document, and to embrace in it their teaching on all essentials of doctrine. Despite Luther's avowal as to them, the Elector's favorite Schwabach Articles were fallen back upon, and Melanchthon's pen was most busy during this week in incorporating the new material, as we can easily imagine when we recall what it meant to transform the Electoral Apology into a Confession containing all the doctrines of faith. "I have embraced nearly all the Articles of Faith, for Eck has put forth the most diabolical slanders against us."

May 11th.

By the middle of the week, May 11th, the Apology, revised and developed into a Confession,[75] was again completed in the eyes of the little Electoral party at Augsburg. The Confes-

---

[71] Täglich in den Kirchen unverstört; dazu kommt sehr viel Volks.—*C. R.,* II, 53.

[72] *C. R.,* II, 86.

[73] *Scultet.,* 271.

[74] *Ib.,* 269.

[75] Sleidanus in his seventh book calls it the Saxon Confession, and Cyprian reports that this Saxon Apology was sent to Luther on May 11th without realizing what we now know as to the content of this Confession.

sion shows that Melanchthon, in selecting the material, had his eye upon Eck's Articles, and that Melanchthon was particularly anxious to show that the Elector was no heretic, and had no connection with the heretics of earlier ages. The Confession is not to be offered to the Emperor without first having been forwarded to Luther, who was the final authority.

But tidings of the Emperor's coming were expected any day. The business required haste. Melanchthon would write a personal letter to Luther with all explanations; and the Elector would send the document with instructions that Luther make his emendations in the margin of the document itself, so (doubtless) that the text would be final as it came from Luther's hand, and perhaps, if the case should be urgent, the paper might be handed in as revised, without the loss of time in re-writing and incorporating Luther's corrections.

The Elector also desired an Opinion from Luther on what proved to be the great test question of the Diet—the one by which, in our judgment, apart from the Confession, the Elector won the cause for Protestantism.

MELANCHTHON TO LUTHER AT COBURG

When the Elector Sent Luther the Augsburg Confession for Revision.

Original in the Hof and Staatsbibliothek in Munich.
Printed in Mel. Epp., I, 18; C. R., II, 45.

May 11th.

To *D.* MARTIN LUTHER, HIS VERY DEAR FATHER.

Greeting! Our Apology is being sent you, but in truth it is rather a Confession. For the Emperor has not time to listen to lengthy disputations.[76] Yet I have said that which I believed most useful or proper. On this ground I have succinctly given nearly all the Articles of Faith, since Eck has circulated the most Satanic slanders against us. Over against these, I wished to oppose a remedy. Please give judgment on the whole writing according to your spirit.

Duke George and Margrave Joachim have gone on to meet the Emperor. Now a Diet will be held *über unsern Hals.* Therefore pray God to bring the counsel of the heathen to nought. (Ps. 33:10.)

A question is referred to you, to which I greatly desire an answer from you. Beyond doubt the Emperor will prohibit the Zwinglian sermons. We judge from

---

[76] *I. e.,* such as Eck's Theses would introduce, and we have therefore placed our doctrine, compactly and quietly, into this Apology.

this, that under this pretence our sermons will also be forbidden, for Eisleben is already preaching publicly in a church. Now what is your opinion? Is not the preaching in a public place to be given up, in case the Emperor desires this: if he should wish this in order that the Zwinglian preaching might also be prevented without disturbance? I have answered: one must yield to the will of the Emperor, in whose city we now are guests. But our old man is difficult to soften. What therefore you think, I beg that you will write it *in German* on separate paper. Please answer concerning this matter.

We reckon that the Emperor cannot arrive within fourteen days. In such a great divergency of opinions it is not possible to judge what can be hoped for from the deliberations of the Emperor, but we await help from Christ. Eisleben greets.

PHILIPPUS.

The Elector's letter points clearly to the "Articles of Religion" drawn up at Wittenberg at the Elector's command as the basis of the Confession:—

THE ELECTOR JOHN AT AUGSBURG TO LUTHER.

Asking Luther's Opinion of the Confession Worked Over by Melanchthon.

Original in the Weimar Gesammt-Archiv.
Printed in Wittenb. ed., 1569, IX, Bl. 405 b; C. R., II, 45, 47.

May 11th.

JOHN SC.

First of all our Greeting, Honorable, Learned and Devout [Friend]! After you and our other learned men at Wittenberg had, at our gracious thought and desire, made a draught of the Articles of Religion concerning which there is now strife, it is our wish to let you know that Melanchthon has further revised the same, and drawn them up into a Form, which we are sending you herewith.

And it is our gracious desire that you would feel free to further consider and revise the same Articles; and, where you deem it wise and well to take away or to add anything, please do so in the margin. Send back the same carefully secured and sealed, without delay, that we may be ready and prepared for the arrival of his imperial Majesty, whom we expect in a short time.

We also desire you to know that our representatives at the imperial court at Innsbrück have written that it is the plan to deal with us on the arrival of his imperial Majesty, that we should not permit preaching in the churches, as we have begun it. This you will infer from the enclosed statement. And although I have drawn up an Opinion on this subject, yet I wish your further opinion, that we may do right in the sight of God and our conscience. In this you will do our gracious pleasure. . . . Wednesday after Jubilate, A. D., 1530.

To Dr. Martin.

As to the Protestant preaching, Melanchthon was eager from first to last, that is from May 11th to June 20th, that it cease. He was eager to please the Emperor and Rome, and he did not realize that on this point, viz., of the Protestants' right to clear public testimony of one's faith according to one's conscience, the whole battle for Protestant liberty at Augsburg would be fought. Neither did he see that compromise on this small point meant the extinction of Protestantism. The means he used to oppose the Elector's decision were perhaps characteristic. There is a marked contrast between his letter and that of the Elector in alluding to the issue. Melanchthon puts his own wish into Luther's heart, and then asks Luther to write back *in German,* and on *a separate paper,* so that he can show Luther's words to "the old man who is difficult to soften." The Elector states that he has formed his Opinion, and does not reveal it; but says, "I wish your Opinion, that we may do right in the sight of God and our conscience."

WHAT CONFESSION DID LUTHER SEE ON MAY 11TH?

What Luther received with the letters of the 11th of May was the Elector's Confession. It contained a Preface in praise and defence of the Elector, the Articles of Faith, recently introduced on account of Eck's attack, and the Articles on Abuses. Its most striking fact is that the whole document centres in and revolves about John of Saxony, somewhat after the substance and form of Luther's Opinion of the preceding year at Rotach, as to "what should be said to the Emperor." The Elector's name is found in the first line of the Preface, and he and what he has done are mentioned in almost every paragraph of the Preface. The Articles of Faith are introduced as follows: "Now we will speak of the doctrine, and first of all recount all the most important Articles of Faith, that his Majesty may perceive that the Elector of Saxony has not permitted anything unchristian to be preached in his dominion, but has diligently held to the common pure Christian faith."

The Second Part on Abuses reads as follows:—

"Since Electoral Saxony has not varied from the Scripture or from the common Christian Churches in any Article of Faith, but has simply abolished certain abuses." . . . This Apology-Confession was by no means a Romanizing document—unless the completed Augsburg Confession of June 25th is to be regarded as such—though it was as irenic and as particularistic as possible. It was the final Confession "im Werden," more and more unfolding its own inner strength, and more and more transforming itself from an Electoral Apology to an Evangelical Confession.

Luther was a born Confessor, and, so far as we can see, his reply to the Elector expresses his exact feelings." *As the Elector's* Confession, he was very much pleased with it— Melanchthon had expressed the Electoral situation—; but for his own Confession—as the Confession of a Minister of the Gospel or of the Churches—it was treading too softly.

We base our judgment, as to what Luther saw, on the document delivered to the Nurembergers, two weeks later; for while changes were going on in this Apology-Confession between the 11th and the 25th, they could not have been of a more or less Romanizing or particularizing character between those two dates, nor were they other than in the line of a more normal unfolding.

As to the difference between the Apology-Confession sent to Luther on May 11th, known to us as of May 25th, and the final form of June 25th, we know that Articles XX, on Faith and Good Works, and XXI, on the Worship of the Saints, were then yet missing; that Articles XXVII and XXVIII had not assumed their final form; that nothing is positively ascertained as to the nature of the detailed changes Melanchthon was making in the text; that sometime after the opening

---

" *Cp.* Kolde in *Herzog-Hauck:* " Despite the ironical play on Melanchthon's well-known efforts never to give offense, . . . Luther desired in this remark to express his complete agreement."

of the Diet on the 15th of June, Melanchthon had cast the Confession aside as probably never to be used, until he was compelled to take it up again the following week, and that then his private judgment was no longer consulted as to what should be finally altered or added.

As to Melanchthon's part in the work, we may say that his judgment was bad, and his skill great. He was a wretched designer and an exquisite modeler. As Kolde[78] says: "Nothing un-Lutheran, much less Melanchthonian, entered the Confession—as has been supposed—through the various changes undertaken by Melanchthon, which would not have been agreeable to Luther if he had been able to observe them in detail, most of all, because he was never sympathetically disposed toward such changes, and they assuredly greatly concealed the antithesis,[79] and there is not a little which he would have expressed more sharply." As for the result, we may be thankful that Melanchthon rounded out into objective principle, and moulded into classic form the aspirated edges of Luther's teaching, and Brück braced up the inner weakness of Melanchthon's principles; while, later on, the Apology, the Schmalkald Articles and the Formula of Concord completed such teaching as was not thoroughly wrought out at Augsburg.

May 12th.

THE KNIGHT MILITANT OF THE REFORMATION ARRIVES.

The post had scarcely left Augsburg with the two letters and the Confession for Luther, before Philip of Hesse, the Knight Militant of the Reformation, who was not expected at this Diet, since he had no heart[80] for the Emperor's plan, and since also he had failed to unite Luther and Zwingli at

---

[78] *Alt. Red.*, p. 75.

[79] "*Den Gegensatz.*"

[80] "Der weitblickende Landgraf von Hessen blieb auch jetzt argwöhnisch und schwankte."—*Kolde.*

Marburg, came marching into the gates of Augsburg with an escort of one hundred and ninety horsemen.[81]

May 13th, Friday.

Restive Philip could not remain many hours in the imperial city before involving himself in some sensation. And sure enough, the next day he opened the gates of the Cathedral,[82] and his theologian Schnepf preached the Protestant doctrine there. Later in the season, Philip had preaching every day in the Church of St. Ulrich.

On the same day also Duke Frederick of Saxony, Duke George's prince, came with Prince Joachim of Anhalt and many horsemen, while the Elector Joachim of Brandenburg, Duke George of Saxony and Duke William of Bavaria went on towards the Emperor to Innsbrück.[83]

May 15th.

LUTHER TRIES TO RESPOND TO AND CONSOLE THE ELECTOR.

Meantime the two letters, and the Confession, had reached Luther, and his reply was prompt—too prompt and brief no doubt to please the small party at Augsburg. He had no emendations to offer. He was pleased; but it was not after his style to confess so softly.

However, he did not know that the crisis now closely impending would rub out some of the softness, and that the Lord Himself would bring about some emendations, before the Confession was put forth.

LUTHER'S REPLY TO THE ELECTOR, CONCERNING THE CONFESSION.

Original in the Weimar Gesammt-Archiv.
Printed in Wittenb. ed. 1569, XI, Bl. 406; Er. LIV, 145.

May 15th.

Grace and Peace in Christ our Lord! . . . I have read over the Apology of M. Philip. It pleases me right well, and I do not know what to improve or

---

[81] *Salig,* II, 162, says, " Mit 120 cuirassiers."
[82] " In the chapter of St. Moritz."——*Augsb. Ev. Kirchen-chronica.*
[83] *Salig,* II, 162.

change in it; neither would it be proper, for I cannot tread so gently and quietly. Christ our Lord help that it bear much and great fruit, as we hope and pray. Amen. On Sunday Cantate, in the year 1530. . . .

E. K. F. G.,

Obediently,

MARTINUS LUTHER.

The perilous test question of the Diet, whether the Protestants should preach their doctrine in the city of Augsburg during the Emperor's presence, had been referred to Luther for advice, and now on this very day (May 15th), when Luther is writing his reply, and the Elector and Melanchthon are eagerly awaiting it, Philip of Hesse rushes them all to the verge of ruin by commanding Cellarius, a *Zwinglian,* of Augsburg, to preach *in the Cathedral!*

The wise Elector had seized on this liberty of preaching as the one serious initial problem. Any utterance from the other side, concerning it, would be the first indication of the imperial mind as to how it intended to deal with the Evangelical cause, and as to whether the promises of fairness to all parties, made in the Call, would really be redeemed. The dispatches from the Emperor's Court were full of rumors to the effect that the Emperor had shifted his position. Chancellor Brück and the Elector, recognizing the test character of this question, and the unfavorableness of a prohibitive omen, took a more stubborn stand against yielding the cause in advance than did Melanchthon or Luther under the influence of Melanchthon's suggestion. Luther, on the hypothesis of the Emperor's guilelessness, replied on the 15th that he would like to have his Majesty dissuaded from this prohibition and induced to send some one to hear what is really being preached; but if that prove of no avail, one must allow force to take the place of right, for Augsburg is an imperial city.

May 20th.

Luther's reply of May 15th to the Elector had been very brief; and, on reflection, he may have felt that in this trying hour he had not given the Elector that hearty sympathy and support which "the old man" truly deserved.   At all events, five days later, Luther again wrote the Elector, and this time a longer and hearty letter of encouragement.

Chyträus puts the occasion of this letter as follows: Since his Majesty was delaying his coming, and the Elector of Saxony was deeply agitated not only because of his vexation at the lengthy delay, but also because of the threatening and the terrifying attitude of the enemies, who assured themselves of certain victory when his Majesty arrived, Luther wrote the Elector a comforting and lovely letter:—

LUTHER TO THE ELECTOR.

MS. in Wolfenbüttel.
Flacius Deutscher Br., Altenburg, V, 23; Erl., LIV, 146.

May 20th.

It is indeed a glorious and great honor that God has chosen His gracious Prince, who has devoted everything to God's service, and that His holy Word is not only not abused, but supported and upheld.   It is also immaterial that some of us feel depressed about the situation; only let your Grace continue in the furtherance and protection of the work in maintaining the Word.

May your princely Highness graciously receive my letter.   God knows that I speak the truth and do not dissemble; for it pains me that Satan could cause concern and sorrow in your gracious heart.   I know him well, and realize how he tries to have me play with him.

Hence it is the duty of us all to loyally stand by his princely Highness with prayer, comfort, love, which we always can; for when your Grace is happy we live, but when you are sorrowful we are sick.

But may our Lord and Saviour Jesus Christ, Whom the Father of all grace has so freely revealed and offered for us, send your Grace, above all my words, His Holy Spirit, the true eternal Comforter, and uphold, strengthen and preserve your Grace against all the poisonous fiery darts of a sour, heavy, fearful spirit. Amen, beloved God, Amen.   Given May 20th, 1530.

E. K. F. G.,
Obediently,
MARTIN LUTHER.

May 12th.

THE EMPEROR SETS UP COURT AT INNSBRÜCK.

And now about a fortnight after the Elector reached Augsburg, the Emperor, with Ferdinand and the queens of Hungary and Bohemia; the embassadors of France, England and Portugal; with Campeggius, the Papal Legate, and other cardinals; the Spanish nobles and many princes from Italy and Germany, entered Innsbrück, and settled down to study and master the religious situation in Germany.

Italian gold was freely scattered to gain the German favor. The court was split into a Roman and a Protestant party. The Romanists urged his Majesty to stand by the edict of Worms and condemn the Evangelicals without a hearing.[84] Campeggius advised even the inquisition, confiscation of property, and punishment with fire and sword.[85]

The Evangelical cause had a defender in the person of the imperial chancellor, Mercurinus Gattinara. Although he was ill, he had managed to follow the court of the Emperor to Innsbrück in order to neutralize the influence of Campeggius. "There is nothing I desire so much," he is said to have declared, "as to see the Elector of Saxony and his allies persevere courageously in the profession of the Gospel, and call for a free religious Council. If they allow themselves to be checked by promises or threats, I hesitate myself and I doubt of the means of salvation." [86]

GEORGE AND JOACHIM AVOID AUGSBURG, AND RIDE ON TO INNSBRÜCK.

The Elector John, the chief of the princes, and the first of them to arrive at Augsburg, had courageously begun preaching; and when the Roman princes, Duke George of Saxony, Duke William of Bavaria and the Elector Joachim, heard that John was preaching the Evangelical faith at Augsburg, filled with consternation, they passed Augsburg by, as we

[84] *C. R.,* II, 57.

[85] Instructio data Caesari dal Reverendissimo Campeggio.—*Ranke,* III, 288.

[86] *Seck.,* II, 57.

have seen, and proceeded direct to the court of Charles, reporting that the Elector John had ulterior designs, and offering the Emperor a guard of six thousand horse.[87]

The false news thus brought to Innsbrück led to repeated conferences there as to what to do. Melanchthon, alluding to these, declared that there was a Diet now being held at Innsbrück on the best way of getting the heads of the Evangelicals. Mercurinus finally succeeded in persuading Charles to remain neutral.

THE ELECTOR INVITED TO INNSBRÜCK.

Yet Charles was determined to avoid the free religious discussion he had promised for Augsburg. If the matter could be quashed in advance, it might not be necessary for him to enter Augsburg at all, and he could proceed direct to Cologne and have Ferdinand crowned. What should he do? His first recourse was a pressing invitation to the Elector John to come from Augsburg to Innsbrück, where he would receive the Emperor's particular favor, and where they might personally confer together concerning the religious situation. It was a shrewd move to draw the Elector away from his base, and to cut off the legal, moral, political and personal strength that base assured him.

But Brück and the Elector instinctively realized that to yield in this or any point would be fatal; and sent back word that it was not proper to discuss the business of the Diet in any other place than that which the Emperor himself had appointed, and therefore begged that his Majesty would hasten his arrival at the city where the Diet should, *ere this,* have been convened. Doltzig presented the following grounds why John could not come: 1. Because the Elector's departure would only awaken suspicion in those remaining. 2. Because the harmony and mutual confidence of the other estates might

---

[87] *Seck.,* II, 156. Salig, following *Augsb. Ev. Kirchen-Chron.,* says "filled the Emperor with all kinds of suspicion because of the early arrival of the Elector."

thereby be disturbed. 3. Because in affairs of the realm no valid action could be taken outside of the Diet.[88] Doltzig's presentation was received graciously by the Emperor.

It was a bold but rightful declaration of independence from the Emperor's shifting program of manipulation, by asserting dependence on the Emperor's original plan and promise, and by insisting on the stable law of the realm. The Elector's position was sound. The situation was now in bloom, all Augsburg was full of newly-arrived soldiers, and the flower of the German nation, princes, nobility and warriors, were to be seen together here in this one city.[89]

May 19th-22nd.

A NEW REVISION OF THE CONFESSION FOR LUTHER.

It is possible that the Confession, returned by Luther on the 15th with his reply, arrived in Augsburg on the 19th. On the 20th he wrote his second and longer letter to the Elector; and by the 22nd Melanchthon was ready to send Luther the Confession a second time with the changes that had been made in the last ten days, together with various items of startling news from the imperial Court at Innsbrück, whence the Emperor was not disposed to come to Augsburg.

The changes in the Confession that were made between the 10th and the 22nd, though continuous, were not material as to doctrine. It was the Elector's personal, and not the confessional situation that now was uppermost. At all events, we may be sure that Melanchthon in his letter of the 22nd mentioned all the *most important changes* in the Confession. It is maintained by some that Luther never received this letter, and the revised Form of Confession. This point will be discussed a little later.

---

[88] *Salig,* II, 162.

[89] *Ib.*

Manuscript in MS. Manlianum, p. 15.
Printed in Melanchthon's epp. lib., I, ep. 2; ed. Lond., I, ep. 2; Cölestin, I, p. 44
(incomplete); C. R., II, p. 59; Erl. Br.-W., VII, p. 342; German, Chyträus, Hist., p. 62 (in
part); and Wilhelm a Vallo, II, b. p. 56.

May 22nd.

1. Hail! We had already hired a messenger, who was to start for your place and thence for Wittenberg, for Jonas learned of the death of his son from the letters of Viola. But while writing I received your letters through *D.* Apel's messengers. Jonas is content since he learned that his wife is well.

2. The Emperor is not yet here, and, it appears to me, will scarce arrive ere Pentecost. He has drawn neither the Dukes of Baiern nor the Duke of Saxony into consultation about the religious affairs, for he wants to remain impartial. It is reported that there are two opinions in the Emperor's council: one, that he should not hear the Lutherans, but have them speedily condemned in a public decree; the other, that he should hear them regularly and remove the abuses of the Church. This latter is said to be the opinion of the imperial chancellor Mercurinus, an exemplary and very reasonable man, who is reported as saying that, in his weakness, he followed the Emperor, inasmuch as he thought that the religious matters would end well, and consequently he would not be participating in compulsory measures. We have heard nothing here which we think more worthy to communicate. And I myself have a special admiration for this utterance and judgment of this very sensible man. May Christ be with us and support us, and so rule all counsels that they may serve for peace and the general welfare. Mercurinus has also said this: "The Diet of Worms proved that nothing substantial can be accomplished with compulsory measures." For he was at Worms in the Emperor's retinue and council.

All of us, the Elector too, are much concerned about your health; and have therefore prayed God that He preserve you for the sake of His Word. We also request that you take good care of your health. Doctor Caspar sends you, through the Elector's messenger, different medicines which strengthen head and heart. For he loves you much.

3. In the Apology, we daily change many things. The article on Vows, as it was more meagre than it should be, I have removed, and supplied its place with a complete discussion. I am now treating of the Power of the Keys. I wish you had examined the Articles of Faith; if you shall have found in them nothing wanting, we will treat the remaining ones quite extensively. For we must change them from time to time, and adapt them to the occasion.

4. The Landgrave of Hesse now publicly says that he will subscribe our address, and it seems that he could easily be brought to our side; but to do so, it is necessary for you to write to him. Hence I most earnestly request you to write to the Landgrave and admonish him not to burden his conscience by defending a false doctrine. I wish you would not write again to the younger prince; for he now hates no one more than you, whom he formerly appeared to love more than the apple of his eye. But his nature is very changeable, and it does not so much come from his tender age as much more, as I think, from nature.

Schnepf is a very good, sensible man. I wish you, to honor him, would write him at a convenient opportunity. As far as the Friesians are concerned, the elector has instructed Pomeranus to find a competent man, who understands the Saxon language, and send him to them. Upon this opinion you can answer.

I send you a painting of the fortress of the city of Wien. Through Apel's messengers we will write more. In the meantime, send our letter to your excellent wife with the messenger, for he can bring back the answer.

Keep well, and pray to Christ, our Lord, for us. Given on the Sunday, *Vocem Jucunditatis.*

May 22nd.

A DISCUSSION OF MELANCHTHON'S LETTER OF THIS DATE.

This was the third Sunday for the Electoral party at Augsburg. Just one week ago Luther had written returning the Apology-Confession, with a note that he was pleased. It had reached Augsburg perhaps on Friday. Meantime the occasion for haste in completing the document had disappeared, since news had come that the Emperor would probably not arrive before Pentecost, and that meanwhile Mercurinus was championing the Protestant cause.

Melanchthon writes this news to Luther to-day, closing with the information that the Landgrave of Hesse probably could be brought to sign the Confession if Luther would write him. To draw Philip away from the Reformed and bring him to adhere to the Confession, was one of the main points in Melanchthon's policy at the Diet.

In the midst of this news, at the least conspicuous place, as the third out of four points touched on by the letter, Melanchthon reports on the Confession, which evidently has receded from its all-absorbing importance of ten days before, when the Emperor was expected to arrive at any day.

Melanchthon tells Luther that in the "Apology," that is, in the Torgau Articles,[90] treating of Abuses, "we are making changes every day. I have taken out the Article on Vows,

---

[90] The Torgau Articles are found in the Beilagen to Brück's *Gesch. d. Religions-Randlungen in 1530*, in Archives at Weimar, fol. 311-323b, where Förstemann discovered them and printed them in his *Urkunden Buch*, I, 68 sqq.

27

because it was too meagre, and in its place I have inserted a more detailed explanation. I am now composing the Article on 'The Power of the Keys.' " So much Melanchthon reports as to the work he had done on the Torgau Articles since he had sent them to Luther ten days ago. He then speaks of the Schwabach Articles' foundation, as follows: "I wish you had examined [or, I wish you would examine] the Articles of Faith. If you find that there is nothing wanting in them, we will take the remaining ones in hand as best we may. For it is ever necessary to change something in them and adapt one's self to the occasion."

What Melanchthon meant to say here is a problem. His words are, "Vellem percurrisses articulos fidei, in quibus si nihil putaveris esse vitii, relinqua utcunque tractabimus." He opens with an unfulfilled wish ("vellem"), and yet closes with a definite future intention ("tractabimus"), apparently based on the fulfilment of the wish. The meaning would be clear if Knaake's hypothesis that Luther had not yet returned the document sent on the 11th, were true; or it would be clear on Kolde's suggestion that M. had not yet looked at the document, returned by Luther and coming perhaps just while M. was writing. Or, if Luther had sent back the Apologia, and not the Articles of Faith; or if M. *were sending Luther the Confession a second time,*[91] M.'s words would be clear. They would also be clear if M. were referring to the original Schwabach Articles, of which Luther would have a copy in his possession, and Melanchthon was here saying he would add such points of doctrine as they lacked, to render them complete for Augsburg..

Whatever interpretation may be placed upon this letter, and whether Luther ever received it or not, does not materially affect the relation of Luther to the Augsburg Confession.

What Luther had in hand on the 15th was the Apology-Confession discovered at Nuremberg by Kolde, and the

---

[91] Krauth, *Chronicle of Augsburg Confession,* 26-31. Possibly Melanchthon was elliptical. [If it be not asking too much,] I wish you would examine the Articles of Faith [whether or not you think there is something defective in them ; and] if you should think there is nothing wanting in them, [then] we will elaborate the remaining ones in like manner [as we have already treated the Articles on Abuses].

changes referred to by Melanchthon, as having been made up to the 22nd and after the 11th, referred chiefly to several articles in the Abuses; whereas the far greater change, which converted the Saxon document into our common and abiding testimony of historical Christianity to the content of Christ's Gospel, was not brought about till the middle of June. The one striking fact in this letter of the 22nd is that Melanchthon, as in his and the Elector's letters of the 11th, still defers absolutely to Luther as to the substance of the doctrine to be embodied; and that it was open and understood between him and Luther that he was to elaborate and adapt the mode of stating the doctrine to the situation under which the Confession would be made.

We see no just reason for the theory that this letter failed to be sent to Luther. It was to go by a special express through to Wittenberg, carrying letters to Luther's wife and others, to which allusion was made in this, and perhaps in the other letters. We know that Luther received the painting of Vienna which probably accompanied the letter, or of whose coming this letter at least advises Luther. And the line of connection which "The Conservative Reformation" has established has not been successfully broken. In it Krauth says:—

" But the fact is that Luther did receive Melanchthon's letter of the 22nd. The letter was not lost, but appears in all the editions of Melanchthon's letters, entire,[92] and in the earliest histories of the Augsburg Confession, without a hint, from the beginning up to Rückert's time, that it had not been received. When we turn to Luther's letters, complaining of the silence of his friends, we find no evidence that Melanchthon's letter had not been received. They create, on the contrary, the strongest presumption that it had been received. As it was sent at once (Melanchthon says that he had hired a letter-carrier before he began the letter), it would reach Luther about May 25th.

" Luther's letter of June 1st to Jacob Probst, in Bremen,[93] shows that he had intelligence of the most recent date from Augsburg, that he was sharing in the cares and responsibilities of what was then passing: ' Here, also, I am occupied with business for God, and the burden of the whole empire rests upon us.' He then uses, in part, the very language of Melanchthon's letter of May 22nd, as to

---

[92] Original Latin in *C. R.*, II, No. 698 ; German in Walch, XVI, No. 927.
[93] De Wette, *Briefe*, No. 1217 ; *Buddeus*, Suppl., No. 123.

the time when the Emperor would be at Augsburg.[94]   He quotes from that letter Melanchthon's very words in regard to Mercurinus :—[95]

'He would have nothing to do with violent councils—that it appeared at Worms what violent councils would do.   He desired the affairs of the Church to be peacefully arranged.'   He closes his account of things at Augsburg by saying : 'You have an account of matters now as they *are to-day* at Augsburg' (*hodie habet*).

"Luther did receive Melanchthon's letter of the 22nd, and on June 1st quotes largely from it." [96]

"Luther's letter of *June 20th*, to Justus Jonas,[97] gives direct evidence how long the interruption of correspondence continued : 'Your letters have come at last, my Jonas, after we were well fretted for *three whole weeks* with your silence.'   The period, therefore, did not embrace May 22nd, but only the first three weeks in June.   There is no reason whatever, therefore, for doubting that Luther received Melanchthon's letter, and the Articles of Faith of May 22nd." [98]

May 24th.

BRÜCK BUSY ON THE CONFESSION.

Meantime there was another hand busy on the Augsburg Confession, as important to the final issue as that of Melanchthon himself.   It was the hand of Chancellor Brück.   On May 24th, the Nuremberg delegates wrote home: "The Saxon Counsel has returned from Dr. Luther; but Dr. Brück, the chancellor, has to recast it from beginning to end." [99]

---

[94] *Mel.:* Vix ante Pentecosten ; *Luth.:* Forte ad Pentecosten.

[95] *Mel.:* Nolle se violentis consiliis interesse ; *Luth.:* Se nolle interesse violentis consiliis.   *Mel.:* Wormatiae apparuisse, quam nihil proficiant violenta consilia ; *Luth.:* Wormatiae vidisset, quid efficerent violenta consilia.   *Mel.:* Vir summus Mercurinus ; *Luth.:* Summus Mercurinus.   *Mel.:* Res ecclesiasticae rite constituerentur ; *Luth.:* Ecclesiae res cum pace constitui.

[96] *Con. Ref.,* p. 230.

[97] *De Wette,* No. 1232 ; *Buddeus,* No. 127.

[98] *Con. Ref.,* p. 232.

[99] *C. R.,* II, 62.—"Hinten und vorne daran zu formen habe."   Perhaps this refers to the Preface and the Conclusion : it may include the phraseology and the line of argument of the Articles.   For we know that Brück had a close hold on the substance of the Reformation doctrine, and was on the watch lest Melanchthon should yield in the substance ; and was determined that there should be a square presentation, such as would afford a solid foothold for argument, of the Evangelical doctrine, and for the preservation of civil rights. *Cp.* also the report of the Nurembergers later in the Summer :   "The Elector in this business has no one more sensible than the one and only Dr. Brück."

THE OLD MARGRAVE GEORGE OF BRANDENBURG ARRIVES.

On this day, May 24th, the Protestant forces were augmented by the arrival of the Margrave, who was an important factor in the change to come over the Apology-Confession, since he came expecting to fulfil his original intention[100] of associating himself before the Emperor with the Elector and the city of Nuremberg.

May 24th.

THE EMPEROR SENDS AN EMBASSY TO AUGSBURG.

While the Apology-Confession was proceeding toward completion, and the Elector was seeking the advice of the theologians as to the preaching, Charles made one more attempt to settle things from Innsbrück. On May 24th, two of his important officials, friendly to the Elector, the Counts of Nassau and of Neuenar, appeared before the Elector, with a letter[101] of secret instructions in their pocket.

They stated that the Emperor was very sad at the thought that religious controversies should have broken the good understanding that had existed so long between the houses of Saxony and Austria; that he was surprised to see the Elector rising in opposition to the Worms edict, which had been passed unanimously by all the imperial estates; and that his newly-made alliance would tend to disrupt the German nation and cause bloodshed. Last of all, the embassadors insisted that the Elector bring the preaching to an immediate end, else, in their judgment, there would be serious consequences.

---

[100] *Först.,* I, 119 sqq.

[101] A copy in the archives at Weimar. Printed in *Först.,* I, 220; *Cölest.,* I, 50.

Imperial Instruction, with which the Counts of Nassau and Neuenar
were Sent to Augsburg to the Elector John, to Pray that Either
He or His Son, the Prince, Should Journey to the Emperor, or
that at Least the Protestant Preaching Should be Intermitted
Until the Arrival of His Majesty.

A copy in the Archives at Weimar.
Printed in Förstemann, Urk., I, 220; Cölestin, I, 50.

May 24th.

Carl, by the Grace of God, Roman Emperor, at all times promoter of the
Empire.

First of all, they are to convey to him our kingly grace and all good, and
then to narrate how we have perceived his obedient Christian and faithful tender.

He is to be reminded that he shall remember the close relations between
the houses of Austria and Saxony ; and he knows how the troublesome affairs of
our holy Christian faith originated, out of which so much dissension has grown.
He also knows that those who have separated themselves in this matter from us
and the other five electors of our holy Empire, have ignored and despised the
edict ; and that we and all six electors and other princes and estates of the holy
Empire did unanimously resolve on what is for the best, which, together with the
error and dissension touched on above (despite the highest disgrace I as a Roman
emperor have thereby suffered), has brought the holy Empire and almost all
Christendom to such a condition that it can not again be easily restored.

And, further, that he has made and still maintains a special understanding
and compact with those who have been disobedient and obstinate toward us in
this matter, against us and our edict ; and that he as the head of the opposition
is still supporting it.

So far as the shedding of blood is concerned in the past, as also in the future,
he knows that we will spare no diligence that it shall not occur.

THE SECOND IMPERIAL COMMAND TO SILENCE THE GOSPEL.

The Elector had already declined to put a stop to his
preachers' sermons; but this embassy more persistently than
ever urged that the preaching cease. The Elector was taken
by surprise, and exclaimed: "If the Emperor forbids the
preaching of the Gospel, I shall immediately return home." [102]

Though the full significance of his position may not have
been clear to him at this time, the whole Confessional question
at Augsburg was wrapped up in his right and duty as to this
one thing.

He was standing here on the edict of 1526, as over against

[102] *C. R.,* II, 88.

that of 1529. In 1521 Luther, at Worms, was asked to recant, while in 1530 the Elector at Augsburg was asked to refrain from giving testimony to that which he believed. The guise of propriety as to a disputed question was assumed by the Roman demand made through the Emperor, but without any guarantee that the right, once lost, would be restored by a fair investigation. If confession in the pulpit could be shut off ahead of trial, then confession in the Diet could similarly be suppressed without trial. The importance of the principle of preaching became more and more clear as the days passed. It was really the basal question of the hour. Put in general terms it amounted to this: Are the German nation and the Lutheran Faith standing to-day on the Diet of Spires or on the Diet of Worms?

The Elector's firmness was admirable, and all the more so because his theologians—even Luther—had yielded.[103]

We do not believe that this point has been given consideration, as a key, in the attempted unraveling of the mystery of the silence between Augsburg and Luther for the coming month, and of the independent diplomacy of Melanchthon during part of the same period. Is it not possible that some of Melanchthon's agony was due to the Elector's loss of confidence in him as a counsellor? And is it not possible that the disappointing advice of Melanchthon and Luther, in the present emergency, had caused "the old man" to confide more fully in the common-sense wisdom and faith of Brück and to seek less counsel from Luther—who in his isolation had not discerned the import of the Roman imperial pressure—, and from Melanchthon—who was willing to yield the greater part of the cause, to keep the peace?

Melanchthon, on May 22nd, does not write to Luther as an inner counsellor of the Elector; and it is to be noted that,

---

[103] Luther's reasoning expressed in his letter of May 15th, based on the fact that Augsburg was an imperial city, is more than counterbalanced by the fact that the city, the Diet and the Emperor himself were on *German soil.* Any weight that this latter fact might have on the day of the reading of the Confession, applied with equal force to the preaching; and the Elector, and Brück, realized it. Besides, preaching is testimony for God's Gospel, and Cæsar is not lord of God's Gospel.

excepting his letter of June 1st, we know of no other letter of the Elector to Luther during the rest of May and the whole of June. The Elector was disappointed in the yielding of his theologians: he was now keeping his own counsels. Melanchthon was frightened; and, having been approached by the German Catholic party before the Emperor arrived, and by the Imperial party on June 15th or 16th, was going his own dangerous way.

Melanchthon had appealed to Luther's favorite civil doctrine of obedience to authority; and Luther, still trusting the Emperor, and not knowing that the civil authority was warped on this point by Roman ecclesiasticism, nor realizing that the question of conscience in confessing the Gospel and of liberty in worship was at stake, had given the exact reply that Melanchthon desired,—on a separate sheet of paper, which could be shown the Elector.

While it is true that a month later, on June 19th, at the last moment, the act of preaching was temporarily suspended, and that this concession on the part of the Protestants made the peaceful reading of the Augsburg Confession to the Diet possible; yet by that time, the action of the Elector had rescued the question from compromise. The suspension was now a judicial one, pending a decision. It affected both parties equally, infringed on no liberty of conscience, and permanently yielded no rights of testimony. But his theologians had advised an unconditional surrender of this position at the start, and the Elector shook his head.

"Our old man is intractable," wrote Melanchthon to Luther. Brück and the Elector, the two laymen, were a unit against the theologians. They were determined not to compromise. Said Brück: "The Emperor's demand is but a suitable beginning to bring about the destruction of the Gospel.[104] If we give in now, they will crush us hereafter. Let us humbly beg his Majesty to permit the sermons to continue."

---

[104] " Ein fügsamer Anfang der Niederbringung des Evangelii."—*C. R.,* II, 76.

May 31st.

Seven days after the embassadors of Charles appeared the Elector sent in his written reply:—

"It is not true," he said, "that the edict of Worms was agreed to by all the electors. How could my brother and myself, by approving it, have placed ourselves in opposition to the everlasting Word of God? Moreover, succeeding Diets have declared this edict to be impossible of execution. As for my friendly understandings, their only aim is to protect me against acts of violence. Let my accusers lay before the eyes of his Majesty the alliances they have made. I am ready to disclose mine; and the Emperor shall decide between us.

"Last of all—in respect to the preaching—nothing is proclaimed in it but the glorious truth of God, and never was it so necessary to us. We cannot, therefore, do without it!"

This was the brave Elector's bold ultimatum; and it would work its share in bringing the Emperor speedily to Augsburg.

Six days later, his Majesty had not only received the Elector's answer, but had already started on his way to Augsburg.

May 29th.

DISUNITED LUTHERANS NOT PREPARED FOR THE DIET.

The Lutheran estates, since the Elector kept himself aloof, were at a loss and felt themselves to be without leadership. The Landgrave had no Confession, for he had been opposed to deciding the religious question at a Diet. As early as May 22nd, he had been making efforts to be allowed to participate in the Confession of the Elector, for Melanchthon then wrote: "Nunc Macedo agit ut orationi nostrum subscribat." [105] The Margrave had no Confession, for he had intended as early as March 24th to cast in his lot with the Elector. Nuremberg had an "Opinion," but the delegates were instructed to remain in close touch with the Saxons. Ansbach and Reutlingen doubtless also desired to unite with the Elector.

---

[105] *C. R.,* II, 60.

But, despite his danger in disobeying the instructions of the Emperor, "the old man" did not wish to be bound up with or be interfered with by the others. The Emperor was addressing him alone, was making him responsible, and was charging him with disloyal alliances. He would not give the Emperor cause for such charges, but would continue loyally on the line he had originally followed, and insisted on, in accepting the Call to the Diet. Luther was opposed to all alliances. The Elector therefore sent Nuremberg word through Brück, in a very Luther-like utterance, that, "His electoral Grace did not like many counsellors in such an affair, for the devil was fond of too much counsèl!"

Nevertheless Nuremberg requested at least a copy of his Apology-Confession, and received it very promptly. For the interview with the embassadors, Nassau and Neuenar, had convinced the Elector that the Emperor was hostile, and that the Protestants needed each other's strength. The arrival of the Margrave George without a Confession on that very day, and the position of the Margrave's Chancellor Vogler, with the agitation of Philip of Hesse, led, we believe, to an examination of the Confessions of the other Estates, and to a consideration of the opinions of the other theologians on the Augsburg Confession.[106] Nuremberg had such a "Rathschlag;"[107] and so had Reutlingen.[108] The old accounts of the reading and use of these Confessions by Cyprian and by Salig, and especially the statement made by Melanchthon himself, in his account of the origin and presentation of the Augsburg Confession, a few months before his death, in 1560, should, we believe, be taken as applicatory in summing up the general situation between May 24th and June 25th, with the details referring at times to the earlier and at times to the later date.

---

[106] *Salig*, II, 168.

[107] *Cp.* W. Möller, *Osiander*, Elberfeld, 1840, p. 128 sqq.

[108] Gayler, *Hist. Denkwürdigkeiten der Reichstadt Reutlingen*, 1840, p. 350 sqq.

COMPOSING AND REVISING THE CONFESSION.

The story of Melanchthon, which has been analyzed exhaustively by Dr. Krauth,* begins with the Emperor Charles, as follows:

"On his return to Germany, 1530, he called the Princes to Augsburg [these, the Elector and Princes and cities] that a Confession should there be presented. Of this a narrative ought to be given, inasmuch as it is necessary that posterity should know that our Confession was neither written of individual purpose, nor thrust upon the Emperor not demanding it [this Confession which was delivered to the Emperor in the Diet, 1530]. But either some Confession had to be presented, or it would have to be shown by dissembling, that the doctrine which had already been received, had been abandoned, and there were also some at that time who wished to avoid the perils of Confession. But others, *the Princes and Officials* (Gubernatores), *whose names follow the Confession* [the Elector and Princes and cities], believed that the Confession should be offered as evidence that they had not acted in levity, or impelled by any unlawful desire, but that for the glory of God and the salvation of their own souls, and the souls of many, they had embraced the purer doctrine. I brought together, therefore, in singleness of purpose, the principal points of the Confession, which is extant, embracing pretty nearly the sum of the doctrine of our Churches [this Confession, as God had ordained and given it, was drawn together by me]. I assumed nothing to myself, for in the presence of the Princes and Officials [the Elector, and Princes and Legates, who subscribed it] and of the preachers [with their Counselors and preachers who were there], it was discussed and determined upon [diligently pondered], in regular course, sentence by sentence [all the Articles]. The complete form of the Confession was subsequently sent to Luther, who wrote to the Princes that he had both read this Confession and approved it. That these things are so,

---

*v. A Chronicle of the Augsburg Confession, 1878, pp. 54-61, pp. 83-86. v. also First Lutheran Diet, 1877, pp. 238, 242. v. also Con. Ref. pp. 232, 233.

the Princes, and other honest and learned men yet living, will remember [gracious Princes and Counts, and other honorable men, who by God's grace are yet living, can testify].

Salig says: "We now come to the composition of the Augsburg Confession itself. That the Seventeen Articles composed by Luther form its basis has already been alluded to several times. But Melanchthon now was obliged to elaborate them further, and, as he possessed a beautiful, perspicuous style, to form the Confession out of them. He had already made the beginning at Coburg. And at Augsburg there was more time to work upon it. But he did nothing by himself in so important an affair, concerning as it did the Faith of the whole Lutheran Church. To give over to a single man so important a work showed that there was the greatest confidence in his suitability.

"Nevertheless the fact that this work was to pass through the experienced hands of many other people demanded the foresight and watchful care of all the Protestant estates. Melanchthon handed over his writing from article to article to the censorship of the estates, their counsellors and theologians (Der Leipzischen Theologen Historie der Augsp, contession oder des Sacraments Streits, p. 109) ; as then *D.* Erhard Schnepf, who himself was present at the deliberations, writes in his confession issued in 1655 (*ib.* f. 109) ; and as Melanchthon testifies in the preface of the first volume of his complete works, that he had done nothing at all by himself, but had received the opinions [Gutachten] of other theologians concerning all the articles." [109]

"The pious Elector John was particularly concerned for the Tenth Article, which treats of the Holy Communion, that the same might be composed and completed in the most accurate and faithful manner, since among all the disputed points of doctrine, it was the chief article that marked the difference of the Lutheran from the Swiss and Highland doctrine. When now the confession was completed, the Elector sent it with a letter of his own to Luther, etc."[110]

In weighing the testimony of Salig, it should be borne in mind that he lacked the knowledge gained by the method of critical research from the days of Weber down; but, on the other hand, that he cannot be accused of favoring the ultra-Lutheran position, since he was a pietist, whose natural judgment would be regarded as favorable to Melanchthon. Kolde's estimate of Salig as an authority is just.

Cyprian also rests on solid sources and a sound judgment. He says:

"After the Emperor had assured the evangelical estates in his Call that he would graciously hear their Opinion of Religion at Augsburg, all who did not wish simply to lean upon the Elector had their theologians draw up a short Outline of the Doctrine which was then in use in the churches of his territories, and brought it along to Augsburg. This was a very easy matter, since now for the

---

[109] *Salig,* II, 168.
[110] *Ib.*

past thirteen years everything had been pretty well cleared up and deliberated on through the various propositions, books and doctrinal documents; and since the Seventeen Articles which the Elector John and the Margrave George of Brandenburg had laid before the assembly of the Protestants, were in their hands (*Müller*, c. l., p. 302.) Of these outlines brought to Augsburg, Camerarius in his *Life of Philipp*, p. m., 124, says: 'There were very many descriptions set forth, some of them verbose. For those who were being associated in this cause had each ordered their own theologians to compose something in writing. These had to be read and known by Philipp.'

"In Augsburg, the Saxon and other theologians conferred as to their views on the Outline of Doctrine, and at last completed the confession of faith: with Melanchthon putting it on paper (*wobey Melanchthon die Feder führete*). The Seventeen Articles, shortly before delivered at Torgau, as is evident, and as the Elector himself testifies, were made the basis.

"Not only the theologians, but also the civil counsellors, considered the Confession, even to the smallest points, as the word 'truly' in the Tenth Article can give evidence. Of this Erhard Schnepf, the theologian of the Langrave of Hesse, who was of use in these transactions, gives the following information, in the beginning of his *Bekäntnis vom Abendmahl*, edited in the year 1555:

"'Now it is known to all who were present at that Augustana deliberation in the year 1530 in which the Confession was written, that before it was offered to the Roman Emperor Charles V., it was subjected to the censure of the theologians of the princes, and of those also who were the counsellors to our princes, and of the legates of the two cities, on account of which it was at that time determined to use only the adverb *truly*, although ambiguous as then discussed by many; since no one then of all those who were committed to the Augsburg Confession and who had been admitted to this meeting of deliberation was of the same view with the Zwinglians. For I was present and . . . this work was dangerous, very important, and for many reasons, especially so far as concerned the point of the power of the bishops, very delicate; for it went straight to the heart of those heads of benefices and the bishops who were almost all of them worldly princes, and were present in great splendor, and who could besides place a large army in the field against the Evangelicals, and who were weaponed by the doctrine of purgatory and the mass, of oral Confession, by the superstition of the people, by the indulgence, by the interdict, and by the Pope."—*Cyprian*, pp. 55-56.

Cyprian claims co-operation from the beginning:

"In one sense of the word it was a matter of good fortune that the Emperor had delayed, which delay was falsely ascribed to the honors shown to him in the Venetian, Tyrol and Bavarian regions. For the estates could consult confidentially with each other, and the theologians who discussed the articles anew and worked them over with all brotherly freedom, became more and more certain in the points of teaching out of God's Word, and could draw up their sentences carefully. Melanchthon made his daily changes with the advice of the others. Camerarius vita Philippi, pp. 123; Post diligentissimam consideralionem compssitum est scriptum etc.—*Cyprian*, p. 57. [*Vid.* also Mel.'s Pref. to *C. R.*]

Yet we are in doubt to-day as to how far the estates participated in the framing of the Saxon Confession prior to the 15th of June and the crisis at Corpus Christi. Melanchthon probably had gone through all the Confessional documents, and gained hints for his daily changes. Cyprian, largely quoting *ex diario* gives us the following succinct information:—

"Already on the 16th of May the Elector announced to his Mittverwandten at Augsburg that the Confession was then just completed, but not yet finally decided on; but had been sent to Dr. Luther for examination.

"On the 31st of May, the Confession was communicated, in Latin, but without Preface and Conclusion, to the delegates of the cities. For Melanchthon had composed it in the name of the Elector alone.

"On June 8th, the chancellor of the Margrave announced to the representatives of the cities:—

"'His preacher and his counsellors had gone over the Articles of Faith which the Saxons had composed, but they found just that lack which others had already remarked: that they were written in the name of the Elector alone—they must be composed in the names of all the princes and cities who were in unity on the Articles of Faith.'

"On June 14th, the representatives of the cities received the Saxon Outline of the Faith in German, in which Philip had already made a change, namely, where it had been stated in Latin that this or that was preached and held in the electorate of Saxony. In the German, he had omitted the electorate of Saxony and used a common word that might be taken to denote all the estates. (*Ex diario.*)

"According to this, through all these days, the work was given the best possible consideration. They labored in common counsel upon the Confession, and it was composed in the names of all the Evangelical estates."—*Cyprian*, p. 179.

However this may be, it is at least certain that during this week (June 23rd), two days before the delivery, all the estates were called in and all doctrinal matters were decided on conjointly. Melanchthon, with the discredit of his private negotiations upon him, stood more in the background. Frightened by Valdés, he softened expressions wherever he could, and unsuccessfully attempted to retain the jurisdiction of the Roman bishops; but he had the satisfaction of seeing the Tenth Article retained in its strength and the Swiss thrown out (Kolde). Neither he nor any of the theologians —except Jonas—were present at the delivery of the Confession, nor were they allowed to sign it. The matter was in the firmer hands of the Princes and their counsellors, who were unwilling to give up the solid public rights on which they stood from previous Diets, and particularly from the imperial Call; and who insisted that the Confession must be delivered to the Emperor in the Latin and in the German language.

After the delivery of the Confession, which Melanchthon regarded as a temporary widening of the breach, he, instead of standing on the positions taken, insisted on going back to his old hope of compromise and in bringing forward the question, "How much was to be yielded to the Romanists." [110a] In the Committees of Compromise that were appointed after the Confutation came in, he became more and more dictatorial, and all feared to withstand him. The Nurembergers reported[111] that "The other Saxon theologians dare not speak openly against Philip, for he has gone so far recently as to say against the Lüneburg chancellor: 'He who dares assert that the recent concessions made [to the Romanists] are not Christian, lies like a villain.'"

They reported that the pious Vogler was much maligned, after he left Augsburg, for having been unwilling to compromise, and continue: "The Elector in this business has no one more sensible than the one and only Dr. Brück; but they have brought him to the point where he now also grows anxious in business, since there is not a soul to give him any support."

[110a] To be fully just to Melanchthon, we point out that, for this, Luther's " Admonition " and other declarations at the start might be looked upon as affording some precedent.

[111] *Salig*, II, 332.

But we have greatly anticipated the course of events, and must return to the end of May and the first day of June.

May 31st.

THE OLDEST REDACTION.

The Nuremberg delegates received the Latin Version of the Apology-Confession, and sent it home on June 3rd. This was the document which has been termed by Kolde, "The Oldest Redaction of the Augsburg Confession." In it, we find Melanchthon still manifesting complete confidence in the Emperor, praising him in the article on the Marriage of the Priests, and upholding his authority in spiritual things and his power to decide for the Church. It was a royalist and a Romanistic document conceding, for the sake of apparent unity, those Germanic qualities of right and liberty, which finally gave substantial basis to Protestantism in the real Augsburg Confession. The weakness of " stepping softly" can be studied to advantage in this proposed Confession of Melanchthon. Its study as a step in the development of confessional doctrine is also most instructive. We see how the development originally was attempted on the basis of the Apostles' Creed, how clear and apt and full some of the doctrinal confessions were before having been filed down into our present Confession, and how Zwingli was condemned at the end of the short article on the Mass.

On the same day the Confession was made known to the other states, who demanded that it should be presented in common in the name of them all.[111a]   But at the same time Philip's plan of appeal to a council gained strength. " We appeal to a Council. We will not receive the Emperor as our judge; the Ecclesiastical Constitutions themselves forbid him to pronounce in spiritual matters."[111b]   Moses declares

---

[111a] " In gemein in aller Fürsten und Städte Nahmen."—*C. R.,* II, 88.

[111b] " Die *Constitutiones canonicae* den Kaysern verbieten zu richten und sprechen in geistlichen Sachen."—*Ib.,* 66.

that it is not the civil magistrate who decides, but the sons of Levi. St. Paul also says (1 Cor. 14), *'let the others judge,'* which cannot be understood except of an entire Christian assembly; and the Saviour Himself gives us this commandment: *'Tell it unto the Church.'"*

THE SILENT INFLUENCE OF LUTHER.

Luther did not realize that his silent influence, as the watchman on the mountain, as Moses stretching out his arm over the field of battle that the issue might be on the side of the Lord, was of more weight than his words, and perhaps than his personal presence in the mighty contest. Had he come to the Diet, the Augsburg Confession would not have been delivered, and Protestantism would have paid for his presence with his life, or with bloody war. Had he remained teaching in Wittenberg, Melanchthon would before the Summer was over have betrayed the whole cause into the hands of the Romanists. Providence had placed him, the invisible prophet, on the Mount, and within the mighty Fortress where his prayers arose uninterruptedly. Yet he could feel that he was of no use!

LUTHER TO LINK

Wolfbütt. Cod. Helmst., 108, f. 30b.
Cölest., I, 37; Erl. Br. W., VII, 345.

May 28th.

. . . I also know very well that I am entirely useless on this trip, and would perhaps have accomplished much more at home by teaching, but I could not withstand him who summoned me. . . .

I fear very much that Germany, especially the Upper, deserves from God a severe judgment on account of the abominations, murders, deceptions and other outrages against God's Word which daily increase; and the Turk puts on his armor not in vain. God have mercy upon us. . . .

The 28th of May, 1530.

YOUR MARTIN LUTHER.

28

June 1st.

A few days later, in the beginning of June, the Elector sums up the situation briefly and admirably in a letter to Luther:—

JOHN TO LUTHER.

Chyträus Hist., p. 11.

June 1st.

Our greeting, Reverend and Learned, Dearly Devoted. We received your last letter, and interpreted the Christian consolation you addressed to us to our great satisfaction. It shall also, if God will, be highly consoling in these very important transactions.

We wish to inform you confidentially that his imperial Majesty has here served upon us an Instruction in which we are sharply taken to task respecting his Majesty's edict[112] and certain other things.

Likewise (although mildly) there is therein also demanded of us that we shall discontinue preaching until his imperial Majesty will arrive and restore order in these matters. But we have given his Majesty an answer to this, from which his Majesty must graciously realize that we, as we have determined, cannot yield in this matter. What may happen in consequence thereof, we will, God willing, endure.

The report is that his imperial Majesty left Innsbrück, is moving to Munich, and will thence come here after Pentecost.

Dated Augsburg, on the first of June, Anno 1530.

We wonder how Luther, who had yielded to Melanchthon and to his regard for imperial authority, felt when he read this letter from John the Steadfast, who could not spare the preaching of the Word, and who said " It would be terrible to give up God's Word and truth." Concerning Luther's and Melanchthon's advice on the preaching the Elector is reported to have remarked, " I do not know whether I or my learned ones are becoming foolish."

Without the Word of God and prayer, Luther would have been sad and lonely enough at Coburg, even before the period from May 26th to June 19th, in which letters failed to arrive. On May 29th, his aged father died. On June 1st, he sends Probst a resume based on Melanchthon's letter

---

[112] The Edict of Spires, 1529.

to him of May 22nd, of the situation at Augsburg as he then understood it.

LUTHER TO JACOB PROBST.

Wolfb., Cod. Helmst., 108, f. 112.
Cölest. Hist. Com. Aug., I, f. 54; Erl. Br. W., VII, 352.

June 1st.

To-day, on the first day of June, the Emperor is still at Innsbrück, and will perhaps get to Augsburg towards Pentecost.

We have great hopes that the Emperor will act graciously, and he has in fact up to the present[113] written two or three times to our princes in a kindly way, as others of his court also have done, particularly Henry, duke of Nassau. He has also revealed this token of his gracious feeling that, when the dukes of Bavaria, Duke George and Margrave Joachim, had passed Augsburg by, and hastened to Innsbrück to the Emperor, that they might win the Emperor, and, by gaining his ear in advance, enrage him against our princes, the Emperor was unwilling to yield to them, since he wished to remain impartial to the others. And the highest Chancellor Mercurinus did openly say that he would not participate in compulsory measures, because he had sufficiently experienced at Worms what such action would accomplish. He wished that the difficulties of the Church would be peaceably settled. This Naaman (2 Kings 5) God has perhaps raised up for us.[114] Let us only pray. Our praying has begun to be heard, and we will not discontinue it.

There is great scarcity at Augsburg, so that our Elector pays one hundred florins every week for bread alone, and expends weekly two thousand florins.

This Diet will not continue long. Eck has distributed Forty Theses against us, which are full of the devil, and he offers himself to dispute with everybody except himself. We deride the fury of this person; there will now be no chance to dispute after the enemy has killed so many; neither will there be, for this purpose, any time at Augsburg.

I tarry upon the border of the Saxon territory, halfway between Wittenberg and Augsburg. For it was not safe to take me along to Augsburg.

Thus you have very nearly the whole matter, as it just now presents itself at Augsburg. Philippus, Jonas, Spalatin and Agricola went with the Elector to Augsburg.

By the next day Luther is more pessimistic, and less hopeful of the Diet, despite the temper of Gattinara and the Emperor. Visitors, unbidden, had been trespassing upon his time. He did not wish to hold public court at Coburg, and he seems to have felt that the news of his presence there

---

[113] He had not yet heard of the Nassau embassy of May 24th.
[114] He died three days after this letter was penned by Luther.

had leaked out through the traveling messengers. He re-
quests his friends at Augsburg to write less openly, but lo!
they do not write any more at all!

LUTHER TO MELANCHTHON

Wolfb., Cod. Helmst., 108, f., 22b.
Cölest. I, fol. 60b; Erl. Br. W., VII, 361.

June 2nd.

Grace and peace in Christ! Hans Reynick, of Mansfeld, and George Romer
were with me yesterday, and Argula von Staufen to-day. But as I see that this
place will be visited all too much, I have resolved, following the example of your
Stromer, to travel elsewhere, either apparently or really, in order that it may be
rumored that I am not keeping myself here any longer.

I beg of you, and the others with you, in future to speak and *write* so that
no one will seek me here any longer. This I am announcing to you in a Jonas-
like hurry, *for I wish to remain concealed,* and to have you, at the same time,
to keep me concealed, both in your words *and letters.*

Here they begin to make us believe that your Diet will achieve nothing; and
that the Emperor will, through the deceit and skilful manipulation of the bishops,
be detained, until you shall have spent all, and will be obliged to return home.
For it is not thought that the archbishop of Treves and the elector of the Palatinate
will be present; and that the Emperor, induced through the skill of the papists,
will seek reasons to be prevented from coming to Augsburg. These matters and
utterances cause me to have curious thoughts. But the messenger is in haste. Be
well in Christ. June 2nd, 1530.

YOUR MARTIN LUTHER.

June 2nd.

MELANCHTHON FLATTERED BY THE ROMANISTS.

At Augsburg, meanwhile, Melanchthon was tampered
with by the chaplain of Duke George, Cochlaeus, who sent
Philip a private note (*Cölestin,* I, 55), expressing a desire
to speak with him alone in the presence of Arnoldo Wesa-
liensi.[115] Melanchthon, who felt himself cut off and solitary
at Augsburg,[116] was softened by this approach, and felt that
the negotiations should be conducted as mildly as possible.
He asked the Elector to refrain from the use of meat on fast

[115] *Salig,* II, 175.
[116] Nos non minus sumus monachi quam vos in illa arce vestra.—*C. R.,* II, 46.

days in his court, because the Romanists were speaking about it. But the Elector did not yield.

Just before the Emperor left Innsbrück, Melanchthon entered into a secret correspondence with the other side as represented by Albrecht, archbishop and cardinal of Maintz, who proved somewhat more friendly than the other cardinals. All that is known as yet of this strange transaction is to be found in a sentence in a letter of John Rurer, the court preacher of Ansbach, who was at Augsburg on the Evangelical side with Andreas Altheimer. The letter[117] is dated June 4th. The following is the sentence: Scripsit Philippus litteras ad Archiepiscopum Moguntinum, quibus petit, quo operam det ne res ad arma deducatur, quid is responderit, aliquando cognosces, nondum Philippus responsionem sed solas suas literas nobis communicavit.

June 4th-6th.

THE HAND OF ROME SHOWN IN PREPARATIONS FOR THE DIET.

We already have seen that the Emperor's policy was delay, and an atttempt to persuade the Elector to settle things privately at Innsbrück. But the Elector's declaration of independence, and his refusal to treat except at Augsburg, together with a letter sent the Emperor by the estates impatiently awaiting him at Augsburg, brought his Majesty on at once toward the gates of the city. In the letter just alluded to, the estates said:—

" Since, in accordance with your Majesty's Call, we have most obediently come here with other Princes and Estates of the realm, and some of us have now been lying here a long while, under great difficulty and expense, we most obediently beseech your imperial Majesty to make haste to get here as soon as possible, considering that the importance of the case and necessity itself highly demand it, so that there be no failure in meeting you at your entry, and your Majesty be not delayed for a long time in the country, but everything proceed in good order as befits the occasion."

---

[117] The letter is printed in the Appendix of Kolde, *Alt. Red.,* p. 107.

His Majesty responded to this, and was coming now—but under Roman control; for Gattinara on June 4th had succumbed to death, leaving not one person in the imperial train to advocate the Evangelical cause. The delegation which was sent forward to arrange for the imperial arrival declared that, as an Emperor crowned at Rome,[117a] Charles would settle religious controversies at the Diet; and would necessarily admit the papal legate in his full character and commission, with precedence over all other embassadors. Hence the civil Electors should precede the Emperor in the entry, the cardinals, archbishops and bishops should ride alongside of him, and the papal legate should enter with the Emperor and King Ferdinand and beneath the same canopy.[118]

The Electors remonstrated against this order, as an infringement on the privileges granted to them in the Golden Bull. Still this matter could be settled; but as the Emperor was coming to celebrate the festival of Corpus Christi with all the estates according to the usual papistic ceremonies, the far more important question arose, whether the Protestants, if the Emperor should command them to do so, could participate in the procession with a good conscience. The Saxon theologians on request prepared the following Opinion:—[119]

"It would be the safest to withdraw entirely from the procession, and upon the way consider how best to excuse themselves to the Emperor, with the acknowl-

---

[117a] THE POPE AND THE EMPEROR AT BOLOGNA.

"Herod and Pilate soon became friends, when Christ and His Word were to be attacked. The Emperor desired to be crowned and had thenceforth to live to please the Pope. Bologna was chosen as the spot where this solemnity was to take place. . . . The Pope arrived first, but the Emperor made his entry on Nov. 5th, 1529, and remained there four whole months, and lived in one palace with the Pope, and desired a free General Council."—*Salig*, II, 154.

"At Bologna the Emperor attended a congregation of the Pope and the Cardinals, and also used this opportunity to consider his mild methods, selected from many others, of bringing about religious peace."—*Ib.*

The Pope persisted until the Emperor was obliged to promise that he would first bring the Lutherans to obedience to the Papal chair in a gracious way; and if this proved fruitless, he would compel them to it by force of arms. To this end the Emperor, on the 21st of January, wrote a Call to a Diet to be held at Augsburg on the 8th of April."—*Ib.*, 156.

[118] *Cölestin*, I, 58b sqq.; *Müller*, III, 521 sqq.

[119] *Cölestin*, I, c. 67.

edgment that however they did not despise the most honored sacrament; for, first, such processional misuses are against the Scripture and the command of God; and, second, the sacrament was not ordained for the purpose of praying to it. If they should accompany these processions, the abuses against which they were teaching would be countenanced by them.

June 4th.

GATTINARA DIES; THE EMPEROR LEAVES INNSBRÜCK.

Mercurinus Gattinara, the imperial chancellor and the staunch friend of the Evangelical cause, who had kept Campeggius and the Romanists in check up to this time, and who, though ill, had accompanied the Court of Charles to Innsbrück, died to-day. Luther had just compared him to a Naaman "raised up for us in the Court of the King of Syria." At every step the chancellor[120] had resisted the Pope. The Emperor would bring to him the papal propositions, and the chancellor would say, "Remember that you are master!" But with his death, on the 4th of June, the last advocate of the Elector vanished from the papal court, and henceforth the Romanists alone had the ear of the Emperor.

Two days after his death the Emperor was already on his way to Augsburg; and when, on the Emperor's arrival, the Elector learned that Mercurinus was dead, his eyes were opened to the necessity of giving up all hopes of a fair hearing for his personal Confession, and of uniting with the other Lutheran estates to form a Protestant party.

June 6th, Monday.

To-day the Emperor and his court broke up at Innsbrück, and on the following Friday[121] arrived at Munich. Here it was planned by the enemies of the Protestants that the Emperor should reach Augsburg on the very eve of Corpus Christi day.[122]

[120] *Cyprian* briefly describes this influence, and the consequent mildness of Charles, on pp. 7 and 8 of the Introduction to his *Historia.*

[121] *Salig,* II, 177.

[122] *Ib.,* 181.

June 7th.

LUTHER STIRS AUGSBURG WITH HIS PERSONAL CONFESSION.

The Emperor would be here in a week, but Augsburg was to experience a great sensation previous to his arrival. Luther's personal Confession—his " Admonition to the Catholic clergy of the Diet "—reached Augsburg in print on the 7th of June. It surely added oil to the flame. It was immediately sent to the imperial Court and Charles in a command to the magistrate prohibited it·from being offered for sale in Augsburg.[123] Luther had told Melanchthon as early as the 12th of May that the copy had been sent to Wittenberg to be printed.

It was Luther's wish to appear at the Diet in this writing, since he could not be there in person. His personal presence, he felt, would be of no value. He still sees a day of salvation in the Diet, which God offers. He will pray, beg and advise the clergy there assembled that they do not use the day thus given in vain.

Though everlastingly set against those who ridicule Evangelical preachers for their family life, while they themselves lived in sins, he says: " Give us the doctrine of the Gospel free, to comfort pious consciences, and we will not disturb you in your property and your jurisdiction."

It will be well to present an abstract of parts of this vigorous document, which reached Augsburg just ahead of the Emperor:—

ADMONITION TO THE CLERGY ASSEMBLED AT THE DIET AT AUGSBURG.

" Et nunc, reges, intelligite, erudimini, judices terræ."—Ps 2 : 10.

Grace and peace in God, our Father, and the Lord Jesus Christ ! Since it is not fitting that I appear at this Diet, and if I did, I could not be of service there, as I am not adapted to pomp and formalities, I have undertaken to be among you with my spiritual presence (which I shall prove by diligent petitions to my God) and through this my feeble message.

---

[123] Jacob Sturm at once sent it to the Reformed at Strasburg.

My conscience compels me to admonish you, in a friendly way, not to misuse this Diet. God has given you great opportunity, through our most gracious Lord Charles, to accomplish much good. Now is the accepted time and the day of salvation for you. The hearts of all the people are waiting with great expectancy that this Diet prove good.

But should it dissolve without deeds, since all the world has for a long time been pinning its hope to diets and councils, despair would result. For things can not exist any longer as they are. This you know and feel better than I can tell you.

Some will say I have intruded. Yet the foolish man oft gives better advice than many wise. It is the wise men who have done the greatest harm upon earth, especially when they have depended upon their wisdom, and have not dealt in the fear of God.

Of this all history, in and out of the Scriptures, is full ; and if there were no other example, look at your own case. For almost ten years you have tried your wisdom in so many diets, so many propositions, so much diplomacy, with force and anger, with murder and punishment, that I have wondered at you ; and yet nothing has come of it.

This is the result of wisdom without humble prayer. You are not willing to fear God and to humble yourselves. If you still attempt to threaten and do not beg God for help, you shall not now accomplish anything, though you be as wise as Solomon. But I am praying diligently for God's grace. My prayers are heard, which, I fear, is not the case with you.

God grant that you do not oppose Him, and that my prayers may not be lost on you, for I see that the devil wishes to be on the ground, together with the Turk, and is stirring up one faction against another, and would rejoice to ruin everything.

Do not try to save me. For though I should be set in the midst of Turks and Tartars, the Pope or the devil, my cause is sure ; so that I know where I shall finally abide, according to Romans 8 : 28, "All things work together for good to them who are called according to his purpose." This has been confirmed by the blood and martyrdom of many pious people.

But for you and the poor, ignorant people I have concern, and would gladly aid with prayer and admonition, for I fear you have forgotten humility toward God, and that you key your strings too hard, whereby some disturbance may arise, so that both we and you will fall into deep need, as has before occurred. For you know how all the world was looking and waiting with hope for the Diet at Spires. Your proposals there were so wise ! Then immediately came the rod, namely, Münzer, and from his harmful tumults we have not yet recovered. This is what it means to attain everything by force and self-will.

Therefore, at Worms, our dear Emperor Carl was obliged to do what you wished, and to condemn me with my whole teaching, which you have, nevertheless, yourselves accepted and used secretly in many parts. And your preachers would have nothing to preach now if it were not for Luther's books; for they let their sermon-book lie under the bench, and begin to preach against us about faith and good works. Meanwhile you forced an edict to put Lutherans to death, which was so terrible that you yourselves could not endure it, and it had to be altered at the Diet at Nürnberg.

I am not telling this to ridicule you, but to admonish you to learn from experience to discontinue the use of threatening, and act toward God in fear and humility. Truly the problems are too great for human wisdom and power. God must help, or else the evil will grow worse. The spirit of Münzer will live, and I fear more powerfully than before.

You know how faithfully I held the ground against all fanatics, and have protected you. Some will say, " This is all the fruit of your teaching," but there are many pious persons among you who know it is not true. Have you forgotten what the German nobility at Worms said to his imperial Majesty, and have you forgotten how at first my doctrine was preached by nearly all of you? At the time, Luther was a fine teacher, aptly attacking the indulgence. Afterwards I attacked the cloister-life, and the monks became fewer; but I never, not to this day, heard of a bishop or priest who wept on that account. There is now scarcely a soul at Augsburg who would elevate the monks to their former position. The bishops will no longer endure such bedbugs and lice in their furs, but are glad that I have freed them.

If our Gospel had done nothing but relieve the conscience from idolatry of the indulgence, it should be recognized as the Word and power of God. Who is there among you who has repented of his great sin? Now you wish to come to Augsburg and tell us that the Holy Ghost is with you, that you think you never did any harm to Christianity, that you accomplished great things, whereas you have desolated the Church.

[Here Luther goes on to describe the Confessional, the Beicht, Penance, the Kaufmesse, Excommunication, both forms of the Sacrament, and Celibacy.]

The points which are necessary to be taken up in the true and right Christian Church, if we are to continue therein, are these: What a Lie is, what the Gospel is, what Sin is, what Grace is, what a Gift of the Spirit is, what right Repentance is, how one Confesses aright, what Faith is, what the Forgiveness of sins is, what Christian Liberty is, what Free Will is, what Love is, what the Cross is, what Hope is, what Baptism is, what the Masses are, what the Church is, what the Bishop is, what the Office of Preaching is ; what the right Catechism, namely, the Ten Commandments and Lord's Prayer and Faith; the right Prayer, the Litany; Reading and Exposition of the Scriptures; what Good Works are; Instruction for the Married; for Children; for Man and Maid Servants; to Honor Authority; to Visit the Sick; to Care for the Poor and for Hospitals; to Instruct the Dying. These points have never been thoroughly handled and taught by any of you.

But that we old fools should go about in bishops' hoods and priestly raiment, as though externals were articles of faith, that is the devil himself. You know full well that Pope Adrian through his legates at Nürnberg admitted that the Roman Church was the cause of much woe, and offered to make it better. Why are you ashamed to acknowledge this? Why do you stand fast in your pride?

You cannot spare the prayers of the Lutherans, the pious heretics, if you are to effect anything of value. But if you carry matters through by force, your blood be upon your own head. We are and desire to remain in unison. We have faithfully admonished you to repentance, and have said we desire nothing but the pure Gospel. But the God of peace and consolation give you His Spirit, Who will show and lead you to all knowledge, through our Lord Jesus Christ, to Whom be praise and thanks for His unspeakable grace throughout eternity. Amen.

Wednesday, June 8th, to Wednesday, June 15th.

While the public were filled with the sensation created by Luther's Admonition, and the news of the Emperor's approach, the Protestant princes were busy considering what position they should take at the Diet so close at hand.

Melanchthon was in favor of leaving all to the Emperor's good will—even though no Confession should be forthcoming.

Philip of Hesse was opposed to dealing with the question of religion in a political Diet, and wished to unite the Lutherans and the Reformed in a common appeal to a Council. The Elector was averse to uniting with anyone (he was the chief offender in the Emperor's eye), and, until recently at least, had hoped to be able to present his Saxon Apology-Confession in defense of himself and Lutheran doctrine. The other estates were perplexed. On June 8th, the Margrave of Brandenburg's Chancellor, Vogler, had a talk with Kress, one of the Nuremberg delegates, in which he pointed out the defect of the Saxon Apology-Confession, viz., that it was made only in the name of the Elector of Saxony, while the Margrave thought it ought be offered in the name of " all the princes and cities that are *in unity on the Articles of Faith,"* so as to be the common Confession of the Evangelical estates of Germany. He said that, " the Introduction might separately specify, where it could not be done in common, what every prince or estate had done for his imperial Majesty." For the Call had specified that *each* estate should prepare its own Statement, and, according to Cyprian, every one of them who did not simply lean upon the Elector had ready a short outline of the doctrine which was taught in his lands.[124] Camerarius says, "Those who were joined together in this cause had ordered their own theologians also to compose something, which was read by Philip." [125] " This was not a difficult task," says Müller.[126]

---

[124] *Hist.,* p. 55.
[125] *Vita,* 124.
[126] *c. l.,* p. 302.

But to return to the situation before us. During the period between Wednesday, June 8th, and the following Monday, the 13th, Nuremberg and Brandenburg appear to have been agitating for this change in the Preface of the Apology-Confession, in which all the estates should be recognized.

Between Saturday, the 11th, and Monday, the 13th, Philip of Hesse seems to have become very active again, especially with the Margrave, in opposing the intention of submitting the religious question to the Diet. He once more was agitating for a confederation with the Zwinglians, and the postponement of the religious question to a Council. Meantime Melanchthon probably was changing the Confession in accordance with the enlarged horizon gained in the Protestant negotiations, although it still stood as a Saxon document.

On Monday, the 13th, Melanchthon had a conversation with the Roman Henry of Brunswick.[127] The Landgrave Philip was pressing for confederation, but Henry told Melanchthon that the Landgrave was a plotter; and Melanchthon expressed himself as opposed to Protestant confederation, and as willing to harmonize with the Romanists if, as the Duke said, the twofold form of the sacrament, the marriage of priests, monastic liberty, abolishment of paid masses and freedom of foods were not condemned.

On this very day, June 13th, Melanchthon wrote to Luther[128] his opinion, gained from the Elector's correspondence, that Charles would make peace with the Elector, provided that he kept himself free from alliances.

Here then was Melanchthon's dilemma: he wanted Philip to unite with the Lutherans, else he might join the Zwinglians; but he wanted the Elector to have no allies, that the Emperor might be pleased and settle the matter. Which horn should Melanchthon take? He wrote to Luther: Paene consumor miserimis curis; and a few days later he took the plan of acting on his own responsibility, and negotiating secretly with the officers of the Emperor!

---

[127] Jonas to Luther, *Enders,* VII, 380.
[128] *Ib.,* VIII, 383.

June 12th, Pentecost.

WHITSUNTIDE, JUST PRIOR TO THE DIET.

The Emperor is spending this day at Munich, while at Augsburg the Elector is attending the preaching of Urbanus Rhegius in the church of St. Catharine.[129]

June 13th.

On Whitmonday the Emperor broke up at Innsbrück, and traveled slowly toward Augsburg, the seat of the coming conflict.

June 15th-25th.

II. PERIOD OF ACTIVITY AND SUSPENSE.

June 15th, Wednesday.

RECEIVING THE EMPEROR.

ACCOUNT OF THE MEETING AT THE BRIDGE OF THE LECH, AND OF THE PROCESSION.[130]

This was the day on which the Emperor would come. For the past week his baggage trains[131] had been making a din in the waiting city—the home of the Welsers and Fuggers, the great capitalists of Europe, and the great trading centre between Italy and the Levant, and the towns of Northern Europe.

At five o'clock[132] on the morning of the 15th, the Elector and the princes assembled in the town hall. At one in the afternoon, they went forth on horseback to meet his Majesty, and stood ready for his coming at the bridge of the Lech.

---

[129] *Salig*, II, 163.

[130] " Des Allerdurchlauchtigsten, Grosmächtigsten Fürsten und Herrn, Hrn. Carolen, Römischen Kaysers, etc., am Nahman des V., einreitend auf den Reichstag zu Augspurg, an Mittwochen, St. Veits Tag, der da war der 15. Tag im Brachmonat. Ann. 1530."—Hardts, *aut. Luth.*, I, 267. *Cp.* Cyprian *Beilagen z. Hist. d. Augs. Conf.*, p. 60 ; Cölestin, *hist. comit. Aug.*, I, p. 68 ; Schirrmacher, *Briefe u. Acten*, 54 to 57.

[131] *C. R.*, II, 90.

[132] *Först.*, I, 263.

After some hours waiting, clouds of dust and much noise on the other side of the bridge heralded the approach of the Emperor's soldiery. The Electors and princes were recognized by Charles with an amiable smile, and he very graciously shook hands with each. He had no sooner alighted from his horse for the greeting, than he expressed the desire to the Elector that he cause the preaching to cease.[133]

The archbishop of Maintz delivered the address of welcome. Apart from the group, on a little elevation,[134] sat the Roman Legate in purple, supported by two cardinals, the archbishop of Salsburg, and the bishop of Trent. When Campeggius the Legate saw the Emperor and the princes dismounted and greeting each other, he lifted up his hands and blessed them. They, with the Spaniards, Italians, Netherlanders and Germans in the train, fell on their knees; but the Elector John and his fellow-Protestants stood bolt upright and refused the papal benediction.

The magnificent procession, eclipsing[135] anything heretofore seen in the empire, now entered[136] the city, with the soldiers of the six electors in advance. After the princes and electors, came John of Saxony bearing the glittering naked imperial sword before the Emperor, on whose right was Maintz and on whose left was Köln, with King Ferdinand and the Papal legate Campeggius[137] immediately following.

The procession [138] wended its way to the Cathedral, where the bishop of Augsburg and his white-robed clergy struck up

---

[133] This was practically his first word to the Protestants. The Elector himself tells the story in his letter to Luther of June 25th. He says: "So soon as his imperial Majesty came here to Augsburg and alighted from his horse, he desired from us, and those with us, that we cease the preaching."—*Cölest.*, I, 139. The account of Chytraeus confirms this scene and its request as having taken place on the banks of the Lech.—*Hist. Augsp. Conf.*, p. 54b.

[134] *Först.*, I, 256.

[135] *Seck.*, II, 160.

[136] Melanchthon says it was 8 P. M. when the entry was made, and that the procession moved very slowly. *Vid. Melanchthon to Luther,* about June 20th.

[137] It is recorded that when the procession started, the legate made an attempt, frustrated by the Electors, who told the Emperor to ride alone, to move forward under the same canopy with the Emperor.—*Salig,* II, 178.

[138] For a list of the bishops, etc., who participated, and were present at the Diet, see *Cölest.*, IV, p. 121b.

the *Advenisti desirabilis.* The Emperor entered the Cathedral and knelt before the altar with hands extended to heaven. During the *Te ergo quaesimus,* he again knelt on the bare stones, and all the assembly with him. But the Elector and the Landgrave remained standing. Campeggius pronounced the benediction, and the procession resumed its march to the bishop's palace, which had been prepared for the Emperor's use, and reached there after ten o'clock at night.[139]

THE NOCTURNAL INTERVIEW IN THE PALACE.

From five o'clock in the morning until ten at night the old Elector had been kept on his feet, and now the surprise of the day was to be sprung—"the nocturns of treason were about to begin." [140] Charles had dealt with the Protestants with great personal grace; but, after waiting till evening for his appearance, they had been hurried along into the ceremonies of state under the auspices of the Church. It was almost impossible to distinguish between civil and religious duty. To-morrow the Emperor must celebrate Corpus

---

[139] *Salig* (II, 179, 180) says: " For it is doubtless undeniable that scarce any Diet was held in Germany which compared with this Diet in multitude of people, splendeur and other advantages. The Augsburg Confession was given the honor by God of being heard by Emperor, Kings and Princes, by embassadors from all the lands in Europe, and of being read by an indescribable multitude of people. Hitherto God's Word had lain concealed beneath the bench, and was unknown to Princes and Lords, to clergy and laity. Now it resounded in the whole world . . . so that at a Diet, the like of which Germany never saw before, and probably also will never see again, it sounded in all ears, and became the sensation of the hour. The Word of Christ (Matt. 10:26, 27), was perfectly fulfilled: ' There is nothing concealed, that shall not be revealed. What I say unto you in darkness, that speak in light; and what you hear in your ear, that preach from the house-tops.' . . . At Nice the Emperor Constantine the Great was present with 318 bishops. Chalcedon shone with a splendor of 630 bishops. But at Augsburg there was an Emperor, a King, and the flower of the Princes of the German nation. At the earlier Councils, innocence was at times suppressed, and the truth darkened; and results dwindled down into a war of words. At Augsburg great Electors and Princes themselves were the confessors of divine truth, and bore the Holy Word to the ears of all men. . . .

" Where then is there a Council which can be compared with this Diet? At the Diet at Worms the truth was still greatly oppressed, and Luther stood there alone and confessed it. But within only a few years the Gospel had been so blessed that now the greatest Princes in Germany confessed it, and the kingdom of Heaven was now like a grain of mustard seed, which a man took and sowed in a field."

[140] *Spalatin.*

Christi; and the procession of the holy sacrament was even then being arranged. The Lutherans were to be given no time to think, to consult, or to appeal, but were to be involved by the swiftness of events, the exigencies of their civil positions, the personal favor and grace of the Emperor, in such a way that later on they would not consistently be able to take a stand against the Church.

Charles had made several attempts at a distance to get them to yield, now he would meet them on the spot, and try his diplomacy face to face. After the Cathedral service the princes entered the palace with the Emperor. Then the Romanists were told to depart, and Charles invited the Elector, George of Brandenburg, Philip the Landgrave, the Prince of Anhalt and the Duke of Lüneburg to follow him into his private apartments.[141] King Ferdinand accompanied the party as interpreter.

The reader should notice an important historical fact at this point, and one that has a vital bearing on the most important change in the Augsburg Confession. Up to this moment, the Emperor had dealt with his beloved uncle, the old Elector, as a person apart from the other Protestants. He had promised the Elector special favor if he would keep himself free from all alliances. The worthy and faithful old prince had endeavored punctiliously to live up to this understanding. Even his Augsburg Confession was to have been only that of the Elector of Saxony.

But on this night the Emperor was unconsciously or deliberately sweeping all the past away. He was not dealing with the Elector in person, but he singled out a party of Protestants, brought them into his own house, and dealt with them *together*. That act released John; it actually placed him—whether he would or no—on a level with all the other Protestant princes. The Emperor himself made the Protestant princes co-defenders: he united them; and his act, considered as an external act—not the Elector's, nor Melanch-

---

[141] *C. R.,* II, 106, 114.

thou's—took the taint of Saxon particularity out of the Confession, and lifted it to an œcumenical height.

Behind closed doors, Charles through Ferdinand "requested of their electoral and princely Graces that they henceforth should not permit preaching in Augsburg" [142] during the sitting of the Diet. So this meeting, instead of manifesting the imperial favor, promised in the "Call" and looked and hoped for ever since, was only to reopen the one throbbing sore spot. [143] The Elector and the Margrave turned pale. There was silence. " Die beede älte Fürsten zum höchsten entsetz." [144] The Margrave spoke up: " We beg your Majesty not to insist on your request," he said, " for we preach only God's pure Word, as did Augustine, Hilary and the ancient doctors. Of this your Majesty may convince himself. We cannot do without the food of God's Word, or deny the Gospel with a good conscience." [145]

When Ferdinand told Charles how old George had quoted the ancient doctors, the Emperor flashed up in anger, and insisted on his demand. "But," said Hessian Philip, "the conscience of his imperial Majesty is not the lord and ruler over our conscience." Twice was the request repeated; twice was it refused. Then Ferdinand said, "The Emperor will not withdraw his demand." Turning to Charles, the old Margrave of Brandenburg exclaimed: "Before I would deny my God and His Gospel, I would kneel down here at your Majesty's feet and have my head struck off."

This was the climax that night. It was *the* great confession at Augsburg that it is better to die than to compromise; and it foiled the Emperor for a moment. He directed the

---

[142] *Chytraeus,* p. 40.

[143] "When we came to the Emperor's lodging, the very first point was that the preaching should be stopped. This matter was disputed over for three successive days. For our side would by no means agree to demit the preaching, until, after a lengthy conflict, it came to the point that the Emperor deprived both parties of the sermons. He himself had someone to read the Gospel and Epistle without explanation."—*Melanchthon to Luther,* about June 20th.

[144] *C. R.,* II, 106, 114.

[145] *Ib.* 115.

29

princes to transmit in writing the reason why they were unwilling to dispense with the preaching.[146] Old George's "short and rugged speech, though eminently respectful, ended with words which flew over Germany, kindling hearts as fire lights flax."

But Ferdinand was ready with the second trap. "Since his Majesty," said he, "is unable to stop your preaching, he asks that you will at least observe the custom of accompanying him in the procession of the sacrament."

The princes refused unconditionally. "Christ," said they, "did not institute His sacrament to be worshipped." Charles persisted in this demand, and the Protestants persisted with equal tenacity in their refusal.[147] Finally the Emperor declared that he would not accept their reply, and that they should think the matter over during the night, and be prepared to reply early the next morning.[148]

This day and night of June 15th settled the future of Protestantism and the fate of the Augsburg Confession in the mind of the Elector. The death of Mercurinus at Innsbrück ten days earlier, had already been a note of warning as to the danger in which they stood; and this night convinced the Elector that there was nothing to hope for from the Emperor, though Melanchthon still put his trust in him. Already earlier in the day, the Elector and his advisers had adopted the principle of admitting the other Estates to the Confession, and a German text, sent to Nuremberg, now already contained the phrase, "A common word which can be applied to all Estates," [149] at the places where the Latin text still confined the Confession to Saxony. No doubt the admission of the other Estates would have been consummated at once, if it had not been for the embarrassment and confusion this caused the Elector respecting Melanchthon's Introduction to the Confession, which would then have had to be given up.[150]

---

[146] *Chytraeus.*
[147] *C. R.*, II, 115.
[148] *Salig*, II, 182, says, "Six o'clock."
[149] *C. R.*, II, 105.
[150] *Ib.*

The princes left the Emperor's palace that night deeply stirred in soul, and the Emperor was almost beside himself with rage,[151] which Campeggius endeavored to fan into more lurid flame. Seckendorf[152] narrates that the Emperor, too impatient to await the Protestant answer, sent to the Elector for the decision during the middle of the night. "At the present moment we need sleep," exclaimed the Elector; "to-morrow we will advise you of our decision."[153]

A DEMAND FOR COPIES OF THE PROPOSED CONFESSION.

Quite naturally, as all the princes were now co-operating, and as Vogler proposed to at once hand the doctrinal articles to the Emperor, there arose an unusual demand for the Confession just at this time. It is natural, too, that the copies made and placed in the hands of the princes, should be retained by them for consultation during the Diet, and should afterwards be taken home. And as a matter of fact all the copies of the Confession that are extant from the time before its presentation, including Spalatin's written in his own hand, do go back to this very period.

Thursday, June 16th.

REFUSING THE IMPERIAL REQUEST ON THE MORNING OF CORPUS CHRISTI.

It was no wonder that the poor Elector, now thoroughly worn out, became ill during the night, and could not mount his horse next morning at seven[154] o'clock, with the princes and the counsellors who went back to the Emperor's palace. It is little wonder that the restless Landgrave of Hesse was as deeply stirred as the Emperor. As soon as he reached home

---

[151] *C. R.,* II, 116.

[152] II, 161.

[153] About June 20th, the Elector wrote to Luther: "We plead with his Majesty the same evening, also the following day, respectfully, but giving many good reasons. But we were not able to succeed."—*Cölestin,* I, 139.

[154] *Salig* says they were to be on hand at "Six o'clock."

that night, he sent his adviser to wake up the Nuremberg delegates and let them know all that had occurred.[155]   The demand of Charles had that night yet been placed before the Lutheran theologians, and Spalatin wrote out the Protestant Opinion before morning.   It said: "The sacrament was not instituted to be worshipped like the brazen serpent of the Jews.   We are here to confess the truth, and not to confirm abuses."

When the little party arrived at the Emperor's palace the next morning, George, the old Margrave, was their spokesman, the Elector being represented by his son.   Said George to the Emperor: "My ancestors and I have always supported you; but in the things of God, the commands of God compel me to put aside the command of man.   If, as we are told, death is to be the fate of those who persevere in the true doctrine, I am ready to suffer it."   Offering the Emperor the Opinion[156] of the Protestants, he said: "We will not countenance these human traditions, opposed to the Word of God, with our presence; on the contrary, we declare unitedly that we must expel them from the Church, lest those of its members that are still sound should be affected with this deadly poison."[157]

To this Ferdinand replied: "If the love of God will not impel you to go with the Emperor, then do so for the love of the Emperor, and as vassals and princes of the Empire.   His Majesty commands you.   He begs you."   The Princes replied: "This is an act of worship, and our conscience forbids it."   The Emperor had taken his last step and exhausted his last resource; and now, after all the planning from Innsbrück down, had lost the cause.   Saying, "We wish to see whether you will obey his Majesty or not,"[158] Ferdinand, with the Emperor, left the room, and the princes, instead of following, *returned to their quarters.*

---

[155] *C. R.,* II, 106.
[156] The Document is found in *Cölestin,* I, 82.
[157] *Ib.,* 84; *Chytraeus,* p. 41.
[158] *C. R.,* II, 108.

That day at noon, behind the host, carried by the Archbishop of Maintz, the Emperor marched alone with his head bare, and a taper in his hand, with scarcely one hundred citizens of Augsburg following him in the procession of Corpus Christi. So irritated was he on his return to the palace that he threatened that he would dismiss the Lutherans to their homes with a safe-conduct next day,[159] and the Diet would uphold the Church and the empire without them. But the German Catholic princes saw that this would lead to terrible war, and they supplicated his Majesty, asking him to wait till his anger should cool.[160]

MELANCHTHON'S SHORT-CUT.

In this crisis, with that sad and unconscious lack of a sense of public loyalty to those who were near him, between Corpus Christi day and the following Saturday, that is between the 16th and the 19th of June, when the princes in the contest with the Emperor were staking their very lives for the Truth, Philip Melanchthon, who was always terrified at the mere thought of war, went privately, on his own responsibility, and without the knowledge of the Elector, into negotiations of his own[161] with the Spanish imperial secretary, Alphonso Valdés, and through him with the Emperor, for the express purpose of convincing the Emperor and the legate of the Pope that the Protestants were not as bad as they looked, and of arranging a way in which a public Confession of the Lutheran Church might be avoided and the whole Church brought back into the bosom of Rome.[162]

---

[159] *Cochlaeus*, 193.

[160] *Ib.*

[161] "In his anxiety he sought to gain touch with the imperial secretaries, immediately after the arrival of the Emperor. For Melanchthon's initiative against Maurenbrecher, *Kath. Ref.*, p. 284, see my information in *M. Luther*, II, 592."—*Kolde.*

[162] The details of this secret movement are described in the Chapter on "Melanchthon's Unsuccessful Attempts as a Diplomatist." *Vid.* also Kolde, *Luther, II,* 343 ; Virck, *Mel. polit. Stellung auf d. Reichstage zu Augsburg,* Z. K. S., IX (1888), pp. 92 sq.

The terrible clash of the night of the 15th, with the Emperor's attempt to force the hand of the Evangelical party by a cessation of preaching and a participation in the feast of Corpus Christi, had impressed the fearful Melanchthon so deeply that he was consumed with the desire to settle the matter himself and as soon as possible. He had sought to get into touch with both the imperial secretaries. With the Flemish secretary, Cornelius Schepper, he had held his first conversation the next day, June 16th, but Schepper was reticent and gave him to understand that the Emperor was determined to move against the Lutherans.[163] Though Melanchthon was told there was no hope for peace, as, since the death of Mercurinus, no one of authority in the imperial court leaned their way, he took the one last recourse. After Schepper's rebuff, he went to the Spanish secretary, Valdés,[164] and succeeded in making him feel that the main points for which the Lutherans would contend were only the twofold form of the sacrament, the marriage of the priests, and the abolishment of private masses.

Thursday, June 16th (Continued).

THE PROTESTANTS NOW FORM A CLOSED PARTY.

From this day on, the Evangelical princes act together as a common party. The night before they had together determined not to omit the preaching, and refused to participate in to-day's procession.[165] That they regarded themselves as a closed party[166] may be seen from the title of the document

---

[163] " Aneas Silvius himself," said Schepper, " before he became Pope, had written: The Roman Court gives nothing without money: even the gifts of the Holy Ghost are being sold.' "—*Epist.* 66, Ed. 1496. *Noribergae publicata per Antonium Koberger. Vid. Cyprian,* p. 8.

[164] *C. R.,* II, 118 sq., 122.

[165] *Ib.,* 106.

[166] *Förstemann,* I, 215.

which the Margrave of Brandenburg's Chancellor, Vogler, presented at their common meeting to-day. The title reads: "Certain considerations why my clement lord, the Elector of Saxony, Margrave George of Brandenburg, Duke Ernest and Duke Francis of Brunswick and Lüneburg, Philip, Landgrave of Hesse, and Wolfgang, Prince of Anhalt, has given consent to set aside the party of his electoral, the present Grace."

Vogler actually proposed that the Evangelical Party at once hand over the doctrinal articles of the Confession to the Emperor so as to convince him that their party was really orthodox. But the old Elector, who had now had experience after experience with the Emperor, and who possibly recalled how little his own effort in this direction had accomplished when he sent up the Schwabach Articles to the Emperor, negatived the proposition.

THE QUESTION OF PREACHING ONCE MORE.

Thus had passed the feast of Corpus Christi. The Protestants did not celebrate. But the preaching in the churches was a more serious matter, for it continued every day, and was creating excitement among the public. Some of the Zwinglian sermons were very bold in their veiled allusion to present events. On the night of June 15th, the Emperor had insisted on a written reply to his demand. The Princes, at their meeting of June 16th, determined not to omit the preaching, and that on the following day they would deliver a written explanation to his imperial Majesty.[167]

Friday, June 17th.

Accordingly, on the morning of June 17th, before breakfast, and doubtless after the Landgrave of Hesse had transmitted to them his explanation to the Lutheran position to be

---

[167] *Report of the Nurembergers,* June 16th, *C. R.,* II, 108.

given to Charles on the matter of preaching, the Princes handed in their reply, written by Brück, to the Emperor:—

THE ANSWER OF THE PROTESTANT ELECTOR AND PRINCES TO THE REQUEST OF HIS ROMAN IMPERIAL MAJESTY THAT HIS ELECTORAL AND PRINCELY GRACE SHOULD NOT ALLOW PREACHING DURING THE DIET.

Original in Archives at Weimar.
Printed in Först., I, 283; Chytr., 88.

1. Most excellent, mighty and invincible Emperor, most gracious Lord. Since your Majesty to-day gave us an instruction that we should transmit our conclusion in writing, for your further consideration: in obedience thereunto we now announce and repeat in this our writing, that your Majesty should graciously note, that if we find our preachers proclaiming new things, and teaching what is not grounded in the Holy Scripture or is contradictory to our holy Faith, we shall not willingly permit it, but will array ourselves against it. We wish them to preach and explain the Gospel clearly and purely, and even as it was preached and taught by the worthiest and most faithful Fathers in the holy Christian Church, as your imperial decree, at your Majesty's Diet in Nürnberg, in 1523, publicly declared should be the case.

If now such preaching of the holy Gospel were discontinued, as though it were false doctrine, it would be terrible. It would stand before God (Who does not want His holy Word bound) as a sin against the Holy Ghost.

We also, as poor sinful people, need such preaching and proclaiming of God's Word, to console our conscience, and to find help therein from God in our daily necessities and obligations. As little as we can forbid the daily food of the body, so much less can we be without the sermon and proclamation of the Divine Word, since man liveth not by bread alone but by every word that proceedeth out of the mouth of God. As we also declared to your brother, King Ferdinand, and the appointed commissioners, four years ago at your imperial Majesty's called Diet of Spires.

2. And even if the preaching were different, yet your imperial Majesty and everybody knows that there is *a dissension* in doctrine. Wherefore and for other reasons your Majesty called this Diet, that each one's opinion and meaning should here be heard, and, if error be found, it should *on both sides* be settled and brought into Christian unity.

3. On this account we ask your Majesty to graciously consider how our consciences could be satisfied if, while there was other preaching elsewhere, we had none, and could hear only the other preaching.

4. This would compel us, against our conscience, if we consented to it, to adjudge our doctrine as wrong, and the opposite as right, *before*, according to your Call to this Diet, the matters not right *on both sides* were adjusted. For it must follow, if we give up our preaching and hear another, that we are in essence and in effect compelled to acknowledge that our doctrine, since it is done away with, would be erroneous; and the other, since we are hearing and accepting it, would be right.

5. For what is done away with must, according to your own Call and all human reason, be wrong at that time, and that which is ordained must be right.

And if there should be, as we can well judge, little further done in these most weighty matters relating to our salvation, it would be directly against your own Call, which so clearly involves that each one shall be *heard first*, and then that which has not been done right *on both sides*, on the other no less than on this, and not only on our side, shall be done away with.

6. If your Majesty should be informed by anyone that we preach novelties, it is our judgment, as we yesterday declared, that the clear Gospel is preached and explained by us as it was by the most worthy and prominent fathers of the Church according to the Scripture, and that neither anything else, nor any novelty is being preached.

7. And suppose there were novelties or abuses in our preaching, your Majesty nevertheless knows what terrible novelties in doctrines, customs and life have been introduced against Scripture and the Fathers, on the other side, and are still being practised, so that the whole world, and the pious before our age, have lamented and complained, and do so to-day. Let your Majesty recall what remarkable abuses were brought before you at the first Diet at Worms, which are unchanged to this day.

8. And we state all this simply to indicate to your Majesty what partial and unequal treatment the opposite party expects and demands from you.

9. We know that our preachers give no offense to the conscience. But, as we said yesterday, if there be any one whose conscience has been given offense, we will require a report of our preachers concerning it.

10. But what offense would we not give to our neighbor's faith and love, if the report went out that we were willing to cease preaching the Gospel, and thus in essence condemn our own doctrine as wrong? How could we give answer to God our Judge?

11. We have also admonished our preachers and people, after the sermon, to pray diligently for grace for your Majesty as the divinely ordained authority, and for the Electors, princes and estates that the business transacted at this Diet would eventuate, to the praise of God, in Christian peace and Christian unity.

12. The people are also faithfully instructed against certain doctrines concerning the Sacrament, which would be much more dangerous if our preachers were silent.

13. If we should cease preaching, we would be condemned by our own consciences, as being responsible for the ruin of those who were thus misled. For these disputed matters have been discussed for some years past; and at both the Diets of Spires the doctrine of the Gospel was preached openly and in an orderly way, with which it was impossible to find fault.

14. To this all, we did not take it that the edict of the Diet of Spires of one year ago required that we should now agree to the cessation of the preaching of the Gospel.

15. It has also been the free and undisputed right of your ancestors, and of those of the Electors and Princes (except that at both the last Diets of Spires the churches were denied us for the free preaching of the Gospel), that each one might order his preacher to preach the divine Word publicly in the Church before him and all others who should attend.

16. If we should yield to the abolishment of the preaching, this would be understood by many that your Majesty had decided against us unheard, after your

Call has been published throughout the Empire, and every one, no matter of which estate, is looking toward God and yourself in the hope that these most serious matters will be disposed of aright and according to God's unchangeable truth.   We also are assured that your Majesty will act in no other manner than your Majesty has announced in his Call.   We therefore most humbly pray your Majesty, as we have done the past two days, that you would graciously regard this explanation as coming from obedient and well-meaning hearts, and would venture to spare us from the intended prohibition of our preaching, and would permit us, as at Spires and here up to the present, to let our preachers preach.

All the more will we confess ourselves, in matters that pertain to our body, property and means, as your obedient electors and princes.

Datum, Friday after Corpus Christi (June 17th), year, etc., 1530.

> JOHN, Duke of Saxony Elector,
> GEORGE, Margrave of Brandenburg,
> ERNEST, Duke of Brunswick and Lüneburg,
> PHILIPP, Landgrave of Hesse,
> WOLF, Prince of Anhalt.

THE ASSEMBLY ON FRIDAY, JUNE 17TH.

This was the morning of Friday, the 17th.   Charles at once convened the electors and princes to deliberate concerning this answer.   They assembled after noon,[168] and remained in session until evening.   The Emperor was very much stirred against the Evangelicals at this meeting, and seemed determined to repeat and enforce his command against the preaching.   For, contrary to the judgment of the milder ones of our party—who had advised that the preaching be held off for one day longer, in anticipation of the imperial reply— that very morning the preacher of the margrave George, whose turn it was, had preached before the Evangelicals in the Church of St. Catharine.[169]   This so incensed the Emperor that the Diet would probably have come to nothing, had not several Princes leaped into the breach to make matters right.

---

[168] *Chytr.*, 42 ; *Seck.*, 165 ; *C. R.*, II, 113.   *Salig*, II, 183, says " forenoon," but the two statements are reconcilable.

[169] *Salig*, II, 183, 184.

" At last the mediators chose a committee [170] from among themselves which came [171] to our princes on Saturday noon, and urgently begged them to yield to his Majesty and silence the preaching. For his Majesty desired this *from the opposite party also;* [172] and if both parties would cease from preaching, his Majesty himself would undertake to handle the affair in accordance with the Call." [173]

It was proposed that Charles himself appoint persons who would read nothing but the text of the Gospels and Epistles, and a general confession of sins. " Our party," says Chyträus, " emphasized their Christian need, as rendering them unable to assent; but since his Majesty has given notice that he is in authority in this city, and the decree of the first Diet of Spires decided that every authority should decide in this matter as they would be able to give answer to God and his Majesty, and since our princes are outside their domain, they would not oppose his Majesty, although they were not willing to do without preaching, but had to do and suffer his Majesty's affairs. [174]

Friday, June 17th.

A PRIVATE PROTESTANT SEANCE.

While the stately, discriminate and enduring reply of the Lutheran princes was being given to the Emperor, and devoted old Duke George of Brunswick was again offering to

---

[170] The Committee was composed of the Archbishop of Maintz (according to *Cölestin,* p. 89 ; *Müller* makes it the Elector of Cologne, p. 548), the younger Margrave Joachim of Brandenburg, the Electoral Palatine, Master of the Court Lud. v. Fleckstein, Duke George of Saxony, Albert of Mecklenburg, and Ludwig of Bavaria.

[171] For a difference on this point, and for a clear, detailed description of these negotiations, *vid. Salig,* II, 184, 185. But Salig's date on p. 185 is a typographical error, and should read June 17th, not 10th.

[172] To "the opposite party" it was not a great hardship, since Rome does not lay stress on preaching.

[173] *Chytr.,* 44-45.

[174] *Ib.,* 45. Chytraeus adds that the Duke of Brunswick and the Archbishop of Maintz were unusually well-disposed in this matter—more so than could have been expected.

die for his faith, Valdés came[175] hurrying to a private seance with the Emperor, bearing a tale, concerning the Lutherans, of a different kind. He reported that the Elector's leading theologian had approached him privately on behalf of the Protestants with a way of bringing the whole trouble to a close, if the Romanists would but yield on a few points. Such an offer was most opportune for the Emperor, and he promptly grasped it. The presentation of Melanchthon was transmitted to the papal legate Campeggius for consideration.

Saturday, June 18th.

MELANCHTHON HEARS FROM VALDÉS, AND THE ELECTOR HEARS FROM THE EMPEROR.

Valdés' negotiations move swiftly. He has seen the Emperor and Campeggius, and the Emperor again, and this morning has a message from Melanchthon; for the Nurembergers write home, " Above-mentioned Alphonse undertook to deliver said report, and on Saturday invited Philippus again." And Melanchthon himself wrote to Luther, probably on June 20th, in his usual tone, in corresponding with Luther, of disarming suspicion: " A certain Spanish confidential secretary has also promised everything good, and has just held a conference with the Emperor and Campeggius concerning my Opinion; but everything lies with God."

Philip is told by Valdés that the Emperor had long been desirous of effecting harmony without extended discussion; that the Emperor is pleased and the Papal Legate looks with favor on his private proposition; and, that they may come at once to a definite transaction, the Emperor commands him to present the points of controversy in briefest form, "in order to be able to consider the matter if possible in all privacy and quiet." [176]

---

[175] There is no proof positive that Valdés' interview with the Emperor took place on the 17th, but the probability that this was the date is strong.

[176] Lämmer, *Monumenta Vaticana,* 43 sq. ; *Schirrmacher,* 71 sq.

REPORT OF THE DEALING OF VALDÉS WITH PHILIP MELANCHTHON.

From an old anonymous Report of June 18th, ascribed by Walch to Spalatin.
Wittg., IX, 409b sqq.; Leipz., XX, 202 sqq.

Alfonso, his Majesty's Spanish chancellor, also Cornelius, have held several friendly conversations with Philip, have shown him that the Spaniards are persuaded that the Lutherans do not believe in God [etc.].

On Saturday evening Alfonso sent for Philip and announced to him that he had been with his Majesty that morning, and for a long time had not had a more comfortable time and place to speak with his Majesty; that he had given his Majesty instruction concerning all the Lutheran Articles; and that they do not believe anything against the church. His Majesty then said, "Quid volunt de monachis?" and ordered Alfonso to tell Philip that he should transmit a very brief description to his Majesty. This Philip accordingly did, and therefore he also ordered Alfonso to go to the Legate and to come to agreement with him concerning the matter. This also happened, and the hitch is by all odds the greatest in the matter of the mass. God be praised, there is good hope. The Emperor would gladly help in the matter, and God has also given him means thereto.

So Melanchthon's eye is filled with a brilliant rainbow of peace which he has spanned between Wittenberg and Rome, and looks to see the dark bosom of the cloud dissolve, even though his own Electoral superiors are madly persisting on this very day in their refusal to desist from preaching in the Emperor's city.

AT PROTESTANT HEADQUARTERS.

And the skies seem to brighten. By noon a Committee of German Catholics appointed by the Emperor arrives and offers to forbid the Roman preaching during the Diet, if the Lutherans will agree to cease theirs. The proposition does not suit the Elector: as a spiritual man he needs his preaching, and now more than ever; but as a judicial offer of the common ruler, it is fair. What shall be done? Melanchthon is ready with an Opinion [177] in five brief points, showing why the temporary cessation should be agreed to; and in the end the Elector and the Lutheran princes yield to the committee. There is to be no preaching at all in the

---

[177] *Cölestin,* I, 89; *C. R.,* II, 111.

churches of Augsburg to-morrow. This does not mean compromise with Rome, but respect for pending judicial process.

His Majesty acted with celerity; and in a few hours he had
appointed preachers, with fixed instructions to only read the
service. That evening heralds went through all the streets
and cried[178] that no one should preach in Augsburg except
those appointed by the Emperor, under penalty of corporal
punishment.[179]

This created a great sensation, and all were eager to know
what would happen on Sunday.[180]

At the Lutheran headquarters, meantime, the Elector and
the Margrave were promising to receive the Nurembergers
into the Confession; but Jonas, who knew from Melanchthon
of the latter's conversation of two days ago with Valdés, sat
down and was reporting it to Luther.

The Emperor had become deeply concerned in the situation; and when, on Saturday evening, the Augsburg Chapter
came to him with the customary gift, he not only received
them in person, but requested them to pray God for him a
poor sinner, that he might be guided by the Holy Ghost to
establish one common Christian order, and not anger God.
"Wobei ihm die Augen übergangen." [181]

Sunday, June 19th.

NO PREACHING IN AUGSBURG.

The churches were filled, and the Roman sermon was gone
through without preaching, according to agreement. The

---

[178] " Hear, hear, hear what his Roman imperial Majesty commands: No
preacher here at Augsburg, be he who he may, shall hereafter preach, except
those appointed by his Majesty, to avoid his Majesty's greatest punishment and
disfavor."—(German) *Seck.*, p. 1039.

[179] *Chytr.*, p. 45. The Elector, in agreeing to the measure reluctantly, had
remarked that he expected to hear preaching in his own quarters when he so
desired.—*C. R.*, II, 113. The prohibition was to have been only temporary,
but it continued throughout the Diet.—*Salig*, II, 185.

[180] Omnes hunc avidissime expectant.—*C. R.*, II, 116.

[181] *Chytr.*, p. 46 ; *Salig*, II, 186.

people were moved to laughter.[182] After the sermon, the mass
was celebrated. The Emperor was strictly obeyed, and most
of the Protestant preachers had left the city to preach where
they were wanted.[183]

The Elector was downcast without the preaching of God's
Word. "Silence is imposed on the Word of God itself," he
said.[184]

When Luther heard[185] of these proceedings, his favorable
opinion of the Emperor was somewhat modified at last, and
on June 30th he wrote:—

LUTHER TO AGRICOLA.

Cod. Jen. B. 24, n. fol. 163; DeWette, IV, p. 57; Buddeus, p. 119.

My thought of the situation is thus: that the end of the Diet will be that the
Emperor will try and compel the Elector to renounce the whole doctrine. That
is my opinion, and it will be the severest result of this Diet. Admonish Philip
that he moderate the offering of an anxious spirit, so that at least he may not be
lacking in that wherewith to offer. It is no doubt a great comfort to know that
he is worrying himself in a good cause and for God's sake, since he cannot doubt
that it pleases God as a sweet incense. But moderation is good in all things:
sacrifice pleases God, but not grieving one's self to death. For God takes no
pleasure in our destruction. To think so comes from Satan.

For to put hope in the Emperor's good will amounts to nothing.[186] In my
belief the Pope and the bishops have influenced the Emperor, so to hear the case,
that, after our reply is made, they can still conclude what they desire, and nevertheless preserve the reputation of having given us a gracious hearing. Thus they
will be able to complain more plausibly of our obstinacy, as though we had been
patiently heard on our side, but in the end were unwilling to hear the Emperor.
. . . In very truth, you have not to do with men at Augsburg, but with the

---

[182] *C. R.,* II, 117.

[183] One Roman priest, for breaking the rule in the Church of the Holy Cross,
was placed in prison by Charles (and then allowed to escape).

[184] *Seck.,* II, 165.

[185] The Elector himself wrote to Luther, on June 25th, as follows: "At last
it was announced to us that his Majesty would forbid preaching on both sides,
and appoint preachers who should preach the Gospel pure and clear, so that
no one would be in want of spiritual nourishment; and his brother, the King,
should also not let Faber preach. . . . Now we are informed that the appointed preachers usually speak no more than the text of the Gospel; what
they teach in addition is said to be childish. So our Lord God must keep
silence at this Diet. We do not blame the Emperor, but rather our enemies
and those unfavorable to the Gospel."—*Cölestin,* I, 139.

[186] About June 20th, Melanchthon wrote to Luther: "At the same time, in
the whole court there is no one more mild or gracious than the Emperor himself, since he, as Henry the Duke of Brunswick tells me, is toning down the
bitter attacks of the princes. We have only two princes who are concerned
about our danger, the Archbishop of Maintz and the Duke of Brunswick. The
Elector of the Palatinate and the Margrave of Baden are not present."

gates of Hell itself. . . . But God blinds the wicked spirits in their rage, and they dash themselves against the wisdom of God and deceive themselves in their prudence. Amen. Amen.

The Lord Jesus Who has sent you all thither to be his confessors and servants, for Whom you are also offering your necks, be with you and give you with His Spirit a sure witness, that you know surely, and do not doubt, that you are His Confessors. This faith will fill you with life, and will comfort you, for you are Embassadors of a great King. This is His true Word. Amen.

LUTHER'S LETTERS OF THE 19TH.

Luther, up to the 19th, had still hoped well of the friendly Emperor. He had heard no more than that his Majesty had reached Augsburg, and that of all the Romanists he seemed to be the mildest toward the Protestants. Luther up to now saw no human help except in the Emperor,[187] but he feels his lack of knowledge. To-day he writes to Cordatus:—

June 19th.

We have *no news* from Augsburg. Our friends at Augsburg write us none.

And the same thing to Zwilling:—

June 19th.

You will, perhaps, get *the news* from Bernhardt, for our friends have not answered our letters through the whole month.

The next day, however, June 20th, the silence was broken. He hears from Jonas:—

LUTHER TO JUSTUS JONAS.

June 20th.

Your letters have come at last, my Jonas, after we were well fretted for *three whole weeks* with your silence.

We have already alluded to this mystery. What was there to say? The Elector was pursuing his own plan as to the

---

[187] On this day Luther writes from Coburg the celebrated letter on Heaven to his little son.

maintenance of the preaching, and Melanchthon his own plan as to the abandonment of the Confession. Neither were in touch with Luther, and Luther himself had written in the beginning of June that letters should not be sent him too freely and openly. The status at Augsburg was changing hourly. Consultation had followed consultation. All were weary. The Emperor had been present a week—nothing had been accomplished—who knew what the morrow would bring forth? The spirit does not move to correspondence under such circumstances.[188]

And yet Melanchthon had visitors and correspondence to attend to on this 19th of June. To the Nuremberg delegates he now reports the result of the meeting he yesterday had with Valdés, and informs them that it would probably not be necessary to present the Confession. The Nurembergers the same day write:—

June 19th.

"For, as Philippus Melanchthon reports, the matter will perhaps not be carried so far, but will probably be narrowed down to a few points, and written and treated more briefly. Whatever action shall be taken, whether the former (scil. Confession) be completed or a new one drawn up, shall be reported by us to your worthies."[189]

To his intimate friend, Camerarius, he writes:—

June 19th.

I got hold of the Spanish Secretary, who promises faithfully and has already spoken concerning my view to the Emperor and Campeggius.[190]

To Myconius, Melanchthon disclosed:—

June 19th.

Ego pertentavi unius, atque alterius ex Hispanicis scribis animum ; quantum proficiam videro.

---

[188] *Vid.* June 30th, for the further discussion of this subject.

[189] *C. R.,* II, 112 sq.

[190] *Ib.,* 118 sq.: "Nactus sum Hispanum secretarium, qui benigne pollicetur, et jam de mea sententia cum Cesare et Campegio collocutus est."

Sunday, June 19th.

PRELIMINARY TO THE DIET.

Early on the morning of Sunday, the 19th, about seven o'clock, the princes appeared at the palace and escorted the Emperor[191] to the Cathedral, where he received the sacrament. After the close of the service, the princes went to the Rathaus where Frederick of the Palatinate read off the Propositions of the Diet, which in the afternoon were dictated to the secretaries of the estates.[192]

The Emperor called all the princes to him in the afternoon, and, at the instigation of the Papal Legate, ordered the Elector, as marshal of the Empire, to carry the sword[193] before him in all the ceremonies of the Diet, and particularly at the mass of the Holy Ghost which would open the session on the morrow. The Elector received this message and called together his theologians. He could scarcely refuse, neither could he obey, without dishonoring the Gospel. But the theologians said: "This is a ceremony of the Empire, and you are summoned as court marshal. The Word of God itself, in the case of Naaman, affords you precedent."[194]

Monday, June 20th.

THE OPENING OF THE DIET.[195]

The Emperor and his brother, together with the electors and princes, entered the cathedral and took their seats on the right side of the choir. Opposite them were placed the

---

[191] "The Emperor is said to have prayed very faithfully these days" [*i. e.,* before he took Communion on June 19th].—*Cyprian,* 64.

[192] *Ib.*

[193] Non gratiae missae, sed officii, quod gladium Cæsari præferre ad ipsum pertinet.—*Comment. rerum August. Vindelicar,* II, cap. 65.

[194] *Seck.,* II, 167.

[195] Schirrmacher, *Briefe und Acten;* Förstemann, *Urkundenbuch zu der Geschichte des Reichstags zu Augsburg,* 2 vols. (Halle, 1833-1835); and *Archiv für die Geschichte der kirchl. Reformation* (Halle, 1831); Moritz Facius, *Geschichte des Reichstags zu Augsburg* (Leipzig, 1830).

Legate, the archbishops and the bishops. The ambassadors were in the middle. The Landgrave of Hesse and other Protestants, to abstain from the adoration of the Host, were in a gallery that overlooked the choir.[196] The Elector bore the sword before the Emperor, but remained standing at the moment of adoration.

The Archbishop of Salerno preached the sermon, first against the Turks, and then against the Germans, whom he described as in some respects worse than the Turks. "They tear the seamless coat of Christ: they abolish the sacred doctrines and substitute for them buffoonery."[197] Turning toward the Emperor and his brother the preacher said, "Sharpen your swords against these perverse disturbers, and bring them back into the fold of the church.[198] Germany will have no peace so long as this heresy is not eradicated by the sword. St. Peter, open the stony hearts of these people with your keys. St. Paul, if they become too rebellious, cut their hardness of heart into pieces with your sword." The sermon did not please the Germans. Even the Archbishop of Maintz was offended. But the words of the preacher did not reach the body of the building, and were inaudible to the people.

The Emperor now proceeded to the town hall in his carriage, and sat down on a throne covered with gold. In front of him was Ferdinand, on a bench. Round about him were the electors, forty-two princes, the delegates from the cities, the bishops and embassadors. The Diet was formally opened by a "Speech," or "Proposition," from the throne, in which the Diet was informed (through Count Palatine) that the business was in two parts, first the armament against the Turks, and second that his Majesty desired by fair and gentle means to end the religious differences which were distracting Germany.

The Emperor declared that if the edict of Worms had been observed, the religious difficulties of the realm would not

[196] *Seck.*, II, 119.
[197] Pallavicini, *Hist. Trid. C.*, I, 23.
[198] *C. R.*, II, 120.

have taken on such ! proportions; but that he wished careful consideration be given to the matter now. In form, he adhered to tl plan laid down in his Call, but substantially he was at th mercy of the Romanists.

Referring to the res of the edict of Worms, he asserted that it had led not onl o the contempt of the Emperor himself, but also of Almighty God, to a decline of divinely ordained authority, to the great disadvantage of the estates themselves, and which would result in conflagration, war, and death, as has shown itself in various ways in the German nation, especially in the Peasants' War, and in the disorders of the Anabaptists.

Therefore the Emperor, who perceived these conditions with great sorrow, undertook, in his native goodness and grace, and in accordance with the Call, to guide all things into a better way. Accordingly his Majesty is willing to take up this matter and to deliberate and conclude how both the invasion of the Turk and also the errors and divisions in the Holy Faith may best be handled. In a very friendly and gracious way he now earnestly desires that the electors, princes, and the common estates, in so far as each one of them is concerned, may now present in writing in the Latin and in the German language their opinion and view concerning the error, division, and abuses, in whatsoever the clergy may have grievances against the civil power or the civil power against the clergy or among themselves, in order that the conditons may be harmonized and compared and brought into Christian unity.

After the Speech, the Diet was free for the day. The Elector called a meeting of the Protestant party—its members were excited by the speech—and told them not to turn aside, and exhorted them to be intrepid in maintaining the cause of God.[199] They then made the necessary agreement.[200] Thus ended the first day of the Diet, on Monday night.

---

[199] *Seck.,* II, 108.

[200] *" Nahmen die nöthige Abrede."—Cyprian,* p. 65.

Tuesday, June 21st.

THE ELECTOR PREPARES FOR THE GREAT EVENT. MELANCH-THON'S DISCLOSURE REJECTED.

The Elector arose early this morning and sought spiritual strength in the Word and in fervent prayer to God.[201] He then took up the imperial "Proposition" of the day before for consideration, with his son, Brück and Melanchthon, and came to the conclusion that the Diet ought to attack the religious issue first of all.

"In the afternoon he called his brethren in the faith—the Protestant allies—and consulted with them as to his idea that it was necessary to give the matter of religion precedence in the Diet. He asked them to bring him their views"[202] the next day.

Melanchthon must have felt uneasy at this interview. He had laid his underground line to the heart of the enemies' country—yea, to Rome itself—for the purpose of obviating the very crisis which the Elector and his counsellors had now decided to bring about, viz.: an open Confession and an immediate public discussion in the Diet. He had thrown the Confession aside, and was even not prepared to furnish a copy of it. In consequence of his secret negotiations, the imperial Secretary, the Emperor, and the Papal Legate were now expecting that any public disturbance would be hushed up, and that a settlement would be made in private. In truth Melanchthon was at this moment under imperial instructions to write out a *draft* containing the maximum of Lutheran differences *for the Elector to sign,* and after securing the signature was to hand it, with the approval and consent of the princes, to Valdés, the Spanish secretary.

To carry through such a plan, it was imperative, without an hour's delay, to convince the Elector and the chancellor that the discussion on the subject of religion, and the delivery

---

[201] *Seck.*, II, 169.
[202] *Cyprian*, p. 65.

of a Protestant Confession at Augsburg should be given up, and that a settlement ought to be made in private, as the Emperor requested. The moment had come when Melanchthon must speak.

How Melanchthon broached the subject does not appear. But after hearing the project, Brück waved it aside, if for no other reason than that the abandonment of a public procedure to which they had gained undisputed right, for a private and unguaranteed procedure, might imperil their whole standing before the Diet, and consequently their cause, their churches, and their faith. The strength of their position lay in strict obedience to the Call.[203] This summary rejection of Melanchthon's plan put an immediate end to the private imperial negotiation.

But there was another important matter to consider this morning. It was what the Protestants should do in view of the evidently unfavorable tone of the imperial "Proposition" of yesterday. The Evangelicals decided that it was necessary for them to deny the right of the Diet to come to a final decision on a matter of religion; and to insist that the possibility of appeal to a General Council of the Church must be left clear and open.

In addition to these two points, it was, further, decided to complete a common Confession for the whole Lutheran party, and to draw the counsellors and theologians of the separate Lutheran estates into consultation. And since the Confession was to be that of the whole Church, it was now necessary to lay aside Melanchthon's long Introduction, which he had elaborated so rhetorically, and to substitute a German preface which embodied the relations of all the estates toward the Emperor, written by Chancellor Brück, and translated into German by Jonas.[204]

---

[203] The Nuremberg *Rath* therefore declared that it was necessary to insist on the delivery of the Confession in the *German and Latin* languages.—*C. R.*, II, 123 sq.; *Vogt*, 18, cited by *Kolde*.

[204] *Först.*, I, 460. No copies were made of this translation. Kolde estimates Brück's Preface (which Weber derides) thus: It was composed with much skill, and recapitulated the transactions of the previous decade.

The meeting of the Protestants on this 21st of June, despite the thrilling scenes through which they had already passed, must have been most memorable. With the plan for the future now firmly mapped out, and with the revelation of what Melanchthon had been trying to do during the past week, it left a deep impression on the minds of the estates newly admitted to the consultation. The Nuremberg delegates immediately wrote home and sent a long report of the negotiations that had taken place between Melanchthon and Valdés. Kress had first reported that Melanchthon would "to-day converse" with Brück. But later, in the postscript to this letter, he stated that he had just been called into the hotel of the Elector, where in the presence of the counsellors of Saxony, Brandenburg, Hesse, and Lüneberg, he was informed that they were on the point of "revising, writing, and completing the Articles." Thus the laymen once more set the confessional situation in the centre as the real thing, and went to work immediately to put the Elector's document into such shape that it would become a common and permanent Confession of their Faith.

At this meeting, then, the Emperor's original plan of settling the religious difficulty *in the Diet* was dropped; Melanchthon's plan of placing it into the hands *of the clement Emperor* was providentially frustrated; and the Landgrave's plan of appealing to *a General Council,* together with the completion of *a common Confession* which set forth the Lutheran teaching, and which should contain *the appeal,* was adopted. To harmonize their position with that of the Diet at Spires, on which they had fallen back, the attacks that Melanchthon had made in the Confession upon the "Sacramentarians," and the expressions concerning the "Jurisdiction of the Bishops," were also dropped; but the Landgrave was unsuccessful in gaining a reconsideration of the Tenth Article on the "Mass."

Wednesday, June 22nd.

THE CONFESSION CALLED FOR UNEXPECTEDLY.

The private negotiations, which the Emperor favored so highly, had fallen through. All that Melanchthon was allowed to do was to show Valdés the Confession that had been drawn up for public presentation. Since the Protestants would not take his way, the Emperor would surprise them by calling on them very suddenly for their own way. This was what happened.

To-day the Emperor ordered that the Elector and his party should have their Confession ready by day after to-morrow, Friday. In accordance with the plan of his original Call, the Roman party also were invited to present a Confession, but the Romanists told the Emperor that it was not necessary: they were satisfied with the edict of Worms.[205]

Not since the 11th of May, when Luther was asked to return the Confession with all haste, had there been such pressure put upon the Protestants. During the interim between the negotiations of Melanchthon and the imperial secretary, it had lain neglected. Only yesterday the German Introduction was submitted; and other changes were made. The whole document, and especially the beginning and the ending, were lacking in definite form. Perhaps the archbishop of Maintz[206] could secure for them one day more in which to properly complete it, but this was refused.[207]

So what was left of Wednesday and Wednesday night was given to completing, correcting, and transcribing the Confession.

---

[205] *Wednesday, June 22nd.* "The Romanists declared they had no Confession to hand over. The Evangelicals pointed out that in the Call it was made the duty of both sides to offer a statement on the matter of religion; but the Romanists by no means and in no way would yield to this."—*Cyprian*, p. 65.

[206] When the Elector of Maintz was asked to gain one day's delay, he replied that there was nothing to be asked for, since the Emperor was already disposed to hear the papal legate, Campeggius, and the Evangelicals on that day.—*Ib.*, p. 66.

[207] *C. R.*, II, 127.

THE VERDICT OF VALDES.

Undoubtedly when Melanchthon showed the Confession to Valdés, V. not only declared it too bitter, but reported to the Emperor that the Protestants were going to stand for a Council; and reported the whole Protestant position to Campeggius, who sent it to Rome, where it was discussed by the consistory on July 6th as "The Articles of Melanchthon." The verdict of Valdés served to bring Melanchthon back to work on the document with redoubled zeal, and up to the last moment, in order to smooth out every trace of unnecessary roughness.

Thursday, June 23rd.

REVISING AND SIGNING THE DOCUMENT.

To-day the last reading and the final fixation of the text was undertaken. Bright and early the Lutheran princes, counsellors and theologians assembled at the Elector's hotel.

"On Thursday, the 23rd of June, the representatives of Nuremberg and Reitlingen were requested to come to Saxony, Hesse, Margrave George and Lüneburg; and there the specified Instruction concerning the Faith was read, heard and deliberated on before all the Princes, their counsellors and theologians, whose theologians were twelve, without the other learned men and doctors. The same was to be ordered to be read to-morrow afternoon to his imperial Majesty before the Diet."[208]

The whole Confession, with the new German Preface was read in German and revised. The Epilogue probably was added at this final revision. According to a later communication of Melanchthon the single articles were discussed in order. "Nihil mihi sumpsi. Praesentibus Principibus et aliis gubernatoribus et concionatoribus disputatum est ordine de singulis sententiis."[209]

As Melanchthon wrote to Camerarius on June 26th, he

---

[208] (*Ex diario* f. 31b) *Cyprian,* p. 179.
[209] Mel. in the Vorrede zur *Sammlung s. Reden.*

was changing and improving much on the Confession to the last, and was putting things more mildly because he had learned from Valdés, to whom he had shown it, that it was much too bitter. He says to Camerarius: "I would also have made more changes, if our advisers had permitted. So far from thinking it was written too gently, I am, on the contrary, worried lest some might take offense at our freedom." Finally the whole document was once more discussed and reviewed. All concurred in it except the Landgrave of Hesse and the delegates from Strasburg, who wished the article on the Lord's Supper changed. The princes would not concede this.

The moment was at hand when the document was to be signed. The Elector was about to put his name down, when Melanchthon interposed, and said that the teachers and theologians, as representatives of the Church, should sign the document; but the Elector persisted that his faith was more precious to him than his earthly authority. "I will confess my Christ," said he. Thus John the Steadfast attached his name to the Confession.[210] Sign he would, and did.[211]

John Frederick signed next, but only the Latin text. He was followed by the Margrave George, Duke Ernst, Franz of Lüneburg (the Latin text only). The pen was handed to the Landgrave, who, after some objection, signed, but said to himself at the same time that he was not satisfied with the statement of the article on the sacrament.[212]

The Prince of Anhalt, and the cities of Nuremberg and Reutlingen attached their signatures. "The representatives of Hailspron, Kemten, Winszheim, and Weiszenburg were willing also to confess along side of Nuremberg and the representative of Reitlingen, in the delivered Instruction of

---

[210] Charles, later, refused to invest John with his Electoral dignities in the usual feudal fashion ; and his entourage whispered that if the Elector was not amenable to the Emperor's arguments, he might find the electorate taken from him and bestowed on the kindred House of Ducal Saxony, which in the person of Duke George so stoutly supported the old religion. The threat is recorded in *Archiv für Schweizerische Geschichte und Landeskunde,* I, 278.

[211] *Camer.,* p. 120.

[212] *C. R.,* II, 155.

Faith of the Elector and the other Princes, and they were also ready to sign it; but after taking counsel among themselves, they asked permission for several days' delay." [213]

This small but determined party of Protestant Confessors, who knew that they might be laying down their property, their lands and their lives for their faith; and who would be obliged to appear as an insignificant minority before the combination of the Roman Church and the greatest civil power in Europe, but who desired nothing so much as an open vindication of the truth, their faith, and their honorable name, now determined that they would petition as a concession from the Emperor, that the Confession should be recited forth in public. [214]

Thus these Lutheran laymen, standing squarely for their liberties and their faith, pushed aside the milder plan, and left the Melanchthonian advisers in the background, while they went before the Diet and stood their ground in the sense and spirit of Luther, and not in the sense and the timidity of Melanchthon. When we are told that the Augsburg Confession is not Luther's Confession, and that he was rather its unfriendly critic than its creator; let us at that moment remember that Melanchthon had abandoned it, that he never signed it—was not permitted to become one of the signatories —that, though miles nearer than Luther, he was not present with that little party of heroes on the 25th of June in the bishop's palace when it was given to the world, and is not therefore numbered among its primal Confessors.

Friday, June 24th.

PREPARED, BUT PUT OFF FOR ONE DAY MORE.

The Lutherans came to the Diet to-day ready with their complete "Statement of Grievances and Opinions" relating to the Faith, but they were not permitted to read it, the

[213] (*Ex diario* f. 31b) *Cyprian,* p. 180.
[214] *Seck.,* II, 169.

Romanists seeming to have taken measures to try to crowd it out. First of all, the sitting of the Diet did not begin until three o'clock in the afternoon. The Papal Legate was then announced, and the Emperor went to the top of the staircase to meet him. Taking his seat in front of the Emperor, Campeggius arose to speak. "Never before," said he, "has the ship of St. Peter been so violently tossed in the waves." [215] Then addressing the Emperor, he implored his Majesty to get rid of the Protestant errors, to deliver Germany, and to save Christendom. The Archbishop of Maintz replied to him, and the Legate left the Diet.

Now the Evangelical princes arose to plead their cause, but delegates from other countries who were present were given a hearing. At last the princes arose again,[216] and Chancellor Brück declared that his party was accused of supporting heresy, their good name was compromised, and their souls were in danger, and he therefore begged his Majesty to hear what the doctrines are which they profess. The Emperor declared that the hour was too late,[217] and they should be satisfied to have their Confession delivered in writing. They declared that their souls and their honor were at stake.[218] They were accused publicly and they ought to answer publicly. Charles seemed ready to yield, but Ferdinand[219] prevented him.

Then, for the third time, the Elector and his party vehemently and persistently demanded that they should be allowed to read their Confession for the love of God, and declared that no person was insulted in it. The Emperor was surrounded with a great number of guardians and ecclesiastics;[220] but he finally granted their request, yet said that

---

[215] *Seck.*, II, 169.

[216] " Although evening was already breaking in, they persistently petitioned that their Confession should be heard."—*Cyprian,* p. 67.

[217] "After counsel had been taken with the King and the other Catholic estates."—*Ib.*

[218] *C. R.,* II, 128.

[219] *Seck.*, II, 169.

[220] *Ib.*

as it was now too late, they should send him the written document, and that the next day at two o'clock the Diet would hear it privately in his own palace.[221] The princes refused to give up the Confession on the ground that the work had been done in great haste, and that, before formally giving over the document, it needed revision, which they would undertake during the night.[222] The Emperor yielded, and the Protestants left the Diet with a thankful heart.

Saturday, June 25th.

PRESENTATION AND READING OF THE CONFESSION.

The presentation of the Confession took place in a small chapel, but a great crowd thronged the court without.[223] Only those officially concerned and their attendants were admitted.[224]

It was in the afternoon. There sat his imperial Majesty upon the throne, flanked on either side by the electors, princes and states of the empire. Some of the dignitaries of the Church were there. The scene was impressive.

The Emperor requested the Confession to be read in Latin.[225] "We are Germans," said the Elector of Saxony, "and on German soil; I hope therefore your Majesty will allow us to speak in German". His Majesty acquiesced in his Grace's request. And then Dr. Beyer, one of the Elec-

---

[221] *C. R.,* II, 124.

[222] "But all this was refused, and the immediate delivery was insisted on; but at last, after much deliberating, the Emperor agreed to hear the Confession the following afternoon.—*Cyprian,* p. 67.

[223] *C. R.,* II, 157.

[224] "On Saturday, June 25th, the Emperor, the King, and all the estates, betook themselves, in the afternoon about four o'clock, to the corbeled hall in the court garden of the Bishop of Augsburg, where his Majesty was accustomed to hold the service. . . . No one but the estates and counsellors were permitted to remain. The Evangelical princes arose, to make their Confession standing, but were prevailed on by the Emperor to sit down. The two Electoral Saxon Chancellors then stepped into the middle of the room."—*Cyprian,* p. 68.

[225] *Seck.,* II, 170.

tor's chancellors, read the Confession so loudly and distinctly that the multitude gathered around the outside of the building heard every word.[226] The eyes of many a Roman Catholic were opened. The bishop of the city said, "What has here been read is the pure and unadulterated truth; we cannot gainsay it." [227] The Legate had absented himself, lest his presence be interpreted as authorizing the reading of the Confession;[228] and many others of the Roman clergy did not attend for fear their Church would be sharply criticised.

Charles V. accepted of Chancellor Brück the two copies, handing the German one to the Elector of Maintz and keeping the Latin for himself.[229] The reading had consumed about two hours. The Lutherans rejoiced in having been able to make a good confession before many witnesses. The Emperor's reply was that he would further consider the matter.[230]

The Emperor extended his hand to the Elector and said tenderly, " Uncle, I would not have expected this from you ;" and silently the Elector bowed and, with his eyes full of tears, left the Diet with the Duke of Lüneburg and the Prince of Anhalt. The Emperor departed dissatisfied and resolved to bring the Protestants to obedience both by law and force of arms.

Before parting the Emperor descended his throne, approached the Protestant princes, and earnestly requested them in a low tone not to publish the Confession.[231]

---

[226] Chytraeus, *Hist. Augs. Conf.*, p. 56.

[227] *C. R.*, II, 154.

[228] Sarpi, *Hist. Council Trent*, I, 101.

[229] Neither of them have as yet ever come to light again.

[230] " After the reading of the Confession, which continued for almost two hours, the Emperor, through Frederick Count Palatine, announced to the Evangelicals, in the full Diet, that he would take this important matter into consideration. Hereupon the Evangelicals thanked most obediently for the hearing, the chancellor Brück wished to hand over the German and Latin copies of the Confession to the Imperial Secretary, Alexander Schweisz, that he might place it into the hands of the Elector of Maintz, as the Chancellor of the realm: but the Emperor reached out for them himself, and took both copies, and gave the German to the Chancellor of the realm, but kept the Latin copy for himself."—Spalatin, *Annal. Luth.*, p. 139 ; *Müller*, p. 587 ; *Cyprian*, p. 71.

[231] *C. R.*, II, 143.

THE TOWERING SUMMIT.

The good fight was made, the faith was kept. The Protestants had completed their Evangelical Confession before the Holy Roman Empire. They had stood for truth against the world. The united power of this world's Church and State had failed to move them. Their Confession was the immutable Rock. It was a finality that might be added to, but not taken from. It was a broad and sure foundation to build upon. It was not the building, but the Rock; it was not the full-blown tree but the germ. It was Lutheranism brought to a minimum upon which, when Providence provided a season for inner development, should rise Lutheranism brought to a maximum. Anything less was not the Lutheran Faith; anything more in the line of *legitimate* development, whether it were an Apology or a Formula, would be the Lutheran Faith more highly unfolded.

The real power in the Augsburg Confession lay not in its writing, whether the pen employed were that of counsellor or theologian, but in its content. Its power was not the power of its subjects or phrases, but the power of its truth. Its content was made effective and final by its delivery. It thus became *testimony,* which could not be afterward modified or changed even by the authors, except upon a recantation from conviction of former mistake, or from treachery to the truth brought about by the pressure of practical considerations. He who allows practical considerations to modify the testimony of his conscience is not a confessor of the truth.

The Augsburg Confession was the truth. It was formally and solemnly subscribed. It was delivered, by that heroic electoral group, at the peril of position, popularity and life, because it was the truth. Any subsequent yielding in the men to the terrors of Roman pressure could not alter the testimony to the truth. Nothing done later ever changed it; and even if the mediating efforts of Melanchthon and his committee, in subsequent negotiations, should have modified or overthrown it, its testimony would have towered triumphantly above the succeeding waves of variation stirred up by its unstable confessors; and it would have remained an œcumenical monument of the Gospel Faith of the great Reformation, buried or washed, defaced, scarred, spurned, betrayed; but not injured nor torn from its Scripture pedestal, by those who, like Peter of old, had been so moved by their surroundings as to deny their Faith and their Lord.

IGNORING THE IDEAL IN HISTORY.

As is the case with every other noble work of God and every other noble product of time, it is possible to write down the Augsburg Confession to the level of a mere historical document, transient and temporary, and filled with the imperfections, the lower motives, and the ambiguities of its occasion. But this attempt, like that of all similar effort to weaken and disfigure the great and authoritative monuments and abiding instruments of the race, such instruments as the Magna Charta, the American Declaration of Independence, by overlooking the permanency and overestimating the occasional character of their causes, is a historical perversion.

The attempt to drag down and cheapen the great Confessional standards of our faith, by pointing out and emphasizing the human passions and motives that may have animated the men who were active in their formation, by elaborating and laying stress on the incidental occasions, which, in the hand of Providence, are often slight and minor or even unworthy, instead of upon the real underlying cause; and by surrounding the real standard of Truth attained and confessed, with the great multitude of inferior, unfinished and unsuccessful propositions, and the counterfeits, which nearly always swarm round about a genuine and great work of truth, is not a worthy one, and is not writing history in the true sense of the term.

This attempt has been made against every standard of historical greatness. In our own country, George Washington has been written down to the level of a common, coarse, and unworthy humanity. Cheap side-lights thrown upon the framing of the Declaration of Independence and the Constitution of the United States often have set these instruments in the glare of an unworthy and common-place coloring. The attempt has been made to reduce the divinity of our Lord to an elevated humanity by gathering round about Him great men, *e. g.,* the religious founders of a hoary orient, who apparently stand forth as His equals. The same attempt has been made to write down the history of Israel and its religion to the level of the other ethnic communities around it. The Sermon on the Mount itself, has, according to these depreciators, been proven to be no more than a chrestomathy of the choicest sayings of pagan antiquity.

In any sphere, it is nearly always possible, by judicious selection, to raise up a multitude of the second best and the counterfeit productions of a people or a religion in such a way as to disparage, and apparently to take away the supremacy of the original. For the original, despite its greatness, its truth and its purity, cannot escape, so long as it is in this world, showing some contact with the sin and weakness of human nature.

But the great question in deciding on the real merits of an acknowledged standard is not how far it can be weakened down, or how near it comes in certain points to its inferiors. To attempt to show this is not in accord with a true historical method, but is essentially the method of skepticism, used for purposes of undermining faith in that which is really good. The question is not whether the foundation is covered with the shifting sands of time, or is strewn with the defective spawls and rejected boulders of the workshop, but the question is whether, beneath all these, the real solid rock is still standing. The effort to level and destroy men's faith in the Word of God, in miracle, in the Person of Christ, in the Lord's Supper, in the great and wholesome political, historical, or

31

Confessional foundations of the past, is at the very least pessimistic, and owes its origin to something outside of genuine Faith.

If the comparative method is to be applied to the Augsburg Confession and the Symbols of the Church, let it bring forth the clear distinction between the genuine Confession and the defective compromises that were constantly being put forth by wavering confessors within the Church.

He is a poor interpreter of pure art who would set up the perfectly chiseled and immortal statue amid the partly hewn and rejected blocks that had been its companions previous to its completion; and would strew it over with the chips and the dust which had fallen from it in the sculptor's shop, and would say to us: See, it is no more and no better than the varied and motley stones from which it has sprung.

THE TWO PERSONALITIES OF THE REFORMATION.

The unpartisan historian, the unprejudiced Lutheran and the true Church will recognize that there are virtues and faults in both of the leading historical characters of the Reformation. They will seek to appreciate and appropriate the virtues, and not to combine and propagate the faults of both. Luther's sound and uncompromising confessional faith, his complete subjection to God's Word, his deeply spiritual and peaceful spirit, his reliance on prayer rather than on human propositions and combinations in time of crisis and danger; united with Melanchthon's moderation and inoffensiveness in public statement, and his veneration for the catholic past, will develop for us the Lutheran Church at its best. On the other hand, to combine Melanchthon's spirit of compromise in faith, his evasiveness and use of ambiguous forms in confession, his desire to be with the stronger party and his wish for external union, with the violence, heated zeal and spirit of personal attack of Luther is to give us a church with all the faults and without the virtues of both Reformers.

The Lutheran Church has suffered much by making of her Confessional question a case of credit in authorship, rather than a case of Confession of truth. Individuals do not figure here. In the last analysis, temperaments, accidents of history, and elements underlying a human situation, turn out to be but instruments of Providence for the establishment of God's immutable purpose. In the establishment of the Lutheran Confession, let each man have his credit, but let it not be forgotten that Providence overruled the weakness of every man, and overcame the human probabilities of every situation, and that nowhere in history does the glory belong more clearly to God alone.

Luther was not a narrow-minded man. He prized the powers of Melanchthon above his own. It was he who said: "All the Jeromes, Hilarys, and Macariuses together, are not worthy to unloose the thong of Philip's sandal. What have the whole of them together done which can be compared with one year of Philip's teaching, or to his one book of Common Places? . . . I prefer Melanchthon's books to my own. . . . It is my work to tear up the stumps and dead roots, to cut away the thorns, to fill up the marshes. I am the rough forester and pioneer. But Melanchthon moves gently and calmly along, with his rich gifts from God's own hand, building and planting, sowing and watering." [232]

He also said: *"Res et verba Philippus; verba sine re Erasmus; res sine verbis Lutherus; nec res nec verba Carolostadius."* Such an estimate, declares Warfield, who is not a confessional Lutheran, but a Presbyterian, "was more than kind to Melanchthon, in so far at least as the comparison with Luther himself was concerned. It was to Luther in no small measure that Melanchthon owed his capacity for deeds; without Luther to wield the weapons which he forged in his intellectual armory, it is to be feared that the fires in the forge would often have gone out. He

---

[232] Pref. to Melanchthon, *Colossians.*

shares from their close comradeship a large part of Luther's fame as the herald of intellectual and religious freedom, yet, by the temperate spirit which animated his words and acts, escapes the hostility so often stirred by his rash and rough-spoken leader." [233]

Plitt puts the situation more pointedly. He says that Luther was not the composer of the Confession, but in full justice he can be called 'the father of the Confession,' and Melanchthon himself, 'the composer of the phraseology.' [234] "Looking at it in this light, the view now current, which has desired to speak of a Melanchthonian character of the confession," says Plitt, "in order thereby to depreciate its Lutheran character, is thoroughly unhistorical and groundless."

THE HAND OF PROVIDENCE.

When we come to sum up the creation of the Augsburg Confession, with its question of authorship, we can scarcely fail to see that rarely in the history of the world or the Church has the Hand of Providence guided the principals in a great act of testimony so evidently, and so apart from their original intention, and so completely eliminated that which was partial and unfit and retained that which was the clear, full and objective truth of God, as has been the case in the elaboration of the Augsburg Confession.

The Emperor was the impelling cause of its origin. He ordered the Elector to prepare an irenical statement of his differences in religious faith and usages, in writing, and in

---

[233] *Pres. and Ref. Rev.*, 29. 1.

[234] This is also the phrase used by Lindsay, *Hist. of the German Reformation.* We do not, ourselves, believe that this phrase does Melanchthon proper justice. While felicity and objectivity of statement were Melanchthon's forte, and his creative power was weak, he nevertheless was the prince of diplomatists and adjusters. In addition to the phraseology, to Melanchthon belongs the credit of the effective disposition, and even of the partial selection of material; of the general spirit of moderation and breadth, the entire absence of personal sting, and the perfect adaptation—except a number of egregious failures where he was checked by Brück and the other counsellors—to the situation.

But to orate as the illuminated rational critic Weber does, in behalf of the Melanchthonian authorship of the Augsburg Confession betrays a bias in a professedly impartial investigator which is only surpassed in that prince of

two documents, the one in the Latin and the other in the German language.

The Elector was its executive and directive source. He decided that Luther and the other theologians should furnish the material. He decided that he would stand all alone in this matter, and he perhaps decided that it should be an Electoral Apology, and not a common Protestant Confession. He also decided for reasons previously given that Luther should remain at Coburg, and that Melanchthon should accompany him to the scene of the Confession. He was opposed to admitting Philip of Hesse and the Bavarians, and still more so the Zwinglians, to his Apology.

Luther was the substantial cause and author of the Confession, not merely in the sense that the Lutheran doctrine was his, but that he was the chief personality in the composition of both the Schwabach and the Torgau Articles, which constitute the substance of the Augsburg Confession.

Melanchthon was the framing and adaptive author. He was not the mere scribe or secretary of the Elector, but he had the serious constructive responsibility of taking the cue from the situation, of eliminating polemic, temporal and subjective elements from both the faith and the situation, and bringing them face to face at the right point of contact. His higher and independent work, however, was a failure and had to be rejected; and the Confession ultimately reverted to the old foundation of Luther.

John Eck and the Roman enemies of Protestantism were, in the hand of God, directly responsible for turning the

partisan Confessional historians, Dr. Johannes Wigand, Bishop of Pomesan in Prussia (*Historia de Augustana Confessione, breviter* recitata in Academia Regiomontana) (1574). For instance, Weber says, " When did it ever occur to anyone to derogate from La Fontaine or from Racine or from Corneille, because they borrowed their material, the one from fables, the others from history? Yet this is just the tone which so many older and newer theologians have struck since the exaltation of 'the Bergian Book of Concord.' All sorts of grounds have been suggested to detract from Melanchthon's work and to turn it into the service of a secretary. Thus Melanchthon is supposed simply to have put the Confession into a certain form from the Seventeen Articles, which the highly illumined man of God, Mr. Luther, had composed beforehand. . . . I account it as one of the consequences of the Bergian Book of Concord, that men, since its day, have attempted to make Melanchthon's part in the Augsburg Confession smaller and smaller, and to derogate from it."

Apology as a mere explanation of ecclesiastical customs and a plea for imperial grace into a full-orbed Confession of the Lutheran faith. Philip of Hesse and the other Protestant estates contributed their important share to the confession in changing it from a private Electoral document into a Common Confession of the Lutheran Churches, against the Elector's will and against Melanchthon's desire and judgment.

The Chancellor Brück was the author of the policy of the Confession, and its revising editor. He was the man who insisted on giving it full and independent standing as a Confession of faith, and who would not yield to Melanchthon's desire to abandon the public Confession and commit, in a private manner, the future into the Emperor's hands. Thus was the Emperor's original plan as to the document which after a friendly comparison was to bring back Protestantism into the Roman Church, and which gained the sympathy and approval of Melanchthon, offset by Luther and by the sturdy Elector. Thus also were Luther's personal and polemic tone (*Vid.* the *Admonition*) and lack of judicial attitude offset by the Elector; while the Elector's narrowness and isolation, as well as Melanchthon's unwillingness to openly confess regardless of consequences, were checked by the Emperor's passion stirred by Eck and Wimpina; and by the firmness and insistency of the Protestant Estates thrown together into a common danger.

" He who in all this," says Cyprian,[235] after showing that the Confession was prepared by the aid and participation of all the estates, " does not recognize any Divine working, support and encouragement, must if he be acquainted with the history, surely be setting himself against the testimony of his own conscience."

It is clear as day that Providence, in the course of events, eliminated the imperfections in the mind and plan of every one of the principal parties, and allowed that which was true, sound and catholic in their purpose to abide. We may

[235] *Hist.,* 57.

thank the Emperor, as the instrument of God, for the Confession; and the Lord Himself for its unyielding independence. We may thank the Elector for the fidelity of the Confession, and the Lord for its universality. We may thank Luther for the sound Faith of the Confession, and the Lord for its impersonal objectivity. We may thank Melanchthon for the selection and adaptation of material, and for the perfect and abiding form of the Augustana, and for its exclusion of the Reformed teaching, and the Lord that Melanchthon was not left to his own judgment on any point connected therewith. We may thank Brück for keeping the Confession out of imperial politics; and Philip of Hesse for making it a common Lutheran document. And no matter how we approach the Augsburg Confession, the quarrels as to individualities sink into insignificance before the great Confessional fact itself, and the Hand that guided it through dangers on every side to a triumphant completion far above the expectation of participating friend or foe. *This is the Lord's doing,* and it is marvelous in our eyes.

CHAPTER XX.

THE LUTHERAN CONFESSION.

THE AUGSBURG CONFESSION PRESERVED UN-ALTERED.

Melanchthon in Tears: Their Cause—Luther in Peace, Its Cause; Ready to Stand by the Confession even to Martyrdom—Was Melanchthon Open-hearted to Luther?—The Correspondence between Augsburg and Luther from June 25th to July 1st, and Luther's Attempt to Counteract Melanch-thon's Lack of Faith—The Diet—The Course of Events to the Confutation—The Attempts at Compromise under Melanchthon—Their Failure, and the Departure of the Elector.

III Period. The Summer at Augsburg.[1]

THE MYSTERY OF MELANCHTHON'S TEARS.

THE Confession was delivered. The Protestant cause had triumphed. One might suppose that above all others, Philip Melanchthon would have been exultant in spirit, and would have shared in the universal rejoicing. But it was not so. Strangely enough he was plunged into the deepest woe, and his eyes were *fountains of tears.*[1a]

Anyone who ponders this phenomenon, will gain an insight into the character of Melanchthon, which will go far to explain much that occurred in the history of the Lutheran Church for the next thirty years, that is until the death of Philip.

In the first place, we find here the situation of a man who is the unwilling author of an immortal work, and who would have prevented its appearance .if he could. Not only had he thrown aside the Confession during the last ten days, but

---

[1] For the three periods, *vid.,* p. 342.
[1a] *Melanchthon to Luther,* June 26th.

from the very start he had preferred not to have an open Confession of differences, and was hoping against hope for a return of Lutheranism into the bosom of Rome.

Further, we see here a man sought out by the Romanists shortly after his arrival at Augsburg, and he had all these days been cultivating relations with them, and from him they had gained the impression that only a few changes were necessary in order to restore harmony and unity. His reputation for insight as a prophet, and his character as a man of influence among his own people, were, so to say, at stake before the other side, from the Emperor and the papal Legate at the head, all the way down. While his gifted and balanced mind was revealed in the Confession, *his heart* was outside of it, so far as it was a document to be adhered to in practical life. Like other pragmatists or theologians of expediency, he did not see the inconsistency between officially confessing one set of truths, and practically tolerating another. As he had made the effort of his life to prevent its appearance, he would not rejoice at its delivery, on which occasion he was not present, as he intimates in one of his letters to Camerarius.

But above all, it was his fear lest an open statement of the truth bring about war, for which he had a mortal terror, and his thought that the Protestants were few and in the minority, and his party despised at court, that caused him anxiety.

To this, fourthly, must be added the fact that the poor man was nervous and worn to the last extreme. Every effort and every change of tactics had burned its way through his soul: for he was in theology and letters the leader of his party. He had been carrying on a double policy, one private and the other public, each contradictory of the other, at one and the same time. Now, against his will, the Confession was made, and to him it looked as though the Protestants might fall into great straits. He was fatally possessed of the idea that the two parties in the church must get together.

In order to do this, however reluctant, he was willing to

pay the price, to sacrifice some truth. He knew that Luther was not willing, and this increased his difficulty. To him a united church, that is union with Rome, was of more account, under the pressure of political emergency, than mere theoretical principle. When it came to the question between breaking the peace or sacrificing the doctrine he was ready, in order to gain the former, to bargain for a compromise which would hold on to as much of the latter as possible. With him a platform on which the Protestants might stand was something to negotiate for, and was not purely a testimony of conscience. The Confession was something to be adhered to abstractly, but which, for the sake of unity, could be modified in actual practice. Thus he prefigured that element in the Lutheran Church, which, in order to preserve peace and a visible ecclesiastical unity, is ambiguous in its Confessional principle, and does not regard the Lutheran Confession as a testimony of conscience.

Since the peace to be secured was a matter of bargaining in doctrine and usage, and the question was how great a price the Protestants were willing to offer, his very first inquiry of Luther was, what Luther would be willing to give up in the Confession which had just been made, for the sake of peace with Rome. This inquiry went forth at the time of the delivery of the Confession, and four days later, as soon as Luther received it, he hurried the reply back to Melanchthon, "So far as I am concerned, more than enough has been yielded in that Apology. . . . I am more and more confirmed in the purpose that I will yield nothing more, come what may."

As to the *further course* of the Confessional struggle itself, Melanchthon had reason to be troubled. This was a fifth cause for despondency. The Romanists would give answer; and who would there be at Augsburg to prepare a theological defense but poor Melanchthon? His intuition proved to be correct: for he quickly resumed further negotiations, and on his weary shoulders fell the burden of preparing an Apology to the Confutation; and thus when the cause, as a matter of testimony, had triumphed on June 25th, Melanchthon was but entering the crisis out of which, by the grace of God, there arose the crowning work of his life.

Another important fact is this, that Melanchthon was much concerned for the immediate visible future and for posterity. He was one of those mortals who seem to feel that the world will go to ruin unless things are decided in accord with their judgment. Luther wrote to Jonas that he should try to dissuade Melanchthon from the thought that he was the regent of the whole world. Nowhere does the distinction between Luther and Melanchthon loom up more clearly than in a great crisis. Luther gave himself with all his soul to communion with the Lord: Melanchthon gave himself to innumerable consultations, plans, policies, and arrangements for turning the tide of events in accord with the methods of men. As a result, Luther was mighty in the strength of God in every critical moment: Melanchthon was weak, careworn, unsettled, and unnerved, fearful lest the plans he had laid would miscarry, and the worst would befall. Round about the soul of Luther there swayed the atmosphere of Heavenly peace.

LUTHER'S SATISFACTION.

Luther cared little for the political adjustment and defense of his cause. Consequently he had taken so slight an interest in the Electoral Apology, and in the Diet itself. With him faith was a question of conscience, and he did not want it to be hampered or adjusted by imperial politics. He was overjoyed therefore when he heard the tidings of a public and uncompromised delivery of the full Evangelical Confession of Faith. "I am exceedingly happy," he wrote to Cordatus,[2] "to have lived to this hour, in which Christ has been preached through His valiant confessors, in such open manner and in so great an Assembly, by means of this really extraordinary

---

[2] *Luther to Cordatus,* July 6th.

beautiful Confession, and the word is fulfilled: 'I will speak of thy testimony before kings;' also this is fulfilled: 'I was not put to shame.' For 'Whosoever shall confess me before men, him will I confess before my Father which is in Heaven.' "

Just as he would not and could not recant at Worms, so a step backward would be impossible at Augsburg. "Our Confession," he said, "will penetrate into every court, and the sound thereof will spread through the whole earth." [3]

Though Luther, if it had been his own, would have set the Confession in a different frame, and would not have brought down the Evangelical doctrine to a minimum, now that the Confession was accepted by him, and had become history, he held it as the final answer of Protestantism to the Roman Emperor. He was the one of all others who saw that the work was done. In his eyes it was not merely final, but glorious. There was nothing more to be said, nothing to be added, and nothing to be taken away.

Above all other things, his clear insight told him that there was nothing to be negotiated. He knew that the Romanists, even if they were beaten in diplomacy, would not do more than pretend to yield. He saw that the break must come. He wanted it to come before the conscience of Protestantism was defiled by insincerity.

He was ready for martyrdom or war as the case might be. With far-sighted intuition, he pressed it into the soul of his party at Augsburg that this was not a time for parley. Melanchthon's first words to him, in conveying the tidings that the Confession had been delivered, revealed the fatal misconception that was swaying the mild but head-strong Præceptor. If Melanchthon were allowed to remain at the Diet, he would continue to exercise his fatal propensity for diplomacy, and would yield compromise after compromise.

---

[3] Copies of the Confession were sent by the Emperor to all the Courts of Europe, and he himself had it translated into Italian and French (*C. R.*, II, 155). It was also translated into Spanish and Portuguese, and, later, in 1536, by Taverner, into English, American ed. edited by Jacobs.

There was only one thing to be done, and that was to get the electoral party away from Augsburg. "I absolve you from this Diet in the name of the Lord," he wrote them. "Come back home. I want to be the sacrifice of this newest Council as John Huss was at Constance." He foresaw that Melanchthon, in his present temper, and with his dread of war, would give up everything for the sake of peace.

Already on June 29th he wrote Melanchthon, " so far as I am concerned, *more than enough has been yielded in that Apology,* which if they refuse, I see nothing more which I can yield, unless they furnish clearer reasons and Scripture proofs than I have yet seen. Day and night I am occupied with the matter, thinking over it, revolving it in my mind, arguing, searching the entire Scriptures, and there grows upon me constantly that *fulness of assurance in our Doctrine, and I am more* and more *confirmed in the purpose, that I will yield nothing more, come what may.* . . .

The next day, on June 30th, he wrote Brentz that he was afraid that Brentz too would weaken, under the influence of Melanchthon in the presence of the Diet.

Luther has no dread of martyrdom: "God will rule the world better when I am dead than if I should continue to live, since I am hindering Him by my life." On the same day he wrote Agricola:—

"I judge that the Diet will have a bad end. The Emperor will ask the Elector to give up the whole doctrine, as they gave up the preaching ; if he refuses, there will be an interdict against the doctrine. This will bring on the real crisis of the Diet. For it is quite certain that the papists, who are under the control of the devils, are furious. . . . I believe that they have incited the Emperor to grant us a hearing, so that after they have heard our defense they can carry out what they please, under the excuse that they had given us fair enough chance. You have to do at Augsburg not with men but with the gates of hell itself."

To the Elector he wrote on the same day, "I admonish you not to be stirred by their wicked assaults." On June 30th, he writes, "I am filled with joy and rejoice exceedingly at the extraordinary and great gift of God, in that our Prince is so steadfast and composed in his disposition, for I regard my prayers offered for him as having been pleasing to God and prophesy that they will be heard in other things."

To Jonas he wrote of the Roman party, "There is no hope that they can be changed. I am glad that they are growing more obstinate. Let us only remain bold in Christ. He lives, and we shall also live, even though we shall be dead. He will care for the children and wives of those who are martyred. If I am called, I will surely come." This was on June 30th, immediately after he had received the tidings of the delivery of the Confession. But Melanchthon, while he felt that he was being martyred daily, as he expressed it, had no desire or taste for the real sacrifice which a heroic faith is willing to make. In his heart there rose a reign of terror, and in times such as these, he felt it almost impossible to sustain himself without leaning on the stronger faith of Luther.

WAS MELANCHTHON FRANK TOWARD LUTHER IN HIS REPORTS OF THE DIET?

Was Melanchthon frank toward Luther during the month of June? Did he have a good conscience as to the advices he had sent Luther?

Whether he sought to conceal his plans from the Elector, "the old man,"—of whom he writes disrespectfully, "who is hard to soften,"—and whether his private policy by which he entered into an understanding with the Emperor and the papal legate were marked by duplicity, does not clearly appear. He did take Jonas into confidence, and the Protestant party was acquainted with his ideas, and possibly his actions, to some extent. The question is, to what extent? But we do know that Luther was not dealt with squarely in this matter. A careful examination of Melanchthon's letters to Luther will show that Melanchthon was accustomed to understate or discount his own desire and plan as much as possible, so that, although his plan was quite contrary to Luther's nature, yet, in his account of it, it was made to seem to be harmless; and Luther was pressed to grant permission or give approval by return post on insufficient knowledge of the case. A study of Melanchthon's method of communicating information to Luther will repay the reader, and will doubtless satisfy his mind as to whether Melanchthon's reports of the situation were unbiased and open.

So far as we know, no one has ever questioned the openness and the thorough veracity of Luther; but Luther himself seems, at last, to disbelieve the statements that Melanchthon was making to him respecting the misunderstandings connected with the mysterious difficulties of correspondence that occurred several weeks before and during the meeting of the Diet. How could Melanchthon write to Luther with a good conscience when he was intriguing with Rome, and when he was trying to hush up the truth concerning which Luther was so eager to testify? When it comes to the unpleasant need of falling back upon the rock at Coburg, when Luther is to write and influence others, or when his permission on any point is to be gained, then Melanchthon approaches Luther with evaluated statements, and places the answer he wants from Luther into Luther's mouth.

The break in correspondence during the month of June is a mystery. Some wrongly have supposed that Brück or the Elector prevented the delivery of letters between Luther and Melanchthon during this interval. We have pointed out physical causes for the delay, and among these are to be reckoned the great amount of work which fell upon Melanchthon during this time; but after all, there is something additional, as Luther surmises, and from which Melanchthon tries to defend himself.

It is natural that at the close of the Delivery of the Augsburg Confession, the party in Augsburg should wish to communicate the fact to their friends, and we find more letters written in the several days following the Delivery of the

Confession than had passed between Coburg and Augsburg during the whole month of June.

The letters of Jonas disclose the fact, that, if those of the Protestant party who were afraid of the danger could have been convinced, Luther might have been called to the Diet by a special herald, and that Luther was holding himself in readiness to come. It was probably his sense of obedience to his civil ruler, protector, and friend, who had placed him at Coburg, that held him back from a sudden appearance in the midst of the danger. While the appearance of Luther would have acted as a bomb to Melanchthon's plans, yet it is not likely, even if Melanchthon and the Elector had been willing to bring him, that the Emperor could have been persuaded to admit his presence. Luther would have gone the way of Huss. He was prepared for this, but Melanchthon shrank from it.

A charitable view of Melanchthon's case is that expressed by Luther himself in the letter to Jonas on June 30th: " It is Philip's philosophy and nothing else that gives him trouble. For the matter is in the hand of Him Who is able to say to the proudest: 'No one shall pluck them out of my hand.' "

June 25th.

THE FLOOD OF CORRESPONDENCE.

Let us attempt to follow the correspondence as it flowed out from Augsburg on the glorious 25th of June. First of all in the morning, Jonas, the favorite correspondent of Luther, had written him a full running account of events of the day before, and of what would probably to-day come to pass. Listen to his warm-hearted narrative:—

JONAS TO LUTHER.

Cölestin, I, 135.

June 25th, 1530.

Yesterday [June 24th] the Emperor met with the electors and estates of the realm in the town hall and heard Cardinal Campeggius speak. His address was not long. He admonished the Germans to peace, and that they should fight the Turks. He did not allow anything adverse to the Lutherans to enter his speech. Just about this time an embassy from Austria appeared showing how their property and families were placed in peril of their life every moment through the Turk. Their complaint was read while Ferdinand was sitting by.

This day had also been set apart for our princes that they might bring in the articles of their Confession; and they have subscribed it: our Elector, the young princes, then the Margrave George, Duke Ernst of Lüneburg, the prince of Hesse, the prince and lord of Annhalt, the council of Nuremberg and the council of Reutlingen.

The Landgrave insisted strongly that the articles should be read loud and clearly before his Majesty and the estates, but King Ferdinand, during the session, brought first this and then that item upon the tapis. He whispered into the ears of others, and did not cease until the reading was hindered for this day.

Nevertheless this afternoon at two o'clock, when the meeting will not be largely attended, our articles are to be read before some of the princes in the imperial chamber.

We still hope, if his Majesty will graciously investigate the matter, although I do not know whether it will happen, since he has so many cardinals about him; yet we still hope that you, dearest father, will be summoned hither by a herald. I cannot say how many words of fleshly prudence are being used, as though you would not be safe here from secret violence; but as God has already done great wonders we will now not let our courage sink. Although I myself would not like to cause you suffering in such a difficult affair and to undertake the dangerous journey, but the Lord will rule everything.

There are six cardinals here, and many theologians and Spanish bishops. The cardinal and bishop of Trient and Salzburg, the cardinal of Maintz, the bishop and cardinal of Rasano, the Pope's legate to King Ferdinand: these all are in the Emperor's palace every day, and besides these there is a whole swarm of clergy who encircle his Majesty like bees and are daily enkindled with new hatred against us and you, and do nothing else but burn like fire among the thorns.

At exactly the same time, viz., on the 25th, before the delivery of the Confession, the Elector informed Luther of events up to the hour of writing, as follows:—

THE ELECTOR TO LUTHER.

Chytraeus, p. 54; Cölestin, I, 139.

June 25th.

We were ordered to deliver our Opinion and Confession of Faith in common with the other princes and estates. The opposite party, it is reported, will not deliver a Confession, but will announce their intention to abide by the Edict, and by the faith which they have inherited from their fathers. But if the Pope or his legate, together with his Majesty, should ask them to accept a new faith, very graciously would they be willing to do so.

32

Accordingly we appeared on the day of John the Baptist with ours before the Emperor and the King in open audience, and offered our Articles in Latin and German, the German to be read publicly.

In spite of our persistent appeal, we could not attain to the point of having the Articles read openly. The King and the other party most actively opposed us, but we gained so much, that his Majesty will hear these same Articles in his palace. This is arranged thus to prevent the presence of a multitude.

Almighty God, grant us Thy grace, that matters will result to Thy honor. Pray God diligently for us.

We will let you know further how matters develope, for we are most favorably disposed toward you. Datum, Augsburg, June 25th, 1530.

June 26th.

WHY LUTHER FELT HURT.

The day after the reading of the Confession was Sunday. But it brought no peace to poor Melanchthon. It was a day of woe. For he learned that Luther was seriously offended at him—so stirred in fact that he would not even glance at the letter which Melanchthon had written him a week ago. Dietrich had sent this news down from Coburg.[4]

Luther had his reasons for feeling hurt. Matters at Augsburg were approaching a crisis, but during all these days Melanchthon had proceeded according to his own judgment, and, instead of advising with Luther, had observed absolute silence.[5] It was now the 26th of June. Melanchthon had written him on the 22nd of May.[6]

Luther had received this letter, but no more. When Apel's express drew up at Coburg en route for Wittenberg, Luther found not a line for himself, "Do you bring no letters?" the messenger was asked. "No," said he. "How

---

[4] *C. R.,* II, 140 sq.

[5] On Melanchthon's behalf it should be said that the situation changed so rapidly, that advice from a distance would only add to the confusion ; and this would be an adequate explanation if Melanchthon had fairly reported and discussed the greater questions which did not change so quickly.

[6] *C. R.,* II, 59. This letter went to Coburg by special through-express to Wittenberg.—Kolde, *Analecta,* p. 126. Luther had received it, and referred to it in his letter to Probst of June 1st, already given. See footnote on the Luther-Mel. correspondence for the letter Melanchthon wrote Luther on June 13th.

are the men at Augsburg?" said Luther. "Well," ' said the messenger. Then Luther sat down on the 2nd of June and wrote Melanchthon that he was receiving too many visitors, and that their Augsburg friends should keep quiet about him in their letters.

The next day, June 3rd, he wrote Melanchthon again, but not a line came in from Augsburg. One day there came riding in an "express on horseback whose destination was Torgau. He brought a letter from the Prince, and was asked—

" 'Did you bring letters?' He answered, 'No.' 'How are the men?' 'Well.' Then, as a wagon with venison left here, I again wrote to Philip. *The man returned likewise without an answer.*

"Now I began to entertain sad thoughts, and supposed that you wished to conceal from me something evil.

" In the fourth place, came Jobst Nymptzen. When asked, 'Did you bring letters?' he answered, 'No.' 'How are the men?' He answered, 'Well.' I told him how our laborer here received letters from his brother, the Marshall of Falkenstein, while we in the meantime hungered and thirsted over three weeks during your kind silence. Out of this laborer's letters we were obliged to gather such information as we could when we wished to know anything of affairs at Augsburg." [8]

On the 18th or 19th, Melanchthon did at last get off a letter to Luther. It was four days after the imperial entry,

---

[7] Thus *Luther* himself to *Spalatin,* June 30th.

[8] The quixotic supposition of Rückert and others that some of the letters of Melanchthon to Luther were intercepted by Brück, is groundless. (See Kolde, *Ztschr. f. h. Th.,* 1874 H. 3). Melanchthon had really neglected writing from May 22nd to June 13th (compare also his own admission, *C. R.,* IV, 1008). Rückert has entirely overlooked this letter of June 13th; and the assertions of Jonas (Kolde *Anal.,* 139). Melanchthon's neglect is to be explained by his being overworked and driven from post to pillar. How he could say on June 25th, that he had written singulis septimanis, has been explained. That he had not written for some time *before* June 13th, he overlooked in thinking of the letter of the 13th, which he believed to be in the hands of the nevertheless angry Luther, and probably he could not exactly recall the dates of the earlier letters. Moreover Brück, who was so often offended at Melanchthon's wavering attitude, would be the last man in the world to intercept a correspondence that would brace up Melanchthon as did the letters of Luther.—Köstlin, *Martin Luther,* II, 656.

which Melanchthon pictured, with the three days' disputation on the preaching and its result, and the unfavorable complexion of the Diet. He closed with the statement, " that a certain Spanish confidential secretary has promised everything good, and has already held a conference with the Emperor and Campeggius concerning my Opinion. Everything depends on God. Keep well."

This was the letter that Luther refused to open and read, which fact reported by Dietrich reached Melanchthon on June 25th, and which caused him to turn to Luther in tears. Melanchthon's misery appears more clearly in his letter, which we append, than we are able to describe it:—

MELANCHTHON TO LUTHER.

Cölestin, II, 196.

Sunday, June 26th.

We are here in the greatest distress, and must constantly shed tears; and to-day, in addition, our spirits were cast down to the deepest extreme, for we have read the letters of M. Veit, in which he gave us to understand that you are so angry at us that you are unwilling to read our letters.

Now my dear father, I will not still further increase my pain with words, but I beg you to consider in what place we are, and by what dangers we are surrounded, and that without your encouragement we can have no source of strength. The sophists and monks are running about every day and try to prejudice the Emperor against us. The bishops with one accord hate us awfully. Those who were on our side before, are so no more, and we are swaying in endless dangers, altogether forsaken and despised.

I therefore beg you that you will have regard for us, who follow your judgment in such weighty matters, or for the common good, and will read and answer our letters, so that you may support us with good advice, and uphold us with encouragement.

We have handed our Defence over to the Emperor, and I am sending it herewith for you to read. So far as I can see, it has been made sufficiently sharp; for you will note that I have painted the monks in living colors.

But now the point is, as I believe, how to reach a decision, before our antagonists answer it, *as to what we are willing to yield* in the matter of two forms, of marriage, of private mass. The whole transaction will probably turn upon these points. Answer concerning this, and particularly concerning the private mass, as it probably will not be allowed to drop out of sight.

I have sent off this messenger at my own expense, and not long ago I sent a special one, but he came back again empty. Our antagonists are al eady taking counsel as to what they will answer. Therfore everything is uncertain. Sunday.

PHILIPPUS.

FROM COBURG TO CAMERARIUS.

There was urgent need of writing this letter. It bears the new Confession delivered the day before, and with it, in the same breath, a request to answer *as to "what we are willing to yield"* in the two forms of the sacrament, as to the marriage of priests, and as to the celebrating of private masses.

In writing to Camerarius that day Melanchthon had a more congenial task, and we feel that the letter, though anxious, is in a different tone. It reads as follows:—

MELANCHTHON TO CAMERARIUS.

Printed in Mel. Epist. ad. Camerarius, p. 139; C. R., II, 140.

June 26th.

Yesterday by the grace of God our Confession was delivered to the Emperor, and was read openly ; and it is said that there was an unexpected silence and attention among the princes. I was changing and improving it much every day, and I would also have made still more changes, if our counsellors had allowed it ; and so little do I think that it has been written too mildly that I am much more concerned lest some will take offense at our liberty; for before we delivered it, the imperial secretary of Valdés saw it and pronounced the judgment that it was much too bitter and biting for the opposite side to be able to endure.

My soul is filled with great and terrible anxiety, not concerning our affair, but concerning the absence of concern in our people. Only do not be anxious as to me, for I have commended myself to God.

But there is something peculiar that has given me much to think about; but of which I can only speak to you by word of mouth. I wish you could get our Apology to read, but the Emperor forbids that it be printed. Again commending you to God.

PHILIP.

June 27th.

A STUNNING SURPRISE.

The next day, June 27th, Monday, Melanchthon had another stunning surprise. In an interview with Schepper, the German Secretary, he learned that the intentions of the imperial court were to deal sternly with the Evangelical party, and to grant no concessions at all. It had a crushing effect on him.   Jonas tells the whole story just as it occurred:—

JONAS TO LUTHER.

Enders, VII, 387.

Recently the cardinal of Salzburg summoned Philip to a confidential interview, through Wolfesgang Stromer of Nuremberg; and when Philip came back from him in a very much heated condition he told us, although it was at two o'clock in the morning, what they had spoken of to each other. "I have," said Philip, "heard the most extreme threats, and everything but a sentence of death. . . . The Emperor will not tolerate us, the disturbers of the common peace. They are as sure as though there were no God. It is surprising how they trust to human might, and how we are nothing but ants in their eyes."

Philip and I were with Cornelius Schepper, who is now the imperial secretary, who said: If you have money, it will be easy for you to buy from the Italians whatever religion you like; but if your coffers are empty, your cause is lost. He also said: It is impossible that the Emperor, who is now surrounded by cardinals and bishops, would accept any other religion, or content himself with any other than that of the Pope. So thoroughly has the old faith been drilled into his head.

Melanchthon had written Luther on the 26th, but uneasy at the attitude of Luther, he follows it up with two others on the 27th. The one he sends with Hornung (who was off to Coburg), feeling that the latter might perhaps reach Coburg ahead of the messenger who had started the day before. It reiterates the feelings of the day before, and is enclosed in a letter to Dietrich, so that Luther may be stirred to read it. It runs as follows:—

MELANCHTHON TO LUTHER.

Melanch., Ep., I, 9; Cölest. II, 196; Chytr., Lat., 139,—Ger., 228; C. R., II, 145; Cyprian, Beilag., 182.

June 27th.

I cannot express the great grief into which we are plunged by M. Veit's letter, who has informed us how violently angered you are because up to this time we shall not have written often enough. Never have we been in greater need of your counsel and comfort than now, since up to the present we have, in all the most dangerous matters, followed you as our leader.

Therefore I pray you for the sake of the honor of the Gospel that you will interest yourself in us for the sake of the common good, which, unless you sit at the helm, apparently must endure very severe storms. Christ allowed Himself to be awakened in the ship which was in danger. We are verily in much greater danger, in which nothing more painful could happen against us than if you would forsake us.

I dare not complain about this to D. Brück so as not to make him feel worse. Up to the present matters have been in such a state that we have spent much time in weeping. Hence you must not think that we, as though we were Ulysses' associates, had willingly forgotten you; and we have also often written, which we can truly prove.

PHILIPPUS.

The hopelessness of the tenor of Melanchthon's mind is pictured in a second letter to Luther written the same day:—

MELANCHTHON TO LUTHER.

Cölest. II, 197; C. R., II, 144.

June 27th.

Our Confession was delivered last Saturday evening. Now the opponents are counselling as to what their answer shall be: they congregate, labor in united effort, and incite the princes, who previously were sufficiently prejudiced against us.

Eck[9] spares no pains in dissuading the archbishop from further investigation, since the matter is already condemned.

Our party is small; the number of those contrary-minded, on the other hand, is incomparably greater. The archbishop of Mayence,[10] the bishop of Augsburg[11] and the duke of Brunswick[12] avail for us, although they do not fight valiantly enough. It is rumored that the dukes[13] of Baiern, since they have heard the Confession, have become more lenient; at the same time, however, they are not deserting duke George[14] and margrave Joachim.[15] These are the shrewdest leaders of the other party.

The Emperor has written to Erasmus[16] and called him to the Diet. I cannot perceive what good we have to expect from the very bitter hatred of our enemies. Not sure of the demagogues to whose perverted judgment we are subject, we must take our refuge in God and expect help from Him. Only pray to Him for us that He may direct our cause and grant us peace.

At Altenburg[17] there was for three days a terrible electrical storm. The lightning struck two towers, those of the fortress and the church, whereupon a great flood followed. It terrified me very much.

But let us turn to Luther in his lonely fortress on this Monday, June 27th. He had received Melanchthon's letter of the 19th, and sits down to pen a reply, the first one he

---

[9-16] A picture of the German leadership of the age.
[17] Twenty-four miles from Leipzig.

had written to Melanchthon since the beginning of June. It is a mighty epistle:—

LUTHER EXHORTS, ENCOURAGES AND WARNS.

He tries to draw the fangs out from Satan's mouth for the sake of comforting the terrified Melanchthon. He says:—

LUTHER TO MELANCHTHON.

MS. Cod. Jen. b. fol. 110.
Cölest., II, 198; Chytr., 135.

June 27th.

Grace and Peace in Christ! In Christ, I say, not in the world. Amen.

Concerning the excuse for your silence, another time, my dear Philip. The messenger can scarcely wait till I write. . . .

I very much hate your exceeding solicitude, by which, as you write, you are being consumed. That these cares so rule your heart is not due to the greatness of the cause, but to the greatness of our unbelief. For the very same cause was still greater in the time of John Huss and many others. . . .

It is not our cause. Why do you thus torture yourself without end? If the cause be false, then we wish to renounce it; but if it be true, why do we, with so great promises, make Him a liar Who commands us to have a confident and intrepid heart [Ps. 55 : 23]: "Cast your burden upon the Lord." The Lord is near those who are broken-hearted [Ps. 34 : 19], who call on Him. Does He, then, speak this to the wind, or cast it before beasts?

I am also sometimes cast down, but not always. *Your philosophy worries you so, it is not theology.* And your Joachim seems to me to be gnawed by the same care. As if you could really accomplish anything by your taking anxious thought. What in the name of sense can the devil do more than strangle us? What more? I beg you—who in all other things are ready for the fray—to take a stand against yourself, your greatest enemy, since you furnish Satan with so many weapons against you.

Christ died once for sin; but for righteousness and truth He will not die, since He lives and rules. If this is true, what is to be feared for the truth? But if you fear, the very truth will come to nought, through God's anger. . . .

He Who has become our Father, will also be such for our children. I indeed pray diligently for you; and I regret that your obstinate anxiety renders my prayers ineffectual. I for my part am, so far as the cause is concerned, not very much disturbed—yes, of better hope than I had expected. God is able to raise the dead. He is also able to sustain His cause when it wavers; when it has fallen, to raise it up again; when it stands, to further it. Should we prove not to be worthy, let others be to blame for it. For if we are not strengthened by His promises, I pray you, who then are the other people in the whole world to whom they really apply?

But about this more another time. I am, at any rate, only carrying water into the sea.

Your letters concerning the Emperor's arrival went to Wittenberg yesterday. For they too are very much worried at your silence, as you will discover from the letters of Pomeranus. It is not the fault of the messenger, whom Jonas blames, but altogether yours, and yours alone. Christ comfort you all through His Spirit and strengthen and instruct you. Amen.

If I should hear that affairs and the cause are in a bad way, and that they will be in danger, I will come in a hurry to see the terrible teeth of Satan eager to snap their prey, as the Scripture says (Job 41 : 5).

Meanwhile greetings to all. We shall send other letters as soon as possible.

MARTIN LUTHER.

This is a perfect letter, considerate, consoling and full of comfort; yet filled with warning and blame, and threatening that he would come to Augsburg himself and face the teeth of Satan that were throwing everybody there into consternation.

June 29th.

A RED-LETTER DAY AT COBURG.

More Admonition for Melanchthon

Wednesday, June 29th, was a red-letter day at Coburg for lonely Luther. First of all he received the messages that Jonas and Melanchthon had sent him on the 26th. He, further, received letters from Brentz, Spalatin, Agricola, and John Frederick. Melanchthon's letter sent by special messenger, because Dietrich had told him Luther was angry, also came in. How should Luther answer it? It was an important missive, and betrayed Melanchthon's lack of Confessional spirit. Luther sat down and wrote the following words of admonition and comfort:—

LUTHER'S LETTER OF COMFORT TO MELANCHTHON.

MS. in Cod. Closs.; Cod. Jen. B. fol. 117.

June 29th.

Grace and Peace in Christ! I have read, my dear Philippus, your rhetorical letter, which wears the garb of innocency concerning your silence. But meanwhile I have twice written letters to you, in which I have sufficiently (at least in the second letter, which the messenger will bring, who has been sent by our laborer to the princes) presented the reason for my silence.

To-day your latest letters have been delivered to me, in which you remind me of your labors, dangers and tears in such a manner, that I appear to have afflicted you unjustly with grief upon grief through my silence, as if I had not known your troubles; or was sitting here in the midst of roses and was not bearing with you any of the cares.

And yet would to God that my cause were such as would permit tears to flow. Yes, I also had resolved to send a messenger to learn whether you were dead or alive. M. Veit will testify to this; and nevertheless I believe all your letters were delivered to me. For the letters, which finally arrived late, concerning the arrival and entrance of the Emperor, came almost simultaneously. But this may have been the "Ate," or any other satan, "and let him have what he deserves."

I have received your Confession (Apology) and am wondering what you might like to have changed, *since you are raising such a question as, What and how much should be conceded to the Papists.* With reference to the Prince, that is another question—what he could concede, if danger threatened him.

So far as I am concerned, *more than enough has been yielded in that Apology,* which if they refuse, I see nothing more which I can yield, unless they furnish clearer reasons and Scripture proofs than I have yet seen. Day and night I am occupied with the matter, thinking over it, revolving it in my mind, arguing, searching the entire Scriptures, and there grows upon me constantly that *fulness of assurance in our Doctrine, and I am more and more confirmed in the purpose that I will yield nothing more,* come what may. . . .

I am offended at your writing, that you are following my authority in this cause. I will not be, nor be called, author in this cause. If it is not equally your cause, it shall not be said that it is mine, and was imposed on you. If it be my cause alone, I will manage it alone. . . . *If we be not the Church,* or a part of the Church, where is the Church? If we have not the Word of God, who has it? . . . I have consoled you in the last letter. May God at least grant that He is not death-dealing but life-giving. What further can I do?

The end and the result of the matter worry you, *because you cannot grasp it with your hands.* But if you could apprehend it, I would not wish that I had anything to do with it, much less be its originator. God has comprehended this matter in a certain general doctrinal article, *which you do not have in your rhetoric, nor in your philosophy:* and which is *called Faith.*

In this article of doctrine everything is contained which man does not see and which is not visible to the eye [Heb. 11 : 1, 3]. If anyone attempt to make it apparent to the eye and comprehensible, as you do, he will receive for his effort cares and tears, as you have received them. "The Lord hath spoken, He desireth to dwell in darkness" [1 Kings 8 : 12], and " He hath made the darkness for his habitation " [2 Sam. 22 : 12]. "He who so wills, changes it." Had Moses resolved ·first to understand the end, how he might withstand the host of Pharaoh, Israel might to-day yet be in Egypt. The Lord increase your and the faith of us all.

If one has this, what can Satan and the whole world accomplish? If we ourselves have no faith, why do we not at least comfort ourselves through another's faith? For there are others who believe in our stead, unless it be that there is not any more a Church on earth, and that Christ will discontinue His presence among us before the end of the world. For if He is not with us, I pray where then in the whole world is He? If we are not the Church, or at least a part of it, where then is the Church?

Or are, perchance, the dukes of Baiern, Ferdinand, the Pope, the Turks, and the like, the Church? If we have not the Word of God, who then are the people who do have it? If, therefore, God be with us, who can be against us? Our sinfulness and ungratefulness do not make Him a liar. But you will not listen to this—so discouraged and weak does Satan make you. May Christ heal you. For this I pray earnestly and continuously. Amen.

Greet all, for I also cannot write the latest to everyone. I wish opportunity would be given me to come to you, indeed I have great desire to come without being commanded or summoned. The grace of God be with you and you all. Amen.

On St. Peter and St. Paul Day [the 29th of June], Anno 1530.

MARTIN LUTHER.

Postscript.

After I had finished the letter the thought occurred to me that it might perhaps appear that I had given too little attention to your question, how much and how far one could concede to the opponents; but you have also asked too little. You have not indicated what and what kind of concession you think would be required of us.

As I have always written, so I now write, I am ready to concede to them everything, provided only that the Gospel be left free to us. But *that which conflicts with the Gospel I cannot concede.* What else can I answer?

Luther always has faith and peace, and comfort from the Scripture. He shows Melanchthon kindly that he understands the latter's duplicity, and reveals that Melanchthon would have yielded up much more to Rome in the Augsburg Confession, if he had been permitted to do so. Most clearly does the contrast come out between Luther the strong confessor, and Melanchthon the timid temporizer. The situation in the letter opens to us the nobility, devoutness and manly honor of the Lutheran principle, and the effeminate, crafty and complaining traits of the Melanchthon principle.

June 30th.

ANSWERING THE FLOOD OF LETTERS.

Thursday, June 30th, was a full day for Luther.   He had grave replies to make to the remaining letters of yesterday— to Spalatin, Brentz, Agricola, John Frederick, and Jonas. To Spalatin he tells the full story of the letters that never came to Coburg.   He shows his joy that the Romanists have become bitter, and regards it as a good sign.   He asks Spalatin to hold Melanchthon's pride in check.

LUTHER TO SPALATIN.

Cölestin, II, p. 200; Chytraeus, Lat., p. 142—Ger., p. 233.

June 30th.

To Mr. George Spalatin, my brother in Christ.

Grace and peace in the Lord!   You say, my dear Spalatin, that I am unwilling to be considered negligent in corresponding; but you are the same.   For of Dr. Jonas' messenger, through whom you promised to write copiously to us, and to the Wittenbergers, by Apel, so that we had anticipated forests of letters and feared that you might become more noisy than our jays [we have received not one letter].

When Apel's messenger came with only Jonas' letters for Wittenberg, he was asked, "Do you bring me no letters?"   He answered, "No."   "How are the men?"   "Well."   Concerning this first disappointment I at once made complaint against Philip.   Afterwards there came a messenger on horseback who was dispatched to Torgau, who brought me a letter from the princes themselves, and was asked, "Do you bring letters?"   He answered, "No."   "How are the men?"   "Well."   Then, as a wagon with venison left here, I again wrote to Philip.   The man returned without an answer.

Now I began to entertain sad thoughts, and supposed that you wished to conceal from me something evil.   In the fourth place, came Jobst Nymptzen. When asked, "Do you bring letters?" he answered, "No."   "How are the men?"   He answered, "Well."   I communicated how our laborer here received letters from his brother, the marshall of Falkenstein, while we in the meantime were hungering and thirsting for more than three weeks, during your kind silence; out of which letters we were obliged to gather information when we wished to know anything.

Would you not say I were negligent, if you had such an experience with me? I admit I was moved with anger and fear, as I learned of Philip's cares and the Prince's trials.   Yet I was relieved of my fear when I heard you were well, but I could not fully believe it.   But enough of this.

That the kings and princes are raging against the Lord's Anointed, I consider a good omen, much better than if they were dissimilating. For Ps. 2 says, "He that sitteth in the heavens shall laugh." Since our Prince laughs, I see not why we should weep: we also can comfortably laugh at their vain resolves. Faith only is necessary.

He Who began this work, has begun it without our counsel. He has also sustained and ruled it. And it is He Who will perfect and execute it without and beyond our counsel.

I know and am sure Whom I have believed, for He is mighty to accomplish above what we petition and understand, although Philip thinks and wishes to be doing it according to his own counsel, so that he may gloriously exclaim: "Surely, so it had to happen, so have I made it."

No, it must not be said: "*So I.*" Admonish Philip constantly not to become God, but to fight against what is inborn in him; for this is not for our good. It drove Adam out of paradise, and only disturbs us, and robs us of our peace. We want to be men, not God. On the last of June, 1530.

YOUR MARTIN LUTHER.

To Brentz, Luther appeals and begs that Brück or some-one else will, like an angel from Heaven, take Melanchthon in charge, and guard him from the mistakes of his weak nature. He says:—

LUTHER TO BRENTZ.

MSS. in Cod. Closs.; in Cod. Jen. b, fol. 133.
Cölestin, II, 201.

June 30th.

Grace and peace in Christ ! I learn, my dear Brentz, that you likewise are being worried in that Assembly of the gods. It is Philip's example that is moving you. He is zealously concerned for the public peace and for posterity, but his zeal is not wise;—as though our ancestors, by their anxiety and care, had brought it to pass that we are what we are, and this had not come about only through God's wisdom, Who will continue to be God after we are gone. For He will not die with us. . . .

I am writing this in order that Gregorius Brück or some one else among you may speak to Philip and get him to cease being regent of the world, that is, may cease making a martyr of himself. . . . God will rule the world better when I am dead than if I should continue to live, since I am hindering Him by my life

Try to see whether Philip cannot be persuaded through you,—of whom he must believe that you are men of God,—though he is not moved by my words. He is not so perverted that, if God should command him by an angel from Heaven to be of good cheer, he would despise the command. He will not despise us, if we all admonish him thus. . . . The grace of God be with you. The last of June, 1530.

YOUR MARTIN LUTHER.

The agony of Melanchthon has become a matter of public knowledge, and Luther, on the same day (June 30th), asks Agricola to admonish and encourage Philip.   He also praises the Elector's steadfastness, and predicts that the Diet will come to an unhappy termination.

LUTHER TO JOHN AGRICOLA.

Cod. Jen., Bl. 24.

June 30th.

Admonish Philip that he moderate the offer of an anxious spirit, so that at last he may not be lacking in that wherewith to offer.

It is indeed a consolation to know that he is troubled in spirit for the sake of the cause; we cannot doubt that it is pleasing to God as an exceedingly pleasant savor.

But in these matters there must be temperance.   While the offering of self is acceptable, self-destruction is not; and God does not wish that souls be led to ruin.   This is an additional Article from the Devil.   For to put one's hope in the grace of the Emperor, is idle.

YOUR MARTIN LUTHER.

John Frederick is evidently deeply stirred by the violence and treachery of Duke George and the German Catholic Princes, and Luther, with the same masterly hand with which he consoles and establishes the weak in greater determination, now moderates the wrath of his superior, and counsels quiet strength and patience.   He says:—

LUTHER TO DUKE JOHN FREDERICK.

Cölestin I., 202; Erlangen 54. 157.

June 30th.

Grace and peace in Christ !   Your Grace now sees right before your own eye what kind of a master the devil is, who leads such wise great people captive in his service, and undertakes all that he does in swift deceit.

And although I know that your Grace—praise God !—is well fitted out against it, and can understand and pass judgment on all their machinations, yet I respectfully admonish you not to allow yourself to be stirred by the wicked assaults against you made by your nearest blood relatives.   When the devil is defeated, he still works to stir up our heart to bitter feeling.   For this the Thirty-seventh Psalm is a good medicine.

The Emperor is a pious soul, worthy of all honor personally, but good God ! what can one man do against so many devils, unless God bring him mighty help.

It vexes even me that your blood relatives carry on so obstinately ; but I must restrain myself, else I would be wishing them this and that. I can easily believe how much more this vexes and moves your Grace. But for God and the dear Emperor's sake, your Grace will have patience, and will also pray with us for the wretched people.

If I have made a mistake in saying that your Grace is vexed at the deceitfulness of friends, I am glad, for from my heart I mean it well. I am commending your Grace to God. Amen.

Coburg, the last day of June, 1530.

YOUR OBEDIENT MARTIN LUTHER.

LUTHER TO JONAS.

Cölest., I, 136 ; Chytraeus, 141.

June 30th.

Grace and peace in Christ ! At last your letters have arrived, my dear Jonas, after you have worried us for three full weeks by your silence. . . . Time of prayer left me no opportunity for anger. But I have been busy giving you a bad name for this silence, especially at Wittenberg.

It does no good to complain against the messengers. They have delivered the letters faithfully, especially the one you hired. From the time he delivered your letter I received nothing except this last one concerning the arrival and the entry of the Emperor, and yesterday the one with your complaints, but I will avenge this in due time.

I am filled with joy and rejoice exceedingly at the extraordinary and great gift of God, in that our Prince is so steadfast and composed in his disposition, for I regard my prayers offered for him as having been pleasing to God and prophesy that they will be heard in other things. This joy of mine has been increased in that I recognize that you are very reliable in the Lord against this raging of Satan.

Philip is worried by his philosophy, and by nothing else; for the cause is in the hand of Him who dare say to the very proudest: "No one shall pluck them out of my hand." Those things that I have been able to take out of my own hands and cast upon Him, have been preserved by Him safe and sure, for "God is our refuge and strength."

I am glad the Pope has received a new sign. He will have something by which to despise God still more, and will go to ruin all the more quickly.

I cannot cease wondering that Ferdinand has forgotten the Turk and the wretchedness of his people. If I were responsible for so much destruction of human life, I would die in an hour, especially if my conscience added that my neglect had been the cause of it.

Our bishops will surely be destroyed. As there is no hope of changing them, I am glad that they are growing more obstinate.

Let us only remain bold in Christ. He lives, and we also shall live, even though we shall be martyred, and He will care for the children and wives of those who have died. He rules, and we shall rule, yes, we rule already.

If I be called to Augsburg, I will surely come, for Christ wishes it so, and indeed I am filled with the desire to come unsummoned and undemanded.

The grace of God be with you. Out of the wilderness, on June 30th, 1530.

YOUR MARTIN LUTHER.

Finally, on this last busy day of June, although it was only yesterday that he had braced up Melanchthon, Luther feels constrained to write him one more letter, and this time to speak more plainly than ever as to the need of firmness and faith in Confession.

When we recall that it was only five days ago to-day, that the Confession was delivered, the greater part of which interval was consumed in getting the news to Coburg, and when we think how Luther immediately sits down and in these two days sends back a whole "forest" (his own term) of letters, in everyone of which extreme efforts are made to hold Melanchthon firm and true, we see not only that Luther recognizes that the great Confessional moment had arrived for the Church; but that he also fears that the summit which had been attained, would again be lost by the ecclesiastical manœuverings of Melanchthon who could never be pinned down to the immutable truth, but was ever modifying it under considerations of worldly prudence. How well Luther knew Melanchthon—how near the Church came to being totally wrecked, despite the glorious Confession of June, by the concession of Melanchthon in July and August —and how wonderfully Luther forecast this outcome, as soon as the glad tidings of June 25th were brought to Coburg— the following history of the Diet will show.

We turn now to his last strenuous appeal to Melanchthon:

LUTHER TO MELANCHTHON.

A contemporary copy in Weim. Archiv.; Cod. Jen. b., fol. III.

June 30th.

Grace and peace in Christ! What first of all to write you, my dear Philippus, I positively do not know. For my thoughts rush and surge at your exceed ingly wicked and perfectly useless cares, *and I know that I am telling a story to one who is deaf.* The reason for this is that *the only one you have faith in is yourself.* You have no faith in me, and, unfortunately, not in others.

In personal conflicts I am weaker, but you stronger ; on the other hand, you are in public as I am in personal matters, and I in public as you in personal matters (if in truth that can be called a private affair which takes place between Satan and myself). For you despise your life, and your fear is for the general cause ; as far as the general cause is concerned, my spirit is strong and undisturbed, for I assuredly know that it is righteous and true, yea, also the cause of Christ, which will not fail. Hence I am a very safe spectator, and can disregard the furious and threatening Papists.

If we fall, Christ will fall with us, and He is the great Ruler of the whole world. And if it were possible for Him to fall, yet I would rather fall with Christ than stand with the Emperor. But there is little use in my writing this, for you will continue to run these affairs as a rationalist, and in accordance with your philosophy. You will continue, that is, as the saying goes, "with reason, to be irrational." You are killing yourself and utterly fail to see that the matter lies beyond the power of your hand and counsel, and that it will be carried on regardless of any concern which you may feel. And *my prayer is that Christ may prevent it from coming into your hand or counsel, although you are so obstinate in desiring to control it.* For if you did succeed in getting your hand upon the lever, we would go down to ruin beautifully indeed and with one crash.

I pray for you, have prayed, and will pray, and I doubt not that I am heard, for I feel the Amen in my heart.

Your Martin Luther.

June 26th-30th.

THE SITUATION AT AUGSBURG.

While this voluminous and animated correspondence was flowing between Luther and the little party at Augsburg, the Emperor was trying to recover from the effects of the Delivery of the Confession, and to decide what should be done.

The next morning, before breakfast,[18] he gathered the weaker Protestants, the representatives of the cities, to his ante-chamber and sought to gain their submission to the Diet of Spires; but they sent word on Monday that they could not adhere to the Recess of Spires "without compromising their conscience before God."[19]

---

[18] *C. R.*, II, 143.
[19] Först., *Urk.*, II, 6.

33

Though it was Sunday, he also summoned the Roman Estates and Princes, and asked them what reply should be made to the Confession. The strict Papists said : Execute the Edict of Worms by force. The Princes said: Submit the Confession to impartial judges and let the Emperor finally decide. A third party said: Let a Confutation be composed by the Roman doctors.

George of Saxony and Joachim of Brandenburg were violent in denouncing the Protestants; but the archbishop of Maintz, the bishop of Augsburg and the Duke of Brunswick were favorable to them.

July 1st-6th.

THE CRISIS OF THE DIET—ROME WINS.

The Emperor wished the Romanists to offer their Confession in accordance with the terms of the Call; or, if not, that they bring in accusation against the Protestants. But they refused to be regarded as a party, or to have the Emperor judge between them and the others. That there was nothing to arbitrate, was their claim. The question, they said, was one of crushing persons in rebellion. The Emperor was obliged to accede to this view, and, thereafter, instead of assuming an impartial attitude, to range himself on their side. This, diplomatically, was the crisis of the Diet. By this step the Pope won, and the Emperor lost, everything. Rome again was in complete ascendency, and the Emperor was her servant and vassal. The whole independent attitude of Charles, supported by Mercurinus, and the corresponding basis of the Diet proclaimed in the Call, were obliterated. Not only had Rome prevented a Council but it had conquered a Diet. The Archbishop of Maintz was so disgusted that he did not come to the meeting.[20]

Twenty of the most violent enemies of the Reformation

---

[20] *C. R.*, II, 175.

were selected to confute the Confession in the name of the Emperor and Rome. They are said to have understood their work to be not a matter " of refuting the Confession, but of branding it."

COULD THE EMPEROR BE JUDGE?

Ostensibly still impartial, the Emperor asked each party whether the Diet and he himself possessed the right of pronouncing in this matter of religion.[21] The Elector consulted Luther. Luther answered:—

"The Emperor should be held to his Call. For if he decide without a hearing, no Diet would have been necessary, but he might have settled the affair in Spain. He cannot be accepted as judge, *unless he does not judge anything against the Scripture, or the clear Word of God.* For no Emperor and no earthly judge can be set above God. If the Emperor should receive this ungraciously, as though we were not recognizing him as a Christian Prince, he can be reminded of God's command that we are not to put our trust in princes and in human beings. Judgment and condemnation without Scripture, are like a lord without a country, a kingdom without money, a learned man without an art.

"Let the Elector only be full of confidence. For Christ is here, Who will confess him before His Heavenly Father, even as he has now confessed Christ before this wicked generation."

The Romanists unreservedly accorded the Emperor the right to proceed, as Roman Emperor and Guardian, Advocate and Sovereign Defender of the Church,[22] since he was definitely ranged on their side.

July 9th-12th.

HAVE THE PROTESTANTS ANY MORE PROTESTS IN RESERVE?

On the ninth of July the Lutherans were asked whether they had presented their whole Confession, or whether they

---

[21] Först., *Urk.*, II, 9.
[22] *Ib.*, 10.

were not holding some articles in reserve. "I perceive what they mean by this question," wrote Luther to Jonas. "The Devil has noticed that your Apology, the Soft-Stepper, has kept silence on the Articles of Purgatory, the Worship of Saints, and on the Pope the Anti-Christ."

On July 10th, the Protestants made reply to the Emperor's question in one of the most open, truthful, logical, noble and courageous documents ever presented to an earthly ruler. It seems to have been drawn up by Brück, is duly signed by the Princes, and speaks as plainly, yet respectfully, to an Emperor as was ever ventured by loyal subjects, intimating that the Emperor had better hurry on to the proper business of the Diet, and permit the estates to return home; but that if it is the Romanists who wish to raise the question of Papal Abuses, the Protestants are ready to give them all the answer they desire. We do not believe that the document, which again emphasizes the rights and the good faith and persistency of the Lutherans in adhering to the Emperor's own Call, and which convicts him of having broken his own word under the influence of the Romanists, has been sufficiently emphasized by historians. While its positive effects were not perhaps so visible, it served to render the stand taken in the Confession permanent. It reads as follows:—

The Explanation of the Protesting Estates that no More Articles Will be Handed In.

Cölest., II, 118; Först., Urk., II, 17.
Chyträus, Ger., 196; C. R., II, 184.

July 10th, 1530.

Prince of Noble Birth and Dear Uncle, etc.

Since you bore his Majesty's command to us, yesterday at seven o'clock, that we tell whether we intended to hand in more Articles or whether those already delivered would be allowed to suffice ; we present this friendly reply:—

Whereas it is notorious that there are many great and serious Abuses in the Church, relating to doctrine and the spiritual rule, which have given cause to us and many others to preach against them for the edification of consciences burdened to the imperiling of their salvation.

And inasmuch as his Majesty has graciously given assurance, in his Call, that these matters of religion should be taken up among ourselves in love and good will, and be settled in accordance with the truth (which indeed is God's pure Word alone), as is now taking place in a Christian and proper manner ; therefore,

1. We did not specifically mention all the Abuses in the writing you allude to, but we delivered over a Common Confession and Testimony, in which is summed up about all the doctrine preached among us as useful to salvation, in order that his Majesty may fully know that no unchristian doctrine is taught among us.

We have deemed it needful rather to emphasize those Abuses concerning which the consciences of our people were burdened, than other Abuses, relating to the walk of the clergy, for which they must in any event themselves give account to God.

2. In order that this matter might be dealt with in charity and be resolved with God's Word by the truth, and that the most prominent parts in which a change has occurred, and the reasons therefor, might be recognized more clearly, we have avoided the attempt to catalogue each and every Abuse.

3. In these Articles we hoped to have refuted such uncertain and unrighteous doctrine together with the Abuses antagonistic to it, and therefore we deem it unnecessary to bring in more Articles.

4. But if the opposite party raises the question of further Abuses as its "opinion and meaning", in virtue of his Majesty's Call and the resulting presentation, or undertakes to attack our Confession, or advance any new position, we are ready herewith to give further report on the same, according to God's Word, as indeed we offered to do at the end of the Confession already delivered.

5. And therefore we most respectfully urge, as we came here to Augsburg in good season, in obedience to his Majesty, and have been burdened with heavy expenses now for a long time, that his Majesty would arrange to proceed in accordance with and live up to his Majesty's Call, as touched on above, without further delay, as there has been no falling short on our part, and also, if God will, shall be none in the future.

Actum, Augsburg, 10th day of July, 1530.

By God's Grace,

JOHN, Duke of Saxony, and Elector,
GEORGE, Margrave of Brandenburg,
ERNEST, Duke of Brunswick and
Lüneburg,
PHILIPP, Landgrave of Hesse,
WOLFGANG, Prince of Anhalt, together
with those Associated with us.

July 1st-6th.

LUTHER SPREADING THE NEWS OF THE CONFESSION.

Meanwhile, in these first days of July, Luther was still living over again the heroic moments of the delivery of the

Confession, and describing the important scene to his friends. He criticised one point in it, viz., that it left open the possibility that such confirmed enemies of Christ as the Romanists who made the Pope their corner-stone and who were to be compared with the Jews that rejected our Lord, might after all be confessors of the pure doctrine. He says:—

LUTHER TO MELANCHTHON.

Cölestin, II, 204.

July 3rd.

Grace and peace in Christ !
My dearest Philip:—
Yesterday I most carefully read through your Confession. I am much pleased with it. But it errs in one point, in which it is contrary to Scripture, since Christ predicts of Himself (Luke 19:14), "We will not have this man to reign over us;" and it collides with the judgment (Psalm 118:22); "The stone, which the builders have rejected." What can you expect in so great blindness and obstinacy, but that it would be rejected ?

They do not grant us the name of builders. We should glory in being counted with the wicked, as that stone itself was counted with thieves and condemned with them.

Therefore we have hope for salvation only with the Lord; and He will not forsake this stone, as it says: "It has become the head of the corner." But this is the Lord's doing and not ours. Therefore it is marvelous before our eyes. Christ strengthen you with us, and comfort you with His Spirit, and deal with us according to all His wonderful powers. Amen. July 3rd, 1530.

YOUR MARTIN LUTHER.

To the heroic Cordatus, Luther describes the Confession and the scene of its delivery as follows:—

LUTHER TO CORDATUS.

Cölestin, II, 207.

July 6th.

Grace and peace in Christ! . . . Jonas writes that he was among the auditors, when our Confession was read by Dr. Christian for two whole hours, and he saw the features of all that listened, concerning which he has promised to tell me by word of mouth. I have a copy of this Confession here, but must hold it subject to order. Our antagonists surely have used every effort to prevent the Emperor from hearing it. . . . On order of the Emperor it was read before the whole Diet, that is before the Princes and Estates of the Empire.

I am exceedingly *happy to have lived to this hour,* in which *Christ* has been preached *through His so great Confessors* publicly in so great an Assembly by means of this really *extraordinarily noble Confession,* and the word

(Psalm 119 : 46, Vulg.) is fulfiled: "I will speak of thy testimony before kings;" also this is fulfiled: "I was not put to shame." For (Matthew 10 : 32) "Whosoever shall confess me before men (so He speaks Who does not lie), him will I confess before my Father which is in heaven."

I believe you already have heard everything else from the others. The splendor of the imperial entry has been set forth in print. . . . Continue to pray, and urge all to pray, particularly for the excellent Emperor, the young man who is worthy of the love of God and man; also for our not less excellent Prince, who carries a very heavy cross, and for Philip, who is making a martyr of himself, with cares, in a most deplorable way. If I should be called [to the Diet] I shall also call you. Do not doubt this. The Lord be with you. Amen. Out of the wilderness on the 6th of July, 1530.

YOUR MARTIN LUTHER.

To Melanchthon, on July 5th, he writes:—

LUTHER TO MELANCHTHON.

Cölestin, II, 206.

July 5th.

Grace and peace in Christ! . . . We are, thanks be to God, in good hopes, not because of your Diet or your deliberations, but because of the power and presence of Christ, to use the word of Peter. They write from Wittenberg that they are praying there in the churches so earnestly that I am convinced that something good will be accomplished at this Diet. Greet Jonas, Agricola, Spalatin, Brück, Dr. Caspar, and all that are ours. July 5th, 1530.

YOUR MARTIN LUTHER.

On July 6th, Luther described the Diet to Hausman, and "*our* Confession which *our Philip* has *prepared.*" On the same date, having heard how ill-pleased the most powerful Catholic ecclesiastic in Germany was with the fiasco in which Charles had surrendered to Rome, and having been told it might be well to address the Archbishop, Luther writes the following letter, which quickly appeared in print at Nuremberg, and was circulated freely:—

LUTHER TO CARDINAL ALBERT, ARCHBISHOP OF MENTZ, PRIMATE OF GERMANY.

Printed at Nuremberg, 1530; Erl. XLIV 159.

July 6th.

Your Highness, as well as the other orders of the empire, has doubtless read the Confession, delivered by ours, which is so composed, that with joyous lips it may say: "If I have spoken evil, bear witness of the evil; but if well, why smitest thou me?" It shuns not the light, and can sing with the Psalmist: "I will speak of thy testimonies before kings, and will not be ashamed."

But I can well conceive that our adversaries will by no means accept the doctrine, yet much less are they able to confute it. I have no hope whatever that we can agree in doctrine; for their cause cannot bear the light. Such is their bitterness, with such hatred are they kindled, that they would endure hell itself, rather than yield to us and relinquish their new wisdom. I know that our doctrine is true and grounded in the holy Scriptures. By this Confession we clearly testify and demonstrate that we have not taught wrongly or falsely.

July 9th.

After two days, July 9th, Luther wrote a strengthening letter to the Elector in reply to the Elector's letter of July 4th, which he had not received until the 9th. "God knows," says he, "he is writing the Elector only because he fears Satan may overcloud the Elector's heart."

LUTHER TO DUKE JOHN, ELECTOR OF SAXONY.

Erl. XLIV, 169.

July 9th.

Our adversaries thought they had gained a great point in having the preaching interdicted by the Emperor, but the infatuated men did not see that by this written Confession, which was offered to the Emperor, this doctrine was more preached, and more widely propagated, than ten preachers could have done it. It was a fine point that our preachers were silenced, but in their stead came forth the Elector of Saxony and other princes and lords, with the written Confession, and preached freely in sight of all, before the Emperor and the whole empire.

Christ surely was not silenced at the Diet, and mad as they were, they were compelled to hear more from the Confession, than they would have heard from the preachers in a year. Paul's declaration was fulfiled: "The word of God is not bound." Silenced in the pulpit, it was heard in the palace; the poor preachers were not allowed to open their lips, but great princes and Lords spoke it forth.

Luther then answers the Elector's question as to whether the Emperor had the right to decide the matter before the Diet. We already have set forth his words. Luther continues:—

Let your Grace be assured, Christ is here; and He will confess your Grace again before His Father as your Grace has confessed Him before this wicked generation, as He says : Them that honor me, will I honor.—1 Sam. 2 : 30. The Lord Who has begun this matter will undoubtedly complete it. I am praying earnestly and diligently for your Grace. If I could do more, I would, for I owe it to you. God's grace be with you, as hitherto, and increasingly. Amen. Saturday, July 9th, 1530. Your obedient

MARTIN LUTHER.

On the same day Luther replies to Jonas, and tells him, as he told Melanchthon the day before, that Rome never will agree with the Evangelical Faith. He says:—

LUTHER TO JONAS.

Cod. Closs.; in Cod. Jen. b, fol. 130.
Printed in De Wette, IV, 85.

July 9th.

Grace and peace in Christ ! In these days we have received very many letters from you, dearest Jonas, and since that time of silence we have answered four times, yes five times. This we are now writing for the sixth time. Your letters have been exceedingly satisfactory to me.

I see, indeed, that now after the argument, the prologue of the Diet is being recited. The act itself, and the crisis will follow ; but they [the Romanists] have a sad finale to look to, we a joyous one.

Not indeed that unison in doctrine ever will be restored, for how can anyone hope that Belial will come into concord with Christ? Except that perhaps marriage, and both forms of the Sacrament may be yielded by them—perhaps !—but I wish and almost hope that "the difference in doctrine may be reconciled, and a political unity may be made possible." [23] If this should come to pass through the grace of Christ, more than enough will have been accomplished at this Diet.

For first, and greatest at this Diet, Christ has been proclaimed in a public and glorious Confession. He has been confessed in the light, and to their face, so that they cannot boast that we fled, or that we feared, or concealed our faith.

My only unfulfilled desire is that I could not be present at this noble Confession. I am like the generals who could take no part in defending Vienna from the Turks. But it is my joy and solace that meanwhile *my Vienna* was defended by others.

It is certain that we have always sought peace. If we now can reach the point *of dissolving the Diet* and *separating in peace*, we shall clearly have triumphed over Satan this year. For there is no hope that the enemies will do any good. What can I hope from the Emperor, good as he may always be, since he is possessed ? Christ lives and sits at the right hand, not of the Emperor (for then should we have gone to destruction long ago), but at the right hand of God. This is something incredibly great. But I am drawn to this incredible truth, and am

---

[23] The reader should note that this is the original basis of the Diet as found in the language of the Emperor's Call.

willing to die upon it, and why should I not therefore also be willing to live upon it? Would God that Philip would believe this at least with my faith, if he has no other. . . .

YOUR MARTIN LUTHER.

July 8th-12th.

THE MELANCHTHONIAN SIN AGAIN.

But during these early days of July, there was one man at Augsburg who was filled with fears, and who was again ready to attempt a negotiation which would undo the good work accomplished, and betray and bring back the Protestant party to Rome.

Not that Melanchthon thought of yielding in doctrine, or of changing the first part of the Confession at this time. But as customs and institutions were matters of Christian liberty, he thought much could be yielded in the matter of Abuses, and that thus the opposite party might be conciliated.

There seem to be men in the Church in every age so eager for peace and unity that without actually meaning to be disloyal, they take the supposed salvation of the whole ecclesiastical situation into their hands and make ambiguous advances to the enemy without realizing all the painful consequences that are thus brought on the Church indirectly and gradually, and from which she often must suffer in subsequent generations and perhaps to the end of time.

Melanchthon had been deceived once by the Romanists, on the 19th of June. Now he remained without hope and believed the threats of the Romanists. Luther had all along taken the position that, despite what the Emperor might perhaps try to do on the Protestant behalf, Rome would admit nothing. " You are waiting for the answer of Rome," he wrote. " It is already written: Patres, Patres, Patres; Ecclesia, Ecclesia; usus, consuetudo, praeterea e Scriptura nihil.[24] The Emperor on the strength of this testimony will pronounce against you."

---

[24] Lutheri *Epp.,* IV, 96.

But Melanchthon was seized with gloomy desperation. He could not sleep. He saw no more hope,[25] except in God. As we already have found, he had, from the very Delivery of the Confession, set his heart on making further concessions.

After the Emperor was exerting all manner of threats and promises to cause the individual Evangelical leaders to abandon the Confession, Melanchthon came to the Elector and begged him to yield on all the Abuses, and go back to Roman customs and the jurisdiction of the bishops, provided that Rome would grant the two forms of the Sacrament and the marriage of priests. He argued this at length with the Elector,[26] and finally seems to have secured his permission to present the matter to Campeggius.[27]

Melanchthon, asking for an interview with Campeggius,[28] says, "We have *no dogma which is diverse* from that of the Roman Church. . . We *venerate the authority* of the Roman Pope, and *are ready to obey him,* if he does not reject us, and *if he will pardon* or approve certain small matters which we cannot change. Will you reject those who *come before you as suppliants?* Will you pursue them with fire and sword? Nothing brings so much hatred to us in Germany as the firmness with which we maintain the doctrines of the Roman Church. But with the aid of God, *we will remain faithful, even unto death, to Christ and the Roman Church,* although you should reject us."

This humble and obsequious letter seems to be almost beyond the bound of credibility, and its authenticity has been questioned, but we believe without good reason. Well does a Reformed historian comment on this passage: "Thus did Melanchthon humble himself. God permitted this fall, that future ages might clearly see how low the Reformation was willing to descend in order to maintain unity, and that no one

[25] *C. R.,* II, 145.
[26] *C. R.,* II, 162.
[27] " Principes nostri miserunt nos."—*C. R.,* II, 171.
[28] *C. R.,* II, 168.

might doubt that the schism had come from Rome; but also, assuredly, that they might learn how great, in every important work, is the weakness of the noblest instruments."

We must, however, be just to Melanchthon. He was surrounded by most bitter enemies, and threatened with the wrath of the Emperor and his most powerful princes; and in his interview with Campeggius, he had declared, "We cannot yield nor be unfaithful to the truth. We commit our cause to the Lord God."

This interview, for which Melanchthon had begged, took place on July 8th. Melanchthon thought that he had received assurance that the Legate would yield to the celebration of the Sacrament in two kinds and to the marriage of priests. If the Legate had yielded to him, Melanchthon would thus have changed the whole history of the Church, and, thanks to Melanchthon, Lutherans might to-day be safe back in the bosom of Rome. But the Legate humiliated Melanchthon, and said that he would not be able to make concessions without the consent of the German princes.[29]

On this 8th of July Melanchthon wrote to Luther, saying that he would tell him briefly what was going on at Augsburg. He then describes the three opinions that prevailed among the Romanists and declares that the Emperor reserves the right of deciding the matter according to his judgment, in the failure of which everything would be brought back to the old situation until the calling of a Council.

"'This last view has not been made known openly. We have not yet been answered. But I hope that it will be proclaimed on the coming Monday. I am waiting for it with great desire for I have learned by experience how the Legate Campeggi is disposed. When the archbishop of Maintz saw that he could not accomplish anything by much controversy, he remained away from the meeting the next day.

I have now given you not only the transactions up to date, but also told you what is still to be expected, without any addition of my own. For I see in advance, what a sad tragedy the intention of our opponents will occasion. The

[29] *C. R.,* II, 174.

farmer (Duke George) whom you know, is at the head of the play, and is incited by certain hypocrites among the theologians. I cannot write more. Keep yourself well and pray for us.''

July 13th.

LUTHER WRITES STRONG TO AUGSBURG.

Despite the meagre information that Luther received from Melanchthon, whose want of frankness seems incredible at this distance, Luther from now on floods Augsburg with letters, begging the men there to remain true to the cause.

To Jonas he writes:—

LUTHER TO JUSTUS JONAS.

Cölestin, II, 228.

July 13th.

Who does not see that the Emperor is *being driven and led*. If you *now stand firm*, and *yield in no point*, you will compel them to change their present propositions into wrath. . . . You long already have had other plans, and what you have written me is already old. But I hope that my letters (for I have written at least five times,—to Philip I have written that often) have been delivered. The Lord Jesus Himself, our salvation and life, our love and trust, be with you, as I hope. Amen.

YOUR MARTIN LUTHER.

To Philip he speaks most plainly. This letter of his comes from the heart of a hero, and shines with confidence in the Confession of the truth:—

LUTHER TO MELANCHTHON.

Buddeus, 49, from the Jena MS.
Cölest., II, 229b; Chytr., 105b.

July 13th.

Doctor Martinus Luther, to the faithful disciple and witness of Christ, M. Philipps Melanchthon, his brother.

Grace and true peace of Christ ! I believe, my dear Philipps, *that you in many ways now realize from experience* that *Belial can in no manner be united with Christ,* and that one can entertain *no hope of concord,* so far as the doctrine is concerned. I wrote about this to the princes that our cause cannot be left to the Emperor as judge. And now we perceive the purpose of the writing that contains the so-gracious Call. But, perhaps, the matter had already progressed too far before my letter arrived. But at least for myself I WILL NOT YIELD A HAIR'S-BREADTH,[30] nor allow that the matter be again brought into the former situation [restitui]; I will rather await all external danger, since they proceed so determinedly.

The Emperor may do what he can. *But I wish to know what* YOU *have done.* I wish that you would not permit yourself to be disturbed on account of the victory and boastfulness of the enemies, but that you would establish yourself against it through the power and strength and might of Him Who raised Christ from the dead and will quicken us with Him and raise us.

MARTIN LUTHER.

THE CONFUTATION FINISHED.

On the 13th of July, the Roman Confutation was completed. " Eck with his band,"[31] said Melanchthon, " transmitted it to the Emperor." It was found, by all, to be confused, violent, thirsting for blood.[32] The Emperor turned from such an impossible document, to the plan of sending delegations to visit each of the Protestant leaders alone and subdue them singly by threats.

July 15th-20th.

THE PROTESTANT PRINCES THREATENED.

The Margrave was approached by his two cousins, the archbishop of Maintz and the Elector of Brandenburg, and by his two brothers, but without effect. Another delegation waited on the Elector John and attempted to compel him to renounce the heresy of Luther with many threats. He was accused of being in league with the Swiss (whose Confessions were just at this time being laid before the Emperor). He was threatened with a refusal to confirm his son's marriage and with the loss of the electorate, and that Duke George of Saxony would be made elector in his place. The Elector

---

[30] Ne pilum quidem cedam.

[31] *C. R.,* II, 193.

[32] Adeo confusa, incondita, violenta, sanguinolenta et crudelis ut puduerint.—*Ib.,* 198.

wrote a brief and calm note to Luther on this day, simply saying that they were still waiting to hear from the Romanists, who are not in unity with each other. On this day Melanchthon also wrote to Luther as follows:—

MELANCHTHON TO LUTHER.

Cölest., II., 233; Chytr., Ger., 215.

July 15th.

I have written to you that new plans are frequently undertaken. Yesterday it was decided in the electoral and princely counsels, that the Emperor should again be petitioned to bring about a Council for the whole German empire.[33] To this it was added that the purpose should be made that the peace should not be broken. Our people were not in unison as to including the second point, although they have decided on this, and have given certain reasons. The reasons do not particularly please me. We desire to seem to be too prudent.

I am sending you a list of the writings which our enemies have delivered to his imperial Majesty. You will see there that they have appended some contradictory articles to the Confutation with a bad design, namely, that they may embitter his Majesty's gentle heart against us. Such stabs in the dark these wicked ones make against us. If it comes to answering them, I shall indeed repay these wild bloodhounds.

I have several times visited the intimate companions of our enemy Eck. It is impossible to say how deeply embittered that pharisaic hatred is which I have noticed in them. They are doing and thinking of nothing else than of stirring up the Princes against us, and of causing the pious Emperor to enter into a godless work against us. Pray for us. Friday, July 15th.

---

[33] " The Emperor wanted a Council, and even the Catholic Princes thought a General Council necessary," Campeggi wrote to Rome. In the imperial Instruction given to the commissioners at the Diet of Spires in 1526, it had been expressly stated that " His Majesty would not decide at the Diet any matters of religion, but would continue to petition the Pope for a Council." In the Preface to the Augsburg Confession in 1530, the stand was taken that at the Regensburg Diet in 1527, a Council was appealed to, with the approval of the Emperor. Although the document is no longer in existence, it cannot be doubted, since nearly all the men who had been present at Regensburg three years earlier were still living and most of them were present at the Diet of Augsburg. Moreover Cardinal Campeggius himself wrote to Clement VII. from Augsburg in 1530, that all the Catholic Princes at the Diet at Augsburg maintained that a Council was necessary.—Raynaldus, *an.*, 1530, n. 171. Raynaldus further writes of the Pope, that, although he had been petitioned by the German assemblies of the Nation, and by the Emperor himself in the year 1529, yet he had an antipathy to the Council.—*An.*, 1529, n. 48 ; *Cyprian,* pp. 42-43.

On July 14th Melanchthon had also written to Luther a letter as follows:—

MELANCHTHON TO LUTHER.

Cölest., II, 288; Chytr., 161.

July 14th.

Yesterday I received two letters from you. You write more frequently and of more pleasant matters than we. Nothing has been decided in our affair up to now. At present deliberations are being held daily. Christ grant that they may bring about peace. Eck has handed in a Confutation of our Confession. It is not yet come to light, but I hear from good friends that it is a long document full of libel.

Zwingli has sent a printed Confession here. People are ready to swear that he is entirely insane. In dealing with Original Sin and the use of Sacraments he revamps the old errors. As to Ceremonies he talks like a barbarian, and would have them all put aside. He insists on his [erroneous] teaching on the Lord's Supper. He also wants to root out all Bishops. I will send you a copy of the writing when I receive it.

I am sending you the Questions concerning Traditions, and asking you to write in full regarding them, for nothing in all our disputations gives us more trouble than that which seems the easiest. And indeed it is a small matter. The doctrines of men are but traps for the conscience, whether they are adhered to, or whether they are abolished. We have a sure foundation in Justification; but that in the other Article of Liberty—that one must also maintain external liberty—gives much offense. I am naming Liberty, as even Paul adhered to the Law among the Jews. I have set down many of the causes of human Traditions, how they originate, so that you may better see what is the matter with me.

In the matter of the Mass and in the first draft of the Articles of Faith, I think I have been careful enough; but in the matter of Traditions, I am not yet satisfied with myself in this writing [the Confession]. I believe also that our enemies will make a great noise concerning the spiritual orders. Keep well, July 14th, 1530.

With this came five Causes of churchly Traditions, and Melanchthon says: "Answer me whether it is necessary to adhere to Traditions because of the power and word of authority, and whether such Traditions bind the conscience".

Luther replies to Melanchthon in an extended treatise of July 21st, which he closes as follows:—

LUTHER TO MELANCHTHON.

"But these things you despise as coming from a mere coarse farmer. Nevertheless they are worth a good deal in answer to your precocious and useless questions. You see this, that those Romanists do not want any less, and can want nothing less, than that they may rule over the churches according to their worldly right, and only so that they are regarded as Princes of the world. They want to be Bishops, and if they did not want to be that, what would they be? What would they remain?

" Therefore, I wish you were of a little quieter disposition. You worry even me with your vain anxiety. It almost vexes me to write to you, when I see that I am accomplishing nothing with my words. Though I be rude in speech, yet I am not in knowledge. II Cor. 11:6. Christ be with you. Amen. July 21st. Your Martin Luther."

Meantime, on July 16th, the Count Palatine Frederick and Count Henry of Nassau came to the Elector and declared that the Emperor would probably not grant him the investiture to the electorate.[34] To this the Elector made reply on July 21st.[35] The reply touches, first, the question of the investure; second, the question of faith; and third, the question of the league with other Protestants.

In the letter written to Niclas von Ende on July 28th,[36] the Elector says that he had received no answer from the Emperor up to date although to-day or to-morrow it would be five weeks since he had answered the Emperor, that he had requested that he be invested with the electorate, and that this was declined. That he had asked for the investiture a second time, and had not yet received any answer. He concludes that the Emperor is offended at him, and that his own

---

[34] The document is found in Müller, *Historie*, III, p. 671.

[35] Found in *Cölest.*, II, 245 ; Chytr., Lat., 125.

[36] Müller, *Hist.*, III, p. 685.

34

friends (blood-relatives) have caused this "for his imperial Majesty has not yet vouchsafed us one word. So we wait here at great expense. We have to-day with us one hundred and fifty horses, and have consumed a great amount of money, and have had to borrow 12,000 gulden here."

Everywhere it was said that George would be proclaimed Elector instead of John. On the 28th of July many princes were invested with their dignities, but the Elector was excluded. Before long he even was informed that, if he did not yield, the Emperor would expel him from his estates and inflict the severest punishment on him.[37] It was a dreadful ordeal for the faithful man, but the Elector finally made the right choice. He declared that he intended to confess his Saviour.

On the 21st of July he replied to Charles' arguments. He proved that the Emperor could not refuse him the investiture, and that the Diet of Worms had secured it for him. As to faith, he said that in the Confession he was not merely adhering to what his theologians said, but that he himself recognized that God's Word was not based on Rome's teaching, and that *here and now* he *once more confessed all the articles of the Confession,* and he entreated the Emperor to permit him and his to be accountable to God only in matters pertaining to the salvation of their souls.[38]

August 3rd.

CONFUTATION READ IN THE DIET.

At last, on the 3rd of August, the new Confutation was read before the Diet. It approved some articles of the Confession and condemned others. It declared that the doctrines, on the Trinity, on Christ, on Baptism, on eternal punishment, on the origin of evil, and the assertion that faith was

---

[37] Müller, *Gesch., d. Protestation.*
[38] Först., *Urk.,* pp. 80-119.

necessary in the sacrament, in the Protestant Confession, were right.

Camerarius, concealed in the chapel of the palace, heard the Confutation read and reported verbally to Melanchthon. Melanchthon was still very much frightened and once again interviewed the papal Legate on August the 4th, asking him to grant the two points of the mass and marriage, and declared that then the Lutheran pastors would return to the government of the Roman bishops.

Melanchthon had an idea that if the Protestant Church were returned to the Roman Bishops, it would nevertheless not be subject to the old Roman usages, just as little as the New Testament, as St. Paul says, was subject to the Old Testament ordinances. This clever notion assumed great importance in Melanchthon's mind, and he persisted in thus attempting to point out the solution, especially in his correspondence with Luther. The letters of July 27th, August 3rd and 4th, and others, between the two men, are occupied with this discussion.

July 19th-August 4th.

LUTHER'S CORRESPONDENCE, UP TO THE CONFUTATION.

Melanchthon is a reed shaken by the wind, which Luther must steady.

LUTHER TO MELANCHTHON.

Cölestin, II, Bl. 231 b.

July 19th.

Grace and peace in Christ! You do not write, my Dear Philip, but I do.

The matter tends toward an outcome similar to that at Worms, viz., that the Emperor is to be the judge. So far as I see, the other side offers nothing but mere threats, threats against the Lord and His anointed. David, the victor of Goliath, calls threats vain. He who dies because of threatening, shall surely be brought to the grave. You are not conquered by others, but by yourself. Though we constantly hear threats, threats are nothing but stubble and reed, which the Lord knows and perceives.

But grant that war and violence should follow ; it has not actually begun ; and meanwhile something may happen ; and even when it begins in fact, it has not yet had a continuation, and if it should have a continuation, it has not yet triumphed. *Do be strong in the Lord.* Amen.

July 19th, 1530.

YOUR MARTIN LUTHER.

LUTHER TO MELANCHTHON.

July 20th.

It was a great affliction for me that I could not be present with you in person at that most beautiful and holy Confession of Christ (*pulcherrima et sanctissima*).

But though he had a warm heart of praise for Melanchthon, Luther's wisdom and word always struck at the main root of things. The Papacy had been passed by in silence in the Augsburg Confession, with the result of saving up the Thirty Years' War for the next century. Luther believed in dealing with the Pope straight from the shoulder. He mentions the matter to Jonas at this time :—

LUTHER TO JUSTUS JONAS.

MS. in Wolfbüt., Cod. Helmst. 108, fol. 67; Cod. Jen. b. fol. 194.
Cölest., II, 233 b; Erl., VIII, 133.

July 21st.

Grace and peace in Christ ! At last you have awakened. Philip is very skillful in excusing you, but it is easy to deceive a man like myself, who is neither a rhetorician nor a dialectician, with these arts.

But I am deceived in my hope, as I thought you would come, struck long ago by an Edict of the Emperor.

Satan still lives, and has observed that your Apology, treading softly, has passed over the Article of Purgatory, of the Worship of Saints, and most of all *of the Pope as Antichrist.*

Unhappy Emperor, if he proposes to give up the Diet to listening to Confutations of Luther, as if the present Apology did not give them enough to answer !

As to the bold Reformed Confessions that had come in, and which Melanchthon and Jonas deplored because they stirred up the Emperor and the Romanists to enmity, Luther writes:—

LUTHER TO JONAS.

July 21st.

I really like Zwingli and Bucer ! Thus also shall God bring them forward at that day ! Indeed, we might now enter into a brotherhood with these persons ! But after the departure of the Emperor, they will again be different people.   If you are not satiated with the Diet, then I am astounded : I am tired.   I desire to be the sacrifice of this last Council, as John Huss at Constance was the sacrifice of the last papal triumph.

YOUR MARTIN LUTHER.

Six days later, Luther wrote to Agricola urging loyalty and steadfastness.   This strong letter runs as follows:—

TO JOHN AGRICOLA, EISLEBEN.

Tr. by *Currie.*

July 27th.

It is an old device of Satan that when he is beaten by the truth he diverts people's attention to secondary matters, so preventing them attending to the main thing.

Let us therefore *cleave to our cause* and *not yield.*

I am sure their eyes are shut, for I regard them as *devils incarnate.*

No more senseless demand has ever been made than that everything should remain as it was and their ideas be accepted, while ours are cast aside, especially as they themselves admit that we are right in many respects.   For this is tantamount to expecting that *our Apology,* which even they praised, *should be disavowed* by us before the whole world.

MARTIN LUTHER.

July 27th-August 4th.

MELANCHTHON PUSHES HIS PLAN.

MELANCHTHON INQUIRES CONCERNING RITES AND ORDINANCES.

Cölest., II, 291 ; Chytr., Ger., 261 ; C. R., II, 229.

July 27th.

1. The Confutation is being shorn of its abusive expressions, and to-day I understood from Campeggius that it would be forthcoming in a few days.   When it

appears, we can approximately decide *the time of our departure.*   If they agree to our answering it, *we will not stay much longer.*

2.   Erasmus has again written to the Emperor, and he is evidently pleased with our cause so far as the marriage of the priests, vows and the two-fold mode is concerned.   For he specially mentioned these Articles.

3.   It appears to me that you are somewhat stirred up in your answers concerning human ordinances.   But I pray that you will *approve my Disputation.* These are great matters, and *those who are here give me little help.*   I am of the full assurance that the bishops dare not encumber the Church with their ordinances, and I also have thus written in the Confession, and will not alter the same. . . .

At Augsburg, July 27th, 1530.

LUTHER TO MELANCHTHON.

MS. : Aurifaber's unprinted Collection, III, Bl. 72.

July 30th.

To Philip Melanchthon, the faithful confessor of Christ, and genuine witness: Grace and peace in our Lord !

I am thinking that you have battled sharply with the bad spirits this week. . . . I am with you in faith and spirit as much as I can be ; but I believe that a very weak faith in Christ is with you more.   I am praying Him in sobs and words which He Himself has commanded and given.

The Lord grant that you abide *steadfast in the cause,* and do not allow yourself to be drawn into *a war of accusations.*   I believe that the opponents are aiming at that very thing since they are not fully sure of their cause.

But what will the end be, *if you begin to excuse and cover over the abomination of the Pope* against God and the civil rule?   By God's grace you will know better how to avoid this.

If I cannot read and write, I am able nevertheless to think and pray, and thus in this way work powerfully against him.

My dear Philip, see to it that you do not torture yourself in this affair, which is not in your hand but in the hand of Him Who is greater than the world, and out of Whose hand no one can tear it away.

YOUR MARTIN LUTHER.

LUTHER TO MELANCHTHON.

Jenaer MS. : Flacius, Lat., Briefsam.
Cölest., II, 292 ; Chytr., 168.

August 3rd.

To his exceedingly dear Brother :—

Grace and peace !   Now you are writing me already for the third or fourth time concerning the Ordinances, my dear Philippus.   Either I do not understand you, or you argue about an impossible thing. . . . I could not at this time comprehend your words otherwise. . . . May the Lord soon transform you into such persons *who will return.* The grace of God be with you all. Amen.

The 3rd of August, 1530.

MARTIN LUTHER.

LUTHER TO MELANCHTHON.

MS. in Rhedig. Brief. in Breslau; Cod. Jen. b, fol. 76. Cölest., II, 293.

August 4th.

Perhaps I am so distracted through other thoughts that I do not properly comprehend yours. I am astonished why you should inquire after such matters as though you did not know them, while I nevertheless know that you most thoroughly understand everything pertaining to our cause. . . . So that among ours at Augsburg, viz., Philippus and Jonas and the whole society (Collegium), there are great disturbances.

THE CONFUTATION READ.

But before Melanchthon was fully informed, it seems, as to the acerbity of the situation from a political point of view in the Diet, on this 6th day of August he sat down and wrote the following account of events to Luther:—

MELANCHTHON TO LUTHER.

Cölest., III, 25; Chytr., 215 (Ger.), 317.

August 6th.

1. At last, on August 3rd, we heard the Confutation, together with the Emperor's Declaration, which was quite severe. For before the reading of the Confutation, the Emperor had said he wished to continue in his recorded Opinion, and desired that our princes would unitedly reconcile themselves with him therein. If not, then he, as a Protector of the Church, would no longer suffer such a division in Germany.

2. This is the summary of the address. While this sounded very severe, yet we were all very happy after the reading of the Confutation. For it is childish and silly. Concerning the two kinds, Faber applies the history of the sons of Eli, that they asked of the priest a little bread, and shows from it that the laity shall receive only the form of bread. The Mass is justified in a particularly lame and deceitful manner.

When Joachim returned after the reading of the Confutation (for I was not there), he said, It is a great mistake that I concern myself so much about the different arguments as to human Tradition.   For such thoughts never entered into their head.

3. Our party requested a copy of the Confutation, but the imperial Majesty took it under advisement, and on the following day again admonished our princes that they unite and reconcile themselves with him on the basis of this document.

His imperial Majesty is willing to permit the writing to be delivered to them, but on condition that it be not printed nor copied. About this there was much debate, until finally the archbishop of Maintz, and his brother, the elector of Brandenburg, and the duke of Brunswick coincided with our princes, and requested that they should not any further insist on their position, so that the imperial Majesty might not be more intensely moved. They desired to think out more agreeable means and ways, how the whole matter might be considered and conducted in a friendly manner. Thus we could not yet see the Confutation, and to-day shall be present (to learn) what means the princes will propose. Here you have all our news.

4. All good and considerate persons are now much more hearty and friendly, since they have heard the childishly framed Confutation. [Melanchthon did not yet realize that the intervention of the German princes at this moment had brought back better feeling. He apparently had heard the account of only one informant, like himself interested chiefly in the Confutation.] *Our princes could more easily attain peace, if they would assiduously approach and faithfully petition the Emperor himself and certain sensible princes in the matter; but they are entirely negligent in this and, as things appear to me, it inwardly angers me that they do not do this.*

The whole matter stands in God's will, and will not be governed through human flesh. Meanwhile *I become impatient about our negligence;* I think that God withholds from us this human help so that we will not confide in ourselves. Hence you will diligently pray that God may sustain and protect and *grant us universal peace: The Landgrave keeps himself under perfect control.* He explicitly told me that he too would, for the sake of peace, accept very burdensome conditions, in so far only as they can be borne without any reproach and disadvantage to the Gospel.

Herewith commended to God.   The 6th of August, 1530.

LUTHER TO MELANCHTHON.

Jen. MS.
Cölest., III, 28 b; De Wette, IV, 133.

August 15th.

I praise God, who has permitted the Confutation of the opponents to take such a stupid course. Now then, for a strong pull through to the end ! Having read Eisleben's letter. which treats of disturbances and devils, I had been fearing that dreadful things would happen.   MARTIN LUTHER.

August 6th.

THE LUTHERANS' DARKEST HOUR.

On August 6th, as Melanchthon narrates just above, the Lutherans were offered a copy of the Confutation on condition that they agree with the Emperor, and refrain from printing the document. They declined the offer. The refusal of the Lutherans to receive the Confutation on the imperial terms, their appeal to God and to his Majesty [39] brought on a scene of excitement and confusion. The Romanist Princes, especially George of Saxony, declared that this reply was rebellion, and it seemed for a time as if war would begin on the very floor of the Diet.[40] The Papal Legate, spurred on by tidings he had received from Rome, urged Charles to seize fire and sword and take possession of the property of the heretics, and put the heretical University of Wittenberg under the ban.[41]

The Lutheran party held their peace, though filled with indignation.[42] Melanchthon, in great fear, fell back on Luther's prayers.

But Luther himself was full of faith and courage. Already on August 5th he had written his famous letter concerning the two miracles he saw at his window, the one of the stars in the magnificent firmament whose immense vault the Lord supported by his power, and yet the heavens did not fall; and the other of the great cloud hanging over our heads, which was not suspended by cords, and yet did not collapse. He wrote to Augsburg: "God will choose the way and the time of deliverance, and He will not tarry. What the men of blood have commenced, they cannot finish. Our rainbow is very faint, and their clouds are very threat-

---

[39] Först., *Urk.*, II, 181: "Dass sie es gott und S. majestät befehlen musten."

[40] *Ib.*, *C. R.*, II, 254.

[41] Instructio data Cæsari a reverendissimo Campeggi in dieta Augustana, 1530.

[42] *C. R.*, II, 254.

ening, but ours will be the victory. No matter if Luther perishes, Christ will be the conqueror. And then Luther will also be conqueror." [43]

It is said that when at the meeting the Emperor called upon the Protestants to submit to the Confutation, and then looked knowingly at his sword, the Elector of Saxony took him up at his own meaning and replied, " The straight line is the shortest road." It might surely have been war, if the archbishop of Maintz, the Elector of Brandenburg, and other German Catholic Princes, who knew the strength of the Protestants and were fearful of an invasion of their own dominions, or who sympathized with them in their position, had not intervened and offered themselves to the Lutherans to mediate their cause. The Elector declared that it was not the Emperor with whom the Lutheran quarrel lay. They had come in response to his Call, and they were ready to have unity of faith restored on the basis of that Call.[44] This was the position the Lutherans had taken all along, and with this in view the Augsburg Confession was framed, viz., the possibility of a purification of the old church in doctrine and abuses; but not a unification at the expense of any point of the Gospel doctrine.

The Emperor accepted the offer of these Princes, and consequently sixteen German Catholics were appointed as mediators between the Romanists and the Protestants. This was still the morning of August 6th, and the mediators met immediately. The morning they spent in internal struggles and disputes, the bishop of Augsburg speaking in favor of the Lutherans, and the archbishop of Salsburg against them. These Catholic Princes met in the afternoon again, but instead of mediating between others, almost came to blows [45] among themselves.

---

[43] MS. in *Cod. Jen.* b. fol. 306. *Chytr.,* 96 b ; *Erl.,* **54** : 183 ; *Cölest.,* II, 275.

[44] *C. R.,* II, 254.

[45] *Chytr.,* Ger. 215 ; *Salig,* I, 277.

HEROISM OF THE LUTHERAN REFUSAL.

This refusal of the Lutherans to accept the Confutation and return to the Roman Church was one of the boldest of the many perilous acts of these heroes on behalf of their Faith. Up to now, Melanchthon (who from the very start was averse to a frank and open Confession, and who seemed as one possessed with the demon of negotiation and compromise rather than with the spirit of Confession) alone excepted, all the princes and theologians had stood squarely on the Confession, deliberately preferring to take the consequences of excommunication from the Catholic Church, loss of position, loss of property, loss of life, and open war itself, rather than yield one point of the pure doctrine. They stood for their rights under the Call, and they had hope in the Emperor as one who felt the power of the truth.

To paint them,—even in the darkest days of this dark month of August, when under the fearful, if not perfidious, leadership of Melanchthon, they came near making shipwreck of the whole cause for which they had sacrificed so much,—as willing to secure peace at any price, as being unable to endure the idea of parting from the Roman Church, or to go to the still more untruthful extreme of intimating that they were worried by the fear that there was "no salvation for them outside of the Roman Church," is not only a perversion of the facts, but is an injustice to men who were literally giving their life for the cause.

Of the Lutheran part of the Committee that subsequently brought the doctrine into compromise, the old Margrave, who had offered his head at the block eight weeks earlier rather than give up his faith; the timid Heller; with Schnepf, the theologian of Philip of Hesse, and a sound man; Brentz and Melanchthon, were members. We believe it can be shown that the plan, the method, the stubborn insistence on compromise, and the results, were, under the manipulation of Rome, those of Melanchthon; and that of all the party—

the Elector, Brück, Schnepf, the Margrave and the Nurembergers,—he was the only one who was really willing to
wreck any part of the doctrine of Luther for the sake of
remaining with Rome. And he had even tried to justify
the compromise to his own conscience. As he made Luther
weary by the constant proposal of Roman approximations,
which were not however put squarely, in the actual historical form in which he intended to avail himself of them,
so by dint of persistent dictation and assumption of authority
he brought down the situation here, as he did years later
in the Leipzig Interim, to a surrender of Justification by
Faith, the great Article of the standing or falling church.
For anyone, in face of the persistent evidence of the constant leaven of the Melanchthonian principle of compromise
of doctrine before the Confession, after the Confession, in
the Variata, and during the whole generation of Melanchthon's leadership, to say that this was the position of Luther, or of the Elector, or of Brück, or of the Electoral party
at Augsburg, or to represent these men as being willing to
secure peace from Rome at any price, is to cover the shame
and to attribute the principles and motives of one unionistic Lutheran to men who all their life stood firm against
union of any character at the expense of doctrine. If any
one thing is revealed clearly in Melanchthon's correspondence, it is that he finds little sympathy (outside of Jonas),
in the Electoral party for his views and plans.[46]

August 7th.

A DAY OF SENSATION FOR BOTH SIDES.

The Lutheran Princes were still asleep the next morning

---

[46] To cite only two instances: Mel. to Luther, July 27th: "Those who are
here help me little ; " Aug. 6th, Mel. to Luther: "Our princes could secure
peace much more readily, . . . if they diligently begged for it; but they are
altogether neglectful as to this, and as it looks to me, secretly irritated, so
that they do not undertake this." Here we have Melanchthon's own testimony
not only to the fact that the princes are of little help to him and out of sympathy with his plans ; but that, while he is eager for peace, the princes are
apathetic. What further proof is needed as to the difference in attitude between himself and the Electoral party !

when they were ordered to come immediately to the chapter hall.[47] They arrived at eight o'clock. The mediators appointed on August 6th met with them and demanded that they give up their false doctrine, and come back to the bosom of the church. The Elector of Saxony asked for time. Then Joachim turned upon him savagely and said that unless he gave up the doctrine of Luther, the Emperor would use force against him and subjugate him, deposing him from his position, despoiling his possessions, laying waste his country, and taking away his life, and would force his subjects back to the old faith. Turning toward the Elector, he said: "All will be torn from you, swift ruin will descend upon your subjects, and even upon their wives and children."

The Elector showed no sign of movement. His friends now saw why it was that the guards of the Emperor occupied the gates of the city:[48] the Emperor intended violence.[49] The Elector was stunned as by a thunder-bolt, and returned home in distress.[50] Those historians who fail to present the whole truth, and make it appear that this distress was a sign of yielding, are not to be trusted. However terrifying the threats, the Elector and his party stood firm, and did not recede one step. "Sed hae minae nihil commoverunt: perstant in sententia, nec vel tantillum recedunt."[51] On that same afternoon Brück prepared a firm answer to these dreadful demands. This answer stated that the Lutherans could not yield to the proposals made by the Catholic commissioners, that their side had not been properly heard, as the Emperor had promised it would be in the Call, that they had not received a copy of the Confutation, and that

---

[47] *C. R.*, II, 254; Brück, *Apol.*, f. 79.

[48] *Ib.*, 277.

[49] *Ib.*

[50] *Cölest.*, III, 26b.

[51] *C. R.*, II, 277.

the Emperor had promised to call a national Council to take up these matters.[52]

But it proved to be not necessary to read their answer that day in the Diet. A tremendous sensation had occurred. The evening before, on August 6th, at eight o'clock, Philip of Hesse had succeeded in leaving Augsburg in disguise, and in escaping to his dominions. He had said, " I shall fight for the Word of God, at the risk of my goods, my estates, my subjects, and my life." The news travelled through the city like the report of a volcano. The Emperor was shaken to the bottom of his heart.[53] The Elector and his firm but down-hearted band of heroes were as much astonished as the Romanists themselves. Luther, as soon as he heard it, highly approved of the Landgrave's departure, and exclaimed, " Such delay and indignity are enough to tire more than one Landgrave."

August 8th to 15th.

THE ROMANISTS CONCILIATE AND ASK FOR A COMMISSION.

The effect on the Diet of the Landgrave's departure was instantaneous. The German Catholic Princes thought they already saw him at the head of an army and feared lest their territories would immediately be invaded by the bold knight. All threatenings in the Diet against the Lutherans ceased, and they were treated with respect. As the cry had a day ago been violence and war, it now was compromise and peace. So great was the reaction, so full of anxiety was the Emperor, so meek was the Papal party, that, though Brück had handed in his defiant answer, subscribed by eight Princes and six cities on the 9th of August, and the Elector Joachim had replied to it as the spokesman of the

---

[52] *C. R.,* II, 266 ; *Chytr.,* Lat., 221.
[53] *Seck.,* II, 172.

Catholic commisson on the 11th of August,[54] when, on the 13th of August, the Protestant Princes made their counter reply,—and declared that they were willing to go as far *as was consistent with God's Word,* and to unite with others *so far as their consciences would permit,* if the method originally proposed by the Emperor in the Call were followed, and a small number of commissioners were chosen (not from the Catholic side exclusively as had been done but) from both sides, who would consider the articles in dispute and endeavor to bring about an agreement, as the Call intended,—the Romanists were only too glad to adopt the method originally proposed by the emperor, and, wonder of wonders! *to make the Augsburg Confession itself the basis* of consideration.[56]

On the next day, the Emperor appointed a commission of an equal number of representatives from both sides. The reader should note that all three of the theologians representing the Catholic side were the most bitter and venomous enemies of the Lutherans, viz., John Eck, Conrad Wimpina and John Cochlaeus. He will also see, if he studies the situation, that the Romanists suddenly became wolves in sheep's clothing, that the commission would proceed on its downward path under the leadership of Eck on the one side, and the still once again miserably deceived Melanchthon on the Protestant side. He will see too that the protestant theologians were not our leaders in the true sense of the word. Eck knew in advance that Melanchthon could be gained over to the Roman side, and knew that the Princes did not sympathize with Melanchthon on this point; and, therefore, he said as early as the 14th of August that, " They did not want any Princes on the commission; for the Princes

---

[54] Even Joachim had wound up his reply by saying that *" for the present* it would be wiser to propose means and ways for concord! " [55]

[55] *Chytr.,* 222 sqq.

[56] For this counter reply of the Protestants, see *Chytr.,* (Ger.) 130, (Lat.) 225 ; *Salig,* I, 282-284.

are self-conceited fools." [57]   The Lutherans were appointed by the Emperor.

Already on August 15th the Lutheran theologians had presented to their Princes an Opinion on the subject of " concord," which reproduces, word for word, and almost clause for clause, the favorite thought of Melanchthon; and in which he has evidently embraced the opportunity to chastise and warn the Princes against supposed apathy toward war.   In this Opinion, in which Melanchthon tries to train and school the more sturdy princes to his own more timid views, as being those of the Word of God, by arguments which he has been attempting also to force upon Luther in his correspondence with him, perhaps the most remarkable of all the Melanchthonian statements is this: " Therefore we most humbly beg the princes, for the sake of God and for their own good, to try to make peace, and to see to it, that *if the enemy should become too severe, our consciences should become more easy."*   Thus does the unionistic theologian graduate his conscience, not according to the teaching of the Word of God, but inversely according to the severity of the enmity.   No wonder that pure Lutheran doctrine was in danger of being sacrificed under a theologian animated by this principle. [58]

August 16th.

GREAT CONCESSIONS PROPOSED.

On August 16th the commission consisting of two princes, two lawyers, and two theologians from each side went to work.   The Protestant theologians were Melanchthon, Brentz, and Schnepf.   The Evangelical Confession was taken as the basis of discussion.   Of the twenty-one articles, the Romanists finally objected only to penance, invocation of saints, and justification by faith.   Rome *could* not yield on this latter

[57] *C. R.,* II, 279.
[58] *Ib.,* 281 sqq. ; *Chytr.,* Lat., 236 sqq.

point: it *must* maintain the meritorious influence of works. As to government, ordinances, and abuses, the Protestants, on their part, went so far in their concessions as to agree to restore the bishops, and even to agree to acknowledge the Pope,[59] while the Romanists yielded the marriage of priests until the next Council. But Brentz wrote, "we cannot acknowledge the Pope, because we say he is Antichrist";[60] and, two days later, when the others seemed on the point of yielding, Brück wrote on the margin of the document, "We cannot acknowledge the Pope because we say he is Antichrist, and because he claims primacy by divine right."[61] We have reason to believe that of the six Protestant commissioners, Brück, Brentz and Schnepf protested and were unwilling. Melanchthon was able to manage the brave old Margrave and the timid Heller. The committee not only agreed to go back to the jurisdiction of the Pope and the bishops, but also to return to the Roman customs and ceremonies. How astonishing it is that sixteen years later, as soon as Luther was dead, Melanchthon again put the Church into this very position; though meantime he had been veering and temporizing toward the Reformed position.

On August the 18th, the commissioners issued an "Explanation" of the articles to which both commissions had agreed. This "Explanation" raised a storm outside the committee. The lay Protestants were disgusted with the theologians. We are told that all Augsburg[62] declared, "It is better to die with Christ, than to gain the favor of the whole world without Him."

---

[59] All this was in accordance with Melanchthon's program of concession, made before even he knew there would be an opportunity to concede. This put his informal concessions to the Legate into fixed shape. He had been preparing for it in the correspondence on Ordinances of which Luther grew weary, and Luther had been unable to shake him in this purpose. The discussion in the Commission on the Protestant side proves all this. Thus, they said, "Although the pope is Anti-Christ, we may be under his government, as the Jews were under Pharaoh, and in later days under Caiaphas." "Only," said the Lutheran theologians, "let sound doctrine be fully accorded to us."

[60] Först., *Urk.,* II, 249.

[61] *Ibid.,* 247.

[62] "Die ganze Stadt sagt."—*C. R.,* II, 297.

It was indeed a great Melanchthonian treachery, in which Melanchthon had involved his commission. The theologians with him were Heller, Brentz, and Schnepf. Schnepf, according to certain accounts, seems to have remained steadfast, and Brentz seems to have become confused.

To make these men the representatives of the whole Lutheran party at Augsburg, is not to write history. They had been appointed by the Emperor: they had been dictated to by Melanchthon. His fear of war, his desire not to break with Rome, his lack of faith, his respect for worldly power, and all the worse sides of his mental character entered in as the controlling element. In the article on the Lord's Supper,—just as later on, he had in his 'Loci' and in the 'Variata' of the Augsburg Confession used ambiguous language,—he was now using ambiguous language to cover both the doctrine of transubstantiation and the Lutheran doctrine of the sacrament.

For any historian to conclude, after all that Luther had been writing since 1527 on the Sacrament of the Altar, after the severe examination of the doctrine of the mass during the struggles of the Sacramentarians, that the Lutherans themselves at this time maintained a view of the sacrament which could be harmonized with the Roman teaching of transubstantiation, is an insult to the early reformers. Melanchthon understood Eck's meaning in the statement which he here accepted, but he, for the sake of peace, and with that inability to appreciate the immutableness of the teaching of the Word of God, was willing to gloss over a fundamental difference in this doctrine with Rome, just as he afterwards was willing to gloss it over in connection with the teaching of Bucer and Calvin. There was the same inconsistency on his part as to Protestant concession in the doctrine of Private Confession.

Eck had managed things so wonderfully that he had succeeded in gaining from Melanchthon almost every point vital to the Romanists. As to justification, Cochlaeus reported thus: "The Lutherans of their own accord gave up and renounced this word *Sola,* and no longer said that we are justified by faith alone. Hence, a short statement of Concord was at once drawn up in the briefest possible form of words, and, unless my memory fails me, it was written by Philip himself, namely, that justification or the remission of sins takes place " per gratiam gratum facientem et fidem formaliter, per verbum vero et sacramentum instrumentaliter." [63]

But great bomb-shells, as we shall see, were soon dropped, by Luther, into this beautiful peace, mediated by Melanchthonian treachery.

MELANCHTHON AND HIS COMPROMISE.

That Melanchthon has been recognized in history as responsible for thus attempting to strangle the Lutheran Church, the report of the proceedings of this Commission given by even such a mild, tolerant, pietistic, and moderate historian as Salig [64] will show. Salig excuses himself at the start by saying, "Whether Melanchthon was to blame or not, I shall not say at this time. Luther at least praised his transactions and freed him from blame." He then tells the following story, put together from Vita Phil. Mel., Coelestin, Chytræus, Mueller, Sleidanus and other early historians:—

"At that time Melanchthon was under very great pressure and subject to many criticisms from his party. Camerarius reports that frequently he saw Melanchthon sobbing and crying, [65] and had heard many complaints. The causes of the adverse remarks were chiefly these: —

" (1) That in all things he caused himself to appear too mild and fearful.

---

[63] Plitt, *Apologie der Augustana,* p. 49.

[64] *Salig,* I, 318.

[65] Melanchthon wrote to Camerarius : " Not a day passes in which I do not wish that I might leave this world."

" (2) That he wrote letters that were too humble, to the cardinals, the legates, and other bishops, such as Luettlich, and Augsburg, and to the Venetian orator, Nicholas Teupolus."[65][65½] That his letters were now being carried around in print at Augsburg to the greatest shame and reproach of Melanchthon, which were not a little increased by a letter of Luther in which this softness of Melanchthon was chastised in caustic words.

" (3) That he would have been glad to give back their jurisdiction into the hands of the papal bishops, and therefore had yielded more than could properly be done without injury to the Confession, although he had at the same time laid down the condition that the bishops should leave the pure Gospel free. Yes, one of the Evangelicals went so far as to speak these hard words of Melanchthon: If Melanchthon had been hired at the price of a great sum of money by the Papists, to defend their cause, he could not have gone about it in a better way. Melanchthon was to be held, not as a patron of the Evangelicals, but of the Papists.

"Melanchthon complained to Camerarius, that many Evangelical representatives were angry at him on this account, and that others had charged him of these things in bitter words. Luther wrote,[66] September 2nd: It is not possible to say how much he was hated by the Nurembergers, because he had again yielded the power to the bishops.

" (4) For the Nuremberg Theologians had diligently reported the opinions and actions of Melanchthon back home. The Council at Nuremberg passed a special resolution with respect to the inconceivable reply of the Protestants.

" The instrument drawn up seemed to have yielded very much, and to have given into the hands of the Papists that which was either injurious to the conscience, which could not be maintained with Scripture, or burdensome and offensive to those who up to now had confessed Christ and his Gospel.

---

[66] Cölestin, III, 63.   [65½] Not a Letter, but a Conversation. v. p. 216.

" (1.) In the first place, it would be a great disadvantage to the Christian authorities to be obliged after all to allow all Monks and Nuns and their cloisters with all their manners and ceremonies to continue peacefully in the old lines. . . .

" (2.) In the second place, it would not be well to admit to the Papists that there are three parts in repentance.

" (3.) In the third place, to say that the Sacrament should be administered to none without previous auricular Confession would not only lead to much misunderstanding of the matter, but would also be dangerous. . . .

" (4.) The article of fasting and the eating of meats had been so composed as to give up Christian liberty under the appearance of peaceful unity and uniformity.

" (5.) The intercession of the saints or of angels in Heaven is not to be proven out of the Scripture.

" (6.) The quickest way to suppress and extirpate the Gospel was to give the bishops spiritual jurisdiction to a much greater extent than they up to this time had dared to ask for, and than they actually had formerly possessed.

" (7.) Further, it was a crafty stroke by which the Papists had postponed all the other articles which had not been discussed, to a future Council, and wished that this single one alone, of the jurisdiction of the bishops, should be at once thus accepted. They had reached a path and a method by which they would soon be able to become masters of the Gospel and of those who proclaimed it.

" If such articles were now accepted, the Christian Estates could not be acquitted of acting against the Scriptures. Although one would do much for the sake of peace, it is necessary, in order not to bring about war in the heart and conscience, to do right as a Christian, and commit the serious question of peace or war to God.

" Further, if the articles referred to should be adopted, and Luther and other preachers should preach, teach, and write against them, and they could not do otherwise, one should stop to consider what sort of a peace had been attained by such yielding up of the cause.

" In earlier days, the Christian Estates had proven themselves so brave and steadfast, and now, without necessity, they yielded as much as they could. . . . Moreover, in such important affairs, one must not act in a perplexed and uncertain way, but must place everything beyond the possibility of being disputed and doubted. No matter how it now went with this plan of mediation, the Christian Estates would awaken the suspicion and dislike of friend and foe, while the Papists would be greatly strengthened in their abuses, and would shout aloud their victory, as Cochlaeus had already written to Nuremberg, and had praised the yielding of the Evangelicals to the highest degree. All this was, accordingly, to be announced by the Nuremberg representative to the Elector of Saxony.

" When the matter reached them by post, they were said to have answered: That not only they, but their Theologians, from whom they had secretly taken counsel, had found all sorts of difficulty in some of the methods and articles. If the same had been sent to them before they were delivered to the Committee, they would have spoken out their difficulties to the Elector and other Princes and the honorable Council. Therefore, they regarded the transactions of the Committee as altogether inconceivable and invalid, and begged that the Estates would allow the whole matter to go to Dr. Luther, and would deliberate with him, so that nothing would be agreed upon to the disadvantage of the Gospel, for if anything final should be undertaken without his knowledge and will, and Luther should afterward preach against it, the matter would become much more confused than beforehand.

" If it should be a difficult matter to recall the points which had been agreed on, the Papists could nevertheless not demand acceptance without ratification, just as they themselves would not accept without the approval of the Emperor and the other Estates, anything that the Evangelical theologians should bring to a final conclusion without the consent of the Estates.

" (8.) All this was the consequence, chiefly of the mild propositions and the wide correspondence of Melanchthon, which however he never was willing to admit. But, in order to understand the cause and the occasion of this Nuremberg opinion more fully, we shall present a short extract from Hieronymus Baumgartner, who was at that time present at the Diet at Augsburg, and who wrote to Lazarus Spengler, Secretary of the Nuremberg Council. From this correspondence one can see how the other Theologians were not satisfied with the mediators at the Diet.

" ' In the first letter, Baumgartner writes: I must give my opinion of the action of this Diet in matters of faith. God grant that in this I shall not become a true prophet!

" ' First, you know what persistent opposition there has been against us in past transactions first by this and then by another devil, who at times transformed themselves into angels of light. Although the Romanist party failed to attain its desire, and the measures proposed on our part were accepted, we nevertheless are finding out that even now the idea is to place their measures in the decree at once as having been agreed to.

" ' Even if such an extreme should not happen, the Romanists have never entered into any dealing in vain, but they always forced some concession from us, which we have been obliged to grant. This yielding they always hold ready to spring upon us and, at sometime when it is least desirable, they will use it. But by His special grace God has ordained that the Confession has been delivered over once for all in full:—else our Theologians would have confessed another one long ago, which indeed if they had been supported, they would gladly have done, although they are not all of the same mind.

" ' *Philip has become more childish than a child. Brentz*

is not only unskillful, but also rough and coarse. Heller is full of fear, and these three have caused the pious Margrave to be quite distracted and discouraged, and have persuaded him to do what they desire, although I perceive that he would gladly do right. The pious Vogler is much abused in his absence, as though, if he were still here [Baumgartner writes from Augsburg], so much that is good [in their eye] would not have been accomplished.

" '*The Elector in this business has no one more sensible than the one and only Dr. Brück; but they have brought him to the point where he now also grows anxious in business, since there is not a soul to give him any support. The other Saxon theologians dare not speak openly against Philip,* for he has gone so far as recently to assert against the Lüneburg chancellor: ' He who dares to say that the remedies last yielded to are not Christian, lies like a villain. . . .

" ' In fine: if that rough and ungracious decree of his imperial Majesty had not soon failed, the Romanists would not have ceased with us until they had brought us into the net. So greatly have we needed God's protection, and have not received the Emperor's: for this affair has continued constantly up to this time.

" 'As often as the princes assemble, one comes riding up to the Elector and tells him, ' *how faithful and well disposed he is, etc., that he has heard this or that from the Emperor, and if one would only yield in this or that point, the affairs might still be adjusted.*' Immediately Philip is on hand, writes up an article, comments on it, etc. This is then carried by Heller and Brentz to the Margrave. When then we have been consulted, and we declare that the predigested broth does not taste good, offense is given and the theologians go about and say that we do not desire peace, as though peace were indeed to be surely preserved by our yielding.

" ' Let us only make attack with the Landgrave, whom they defamed most sadly in this matter. What will come of all this at last, you can well perceive as an experienced man, if force be used, as the Emperor intends. The effort will be to take away the Gospel from us by violence, as we well deserve; and although this is very oppressive, yet it is easier before God than that we should voluntarily enter those paths in which it will surely be stolen from us by treachery. It is indeed necessary to call on God continuously. . . . Schnepf alone still has a voice to sing in a firm and Christian way, on which account he is often mocked scurrilously by the others. Without him we would be, as far as all the theologians are concerned, at one with the other side.' "

LUTHER TO SPENGLER.

Wolfenbüttel.
Erl., 54, 188.

August 24th.

We have heard of the new committee at Augsburg and of the Landgrave's departure, and it is something wonderful for us to look upon. God give further grace. Amen.

MELANCHTHON TO LUTHER.

Chytr., Ger., 400.

August 22nd.

Yesterday we brought the disputations to an end. Eck ridicules the word *sola*, although he has not rejected the doctrine as such.

When we came to the disputation as to both forms, I could not accept the doctrine that there is no commandment to receive it in both forms.

Spengler wrote to Luther concerning the lack of unity and the too great mildness of the theologians at Augsburg. Luther answered him on August 28th, saying that they should consider how much the theologians at Augsburg had been obliged to endure, and should not blame them for the reason that, despite their yielding, up to this moment the truth had remained unharmed. Even if somewhat too much had been yielded, which he nevertheless hoped was not the case, yet the matter was not lost, but it was still possible to begin a new conflict. Spengler should rest assured, that he, Luther, would yield nothing pertaining to the Gospel. And if his men at Augsburg yielded anything, it would go bad with the Roman party.

To Jonas, Luther wrote that he had received many letters in which it was stated that the Lutheran side had been betrayed, and that too much had been yielded for the sake of peace: but that he himself relied on the reaction. He said further that he would not endure the inconceivable and impossible Articles which the mediation committee had composed, even if an angel of Heaven commanded him to do so. The Roman party would never yield a hair's breadth. There was not much need of composing many articles. If the Canon were yielded to Rome, the whole Gospel would be denied. If the jurisdiction of the bishops were yielded, our denial of the Gospel would be so much the greater. Peace might charm with its syren tones, but God must be obeyed. This is not a matter of prophesying war, but a matter of believing and confessing. He knew Eck's intention very well. The thing to do was to terminate matters and only come back home again. If a war followed, it would follow. God would deliver His people, even out of the Babylonian furnace of fire.

The kindliness, the patience, the unfaltering friendship, the toleration of Luther for Melanchthon during all these days is marvelous. He loved, he pled, he pitied, but the words of thunder and the bolts of lightning which he hurled so fearlessly upon the enemy did not descend upon the weary, worn, and erring head of his disciple and follower. To the end of his life Luther constantly overlooked the aberrations of Melanchthon with a self-denial, a composure, and a taciturnity that are remarkable.

Salig's opinion of Melanchthon is as follows:—[67]

" We will not excuse Melanchthon in all things, since it is known that he was not indeed the most steadfast sort of a person. But that Baumgartner perhaps wrote much from jealousy, is also no doubt not to be denied. At least Luther

---

[67] I, 335.

always knew how to recognize Melanchthon's great services and his excellent adaptability, and praises him in a way he would not have done, if he had not been satisfied with his leadership."[68]

Cyprian's judgment on Melanchthon is more serious than that of Salig. In one place he quotes an estimate by Cochlaeus, which we give, not because we believe it really characterizes Melanchthon, but because it so graphically depicts the impression that men of compromise—especially if they be theological diplomatists—make even upon their enemies, though the latter be their equals in negotiative craft. Cyprian says:—

" Therefore Cochlaeus wrote to the Emperor concerning Melanchthon:—Your Majesty clearly understands that that man, by his bland speech and his wolflike hypocrisy, conducted himself more disgracefully at the court at Augsburg than the absent Luther did by open taunts and bitter words. For Luther railled in his customary manner; but he, indeed, like a deceitful serpent, intending frauds, endeavored to overcome not the people but the prominent men by his hypocrisy. By so much as Philip is more agreeable to learned men than Luther, and by so much as he is more modest in teaching, so much the more grievously did he harm the Church: it was his habit to reply that they need not await what Luther would write, but what the prince would propose to the Emperor. How craftily he acted with the legate (Campeggi), no one knew better than the legate himself, who, not sufficiently trusting his tears and entreaties, at first, ordered him to put his petition in writing, and yet was not able to preclude all deception by this species of cunning. For he said some time after that he could not trust him in any respect after he had heard him." [69]

---

[68] This is a mistake on the part of Salig. Luther never had blame for Melanchthon, but was silent, even where the younger disciple, by his inconsistency, placed him in a position of great peril.

[69] *Cyprian,* p. 107.

Even Hofstätter [69a] writing on the anniversary of Melanchthon, and in his praise, admits all the facts respecting the failings of the great Præceptor. He says:—

" We see his failings not only in the Melanchthon of the Variata and of the Interim, in his various attempts to greatly weaken the original doctrine as toward Rome and Calvin, and to again veil the truth that had become recognized : we also know quite well how he, to start with, lacked competency to cope with the many works that crowded him in ecclesiastical and governmental polity. Moreover we realize that in the timidity of his nature, in his susceptibility toward hierarchical power and an outward ecclesiasticism, he did not consistently follow the Reformatory views out to their consequences with the bold determination of a Luther. We may perhaps also deplore the fact that such a man of learning, and of the cathedra, was drawn so inextricably into the practical affairs of the Church and was so restrained in a free scientific development of the new ideas. But all that does not lessen his merit nor our gratitude. All that cannot make us forget what the same Melanchthon gave our nation and our Church."

Again Hofstätter says:—

" But now Melanchthon did not abide by it [the Augsburg Confession]. His anxious looking to see which way the wind blew at the imperial court, the feeling that he was responsible for an unfortunate issue of this Diet, from which so much was promised for the evangelical cause, led him, at Augsburg, into many a crooked way and into much deplorable yielding. He invites Cochläus to dine, and negotiates with the secretary of the Emperor. Responding to the wish of the Emperor, he declares himself ready to settle the whole matter privately, and not to insist upon the public discussion. After this he turns to the Legate of the Pope and intends not to decline any conditions of peace that may be at

---

[69a] *Die Augsburgische Konfession in ihrer Bedeutung für das kirchliche Leben der Gegenwart. Leipzig, 1897.*

all possible. He proclaims the mildness of Rome and at
last discovers only a slight deviation in ceremonies [between
Rome and the Evangelical side]. He does not venture any
longer to demand the abolition of the mass, and while the
Romish Confutation with its groundless complaints and the
demand of the Emperor, sharpened by threats, to return to
obedience to the Church, was the very thing to strengthen
the Evangelical Princes in their Faith and to fill them with
immovable courage; while Luther who from the very start
had been moved by doctrinal and not by political considerations, not only failed to grieve over such a termination of
the Diet, but bluntly rebuked Melanchthon for his lack of
Faith, Melanchthon again brought up his concessions in the
presence of the Legate, and stipulated, for his part, nothing
but the marriage of priests and the cup for the laity, giving
up all the rest of the Reformation as a temerarii motus.

"It was only the Evangelical princes who at that time
preserved the Evangelical honor and faith. They courageously and beautifully confess: 'Better perish with Christ,
than without Him gain the favor of the whole world.' So
also it was they who declined the decree of the Diet with its
humiliating conditions; and the cause of the Gospel was not
lost, despite the enmity of Emperor and Pope, despite the
disposition to concede and the faint-heartedness of Melanchthon; and the Confession delivered in Augsburg remained
the Creed of the Reformation."[69b]

"But," says Hofstätter, "what estimate shall we then
make of Melanchthon, of him who by his anxious compromising and yielding threatened to pour away the great
blessing that was contained in his own Confession? We
neither conceal nor palliate this. We do not even wish to
make the excuse for it that a fateful conflict in his life
caused him to be drawn to tasks for which he was not at
all fitted. Nevertheless we will not indeed forget that the

[69b] *Die Augsburgische Konfession in ihrer Bedeutung für das kirchliche Leben
der Gegenwart,* p. 4-7.

hours of vexation and weakness disappeared, and that the very days at Augsburg brought forth that other Confession, which, free from all compromises, again defended the jewel of the Reformation with fresh clear words, which because of its tone and its witness soon became the symbol of the Evangelical side and the Confession of our Church, and which to this day remains an eloquent defense even for Melanchthon. In addition to this, the Augustana is and indeed remains his work, and this work praises its master."[69c]

Professor Loy, in his history of the Augsburg Confession,[70] pronounces a just judgment on Melanchthon as follows:—

" He was a man of peace and unduly timid withal. It is difficult to speak of the work of this commission without censuring his weakness at a time when the occasion demanded unflinching strength. He hesitated when he should have stood forth as the bold confessor of eternal truth.

" The fact is undeniable that his lack of qualification for leadership . . . threatened disaster to the whole cause of the Reformation. He did not show the firmness against men so resourceful in subterfuge as Eck, which was befitting the humble disciple of Christ who bowed to the Lord's Word, whatever might come of it. . . .

" Peace seemed secure without a distinct declaration of the Evangelical truth. Luther who always looked at things in the clear light of the Gospel, replied to Melanchthon: ' You write how Eck was forced to confess that we are saved alone by grace; would to God that you had forced him to quit lying.'

[69c] *Die Augsburgische Konfession in ihrer Bedeutung für das kirchliche Leben der Gegenwart,* p. 7.

Hoffstätter errs in supposing that Melanchthon, if not restrained and hemmed in, would have been more free and scientific in the development of the Church's doctrine ; and that we owe to him entirely the change in the Confession from a mere paper on Ceremonies to an "Apology" of the most weighty articles of faith.

[70] *The Augsburg Confession,* p. 52-53.

" Unable in his weakness to withstand artifices, Melanchthon was allured into concessions which were not even in accord with the faith even of his soul. But God still ruled, and He had no concessions to make. When the Papists insisted that the Protestants must not teach that the Holy Supper is administered in both kinds by divine command, Melanchthon's conscience overcame his love of peace, and neither he nor his colleagues could be induced to make a concession. . . . The Lutherans declared that the people must be taught what the Scriptures teach. The negotiations were thus brought to a close, and the commission reported that no agreement could be effected."

August 26th.

FIRE OPENED FROM COBURG.

But Luther, though he was so patient with Melanchthon and the Augsburg party, and so apologetic on their behalf in all complaints from outside, took positive and radical action when the tidings came to him on August 26th concerning the proposed compromise. He wrote no less than five letters, one to Melanchthon, one to the Elector, one to Spalatin, one to Jonas and one to Brentz, on the 26th, and three more on the 28th.

So far as we recall, Luther had been kept in ignorance of this new move. Melanchthon had not written to him from August 8th to August 22nd. Before this letter came, Luther had heard some rumors via Wittenberg which seemed quite incredible, and of which he spoke ironically to Melanchthon in a letter on the 24th. Besserer reports to Ulm on this date that Luther already is exceedingly wrought up.

LUTHER TO MELANCHTHON.

Cölest., III, 50.

August 24th.

I believe you have long ago heard the latest news from Augsburg, my dear Philip, viz., that fourteen men have been chosen anew as new mediators, all of whose names we know, and that you, with Eck, are the principal speakers, but

Spalatin is the secretary. If this is true, it is wonderful. The Lord, who sent you to Augsburg, make you great and glorious there ! . . What shall we travelers do but show our skill in announcing the news, while meantime, you remain as disposed to silence as the frogs in Seriphus.

August 22nd.

Melanchthon had written to Luther on this day,[71] and had told him of the happenings in the larger Commission. Luther was stirred, and sat down and told Melanchthon that the Papacy and the Gospel doctrine could not exist together, much less be reconciled; that he had a crafty set to deal with, whose aim was to suppress the Evangelicals; that Melanchthon's defence of justification, and the two modes was good, but that he could not have done worse in inviting a severe and dangerous war by again yielding to the authority of the bishops, and returning to the old rites.

LUTHER TO MELANCHTHON.

Cod., Jen., b. fol. 114.
Cölest., III, fol. 50b.

August 26th.

I pray you, is not everything deception there? You now have Campeggi, you have the Saltzberger, you have the silenced monks who crossed the Rhine to Spires. . . .

What have I ever hoped for less, and what do I now wish less, than transactions concerning a union in doctrine? As if we really could destroy the Pope, or as if as long as popery remains unharmed, our doctrine could be unharmed. Of course there can be union and compromise, in order that he may remain pope. He will concede and allow, if we do thus. But God be praised that you have not accepted anything from them.

You write that Eck has been forced by you to confess that we are justified by faith ; would to God though that you had also compelled him not to lie. For Eck confesses that righteousness comes from faith, but at the same time he defends all the abominations of popery, kills, persecutes, and condemns those who confess this doctrine of the faith. He is not repenting, but continues.

The whole of the Roman party does the very same thing, and with these people you are seeking conditions of unity and worrying yourself in vain, until they shall find something plausible by which they can destroy us. In the matter of the two forms you have done right. . . .

It is not in our power to place or tolerate anything in God's church or in His

---

[71] *Chytr.*, p. 265.

service which cannot be defended by the Word of God, and I am vexed not a little by this talk of compromise, which is a scandal to God. With this one word "mediation" I could easily make all the laws and ordinances of God matters of compromise. For if we admit that there is a compromise in the Word of God, how can we defend ourselves so that not all things become compromises. . . .

As to the restoration of obedience and jurisdiction to the bishops and to the common forms and ceremonies, as you write: " Take heed, and do not give more than you have," so that we are not forced into a serious and dangerous war anew, to defend the Gospel. I know that you always except the Gospel in these dealings, but I fear that they might blame us as a faithless and unreliable people, if we do not uphold what they desire, for they will take our admonitions in a wide, ever wider, the widest possible sense; but give to their own a narrow, ever narrower, the narrowest possible sense.

In short, I am thoroughly displeased with this negotiating concerning union in doctrine, since it is utterly impossible, except the Pope wishes to put away his power. It was enough to give account of our faith and to ask for peace. Why do we hope to convert them to the truth? We have come, to hear whether or not they will assent to our Confession, and they be free to remain where they are. And we ask whether they reject our side, or acknowledge it as right. If they reject it, of what use is it to try to enter into harmony with enemies? If they acknowledge it as right, why should we retain the old abuses? And since it is certain that our side will be condemned by them, as they are not repenting, and are striving to retain their side, why do we not see through the matter and recognize that all their concessions are a lie?

We present some further extracts from this powerful battery that was now directed from Coburg against the compromises at Augsburg:—

To Justus Jonas.

Tr. by *Currie.*

August 26th or 27th.

I got a sight of our people's opinion concerning our affairs, but what I wrote Philip I write to you, that for Christ's honour and to please me you would believe that Campeggius is a perfect devil.

I have been much upset through our opponents' propositions. As sure as I live this is a trick of Campeggius and the Pope, who first tried by threats to ruin our cause, and now by artifice. You have resisted force and withstood the Emperor's imposing entry into Augsburg ! And now you must put up with the tricks of those cowled monks which the Rhine conveyed to Speyer, and their arrival is closely associated with this talk of unity of doctrine.

This is the whole secret. But He who enabled you to withstand violent measures will strengthen you to overcome feebler. But more of this to Philip and the Elector. Be valiant and concede nothing which cannot be proved from Scripture. The Lord Jesus be with you. Amen. From my hermitage.

Martin Luther.

36

Cod., Jen., b., fol. 225 b.
Aurifaber III, fol. 86.
Cölest., III, fol. 59.

August 26th.

I have heard, certainly not with pleasure, that you have begun a marvellous work, namely, to unite the Pope and Luther. But the Pope will not desire it, and Luther forbids it ; see to it that your pains are not in vain.

Continue to defend the doctrine of justification by faith with courage. It is the heel of the seed of the woman that shall bruise the head of the serpent.

MARTIN LUTHER.

[And see the letter of Besserer to Ulm, of Aug. 24, in Kolde, *Analecta,* p. 148.]

We also have two Opinions of Luther concerning the means of compromise by both these commissions. The first is written for the theologians. In the doctrinal articles he writes there is nothing to yield. Then he shows that in the articles of abuses nothing of all that which was proposed by the Papists can be yielded with a good conscience. (Luther goes into detail on each of the abuses.) This Opinion of Luther was as hearty as thorough, and was according to the Word of God.

Cod., Jen., b., fol. 114.
Aurifaber III, fol. 79.
De Wette IV, fol. 156.

August 28th.

Grace and peace in Christ ! My dear Philip, I gave answer to these questions yesterday. And what is this, that they undertake to aid such openly godless affairs, when they themselves did not teach thus before. . . . You could do nothing more right, in my opinion, than to *free yourself from these gross intrigues* by saying that you would give to God what belongs to God and to the Emperor what belongs to the Emperor. . . . *Deal in a manly way,* and let your heart be comforted.

MARTIN LUTHER.

The other Opinion he wrote to the Elector John on August 26th, concerning the proposed methods of the other party and particularly concerning private masses, communion in one form, and the canon. For the Elector had written to Luther and sent him both copies of both sides of the commission and asked his opinion on it. In it Luther is amazed at the Papists, that they regarded the communion in one or both forms as a matter of indifference. If private masses were to be continued, the Gospel must be given up, and mere good works of man must be accepted. He decides in the same way as to the Canon, and then concludes: " Finally, we will suffer and yield everything that lies in our power. But what does not lie in our power we ask that they will not desire of us. What is not in accordance with the Word of God, it is not in our power to accept; and what has been established without the Word of God, in the matter of service, is also not in our power to accept."

THE CONFESSION TO STAND UNALTERED.

But before Luther's latest letters could reach Wittenberg, the Electoral party at Augsburg had decided to terminate the Commission's negotiations. Their decision is of August 28th, and in it they declare they will adhere to the Original Confession without any " Weiterung." The Elector said he would depart from Augsburg, as he saw very well that the deliberations were in vain. On August 29th Melanchthon and certain others were commanded to prepare an Apology to the Augsburg Confession refuting the Confutation.[72]

But the Emperor was determined on an agreement, and as it was supposed that things would go better if some of the more violent individuals, such as Duke George, were set aside, he resolved to name a smaller body, with only Eck on the one side and Melanchthon on the other. The two other Protestant members were Brück and Heller.[73] This last committee was short-lived.

---

[72] Preface to Apology.

[73] On the 23rd of August the Catholic estates sent some of their counsellors to the Elector to say that they were willing to ordain a smaller commission, and with the prayer that the Elector should not depart. The Elector promised to communicate this to those associated with him and to reply to the Elector of Maintz. Although the Evangelical princes at first declined in view of the former experience, yet to avoid trouble, it was at last yielded to. Three persons were appointed on each side. The following day, the 24th of August, this conference began. The Papists sang their old song. The Lutherans replied that further deliberations might have been spared if there was nothing new to

This new move awoke the indignation of the Nuremberg deputies, as we saw above, and of the Landgrave Philip. "Melanchthon," wrote the Landgrave to Zwingli, "walks backward like a crab." To his delegates at Augsburg the Landgrave said, "Overcome these dreadful combinations of Melanchthon, tell the deputies to be men, and not women."[14] Melanchthon endeavored to defend himself by prophesying anarchy, and a spoliation of the church, owing to the cupidity of the secular Princes, if the spiritual jurisdiction of the bishops were withdrawn. And, in the future, tyranny would reign worse than that of the present.

Under the new commission the Romanists yielded everything except the three points: penance for the remission of the penalties of sin; merit of good works; and validity of the private mass; but the Protestants would not agree, and the negotiations came to an end on August 30th. The Roman part of the commission reported the failure to the Emperor.

be brought forward, and referred to their former answer. The Papists then introduced other measures, that were, however, essentially the same as the old ones. They said they desired only to save the Abuses. They flattered the Lutherans with the promise of a Council. They declared that as there was no promise of unity, they understood that the Emperor would hold such a Council as would restore a common church without any of the new doctrines and customs. The Protestants answered that they had not broken away from the Christian and good order of the church. On the 28th of August they gave their final explanation.

On the 25th of August Melanchthon wrote to Luther what had happened in the smaller commission, and since the letters of Luther referred to before had not yet arrived, asked him again whether they could not yield to the Catholics if they would not reject communion under the one form so that they would again get both forms. He reported that the Papists had now ceased to press the private masses upon the Lutherans but that they were all the more stubborn with reference to the Canon which the Lutherans should accept with a comfortable interpretation. He recognized the deceit that lay beneath this. He complained that he was in bad repute because he had wished to give back the jurisdiction to the bishops, and he sent a copy of the points that were taken up at the last commission. In another letter he wrote that although he was now threatened with danger, he was not afraid for his own person, but was nevertheless anxious because of the weakness of our princes.

Luther replied that he was very sorry that he could not be present with him in the most beautiful and the most holy confession of Christ. He made no question of rejecting the mass. Hezekiah broke the brazen serpent notwithstanding the fact that it had been made for the memory and praise of the divine work. The Papists ought first of all be restored to the doctrine of faith and works, and the church be restored to her right customs again and then the ceremonies would take care of themselves.

In another writing he painfully awaits Melanchthon's either secret or open return, as of a Lot in Sodom, and admonishes him to hold out since great joys would follow his suffering.—*Salig,* II, 314-328.

[14] *C. R.,* II, 327.

The Elector and the Margrave now determined to negotiate no further concerning the Confession, and asked the
Emperor's leave to depart. Charles refused, and then sought
to win the Lutherans by kindness, and later, early in September, by threats of summary measures.

September 7th.

On this day, Wednesday, at two o'clock in the afternoon,
the Lutherans were summoned to the Emperor, and Count
Palatine told them, " That the Emperor, considering their
small number, had not expected that they would uphold new
sects against the ancient usages of the Universal Church;
but that desirous to the last of being kind, he would require
of the Pope the convocation of a Council; and that, in the
meantime, they should return into the bosom of the Catholic
Church, and restore everything to its ancient footing." [15] The
Protestants replied that they had supported no new sects
contrary to Scripture; [16] that if they had failed to agree, it
was because they must remain faithful to the Word of God;
that if the Emperor would convoke a general free and Christian Council in Germany, he would be carrying out the
promise of preceding Diets; but that nothing could compel
them to again set up any ordinances in their churches that
were opposed to God's commands.

At eight o'clock in the evening, the Lutherans were again
called before the Emperor and informed of his astonishment
that after so much concession on the part of the Catholic
commission, the Protestants would yield nothing. Their
comparative significance in comparison with the church and
the Emperor were pointed out. It was said to be no more
than right that they as a minority should yield to the majority. The Emperor would give them until to-morrow at
one o'clock to decide whether they would persist in refusing
further means of conciliation.

---

[15] *C. R.,* II. 355 ; Först., *Urk.,* II, **391**.
[16] Brück, *Apol.,* p. **136**.

September 9th.

Another day was given for deliberation.

September 10th.

THE FINAL REPLY.

The Protestants replied to the Emperor that new efforts at conciliation would only bring fatigue to the Emperor and the Diet, and that all that was needed were rules for political peace until a Council should assemble.[77]

The Emperor forbade the Elector to leave Augsburg, and this led to personal rejoinders between the two, with great disturbance in the city of Augsburg.

September 12th.

Prince John Frederick left Augsburg.

September 13th.

At six A. M., Brück and Melanchthon met a Roman committee to settle details. The Lutherans, including Jonas and Melanchthon, now saw the abyss into which they had well-nigh fallen, and the reaction which Luther had prophesied set in against the dreadful articles to which they came so near yielding. Luther had written to them to return from Augsburg, even if they were cursed by the Pope and the Emperor.[78]

Here comes the letter in which Luther says he will canonize them for confessing Christ:—

LUTHER TO MELANCHTHON.

MS. in Wolfenbüttel, Cod. Helmst. 108, f. 96.
Cölest., III, 87b ; Erl., Br. W., VIII, 258.

September 15th.

Yesterday our young prince came, arriving suddenly. I was glad they had fled from yonder commotion. God grant I might see you soon as one escaped, if

---

[77] Först., *Urk.*, II, 410 ; Brück, *Apol.*, p. 139.
[78] Vel maledicte a Papa et Cæsare.

I be not permitted to await you as one released.   You have done enough and more than enough : now the remaining time is for the Lord, that He accomplish it ; and He will also do so.   Only be a *man*, and hope in Him. . . .

Remember that you are one of those who are called Lot in Sodom, whose souls are tormented day and night by godless deeds. . . .

May the Lord shortly get you loose from Augsburg.

You have confessed Christ, you have offered peace, you have obeyed the Emperor, you have endured injuries, you have been drenched in revilings, you have not returned evil for evil.   In brief, you have worthily done God's holy work as becometh saints.

Be glad, then, in the Lord, and exult, ye righteous.   Long have ye borne witness in the world, look up and lift up your heads, for your redemption draweth nigh.   *I will canonize you faithful members of Christ*, and what greater glory can ye have than to have yielded Christ faithful service, and shown yourselves members worthy of Him.

YOUR MARTIN LUTHER.

Melanchthon was already engaged, heart and soul, in defending the Confession.   The reaction had come to his nature.   His zeal in mediating had become zeal in defense. In a few days his "Apology" would be completed.   The Elector was deaf to all further appeals and threats of the Emperor.   He was determined to abide by the Confession, *unaltered,* after all these experiences at variation, and to leave Augsburg.

There is no question in the mind of the writer that the Augsburg Confession gained its immeasurable influence in the whole Protestant world, as the charter of the Reformation, not simply because of what it contained, but because that which it contained both *in expression, and in implication,* was so stubbornly fought for against the combined civil and religious tyranny of Europe; and that the impression made by this handful of contestants, for the pure Word of God, which they would 'neither compromise nor change under flattery or threats, in addition to the Faith and the Document itself, combined to produce results accepted, but scarcely recognized in some of their main features by all subsequent generations.

September 15th.

To Katherine, Luther's Wife.

September 15.

God's will be done, if only the Diet were at an end. We have done and conceded enough. The Papists will not yield a hair-breadth, but one will come who will compel them to do so.

MARTIN LUTHER.

Hieronymus Baumgärtner [78] to Lazarus Spengler.

In J. F. Meyers dissert. de lenitate Phil. Melanchthonis, p. 48.
Salig, II, p. 334.
C. R., II, 372.

September 15th.

It is often cast up to us openly that we are constantly taking our stand upon our theologians and learned men, whereas it turns out that our theologians are altogether '*schiedlich*,' but we are unwilling to follow them.

Then manuscripts of Philip are shown us, which he sends to them secretly, often unrequested, and in which he makes propositions that are not only unchristian, but which it is also entirely impossible to take up, especially for the princes. Then he says : Oh, if only we were away, as though they would then afterward do what they wished. . . .

Therefore, I pray you for the sake of God and His Word that you will also do your part and write to Dr. Martin Luther that, as to one through whom God again restored His Word to the World for the first time, he would restrain Philip by force, and would warn the pious princes, and especially his own lord, against him, and admonish to steadfastness.

For at this Diet there is no human being up to the present moment who has done the Gospel more harm than Philip, who has fallen into such presumptuousness that he not only will not hear any one speak and advise otherwise, but bursts out into ill-devised swearing and scolding that he may terrify every one and suppress him with his own opinion and authority.

I do not like to write this of him, since he has always been esteemed highly by many, and I have acquiesced in this, and at the same time have yielded much to him against my conscience. But now the time of crisis has come, so that to me, if God will, neither Luther nor Philip shall be so dear that I will try to please them against God's Word.

Dated. Augsburg in haste, Thursday, September 15th, 1530.

HIERONYMUS BAUMGÄRTNER.

September 17th.

In response to Luther's appeal, the Elector prepared to

---

[78] On Jerome Baumgärtner see article in the *Deutsche Allg. Biog.* II, p. 169 and Nik. Müller, *Beitr. z. Briefwechsel des älteren Hieronymus Baumgärtner. Mitt. d. Ver. f. Gesch. Nürnbergs,* X (1893).

quit Augsburg on this Saturday; but the Emperor obliged him, under various pleas and in the midst of many interviews, to delay his departure.

September 19th.

On this Monday, Charles requested the Elector to remain some days longer. The Elector was not sure that he was not now a prisoner, but said he would wait till Friday; and if nothing was done by that time, he would leave Augsburg at once. The party felt they might be doomed to be hanged.

Luther, meantime, defends Melanchthon before outsiders, and absolves him from having yielded too much:—

September 20th.

TO PHILIP MELANCHTHON.

Tr. by Currie.

September 20.

To the learned Philip Melanchthon, servant of the Lord.

Grace and peace in Christ ! You could not credit, my Philip, what a swarm of verbal and written complaints I received after I got your letter, and very specially concerning yourself. I tell you this most unwillingly, for I am tenderly solicitous not to grieve you in the slightest, for you should receive only consolation from me, who have always tried to do so. But now I have our people's letters and the other party to contend with.

I defend myself thus. At first our Augsburg friends sent me very different accounts.

But I am determined rather to believe you than others, and hope you will conceal nothing pertaining to the cause from me.

For I am convinced that you will concede nothing which could injure the confession and the gospel.

But to begin with, it is not necessary to explain explicitly what the gospel and our confession really are !

But we must abide by our old agreement—to concede everything in the interests of peace which is not at variance with the gospel and our recent confession. I have no fear for the good cause, but dreaded force and cunning on your account.

Pray write, *via* Nürnberg, all that has happened since I got your last letter. For the tragic letters of our people would make us fancy that our affairs have assumed a serious aspect. The night before last some one mumbled something like this before the Prince at supper, but I said, with assumed indifference, that no one had written me about it. So I long for letters. Give me a true account to stop their mouths. They pay no attention to me. May the Lord guide and maintain you. Amen. From the desert.

MARTIN LUTHER.

LUTHER TO LINK.

MS. in Aurifaber, III, 200.
Cölest., III, fol. 88b; De Wette, IV, 167.

September 20th.

I have read your very serious complaints against my Philip, my dear Link, and if I had not found, from the letters I received last Saturday (Sept. 17th) from our party at Augsburg, that our case went into the hands of the Emperor [*i. e.*, for his final rescript], I should have been very uneasy. But I hope that meantime you have perceived that the case is different from what you write.

If it is not, I will write pointed letters to them. But I have already indicated sufficiently that it is not my intention to endorse such conditions and articles. Whether they have been influenced to decline those methods through such letters, I do not know.

I take it that they also see how shameful, disgraceful, and dishonest toward God, those methods are with which our enemies boastfully get the better of and ridicule our weak little flock.

But Christ who is blinding and hardening the enemies not to believe the Gospel, is preparing them for the Red Sea. . . . Let them go to the bottom, if they wish it. The Lord will be with us. Dismiss your feelings. Although Philip has perhaps made a mistake concerning some methods, yet up to now there has been no agreement on any of them, not even on those to which he has given his consent. But I hope that Christ has used this masque to scoff at our scoffers, and that their iniquitous joy that we would yield will give place to their discovery that they themselves have become the objects of ridicule. This is my interpretation ; and I am sure that without my consent, their consent is of no value. But even if I (God forbid !) should agree to those godless, inhumane, and faithless monstrosities, the whole Church and the doctrine of the Gospel would not agree. But pray for me.

MARTIN LUTHER.

September 22nd.

APOLOGY OFFERED TO THE EMPEROR.

The Emperor to-day had the Recess read to the Elector. The Edict of Worms would be enforced: the public prosecutor was commissioned to put the disobedient ones under the ban. They were to be allowed until the 15th of April of the following year for reflection, and, meanwhile, should not introduce any innovations, and should allow confession and the mass in their territories. A General Council of the Church was to be called.

Brück, in reply, maintained that the Confession of the Lutherans was so based on the Word of God that it was impossible to refute it. " We consider it the very truth of God, and hope by it to stand before the Judgment seat of Christ."

Brück then announced that they had refuted the Confutation and offered the Emperor the Apology, which Melanchthon had already written by that time. The Emperor would have received it, but Ferdinand prevented, and it was handed back.

September 22nd.

Already on his journey home, Melanchthon began to enlarge and deepen his Apology. He undertook a thorough refutation. The transactions of the Diet had demonstrated to him that a compromise was not to be thought of. Having no reason therefore to conciliate, he spoke the truth with a sharpness that was wholesome and necessary.

SEVERAL LETTERS AT THE CLOSE.

LUTHER TO CORDATUS.

MS. in Wolfenbüttel, Cod. Helmst., 108, f. 108.
Cölest., III, 89 ; Erl. Br. W., VIII, 271.

September 23rd.

The princes are leaving one after another, but Satan, extraordinarily wicked, is holding ours there yet tight.

MARTIN LUTHER.

TO KATHERINE, LUTHER'S WIFE.

Tr. by Currie.

September 24.

Grace and peace in Christ, my dear Käthie ! I hope, by God's grace, we shall be with you in fourteen days, although I fear our cause will not remain uncondemned. Efforts are being made towards this end. They will have difficulty in forcing the monks and nuns to return to the cloister.

Still —— —— has written ; he hopes all will end peacefully in Augsburg when they disperse. It would be a mercy if God granted this, for the Turk is determined to be at us.

I herewith commit you to God. Amen.

MARTIN LUTHER.

Original in Coburg Castle Erl. 54, p. 194.

September 28th.

Grace and peace in Christ. Honourable, prudent, dear sir and friend! I have again received my letters, that I had sent to you through M. Veit. In that you are anxious that M. Philippus should be still more careful, you are doing as a good friend. . . . but God be praised that our dear prince is now for once freed from hell. Let things happen as God desires. He is the author of peace and the arbitrator of war. We have done nothing. He who does not desire peace, to him God can make things unpeaceful enough. I will also, as you desire, write to the pious prince, Margrave George, and will admonish and comfort. The merciful God strengthen our dear prince, together with you, your preachers and the whole congregation. Amen.

MARTIN LUTHER.

TO THE ELECTOR JOHN.

Original in Archives at Weimar.
Cyprian Beilage, p. 209.

October 3rd, 1530.

To the High-born Elector John. Grace and peace, most gracious Lord! I am delighted that your Electoral Highness is emerging from the Augsburg hell, and although the eye of man may be displeased with this, still we hope that God may finish the work He has begun in us, and strengthen us more and more. You are in God's hands, even as we are, and our enemies cannot hurt a hair of our heads except God wills it. I have committed the matter to the Lord, who has begun it, and will complete it, I fully believe.

It is beyond man's power to bestow such a gospel (*Lehre*), so I shall watch to see who dare defy God in these things, for "bloody and deceitful men shall not live out half their days." They may threaten, but to carry out is not in their own power. May your Electoral Grace be strong in the spirit of joy and steadfastness. Amen.

MARTIN LUTHER.

September 23rd.

THE ELECTOR DEPARTS FROM AUGSBURG.

At five o'clock in the morning, the Emperor's Rescript was read to the Electoral party; and at eight, they saw the Emperor, who made great threats. But in spite of all threats, they rejected the Rescript, and parted.

At three in the afternoon, *the Elector* and his party *left Augsburg!*

Thus the mighty deed done for Truth in this ancient city, escaped a landslide back to Rome. The pathway to the few really great peaks of history is strewn with the boulders of failure. Behind and beneath every towering height that lifts itself clear into the sky—we find hundreds of smaller and indeterminate hillocks swarming upon its shoulders. It is a pity that many historians magnify these minor hills until the mighty mountain fades from their vision.

The pathway up to and down from the height of the Augsburg Confession is not important except as it exhibits the difficulties and the dangers of the true and heroic Confessional undertaking. With yawning chasms on either side, the ascent went upward until the height of Testimony had been reached and fixed by Providence, when the pathway again gravitated downward toward the plains of commingled truth and error.

The Confession was no sooner made, than Melanchthon began writing to Luther as to what in it, in further discussion, they had better concede. " Concede! " said Luther. " You have already conceded too much."

Through the guidance of Providence, down this slippery pathway, all other propositions and Confessions were left by the roadside as historical wrecks; while the real Word of Augsburg has continued to stand in its own native power, until this day. *It will abide forever.*

CHAPTER XXI.

THE LUTHERAN CONFESSION.

THE AUGSBURG CONFESSION: THE FURTHER HISTORY OF ITS EDITIONS AND MANUSCRIPTS.

Kolde's Essay,

WITH A SUMMARY OF THE ARGUMENT AS IT BEARS ON THE CONFESSIONAL QUESTION, BY T. E. S.

The First Prints—The Editio Princeps—The Variata of 1540 and its Influence—The Corpora Doctrinæ—The Original Manuscripts of the Augsburg Confession. The Lack of a Perfect Copy of the Augsburg Confession—Its Text in the Situation of Many Historical Documents, and of the Scriptures—The Difference between a Variant and a Variata Edition—The Attitude of Luther and of the Elector toward the Variata—The Attitude of Eck and of Rome—The Difficulties of the Colloquy of Worms and of the Frankfurt Recess—The Significance of the Convention at Naumburg—The Texts of the Augsburg Confession as Related to the Book of Concord—The Relation of the Manuscripts and Prints to the Augustana as a Confessional Standard.

ALTHOUGH the Emperor had prohibited the publication of the Confession, to which in the middle of July the imperial cities of Windsheim, Heilbronn, Kempten and Weissenburg (in the Nordgau) acceded,[1] yet

---

even during the Diet, as far as is known now, there appeared six German editions and one Latin.[2] Their inexactness, which might easily cause bad repute, induced Melanchthon, notwithstanding the imperial prohibition, to enter upon an official publication of the Augustana immediately after his return from Augsburg. In fact it was at once undertaken, and, as a remark in the preface shows, according to which it was to displace the editions published *ante duos menses,*[3] it was to be published at once. But the intention to add to it an apology of the Confession, the completion of which was delayed by ever renewed recasting, prevented the execution. *There is therefore no official*[4] *edition of the Confession alone that appeared in the year 1530.*

It was published by George Rhau, in Wittenberg, together with the Apology, toward the end of April or beginning of May, 1531, and that in such a manner, that since the German translation of the Apology, by Justus Jonas, was not yet ready, the Latin text was first published alone and the German probably not until the Fall. The latter was partly furnished to the subscribers as a supplement, and partly delivered in the same binding with the Latin.[5] The title was as follows: CONFESSIO FIDEI / *e x h i b i t a   i n u i c-l i s s.   I m p.   C a r o l o   V.   / Caesari Aug. in Comicijs / A n n o / M. D. XXX. // Addita est Apologia Confessionis.* **B e i d e ,   D e u d s c h /   V n d   L a t i n i s c h.** / *P s a l m.   1 1 9. / Et loquebar de testimonijs tuis con-/ spectu Regum &° non confundebar.*

Of this so-called *editio princeps* at least two principal kinds must be distinguished[6] that must have originated from the fact that during the printing slight divergencies occurred in

---

[2] B i n d s e i l *C. R.* XXVI, 478.

[3] As this no longer applied at the time of the real appearance, **Melanchthon** in the second edition of 1531 substituted : " ante semestre."

[4] K o l d e. *Neue Augustanastudien,* p. 729 sqq.

[5] Sept. 26th, Melanchthon still wrote about being busy with the **correction** of the German Apology which was then in print.—*C. R.* II, 541 sq.

[6] On this and the titles see *C. R.* XXVI, 235.

separate sheets, or changes were made necessary through corrections,[7] while the printer, as was frequently done during that period, circulated copies without the corrections.

Melanchthon asserts that he drew his text from *exemplari bonae fidei,* and the fact that here he does not style himself the author, as he does in the case of the Apology, shows that he regarded the Augustana as an official document. Nevertheless, as a comparison with the copies nearest the time of the presentation irrefutably proves he undertook so many changes in his edition, and in the German text even comprehensive rewritings,[8] that it presents nothing less than an authentic text. And also since the copies presented (of which we shall speak below) have never been found again, we do not really know the text actually presented, notwithstanding all the valuable attempts to determine[9] it, by means of critical methods from the extant oldest copies.

On the other hand, it must also be emphasized that the changes apparently made in the interest of instructiveness and clearness in the *editio princeps* and Melanchthon's many explanatory additions[10] are in a sense noteworthy as the author's authentic explanations, and can hardly in any place be regarded as actual alterations of the doctrinal substance. Further, that of the evangelical estates—and theologians—although they might have recognized these divergencies very easily from the copies at hand, which must have been much more numerous than we know, no one took

---

[7] Thus in one recension of the Summary: "vel ab Ecclesia Romana" and " Tota dissensio est de quibusdam abusibus." This form by which Melanchthon returned to the oldest redaction, probably gave offence, hence the first sheets were reprinted, and the current *editio princeps* reads: " Vel ab ecclesia catholica vel ab ecclesia Romana," and further: " Sed dissensio," etc.

[8] Less in the Latin text. Here the most important changes are in the 13th and 18th articles. That the Damnationes in the *Ed. princ.* were not in the copy presented, appears from the fact, that they are not known to the *Confutatio Pontifica. Cp.* F i c k e r, *Die Confutatio des Augsburger Bekenntnisses.* Leipzig. 1891, p. 48, 60.

[9] P. T s c h a c k e r t. Die unveränderte Augsburgische Conf. deutsch u. lateinisch, etc. Leipzig, 1901. V. this also for a discussion of the most important manuscripts.

[10] T h. K o l d e, *Die Augsburgische Confession* etc.

exception to them, and the *editio princeps for decades was regarded as the authentic edition.*

While the next editions—as early as 1531 a Latin octavo edition appeared—upon which we do not need to enter individually here, where we are treating of the Augustana as a Lutheran Confession, show only unimportant corrections and alterations, the German octavo edition of 1533[11] deserves a special significance, for it experienced various amplifications in a series of articles, *e. g.,* iv, v, vi, xiii, xv, and especially xx. Thus it becomes a sort of preliminary work to the Latin text of 1540, as Melanchthon, for the sake of greater clearness, inserts thoughts from the Apology. It might already be described as a kind of Variata; but, so far as we know, that never was done in those days, because it does not present any alteration in the substance of the doctrine.

On the basis of several passages from letters of the year 1535, in which Melanchthon announces a revision of the *Loci* and the *Apology,* it has been repeatedly assumed[12] that a Latin Variata of the Confession appeared as early as this year. But as such a one cannot be proven, and as Melanchthon from 1531 understands by the Apologia nothing else than his refutation of the Confutatio Pontifica, these announcements mean nothing more than that Melanchthon in those days, beside the revision of the Loci, was also busy with one of the Apology, which was never published.

Neither can the objection of the Elector John Frederick to Luther and Melanchthon of May 5th, 1537, be adduced as

---

[11] Confessio | odder Bekentnus | des Glaubens etlicher Für— | sten vnd Stedte, vber antwort | Keiserlicher Majestät auff | dem Reichstag ge— | halten zu Augspurg, | Anno M. D. XXX. | Apologia der Confessio, | mit vleis emendirt. || The Apology which is added, shows it to be the edition of 1533: Apologia | der Confession | aus dem Latin | verdeudschet durch D. | Justum Jonam | Witeberg.—M. D. XXXIII. Gedruckt zu Wittemberg | durch Georgen Rhaw. ||

[12] Thus B i n d s e i l *C. R.* XXVI, 339 : "I am printing the Apology and the Loci, and desire truly to explain simply the principal passages." And p. 871 : "And now I am printing both the Loci Communes and the Apology." A third passage in an undated letter to Menius, ibid., p. 873 : "My Apology has been born again and improved in the passage concerning justification." It is evidently of the year 1531.

proof for the existence of a Variata at that time. He says there (C. R. III, 366): *"It is also said that M. Philipp undertook in several points to alter, soften and publish with other changes the Confession made by Your Electoral Highness and other princes and estates before his Imp. Maj. at Augsburg."* The latter evidently refers to the fact that probably without any doings of Melanchthon, in the year 1535, a reprint of the Latin octavo edition of 1531 appeared in Augsburg (now in the Nuremberg city library), and a second one in Hagenau. And if the assertion that Melanchthon altered and softened the Confession does not merely rest on rumors brought to the Elector, we may remember that at that time, in circles unfavorably disposed toward Melanchthon, notice was first directed [13] toward the alterations in the octavo edition of 1533.

From the beginning the Augustana served as the articles of confederation of the Schmalkald League, and the Diet of Schmalkald in 1535 obligated the members to be received, to see that preaching and teaching be uniformly done according to the Word of God and the pure doctrine of our Confession.[14] Still more important for the history of the Augustana and probably also of its text was the Diet of Schmalkald of 1537. For there, as must here be mentioned, the theologians received the commission to revise the Augustana and the Confession and confirm it with new arguments from the Scriptures and the Fathers, although not contrary to its contents or the substance of the Wittenberg Concordia, but only to speak somewhat favorably of the papacy.[15] This proves what we know otherwise also [16] that an expansion and amplification of the

---

[13] There is evidently no reason to doubt with W e b e r II, 356, and others, that the Elector's intended representation to Melanchthon really occurred.

[14] W i n c k e l m a n n, Strassburg's politische Korrespondenz, II, 322. The Wittemberg doktoranden were obligated to the Augustana as early as 1533.—F ö r s t e m a n n, lib. Decanorum Facultatis Acad. Vittebergensis Lips. 1838, pp. 152, 158. Cp. also P a u l D r e w s, Die Ordination, Prüfung und Lehrverpflichtung der Ordinanden in Wittenberg, 1535. Giessen 1904. Also the theologians participating in the Wittenberg Concordia acknowledged the Augustana and the Apology. C. R. III, 76.

[15] K o l d e. *Analecta Lutherana*, 297. C. R., III, 267.

[16] Cp. the answer of the evangelical estates to the English representatives

text of the Augustana was not regarded as excluded. Thus the Augustana might have been altered at that time and offi cially at that.

But, as it is said, from lack of books the task was given up, and, beyond adopting Melanchthon's Tractatus de Potestate Papae (see below), they were content to witness anew to their assent to the Augustana and the Apology by their signature. Thus the Confession—most likely on the text of the *editio princeps*—was again confirmed as the common basis of the Schmalkald League, and, materially at least, as symbol of the ecclesiastical territories concerned. If then the Confession was not amplified, the supposition can at least not be set aside, that the desire expressed at Schmalkald to confirm the Confession with further arguments from the Scriptures and the Fathers and to see the Wittenberg Concordia acknowledged besides, may have helped to induce Melanchthon to undertake a revision in this sense on his own part." [17]

This undoubtedly long-prepared revision is the Latin quarto edition of 1540, [18] which afterwards, on account of the many alterations contained in it, received the name *Variata.* These alterations are partly of a formal nature, inasmuch as the articles in the second part are placed in a better and more logically correct order; partly, however, they consist of frequently comprehensive amplifications, which

---

at the Diet of Schmalkald in 1535: "Let the most serene King promote the Gospel of Christ and the sincere doctrine according to the manner by which the princes and the confederated estates confessed it at the Diet of Augsburg and guarded it according to the Apology, unless perhaps, in the meantime certain things from them by the common consent of said King and the princes themselves, will seem to need change or correction from the Word of God."—*C. R.* II, 1032.

[17] This would offer a way to harmonize C. Peucer's oft-mentioned remark, *C. R.* XXVI, 342 (Opera Melanchthonis Witt. 1562 praefatio), and Selnecker's remark which probably rests upon it (Catalogus brevis praecipuorum Conciliorum, Francof. ad Moen. 1571, p. 97), that it was written as early as 1538. But since both connect with it the assertion of Luther's approval, we can not depend much on it.

[18] While the Apology, which is again connected with it, is denoted as *diligenter recognita* (Cp. *C. R.* XXVI, 343), the author shows neither in the title nor the preface, that the Augustana is also revised.

evidently originated from the desire of clearness and distinctness (while also making use of many statements in the Apology, they aim at greater sharpness in combating the Roman opponents and a richer Scriptural proof as had been desired at the Schmalkald Diet); and, thirdly, they are real alterations or at least softenings of a dogmatic nature. To these must be counted the amplification of articles V and XX, with the emphasis upon the necessity of repentance and good works, and that of article XVIII (de libero arbitrio) which not so much in their wording as in connection with the changed attitude of Melanchthon in the later revisions of the Loci Communes (since 1535) may be interpreted synergistically.

The special cause of offence [19] later, not at once, was the new statement of the X. article on the Lord's Supper. Where the previous statement was: *De coena Domini docent, quod corpus et sanguis Christi vere adsint et distribuantur vescentibus in coena domini, et improbant secus docentes;* the statement now read: *De coena Domini docent, quod cum pane et vino vere exhibeantur corpus et sanguis Christi, vescentibus in coena Domini.*

It ought never to have been denied that this implied actual alterations. What motives impelled Melanchthon can be determined [20] neither from his own statement nor from contemporary reports from the circle of his acquaintances. A comparison with the Wittenberg Concordia of May, 1536 (*Cum pane et vino vere et substantialiter adesse,* C. R. III, 75), justifies the assumption that by the formula, *Cum pane et vino vere exhibeantur,* he desired to yield to the actually existing union with the Highlanders; but if at the same time he omitted the *vere et substantialiter adesse* and the

---

[19] For us moderns it seems strange (though not so in the era of the Reformation), how Melanchthon in the article on the marriage of priests so enlarged the apostrophe to the Emperor that it actually constituted an article of faith on the ecclesiastical rights of princes. Cf. also *C. R.* III, 240 sqq.

[20] I would not leave without mention, that it was asserted *afterwards* that Melanchthon acted under the direct influence of Landgrave Philipp, of Hessen. Thus S e l n e c k e r in his *Historica narratio et oratio de D. D. Martino Luthero,* Lipsiæ 1575. But no importance is to be attached to this anecdote.

improbatio, we need not harbor any doubts that with the gradually changing conception in his mind about the Lord's Supper he desired to leave a possibility open for himself and others to go along with the Swiss theologians. Although now the Elector (as reported) already in 1537 had reproved Melanchthon's alterations in the Augustana text as a presumption, and even in those days everybody in Wittenberg anxiously watched every variation, it cannot be proven, that the "Variata" had caused any offence when it was first published. The oft-time repeated assertion about Luther's condemnation of it, as it was peddled about later during the times of the controversy by the Gnesio-Lutherans, is not confirmed by Luther's letters and other well-authenticated[21] statements of contemporaries. On the other hand, there is certainly no foundation for the statement that Luther approved of these alterations, or that they were made with his co-operation.[22] It is self-evident that Luther knew of them, and, with his well-known character, we must assume that he disliked Melanchthon's procedure exceedingly, but had to suffer it, like many other things.[23]

If this is only a supposition, it is a fact that the new edition was used unsuspectingly as a new edition receives

---

[21] Explicitly and impartially examined in K ö l l n e r *Symbolik* I, 237. Many things related afterwards probably rest on faint memories of the occurrences of 1537. K o l d e , *Martin Luther* II, 461 sqq. For the moral appreciation of the fact (which can not be measured by modern standards), that an author may not make any changes in a production of his own that has become an official document, it must be said, that more freedom was granted an author in those days. This is proven by the circumstance to which no exception was ever taken, that Luther in the published edition of the Schmalkald Articles, which he considered though erroneously, to be a document formally adopted by the Evangelical estates, made amplifications (See below).

[22] *E. g.,* C . P e u c e r , *Opera Melanchthonis,* Witteb. 1562, Vol. I, præfatio : " But there was a later confession written at the suggestion, recognition and approval of Luther." Thus also S e l n e c k e r , *Catalogus Conciliorum.* Francof. 1571, p. 97 : " A later Augustana Confession reviewed and approved by Luther," etc.

[23] How far Luther could go in this respect, is shown among other things by the circumstance that he speaks of the articles of union with the English of 1536, which just recently have become fully known to us, and which aside from the X. article which can be understood in a Romish sense, moved entirely in line with the Variata, in his letter to the Elector (May 28th, 1536, De Wette IV, 683), as such " that will accord with our doctrine." *Cp.* G . M e n t z , *Die Wittenberger Artikel von 1536,* Leipzig 1905.

the preference over against the older one. And although John Eck in the Worms Colloquium of January, 1541, objected to the alteration of the original text, and this led to discussions,[24] in which Melanchthon declared that he had "made no changes in the matter, substance and meaning," this attack upon him made so little impression upon him, that when a new edition became necessary in 1542 he made new alterations, a thing which would be utterly incomprehensible, if he had been attacked in his own camp on account of the alterations in the edition of 1540.

This state of affairs changed when the gradually growing difference in the manner of teaching between Melanchthon's special disciples and the later so-called Gnesio-Lutherans became more evident after Luther's death, and the unfortunate period which began with the battle about the Interim more and more fixed the gulf between both parties, and the edition of 1540 (1542) was elevated to a party signal by the Melanchthonians and the Highland congregations which were already influenced by Calvinistic ideas. At the Augsburg negotiations for peace in 1555, through which the Augustana also publicly received legal standing in a formal way, did the matter come to be discussed.

But the attempt made by the Catholics, especially Treves, to exclude the Calvinists and grant peace only to the confessors of the Augustana of 1530, was at that time repulsed by all Protestant estates.[25] But after a short time, amid the ecclesiastical confusion in Thuringia, complaints were multiplied that all kinds of pernicious sects were entering the Empire under the cloak of the Augsburg Confession. And the scandalous proceedings at the colloquium of Worms in 1557, which had been called for the purpose of uniting Catholics and Protestants, and from which the Protestant

---

[24] *C. R.* IV, 34 sqq. H o r t l e d e r Von den Ursachen des Teutschen Krieges, etc. Book I, p. 177.

[25] *Cp.* L . S c h w a b e , Kursachsen u. d. Augsburger Religionsfriede in Neues Archiv f. sächs. Geschichte. X. Bd. p. 221. G . W o l f , Der Augsburger Religionsfriede. Stuttgart 1890, pp. 47, 61.

parties mutually strove to exclude each other, and at which the Jesuit Canisius, not uninfluenced by their mutual accusations, already spoke of a pure and an impure Augustana [25] actually forced an explanation of the subject.

At the Naumburg Diet of Princes in 1561, which was to prepare a new common utterance in view of the newly convening Tridentine Council, this question, too, was to be settled by a new subscription to the Confession. The result of the wearisome negotiations, during which the endeavor to retain the wavering Elector Frederick III. of the Palatinate for Lutheranism, led to many illogical acts, was as follows: The German text of the Editio princeps was subscribed to and the Latin of the octavo edition of 1531. The essential reason for this incongruity lay in the fact that in the Apology, which was bound together with the latter, the quotations in the first edition from Vulgarius (*i. e.,* Theophylactus) which were objectionable to the Palatine Elector and others, because they permitted an interpretation of the X. article in the sense of Transubstantiation, were omitted. [27] At the same time the declaration was made in a preface to the Emperor, that they would abide by the Confession originally presented, but by signing the edition of 1531 would not reject those of 1540 and 1542—which latter " was more explicit, so that the divine truth should the better be brought to light, and faith and trust in the satisfaction and merit of Jesus Christ, with the rejection of all human tradition and ordinance should be delivered pure and undefiled to posterity"—especially since this edition "was now in use among the majority of our churches and schools."

Through this declaration, which was influenced by circumstances and composed by laymen, the Variata was recognized as another form of the Confession; but the opinion was contradicted, according to which the attempt was being made through it " to defend another or new and unfounded

[26] C . A . S a l i g , Vollständige Historie III, 308.
[27] R . C a l i n i c h , Der Naumburger Fürstentag. Gotha 1870. p. 165.

doctrine;" but the question, what to do in view of the really existing differences, was evaded.[28] The result was, that the strictly Lutheran Duke Frederick of Saxony, who had in vain demanded a mention of the errors that had arisen against the Augustana of 1530, seceded and wanted to abide by the original Augustana and its own "real Christian declaration and rule," the Schmalkald Articles. Now, almost all princes present or their counsellors subscribed to the above-mentioned preface; but, under the influence of their theologians, they gradually withdrew their signatures and united with the declarations of the Saxon duke, with the exception of the Elector Palatine, who, completely isolated, united with Calvinism by introducing the Heidelberg Catechism.

Notwithstanding all this, the Variata for a while enjoyed recognition in wide territories, through the Corpus Doctrinæ Philippicum, a private undertaking of the Leipzig bookdealer, E. M. Vögelin, which appeared in 1560 in German, and soon after in Latin.[29] Beginning with a preface of Melanchthon, dated Sept. 29th, 1559, resp. Feb. 16th, 1560 (*C. R.* IX, 929 and 1050 sqq.), the work contained only the three ancient symbols, and beside them nothing but writings of Melanchthon, the Augustana, the Apology, the Confessio Saxonica of 1551, the Loci, the Examen Ordinandorum, the Responsio ad Articulos Bavaricae inquisitionis and the Refutatio Serveti, to which was added in the Latin editions the Responsio de controversia Stancari.

---

[28] H e p p e ' s assertion (Gesch. d. deutsch. Prot. Marburg, 1852 I, 406, and again in: Die Konfess. Entwicklung der altprot. Kirche Deutschlands. Marburg 1854. p. 169), that the Variata was at that time recognized as an authentic interpretation and Melanchthon's theology was exalted to front rank, needs no further disproof. Just as erroneous is C a l i n i c h , Naumburger Fürstentag, p. 175, that it was not clear to the princes, with the exception of Frederick of the Palatinate and John Frederick, that there existed principal differences between the various editions. There had been negotiations enough on that point.

[29] The first German edition is entitled: Corpus Doctrinæ Christianæ, d. l. gantze Summa der rechten waren Christlichen Lehre des heiligen Evangelii. . . in etliche Bücher verfasset durch den ehrwürdigen Herren Phil. Melanchthonem etc. (the complete very long title in *C. R.* XXII, 35; Latin XXI, 587).

In this the German text contained the Augustana of 1533, while the Latin edition offered a mixed text, giving with every article the later recension of 1540 (resp. 1542) first, and the original one after. This book of instruction, of which a number of editions soon became necessary, was authorized by the church authorities in Electoral Saxony (hence Corpus Doctrinæ Misnicum), in 1566, and generally used in the schools. In Pomerania it was authorized in 1561, but in other lands only in such a form, that Luther's Catechism and the Schmalkald Articles were added to avoid the suspicion of Philippism.

But there was a still larger number of Corpora Doctrinæ, either framed after the Philippicum, or produced in opposition to it, that rejected the Variata and beside the Invariata authoritatively spread writings and opinions of Luther as standards of instruction.[30] And although recognized Lutherans like Nicholas Selnecker and David Chytraeus then spoke mildly of the edition of 1540 and thought to find in it no variation of the essential doctrine,[31] yet others attacked it all the more violently and loudly, among which especially the so-called Reuss or Reuss-Schönburg Confession of 1567.[32] The authors therein acknowledged "*the old true unaltered Augsburg Confession . . . which we hereby distinguish and separate from the supposed Augsburg Confession which was afterwards in many places changed, mutilated, misinterpreted, falsified by the Adiaphorists in words and acts, and that simultaneously became a cothurnus, a Bundschuh, a slipper and a Polish boot, equally good on either foot, or a cloak or changeling skin with which the Adiaphorists, Sacramentarians, Antinomists, new teachers of work-righteousness*

---

[30] They are enumerated in G. K a w e r a u 's article: Corpus Doctrinæ Prot. Realencykl. 3. Aufl. Vol. IV, 293 sqq.

[31] W e b e r , II, 301 sq.

[32] Konfessionsschrift etlicher Prädikanten in den Herrschaften Greiz, Geraw, Schönburg, etc., 1567. *Cp.* O. M e u s e l Die Reussisch oder Reuss.— Schönb. Konfession von 1567 in Beitr. zur sächs. Kirchengesch. 14. Heft. 1899, p. 149 sqq., and B e r t h. A u e r b a c h , Die Reussische Konfession im Thüringer Kirchl. Jahrb. X. Bd. 1905, p. I, sqq.

and the like, under the semblance and name of the true Augs-
burg Confession cover, adorn, defend and confirm their errors
and falsification, and assert that they, too, are adherents of
the Augsburg Confession, for this one reason that under
its cover against hail and rain they may also enjoy the com-
mon peace of the Empire, and may peddle further and spread
their errors the more freely under the semblance of friends,"
etc.[33]

Such statements could find willing soil the more readily
since Calvin had repeatedly emphasized his assent to the
Augustana of 1540.[34] Then came the crypto-calvinistic
disturbances in Saxony, which convinced Elector August
that the plan was to lead him and his country into Calvinism
by means of the Variata.[35] The final decision for large territories came through the activity of Jacob Andreae, who, as
may be seen from the history of the Formula of Concord,
thought, when all attempts to effect harmony between the
controverting parties had failed, that union could only be
brought about if the Philippists and the Variata were suppressed. A sermon delivered by him in Wittenberg, in the
year 1569, was characteristic of this effort. In this—of
course, yet with the opposition of the students—he inveighed
against the Corpus Philippicum and its "knaveries and
falsifications of the Latin Augsburg Confession and Apology."[36] Under these circumstances it was a matter of course
for the Formula of Concord to acknowledge the first unaltered
Augsburg Confession and for this edition to appear to the
Lutherans as the only genuine one. Hence their effort had to
be, when they compiled the Lutheran symbols, to print the
text if possible just exactly as it had been presented to the
Emperor in 1530. But where could that be found?

---

[33] Reussische Konf. according to the third (and last, first paged) edition of
1699, p. 23 sq.

[34] K ö l l n e r , 241.

[35] R . C a l i n i c h , Kampf u. Untergang des Melanchthonismus in Kursachsen, etc., Leipzig, 866.

[36] L e o n h a r d t H u t t e r , *Concordia Concors*, Witeb. 1614, p. 410 sq.

THE ORIGINAL MANUSCRIPTS.

THE old tradition that the *German* copy of Albrecht of Mayence was deposited in the imperial chancery at Mayence must be considered correct. There is documentary proof that John Eck, when, on Dec. 4th, 1540, he demanded permission to compare the Mayence copy with the Variata, was granted the privilege.[37] Probably it never returned to Mayence and was lost at that time, for according to the researches of G. G. W e b e r [38] it may be considered established that when, in 1545, it was necessary to send away the Augsburg religious documents for the use of the Tridentine Council, it was no longer there. It is easy to understand that this was not readily admitted at the imperial chancery.

Thus it happened that when Elector Joachim II., in 1566, to obtain the genuine text had his court-preacher George Coelestin and the counsellor of the Archbishop of Magdeburg Andreas Zoch prepare a copy of the original manuscript supposed to be at Mayence, the copy of a poor copy (probably antedating the presentation of the Augustana) was presented them as an authentic text (likely without their knowledge). This then was received into the Corpus Doctrinæ Brandenburgicum as authentic in 1572, and printed separately[39] by Chytræus (1576) and again by Cölestin, (1576 and 1577).

It was thought that this text must be made the foundation, and after Elector August of Saxony in 1576 had obtained a new certified copy of the Mayence text, which of course agreed essentially with the one previously obtained, this recension was made the basis of the German text of the Book of Concord.

According to all this, which was only gradually deter-

---

[37] *Cp.* K o l d e , *Neue Augustanastudien,* p. 739. There also on the circumstance that Eck, because he wished to compare the manuscript with the Latin Variata, supposed the Latin manuscript to be in Mayence.

[38] Kritische Gesch. d. Augsb. Konfession. II. Preface.

[39] A description and valuation of these editions in W e b e r I, 121 sqq.

mined [40] by careful research, which need not be detailed here, this text with its many errors, omissions and sentences warped by transpositions has very little claim to come near the original; but by its reception into the Book of Concord it became the Textus receptus and has remained so to the present day.

The Latin original, too, must be considered lost forever, and unfortunately not one of the many copies caused to be made by the Emperor and Cardinal Campeggi immediately after the presentation has come to light again; but we know at least a little more as to its whereabouts.[41] It was in its day deposited in the imperial archives at Brussels. There it was examined in 1562 by William Lindanus, Bishop of Roermund († as Bishop of Ghent, Nov. 2nd, 1588), in company with Joachim Hopper, afterward state secretary for Netherland affairs in Madrid, and compared with the edition of 1531. As late as 1569 it was still there in the keeping of the highly esteemed member of the Staats-rat Viglius Zuichem. Then King Philip of Spain, having learned of the story first brought up by Lindanus as it appears and considered credible, that the Augustana original preserved in Brussels was written by the hand of Melanchthon,[42] on Feb. 18th, 1569, gave command to Duke Alba to seize the Book of the Confession [43] lest "they (the damned) consider it a Koran," to "take it with you when by a favorable chance you return to this country, and you shall take care lest they give you a copy for the original, and that no copy remain, not even a trace of it, so that such a destructive work may be destroyed for ever." [44]

That Viglius Zuichem thereupon surrendered his precious document to the Duke, is attested by himself in a letter to

[40] W e b e r; also the good review of the literary transactions of the 18th Century in O. Z ö c k l e r, Die Augsb. Konfession, p. 74 sqq.

[41] K o l d e, *Neue Augustanastudien*, p. 740 sqq.

[42] W i l l i a m L i n d a n u s, Apologeticum ad Germanos etc. Antverpiae 1568. Vol. III, p. 92. Concordia Discors etc. Coloniae 1583, p. 185.

[43] The other view in *Neue Augustanastudien*, p. 737.

[44] The Spanish original of this letter in J. D ö l l i n g e r, Beiträge zur politishen, Kirchl. u. Kulturgesch. der sechs letzten Jahrhunderte. Regensburg 1862. Vol. I, p. 648.

Joachim Hopper,[45] and there is no doubt that Alba, when he returned to Spain in 1573, took the Latin original of the Augustana with him, and that there the wish of the king to have it destroyed entirely was complied with.

It is striking that although Lindanus in 1568 treated of the treasure at Brussels, people in Germany thought they must look in Maintz also for the Latin original, and Cölestin even claimed to have found the genuine text there. But he was not trusted, and when Elector August, on the foundation of a personal inquiry with Elector Daniel of Maintz, was probably confirmed in his suspicion against Cölestin's copy,[46] the compilers of the Book of Concord refrained from basing anything on a manuscript text. *Privato et festinanti instituto* Selnecker, as he himself acknowledges,[47] even because the rather rare quarto edition could not be obtained, set up the octavo edition of 1531 as authentic or editio princeps; but in the second edition of the Book of Concord he replaced it by the real *editio princeps, i. e.,* the quarto-edition of the spring of 1531. In this form the Latin recension has maintained its place as normal text in all editions of the Book of Concord up to the present.

SUMMARY AND ARGUMENT,
AS BEARING ON THE CONFESSIONAL QUESTION.

(ESSAY BY T. E. S.)

After June 25th, 1530, the two originals of the Augsburg Confession were in the hand of the Holy Roman Empire. Its publication was forbidden by the same authority. Its

---

[45] *Viglii Zuichem ab Aytta* epistolae ad virum Joachimum Hopperum etc. Leonardiae 1661, p. 143. Reprinted in *Neue Augustanastudien,* p. 744 sq.

[46] *Cp.* Z. K. G. IV, 626.

[47] In the *Postfatio* of the edition of the Latin Book of Concord, of 1584.

authors, including Luther, laid chief stress on its vocal deliverance as a public act of Confession, and a more permanent preservation or publication was not premeditated by them.

As not only their Faith, but their lives and their fortunes seemed to be at stake, the events of the moment, the expectancy of a Roman Confutation, the Compromise Measures, and the Defense, or Apology, of the Confession, with a growing desire to get away from their prison-position in Augsburg, so occupied their attention, that, as they departed one after another, each prince took with him for future use or preservation only such a copy of the Confession as he happened to already possess, dating from the period before the final changes, when others than the Elector were admitted to participation in the coming Confession.

Thus the failure to supply the Lutheran Churches of the realm and the future Lutheran Church of the world with a standard copy, transcribed from the originals, of its birthright charter, for which its principals had imperiled their lives and their all in withstanding the final Rescript of the Emperor at Augsburg, and by which they had forever defeated his policy, and foiled the compact between Rome and the imperial power at Bologna, rests, so far as there is any responsibility connected with it, on the Emperor himself, on members of the Church of Rome, and on Melanchthon.

Melanchthon's portion of the responsibility was not that he failed to duplicate the originals in a faultless transcript just prior to the Confession's Delivery, but it lay in two other acts. The first of these was that he left both the Emperor and the Legate under the impression that no Confession would be produced. He left them under the impression that a short private agreement, conceding almost everything to Rome, would be arranged through himself. When then the Emperor found that this was not the case, that he had been deceived, and that the Lutherans would insist on producing a Confession after all, he demanded it immediately, and barely allowed time for even the original copies to be presentably engrossed.

The second reason why Melanchthon was responsible is that, during the negotiations with the Legate, for a period of a week before the Delivery of the Confession, he cast its further preparation aside, since its presentation did not meet with his approval and would not in his judgment occur. When this plan was reversed by the Elector and the Estates, he was caught so short by the Emperor's demand, and continued to be so busy up to the last hour in making changes of greater mildness toward Rome, that the idea of a Lutheran official duplicate, if it occurred to him, could not be carried out.

The Emperor's part in preventing an official copy was that he forbade the publication of the Confession after its Delivery, and the Lutherans were so loyal to him and so busy in the further progress of affairs that they unconsciously or deliberately delayed the matter of publication for many months, until the various personalities, documents, and early transcripts centreing in their presence at the Diet had been scattered.

It was not before November that publication was provided for, although the document had been delivered in June. The fact is that the Evangelicals *were driven* to publication, notwithstanding the imperial command, because the market had been flooded with unauthorized and faulty prints of the Confession. While the Diet was in session, the German text of the Confession had been printed, probably in Switzerland, with many mistakes. Thus the trouble concerning the textual Variata arose from an act of the Highlanders. In the course of the year, five such incorrect and unauthorized editions of the German text, and one of the Latin, followed.

These were the reasons for the confusion in the early prints of the Augustana; and, in this situation, Melanchthon did the right thing, when, some time in November, he superintended the printing of an authorized edition of the Augustana in Wittenberg, in the German and Latin texts, to be followed and bound up with the Apology, and which became the Editio Princeps of 1531.[48] The several forms of this Editio Princeps are well accounted for by Weber. For the relation of the Latin and German texts of this edition, and their relation to the German text in the Book of Concord, see Kolde earlier, and Weber later in this chapter.

The third fact responsible for the failure of the Lutheran Church to possess a faultless copy of the original of the Augsburg Confession is the craftiness of certain members of the Roman Church. Rome controlled both of the originals of the Confession, though both were state documents. The German original disappeared from the chancellery at Maintz between the time when John Eck examined it in 1541, for the purpose of comparing the original with Melanchthon's Variata of 1540, and the year 1545, when it was to have been sent with other relevant documents to the Council of Trent. The Latin original lay in the archives at Brussels as late as 1569, and was taken subsequently by the Duke of Alba to Spain, and doubtless destroyed.

But though the Lutheran Church is thus without a faultless original of the Augsburg Confession, it is not without a Textus Receptus, a standard, authorized, and approved First Edition; and in which all agree, both the original signers and survivors, the contemporaries, and subsequent scholarship, that there are no changes in substance ·from the original, and that whatever the variations may be, they are textual. The existence of hundreds of variants, concerning which it can probably never be decided as to what precisely the original contained, even though many of these variants are found in the Textus Receptus, or Editio Prin-

---

[48] It probably would be putting the case more exactly to say that Melanchthon, on behalf of the Reformers, was interested in giving to the world the Apology for the Confession, which was the official reply to the Confutation, but which the Emperor had, at the instigation of Ferdinand, refused to receive; and which needed the Confession itself to appear with it as a starting-point and a basis; in addition to the reason given above.

ceps, itself, does not destroy the authority or the fixed character of the substance and the form of the Confession itself. The work of Tschackert itself is subject to this principle.

The Augsburg Confession is in the situation of a great many famous historical documents. It was not inspired, either in origin or in preservation, and is subject to the immediate course of historical law. So far as a standard text is concerned, it is not as badly off as the Holy Scripture, which is inspired, and of which, while we admit that there are hundreds of thousands of variants in the texts, we do not admit that there are Variata in the versions and editions.

The *original manuscripts* of the Scripture have all disappeared. Many of the Old Testament rolls were destroyed during the Jewish exiles and persecutions. Of the later manuscripts that remain there are no less than 1300 or 1400, and they are mediæval. The Greek manuscripts of the New Testament also suffered in the early Christian persecutions, but we still have more than 125 Uncials and 2500 Cursives, the oldest of the Uncials dating back only to the Fourth Century.

The difference between a version full of variants, and a Variata Edition, is that the mistakes in the first case were unintentional, and that in the second case the mistakes are not unintentional, but are intentional changes in an historically accepted document. If a scholar in the Roman church should discover a manuscript of the Vulgate full of variant readings and publish it, it would be a variant edition; but if he should himself make ever so small changes for the purpose of influencing the standard in a question of disputed doctrine, it would be a Variata Edition. The distinction between the two, as can readily be seen, is not only very clear, but also very important.

By the " text " of an historical document the total contents of any particular copy or family of copies of the document is meant. The ascertainment of the true text of any great historical document, where the original no longer exists, is generally attended with great difficulties so far as details are concerned, yet it is usually accomplished so far as the fixed form on the whole, and the complete substance

38

of the truth, are concerned. There is no special providence which protects the documents and the printing of even the Scriptures from variants.

Obscure letters, unintentional omissions by scribes, or the inclusion of a note or a correction written in the margin, or undesigning insertions in a text for supposed completeness, an abbreviation made by the copyist because he deems it important to economize space, a greater or a less realization of the worth of literal exactness in copy, cause variations in everything that is re-written by the hand of man. With all our modern skill applied to the securing of mechanical accuracy, there are very few letters written to-day, and almost no books printed, which are absolutely accurate.

But to confuse unintentional mechanical or editorial deviation in various editions of a work with variations which are made under the influence of a purpose, or which result in a deflection, however slight, from the truth of the original, is neither historical nor just. Melanchthon himself (and other persons mentally constituted as he was) did not see this point. His pragmatic instincts were so great, as we are driven to show in our discussion of the Melanchthonian temperament, that he did not hesitate to interfere with and modify objective standards for the purpose of " improving " them into accordance with his own more recently gained ideas or objects. His variations in the " Loci," which was his own personal work of doctrine, and in the Augsburg Confession, which was the Church's official creation and possession, went hand in hand. The strange thing is, as Melanchthon made his changes in the Confession in all innocency, that he did not indicate what he had done to the official work in the title. Thus we find in the edition of 1540 that he announces revision in his Apology, but fails to announce it in the Confession. Kolde puts this fact very forcibly when he says :—

" While the changes in the edition of the Augustana of 1533, as well as those undertaken in the following editions, are of no importance dogmatically, this is not the case in the new Latin quarto edition of 1540. Although the author in no wise prepares the reader for it,—the Apology bound in the same edition is characterized as *diligenter recognita* (there is no such characterization in the Augustana),—this edition, which well receives the name *Variata,* shows that it is partly a new elaboration with very weighty changes." [49]

It is quite true that a consciousness of historical accuracy, judged by strict standards, was more or less dim in the minds of all the Reformers, and that between the years 1535 and 1540 they not only allowed but suggested various expansions and improvements in the Augsburg Confession and in the Schmalkald Articles; but if their conscience was primitive in this historical technicality, it was true and strict morally. They never contemplated any changes of doctrinal basis or Confessional principle, but only a more full explanation and maintenance of the same real and identical principle.

And though Melanchthon denied before Eck, that he had made any changes of substance in his Variata of 1540, this denial cannot be accepted as a just and accurate judgment of his work, for the reason that throughout his life he was given to pragmatic formulation of statement in the interests of the immediate object to be subserved, and was not chiefly concerned with the exact presentation of historical fact unfavorable to himself or to his position.

When we consider Melanchthon's persistent attempts at variation in the Diet at Augsburg, and the lessons he had been taught there by his sad experience in the deliberations of the Evangelical party, and through the warnings in the letters of Luther; and, when, futhermore, we recall the weight with which the Tenth Article of the Augsburg Confession was regarded at Augsburg, so that, as Cyprian tells us, the Elector was chiefly concerned that this article might appear in right form, and that, despite all the threats and pleadings of Philip of Hesse, the article was written to ex-

---

[49] " Augsburg Confession," in *Herzog-Hauck.*

clude any possible participation in it by the Highlanders; and when, further, we recall the history immediately behind the Augsburg Confession, of which the Schwabach and the Marburg articles were the visible testimony, we cannot fail to see how great was the responsibility which Melanchthon took in giving to the Lutheran Church a Variata Edition, in addition to the standard edition and all the textual variants that had hitherto obtained.[50]

The passing of years and the change of circumstances between 1530 and 1540 had cast upon the principles of the Augsburg Confession a changed shading and perspective, but not a different value. It was quite natural, therefore, that when Melanchthon sought to bring up the Confessional document and teaching of past years to conformity with the demands of the present age, by newly revised and improved editions, there would be so much that seemed helpful and instructive, especially to the rising generation, which enjoys books that are up-to-date, that the newer works of Melanchthon should be preferred to the older ones, which no longer corresponded precisely to the temper of the moment; and that even changes of substance were more or less laxly regarded, for the time being, because of the supposed advantage accruing from the newer work on the whole.

But though the majority were carried away by this point of view, and did not think of raising objection to the changes made in doctrine in the Variata, there were two classes of individuals who could not fail to be affected by

---

[50] Plitt puts the Lutheran position strongly, as follows: " As Melanchthon has continued to make changes in both works up to the moment of printing, so he did not cease in new editions ; and as he thought to improve, although his works had not indeed become public writings, this was at first allowed him, since he always explained, and we may be sure out of an honest heart, that his changes did not concern the meaning, but the expression. This also was to have been the case in the change which he made in 1540, and especially in the X. Article of the Lord's Supper. But soon others attempted to make this new setting authoritative in the sense of divergent teaching against the original text and, since it was the later text, to set it up as the decisive one. This led to a conflict concerning the Confessio Invariata (1530), and the Variata (1540) ; and the more it appeared that the latter was to be made to serve a widespread misuse, the more decidedly it was declared in the Lutheran Church, and this was the natural thing, that the text of 1530 was the decisive and official one of the Confession."

it. One of these two classes was composed of those who had contended and suffered for the faith once delivered to the saints, for the old principles held on to at Augsburg. Among these, especially, were the Elector and Luther.

Luther's bearing in this matter is a credit to his patience, to his love, and to his devotion to his great friend and co-worker Melanchthon. His attachment and sympathy for Melanchthon seem to have been so great that he passed over much that Melanchthon did, in silence. The whole plan of Melanchthon of upholding the truth by conference, by an arrangement, and by negotiation, and of seeking to combine different parts of the church into unity where there were differences, did not approve itself to him. He believed in full and open Confession of the truth, and in leaving the course of history to Providence. It was for this reason, doubtless, that he was not entirely satisfied with the gentleness of the Augsburg Confession toward Rome, so that he spoke of writing a German "Apology" himself.[51] But the universal approval which the Augsburg Confession received everywhere after its delivery and the rise of the Schmalkald League gave matters a direction confessionally and politically which caused Luther to be more reticent. Yet there seems to be little doubt that Luther was worried, though he restrained himself marvellously, concerning the Variata, and that for a time there was some feeling, which did not come to words, between him and Melanchthon on this account.[52]

As for the new Elector, it is admitted on all sides that he had a keen eye for the preservation of the original Con-

---

[51] *Cp.* Kolde, *Luther*, II, 382.

[52] The condemnation of the Variata by Luther as circulated by the Gneslo-Lutherans, does not find any confirmation in the letters of Luther and other accredited deliverances of that time (Köllner, *Symbolik*, I, 239). It was even approved of by such decided Lutherans as Brentz (*C. R.*, IV, 737).

It may seem strange that the Variata of 1540 caused no criticism on its appearance. Yet we must remember the experience of 1537, when the rebuke of the Elector John met with no success, and that the sympathies of the whole rising generation were with their popular teacher and the great Protestant diplomat, Melanchthon.

fession, and that already in 1537, he suggested that Melanchthon be rebuked, and that he termed the alteration a presumption. There is no doubt, as even Weber admits, of the
genuineness of this fact; and we question whether, in view
of the circumstantiality of the account (Kolde cites *C. R.,*
III, 366), the Elector knew of nothing more than rumors.[53]

The statement of it is to be found in *D. Gregorii Brucken
Schrifften* in unterschiedlichen jahren in religionssachen
ergangen, and which bears the following title: " Furhaltung,
so Doctori Marthino und Doctori Pomerano, durch Doctor
Brucken, in beysein und in gegenwertigkait unsers gene-
digsten Herrn des churfursten zu Sachssen ic zu Witembergk bescheen, Sonnabendt Nack Cantate Ano Dnj
XVXXXVij."

The old document reads as follows:—" Magister Philip
is said to have assumed the authority to alter, render milder,
and to print, with other changes, the Confession, made by
your Electoral grace, and the other princes and estates, without previous knowledge and consent of your Electoral grace
and the others, which it was reasonably due that he should
have received from your Electoral grace, since the Confession emanates principally from your Electoral grace and
from the other estates.

" The result of this was that your Electoral grace and
the other estates connected with you were charged that you
are not sure of your doctrine, and that you also do not defend it consistently, at which the people then take offense.

---

[53] Kolde says: " Neither can the objection of the Elector John Frederick to
Luther and Melanchthon of May 5th, 1537, be adduced as proof for the
existence of a Variata at that time. He says there (*C. R.*, III, 366): ' *It is
also said that M. Philipp undertook in several points to alter, soften and
publish with other changes the Confession made by Your Electoral Highness
and other princes and estates before his Imp. Maj. at Augsburg.*' The latter
evidently refers to the fact that probably without any doings of Melanchthon,
in the year 1535, a reprint of the Latin octavo edition of 1531 appeared in
Augsburg (now in the Nuremberg city library), and a second one in Hagenau.
And if the assertion that Melanchthon altered and softened the Confession
does not merely rest on rumors brought to the Elector, we may remember
that at that time, in circles unfavorably disposed toward Melanchthon, notice
was first directed toward the alterations in the octavo edition of 1533."

"And especially did your Electoral grace desire that
both of these confidential and necessary announcements to

und Cyprian *a*) ſtellten nachher das Faktum anders, und
zeigten aus einem im Herzogl. Weimariſchen Archiv vor-
handenen Protocoll, daß der Churfürſt nicht Philippum
durch den alten Canzler Brück beſprechen, ſondern daß er
durch ſeinen Canzler Luther und Pomerano in ſeiner
Gegenwart einen geheimen Vorhalt habe thun laßen,
weil Melanchthon die A. C. gemildert und geändert,
und ſolche ohne ſein Vorwißen zum Druck befördert
haben ſolle. Auch ſetzen ſie das Faktum nicht nach
dem Regenſpurger Colloquio ins Jahr 1541. wie Kirchner,
Selnecker, Chemnitius und andere, ſondern 1537. welches allerdings der Sache eine ganz andere Wendung giebt.

Es hat der verdienſtvolle Herr Paſtor Strobel mich
vor einiger Zeit um treue diplomatiſche Abſchrift dieſes
Protocolls gebeten: und ſo ſehr ich mirs würde zum Ver-
gnügen gemacht haben, ihm hierin zu dienen, ſo konnte
damals das Protocoll nicht aufgefunden werden, wie denn
ſolches der Herr geheime Hofrath H. Eckardt, als dama-
liger Archivarius des hieſigen Herzogl. Archivs, hat drey-
mal vergeblich auffuchen laßen. Endlich fand ſichs im May
voriges Jahrs in einem Lokat, wo mans nicht erwartete.
Es befindet ſich in einem Convolut Acten, welches rubri-
cirt iſt: D. Gregorii Brucken Schrifften jn vn-
terſchiedlichen jahren in religion ſachen ergangen *b*), und führt auswendig die Auffchrift:

Furhaltung, ſo Doctorj Marthino vnd
Doctorj Pomerano, durch Doctor Brucken, in beyſein vnd in gegenwertickait vn-
fers genedigſten herrn des churfurſten zü
Sach-

a) Hiſtorie der A. C. C. 160. f. f.

your Electoral grace should be kept secret and that I should not say anything to any one concerning it at the time."

WEBER II.

Sachssen rc zu Witembergk beschcen, Sonnabendt Nach Cantate Anno Dni XD XXXVij a)

Eine spätere Hand, die aus dem Zeitalter herrührt, wo unter der Vormundschaft Churfürst Augusts zu Sachsen das hiesige Herzogliche Archiv inventirt ward b), hat verstehende Aufschrift folgendergestalt fortgeführt: Der zweiung halben, So sich zwischen gedachten beiden Theologen an einem vnd den dem Philippo vnd Doctor Creuziger anders theils vber etlichen Artickeln der Religion wider die Augspurgische Confession, welche Philip, in vielen Punkten geendert haben solle, Item belangend der Juristen Zweiung wegen der Priester Ehe, vnnd dergleichen Irrige sachen mher, Daraus die Universität spaltung vnnd Vntergang zu besorgenn welchem zuuorkommen, Er Doctor Luther neben Pomerano jr vertraulich bedencken anzeigen sollenn. rc. Inwendig beginnt das Protocoll, welches aus 8 gebrochenen Folioblättern besteht, mit folgenden Worten: Der hanndel solte Doctorj Marthino vnd pomerano also anzuzaigen sein. Da Cyprian das Protocoll hat abdrucken lassen, so gebe ich hier bloß die Stelle, die die A. C. betrift, wie auch den Schluß des Fürtrags:

So solt sich auch magister Philip angemast habenn, Euer churfl. gn: vnd der andern Fursten vnd Stende, Confession, vor Kay. mt zu Augsburg beschcen, in ezlichen

B 2

a) Diese Aufschrift rühret von eben der Hand her, so das Protocoll geschrieben.

b) Nach Müllers Annalen des Churf. und Fürstl. Hauses Sachsen C. 167 ist das Archiv vom Jahr 1574 — 1581 inventirt worden.

" Seckendorf and Cyprian have shown that the Elector did not have Philip spoken to through the old chancellor Brück, but that he made an indirect charge through the chancellor

WEBER III.

lichen puncten zu endern, myltern, vnd — anderweit drucken zu laſſen, one Euer churfl gn. vnd der andern vorwiſſen vnnd bewilligung, des er ſich Euer churfl, gn, etachtens; je billig ſolt enthalten habenn, Nach: dem die Confeſſion, Euer churfl. gn. vnnd der andern Stende furnheinlich iſt.

Dauon euern churfl. gn, vnd den andern jren mituer: wandten Stenden auferlegt wurde, Das Sie jrer There nit gewiß, auch vnbeſtendig wheren, Doran ſich dan auch das volk ergert — . — — —

Vnnd jnnſonderheit begherteu eure churfl gn, das Sie beyde dieſe euer churfl gn. vortrauete vnnd notwendige antzaige, bey ſich jn geheim wolten vnnd niemands hieruon ich was noch zur Zeit antzaigen

An der Authenticität des Protocolls iſt nicht zu zwei: feln, theils weil ich das Papier, worauf es geſchrieben, und die Hand deſſen, der es aufgenommen, noch mehrmals in Acten aus dem damaligen Zeitalter wahrgenommen, theils weil Churfürſt Johann Friedrich eigenhändig Mar: ginalien dazu geſchrieben *a*). Gleichwie nun das ganze Pro: tocoll, welches man beym Cyprian nachſehen kann, ſchö: ner Beytrag zur Charaktergeſchichte Churfürſt Johann Friedrichs iſt, und von ſeiner Leichtgläubigkeit und Furcht: ſamkeit, aber auch Eifer und Treue für die erkannte Wahr: heit zeuget, die jedoch nicht immer mit Klugheit und Politik, ſondern zuweilen mit Härte, Intoleranz und Un-

a) Cyprian ſagt in der Geſchichte der A. C. S. 161. daß auch Summarien von der Hand des Canzlers Brücks darin anzu: treffen. Hier hat er ſich aber geirrt: Denn Brückens Hand habe ich nicht gefunden.

to Luther and Pomeranus, in his presence, because Melanchthon had made the Augsburg Confession milder and altered
it, and had put it in print as such without his knowledge.
They do not place the fact in the Regensburg Colloquy after
1541, as do *Kirchner, Selnecker* and *Chemnitz* and others,
but in 1537, which gives quite another turn to the affairs."

Weber admits the authenticity of this minute, both because the paper and the handwriting correspond with the
time from which they profess to emanate, and also because
the Elector John Frederick annotated the margins with his
own hand.   Weber also admits that this is a fine contribution
to the history of the character of the Elector John, it testifying of his "superstition and fear, but also of his zeal
and faithfulness for the recognized truth."

Here is direct testimony that Melanchthon was blamed by
the Elector for "assuming the authority to *alter, render
milder,* and *print with other changes*" a Confession that was
not his own property; and that he had done this "*without the
previous knowledge and consent*" of the Elector and "the
others," among whom Luther is to be included.   Weber is
interested in showing that the said interview did not take
place in 1541; and hence he is obliged to admit that it did
take place in 1537.   It proves both an exact knowledge, and
a displeasure on the part of the Elector as early as this year.

We have seen that the one class of persons interested in
keeping the Church safely anchored on the doctrine and the
Confession which had been gained at Augsburg were the
original signers and participants in it at the Diet.

The other class of persons interested in the exact nature
of the Lutheran Confession, and waiting with eagle eye to
point out weak spots and inconsistencies in the Evangelical
Confessional principle, was the Roman enemy.   And so it
happened that the original antagonist of Luther and his
doctrine, John Eck, had the satisfaction and the honor of

pointing out to the world and of publicly awakening the Lutheran Church to the fact that in the Variata of 1540 it was declaring a doctrine for which it had been unwilling to stand at Augsburg. This was denied by Melanchthon, but various elements in the Evangelical Church now began to see that such was really the case.

This Confessional discovery came at a time when other conflicts, some of them very bitter and unwarranted, and others inevitable and based on the general situation, were beginning to break out; and when the political complications, arising shortly after Luther's death, revealed more clearly than it is possible for words to do, the need of a standard Confession, and the great peril in which the Evangelical Church was then being placed by its substitution of indefinite and individual interpretations for the real word of Scripture.

The Confessional difficulties brought about by the introduction of the doctrines of the Variata, which had slumbered for years, sprang up into the clear light at the Colloquy of Worms in September, 1557; and all attempts at reconciling the Confessional differences failed. The Frankfurt Recess in March of the following year only served to emphasize the sharp contrast that was already drawn between the two parties. To solve the problem a proposition was made to hold a General Synod, but Melanchthon objected to this in May, 1559, and Brentz likewise in December of the same year. Then the Count Palatine, Duke Christopher, and the Landgrave Philip made a proposition to the Elector Augustus, to hold a common meeting of the German princes adhering to the Augsburg Confession, together with a few theologians, but this was also rejected.[54]

In the midst of all this Melanchthon died on the 15th of April, 1560. King Ferdinand was casting it up to the Elector Augustus that the Lutheran doctrine on the basis of the Augsburg Confession was no longer being taught

---

[54] *Kalinich*, p. 49 sqq.

either in his university at Wittenberg or in his university at Leipzig. Pius IV. was expected to reopen the Council of Trent. Threatening reports were scattered far and wide that there would be an outbreak of a new religious war whose object should be the forcible suppression of Protestantism. It was openly declared that as the Protestants no longer confessed the original Confession, but as they tolerated all sorts of innovations and divisions among themselves, they no longer possessed a right to the concessions made by the Religious Peace of Augsburg.

Therefore Duke Christopher of Würtemberg, despite the failure of previous efforts of his, on the 29th of June, 1560, suggested to the Elector Frederick III. of the Palatinate and his son-in-law Duke John Frederick of Saxony the necessity that the Protestant princes re-confess the Augsburg Confession together, and write a proper Preface and Conclusion showing their unity in such Confession. They agreed to invite the remaining princes and estates to participate in this work. All the estates of the Augsburg Confession were to solemnly promise to remain firm and loyal to the Confession, and not to tolerate any revolutionaries or sectarians in their countries, and not to permit the theologians to enter into disgraceful polemics. The newly-subscribed Confession was to be delivered to the Emperor.

Duke John Frederick, who hitherto had been one of the chief obstacles toward union, because he favored Flacianism, not only agreed to this proposition, but expressly declared that " he desired a coming together of the princes; that theologians were not necessary at the meeting, and that he would control his own theologians so that they should not write and scold against each other." [55]

Duke John Frederick then undertook with Count Palatine and Christopher to win the Landgrave Philip and the Elector August of Saxony for the project. The Elector Augustus said he was agreed, and remarked that the coming

---

[55] *Kugler,* II, 188 sqq.

assembly would be a fitting occasion to come to an under-standing concerning a unanimous Confession in view of a future Council of the Church. At the same time he made it a prerequisite that no other Confession should be sub-scribed than the one handed to the Emperor in 1530, which had been used in the visitation in these countries and upon which the former treaties of peace had been founded.

Yet he connected his participation with the condition, (1) that no political transactions should take place at this con-ference; (2) that there should be no condemnations of the sects. The Convention at Naumburg began on the 21st of January and lasted until the 8th of February, twenty-one sittings in all.

At the opening session a difference occurred between Elector Augustus and Duke John Frederick concerning the call to the Assembly, the Elector charging the Duke with having omitted from the invitation the clause which said that there were to be no condemnations, and no political matters discussed at the Assembly. Duke Christopher brought with him a memorial card concerning the setting up once again of a unanimous Norma Doctrinæ.

At the third session, the Elector Frederick read the invitation and based upon it four propositions :—

(1) As the various editions of the Augsburg Confession contained many devi-ations, it would be well to compare the various editions in the presence of all the princes and then to decide which copy was to be subscribed.

(2) A preface should be prefixed to the newly subscribed Confession in which the occasion should be clearly explained.

(3) There should be a writing or an embassy to the Emperor which would explain the purpose of this Diet at Naumburg.

(4) It should be considered whether and in how far the remaining estates of the Augsburg Confession who had not yet been invited should be moved to a sub-scription.

The great question was, which edition of the Augsburg Confession should be subscribed. The Elector Palatine and the Elector of Saxony spoke on behalf of the edition of 1540, as this did not deviate in substance from the original edi-tion, but was composed with greater clearness and dexterity. The other princes were against this, falling back upon the wording of the invitation, which declared that the subscrip-tion was to be the Confession that had been delivered to the Emperor in 1530. The Elector of Saxony also declared that he was ready to agree to this, on the condition that in the Preface the harmony of the later edition with the earlier edition should be expressed.

The Elector Frederick remained in his first opinion. Duke John Frederick, together with Ulrich of Mecklenburg and the Count Palatine Wolfgang, now declared that the Schmalkald Articles should also be subscribed at the same time, but this proposition found no response with the remaining princes.

The representatives of the absent princes were invited, after deliberation, to express their view of the proposed points. The question concerning the Confession to be subscribed actively busied the theologians who had followed their princes to Naumburg. David Chytræus,[56] who had come with Ulrich from Rostock, as well as the Saxon theologians Mörlin and Stössel warned against the acceptance of the later editions and the corruptions of Melanchthon. The Jena-Lutherans also were active against the supposed heresies of Melanchthon, and sent in an opinion against subscription, and against the petition for a General Synod.

In the fourth sitting the delegates of the absent Estates said they were authorized to sign only the original Augsburg Confession in the same form of words in which they had been delivered to the Emperor.

Therefore the assembly now proceeded to a comparison of the various editions that lay before them, and first of all of the Latin text.[57]

The comparison was made in this way: the counsellor of the Count Palatine read the copy of 1531, the chancellor of the Elector of Saxony repeated the corresponding article of the edition of 1542. The Elector Frederick had the edition of 1540 in his hand, Duke Christopher had the copy written by the hand of Brentz. The Saxon chancellor Brück had a

---

[56] *Salig,* III, 669 sqq.

[57] Only the Elector Frederick and the Duke Christopher, and in part Duke John Frederick and the Count Palatine Wolfgang participated personally in this matter: the rest were represented by their counsellors.

supposed original copy coming from Spalatin. As many differences of form became manifest already in the first articles, it was resolved to ask counsel of some of the theologians present. At the fifth sitting the comparison of the Latin editions came to an end, and in the afternoon the German editions were collated in the same way.

In the sixth sitting five questions were set up for a discussion:—

(1) Whether the edition of 1531 or that of 1540 or 1542 should be adhered to.

(2) Whether the phraseology of the Tenth Article in the edition of 1531 contained a confirmation of the Papal doctrine of transubstantiation.

(3) Whether according to Article XXIII, it would be permissible to dispense the sacrament in both forms.

(4) Since Article XXV said "The mass is retained among us," the Elector Frederick said he could not sign, since in the Palatinate the mass and all Papal ceremonies had been abolished.

(5) Whether in the new Preface, in place of the Schmalkald Articles, the Saxon Confession of Melanchthon, which stood in the Corpus Doctrinæ Sax., should not be mentioned, and the articles of the sacrament, the procession and mass should be briefly explained.

In the seventh session the question came up as to what copy of the Augsburg Confession should be subscribed.[58]

The Elector Frederick voted for the subscription of the Latin and German text of 1540 "since this according to its meaning was not only the same as that of the Confession delivered over, but also explained it more fully ; but in the preface certain necessary opinions were to be noted."

The Elector Augustus would likewise have been for the Confession of 1540, as this was composed in the lifetimes of the Elector John Frederick, Luther and Melanchthon, since it accorded with the true sense of the Confession of 1530, and since it had been used in church, school and house without a doubt ; but as the invitation and the instruction of the delegates limited them to the Confession of 1530 and as the religious peace was founded upon the Confession given over to the Emperor, he was in favor of subscribing to the edition of 1531 as being of nearest

[58] Kluckhohn, *Briefe,* I, 158 sqq.

form to the original ; but in the preface the Confession of 1540 should be mentioned as an explanation of the previous Confession.

The delegates of the Elector of Brandenberg voted in the same way.

The Duke John Frederick of Saxony would have preferred subscription to the Latin and German texts that he had brought with him and reported to have come from Spalatin, but as the princes and delegates did not credit any authority to it, he was satisfied with subscribing the printed copy of the year 1531, "together with the Apology and the Schmalkald Articles and the mention of the Locupletirten Confessions in the preface."

For the editions of 1531 Count Palatine Wolfgang, Mecklenburg, Würtemberg, Hesse, Baden, etc., voted.   The discussion was not ended.

On January 28th in the eighth sitting, although the Elector Frederick attempted to force his demand through, the Confession of 1531 was adhered to, but now there was still a difference as to whether the Apology, and the Schmalkald Articles were to be added as Christian explanations, or whether the Saxon Confession and the Frankfurt Recess should be added as such, and as to whether explanations concerning the Lord's Supper and the mass should be given. On January 28th, a compromise was arranged. The Schmalkald Articles were withdrawn on the one side, and the Saxon Confession and the Frankfurt Recess on the other. Only the recognition of the Apology and of the Augsburg Confession of 1540 should be mentioned in the preface. The two Electors were charged with the drawing up of the Preface, the counsellors and theologians of the three Electors were to make a still more exact comparison of the Latin and German copies which had been selected for subscription; for the German Confession the text of the *quarto* of 1531 was selected, for the Latin the text of the *octave* edition of 1531, which omitted the quotations in the Apology from Theophylact that permitted Art. X to be interpreted in the sense of Transubstantiation.

By the morning of January 29th the collating of both editions was finished. On the afternoon of January 29th the new Preface, which with the newly subscribed Confession, was to be handed to the Emperor, was reported to be subscribed. The Estates defended themselves in this Preface

against the imputation that they had departed from the
original Augsburg Confession, or were no longer in unity in
the explanation of the same. On the contrary they had referred to this Confession continually at the Diets, as well
as to the Scripture, last of all in 1559 at Augsburg, and had
again compared the same. It is true that the Confession
of 1540 and 1542 was composed in a somewhat more extended manner, and was explained upon the basis of the
Holy Scriptures; yet they would abide by the Confession
of 1530, in order to show that they do not defend new or
ungrounded doctrines; at the same time they desired to
have other writings especially repeated which corresponded
with the Holy Scriptures, the Augsburg Confession, and the
Apology, for the turning away of false teachings and abuses.[59]

This was signed by the Elector Frederick, the Elector
Augustus, the Count Palatine, Duke Christopher, the Margrave Carl, Landgrave Philip of Hesse, by their own hands,
and by delegates. The Duke John Frederick of Saxony
and Ulrich of Mecklenburg did not sign, but asked time
for thought.

On the afternoon of January 31st those who had not
signed declared that they could only do so if the errors rejected by the Lutheran Church, especially as to the sacrament, were expressly condemned. There was a violent conflict between father-in-law and son-in-law—the Elector Frederick and the Duke John Frederick. In the fourteenth
session on February 2d John Frederick gave a decided written protest against the Preface to be subscribed, which was
answered on the same day, and he was asked not to further
delay the highly important matter. The next morning between five and six o'clock, Duke John Frederick left Naumburg suddenly and returned to Weimar.

On the evening of the same day, the Elector Frederick

---

[59] Through this declaration, influenced by circumstances and composed by
laymen, the Variata was recognized as another form of the Confession: but
the question what to do in view of the really existing differences was evaded.—
Kolde.

39

in the fifteenth sitting repeated his Melanchthonian Confession on the Lord's Supper with which the remaining princes declared themselves to be satisfied. An attempt was made to reconcile the Duke John Frederick, but he abode by his demand for a satisfactory declaration concerning the doctrine of the Lord's Supper, for a full explanation of the difference between the Augsburg Confession of 1530 and 1540, for a recognition of the Schmalkald Articles as the "real Christian Declaration and Rule of the original Augustana," and was willing to delay the matter of the sects and the corruptions to a later Synod, but this reply came in too late for the meeting.

The resolutions were sent out to the remaining Protestants, Estates, Counts, Lords, and cities for subscription.[60]

Under the guidance of the theologians the princes subsequently withdrew their signatures and joined in the Declaration of the Duke, except the Elector Palatine, who became a Calvinist and introduced the Heidelberg Catechism.

The results of the Diet were a decided declination to participate in the Tridentine Council and the growth of a Protestant consciousness. Peace in the church was by no means brought about: the division only became more open, especially between the houses of Saxony and the Palatinate, and between both lines of the Saxon houses. Even the presence of a common enemy could not strengthen any feeling of unity between the confessors of the Augsburg Confession. The Naumburg Convention had only more prominently exposed the inability of the princes to come to a unanimous subscription.

The Naumburg Convention with its discrimination, but also its authorization, of both editions of the Augustana forms an important epoch in the development of the confessional and political history of German Protestantism, a connect-

---

[60] On the significance of this Diet at Naumburg, compare the declaration in the Preface of the Book of Concord of 1680, together with Salig, Planck, Heppe and Calinich. The judgment in each case is according to the confessional standpoint of the writers.

ing link on the one side between the Augsburg Confession
and the Book of Concord, on the other side between the
Religious Peace of Augsburg and the Peace of Westphalia.
For through this Convention at Naumburg the Invariata
of 1530 is indeed recognized as the authentic fundamental
Confession of the Lutheran Church, and through it the basis
of the Formula of Concord was won for the Lutheran Church;
but on the other side the political equality of the confessors of the Variata with those of the Invariata, and thus
the extension of the benefits of religious peace to the German Reformed church were prepared for.

This Naumburg Convention, in which Melanchthonians
and stricter Lutherans participated, set the current toward
the future and established many things. The Book of Concord was but the execution on the sound Lutheran side of
that step which Naumburg, which was prevailingly Melanchthonian, had recognized as imperatively necessary.
The repeated re-affirmation of the Formula of Concord, as
being the very Confession, " word for word " with the one
" delivered to the Emperor Charles in 1530," dates back
to Naumburg. The " Preface " and the " Conclusion "
written in the name of the Princes rather than of the theologians go back to the ideas of Naumburg. Naumburg
even suggested the preparation of *a new Confession,* and
this was ultimately undertaken in the Formula of Concord. It suggested the condemnation of sectarians, and
the mode of securing subscriptions for the Formula. The
Elector Augustus, so active on the Melanchthonian side at
Naumburg, afterward became the leader of the princes in
having the Formula prepared, and it is natural that he
should have used these methods (which the Melanchthonians
did not object to at Naumburg) to secure the completion
and adoption of the Formula later on. Naumburg is
strong testimony of the need of the Formula.

One of the very first necessities of the Lutheran church,
as we have now seen, if there was to be harmony and unity,

was an established and acknowledged standard for the Augsburg Confession. The authors of the Formula of Concord, to their great credit, saw the importance of getting such a standard text, and they took sound means of securing it; but, owing to the surreptitious removal of the German original from the Maintz chancellery, with the substitution there of a copy in its place, coupled with the declaration that this was the authentic original, and owing to the mistake, or possible duplicity of the ambitious Cölestin, the compilers of the Book of Concord, not being inspired, were led into a mistake. So sure had they been of their discovery of the original German copy at Maintz, that even the mild Melanchthonian Chytraeus, who would never breathe a word against his beloved Melanchthon, writes as follows respecting the supposed original copy that had been rediscovered at Maintz:—

"In order that the Christian readers of this book may be sure that all the documents and transactions occurring before, during, and after the Diet at Augsburg in 1530 are genuine, and that no doubtful or suspicious acts are mingled among them ; I will distinctly indicate where in the volumes of Luther and other credible books the most important parts incorporated into this work are to be found.

" But as the Augsburg Confession of the Elector of Saxony and the Princes and Estates then connected with him, delivered over to the Emperor, is the most important part of this whole book, I will first of all report concerning it, for every one knows that among the copies of the Augsburg Confession, which has been so many times reprinted, enlarged and changed, there seems to be not a small degree of dissimilarity.

"But after all, these churches always undoubtedly referred and appealed to the Confession that was delivered to the Emperor Charles at the Diet at Augsburg : I have had the first copy of the same, as it was delivered at that time to his imperial Majesty, word by word, and from the original that was preserved in the imperial chancellery of the archbishop at Maintz, copied off, the one examined by Dr. Henry Zoch, upon the order of Margrave Joachim, the Elector at Brandenberg, and have given the same in the Kirchenordnung of the Elector of Brandenberg some years ago.

" I have myself seen the examined copy in the chancellery at Maintz. Which also corresponds entirely, word for word, with the oldest Latin quarto of the Confession printed by George Raw at Wittenburg : and with the written copy which Duke Henry of Mecklenburg and certain other princes copied off and sent there during the sessions of the Diet in 1530 : likewise with the copy written off by his own hand of M. George Spalatin who at that time was present at Augsburg as one of the court preachers of the Elector of Saxony and which is still in existence in the Saxon Electoral chancellery.   So that therefore there is no doubt that this is really and truly the right and genuine first copy of the Confession, as it reads word by word, which was delivered to his imperial Majesty at the Diet in 1530.''

But the copy at the Maintz chancellery was not the German original, only a copy.   Thus the German text of the Augsburg Confession in the Book of Concord, while it is not a Variata, and is eminently sound in the principles of the Augsburg Confession, to use the worst expression that can be employed against it, namely, that of Weber, swarms ("wimmelt") with textual errors.

The writers of the preface of the Book of Concord say:—

" Not without agitation of mind we were informed that the adversaries of the true religion received our work in such a way, as though we were so uncertain concerning our Confession of faith and religion, and so often have transfused it from one formula to another, that it is no longer clear to us, or our theologians, what is the Confession once offered to the Emperor at Augsburg.[61] . . .

"Accordingly in order that no persons may permit themselves to be disturbed by the charges of our adversaries . . . that there is not even agreement among us as to what is the true and general Augsburg Confession, but that both those who are now among the living, and posterity also may be clearly and thoroughly taught and informed what that godly Confession is . . . we emphatically testify, that we wish to embrace the first Augsburg Confession alone which was presented to the Emperor Charles V. in the year 1530 at the famous Diet of Augsburg (alone we say), and no other, copies of which deposited in the archives of our predecessors of excellent memory, who presented it in the Diet to Charles V. himself, we caused to be compared by men worthy of confidence (lest in us something with respect to most accurate regard for diligence, would be wanting) with the copy which was presented to the Emperor himself, and is preserved in the archives of the Holy Roman empire, and we are sure that our copies, both the Latin and the German, in all things correspond to it, with like meaning.''

These men were right in all points save their premise, viz.: that the Maintz chancellery in the Roman Church had really preserved the fundamental Protestant charter for a half century, and that what was there called an " Original " was an " Original " in the real sense of the word.

Thus a German copy, with many textual variants, and

---

[61] Jacobs, *Book of Concord*, I, p. 11.

not the lost German original, became the German text of the Book of Concord. The first Latin text published in the Book of Concord was the octave edition of 1531, because there was haste in getting the Book out, and the quarto was not to be had. But in the next edition of the Book of Concord, the quarto of Editio Princeps of 1531 was inserted, and has been the standard ever since.

For over a century and a half the German text was supposed to have a superior authenticity to the Latin text, as being an exact copy to the very letter of the German original, and was regarded with great textual reverence. But Pfaff already at the end of the first quarter of the 18th Century had failed to find the original at Maintz, and Weber at the end of the same century finally brought the truth to light that there had been no original at Maintz as early as 1545. That the authors of the Formula of Concord were deceived as to the original German text of the Augsburg Confession, no more proves the lack of authority of the Confession as a confessional standard, or its lack of a fixed doctrinal and general textual form, than the fact that many scholars of the 17th Century were deceived as to the inspiration of the letters and vowel points of the Hebrew manuscripts of the Old Testament proves that the Old Testament is thereby to be discredited, or that it is not a sufficient standard in its own plane of authority; or that, because the New Testament contains certain passages, which are now regarded as spurious on the authority of the best manuscripts, and because texts have been discovered which completely change many of the readings of the old Textus Receptus, it therefore is no longer to be found in standard form, and has only a passing and changeable value for those who believe and confess it.

This story of the German original is an old one, but has been brought forth recently under the guise of novelty. It is given in toto already in *The Conservative Reformation,* as follows:—

"The first authorized edition, the Editio Princeps, coming from the hand of its composer, and presenting not only in the nature of the case the highest guarantee for strict accuracy, but surrounded by jealous and watchful enemies, in the very Diet yet sitting, before which it was read, surrounded by men eager to mark and to exaggerate the slightest appearance of discrepance, was received by Luther and the whole Lutheran Church. Luther knew no other Augsburg Confession in the German than this. It was received into the Bodies of Doctrine of the whole Church. It appears in the Jena edition of Luther's works, an edition which originated in the purpose of having his writings in a perfectly unchanged form, and was there given as the authentic Confession in antithesis to all the editions of it in which there were variations large or small.

"In the Conventon of the Evangelical (Lutheran) Princes at Naumburg in 1561, among whom were two of the original signers, this edition was declared to be authentic, and was again solemnly subscribed, and the seals of the signers appended. Nothing could seem to be more certainly fixed than that this original edition of Melanchthon presented the Confession in its most perfect form, just as it was actually delivered in the Diet.

"But unhappy causes, connected largely with Melanchthon's later attempts to produce unity by skilful phrases and skilful concealments, led to a most groundless suspicion, that even in the original edition there might be variations from the very letter of the Confession as actually delivered. That there were any changes in meaning was not even in those times of morbid jealousy pretended, but a strong anxiety was felt to secure a copy of the Confession perfectly corresponding in words, in letters, and in points, with the original. The original of the Latin had been taken by Charles with him, but the German original was still supposed to be in the archives at Mentz. Joachim II., in 1566, directed Coelestinus and Zochius to make a copy from the Mentz original.   Their copy was inserted in the Brandenburg Body of Doctrine in 1572.

" In 1576, Augustus of Saxony obtained from the Elector of Mentz a copy of the same document, and from this the Augsburg Confession as it appears in the Book of Concord was printed.   Wherever the Book of Concord was received, Melanchthon's original edition of the German was displaced, though the corresponding edition of the Latin has been retained.   Thus, half a century after its universal recognition, the first edition of the Augsburg Confession in German gave way to what was believed to be a true transcript of the original.

" Two hundred years after the delivery of the Confession, a discovery was communicated to the theological world by Pfaff, which has reinstated Melanchthon's original edition.   Pfaff discovered that the document in the archives at Mentz was not 'the original, but a copy merely, and the labors of Weber have demonstrated that this copy has no claim to be regarded as made from the original, but is a transcript from one of the less-finished copies of the Confession, made before it had assumed, under Melanchthon's hand, the exact shape in which it was actually presented. While, therefore, the ordinary edition of the Augsburg Confession, the one found in the Book of Concord, and from which the current translations of the Confession have been made, does not differ in meaning at all from the original edition of Melanchthon, it is, nevertheless, not so perfect in style, and where they differ, not so clear.   The highest critical authority, then, both German and Latin, is that of Melanchthon's own original editions.[62]

" The current edition of the German, and the earlier edition of Melanchthon, are verbally identical in the larger part of the articles, both of doctrine and of abuses.   The only difference is, that Melanchthon's edition is occasionally some-

---

[62] For the facts here presented, *Cp. Weber, Krit. Geschichte;* Hase, *Lib. Symb.;* Francke, *do.;* Köllner, *Symb. d. Luther. Kirch.,* 342.

what fuller, especially on the abuses, is more perfectly parallel with the Latin at a few points, and occasionally more finished in style. When the question between them has a practical interest, it is simply because Melanchthon's edition expresses in terms, or with greater clearness, what is simply implied, or less explicitly stated in the other." [63]

In conclusion we may sum up the matter of the relation of manuscripts and the printed editions to the Augustana as a Confessional Standard as follows:—

(1) The Augsburg Confession was largely drawn up from previous manuscripts, notably the Schwabach and the Torgau Articles. While it was still a proposed draft, and before it attained its final fixed and signed form, it was revised incessantly, chiefly by Melanchthon, its personal composer, but also by the Elector, Brück, and the Estates at a late date allowed to participate in it. Manuscript copies were made of it, some of them used by the Princes at the Diet, and at least one sent home by the representatives of a municipality reporting to their fixed authorities, before it reached its final form.

(2) As final, fixed, and signed, it existed in two manuscripts, the German of which was read at the Diet and which was deposited in the Maintz chancellery, whence it disappeared, after Eck had compared the Variata of 1540 with it, before 1545; and the Latin original which was deposited in Brussels until 1567 and then disappeared.

(3) The Emperor had forbidden the publication of the document. But it was published surreptitiously in a number of editions by various irresponsible parties, and Melanchthon was obliged to prepare a form which represented the convictions of the Lutheran Estates. No blame can be attached to him if the text of this Editio Princeps differed textually in a number of ways from the originals handed in to the Emperor and as the edition thus issued was ac-

[63] *Con. Ref.,* p. 251-253.

cepted as authentic by all the original principals and signatories, it must, in the absence of the original, be so regarded, not only because it was the first official text drawn up, and was declared by Melanchthon to have been drawn from good authorities, but also because it was accepted by all the parties in interest, as the Standard Edition, even though here and there, and in many places, we may firmly believe, from our knowledge of the private manuscripts of the Princes, that it does not bear the exact external text of the original document. Kolde is entirely right when he says: " This must be emphasized, Melanchthon's edition was taken and regarded as the authentic reproduction of the faith confessed before the Emperor and the realm, in spite of the fact that they had in their hands many kinds of copies reading otherwise." [64] Kolde also draws attention to the fact that in this First Edition of the Augustana, which was bound up with and issued simultaneously with the Apology, the book shows an official character because Melanchthon does not call himself the composer, while he does state in the title that he is the composer of the Apology, because, even though in its first outline it was composed at the request of the Evangelical Estates; yet it was never delivered, and was greatly enlarged by Melanchthon, and therefore was merely a private work at that time.

(4) Even the most numerous textual variations in various copies of the Confession would not justify us in abandoning an edition thus received as Standard, on the ground that it was a Variata. The corruptions of the Textus Receptus, though they run up to over a hundred thousand, in the New Testament would not justify us in saying that the world has been obliged to depend upon an "Altered Bible." In this case, the Received Text has the sanction and has enjoyed the use of the original writers themselves, as the Standard Copy.

---

[64] Article on Augsburg Confession in *Herzog-Hauck.*

As to Cölestin and the imperfect readings of the German edition in the Book of Concord, it only can be said, that later discovery destroys the claim of those who wrote the Preface of the Book of Concord that the German text is correct word for word, but does not invalidate the substance of that text, and it all the more firmly establishes the Latin text of the Editio Princeps as the standard of the Augustana *Invariata.*

The confirmation of the Latin Text of the Quarto of 1531 as a Standard is admitted by Weber, as the following conclusions (I, pp. 46, 47) show:—

1. That the text of the Latin Quarto Edition of 1531 still bears undeniable marks of recognition from the earliest draft of the Confession. This is probably the only right explanation why it still differs here and there, and particularly in the first of the contested Articles from the manuscripts in the archives, as well as the Maintz copy, and if you desire to say so, also from the German Melanchthonian Edition of 1531. I do not deem it necessary to give examples. Every one can find such who takes the trouble to compare the before-mentioned text with the Maintz copy.

2. That the text of the Latin Quarto Edition of the Augsburg Confession of 1531 cannot be taken as a touch-stone by which to discover the original German text; for this did not receive the last touches from Melanchthon's hand.

3. It is historically certain that Melanchthon elaborated the German Confession more diligently than the Latin, and it is probably historically certain that not all the changes which Melanchthon introduced into the Confession from May 22nd to June 22nd were transferred to the Latin.[65]

4. Weber explains that the " Written Original Confession " of which a copy was sent by the Elector Daniel of Maintz to the Elector of Saxony on the evening of August

---

[65] " As I have shown in the preceding example on the Article of the marriage of priests."

19th, 1576, was a copy of the Augsburg Confession in the already copied "*Religious Acts,*" which writing had already been called the "*Protocol*" by Cölestin. He says that in the Maintz chancellery it was the custom to call every copy which took the place of the original an "Original." Thus he declares that Spalatin's manuscript of the Augsburg Confession which Duke John of Saxony took to the Confession in Naumburg in 1561 was called "Original". He believes that the chancellery applied the word "Original" to written documents as in contrast with printed volumes. He also believes that the document sent to the Elector Augustus had the signatures, and that they had been transferred to the copy in question from the Brandenburg document.

But while Weber deprecates the authority of the German text in the Book of Concord, he places highest value on the Latin Editio Princeps. He says: "I do not wish to declare that the highest authenticity is to be ascribed to Melanchthon's first Latin Edition, *i. e.,* looking at it critically, that it is the same as the original writing delivered to the Emperor. For Melanchthon himself admits that his Edition was not prepared in accordance with the original writing, but according to a trust-worthy copy; and . . . it may be that Melanchthon here and there interpolated something in his Edition." But Weber is unwilling to allow either the Fabricius copy or the manuscripts in the archives to have higher authority than Melanchthon's Latin copy, and he desires his readers to give preference to this Latin text of the Editio Princeps, "which the Protestant church has also ascribed to Melanchthon in that it has taken up this his chief edition into the Book of Concord, rather than to adhere to the text of Fabricius and the manuscripts of the archives."

"If the editions of the Augsburg Confession," says Weber, "are to be distinguished from one another without our falling into confusion, it is necessary to give the higher authority to the first one, which according to Melanchthon's admissions was printed critically and according to a good and trustworthy copy, from the later ones which contain his further elaborations and elucidations."

Weber also calls the Latin quarto edition of 1531 the "Melanchthonische Haupt-Ausgabe." He says: "This investigation . . . at every point maintains the authenticity of the Editio Princeps. It remains the most precious treasure of the Evangelical Church." [66]

In conclusion, we may add that the delicate accuracy of the Invariata is that of a standard watch movement, rather than that of an exquisitely chased watch-case. The question of the Variata is not a question of the letter, but of substance. The original letter becomes important only where it is actually the bearer and the arbiter of original substance.

---

[66] We have quoted Weber so fully because he is the leading critical Melanchthonian authority.

CHAPTER XXII.

THE LUTHERAN CONFESSION.

PROTESTANTISM UNDER THE AUGSBURG CONFESSION TO THE DEATH OF LUTHER.

The Apology and its Confessional Import—The Schmalkald League—The Princes and Estates—The Faith Taught in the *Loci*—Melanchthon Waves the Olive Branch to Bucer—The Wittenberg Concord—The Schmalkald Articles—The Marriage of Philip of Hesse—The *Variata*—The Regensburg Interim—The Reformation of Cologne—The Death of Luther.

LET us turn from the history of the Augustana manuscripts and editions, to witness the development of the Protestant principle, and to watch the men and movements under which it occurred.

On the third of August, 1530, the Roman Confutation[1] of the Augustana was read before the Diet, and on the twenty-second of September, just before the Diet adjourned, Melanchthon's Apology was offered to the Emperor; and now Melanchthon spent the remainder of the year and the beginning of the next, to April, 1531, in making his Apology more thorough and elaborate. In mild and flowing language, rising at times to heights of passionate eloquence, it pours forth treasures of Scriptural and historical learning, to defend and elucidate the great Protestant doctrine of justification by faith alone, without works, from every possible point of view.

The Apology, far more[2] than the Augsburg Confession,

---

[1] Given in full, tr. by Jacobs, in our English *Book of Concord* II, p. 209-241.

[2] The Apology is "seven times as large as the Confession itself. It is the most learned of the Lutheran symbols."—Schaff *Creeds* I, p. 244.

is the great Lutheran monograph on the cardinal doctrine of Reformation, written under the actual attack of the Roman theologians, and confessing,[3] with heart and soul, this fundamental truth of Scripture. It opened all eyes, except, perhaps, its author's, to the permanency of the gap between the Evangelical Faith and Rome.

But the Emperor was ill-pleased with this success, and the Protestant states felt it necessary to form a league among themselves. For it now appeared " that those who had the pure Word of God preached in their territory, were to be restrained by force from continuing this God-pleasing undertaking, and, since it was the duty of every Christian government to prevent its subjects from being compelled to fall away from the pure Word of God, they, solely for the sake of their own defence, had come to the agreement that, whenever anyone of them was attacked on account of the Word, or anything connected therewith, they would immediately all come to his assistance. This alliance should not be regarded as in opposition to the Emperor, since it was simply intended for the protection of Christian truth and peace, as also for defence against unlawful violence."

Thus [3a] was the Schmalkald League brought into life, with

---

[3] " To one charged with the care of souls the frequent reading of the **Apology** is invaluable on account of the manner in which it solves difficulties connected with the most vital points in Christian experience ; while the private Christian, although perhaps compelled to pass by some portions occupied with learned discussions, will find in many—we may say, in most—parts what is, in fact, a book of practical religion. The chapter ' Of Love and Fulfilling the Law,' with the preceding more learned and technical one on Justification, Philippi aptly remarks, bears to the entire contents of the Confessional writings the same relation the Epistle to the Romans has to the entire Scriptures their ' kern and stern,' so clearly are they grounded in Scriptural experience, so triumphant, edifying and consoling is their development."—Jacobs, *Book of Concord* II, 41.

[3a] They met, princes and delegates of cities, in the little upland town of Schmalkalden, lying on the south-west frontier of Electoral Saxony, circled by low hills which were white with snow (December 22nd-31st). They had to face at once harassing litigation, and, after the 15th of April, the threat that they would be stamped out by force of arms. Were they still to maintain their doctrine of passive resistance? The question was earnestly debated. Think of these earnest German princes and burghers, their lives and property at stake, debating this abstract question day after day, resolute to set their own consciences right before coming to any resolution to defend themselves !

Many towns now joined the Schmalkald League. Brunswick joined. Hamburg and Rostock in the far north, Goslar and Göttingen in the centre,

restive and radical Philip of Hesse as the moving, and the Elector[4] of Saxony as the substantial, spirit. That Fall, Zwingli was killed upon the battlefield, and Oecolampadius died; and the following June, the Emperor's difficulties with the Turks influenced him to grant the Protestants the religious Peace of Nuremberg. Leonard Kaiser perished in the flames, a Lutheran martyr; and, during that same season, the Elector was stricken with apoplexy, and was succeeded by his son, John Frederick.

The princes and estates were looked to as the Powers to carry out the Reformation, each in his own territory. While the congregations possessed the right of passing judgment on doctrine, the princes were regarded as representative of the congregation-at-large (Christianity), and as "præcipua" in it.

Thus the princes and magistrates were the official representatives of the Reformation. They became the public defenders of the new doctrine,[5] framed by the theologians, *but legalized only when adopted by the secular government.* This accounts for the importance attached, by all church parties, to subscription to the Confessions legally adopted on any territory; which has followed the State faiths of Germany as an incubus, through succeeding centuries; and which, as underlying a State form of religious organization, must be divorced from a consideration of the Confessions

---

joined. Almost all North Germany and the more important imperial towns in the South were united in one strong confederacy by this Schmalkald League. It became one of the European Powers. Denmark wished to join. Thomas Cromwell was anxious that England should join. The League was necessarily anti-Hapsburg, and the Emperor had to reckon with it.

When the Diet met at Nürnberg in 1532, the Emperor knew that he was unable to coerce the Lutherans, and returned to his earlier courteous way of treating them. They were more patriotic than the German Romanists for whom he had done so much. Luther declared roundly that the Turks must be met and driven back, and that all Germans must support the Emperor in repelling the invasion.—Lindsay, *Hist. Ref.,* p. 373 sq.

[4] "When warned by Melanchthon of the possible effects of his signature, the Elector John of Saxony nobly replied: 'I will do what is right, unconcerned about my electoral dignity; I will confess my Lord, whose cross I esteem more highly than all the power of earth.'"—Schaff *Creeds* I, p. 226.

[5] First recognized in the decree of the Diet of Spires; and receiving legal imperial sanction at the Peace of Augsburg.

proper. It is only a secondary matter in a country where the legal aspects of a religious faith are not primary, and where the legal sanctions of the State are separate and apart from the faith and the constitution of the Church, and are applicable only in the solution of questions pertaining to property and disputes as to compensation of officers. " Originally intended merely as testimonies or confessions of faith, these documents became gradually binding formulas of public doctrine, and subscription to them was rigorously exacted from all clergymen and public teachers in Lutheran State churches." [6]

While the princes were defending the faith, and Luther was witnessing to it and translating the Scriptures, Melanchthon was at work framing the forms for its permanent embodiment, and passing them down to the next generation of scholars who now sat, as students, at his feet. Luther was the Confessor, and Melanchthon was the theologian, the systematizer, of the evangelical doctrine. Luther found the truth; Melanchthon harmonized it with philological, logical and philosophical knowledge, and put it into text-book form. Luther was not slow in declaring that " All that we know in the arts and in philosophy, we owe to Philip. He has only the degree of Majister, yet he is a doctor above all doctors."

As a true humanist, Melanchthon would have preferred to remain in these realms of " the arts and philosophy," in which he was the first great modern text-book maker. But Luther insisted that he must enter the sphere of theology; and after various theological lectures, he gave the Church the first great Protestant text-book of Theology, in 1521, which ran through no less than fifty editions during his

---

[6] " As early as 1533, a statute was enacted in Wittenberg by Luther, Jonas, and others, which required the doctors of theology, at their promotion, to swear to the incorrupt doctrine of the Gospel as taught in the symbols. It was only a modification of the oath customary in the Roman Catholic Church. After the middle of the sixteenth century, subscription began to be enforced on pain of deposition and exile. See Köllner, *Symb.*, 1 p. 106 seqq."— Schaff, *Creeds* I, p. 222. Its introduction at this time, after the organization of the Schmalkald League, is significant.

lifetime, and which brought his power of systematization, his stores of knowledge, and his dialectic skill of statement, to bear upon the evangelical doctrine discovered by Luther. The "Loci" had thus become the first and, for a long time, the only attempt at a systematic presentation of conservative Protestant dogmatics. Luther, in his hearty way, declared the book " invincible, worthy not only of immortality, but of being placed in the inspired canon."

This unstinted commendation of the "Loci" was of its first edition. It was the later editions, from 1535 and subsequently, in which Melanchthon made doctrinal changes in the material of the "Loci," corresponding to the changes in his teachings, that indicate the growing difference in doctrine between Luther and himself.[1]

But the year 1532 was a peaceful one—a rainbow between the storms—for Melanchthon; and his Commentary on Romans appeared. It was probably the last year of real concord and rest for the gentle Preceptor: 1533 ushered in the gathering darkness. Luther and Melanchthon " represented in their later period, which may be dated from the year 1533, two types of Lutheranism, the one the conclusive and exclusive, the other the expansive and unionistic type.[2] For Melanchthon, who had opposed the Swiss Reformed consistently, and especially at Augsburg, in the lingering hope of a restoration of Lutheranism to Rome, and whose heart had clung to a visible external unity of the Church under a uniform rule culminating in the Papacy, now became a convert to the persuasive powers of Martin Bucer, the most diplomatic of all the Reformers, who gave his busy life and enormous strength to the cause of a great Protestant Union; and who managed by sacrificing parts of his own doctrine of the Lord's Supper to Lutheranism—which he felt he could readily do, since, as is the case with the Re-

---

[1] " In the first edition of the ' Loci,' Melanchthon's monergism is entirely out of harmony with the synergism which our author advocates."—Jacobs on Valentine, *Christian Theology.*

[2] Schaff, *Creeds* I, p. 259.

formed, it was not such a vital truth to him—not only convinced even Luther for a time⁹ that union on the doctrine of
the Sacrament was possible, but by repeated interviews and
writings to the radical Swiss held them in check in their
extreme views, and thus probably, brought Protestantism as
near together, temporarily, as it ever has been in the past,
and nearer than it ever will be in the future.

This quiet forsaking of Luther, and of the Lutheran
doctrine of the Lord's Supper,¹⁰ under the influence of Bucer,
and this coming into agreement on the sacrament with Bucer
and Calvin, was connected with and furthered by several
other developments in Melanchthon's mind. In the first
place, he had found that some of the Church Fathers, whose
authority he ever respected highly, had sanctioned the fig-
urative view of the Supper; and, in the second place, he was
just at this time filled with the delusive idea of uniting the
whole Protestant world into a visible Church, just as earlier
he had hoped for such a visible reunion under Rome. In
sympathy with Bucer, he was engaged in negotiations not
only to bring south and north Germany together into the
unity of one Protestant bond, but he was negotiating with
Francis, King of France, and Henry VIII. of England to

---

⁹ In the Wittenberg Concord.

¹⁰ The Reformed, at least, claim that Melanchthon was agreed with Bucer,
and later with Calvin, on this doctrine. Schaff says: "He [Melanchthon]
gave up the peculiar features of Luther's doctrine, viz., the literal interpretation of the words of institution, and the oral manducation of the body of
Christ. . . . Calvin publicly declared that he and Melanchthon were inseparably united on this point: '*Confirmo, non magis a me Philippum quam a
propriis visceribus in hac causa posse divelli*' (*Admonitio ultima ad Westphalum, Opp.* VIII, p. 687). Galle maintains that Melanchthon stood
entirely on Calvin's side (I. c. P. 445). So does Ebrard, who says: '*Melanchthon kam, ohne auf Calvin Rücksicht zu nehmen, ja ohne von dessen Lehre
wissen zu können, auf selbständigem Wege* [But recall Bucer's previous influence.—T. E. S.] *zu derselben Ansicht, welche bei Calvin sich ausgebildet
hatte*' (*Das Dogma v. heil. Abendmahl*, Vol. II, p. 437.) He also repeatedly
rejected (as, in fact, he never taught) the Lutheran dogma of the ubiquity
of Christ's body, as being inconsistent with the nature of a body and with
the fact of Christ's ascension to Heaven and sitting in Heaven, whence he
shall return to judgment. But he never became a Zwinglian; he held fast
to a spiritual real presence of the person (rather than the body) of Christ,
and a fruition of his life and benefits by faith. In one of his last utterances,
shortly before his death, he represented the idea of a vital union and communion with the person of Christ as the one and only essential thing in this
sacred ordinance."—*Creeds* I, p. 264 sq.

the same end. Poor Melanchthon! How little he understood human nature, both that of kings, of theologians and
of common people, and how much confidence he placed in
idle promises of nearer union that never were intended to
compass more than the self-interest of those that made them!

Bucer was unwearied and undaunted in his efforts to bring
the Protestants together. In 1529, he had succeeded in com-
pelling the two Protestant parties to face each other at
Marburg. And though he could not, even with the aid of
Philip of Hesse, persuade the Elector and Melanchthon to
allow the Reformed to join in the Confession at Augsburg,
but was obliged to frame and hand in one representing four
Reformed cities, the *Tetrapolitana,* separately, to the emperor (July 11, 1530), yet he remained undismayed; and,
before he left Augsburg, sought and gained an interview
with Luther at Coburg (Sept., 1530), in which Luther good-
naturedly promised to read a new Confession which Bucer
would prepare. As Melanchthon also seemed more disposed
to listen to him, he now undertook an extensive journey
through upper Germany and Switzerland, to make it clear
to the Reformed that they should prepare for an approach
toward the Lutherans. The political situation was such that
both the Swiss above, and Strasburg below, were most willing to do this, in order not to be separated from the powerful Elector of Saxony. It was thus that Strasburg succeeded
in being admitted into the Schmalkald League. By 1534,
Bucer had pushed his life-effort at Concord so far that, in
December, the Swiss accepted a doctrinal compromise and
authorized Bucer to enter into unionistic negotiations with
Luther.

Just at this juncture, in Dec., 1534, Philip of Hesse[10a]

[10a] In the Spring of 1534, Philip, at the head of the Schmalkald League, had
driven Ferdinand and the imperialists out of the Duchy of Wuertemberg and
made it a Lutheran State. As a result of this Protestant victory of Philip,
Ferdinand was obliged to agree that the Imperial Court would try no Protestant for a matter of faith. The victory also led to the dissolution of the
Swabian League in 1536, and thus the Schmalkald League was master of the
German situation.

arranged a meeting at Cassel between Bucer and Melanchthon—and Melanchthon came back to Wittenberg, a supporter of Bucer. A week or two later, on Jan. 10, 1535, we find Melanchthon privately renouncing Luther's doctrine, in a letter to Camerarius in which he says: "*Meam sententiam noli nunc requirere, fui enim nuncius aliae*," [11] *i. e.,* Luther's. And only two days later still, he wrote confidentially to Brentz, that many of the Fathers interpreted the Supper typically. No wonder, then, that the new edition of the "Loci," just now in press (1535), came out with its changes not only on the doctrine of the Lord's Supper, but also on Free Will; and that the "Variata" appeared later with its significant changes. It becomes a question as to how far Melanchthon was only expressing his private opinion, and relieving a burdened conscience, in these changes; and in how far he was intending thus silently and diplomatically to prepare the way, even at that day, for Bucer's cherished scheme, furthered by himself, of uniting the Reformed and the Lutherans on a basis acceptable to both.

At last, in 1536, Bucer's long-prepared-for scheme to unite Reformed and Lutherans reached its head in a meeting at Wittenberg. Luther was sick, and at first opposed the holding of the meeting. After Bucer's earnest efforts, this conference between the Reformed and the Lutherans took place in Luther's own house. Here the *Wittenberg Concord* was signed by Bucer, Capito and Albert, on the Reformed side, and by Luther, Melanchthon, Bugenhagen, and others on the Lutheran side.[12] (The Wittenberg Concord with Bucer's Exhortation and Explanation, is to be found in our English Book of Concord.[13])

[11] *Corp. Reform.*, II, p. 822.

[12] Though the refusal of Luther at Marburg is always referred to by Unionists, it is sometimes overlooked that three Reformed leaders, Bullinger, Myconius, and Grynaeus, seceded from the Union effort of Bucer and defended themselves in the *Confessio Helvetica prior*, which, in temperate manner, maintains firmly the doctrine of Zwingli.

[13] II, p. 253-260.

This Concord declares that "we must affirm that the true body and blood of the Lord are truly given and received in the Holy Supper," and that "Dr. Luther and his colleagues do not teach that Christ is naturally united with the elements, or offered after any mode of the present life. It is a heavenly object and is offered after a heavenly mode." "Since such is your position," said Luther, "we are one, and we recognize and receive you as our dear brethren in the Lord, so far as concerns this article."

The spirit of Luther was admirable. The Marburg Colloquy and the Wittenberg Concord belong together, and, with Luther firm as a rock in both, must be judged together. Luther's love for true union in unity, his steadfastness, and moderation; and yet, in the end, the vindication of his Marburg judgment—are most remarkable.[13a]

At Wittenberg Bucer sacrificed Reformed doctrine; and the inconsistency of Unionists, in professing to be willing, on their side, to compromise on non-essentials, if they can unite in fundamentals, has never been more strikingly shown than is done by Schaff, who condemns Luther at Marburg for not yielding, *and yet condemns Bucer (and the whole compromise plan), at Wittenberg, for yielding.* Schaff's words, written in describing the Reformed church, deserve to be pondered. He says: "Bucer labored with indefatigable zeal for an evangelical union, and hoped to attain it by

---

[13a] Luther's original view, at the end of January, 1535, of this whole situation brought on by Bucer, Philip of Hesse and Melanchthon at Cassel, is so sound and sensible, and so pertinent to-day yet, that we have translated a part of it, as follows:—

"With respect to Bucer's Opinion that Magister Philip has brought from Kassel this is my Opinion: First, since it is conveyed therein that those who speak, wish to and shall teach according to the Apology or Confession, I cannot and do not know to reject such a Concordia for my own person.

"Second, since they clearly confess that the Body of Christ is truly and essentially offered in the Lord's Supper in the bread, that it is received and eaten, etc.; in case their heart stands as the words read; I also this time do not know to cast blame upon the words.

"In the third place, since nevertheless this matter has from the beginning made a deep and wide rent, and because even at the present time, it is scarcely believed on our side that the others mean it as purely as the words read, and the fear is still strong that some of them are almost enemies of our name and faith, I regard it as useful and good, that the Concordia be not so suddenly concluded, in order that their party does not hasten too quickly

elastic compromise formulas (like the Wittenberg Concordia of 1536), which concealed the real difference, and in the end satisfied neither party. . . . We may regard the Strasburg Confession as the first attempt at an evangelical union symbol. But Bucer's love for union was an obstacle to the success of his confession, which never took deep root. . . . Bucer himself remained true to his creed, and reconfessed it in his last will and testament (1548), and on his deathbed." [14]

Because of the various alterations Melanchthon had made in his writings, and his compromising attitude with the Reformed, as well as the fact, no doubt, that he had not been quite open and true to Luther, in his growing relations and doctrinal agreement with Bucer, the years 1536-1538 were exceedingly uncomfortable for Melanchthon, on account of the strained relations; so that he compares himself to *a Prometheus ad Caucasum alligatus* (C. R. III, 606), and writes to Camerarius (Nov., 1539): "Me dolores animi, quo tuli toto triennio acerbissimos et continuos, et caeterae quotidianae aerumnae ita consumserunt, ut verear me diu vivere non posse."

By 1539 Protestantism had become mighty. Duke George had died and his brother Henry introduced the Evangelical faith into Sachsen, to the great joy of the people. The three clerical Electors, the archbishop of Maintz, Köln and Treves, were speaking of making their provinces secular and joining

---

and that division does not arise among ourselves. For our people also have a right in the matter which is not my own or that of any one else alone; but if a more friendly manner were to arise toward each other out of the words laid down, it would readily show itself in time, whether their meaning was pure and right, or whether there was something more behind, in order that such a concord would not later turn into a worse discord.

" They could meanwhile soften the suspicion and rancor for our party, and then at last drop it; and after the turbid water had then settled itself on both sides, one could conclude a true and stable unity, which would be accepted willingly and spontaneously by all, with the good of all, without suspicion, and from the right ground, and which probably cannot, at least not easily, come to pass without further interviews and experience."—*Hist. d. Sacramentsstreits*, 216; *Walch*, XVII, 2496; *De Wette*, IV, 589; *Erlangen*, LV, 85.

[14] Schaff, *Creeds* I, p. 526, 529.

the Protestants, thus bringing a Protestant majority into the Imperial Electorate, so that the next Emperor would be a Protestant. Breslau, Bavaria, Austria and Bohemia were rapidly becoming Protestant. The Emperor Charles was thoroughly alarmed, and he instituted the compromise Conferences at Hagenau, Worms and Regensburg.

In 1539-1540 Melanchthon was still most busily engaged in ecclesiastical work, at the convention in Frankfort, in the introduction of the Reformation in the Duchy of Sachsen and Meissen, at the second convention in Schmalkald, as also with the founding of the Leipzig University.

The Schmalkald League had, some time before, requested the theologians to confirm the Augsburg Confession with further arguments from Scripture and from the Fathers; and on the heels of the Wittenberg Concord, *i. e.,* not very long thereafter, Melanchthon made the famous alteration in the tenth article of the Augsburg Confession. A comparison with the Wittenberg Concord will justify the assumption that Melanchthon desired to yield to the actually existing union with the Highlanders; for, as Kolde says, " if at the same time, he omitted the *vere et substantialiter adesse* and the *improbatio,* we need not harbor any doubts that with the gradually changing conception in his mind about the Lord's Supper, he desired to leave a possibility open for himself and others to go along with the Swiss theologians."

We have seen that the Elector disapproved Melanchthon's alterations in 1537 ; but Luther remained silent, except that the situation with respect to the Pope had called forth from him, at the request of the Elector, the Schmalkald Articles, in the signing of which, Melanchthon gave offence to the other Reformers. Melanchthon's signature reads thus : " I, Philip Melanchthon, also approve the above articles as right and Christian. But concerning the Pope, I hold, that if he would allow the Gospel, for the sake of the peace and general unity of Christians who now are under him, and may be under him hereafter, his superiority over the Bishops, which he otherwise possesses, should also be conceded by us *jure humano.*"

Luther no doubt felt much grieved at the changes of Melanchthon toward him and his teaching, and, says Schaff, " was strongly pressed by contracted and suspicious minds to denounce them openly; but he was too noble and generous to dissolve a long and invaluable friendship, which forms one of the brightest chapters in his life and in the history of the German Reformation." [15]

However, the friendship of the two Reformers was suspended for a time. In 1537, the chancellor, Brück, reported to the Elector of Saxony, that " Luther seemed to be troubled because he could not tell how Philip regarded the sacrament, and because it looked as if Melanchthon, since his return from Cassel, had become almost Zwinglian in his views. Luther did not know what Philip believed in his heart, but it seemed strange that he should recommend the giving of the sacrament in one kind. If Melanchthon persisted in his opinion, then the Word of God must come first. He would pray for Philip. If, for the sake of tyrants and of the preservation of the peace, the sacrament might be administered in one kind, it would be necessary, on the same principle, to concede justification by works." " I think," added the chancellor, " that it would do no harm if Dr. Martin should speak earnestly and cordially with Philip."

Meantime, trouble had arisen from another source. The doctrines of sin and grace, of faith and justification in the Augsburg Confession, and the doctrine of the Law and the Gospel in the Catechisms, were being menaced by Agricola of Eisleben, who had removed to Wittenberg. Luther very sorrowfully and unwillingly testified publicly against the false teaching in 1538 and 1539, and published his book against the Antinomians. Agricola abused Luther for his utterances, but left Wittenberg before the case came to trial.

---

[15] Schaff, *Creeds* I, p. 265.

The controversy broke out again later in the middle of the century.

In the midst of many labors and travels, and terrible self-reproaches and fears regarding the second marriage, at which he was an unwilling guest, of his and Bucer's friend, the restless Reformer, Philip of Hesse, Melanchthon suddenly grew sick unto death, at Worms, but was recalled to life by the mighty faith of Luther, and, in this same year 1540, gave to the press his "Variata." [16]

It would be interesting to know whether Luther's words to Melanchthon of June 18, 1540, "*Nos tecum et tu nobiscum, et Christus hic et ibi nobiscum,*" were written with or without a knowledge of the "Variata."

The difference in Melanchthon's text was first pointed out to the shame of the Lutherans by a Roman Catholic, in 1541. The man who had the satisfaction of putting his finger on this breakdown of Lutheran doctrine was no other than John Eck, the old enemy of Luther, in the discussion with Me-

---

[16] " Melanchthon himself *materially changed the tenth article* in the edition of 1540."—Schaff *Creeds* I, p. 232.

" The strong opposition of Melanchthon to Zwingli's theory before 1536 or 1540, *when he modified* his own view on the Eucharist."—*Ib.*

" The explanations and modifications of Melanchthon himself in the edition of 1540, extended, as it were, the hand of fellowship to them."—*Ib.*, p. 235.

" The altered edition of 1540 . . . represents . . . *the present theological convictions* of a very large party in that [Lutheran] denomination."—*Ib.*, p. 242.

" The edition of 1540, which appeared in connection with an improved edition of the Apology, differs so widely from the first that it was subsequently called the *Altered* Augsburg Confession (*Variata*), in distinction from the *Unaltered* (*Invariata*) of 1530 or 1531.

" It attracted little attention till after the death of Melanchthon (1560), when it created as much trouble as the insertion of the *filioque* clause in the Nicene Creed. The Altered Confession, besides a large number of valuable additions and real improvements in style and the order of subjects, embodies the changes in Melanchthon's theology, which may be dated from the new edition of his *Loci Communes*, 1535, and his personal contact with Bucer and Calvin. He gave up, on the one hand, his views on absolute predestination, and gradually adopted the synergistic theory (which brought him nearer to the Roman Catholic system) ; while on the other hand (departing further from Romanism and approaching nearer to the Reformed Church), he modified the Lutheran theory of the real presence, at least so far as to allow the Reformed doctrine the same right in the evangelical churches. . . . In other words, the article is so changed that Calvin could give it his hearty consent, and even Zwingli—with the exception, perhaps, of the word *truly*—might have admitted it."—*Ib.*, pp. 240, 241.

lanchthon and Bucer at Worms,[17] which was continued at Regensburg.

The discussion was at the request of the Emperor, and resulted finally in the Regensburg Interim, which granted peace to all Protestants in the League, but also obligated them (and them only) to all articles on which agreement had been reached with the Roman Catholics. Melanchthon was the principal theologian of the Protestants.

As Melanchthon was a dialectician in dealing with truths, so he was a diplomat in dealing with men. Now a diplomat looks at movements and at truth itself, pragmatically, rather than intrinsically, that is, he looks at it for what it will yield him in his present situation, and not for what it commands him in every situation. A humanist who is a diplomat must be an unswevering man of grace, if he can preserve his mental habit unspotted, and retain it in loyal allegiance to the sharp corners of truth, without trying to file down and accomodate.

At Regensburg, Melanchthon was, for once, disgusted with conciliatory diplomacy;[18] the Lutherans were disgusted at the compromising formula agreed on in phrasing the cardinal principle of the Reformation;[19] and the Emperor was disgusted with the obstinacy with which Melanchthon clung to the evangelical position in the articles of the Sacraments (this pleased Luther), Oral Confession, and the Church.[20]

By 1543, the unionistic understanding of Melanchthon and Bucer had gone so far, that, in the Reformation of

---

[17] Melanchthon desired to base the discussion on the 'Variata' of the Augsburg Confession. Eck objected because it was altered. Melanchthon replied that there was no alteration in the substance, but only that language milder and clearer had been used. Then Eck put his finger on article X.

[18] "Conciliationes, quae nullae fieri possunt, nisi fucosae, sycophantias, sophismata, quibus vel Principes ipsi vel eorum theologi insidias nobis struent" (*C. R.*, IV, 116).

[19] "Justificari per fidam vivam et efficarem."

[20] Melanchthon had come to Worms with the intention of defending the doctrine of the Augsburg Confession, and of not conceding to Rome, and he was quite successful.

Cologne, to which Melanchthon had been repeatedly invited,[20a] he prepared the articles on the Trinity, Creation, Original Sin, Justification by Faith, the Church and Repentance, which were assigned to him; while Bucer—certainly with Melanchthon's approval—wrote the articles on Baptism and the Lord's Supper!

Luther had borne much in silence up to this time, out of regard for the feelings and the great services of his friend; but now he was openly provoked by the way the doctrine of the Lord's Supper was dealt with in the Cologne Book.[21] It was Bucer's, but Melanchthon had approved it, and Luther was indignant because of what it failed to say. He looked in it in vain for any positive statement of the real presence.[22] Luther strongly censured Bucer from the pulpit,[23] though he did not even at this time mention Melanchthon's name. But it was felt that his blame was for more than one. All intercourse between the two Reformers ceased, and Melanchthon lived in daily dread of an open rupture. Luther soon thereafter published his "Short Catechism Concerning the Lord's Supper," against the Zwinglians, though it contained no word or thought against Melanchthon.

Melanchthon, on his part, privately " complained at times of Luther's overbearing violence of temper, and thought once (1544) seriously of leaving Wittenberg as a ' prison.' "[24]

But in November of this year (1544), Chancellor Brück reported to the Elector: " I can not learn anything from Philip, but that he and Luther are good friends." This was Melanchthon's year of personal affliction and personal sorrow. In quick succession came the Diet at Worms, the writ-

---

[20a] By the archbishop and elector of Cologne to superintend the introduction of the Reformation into these territories.

[21] For the language itself of the Cologne Book, see Seckendorf, *Hist. Luth.*, p. 446.

[22] For Luther's remarks, see *Luther's Letters*, De Wette V, 709.

[23] For Luther's utterances from the pulpit, see *C. R.*, V, 478.

[24] Schaff, *Creeds* I, 265.

ing of the Wittenberg Reformation,[24a] and the Conference at
Ratisbon. Luther wished to keep Melanchthon away from
Ratisbon. " The ceaseless round of fruitless colloquies, discussions, disputations, and the vain attempts at accommoda-
tion or compromise in which the mild-mannered Melanchthon, who enjoyed nothing so much as the privacy of the
study, had been engaged for the last fifteen years, were
enough to move the heart of . . . his noble minded friend
. . . to desire that he might at last be spared the useless
infliction. . . . The fact is that the two great champions
of the Reformation were at this time on good terms with
each other. . . . Philip frequently came as of old and
dined at Dr. Martin's table, and twice they journeyed in
each other's company to Mansfeldt." [25] Luther " spoke very
highly of Melanchthon's ' Loci ' in March, 1545, and in
January, 1546, he called him a true man, who must be retained in Wittenberg, else half the university would go off
with him." [26]

Yet the sky darkened on all sides. Not only was a new
generation growing up with modified views, but the Emperor was following hard on the trail of Protestantism, the
Schmalkald League was injured and weakening, soon would
come the ban against Philip of Hesse and the Elector John
Frederick, with the treachery of Maurice and the opening
of the Schmalkald War. Luther's " dissatisfaction with the
affairs in Wittenberg (which he threatened to leave permanently in 1544) cast a cloud over his declining years." [27]
Thus Luther died. On the day following his death (Feb. **18,**
1546), Melanchthon said to his students: *" Obiit auriga et*

[24a] This was a pamphlet prepared at the request of the Elector, and sent
to the Council of Trent as a summary of the doctrines of the Lutheran
Reformation.

[25] Stump, Melanchthon, 183, 184.

[26] Schaff I, p. 265, referring to *Corp. Reform.*, VI, p. 10; Gieseler IV,
pp. 432-435.

[27] *Ib.*, I, 260.

currus Israel, qui rexit ecclesiam in hac ultima senecta mundi," and added, *"Amemus igitur hujus viri memoriam et genus doctrinae ab ipso traditum, et simus modestiores et consideremus ingentes calamitates et mutationes magnas, quae hunc casum sunt secuturae."*

CHAPTER XXIII.

THE LUTHERAN CONFESSION.

PROTESTANTISM FROM THE DEATH OF LUTHER TO THE DEATH OF MELANCHTHON AND TO THE DISINTEGRATION OF LUTHERANISM.

Years of Reaction—Melanchthon Leader—Political Events, 1546-1555—Augsburg and Leipzig Interims, Maurice—The Papacy and the Empire in these Events—The Controversies :—Adiaphoristic—Osiandrian—The Two Great Parties—Majoristic—Antinomistic—Crypto-Calvinism—Eucharistic—Synergistic —Melanchthon a Synergist—Corpus Philippicum—Partisan Warfare—Dire Results.

THE death of Luther, on " Concordia " day, ushered in years of reaction and internal weakness—years of external pressure and oppression: the second generation of Lutheranism came to the front, with waverings toward the common foe without, and disintegrations and hardenings into local territorial units, under the separatistic action of the princes and their theologians.

Providence sends one great leader, but rarely continues the succession. The work in this instance was left to Luther's contemporaries, and their successors. Of his contemporaries, Melanchthon was chief. The spirit of Melanchthon was not that of a witness or confessor, but that of a scholar and teacher, a definer, a discriminator, and a systematizer.

Melanchthon was now the acknowledged head of the Reformation. He became again involved in negotiations with

587

the Papists, to whom he made the most remarkable concessions. His connection with the Leipzig Interim (1548), was the most unfortunate act of his life. Under the form of an apparent compromise, he yielded many of the most essential points of difference. " He was willing to tolerate both a popedom and a hierarchy, stripped, however, of divine rights, and deprived of all power in matters of faith. The relation of faith to works, and the doctrine of the sacraments, might, in his estimation, be veiled in a judicious obscurity of phrase."

In every part of the evangelical Church the *Interim* was most violently resisted, and Melanchthon's connection with it strongly condemned. In addition to private rebukes from Calvin and Brentius, Agricola, Flacius, and others, publicly attacked him.

In 1550, Melanchthon published his *Explanation of the Nicene Creed;* and in the succeeding year, the *Confessio Saxonica,* in which he had gained courage to entirely repudiate the concessions of the *Interim.* In 1552, he was engaged in a controversy with Osiander, who had confounded justification with sanctification; in 1553, he published brief treatises against Schwenkfeld and Stancar; and in 1554, his *Examen Ordinandorum,* a brief outline of doctrinal, ethical, and polemical theology, for the use of candidates for the ministry.

Even during Luther's life, where the gap left by Luther's Living Witness seemed too abrupt, Melanchthon had busied himself, not solely with the amplification of the pure doctrine, but also in the attempt to build bridges between it and Roman or Reformed doctrine. Melanchthon, the harmonizer, had an eye to connections without, especially in times of danger, rather than an eye single for the inner strength. More and more during Luther's later life, in order to make connections with those without, he came near boring holes in the side of the newly launched vessel which, nevertheless, continued for a time to hold together after

Luther's death, through the power of the truth and of Luther's testimony.

As the chief teacher and trainer of the rising generation, exceedingly attractive to young men, by his learning, his affection, his piety and his admirable spirit, Melanchthon threw into the Church a race of leaders, that were not Scriptural confessors of the faith chiefly, like Luther, but definers of doctrines, makers of formulas, and repairers of ravages created by disputations.

Up to the death of Luther, speaking roughly, the positive building process, as to inner doctrinal construction, and as to outer constitutional organization, had made progress in the conservative Evangelical Church with the valuable help of Melanchthon himself. The great living doctrines were being turned into literature, into life and into praxis. The tree was growing from its own inner sap, and was becoming all the more hearty in standing by itself, in the healthful openness of wind and sun and storm, and apart from the shadows of the surrounding forests.

But Melanchthon's mind, even at this time, like that of conformable natures, whose instinct it is to grow by leaning on supports, rather than by being braced up in the strength of the life-blood within, was busy in throwing out tendrils toward trellises and walls rising on foundations without the pale of Lutheranism. A great exterior harmony of the whole, especially under political persecution, to such natures, is more to be desired than inner solidity that slowly wins its way through the compact growth of a self-consistent life.

THE BREAK-UP OF PROTESTANTISM.

From the death of Luther, the concord that had existed, externally, in the Evangelical Lutheran Churches died away. He had hardly closed his eyes before discord, apparently at times a sign of coming dissolution, broke out on every hand. The fact is that Luther himself had foreseen the arrival of

41

this reaction.[1] Schaff admits that Luther had kept down the rising antagonism against Melanchthon " by the weight of his personal authority, although he foresaw approaching troubles."

Luther had scarcely been dead for four months before the Pope entered into a secret covenant with the Emperor to exterminate Protestantism in Germany, and to forcibly compel the Protestants to return to the allegiance of the Pope, binding himself, on his part, to help defray the expenses of a resort to arms against the evangelical states. This was in June, 1546. The Emperor also made a secret treaty, a few days before, with Duke Maurice of Saxony, who, to gain the electorate of Saxony, now agreed to submit to the coming decree of Trent.[2]

The two foremost political leaders of the Lutheran Church, the elector John Frederick of Saxony and the Landgrave Philip of Hesse were captured and imprisoned as rebels and vassals. The whole of South Germany and, except a few Protestant cities, north Germany also, was conquered by the emperor. Thus misfortune followed mis-

---

[1] The year after the presentation of the Confession at Augsburg (1531), Luther, preaching on John VI and VII, had declared that " the Gospel will abide among you for a short time only, after the heads of those who preach it now have been laid in the dust. After our death it will not remain ; for it is not possible that it can remain. The Gospel has its course, runs from one city to another, is here to-day and at another spot to-morrow. Believe it and honor it while you have it. It will not abide with you always. Tell me again in twenty years from now, how the matter will stand. Others will come and preach to please the devil."—Walch VII, p. 2306-2308.

When Luther was sick at Schmalkald in 1537, he told the Elector of Saxony that after his death, discord would break out in the University of Wittenberg, and his doctrine would be changed.—Seckendorf *Com. de Lutheranismo* III, 165.

Nine years later, shortly before his death in 1546, he preached at Wittenberg, saying : " Up to this time you have had the real and true Word ; but beware of your supposed prudence. The devil will light the light of reason and lead you from the path of Faith. I see before my eyes that if God does not give us true preachers and servants, the devil will tear our church to pieces by evil agitators. That is his definite object. If he cannot do it by the hand of the Pope and the emperor, he will accomplish it through those who are in agreement with us in doctrine. Pray earnestly that the Word may be left to us, for things will come to a dreadful pass." Walch XII, 1534. To Schurf Luther is reported to have declared : " After my death, none of these theologians will remain firm."—*Ib.*, p. 1538.

[2] Reserving the points, justification by faith, the cup for the laity, and the marriage of priests, as permissible in his own domain.

fortune for the Lutheran Church, until, nine years later, the religious Peace of Augsburg (1555) was secured against Rome, assuring all adherents of the Augsburg Confession of religious freedom, in which benefit the Calvinists also were rightly included.

During this period, the Pope had proposed to win over the Protestants, now broken in spirit and shorn of their power, by the Augsburg Interim, in which the doctrine of justification was sacrificed, seven sacraments were recognized, the doctrine of transubstantiation was maintained, and the mass was interpreted as a thank offering. All the Roman ceremonialism was retained. Most Protestant princes accepted the Interim, but the faithful pastors, especially in Southern Germany, did not, and were banished by hundreds.

Melanchthon, the surviving leader, valiantly attacked the Interim, and in 1548 published the first public writing against it. He also declared that if Luther had lived, this change of doctrine would not now threaten the churches, which are being destroyed, and the conflicts, which are now raging, would not have arisen. But before long, Melanchthon became terrified at the threats of the emperor's anger, and paved the way for the Leipzig Interim, which was based, ostensibly, on the principle that the pure doctrine of the Gospel was to be maintained, and that concessions to Rome were to be made only in regard to adiaphora. The effect of this Interim was to obscure the cardinal doctrine of the Reformation, viz., that of justification by faith, and to express it in an indefinite formula; to readmit episcopal jurisdiction, and all Roman ceremonies and observances. Melanchthon thus became the author of a movement which not only almost wiped out the specific character of Protestantism in the eyes of the people, but which at once gave rise to the adiaphoristic and the other controversies, which the Formula of Concord was obliged to settle. Schaff admits that Melanchthon, " not without blamable weakness, gave his sanction to the Leipzig Interim, and undertook to act as a mediator between the

Emperor, or his Protestant ally Maurice, and the Protestant conscience. It was the greatest mistake of his life. . . . The venerable man was fiercely assailed from every quarter by friend and foe.[3]

It is usual to attribute the dreadful controversies of these dark days to the doctrinal extremists, and to the polemical spirit of a more rigid Lutheranism; and to assume that if the ways of the peace-loving Melanchthon[4] had been followed, the whole Lutheran Church might have lived then, and thenceforward thereafter, in harmony and peace. The real fact is that the peace-loving Melanchthon was partly the victim, and partly the author not only of such theological controversies as that of the adiaphora, but of conditions inviting actual war; for internal weakness invites war. And to some minds it is a question, whether, if Melanchthon's method had ultimately prevailed, there would be any Lutheran Church to-day; not because Melanchthon himself would have surrendered it, but because his method was one that leads to the destruction of Lutheranism. As it was, in the Interim Melanchthon came very nearly sacrificing at Leipzig all that had been gained in the struggle with the papacy at the Diet of Augsburg.[5]

However, let us not be unjust to Melanchthon; as we ask

---

[3] Schaff also mentions the *temporal* gains and *incidental* advantages of Melanchthon's course.—*Creeds* I, p. 300.

[4] For instance, Schaff, in his *Creeds* I, p. 266, says: " After his death (1546), the war broke out with unrestrained violence. Melanchthon was too modest, peaceful, and gentle for the theological leadership, which now devolved upon him; he kept aloof from strife as far as possible, preferring to bear injury and insult with Christian meekness."
On this we would remark: 1st, That Melanchthon and his principles were in large measure responsible (barring Osiander) for the internal strife of this period, and that he failed to realize the unfitness of his own principle for leadership; 2d, That Luther had been a restraining influene to shield Melanchthon for years; 3d, That while Melanchthon did not engage in bitter strife, he still desired to lead, and did lead, in negotiations that resulted in obscurity and strife; 4th, That " preferring to bear injury and insult with Christian meekness " is often the outer attitude of men who nurse defeat in their heart, and in private censoriously and bitterly condemn those from whom they differ. This was not so fully the case with Melanchthon, but the Schaffian " meekness " has its types in every age.

[5] Comp. Seeberg. "Melanchthon had two souls;" and Kolde (*infra*, p. 643), "His weak conduct in the Interim matter and the controversies arising therefrom, changed the entire state of affairs."

all others, that they be not unjust to those later leaders who saw the necessity for another general Confession of the Church, and who brought about the existence of the Formula of Concord. Even the strongest men do not really uphold and preserve the Church, and cannot spare it from meeting its appointed testing. Sooner or later the Church must pass through the darkness of inner and outer crisis. Like the Confession of Augsburg, the Formula of Concord was the result, not of men's contrivings, but of the Lord's doings, Who enabled the Church to work out, resume and reassert her integrity after forty years of civil, political, and religious anarchy.

We must never forget that the strong hand of the papacy and the strong arm of the empire were unitedly arrayed against Protestantism, which was not yet thirty years old when Luther died. After the power of Luther's presence was withdrawn from the field, these foes from without made their advances on the Church, employing not only arms, but, as is always the case with Rome, the insidious means of theological and political diplomacy. Theological strife and rebellion were stirred up within by the agencies of the Pope, and imperial pressure was put upon the Church without. What had been stayed temporarily by the strong hand of Luther, and by the Confession at Augsburg, now broke like a storm over the Church in her period of weakness and reaction. Neither a rigid Lutheranism, nor a softer Melanchthonianism, was responsible for that part of the situation which arose from the historically necessary unfolding and permanent application, under outward pressure and by a second generation, of the principles of the Augsburg Confession to existing theory, institutions and ecclesiastical practice. And what came forth from this time of terrible testing, should, in all justice, be regarded as not less precious in result than that which came forth in the earlier struggles culminating in Augsburg.[8]

---

[8] Schaff, speaking of the Formula of Concord, admits that, "These con-

To suppose that the conditions in the Lutheran Church after the death of Luther and prior to the internal and theological peace brought about by the Formula of Concord, were the result of an over-emphasis of the Confessional principle, whether by Luther himself, or by second-rate controversialists who followed him, is as far away from the truth as it is to suppose that this mighty crisis might have been averted and this impetuous torrent stemmed, if the Church had followed the way of Melanchthon.

Dr. Krauth truly says, " The time of deluge had come, the world had to be purified; and it was useless to send out the dove till the waters had passed away. The era of the Reformation could not be an era of Melanchthonian mildness. To ask this, is to ask that war shall be peace. . . . The war of the Formula was an internal defensive war; yet, like all civil wars, it left behind it inevitable wounds which did not at once heal up. The struggle in churches or states, which ends in a triumph over the schism of their own children cannot for generations command the universal sympathy with which the overthrow of a common foe is regarded."

But, let us add, the value of the results is none the less. The contrast between the conditions that led to the Augsburg Confession and those that led to the Formula of Concord are strikingly like the contrast between the conditions that led in our land to the Revolutionary War, and those that led a century later to the Civil War. There may be those who regarded the Civil War as unnecessary, and as the result of an over-rigid and fanatical social standard, and an over-zealous spirit, but the more we look beneath the surface, the more we see that it was the inevitable setting in and culmination of a reaction in a century of freedom, within and during which, after the pressure of external necessity

---

troversies *were unavoidable* in that age, and resulted *in the consolidation and completion of the Lutheran system of doctrine.*"—*Creeds* I, p. 259.

was removed, unsettled internal causes arose, and would not be silenced, until a final settlement was made.

Do not those who accept the results at Augsburg as confessional, but deny the results brought about by the Formula as confessional, bear some striking resemblance to Americans who would accept the results of our war against those without, and who exult in our original constitution in the Eighteenth Century; but who deny any necessity or validity in results brought about by the culmination of the internal process of construction, and by the conflict from which they issued a little more than a half century later. In both cases, the first result seems more epochal and decisive, because the foe is an external one, and we hear no more of his victories. But in both cases, no matter how or by what process it may have been reached, some settlement of the problems, some inner reconstruction, which would at once maintain the older principle in all its strength, but at the same time apply it to the new conditions, was unavoidable.

The Leipzig Interim was of date of Dec. 22d, 1548, about two years after Luther's death. So thoroughly was Melanchthon under a cloud from his position taken as to this Interim, that the sound doctrine which he enunciated in the Saxon Confession, in 1551, and which was unanimously adopted by the Wittenberg theologians, did not remove the suspicion with which he was regarded.

THE CONTROVERSIES ARISING OUT OF THE LEIPSIG INTERIM.

The seeds of the subsequent controversies, often alluded to in connection with the depreciation of the Formula of Concord, are all to be found *in the Leipzig Interim* (given in full in our English Book of Concord),[1] which Melanchthon and the Wittenberg theologians announced themselves as prepared to accept after Luther's death. Justification by faith is there so changed as to mean, " that man is renewed by the

---

[1] II, p. 253-260. Tr. from C. R. VII, 259 sqq. by Jacobs.

Holy Spirit, and can fulfil righteousness with his works, and that God will, for His Son's sake, accept in believers this weak beginning of obedience in this miserable frail nature." [8]

In the Leipzig Interim it is also asserted that " God does not deal with a man as a log, but draws him in such way that his own will also co-operates." [9]

Here we notice that the ground is Melanchthon's own ground, that the mistake is Melanchthon's, and that the doctrine of Luther had nothing to do with the matter except that Luther's is the true principle. In addition to this yielding on justification, the proposed re-introduction of the Romish ceremonies and restoration of the jurisdiction of the bishops led to bitter conflict, in which many of Melanchthon's best friends deserted him.

The great question in this controversy was whether it is ethically proper to yield any such unessential matter as ceremonies and government, provided that the pure doctrine be maintained. Melanchthon and his fellow-Wittenbergers declared it was. Flacius [10] upheld the principle, " Nothing is indifferent *in casu confessionis et scandali."*

We have already seen that the restoration of Roman ceremonies was a part of the Leipzig Interim. It was the most visible and striking part to the Protestant Churches. It is no wonder then that the Adiaphoristic controversy sprang up immediately upon the adoption of the Interim. Some months later the Osiandrian controversy arose, and several years later (1551) still another controversy, the Majoristic, developed, while the Eucharistic controversy (1551) followed hard upon its heels.

The personalities of those engaging in these controversies deserve a moment's attention. Of the older friends of Luther there were two still living, viz., Justus Jonas and Nicholas Amsdorf. The latter was the head of the rigid Lutheran

---

[8] Bieck 372. *Das dreifache Interim,* Leipsic, **1721.**

[9] *Ib.,* 362 ff.

[10] Praeger *Flac.,* I, 142 sqq.

party which included a younger and more disputatious generation, viz., Flacius, Wigand, Gallus, Judex, Mörlin, Heshus, Timann and Westphal. These men were right in being unwilling to turn either toward Rome, on the one side, or toward Calvinism, on the other side, and in attempting to neutralize the weaknesses of Melanchthon in these opposite directions; but they were wrong in the violent and partizan manner in which they maintained their positions. The other party, the extreme followers of Melanchthon, was composed of Camerarius, Bugenhagen, Eber, Crell, Major, Cruciger, Strigel, Pfeffinger, and Melanchthon's son-in-law, Peucer. This party was termed the Philippists, and included all those who embraced the synergism of Melanchthon, while among them there was a smaller party who secretly held the Calvinistic doctrine of the Lord's Supper, and were called Crypto-Calvinists.

The Philippist party was entrenched in the old centre at Wittenberg and in the newer vicinity of Leipzig, while the ultra-Lutheran party, often called *Gnesio* (that is, genuine) Lutherans, had their seat at Jena.

In the midst between these two parties, stood those milder men, of more judicial frame, many of them pupils of Melanchthon, imbibing the sweetness of his spirit, and the excellence of his method, but avoiding his error and clinging to the doctrine of Luther. Some of these men, namely, Andreæ, Chemnitz, Selnecker and Chytraeus, later on, became the framers of the Formula of Concord and brought peace to the Church. Even Schaff gives them the central position in Lutheranism, saying that they stood mediating between ultra-Lutheranism and Melanchthonianism.[11]

The extreme Lutherans held fast to the principle of stability, and the extreme Melanchthonians clung to the principle of change. The extreme Lutherans held to a sharp and positive outline, the extreme Melanchthonians believed rather in

---

[11] *Creeds* I, p. 267. Yet some writers still insist on identifying the Formula with the extreme of Flacianism!

breadth, mildness, compromise and union. The extreme Lutherans held to the articles of faith as complete, established and unchangeable. The extreme Melanchthonians believed them to be elastic and adaptable.

Melanchthon had declared good works to be necessary, while Luther had paradoxically said that "good works are a hindrance" to justification. George Major and others developed the view of Melanchthon to the limit, and raised this controversy—from the Melanchthon side—and in line with the treatment of justification in the Leipzig Interim, and declared that good works are necessary to salvation. Major was vigorously combatted by Nicholas von Amsdorf and by Flacius. Melanchthon attempted to settle the matter by dropping the two words, " to salvation; " but this led the Flacian party to the extreme statement that " renewal is an entirely separate thing from justification." [12] Both Melanchthon and the Gnesio-Lutherans opposed the Flacian position.

Immediately out of the Majoristic controversy arose the Antinomistic controversy, in which some of the teachings of Agricola, who had been firmly opposed by Luther years before, continued to reappear.

Meantime, that is between the death of Luther and 1552, Calvin's doctrine of the Lord's Supper, to which Melanchthon and his followers had become friendly, was being silently propagated in Germany. Melanchthon possessed a kindly feeling for Calvin. Calvin, not a contemporary of Luther, was a member of the second generation of Reformers, who fell heir to the mediating theology of Bucer, and was successful in planting a Calvinistic church upon German soil, and in winning the allegiance of many Melanchthonians and Lutherans.

Ever since his change of the tenth Article of the Augsburg Confession, and since the Wittenberg Concord, Melanchthon

---

[12] Seeberg finds in this Flacian extreme position simply a logical inference from the Melanchthonian conception of the doctrine of justification, to which Melanchthon himself had a corrective in his theory of the ethical necessity of good works, but which corrective these extreme Flacians lacked."

had been teaching a different doctrine from Luther on the Lord's Supper, somewhat approximating Calvin's, which rejected the omnipresence of the human nature, and the *communicatio idiomatum*. For years the effect of the difference was not noticed; but the teaching went on, and the approach of Lutheranism, as found in Melanchthon's pupils, toward Calvinism became nearer and nearer.

At last, in 1552, Joachim Westphal, pastor in Hamburg, pointed out that the Calvinist teaching on the Lord's Supper was not that held by Luther. Westphal's declaration awakened great excitement in Bremen, in Heidelberg, and especially in Württemburg. In 1559, under the leadership of Brentz, the Church of Württemburg pronounced in favor of the Lutheran doctrine. Melanchthon carefully avoided committing himself on this subject. To Hardenburg in Bremen, he wrote,—"I beg of you dissimulate" ("Multa dissimules"[13]); and to Brentz,—"To answer is not difficult," but dangerous."[15] This was in 1559, the year before Melanchthon's death.

Two years before this Eucharistic controversy had broken out at Hamburg, Andrew Osiander put forth his new disputation (1550-1552) concerning justification. Osiander was opposed by both Philippists and Lutherans. Yet it is held by some that he performed a service to the church " by ad-

---

[13] *C. R.*, VIII, 736; Cf. IX, 960.

[14] *Ib.*, 1034 sq.

[15] We quote Melanchthon to Brentz :—

Responsio Phil. Mel. ad quaestionem de controversia Heidelbergensi (*C. R.*, IX, p. 961) : *Non difficile, sed periculosum est respondere.* . . . *In hac controversia optimum esset retinere verba Pauli:* " *Panis, quem frangimus.*" *Et copiose de fructu Caenae discendum est, ut invitentur homines ad amorem hujus pignoris et crebrum usum. Et vocabulum declarandum est. Non dicit, mutari naturam panis, ut Papistae dicunt; non dicit, ut Bremenses, panem esse substantiale corpus Christi; non dicit, ut Heshusius, panem esse verum corpus Christi: sed esse, hoc, quo fit consociatio cum corpore Christi, quae fit in usu, et quidem non sine cogitatione, ut cum mures panem rodunt.* . . . *Adest Filius Dei in ministerio Evangelii et ibi certo est efficax in credentibus, ac adest non propter panem, sed propter hominem, sicut inquit:* " *Manete in me, et ego in vobis.*"

According to Heppe, Melanchthon taught the sacramental communication to be that of the living body of the divine-human Person, resulting in a personal communion, an indwelling of the God-man in the believer.—Heppe, *Dogmatik des deutschen Protestantismus*, III, p. 150.

vocating ideas embraced in original Lutheranism as against Melanchthonianism." This is the view of Seeberg, who praises the broad, systematic instinct that permeates the discussions of Osiander.[16]

No sooner had the controversy on Adiaphora ended than the controversy on Synergism began,—a heresy which is always with the Church, and not least in the Protestantism of to-day. In 1555 Pfeffinger of Leipzig, a follower of Melanchthon's teachings, put forth the doctrine that man is not "purely passive" in his conversion, as a statue, but that he must do his part. Thus arose a controversy full of sensations, in which Flacius fell into heresy, and Strigel, in the very heart of the strictest Lutheranism, suddenly became a Synergistic convert.

Even Schaff admits, in this connection, that Melanchthon was a Synergist, and says, " The defect of the Synergistic theory is the idea of a partnership between God and man, and a corresponding division of work and merit. Synergism is less objectionable than semi-Pelagianism, for it reduces cooperation before conversion to a minimum, but even that minimum is incompatible with the absolute dependence of man on God. It touched the central doctrine of Evangelical Lutheranism, *justification by faith,* whether it is a mere declaratory, forensic act of acquittal from sin and guilt, or an actual infusion of righteousness."[17] Schaff terms " the later Melanchthonian Synergism," " a refined evangelical modification of semi-Pelagianism." This was a teaching which threatened the fundamental doctrine of the Reformation, that of salvation by grace through faith alone. In the

---

[16] Says Seeberg, " He had a general theory of Christianity such as no other among the theologians succeeding Luther possessed, until Calvin appeared. Among the men of second rank of the Reformation period he was perhaps the greatest. Viewed historically, his attempt constitutes the contemporaneous counterpoise to the doctrine of justification taught by the later Melanchthon. Both men gave one-sided interpretations of ideas of Luther's. . . . But it must after all be counted a blessing that the Melanchthonian and not the Osiandrian scheme met the approval of the Church."—*Hist. of Doctrines* II, pp. 372, 373.

[17] Schaff, *Creeds* I, 271.

Adiaphoristic controversy, and here also, the trouble was a fruit of the teaching of Melanchthon.

Several qualities and motives in Melanchthon's nature, including his humanist outlook on free will, and his tendency to emphasize the necessity of good works, contributed to inspire him with erroneous views, when the evangelical doctrine began to be wrought out more expansively; and led him to find the cause for the actual variation in the working of God's grace, in man, its object.

This subtle Synergistic spirit attacks the very foundation of Lutheranism, flows out into almost every doctrine, and weakens the church at every point. And it was particularly this weakness, which the great multitude of Melanchthon's scholars, who become the leaders of the generation of which we are speaking, absorbed; and which rendered it difficult to return, finally, and after years of struggle, to the solid ground, once more recovered in the Formula of Concord.[18]

A number of the Lutheran leaders, including Chemnitz and Selnecker, who gave us the Formula of Concord, were infected originally with the Synergistic teachings of Melanchthon, and had by a living experience in this error, to work their way through to more solid ground. The Synergistic teaching, added to the indeterminateness reopened by the changes of Melanchthon on the Lord's Supper, reduced the inner strength of the work wrought by the Augsburg Confession to a minimum, and invited men of arbitrary, passionate and polemical nature to enter into minor controversy of various kinds, and thus increase the divisions and confusion within the conservative evangelical churches.

THE SCHOLASTIC METHOD OF MELANCHTHON.

All the efforts of poor Melanchthon to attach the Lutheran

---

[18] Schaff fully admits this: "The 'Form of Concord' settled the controversy by separating good works both from justification and salvation, yet declaring them necessary as effects of justifying faith."—*Creeds* I, p. 277.

Church, whether to Rome or to Calvinism, proved unsuccessful. He was misunderstood and misrepresented. Amid the attacks of partisan enemies, who regarded him as having betrayed the Lutheran cause, he died, in 1560, brokenhearted.

He was the great theologian of the Lutheran Reformation. His gifts reduced the purified doctrine to a connected system, and organized the outward form of the Church. His mind was so constituted that he was accustomed to generalize his convictions in such way as to bring them into a wider harmony with those outside him, without loss of essence perceptible to himself. He declared always that he taught Luther's doctrine and, to the end, that his faith was unchanged.

His broad humanism, fostered by classical tastes and natural amiability and timidity, rendered him unsafe as a leader, although strong under a firmer will. It is to this that Calvin referred when he heard of Melanchthon's death : " O, Philip Melanchthon! for it is upon thee whom I call, upon thee, who now livest with Christ in God, and art waiting for us, until we shall attain that blessed rest. A hundred times, worn out with fatigue and overwhelmed with care, thou hast laid thy head upon my breast and said, Would God I might die here. And a thousand times since then I have earnestly desired that it had been granted us to be together. Certainly thou wouldst have been more valiant to face danger, and stronger to despise hatred, and bolder to disregard false accusations."

At this point we must say a word concerning one of the strangest of paradoxes, namely, that Melanchthon's exaltation, as a teacher, of the doctrina Lutheri, before Luther's death, brought on the clash with the Melanchthonian doctrine in the controversies after Luther's death. Thus Melanchthon was the father of both parties in the controversies. The earlier, or strictly Lutheran scholars, had been started out on the correct conception that the two marks of the Church are the pure doctrine and the right administration of the sacraments.

But to this Melanchthon added a scholastic conception of the pure doctrine. He taught his older scholars that the pure doctrine is the teaching of the three old church symbols, the Augustana, and the doctrine of Luther as taught at Wittenberg. " Lutherus veram et necessariam doctrinam patefecit." In other words, as has been said, Melanchthon dogmatized the authority of Luther, so that the young theologians went forth from Wittenberg with the scholastic idea that the Gospel is the sum of the correctly framed articles of faith, and that the doctrine of Luther is the external authority, determinative of the Faith. How could anything else be possible under such teaching than the rise, after Melanchthon wavered in doctrine, of the Gnesio-Lutheran school?

When Melanchthon came finally to an openly independent development, emphasizing the facultas applicandi se ad gratiam in the sinner, the necessity of good works in the state of grace, and contending against the scholastic conception of the "ubiquity" of Christ in the Lord's Supper, which he had himself previously wrought into doctrine; and allowed the changes in the Variata to become manifest, and in his dealing in the Interim, the avoidance of theological conflict was evidently impossible, especially as Melanchthon's conception of the Church required a decision of such doctrinal differences.

Melanchthon himself had canonized the doctrine of Luther, and was now departing from it. Was it any wonder that the Gnesio-Lutherans turned back to Luther as against the more newly manifest Melanchthon? And as they were a party, was it any wonder that they combined the coarsest and sternest part of Luther's personal qualities with the most abstract and scholastic method of Melanchthon's teaching?

" It is unreasonable to condemn the lack of piety and the controversial spirit of these circles. Through the Melanchthonian conception of the Church, suspicion appeared to become the most holy duty. They served God and the Church in all earnestness as they understood it."

"Neither party was willing to give up or to diminish the authority of Luther. The situation was really this,[19] that the majority of Churches within the Saxon Reformation at first did really not know that there was a Melanchthonianism being set up alongside of the doctrine of Luther, and that later they did not wish to know it."[20] When Flacius awoke them, they were in a great strait as to how to combine piety toward the great Praeceptor with piety toward the Great Confession.

There was no contemporary leader on whom they could rely, and they floundered blindly in search of a secure authority. "Nothing[21] throws clearer light upon the complicated situation, which it is important to understand and to appreciate, in order to perceive the necessity and the difficulty of establishing a final and decisive Confession, as well as a universally acknowledged corpus doctrinæ, than the transactions of the Naumburg Fürstentag of 1561, where, in view of the charge made by the Roman Catholics that the Lutherans had departed from the original Augsburg Confession, they confessed their adherence to the edition of 1531 with the express remark, that they did not at all mean, in this new subscription to depart from the Confession of 1541, which made certain articles more clear, and brought the divine truth to light, and therefore they could as little depart from this as from the first Confession."[22] This impossible solution is the only possible solution outside of the Formula of Concord.

After the death of Melanchthon in 1560, came the natural

---

[19] Calinich on *The Naumburg Fürsten Tag.*

[20] "Formula of Concord," *Hauck Encycl.*

[21] *Ib.*

[22] This naive contradiction has inhered, often with the same unconsciousness, in Melanchthonian Lutheranism ever since, and is giving the Church her troubles to-day.

tendency to exalt his writings (*Corpus Philippicum*[23]) to symbolical authority. The attempt, made already in 1560, to force this Corpus upon the churches in the electorate of Saxony aroused the deepest feeling.[24]

Here we have the earliest set of Symbolical Books, proposed as a norm, which, though more bulky than the Book of *Concord,* contained not one of Luther's writings, but was largely composed of private writings on which no official action of the Church had been taken.

It is worthy of note that this first effort to use symbolical Books in the Church, in order to cover the controversies since the death of Luther, arose on the Melanchthonian and Unionistic side, and not on the strictly Lutheran side. These bulky Confessions first appeared among the Unionists; and to reduce them, and bring the teaching of the Church within a really confessional compass, was one of the great objects of the Book of Concord.

At least twenty different Lutheran Confessions of faith, most of them bulky, appeared between the death of Luther and the adoption of the Formula of Concord. The best known of these were the Philippicum (1560), just mentioned, the Brunswick (1563), the Pomeranicum (1565), the Prutenicum (1567), the Thuringicum (1570), and the Brandenburgicum. The Corpus Julium (1576) stood in a class by itself.

In 1566, the Reformed Theologians (Heidelberg) assailed the *Communicatio Idiomatum* and the ubiquity in connection with the Lord's Supper, and Brentz expecially, defended the doctrine. In Saxony the Crypto-Calvinists[25] rejected the

---

[23] The *Corpus Philippicum* was a private undertaking of the book dealer Vögelein in Leipzig, who in 1560 edited a collection of Melanchthon's doctrinal writings. This was not only introduced into electoral Saxony, but into Hesse and Pomerania, and called forth strictly Lutheran *Corpora Doctrinae* in opposition."—*Seeberg,* II., p. 380.

[24] Einleitung to Koethe's *Concordia,* LXXXVIII sqq.; Proleg. to Hutter's *Explicatio Libri Chr. Concordiae,* Francke's *Libri Symbolici,* Prol. III. v; Köllner, i 524.

[25] Eber, Major and Crell.

42

doctrine in 1571, and were replied to by Chemnitz.[26] **Thus** the controversies concerning the Lord's Supper and the Person of Christ were added to the previous array of theological differences.

During all this time the combination of State and Church in one faith, and the fixation of the religion of the state by means of dogmatic formulas, together with the customary academic form of disputations, aided in creating the most bitter contention. Seeberg declares that "the passion displayed and the worship of formulas reminded of the worst periods of the dogmatic struggles upon Byzantine territory."[27] This was true no less of the Melanchthonians than of the stricter Lutherans.

The attempt of the princes to restore peace in the Frankfort Recess in 1558, with the Weimar confutation in 1559, and the condemnation of the latter by the Philippists, the Naumburg Diet with its unsuccessful results in 1561, the conflict in regard to the "Invariata" and the "Variata" editions of the Augsburg Confession the same year, and now later, the controversies upon the doctrine of the Lord's Supper, broke the Evangelical Lutheran confession into many fragmentary parties.

THE PART OF POLITICS.

The political situation also contributed its full share toward the disintegration of Lutheranism. The Protestant victory over the Emperor and the Passau agreement of 1552, led to the Religious Peace of Augsburg in 1555, in which all adherents of the Augsburg Confession, Lutherans and Calvinists,[28] were assured religious freedom; but the further

---

[26] In his *De duabus naturis in Christo.*

[27] In speaking of the need of the Formula of Concord, *Hist. of Doctrines* II, 378.

[28] "Calvin wrote to Rev. Mart. Schalling, at Ratisbon, 1557: *'Nec vero Augustanam Confessionem repudio, cui pridem volens ac libens subscripsi, sicut eam auctor ipse interpretatus est'* (Epp., p. 437). Similarly in his

spread of Lutheranism was checked by the *reservatum ecclesiasticum.* As only one-tenth of Germany was Roman and seven-tenths Lutheran, the results gained by this Peace were meagre. But this signing away of a large part of Germany to Roman Catholicism, and the closing of the possibility to Protestantism of extending itself to a wider territory, was not, it is agreed, the saddest part of this Religious Peace. This was the tragedy, namely, that the Reformation scarcely begun came to a halt, and that Lutheran Protestantism proceeded no further in its work. Since outer expansion was no longer possible, Lutherans seemed to think that the internal work also was finished, and were satisfied to make permanent the little that had been thus far gained. The controversies arose, and also the state-churches (Beamptenkirchen), that busied themselves chiefly in these controversies.[29]

Already in 1556, things had come to such a pass, that the old Evangelical doctrine was taught openly only in a few places, particularly in north Germany. The Reformed Palatinate thanked God in her churches, that Saxony, the mother of the Reformation, had now become Reformed; the Jesuits rejoiced that the Lutherans were no longer real Lutherans, and the noble and earnest leaders of all sides, including Melanchthon, fell into trembling and despair. Thus was the edge of the Confession of Augsburg bent and broken; and none can say what the result would have been, had the tide, in the Providence of God, not once again turned back toward the true faith.

In this chapter we have tried to follow the thread of history

---

Ultima Admonitio ad Joach. Westphalum, Genev., 1557. It is not quite certain whether it was the Altered or the Unaltered Confession which Calvin subscribed at Ratisbon, but probably it was the former, as he says that it contained nothing contrary to his doctrine, and as he appealed without fear to Melanchthon himself as the best interpreter. The Altered edition had appeared a year before, and had been actually used at the previous Conference at Worms, though Eck protested against it. See *Köllner* p. 241; *Zöckler,* pp. 40, 41; Ebrard, *Dogma vom heil. Abendmahl,* II, p. 450; Stähelin, *Joh. Calvin,* I, p. 236; G. v. Polentz, *Geschichte des französischen Calvinismus,* I, p. 577; II, p. 62."—*Schaff,* II, p. 235.

[29] "Formula of Concord," *Hauck Encycl.*

as it frayed out into controversies, and as these arose out of each other, from Luther's death to the death of Melanchthon, and into the following decade, where we found conflict and disintegration. Before scanning the horizon for hope of relief, it will be useful to take a more thorough look backward at the great man whose word and deed, whose personality and principle are interwoven as the leading figure into every page of the history through which we have passed.

CHAPTER XXIV.

MELANCHTHON AND THE MELANCHTHONIAN PRINCIPLE.

Luther the Confessor, not the Hero—Melanchthon's Gifts and Gracious Nature—
Luther's Loyalty to Melanchthon—Melanchthon as a Teacher and Writer—
His Philosophy and Theology—His Practical Tendency—The Lumen Naturale
—His Two Contradictory Principles—The "Loci Communes"—Its Effect on
Lutheran Seventeenth-Century Theology—His Clear Understanding of the Fun-
damental Principles of the Reformation—Melanchthon's Lack of Faith in Crisis
—His Mild Rationalism—Makes Confession a Problem of Adjustment—Willing-
ness to Enter Compromise—Timidity—Desire for Union—Diplomacy—Anxiety.

THE Confessional principle of the Church is the *principle of Scripture.* In essence it is divine. The men
who discovered or elaborated it, are not its authors; and
their words and opinions, whether in consonance or in dis-
sonance with it, do not affect it.

Doubtless it will be conceded that of these men, in modern
days, Luther was chief. Drinking in the word of forgiveness and salvation, he gave forth his confession to an
eager world, in great columns of testimony, as a gushing
geyser rises into evidence from the power and pressure of
the inner movement that sends it forth.

It would be a pleasure to set forth Luther more fully, in
the childlike simplicity and heroic trust of his rugged faith,
as bearing upon the Confessional principle. But since the
personal traits of the Reformation Elijah are so deeply
graven on every Lutheran mind, and to avoid the impres-

sion of a purpose on our part to exalt Luther[1] and depreciate Melanchthon, Luther's faithful and angelic second self, we shall confine our praises, as also, in the nature of our subject, we are compelled to concentrate our analysis upon the exquisite personality of the faithful Elisha, Luther's own "Magister Philippus."

He was the crystal stream that dissolved the rough, mighty, ferruginous, boulder-like rocks of the Reformation, and held their salutary elements in its silvery body, and bore, in sweet and gentle flow, the new invigorating waters, rich and ruddy, charged with restorative tides of healthier life, to the eager, thirsty souls of the youth in every niche and corner of the great German Empire.

Melanchthon came to Wittenberg with a classic ancestry in his veins.   A humanist by nature and education, and a Christian by grace—if we were synergistic, we should be

---

[1] This volume has no interest in the hero-worship of Carlyle, often attributed—unjustly, we believe—to Lutherans of solid faith and earnest conviction.   Thus Schaff, with all his love for the Lutheran Church and desire that they come into federative union, or, at least, brotherly fellowship, with the Reformed, adds these words to his estimate of the "mighty genius of Luther": "The towering greatness of Luther is to the Lutherans a constant temptation to hero-worship, *as Napoleon's brilliant military genius is a misfortune and temptation to France.* . . . There are not a few Lutherans who have more liking for Luther's faults than for his virtues, and admire his conduct at Marburg as much, if not more, than his conduct at Worms."

And again Schaff says elsewhere: "The overestimate of Luther is well explained in the lines,—

'Gottes Wort und Luthers Lehr
Vergehet nun und nimmermehr.'"

Schaff's estimate is apparently a miscomprehension of the intent of these classic lines.   In any case, the Schaffian school should be willing to take the judgment of the mild, moderate and admirable Melanchthon on this point. Melanchthon said: "Luther brought to light the true and necessary doctrine" (*C. R.*, I, 728), and "We must hold fast to the pure doctrine, namely, the *Confessio Lutheri* (*C. R.*, XI, 272 sq.; VIII, 49).   On which Seeberg (II, 353) remarks: "The co-ordination of '*Gottes Wort und Luthers Lehr*' is perfectly in accord with Melanchthon's feeling."   It is the doctrine *of Christ,* and of justification by faith, to which the couplet refers.

The present writer is no admirer of the Napoleonic in Church or State. To him, in this examen as to the inner nature of the Lutheran faith, and its genuine and complete confession, the personal traits and partisan espousal of Luther are little or nothing.   Our one concern here is in and for the principle of the real Scriptural Faith, and its Confession.

Any stage of the investigation in this work will not therefore be justly met by attributing to it the motive of a championship of the cause of Luther, as in contrast with that of the more delicate and altogether lovable Melanchthon. It may be suspected, that the pen moving on these pages is capable, on occasion, of volcanic outburst; but this volume should be its own witness that the pen is flowing, if not with the sweet and clear, yet with the quiet point and

tempted to say by temperament and grace,—his culture had rendered him uncomfortable at Tübingen, prior to his grand-uncle Reuchlin's recommendation of him to Luther.[2] The wonderful intellect was enveloped in a timid and shrinking, yet gently persisting disposition; and enshrined in a physical frame so frail that it, even in health, seemed likely, at any moment, to give way under the strain of thought within. Luther said of Melanchthon, after he had reached Wittenberg: " There is but one thing I fear, namely, that his delicate constitution will not be able to endure the manner of life in this region."

Peculiarly tender and feminine in the perfection of his intuitive insight, the clearness of his reasoning, the persistency of his inner determination, itself sufficient to make himself and those around him miserable[3] under adverse

measured scale of Melanchthon's soft and tender quill. Whatever Luther-like eruptions may startle the tranquillity of any clear American night, from any other sources, the utterances in this work, if they offend, will probably do so because they are sedate.

[2] Reuchlin had learned to know Melanchthon as a school-boy at Pforzheim, and took great delight in him. It was impossible not to love the lad, so amiable, so thoughtful, and so modest. Even his stammering tongue, which prevented him from talking freely, was no obstacle to those who knew him.

His quick perception, retentive memory, marvelous acuteness, sagacity in argument, purity in expression, rare and extensive knowledge, delicate and elegant taste, commended him to every educated man. Erasmus said of him, " He not only excels in learning and eloquence, but by a certain fatality is a *general favorite.* Honest and candid men are fond of him, and even *his adversaries* cannot hate him." And nearly four centuries later, the English translator of his biography, G. F. Krotel (*Life of Ph. Melanchthon*, by C. F. Ledderhose, Phila., Lindsay and Blakiston, 1855), says : " Melanchthon has been called the most amiable, the purest, and most learned of the celebrated men of the Sixteenth Century. And he has succeeded in securing the affections of posterity, and more than any other one of the valiant champions of the Reformation, is the general favorite of all evangelical Christians, and still seems to stand as the gentle mediator between the two great divisions of the Protestant Church formed at that time, claimed and loved by both."

[3] The weight of Melanchthon's disposition was against discord and in favor of peace. He hated the rough, the violent, the crude, the immoderate (*immanitas horridum nimium, Postil,* II, 552). Yet, as is so often the case with very gentle people, there was an irritability, and a susceptibility to exasperation in his own nature. He himself confesses this : *sæpe ex animo indignor, scis enim me esse iracundum (celeris sed brevis iræ).—C. R.,* III, 1172. And his friend Camerarius tells us: *affectionibus animi vehementibus ; graviter ergo commovebatur, eratque in eo impetus hic repentinus, qui tamen sedabatur celeriter.* Further, Ratzeberger (92) alludes to Melanchthon's being stirred up in his public lectures and his private teachings because " he wished to have his *rationem docendi* " observed " *exacte ad unguem.*" " Melanchthon was gentle by nature only in the sense that he was not capable of deep and lasting passion, and that the rising waves of anger were always brought to calm again by his good-heartedness and his benevolent and loving disposition,"

conditions; peculiar in the charm of his personal, and the failure of his negotiative, contacts; and peculiar also in the almost unaccountable inability to see the necessity of strict fidelity to an original faith or a primal understanding, when he functionated as the representative of conjoint action, and to realize that changes in public declaration of position [4] are destructive of historical accuracy, stability and confidence; Melanchthon, with all his genius, acted most wisely when in a supplementary station, under the direction of a positive guide.

Barely more than a mere lad at school was he, when he offered the classical world a grammar of the Greek language, and an edition of Terence, which brought the commendation of Erasmus. Reuchlin said of him, "Among the Germans I know of no one who excels him, except Erasmus of Rotterdam, and he is a Hollander."

Wittenberg soon discovered that it possessed a treasure of the most rare kind in this frail-looking new-comer, "the Grecian," as he had been known in earlier days by his schoolmates. "A wonderful man, in whom everything is well-nigh supernatural,—my most cherished and intimate friend," wrote Luther to Reuchlin, less than four months after Melanchthon arrived in the city of the Reformation.

Melanchthon received the degree of bachelor of divinity in 1521, but his modesty prevented him, throughout his life, from accepting the Doctor's degree,[5] though, as a teacher, no other man of the Sixteenth Century was held in such high honor. It is sad, indeed, to think that this delicate and finely strung harp, this classic voice, this sensitive soul was

---

says Herrlinger. But he was sensitive to a point, and no wonder, in view of the delicacy of his temperament, and of the many terrible rebuffs and insults he was obliged to endure. It is important to bear this peculiar temperament of Melanchthon,—which characteristically manifests itself in peace-loving and temperamentally unionistic theologians,—in mind.

[4] And still more so, changes of position itself.

[5] " Titulus aliquid oneris habet. Vides meum exemplum ; nemo me perpellere potuit, ut illum quamlibet honorificum titulum Doctoris mihi decerni sinerent ; nec ego gradus illos parvifacio ; sed ideo, quia judico esse magna ornamenta et necessaria Reipublicae, verecunde petendos esse et conferendos censeo."—*C. R.,* IV, 811.

torn out of the professional chair, to enter the mighty conflicts and struggles of a rude political world for which he
was not fitted; and to become the leader of the Christian
faith in trying times, when sturdy confessors and not tim-
orous professors were needed to declare, cling to and stand
by the Word of God, without fear and trembling; and when
the faith required was that in an objective reality, and not
that of a believing rationality.

That Melanchthon was not fitted to stand steady amid
the sweeping currents of religious error, was shown as early
as 1521, when the Zwickau prophets appeared in Wittenberg and he, as a theologian, was unable to control the situation. On Dec. 27th, 1521, he wrote to the Elector:—

"I have conversed with them myself, and they declare most wonderful
things concerning themselves, viz., that God with a loud voice sent them forth to
teach, that they enjoy most intimate conversations with God, behold future events,
and that they are, in short, prophetic and apostolic men. I cannot describe how
all this moves me. That spirits possess them, seems to be established by many
reasons, concerning which no one can easily form an opinion but Martinus. If
the Gospel and the honor and peace of the Church are in any danger, it is absolutely necessary that these people should have an interview with Martinus, especially as they appeal to him."

Melanchthon was not a man for crisis, nor for theological
utterance in the sense of declaring and establishing the Faith
in public difficulty. His examination, apprehension, estimation, expression, and even use of faith, in public affairs,
were of the school,⁶ and not of the apostolic order.

---

⁶ Compare Melanchthon's **Preface** to the **third edition of** the *Loci:* **Cum**
viderem res magnas et necessarias divinitus patefactas esse in nostris ecclesiis
per viros pios et doctos, duxi materias illas in variis scriptis sparsas colligendas
esse et quodam ordine explicandas, ut facilius percipi a juvenibus possent.
Hoc velut pensum debere me in hoc scholastico munere, quod gero Ecclesiæ
judicabam.—*C. R.,* XXI, 341. Melanchthon was one of those practical men
who desire to make truth clear and easy, and whose purpose as theologians
is not so much the apprehension of doctrine in its greatness, as the reduction
of doctrine to terms of easy and clear theological construction. Kahnis is
right in his remark that Melanchthon was "not a theorist but a teacher."
Speculation was entirely foreign to Melanchthon and his mode was the reasoning of the schoolmaster, who "defines precisely, divides justly and combines appropriately."—*C. R.,* XI, 654. This is one of the reasons why Melanchthon's work is not particularly creative, but elaborates elements of knowledge
that have been handed down by another; and why his Loci are "a sum-

The much appreciated practical character of Melanchthon's theology—which avoided the deeper problems, and confined itself to those *quae aedificationem conducunt, quae ad vitam accommodata sunt;* and which connects Melanchthon with the moderate theologians in the beginning of the Eighteenth, and the supernaturalists in the beginning of the Nineteenth Century, and with that school in our own century which feels that the religious rather than the theological interests of the church should be emphasized, proved itself to be unequal to dealing with the critical situations and the grave problems that arose in the Church throughout Melanchthon's life. As Plitt says: "In place of dealing with difficulties, Melanchthon always tried to evade them." [7]

It was just about the time when Melanchthon had brought forth his first dogmatic system, the 'Loci,' that Carlstadt came to Wittenberg; and rendered the situation so overwhelming for Melanchthon that he longed and prayed for the return of Luther from the Wartburg.

Nevertheless this same blessed man was personally great and honorable in adherence to conviction. When tempted, not long afterward, with the promise of a high position within the Roman camp, in exchange for desertion from the Lutheran ranks, he declared to Campeggius, the papal legate in Germany: "If I discover anything to be true, I hold it fast, and maintain it without any regard to the consequences to any mortal, without any regard to advantages, honor or gain."

---

mary of Christian doctrine, which *all* men ought to know." Preface to the German 'Loci,' *C. R.*, XXII, 47.

In this sense, it is instructive to compare the idea and method of Melanchthon with those of Luther in his popular Catechisms. In thus narrowing his theology to school purposes, Melanchthon seemed to be more concerned with the careful elaboration of single points, and their defence and with the combination of single doctrines that belong together, than with the building up of the whole into a system, says Herrlinger, thus leading finally, in confining investigation to the important needs of the situation—the great fault of Melanchthon also in his negotiations on behalf of the Church—to a low scientific ideal. Hence Erasmus wrote him: *In scriptis tuis, in quibus mihi multa arrident, interdum desidero plus circumspectionis. Frequenter enim sic leviter capita rerum attingis, ut negligere videaris, quid arguto lectori venire possit in mentem.*—*C. R.*, III, 87. *Cp. Herrlinger.*

[7] Introduction, *Augustana*, I, 537.

But those strong, sententious words were uttered in reference to his own personal character as a scholar and teacher. So soon as the welfare of the Church was concerned in any movement, or so soon as ties of sympathy and friendship appealed to him from an opposite party, Melanchthon was at sea, miserable and dejected in his own mind, and filled with some plan to extricate the cause or the man to whom he wished to be a friend, by the devices and diplomacy of human reason, rather than inspired by the endeavor simply to do the right thing, and then leave the final issue to the Lord.

In many of the Confessional movements in which Melanchthon was concerned, his first and foremost wish was for tranquillity—of the Church, and of his own mind; and his first effort was to secure it. He was, more than a few times, in the wretched plight of not being able either to stem the tide of difficulty in the Church, or to persuade himself of the desirability of betaking himself out of it. We occasionally find men of this temperament in affairs of state, brilliant in gifts, fertile in the conception of plans, weak and near-sighted in execution, and yet, by some strange fascination, unable to restrain themselves from participation in the progress of a matter in which they are deeply interested. The type is also sometimes found in womanhood— where we characterize it as weak and meddlesome, although, strictly speaking, this is not correct; since there is in such character a strength, or bravery, of a minor order, prone to persist, but neither efficient to resist, nor sufficient to conquer.

Nevertheless, Luther rightly estimated the gifts, the labors and the spirit of Melanchthon, as of the most incalculable value. Luther recommends him to Spalatin as follows: "I would most heartily commend to you Philip, the great Grecian, the thorough scholar, and most amiable man. His lecture-room is crowded with hearers. It is owing to him, principally, that all theologians, the first, middle, and lowest class, are studying Greek."

And when John Eck obtruded his vainglorious learning upon the scene, Luther again wrote to Spalatin: "I again come to speak of Philip, whom no Eck can bring me to hate, and whose testimony in my favour I always esteem higher than anything else. The judgment and opinion of this single man is of more value to me than that of many thousand worthless Ecks, and I would not be ashamed, although I am a Master of Arts, of Philosophy and Theology, and am adorned almost with all the titles of Eck, to leave my own opinion, if this Grammarian could not agree with it. I have often done this, and do it still, because of the divine gift which God has deposited in this frail vessel. . . . Philip I do not praise, he is a creature of God."

This opinion of Luther continued. Early in 1530, he wrote to Jonas: "All the Jeromes, Hillarys, and Macariuses together, are not worthy to unloose the thong of Philip's sandal. What have the whole of them together done which can be compared with one year of Philip's teaching, or to his one book of Common Places? I prefer Melanchthon's books to my own, and would rather have them circulated than mine. I was born to battle with conspirators and devils, therefore my books are more vehement and warlike. It is my work to tear up the stumps and dead roots, to cut away the thorns, to fill up the marshes. I am the rough forester and pioneer. But Melanchthon moves gently and calmly along, with his rich gifts from God's own hand, building and planting, sowing and watering."

Melanchthon was not a mere "Grecian," but a true and learned Christian, having become such early from his constant reading of the Scriptures. The doctrine of justification by faith was his before he reached Wittenberg.

The ethical earnestness of his thoughts, the purity of his style, and the marvelousness of his gifts of apprehension, order, and expression, the wonderful clearness of his presentation and the subtle taste of the true litterateur drew crowds of students from all parts of the German empire.

Heerbrand, in an oration to his memory, declares that Melanchthon had as many as two thousand pupils and hearers, among whom were princes, counts, barons and other noblemen.[8]

Melanchthon's public grasp of subject-matter even in his more free and facile moods[9] was that of epitome.[10]

The mind of Melanchthon was assimilative, not creative,[11] judicial in the weighing of materials with painful anxiety, illuminative, summaristic and naturally expressive. He gathered the principles of the two great classic languages into a simple unity; and his grammars continued to pass through new editions from the start of his academic career until long after his death.[12] After receiving the degree of

---

[8] Reuchlin and Erasmus became famous by their editions and writings on the classics, but Melanchthon attracted young men by his lectures as well as by his writings.

[9] Not so in private correspondence, when his wealth of expression and detail of learning tempted him to unburden himself with almost unmeasured fullness.

[10] It would be interesting to know in how far the rejecting of the earlier frames, and the casting of the final form of the Formula of Concord were due to the fine, clear-cut and orderly influence of Melanchthon upon the minds of those who wrote the Formula.

[11] Melanchthon was not an original spirit, drawing his strength out of the great deeps. His nature was prevailingly receptive, and the extraordinary versatility of this receptivity, by which he combined in himself all the elements of culture in his day, could not, despite his undeniable effort to relate all the sciences to theology, be favorable to that concentration of thought in the realm of theology which is necessary for the formation of a complete and consistent system. But Melanchthon's receptivity is always turned first and foremost to theology, especially to the Scripture. The doctrine of the Church is indeed to be a *grammatica sermonis divini.* And, further, Melanchthon never conceals his theological dependence upon Luther. *Cp.* his words even in his last Testament, *C. R.,* III, 827 : ago gratias rev. Doctori Luthero, quia ab eo Evangelium didici ; also VII, 479.—*Herrlinger.*

[12] " His *Latin Grammar,* prepared originally for his private pupils, was almost universally adopted in Europe, running through fifty-one editions, and continuing until 1734 to be the text-book even in the Roman Catholic schools of Saxony. His *Greek Grammar* also enjoyed great popularity. Of his *Terence,* 73 editions had been published within 106 years of its first publication. He also published either scholia upon or expositions or paraphrases of the *De Officiis, Laelius, De Oratore, Orator, Topicae, Epistles;* and 19 *Orations* of Cicero, Porcius, Latro, Sallust, the *Germania* of Tacitus, Pliny, Quintilian, l. xii, six orations of Demosthenes, one of Aeschines, Lycurgus, Stobæus, Aelian, Lucian, Thucydides, Xenophon, Plutarch, Lysis, Ptolemæus, selections from Homer and Sophocles, 18 tragedies of Euripides, Aristophanes, Menander, 19th Idyl of Theocritus, Tyrtæus, Solon, Theognis, Calimachus, Pindar, Empedocles, Virgil, Ovid, the *Miles* of Plautus, and the *Theognis* of Seneca, in addition to composing 391 Latin and Greek odes. His style *(genus dicendi Philippicum),* which is said, in purity of diction and correctness of classical taste, to excel even that of Erasmus, for a time was regarded in the schools as a model, even to the exclusion of Cicero and Quintilian."—**Summary by** H. E. J., in *McClintock & Strong.*

Master of Arts, he lectured chiefly on the Latin classics, Virgil, Terence, Cicero and Livy.[13]

But he was interested as well in the forms of thought, as in the art or form of expression, and in all that goes to make up the personality of man; and he wrote the philosophical text-books of his day,—the *Epitome Philosophiæ Moralis,* the *De Anima,* and the *De Dialectica.*

For Melanchthon was not a mere stylist, but a born dialectician. His definition of logic as " the art of speaking by *defining, dividing,* and *arguing* ", reveals his mind and method in theology.[14]

It was he, and he alone, who impressed the dialectic and text-book stamp upon the form of Lutheran theology, from its first beginning to the very end of its highly wrought-out orthodox and classic period, in the Seventeenth Century.[15]

The complete departure of the early and later Lutheran theological form from the method and the more vital and germinal insight of Luther, into the modified Aristotelian frame of logical definition, and into a continuance of the academic disputation of the mediæval schoolmen, was mediated, as well as simplified and modernized, by Melanchthon. This was Melanchthon's " Rhetoric ", which Luther and the other Reformers refer to as hindering Melanchthon's faith.[16]

---

[14] He began lecturing on the Scriptures during his first winter at Wittenberg, taking up Titus, Psalms, Matt. and Rom. His published lectures on Scripture embrace Gen., Prov., Eccl., Isaiah, Jer., Lam., Dan. Hag., Zech., Mal., John, Rom., Cor., Col., and Tim.

[14] At the University of Heidelberg he had heard the *garrula dialectica et particula physices,* and had worked himself with youthful enthusiasm into the Grammatik, Rhetorik, and Dialectik of the day.

[15] The tendency to reduce Theology to a philosophy, and to its humanistic and practical value—among some of the Melanchthonian theologians in the Twentieth Century, could probably be traced back to Melanchthon, indirectly through the pietistic and rationalistic influences of the Eighteenth Century, and through the mental frame and phrase of the great American Melanchthonian, S. S. Schmucker; but it is also due to contact with humanistic sources in typical American religious denominations, and to contact with the influence of common American Christianity.

[16] *Vid.* the correspondence concerning the Augsburg Diet in *Chapters XIX and XX.*

But the Melanchthonian principle embraced more than the logic of simplified definition, and the rhetoric of its clear and harmonious setting forth. Unlike Luther, Melanchthon, following the bent of his nature and his humanistic education,[17] laid stress on *Philosophy*[18] (it was a simplified Aristotelian type)[19]—based on the *lumen naturale*,[20] on a natural religion, and a natural law; which, though beclouded by sin, is a real gift and power in human nature. In his '*locus*' on the nature of God, for instance, he starts with the "true, pertinent thoughts" of Plato, which are founded upon mature reasonings, and says they "must *still have added* to them the attributes which God himself has revealed."[21]

The *lumen naturale* is practically a foundation and a

---

[17] Melanchthon approached philosophy *through philology*.

[18] To philosophy Melanchthon reckoned the formal arts, and also found *admincula* for theology in the metaphysical material of philosophy. He took from the old church philosophy, his psychological and ethical conceptions, and sought to fill them out with an evangelical experience. In such doctrines as those of the trinity, justification, the sacraments, he sought to find points of connection between the revealed, or dogmatic, and the natural, or humanistic, idea. He regards philosophy as *moderata investigatrix veritatis*, but he warns against confusing the two spheres, and places philosophy beneath the revealed truth which is the *præcipua rectrix opinionum* [sic] *et vitæ*. He was a pronounced Aristotelian, and successfully turned that system into a *philosophia simplex, vitæ utilis.—C. R.*, XI, 344.

Yet Melanchthon purified his teachings from the speculative elements of the schoolmen. He depreciates the undue ascendency of Aristotle instead of Christ in his own day, as he also does the undue influence of Platonism in the Ancient Church.—*Loci* (Plitt-Kolde), p. 37.

[19] " Among his philosophical works were an *Epitome of Moral Philosophy; Elements of Ethics; Commentary on Aristotle's Politics; Elements of Rhetoric; Logical Questions;* and dissertations on ethical subjects, such as oaths, contracts, etc. For many years instruction in these works was the regular course in ethics in most of the schools of Protestant Germany. Hallam pronounced them " more clear, elegant, and better arranged than those of Aristotle himself or his commentators " (Hallam, *Literature*, ii, 50). He was the author, also, of an elementary text-book of physics, and a sketch of universal history, from the creation to the Reformation, *Chronicon Carionis*."—Summary of H. E. Jacobs, in *McClintock & Strong*.

[20] XII, 514, 577, 648.

[21] " The possession of this *additional* and unique revelation, of course, does not annul or displace the data from which *natural theology* derives its *invaluable* theistic and religious truth. These continue in *their own rightful force* and *validity*, for full consideration in theological grounds and verifications. The disposition, sometimes shown, to contemn and exclude from Christian theology the data that have *illuminated the way of natural theology into the great fundamental realities* of the divine existence and many of the divine prerogatives and attributes and of the religious nature and responsibility of man, is manifestly unjustifiable. These have lost none of their intrinsic legitimacy by reason of the *added* light, and rightly form auxiliary sources in theological determinations."—Valentine, *Christian Theology*, I, 22, 23.

frame—not however here in a synergistic sense [22]—on which theology is to be built. Theology is to be put into form and taught—rather than to rise out of the Word into faith, and through faith to be expressed in every act of life. We are dealing with *statements* of principle, rather than with principles. The academy takes the place of the battle-field. Reason enters theology at the lower root, and orders it; and ethics takes theology in the upper branch, and applies it. In Melanchthon's use of the rational frame, we must, however, remember that speculation and rational substance have have no place.

Melanchthon is guided, throughout his long life of thought, by two leading principles, both practical,—first, to preserve the historical continuity of the church, *i. e.,* the visible church; and second, to re-frame and re-state the doctrine, according to new light and the latest need. In these two principles there lies concealed an antithesis or contradiction on which the Melanchthonian theology shatters itself. " Historical continuity " and " unbroken visible unity " require stability; while "restatement" involves the possibility of constant fluidity, breaking up, and change. We cannot have the fixed and the variable together. [23] We cannot " be firm " and " accommodate " at the same time. We must give up either " continuity " or " changefulness." The many seemingly contradictory theological frames and actions of Melanchthon whether toward the Roman or the Reformed extreme, are rendered intelligible when we find his mind possessed of both these principles, the one or the other of which is called forth by the situation immediately before him.

As a teacher of logic, and in theology—except as to form of discussion—Melanchthon was not germinal, but reflexive

---

[22] In Paul, Melanchthon finds the way to *Justitia,* that is, to *perfecta virtus, quæ ex animo beat nos.* Unlike Luther, Melanchthon found his inner peace on the way of moral perfection. But he had learned from Paul that Christ is our righteousness, and that the power and joy of virtue follows only from the certitude of forgiveness.—*Institutio theologica* of 1519. *C. R.,* XXI, 49 sq.

[23] *i. e.,* on parallel lines.

and practical, without an inner and constant principle of organic unfolding. He was progressive in the *apprehension* of philological, historical and logical investigation. That Melanchthon was variable, or changeful, that is that he regarded the inner principle not so much in its objective being as in its outer form of statement, on which he constantly sought to " improve ", needs no demonstration. His unreliability in the earlier stages of the Augsburg Confession; his habit of apprehending truth in itself indeed, but also in its propinquities and relations to his ecclesiastical environment; and his free shifting of the point of view, especially when and where he was not steadied,—constituted his weakness.

The Lord's Supper, with him, for instance, was a matter of logical conception. " For ten years neither day nor night has passed," he wrote in 1537, " in which I have not reflected on this subject." In 1529, he would rather die than be contaminated by union with the Zwinglians.[23a] In the Augustana he reflected and expressed Luther's teaching. In Augsburg, a month or two later, in his *Opinion Concerning the Foundation of the Doctrine of the Sacramentarians* (found in English *Book of Concord,* II, pp. 241-243) he declared that " Bucer is wrong in contending that he agrees with us. . . . Bucer diffuses mist. . . . We require not only the presence of the power, but of the body. This Bucer disguises purposely. . . . Bucer seems to me to be preparing a plot when he says that we agree. . . . We deny transubstantiation and that the body is locally in the bread.

[23a] " Cheer up about the Zwinglian ' Rotte.' I myself experienced, when their wheelhorses were (at Marburg), that they have no Christian doctrine. .
I would rather die than to hold wth them and say that the body of Christ must and can be only at one place. Therefore only go ahead and censure them, publicly and privately, when and where there is opportunity. Censure this in them, that they teach nothing right of the use of the sacraments. There is found indeed in all the Zwinglian books not a single annunciation of faith, by which we become righteous before God. Even when they mention the faith, they do not mean the faith which believes the forgiveness of sins, and is sure that we are received into grace, heard and protected and kept by God; but they only mean a historical faith (which also the devils have), a mere empty knowledge."—*Melanchthon to Martin Görlitz,* about March, 1530.

43

. . . We declare confidently that the present Christ distributes his body and blood for us to eat and drink." In the first edition of the Apology, " he at least approximated very closely to the doctrine of transubstantiation. In 1531, he gave up the theory of ubiquity; under studies of the Church Fathers, he more fully abandoned Luther's teaching, and finally in the edition of the Confession of 1540, he approximated to that of Bucer and Calvin." [24]

When he came to Wittenberg, Melanchthon was filled with the idea of a Reformation in the Church by a renaissance of science and learning.[25] Under the impetus of this humanistic ideal, he began his multitudinous literary labors by lecturing on Homer, and on the epistle to Titus. Side by side the classical and the confessional principle lived and grew in his mind, and bore, in their union, their first fruit in a brief statement of the Scripture doctrines in the new, clear form, for his own private use. This statement of doctrines he used as an introduction in lecturing on Romans, and his students thought it so good that they published it unrevised, and without his consent.

Then Melanchthon, though in the midst of the Zwickau difficulties, published this first evangelical dogmatics under the title *loci communes rer. theologicarum, seu Hypotyposes theologicæ,* Dec., 1521.

Luther was so pleased with the book that he called it " liber invictus, non solum immortalitate, sed et canone ecclesiastico dignus."

Of it, the Romish Alphonso de Zamara is said to have declared: " It explains its doctrinal statements in such appropriate and accurate terms, and, by a methodical treatment, renders them so clear and strong, that it is injuring the papal power more than all other writings of the Lutherans."

Calvin, later, wrote, in line with Melanchthon's main purpose, and revealing in a word or two the great difference

---

[24] From Schaff, not strictly correct, but sufficiently so to illustrate the point.
[25] Plitt, *Mel. loci comm. in ihrer Urgestalt,* 1864, p. 34.

between Melanchthon's life-aim as a theologian, and a truly *scientific* inquiry or construction of the Christian doctrine: " So beautiful is the proof that it affords, that the most perfect simplicity is the noblest method of handling the Christian doctrine."

This sudden and complete Protestant theological pedagogik was of such value to the Reformation, and seemed to reveal such powers in its author, that Luther tried to have Melanchthon relieved from his work on the classics, in order that he might give his whole strength to theology. Melanchthon himself objected, and intimated that if it were necessary to choose between the two, he would demit theology in favor of the classics.

But he now plunged with Luther into the task of translating the Scriptures, the inner basis of the Reformation; and then came the Diets, and Conventions, and doctrinal statements, the outer basis of the Reformation. The almost unbearable burden of framing these many statements fell upon the frail shoulders of our wonderful thinker and scholar.

It therefore was 1535 before a second main edition of the ' *Loci* ' was published, by which time the humanistic seeds in Melanchthon's mind had so far developed into theological substance, that the predestinarian sentence, "All things happen necessarily," was removed, and room was left for the synergistic growth,[26] which the mind of Melanchthon manifested in the next decade.

By 1543, when the greater differences in thinking between Luther and Melanchthon had come plainly to the surface, and Melanchthon had been in constant communication with the Reformed divines concerning the doctrine of the Lord's Supper,[27] while at the same time he had advanced so far as to lean toward Rome in the synergistic doctrine of free will and good works; and after the *Variata* of the Augsburg Con-

---

[26] *Cp. Chap. XXII.*

[27] *Ib.,* and also following chapters.

fession had appeared, he issued the third main edition of his
' *Loci,*' [28] in enlarged form in which he, to use the words of
Jacobs,[29] " so far changed on that subject as to seem far more
in harmony with the teaching of Erasmus than that of Luther." In the edition of 1548, Melanchthon went so far as
to boldly say, " Liberum arbitrium est in homine facultas applicandi se ad gratiam." The opinion has been advanced,
and indeed with some degree of truth, that without the association with Luther, Melanchthon, in his reformation of
doctrine, " would have become or remained a second Erasmus ", *i. e.*, not in the worst Erasmian, but in the religious
Erasmian sense.

It was Melanchthon's contradictory principle of ecclesiastical conservatism and intellectual change, together with
the intimacy with Bucer, the cross-field thinking of Osiander,
and the onward development of the external situation, that
introduced and prolonged the many controversies into which
he was plunged. The method, and, in part, the content of
the controversies, as well as the form of the later Lutheran
system, were furnished by Melanchthon.

Thus in a most important sense, the spirit of Melanchthon,
and not that of Luther, led to the doctrinal formularies of
the Sixteenth Century and to the ultra-orthodoxy of the
Seventeenth, after the original spirit of free investigation
had died away. Dilthey and Hartfelder have pointed out
that the theology of Melanchthon combines the articles of
faith with ancient cosmology in the scholastic style of

---

[28] According to Chemnitz, Luther often said, that there was more solid
doctrine in the ' *Loci* ' than in any other book that had appeared since the
days of the Apostles.

When the changes came in the Augsburg Confession and in the '*Loci*' Luther
was *silent,*—to avoid a personal break between his friend and himself, and a
public break in the University, the State, and the Church.

When Luther revised the German translation of the ' *Loci* ' by Jonas, he
suggested that " Justification " and " the Holy Supper " were not treated with
sufficient fulness.

Jacobs says, " The renowned *Loci Theologici* of Chemnitz is a commentary
upon Melanchthon's *Loci.* Similar commentaries were written by Prætorius,
Pezel, Strigel, and Fabricius; while Spangenberg, Sohn, Mayer and Hem-
mingius have prepared abridgments. For many years it continued to be a
text-book in the Lutheran schools, until supplanted by Hutter's Compend."

[29] Melanchthon in *McC. & Strong.*

Thomas Aquinas;[30] though, unlike Thomas, Melanchthon does not go so far in uniting the two as to construct a system of metaphysics, but limits himself to man's natural consciousness as a point of departure. Yet Seeberg is sure that this combination made by Melanchthon led historically to the orthodoxy of the Seventeenth, as well as to the illumination of the Eighteenth Century.

"It may be said," declares Seeberg, "that the maintenance and spread of 'pure doctrine' is the great motive which inspired Melanchthon's life-work, as a Reformer of the church and of the universities, as a theologian, philologian, and teacher.[30a]

"On the other hand, we may thus also understand his fatal attitude toward the Interim, *C. R.,* VII, 382 sq., 322 sq., and toward Calvin and his party; for, aside from the deviations which had separated himself as well from Luther, he believed himself to be in doctrinal accord with Calvin—and everything to his mind depended upon doctrine.

"This involved again, as compared with Luther, a narrowing of the horizon, resulting not merely from the great importance attached to the 'pure doctrine', but from the fact that the life-giving energy of the church was attributed to the latter. It cannot be denied that in these views are to be found the germs of the errors of the orthodoxy of the Seventeenth Century."[31]

Seeberg is partially conscious of Melanchthon's inconsist-

---

[30] But in simple form and with a purely practical view.

[30a] This explains his great severity toward heretics [*e. g.,* Servetus].—*C. R.,* II, 18; III, 197 sq., 199, 241 sq.; VIII, 520 sq.; IV, 739; XII, 699; XXIV, 375, 501.

[31] Seeberg, *History of Doctrines,* II, pp. 355-356. Seeberg disclaims novelty for this position, and points to Gottfried Arnold, Zierold (1700), and Ritschl (*Die Entstehung der luth. Kirche*), as its earlier exponents. *Cp.* also p. 363:—
"The practical application of these principles and views led to the lamentable doctrinal controversies in the period from the death of Luther to that of Melanchthon. Both the unfortunate wavering of Melanchthon in connection with the Interim—when the doctrine appeared to him to be sufficiently guarded—and the bitter assaults made upon him by the so-called Gnesio-Lutherans for his lack of firmness upon that occasion and for his doctrinal divergencies find explanation in the one-sided character of his later conceptions of the church and of doctrine."

ent double principle,—pure doctrine as manifested historically in the outward unfolding of the church, and pure doctrine as mediated inwardly by the logical thought of the individual investigator; but, while he emphasizes the permanency of Melanchthon's form, he makes no allusion to the
contradiction in the substance of the Melanchthonian principle.

The Melanchthonian nature, principle and practice, though
of such well-meant and kindly intent, operated unfortunately
throughout all the great events of the Reformation; and it
will be of great service to the ultimate purpose for which this
work has been written, if we shall be able to make a true
analysis of it, which will be appreciative at once of its elements of strength, and of its disastrous elements of weakness.

In personal intellectual bravery, Melanchthon was unflinching. His masterly defense of Luther against the Sor-
bonne, and before his old friend Erasmus, prove this fact.
His personal loyalty is also unquestionable. For many
years he clung to Luther with all his heart. He most faithfully reproduced and elaborated the doctrine of Luther. He
was the first one [32] to understand the great service of Luther
in the historical development of Christianity; and he counts
Luther among the mighty heroes of the faith, among Isaiah,
John the Baptist, Paul and Augustine. He tells us that
" Luther brought to light the true and necessary doctrine,[33]
and that we must hold fast to the pure doctrine, viz., the
Confessio Lutheri."

He clearly understood and assiduously applied the cardinal principles of the Reformation, in a mild, considerate,
courteous and admirably thoughtful way. We already have
alluded to his ' *Loci.'* In addition, we may cite his Work on
the Saxon Visitation, sometimes called the *First Confession
of Faith of the Lutheran Church,* in which he had presented
a most sound and discriminating application of Lutheran doc-

---

[32] Seeberg, *Hist. of Doctrines,* II, p. 352.
[33] *C. R.,* XI, 728.

trine, though in such mild form that he was supposed by the
enemies of the Reformation to be yielding to Rome, and was
obliged to suffer much pain of mind in consequence." Then,
there follows his great Augsburg Confession and his great
Apology, with all the multitude of his teachings and lectures.

The first startling weakness that we come upon, in Melanchthon, is that on nearly every great occasion, he *lacked
the strong faith of Luther;* and the cautious operation of his
intellect—his distrust of the power of triumph in the right—
his apparent inability to take an age-long look, to see the
eternal view of his work—and his desire for immediately
favorable results—together with his apparent inability to
trust Providence in the midst of clouds because of a temperament that went to pieces under unfavorable conditions, made
him wretched. He depended too much on the opinion of
others, and seemed to be unable to stand on his own feet no
matter what Rome says or does. So he wrote from Spires
to Myconius, " for here we are objects of scorn to the proud
spirits, and of derision to the rich "—not such a dreadful
thing for a follower of Christ,—and a Lutheran at that!

But let us proceed to a second point. Melanchthon's faith
was not firm and great, because his reason was always in-
terfering with his faith—and he, in a sense, followed his
reason. His scholarly instincts were all conservative, and
his ripe judgment was ever preservative, but his prime point
of contact was rationalistic. He walked by faith indeed,
but faith that was dependent upon reason; upon sight, and
not upon insight. Hence when sight and reason wavered
or shifted, faith followed in its wake.

Melanchthon was already worrying about the doctrine of
the Lord's Supper at Spires in 1529, and wrote to his close
friend Oecolampadius: " It is very painful to me that discord

---

[34] Melanchthon to Camerarius : " Indeed my defection is publicly reported
as a fact, because in the little book written for the Reformed Churches, I
have shown an increased degree of moderation ; and yet you perceive I have
really inserted nothing different from what Luther constantly affirms. But
because I have employed no asperity of language, these very acute men judge
that I necessarily differ from Luther."

should have arisen in this matter, ordained by Christ Himself to establish an indissoluble love. Never has anxiety for any matter disturbed my heart more than my anxiety in this. And I have not only myself considered what might be said for and against this matter, but I have also examined the opinions of the ancients." [35] His faith was not firm, *because his reason was busy and halting* in a mystery which it had not solved, and which it never would solve.

At Marburg, he strongly supported Luther against Zwingli. Not only did Melanchthon [36] *agree with Luther in withholding* the hand of fellowship from Zwingli, a fact which is often overlooked; but he wrote to a friend concerning the Zwinglians: " They seemed to be more trifling even than they had been before this conference. They contended very strongly that we should we call them brethren. But look at their stupidity: when they condemn us, they yet desire to be considered by us as brethren. We cannot give our consent to this." [37]

Yet when he came under the less gross rationalistic influence of Bucer, and found what seemed to be a pathway of reason through the Sacrament, supported by some authority of the Ancients, held by others outside of his own Church, and more defensible along the line of the *lumen naturale,* not all his respect for pure *doctrine,* nor all his attachment and gratitude to Luther could keep him from lowering faith to the plane of scholarly opinion, and from resting finally in the most reasonable " opinion." This leads direct to the third weakness of the Melanchthonian principle, to the great and far-reaching mistake in all ages, of the milder rationalism.

Melanchthon's fatal error lay in the mental attitude with which he approached the problem of Confession. He made it a mental problem, one in which *the adjustment* of truth

---

[35] Krotel-Ledderhose, *Life of Melanchthon,* p. **82.**
[36] *Vid.* also *C. R.,* I, 1098, 1108 ; II, 25.
[37] *Melanchthon to-Agricola,* Oct. 12th, 1529.

played too great a part. He had fallen into the inveterate habit of seeking to conciliate differences in the thoughts and actions of men, by shaving off offending edges of doctrinal substance. He dealt with the confessional principle, not as with a fountain of testimony, that springs, pure, clear, and inviolate from the bed-rock of Scripture; but as an apothecary's compound to be so skilfully composed that it would be mediating between the different convictions, opinions and practices of men. In this way the intellect and the conscience become confused, and the near and pressing advantage of the politician often seem of more import than the ultimate advantage of the pure confessor. Therefore Melanchthon continuously exposed the Reformation and its Confessional principle to the peril of ruin by compromise, instead of bringing it bravely to do its duty in open utterance, and allowing Providence to take care of the future.

The fourth peculiar propensity, on the part of Melanchthon, which was an instinctive willingness to enter into compromise, was due to the combination of two marked elements in his nature. The first of these—the love of union [38] and agreement, and the cultivation of amiable relations of concord with the personalities in his present environment—over-weighed the strength of his faith in the exact Word, which was conceived of subjectively as " doctrine " and was mediated by rational processes. [39]

The other element that united with the rationalistic testimony to interfere with untrammeled and open confession, was the great timidity, or cowardice, of Melanchthon—not a personal fear, for, though he was always trembling with apprehension, it was for the fate of the cause which he represented, and because of his great aversion to conflict and

---

[38] This love arose in large measure from one of the fundamental principles or instincts discussed above, viz., the desire to preserve the visible Church of Christ intact in his own age, and thus connect it in outward completeness with preceding ages.

[39] This same rationalism within the Word, without Melanchthon's love of union, came to full expression in the dogmaticians in the Sixteenth Century, and still comes to such expression in the absolute syllogisms underlying the doctrinal elaborations of one of the Lutheran theological schools.

his horror of war. It was this particular weakness of cowardice, and lack of objective trust, in Melanchthon's character, which is traceable ultimately to his rationalism, that
threw the unhappy man, the man of peace, who longed for
quietness and order, into continuous conflict within and
without, during the whole of his long period of public activity. Unutterably pitiable is it to see a man of this gentle
and lovely temperament, thus constantly contributory, by the
imprudence and failings of his own virtues, to the growth
of the very dissensions and bitternesses which he hoped to
bring to an end.

How exceedingly tragic that his scholastic habit of re-
weighing and re-formulating the conclusions of his reasoning; that such heavenly gift of expression in this divinely-
chosen instrument of the Reformation, which ought to have
brought more permanent stability of substance and sharper
and ever less subtle outline of form into the Confession of the
Church,—how tragic that such habit of foreboding, in such
gift of precision, should become so detrimental to the witness of God's truth: as happens with men who weigh and re-
weigh all things with their reason so continuously that di-
vinely-wrought faith in the Word seems secondary!

Great masters of form often come to consider it as lawful
to touch the integer of substance, and to smooth down super-
fluities and excrescences, as they would say, so that the truth
may be more acceptable to the understanding; and thus—
to change the figure—polish away the very pivots, so small
and yet so essential, upon which the sphere of doctrine bears
down upon the bed-rock of its foundation, and set the ball
of teaching a-rolling down an endless groove of change.

How tragic that this restless spirit of change, so characteristic of Protestantism and so destructive of the only premises upon which Protestantism can permanently stand, should
have entered, as a new, separate, and minor, but persistent
principle, so early, and for years so unobservedly, into the
career of the Evangelical Reformation!

Thus, in the fifth place, all the qualities—and some of them in their paradox, *e. g.,* his love of change (rational), and his fear of change (historical); his desire to be independent as a teacher and his love of dependence on authority; his wish to win those without, which led him to take the risk of offending those within,—are contributory to the most marked and unfailing instinct of Melanchthon, viz., the desire for union. It is the weaker, the secondary, the unsatisfied, the longing and changing nature that needs and is driven to seek union.

The instinct of union was fundamental in Melanchthon's nature. It sprang not simply from the desire for immediate concord, and from the wish to avoid strife, which was a strong trait in him, but also from the still greater desire on his part to preserve the unity of the visible church. He strove most valiantly in his own way to prevent the visible church from going to pieces. On the one side he held on to the Roman Church with almost inconceivable fidelity, and on the other side he reached out toward the Calvinistic Church with tenacity, though he consistently and continuously hated Zwinglianism (with which much modern Protestantism is to be compared), and would have nothing to do with it. To this desperate effort of Melanchthon, to keep the Christian Church united in a visible unity, many of his apparent sacrifices of principle in ambiguous formulas, much of his waste of energy, and his most serious troubles are due. Down to the very last, even subsequent to the Convention of Worms in 1557, he hoped for a reconciling union of the visible Church.

This consistent and continuous unionistic effort of his was doomed to fail. He conciliated the Romanists, but offended the Protestants in his gentle and generally admirable Saxon Confession, in 1527. He was obliged to change his own position at the Diet of Spires in 1529. He came near overturning the whole Protestant foundation by his concessions to Rome in connection with the Confession at Augs-

burg in 1530. In his earlier friendship with Oecolampadius and his later friendship with Bucer, the great mediating
theologian, he brought harm and discord into Lutheranism,
and yet did not unite even the looser and more liberal
Lutheran elements together organically with Calvinism, in the
most prominent point of separation, viz., the doctrine of the
Lord's Supper. Melanchthon's efforts toward unionism on
this doctrine were not to develop a theory of his own, but to
find a common basis for all evangelical Christians (in which
the Zwinglians were however excluded), who held fast to the
real objective presence of Christ in the Supper, as opposed
to the Supper as a *memoria hominis mortui,* and a mark
merely of human fellowship (which Melanchthon always
continued to regard as Zwingli's view). Melanchthon had
no idea either of drawing all Protestant sects more closely
together, or of having fellowship in the Lord's Supper with
those who hold it as a mere memorial.

But he supposed it possible to preserve church unity by an
agreement of the more conservative Protestants, such as
was attained later through the mediation of Bucer and his
own agreement with the Swiss Reformation through the
Wittenberg Concord. *Conjunctionem nostrarum ecclesiarum retineri volui et domestica quaedam vulnera tegi.*[40]

Both Calvin and Melanchthon made the mediæval mistake of presuming that such concord could be arranged by
formulas of union, whose words would cover up minor differences and limit unnecessary disputes, and thus preserve
the unity of the true doctrine. It would not however be
just to conclude, much as the words of the two men seem at
times to indicate the fact, that Melanchthon could find himself in hearty and permanent agreement with the formulas
of Calvin, respecting the Lord's Supper. He probably
never used them.[41]

The sixth point in our analysis of Melanchthon's prin-

---

[40] *C. R.,* XXI, 346.
[41] Yet *cp. Schaff in loco.*

ciple and character brings us to his trait of diplomacy. Is it any wonder that a mind that worked by reason rather than rested in faith alone; that believed it possible to eliminate differences by the introduction of harmonic formulas; that longed for outside attachments, and feared the public consequence of isolation, should, in the name of the Lord, take a hand in the diplomacy of the day to bring about in Church affairs that which he so ardently desired? Thus, while Luther remains the mighty preacher, and pins his whole faith to the Word, Melanchthon becomes *the ecclesiastic,* and assists in putting the Lord's work on its feet by his own schemes and plans.

Kolde, in several of the preceding Chapters,[14a] has made clear how, at the Diet of Augsburg, while Brück and the Elector proved themselves to be the real confessors, Melanchthon was engaged in politics. His conduct on this occasion seems incomprehensible: that he should have continued in such a guileless faith in the open-mindedness of the Spanish Emperor—that, with all his experience with Rome at previous Diets and Conventions, he should still trust the Papal legate—that he should enter into and carry on negotiations of greatest political import, without any commission from the Elector, whose servant he was; and without any consultation with the Elector's chancellor, who was the proper official advisor—and that he should be willing to modify the theological outcome without consulting Luther, or the other theologians, in witness of which is his persistent silence toward Luther during the period in which he was engaged with negotiations with the Papal legate—and that he should take into his own hands the settlement of the future of Protestantism, in a way different from that projected and planned by the body of advisers; and thus neglect the proper work, viz., the completion of the Confession of the Evangelical Faith, until the last moment, when there was barely time left to make a respectable copy of the man-

---

[14a] *XV* and *XVI*.

uscript,—are, each and all, testimony and evidence of the peculiar and unfortunate Melanchthonian method, which brought disastrous results to the Reformation.

Not only during the days preceding the Confession at Augsburg, but also during the long Summer of 1530, when weary and fruitless negotiations were being held with the Roman Pope on the basis of the Confession, which culminated, on the one side, in the Romish Confutation, and on the other, in Melanchthon's glorious Apology; Melanchthon's vain hopes for peace and his willingness to concede parts of confessional substance, or, at least, to veil them in a formula of agreement which represented verbal harmony, but covered actual difference, were in evidence.

The seventh and last characteristic of Melanchthon's nature was his dreadful fear and trembling (already alluded to under point four above), and his lack of trust and confidence, in the crises of the Church through which he passed. We recall his anxiety and helplessness at Wittenberg when the fanatics appeared during the absence of Luther. Worry and care seem never to have lifted their clouds from his soul. The result of the Diet of Spires, in 1529, which insisted on the enforcement of the edict of Worms, filled the spirit of Melanchthon with dismay. He trembled for the safety of the evangelical cause, and felt that a more conciliatory course would have avoided the dire result. " Perhaps the excessive anxiety which took possession of him may account for the unjust censure which he passed upon the conduct of the Lutheran princes in this Diet. He vainly imagined that the Roman Catholics would not have passed the obnoxious decree at all, or would have annulled it again, if some minor and unessential points had been conceded to them. But he credited the Roman Catholics with good intentions which they never possessed. They were bent on crushing out the Reformation. The princes judged far more correctly than he of the temper and spirit of their foes, and of the course which had to be pursued in dealing with them. Yet it must be said to Melanchthon's credit that after the decree of the Diet was passed, he was as much opposed as any one to yielding obedience to its unholy demands, and that he advised, as a last resort, the presentation of a formal protest against the resolution of the Diet.

"Accordingly, on April 15th, 1529, the Lutherans presented their celebrated *Protest* (written by Melanchthon himself) and Appeal. On the sixth of May, Melanchthon arrived again at Wittenberg. Both he and Luther expected that a religious war would follow. Melanchthon was so troubled at the prospect that Luther wrote: 'Philip worries himself so much about the Church and the general welfare, that he is injuring his health.' " [42]

The same incubus followed Melanchthon to the Diet of Augsburg, and rendered him miserable and hopeless during the greater part of that memorable Spring and Summer. He toiled incessantly, but always in fear and trembling and on the edge of despair. We have described his vain hopes, and his schemes to avert disaster, and their failure elsewhere. But most graphically does his weakness and misery come out in his correspondence with Luther during that Summer. Luther was being held at Coburg. He was like a lion in the cage, and comparatively little information reached him as to doings in Augsburg. Melanchthon's plan was to patch up a peace which he knew Luther would frown upon, and he stopped writing to Luther and then complained that Luther did not write to him.

After passing the Melanchthonian principle and temperament under such searching review, we cannot avoid asking the question, Is this the proper principle and temper for the Lutheran Church to assume in our day? Was the Melanchthonianism of the sixteenth century, or of the eighteenth century in Europe, or that of the nineteenth century in Europe or in America, promotive of the peace, the strength,

---

[42] Stump, *Life of Melanchthon,* p. 89.

and the life of the church? In the sixteenth century, it, first, had its trial, and, after a generation, brought the church to the verge of shipwreck. We believe it has done this in later days, and will always do so. The Melanchthonian principle left to itself will merge a weak Lutheranism into a common Protestantism, which the Lutheran essence will not leaven, but in which it will, as Schaff intimates, be swallowed up of the Reformed principle. The operation of this principle in the sixteenth century Schaff describes as follows:—

" The Melanchthonians . . . maintained, with less force of will and conviction, but with more liberality and catholicity of spirit, the right of progressive development in theology, and sought to enlarge the doctrinal basis of Lutheranism for a final reconciliation of Christendom, or at least for a union of the evangelical churches." [43]

Even the genially discriminative Kahnis has said, " There have been those who lamented that it was not conceded to Philippism to speak the final word. But before a tendency can impart character, it must have character, and this was wanting in Philippism. Nothing but a positive Lutheranism had the theological potencies, the firmness and definiteness of doctrine, the energy of witness, and principles on which established Churches alone can rest, which was the problem to be solved." [44]

[43] *Creeds of Christendom,* I, p. 267.

[44] Kahnis, *Innere Gang.,* I, pp. 54, 55.

CHAPTER XXV.

THE LUTHERAN CONFESSION.

THE NEED OF A CONCORDIA REALIZED, AND ITS ORIGIN ATTEMPTED.

Four Periods of Development—The Variata Insufficient—The Situation 1560-1576—The Statements of Andreæ in 1569—The Six Sermons sent to Chemnitz in 1573—The Commission of Augustus—The Torgau Book—The Bergen Book—The Calvinistic Protests.

LOOKING backward, from that point in the history of the Sixteenth Century to which we now have attained, we find the Lutheran Confession[1] to have passed through four periods of development. The first period comprises its birth and youth, 1517-1530. The second period embraces the years in which the Confession was publicly established and regularly taught to the rising generation as a system of doctrine, 1530-1546. The third period includes those dark years between the death of Luther (and the Leipzig Interim) and the Peace of Augsburg, during which the Lutheran doctrine suffered much from oppression, curtailment and schism (1546-1555). And the fourth period represents the results of schism in separating and widening the breach between the external units, and embraces the unsuccessful Diets of the Princes, and the introduction of the *Corpora Doctrinae,* whose common Confession was the Evangelical Lutheran Faith (1555-1560-1567).

The events from 1555 to the death of Melanchthon have

---

[1] *i. e.,* the Catholic Confession with the errors of Rome expurgated.

44

already been treated. Those from 1560 to 1567 and later, the rise of the *Corpora Doctrinae,* the subsidence of the Majoristic, Synergistic and Osiandrian Controversies, and other movements, will be alluded to and discussed in various subsequent chapters in their relation to our examination of the Formula of Concord.

The true Lutherans who remained steadfast throughout these years of darkness, and who were not so narrow and so embittered as to prefer their own little party or their own personal liberty, and a continuance in conflict, to a knitting together of the whole evangelical Church of the clear Augsburg Confession upon its sound, complete, normal and original basis; gradually came to the conclusion, in view of the shadows, obscurities and uncertainties that had gathered about the Lutheran Confession during the generation of Melanchthonian activity, because it was Variate, and because of the strains imposed upon it and the liberties taken in diverse development, that the only way to bring the Church back to the whole Faith, and anchor it on a truly catholic basis, able to meet the catholic claim of Rome, was to re-affirm all the earlier Confessions of the Catholic Christian Faith, with the Augsburg Confession, and to unfold the full Faith of these Confessions more fully under the guidance of God's Word at any points which had become obscured and contorted during this period.

The first of the theologians to attempt this work was a pupil of John Brentz, one of the original Confessors and professor of Theology of Tuebingen.[2] In 1569 he wrote a Confession in five statements,[3] one on Justification, one on Good Works, one on Free Will, one on Adiaphora, and one on the Lord's Supper, each of which had been the subject of a controversy, and doctrines of which had been obscured; and sent them around to other theologians in other parts of Germany, asking whether these statements would not be

---

[2] For a fuller account of Andreæ, *vid.* chap XXX.

[3] For title, etc., *vid. ib.,*

suitable as a Confession, to set Lutheran doctrine in the clear, and bring peace to the troubled Church.

Many theologians were ready to accept these statements of Andreae, but some saw that they were not sufficiently distinctive and complete, and that they probably would be subscribed by men who would continue to hold false views privately, but who would recognize the prudence of outwardly accepting the new Confession.[4] In journeying through north Germany, Andreae happened to meet the theologian Chemnitz, who was superintendent in Braunschweig, of whom the Romanists later said, "You Lutherans have had two Martins (Martin Luther and Martin Chemnitz); if the second one had not come, the first one would not have remained standing."

As a result of the interview between Andreae and Chemnitz, Chemnitz drew up and circulated a form of Confession of those articles in the Augsburg Confession that had been falsified. This was to be added to the Confession of Luther.

Following this, in 1573, Andreae sent Chemnitz six sermons concerning the divisions that had arisen in the Church of the Augsburg Confession between 1548 and 1573; and subsequently prepared the eleven Swabian articles, which were endorsed in Württemberg, and which Chemnitz and Chytraeus corrected and worked over.[5] Then the eyes of the Elector Augustus of Saxony were opened, and he called a Conference of twelve theologians, praying that the Lord would enlighten their hearts with his Spirit, and thus bring them to the truth, and to godly unity.

The decision of this Conference was, first, that all bad feelings arising in past controversies should be forgiven and forgotten; second, that no one was bound any longer to the Corpus Doctrinae of Melanchthon; third, that men like Chemnitz, Andreae and Chytraeus should be commissioned to

---

[4] *Vid.* chap. XXX.

[5] For a fuller account of the Swabian Concordia and what followed, *vid.* chap. XXVI.

compose an explanation of all doctrines that had arisen, which were contrary to the Augsburg Confession.

This commission after much deliberation produced the Torgau Book, which became the Bergen Book, or Formula of Concord. Chemnitz, who had been doubtful of the result, said at the end of the deliberations, that the whole matter seemed to him like a dream, since everything that had happened had been so far above his hope and expectation; and the news went throughout all Germany that, after so long a time, the confusion and division had given way to unity.

As a result of these tidings the Elector of Saxony received many letters of protest from Calvinistic princes and from Crypto-Calvinistic sources; and even Queen Elizabeth of England sent over a deputation in the interests of Calvinism not to allow this book to be promulgated. Many Reformed proposed that a common Reformed Confession should be set up over against the Formula of Concord, and that the Reformed should withdraw from their acceptance of the Augsburg Confession; but Ursinus, the author of the Heidelberg Catechism, wrote to Beza to the effect that it would be better to continue to accept the Augsburg Confession (and to agitate against the Formula).

Thus the Formula originated. It came forth after many efforts, as the work of a larger number of men, of more representatives of the Church as a whole, than the Augsburg Confession.

It was the triumph of Luther over Eck and Erasmus, of Protestantism in stable equilibrium over Protestantism in strife, of Faith over reason, of divine Reality over the human idea, of Grace over legality, of consistency over expediency, of honesty over evasion, of principle over politics, of the golden mean over its two extremes, of Christ in His real presence over Christ's image in a spiritual imagination, of the Gospel as a power, over the gospel as a philosophical doctrine.

CHAPTER XXVI.

THE LUTHERAN CONFESSION.

THE FORMULA OF CONCORD.—ITS ORIGIN, BASED ON KOLDE'S INTRODUCTION AND ON THE ARTICLE ON THE FORMULA IN HAUCK.

The Six Controversies and Points at Issue—The Pliant and Scholastic Nature of Melanchthon—The Rise of Calvinism—The Disruption of the Schmalkald League and the Helplessness of the Protestants—The Corpora Doctrinæ—The Efforts of Andreae—The Effort of Chemnitz and Duke Julius—The Effort of Augustus—The Swabian Concordia sent to Augustus by Julius, and the Maulbronn-Formula sent by the South Germans—Recast into the Torgian Formula and the Bergen Book—The Subscription to the Formula.

A NEW Confession was a historical necessity. There was only this one alternative, either to let the division and confusion remain which resulted from the six controversies concerning the Interim and Adiaphora, Major and his doctrine of Good Works, the Antinomia, Westphal and the Lord's Supper and Christology, Osiander and his doctrine of Justification, and Synergism with Pfeffinger on the one extreme and Flacius on the other; or to bring these controversies to an end by a Confessional decision as to the differences of doctrine. With this naturally came the further necessity of rendering the Confessional foundation sure by means of a common Corpus Doctrinae.

THE INNER AND OUTER CAUSES OF THE CONTROVERSIES.

We shall understand the various efforts made toward this

641

final end, and the result itself, the Formula of Concord, if we first of all point out the external and internal causes of the controversies and the resulting confusion. In reality the causes were not only, as is often affirmed, *the theological divergencies of Melanchthon* in the doctrine of the Lord's Supper, of grace, of the church, of the ecclesiastical rights of the government, etc., *or his pliant nature* which constantly yielded to prevailing conditions, and called forth the opposition of those who had long remarked these things and now arose with Luther's word against the Philippists. The final causes lie much deeper and penetrate to the difference between faith, divinely born; and truth, humanly grasped, as ultimate sources of spiritual life.

Luther was universally conceded to be the hero of the Evangelical *faith;* but Melanchthon, the schoolman, was the *preceptor of the church* that was becoming evangelical. In his school the gospel became the *doctrina* evangelii. He coined the evangelical dogma, and also stated it, *many times changing formulation* to no small degree for the sake of perspicuity, *and it was only later* that this habit was found *to involve many contradictions.* And (this is a second important point), *under his influence* the conduct of theological science had entered upon *pathways that were destined to become disastrous.* Above all else, the regular disputations that had been resumed in Wittenberg in 1533 inevitably led to a new scholasticism and actually fostered the tendency to constantly originate new theories by making finer and ever finer distinctions. There is a peculiar tragedy in the fact that *Melanchthon himself* who was always averse to such acuteness of doctrinal statement, did, against his own will and *by his own method,* further the tendency to *spin out* a theological thought *to its very last consequences.*

When Luther died, Melanchthon became in reality the recognized leader. What we actually know, gives us no reason to assume that the number of his opponents, or even of those who regarded his theological development with apprehension, was at all considerable. But his weak conduct in the Interim matter and the controversies arising therefrom, changed the entire state of affairs. Faith in the orthodoxy of Wittenberg was shaken in wide circles, and, while Luther was now emphatically trumped out against Melanchthon, others, too, who heretofore had kept in the background, thought the time had arrived for them to come forth with their own private opinions. Among these the foremost was Andrew Osiander.

To this must be added the gradual rise of the Highland " Richtung," which became more independent under the influence of Calvin, deepened, won great regions of the West and a considerable number of Melanchthonians as adherents, and finally carried the controversy concerning the Lord's Supper into the very mother-country of the Reformation. This in the last instance was to no small degree conditioned by political circumstances.

When the Schmalkald League was disrupted, a bond of ecclesiastical union of no small importance had been severed. It is unquestionably true that from the time of the Interim, to which every little state church accommodated itself in its own way, and after its revocation, in the readjustment to evangelical forms of worship and faith, the specific system of state churches really had its actual beginning. Thus at the same time the self-consciousness of the state clergy grew stronger and with it the consciousness of the right to possess an individual opinion, which of course must be the right one. And the strife between the universities of Jena and Wittenberg, which degenerated into actual hatred, found increasing nourishment in the contention between the two Saxon lines.

These are the internal and external conditions of the theological controversies, and in part, even of the forms in which they were manifested. As old as these causes are the attempts to overcome them. They became more definite and more general after the year 1555. In the religious peace of Augsburg, the Augustana had become the charter of German Protestantism, a real symbol. Now the question arose as to which of the opposing parties had a right to appeal to the Augsburg Confession and thereby possess a claim to the peace of the realm. This called forth the endeavor of the princes, to secure the unity of Protestantism and its chartered existence in some form, by acknowledging the Augustana.

THE EARLIEST EFFORTS OF THE THEOLOGIANS TO SECURE CONCORD.

Already in 1556, Flacius himself had made his " Linde Vorschläge," rejecting the teachings of Zwingli, Osiander and Major, and demanding that those in error should openly retract the same: " Discerning and God-fearing people, to whom religion and pure doctrine are an earnest matter, will understand that it is necessary to act differently in matters of faith than we do in civil transactions, where one often makes amnesty, that is, causes errors to cease by forgetting them, by letting them go, and that by no other milder means can the divisions in the churches be silenced and brought to an end."

The next year Flacius again suggested mediation between Melanchthon and himself. Melanchthon set up as conditions a being united on the whole corpus doctrinae, and an obligation to ignore the controversy concerning the adiaphora; the unity was to be a unity of the confession: " et simus conjuncti ad defensionem verare doctrinae juxta symbola et certam confessionem." The issue of the controversy is here foretold almost prophetically. The Flacians adhered to the demand of an open declaration concerning the adiaphora and the theses of Major. As the rule of the consensus they set the Schmalkald Articles in addition to the Augustana and its Apology. These were all impossible in that they taught Luther's doctrine of the Lord's Supper.

Flacius passed a sleepless night concerning the unrepentance of Melanchthon, but he thought the dog would have to bark sufficiently long to wake up the fox.

The religious Gespräch at Worms brought the differences to a head. The Flacians questioned the right of the Philippists to call upon the Augustana. The princes attempted to restore peace at the Frankfurt Recess, through Melanchthon's Opinion, which finds the pure doctrine in the three chief symbols, the Augsburg Confession and the Apology; and in which Melanchthonian formulas are used in reference to the new obedience and to the Lord's Supper. Unity was to be obtained by means of a censor, who should suppress all religious writings " not found safe by the regularly appointed censor in accordance with the true [Melanchthonian] confession of faith." The Flacians declared this was " binding the mouth of the Holy Ghost."

The idea of securing unity by a General Evangelical Synod was dropped, as new controversies were feared. For, as Brentz said, there was no Elector John the Constant, and no Luther, living any longer. Against the Frankfurt Recess, the Weimar Confutation condemned Philippism (1559), but the Diet of Princes at Naumburg (1561) confirmed the Frankfurt Recess. The Schmalkald Articles were not included by it among the symbols, and the great speaker was the Calvinistic Frederick III. of the Palatinate. Because this Diet evaded a clear Confession concerning the Lord's Supper, the latter was at once brought into prominence as an additional subject of conflict. Many who had been neutral, now joined the Gnesio-Lutherans, believing Luther's doctrine of the sacrament in danger.

And at this point they realized that the Augustana in itself did not offer a sufficient confessional basis. A Convention at Lüneburg asked for a Corpus Doctrinae that, in addition to the Augustana, should also include the Apology, the Schmalkald Articles, Luther's Catechism, and his remaining writings; and that Osiandrists, the Majorists, the

Sacramentarians, the Adiaphorists, and the Synergists should be condemned. This was still in 1561. In Lower Saxony, especially, great stress was laid upon Luther's orthodoxy and upon the right doctrine of the Lord's Supper.

And just at this time John Frederick resolved to break with the radical Flacians. Flacius and Wigand were deposed and exiled. This was in the end of 1561. This new turn of affairs, while causing the Gnesio-Lutheran ideas no longer to be the matter of a single theological party, brought wide recognition for them throughout the church.

The Reformed Church also showed its object far more clearly. Frederick III. went over to Calvinism entirely, and adopted the Heidelberg Catechism in 1563. Electoral Saxony had adopted the Melanchthonian Corpus Doctrinae Christianae. It also was adopted in Hesse and Pomerania, and a number of other territorial churches.

But in the strictly Lutheran countries and cities nothing Melanchthonian except the Augustana and the Apology was adopted. The Corpus Doctrinae of each contained the writings of Luther. Thus each territory now had its norm of doctrine. But the problem was to establish a common Corpus Doctrinae for the whole Lutheran Church of Germany. This problem was solved through the Book of Concord. The Corpus Doctrinae of each territory issued finally into the Book of Concord.

For the single territorial confessions could not dispose of the old conflicts brought on by the Philippistic teachings. The Gnesio-Lutherans were recalled to Ducal-Saxony, and a hot conflict arose with Electoral Saxony on the old subjects. The Colloquium at Altenburg, continuing from October, 1568, to the Spring of 1569, could not restore a good understanding. Everyone recognized the ruinous consequences of conflict, and though efforts to reconcile were made, they did not succeed. There was only one way to restore peace. The source of conflict must be considered, and a solution that would satisfy must be sought. In the nature of the case this could only occur by means of theological formulas, and it could only be executed by having the territorial churches recognize these formulas. It is this fact which gave the Formula of Concord its outer form, and which determined its territorial mode of subscription. ,

The Naumburg Diet of Princes in 1561 and its immediate results, had revealed how unsuccessful such attempts were. Every political organism now went its own way. The introduction by the state churches of their own *corpora doctrinae* and similar standards of doctrine, to protect the doctrinal unity of their *own* State church, at the same time showed more and more clearly the internal disruption of Protestantism as a whole, and its separation into Philippistic and Lutheran State churches.

In the meantime, as we have seen, the idea was pondered of stemming the evil in another way, by setting up a new confession which was to level the differences, and by introducing a *Corpus doctrinae* common to and uniting all evangelical state churches. This thought would not have been possible, had not conditions at the end of the sixth decade begun to change materially. The Gnesio-Lutherans who had to sacrifice their leader Flacius on account of his Manichaizing doctrine of original sin, still maintained their position, but had lost their influence to a great extent and finally died out. The same was true of the Old Melanchthonians. Quite a number of those who had come forth from Melanchthon's school, remembered their Lutheranism when the controversy of the Lord's Supper became a question not between Luther and Melanchthon, but between Luther and Calvin. Among these were the leading theologians of Lower Germany: Martin Chemnitz in Braunschweig (†1586), Nicholas Selnecker, (Superintendent of Wolfenbüttel 1570-1574, professor in Leipzig 1574-1589, and † 1592 in Dresden) and David Chytraeus (professor in Rostock in 1551,† 1600), who, without denying their Melanchthonian training, claimed to be Lutherans.

Above all, it was an important thing that Württemberg under the powerful influence of John Brentz († 1570), through the " Stuttgart Theologians' Confession " of Dec. 19th, 1559, had stated the doctrine of the ubiquity [taught by Brentz, but not taught by the Formula of Concord,'] in such a manner as to bring out the antithesis to Melanchthon still more sharply, had been relatively untouched by the controversy and could thus become the rallying centre of the Lutherans. Accordingly it was a man of the Church of Württemberg who made it his life aim to unite the contending parties. He was employed by his prince in numerous diplomatic and ecclesiastical embassies, was most versatile and much calumniated, and from 1562 on, professor, provost and chancellor in Tübingen. This man was Jacob Andreae.

THE FIRST ATTEMPTS TO UNITE, 1567.

The first new attempt at unity dates from 1567. To draw up a formula of harmony, the Duke Christopher of Württemberg commissioned Jacob Andreae, in consequence of a colloquium with respect to doctrinal differences which he had with the Landgrave William IV. of Hesse Cassel. This formula of confession, laying aside all personalities, in a purely objective way, confined itself to the five controversial articles of justification by faith, good works, free will, adiaphora, and the Lord's Supper. It claimed to be a " Short Elucidation in the form of a Confession, according to which Christian unity may be attained in the churches devoted to the Augsburg Confession, and the scandalous and protracted schism may be ended." [2]

But the situation was not favorable for success. Duke Christopher, who first had broached the idea of such a work

---

[1] *T. E. S.*

[2] " *Bekenntniss und kurze Erklärung* etlicher zweispaltiger Artikel, nach welcher eine christliche Einigkeit in den Kirchen, der Augsb. Konfession zugetan, getroffen und die ärgerliche langwierige Spaltung hingelegt werden möchte."

of concord, died on September 15th, 1568, and Landgrave William of Hesse Cassel to whom Andreae was then obliged to report, proposed to extend the union not only to all the various parts of Germany, but even to the Reformed Churches outside of Germany. Moreover a unity was not to be thought of as long as Philippism reigned supreme in Electoral-Saxony, while the Ducal-Saxon theologians, as was shown at the Altenburg Colloquium, were unbendingly and extremely Lutheran. And when Andreae, in his article on the Lord's Supper, which taught the Lutheran type of doctrine in a moderate manner, without reference to its relation to Christology, gave an "Explanation" to it, in which the consequences of this teaching were extended to the doctrine of the Person of Christ, he came into decided conflict with the Philippists. Both parties suspected him, and the Landgrave of Hesse became still more distant.

THE SECOND ATTEMPT AT UNITY, 1569.

The first attempt in 1567 failed. In 1569, Andreae journeyed to Saxony, but both the theologians at Jena and those at Wittenberg turned him back. On a new journey in 1570, he succeeded at Zerbst in moving the theologians present to a recognition of the first edition of the Augustana as well as the Apology, the Schmalkald Articles, and the Catechisms of Luther as the regulative norms; but he gained all the less by this, since the men of Wittenberg and of Leipzig now formally characterized the Corpus Philippicum as their norm of teaching. In 1571, almost every hope of uniting vanished. Having been impressed with the fact that the Philippists were adverse to all union, and that his attempts at reconciliation only had served to arouse the suspicion of the Lutherans against him, he undertook to give his efforts a different direction. From henceforth he strove to unite all Lutherans against all Philippists and Calvinists.

THE THIRD AND MORE SOUND ATTEMPT AT UNITY.

In 1573 and 1574, the relations of the parties in Saxony, which up to this date were the greatest obstacle in the way of the work of Concord, essentially changed. The decided Lutheran party in Ducal-Saxony (Jena) was split, when, after the death of Duke John William, the Elector Augustus undertook the rule of the Thüringian Province and introduced the Wittenberg type of doctrine by force (1573).

The Philippistic party in Electoral-Saxony, up to now protected by the Elector Augustus, who was not versed in theology and who, despite his ardor against Flacius, never desired to be anything else than "good Lutheran" and, up to this time, never felt any intimation that the Philippistic type of doctrine dominant in his country departed from the Lutheran standard, was at last thrown from its power, when the Philippists, made too bold by their momentary victory, proceeded openly in the prosecution of their plans and could not any longer keep the Elector deceived as to the departure of their doctrine from the Lutheran doctrine (*Exegesis Perspicua,* 1574). Nothing is better fitted to show the impending historical necessity of a final Lutheran confession than just this temporary dominion of Philippism in Electoral-Saxony, which, possible only under the guise of Lutheranism, broke to pieces the moment that that dishonorable guise, hitherto maintained, was torn away.

SIX CHRISTIAN SERMONS.

Already in the year 1573, before the catastrophe in Electoral-Saxony made its appearance, Andreæ, who had been encouraged to further effort by Selnecker's dedication of his "Instituta Religionis Christiana," published "Six Christian Sermons, concerning the divisions among the theologians of the Augsburg Confession, as they arose from the year 1548 up to this present 1573d year, how a plain pastor and a common Christian layman who might be scandalized thereby, might be set right through the catechism." [2]

Freed now from the suspicion that had fallen on him from the extremes of both sides, Andreae undertook to define his position to the controversies in a precise manner. If in his earlier "Confession," he had omitted all controversy on the Person of Christ, he not only made good the mistake this time, but added, in addition, several discussions on the relation, and on the third use of the Law.

The six sermons treated: (1) the righteousness of faith and the essential indwelling righteousness of God; (2) the necessity of good works to salvation; (3) original sin; (4) the free will of man in divine things; (5) church ceremonies which are called adiaphora; (6) the law of God; (7) the distinction between Law and Gospel; (8) the third use of the law; (9) whether good works are necessary; (10) the person and majesty of Christ, the Son of God and the Son of Mary.

He dedicated the sermons to Duke Julius of Brunswick, to whom Andreae had rendered distinguished service in the ordering of ecclesiastical matters in his country. Martin Chemnitz in Brunswick, Joachim Westphal in Hamburg, Chytræus in Rostock received these sermons with favor, and endeavored to obtain recognition for them from various ecclesiastical ministries of Lower Saxony.

The sermonic form which Andreae chose shows us that in his conception the salvation of the church must be found in the *common evangelical Christian* consciousness as it exists *in the catechism,* and not by means of scientific theological investigation. And not only his good Lutheran way of thinking, but also his farsightedness was shown,

---

[2] *"Sechs Christlicher Predig,* Von den Spaltungen, so sich zwischen den Theologen Augspurgischer Confession, von Anno 1548 bis auf diss 1573. Jar. nach und nach erhoben, wie sich ein einfältiger Pfarrer und gemeiner Christlicher Laye, so dardurch verergert sein worden, aus seinem Catechismo darein schicken soll " etc.—Printed entire in H. Heppe, *Geschichte des deutschen Protestantismus* III, Appendix I, pp. 1-75.

when he this time passed the Wittenberg theologians by, awaiting that God "would surely in His own time open the eyes of their Lord the Elector and through him afterward set for them a goal."

Thus Andreae's original plan of uniting the Lutherans and Philippists, which had proved to be Utopian and only heightened the antithesis, was cast aside. A formula was now to be found which would unite all Lutherans and which should be used as a means of conflict against the Philippists and the Calvinists.

The sermons, as we have seen, were favorably received by the Faculties in Tübingen, and in Rostock with Chytræus as its head. But Chemnitz was right in showing Andreae that the sermonic form was hardly adapted to confessional purposes, and a summarizing according to articles in "thesis and antithesis" was called for.[3]

THE SWABIAN CONCORDIA.

Andreae at once agreed with Chemnitz. Thus a new draft was prepared, which was approved by the Tübingen Theologians and the Stuttgart Consistory. This was known as the *"Swabian Concordia."*[4] It contains: 1. Original Sin. 2. Free Will. 3. Justification before God by Faith. 4. Good Works. 5. The Law and the Gospel. 6. The Third Use of the Law. 7. Churchly Usages called Adiaphora. 8. The Lord's Supper. 9. The Person of Christ. 10. Eternal Providence and Election of God. 11. Other Groups and Sects that never accepted the Augsburg Confession. It is important to note that Andreae in the Introduction emphasized the necessity of accepting confessionally those symbols and writings that were afterward received into the Book of Concord.

---

[3] *Cf.* the letter of Duke Julius to Andreæ Oct. 4th, 1573, in H a c h f e l d , *Zeitschr. für hist. Theol.* 1866, p. 231.

[4] It is reproduced in H a c h f e l d , *Zeitsch.*, 1866, pp. 234 sqq.

On March 22nd, 1574, the document was sent to Duke Julius, and Chemnitz endeavored with the authorization of the Duke to win acceptance for it. This resulted in repeated revision by the theologians of Lower Saxony, Chemnitz being the principal agent, and finally in the much more compendious and considerably more theological *"Swabian-Saxon Concordia."* [5] When this was accepted and subscribed by the theologians and pastors in the duchies of Brunswick and Mecklenburg, and the counties of Mansfeld, Hoya and Oldenburg, the Lower-Saxon countries, they regarded the Concordia with Württemberg as sealed. But the Swabians were not at once satisfied with this complete recasting. They objected to the unevenness in style caused by working in the wishes of the individual theologians, the Latin technical terms and the theological and polemic tenor that did not fit into a work intended for the laity. Above all else they feared the arising of new controversies on account of the citations from Melanchthon, who was now approved and now condemned in the document. They would have preferred it if all quotations had been limited to Luther's works. [6]

They had hardly reached the point of official explanations when the events in Saxony gave a new turn to matters. After the appearance of the *Exegesis perspicua controversiae de coena Domini* published by the Silesian physician Joachim Curaeus in 1574, the Elector August became persuaded of the Crypto-Calvinism of his theologians and proceeded very sharply against the Philippists and was now won, for the securing of the orthodoxy of his country, to the thought of a union on a Lutheran basis. In a rescript to his councillors dated Nov. 21st, 1575, [7] he presented his

---

[5] H e p p e as above, III, Appendix, pp. 75-166, the final revision 116-325. H e p p e erroneously takes the first shorter revision for the Swabian Concordia.

[6] This appears from Andreae's Opinion delivered to Prince Elector August of Saxony H u t t e r , *Concordia concors,* fol. 86 sq.

[7] H u t t e r as above, fol. 76.

45

views as to *" whether there might not be a mode by which
we who doctrinally accept the Augsburg Confession might
not in a friendly way get together* and agree that every
prince should appoint several peace-loving theologians, about
three or four in number, and an equal number of political
councillors, and that these gentlemen should convene and
that every one should bring his corpus doctrinæ with him
and then deliver it to all theologians and political councillors in such a manner as to make the Augsburg Confession their guide. Then they should look up in their corpus
doctrinæ, discuss and deliberate how, by the grace of God,
they might make one corpus out of all, to which we might
all subscribe, and this book or corpus doctrinæ should be
printed anew and given in the land of every prince to his
theologians to be guided thereby."

THE MAULBRONN FORMULA.

Even before this, on the suggestion of the Elector, Count
Ernest of Henneberg, Duke Ludwig of Württemberg and
Margrave Charles of Baden requested of the Württemberg
Court-preacher, Lucas Osiander, Provost Balthasar Bidem-
bach in Stuttgart, the Henneberg Court-preacher Abel
Scherdinger and several Badensian theologians an opinion
on the production of a Concordia. Their opinion,[8] delivered
Nov. 14th, 1575, was approved, and Osiander and Bidem-
bach were commissioned to work out a formula of union.
This formula being once more discussed with several Henneberg and Badensian theologians in the Convent of Maulbronn and subscribed, Jan. 19th, 1576, was called the *Maulbronn Formula.*[9]

Here the Swabians avoided all the things which they disliked in the Swabian-Saxon Concordia, such as the Latin
technical terms and the mention of Melanchthon, and con-

---

[8] H u t t e r as above, fol. 89 sq.
[9] Printed by T h . P r e s s e l , *Jahrbücher für deutsche Theologie,* II (1866),
pp. 640 sqq.

fined their quotations to Luther's works. The arrangement of this much briefer confession was essentially different. To express the thought more clearly that the object was to unite the confessors of the Augustana, all heresies equally condemned by the contending parties were excluded, the individual points were arranged in the same order as in the Augustana and before every section was placed the corresponding statement of the Augsburg Confession. Thus the Formula contained the following sections: 1. Original Sin. 2. The Person of Christ. 3. Justification by Faith. 4. The Law and the Gospel. 5. Good works. 6. The Lord's Supper. 7. Of churchly rites or things called Adiaphora. 8. Free Will. 9. The Third Use of the Law of God.

The Saxon Elector received the Maulbronn Formula about the same time as the Swabian-Saxon Concordia sent him by Duke Julius of Brunswick. He asked an opinion on both of Jacob Andreae. Andreae gave the Maulbronn Formula the preference for formal reasons—the substance was the same in both. He was also willing that the Swabian-Saxon should be laid as a basis. There was not much more need of disputing concerning the doctrine in itself "which had been so thoroughly disputed all these years that people doubtless well understood; and that not many misunderstandings occurred any more." Deciding thus for the Maulbronn Formula as the basis of the work of Concordia, he advised at the same time to arrange a convention to which not only theologians from the Electorate of Saxony and from Württemberg were to be invited, but also Chemnitz and Chytræus the principal authors of the Swabian-Saxon Concordia. The Elector interpreted this to be an approval of his own plan and engaged in the matter with great zeal. This gave rise to the danger, under the political constellation of the Empire, of preventing some governments from joining of which it had been expected that they would.

The Duke desired to hold a convention of reputable theologians, and selected Chemnitz and Chytræus from North Germany. Augustus agreed thoroughly to this plan: "Although every authority must now be timid in mingling in among the confused minds of the theologians, nevertheless, as there is no Pope among them, he feels anxious lest it will grow worse and worse in their acts, if the civil authority does not enter into the matter from every side." Therefore the theologians should gather to establish a common Corpus Doctrinæ. Moreover "certain controversial theologians such as Illyricus and others" have died, "the rest are wearied in part with disputing and scolding, so that it will be easier to come to a conclusion." This was true. The younger generation had attained—in so far as they did not follow the recoil of Melanchthon toward Calvin—a certain unified Luther-Melanchthonian view.

THE LICHTENBERG AND TORGAU CONVENTIONS, 1576.

Things went forward. Selnecker had been working in Leipzig since 1574, and through his influence the theologians of the Elector were won in a body at a convention in Lichtenberg in February, 1576; and upon their request Jacob Andreae himself was called to Saxony, and on May 28th (to June 7th) a more general convention of theologians met in Torgau. This was attended by the Saxon theologians led by Selnecker, Andreae and Chytræus and two representatives of the Electorate of Brandenburg, the general superintendent, Andrew Musculus and the Frankfurt professor, Christopher Körner. Here, with the final consent of Andreae, they returned to the Swabian-Saxon Concordia and its divisions, but re-cast it according to the wishes of the Swabians with due consideration of the Maulbronn Formula. The work thus produced, the *"Torgian*[10] *Book,"* contained

---

[10] The title in the manuscript copies reads: "Opinions as to how the divisions among the theologians of the Augsburg Confession may be reconciled and settled by means of God's Word." Compare H e p p e , as above III, 118 ; and the same, *Der Text der Bergischen Concordienformel* &c.

twelve articles, the same that are found in the finally adopted Formula of Concord. The reason for this number of articles was, that in reference to the controversy called forth by Aepinus in Hamburg, a new article entitled Christ's Descent into Hell was inserted as the eighth article.

THE TORGAU BOOK AND ITS CRITICISMS.

With the completion of the Torgau Book an important step forward toward union was taken, and the Elector Augustus exerted himself to the further progress of the work. At his suggestion copies of the Formula were sent to the most of the Evangelical Estates in Germany, with the plea that the same be tested by the Theologians there, and that the result of this test be returned to Dresden. The criticisms that came in, which mostly harmonized with each other, afforded a characteristic picture of the ecclesiastical situation. The Anhalt theologians frankly declared the whole undertaking to be useless: " Why make a confession which is at least ten times more expanded than all the conclusions of the Ancient Church ? " Above all, Luther and Melanchthon dare not be separated. But on the other side there were zealous Lutherans like Heshusius and Wigand in Prussia, who found it difficult to lay down their exceptions against this work of mediation and its author Andreae, and who wanted to insist that the names of the heretics, with Melanchthon at the head, be cited in the Book. On the other hand, there were territorial churches like those of Pomerania and Holstein in which the situation with respect to the divisions in doctrine had not penetrated into the common consciousness and therefore declared that they felt it strange that Melanchthon's authority was not expressly recognized along side of Luther's. They had no idea of deviating from Luther's authority. The same Pomeranian theologians who accepted Melanchthon's authority in this way, declared themselves to be a unit with the Articles of the Torgau Book concerning the Lord's Supper and the Person of Christ; and the same Holstein theologians who denied the necessity of a new Confession (since new ones would eat up the old ones and stir new strife), and took offence at the new treatment of Christology, were in favor that everything that was in their own favorite Corpus Doctrinæ including the Schmalkald Articles, should in future disputation be decided out of Luther's writings along side of the Scripture.

By the end of February, 1577, most of the criticisms concerning the Torgau Book had come in to Dresden, and the Elector Augustus commissioned Andreae, Chemnitz and Selnecker to consider the criticisms and finally edit the work.

THE BERGEN BOOK.

They convened March 1st, 1577, in the convent of Bergen. When still further criticisms were received, further deliberations became necessary. To these Musculus, Körner and Chytræus were also invited.

There could be no mention of a change of the original program which was to give expression to the genuine Lutheran doctrine. They confined themselves to greater precision in some of the dissertations and to meeting ambiguities. Many objections had been made against the great compass of the Formula which made it unfit for a confessional symbol. To satisfy these Andreae had composed—

THE EPITOME.

" *Comprehensive summary* of the articles in controversy among the theologians of the Augsburg Confession, set forth and reconciled in a Christian way, according to God's Word, in the following recapitulation."

Probably this, though afterward revised, was adopted at the first convention in Bergen.

At the last convention toward the end of May, they quickly agreed on the chief part, eventually the second part of the work, *The Solid Declaration:* "Solid [originally "general"] plain and clear repetition and declaration of certain articles of the Augsburg Confession concerning which for some time there has been Controversy among some Theologians who Subscribe thereto, Stated and Settled according to the Analogy of God's Word and the Summary Contents of our Christian Doctrine." The "*Catalogue of Testimonies* of the Holy Scriptures," added first with the caption "Appendix" and later without the same, and which was composed to prove that the Formula of Concord does not teach any new thing on this point, and brought testimony from the Fathers on the Doctrine of the two natures and the *Communicatio Idiomatum,* is a private work of Andreae and Chemnitz. On the 28th of May, 1577, the finished Bergen Book was laid before the Elector Augustus. This is the *Solida Declaratio.*

Thus originated the "*Bergen Book*" or, as the Lutherans usually named it in reference to its object and what it finally became to them, the "*Formula of Concord,*" the result of years of discussion and of many considerations not always of a theological nature, and of the collaboration of many theologians who were animated by the same intention, but only gradually walked the same pathways. That determined its character.

The original thought of laying the Bergen Book before a general convention of the Evangelical estates was regarded as too dangerous. Both the electors of Saxony and Brandenburg undertook to send copies of the Bergen Book first of all to those estates for their approval and signature whose co-operation one could regard as sure.

That the Confession was not accepted on all sides with equal willingness, that those churches which had had a different development of the process of confessing and especially had connected themselves with the later mode of Melanchthon's teaching, in order to maintain the bond of connection with the Calvinistic Reformed Church, should have rejected the Bergian Confession, and thus be pressed to approach the Reformed Confession more closely, is so natural, that one would only be astonished if it were otherwise.

For the very object of the Confession was to establish the genuine doctrine as over against the Melanchthonian divisions. It was a consequence of the leading ecclesiastical conception, that new ecclesiastical separations must also take place, where they remained in disunity in the doctrine.

It is also easily comprehensible that the Formula of Concord would become a rock of offense to all those who believe that a covering over of doctrinal differences which were already existing, and a regarding them with indifference was the right way for the restoration of the peace of the church.

CHAPTER XXVII.

THE LUTHERAN CONFESSION.

THE INTRODUCTION OF THE CONCORDIA, AND THE AUGUSTANA CONSERVED.

Not Introduced by Papal or Imperial Mandate—Sent Forth and Discussed Throughout Germany—None Other so Fully Tested—The Quedlinburg Declaration—A Good Cause not Accountable for the Sins of Individuals—The Signatories not Condemnable—Planck—More Democratic and Unanimous Than Would be Possible in America To-day—No Creed really Œcumenical—No undue Political Influence—The Opinion of Kolde and of Müller—The Extent of the Adoption—Rejected by Calvinistic States—Lutherans Who Failed to Subscribe—The Opinion of Thomasius, Planck and Köllner—The Real Confessional Validity.

THE question of introducing the Formula was difficult. The Augsburg Confession arose out of a historical and heroic occasion, in the midst of popular excitement, and in response to the demand of Pope and Emperor. But Pope and Emperor had no concern for the healing of Protestant, internal dissensions, or for the putting forth of a constructive Declaration of the Lutheran Church's Faith. Popular excitement, too, was lacking, for the people were weary, hopeless, and separated. Yet, it scarcely will be accounted against the Confessional character of the new Confession, that its appearance was not mediated by a mandate of Pope or Emperor;[1] and that it addressed itself, in appealing directly to the people of God—to "those now

---

[1] *Vid.* Chap. XXIX, p. 711.

661

living, and those who shall come after us ",—to the less heroic and more humble, but equally necessary task of probing and rightly binding up the wounds of a weak and helpless Zion.

The Confession was sent forth into every part of Germany, and was discussed and examined by ministers and teachers in Conferences or Synods called for the purpose of testing it. Twenty-five criticisms came in to the theologians who devoted nine days to considering them and details of language. At last, on May 29th, 1577, the six theologians signed the Confession with the following words:

" Therefore, in the sight of God and of the entire Church of Christ, we wish to testify, to those now living and to those who come after us, that the above Declaration . . . and no other is our Faith, Doctrine and Confession, in which we also will appear, by God's grace, with unterrified hearts, before the judgment seat of Christ and for it will give an account. Nor will we utter . . . anything contrary to this Declaration, but, by the help of God's grace, intend to abide thereby. After mature deliberation, we have in God's fear and with the invocation of His name, attached our signatures with our own hands."

That such a great wonder should have been wrought by the grace of God, in bringing into internal concord the conservative evangelical Churches on the basis of the old Augustana was not satisfactory to those without—as little to the Protestant communions closest to the Lutheran Church, as to those who constituted its complete antipode. Those nearest were the loudest to decry the validity of the result.

" The Reformed Count Palatine, John Casimir attempted to hinder the acceptance of the Formula of Concord by seeking, at the instigation of the English Queen, to organize a union of all the Reformed against it (1577 Convention at Frankfurt). The embassador of Queen Elizabeth of England raised energetic objection that several of the German courts must be encouraging separation of the Evangelical churches.

" But in the very nature of things this could not have any success, neither did anything come of the attempt resolved on at Frankfurt to establish a national Reformed confession which should show the unity of the Augustana and the Helvetica.

"Against this on the side of the Lutherans it was sought to do what was possible under the given circumstances to be friendly to the uncertain estates, such as the Elector Louis of the Palatinate, the Landgrave William of Hesse, the Princes Joachim and Ernst of Naumburg, and others, to make them friendly to the work of Concord." [1a]

The Calvinists complained that *a General Council* should have been held before the Concordia was formally accepted. Had this been done, the Calvinists, calling themselves Lutheran, and the Philippists, would have gained an opportunity to stir up new strife.

In reply to the criticism that it was unjust for only six theologians to write a Confession for the whole Church, and that a General Synod should have been held before the signing of the Confession, the Convention at Quedlinburg, in 1583, declared it untrue that the Formula of Concord had been composed by only six theologians, and reminded the critics, how, on the contrary, the articles had first been sent a number of times to all the Lutheran Churches in Germany—how, in order to consider them, Synods and Conferences had been held on every side, and the articles had been thoroughly tested—how criticisms had been made upon them—and how the criticisms had conscientiously been taken in hand by a special commission.

The Quedlinburg Convention therefore declared in its Minutes, that, indeed, " such a frequent revision and testing of the Christian Book of Concord, many times repeated, is

---

[1a] *Hauck Encyc.*

a much greater work, than if a General Synod had been
assembled respecting it, to which every province would
commission two or three theologians, who in the name of
all the rest would have helped to test and approve the book.
Since in that way only *one* Synod would have been held,
for the comparing and testing of this work, but, as it was,
many Synods were held; and it was sent to many provinces
who had it tested by the weighty and mature judgment of
their theologians; in such manner as has never occurred in
the case of any book or any matter of religion since the
beginning of Christianity, as is evident from the history
of the Church."

In planting Christianity,[2] in founding the Church,[3] in
introducing the Confession, the good cause should not be
held responsible for sins of individuals who act against the
spirit and intent of the movement. We are solemnly told
that no one was forced by threats to sign the Formula of
Concord, and that no one was tempted to do so by promises.
We know that no one was taken suddenly by surprise.
Every one was given time to think. As the work of composition extended through years, so several years were given
for the work of signing. Some objection has been lodged
against the means used to secure the completion and assent
to the Book of Concord.[4] There always is a small, narrow
and petty way of looking at historical personages, events
and movements; and there is a large, just and sympathetic
way of making the estimate. It is easy to impugn even the
New Testament by saying that John was vindictive, James
was ambitious, Peter was impetuous, and Paul was narrow
and rabbinic. It is not difficult to find the supposed unworthy motive in the noblest deeds and events that are
chronicled in the annals of human history; and so, it is easy,
after the manner of the historian Planck, to apply the
smaller defects of the principal men in our confessional

[2] John 6:70.
[3] Acts 5: 1-4.
[4] *Cp.* the imputation in footnote of Schaff, *in loco.*

history to their chief actions, and to put the least charitable construction on all their words and deeds.

Our poor human nature, common to all of us in the Church, is so weak, that nothing is done by us which does not seem to bear the stamp of evil upon it. But to point out these stains is not to justify or condemn an act. If it were, all ecclesiastical action and writing must cease or be condemned even in the saints of this latter day.

It may be regarded as reasonably certain that not all the vain-glorious men, nor all the party-workers, who prefer their own organization and name to the cause of the truth, nor all the pugnacious men, nor all the narrow-minded men, nor all the men of religious deadness and theological fury, lived in the Sixteenth Century. Nor are all those to whom such a despicable character can justly be attributed, to be found in the Lutheran Church of that Century, as little as all the true saints were to be found within the borders of Lutheranism, and all the doubtful saints were to be looked for in Geneva or Rome. There was a deep piety of many in Rome, and in the Reformed Churches, and of many also in the Lutheran Church. Perhaps the piety and honesty of the old and the mediating Lutherans in that century, would compare favorably with that of the two schools of to-day. That there are the impious, at least those who are not models, in both schools, in both ages, must be admitted. The question before us then is not to be decided by looking at the weak human nature on any side, but by an examination of the principles beneath it.

If some were coerced into signing the Book of Concord by moral suasion, or otherwise, it is at least a fact that there were many more who were not thus coerced. If there was some bitter feeling on both sides in the Sixteenth Century, surely there has also been some bitter feeling on both sides in the Nineteenth Century, in time of confessional activity and excitement. If the Concordia was not universally accepted, let it never be forgotten, that this very thing was also the case with every other creed in Christendom; and that it became more conspicuous in the case of the Formula, because of the greater pains taken to secure the approbation of every individual in truly democratic manner.

Had the Elector Augustus and a few other statesmen signed it, as was done in the case of the Confession of Augsburg; though they might not have been able to cause the clergy under them to obey so readily as occurred after the signing at Augsburg, the clergy being now more enlightened, the question of improper subscription could not have been raised. A moment's thought should convince every reasonable mind that the average human nature of the day will probably control the average securing and signing of documents. We very much doubt whether the Lutheran Church to-day could secure any democratic subscription so clean, so conscientious, so united, or so large, as that which was given to the Book of Concord.

It would require the name of every Lutheran clergyman in North America, secured without undue influence, to gain such a result. And when we consider the nature of Twentieth-Century Lutheranism, and how many nominal Lutherans, on the ground of personal liberty, or because they do not deem united effort necessary, or from indifference, would fail to append their signatures to a document; and, on the other hand, how many otherwise excellent Christians think so little of their signature in our day that they will sign any paper presented to them, we may feel sure that no new creed of the Church to-day could be so unanimously and yet so genuinely accepted.

No Creed of the Church, in any age, has ever been unanimously accepted. The Apostles' Creed was not universally accepted; and its final prevalence was not entirely apart from political movement—Harnack would say, was due to political movement—in the Church. If the history of the Nicene Creed were entered into in detail, it would reveal conditions in the Church beside which those surrounding the Formula of Concord were heavenly. The same may be said of the Athanasian Creed. Neither the Apostles', nor the Athanasian Creed is really œcumenical. Neither of them was known to the Greek or Oriental Church, which abode faithful to the faith "settled by the Holy Fathers at Nicaea."[5] And can we say that the conditions surrounding the composition of the Augsburg Confession were ideal? The chapter in this book on Melanchthon as a diplomat and the one on the Melanchthonian Principle will answer the question.

The churches were not given an opportunity to discuss the Augsburg Confession, as they discussed the Book of Concord. What the result at Augsburg would have been if the personality of Luther had not been standing in the background, and the Church had been torn by dissensions, and every article had had to be canvassed and agreed on in advance by all the churches, no man can forsee.

That the Confession of Augsburg achieved so much, is a glorious tribute to the confessional truth in it. And the same is true of the Formula of Concord. If the Formula had not embodied the Confessional Principle of the Church, the real development of the inner nature of Lutheranism stated in Confessional manner, it would not have been accepted in the wonderful way it was, and amid the bafflings and discouragements of the period, and would not have achieved what it did.

Where religion is introduced and upheld by political

---

[5] *Cp.* Principal John Tulloch of St. Andrews: "Of all Christian creeds, the Nicene, or Niceno-Constantinopolitan, is the only real œcumenical creed, deliberately discussed and adopted by the representatives of the universal Church. The two others associated with it in the services of the Western Church have not only never had acceptance beyond the range of that church, but are very gradual *growths* within it, without any definite parentage or deliberate and consultative authority. They emerge gradually during many centuries from the confusions and variations of Christian opinion, slowly crystallizing into definite shape; and such authority as belongs to them is neither primitive nor patristic. It is the reflected assent of the later church in the West, and the uncritical patronage of a comparatively ignorant age, which have alone elevated them to the same position as the faith defined at Nicaea, which is the only truly Catholic, or universal, symbol of the universal church."

authority, as it was on all sides in the days of the Reformation, with the consent of both Luther and Melanchthon, and of all parties, since none knew any better, and the principle of individual Protestant freedom of conscience had not worked itself out into the State as it has to-day,[6] it is almost inevitable that religious measures will to some extent, at least indirectly, be affected by political authority.

If political authority was permitted to show itself in behalf of the Formula of Concord, as also had been the case for and against the Augsburg and the other Protestant Sixteenth-Century Confessions, it is to be regretted; yet it does not invalidate, nor necessarily tarnish the Confession as such. Neither did it really contribute, we may be sure, to the actual influence of the Formula.

" To persecute errorists, is only another mode of disseminating and strengthening their cause. It gives them importance; it excites sympathy in their behalf; and whilst it may reclaim the timid, it makes others ten-fold more firm and active. Nor was the effect to be different in the cases of those princes and rulers who employed severe and bloody measures against the Crypto-Calvinists and others three hundred years ago. When carried so far by theological disputes as to behead Horst and Funk, imprison John Frederick, quarter Grumbach and Brück, hang their adherents, confine Peucer in a loathsome dungeon, banish Rüdiger, Crell, Wiedebram, Cruciger, Pegel, and Moller, and to commit other deeds of violence against dissenters, no wonder that confidence was destroyed, hearts alienated, and multitudes driven to array themselves under another standard. And yet, such was the stormy aspect of things years before the Form of Concord was written.

" It was not the Form of Concord that originated these scenes of strife, bitterness, and blood. On the contrary, this

---

[6] Yet the German emperor would even to-day be pleased to unite church and state more closely in a national religion, on the basis of a national Germanic " Union."

new and valuable symbol, naturally and necessarily, grew out of these lamentable religious disturbances. It was framed with reference to their settlement. It was designed, as its name imports, to bind-together the distracted church, to cast oil upon the troubled waters, and to save the precious ark of God from being dashed into irrecoverable fragments. It was for this that Augustus and his coadjutors instituted measures to bring it into being. It was for this, that it was submitted to the church for examination and criticism before its completion. It was for this that Chemnitz, and Andreae, and Selnecker labored upon it with so much assiduity and prayer. And it was for this that it was at once acknowledged and subscribed by three electors, twenty princes, twenty-four earls, the lords of the four free cities, thirty-eight members of the Diet, and about eight thousand office-bearers in the churches and schools." [6a]

So little was there thought of using force [7] that those who showed that they believed otherwise were not allowed to subscribe. Andreae himself testified: " I can truly say that no man has been forced to sign, nor has been driven away on this account." [8] In Berlin, the commission found two hundred ministers assembled. The Formula was read word by word. Criticisms were heard and explained, and finally all were agreed to it, so that the president of the Commission thanked God for the true doctrine thus given, and the whole assembly cried "Amen."

We believe no instance is known in which it is of record that compulsion was used to secure the adoption of the Formula. Doubtless moral suasion of a sort that men use to-day in getting out votes on what they deem to be the right side, was busy then as now. It is possible that official zeal may in instances have used political persuasion;

[6a] *The Evangelical Review.*

[7] As even Dr. Schaff admits. *Vid.* footnote 9 in this chapter.

[8] *Vid.* Müller, *Symb. Bücher, Einleit.* CVII.

46

and that there may be some weight in Hutter's inference from the arrangement of the signatures.

But after due allowance for such possibilities, the great fact that is decisive is that the Formula was adopted by an overwhelming part of the Church, and that the bulk of these signatures were given with heart and soul. As over against Planck's prejudiced assertion that the general reception of the Formula was obtained " by actual compulsion," let us plance the balanced historical verdict of Kolde:—

" Naturally enough, the churches leaning toward Calvin allied themselves more closely to each other over against a formula which excluded them. Every formula of union, like every confessional symbol, has ever had a separating influence.

" It was not to be wondered at if many hesitated, especially in Saxony [the seat of Melanchthon's strength], and that the electoral commissaries, who traveled from place to place, experienced many objections and had to quiet many misgivings. It can not be denied that the desire of the ruler of the land played its part in influencing them. . . . But on the other hand the influence of the ruler must not be estimated at too high a rate, as many of the opponents of the Book of Concord have endeavored to do. Among other reasons, this fact is borne out by the addition to the signatures 'cum ore et cordo', which occurs with great frequency." [8a]

To this may be added the older words of Mueller in his Introduction to the Symbols:—

" The oft repeated offences and reproaches of this Symbol, were listened to and corrected, with moderation and patience. Time was allowed to every one to consider. Indeed each one was admonished, in the name of the Elector, not to subscribe against his conscience. And, although Hutter contends that many subscribed it reluctantly, it is a

---

[8a] Close of Kolde's *Introduction to the Formula.*

mere conjecture drawn simply from the arrangement of the signatures, which is no proof that the signatures themselves were obtained by force. Andreae confidently asserts, at the convention of Herzberg, in 1578, 'I am able to declare most truly, that no man was compelled to give his signature, nor subjected to any undue influence. If this is not true, the Son of God has not redeemed me with His blood.' In consequence of this declaration, the opponents were challenged to name but one who had been compelled to subscribe, and they were unable to do it; on the other hand, it was acknowledged by the theologians of Nuremberg themselves, who rejected the Form of Concord, that the signatures were obtained without compulsion."

Turning now from the mode and the heartiness, to the territorial extent of the subscription, we find that, with a few exceptions to be immediately referred to and explained, the adoption of the Formula covers the greater part of the imperial Protestant territories.[9]

It was adopted in the three Electorates of Saxony, the Palatinate, and Brandenburg; the Duchies of Prussia, Wuertemberg and Mecklenburg; the Margravates of Kulmbach, Baireuth, Ansbach and Baden; also in the Upper Palatinate, Neuburg and Sulzbach; in the Principalities of Brunswick and Lüneburg, in Thüringia, Koburg and Weimar, in Mömpelgard; in the regions of Magdeburg, Meissen, and Quedlinburg; in the earldoms of Henneberg,

---

[9] Schaff, in his *Creeds of Christendom* I, p. 331, note 3, says: "It was adopted by the majority of the Lutheran principalities and state Churches in Germany; also by the state church of Sweden, the Lutherans in Hungary, and several Lutheran synods in the United States. On the other hand, it was rejected by a number of Lutheran princes." In a footnote, Schaff continues: "The Preface of the Book of Concord is signed by eighty-six names representing the Lutheran state churches in the German empire; among them are three Electors (Louis of the Palatinate, Augustus of Saxony, and John George of Brandenburg), twenty Dukes and Princes, twenty-four Counts, thirty-five burgomasters and counsellors of imperial cities. The Formula was also signed by about 8000 pastors and teachers under their jurisdiction, including a large number of ex-Philippists and Crypto-Calvinists, who preferred their livings to their theology; hence Hutter was no doubt right when he admitted that many subscribed *mala conscientia.* Yet no *direct* compulsion seems to have been used. See Köllner, p. 551, and Johannsen, *Ueber die Unterschriften des Concordienbuches,* in Niedner's *Zeitschrift für histor. Theologie,* 1847, No. 1."

Oettingen, Castell, Mansfeld, Hanau, Hohenlohe, Barby, Gleichen, Oldenburg, Hoya, Eberstein, Limburg, Schönburg, Löwenstein, Reinstein, Stolberg, Schwarzburg, Leiningen, and others. Also in the cities of Lübeck, Hamburg, Lüneburg, Regensburg, Augsburg, Ulm, Biberach, Esslingen, Landau, Hagenau, Rothenburg, Goslar, Mühlhausen, Reutlingen, Nördlingen, Halle, Memmingen, Hildesheim, Hannover, Göttingen, Erfurth, Einbeck, Schweinfurt, Brunswick, Münster, Heilbronn, Lindau, Donauwörth, Wimpfen, Gingen, Bopfingen, Aalen, Kaufbeuern, Kempten, Issny, Leutkirch, Hameln, and Nordheim. To these' subsequently have been added, Lauenburg of Saxony, Holstein, Pomerania, Krain, Kärnthen, Steiermark, and Hungary. And even in Denmark, where it was once forbidden on pain of death, it soon obtained a high authority, and was really used as a symbol though not officially acknowledged as such. It was also accepted in Pomerania and Hörnia.

By June 1580, when the Fiftieth Anniversary of the Augsburg Confession was celebrated with a great festival, eighty-five Stände had signed it, and three years later the number ran up to ninety-six. Sweden accepted the teaching of the Formula in 1593 in the Council of Uppsala, and the Formula in 1647-1663. Hungary adopted it in 1597.

We already have alluded to the fact that a united general subscription to any new confessional document is not to be thought of in America to-day;[10] and that many who approved all the principles of a document would, for various reasons, fail to sign it. This happened to some extent in the case of the Formula. Of those who rejected the Formula, first come those few states, which did so for real confessional reasons, and which were not Lutheran at all in their convictions, but Calvinistic; and of which it was the intention of the Formula, for the sake of truth and peace, to rid the Lutheran Church. This was the disturbing element in

---

[10] *Cp.* the debates of Inter-Synodical Conferences.

the Church, an element which belonged elsewhere, and which the Formula of Concord placed elsewhere. " It was not a loss, but a riddance; not a dismemberment, but a superior consolidation, which the Church effected by this proceeding."[11] These Calvinist Lutherans comprised Anhalt, Lower Hesse and Bremen. They did the right thing in withholding their signatures. Zweibrücken and Anhalt went over bodily to the Reformed Church in 1588, and Hesse followed in 1604. The Palatinate with Louis as ruler, favored the Concordia, but Louis died in 1583, and then his successor Casimir introduced the Reformed Faith.

In Denmark, which had been free from controversy, the Formula had a curious fate. The wife of Augustus of Saxony, it is said, sent her brother Frederick II. a handsomely bound copy of the Formula; but inspired by some of his theologians, who were Philippists or Crypto-Calvinists, Frederick not only threw the book into the fire without reading it or having it read by his theologians; but he issued an edict on July 24th, forbidding anyone to bring a copy of the book into the kingdom, on penalty of execution and confiscation of property. Thus the legal suasion of the ruler, so common in that day, was not on any one side of the question. Ministers and teachers were to be deposed from office if they were convicted of harboring a copy in their houses. Yet the Formula " came to be regarded in Denmark with the highest reverence; and, in fact, if not in form, became a Symbol of the Danish Church."

Then we reach Brunswick, whose Duke Julius was most active in behalf of the Book of Concord in its initial stages, and whose Corpus Julium embraced everyone of the Symbolical books but the Formula, and who had failed to sign it for personal reasons.[12]

---

[11] *Sciss.*

[12] He was greatly offended at Chemnitz for having rebuked him, because he allowed his son to enter the Roman priesthood. Thus Julius was animated by a very " practical " reason for being more " liberal " than the Formula.

The Brunswick theologians do not object to the article on the Lord's Supper in the Formula, but they desire that the 'absolute ubiquity' be not asserted (August 15th, 1576) ; and they desire a General Synod to inquire, since the communication is applied by many to the first genus, and the others are excluded, whether the term was used as a " commune genus " under which all three were embraced, with a special definition and appellation attributed to each one. But some of the Brunswick theologians, with divines from Goslar, Göttingen, and Hannover in lower Saxony, ventured to declare :—

" We have discovered that, nearly throughout, the Formula is word for word, what was before this, a year ago, decided in these churches, and unanimously approved, except some small additions made in the conference at Torgau, which were properly added for elucidation from Luther's writings, and we declare that in the churches we maintain the doctrines in regard to controverted articles as they are set forth in this Formula, and therefore coincide with, and are satisfied with this Formula ; it is our purpose too, by the help of God, to adhere to the form of doctrine, and are resolved not merely in our ministry, but before our Christian magistrates so to uphold them, that not only in churches and schools, with the present generation they may be received, but that this deposit may be transferred to posterity."

Thus it came about that in that part of Brunswick, whose Confessional symbol was the Wilhelminum, the Book of Concord and the Corpus were both received as symbolical.

As Chemnitz had offended Julius in Brunswick, so Andreae had given offence [13] to Paul von Eitzen. Holstein therefore reports that it does not feel the need of a new symbol " because all the controverted articles dealt with in

---

[13] *Vid.* Löscher *Historia motuum,* III, p. 262 ; Walch, *Einlt. in d. Rel. Strtgktn. d. ev. L. Kirche,* IV, p. 450 ; *Planck,* 494 ; and Hutter, *Concordia Concors.*

the new Formula are clearly explained in the old symbols."
To show that its faith is the same as that of the Formula,
it offers its formula of ordination as follows:—

"I swear fourthly, and particularly, that the words of my Lord and Saviour,
Jesus Christ, in his Holy Supper and Testament, namely, 'This is my body which
was given for you, this is my blood of the New Testament which was shed for you
and for many, for the forgiveness of sins,' I hold and believe truly in the simple
true sense of the plain words, namely : that the true actual body of my Saviour,
Jesus Christ, Who gave himself to death for me on the cross ; and the true actual
blood of Christ, my Saviour, which was shed for me, is truly present in the Lord's
Supper, and is really distributed in every part of the world, where the Lord's
Supper is administered according to the institution of Christ and is received by all
who go to the Lord's table, as the Lord's words express. As this doctrine of the
Holy Sacrament is explained in the Augsburg Confession, the Apology, the
Schmalkald Articles, and the two Catechisms of our holy Father and Teacher, Luther, which Confession and writings, I hold and believe in this article, rightly and
truly, and obligate myself, by this, my oath, by the help and grace of God, to
present to my congregation the same true simple doctrine of the Lord's Supper,
without perversion and change, and to teach it till my death. Sixthly, and
specially, I hold and declare that the doctrine of the Anabaptists, and the per-
verters of the Sacrament, Carlstadtians, Zwinglians, Calvinists, Bezaites, or by whatever name they are, or may be called—in opposition to the necessity and power of holy
baptism, and against the true presence, distribution and reception of the true actual
body and blood of Christ in the Holy Supper, wherever it is properly administered throughout the church, according to the institution of Christ—is wrong,
false, untrue and deceptive. But I will help to uphold and to propagate, by the
grace of God, and the Spirit's aid, the unchangeable, true doctrine and faith concerning the truth and Omnipotence of our Lord Jesus Christ, and the inseparable
union of His divine and human natures in the one undivided Person of Christ,
and the true actual presence of the true body and blood of Christ in the Holy
Supper."

The Pomeranians, finally, who were mainly concerned
about the defence of their Corpus Doctrinæ, started a difficulty in regard to the article on conversion, which grew out
of a misapprehension,[14] but professed themselves satisfied
with the article on the Lord's Supper and the Person of
Christ; only they desired a *very copious* exposition, as they
belonged to the most decided friends and defenders of

---

[14] *Cp.* J. G. Walch, *loc. cit.*

church orthodoxy. The Pomeranian Church Order of the
year 1563, confesses:—

"In regard to the Lord's Supper it should be taught harmoniously, that we
receive in it the true body and blood of our Lord Jesus Christ with the bread and
wine, and that the Lord Jesus Christ is present in the Sacrament, not merely with
His grace, spirit and power, but really with His body and blood, as the words of
Christ express: 'This is my body, this is my blood,' which believers receive to
life and the unworthy and impenitent to condemnation."

Further, the Pomeranians in the year 1593 assumed the
three articles of the Formula of Concord— in respect to
the Lord's Supper, the Person of Christ, and the election
of grace—as their standard in the controversies with the
Reformed; and signed the whole, at a later period.

In Holstein, and in the cities of Magdeburg and Frankfurt-on-the-Main and Nuremberg, some of the Philippists,
who were not pleased with the Formula because the Melanchthonian errors were rejected in it, opposed its introduction. These cities, with Strasburg, Spires, Worms and
Bremen, felt hurt that they had not been asked at the
start to participate in the work, and failed to sign, though
most of them testified that they were at one in the faith
of the Book of Concord.[15]

As in Pomerania and Holstein, the Hesse-Cassel theologians are not satisfied with the Formula as a Confession.
They say: "Our churches do not teach otherwise . . .
than that, in the true use of His Supper, together with the
bread and the wine [is] the true, essential, present body
of Christ . . . not nevertheless . . . in an external
natural, but in an internal mode comprehensible to faith
alone, by worthy and unworthy equally, by the worthy indeed in the confirmation of faith, and thus to their salvation; but to the unworthy to their judgment."

It was Crypto-Calvinism that kept part of Schleswig, especially the principalities of Liegnitz, Brieg and Wohlau;

---

[15] Müller, *Einleit.*, p. **CX.**

also Hesse-Cassel, Zweibrücken, Nassau, Bentheim, Tecklenburg and Solms, from signing. On the other hand, the Roman Catholic government in the Duchies of Cleve and Berg, in the earldoms of Mark and Ravensberg, in the Principality of Halberstadt, in Osnabrück, in the region of Ortenburg, in Austria (in the beginning), in Bohemia, and in part of Schleswig and Lausitz, prevented the pastors and schoolteachers from signing.[16]

This then is the remarkable fact, that the greater part of those Lutheran magistracies that declined to sign the Formula were satisfied with its doctrine, and with its conformity to the older Confessions.[17]

These objectors concurred with Luther against the doctrine of synergism and in that of the Lord's Supper; though in some cases the conception of the doctrine of the Person of Christ appeared too subtle to them, and in others there was dissatisfaction that several Melanchthonian expressions had not been retained. Still others considered an additional Confession unnecessary. Others again declined, partly from wounded pride, and partly because, though they themselves were favorable to the doctrine of the Formula, yet their leaders were Calvinistic.

This is the conclusion of Kolde (see close of Chapter XXVI); and also of such widely differing investigators as Thomasius, Planck and Köllner. Says Thomasius:—

" To this candid judgment, we annex that of one of the most determined opponents, Planck, who took pains to exercise impartiality towards all except the Lutherans, who poured contempt and sarcasm on the entire work of pacification, and knew how to place it in the most unfavorable light; this historian feels himself compelled to acknowledge, ' It is almost beyond controversy, that in the Formula, in every controverted doctrine, precisely the view was intro-

---

[16] Müller, *Einleit.,* p. CIX.

[17] Köllner, *Die Symb. der Luth. Kirch.,* Hamburg, 1837, pp. 556, 573.

duced and sanctioned, which was most clearly sustained by the Augsburg Confession, by the Apology for it, by the Schmalkald Articles, and by the Catechisms of Luther. At most, the article in regard to the Person of Christ alone admitted of plausible doubt, whether it was presented in the Formula as it had been in those writings; but even here it was not very difficult, by a succession of deductions, to prove that it was involved in them. (*Protest. Lehrbegr.,* vi, 697).'

"Little as we approve of the manner in which Planck expresses himself, we wished to direct attention to this acknowledgment, particularly with a reference to those who regard him as the highest authority when he treats so slightingly, the Formula of Concord."[18]

"The symbolical authority of the Formula of Concord for the Lutheran Church, as such," says Köllner, "can hardly be doubted. By far the largest part of those who regarded themselves as belonging to the Lutheran Church received it as their Symbol. And as, to use the words of the Elector Augustus, we have no Pope among us, can there be any other mode of sanctioning a Symbol than by a majority? To this is to be added, and should be especially noted, that the larger part of those who did not receive it, objected to doing so, not on doctrinal grounds, but partly for political reasons, freely or compulsorily, as the case might be, partly out of attachment to Melanchthon, partly out of a morbid vanity, because they had not been invited early enough to take part in framing the Concordia, and had consequently not participated in it, and partly because, in one land, those who had the most influence were Calvinistically inclined, although a large majority of the clergy approved of the doctrines of the Formula."[19]

We have dwelt on the fact of this heavy majority vote in favor of the Formula, in reply to criticisms that the

---

[18] *Thomasius Trans.* in *Ev. Rev.,* II, 218 sqq.

[19] *Köllner,* p. 575 (Trans. by *Philip Krauth*).

Formula is not a Lutheran Confession because it was not adopted universally in the Church. We have tried to show how impressive was the extent of its adoption; and how, if it were a question to be decided by majorities,[20] its adoption could be regarded as almost overwhelming. But it must not be forgotten that a Confession can never become a symbol of the Church by a majority vote. The Confessional principle is one of conscience, and the conscience of the minority is not to be overruled by that of the majority.

Still further, the Confessional principle is the truth of Scripture; and agreement in it is not to be reached by a majority, or even by a unanimous vote. The Confession of the Lutheran Church is what it is, not because Lutherans have agreed to make it so, but because Scripture has made it so. The Lutheran Confession cannot be altered, modified or abrogated by any part or by the whole of the Lutheran Church in any age or any country. " If all our general bodies, . . . were to unite in a unanimous rejection of some distinctive feature of the Lutheran Church of the Reformation period, they could not change the faith and confession of the Lutheran Church, but would simply demonstrate that, in such action, these bodies were no longer Lutheran, but had broken with the unity of the Lutheran Church." [21]

What we have, therefore, discussed here is simply the historical question of the extent of the adoption of the Formula of Concord, and not the supposition that that extent could become the determinative of its validity. If the Formula really embodied the Lutheran principle, and yet failed of a majority adoption, it would nevertheless be a true Confession of Lutheranism, especially for those who confessed it.

The effect of the introduction of the Formula is impor-

---

[20] The Thirty-nine Articles are not on the same plane as the Lutheran Confessions. The *mandate enjoining subscription to the former was granted by the King*.

[21] Jacobs, in *Distinctive Doctrines,* pp. 95-96.

tant.   It separated out the non-Lutheran elements from the Lutheran Church.   It disposed of the vague position of the Philippists; and because they were obliged to decide either for or against a clear-cut confession, it precluded the misunderstandings and bitter controversies of the past within the Church.   It thus solidified the Church, and prevented its disintegration.

CHAPTER XXVIII.

THE LUTHERAN CONFESSION.

IS THE FORMULA OF CONCORD A CONFESSION?

Who Made the Negative Reply?—Zwinglians, Calvinists, Roman Catholics, Philippists, Church of England, and Eighteenth Century Rationalists—Objections Usually Offered—The Answer to Our Own Times : The Formula Does Not Throttle the Freedom of the Twentieth Century—The Answer of History : The Formula is a Confession Historically—The Answer to the Objection of Multiplicity, and that the Augsburg Confession is Sufficient : Has the Latter Sufficed, and the Former Multiplied the Confessions of the Church?

THE testimony in the preceding chapters of this book has gradually been leading up to one question: Is the Formula of Concord a true Confession? A negative reply was sounded loudly from the beginning, by Ursinus,[1] the pupil and friend of Melanchthon, and the friend of Calvin, by the Philippists,[2] by Roman Catholics,[3] later on, conjointly by Zwinglians and Calvinists—and by Hospinian[4]

---

[1] *Admonitio Christiana de libro Concordiæ*, 1581.

[2] *The Anhalt Opinion*, 1581 ; *Reply of the Bremen Preachers*, 1581 ; Irenæus, *Examen*, 1581 ; Ambrose Wolff, *History of the Augsburg Confession.*

[3] Cardinal Bellarmin, *Judgment on the Book of Concord*, Cologne, 1589 (*Controversies*, IV).

[4] Beza, *Refutatio dogmatis de ficticia carnis Christi omnipræsentia.* Rud. Hospinian, *Concordia Discors* (Zurich, 1607).—This bitter polemic was preceded by a folio in 1602, *De origine et Progressu Controversiæ Sacramentariæ de Cœna Domini inter Lutheranos, Ubiquistas et Orthodoxas quas Zwinglianos seu Calvinistas vocant* which readers will not find overflowing with love for the Lutherans ; and was followed by his *Sacræ Scripturæ, orthodoxis symbolis, toti antiquitati puriori, et ipsi etiam Augustanæ Confessioni repugnantia*, in 1609. This work introduced heavy controversy. Hospinian was answered by Hutter, from Wittenberg in 1614, in the folio, *Concordia Concors.* H. L. J. Heppe, *Geschichte der lutherischen Concordienformel und Concordie;* also the latter's *Die Entstehung und Fortbildung des Luthertums und die kirchlichen Bekenntniss-Schriften desselben von 1548-1576*, Cassel, 1863.

especially,—by the Church of England people,[5] and then still further re-echoed by both Synergistic, Pelagian and rationalist historians and symbolical writers;[6] and has, in these latter times, been ringing again in the ears of the Church. It declares in substance: "The Formula of Concord is a theological form, a dogmatic treatise, a commentary, the shibboleth of an extreme party, but it is not a Confession!"

OBJECTIONS TO THE FORMULA.

When we ask the reasons assigned for excluding the Formula from a Confessional position, we find many. The Concordia is not a true Confession, it has been said, because it fixes doctrine in a scholastic frame, and therefore constricts the truth. The Lutheran Church is a Church of freedom and of progress. The Word of God in the Church can not be bound, especially not in this Twentieth Century. The world has learned to look to development rather than to dogma.

In the second place, the Formula is not a true Confession, it is said, because the doctrine which it teaches of the ability of Christ to be omnipresent in His human nature is so unscriptural and (what is more to the objector) so incredible to human reason, that it cannot be true.

More than this, the Concordia is not unanimously regarded as a Confession of the Lutheran Church, and large parts of the Church ignore or repudiate it. And, after all, the Augsburg Confession is the one great Confession of the Church, and is sufficient for its confessional needs. The tendency to multiply symbolical writings should be discouraged. The Formula has added greatly and unneces-

---

[5] Queen Elizabeth of England sent embassadors to the Elector Augustus and several of the Evangelical Estates, to head off what she supposed would be a condemnation of the English Church; and also delegates to the Reformed Convention at Frankfurt-on-the-Main in 1577.

[6] G. J. Planck, *Geschichte der Entstehung . . . unseres Prot. Lehrbegriffs . . . bis zur Einführung der Concordienformel*, Leipz. 1791-1800. *Cp.* also such writers as Mosheim and Gieseler.

sarily to the bulk of our Confessions. In creeds, as in all other axioms, the rule of paucity should prevail.

Still further, the Formula is no Confession because there was no sufficient Providential stress, no trying inner need, and no outer crisis at hand, sufficiently grave to justify its appearance; and the means used to gain subscription to it, were not such as the Church can approve.

Finally, objection is made to the use of the Formula of Concord as a Confession of the Church because it does not really present Lutheran doctrine in its broadest extent, for Melanchthon and the Melanchthonians were slighted in it. It is claimed also that the subjects distinctively treated in it are not properly Confessional subjects; that the points of difference which it touches are too fine and hairsplitting to be a part of the Evangelical faith; that the method which it employs is too Romanistic and too scholastic. And it is suggested, in general, that the Sixteenth-Century spirit of theology which it breathes is not suitable for the Confessional use of the Church to-day.

THE ENLIGHTENMENT OF THE AGE.

Dwelling for a moment on the last of these objections, no one can deny that during the past two hundred and fifty years the human mind has been exceedingly active. More discoveries and more thorough investigations of every department of science were made in the Nineteenth Century than in all the ages that preceded it. The confining bonds of the traditional knowledge that has been handed down to us from the ancients have been broken, and we are living in a new era of thought and life.

But we are not living in a new era of revelation from God. If we believe that the full Gospel has been revealed and preserved to us in the Scripture, we must admit that the progress of humanity does not apply to the content of our faith, no matter how much it may be possible to make improvement in form. With J. A. Seiss we exclaim, " We should like to know who has invented *improvements* on Christianity! "[7]

" Have we really," said Charles F. Schaeffer, "made such progress in the discovery of truth since the era of the Reformation, that we understand the Scriptures more thoroughly than those who framed the Symbolical Books? When Luther and his associates were prepared to surrender their lives, but not the doctrines of the Augsburg Confession, the Apology, the Schmalkald Articles, and the Catechism, had these men of faith and prayer discovered treasures of divine truth of less extent and less value than we possess in modern times? When the Elector Augustus with holy fervor prayed to God that the authors of the Concord-Formula might be guided by the Divine Spirit in the preparation of that admirable work, was his prayer for the illumination of the Spirit less efficacious than modern prayers are? If the writers of the Symbols were unworthy of regard, or are erroneous in their exhibition of truth, who are the men that are more competent to unfold the Scriptural doctrine? What palliating features have they discovered in man's corruption, in more recent times? What useful changes do they suggest in the doctrine of the atonement? What improvement do they propose in our old doctrine of justification by faith? What more ready access to the throne of grace have they discovered? Are we wiser, more holy, richer in divine grace, more useful through the inspiration of the 'spirit of the times' than our pious fathers were? We are weary of the superior intelligence of the Nineteenth Century in matters of Christian faith."[8]

The content of God's Word to man, and of man's saving faith in Christ, does not change; but, like Christ, it is

---

[7] *Ev. Rev.*, IV, p. 20.

[8] *Ib.*, I, p. 482.

"the same yesterday, to-day, and forever." [9] And even the sound old forms, in so far as they embody the true development of the Church in its witness to the Gospel are to be held fast to and appropriated. Nicholas Murray Butler, President of Columbia University, has defined education as "the appropriation, by the individual, of the spiritual possessions of the race." The appropriation of the spiritual possessions of the Church, in her Testimony to the truth which is preserved for the future by the maintenance of stable Symbols, that embody these Scriptural possessions, is the Church's first and most important duty toward the rising generation.

The modern radical spirit which would sweep away the Formula of Concord as a Confession of the Church, will not, in the end, be curbed, until it has swept away the Augsburg Confession, and the ancient Confessions of the Church—yea, not until it has crossed the borders of Scripture itself, and swept out of the Word whatsoever is not in accord with its own critical mode of thinking. The far-sighted rationalist theologian and Dresden Court preacher, Ammon, grasped the logic of a mere spirit of progress, when he said: "Experience teaches us that those who reject a Creed, will speedily reject the Scriptures themselves." With the radical Church in America, progress has already ceased to be a question of Creeds, but has become a question as to the Scripture itself.

A recent writer, replying to an epigrammatic statement of the position we are discussing, viz., that "The Lutheran ecclesiastical sun did not stand still in 1580," correctly points out, "that the sun did not stand still on the 25th of June, 1530; and that the implied certainty that modern Christian thought cannot express its faith in the categories

---

[9] Our *apprehension* of the content changes; but it grows deeper with our submission to the Word, and more shallow from our exaltation of our own intelligence. Our development of Scriptural Truth is also enriched under the influence of the Holy Spirit through the Word in the Church; but this is an organic inner unfolding, and not an external and critical overturning of the old Faith.

47

of mediæval and primitive thought tells just fifty years
harder against the Augustana, and more than a thousand
years more against the Nicene Creed." " Certainly," it says,
" there are some things in Christian thinking that have the
attribute of stability, some things that cannot be shaken. . .
No one who is qualified to pronounce judgment, believes
that the theological sun stood still in 1580 or, further back,
in 1530.   There is but one authentic account of the sun
standing still, and that was a miraculous occurrence recorded
in the book of Joshua." [10]

Sartorius [11] points out that the obligation of the Symbolical Books, and our duty of co-witnessing with them in the
testimony of the truth, *does not stand in the way* of our
developing the Christian faith.   This, he says, is shown by
the Formula of Concord itself.   That document takes pains
to exhibit the order of the formation of the symbols, as the
result of a great process of spiritual *progress*.   They are
testimonies and declarations of the faith, showing how, at
any time, the Holy Scriptures were understood and interpreted on controverted articles, and the doctrines contrary
thereto rejected and condemned by those who then lived.

The giving up of these symbols by the friends of light and
progress has in the past been a sad relapse from the religion
of the Church of the New Testament, into the religion of the
Old, or still deeper, into that of the natural man; and has
attempted to make null and void the mighty spiritual movement, which flows through all ages of the Christian Church,
and has preserved its great results in the Confessions that
mark its most significant epochs.   " As if these men of
progress were the first to be enlightened by the Spirit to
understand the Scriptures, and to define what Christianity
is, they have cut off the entire organism of the doctrinal

---

[10] We might add that while the earth (not the sun) *does move,* it does so
only in its orbit.

[11] *Ueber die Nothwendigkeit und Verbindlichkeit der kirchlichen Glaubens-
bekenntnisse,* von Dr. Ernst Sartorius, General superintendent der Provinz
Preuszen. Stuttgart: Verlag von S. G. Liesching, 1845, p. 59.

development of the Church, to reduce all God's truth to a few simple and general sentences." [12]

Sartorius proceeds to say that the advance from one symbol to another has not come to a necessary stop, but "that there is still room for further development, as new spiritual movements in or out of the Church may render necessary. New symbols were added to the early ones, and the occasion may arise for adding to and defining the symbols which we now possess. . . . The truth must ever be brought forward in forms more definite against error, and be established against shiftings and change, and have the reasons as well as the consequences of its own statements further explained. In a word, it must *live,* and *live on* in its confessors as a common testimony of the fellowship of Spirit and truth among Christian believers. . . .

"The obligation of the symbols involves neither a dead stability, nor a backward movement towards inadequate or extinct forms of the past. Just as certainly as the history of the Church has not remained stationary for the last eighteen centuries, so certainly has she not yet reached a point upon which she may rest without advances. Thus the church connects stability with progress, and the old is united with the new as in one family." [13]

---

[12] *Ev. Rev.,* IV, p. 27. The last statement above sufficiently describes Denney's surprising and superficial attempt in 1908 to make the Christian Confession more brief than the Apostles' Creed by eliminating all reference to the Holy Spirit.

Canon Henson, at the National Episcopal Congress, Boston, 1909, said: "The old ruthless doctrine which separated Christianity sharply from all other religions, and limiting the notion of divine revelation solely to the religion of Christ, cannot maintain its ground. Either all religions exhibit the action of the Holy Spirit or none. The difference between them is one of degree, not of kind.

"The machinery of religion—priesthood, sacraments, liturgies, ascetic disciplines—is everywhere similar, showing plainly that these have their origin in common needs rather than in any 'pattern in the mount' supernaturally communicated to the founders of the Church.

"There is in the world a force superior to man, yet kindred with him, which forever makes appeal to him, which wins his free allegiance and transforms him visibly. The holy Spirit of God has been active in the world since men were; humanity is unthinkable apart from His influence. Every religion worthy the name is His origin, addressing itself to the conscience, reordering and exalting conduct, making men, under whatever descriptions they may pass, 'friends of God and prophets.' " Thus does modern Christianity progress to naturalism.

[13] *Cp. Ev. Rev.* IV, p. 26.

THE QUESTION OF HISTORY.

Up to this point, we have been considering the objection made to the Formula of Concord as a Confession, on the ground that the wider twilight of the Twentieth Century cannot be bound by the narrower noon of the Sixteenth Century. But this is a theoretical objection. Let us pass to the solid ground of history.

Though the Confessional development of the Church has not come to a *stop* with the year 1580, it nevertheless left an *ineradicable mark* of importance on the dial *at that point* in the history of Christianity. If the question, " Is the Formula of Concord a Confession?" is to be answered from and according to the record of history, that answer will be, " It is a Confession." There is no doubt on this point. It is the historical fact. The Formula of Concord cannot, historically, be denied to be the Confession of those who wrote it—and they were not the least of the men of the Lutheran Church in the Sixteenth Century,—and the Confession also of some other Lutherans who joined with them in this Confessional utterance. The Formula may not be your Confession, or my Confession. It may not be the Confession of the whole Lutheran Church because it was agreed to and signed by a very large majority of the Lutherans of that day—since we at least do not admit the American principle of majority-rule in deciding the Confessional matters of the Lutheran Church; but this much cannot be gainsaid, that if those people who put the Formula forth, and uttered it " with mouth and heart," made it their Confession, *it is* their Confession. It may be a poor Confession, a clumsy Confession, an injudicious Confession, but these defects could not deprive it of its Confessional character. History shows that it was given to the world as a Confession, and the question is a historical one.

The men who felt its need, the men who wrote it, the men who intended it to fill a want, and the men who accepted it, gave it forth *as their Confession.* They say, " We *believe,* teach and confess that the only rule and standard are the Scriptures. We *believe, teach* and confess that there is a distinction between man's nature and original sin. Our *doctrine, faith* and *confession,* is that the understanding and reason of man are blind. We unanimously *believe, teach* and *confess* that Christ is our righteousness. And so the confession of faith runs through all the articles. And, last of all, they " desire to testify that this is our *faith, doctrine and confession.*" " If the Christian reader will carefully examine this declaration, . . . he will find that what was in the beginning *confessed,* . . . in the comprehensive summary of our religion and faith, . . . and afterward restated, . . . is . . . the simple, immutable, permanent truth."[14]

It is an incontrovertible fact, then, that the Formula is the Confession of that part of the Lutheran Church which then believed and now believes in its doctrines. It further is clear that it was not intended to be a Confession simply for theologians, but also for every Christian, including the laymen especially. For it says, " This is a brief and simple explanation of the controverted articles. . . . Hence every simple Christian, according to the guidance of God's Word and his simple Catechism, can distinguish what is right or wrong, where not only the pure doctrine is stated, but also the erroneous contrary doctrine is repudiated and rejected, and thus the controversies, full of causes of offence, that have occurred, are thoroughly settled and decided."

But we have more than the testimony of the framers of the Formula in support of its Confessional character. There is the verdict of history. While general historians, and others, may have doubts as to the appropriateness of the form[15] and extent of the matter as Confessional, there is little or none as to the *nature* of the matter as Confessional;

---

[14] *Book of Concord,* p. 539.

[15] *E. g.,* the last words of the close of the Epitome.—*Book of Concord,* p. 528.

and in dealing with the Formula as a historical factor, they accredit it as Confessional. " The striving toward unity was justified, and necessary. The Church felt that a Confession was necessary in order to conserve the fruits of the Reformation," says Hauck. " The Formula of Concord at once assumed a position among the regulative symbols of Lutheranism," [16] says Seeberg. " The amplest and most explicit of the Lutheran Confessions," says Jacobs. " The Formula of Concord is, next to the Augsburg Confession, the most important theological standard of the Lutheran Church," [17] says Schaff, who justifies the great amplitude of his treatment " by the intrinsic importance of the Formula." [18] Frank in the *Schaff-Herzog,* terms it " the last of the six Symbolical Books of the Lutheran Church." Schaff, in his *Creeds of Christendom,* terms it " The last of the Lutheran Confessions; " and a well-known American theological cyclopedia [19] terms it " the seventh and last symbolical book of the Lutheran Church."

Its Confessional importance speaks for itself when a Presbyterian, [20] though not friendly to it, devotes no less than eighty-two pages of his *Creeds* to it and its exposition. Such testimony is weighty when we consider that, in the same work, the Augsburg Confession itself receives only eighteen pages, the Apology two pages, the Tetrapolitana five pages, the Heidelberg Catechism twenty-five pages, the Thirty-Nine Articles of the Church of England thirty-two pages, the Westminster Confession fifty-six pages, and the Apostles' Creed ten pages. While the Confessional importance of a work is not to be measured mechanically, and while the lack of literature in the English language led the author in question to some degree of fulness in his treatment of this Sym-

---

[16] *Hist. of Doctrines,* II, 382.
[17] *Creeds of Christendom,* I, 338.
[18] *Ib.* 340.
[19] *McClintock & Strong, in loco.*
[20] *Schaff.*

bol, yet the fact that his methodical but unfriendly judgment has given the Formula its proper Symbolical position in the plan of his work and has felt it wise to afford this Confession more space, for the edification of American readers, than he allots to any other Creed in Christendom, should be sufficient testimony as to the Confessional importance of the Formula of Concord in the Symbolical literature of the Lutheran Church.

Continuing to speak historically, and as a matter of fact, the Formula of Concord is the Confession of the largest Lutheran body [21] in America, and of the general body with which the writer of this volume is connected, which also constitutes no small part of the Church in America. Of its theologians, C. P. Krauth [22] has called the Formula, "*The amplest and clearest Confession in which the Christian Church has ever embodied her faith.*" And H. E. Jacobs [23] has stated it to be "The amplest and most explicit of the Lutheran Confessions."

MULTIPLICITY OF CONFESSIONS.

But we are met by another question: Is the Formula of Concord *needed* as a Confession? Is not the Augsburg Confession in itself sufficient to embody and represent and perpetuate the doctrine of the Lutheran Church? Why multiply the symbols of the Church? Why render the apprehension of our faith more difficult and cumbersome by so largely increasing the Confessional literature, as is done when we accept the whole Book of Concord? We have in it a complicated body of human testimony nearly as great

---

[21] "Ich erkenne die drei Hauptsymbole der [alten] Kirche, die ungeänderte Augsburgische Confession und deren Apologie, die Schmalkaldischen Artikel, die beiden Catechismen Luthers und die concordien Formel für die reine, ungefälschte Erklärung und Darlegung des göttlichen Wortes und Willens, bekenne mich zu denselben als zu meinen eigenen Bekenntnissen und will mein Amt bis an mein Ende treulich und fleissig nach denselben ausrichten. Dazu stärke mich Gott durch seinen heiligen Geist! Amen."

[22] *Con. Ref.*, p. 302.

[23] *Lutheran Cyclopedia*, Art. on *Concord*.

in bulk, as the New Testament itself. Why not on the grounds of simplicity, paucity, fundamental generalization, and uniformity confine ourselves to a single Confession, especially since that Confession happens to coincide with the public birth of the Church, and state the doctrines of the church in such a way that, barring the question of variations, all Lutherans can stand upon it?

If we are sure that a single Confession is sufficient to embody the faith in such way that it will be clearly understood, and never be misunderstood by any members of the Church, it will certainly be most desirable to have only one Confession, and that as brief as possible. One might almost go as far as to say, with all reverence, that if it were possible for the Lord to have revealed to us His Gospel so clearly that every one would apprehend it, and that no Christian would ever misunderstand it, in a single book of the Scripture, it would be a great advantage to have only one such book, of small compass, practical, popular, and easy to refer to. Though it does not seem to have been possible with regard to the source of Confession, viz., the Scriptures; is it not, perhaps, possible with reference to the Confessions themselves? Could not the Apostles' Creed, or, if you will, the Nicene Creed, have served the purposes of all the œcumenical creeds; and, in truth, with possibly a little amplification, would it not serve the purposes of all Christendom to-day?

We think not. It is not the way of history and life, to have short, ready-made rules drop down from Heaven, or out of the Scriptures, in order to bring uniformity, simplicity, and clearness to the faith of the human race. God has seen fit to so order our development that our Confessions are attained through dearly-bought historical experience. History teaches that Confessions which are drawn up theoretically, without the marks of the fiery historical trial through which they have passed, prove themselves to be as worthless as paper. And the experience of the Church will show that it is impossible to cut away the genuine Confessional shoots of any part or age of the Church for the purpose of concentrating our utterance upon a single symbol, in the interest of paucity and clearness, however thoroughly desirable that interest may be.

In accordance with the law of history, genuine Confessions are usually so concrete in intention, or so ground down by attrition, before they became a real symbol of the Church, that they completely meet, in outer form, and in the pointing of their substance, only the wants that are felt in their day. New wants, not covered, nor contemplated, nor foreseen in the day of the original Confession *will* grow up; and, if it should so occur that any of these new wants become pivots on which the future teaching of the Church can be diverted to this side or that, a new conflict will arise in the Church and a new Confession may develop out of the conflict.

That the Augsburg Confession did not suffice to maintain the pure doctrine even in the early and golden period of Protestantism, is shown by the dreadful conflicts that arose on its basis, and by the setting up of over twenty exceedingly bulky corpora doctrinæ in addition to the Confession. Instead of restraining the formation of parties and the partizan spirit within the Church, the Augsburg Confession became the subject of the most excruciating controversies that agitated the Church. It failed to prevent the polemic extravagances of the Gnesio-Lutherans, the compromises of the Philippists, and the approaches to the Reformed doctrine by the Crypto-Calvinists.

" In this lies the supreme significance of the Formula of Concord and of the Book of Concord, that through it the Lutheran Church maintained her right to stand for herself (Selbstständigkeit) as over against Calvinism. When we look at the quality of doctrine represented by the Formula of Concord, and at the wide circle within which this became the norm, we perceive that it was not some theological party that had forced its views upon the Lutheran Church, but that the germ of a consensus which had been really at hand had attained to its unfolding in the Formula of Concord. It represented a Melanchthonian Lutheranism."[24] "It established the Augsburg Confession and Apology forever as the Confession of the Church as a whole. . . . Most surely will time bring all that love our Church to feel, that without the second war and the second peace, the war and peace of Conservation, the richest result of the first, the war of Reformation, would have been lost. Hopeless division, anarchy, ruin and absorption, were the perils from which the Formula of Concord saved our Church."[25]

That the golden ideal of a single Confession for the Church, does not meet the Confessional necessity of Lutheranism, is shown again very clearly by the experience of the Church in America in the Nineteenth Century. There is a striking article in one of the old numbers of the *Evangelical Review* under the heading " Dr. Schmucker's Lutheran Symbols," in which it is pointed out that the great leader of the English Lutheran Church, in the Second, Third, and Fourth Decades of the Nineteenth Century, in all his ecclesiastical publications, from the appearance of his *Popular Theology* in 1830, really made the attempt, directly or indirectly, " to introduce a new Confession of faith into the Lutheran Church of the United States." The whole of this American effort " culminated and took its most distinct form in " a confessional statement, still very famous by name.

The *Review* article affirms that the new Confession, " as originally prepared, not only contemplated but almost in so many words proposed a division of the Lutheran Church." According to the view of the writer of this Confession, one of the reasons for the proposed introduction of the symbol was that the Lutheran Church was rendered odious because it had been represented *as holding certain doctrines of the*

[24] Seeberg, in *Hauck.*
[25] Krauth, in *Con. Ref.,* pp. 327-328.

Augsburg Confession, and the other Symbolical Books, and that it was well to show that the Lutheran Church wished to have no connection with so-called " Old Lutherans." [26]

In this instance, the acceptance of the Augsburg Confession by a part of the English Church, and the founding of a Seminary upon it and Luther's Catechism, did not prevent an earnest and brilliant man within the Church from throwing his full life-force against, and from promulgating teachings at the fountain-head which were contrary to, the true Confession of the Lutheran Church. Had the Augsburg Confession been re-enforced by the Formula of Concord, while it might not have prevented the activities just mentioned, it would have brought on a crisis and a reaction that, in our judgment, would long ago have removed the Lutheran Church in this land far from the boundary line of Confessional obscurity.

The Augsburg Confession alone has not sufficed in the history of Lutheranism. This is shown, again, in the fact that the most active Confessional symbol in the Church, the one which has formed the witness among the people, has been Luther's Smaller Catechism. If the Augsburg Confession is sufficient, as a Confession, what shall be done with Luther's Catechism, which is not a private commentary or a dogmatic, nor even a mere text-book based on the Confession, but which is prior in origin to the Augsburg Confession, and is circulated far more widely than the Confession itself; and which in some respects gives a clearer insight into the Lutheran principle of Law and Gospel, and into the Lutheran doctrine of the Sacraments, than the Augsburg Confession itself.

If the principle of simplicity and paucity be really the

---

[26] In this proposed Confession, the Preface tells us that "Any district Synod connected with the ———— Synod may, with perfect consistency, adopt this Platform, if the majority of her members approve of the synodical disclaimer contained in part II." In an Appendix to the third edition, which was a *variata* from the first edition, instead of "the former Symbolical Books" we find a "Definite Platform, being the doctrinal basis or Creed, constructed in accordance with the principles of the ———— Synod."

essential thing in Confessions, the real reduction might, after all, have to be to the Catechism,—not because it is Luther's work, as over against Melanchthon's, although the fact that it is Luther's work is not a special discredit to it; but because it is both the Scripture and the Lutheran Confession in a nut-shell. It is *the real epitome* of Lutheranism in the simplest, the most practical, the most modern and living, and, at the same time, the most radical form. It steers clear of all obscure historical allusions, it contains no condemnatory articles, it is based on the shortest and the oldest of the œcumenical symbols. It is not a work for theologians, but for every Lutheran; and it is not nearly as large as the Augsburg Confession. If our Confessional basis is to be determined on the principle advocated, by the objectors to the Formula, the one Symbol of the Church will be the Small Catechism, and not the Augsburg Confession.

But we have never heard of any objection to either of the Catechisms of Luther, as Symbols of the Church. Historically, in fact, there has not been objection to any of the Symbols of the Lutheran Church (barring the Schmalkald Articles), except to the Formula of Concord. After all, it cannot be the principle of Confessional simplicity that is the real motive for ruling out the Formula. Historically, there is no justification for the emphasis of the principle of paucity. No less than five-sevenths of the Book of Concord was accepted by both Melanchthonians and Lutherans, often together with a great deal of additional material, before the Book of Concord appeared.

The Melanchthonians especially were willing to increase the bulk of their Confessional writings. They did not object to the Apology to the Augsburg Confession, which is five times as large as the Confession, and which is no less than one and one-fourth times as large as the whole Formula of Concord, and over five times as large as the Epitome of the Formula. The Corpus Julium contained the whole Book of Concord, except the Formula; and, so far as we recall, there was not a single State of Germany or surrounding countries, in the Lutheran *or in the Reformed Church,* which accepted simply the Augsburg Confession with no other additional symbolical writings.

The principle of an *unnecessary* multiplication of documents (which we accept), is as valid in the confessional field as it is everywhere in the field of public, solemn testimony. It is a general law which applies not only to the public witness of the Church, but also to the documentary development of the constitution of the State, and to all important historico-practical entities. So averse is the English spirit to the multiplication of documents, that large parts of the English law are still not formulated. But that which has been formulated historically, under the stress of crisis, whether it be the *Magna Charta,* or such a document as the *Constitution* of the United States, abides, and is not reduced on the score of simplicity.

The principle of unnecessary multiplication does not really apply to changing the verdict of time, but to the creation of new symbols in the present. In this sense, the *Conservative Reformation*[27] declares, that the Lutheran Church, as a whole, objects to the multiplication of the number or extension of the bulk of creeds. " For nearly three centuries, no addition has been made to her Symbolical Books; and although it is quite possible that, for local reasons, parts of our Church may enunciate more largely particular elements of her faith, we do not think it likely that the Lutheran Church, as a whole, will ever add to her Symbols, not merely anything which can have such relations to them as the Augsburg Confession has (which would be impossible), but not even such as the Formula of Concord has."

Speaking of the bulk of the Book of Concord, the *Conservative Reformation* further says: " The Augsburg Confession, the Smaller Catechism, and the Epitome, may be

---

[27] P. 273.

regarded as the texts, respectively, on which the Apology, the Larger Catechism, and the Declaration are Commentaries. The whole of these books can be embodied in a fair type in an ordinary *duodecimo* volume. When we think of the space which a minister covers with the words in which, during a single year, he states the sacred doctrines—when we look at the many volumes in which particular authors have presented the results of their labors on Scripture, . . . it hardly seems an excessive demand on the part of the Church that she should ask ministers to study one small volume to reach the official expression of her judgment on the greatest questions, which pertain to pure doctrine, sound government, and holy life. Yet the Book of Concord has been denounced on the ground that it contains so much. Be it right or wrong, be its teachings truth or falsehood, its bulk is sufficient to condemn it."

The Epitome of the Formula of Concord, which is the declarative portion of the Confession, is only six or seven pages longer than the Augsburg Confession, and could be published in a small pocket volume not larger than the ordinary Luther's Small Catechism. The œcumenical Creeds, the Augsburg Confession, and the Formula of Concord, could be published in a small work in large clear type which could readily be carried in the pocket. With the growth of historical and institutional Christianty, and especially with the growth of Protestantism, where the temptation constantly arises of every mind becoming a law unto itself, the complexity of actual theological thought increases. Truth and error both are more fully unfolded; and to cover the more complicated situation, the older symbols must be explicated. A primitive people can do with the multiplication table, and a very simple slate and pencil; but where the astronomic, economic and commercial problems of life rise in bewildering confusion, and in larger proportions, it is necessary to have a whole arithmetic, systems of bookkeeping, tables of logarithms, and even very elaborate, yet, after all, really simplifying cash-registers and adding machines. No one will assert that the Augsburg Confession contains the fully developed doctrine of the evangelical Church. It contains the doctrine developed sufficiently to meet the situation then in hand with Rome.

CHAPTER XXIX.

THE LUTHERAN CONFESSION.

THE ANSWER OF A PROVIDENTIAL ORIGIN TO THE QUESTION, IS THE FORMULA A CONFESSION?

A Crying Need : the Confusion of the Age, the Failure of the Melanchthonian Answer—A Definite and Sufficient Call—The History of its Origin and Completion in the Light of the Call.

IS THE HAND OF PROVIDENCE MISSING?

THUS far we have confined our inquiry as to the Confessional nature of the Formula of Concord to the verdict of history, and to a consideration of the principle of an unnecessary multiplication of symbols. But now we are met by still another objection urged against the Confessional character of the Formula. It has been assumed by us all along that the occasion which called forth the Formula was adequate. " But," we are asked, " was this really a fact?" Was there a need, a providential stress in the Church, at the time of the framing of the Formula, sufficiently critical to call it forth; and was the occasion of its issue of such a character as to warrant its being considered a real Confession?

In reply to this inquiry, it must be said that there was a crying need. Very few men are able to realize the internal confusion into which the Lutheran Church had been thrown in the latter half of the Sixteenth Century. The battle with

700

external foes in the earlier part of the Century, which stirred all Europe, which made the castle-door at Wittenberg ring, which caused the world to thrill at the declaration of Luther at the Diet of Worms, and which inspired the Protestants with faith in their cause as brought to the Emperor in their Confession at Augsburg, was serious enough; but the later situation was relatively worse.

Internal demoralization, all will agree, is the very worst foe against which any large and imperfectly organized body has to contend. " The superstitions of centuries had been over-thrown, and the temple of a pure Scriptural faith was to be reared upon their ruins. Every man was a polemic and a builder. It was an age in which extravagances rose in hostile pairs. Two errors faced each other, and in their conflict trampled down the faith which lay prostrate between them. The controversies which followed Luther's death, arrested the internal development of the Church. The great living doctrines, which made the Reformation, were in danger of losing all their practical power in the absorption of men's minds in these controversies. The Church was threatened with schisms. Her glory was obscured. Her enemies mocked at her. Her children were confounded and saddened. Crafty men crept in to make the Lutheran Church the protector of heresy. There was danger that the age which the Conservative Reformation had glorified, should see that grand work lost in the endless dissensions of embittered factions.

" Hence it is, that while the larger part of the Lutheran Church received the Formula with enthusiasm, some did not accept it. For, while the Confessions set forth the faith of our Church, in her antagonism to the errors outside of her, the Formula, in the main, is occupied in stating the truth, over against the errors which had crept into her. Romanism, with its artifices, had misled some. The ardor of controversy had led others, as, for example, the great and noble Flacius, to extravagance and over-statement. The Lu-

48

theran Church was assailed by intrigue, Jesuitical device, and conspiracy. False brethren endeavored by tricks of false interpretation to harmonize the language of the Augsburg Confession with their errors. The mighty spirit of Luther had gone to its rest. Melanchthon's gentleness sometimes degenerated into utter feebleness of purpose, and alike to the Romanists and the sectarians he was induced to yield vital points.

" Not yet compacted in her organism, living only by her faith, the Lutheran Church was called to meet an awful crisis. No man who knows the facts, will deny that something worthy of the responsibility involved in such great and cogent issues had to be done." [1]

Even Harnack, whom none will suspect of speaking in the interests of a strict Lutheran Confessionalism, has this to say [2] of the Lutheran Church prior to the appearance of the Formula of Concord: " Round about 1570, it seemed that Lutheranism was done for. It was everywhere outside threatened by Calvinism, and then split up by strife and reaction." Prof. Tressler adds, " In face of such a situation and to meet it with Scripture wisdom, the Formula in 1577 appeared."

We have tried to present a picture of the confusion that reigned in the Church after the death of Luther and later of Melanchthon, and before the appearance of the Formula, to show the crying need of some common principle of strength and order. But it was more than a matter of mere confusion that threatened the Lutheran Church. There was a real peril—at least, historians of every school, with Harnack, tell us so—of Lutheranism falling into pieces; and it must be conceded that the good wrought by the Augsburg Confession in 1530 would have been very limited if, half a

---

[1] Condensed from *Con. Ref.*, pp. 306-307.

[2] *Lectures on the History of the Reformation,* quoted by Tressler, one of his hearers.

century later, the evangelical principle had disintegrated into hopeless and waning Protestant individualism.

Schaff, in opening his discussion of the origin and occasion of the Formula puts the deep necessity of the situation in a nutshell. He says, " The Form of Concord, the last of the Lutheran Confessions, completed in 1577, and first published in 1580, is named from its aim to give doctrinal unity and peace to the Lutheran Church, after long and bitter contention. The work was occasioned by a series of doctrinal controversies, which raged in the Lutheran Church for thirty years with as much passion and violence as the trinitarian and christological controversies in the Nicene age. They form a humiliating and unrefreshing, yet instructive and important chapter in the history of Protestantism. The free spirit of the Reformation, which had fought the battles against the tyranny of the Papacy and brought to light the pure doctrines of the Gospel, gave way to bigotry and intolerance among Protestants themselves. Calumny, abuse, intrigue, deposition and exile were unsparingly employed as means to achieve victory. Religion was confounded with theology, piety with orthodoxy and orthodoxy with an exclusive confessionalism. Doctrine was overrated, and the practice of Christianity neglected. The contending parties were terribly in earnest, and as honest and pious in their curses as in their blessings; they fought as if the salvation of the world depended on their disputes. Yet these controversies were unavoidable in that age, and resulted in the consolidation and completion of the Lutheran system of doctrine. All phases and types of Christianity must develop themselves, and God overrules the wrath of theologians for the advancement of truth." [3]

Krauth puts the matter only a little more strongly when he says, " Hopeless division, anarchy, ruin and absorption were the perils from which the Formula of Concord saved

---

[3] *Creeds of Christendom,* I, pp. 258, 259.

our Church."[4]   The Roman Church had made persistent use of every opportunity to recover her outer hold and regain her inner power over the Protestant world. The territorial expansion of Protestantism had ceased. The spiritual life and inner progress of Protestantism had come to a standstill. There was no longer any anchorage to which the Church could cling. Unless the principles of the Evangelical Faith could be gathered into consistency, and set forth in a clearer light than that which now was shining down from a former generation, there would be no teaching sufficiently steady to counterbalance the inner strengthening of the Roman Church, which had come to it as a result of the Council of Trent, and which it had gained through the founding of the Society of Jesus. The ceaseless conflict between Lutherans, which, even in exhaustion, showed no signs of a springing concord, was causing the faith of the Reformation to crumble to dust   Even the political authorities most keenly realized the necessity, if religion was to be preserved, of having the theologians bring their desultory antagonisms to an end, and work out some permanent standard which should become the firm and consistent Faith of the Church.[5]

The very tendency, already alluded to, of undue multiplication of symbols, complained of to-day by those who would cut the nerve of historic continuity in the vain attempt to attain ideal brevity and simplicity in the expression of the Confessional principle, was threatening the Church at the time when the Formula was adopted. There was crying need of a Confession that would compress and unite the many Confessional statements springing up in Post-Reformation Protestantism. One of the Formula's leading objects, and one of those in which it was very successful, was the elimination of bulk and the simplification of the great mass of material that had sprung up in luxuriant profusion round about and all over the original Confession. Who

---

[4] *Con. Ref.*, p. 328.

[5] Tschackert, *Die Enstehung der luth. . . Kirchenlehre,* pp. 570, 571.

can dispute the statement of Krauth that " we have *twenty-eight large volumes* of Melanchthon's writings—and at this hour, impartial and learned men are not agreed as to what were his views on some of the profoundest questions of Church doctrine, on which Melanchthon was writing all his life ? " [6]

Who can question the fact that much that Melanchthon wrote could be taken in two senses, and that his name was used to shield that of which there is no reason to believe that he would have approved ? " Whatever may be the meaning of Melanchthon's words in the disputed cases, this much is certain, that they practically operated as if the worse sense were the real one, and their mischievousness was not diminished but aggravated by their obscurity and double meaning. They did the work of avowed error, and yet could not be reached as candid error might." [7]

We have, then, in the Melanchthonian principle as embodied in Confessional print at this era the two qualities of great bulk and great weakness. The Corpus Philippicum, preceding the Book of Concord, was much more bulky than the Book of Concord and is composed entirely of Melanchthon's writings,[8] many of them his private writings, containing much matter that was cumbrous and unsuited to a Confession.

In addition to these, the Latin Philippicum contains the Augustana, 1542; the Apology, the Repetition of the Augsburg Confession for the Council of Trent; the Loci Theologici, the Examen Ordinandorum, the Answer to the Bavarian Articles, A Confutation of the Error of Servetus, and Melanchthon's reply to Stancar. This constitutes a folio of over one thousand pages. The Corpus Julium, another rival of the Book of Concord, as we have seen, contained everything found in the Book of Concord, except the Formula,

---

[6] *Con. Ref.*, p. 291.
[7] *Ib.*, 291.
[8] Except the three œcumenical Creeds.

and in its place included a work by Chemnitz and one by Urbanus Rhegius!

When the Formula of Concord is spoken of as a good private commentary, but too bulky to be a public confession, it is well to bear in mind the Melanchthonian ideas on this subject which preoccupied the ground before the Formula of Concord came into existence.

Had not the Melanchthonian situation failed so completely, in its confessional development of the Church and its doctrine, it is a question whether the men who undertook to frame a clear, strong, brief Form, to bring harmony, would have been impelled to supply the crying need. The friends of the Lutheran Church "were embarrassed and confounded, and its enemies delighted and encouraged, by perceiving endless diversities of statement in the editions of books, rapidly succeeding each other, books which, in their first form, Luther had endorsed as of Canonical purity and worthy of immortality. The very Confessions of the Church, determined by her authorities, and signed by her representatives, were amended, enlarged here, abridged there, changed in structure and in statement, as the restless spirit of refining in thought or style moved Melanchthon. All his works show the tinge of his mind at the time of their issue, whether affected by his hopes that Rome would be softened, or roused by the elusive prospect of real union with the less radical part of the Zwinglians. Melanchthon fell into a hallucination by which his own peace of mind was wrecked, his Christian consistency seriously compromised, the spirit of partisanship developed, the Church distracted and well nigh lost. This was the hallucination that peace could be restored by ambiguous formulas, accepted indeed by both parties, but understood in different senses." [*]

Here the great error of pure Protestantism, as accepted in Melanchthonianism, comes to light. It is the liberty

---

[*] *Con. Ref.,* p. 290.

claimed for the individual mind to modify the Church's faith in accordance with its own personal views, without clearly and formally submitting such proposed modification to the Church for acceptance and rejection, and without willingness to assume the consequences if there be rejection. To the Melanchthonian mind, the right of the individual to make intellectual progress for himself and for the Church, overtops all rights which are conjoint and historical. To a conservative evangelical Protestant, this private right cannot be carried out to the detriment of other existing rights in the body of the Church, without giving all such rights ample notice and their just power to act. For the individual in a communion to act in and for the communion as he thinks—when the communion and he differ in their thinking—without first influencing the communion to change their thinking to his thinking, nay, even without notifying the communion, is a lack of ethical integrity in dealing with that which is outside of ourselves and to which we have no right.[10] The Melanchthonian principle did not recognize that the rights of individual Protestantism cease where the rights of collective Protestantism begin.

It was this mistaken habit of regarding a Confession as belonging to a changeable—or progressive, if you prefer—individual, to be modified according to new views and circumstances, rather than as necessary testimony, reflecting the unchangeable Word of God in the Church, that brought multiplication, bulk, confusion and peril into the Church; and, in consequence of which, the great and true Confessional witness at Augsburg had not been able to maintain either the pure doctrine or the united Church.

---

[10] It may be urged that Luther was more of a Protestant in this individual sense than was Melanchthon; and that he cared less for the old historical forms than his coadjutor who was always seeking some outer *nexus* with the visible Church of the past. But this objection falls before the fact that, while Luther cared less for the forms, and was more individualistic as to the visible *nexus,* he was conservative to the core on the substance. There was no rationalistic coefficient in his faith. Melanchthon on the other hand was constantly seeking internal or rational freedom, with outer conformity.

This fact is admitted by Schaff, who says: " Melanchthon, . . . with . . . more logic and system than Luther, and with a most delicate and conscientious regard for truth and peace, yet not free from the weakness of a compromising and temporizing disposition, continued to progress in theology, and modified his views on two points—the freedom of the will and the presence of Christ in the Eucharist; exchanging his Augustinianism for Synergism, and relaxing his Lutheranism in favor of Calvinism; in both instances he followed the ethical, practical, and unionistic bent of his mind. . . . These changes were neither sudden nor arbitrary, but the result of profound and constant study, and represented a legitimate and necessary phase in the development of Protestant [not Lutheran] theology, which was publicly recognized in various ways before the formation of the ' Form of Concord.' " [11]   Thus with remarkable admissions as to the Melanchthonian principle does the Reformed historian write, and prove that the author of the Augsburg Confession made progress beyond the Confession, from which it follows that the Confession was not sufficient in itself to maintain the Confessional principle of Lutheranism.

From each and all of the varied considerations before us, we are led to conclude that the crisis at hand in the Lutheran Church was sufficiently grave to demand and to justify a new Confession of the faith. Would the authors of the final Confession, men of temperate judgment, have denied themselves so long and suffered so much; and would the Elector have expended so many thousand dollars in this work of sound unification, if the Melanchthonian principle (and the Confessional corpora doctrinae) had not demonstrated their inability to control the Church, and if a serious crisis were not impending?

Let us briefly sum up the crying necessity, the inability of the helpless Church to extricate herself from the exigency,

---

[11] *Creeds of Christendom,* I, p. 261.

if Providence, by changing the historical situation, by raising up men of insight, perseverance, prudence, and love for the truth, and by removing obstacles on every side, had not ushered in a new and better era.

First of all, the Formula was a *spiritual necessity.* The Melanchthonian principle had been operative now for a whole generation. It had failed at Augsburg in 1530; but still its methods of dealing with the truth, with the Confession, with men, with public policies, and with ecclesiastical difficulties had continued to assert themselves. These methods, though wearing the mantle of peace, had brought no peace anywhere. On every hand, and in every quarter, there was nothing but war; and as Seeberg himself declares, if the Melanchthonian principle had continued in direction of affairs, the conflict in the Lutheran Church would have been eternal. For the suppression of parties, and strife, and intestinal conflict, and peace of mind and heart in the Faith, the Formula of Concord was a necessity. As Seeberg says, " It succeeded in gradually restoring the peace of the Church." [12]

A new Confession was also a *vital necessity.* The right of the Lutheran Church to self-existence had been questioned from the start by Rome, and the progress of that life, as it struck out on its new pathway, after clearing itself from Roman bondage, was eagerly watched by the old enemy. And there was a similar eagerness on the part of the other Protestant parties, who had not been favored as the Lutheran Church was, at Augsburg; and whose hope of becoming the prevalent type of Protestantism lay in dissipating the more conservative elements of Lutheranism, and in absorbing the Church under their own radical principle. There is no doubt that Calvinism, if it had been successful in its use of the Melanchthonian mantle, in possessing itself of the leading citadels of Lutheranism, would have successfully united

---

[12] II, 382.

Protestantism by the destruction of the conservative principle. All divisions in the Protestant Church to-day may be traced back to this deepest one, and the questions of the Sixteenth Century on this point are the questions that Lutheranism must likewise meet to-day.

For the Formula of Concord, there was, in the third place, *a historical necessity.* This point is emphasized by Seeberg. Says he, " A new Confession was a historical necessity. . . . There was only this one alternative, either to let the division and confusion remain, or to bring them to an end by confessional decision of the conditions of doctrine. The situation shown at Naumburg, the situation in the institutions of learning, in the politics of the day, and in the administration of the churches, showed how hopeless the future was, without some common standard of Lutheran agreement, which would resolve the conditions that had arisen within the Church after its period of Reformation and during its period of reconstruction."

The Formula of Concord was also *a confessional necessity.* As we already have seen, through the multiplication of the Corpora Doctrinae, the confessional situation had become so complicated as to be quite intolerable, and with the large number of petty state churches, the frequent changes in the rulers of the state, and the religious confusion ensuing, the Testimony of the Lutheran Church was brought to the verge of contradiction.

But, last of all, a new confession was necessary *to uphold the truth of God's Word.* The Augsburg Confession had spoken, guardedly, toward Rome. The Apology had spoken more fully toward Rome. The Schmalkald Articles had spoken toward Rome. But there was no voice rising up within the Church, as yet, to speak the truth toward Protestant errors against the Word of God. The Word of God itself had not yet been recognized as the supreme rule of faith. The doctrine of free grace, and of Christ Himself, as applied, in our salvation, in Word and sacrament, the whole essence of the real Gospel, as opposed to the apprehension of Christianity as mere reform in body and members, was now at stake. God's Word, for which so much had been suffered, in order to free it from the Church's Word, was in danger from the milder and more humanistic apprehension of a new Protestant scholasticism.

With such a crying need, the need of the spirit for peace, the need and right of the body to self-preservation, the need of historical and confessional strength, and, above all, the need of establishing the truth of God's Word in Christ, who will deny that the Formula of Concord, viewed from the situation out of which it arose, is a real confession of the Church!

WAS THERE A PROPER CALL?

Passing by the need and occasion of the Formula, the objector may turn to criticise its Call. Whence came the authority to issue a new Confession? Who gave its authors the power to propose it to the Church? Did its writers really have a sufficient Call?

The outer Call extended to these men was as clear, more universal, and less individual than that given to Luther to nail up the Theses. We have heard how, in the opinion of its defenders, the Formula was examined in a more thorough manner, and approved more substantially, than if it had emanated from a General Council of the Church. The Call of the writers, in its deliberateness, in its authoritativeness, and formality, was the greatest outer Call given to any body of Lutherans since the days of the Augsburg Confession.

There was no imperial Call. Maximilian II., who reigned as emperor of Germany from 1564 to his death, October 12th, 1576, though himself a Protestant, or at least friendly to Protantism,[13] dealt with the various religious

---

[13] Through the influence of his preceptor in youth. In 1568, he granted the Protestants in Austria liberty to worship God according to their conscience, and commissioned Chytræus to compose a Protestant liturgy for Austria. He opposed and restricted the Jesuits, yet tolerated them in their influence in his own family.

parties in the interests of preserving the empire, and his decisions, as the Protestants were divided, fell more or less in accord with the majority of the Estates, which were Roman in belief. Unlike Charles V., Maximilian was tòo friendly to Protestantism to allow the Pope to put the Protestants on the defensive, which was the case in the Diet at Augsburg, and unlike the Saxon electors, he was too much of a politician to allow religion chief place in his rule. Therefore there could be no Imperial call to a confession.[14] But the Call was issued by the legitimate successor of the political head of the early Reformation activity, by the Elector of Saxony, Augustus,[15] the son-in-law of Christian III. of Denmark. There is nothing but good to be said of the Elector, of his intention, and of his Call. " The Elector was in advance of his time in the principles of constitutional sovereignty. In an arbitrary age, he governed by law. He consulted his parliament on all great questions, and raised no money by taxation without their advice. His edicts were so just that he has been called the Saxon Justinian. His subjects regarded him with peculiar love and reverence. By his skilful internal administration, he raised his country far above the rest of Germany, introducing valuable reforms both in jurisprudence and finance, and giving a decided impulse to education, agriculture, and manufactures. The Dresden Library owes to him its origin, as do also most of its galleries of arts and science.

"Augustus bore a part in the Formula of Concord worthy of him. To meet the necessary expenses connected with the Formula, the Elector himself paid a hundred thousand dollars in gold. His gifts and efforts were unceasing till the

---

[14] Maximilian admonished Frederick of the Palatinate to abandon Calvinism, and become Lutheran again ; and advised the upper Palatine estates to abide steadfast in the use of the Augsburg Confession.

[15] The statement made that the Elector Augustus of Saxony subsequently joined the Church of Rome is an error. Augustus II., who succeeded his elder brother as Elector in 1694, at the age of twenty-four, became a Roman Catholic in order to gain the throne of Poland. His son, Augustus III., also king of Poland, was brought up a Protestant, and became a Catholic on his travels in 1712, and succeeded his father as Elector of Saxony in 1733.

great end was attained. Noble and unsuspicious, he had been slow to believe in the possibility of the treachery of the false teachers, whose mischievous devices he at length reluctantly came to understand. The troubles they brought upon the Church whitened untimely the Elector's head, but so much the more did he toil and pray till the relief from the evil was wrought. While the theologians were engaged in conferences, the Elector and his noble wife were often on their knees, fervently praying that God would enlighten His servants with His Holy Spirit. In large measure, to the piety, sound judgment, and indefatigable patience of this great prince, the Church owes the Formula of Concord," [16] The Preface to the Book of Concord [17] narrates this outer Call in the words of Augustus. It says:—

"And accordingly, we, by the grace of God, Duke of Saxony, Elector, etc., after a council held with some other electors and princes agreeing with us in religion, for the purpose of promoting the godly design of harmony among the teachers of the Church, summoned to Torgau in the year 1576 certain theologians experienced and endowed with pre-eminent learning. When they had assembled, they conferred devoutly concerning the controverted articles and the writing of pacification. And prayers first having been offered, they with extraordinary care (the Spirit of the Lord aiding them by his grace), embraced in a document all those things which seemed to pertain to this deliberation. Afterwards this book was transmitted to some chief adherents of the Augsburg Confession, Electors, Princes and Deputies, and they were requested, with the aid of the most eminent theologians, to read it with godly zeal, to examine it, and finally, to express their judgment and the reasons therefor concerning it collectively and taken part by part." [18]

Much preparation for the work of the Conference, or Synod, or Council, at Torgau had been made at preliminary meetings, just as the Marburg and Schwabach Articles had

---

[16] Hutter, *Conc. Conc.*, ch. XI ; *Anton.*, I, 147, 148 ; *Köllner*, 533 ; Krauth, *Con. Ref.*, p. 308.

[17] *Book of Concord*, p. 12. The occasion for this Preface, the end in view, and the manner of its composition, do not in our judgment reflect upon its testimony or its integrity of purpose. It is a mild, noble and just document, and its defense of the Formula and of the whole undertaking is proper.

[18] Condensed from *Book of Concord*, I, pp. 12, 13.

been prepared prior to the Diet at Augsburg. This previous preparation included the Maulbronn Formula and the Swabian-Saxon Formula, together with the results of the Convention at Lichtenberg.

The Convention, in pursuance of a Call issued by the Elector of Saxony in November, after consultation with a number of the evangelical princes and theologians, met on the Fifteenth of February, 1576. The Elector prepared a memorandum concerning the best means of adjusting the controversies. He regarded the many *corpora doctrinae* accepted by different countries as the chief hindrance to union, and proposed that the princes adhering to the Augsburg Confession should appoint peace-loving theologians, with lay counsellors, to attend a meeting to which each should bring his own *corpus doctrinae*. With the Augsburg Confession as a standard, a new Body of Doctrine should be composed from these, which should be made binding upon all the ministers in their countries. The conference was to determine the number of theologians to be invited to participate in the work, the mode of deliberation, the part to be taken by the Estates, the articles to be treated, etc.

The Convention of Lichtenberg recommended the adoption of three measures to promote peace, viz.: 1. The entire abandonment of all personal rivalries and complaints. 2. The removal of all hindrances to harmony, of which the Corpus Doctrinae Philippicum was mentioned as one, and certain publications, such as the Wittenberg Catechism, the Consensus Dresdensis, through which Crypto-Calvinistic errors were disseminated, as another. Instead of the Corpus Philippicum, the three Oecumenical Creeds, the Augsburg Confession Invariata, the Apology, the two Catechisms and the Schmalkald Articles were recognized as symbolical, with Luther's Commentary on Galatians, if any desire to include it. 3. A conference of theologians is to judge the points in the controversy, according to Scripture and the received Symbols, in the presence of the electors and princes. Chytræus, Chemnitz, Andreae and Marbach were named as theologians well qualified for the work." [19]

On May 28th, 1576, the Elector as recommended at Lichtenberg, convened the Conference, or Synod, at Torgau. It was composed of seventeen theologians from Saxony, Brunswick, Mecklenburg and Württemberg. On June 7th, this body completed the Torgau Book. It was then sent through the Elector to the princes, who gave it into the hands of their theologians for examination and criticism.[20] A committee appointed by the Elector and the princes of Württemberg and Brunswick examined the criticisms, and made corrections in words and style, in several separate revisions.

Finally at Wittenberg, on June 15th, 1777, it was submitted, not to a General Council, but in truly democratic manner [21] to all the teachers and ministers of the Church for their approval and subscription. The ministers of a district would assemble in a Convention and an appeal be made to them to subscribe. The Preface thus describes this procedure :—

" Some of our rank (not all of us were able to do this), have caused this book to be recited, article by article, and distinctly, to the theologians and the ministers of the Church and of the schools collectively and individually, and have caused them to be excited to a diligent and accurate consideration of those parts of the doctrine, which is contained in it.

" When, therefore, they noticed that the Declaration agreed with the Word of God, and with the Augsburg Confession, they gratefully received this Book of Concord as expressing the genuine meaning of the Augsburg Confession, approved it and subscribed to it, and publicly bore witness concerning it with heart, mouth and hand. *Wherefore that godly agreement is and perpetually will be called, the harmonious and concordant Confession not only of some few of our theologians, but, in general, of the ministers of our churches and rectors of schools, one and all, in our provinces and realms." [22]*

---

[19] Condensed from *Book of Concord,* II, Jacobs, Intro., pp. 58, 59.

[20] *Vid. Chap.* XXVI, p. 657.

[21] The wide range of the preparatory work is further proof on this point. " From 1558, at the Frankfort Recess, to 1579, many scores of theological thinkers had labored and prayed toward this end. At least twelve separate conventions, ranging from Faculty Conferences to National Diets, had been utilized in its interests."—*Vid.* G. A. Tressler in *Lutheran World.*

[22] Condensed from Preface to *Book of Concord,* p. 13.

After allowing about two years for the public subscriptions, the rulers and Estates met and signed the Formula and its Preface, now completed, in the Spring of 1579, in all, to the number of eighty-five rulers, nobles and free cities, and between eight and nine thousand theologians[23] (there are at this time, 1909, just a few more than eight thousand ministers in the whole Lutheran Church in America, including all branches).

The historical counterpart to those not participating in the Formula is to be found in the adherents of the Tetrapolitana, who did not participate in the Augustana, but sent in their own Confession. Then the non-partcipants were Zwinglian, and desired to be admitted, but were not. Now they were chiefly Calvinistic, and would not allow themselves to be admitted. The Preface is entitled, "We the Electors, Princes and Deputies of the Holy Roman Empire in Germany, adherents of the Augsburg Confession." Thus was the outer Call complete, in some respects, more so than at Augsburg.

But we lay no stress on the participation of the Civil Authorities, whether Emperor or Elector, in the case of either Confession, except as they represented the duly constituted Church authorities of the day; and as their presence and interest indicated the stress and Providential necessity that brought forth the Confession.

---

[23] For full particulars see Chap. XXVII, p. 671. *sqq.*

CHAPTER XXX.

THE LUTHERAN CONFESSION.

THE ANSWER TO THE CRITICISM MADE ON THE MOTIVES AND MEN, AS TOUCHING THE QUESTION, IS THE FORMULA A CONFESSION?

The Motive of the Formula not a Party One—The Testimony of the Formula Itself —The Men of the Formula : Andreae, Chemnitz, Selnecker.

HAVING concluded the discussion of the Call, we are now brought to the inner motive underlying the Formula. It must be put to the test. " Was not the framing of this Confession *a party measure?* Was it not the final effort of the Lutheran Lutherans to throttle the Reformed Lutherans, and to suppress all liberty of thought? Was the purpose of its framers a genuine Confessional one? Was Confessional Testimony to the Word of God really the underlying motive of the Formula of Concord? "

On this question, the first witness that is entitled to be heard is the Formula itself. What motive can we find in it, in its lines, and between its lines? Is that motive Confessional, or is there a temporal, ecclesiastical, factional, or " sectarian," interest that might seem to have caused it to appear? The Preface to the Formula says:—

" It is a remarkable favor of Almighty God, that, in these last times [*i. e.*, this Sixteenth Century], He has willed, according to His unspeakable love, that the light of His Gospel and Word, through which alone we receive true salvation, should arise and shine after the darkness of papistical superstitions. This brought forth a succinct Confession, prepared from the Word of God, offered at Augsburg in 1530 by our ancestors, presented to the deputies of the Empire, and finally diffused in the entire world. But immediately after the death of Luther, the enemy labored to disseminate the seeds of false doctrine in the churches and schools, and to separate the bond of Christian agreement. Now our chief desire has been that our churches should persevere in the pure doctrine of God's Word, and in unanimity, and that they should be handed down to posterity in a godly way. As, however, we see that corruptions have been introduced by false brethren, just as was the case in the *days of the Apostles,* in those churches in which they themselves had planted the Gospel; mindful of our duty, *which we know has been divinely enjoined upon us,* we think we ought diligently apply ourselves to an aggressive advance against the false dogmas in our realms.[1]

"Accordingly, when an opportunity occurred at the Frankfort Diet, in 1558, a unanimous effort was made to hold a special, general assembly, where there might be a thorough but amicable conference[2] among us, concerning matters maliciously presented by our adversaries; we took the Augsburg Confession of 1530, and all subscribed that godly confession, built upon solid testimonies of truth in the Word of God, with one mind, in order, in this way, to provide for the interests of posterity. It was to be a perpetual testimony, God aiding us, to support no new dogma, but retain the truth which we professed at Augsburg in 1530.

"But when we learned that our Declaration and Repetition of the godly Confession had little weight with our adversaries, and that we[3] were grievously slandered; and the things we did with the best intention were received as though we were so uncertain concerning our confession of faith and religion, and so often have transfused it from one formula to another, that it is no longer clear to us what is the confession once offered to the Emperor at Augsburg; we judged that these slanders and increasing dissensions could not be better met, than by accurately explaining the controverted articles, by rejecting the false dogmas and by lucidly presenting the truth.

"Our theologians then explained the controverted articles from the Word of God and described in what way the dissensions could be settled in a right and good manner; and we were of the judgment that this goodly purpose of the theologians ought to be promoted by us with great earnestness according to the nature of *the office and duty divinely committed to us.* Accordingly, in the year 1576, we summoned to Torgau, certain eminent theologians who conferred devoutly with one another concerning the controverted articles and the writing of pacification. Prayers first having been offered, they embraced all those things

---

[1] These are princes, not theologians ; and under the theory of the day, in which the ruler was responsible for the religion of his people, no fault can be found with this statement. This condition obtained from the start of the Reformation ; but in America, it, happily, no longer exists.

[2] This conference was held at Naumburg.

[3] The princes.

which seemed to be required, in a document;[4] and thus that Book of godly Concord was composed.

"The ministers of the Church with the most ready mind and the testimony of their gratitude toward God, received this Book of Concord, as expressing the genuine meaning of the Augsburg Confession, and publicly bore witness concerning it with heart, mouth and hand. Wherefore that godly agreement is called the *harmonious and concordant Confession* of the ministry of our churches and rectors of our schools, one and all, in our provinces and realms.

"This is the reason why we, with great and godly agreement, have worked out in this Book a Declaration of our perpetual wish, and *a Repetition of our Christian Faith and Confession.*

"The first Augsburg Confession alone (alone we say), and no other, presented to the Emperor in 1530, by the help of God, we will retain to our last breath. We hope, therefore, that our adversaries will hereafter not accuse us of being unable to decide upon anything concerning our faith, as certain, and of fabricating new confessions almost every year. Nor do we judge that other useful writings of Dr. Philip Melanchthon, or of Brenz, Urban Regius, Pomeranus, etc., should be rejected and condemned so far as they agree in all things with the norm which has been set forth in the Book of Concord.

"Although some theologians, and among them, Luther himself, when they treated of the Lord's Supper, were drawn to disputations concerning the personal union of the two natures in Christ; nevertheless our theologians testify that godly men should be led, with regard to the Lord's Supper, to no other foundations than to those of the words of institution of the testament of our Lord Jesus Christ. As to the phrases employed when we treat of the majesty of the human nature in the person of Christ exalted, our theologians wish to testify that this majesty is in no way to be ascribed to the human nature of Christ, outside of the personal union, neither are we to grant that the human nature possesses this majesty, as its own.

"The duty is especially incumbent upon all the theologians and ministers, that they teach from the Word of God those who in a simple or ignorant mind have erred from the truth, to the peril of their salvation.

" By this writing of ours, we testify in the sight of Almighty God and before the entire Church, that it has never been our purpose to occasion trouble or danger to the godly who today are suffering persecution, by this Formula of Union. For as, moved by Christian love, we have already entered the fellowship of grief with them, so we are shocked at this persecution and most grievous tyranny, and sincerely detest it.

"We testify that, in the before mentioned Declaration, we wish to conduct our churches and schools, first of all, to the fountains of Holy Scripture, and to the Creeds, and then to the Augsburg Confession. As instructed from the Scriptures, we are sure concerning our doctrine and Confession. And we have determined not to depart even a finger's breadth either from the things themselves, or from the phrases, which are employed concerning them, but the Spirit of the Lord aid-

---

[4] Afterward this book was transmitted into most able hands for criticism. The responses were suggestive, and were utilized.

ing us, to persevere constantly, with the greatest harmony, in this godly agreement; and we intend to examine all controversies according to the true norm and declaration of the purer doctrine. With the rest of the electors, princes and estates, of the Holy Roman Empire. and other kings, princes and magnates of the Christian state, we also have determined to cultivate peace and harmony." [5]

This is the defense officially made for the Formula. We have given it impartially, and have concealed nothing that might grate on modern ears. No one can fail to find in these words a zealous and a genuine motive—even if it were a piously mistaken one—for the Formula. It was not political considerations, personal considerations, partisan considerations, but the teaching of the pure doctrine to church and school, and the setting it forth in a proper, official and fixed way, so that friend and foe alike might know just what it was at which these official framers aimed.

Their intent is to furnish not private comment, but official teaching that will harmonize the Church. The stress these laymen and rulers lay on subscription (a subscription list is the laymen's way of binding to a declaration or enterprise), the willingness they assume to be responsible for all teaching in their dominions, the sharpness of their reaction against error, and many other things which we would frame and do differently in our age, are readily explainable from the environment of these godly laymen, and from the atmosphere of an age weary of unfair argument and bitter conflict. The tone here, in view of all, is moderate.

When we come to the Formula itself we find it to be a real " Reconciliation in a Christian Way," " according to God's Word, of Controverted Articles " in the Lutheran Church; and in every case the declaration is " we *believe, teach* and *confess.*" The genuine Confessional purpose of the writers of the Formula is not to be disputed. As representing the original faith of the Lutheran Church, these parts of the Church were fully justified and, indeed, as Thomasius says, " bound to proper symbolical decisions in regard to the controverted topics; and if this was done

---

[5] Condensed.

in consistency with the older confessions, so that they were consequences of them, then does it assume the place of a vital continuation of them, and constitutes them an organic whole. He, then, who recognizes them as his faith cannot without inconsequence and without contradiction refuse his belief to the Concordia." [6]

If the objector should consider himself as driven from the ground of historical fact—from the standpoint of the occasion, the need, the call, the purpose and the Confessional motive of the Formula,—he might still perhaps continue his position of objection and inquiry along the line of the character of the men engaged in the work. Were they sufficiently representative, scrupulous, pious and learned to " believe, teach and confess " for the Church?

There is one man who shines out above all others as the practical author of the Book of Concord. The original conception was his, and he, last of all, put the substance of the Formula into the form of the Epitome. His also were the testings of the plan in the scorching fires of experience. To his lot fell the persuasion and conciliation of many parties and partisans in the interest of this higher and real unity; and the return, after defeat, to new attempts. He bore the brunt of battle far more than any other, and the " much hated Book " reflected the great bitterness of its foes upon him.

He was a man of affairs, with a broad grasp of situations, capable of dealing with currents of opinion and representative personalities, of more than great, if not of exhaustive attainments in theology, and one who thoroughly understood the fact that Evangelical Protestantism, if it was to perpetuate itself against the rule of Rome, must not waste its strength in individual and contradictory effort and change, but must hold firmly and distinctly to the substance of the true doctrine of the Word of God. From this position

---

[6] Tr. in *Ev. Rev.*, II, p. 217.

neither persecution nor denunciation could move him. He recognized the doctrine of the Person of Christ as the key of the sound evangelical faith, and in this he lived and died. He began his public activities in 1546 and ended them in 1590 at the age of 62 years, passing away after having received the Sacrament of the Lord's Supper with prayers upon his lips.

Probably no other man of the Sixteenth Century has been so much abused as he, [7] especially by the Reformed writer Hospinian, and others. Let us now say the worst about Jacob Andreae, the projector of the Formula of Concord, and the author of the Epitome. He was of an abrupt and fiery disposition, vehement and vociferous in argumentation, often considering himself to be the only one in the right, peculiar in his feelings, easily stirred to passion, and not always cautious in the use of his language. He probably possessed little of that false modesty which causes a man to be eager to receive the credit for his own actions and to feel hurt when it is not given, and thus also impels him to sit quiet and be sulky when justice is not done him. He was filled with faith, patience and perseverance beyond all possible expectancy. In our judgment, he was not more ambitious, and probably not so much so, as many of the ecclesiastical leaders, servants of God, in our own day. We might mention a whole line of leaders in the Lutheran Church [8] with whom, in spirituality, he would compare favorably.

Andreae was one of those honest souls who erred in all sincerity, from undue persistency, and from passionate ear-

---

[7] "Ungerecht aber sind die maszlosen Schmähungen und Verdächtigungen, womit er von Mit-und Nachwelt ist überhaüft worden."—Wangemann.

[8] When men occupy positions of authority, it seems to become more or less of a second nature to them to speak as with authority, and to tolerate no dissent from their opinion. Even the mild, modest and truly pious Walther, is said, in his later years, to have been no exception to this law.

If we were to select a group of modern ecclesiastics, whose range, attainments and motives were on not quite so high a level as those of Jacob Andreae, the names that occur to us would be Dean Stanley, Stopford Brooke, Philip Schaff, Charles A. Briggs, Leonard Bacon, Phillips Brooks, Bishop Potter; shall we come down a step and say, I. K. Funk, Russel Conwell, Cardinal Gibbons and John Wanamaker?

nestness; and no one was more ready to openly acknowledge his weaknesses and faults than he, to ask the forgiveness of those whom he injured or offended, and to gladly forgive those who had offended him.

Yet he is painted in the blackest colors by contemporaries within and without the Lutheran Church, and by the unionistic and rationalistic Symbolical writers. Planck is particularly scathing in his arraignment of Andreae, and even Kolde has perhaps not thoroughly estimated the value and the nobility of a pioneer of this kind in the kingdom of God.

Andreae was always bold and outspoken. As a young man of eighteen years, he was the only pastor who remained at his post in Stuttgart when the city was occupied with Spanish troops in the Schmalkald war, and here by his conduct he gained the respect of the enemy. When the Interim came, Andreae, then twenty years of age, resigned rather than accept its concessions to Rome. The Interim of 1548 drove him out of Stuttgart. Later he became the fellow-laborer of Brentz, yet was not always of the same opinion with him.

In 1554 he attempted, after the manner of a Calvinistic reformer, to introduce better morals into Württemberg by law. In 1559 he was engaged in a controversy with the Calvinists concerning the presence of the body of Christ in the Lord's Supper, and, when with the Württemberg Church he cut loose from all the Philippistic mediation theories of the Supper, he drew upon himself the ridicule of Melanchthon and the attacks of Beza and Bullinger. He accompanied his prince to Regensburg in 1557 and boldly opposed the Roman preachers at the Diet at Augsburg in 1559.

In 1561 he was engaged in many administrative affairs in the Church, and in 1562 predestinarian and sacramentarian controversy occupied his time. In 1568 he was sent, at the request of Duke Julius, to aid in the introduction of an evangelical liturgy in Brunswick and to represent the South German theologians in conference with the North

German theologians, viz., Chemnitz and Selnecker, in order
to establish a consensus of agreement as to the true faith
of the Church.

From this time on, that is, betweeen 1568 and 1580, he
gave his life to the unification of the Church in a common
faith. He first sought the aid of Duke Julius and the
Brunswick theologians, and then set out for nearly all the
courts, universities and cities in Germany in order to secure
adherents to his Five Articles of Peace, and do away with the
controversies and the errors disrupting the Lutheran Church
since the death of Luther. For this purpose he visited
Brandenburg, Wittenberg, Magdeburg, Anhalt, Hesse, Pomerania, Lower Saxony, Schleswig-Holstein, Mecklenburg,
Lübeck, Hamburg, Lüneburg, Bremen, Denmark, and even
went to the Emperor Maximilian II., in Prague, who encouraged him in his work. He labored to the same end in
South Germany, from whence he hailed.

It should not be forgotten that this first effort at the pacification of the Church was made by Andreae with the idea
of reconciling all the extreme parties and of bringing the
Philippists and the Flacians, as well as the Conservatives,
together into the same faith. By 1570 he came to understand that neither the Philippists at Wittenberg, nor the
Gnesio-Lutherans at Jena, would ever enter into such an
effort to unite the Church; and he quietly projected a new
plan of operations, which would be straightforward and meet
the truth in the middle. He gave up the impracticable idea
of neutralizing opposites or of a compromising of extremes,
but set his heart on bringing together all the sound confessional elements in South and North Germany for the establishment of an orthodox confession which would preserve
the true Lutheran faith throughout all the future.

To this end he prepared Six Sermons * in 1572, and when,
in 1576, the Elector Augustus desired to restore the true
Lutheran faith in his domain, Andreae was summoned. He

---

* Vid. Chap. XXV.

attended the Lichtenberg Convention in the middle of February, 1576.

As the inception, the overcoming of difficulties, and the practical moves in the formation of the Book of Concord, were his, both Catholics and Calvinists, Philippists and Flacians were embittered against him, and even within the ranks of his own fellow-workers complaints were made of his overpowering personality. Yet Planck is obliged to say of Andreae that he " belongs not merely to the learned, but to the liberal-minded theologians of his era. . . . It was not in his nature to hate any man merely because that man was not orthodox. . . . It was not only possible for him to be just at least in the beginning toward those who were in error, but he felt a something to which it is not easy to give a name which attracted him to those that erred."

With Andreae was Chemnitz, the greatest theologian of the Sixteenth Century. " The learning of Chemnitz was something colossal, but it had no tinge of pedantry. His judgment was of the highest order. His modesty and simplicity, his clearness of thought, and his luminous style, his firmness in principle, and his gentleness in tone, the richness of his learning and the vigor of his thinking, have revealed themselves in such measure in his Loci, his Books on the Two Natures of our Lord, and on the True Presence, in his Examen of the Council of Trent, his Defence of the Formula of Concord, and his Harmony of the Gospels, as to render each a classic in its kind, and to mark their author as the greatest theologian of his time—one of the greatest theologians of all time." [10]

" Chemnitz is distinguished as a theologian for his clear and transparent style, his mild but decided spirit, and his sound and discriminating judgment. To the discussion of every subject, he brings the mature fruit of most extensive reading. He belonged to the school of the stricter Luth-

---

[10] *Con. Ref.,* p. 310.

erans, at the same time always retaining the highest respect for his preceptor, Melanchthon." [11]

With Andreae and Chemnitz was associated Nicholas Selnecker, the great theologian of Augustus, the author of the beautiful German hymn, "Ach bleib bei uns, Herr Jesu Christ," and one of the best-beloved hymn writers of that century. Though bitterly attacked, he remained silent under abuse. [12] He was severely persecuted by the Reformed Church for his work on the Formula of Concord. When Augustus died, Selnecker was deposed, his family was harassed, he was reduced to poverty, not being allowed even to remain in Leipzig as a private citizen. With these men were Chyträus, Professor at the University of Rostock, a great and renowned teacher, of naive and gracious mind, of good judgment, and Musculus, earnest, fearless and active.

We doubt whether the Lutheran Church has ever had a body of men greater in learning and piety than those who elaborated the Formula of Concord. Although they were human, and their faults were open and known, as were those of the three chief apostles of our Lord, yet the honesty of their purpose, the depth of their piety, and the sincerity of their conviction cause their life to add to, instead of detracting from, the validity of the Confession.

The Age of Illumination in the Eighteenth Century was, in its superior acuteness of culture very sarcastic as to its judgments on the men, the motives and the value of the Book of Concord. Weber and other Melanchthonian scholars write against the Book of Concord with a bitterness that is amazing. In attributing malice, dishonesty and other of the worst motives of human nature as the moving causes of historical facts, they remind one of Ernest Renan in his treatment of the life of Christ, and of certain negative critics of the Old Testament who reduce the human personalities of the patriarchs and early personages in the

---

[11] Jacobs, *Lutheran Cyclopedia.*

[12] Even Weber a century later, abuses and accuses Selnecker.

Old Testament to a compound of the most selfish attributes of human nature.

The effort of these Melanchthonian liberalists in laying so much stress on the variations of the Augustana in connection with the Preface of the Book of Concord, and with a disparagement of the motives of its writers, is to discredit the strength of the Confessional principle, to undermine the fixed and firm foundation of the Faith in ecclesiastical Confessions, and to make of them the expression of the sum of human opinion concerning Faith at any moment, which changes with every moment.

But these writers seem to forget that the same critical principles which they use against the Confessions, if valid, are also equally operative against the Scripture itself. For every variation in the manuscripts of the Confessions there are perhaps ten in the manuscripts of Scripture. And of all texts of Scripture, the Textus Receptus—the one on which our English Bible is based—is one of the most corrupt.

All scholars recognize that this is not the real point in Scripture; neither is it the real point at issue in the Confessions. If the writer were re-writing this work he might and doubtless would introduce dozens of variations into its mere phraseology; but these changes would not alter any historical values it may possess so long as the facts and positions he maintains remained identical in every writing.

We do not consider such reasoning as that of Weber on the gentle Chyträus as just. Howsoever Cölestin may deserve his condemnation, any one of a hundred circumstances, of which we know nothing, might have existed to change the whole situation. The argument is one of probabilities, re-enforced by appeal to unworthy human motives, such an argument as should not be resorted to by men of really surpassing critical power.[13]

---

[13] Krauth's " Concervative Reformation " is sometimes pointed to as very acute and penetrative in its polemic, but when we recall that Krauth wrote with a full study and mastery of Weber, the biting Melanchthonian, we may

Dr. Krauth was in possession of the researches of Weber as early as 1854, and all his positions with reference to the Augsburg Confession were matured with a full knowledge of Weber's demonstrations as to the texts of the Augustana—demonstrations that with some additions are occasionally given forth to the world under the impression of being new discoveries of more recent scholarship.

In estimating the writings of historians who criticize the confessional value of the Formula of Concord, it should be remembered that the spirit of detraction and hatred shown toward the Formula had been experienced in earlier days by the Augsburg Confession itself. Thus Possevinus declares,[14] " Quamobrem Confessio haec non Confessio, sed infitiatio atq. negatio Evangelicae, Sacrae, Christianae ac Verae Augustanae Fidei jure optimo vocanda est."

The Papists and Fabricius[15] falsely assert that the Elector John denied the Augsburg Confession and ordered his son John Frederick to abolish the Lutheran religion. And Carpzov[16] points that the Calvinists[17] and the Papists[18] affirm that the Augsburg Confession was conscripta and concinnata in the name of a few orders by a few theologians in the greatest haste and under the pressure of dreadful fear. The enemies of the Conservative Evangelical Confession have pronounced malediction upon it first and last—first on the Augustana, and last on the Formula. But its friends, the church of the Reformation, have ever enjoyed the benediction of the Augustana's healthy trunk and ever have sat in safety beneath the shadow of the Formula's protecting branches.

---

well admire the noble objectivity of Krauth's thought.   Of Weber, Krauth says, his work "is classic in the department of the text of the Confession."— *Con. Ref.,* p. 249.

[14] In l. VII. Bibl. 15. f. 298.

[15] *In Præfat, Harm.* Ungersdorfius, Pistor. Jodocus Kedd.

[16] Is. p 127.

[17] Neostadd. *in Admon.* c. 4. p. 143.

[18] Flor. Raemund. *l. 2. Synop.* et Aut. Comp. *c. l. qv. l. n, 3.* Patzm, *in Hodeg.* l. 4.

CHAPTER XXXI.

THE LUTHERAN CONFESSION.

THE ANSWER OF THE FORMULA'S OUTER FORM TO THE QUESTION, IS THE FORMULA A CONFESSION?

The Title of the Formula and its Wording—No Confessional Claim for the Solida Declaratio—Is the Formula a "Commentary"?—In what Sense it is a Mere Repetition, and not a New Confession—Comparison with the Form of the Augsburg Confession—Why the Formula presents doctrine by Antagonism—In what sense the Formula is a Commentary—Is the Formula a Treatise on Dogmatics? —Does the Formula represent All Types of Lutheranism?—Does Sharpness of Logical Form Condemn, with the Epitome as a Confession?

AFTER having examined the Formula in the light of the confessional confusion that preceded it, and of the confessional multiplication it intended to obviate; of the reaffirmation it establishes between itself and the occumenical Confessions, and between itself and the Augsburg and later Lutheran confessions; in the light of its men and motives, of its solemn and oft-repeated, " we believe, teach and confess,"—we cannot do otherwise than conclude that it came into being with a genuine Confessional purpose. Its purpose was to settle, set fast, and bear witness to the real doctrine of the Evangelical Church. This purpose is further evinced in the Title and external form of the work.

The deliberate confessional object of those who issued the Formula appears in the Title which they prefaced to the original symbolical volume. They called the Book of Concord, the " *Christian, Repeated, Unanimous Confession of Faith* of the *Electors, Princes* and *Estates of the Augsburg Confession,* and their Theologians, Subscribed at the end of the book; to which has been added a Comprehensive Declaration, from the Holy Scripture, the only norm and rule of the truth, of Certain Articles that have Come into Controversy since the happy departure from this life of Dr. Martin Luther."

Nothing could mark the intention of its framers and the historical fact itself more formally than the language used in this Title. The Public and Official Confession of those who make it, and who are standing on the Augsburg Confession, is the Book of Concord, from the Apostles' Creed at the beginning to the Epitome of the Formula at the end; to which there has then been added, in the form of proof from Scripture, the more comprehensive Declaration of the Articles in controversy. The Epitome is the confession which they put forth; and the Comprehensive Declaration is its explanation and defense—as the Apology is the explanation and defense of the Augsburg Confession, and the Large Cathechism is the explanation of the Small Catechism.

At this point we are brought face to face with the oft-repeated statement that, " while we are unwilling to ascribe public Confessional value to the Formula as a symbol of the Church, we are willing to accept it privately and for ourselves, and to admit its great value as a private work." The usual form in which this mediate position, ascribing value, but refusing Confessional validity to the Formula, declares itself, is in the phrase, " The Formula of Concord is a 'commentary,' a valuable commentary, on Lutheran doctrine. But it is only a commentary, and not a Confession."

If those who hold to this position were to include the Epitome among the Confessions, as the sixth and last symbol of the Book of Concord, we believe that the Confessional question in the Lutheran Church would quickly resolve itself into a complete and genuine harmony on the basis of the Title just quoted. For the only unsettled question, then, would be as to the formal nature and the position of the Comprehensive Declaration. The substance of doctrine would be exactly the same, no matter what view was taken as to the quality of the Comprehensive Declaration.

Says Thomasius: "The Epitome cannot, with any justice, with its clear and precise form, be exposed to this objection that it wears much more the form of a theological dissertation than that of a Confession. It lays down its positive and negative positions with so much acuteness and clearness, and maintains so happily the didactic confessional manner, that it leaves nothing, in this respect, to be desired; *indeed it surpasses in this the Augustana.* In the Solida Declaratio theological explanation and argument are predominant. . . . Why should the Form of Concord be condemned for that which is admired in the Apology" (*Ev. Rev.* II, 216).

But quite against the intention and Title of the book, against its call, origin and substance and results, the objector declares that the Formula—meaning the whole work— is "only a Commentary."

Is the Augsburg Confession only a Commentary? It was written to bring "back to the one simple truth and Christian Concord"[1] the whole Christian Church. Just so the Formula of Concord was written to "*set forth and reconcile* in a Christian way" the doctrines in the whole Evangelical Faith. The Augsburg Confession offers itself to "Your Imperial Majesty"; the Formula of Concord testifies "in the sight of God, and of all Christendom, to those now living and those who shall come after us." The Augsburg Confession witnesses to "the Confession of our preachers and of ourselves"; the Formula witnesses "that the above Declaration is our Faith, Doctrine and Confession, in which we also will appear, by God's grace, with unterri-

---

[1] Preface to *Augs. Conf.*

fied heart before the judgment seat of Jesus Christ, and for it will give an account."

If the objector, who can hardly maintain standing ground for the proposition that the Formula is only a private writing of some kind, in the face of this language of the Formula, nevertheless desires to persist in his position, he will take one step further and say: " But the Formula of Concord mentions all the Lutheran Confessions, and does not include itself among them. It expressly says that its intention is not to promulgate ' any new Confession.' Why, then, should it be regarded as a Confession ?"

To this objection the reply is evident. The authors of the Formula made clear the Confessional intent of their work, but it was not in their province to set the final and outer seal of value on what they had done. They loyally put the seal on everything that the Church had done up to their day, and they left it to *us,* their successors, with equal loyalty to the testimony of the Church, to affix the seal of value on what *they* had done.

It was not in their province to define the value of their own Confession, nor was it in line with their object. Their object was to show that they were not creating anything new, but merely recovering the one old Confession in the Church, as it manifested itself in *all* the Confessions. Their order is historical, beginning with the Scripture and coming down to the Augsburg Confession, from which departure had been made (especially in the Variata), and to which they were now trying to lead back the Church.

Thus they emphasize the unchanging Confessional principle, the same unchanging germ that unfolds itself in ever-widening circles of growth. As Frank [2] points out, the Confessions of the Ancient and those of the Reformation Church, do not run in parallels, nor stand by themselves as a row of unconnected units; but they concentre about Scripture as

---

[2] *Theologie der Concordien Formel,* I, 7.

narrower and broader circles: the latter of which presuppose and include the former, wherever the development is normal. The inner living and self-centered faith sends forth out of its trunk, in response to solicitation from without, a circle of boughs and branches, which, though turned to various sides, and varying in extent, are yet all expressions of the same inner creative life-power; and as a harmonious whole show forth the one principle within them which causes them to shoot up.

" It is from this view that the utterances of the Formula of Concord are to be measured when it solemnly assures us that it does not desire to constitute any new Confession; but, in bringing the existing conflicts to a decision in accordance with God's Word and the approved writings, it does so only in the power of the divine Word, and of the earlier Confessions. The reference of the Formula of Concord to the Confession, partly of the old and partly of the renewed Scriptural Church, at once transplants us into the organic connection, out of which the truly genuine standards always grow." [2]

Let us look more closely into the supposition that the Formula of Concord claims for itself no Confessional value, because of its repeated statements that it does not intend to make or introduce a *new Confession*. In the opening paragraph of the Solid Declaration [3] it says: " We have declared to one another, with heart and mouth, that we will neither make nor receive any separate or new Confession of our Faith, but acknowledge as Confessional the public common writings which always and everywhere were received in all the Churches of the Augsburg Confession as such Symbols or Public Confessions, before the dissensions arose among those who accept the Augsburg Confession, and as long as there was a unanimous adherence, maintenance and use of the pure doctrine of God's Word as the late Dr. Luther

---

[2] *Book of Concord,* p. 535.

explained it." This is not an utterance as to the nature of
the Formula which they are *now bringing forth,* but an explanation of the reason why they introduce the earlier and
already recognized " Public Confessions " of the Church,
viz., the three oecumenical creeds, the Augsburg Confession,
the Apology, the Schmalkald Articles, Luther's Large and
Small Catechisms, which are to them " the sum of the
Christian doctrine." The Confessors are not here intimating
that their own work is but a private commentary; and is not
to be regarded as a Symbol; but that, in this new Declaration
or Symbol, they are not setting up a new Confession.

The earlier Confessions are introduced as a witness of
the truth in God's Word, and as " a unanimously received
correct understanding of our predecessors." In other words,
they are here, without openly saying it, yet actually, placing
the Formula in line and on a level with the other historic
creeds, in so far as the Confessors touch the subject at all.

But the real point which they are elucidating is the statement that " for thorough, permanent unity in the Church, it
is before all things necessary that we have a Comprehensive,
unanimously approved Summary and Form," wherein are
brought together from God's Word the common doctrines
reduced to a brief compass, the work of previous confessors
in this field, as they state: " By what has thus far been said
concerning the Summary of our Christian doctrine, we have
only meant that we have a unanimously received, definite and common form of doctrine, which our Evangelical
Churches together and in common confess." When, then, they
speak of making no new Confession, they mean to say that
the Formula, as a Confession in line with the Augsburg
Confession and the other Confessions before it, is a Confession of the same old "unanimously received, definite common
form of doctrine." It is not a new Confession, but merely
a repetition of the old Confession, and therefore of the same
authority as the old Confession. "In order that the truth
may be preserved the more distinctly, and be not hidden

under rather general words, we have expressly made a Declaration to one another; so that there might be a Public, Definite Testimony, not only for those now living, but also for our posterity, as to what is and should remain the unanimously received understanding and judgment of our Churches."

This "Declaration," this "Public Definite Testimony," intended for "Posterity" and showing the "unanimous" teaching "of the Churches," guarding against false doctrine and practice in the ministry and in the schools, is not a private writing, but consciously professes the elements of symbolical authority. And can there be doubt as to this authority? We have the judgment of Seeberg: "The Formula of Concord thus at once assumed a position among the regulative symbols of Lutheranism." [4] We have the remarkable testimony even of Schaff:—

"The Formula is the fullest embodiment of genuine Lutheran orthodoxy, as distinct from other denominations. It represents one of the leading doctrinal types of Christendom. It is for the Lutheran system what the Decrees of Trent are for the Roman Catholic, the Canons of Dort for the Calvinistic. It sums up the results of the theological controversies of a whole generation with great learning, ability, discrimination, acumen, and, we may add, with comparative moderation. It is quite probable that Luther himself would have heartily indorsed it, with the exception, perhaps, of a part of the eleventh article. The Formula itself claims to be merely a *repetition* and *explication* of the genuine sense of the Augsburg Confession, and disclaims originality as to the substance of the doctrine." [5]

Schaff here admits that the Formula " is for the Lutheran system what the Decrees of Trent are for the Roman Catholic "; and that the disclaimer of originality (" not a new Confession ") refers to the substance of the doctrine—to

---

[4] *Hist. Doctr.*, II, p. 382.

[5] *Creeds of Christendom*, I, p. 338 sq. Schaff's footnote is discussed **elsewhere.**

the old doctrine—and not to the symbolical form of the Declaration. This is sufficient to convince the discriminating mind that it is untenable to maintain that the Formula is but a private commentary. But, if more evidence be needed, it is to be found in many places in the Formula. Thus the authors bind themselves, saying:—

" We will speak . . . nothing contrary to this Declaration, but . . . intend to abide thereby. . . . We have attached our signatures with our own hands." This is not the language of a Commentary nor of a Dogmatic. It is the language, most solemn, deliberate and final, of a binding Confession.

Let us compare the public forms of the Augsburg Confession with those of the Formula, and see whether these be not of equal symbolical validity. The Augsburg Confession appeals to the Emperor; the Formula, to God Himself and the Judgment Seat of Christ. The Augsburg Confession was intended as part of " a mutual presentation of writings and calm conference between us." It was one of two religious parties appearing before the Emperor, and was not sanctioned by a Council of the Church: " In the event that . . . the difference between us and the other parties be not settled, we present ourselves . . . ready, *though it be beyond what is sufficient,* to . . . defend our cause in a general, free and Christian Council. . . . Nor do we intend to forsake it by this or any other document, unless the matter between us should . . . be compared, settled, and brought to Christian concord." The Augsburg Confession, therefore, was not the Confession of a General Council—was not even laid before the General Council; but it was " a solemn and public protest " by one of two parties before a civil tribunal. The Formula of Concord takes this Augsburg Confession and binds it in with the other symbols of the Christian Church, " as the symbol of our time "; and confessionally acknowledges it and the other Lutheran symbols as binding, in the same way in which it confesses its own Declaration as binding.

On the distinction between a private dogmatic writing and a public standard, Charles F. Schaeffer said many years ago:—

" The Form of Concord, after asserting that the peace of the Church can be permanently established only by the adoption of a compendious statement, or type of doctrine derived from the word of God, proceeds to declare that this compendious form of doctrine ought to consist *not of private but of public writings,* prepared in the name of the associated churches, and sanctioned by them, or, in other words, of symbols or creeds adopted formally by the lawful representatives of the Church as expressive of her real sentiments. [6]

" Even the writings of men like Luther and Melanchthon do not contain our creed unless these writings have been officially recognized and adopted by the Church. It is the extreme of injustice to burden us with private opinions which have never passed the ordeal of a public ecclesiastical revision. We accordingly maintain as a fundamental principle that no doctrine can be considered as a Lutheran doctrine unless it be taught in the acknowledged standards or symbolical books." [7]

The forms used in the Formula are not of a private or dogmatic, but of a Confessional character: " *We believe, teach* and *confess.*" So, also, the rejection or condemnation of false doctrine is symbolic; and in this, too, the exact Confessional form of the Augsburg Confession is followed, only more fully: " They teach."

The Rejection, or Antithesis, is important. Modern feeling hesitates at the bold and outspoken condemnation of error. It would tread more softly; and there are those who stumble at the negative, or condemnative, clauses, even of

---

[6] *Book of Concord,* II, 535.
[7] *Ev. Rev.,* I, p. 464.

the Augsburg Confession, drawn up by Melanchthon him-self. We must not forget that the Scripture[8] is as clear and frequent in its condemnations as in its affirmations—though much modern preaching is not true to Scripture in this respect, but tones down and omits its minatory ele-ment; and that the Confessions are but faithfully following their rule of faith in bearing honest testimony against, as well as in favor of, that which is Scriptural.

In the second place, we must also remember that we learn most by the presentation of a doctrine in its antago-nisms. The mere affirmation is too smooth to stir the activ-ity of the mind and the experience of the soul; but when the false is set in its own glaring contrast to the true, our mind and spirit awaken to the real nature of both. This is doubtless the reason why God permits history to develope by extremes; and why experience, in all its bitter and appar-ently unnecessarily tragic contrasts, is the most effective teacher.

So long as the positive facts were new and not firmly grounded in the Church's consciousness, *i. e.,* so long as Christianity had not yet conquered the world, the positive form of statement, as found in the Apostles' and Nicene Creeds, was most wholesome. But already in the Athanasian Creed, the necessity of impressing the older and more worn truth by contrast began to be felt, and the condemnatory begins to appear.

Much more so would this be the case after a thousand years more of the reign of external Christianity. It was the very hardness and settled character of the traditional wrong in the case of the Pharisees of the New Testament, and of Judaism in the Old Testament, that brought forth the sternest denunciations of the Saviour. He was more earnest and terrible in His denunciation[9] than are any of the Creeds.

---

[8] *Vid.* Chap. VI.
[9] *Ib.*

Moreover, a Confession, in testifying to a doctrine, is expected to *draw the line*. This is the one difficult thing in judgment of the truth. For this purpose, namely, to draw the line, in earthly affairs, the most solemn tribunals, the supreme courts of our land, have been erected; and, if the Church is to be guided aright, this difficult duty should also be undertaken in the symbols that speak for her fundamental and determinative principles. Hence, for these good and various reasons, the " *reaction* " of the doctrine, the *negative declaration,* no less than the *positive,* should be heartily received and openly confessed.

And there is a wider view-point to be taken into consideration in this connection. The Church in her Confessions is always on the defensive. Starting with the substance of Christ in its lowest and most compact terms, her Confessions have never been extended a single point beyond what was needed for protection and defense. They have never been unfolded and expanded *a priori,* that is with a desire simply to cover the field of possible positive faith, but always to check the spread and heal the Church of error.

The spores of error like those of weeds are more prolific than the seeds of truth, and with every succeeding century's development of civilization and philosophy, the sheer burden of education in secular no less than in religious development becomes ever more heavy. This is one of the penalties of life in a world old with thought and action. What was once only a germ becomes multitudinous in its unfoldings and branchings. But in each case, in the Confession, it is those who introduce the variation, the error that requires additional discrimination, that are responsible for the additional bulk of Confessional statement, and not the Church. In reply then to the call for smaller and fewer creeds in our day, a cry often born of modern impatience and ignorance, we say there never were so many errors afloat as now. While modern forms must be met by vital statement, the latter cannot omit or evade the complicated facts as they actually exist, in order to be more popular and more elementary, without suffering from the shallowness that accompanies merely popular forms of statement.

That the Formula is " a Commentary," in the sense that it is an exposition not independent in form and matter, but leaning upon previous Confessions for both—upon what has been made public and acknowledged as standard in the public mind—*i. e.,* that it is *interpretative* and not *constructive,* may be admitted; if, therewith, we accept the interpretation as part and parcel, and as of equal Confessional authority, with the original. [10]

But even here it must be borne in mind that the Formula is not a commentary in the usual sense of the word. It does not " comment " either upon the text or upon the formal material of the Augsburg Confession. It leans only upon the *topics* of the Confession, and its presentation of these topics, both in form and in subject-matter, is independent and whole. It is a " commentary " of the same order as Virgil is a " commentary " on Homer, or as Deuteronomy is a " commentary " on Leviticus and Numbers.

Granting, then, that the Formula is a commentary, it is evident that the work of comment is not its sole, nor its most important and final function. In its own words, it " sets forth," but it also " reconciles " " for all future time." Its intention in doing so is to become a Confessional standard. If it has failed as a standard, it is not a commentary, but a standard only partially accepted, and only partially attaining its object.

In withholding Confessional authority from the Formula, it is possible to vary the descriptive figure applied to the work. Instead of drawing an illustrative term from the exegetical field, and calling the Formula a "Commentary," the term may be taken from systematic theology, and the

---

[10] As an approved judicial decision, and not merely an argumentative opinion on the original.

Formula called a " Dogmatic." " The Formula," says the objector, " is not a Confession, but a good, yet unauthoritative work on the dogma of the Church."

That the Formula of Concord is not a " Dogmatic Treatise " is apparent at the first glance. Dogmatics are not written by half a dozen authors in conjunction; and then sent throughout the Church to be tested and criticised at Conferences and Synods called for that purpose. Dogmatics are not signed and subscribed to by nine thousand confessors. Neither are they written in symbolical form, nor avowedly for posterity. Neither do they depend for their principle of unity upon symbols of the Church, nor do they usually confine their discussion to *loci* that have been the subject of controversy.

There can be no question on this point. The Formula is either a Symbolical Book of the Lutheran Church, or it is a private and party Confession. It is not a Dogmatic. The signers to the Preface declare that " they have been most grievously accused as being unable to decide on anything concerning their faith, as certain"; and as therefore " fabricating new Confessions almost every year, yea, indeed, every month." [11]

Hence they " once more *declare* and *testify before God and all mortals*" that, in their Declaration, they are " not introducing a new Confession, or one different from that presented in 1530," but that they wish " to conduct our Churches and schools first of all, indeed, to the fountains of Holy Scripture, and to the Creeds, and then to the Augsburg Confession." [12] "We mean that doctrine,· which, having been derived from the Prophetic and Apostolic Scriptures, is contained in the three ancient Creeds, in the Augsburg Confession, presented in 1530, then in the Apology, in the Schmalkald Articles, and lastly in both the Catechisms.

---

[11] Preface, *Book of Concord* (Jacobs), p. 15.
[12] *Ib.,* p. 18.

" . . . Therefore, we also have determined not to depart even a finger's breadth either from the things themselves or from the phrases which are employed concerning them; but, the Spirit of the Lord aiding us, to persevere constantly, with the greatest harmony, in this godly agreement, and we intend to examine all controversies according to this true norm and declaration of the purer doctrine."

When it was perceived that the Declaration of the Formula agreed with God's Word and the Augsburg Confession, the signers of the Preface " publicly bore witness concerning it with heart, mouth and hand. Wherefore that godly agreement is called, *and perpetually will be,* not only *the harmonious and concordant Confession* of some few of our theologians, but, in general, *of the Ministers and rectors of schools, one and all,* in our provinces and realms." [13] This language speaks for itself. The real reason for reducing the Formula to the level of a Dogmatic lies in the substance of the doctrine, and does not arise purely from the character of its outer form. The great and substantial objection against the Formula to-day is the objection of the Philippists in the Sixteenth Century, viz., that it does not represent every type of Lutheranism. In shutting out the extreme Philippists, and the extreme Gnesio-Lutherans, and in exposing the waverings of Melanchthon, it has, in the eyes of some Lutherans, narrowed itself from a generic to a party document. Several important facts are not to be lost sight of at this point: The first of these is, that the persistence of Melanchthon and his extreme party followers was responsible for the disintegration that the Formula repaired; the second is, that Andreae actually made his first attempt at union on the broader basis, and failed, because neither the extreme Philippist nor the extreme Gnesio-Lutheran would unite on a central Confession; and, thus Providence so ordered, in the third place, that the

---

[13] *Book of Concord,* p. 13.

Confession in the Formula was to be the *true Word of God* unadulterated with human changefulness; and party expediencies were not to moderate it either in this or in that direction.

Melanchthon was not slighted in the Formula. He is mentioned with respect; but he is not mentioned as an authority, like Luther, because his testimony did not give forth " no uncertain sound." His spirit and method, on their good side, are recognized and employed in the Formula, as might be expected at the hand of Melanchthon's own pupils.

There was one to whom the reputation of Melanchthon was much dearer than to those who, in the Twentieth Century, seem to glory in his doctrinal variations. " No one was in so eminent a sense the pupil of Melanchthon, as was Chemnitz. Connected with him by family ties, and living under his roof, the studies of Chemnitz were guided by Melanchthon, not as a public teacher, but with the close contact of personal interest and intimacy. As a teacher of theology, Chemnitz lectured on Melanchthon's 'Loci,' and Melanchthon himself was occasionally in the audience. The fidelity of the younger theologian to the stricter type of Lutheran theology, and his responsibility as its ablest defender, never led him into harsh denunciations of the man to whom he confesses that he owed so much." And he was the leading theologian of the Formula. He saw its necessity, he guarded its form, he confessed it with heart and mouth, and he explicated and defended its doctrine.

Schaff, defining the nature of a Confession in his Creeds of Christendom, avers that neither the dogmatic, the doctrinal nor the polemic form of a creed renders it any the less a Confession. He says: " A creed may cover the whole ground of Christian doctrine and practice, or contain only such points as are deemed fundamental and sufficient, or as have been disputed. It may be declarative, or indicative in form. It may be brief and popular (as the Apostles' and the

Nicene Creeds), for general use in catechetical instruction and at baptism; or more elaborate and theological, for ministers and teachers, as a standard of public doctrine (the symbolical Books of the Reformation period). In the latter case a confession of faith is always the result of dogmatic controversy, and more or less directly or indirectly polemical against opposing error."

Another objection frequently urged against the Formula is the sharpness and the very evident logic of its form. But when we remember the subtlety and the difficulty of the subject-matter, the emphasis given to just such statement by Melanchthon, and the whole object to be attained, we may be induced to admit that it would have been difficult in that age to embody the substance in any superior form.[14]

The Epitome is the Confession Proper; and the Ample Declaration is its establishment. The material developed is the eleven articles, in the order of the articles in the Augsburg Confession. The Epitome first briefly states the case in controversy (status controversiae); approves the pure teaching (pars affirmativa); and disapproves the wrong teaching (pars negativa). The fundamental exposition (Solida Declaratio) treats of the articles in connection with each other. Then there follows an appendix of heresies.[15]

Thus, the method of the Formula is to present the doctrine, in each case, in simplest witness form, and follow with the larger exposition. It is suitable to *its* purpose, as a Confession, as the varying forms of the oecumenical

---

[14] The form of thesis and antithesis, used by Luther at the opening of the Reformation, and still more so by Melanchthon in his disputations, has been broken by the modern method of induction, but is often employed to-day by the speculative and sketchy theologians of the age. The method in the Formula is a beautiful combination of Luther's frankness with Melanchthon's logic. " As Melanchthon's views of the Teaching and the Church remained the norm, so the influence of his dogmatic is clearly to be perceived in the individual results arrived at in the Formula."—*Seeberg*, on " Formula " in *Hauck*.

[15] The testimony of the witnesses of the Holy Scriptures, etc., in eight articles, by Andreæ and Chemnitz, is not a part of the Formula.

and the other Lutheran Confessions are suitable to *their* purpose.

That the Formula of Concord was not intended to be sharp, controversial and condemnatory, but to draw the teeth out of the highly inflamed and controversial discussions raging in the Church, may be seen from the Preface :—[16]

" Godly men, lovers of peace, judged that the increasing dissension could best be met by an accurate explanation of the controverted articles from the Word of God, which would reject and condemn the false dogmas; and clearly present the divine truth. This would not only silence adversaries, but would show the more simple and godly how to act in these dissensions, and to avoid future corruptions of doctrine."

And could anything be more true of our own day than the following: " Besides, this matter is of importance also in this respect, viz., that troublesome and contentious men, who do not suffer themselves to be bound to any formula of the purer doctrine, may not have the liberty, according to their good pleasure, to excite controversies which furnish ground for offence, and to publish and contend for extravagant opinions. For the result of these things, at length, is, that the purer doctrine is obscured and lost, and nothing is transmitted to posterity except **academical** opinions and suspension of judgment." [17]

---

[16] *Book of Concord,* p. 11.
[17] *Ib.,* p. 10.

CHAPTER XXXII.

THE LUTHERAN CONFESSION.

THE ANSWER OF THE FORMULA'S SUBJECT-MATTER, TOUCHING THE QUESTION, IS THE FORMULA OF CONCORD A CONFESSION?

The Subjects Treated were Subjects of the Day—They were Agitating the Whole Christian World—The Need of Settling them was Felt by the Melanchthonians —The Formula Starts by Planting itself Firmly on Scripture—It Treats the most Vital Doctrines of Christianity, Centering All in Christ—The Formula Treats of Christ: His Work, Presence, Person—It Touches the greater Questions of Christian Faith—Original Sin—Man's Freedom—Infused Righteousness—Law or Gospel—The Person of Christ in the Sacrament.

WE HAVE made our way through many structural preliminaries, and have now come to the heart of the Formula. Is its subject-matter of a weight and fitness to comport with the character of a standard of the Church of the Lord Jesus Christ? Are the doctrines dealt with the right ones for Confessional use? We believe that they are, that they are the great doctrines to which the Church needs to give the Confessional weight of her testimony to-day, in the midst of the errors in which she is living and that are rising around her.

Let us begin by recalling that the subjects treated in the Formula were the problems of the day. The framers of the Formula were not responsible for the subject-matter with which the Confession deals. These questions were in the *times,* and were agitating *the whole Christian world.*

Instead of characterizing these problems as petty controversies within the narrow boundaries of a particular Lutheranism, the profound and broad-minded historian will recognize them as the great religious questions that ever agitate the human mind; and as springing, in the order of a natural and necessary development, from the earlier premises of Protestantism; and as affecting simultaneously not only the Lutheran Church, but the whole of Sixteenth-Century Christianity.

In the Roman Church they took the form of the Jansenist controversy; and in the Reformed Church they came to the surface in the Arminian controversy; while in the deeper bosom of the Lutheran Church, which was sustaining a dual line of development—on the one side, reaching out and attempting to approximate to a common Protestantism; and, on the other side, unfolding, in successive conflicts, the specific and inner quality of its own nature—they came to a head in the Person of Christ, Son of God and Son of Man, and in the most profound sacramental mystery revealed to man.

If the Augsburg Confession flowed forth as the necessary witness, of the earnest soul, awakened by Scripture, against the errors of Rome, the Formula of Concord was the outflow of the same mind and heart, most deeply agitated in attempting to find, for its newly-found doctrine of salvation, a basis sufficiently grounded in the Scripture and sufficiently developed to ward off the extremes of Protestantism's own unfolding life. The Formula of Concord, like other great documentary foundations of history, arose out of terrific conflict and upheaval; for, after the external struggle had been won at Augsburg, the internal weaknesses began to manifest themselves. The Formula was not a book forced upon the Church, nor composed academically in days of peace. It came forth out of much anguish as an inner necessity and as the answer of an obedient Scriptural conscience to the needs of the day. The writers of the Formula say, " These controversies are not mere disputes concerning words." The subjects are great. Their one wish is a practical one, viz., that " the errors and corruptions. that have arisen may be shunned and avoided by sincere Christians who prize the truth aright."

The historian should not overlook the important fact that the need of a Confessional settlement of the problems that were ploughing into the vitals of the Church was felt as well on the Lutheran-Philippist side. The attempt to enlarge and amplify our Confessions first appeared among the Melanchthonians. " It was in the unionistic part of our Church," says Krauth, " that the tendency first appeared to put forth bulky Confessions, and the necessity for the Book of Concord was largely generated by the greatly larger bodies of doctrines which were set forth by the Philippists." The source of the trouble was on the broad side of the house. Its revered head, the excellent Melanchthon, was constantly shifting his ground, treating truth as though it were some human opinion to be modified and adapted to the temper of the hour, and thus destroying its fundamental stability.

While the doctrinal questions undoubtedly would have arisen of themselves within the heart of Lutheranism, the tortuousness, and prolongation, and fierceness of the conflict, was in no small part due to the haziness which overshadowed the whole evangelical field of truth. To again quote Krauth:[1] " We have twenty-eight large volumes of Melanchthon's writings—and, at this hour, impartial and learned men are not agreed as to what were his views on some of the profoundest questions of Church doctrine, on which Melanchthon was writing all his life! "

This same statement, it is true, may also, in some places, be turned against Luther; for he can often be quoted on both sides of the same question. But his utterances, not-

---

[1] *Con. Ref.*, p. 291.

withstanding, were all genuine insights, and not accommo-
dative adaptations; and, therefore, serve, in the end, only
to swell the fuller harmony and strength of the ultimate
principle which the Church maintains.

At its start the Formula plants itself firmly *on Scripture;* and to-day the very first thing we need to know in
any of the movements of our Twentieth Century is the
attitude which their promulgators take toward Scripture.[2]
Without limitation, the Concordia sets up the Holy Scriptures of the Old and the New Testament as the "only
judge, rule and standard by which all other writings are
to be judged." This great principle, not announced in
any of the oecumenical or earlier Lutheran Confessions,
of the *Scriptura unica regula,* disposes of many Sixteenth
Century difficulties; and relieves the Formula of Concord
itself, and the full Confessional principle of our Church,
from the criticism that is often made upon it, viz., that
we lift the Confessions to the place of the Bible. In order
to prevent this very thing, the Formula has declared the
Scriptures to be the only rule, and expressly says that
the symbols of the Church, including itself, ' are not judges,
but only a witness and declaration of the faith.'[3]

It is admitted that the Formula is the only Confession
that brings out the relation of our Church to Scripture.
" The Augsburg Confession," says Schaff, " does not mention
the Bible principle at all, although it is based upon it throughout; the Articles of Schmalkald mention it incidentally; and
the Formula of Concord more formally."[3a] Schaff is per-

---

[2] That this Confession seemed so thoroughly in accord with Scripture as to
have been regarded as semi-inspired by some at a later day, does not militate
against the Confessional strength of the Formula, which has taken unusual
precaution to bear testimony against this very thing. If there are Lutherans
of the Seventeenth Century who have unduly worshiped the Formula of
Concord, are there not Lutherans of several centuries later who pay almost
similar tribute to the Augsburg Confession, as the sufficient fountain and the
palladium of such doctrine as they deem it well to confess.

[3] *E. g.:* " The . . . symbols . . . are . . . a witness and declaration of the faith."—*Intro. to Epit., B. C.,* 492.

[3a] *Creeds of Christendom,* I, p. 216.

haps not quite correct in this statement, for its Preface tells us that the object of the Augustana is to show " what manner of doctrine from the Holy Scriptures and the pure Word of God has been set forth in our lands and churches;" and the conclusion of the Augustana declares that " nothing has been received on our part, against Scripture or the Church Catholic;" and that " we are ready, God willing, to present ampler information according to the Scriptures."

But the Formula explicitly lays down the Scripture principle as the basis for the whole Lutheran Confession. The " Comprehensive Summary " is the teaching or sum of Holy Scripture as it is gathered in the Confessions of the Church. The Formula's Introduction proceeds immediately upon the Evangelical principle of Scripture, and recognizes the Scripture as the one rule and standard of faith, as the touch-stone according to which all doctrine is to be esteemed and judged. The Confessions of the old Church and the Confessional writings of the Lutheran Reformation are acknowledged as the true and faithful extract of Scripture, as the epitomical explanation of the Bible, as the sum and type of doctrine, as the unanimous certain universal form of doctrine ' from and according to which, *because* they are taken out of God's Word, all other writings, *in so far* as they are to be approved and accepted, are to be judged.' All other writings, except the Confessional writings, all ' private writings,' are authoritative only *in so far* as they are proven true by the Confession, only q u a t e n u s. This is the relation particularly to all *Tradition:* it is to be prized as an inherited good, but its value is only q u a t e n u s, that is in so far as it is not contrary to the Scripture. But the Formula of Concord by no means intends to subject the Churchly Confession to a q u a t e n u s. To the Formula the Confession is authoritative *because,* not *in how far* it is in accord with the Word of God. Thus already in the Introduction the Large and the Small Catechisms are expressly recognized as *the Bible* of the laity.

Therefore the Holy Scripture is to be accorded the position of n o r m a n o r m a n s , the standard that rules everything; the Confession as n o r m a n o r m a t a , the standard already judged by the highest standard, which serves as a standard itself just on that account.[3b]

The subjects treated in the Formula of Concord are the most vital doctrines of Christianity. All of them pertain either to man's salvation or to the person and nature of man's Redeemer, Jesus Christ. The Formula begins, like the Augsburg Confession, with man himself, proceeds to what Christ has done for man, and shows how Christ was able to accomplish such a work for man.

Here, then, is the one symbol of the ages which treats almost exclusively of Christ,—of His work, His presence, His person. Here is the Christ-symbol of the Lutheran Church. One might almost say that the Formula of Concord is a developed witness of Luther's explanation of the Second and Third Articles of the Apostles' Creed, meeting the modern errors of Protestantism—those cropping up from the Sixteenth to. the Twentieth Century, in a really modern way.

As usually represented by those unfriendly to it, the Formula of Concord is the product of an extreme, small-visioned sectarian Lutheran ecclesiasticism, under the influence of an abstract theological philosophy. The reverse is the case.[4] The Augsburg Confession has an article on the abstract doctrine of the Trinity; the Formula has none. The Augsburg Confession has no less than two articles on the Church, and one on ecclesiastical order; the Formula has none.[5] The Augsburg Confession has one

---

[3b] Göschel. *Die Concordien Formel nach ihrer Geschichte, Lehre u. Kirchlichen Bedeutung,* p. 42.

[4] Schaff in his extensive treatment of the controversies of the Sixteenth Century undesignedly pays the Formula the highest tribute, as to its handling of these problems for the modern reader, when he says, " We notice them in the order of the ' Form of Concord.' "—*Creeds,* I, p. 288.

[5] Unless the Article on Church Rites be considered one.

article on Private Confession, and one on the Use of the Sacraments; the Formula has none. That the Formula really deals with living and vital issues, as much so as the Augsburg Confession, may be seen from the fact that in the two recent and complete discussions of our Church doctrines, those by Dr. Valentine (*Christian Theology*) and by Dr. Jacobs (*Summary of the Christian Faith*), the Formula of Concord is mentioned as often as is the Augsburg Confession.

The discussions of the Formula of Concord, we repeat, touch the greater questions of our Christian faith. Every one of them is a large and live question in the Protestantism of the Twentieth Century. The subjects treated in the Formula are in truth *the burning subjects in theology at the present day,* the ones on which the Church of the Twentieth Century must speak confessionally. At the head of them we find the question touching the Word of God and the Scripture, whose antithesis to-day is the Negative Criticism and the New Theology. This is followed by the Lutheran teaching on Original Sin, whose antithesis to-day is the Evolution of man's natural powers unfolding to perfection. Then follows, third, the doctrine as to Free Will, whose antithesis to-day is a double one: I.—First, the reign of Natural Law over man; second, man's mind, soul and conscience are a product of heredity and environment. II.— Man's will is able to decide for salvation through new powers bestowed by God. This is the subtle Synergism which has infected nearly the whole of modern Evangelical Protestantism, and which is or has been taught in institutions bearing the name of our own Church. Speaking of this synergistic teaching in the work, *Christian Theology,* Jacobs says:—

"The real question involved in the discussion is this: 'Is faith God's work in

---

* Dr. Valentine puts both on a par, so far as quotation is concerned, in referring to both an equal number of times. Dr. Jacobs refers to the Augsburg Confession fifty-seven times, and to the Formula of Concord forty-four times.

man, or is it a work of man wrought through new powers bestowed by God?' In assailing the affirmation of the former by the Formula of Concord, [the author] arrays himself also against the Augsburg Confession. 'The Holy Ghost is given,' says Art. V, '*who worketh faith* where and when it pleaseth God, in them that hear the Gospel.' It is the question over again of the '*Variata*' as opposed to the '*Invariata*.' "

The fourth living doctrine discussed by the Formula is that of Justification by Faith, the doctrine that is at this moment being completely "readjusted" in English Theology so as to correspond with the old doctrine of "infused righteousness," developed in the Osiandrian controversy, one of the errors that led up to the necessity of the Confession of the Formula.

The fifth subject of the Formula is the Testimony as to Good Works, whose antithesis to-day is reaching one's destiny and salvation by character.

The sixth truth taught in the Formula is the Law and the Gospel, whose antithesis to-day is a modern preaching which places repentance and the punishment of God in the background, and emphasizes only the Fatherly Love of God.

The seventh doctrine of the Formula is that teaching which is often perverted to-day by loose Christians as found in the Augsburg Confession, viz., the Christian's use of the Law, and whose antithesis is that Christian liberty is license.

The antithesis of the Seventh Article, on the Lord's Supper, is the current view that the Communion is chiefly a meal to signify fraternal fellowship among all Christians; and the antithesis of the Eighth Article is that Christ is only a perfect man, inspired and elevated in the order of nature. The antithesis of the Ninth Article, on the Descensus, is the failure to recognize Christ's power over evil. Of the Eleventh Article the antithesis to-day is the over-exaltation of ceremonies and the entrance into liturgical extremes, on the one hand; and, on the other, their complete rejection as foolish mummery. Of the Twelfth

Article, on Predestination, the antithesis is the current belief and assertion that " men have a right to be saved "; and of the last Article, on Sectarians, the present-day antithesis is the position apparently assumed on all sides that the Church is a human organization in which men of one temperament flock together to express their own religious feelings; that every man has a right to utter his own views in every pulpit, that all pulpits should be open to all teachings, since " truth is mighty and will prevail," and that no theological errors are important, nor to be suppressed, since, after all, heresy is only half-truth groping its way through to the fuller possession of all sides of every subject. It would be difficult to find a more modern catalogue of subjects, or one on which the Lutheran Church is more needed for testimony and confession.

Let us look at this important matter somewhat more in detail. The truths testified to and confessed in the Formula are at the very heart of Christ's redemption, and they are treated not only with a face toward Rome, as in the Augsburg Confession, but with a face toward radicalism. They set up the true Faith in the midst of its two extremes. They give us the central view of the questions concerning sin and grace, justification by faith, the use of good works, the Law and the Gospel, the Lord's Supper, and the Person and work of Christ. To these are added a discussion on church ceremonies (a living question to-day, as we have seen), one on predestination (a living question), and a catalogue of wrong doctrines and wrong teachings of all kinds.

The first article goes to the root of humanity's plight. It discusses the source of all the evil in man, original sin —not in the hard and dry scholastic manner of Calvinism, nor in the superficial manner of Romanism, but with a thorough grasp of Scripture and a modern touch. The question analyzed is whether original sin is the nature of man itself, or a corruption of his nature; and the errors disposed of are those which inhere, in large part, in the loose and liberal Christianity of to-day.

No one can discuss theology, especially original sin, without at least stumbling across the theological question of free will. This is not a philosophic doctrine.[7] Valentine himself is not able to omit a consideration of it; and though he believes, as we do, that "the weary metaphysical strife" is unnecessary, yet, of the theological question, he says, "This subject is one of great importance, deeply integrated in Christian theology."[8] The Scriptural teaching as to man's freedom and his relation to the converting grace of God is one of the most fundamental and far-reaching of all the principles of Christianity. The New Testament devotes much space to it. It was the subject of the great controversy between Augustine and Pelagius. All unevangelical and much nominally evangelical modern preaching is vitiated by errors on this subject. The Augsburg Confession had discussed it, and on the right foundation; but, in later years, Melanchthon had taught a form of Synergism, "a refined evangelical modification of semi-Pelagianism."[9]

This doctrine of Synergism, or a partnership between man and God in the work and merit of salvation, is a natural and tempting belief of the human mind, and one which is continuously injurious to the free grace of God, and to a perfectly pure faith in man. The testimony of the Formula on this point is admirably clear, simple and useful; and it leads to the central doctrine of justification by faith.

In the Augsburg Confession justification had been properly treated. Lutheranism had always taught clearly the distinction between justification as an external act of God

---

[7] The philosophic problem of free will or necessity is a question in a different field.

[8] *Christian Theology*, I, p. 464.

[9] Schaff, *Creeds of Christendom*, I, p. 270.

freeing man in his relation to God, and sanctification as an internal act of God in man; and had viewed sanctification as the necessary effect of justification.

But it was a Lutheran university professor, a speculative genius of great learning, who became the first Protestant to assail the forensic conception of justification, and who declared that the sinner is *made* just by an *infusion* of the divine nature of Christ, which is our righteousness. This rejection of justification as a forensic act, and the errors connected with an infused or a developing righteousness in the human soul, is the heart of the New Theology of our day. Since some latter-day Lutherans choose to resort to non-denominational encyclopedias and Bible dictionaries, rather than to the Confessions, for their theology, let us take this cardinal principle of our Church, which Luther calls " the article of a standing and falling Church," justification by faith, and see whether the Lutheran Church does not to-day need the Formula of Concord in the maintenance of this teaching.

The representative English theological cyclopedia of the century, many of whose articles are treatises in themselves— some of them more extensive on a single subject than the whole Formula of Concord with all its subjects, presents the following exposition of justification:—

"One of the commonest views in modern theology makes justification dependent on a real union with Christ, breaking down the sharp distinction between justification and regeneration, and treating them simply as aspects of the same process. Faith, on this view, is to be regarded in justification not simply as the reflex of Divine grace, but as comprehending the spiritual content of union with Christ, and of the gift of the Spirit, which is the basis of the ethical life of the Christian. Hence this view of justification is claimed to be 'ethical'; justification according to it being a recognition of what really is in the believer his new life, as well pleasing to God. A reconciliation with the forensic view is found in the Kantian thought that God judges by the ideal; so that justification appears as a prophetic judgment, which sees in the first germ of the new life its whole fruit.

"This view is closely akin to Osiander's. It has undoubtedly points of contact with the broader use of the word 'faith' in St. Paul, who, as Pfleiderer points out, often uses it as practically equivalent to the whole of Christianity

(*Urchristenthum*, I, p. 250; *cf.* I Cor. 12: 9f; 16: 13). It is further along the line developed in the cycle of passages like Rom. 8: 17; Gal. 2: 17; I Cor. 4: 4; 9: 24, 27; Ph. 3: 10-14, as previously explained."

So, then, it is admitted that the Osiandrian error, which the Formula combats, and which is included in what are often termed those " petty," " dead," and " useless " " Sixteenth Century " " Theological controversies," is *" one of the commonest views in modern theology."* If such is the case, it brings the Formula up to date, as to subject-matter touched on, as the most modern and useful of Lutheran symbols.

It is true that the Augsburg Confession also deals with this cardinal article, but in the cyclopedia referred to, in differentiating the Roman, the Lutheran, and the Reformed doctrines, the Augustana is not mentioned; while the Formula is discussed and criticised at length, as the representative of historical " Protestant Theology." Says the article :—

"The Protestant theology, like St. Paul, found the revelation of the divine grace in Christ, and His work for sinners. Here, however, a considerable development takes place, based upon the mediaeval development of the doctrine of the Atonement due to Anselm. The latter had viewed the death of Christ in the first place as a satisfaction to God's honour, which liberated Him from the necessity of punishing sinners, and in the second place as a merit or work of supererogatory obedience, which could be made available for His followers. The Protestant theology accepted both these ideas, but with such modifications as made it possible to combine them with the forensic idea of justification. The death of Christ was viewed not as a satisfaction to God's honour, but to the penal sanctions of His Law. To this was added His active obedience to the Law in His life as a satisfaction to its positive requirements. The whole was summed up as Christ's active and passive obedience or merit, and regarded as a provision of the Divine grace with a view to the justification of sinners. Justification consists in the gracious imputation of this two-fold merit or obedience to the sinner on the sole condition of faith, so that he becomes not only guiltless before the Law, but also totally free from its claims. This conception is common to both the Lutheran and the Reformed Churches. It did not grow up all at once; but the roots of it can be traced in the earlier Reformers, and it finally established itself firmly in both Churches. It is completely stated in the *Formula of Concord* (pars ii. *Solida Declaratio*, iii, 14, 15)."

This Evangelical doctrine is then criticised at length in the cyclopedia, as follows:—

"The conception of Christ's death as a satisfaction to the penal sanctions of the Divine law, on the ground of which God forgives sinners, may, indeed, be accepted as a natural interpretation of the Pauline conception of Christ's death as an expiatory sacrifice for sin, if this conception is to be translated into terms of law. Whether, however, such translation is desirable, is questionable; as we saw that the forensic point of view is only formally and not materially regulative for the Pauline conception of justification. Thus, instead of seeking to translate related conceptions into legal terminology, we ought rather to seek such an explanation (or, if need be, modification) of them as accords with the material element in St. Paul's idea of justification, viz., that it is entirely the work of grace, 'apart from law.' The Protestant theology, in fact, misinterprets Paul by taking his legal phraseology as essential, and seeking to systematize his whole view of justification and its presuppositions under legal ideas. The attempt of the Protestant doctors to conceive the whole process of salvation in legal forms, made them introduce into theology a number of axioms which are in no way part of the Christian view of the world. Such an axiom is that all sin must be punished; whereas the Christian religion teaches that it can be forgiven, and forgiveness and punishment are mutually exclusive (*Cf.* W. N. Clarke, *Christian Theology,* p. 330). Another axiom is that the punishment of sin may be transferred from one person to another; whereas the very essence of the idea of punishment is its connexion with guilt. The vicarious suffering of the innocent for the guilty is not punishment. A third axiom is that merit may similiarly be transferred from one person to another; whereas the moral result of a life, which is what is meant, is personal, and while it may result in the good of others, cannot be possibly separated from the person of its author, and treated as a commercial asset. That the Protestant doctors had to base their theology on axioms like these, plainly shows that they were on the wrong line in attempting to translate the doctrine of salvation into legal terms. We may no doubt recognize behind the forms of the Protestant theology the intention to show that the Divine grace itself is the grace of a Holy and a Righteous God. But the immediate identification of the Divine Righteousness with its expression in law is fatal to a full and complete view of grace. St. Paul might have taught a better conception of law as a temporary and preparatory manifestation of the Divine righteousness, whose end is fulfilled in a higher way by grace (Gal. 3: 24)."[10]

---

[10] In opposition to this plausible New Theology teaching, we might cite the words of Thomasius on the nature of Justification. He says: "The divine act, in consequence of which this transfer to the sinner occurs, we denominate, distinguishing it from the influences by which the Holy Ghost converts and sanctifies him, a declaratory act (*actus forensis*); not designing thereby, that God in heaven pronounces, in accordance with human usages, a judicial sentence, but in the sense of the earlier teachers of our church, who characterize it as the decision of the divine mind—the determination of the divine mind and will (æstimatio mentis divinæ, relatio mentis et voluntatis divinæ). It is an act of God's intuition, who sees man not as he is in himself and in his sub-

We see that those who follow Ritschl, Kaftan, Häring, Lipsius, and Clarke,—in other words, the most progressive theologians of our day—on the doctrine of "a standing or falling church" find the typical orthodox Protestant confession of Justification in the Formula of Concord, in the article bearing testimony with reference to the Osiandrian controversy; and that they go back to the Formula as the best and most Scriptural Confession of the Protestant or Evangelical development of the doctrine of justification by faith. They recognize that the Formula of Concord is the highest representative of the Scriptural teaching of which they themselves are the antithesis.

The difficulty with many in the Mother Protestant Church who dip into the newer Scotch, British, New England or German streams is that of the near-sighted and deaf octogenarian who lived near but had never seen Niagara Falls, and who swore to and sighed for the superior majesty of a noisy stream called Roaring Run, amid the sylvan scenes of a rich neighbor of his boyhood days. They do not believe how great in volume the Witness of the Formula has shown itself to be, how impregnable, to the believer, its positions are, and how the strength of each and every doctrine in it re-enforces all the rest. Twist or remove the one doctrine of justification, the one doctrine of the Person of Christ, the one doctrine of the Word, the one doctrine of the Sacrament, the one doctrine even of

---

jective condition, but in connection with Christ, as indeed one with Christ, the holy propitiator, with whom he has, on his part, by means of faith, united himself [He sees and loves him in Christ, upon Whom he believes. Compare Luther's declaration : Fides apprehendit Christum et habet eum presentem, inclusum tenet, ut annulus gemmam ; imo vero per eam sic conglutinaris Christo, ut ex te ipso fiat quasi una persona.] ; for though justification on the part of God, results from grace on Christ's account, its subjective condition on the part of man is faith ; and therefore this objective act of God does not remain external to him, but enters directly to his conscience, and thus opens the way, so that the sinner actually perceives within himself the voice of the judging God, who absolves him from his sins, the consciousness of the divine favor and adoption springs up ; here justification coincides with the production by God of justifying faith. It is like the imputation of sin, which is God's condemnation of the sinner, and is so brought home to the heart by the Holy Spirit, that it feels the pain of remorse and the flaming wrath of the judge, terrores conscientiæ (stings of conscience). We go beyond the state-the Church, and you have thrown all the others out of joint.

The Formula is our guarantee against that twist in Lutheranism which prevailed during the reign of the Melanchthonian principle; and against the misarranged and inverted relations in the faith of many Protestants who seem nearest to the Lutheran Church to-day.

A striking illustration of the way in which a misplaced emphasis on one point spreads through, and affects, the whole doctrinal system is to be found in the teaching of Caspar Schwenkfeldt on the Lord's Supper; which led quickly to the rejection of the Lutheran doctrines of justification, of the Word and Sacrament, the Person of Christ, the Church, and the Office of the Word in the Ministry.

Schwenkfeldt's deviation resembles that of Osiander. Starting at the first impulse to salvation, we find in Schwenkfeldt the Outer Word, which is a mere sign. It causes an outer faith; but the Inner Word is the actual substantial Christ Himself, which quickens, enlightens, purifies, saves, and nourishes, without external means. The Scriptures touch only the outer man; and they profit nothing without the spiritual understanding given by God to the elect.

In the sacraments, water, bread and wine are not a medium, but are a mere outer sign of that which is imparted by living inner faith. The Person of Christ is not a union of two natures communicating the *idiomata* of each

---

ment that man is justified by faith ; more accurately to define, we add, ' by faith alone ' (sola fide). By this we exclude from justification all human excellence, works, merit, as effective or auxiliary ; assert, that neither a precursory nor a consequent human love is the procuring cause ; reject the scholastic congruent and coöperating merit (meritum de congruo et condigno) ; the formate faith (fides formata) and the infused justice (justitia infusa), and place our trust entirely and exclusively on the grace which, purchased for us by Christ, is provided and offered in the Gospel. For this very reason is this grace—grace to us sinners,—and therefore accessible and certain, because, on the one hand, independent of an atonement connected with our subjectivity, but positively complete and satisfactory to God, and, on the other, resulting from no condition than faith, otherwise it would be useless. As it is, we extend to it with confidence the hand—the poor, empty hand of faith, and apprehend with it the ' gift of righteousness,' which it offers us in Christ through the word and the sacraments."—*Ev. Rev.*, I, pp. 201, 202.

to the other, but consists in the flesh of Christ deified, and one with God. The union is a transformation or a transubstantiation of the human flesh into the divine nature. This divine flesh, given to man by the inner Word and the inner Sacraments, is the inner faith and brings justification, regeneration, sanctification and glorification. Thus we find here a false unity in the relation of the two natures of Christ, which runs from the Lord's Supper, from the Person of Christ, from justification, clear through all the other doctrines, comes to the surface in the Word and the Sacraments, and, though a unity, introduces a dualism of the inner and the outer, into human nature, into the Gospel, and into the kingdom of God, which accords neither with the healthy balance of the Scripture, nor of the facts of human life. One twist of the central doctrine of the Person of Christ, with its correlate in justification,[11] turns the system of Schwenkfeldt almost as far from Lutheranism as Lutheranism itself is turned from Rome. It is no wonder that the framers of the Formula devoted unusual care to the great central teaching as to Christ Himself.

Turning to the next (third) article of the Formula, we find it reveals the direct line of connection between the doctrine of the Person of Christ and that of justification and faith. Osiander had taught that Christ is our righteousness according to His divine nature—a doctrine which sympathizes with that of infused righteousness; and Stancar had opposed this, claiming that we are justified with

---

[11] " In the fundamental doctrine of justification all the other doctrines of the symbols are involved, so that every one who sincerely believes the one will be compelled to believe the others, if he carry out his faith. Conviction of this, on the part of any one, demands subscription to the entire body of the doctrines of the church, because they contain, developed, the faith which he entertains. Assuredly minor defects in the form would not create difficulty; the less, as in the recognition of the Symbols, what is mere theological elucidation, is not taken into the account, but the ' credimus,' ' docemus,' and ' confitemur.' "—*Thomasius*, Trans. in *Ev. Rev.*, I, p. 200.

Christ as our righteousness according to his human nature. Consequently, here again the question is one of the bearing of the Person of Christ upon other doctrines; and the Formula of Concord, true to its true balance of the divine and the human in the Person of Christ, and true to the golden balance of the whole Lutheran system, has settled the matter right by teaching that the one, whole, and perfect obedience, active and passive, of Christ, as God and man, is our righteousness; and that His whole obedience unto death, is imputed unto us.

Even in the doctrine of good works, which is the next subject of controversy taken up in the Formula, the Formula leads the disputants from the bare bones of the outer frame to the inner grace in Christ Jesus. The Roman Catholic doctrine made much of good works in its system of salvation; and the Reformation's teaching of salvation by faith alone was arrayed directly against it. Yet, up to the appearance of the Formula, Protestantism had not yet finally fixed the exact status of the doctrine of good works, in a positive sense; and in the course of time two teachings concerning them arose: one, that good works are *necessary* to salvation; and the other, that good works are *dangerous* to salvation. Melanchthon strove to solve the troublesome question by saying simply, " Good works are necessary "; but it was the Formula of Concord that finally settled the doctrine, by separating good works from justification and from salvation, yet declaring them necessary as effects of justifying faith.

Among all the effects of the Reformation there is none so popularly lauded to-day as that of the right of freedom of thought, freedom of conscience, and freedom of action. The Augsburg Confession discusses the right indirectly, in connection with ceremonies, traditions, observances, vows, etc.; and the Schmalkald Articles discuss it with reference to the Papacy; but it remained for the Formula of Concord to discuss the doctrine, not with respect to Rome, but with respect to Protestantism itself. The Augustana gives us the doctrine externally, in contrast with Rome. The Formula gives us the doctrine internally in its relation to the Gospel itself.

The Antinomian controversies, usually considered so effete, were nothing but the first cry of the Protestant mind, in its joy for freedom, refusing to be bound by any law. What could be more characteristic of the extreme religious and social democracy of our own day, and of all the individualistic movements of the Nineteenth and Twentieth Centuries, than this unwillingness to abide by the law and command of God?

It is not affirming too much to say that the bulk of our modern religious teaching, the teaching that puts all stress on God's love and mercy; that directs the ministry to preach only of heaven and be silent as to hell; that speaks exclusively of grace, and not at all of penalty,—is, in essence, and at its best, a repetition of the teaching of John Agricola, of Eisleben, who was the first Protestant to declare that the Law is superseded by the Gospel, and has nothing to do with repentance and conversion; but works only wrath and death, leads only to unbelief and despair, and is no longer needed since the Gospel is sufficient both to warn and to comfort.

This error is one of the great weaknesses of a spineless and unionistic Twentieth-Century Protestantism. It was most vigorously combatted by Luther in his catechisms and in his preaching. But the truth was settled finally and confessionally for us by the Formula of Concord, which laid down a three-fold use of the law: first, the political or civil use, to maintain outward order; second, the pedagogic use, to lead men to a knowledge of sin and the need of redemption; and third, a normative use, in regulating the life of the regenerate.

The Old Testament is not Law alone; and the New Testament is both Law and Gospel. It will only be when this

healthy balance of authority and love is universally recog
nized in our own age, that our own theology and religion,
our own training and discipline in home and school, our
own theories of pedagogy, reform and penology, and our
own teaching of ethics and psychology, will return from
the unhealthy extreme into which, in the last generation,
they have been drifting.

The step in the Formula from Law and Gospel, as given
in Christ, to love and life, as manifested and applied in
Christ—is a beautiful upward progression. The Gospel
is most concretely applied in the sacrament of Christ's
body and blood; and the prerequisite of Christ's body and
blood in the Sacrament, is the Person of Christ itself. The
Sacrament of Christ roots itself in the Person of Christ.[12a]
Thus the centre of Christ is Christ in the Sacrament, and
Christ in the Sacrament is the epitome, the summary, the
culmination of the whole Gospel. Says Jacobs:

" Assuming the doctrine of the Real Presence and the
Sacramental Union and Eating, the entire Plan of Salvation and much that it presupposes are most forcibly set
forth in the Holy Supper.

" The proclamation of death and the presence of blood
that has been shed, preach the Law as well as the Gospel,
by arraigning all who partake of the Holy Supper, of a
guilt that called for the death of the Son of God. But
with this announcement of guilt, there is also the proclamation of the remedy which has been provided. While
' without the shedding of blood, there is no remission '
(Heb. 9 : 22), here we are assured that this requirement
has been met, and that blood has actually been shed for
us; and, as a pledge of this, it is actually offered to and
applied to each communicant. The days of Old Testament waiting are over; the promise has been fulfilled; the

---

[12a] " Their [Lutheran and Reformed] controversies clustered around this
article [Lord's Supper], as the Nicene and post-Nicene controversies clustered
around the Person of Christ."—Schaff, *Creeds of Christendom,* p. 216.

sacrifice so long expected is actually here. It is not the body that is to be given, but that has been given. It is not the blood that is to be shed, but that has been shed, of which the cup is a communion. . . Each one, by himself, is made to realize that redemption has been provided for him, and the Son of God belongs individually to him! For this reason, the main stress rests upon those very small monosyllables, ' *For you.*'

" ' All the good things that God the Lord has, belong to Christ, and here become entirely mine. But that I may have a sign and assurance that such inexpressibly great blessings are mine, I take to myself the body and blood of Jesus Christ.' 'If I believe that His body and blood are mine, I have the Lord Jesus entirely and completely and all that He can do is mine, so that my heart is joyful and full of courage; for I am not left to my own piety, but to His innocent blood and pure body which I receive' (Luther, Walch's ed., XI., 842 sq.)." [12]

These are the culminating doctrines of conservative evangelical Protestantism. They are the great bulwarks and preservatives against the rationalism of Zwingli, the humanism of Erasmus, and the shallow work-righteousness of Rome—the Aristotelian excess— on the one hand; and, on the other, against the undue mystical immanence of the eternal in the temporal—the speculative extreme of Plato, Photinus, Gnosticism, Clement of Alexandria, Neo-Platonism, Origen (Augustine), Duns Scotus, Bernard, Hugo, Richard of St. Victor, Bonaventura, Albertus Magnus, Gerson, Tauler, Rüysbrock, Eckhart, Schwenkfeldt, Böhme, à Kempis, Fenelon, Guyon, Swedenborg, Emerson, and the modern pantheists. To the Protestant Church the doctrine of the Person of Christ in His Word and especially in His Sacrament, as found in the Formula, is the one bulwark against a disintegrating religious individualism, the only one which Lutheran Protestantism possesses (since it does

---

[12] Jacobs, *Summary of the Christian Faith,* pp. 356-357.

52

not, like the Reformed Churches, call in the majesty of God's law to preserve itself, nor the principle of the Church as the source of authority, as do Rome and the Episcopalians, who thus bind together minds in disagreement, and varying in conscience, in an outer unity).

The Lutheran bond is an internal one, and not external. And yet it is objective. We are grafted by Baptism into the mystical body of Christ, and in our union with Him become members one of another. In this union, and as full members of it, we receive His real body to eat and His blood to drink, as the dying gift of the living Christ to secure to us in His atoning blood the benefits of remission of sins, life and salvation. With His Word of absolution and the Sacrament of Baptism, the circle of divine power in a human congregation is completed, and each soul is held objectively to the other in Christ.

All worship, up to the Reformation, culminated in the Romish mass—the core of superstition and error, and the stronghold of a priestly order, able, as the Church, to offer sacrifice for the sins of the people.

With the brushing away of the mass as a sacrifice, both the congregation as a communion, and its order of worship, would have lost their highest centre in the true visible Word had not the sacrament of Christ's body and blood been held to as the substantial concentration of the gifts of the absolving Word.

With the Sacrament removed, the Word of absolution could not have maintained its place, and the Word would become a proclamation to the individual, and the sacrament a commemoration by associative individuals of an empty rite, [13] or an act of faith in itself almost sacrificial. [14]

It was Melanchthon, who, trying to bridge the gap be-

---

[13] " The doctrine of the Real Presence of the Body and Blood of Christ, is what gives the memorial all its force."—*Jacobs.*

[14] What *Christ could not do,* in Calvin's view, viz., come to us with His bodily presence, *our faith could do,* viz., come to Him in Heaven, by its spiritual presence !

tween the two Protestant wings by a formula of words,—
the great mistake of his life, which led him to be a maker
of confessions, or rather a confessional dogmatizer, and not
a confessor,—quietly modified the Lutheran teaching of the
real presence in the great Lutheran Confession, without consulting any one, so far as to allow the Reformed doctrine
the same right as his own in the evangelical Churches.
He so changed the tenth article concerning the Lord's Supper, "that Calvin could give it his hearty consent, and
even Zwingli—with the exception, perhaps, of the word
truly—might have admitted it." [25] He omitted the clause
on the real presence, and the disapproval of dissenting views;
and substituted the word *exhibeantur* for the word *distribu-
tantur.*

This one act in itself, done quietly and privately, by a
prominent individual in the church, in a publicly received
Confession, and in the very doctrine in which all the intrinsic divine truth and worship of the Church culminates,
and by which it most of all is openly distinguished from a
legalistic and individualistic Protestantism (with which it
never will be able to combine)—this in itself was sufficient
in our judgment to bring on the years of Confessional confusion that followed; and to justify the Testimony of a
new symbol which should go back to the original teaching
of the Church—especially if such symbol set forth that
teaching in such simple, succinct and complete manner as
is done by the Formula of Concord.

We must digress for a moment. It will be noticed by
our readers that we are confining ourselves to the doctrinal
substance of this discussion.

We do so because it is not textual criticism, but the
inner principle of the truth, which is decisive in a matter
such as this. The question of manuscripts and variations
has exactly as much place, no more and no less, in a con-

---

[25] Schaff, *Creeds of Christendom,* p. 241.

fessional discussion as to doctrine, as the variations in the readings of the New Testament affect the discussion of any such articles of faith as the divine nature of Christ, the existence of miracles, the nature of the Church, etc. The loss of originals or the existence of variations has comparatively little to do with our ascertainment of the doctrinal content of the New Testament, since the facts are not as a rule seriously affected by the changes that came by the mutations of time. But for a Luke or a John, or a Mark or a Paul to have gone through life producing new editions of the Gospels and Epistles, and to have changed the style for the sake of improvement—to say nothing of changing the sense—would have been greeted with amazement. The Witness of the Gospel is too weighty to be made the subject of change in matter and style.

Dr. Schaff claims that Melanchthon's later view of the Lord's Supper essentially agreed with that of Calvin, and that this Melanchthonian-Calvinistic view "was also in various ways officially recognized with the Augsburg Confession of 1540." [16]

The unity of Melanchthon, Bucer and Calvin on the Lord's Supper furnishes the Reformed historian Heppe [17] the foundation for his theory that Melanchthonianism, Humanism and Calvinism together composed a great historical reformatory movement, which was suppressed by the narrowness of the Gnesio-Lutherans. Seeberg, speaking of the situation prior to the Formula of Concord, states that "the peculiar characteristics which marked German Calvinism in many particulars may be at least partly accounted for by this commingling of Humanistic-Melanchthonian and of Calvinistic elements." [18]

---

[16] *Creeds of Christendom,* p. 280.   Schaff adds that this edition "was long regarded as an improved rather than an altered edition"; which is quite natural, since the seeds of error are not detected in their young shoots, but only very late, and after stem and leaf have grown up.

[17] *Geschichte des Deutschen Protestantismus,* 1855-81, 4 vols.

[18] II, p. 381.

At all events, it is certain that the doctrine of the Lord's Supper, as the application of the mystery of the Cross, is the one central and concentrated test of the whole tree of living Faith that lies behind it. The great sensuous Roman system comes to flower in the gorgeous and glittering sacrifice of the mass; the subtle but discerning spiritual system of Calvin, a divine truth in human dialectic, unfolds the Supper into an ethereal fruit plucked by venturesome faith; the rationalism of Zwingli offers in the Supper an empty and withered blossom—ashes of roses; while the believing faith of Lutheranism finds in the Lord's Supper an applied epitome of all redemption, the real and very fruit of the Cross of Christ—the body and blood given and shed for the remission of sins, working deliverance, and bringing life and salvation.

49

CHAPTER XXXIII.

THE LUTHERAN CONFESSION.

THE PERSON OF CHRIST AND THE FORMULA OF CONCORD.

The Person of Christ the Centre—Consequences in Lutheran Theology—"Person of Christ" in the Formula—Not a New Doctrine to Bolster up the Real Presence—The Divergence on this Doctrine between the Two Branches of Protestantism—It is rooted in Luther—Luther on the Person of Christ—Whence Luther Derived fhis Doctrine—Luther's Rescue of the Sacrament—The Communicatio Idiomatum vs. The Zwinglian Alloesis—Misrepresentation of the Lutheran Faith—The Personal Omnipresence a Fundamental Fact—The Most Potent Objection—The Critique of Schaff—Inconsistency of critics of the "Ubiquity"—The Scriptural Origin of the Communicatio Idiomatum—The Ancient Creeds—The Church Fathers—The Formula and the living Christ.

PERSON OF CHRIST CENTRAL IN SCRIPTURE AND IN LUTHERAN

PROTESTANTISM.

THE doctrine of the Lord's Supper is deeply rooted in the Person of Christ. The Person of Christ is the mystery of Christianity and the ages. To-day, yesterday, forever, it is fundamental. Christ is all and in all. The theology of every age is conditioned by its lighter, or its more vital, grasp of this doctrine. No Biblical theme has had such a hold on our own time, except the critical investigation of the Scriptures, as this central one of the personality of Christ.[1] The old

---

[1] Fairbairn, *Christ in Modern Theology;* Noesgen, *Christus der Menschen und Gottssohn,* (1869) ; Grau, *Das Selbstbewusstsein Jesu* (1887) ; Bruce, *Humiliation of Christ* (1889) ; Wendt, *Die Lehre Jesu* (1890) ; Baldensperger, *Das Selbstbewusstsein Jesu* (1892) ; Gore, *Dissertations on the Incarnation*

problems as to the knowledge, presence and power of the Son of God, in relation to the limitations, growth and unfolding of the Son of Man; the psychological inquiry into the mind and the consciousness of Christ, the questions as to the Kenosis, have been pursued with tireless zeal for a whole generation.

The Lutheran Reformation began with the confession of justification by faith, but the leaven at once worked down deeper to the living ground of our justification, which is Christ. Christ is the centre of the Word of God,[2] and the centre of Lutheran theology, as Luther has built it into the explanation of the Second Article of the Creed.

This centre, the Person of Christ, was the most practical and vital part—next to justification—of Luther's Faith. For it was not the philosophy of the incarnation as such, not the speculative mystery of the union of the natures, in which he was interested. His interest lay in the mystery of the active Person. He saw salvation wrought out for himself in the life, death and resurrection of the Divine Person, and he emphasized these personal saving acts, rather than the passive condition of the natures.

From our present point of view, Luther's great work in theology was his re-discovery of the living Christ. Instead of metaphysical analyses of God and definitions of the qualities of the two natures of Christ, which was an intellectual process of the mind, and never touched Christ's saving work, Luther made the Person of Christ a part of the blessed personal experience of justification by faith. Only those who

---

(1895), pp. 71-202 ; Lietzmann, *Der Menschensohn* (1896) ; Powell, *Principle of the Incarnation* (1896) ; Mason, *Conditions of our Lord's Life on Earth* (1896) ; Gifford, *The Incarnation* (1897) ; Dorner, *Person of Christ;* Ottley, *Doctrine of the Incarnation*, Vol. II. Edwards, *The God-Man.* Bruce's several works ; Beyschlag, *Die Christologie des Neuen Testaments;* Forrest, *The Christ of History and Experience* (1897) ; Adamson, *The Mind in Christ* (1898) ; Stalker, *The Christology of Jesus* (1899). Cp. the writings of Schmiedel ; Bossuet (*Jesus*) ; Arno Neumann (*Jesus*), of the critico-physchologico-rationalistic school ; *Das Göttliche Selbstbewusstsein Jesu Nach Dem Zeugnis Der Synoptiker*, Joh. Steinbeck. 1908. A Schweitzer, *Von Reimarus zu Wrede, Eine Geschichte der Leben-Jesu-Forschung*, Strasburg, 1906.

[2] "The chief article is this, that Jesus Christ, our God and Lord died for our sins, and was raised again for our justification."—*Schmalkald Articles.*

know we are not saved by our own person and character, but by the work of Christ, can truly appreciate the Person of Christ. When we know God is working for us, we cease trying to work for ourselves.[3] Therefore the Person of Christ is something more than a doctrine, for the true Christian. It is a part of ourselves, which we carry about with us in our life.

" To know Jesus in the true way means to know that He died for us, that He piled our sins upon Himself, so that we hold all our own affairs as nothing, and let them all go and cling only to the faith that Christ has given Himself for us, and that His sufferings and piety and virtues are all mine. When I know this, I must hold Him dear in return, for I cannot help loving such a man."

In this insight of Luther, we touch the kernel of the Reformation Confession as to Christ Jesus, " the master-truth which distinguishes its theology from all previous teaching about God and the Person of Christ."[4] " The older theology had never grasped the thought that Jesus Christ filled the whole sphere of God. It limited the work of Christ to the procuring of forgiveness of sins, and left room outside of Christ for many operations of Divine grace which were supposed to begin when the work of forgiveness was ended. So there grew up the complex system of expiations and satisfactions, of magical sacraments and saints' intercessions, which made the mediæval Christian life so full of superstitions, and, to all seeming, so empty of Christ."[5]

To Luther—and this is the keynote of Lutheran Protestantism, as distinguished from Calvinism, Zwinglianism, and all other Protestantism—there was room for no other vision of God than that which Christ gives us. This cut away the pagan threads that had continued to form the web of scho-

---

[3] *Erlangen* 12. 244.

[4] *Lindsay* on Luther's Belief in the Person of Christ.

[5] *Cp.* Th. Harnack, *Luther's Theologie.*

lastic theology, and suggested the great vitalization and simplification of Christian dogma.

" ' Luther,' as Harnack says, ' in his relation to God, only thought of God at all as he knew Him in Christ.' Beyond, there is the unknown God of philosophical paganism, the God whom Jews, Turks and pagans ignorantly worship. No one can really know God save through the Christ of history. Hence, in Luther, Christ fills the whole sphere of God : ' He that hath seen me hath seen the Father ', and conversely, ' He that hath not seen me hath not seen the Father.' The historical Jesus Christ is the revealer, and the only revealer of the Father, for Luther. The revelation is given in the marvellous experience of faith in which Jesus compels us to see God in Him—the whole of God, Who has kept back nothing which He could have given us.

" There is only one article and rule in theology. He who has not a full and clear grasp of it is no theologian ; namely, true faith and trust in Christ. Into this article all the others flow, and without this they are nothing."[6] " In my heart there rules alone, and shall rule, this one article, namely, faith on my dear Lord Christ, which is, of all my thoughts on things spiritual and Divine, the only beginning, middle and end." [7]

CONSEQUENCES OF THIS DOCTRINE IN LUTHERAN THEOLOGY.

This mighty Lutheran Confession of the Person of Christ brought about certain important changes in Christian doctrine, principally in Lutheran theology ; but also to a less extent in Reformed theology in so far as it was dependent on Luther. The first of these important consequences was that the Person of Christ itself was endowed with a richer and fuller Scriptural meaning than had ever been the case in the earlier history of the Church. That Christ was God,

---

[6] *Erl.*, 18. 398.
[7] *Ib.*, 58. 63.

in all His acts, brought God on very close and intimate terms with every Christian; and that Christ was man, made God very real, very concrete, very historical and very effective to every believer. Before Luther, the relation of the Two Natures had been so put as to convey the impression that the only use and part of the divine nature in the Person was to reinforce and establish the work of the human nature. Even Augustine and Anselm expressed the matter thus, and the Reformed theology of the Reformation repeats it. But Luther was unwilling to thus crowd the divine nature into a corner. He constantly cautions us against supposing that the " Two Natures " are joined so mechanically that we can consider the one apart from the other.

" This is the first principle and most excellent article, how Christ is the Father: that we are not to doubt that whatsoever the man says and does is reckoned, and must be reckoned, as said and done in heaven for all angels; and in the world for all rulers; in hell for all devils; in the heart for every evil conscience and all secret thoughts. For if we are certain of this: that when Jesus thinks, speaks, wills, the Father also wills, then I defy all that may fight against me. For here in Christ have I the Father's heart and will." [8]

The second of the consequences of the new Reformation doctrine was that Luther restored human reality to the Person of Christ. In emphasizing the powerful and complete Divinity, Luther was the last one to sacrifice Christ's humanity. He tells us that the reason why the Scholastics went so far astray and dealt so artificially with Christ was because they had either dropped the humanity entirely, or had overlaid and obscured it by reasonings and imaginations not found in the Scripture.

" ' The deeper we can bring Christ into our humanity, the better it is,' " he says in one of his sermons. So his frequent pictures of the boyhood of Jesus are full of touches from

---

[8] *Erl.*, 49. 183, 184.

[9] *Ib.*, 6. 155.

the family life of the home at Wittenberg. The boy Jesus lived just like other boys, was protected, like them, by the dear angels, was suckled at His mother's breast, learned to walk, ate and drank like other children, was subject to his parents, ran errands for His mother, brought her water from the well, and firewood from the heap in the yard, and finally, when He grew up and became stronger, began to ply the axe to help His father (*passim*)." And this, Luther asserted against those who had erected it into an article of faith that Christ from the first moment of His life was so full of wisdom that there was nothing left for Him to learn. He will have nothing to do with those who ascribe to Christ only a mutilated humanity. "By humanity I mean body and soul. And this I wish to emphasize because some, like Photinus and Apollinaris, have taught that Christ was a man without a human soul, and that the Godhead dwelt in Him in place of the soul."

"It is," he says in his exposition of John 1:14, "the most precious treasure and highest comfort that we Christians have, that the Word, the true natural Son of God, became man, having flesh and blood, like any other man, and became man for our sakes, that we might come to the great glory: that thereby our flesh and blood, skin and hair, hands and feet, belly and back, sit in heaven above, equal to God, so that we can boldly bid defiance to the devil and all else that harasses us. We are thus made certain, too, that they belong to heaven and are heirs of the heavenly Kingdom." [10]

"It was no mere semblance of a man who was now exalted at the Father's right hand, but one who was bone of our bone, and flesh of our flesh, to whom no human experience, save sin, was foreign,—a boy who enjoyed his play and helped in little household duties, a man who shared the common lot of toil and weariness and temptation, a real man living a true human life under conditions not so far

---

[10] *Ib.*, 46. 12 sq.

removed from our own. Having life—a true human life—
He understands us fully, and we can know Him, and God
through Him. Through Him alone can we come to know
God. 'Outside of this Christ no other will of God is to be
sought. . . . Those who speculate about God and His will
without Christ, lose God completely.' " [11]

The third of the consequences of Luther's Christology was
that, while it accepted, it also put the life of Scriptural
reality, into the old Church doctrine. Luther ever insisted
that he accepted only the ancient Church doctrine on the
Person of Christ.

" 'No one can deny', he says, ' that we hold, believe, sing,
and confess all things in correspondence with the Apostles'
Creed, that we make nothing new therein, nor add anything
thereto, and in this way we belong to the old Church, and
are one with it.' The Schmalkald Articles and the Augsburg Confession begin with stating over again the doctrines
of the Old Catholic Church, founding on the Nicene Creed,
and quoting Ambrose and Augustine; and Luther's contention always was that, if the sophistry of the Schoolmen could
be cleared away, the old doctrines of the ancient Church
would stand forth in their original purity. When he spoke
of the Scholastic Theology as sophistry, he attached a definite
meaning to the word. He meant not merely that the Schoolmen played with the outsides of doctrines, and asked and
solved innumerable trivial questions; but also that the imposing edifice they erected was hollow within, and had nothing to do with the God and Father of our Lord Jesus Christ.
He maintained that in the heart of the system there was,
instead of the God whom Jesus had revealed, the abstract
entity of pagan philosophy, an unknown deity—for God
could never be revealed by metaphysics. All this sophistry
he swept away, and then declared that he stood on the
ground occupied by the theologians of the ancient Church,

---

[11] *Walch,* V, 198.

whose faith was rooted in the triune God, and in belief in Jesus Christ the Revealer of God. . . .

" Luther believed, and rightly believed, that for the Fathers of the ancient Church, the theological doctrines in which they expressed their conceptions about God and the Person of Christ were no dead formulas, but were the expressions of a living Christian experience. Luther took the old dogmas, and made them live again in an age in which it seemed as if they had lost all their vitality and had degenerated into mere dead doctrines on which the intellect could sharpen itself, but which were out of all relation to the practical religious life of men. The *Summa* of Thomas Aquinas gives little insight into the deep and genuine religious experience of the writer, and gets no inspiration there. The efforts of the schoolmen were directed solely to the exposition of the philosophical implications of traditional doctrines; they ignored the relation to actual religious life in the Church, apart from which theology becomes unreal. . . . Through Luther came the discovery that there was theological material in the living experience of Christian souls." [12]

This objective reality of justification through Christ, of faith in Christ, of Christ's sacraments, of Christ's Church, lifts the Lutheran Faith alike above the dead principle adorned with sensuous imagery of Rome; and the subjective idea, and opinion, the vague thought, or natural truth or mere sentiment of a common Protestantism. The Sacrament of Luther, for instance, is not a metaphysical miracle, nor a sentimental memorial, but a mighty and living reality.

The fourth characteristic of Luther's doctrine of the Person of Christ was that it was incorporated into theology in a plain, practical and edifying exposition.

" If Luther accepted the old formulas describing the nature of God and the Person of Christ, he did so in a

---

[12] *Lindsay* on Luther's Belief in the Person of Christ.

thoroughly characteristic way. He desired to state them in plain German, so that they could appeal to the 'common man.' He did not believe that theology, the most practical of all disciplines, was a secret science for experts. He confessed with some impatience that technical theological terms were sometimes necessary, but he did not like them, and he used them as little as possible." [13] He reached the Person of Christ from below, from the redemption of the Cross, and not from any speculative heights above. He does not reason from " what Godhead must be, and what manhood must be," to " how Godhead and manhood can be united." " He rises from the office to the Person, and does not descend from the Person to the office. ' Christ is not called Christ because He has two natures. What does that matter to me ? He bears this glorious and comforting name because of His office and work which he has undertaken.' "

The fifth, and in many respects, the most important change brought about by Luther's doctrine of the Person of Christ was the restoration to its original Scriptural intent and glory, without let or weakening, howsoever, of the doctrine of the Lord's Supper.

THE PERSON OF CHRIST IN THE FORMULA.

The Lutheran doctrine of the Person of Christ we find especially in Luther's Catechisms, as the necessary culmination of the doctrine of the personal union of God and man in Christ. The Third Article of the Augustana pene-

---

[13] (*Erl.* 1st. 36. 506). Like Athanasius, he preferred the word *oneness* to express the relation between the Persons in the Trinity. He even disliked the term Trinity or its German equivalents *Dreifaltigkeit, Dreiheit.* ' Dreifaltigkeit ist ein recht böse Deutsch, denn in der Gottheit ist die höchste Einigkeit. Etliche nennen es Dreiheit ; aber das lautet allzuspöttisch. . . . darum lautet es auch kalt, und viel besser spräch man Gott denn die Dreifaltigkeit. (2 Erl. 6. 358). He called the technical terms used in the old creeds *vocabula mathematica,* and did not use any of them in his Small or Large Catechisms.

trates little further than the Catechism, being only a slight amplification of the clauses in the Second Article in the Apostles' Creed, for the call had not yet come, and the time was not yet ripe for a fuller confessional unfolding of this inner mystery. But the Formula of Concord was driven to the innermost heart of the Faith, and deep below the complicated questions of the day, found it beating in the doctrine of the Person of Christ. This great Confession's most illustrious service is its attempt in twelve statements to confess " the pure doctrine of the Christian Church concerning the Person of Christ." Its wonderful success in opening the full Word of God to our eye as to this mystery of the ages, is a marvel.

The Formula teaches the unity of the personality, the integrity of the natures, the true divinity of the divine, and the true humanity of the human nature, the personal union and consequent communion; the fact that God thus is man, and man thus is God; the virgin birth; the death and resurrection and ascension of Christ, not as mere man, but as the Son of God; the suffering of the Son of God as our high priest; the exaltation of the Son of man at the right hand of God; the possession of divine majesty in the flesh, but the abstinence from it; the substantial, yet not earthly or Capernaitic, impartation of His true body and blood in the Holy Supper; the person of Christ not divided, as it was by Nestorius; nor the natures commingled, as was taught by Eutyches; " but Christ is and remains, for all eternity, God and man in one undivided person, which, next to the Holy Trinity, is the highest mystery, as the Apostle testifies (I Tim. 3:16), upon which our only consolation, life and salvation depend."

As a guide to contemporary religious discussion on the great topics of Christianity, and especially on problems connected with the Person of Christ, the Epitome of the Formula will, we are confident, prove more interesting, and its use of Scripture and of the pure Gospel will be as edifying, to a student and layman, as is the Augsburg Confession. The clearness, calmness, simplicity, and weight of the matter, without repetition of platitudes, fit it for convincing modern use; and we trust that the day will come when it will be published as a tract or pamphlet to be placed in every Lutheran household.

The great stumbling block in the Formula of Concord, to Roman Catholic[14] and Reformed[15] writers of the Sixteenth Century, is the introduction of the new doctrine (thus the objectors put it), of the ubiquity of the Person of Christ. With the philosophical doctrine of " the Ubiquity " as such, we have as little sympathy as these critics. The basing of the truth of the Word upon a philosophical form is foreign to the Scriptural and the Lutheran Confession. It is not " the Ubiquity," but the doctrine which is revealed in the Scripture as a divine fact, and which is applicable as a divinely revealed fact to Christ in all His relations, that is taught most clearly in Luther and in the Formula, and is an essential part of the Lutheran Confession.

We do not find this teaching scholastic, speculative, abstract, or fine-spun, as some writers on the Confessions intimate; but to us the article is filled with the marrow of the Word, more than shares in perspicuity, and altogether outrivals in edification the current ephemeral discussions[16] which seek to illumine the Person of our glorious Redeemer with critical clear lights, or to flash human and psychological[17]

---

[14] Bellarmini, *Judicium de libro quem Lutherani vocant Concordiae.*

[15] *Cp.* Schaff, *Creeds of Christendom,* on the " *Formula.*" Also Lindsay, as given below.

[16] *E. g.,* " *The Christian Doctrine of Atonement as Influenced by Semitic Religious Ideas,*" by Reginald Campbell; " *The Gospel of Krishna and of Christ,*" and " *The Messianic Idea in Vergil,*" by R. S. Conway; " *The Divine Immanence and the Christian Purpose,*" by A. C. McGiffert.

[17] The *philosophical* motive usually attributed to this doctrine's presentation in the Formula is not there except subordinately: the Formula seeks to set forth *only what the Scripture teaches.* The philosophical method of those who complain of the philosophy of the Formula brings a philosophy of its own, whether mediæval or modern, to the Scripture, and *construes the Scripture by it.*

high lights upon it from outside the Scripture. No Confession of the Church of Christ, no private investigation or essay, whether by the Fathers, Luther, Melanchthon, Chemnitz,—shall we come down to modern speculation—to Renan, Strauss, Dorner, Salmond, Schmiedel?—gives so clear a Scriptural insight into the Person of Christ in so few words.

And this doctrine of the Formula is not new. It is not a scholastic subtlety drawn upon in the Lutheran Church by post-Reformation theologians in order to bolster up an anti-Melanchthonian conception of the Lord's Supper.[18] It is not an extreme development deduced by later dogmatists from the earlier Lutheran teaching. It is not a new teaching, but the old faith of Martin Luther himself.

It is not true that the Formula's doctrine of Christ's Person was first taught in the Formula of Concord. The Formula itself emphasizes that this is the doctrine of *Martin Luther.* It is the doctrine which *Melanchthon* had in mind and followed when he wrote the *Augsburg Confession;* it is the doctrine of the *Large Catechism* and the *Schmalkald Articles.* Nay, it is the great central and fundamental doctrine on the Person of Christ, which *separated Zwingli from Luther,* fifty years before the Formula was written, and which still separates the Lutheran Church from the Reformed. Instead of fixing the blame upon the Formula of Concord for introducing an abstract philosophical teaching, in order to bolster up the doctrine of the Lord's Supper, as was done from the start by the enemies of the Lutheran

[18] "The truth is, that when we admit the personal union of the human nature of Christ with a divine nature, we have already admitted the fact, in which the mystery of Christ's Sacramental presence is absorbed. The whole Divine person of Christ is confessedly present at the Supper, but the human nature has been taken into that personality, and forms one person with it; hence the one person of Christ, consisting of the two natures, is present, and of necessity the two natures which constitute it are present."—*Con. Ref.,* p. 459.

53

Church, a study of the facts will show that this doctrine goes *back to the fountain head* of the Reformation, and divides the streams there; that Luther taught positively all that is taught by the Formula, not chiefly in order to support the doctrine of the Lord's Supper, but as a necessary part of the doctrine of the Person of Christ.

The historical situation will show that the real difference between Reformed and Lutheran theology lies in the depth of the Lutheran conception of the reality of the Person of Christ.[19] It will reveal that this is a difference which separated Luther from Zwingli at Marburg, separated Melanchthon from Zwingli at Augsburg, and would have continued to separate Bucerism and Calvinism from Lutheranism forever, if Bucer had not made his great, but not thoroughly open and honest attempt[20] to unite the two churches, to which, not then, but in later days, the words and deeds of Melanchthon lent countenance.

To Calvin, to Bucer, to Zwingli, the Person of Christ, whether in Scripture or in the Sacrament, was *a truth* to be apprehended and worked into our consciousness by a believing faith; but to Luther and to the Formula of Concord, the Person of Christ, whether in Scripture or in the Sacrament, is *a fact,* is the great reality of salvation, which, as a fact, and not as a mere spiritual truth, works itself and its effect upon and into us without the mediative and inter-

---

[19] "In regard to the presence of Christ, our dispute is not as to *how* He is present, which, like the whole doctrine of His person, is an inscrutable mystery, but as to whether there be a *true,* not an ideal presence. It is the *essence* of the doctrine, not its form, which divides us from the Reformed."— *Con. Ref.,* p. 458.

[20] Löscher, *Ausführliche Historia Motuum,* I. 219, according to Jacobs, *Book of Concord,* II, 254, "gives proof of Bucer's sincerity, citing frank acknowledgments of his former error made to others than Lutherans;" and at the conference of theologians at Schmalkald in 1537, according to Melanchthon, *C. R.,* III, p. 292, "Bucer satisfied us all, even the more rigid." "Nevertheless," continues Jacobs, "at Gotha, where Bucer overtook Luther on his premature departure from Schmalkald, Luther arraigned him very plainly for the inconsistencies in which he was involved by his attempts to mediate (*Erl.* 65. 92) ;" "nor have we found any evidence of retraction of the interpretation of 'the unworthy' as given in his 'Explanation.'" For the "Explanation" see the *Book of Concord,* II, pp. 259 and 260.

pretative grasp of our mental processes. Not a logical concept, "the ubiquity," but a living fact divides the Reformed Church from the Lutheran. It is the fact of the Person of Christ. In Rome, the Church reproduces a mechanical reality as the Christ; in radical Protestantism, the human mind and memory grasp after a spiritual reality; but in Luther and the Formula of Concord, the actual and historical Personality of Christ, with its full mystery of strength, grasps and saves the human sinner in the contact of Word and Sacrament.

THE DIVERGENCE BETWEEN THE TWO BRANCHES OF PROTESTANTISM.

It is an act of injustice, oft repeated, to claim that the sharp division between the two evangelical Protestant reformatory movements of the Sixteenth Century was sprung by the Formula of Concord. "The root of the divergence lies in the very nature of Christianity; and there can be no satisfactory solution of the differences between the Zwinglio-Calvinistic, and the Lutheran Reformation, and the Churches which were respectively established upon them, except this, that the one accepted the truth, the other a mistaken meaning of God's Word, on certain points. That is, and will forever remain, the real question between them." [21]

This divergence—divisive at the start—centering always somewhere in the doctrine of Christ or of His Person, fundamental all the way from Luther's early teaching down to the Formula of Concord, affected all the great doctrines, the Law and the Gospel, the Scriptures, the Word and the Sacrament, the Ministry, the doctrine of the Church, and pre-eminently the culminating doctrine of the Lord's Supper. "It has been fruitful in unspeakable mischiefs," and has, more than all

---

[21] *Con. Ref.*, p. 457.

other causes, rendered the struggle against Rome [22] prolonged and dubious.[23]

To know and believe Jesus Christ, true God, true man, as the Scriptures reveal Him, was the underlying task of the Reformation as it is of every other earnest age. Luther, drinking in Scripture with his whole mind and heart, knew and trusted Christ as a real Person, moving freely if incomprehensively as one Person in the spheres of his manhood and of his Godhead. The communication of the properties of the divine nature to the· weaker human nature, not mechanically, but in the vital unity of the Person; and without a weakening of the human by the divine overshadowing; or an abuse of the divine glory and fullness by the mechanical or capricious infringement of the human; was a fundamental doctrine, was a commonplace, was the very staff of life in the Christ-faith of Luther.

THE DIVERGENCE IS ROOTED IN LUTHER.

Yet this basal fact as to the *communicatio idiomatum,* in Luther's doctrine, is rarely recognized by non-Lutheran theologians, and the doctrine is supposed to have been imported from scholastic theology, and forcibly injected into the Lutheran Faith by the Formula of Concord. Despite the abundant quotations from Luther by the Formula, which quotations constitute the substance of the Formula's teaching on this subject, the existence of the fact that the Person of Christ can and does use the divine properties, as being at the call of the personal unity, to enable the inseparable per-

---

[22] Not only in the sense in which Krauth discusses it, as weakening and dividing the Protestant unity; but also in the sense that the apprehension of Calvinism is often Roman rather than Lutheran. " The whole conception of the Christian life as Calvin draws it, is Roman Catholic rather than Protestant. The essential feature of Luther's message was that in Christ we were free to live more and more unto righteousness. . . . On ethical grounds we may say that Calvin was one of the last of the schoolmen. Thomas Aquinas is greatly his superior as an ethical thinker.—*Hibbert Journal,* VI, 1, p. 184 (1907).

[23] *Con. Ref.,* p. 457.

son, divine and human, human as well as divine, to perform its wondrous work of redemption—whether on the Cross, or at the right hand of the Father, or in the Sacrament of the Supper, or in the hearts of believers,—more readily than the sun communicates its properties to the atmospheric ether and is present for creation, vivification, and fructification at any and every point in the planetary system—without at the same time failing or falling short of its central specifically proper presence in the sun itself,—the existence of this fundamental doctrine of Christ in the Lutheran faith, prior to the Formula of Concord, is usually denied by the theologians of the Protestant Churches, English and German.[24] Even Dr. Valentine[25] affirms that the genus majestaticum is peculiar to the Lutheran dogmaticians, though he subsequently admits that its substance was maintained by Luther.

Let us hear what Luther himself has to say on this doctrine, which is so contemptuously characterized as[26] " the

---

[24] *E. g.*, Dorner in Germany, Lindsay in England, and Schaff in America. The shining of the sun upon the earth, as alluded to in the Second Helvetic Confession, confirms the Lutheran, not the Calvinistic doctrine of the Sacrament. " As the sun," says this Confession, " is far away over us in the Heaven [it is not *far away* for a sun, just as a preacher in the pulpit is not absent or ' far away ' from any who come within the range of his powerful voice], yet is none the less efficaciously present [it is *visibly* present, as near in its nature as the gas light over the table is near in its nature] . . . so much the more the Sun of righteousness, absent from us in the Heavens in His Body [are " the Heavens " a room that shuts Him in?] is present to us not indeed corporeally, but spiritually [what becomes of His body meantime] by a life-giving activity."

The presence of the sun upon the earth, is such a Real Presence, in, with and under the atmosphere through which it penetrates, that it not only *appeals to* and *affects* the body, but *is visible in itself* and in its effects of heat. It is not the *spiritual presence* of the sun that overcomes a man with sunstroke, or that prints its glorious image of real light upon the surface of the camera.

[25] *Christian Theology.*

[26] Schaff and all similar writers *in loco*. The insinuation against the Lutheran Faith has filtered down into current modern theology, probably through Dorner. Thus, Gore, on the basis of Dorner, characterizes the Lutheran doctrine as follows:—

" The quasi-Nestorian tendency was checked in Luther by the sacramental controversy. Driven to defend the doctrine of the real presence of our Lord's body and blood in the sacrament of the Eucharist by a theory of the ubiquity of our Lord even in His humanity, he was led to speak of this ubiquity as resulting from the union of the divine and human natures, and of the *communicatio idiomatum* from one to the other as existing from the beginning of the Incarnation. This led to a development of thought in a Monophysite doctrine of the ubiquity introduced into Lutheran theology by the Formula of Concord in order to give support to its theory of the Lord's Supper." The Formula quotes from Luther as follows:—

LUTHER ON THE PERSON OF CHRIST.

"Our reasons are those which Dr. Luther himself, [27] *in the very beginning,* presented against the Sacramentarians in the following words: ' The reasons upon which I rest in this matter are the following:

" ' 1. The first is this article of our faith: Jesus Christ is essential, natural, true, perfect God and man in one person, undivided and inseparable.

" ' 2. The second, that God's right hand is everywhere.

" ' 3. The third, that God's Word is not false and does not deceive.

" ' 4. The fourth that God has and knows of many modes of being in any place, and not only the single one concerning which fanatics talk flippantly and which philosophers call local.'

"Also: ' The one body of Christ [says Luther] has a three-fold mode or three modes of being anywhere.

" ' First, the comprehensible, bodily mode, as he went about in the body upon earth, when, according to his size, he occupied room, and was circumscribed by fixed places. This mode he can still use whenever he will, as he did after the resurrection, and will use at the last day, as Paul says (I Tim. 6: 15) : 'Which in his times He shall show who is the blessed and only Potentate, the King of kings and Lord of lords.' And to the Colossians (3: 4) he says:

---

rather than a Nestorian direction, and this rival tendency, which renders Luther's Christology very difficult to understand as a whole, became dominant in the Lutheran schools. It resulted in the formation of a Christology based on ubiquitarianism, which Dr. A. B. Bruce, without undue severity, pronounces to be, to an amazing extent, 'artificial, unnatural and incredible.' "— Gore, *Dissertations on the Incarnation,* pp. 181, 182.

Thus also Lindsay, as late as 1906, in his *History of the Reformation,* p. 356, will repeat the old slander. He says: " A controversy soon raged in Wittenberg to the scandal of German Protestantism. Luther insisted more and more on the necessity of the Presence in the elements of the Body of Christ ' corporeally extended in space.' "

On page 357 he says again, " Luther, looking mainly at the mediæval doctrine of the Eucharist, taught: (1) . . . (2) That . . there must be in the Bread and Wine the local Presence of the Glorified Body of Christ which he *always conceived* as ' Body extended in space.' . . . (3) That this local Presence of Christ does not presuppose any special priestly miracle, for, in virtue of its *ubiquity,* the Glorified Body of Christ is *everywhere* naturally, and therefore is in the Bread and in the Wine."

Thus also on page 358 he says, " Luther depends on a questionable mediæval idea of *ubiquity,* . . . Zwingli spent all his argumentative powers in disputing the doctrine of *ubiquity* . . . Zwingli maintained that Christ could not be present, extended in space, in the elements." (This is said of the Marburg Colloquy with which compare Luther's and Melanchthon's letter after the close of the Colloquy.)

[27] In his *Large Confession,* concerning the Holy Supper.

'When Christ who is our life shall appear.' In this manner he is not in God or with the Father, neither in heaven, as the wild spirits dream: for God is not a bodily space or place. And to this effect are the passages of Scripture which the fanatical spirits cite, how Christ left the world and went to the Father.

" 'Secondly, the incomprehensible, spiritual mode, according to which he neither occupies nor makes room, but penetrates all creatures according to his most free will, as, to make an imperfect comparison, my sight penetrates air, light or water, and does not occupy or make room; as a sound or tone penetrates air or water or board and wall, and is in them, and also does not occupy or make room; likewise, as light and heat penetrate air, water, glass, crystal, and the like, and is in them, and also does not make or occupy room; and much more of the like. This mode he used when he rose from the sealed sepulchre, and passed through the closed door, and in the bread and wine in the Holy Supper, and, as it is believed, when he was born of the Virgin Mary.

" 'Thirdly, the divine, heavenly mode, since he is one person with God, according to which all creatures must be far more penetrable and present to him than they are according to the second mode. For if, according to that second mode, he can be so in and with creatures that they do not feel, touch, circumscribe or comprehend him, how much more wonderfully is he in all creatures according to this sublime third mode, so that they neither circumscribe nor comprehend him, but rather that he has them present before himself, and circumscribes and comprehends them! For you must place this mode of the presence of Christ, as he is one person with God, as far beyond creatures as God is beyond them; and again as deep and near to all creatures as God is in, and near them. For he is one inseparable person with God; where God is there must he also be, or our faith is false. But who will say or think how this occurs? We know indeed that it is so, that he is in God beyond all creatures, and is one person with God, but how it occurs we do not know; this mystery is above nature and reason, even above the reason of all the angels in heaven; it is understood only by God. Because, therefore, it is unknown to us, and yet is true, we should not deny his words before we know how to prove to a certainty that the body of Christ can by no means be where God is, and that this mode of presence is false. This the fanatics ought to prove; but we challenge them to do so.

" 'That God indeed has and knows still more modes in which Christ's body is anywhere, I will not herewith deny; but I would indicate what awkward and stupid men our fanatics are, that they concede to the body of Christ no more than the first, comprehensible way; although they cannot even prove the same, that it conflicts with our meaning. For I in no way will deny that the power of God is able to effect so much as that a body should at the same time be in a number of places, even in a bodily, comprehensible way. For who will prove that this is impossible with God? Who has seen an end to his power? The fanatics think indeed that God cannot effect it,[27a] but who will believe their thoughts? Whereby will they confirm such thoughts?'

"From these words of Dr. Luther it is also clear in what sense the word *spiritual* is employed in our churches with reference to this matter. For to the

---

[27a] *Cf. Epitome,* vii: 32, 34.

Sacramentarians this word *spiritual* means nothing else than the spiritual communion, when through faith those truly believing are in the spirit incorporated into Christ, the Lord, and become true spiritual members of his body." [28]

WHENCE LUTHER DERIVED HIS DOCTRINE OF CHRIST.

The Formula of Concord proceeds to show how Luther's doctrine is the true *Scriptural* doctrine as over against the rationalistic, scholastic and unscriptural doctrine of Zwingli. Many of our modern writers in Reformed theology will not admit that Luther starts solely with the Scripture, and that his use of the metaphysical modes of presence are but an *illustration of the possibility* of the presence of Christ in such way as Scripture actually reveals it.

Thus Schaff declares the Reformation doctrine of the Person of Christ to have been taken bodily from the Eastern Church, and especially from the symbol of Chalcedon. But the true fact is that the mighty faith of Luther owed very little directly to the oriental formularies. Luther's Christology was rooted in the Scripture itself, of whose depths he was an expounder; in the actual and living Person of Christ as he found it in St. John, St. Matthew, and St. Paul: and in the concrete Augustinian apprehension of the Gospel as salvation by redemption, rather than in the Eastern apprehension of the incarnation.

The East emphasized the union of two natures; the West emphasized the unity of Person; and Luther, starting in Scripture, followed the West.[29] He revitalized the doctrine of the Person, under the powerful and practical aspect of the doctrine of justification by faith, in such way that Christ

---

[28] *Formula of Concord*, p. 620.

[29] *Athanasius* said: " My Saviour must be the great God who made heaven and earth; and He must unite the human and divine natures which He possesses, in a union which for me is a mystery to be believed, but which my intelligence can never explain nor penetrate." But *Augustine* thus beautifully describes Christ, " The Son of God ever, the Son of Man in time, yet one Christ in the unity of the Person. He was in heaven when He was speaking upon earth. Thus He was Son of Man in heaven in the same manner in which He was Son of God on earth ; Son of God on earth in the flesh which He took upon Him ; Son of Man in heaven in the unity of the Person."

was for him not a biography in a book belonging to past ages, whose character and work are to be discussed; but the one Man who now lived and ruled and wrought salvation in human souls; and who though Man was God. He was Son of Man in Heaven in the same manner in which He was Son of God on earth: of God—in the flesh He took upon Him; of Man—in the unity of the Person. He was in Heaven when He was speaking upon earth.

Luther thus followed Augustine, who went back to the old Church tradition of Tertullian through Ambrose. There was no indistinctness, and no fusion in the natures; but the clue to the Person of Christ was to be found in the statement of Paul that Christ existed ' *in the form of God,*' and took upon Him ' *the form of a servant.*' These two forms co-existed in the unity of the Person. Every justified believer feels the power of this unity: " there is a Man in Whom God dwells, and Who is God." " Proprium illius hominis sacramentum est." [30] Hence Luther strongly asserts, " whatsoever I behold in Christ is at the same time both human and divine." [31] " Wherever thou canst say, Here is God, there must thou also say, Therefore Christ the Man is also here. And if thou shouldst point out a place where God was and not the Man, then would the Person be already divided, since I might then say with truth, Here is God, who is not man, and never yet became man. *But nothing of that God for me!* . . . Nay, friend, wherever thou placest God for me, there must thou also place for me the human nature. They cannot be separated and divided from each other. There has come to be One Person." [32]

NOT A POLEMIC NECESSITY.

This is'the inmost faith of Luther's heart trusting in the grace of Christ for his salvation. Such a mighty living faith

[30] *Augustine.*
[31] *Erl.,* 47. 361. sq.
[32] *Ib.,* 30. 211.

in Christ as God had not appeared since the time of Athanasius. Such a help from the mystery of the union of the two natures in Christ had not been known in the Church since the time of Cyril.[33] To say, then, that Luther's doctrine of the Person of Christ was a result of polemical necessity, a means of defending his doctrine to which he had recourse in the controversy with Zwingli, is to place his teaching on Christ under as great a theological misrepresentation, as it is to misrepresent his doctrine of the Sacrament by declaring that he taught transubstantiation or consubstantiation.[34] To know Luther is to recognize the falseness, and indeed the impossibility, of his having built up a Christology by the adroit use of a scholastic mode. Luther's fathom-deep insight into Scripture caused him to discover that the human nature of Christ is there revealed as the organ and bearer of the divine nature, in the whole Revelation and in all the Operations of grace, from the time of His conception, to the time of His Second Coming, and thereafter forever; and this most naturally included the elements of miracle and sacrament. "Luther's most profound ideas concerning the knowledge of God and faith may be understood in the light"[35] of this teaching of Christ.

When, therefore, Luther came to more clearly formulate his doctrine of the Lord's Supper, under attacks from without, what else could he do but present it in the light of its proper background in the Person of Christ? What the Person of Christ was and did on earth it would be and do in Heaven. He would be Son of Man and Son of God in all His acts in Heaven, as He had been on earth; and His presence would be a *presence of the person* on earth, whether spiritual (John 6), sacramental (The Lord's Supper), or local (the Parousia), in the future, as it had been in the past.

---

[33] Harnack, *Hist. of Dogma,* VII, 173.

[34] A stigma fastened on Luther by Schaff. (*Creeds,* I, pp. 232, 316.)

[35] Seeberg, *Hist. Doctrines,* I, 252.

His doctrine of the Lord's Supper, like all his other doctrines, was developed in the process of taking that which he found in the Church, and subjecting it to the test of Scripture.[36]

LUTHER'S RESCUE OF THE SACRAMENT.

Hence his rescue of the Scriptural sacrament of the Lord's Supper from Romish tradition, and his grounding of the true doctrine, were gradual. Under the influence of Scripture, he had to steer clear not only of the false but central fact of the Romish Mass; but also of its antithesis, viz., a false spiritualism, manifesting itself just at this time in the pious mysticism of the later Middle Ages.[37]

In being confronted with the Mass and the other Roman Sacraments, Luther had begun his thought with the Augustinian conception of a sacrament as a "sign which helps and incites to faith,"[38] and even later he still spoke of the sacrament as an "outward sign," a "seal or signet ring."[39] By 1519, he came to be clearer both as to Baptism (*Sermon von dem heiligen, hochwürdigen Sakrament der Taufe*); and as to the Lord's Supper; although in his *Ein Sermon v. d. hochw. Sacrament des Leichnams Christi un. v. d. Bruderschaften,* of 1519, transubstantiation was not yet separated from Luther's original and always abiding belief of the presence

---

[36] This in our judgment expresses in a word all that is to be said as to Luther's dependency on Occam, D'Ailly, Biel and the scholastics. To *derive* a doctrine, and to *illustrate its possibility* from an extraneous sphere are two entirely different methods. The Colloquy at Marburg showed whence Luther derived his doctrine, and *whence Zwingli derived his*. To assert of a modern writer like C. P. Krauth that he derived his *theology* from Berkeley or from Kant, would be on a par with declaring that Luther gained his Person of Christ and his Real Presence aside from, not in Scripture.

[37] Compare especially the "'inner word" of the spirit, which has no need of the "bodily" word; and the "divesting self of material things," in the *Imitation* of Thomas A. Kempis; and the whole circle of mystical, ascetic, apocalyptic and socialistic ideas which broke forth upon him in the Zwickau prophets, Carlstadt and Münzer.

[38] *Walch*, II, 686, 693.

[39] *Erl.*, 12. 178f; 16. 48, 50, 52.

of the body of Christ in the Lord's Supper. But from 1520 on, he definitely rejected transubstantiation as a Thomistic fiction, and laid down his doctrine in his *Sermon on the Mass,* in 1520. The mass *is not a sacrifice,* and the body is to be received in *both* elements. Faith in Christ's bodily and personal presence is everything: "If I believe that His body and blood are mine, then I have the Lord Christ entire, and everything that he is able to accomplish." [40]

It was in 1522 that Luther first heard from the Bohemian Brethren that they held the bread and wine as bare symbols; and that Honius of Holland wrote to him that he interpreted the *est* as equivalent to *significat.* Carlstadt also proposed that "This" refers to the body, but "Take" and "Eat" refer to the bread. Thus was Luther forced to a new investigation, and he decided for an adherence to the very word of Scripture,[41] as well as for the bodily omnipresence, since 'Christ does not continually keep traveling from heaven to earth.' [42] His eyes were opened to the supreme importance of the bodily presence, and he saw that it is not merely a means of realizing the sacramental gift, but the gift itself.

Meanwhile, in 1523, Luther found that Zwingli, who had learned of the correspondence of Honius with Luther, had adopted the interpretation of Honius; and, basing his argument upon John 6, "the flesh profiteth nothing," had used the scholastic conception of the existence of the body of Christ as local, and as not able therefore to be in the Supper. A little later Luther published his work "Against the Heavenly Prophets," in 1524-25,[43] in which the Lutheran doctrine is developed and is practically complete; and his letter to the Strassburgers, 1524.[44]

---

[40] *Erl.,* 11. 187.
[41] *Ib.,* 28. 412f; 29. 329, 331; 393, 396, 398.
[42] *Ib.,* 29. 289, 293f.
[43] *Ib.,* 29.
[44] *De Wette,* II, 574 sqq.

In 1525 Zwingli determined to attack the teaching of Luther and proposed to undermine the authority of Luther.[45] Zwingli sent a fictitious letter to Alberus and attempted in many ways to win the South Germans away from Luther. Oecolampadius, Bucer, and Capito aided Zwingli in this attempt, and unscrupulous means were employed—*e. g.*, the text of Bugenhagen's Commentary on the Psalms, and the notes in the translation of Luther's Church Postils were corrupted—in order to stir up agitation against Luther's doctrine in South Germany.[46] Those who understand clearly what Luther was dealing with cannot condemn his severity " when he finally broke his silence and entered the fray. It is more important to set forth clearly the spirit of these opponents and the historic base of it, than to shudder at the thought of Luther's coarseness in dealing with them." [47] This is all the more true since we now know that Zwingli's dependence upon Luther (notwithstanding Zwingli's protests to the contrary) is a settled fact.[48]

Luther's own view of the morality of Zwingli and his compeers in these transactions is that it is very low. He says, " My free, open, simple snapping at the devil is to my notion much better than their poisonous, plotting, assassination, which they practice against the upright under the pretence of peace and love." [49]

It was in 1525 that Luther first applied the doctrine of the personal omnipresence of Christ to the human nature in the sacrament, and in 1526 he published his " *Sermon on the Sacrament.*" [50] In 1527 he wrote: " *That these Words: This is my Body, stand firm;*" and in 1528, his " *Confes-*

---

[45] *Walther*, l. c. p., 815 sqq., 916 sqq.

[46] *Erl.*, 30. 24, 38, 61, 98, 139, 148 sqq., 160, 205.

[47] Seeberg, *Hist. Doctrines*, II. 320.

[48] *Usteri*, l. c., *Stähelin*, Zw. I. 164ff., 175f., *Kawerau* (Möller, *Kirch. Gesch., III.* 46), quoted by *Seeberg*, II, 308.

[49] *Erl.*, 30. 266.

[50] *Ib.*, 29. 329.

sion concerning the Lord's Supper." [51]   Then came the Colloquy at Marburg,[52] where Luther told the Zwinglians that they had "another spirit," but nevertheless hoped for a "good-natured friendly harmony, that they may in a friendly spirit seek among us for that which they lack;"[53] while Zwingli wrote that "Luther, impudent and contumacious, was vanquished . . . although he declared himself unconquered." The Schwabach Articles follow, making the true doctrine of the Sacrament a part of the faith of the Church. Then comes the Augsburg Confession, Bucer's interview with Melanchthon in 1533, the Wittenberg Concord[54] in 1536, and its failure; and Luther's last work, *Short Confession of the Holy Sacrament* 1545.[55]

THE COMMUNICATIO IDIOMATUM VS. THE ZWINGLIAN ALLOEOSIS.

We have seen that Luther taught the presence of the Body

[51] *Erl.,* 30.

[52] " The Colloquy at Marburg could not, under the circumstances, lead to harmony, although Zwingli, impelled by political considerations (' Burgrecht '), made as large concessions as possible to the Lutherans.   Agreement was indeed reached upon fourteen articles of faith, modeled upon formulas drawn by Luther (Trinity, Christ, original sin, faith, justification, word, baptism, works, civil government). . . Luther, although he had not hesitated to express to the Strassburgers his conviction that they had ' another spirit,' yet hoped for a ' good-natured friendly harmony, that they may in a friendly spirit seek among us for that which they lack ' (E. 36. 322).   Zwingli wrote: ' Luther, impudent and contumacious, was vanquished . . . although he meanwhile declared that he was unconquered ' (opp. viii. 370)."—Seeberg, *Hist. of Doctrines,* II, p. 330.   *Vid.* also the correspondence of Luther and Melanchthon after the Marburg Colloquy, and Article in *The Lutheran Church Review,* " Is there Any New Light Concerning the Schwabach Articles?" 28. 278.

[53] *Erl.,* 36. 322.

[54] " Nor did the *Wittenberg Concord* (A. D. 1536), produce an actual and permanent agreement.   From the time of the Diet of Augsburg, Bucer labored unweariedly to bring about an agreement between the Saxons and the theologians of Southern Germany.   His formula was : ' That the true body and the true blood of Jesus Christ are truly present in the Lord's Supper and are offered with the words of the Lord and the sacrament.'   Both Luther and Melanchthon hoped that an understanding might be reached upon this basis. But Luther did not change his own opinion.   Although he was willing to refrain from laying special stress upon the assertion, that the body of Christ is present also for the unbelieving, yet the formula finally adopted expresses his view : ' That with the bread and wine are truly and substantially present, offered, and received *(vere et substantialiter adesse, exhiberi et sumi)* the body and blood of Christ. ' "—Seeberg, *Hist. of Doctrines,* II, p. 331.   *Cp. Book of Concord,* II, p. 253 sqq.

[55] *Erl.,* 32. 396 sqq.

of Christ in the Supper from the beginning, and that it was a seal to the believing communicant of the forgiveness of sins, wrought by it. We have seen, likewise, how fundamental the Communicatio Idiomatum in the Person of Christ was to the daily, living faith of Luther. As he said, "God 'dwells' in Christ bodily, so that one person is man and God."[56] "The two natures are 'one single person'[57] in inseparable union, so that where the one is the other must also be."[58] "They are to each other as body and soul;[59] and the flesh is a spirit-flesh. It is in God and God in it."[60] "The same Christ who has secured for us grace and the forgiveness of sins is present in the Lord's Supper in order to assure us of His redeeming act."[61] This is the great point, that Christ the actual person, the historical Redeemer, the One well known and Who on earth performed all the acts of redemption is present here in the Supper; and that as He, the God-man, was apprehended historically on earth only in the presence and contacts of His human life, so this same Man Jesus with the human nature, by which He gained our salvation, is present by His body in the Holy Communion to personally seal the salvation He gained. How His body is present (whether by a certain supernatural mode, or in any one of a hundred other ways possible to God—but certainly not in a mechanical ubiquity) is not essential, and does not belong to the doctrine.[62]

When then the discussion of the doctrine of the Lord's Supper with Zwingli was forced on Luther, his faith in the Person of Christ Who was present on earth as a Man to redeem, and Who will be present again as a Man to restore, and Who is present, according to His own word and Testa-

---

[56] *Erl.*, 30. 63.
[57] *Ib.*, 30. 63, 206 sq., 211, 222.
[58] *Ib.*, 211 sq.
[59] *Ib.*, 204.
[60] *Ib.*, 30. 125 ; 48. 28, 58.
[61] *Ib.*, 29. 348 ; 48. 23 ; 30. 85, 134, 137.
[62] *Ib.*, 30. 200, 202, 210, 217.

ment in His Sacrament to seal, was as real and living; as Zwingli's definitions of the two natures were scholastic, abstract and artificial; and, in the Lutheran Faith, as over against the theory of Oecolampadius, Bucer and Calvin, we believers are not merely thinking of Him, as present by an effort of our imagination;[63] nor to see in His Sacrament "a sign of a future or absent thing;" but to hold to it as the presence, under the visible form of the elements, of "His invisible body and blood."

So far then from the particular Lutheran explication of the doctrine of the Sacrament being an invention of the Formula of Concord, the Formula itself draws attention to the Luthero-Zwinglian divergence of half a century earlier, as the final development of the whole matter. It says:—

"Inasmuch as Dr. Luther has written concerning the alloeosis of Zwingli in his large Confession concerning the Holy Supper, we will here present Luther's own words, in order that the Church of God may be guarded in the best way against this error. His words are as follows:—

"'Zwingli calls that an *alloeosis*, when anything is ascribed to the divinity of Christ which nevertheless belongs to the humanity or the reverse. As Luke 24: 26: 'Ought not Christ to have suffered these things, and to enter into his glory?' Here Zwingli triflingly declares that the word Christ is understood with respect to the human nature. Beware, beware, I say, of the alloeosis; for it is a mask of the devil, as it at last forms such a Christ after which I certainly would not be a Christian. For its design is that Christ should henceforth be no more, and do no more with his sufferings and life, than another mere saint. For if I permit myself to be persuaded that only the human nature has suffered for me, Christ is to me a Saviour of little worth, since he indeed himself stands in need of a Saviour. In a word, what the devil seeks by the alloeosis is inexpressible.'

"And shortly afterwards: 'If the old sorceress, Dame Reason, the grandmother of the alloeosis, should say, Yea, divinity can neither suffer nor die; you should reply, That is true; yet, because in Christ divinity and humanity are one person, Scripture, on account of this personal union, ascribes also to divinity everything that occurs to the humanity, and the reverse. And thus, indeed, it is in truth. For this must certainly be acknowledged, viz., the person (he refers to Christ) suffers and dies. Now the person is true God; therefore, it is rightly said: The Son of God suffers. For although the one part (so to say), viz., the divinity, does not suffer, yet the person, which is God, suffers in the other part, viz., in his

---

[63] Just as moderns subjectivize the whole incarnation, redemption, atonement, and the act of justification; and think it into being as an act of the imagination, instead of holding to it vitally as a mighty fact.

humanity; for in truth God's Son has been crucified for us, i. e. the person which is God. For the person, the person, I say, was crucified according to the humanity.'

"And again shortly afterwards: 'If the alloeosis exist, as Zwingli proposes, it will be necessary for Christ to have two persons, one divine and one human, because Zwingli applies the passages concerning suffering, alone to the human nature, and of course diverts them from the divinity. For if the works be parted and disunited, the person must also be divided, since all the works or sufferings are ascribed not to the natures, but to the person. For it is the person that does and suffers everything, one thing according to one nature, and another according to the other nature. Therefore we consider our Lord Jesus Christ as God and man in one person, so that we neither confound the natures nor divide the person.'" [64]

THE MAJESTATICUM BELIEVED BY LUTHER.

Not only did Luther *from the beginning* teach the presence of the body of Christ in the Supper; but that he also taught the Genus Majestaticum, the following words from the Formula of Concord will show:—

"Upon this firm foundation Dr. Luther, of holy memory, has also written concerning the majesty of Christ according to human nature.

"In the Large Confession concerning the Lord's Supper he writes thus concerning the person of Christ: 'Since Christ is such a man as is supernaturally one person with God, and apart from this man there is no God, it must follow that also, according to the third supernatural mode, he is and can be everywhere that God is, and all things are entirely full of Christ, even according to humanity, not according to the first corporeal, comprehensible mode, but according to the supernatural, divine mode.' For here you must confess and say: 'Wherever Christ is according to the divinity, there he is a natural, divine person, and he is

---

[64] Krauth is illuminative: "As these two natures form one inseparable person, the whole person is involved in the acts of each part of it. Everything that the Saviour did and suffered is both human and divine. Every act, indeed, is done, every suffering endured, *through* or *by* the one or the other nature, but not without the personal presence of the other. Jesus Christ wrought miracles *through* the divine nature, but they were wrought *by* the human nature. *Through* His divine omnipotence sight was given to the blind, but His divine omnipotence wrought it *by* his human touch. Jesus Christ died according to His human nature, but His death was the death of a divine person. *Through* his human infirmity He was crucified, but that human weakness wrought *by* His divine majesty an infinite sacrifice. Godhead cannot bleed, but the Church is purchased by the blood of God.

"We Lutherans affirm that there is a real *common participation* of the whole person in the properties of both natures. The Reformed deny it, and say 'that each nature is isolated from the other in its attributes.'"—*Con. Ref.*, p. 476 sq.

54

also there naturally and personally, as his conception in his mother's womb well shows. For if he were God's Son, he must naturally and personally be in his mother's womb and become man. But if, wherever he is, he is naturally and personally, he must also be in the same place as man. For there are not in Christ two separate persons, but only one person. Wherever it is, there the person is only one and undivided; and wherever you can say: 'here is God,' there you must also say: 'Therefore Christ the man is also there.' And if you would show a place where God would be, and not the man, the person would be already divided, because I could then say with truth: 'Here is God who is not man, and who never as yet has become man.'

" 'Far be it from me that I should acknowledge or worship such a God. For it would follow hence that space and place separated the two natures from one another, and divided the person, which, nevertheless, death and all devils could not divide or rend from one another. And there would remain to me a poor sort of Christ, who would be no more than a divine and human person at the same time in only one place, and in all other places he must be only a mere separate God and divine person without humanity. No, friend, wherever you place God for me, there you must also place with him for me humanity ; they do not allow themselves to be separated or divided from one another. They become one person, which as Son of God does not separate from itself the assumed humanity.

" In the little book concerning the Last Words of David, which Dr. Luther wrote shortly before his death, he says as follows: 'According to the other, the temporal, human birth, the eternal power of God has also been given him, yet in time, and not from eternity. For the humanity of Christ has not been from eternity, as the divinity; but as we reckon and write Jesus, the Son of Mary, is this year 1543 years old. But from the instant when divinity and humanity were united in the person, the man, the Son of Mary, is and is called almighty, eternal God, has eternal might and has created and sustains, by the communicatio idiomatum, all things, because he is one person with divinity, and is also true, God. Of this he speaks (Matt. 11: 27): 'All things are delivered unto me of my Father;' and Matt. 28: 18: 'All power is given to me in heaven and in earth.' To what me? To me, Jesus of Nazareth, the Son of Mary and born man. From eternity I had it of the Father, before I became man. But when I became man I received it in time, according to humanity, and kept it concealed until my resurrection and ascension; then it was to be manifested and declared, as St. Paul says (Rom. 1: 4): 'He is declared and proved to be a Son of God with power.' John (17: 10) calls it 'glorified.'

" Similar testimonies are found in Luther's writings, but especially in the book: 'That these Words still stand Firm,' and in the 'Large Confession concerning the Holy Supper:' to which writings, as well-grounded explanations of the majesty of Christ at the right hand of God, and of his testament, we refer, for the sake of brevity, in this article, as well as in the Holy Supper, as has been heretofore mentioned." [65]

Krauth states the point clearly thus: " God became man,

---

[65] *Book of Concord,* pp. 640, 641.

but Godhead does not become humanity. A man is God—but humanity does not become deity. In this aspect the Lutheran Church draws a distinction, total and all-comprehending between the presence of the Godhead of Christ, and the presence of His humanity. Omnipresence is the essential attribute of the divine, and hence His Godhead is necessarily, in and of itself, in virtue of its own nature present. But the essential attribute of the human is to have a determinate presence, and hence the human nature of Christ has such a determinate presence, nor in and of itself would the human nature have any other presence; but as it is in one person with the divine, it is in that one person rendered present with and through the divine. . . .

The human eye, in its own essence or nature, has no power of being conscious of light; but . . . the eye has a real sight *through* the soul, as the soul has its sight *by* the eye. . . . The eye does not become spirit, nor the soul become matter; nor has the soul one consciousness nor the eye another; but . . . there is a common participation of the two natures in the act of the one person; . . . the eye itself really receiving a distinct set of powers, from its union with the soul, and the soul exercising its own essential power, under a wholly new set of conditions, in consequence of its union with the eye . . . There is no transfer of properties; but there is a common participation of them. And so in some sense, and yet with the infinite difference made by the nature of the subjects in this case, we reply to the sophism against the doctrine of our Church: The divine in Christ is forever divine; the human forever human; but as they can never be confounded, so can they never be separated; and the one person participates in both, and each has a personal communication with the attribute of the other. 'Great is the MYSTERY of Godliness: God WAS MANIFEST IN THE FLESH.' " [66]

---

[66] *Con. Ref.*, pp. 479-481.

Luther *always* conceived of the Person of Christ *in its real unity;* Zwingli conceived of it under the two logical categories of finite and infinite. In Luther's doctrine, the whole Christ was in every Word and act, and the Lord's Supper was the culmination and essence of all Words and acts; but in Zwingli's doctrine Christ was differentiated into the abstract quality of the natures. This accounts for the persistent Reformed condemnation of the Formula's teaching "on the Ubiquity," from Hospinian in the Sixteenth Century to Schaff in the Nineteenth.[67] The very term "Ubiquity" betrays a Reformed conception of the subject, non-Lutheran and foreign to the Formula, whose two relevant chapters treat only of the two facts of "The Lord's Supper," and "The Person of Christ."

MISREPRESENTATION OF THE LUTHERAN FAITH.

We are told that the Formula extends the human body of Christ everywhere in a geometric space and in locality,[68] whereas we teach that the human body of Christ cannot be omnipresent by its own nature, but has the majesty of co-presence only from the divinity, and can be omnipresent only in the divine mode, through the unity of the person.

---

[67] *Cp.* Seeberg: "While Luther interprets the traditional dogma from the view-point of personal unity, Zwingli always premises the abstract difference of the two natures. God 'assumed human nature'—the incarnation signifies nothing more than this (ii. 2. 69f). . . . But for the great thought in Luther's theology—that even the human words and works of Christ are a revelation of God—he has no comprehension. *His Christology remains absolutely upon the plane of the mediæval conception.* The divine and human natures are assigned to the opposite categories of finite and infinite nature. The consequences of this position came to light in the controversy upon the Lord's Supper."—*History of Doctrines,* II, pp. 321, 322.

[68] Oil is kept in a lamp or vessel. Its local presence is in the vessel. The oil is never "locally extended in the geometric space of the room" even when burning. But when the higher nature of fire takes the oil up into itself, the presence of the oil, by virtue of the higher attributes of the fire, is diffused everywhere illocally as far as the power of the presence of the fire-nature reaches. Those who misrepresent the Lutheran doctrine say that it teaches that the body of Christ—*i. e., the oil* in the figure, when burning—*extends itself locally through space,* as the oil locally fills the vessel when not burning. One would not suppose that such gross misrepresentation of Lutheranism could manage to live on through the centuries.

We are told that the Formula teaches the corporeal and local presence of the body of Christ, but we really teach a corporeal presence that is not local. Our doctrine is misrepresented. What stronger language could be used than that of the *Conservative Reformation* well known to the author of the Creeds of Christendom: "Of a *local* presence of the body of Christ in, with, or under the bread, there never was any controversy between the Lutherans and Calvinists; that local presence we expressly reject and condemn in all our writings. But a local absence does not prevent a sacramental presence, which is dependent on the communication of the divine Majesty." [69]

In spite of these words, the *Creeds of Christendom,* [70] will persist in the derogatory use of the term ubiquity with reference to the Lutheran doctrine of the presence of Christ in the Lord's Supper, and will insist that it was made a part of the Lutheran doctrine of the Person of Christ in order to support the Lutheran doctrine of the Lord's Supper; that it was unknown to Luther and the earlier theologians; and that it is a metaphysical invention of the theologians of the Formula of Concord. And this is the wide-spread mode of stating Lutheran doctrine among English theologians. Lindsay, the Reformation scholar, does not grow weary of attributing a theory of mechanical and local ubiquity to Martin Luther himself. In his History of the German Reformation he misstates this fact no less than five times within the space of twenty-five pages. The very phrases " Corporeally extended in space," " Body extended in space " are quoted as if from Luther, yet nowhere is there any citation added from Luther's works on this point, and for a very good reason. The following extracts show how positive, detailed and complete is the misrepresentation of Lutheran doctrine on this point.

---

[69] *Con. Ref.*, pp. 131, 132.

[70] It also similarly repeats and affirms the old falsehood that the Lutheran Church teaches the doctrine of consubstantiation in the Sacrament.

THE FORMULA RE-
JECTS AND CON-
DEMNS "THE
UBIQUITY."

A. D. 1580.

Our Church ' rejects
and condemns the error'
" that the human nature
of Christ is *locally ex-
tended in all places of
heaven and earth,*" or
" has become infinite
essence." — *Formula of
Concord*, (p. 520, 642,
Jacobs, in *Book of Con-
cord*).

LINDSAY WOULD FASTEN "THE
UBIQUITY" ON THE LUTHERAN
CHURCH.

A. D. 1906.

1. " Luther insisted more and more on the necessity of the Presence in the elements of the Body of Christ *'corporeally extended in space.'* "—*History of the Reformation*, I, p. 356.

2. " Luther always conceived the Glorified Body of Christ as *'Body extended in space.'* " —*Ib.*, p. 357.

3. " Luther's [theory] depends on *a questionable mediaeval idea of ubiquity.*" —*Ib.*, p. 358.

4. " They met at Wittenberg, and after prolonged discussion it was found that all were agreed save on one small point—the Presence, *extended in space* of the Body of Christ. . . . It was agreed that this might be left an open question; and what was called the Wittenberg Concord was signed, which united all German Protestants."—*Ib.*, p. 377.

5. " Luther's convent studies in D'Ailly, Biel, and their common master, William of Occam, enabled him to show that there might be the presence of the Glorified Body of Christ, *extended in space*, in the elements Bread and Wine in a natural way, and without any priestly miracle: and that satisfied him."—*Ib.*, p. 354.

What the Lutheran Church does teach is not the infinite extension of the body of Christ, but the personal omnipresence of the human nature of Christ, when and as He wills,—and He has willed it in the Sacrament—under the power of the attributes of the divine nature. Our Church does not teach that Christ's human nature is omnipresent in its own right, as His divine nature is omnipresent, in virtue of any property of its own. Nor does it teach that His human nature has been rendered equal to the divine in its essential properties. Still less does it teach that the human nature of Christ is 'locally expanded' in all places of Heaven and earth. God Himself is not present in this manner; and the mode of the presence of the human nature, which, in union with the divine nature, is under the control of the will of Christ, is also not after this manner.

THE PERSONAL OMNIPRESENCE A FUNDAMENTAL FACT.

It is not true that the doctrine of the personal omnipresence was first [71] taught in the Formula of Concord. The foundations of this doctrine were laid in Luther's teaching, in the Augsburg Confession, and in the other symbols; and the Formula pointed out the larger (but consistent) development and the central position of this fact in the Person of Christ.

Jacobs, in discussing the statement in Valentine's *Christian Theology* that the *Genus Majestaticum,* " is peculiar to Lutheran dogmaticians," points out that the statement is modified by the author's own admission that " its substance was maintained by Luther." " The long quotation from Luther in the Formula of Concord concerning the different modes of presence and the meaning of 'the right hand of God' is, in fact," says Jacobs, " the chief part of the argument of that Confession."

Forrest,[72] resting on Bruce and Gore, rises above Schaff and Lindsay in his conception of the doctrine of the real presence, which he characterizes as " illocal," but which he nevertheless regards with a mechanical eye, and disposes of in an epigram based on the theory that Christ was not omnipresent or omniscient upon earth. He says, " The ' il-

---

[71] The tendency of the enemies to the Formula to find and emphasize differences between it and the Augsburg Confession is natural and to be expected. Such differences have been " found " in the teaching of the two Confessions on Free Will. But, says J. T. Müller, " In truth we may call our symbols fortunate that in that their most sharp-sighted opponents can find no other contradictions in them than such whose solution are also to be found within them. If the Augustana and her Apology contain passages which are in need of a justifying explanation, this is given in the later symbols, especially in the Formula of Concord. Therefore the Formula pretends to be nothing else than an explanation of the former, and an introduction to its proper understanding. Such representations are indeed themselves only a testimony for the necessity of the Formula of Concord itself."

[72] *The Christ of History and of Experience,* pp. 194, 195.

local ubiquity' which the Lutherans attribute to His humanity is as fantastic as it is incomprehensible." One might with equal propriety remark that the birth of the Son of God in Bethlehem, or His resurrection from the tomb of Joseph, or His ascension to the right hand of the Father, is " as fantastic as it is incomprehensible."

The contrast in manner in which this doctrine is approached on the Lutheran and on the Reformed and Philippist side is marked. At times this teaching is ascribed to Luther and his scholasticism; and again, it is denied to Luther and ascribed to the Formula. By non-Lutherans it is regarded as a ridiculous human abstraction. By our Church it is regarded as a divine and mysterious fact in the Person of Christ, the crowning, most lofty and most real act of our Lord in His person for us. Compare for instance, the reverence, the restraint, and the objectivity shown in Jacobs' *Summary of the Christian Faith,* and the caustic, rationalizing and almost flippant discussion in *The Creeds of Christendom.* [73]

If this particular form of the communication of divine attributes to the human nature of Christ is a mere theological invention and speculation, and a philosophical abstraction, a pretext of reasoning to help out the Lutheran doctrine of the Lord's Supper, as is so constantly asserted, neither the writer, nor the Lutheran Church, because of her doctrine of the Word, can have anything to do with it. But if the mysteries of the Incarnation, the Redemption, and the Glorification of Christ, are not also mere philosophic figments, and human inventions, but are the great and ultimate facts of history, imperfectly comprehensible by our poor human reasoning, then this particular fact of the genus majestaticum, that inheres in the Incarnation and

---

[73] This is one of the few places in the *Creeds of Christendom* in which Schaff descends from the symbolic standpoint to argue at length, and as a particular member of the Reformed Church, against a particular doctrine ; and he does it in a way which seems to show his intention of giving the Lutheran doctrine a death blow.

Glorification of Christ, is also not a philosophical figment, but an adorable mystery.[73a]

The most potent argument that is advanced by the Reformed and the weaker Lutherans against the genus majestaticum is the rationalistic one, viz.: that it *cannot be true, for it is contrary to human reason,* and human reason *cannot comprehend it.* Thus Schaff says, "How can eternity . . . be really communicated to a being born in time . . . ? How can immensity be transferred to a finite man ? "[74]

And Valentine says, "It is impossible to conceive how the divine properties could be given to the human nature, as real attributes, without making it something else or other than human nature. . It is the essence of human nature to be finite; to add to it omnipresence is, to the necessities of scientific thought, to constitute it *per se* infinitely beyond the self-identity of human nature."[75]

This same argument of transcendence beyond the bounds of what is possible to human thought, can be directed, if it

---

[73a] Everything that the Saviour did and suffered is both divine and human, that is, it is personal. *He* did, and suffered all, and *He* is both human and divine. Every act, indeed, is done, every suffering endured, *through* or *by* the one or the other nature, but not without the personal presence of the other. Jesus Christ wrought miracles *through* the divine nature, but they were wrought *by* the human nature. *Through* His divine omnipotence sight was given to the blind, but His divine omnipotence wrought it *by* His human touch. Jesus Christ died according to His human nature, but His death was the death of a divine person. *Through* His human infirmity He was crucified, but that human weakness wrought *by* His divine majesty an infinite sacrifice. Godhead cannot bleed, but the Church is purchased by the blood of God; for He who bleeds is in one inseparable person, God as well as man, and His blood has efficacy, not because of the properties of the nature according to which He bleeds, but because of the attributes of His whole person, which is divine. Had not He who bled been personally God as well as man, His blood would not have availed. Jesus Christ is essentially and necessarily omnipresent according to the divine nature, but His human nature not of its own essence, or by a necessity resulting from its own attributes, but because the divine has taken it into personal union with itself, is rendered present *through* the divine.—*Con. Ref.* pp. 476 and 477.

[74] *Creeds of Christendom,* p. 324.

[75] *Christian Theology,* II., p. 77.

be valid, with fatal force, against the whole mystery of the Incarnation, the Redemption and the Glorification of Christ. The genus majestaticum is a specific fact in the general union of the divine and human natures in Christ. This union of the finite with the infinite, which is the greatest fact of revelation, is as incomprehensible, as to its possibility, as is the particular fact which is a part of it, which we term the genus majestaticum.

It is, however, admitted by Valentine that if the communication of the divine attributes to the human nature be viewed as " functional," the mild and careful confession of the doctrine in the Formula of Concord can be accepted: " Interpreted in this, its true light or sense, it is really only a necessary explication and issue of the functional action taught in the second kind of communication, arising from the real personal union. . . Looked at in this light, this kind of communication surely belongs to a full Christological view. . . This gives all that is necessary to a correct view of the Lutheran doctrine of the Supper." [76]

This functional action in the communio " gives all that is necessary " to the doctrine of the Supper, but has nothing to spare for the majesty of the Person of Christ, on the ground that " Melanchthon did not accept the idea of a real communication of the divine attributes." [76]

THE CRITIQUE OF SCHAFF.

But the Reformed critique of this doctrine, as represented by Schaff, without entering into the mystery of Christ at all, presumes to judge it from an external and speculative point of view. The very first statement of Schaff, which he supports by a quotation from Stahl, is as follows: " The scholastic refinements of the doctrine of the Communicatio Idiomatum, and especially the ubiquity of

---

[76] *Christian Theology*, II, pp. 79-80.

the body, have no intrinsic religious importance, and owe their origin to the Lutheran hypothesis of the corporeal presence. They should, therefore, never have been made an article of faith. A surplus of orthodoxy provokes skepticism."

If a rationalistic approach such as this were made to the doctrine of Predestination, to the doctrine of the Trinity, and to certain Presbyterian doctrines connected with the organization of the Church, they might be read out of court in statements as curt as these.

In proceeding to show that the Formula overstates and endangers the " central mystery of the union of the divine and human in Christ," Schaff declares, " It leads necessarily—notwithstanding the solemn protest of the Formula to a Eutychian confusion and equation of natures; for, *according to all sound philosophy,* the attributes are not an outside appendix to the nature, and independent of it, but inherent qualities, and together constitute the nature itself."

Schaff's first objection, then, is that the doctrine has no religious value; his second objection is that it is condemned by "all sound philosophy," that is, by human reason. His third objection is that the doctrine breaks down half way, and cannot be carried consistently through all the attributes. This is likewise an objection of the human reason. His fourth objection is that the doctrine has no support in the Scriptures. In reply to this we would say that nearly all the Scriptures which describe to us the manifestation of the divine nature in the human are a proof of this doctrine; not merely such general passages as Matt., 11: 27; 28: 18; John, 5: 26; but Heb., 2: 8; Col., 2: 3; John, 6: 51; I Cor., 15: 45; Matt., 9: 6; John, 5: 27; Phil., 2: 9, 10; Heb., 1: 8; Matt., 18: 20; 28: 20; Eph., 1: 23; 4: 10; Heb., 1: 3; Heb., 2: 9; Luke, 22: 69; I John, 1: 7; John, 17: 5.

The fifth objection of Schaff, namely, " The Christology of the Formula makes it impossible to construct a truly human life of our Lord on earth," is also an objection of pure rationalism. It is not so important for us to be able "to *construct* a truly human life of our Lord" as it is to accept the fact that God "constructed" such a life, and to believe in it whether we understand it or not. As for the "construction," we should remember the words of the Formula, "it shines forth . . . when and as Christ wills."

No time need be wasted on the sixth objection of Schaff, which is illustrative, nor on the seventh, which attributes "consubstantiation" to the Formula of Concord and declares that the ubiquity of the body is *"logically necessary for consubstantiation."* The eighth objection is puerile, declaring that "ubiquity proves too much by extending the eating of Christ to every meal." Christ did not quicken every dead man to life, nor forgive every paralytic his sins, nor heal every blind man he saw, neither is his "ubiquity" a mere mechanical category, which affects all objects automatically, and in which we are, as we are in space and time; but it is under the control of Christ's will, and shines "forth when and as he wills."

The ninth objection of Schaff borders on the absurd. It is that the ubiquity "conflicts with the facts of Christ's local limitations while on earth." As thus conceived by these rationalistic philosophers, the ubiquity indeed would be a terrible burden, a fearful punishment of fate, under which even the Christ of God could not hold himself erect on earth, and which would certainly be a barrier and obstruction to his freedom at the Right Hand of the Father. They so distort the ubiquity mechanically as that it rules the Person and the Will. The Lutheran Church places this Communication of the attributes of the divine nature to the human in proper control of the Person and Will of Christ.

The tenth reason of Schaff is perhaps the real, at least the real historical, reason why the doctrine of the Formula of Concord has been fought so terribly. It is that if this doctrine be true, it requires the presence of the body and blood of Christ in the Sacrament, and would dispose of the

Zwinglian and Calvinistic interpretation of the Lord's Supper.

Thus is the central position of the Formula in the evangelical faith, and the central doctrine of the Formula, which upholds the central fact in the Person of Christ; as acknowledged, in all the greatness of its mystery, by the Lutheran Church, brought out as the real reason for the rejection of the Formula. And thus is the impossibility of union on the part of a real Lutheranism with Reformed Protestantism set forth *in extenso,* by the founder of the Evangelical Alliance.

INCONSISTENCY OF CRITICS OF THE " UBIQUITY."

Those who see in the Lutheran doctrine of the Lord's Supper a philosophical theory of ubiquity, instead of a Christian mystery, seem not to realize that they themselves have lost the true doctrine of the Lord's Supper because they are resting upon a shallow philosophical theory of the Person of Christ. This fundamental distinction could not but come out most sharply every time the Lord's Supper was discussed, beginning at Marburg in 1529; and continuing even when Calvin's view, later, was substituted for that of Zwingli.

For a true presence of Christ on earth, so possible to the glorified Son of Man, the Calvinistic view substitutes " an imaginary presence of the believers in Heaven," so impossible as an actual reality. The Calvinistic view " puts too much upon man who is nothing, because it concedes too little to Christ who is everything . . . With its great advance on the rationalism of Zwingli, the doctrine of Calvin still bore with it the fatal taint of the very view which he calls ' profane.' All that Calvin gained in depth, as contrasted with Zwingli, he lost in clearness. He does not as flatly as Zwingli contradict the text. But he does what Zwingli did not, he contradicts himself. But two views will remain in the ultimate struggle, the rationalistic, Zwinglian, Arminian, Socinian view, which fully denies the whole mystery, on the one side, and the Scriptural, Catholic view, which fully and consistently recognizes it on the other. This is the view of the objective reality of the presence held in its purity in the Lutheran Church, and held in the Roman and Greek churches, though with the rubbish of human additions heaped upon it. The advance of either view presses out the Calvinistic . . . The rigid logic which so wonderfully marks Calvin, in the other parts of his system, [77] seems to fail him here. His sacramental theories were an adaptation of the views of Bucer, which their originator ultimately abandoned for those of the Lutheran Church. They were grafted on Calvin's system, not grown by it, and they fall away even when the trunk retains its original vigor, or are retained, as the Unionistic theology, though with great changes, now retains them, when everything ordinarily embraced in Calvinism, is utterly abandoned." [78]

The most savage assaults upon the Formula of Concord made by Reformed and Philippist are due to its teaching that the human nature in Christ has received the divine majesty according to the manner of the personal union, so that, as the Formula says, " The entire fulness of the divinity dwells in Christ, not as in other holy men and angels, but bodily, as in its own body, so that, with all its majesty, power, glory and efficacy, it shines forth in the assumed human nature of Christ when and as he wills, and in, with, and through it, exerts its divine power, glory, and efficacy."

---

[77] But cp. Prof. Thomas C. Hall of Union Seminary, New York, who says, " The ethical system of Calvin is profoundly reactionary, scholastic, and Roman Catholic in both method and aim.   As a religious force of the first magnitude Calvinism has aided in high degree men's practical ethical life. . . . But on the intellectual and philosophical reconstruction of ethics it has left no such mark as that made by one single work of Luther's, *Die Freiheit des Christenmenschen.*"

[78] *Con. Ref.,* pp. 499, 501.

THE COMMUNICATIO IDIOMATUM ORIGINATED IN SCRIPTURE,
NOT IN THE FORMULA.

This confession, instead of being merely a doctrine of
the Formula of Concord, is the doctrine taught in Scripture,
and did not originate in the necessity of defending the Lutheran doctrine of the Lord's Supper. " The doctrine of our
Church rests upon the true testimony of God's Word, and her
interpretation of the meaning of that Word is not one of her
own devising, but had been given ages before her great
distinctive Confession by the fathers and Councils of the
pure Church." [79]

We have seen that Luther drew the communicatio idiomatum from his profound knowledge of the Person of
Christ as found in Scripture. Its origin is in Scripture,
not in the Formula. John, who tells us that the Word was
made flesh, and *we* beheld *His glory,* the glory as of the
Only-begotten of the Father, presents to us the communication of attributes. Christ Himself teaches this doctrine in
John, 3: 35; Matt., 11: 27; Luke, 10: 22; and John, 13: 3.
One of the most striking of all contrasts between the two
natures in the one Person is this: " Jesus knowing that the
Father had given all things into his hands, and that he was
come from God, and went to God; he riseth from supper . . . and began to wash the disciples' feet." And
here the whole point of the antithesis between *what Christ
was,* and *what He did,* turns upon the *communicatio.*
" That Jesus performed this act of touching lowliness not
in forgetfulness of His glorious majesty and of the plenitude
of His gifts, but fully conscious of them " is the point of
the narrative. But if he had " all things " given unto
Him as a man, as in the consciousness of this glory, He
washed the disciples' feet, then was there real humiliation. [80]
In Him, Who had power to lay down His life and power to

---

[79] *Con. Ref.,* p. 502.

[80] For the discussion of Matt. 28 :18; Matt. 28 :20; John 17 :5; Col. 2 :9;
Matt. 17 : 25, etc., *vid. Con. Ref.,* pp. 502-508.

take it up again, Who offered Himself a ransom for many, Who gave His body and His blood for the remission of sins, Who rose from the dead in the glory of the Father, yet with the nail-prints upon Him; Who is with His disciples even unto the end of the world, the human nature as the personalized organ of the divine nature, experiences, enjoys and uses, according to the wisdom of His own will, the attributes of the divine nature, whether He be on the Mount, upon the Cross or at the right hand of the Father. " So thoroughly," says Krauth, " does this idea of the personal unity underlie the New Testament conception of Christ, that we find it constantly assumed where no formal statement of it is made."

THE ANCIENT CREEDS.

The Apostles' Creed teaches the communicatio idiomatum when it declares that God's " only Son, our Lord," was conceived, born, suffered, crucified, dead, buried, descended into hell, ascended into heaven, and sitteth at the right hand of the Father Almighty." If God's Son was really *conceived* and *born,* and suffered, " if He whom the heaven of heavens cannot contain, was hidden in the grave," there was in the whole earthly life of Christ a communication of natures in their attributes.

The Nicene Creed states the communication of attributes in the one Person with great clearness. "The only begotten, the Eternal Son, Maker of all things, descends from heaven, is made man, is crucified, suffers. He is one Person, to whom is referred all the glory that is divine, and all the shame and pain that are human. The Athanasian Creed witnesses still further: Though He be God and man, He is not two, but one Christ—one, not by the conversion of Divinity into flesh, but by the assumption of humanity to God; one altogether, not by confusion of substance, but by unity of Person. For as the rational soul and flesh is one man, so God and man is one Christ, who (God and man, one Christ) 'suffered for our salvation, descended into hell, rose the third day.' The Augsburg Confession takes up this thread of witness: 'God the Son became man, so that there be two natures, the divine and human, in unity of person *inseparably* conjoined, one Christ, truly God and truly man, who was born, truly suffered, was crucified, dead and buried.' " [81]

THE CHURCH FATHERS.

The participation of attributes in Christ in the sense of the *genus majestaticum* passed from Scripture to the wider territory of the Church Fathers. Was it the Formula of Concord that said, "As the Son of God has been made participant of flesh and blood, so the human flesh of our Lord has been made participant of Deity?" No, it was *St. Basil,* who also says, "When our Lord declares 'All power is given unto me,' the words are to be understood of Him in His incarnation, not *in His Deity.*" [82]

Was it the Formula that said, "Christ according to His humanity shares the throne of God," or "Thou art everywhere, and standing in our midst art not perceived by us," or "One Christ is everywhere; here existing complete, and there complete?" [83] No, it was *Ambrose.* Was it the Formula that said, "He is wherever He wills to be; wheresoever He is, He is entire"? No, it was *Chrysostom.* Was it the Formula that said, "The holy body of Christ . . . is communicated in the four parts of the world . . . He exists entire and undivided in all everywhere"? No, it was *Theophylact.* [84] It was *Jerome* who said, [85] "The Lamb is everywhere."

---

[81] *Con. Ref.,* 316-317.

[82] Basilius *in Homil. de Nativ. Christi.*

[83] Ambrose on Luke X, Lib. VII, ch. 47, and on Heb. IV.

[84] Theophyl., on Eph. IV, 10.

[85] *Adv. Vigilantium.*

55

This confession was not an invention of the Formula. It was confessed by the Formula because it was confessed by Luther. It was confessed by Luther after it was confessed by the Ancient Church, and because both Luther and the Church Fathers found it taught in Scripture itself.

The real objection to the doctrine of the Person of Christ in the Formula was the rationalistic Christology of Zwingli, which he accepted from the schoolmen of Rome, which attempts to limit and confess Christ in the forms of common sense and the human mind; and which was artificial just as the Roman doctrine of justification is shallow; but which has passed into the teaching of Reformed Protestantism. [86]

If it be borne in mind that the Reformed Church, through Zwingli, retained the rationalistic view of the natures of Christ as an heirloom from Rome, it will be understood why the Reformed, the rationalist, and the Roman Catholic have joined hands to extinguish the truth of the Formula.

This truth is the inner citadel of our Faith in Christ our Redeemer, and it is confessed, used and enjoyed in every

---

[86] *Seeberg* speaks even more sharply of Zwingli's theology as follows: " His Christology has the Nestorian tendency of the Scholastics. His interpretation of original sin harmonizes with that of the later Middle Ages. His theory of the sacraments follows the symbolic view not infrequently held in the Middle Ages. He mingles philosophical theories with his presentations of the gospel, lacking Luther's sense of the positive character of revelation— Duns and the Nominalists having here prepared the way. Thus Christianity became a kind of philosophy deduced from the Bible. In view of these characteristics of his teaching, it may be said that the undeniable difference between Zwingli and Luther—despite their common understanding of the gospel—is to be explained by the fact, that Zwingli received his impulse originally from the Erasmian illuministic tendency, and that, in consequence, the medieval ideas continued to exert a greater influence upon him than upon Luther."—II, p. 317.

" Zwingli was from the first conscious of the deviation of his ideas from those of Luther, which explains in part the zealous assertions of his (supposed) independence of the Saxon reformer. If he at first, indeed, represented this difference as a merely formal one, though emphasizing the idea of a repeated memorial (Wiedergedächtniss, i. 257), yet he very soon resolved to assail the theory of Luther, and from the year 1525 built up a carefully planned and vigorous propaganda for the purpose of winning the Southern Germans to his views. . . . There was a feeling of strong confidence that Luther's view could be explained away as simply the product of hypocrisy and timidity (e. g., vii. 390 f). Zwingli and his friends were impatient in their desire to measure swords with Luther and undermine his authority, and counseled against the use of prudent or pious tactics in dealing with him."— *Ib.* I, p. 319.

celebration of the Lord's Supper, which "constantly recalls the minds of those who use it aright to the most central facts and truths of Christianity. In the light of this Holy Sacrament, the proper relation between" the human and the divine, God and man, sin and redemption, "is set forth and maintained. The words of the Gospel which it brings and seals to the individual, every time he communes, condense all that is taught in both Old and New Testament. It is an impressive summary of God's entire revelation of Himself to man. It fixes the lines along which faith moves and according to which it works . . . Nor is its testimony confined to communicants. It shows forth the Lord's death and all that it means to those as yet outside the Church. Without interruption, it has come down from a period before men could read the message of the Gospel in the canon of the New Testament, and even before its very first book was written, and through all these ages it gave the very same testimony as it is giving to-day." [87]

If our faith holds and clings to the living Christ, and is not content with abstract dogma deduced from the mere ideas of a philosophizing Christianity, if we know that our mighty and merciful Redeemer touches God at every point in the heights of heaven and touches our fallen nature at every point in the depths of humiliation; if we know that He is the potent, compassionate, and glorious Mediator, reaching out to us with His flesh and blood, after the manner of the human, and reaching up into the eternal life and equality of His Father in His divinely begotten and eternal nature; if we believe that he has poured out divine powers and treasures of redemption through the human vessels of His own body and blood, and if we believe that these vessels in their union with the divine have become transfigured under its influence; if He, the Mediator is a reality, is a unit in personality, a single entity in the fullness of His own life, far be-

---

[87] Jacobs, *Summary of Christian Faith*, p. 366-367.

yond anything which it hath entered the mind of man to conceive, then how can we be so shallow as to empty the sacramental mystery of His bodily life broken for our sin, of all its reality, and as to deprive His own Church of the one great standing miracle of the real presence of His living and saving Person, unconfused but also undivided.

Well does the Formula of Concord close its wonderful defence of our Lord's Person with the following words:

"We would exhort all devout people not to attempt to scrutinize this deep mystery with the curious search of human reason, but rather with the Apostles of our Lord to exercise a simple faith, closing the eyes of human reason, and bringing every thought into captivity to the obedience of Christ. But most sweet, most firm consolation, and perpetual joy may they seek in the truth that our flesh is placed so high, even at the right hand of the majesty of God, and of His almighty power. Thus shall they find abiding consolation in every sorrow, and be kept safe from every hurtful error."

CHAPTER XXXIV.

THE LUTHERAN CONFESSION.

CONCORDIA IS THE CHURCH'S GREAT CONFESSION OF CHRIST.

The Material of Concordia—Its Field is Salvation—Its Subject is Christ—The Church should never Go Back to the Concordia; but should Stand Upon It—It treats Other Doctrines, but substantially it is the Great Confession of the Person and Work of Christ.

SHOULD our Concordia be the Confession, as is the Augustana, of the whole Conservative Evangelical Church? Its material is that of the Augustana, which it raises to clean, sharp outline and more ample clearness. It eliminates the more earthly and temporal elements found in the Augustana, the Apology, and the Schmalkald Articles. It focuses all the rays of Scripture truth on the field of salvation. It concentrates the whole Lutheran Confession upon Christ, the Son of the living God. It confesses a Christ Who assumed our human nature into the unity of His divine person, that He might be our high priest for our reconciliation with God; and Who, possessing the majesty and power of God according to the personal union, abstained from it in humbling Himself, and grew in all wisdom and favor with God and man; Who exercised this majesty, not always, but when it pleased Him, until, after His resurrection, He laid aside the form of a servant, *and not the nature,* and resumed the use, manifestation and declaration of His own majesty and thus entered into His glory, so that now not only as God, but also as man, He knows all things, is present with all creatures, and has, under His feet and in His hands, everything that is in heaven and on earth.

Present in His whole Person by His divine nature with His Church unto the end of the world, He is also sacramentally present with His Church in His human nature, according to the property of the divine nature, to impart and seal the forgiveness of sins, life and salvation to each believer. This presence of the exalted Christ is not of the earth, or physical, or Capernaitic. Yet it is true and substantial, as He declares in His Testament, " This is my body."

In His incarnation, atonement, resurrection, ascension and impartation of redemption to each believer, the Person of Christ is not divided. Neither are the natures together with their properties confounded; neither is either creature changed into the other; but Christ is and remains, for all eternity, God and man in one undivided person, upon which mystery our only consolation, life and salvation depend.

This then is the sublime Confession, clear and Scriptural, of the Formula of Concord. On its presentation, preservation and protection of the doctrine of the Person of Christ, in which it stands preëminent and unapproachable, even as the Jungfrau towers in her soaring height above the whole circle of her surrounding sisters, the Formula of Concord may rest its case as to whether it is and is entitled to be acknowledged as the Symbol of the Lutheran Faith, and the culminating Confession of the whole Lutheran Church; and whether it is to be thankfully accepted by those who bear the name of Luther and who follow Him in the proclamation of the Word and the administration of the Sacrament.

It is true that the Church of this day will never go back to the Sixteenth Century or to the Formula of Concord. Neither can it go back to the Confession of Augsburg; and still less should it go back to the New Testament of Christ. But only by occupying and standing fully on the sure ground of the past will it be able to build upward to the true pinnacle of the future. A deviation very slight at the start results in a leaning tower at the top.

It is true that the Concordia includes more than the Person of Christ, as the Augustana contains more than the material principle of the Reformation. Thus it settles the principle of things more and things less important in the Christian Faith, the later form which the controversy with Rome took, and which brought the Lutheran states under the control of the emperor and the Roman Church.[1] It takes up the Article of Predestination, which in Lutheran Theology comes after and not before the doctrine of the Person of Christ.[2] But while such Loci as are found in the Augsburg Confession are treated in view of the fifty years' experience since the Confession of Augsburg, the crowning distinction of the Formula of Concord is that it is the Confession of the Work and the Person of Christ—the Work as we find it in saving the lost, the Person as the background and explanation of that salvation. The Formula of Concord is not, like the Augsburg Confession, ecclesiastical or reformatory in its treatment: it is wholly soteriological. It contains no article, like the Augsburg Confession, on the Church, none on Civil Affairs, none on Abuses, none on

---

[1] The emperor requested the Protestants to *submit to compromise* pending the call to a Council. The Augsburg Interim (1548) was the first compromise. It was wholly in favor of Rome, giving to the Protestants only the cup to the laity and the marriage of priests. In south Germany about four hundred Lutheran preachers were expelled or dismissed for non-conformity. Six months later came the second compromise, the Leipzig Interim, for the domain of Maurice of Saxony, of treacherous memory, where the Augsburg Interim could not be carried out. It retained some parts of the evangelical faith, but required conformity to the Romish ritual, including confirmation, episcopal ordination, extreme unction, a large part of the mass, fasts, processions, and the use of images. Melanchthon, here as originally at Augsburg and ever after, compromising, acted as mediator between Protestantism and Maurice.

The Formula in settling this subject, lays down the principle that ecclesiastical rites not commanded in the Word of God are in themselves adiaphora ; but ' the observance or non-observance of them may, under testing circumstances become a matter of principle and of conscience.'

[2] The now famous article on Predestination is introduced by the following paragraph, which shows most clearly the confessional intention and character of the Formula : " Concerning this article no public discussion has occurred among the theologians of the Augsburg Confession. But since it is a consolatory article, if treated properly, and by this means the introduction in the future of a controversy likely to cause offence may be avoided, it is also explained in this writing."

the Bishops, but it confines itself to Christ and to His salvation. The Saviour, the Living Christ, is the centre of the Formula. In this sense the Formula is the return of the Church back to Christ. In a historical sense, it is a return from Melanchthon, for whom the Person of Christ was not the centre, to Luther, for whom the Person of Christ was—in his earlier, and growing ever more intensely, for his later years—the source and centre of hope and faith. The Formula is the Lutheran Church's expansion of the Second Article of the Creed and of Luther's explanation of it, as the remedy for all the errors and conflicts of Protestantism. Luther's theology was the whole Christ and nothing but Christ. His striving was a " profound and earnest attempt to secure full recognition of the doctrine of the truly divine and the truly human natures," especially of the human nature, as enjoying also the fullness of the divine, in the inseparable union of the one Person. By this one fact he felt himself separated from the Roman scholasticism of earlier ages. "The most exalted theologians in former times flew from the humanity of Christ to His divinity, and clung alone to this. I was also formerly such a doctor, and excluded the humanity. But we must ascend to the divinity, and hold fast to it, in such a way as not to abandon the humanity of Christ. Thou shouldst know nothing of any God, or Son of God, but Him who is declared to have been born of the Virgin Mary and to have become man." [3] For Luther, God and man were inseparable in Christ, and that was the mystery of the redemption and of its application in Word and Sacrament. Being inseparable, the man in Christ secures for itself a participation in the loftiest prerogatives of the divine glory; and this fact in Christ is the key that unlocks all the teachings of Scripture as to the One by Whom we are saved. The Sacrament of the Altar and the Formula of Concord, are the two great testimonies, the one divine, and the other human, that Deus et homo unus est Christus.

---

[3] *Erl.*, 47. 362.

CHAPTER XXXV.

THE LUTHERAN CONFESSION.

WHAT THE FORMULA OF CONCORD ACCOM-PLISHED AS A CONFESSION OF THE LUTHERAN CHURCH.

The Substance of the Gospel Set Together after Protestantism had been Tested—
A Confession of Teachers and Congregations—It Rescued the Church from a
Petty Doctrinal Territorialism—It Recovered the Church from the Weaknesses
of Its Friends—The Estimate of Seeberg—It Preserved the Existence of the
Church—It Brought Peace—It Made Possible a Substantial Catholic Evangelical Church—It Guarded the Relation of the Divine and the Human in All
the Great Doctrines—It Settled the Question of Justification, of Synergism and
of the Sacraments—The White Winged Standard of Peace—The First Permanent
Synthesis of Luther and Melanchthon—It Deserves to be Accepted by the Lutheran Church.

THE Formula of Concord was the old Faith of God's
Word summed up for Protestantism, subsequent to
the period of testing, and once again *set together*. It was the
Augsburg Confession reconciled in its own native meanings,
and *repeated reverently* by the *unanimous consent* of the confessors.[1] It was the very substance of the Gospel and
of the Augsburg Confession, kneaded through the experience of the first generation of Protestantism, by incessant
and agonizing conflict, and coming forth from that experience as a true and tried teaching, a standard recognized
by many.

---

[1] *Concordia. Pia et Unanimi consensu repetito Confessio.*

821

The Augsburg Confession appearing in the first flush of heroic reaction from Rome, had proven to be a popular standard. But it was something done *for* the congregations and not by them. Originally it figured as the private Confession of the Elector John. Under stress it was broadened out to include the other territorial heads of Lutheranism. But, whereas the Augustana had seven signers, the pious and unanimous repetition of the Augustana, the Concordia, had over seven thousand signers. After the Augsburg Confession had been delivered for the whole Church prior to its discussion, and had resulted, in part through Melanchthon, in endless and ever weakening post-eventu discussion, the Concordia was signed by the far greater part of the Church, and not until all had participated fully in its discussion, and it thus became the Church's own act and document.

The Formula of Concord was the great Evangelical instrument that rescued the Evangelical Churches from the evils of a petty doctrinal territorialism, from the polemicism of powerfully protected partizanships in isolated institutions of learning, from many princes' individual bodies of doctrine, and brought the men of the Lutheran Faith together on the basis of an internal agreement in the new growth and life that had now sprung up beyond the dark shadows thrown by the closed circle of Rome.

The Book of Concord gave all Lutherans who wish to confess it, not a mere common *corpus,* but a vital and organic *Confession,* and relieved the Church of the numerous collections of confessional and doctrinal writings, bulky and individualistic, which separate territorial churches had drawn up as their standard. In other words, the Book of Concord, notwithstanding the independent Lutherans who did not acknowledge it, accomplished in the Sixteenth Century what the general bodies of the Lutheran Church in America, despite the many independent synods, are attempting to accomplish in the Twentieth Century, viz., protecting the

Church from absorption and furnishing one common centre of strength on which reliance can be placed.

The Augsburg Confession is the Lutheran Faith in the attitude of respectful apology and defence against an open foe without. The Formula of Concord is the Lutheran Faith in the attitude of recovering itself from weaker friends within and devouring friends without. Augustana rescued the Church from decapitation at the hand of the foe; Concordia rescued it from slow poisoning at the hand of its own members.

The two great Confessions are each the result of a great situation for which neither of them was responsible: in the case of the Formula, it was a terrible internal situation in the demoralized Church of Luther. " In forming our estimate of the Formula of Concord, it must be borne in mind," says Seeberg (translated by Hay), " that the problems with which the Formula deals, were *dividing the church* in that age; that it actually gave expression to a consensus already inaugurated; and that it consequently succeeded in gradually restoring the peace of the church. The detailed theological definitions of the pure doctrine which it presented were in keeping with the spirit that had prevailed in the church it represented for about a century and a half. We can, therefore, as little ignore the historical necessity of the enterprise, as we can fail to be impressed with the tactful and energetic literary labor which it reveals. The Formula of Concord did indeed make final the breach between the Lutheran-Melanchthonian and the Calvinistic-Melanchthonian types in the evangelical church of Germany; but this breach was, under the existing circumstances, unavoidable. No reproach can be cast upon a Confession for giving expression to a condition of affairs already existing."[2]

And Seeberg is justified in speaking still more positively. He asserts that the Formula preserved to the Lutheran

---

[2] *History of Doctrines,* II. pp. 382-383.

Church her right of self-existence.[3] Repeating that the Formula arose from an inner historical necessity in the Church, that it solved its own particular task in a prudent and far-sighted way, that the Melanchthonian doctrine, the more thoroughly it was taught, the more decidedly it worked toward a division of the Church, that the nearer Philippism approached Calvinism and the more Gnesio-Lutheranism advanced into party limits, the less was any unity to be thought of, Seeberg goes on to say, " In this lies the supreme significance of the Formula of Concord and of the Book of Concord, that through it the Lutheran Church upheld her ' Selbständigkeit ' as over against Calvinism."

Seeberg declares that " it was not some theological party that had forced its views upon the Lutheran Church," in the adoption of the Formula, " but the germ of a consensus which had been really at hand had attained to its unfolding in the Formula of Concord. It represented a Melanchthonian-Lutheranism . . . The Formula of Concord taught the doctrine which had gradually shaped itself out among the Lutheran theologians. It was therefore able to pacify the Lutheran Church."[4] As showing what the Concordia wrought, Seeberg goes so far as to insist that " historical insight must not allow itself to be darkened to such an extent by subjective inclination as to deny that the situation of the Lutheran Church at that time was such that any unity of the Calvinistic with the Lutheran teaching would have *rendered the destructive ecclesiastical strife within itself eternal.*"[5]

The valuelessness of Dr. Schaff's judgment on the Formula is due to his position on the Union question. The Formula thoroughly blocked the way to union with the Reformed by permanently setting forth the inner strength of a genuine and consistent Lutheranism as the full sum of evangelical faith. Dr. Schaff would have a re-union of the Reformed and Lutheran Churches on the basis that Lutheranism surrender or ignore its central doctrines and come over to a

---

[3] Hauck, *Cyc.*   [4] *Ib.*   [5] *Ib.*

substantially Reformed position. This is always the unconscious position of the unionist with respect to Lutheranism.

The Augustana with the tenth article altered, and the condemnation omitted, might have constituted a fine historical basis for such a union, prepared by Melanchthon himself, and leaving the historical glory to Lutheranism, but taking away the actual substance of its truth.

This glorious re-union of Protestantism at the expense of genuine Lutheranism was prevented by the Formula. Hence Dr. Schaff, and many before and after him, feel that the Formula is sectarian, and that it has prevented the building up of a united Protestant Church with the excrescences of Lutheranism lopped off, and with the Reformed spirit triumphant as a formative factor.

That our estimate reveals the inner standpoint of the harsh judgment voiced by Dr. Schaff against the Formula may be seen from the fact that Dr. Schaff quotes as "not without good reason," the striking statement of Kliefoth, "Mit Spener beginnt *jener grosse Eroberungszug der Reformirten Kirche* gegen die Lutherische, der seitdem verschiedene Namen, erst Frömmigkeit, Dann Toleranz, dann Union, dann Conföderation auf sein Panier geschrieben hat." [5a]

In other words, Dr. Schaff plainly admits that the progress of unionism in the Lutheran Church is an "Eroberungszug," a procession of triumph, for the Reformed Church.

The Formula saved the Church from Roman attacks and Romanizing teachings on the one side and the Reformed tendencies on the other, that were creeping in from without; and it preserved the Church from both the extremely rigid partisans of Luther; [*] and from the compromising Philippists who were agitating and destroying it from within. It proved a solid centre, with substance and strength, which

---

[5a] *Creeds,* I, p. 307.

[*] " Thätsächlich war Luther die höchste Auctorität, obwohl seine Lehre *mit Umsicht und Scheu vor aller Uebertreibung* durchgeführt wurde."—Hase, *Kirchengeschichte.*

gave continued possibility of existence, and prevented the absorption in surrounding faiths even of many Lutherans who would not accept it, but who for various doctrinal and personal reasons rejected it, though remaining benefited by the sphere of its influence.

It settled and set at rest the hidden frictions which remained embryonic in the early years of the Reformation, but which, as soon as opportunity offered, if they had prevailed, would have carried the Church to one extreme or the other, or into unbelief, doubt and despair of ever arriving at a consistent faith. It thus made possible and established a conservative and Catholic evangelical faith which has given rise to no Oxford movements on the one hand, nor Independent sectarian movements on the other.

What has the Formula accomplished for evangelical doctrine? It has settled forever the primacy of the Person and Work of Christ in the Lutheran Faith, and determined and maintained the balance of the divine and human elements in each; thus giving confessional authority to the mystery of the Cross hid from ages, both in predestination, revelation, redemption, the Word and the Sacraments, and in the nature of the Church itself.

It has guarded forever against any confusion as well as any separation of the divine and the human, but has found in the counsels of God, in the Scriptures, in the Person of Christ, in Justification and in Sanctification, and in the Sacraments, a proper point of union in each case, and a mysterious, superhuman, but vital communion.

It taught the Lutheran Church to dwell exclusively neither on the literal nor on the spiritual, but on the underlying unity in both, so that the Word was not without the Spirit, nor the Spirit without the Word; so that tradition and history were not separated from the Holy Ghost; and the Holy Ghost was not separated from the channels and forms in which He operates. It settled for Lutheranism the question as to whether the Law was still to be preached for

repentance, or whether love alone works both faith and repentance,—one of the vital questions in the Protestant world
of to-day. It set forth that Law has not only a *usus politicus*
and a *usus elencticus,* but also a *usus didacticus.*

It settled the vital question, the very foundation of the
Reformation, whether or not the sacrificial death of Christ
is only the negative condition of justification, while the incarnation—as reproduced in the believer, is its positive condition; whether or not justification is a making righteous
by an infusion of the righteousness of Christ.

How cardinal and yet how subtle this error is in prevailing Protestantism in the world to-day may be seen
from the fact that nearly all the newer writers on
doctrine who touch this subject, treat justification as an
infused righteousness, the Osiandrian heresy reproducing
itself in the newer advances of modern denominational
thought and teaching.

It settled for Lutheranism the question of synergism, a
teaching perhaps more widespread to-day than any other
in the Protestant denominations of America.

It also settled forever that the common-sense rationalism
of Zwingli as to the mystery of Christ, in His Word and
Presence, acquiesced in now by the majority of Protestants
outside of our Church; and the Calvinistic idealization of
the Sacramental principle adhered to by the remaining and
more meditative Protestants, run a deep line of separation between themselves and the Lutheran faith. This prevented a
union of the Reformed with Luther and Melanchthon before the Church possessed either the Augustana or the
Concordia, though Melanchthon subsequently wrought misery
in the Church for a generation, and brought on hopeless
internal division, by cherishing the hope of bridging this
gulf; not because he believed the Lutheran doctrine erroneous, but because he felt, synergistic as he was, that the
doctrine of a spiritual reception of the body and blood by
faith, gave up no essential part of religious truth.

The Formula of Concord has opened the eye of faith to this mystery in which the reality of the sacrifice of Christ offered to God, conditions the reality of the sacrament of Christ offered to man, as no Creed or Symbol ever was able to do before.[8] The invisible reality of atonement became visible and actual in the body and blood on the Cross; and the invisible application of the atonement becomes visible and actual in the body and blood in the Sacrament. There is no figure, but an actual divine provision in both. "A presence of the whole Person of Christ, of the divine by its inherent omnipresence, and of the human through the divine—a presence, not ideal or feigned, but most true; not fleshly, but spiritual; not after the manner of this earth, but of the unseen world; not natural, but supernatural—this presence the Lutheran Church maintains, and, God helping her, will maintain to the end of time."[9]

Are not the questions decided by the Formula, on the basis of Scripture, for the Lutheran Church, still burning problems in the wider religious world to-day? Namely,—

1. That there is only one rule of faith and life;

2. That God's Law and authority are needed now as ever to check the evil in our heart and in the world, and to bring a knowledge of sin, even though salvation comes only by the Gospel;

3. That there are things of minor importance, in teach-

---

[8] Compare the beautiful insight of Krauth: " As is the redemption, so is its sacrament. The foundation of both is the same, and lies forever inapproachable by man. . . . In the redemption, nature furnished the outward organ of the divine, in the frail body and the flowing blood of our crucified Lord. Through this organ an infinite ransom was accomplished. In the Supper, the organ of the redemption becomes the organ of its application. With an artlessness which heightens its grandeur, this redemption, which forever centres in Christ's sacred and undivided person, veils its supernatural powers under the simplest elements which sustain and revive our natural life. But faith none the less clearly sees that the bread which we break is the communion of Christ's body, and that the cup of blessing which we bless is the communion of His blood."—*Con. Ref.*, pp. 465 sq.

[9] *Con. Ref.*, pp. 460 sq.

ing, custom and life, but that in crises even such things may assume great importance.

4. That salvation comes not at all from deeds; but that where salvation takes root by faith in the heart, deeds spring up spontaneously in the life.

We do not realize what Protestantism has had protected and preserved for it by the Confession of the Formula.

Luther died with the premonitory clouds of dust presaging the coming storm sweeping his gloom-stricken brow; Melanchthon died terrified and broken-hearted. The gates of hell were opened and the hounds of war were let loose. The Pope and the Emperor conspired to bring the Protestant movement to ruin, and its congregations back to the corrupt old fold. The brilliant lustre of the glorious standard of Augsburg, the *Magna Charta* of the Christian Faith, was being tarnished by its own bearers. The edge of the line was turned, broken. None thought of advance, and none knew how to retreat. Confusion reigned upon the field.

During such times and amid such travail, God set up the Formula—a white-winged standard of order and peace, [10]—round which, after the death of Moses and Aaron, the host of the Lord could flock. This was the conviction of the great multitude of its signatories. It brought light, rule, order and peace into the Lutheran situation; and the storm which Luther foresaw and Melanchthon experienced gave way to calm.

This Formula of Concord is a great symbol. It is nothing less than the first and permanent synthesis of Luther and Melanchthon. It is the teaching of Luther in the spirit and the form of Melanchthon. It has combined the two antagonistic forces of the Reformation.

It has worked its impress into the faith and life of the

---

[10] That anti-Lutheran book, *Der Protestantismus in seiner Selbst-Auflösung;* Schaffhausen, 1843, admits that "after the acceptance of the Formula of Concord, the theological strife receded from the arena of public life."

56

Church as did the œcumenical creeds, which also for ages left parties outside; and time will show, if the Church is true to herself, that this firm but moderate centre, this balance of mutually destructive principles, this source of internal strength, which will make planets and not mere comets of the Protestant churches, will finally prevail in our midst, and among the children of men.

It asks our acceptance and deserves our respect, not as a great theological production, nor yet as a Commentary on the Augsburg Confession, but as the solemn and well-matured testimony of our Church [11] as to the witness and teaching of the Augustana on the great doctrines of Protestantism as they appeared shortly after its birth and will continue to reappear until the end of time.

" But for the Formula of Concord it may be questioned whether Protestantism could have been saved to the world. It staunched the wounds at which Lutheranism was bleeding to death, and crises were at hand in history, in which Lutheranism was essential to the salvation of the Reformatory interest in Europe. The Thirty Years' War, the war of martyrs, which saved our modern world, lay indeed in the future of another century, yet it was fought and settled in the Cloister of Bergen. But for the pen of the peaceful triumvirates, the sword of Gustavus had not been drawn. Intestine treachery and division in the Church of the Reformation would have done what the arts and arms of Rome failed to do. But the miracle of restoration was wrought.

---

[11] " The symbols do not assume to themselves any more than to be witnesses for the truth ; and it is great presumption for a preacher to wish to be more than this, or to raise himself from a witness to be a judge of the truth, above the Scriptures or the church. He is, or indeed should be, only a witness for the truth—not a preacher for himself alone, isolated and separate, as a testator of his own mere private opinion, but in association with the other witnesses and confessors, that is, in fellowship with the church as a co-witness with her testimony, and a partaker in the general confession which she makes. He does not believe *in* the symbols, but *with* them. If he is unwilling to take this position, and wishes with his new spirit to establsh a separate and new congregation, he becomes farther and farther sundered from the common scriptural confessions of the ancient church, and has less and less of the testimony of the Holy Spirit in his favor."—Sartorius, *Ev. Rev.*, IV, 18.

From being the most distracted Church on earth, the Lutheran Church had become the most stable. The blossom put forth at Augsburg, despite the storm, the mildew and the worm, had ripened into the full round fruit of the amplest and clearest Confession, in which the Christian Church has ever embodied her faith." [12]

---

[12] Krauth, *Con. Ref.,* p. 302.

CHAPTER XXXVI.

THE LUTHERAN CONFESSION.

THE BOOK OF CONCORD. THE FACTS OF ITS ORIGIN AND PUBLICATION. KÖLDE'S ESSAY.

Its Publication began in 1578—Adoption of Early Symbols—The Earliest Editions—The Title—The Arrangement—Later Editions.

ALONG with the efforts for recognition of the Formula of Concord went the other task which involved the framing of a *Corpus Doctrinae* that was to unite all the subscribers to the Formula of Concord. The publication of the same was begun in 1578, under the direction of Jacob Andreä, to whom Archdeacon Peter Glaser and a Dean, Kaspar Füger, of the Church of the Cross in Dresden, had been associated as correctors. Their aim was to meet in a preface of some length the many attacks to which the Formula of Concord had been submitted.

Such a preface, prepared as an explanation of the *theologians* on many separate questions,[1] was in the end not adopted. Its place was taken, in accordance with the whole preceding development, by a preface of the Evangelical Estates subscribing to the "Book of the Concordia," with the addition of their subscriptions. To this are added *"The Three Chief Creeds* or Confessions of the faith of Christ, concordantly accepted in the Church."

The adoption of these symbols of the early Church, the

---

[1] Printed by T h . P r e s s e l, as above, p. 711.

Apostolicum and the Nicaenum (more correctly the *Nicaeno-Constantinopolitanum*), occurred as follows. It must be traced back to Melanchthon, who, in order to emphasize the unity with the whole church, declares at once in the first article of the Augustana with especial mention of the Nicaenum, which for centuries was regarded as the foundation of all orthodoxy, that the evangelical churches assent to it and to statements in the Athanasianum.[2] Then too it was important for this question, as well as for all subscription to symbols, that in the Wittenberg doctor's vow, which dates from Melanchthon, those to be promoted were obligated to defend the Apostolic, Nicene and Athanasian Creeds, and that since 1535 this was extended to all ordained in Wittenberg.[3]

The next step was Melanchthon's *Confessio Saxonica,* of the year 1551, written to be presented at the Tridentine Council, and in which he emphatically declares the adherence of the Evangelicals to these symbols.[4] The same was done by John Brentz in the *Confessio Suevica,*[5] which was written for the same purpose, and in the Frankfurt Recess of 1558.[6] In the Corpus Philippicum, accordingly, they preceded the writings of Melanchthon and were received into most of the *Corpora Doctrinae* always in order to establish the connection with the early Church. As the Schwabian Concordia, perhaps with reference to the fact that Osiander had sharply opposed an obligation upon the Symbols,[7] subscribed to them,

---

[2] Cf. K o l d e , *The Augsb. Conf.* etc.. p. 23. Zwingli did the same in his *Fidei Ratio.* Cf. *K a r l M ü l l e r , Die Bekenntnisschriften der reform. Kirche.* Leipzig, 1903, p. 79 sq.

[3] *Liber Decanorum Facultatis Theologicæ Academiæ Vitebergensis* ed. F ö r s - t e m a n n . Lipsiæ, 1538, p. 158, and *C. R.* XII, 5 sq.

[4] *C. R.*, XXVIII, 376, and H e p p e , *D. Bekenntnisschriften der altprot. Kirche Deutschlands.* Kassel, 1855, p. 413.

[5] H e p p e , as above, p. 492.

[6] *C. R.*, IX, 494, and H e p p e , as above, 562. Here they are called the three chief symbols. As to the transactions of the Frankfurt Diet, *Cf,* G . W o l f , *Zur Geschichte des deutschen Protestantismus.* Berlin, 1888, pp. 120, sqq.

[7] *Cf. C. R.*, VIII, 6 sq., and S t r o b e l , *Beiträge zur Literatur d. 16. Jahrh.*, II, 1. Nürnberg, 1786, p. 192 sq., and P . T s c h a c k e r t , *Neue Beiträge zur Geschichte der Symbolverpflichtung.* Neue Kirchl. Zeitschr. (1897), p. 807.

it was only in agreement with the whole preceding development, that they are placed first in the Book of Concord, as being the chief symbols.

When in the title they are described as *"concordantly used* in the Church," an expression used by Luther was adopted, who in his writing, " The Three Symbols or Confessions of the Faith of Christ, Concordantly Used in the Church. Wittenberg, 1538," as a matter of fact had understood the Apostles' Creed and the Te Deum by this expression, and had added the Nicene Creed, by way of appendix, as " a confession also opposed to Arius." [8] It was his German translation as there given that was received into the Book of Concord.

The Latin rendering of the "concordantly used" by "Symbola catholica seu oecumenica," which since then became the usual one in Evangelical theology, must be traced to Nicholas Selnecker, who in three publications of the year 1575 calls the three symbols *" oecumenica "* and after that used this name in his lectures and in catechetical instruction. [9]

The three General Creeds are followed in the order in which they were first placed by the Schwabian Concordia, by:
1. The Augsburg Confession, "as the symbol of our time" to use the words of the Formula of Concord. [10] 2. The Apol-

---

[8] *Luther's Works,* Erl., Ausg., 23, 251. It is therefore incorrect when A d . H a r n a c k says in *Prot. Realenzykl.,* I, 742, 1 sqq.: Luther was perhaps the first to place the three together as expression of the general confessions of the Church. This was done long before, and not at all by Luther. The Te Deum was even in the Middle Ages here and there grouped with the confessions of the early Church. *Cf.* T h i e m e , *Theol. Literaturblatt,* 1892, p. 543.

[9] First in his *Historica Narratio et Oratio de D. D. Martino Luthero,* Lips., 1575, which originated from lectures on Luther's life, delivered in Nov., 1574, where he speaks of the completion of his lectures entitled " *Exegesis Symbolorum Catholicorum et vere O e c u m e n i c o r u m ;* secondly, in his *Catechesis Martini Lutheri Minor Gracolatina,* published 1575 (not 1577 as T h i e m e reports). Here on p. 165 we read: " Quot sunt Symbola fidei Christianae in Ecclesia? Tria sunt præcipua, quæ nominantur *œcumenica,* sive universalia et authentica id est, habentia auctoritatem et non indigentia demonstratione avt probatione, viz., Symbolum Apostolicum, Nicenum et Athanasianum." Last of all, in the published edition of his lectures on the three symbols: Symbolorum, Apostolici, Niceni, et Athanasiani Exegesis etc. Lips., 1575, where on p. 6 we read: Haec tria Symbola sunt *Catholica et Oecumenica.*

[10] In the *Epitome,* p. 518. " Symbolum " for the Augustana was first used in a statement of the Hessian Theologians of the year 1570: " The Augsburg Confession which is our symbol." In N e u d e c k e r , *Neue Beiträge zur*

ogy. 3. The Schmalkald Articles with the subtitle: "Articles of Christian Doctrine, which were to have been Presented on our Part to the Council if any had been Assembled at Mantua or elsewhere, Indicating what we could Receive or Grant, and what we Could not. Written by Dr. Martin Luther in the year MDXXXVII." Immediately following this, as a sort of appendix, came: "Of the Power and Primacy of the Pope. Treatise Written by the Theologians assembled at Schmalkald, in the Year MDXXXVII." 4. The Small Catechism (with the orders for baptism and marriage).[11] 5. The Large Catechism. 6. The Formula of Concord.[12] As an appendix we find the Catalogue of proof passages, etc., and the names of the theologians and schoolmasters who subscribed. On June 25th, 1580, the fiftieth anniversary of the presentation of the Augsburg Confession the work was published in Dresden:

Concordia. Jehovah. Christliche, Widerholete, einmütige Bekenntnüs naçhbenanter Churfürsten, Fürsten und Stende Augspurgischer Confession, und derselben zu ende des Buchs underschriebener Theologen Lere und Glaubens. Mit angeheffter, in Gottes wort, als der einigen Richtschnur, wolgegründter erklärung etlicher Artickel, bei welchen nach D. Martin Luthers seligen Absterben disputation und streit vorgefallen. Aus einhelliger vergleichung und befehl obgedachter Churfürsten, Fürsten und Stende, derselben Landen, Kirchen, Schulen und Nachkommen, zum underricht und warnung in Druck vorfertiget. Mit Churf. G. zu Sachsen befreihung. Dressden M.D.LXXX.

Concordia. Jehovah. Christian, repeated, unanimous Confession of Faith and Doctrine of the after-named Electors, Princes and Estates of the Augsburg Confession and their

---

Geschichte d. Reformation. Leipzig, 1841, II, p. 292. The term "Symbola" for the other writings was perhaps first used by H u t t e r, *Compendium Locorum theologicorum.* Wittenberg, 1610, p. 10.

[11] See on this point below.

[12] The *Epitome* and the *Solid Declaration* both bear a special title-page and the date "Dressden, 1579," which permits the conclusion that, although a separate edition of the Formula of Concord before the Book of Concord cannot be proven, it was yet intended.

theologians subscribed at the end of the book. To which is added a declaration, well-founded in God's Word, as the only rule of certain articles, in regard to which after Dr. Martin Luther's blessed death dispute and controversy have taken place. Upon the common counsel and command of the same Electors, Princes and Estates for the instruction and warning of their lands, churches, schools and descendants, done in print. With Privileges of His Grace, the Elector of Saxony, Dresden, M.D.LXXX.

In all probability, although M. Chemnitz[13] speaks of two editions, there appeared, to be exact, only *one* official Dresden edition in the year 1580; but the copies of the same that have come down to us show in part some very considerable variations.[14] According to the statements of the Saxon court preacher, Polycarp Leiser,[15] which give the impression of complete reliability and in the main agree with those of Chemnitz, the printing was somewhat hastily done and the sheets were printed and sent out separately. Thereupon came objections from theologians and princes, partly on account of the separate parts, partly on account of considerable misprints. This occasioned the reprint of individual sheets, which were again sent out separately, but in the binding were not placed by all recipients in the place of the earlier ones. Besides, the printers may have sent out mixed copies.

Thus, to enumerate only the most important, there occurred the following divergencies: 1. Out of consideration for the Highland Princes, especially for the Elector of the Palatinate, who objected to the exorcism in Luther's baptismal formula (Taufbüchlein), the Dresden Consistory had agreed to omit the Taufbüchlein and the Traubüchlein, on the ground that these things belonged "non ad doctrinalia sed ad

---

[13] In his letter, Nov. 7th, 1580, de mutatione Formulæ Concordiæ, in Hutter, *Concordia concors,* f. 360 sq.

[14] *Cf.* Feuerlini, *Bibliotheca Symbolica,* ed. J. B. Riederer, Normb., 1768, I, 8 sq.

[15] Polycarp Leiser's short and well founded report on the accusation promulgated in public print under the name of Daniel Hoffmann against the Christian *Concordia* printed in Dressden. Dresden, 1597.

caerimonialia." But when the sheets in question were published, the Elector of Brandenburg, Duke William of Lüneburg, and above all Chemnitz, filed objections. Thereupon the Elector ordered them included. This led to negotiations during which Chemnitz, to satisfy all, proposed "One should print the small *Catechismum Lutheri* thus into the *Concordien* that one may lay the Taufbüchlein and the Traubüchlein into it or take it out." This was agreed to and as a result there were copies that contained both parts, others (those printed first) that simply omitted them, and others which marked their absence and the place where they were to be laid in eventually in such a way that the last leaf of the small Catechism bears the page numbers 169, 170, 171, 172, 173, at the same time. 2. Some copies bear as title over the *catalogus testimoniorum* the term "Appendix," while in others, conformably to the desire of the Elector Palatinate, since this was not discussed or, as others thought, so as not to grant them the same authority as to the Formula of Concord, the word "Appendix" is simply omitted. 3. In the Formula of Concord (in *Müller,* 595, *Cf.* variants, p. 824), the quotation from Article XX of the Augustana was reproduced according to the quarto edition of 1531, as it was in manuscript. Chemnitz, who at once observed the discrepancy with the text in the Book of Concord, which rested upon the Maintz manuscript, ordered this sheet to be reprinted, which brought about another difference of copies that was accordingly made special use of by the opponents.[16]

In the same year Selnecker produced a Latin edition of the Book of Concord, which although described as "Communi Consilio et Mandato Electorum, etc., vulgata," was altogether a private undertaking. It contained the first, rather crude,

---

[16] Of less importance was the error called by Chemnitz "pudendum erratum," which was corrected in a reprint (M ü l l e r , p. 539, 33, see variants, p. 824). Some copies also have at the close after the signatures a special leaf with two verses from the 9th Psalm, the book-mark of the printers, Stöckel and Gimel Bergen, and after the print mark the erroneous date M.D.LXXXI, which in other prints was erroneously corrected to M.D.LXXIX.

translation of the Formula of Concord, which had been begun by Lucas Osiander in 1578, and completed by the Tübingen professor, Jacob Heerbrand.[17] As the whole edition was full of errors,[18] it found no favor, and Elector August seems to have prohibited its circulation.[19] Only after a thorough revision of Selnecker's text, especially that of the Formula of Concord,[20] which must be attributed essentially to Chemnitz, had been effected at the convention at Quedlinburg (Dec., 1582 and Jan., 1583), which was especially devoted to the completion of the most important article of defence of the Concordia, the " Apologia or Defence of the Christian Book of Concord," did the Elector command the reprint of the revised text "for the benefit of our student youth and the foreign church." At the same time it was ordered to omit the signatures, so that no one need complain that his name was appended to a book which he had not read or approved.[21] The edition published at Leipzig in 1584 became the *textus receptus* of the Latin Book of Concord.

In a new Latin edition of 1602, the ordering of which became authoritative for most of the later ones, the Preface of the Estates was preceded by an Electoral Mandate (according to the German edition of 1603, in our Ed. III, appendix, p. 785), in which Christian II. of Saxony, orders that all officials be obligated upon the Book of Concord. It afterwards received another addition in the fact that in the Saxon editions the *" Christian Articles of Visitation of 1592 "* were inserted (our edition, p. 778). This was most probably done

---

[17] *Cf.* G. B o s s e r t, *Uebersetzungen d. Formulæ Concordie*, Zeitschr. f. Kirchengesch. XIX, 470. Although according to this by the end of Oct., 1580, the printing of it had been going on for a long time, it seems never to have been published.

[18] Be it again observed that it reproduced the Augustana of the octavo edition of 1531 and contained many typographical errors, among others the much ridiculed one in the *Tractatus de potestate Papæ:* " ultimum f e r c u l u m " instead of " ultimum ius et iudicium."

[19] H e p p e , *Gesch, d. deutsch. Prot.*, IV, 225.

[20] S e l n e c k e r himself furnished a revised text in his *German-Latin separate edition of the F. C.* of 1582.

[21] *Cf.* P o l y c a r p L e i s e r, as above, Diij.

first in the German[22] edition of Henry Pipping of the year 1703.

The *Saxon* Articles of Visitation owe their origin to the Crypto-Calvinistic disturbances that arose again toward the end of the reign of the Elector Christian I. († Sept. 25th, 1591), the victim of which the Chancellor Nicholas Krell († Oct. 9th, 1601) was to become. In order to prevent all agitation, Duke Frederick William, who was regent for Christian II. during the latter's minority, ordered a general church visitation. The theologians called for the same, M. Mirus, G. Mylius, Ægidius Hunnius, Burch. Hebardus, Jos. Lonerus and Wolfg. Mamphrasius composed as a guide for it: *"Articles of Visitation[23] for the whole electoral territory of Saxony, together with the Calvinist's Negativa and Counter-teaching, and the form of subscription in the manner in which they have been put before both parties for subscription."* They treat in four sections of the *Lord's Supper,* of the *Person* of Christ, of *Baptism,* of *Election* and eternal Foreknowledge of God. According to a rescript of March 6th, 1594, all pastors and teachers of Saxony had to subscribe to these Articles, and it was in force up to 1806. For this reason, they possessed a legal and binding importance for Saxony, but only for this country. They have nothing to do with the Book of Concord or with the symbols of the Lutheran Church.

---

[22] I have been unable to ascertain when it first occurred in the Latin text. It does not seem to be in the editions of Rechenberg. [Kolde.]

[23] Printed in 1593. *Cf.* also *Gründl. Verantwortung der vier streitigen Artikeln,* wie dieselbigen inn Theses und Antitheses kürzlich verfasset u. in jüngst verrichteter Chursächs. Visitation zu underschreiben vorgelegt worden, gestellet durch die zu ermeldter Visitation verordneten Theologen. Leipz., 1593, 8. A e g. H u n n i i, *Widerlegung des Calvinischen Büchleins,* so wider die zur Visitation d. Chursächs. Kirchen u. Schulen verfasste vier Artikel ausgesprengt worden, 1593, 8.

CHAPTER XXXVII.

FROM THE BOOK OF CONCORD TO THE PRESENT DAY.

The Story of Unionism and Confessionalism according to Schaff—The Seventeenth-Century Dogmatik—Criticism of the Same—The Reaction in Calixtus—The Modern Individual Philosopher and Dogmatist—The Course of the Church in Europe—In America—Dogmatic System and the Confession.

THE FRATERNAL AND UNION VIEW OF CHURCH HISTORY.

"THE spirit of Melanchthon could be silenced, but not destroyed, for it meant theological progress and Christian union. It revived from time to time in various forms, in Calixtus, Spener, Zinzendorf, Neander and other great and good men, who blessed the Lutheran Church by protesting against bigotry and the overestimate of intellectual orthodoxy, by insisting on personal, practical piety, by widening the horizon of truth, and extending the hand of fellowship to other sections of Christ's kingdom. The minority which at first refused the Formula became a vast majority, and even the recent reaction of Lutheran confessionalism against rationalism, latitudinarianism, and unionism will be unable to undo the work of history, and to restore the Lutheran scholasticism and exclusivism of the Seventeenth Century. The Lutheran Church is greater and wider than Luther and Melanchthon, and, by its own principle of the absolute supremacy of the Bible as a rule of faith, it is bound to follow the onward march of Biblical learning." [1]

This is a typical statement of the consequences and the fate of Lutheran Confessionalism, sketched in the spirit of Zwingli, Beza, Arnold, Zinzendorf, Heppe, S. S. Schmucker and Dorner. It expresses the feelings of the great American writer on the Creeds of the Christian Church, but is out of harmony with a sober judgment found else-

---

[1] Schaff, *Creeds*, I, p. 339 sq.

where in his work. More recent historians have shown that " the spirit of Melanchthon " did not mean " theological progress," but scholastic definition. The freedom and vitality of Luther in his whole-souled and unvaried Confession is in contrast with the confining school-work of Melanchthon. " It cannot be denied," says Seeberg, " that the Formula of Concord by its *classical* theological *manner* has contributed much toward the ossification of Lutheran theology, and has limited and broken its practical working." Let the reader then accept this, once for all, that the scholastic method in setting up dogma by definition and inference, is of Melanchthon, to whom Calvin was a correlate in the Reformed Church.

Neither did " the spirit of Melanchthon " mean " Christian union." It meant an attempt at union by ambiguity of expression, which in time invariably reacted and in place of union brought final dissension and confusion. The entire movement of the Reformed Church under the Augsburg Confession was of this fraternizing but finally disruptive character, and Schaff himself, with feeling, repudiates our Confession as a legitimate expression of the Reformed principle.

" The spirit of Melanchthon " was not revived, so far as dogma was concerned, in Spener or Neander: the great hiatus between Spener and the spirit of Melanchthon is best seen in the mutually hostile attitude of Zinzendorf and Muhlenberg in America. " The spirit of Melanchthon," as shown sufficiently in Melanchthon's correspondence, laid more stress on " intellectual orthodoxy," and less on personal faith and practical piety than did that of Luther. Luther was the truthful, the prayerful, the believing, the resigned, the heroic and the spiritual-minded Christian. Melanchthon's spirituality does not free itself from shrewd manoeuver and logical platitude. " The spirit of Melanchthon " did *not* " extend the hand of fellowship to other sections of Christ's kingdom " at Marburg (the scene probably in the mind of the author), but Melanchthon was more 'bigoted' against Zwingli than Luther. Luther "would gladly have given up his life three times" (these are his own words) to reach harmony in the Confession of the sacrament. "Who . . . that will read Zwingli's *Reckoning* will not see that Luther acted with astonishing moderation at Marburg?"[2] He separated from Zwingli under the assurance of mutual patience and love. But Luther understood thereby the universal Christian and not the intimate brotherly love, because the latter demanded a perfect harmony of faith.[3] The superficiality of the view voiced by Schaff, and prevalent elsewhere, as to "the bigotry of Confessional Lutheranism," is most strikingly seen in his balancing of Lutheran "confessionalism, scholasticism, and exclusivism" on the one side, against "rationalism, latitudinarianism and unionism" on the Melanchthonian side. In reply, it will be sufficient to inquire, Are rationalism and latitudinarianism the company in which unionism wishes to be found! The reader, last of all, will note that it would be difficult to frame a more fallacious statement than the final one of this unionistic historian, in which *" the Bible as the only rule of faith "* is made to appear synonymous with the free *" onward march of Biblical learning"!*[4]

---

[2] Jacobs, Preface to *Book of Concord*, II, p. 6.

[3] The Elector and the Margrave at Schleiz agreed entirely with Luther that full unity in the faith was needed for mutual defence; and when therefore the Schwabach Articles were placed before the Zwinglians as a Confession, *they declined* to sign. This put an end to the proposed federation.

[4] In this discussion, and elsewhere, we have selected and used the classic statements of Schaff by way of illustration, for several reasons. First of all, he is the author of the one standard work on Symbolics in the American Church, and in that work he assigns the first place to the Lutheran symbols, and gives them a more complete discussion than is to be found elsewhere in the English language outside of the Lutheran Church. Second, he was all his life intimately connected with Lutherans and the Lutheran Church, and was a life witness of the Confessional development that culminated in the General Council. Third, his own general doctrinal position, and the tone and spirit of his writings are such as that they would probably meet with acceptance as expressing the views of those of our readers who do not agree with us, both those without, and those within the Lutheran Church. He stood, so long as he lived, both in word and example, at the head of that movement which believes that the days are ripe for advancing to an external Christian union.

Any one who weighs the judgments of Dr. Schaff (taken in connection with

THE DEVELOPMENT IN HISTORY.

From Luther and Melanchthon, the confessional principle
of Christianity developed into that body of truth more pure
and complete, more satisfactory to the mind and the heart,

---

the steps in his own life) respecting the Lutheran Confessions, will find that,
though he is the most voluminous non-Lutheran English commentator on the
Formula of Concord, yet his sympathies were all against it, and its principles,
in consequence of his nature, his training, the denominational changes in his
life, his type of theology, his position in Union Theological Seminary, and in
consequence of all he hoped to accomplish toward the re-union of Christendom
in the fostering of the Evangelical Alliance.

Dr. Schaff's mind on the question before us is revealed by the kind of
solution that he proposes for the reconciliation of the Lutheran and Reformed doctrines. He says, " We firmly believe (*Creeds of Christendom*, p.
327), that the Lutheran and Reformed views can be essentially reconciled, if
subordinate differences and scholastic subtleties are yielded. *The chief
elements of reconciliation are at hand in the Melanchthonian-Calvinistic
theory.* The Lord's Supper is: 1. A commemorative ordinance. (This is the
truth of the Zwinglian view). 2. A feast of living union of believers with the
ever-living, exalted Saviour, whereby we truly, though spiritually, receive
Christ with all His benefits, and are nourished by His life unto life eternal.
(This was the substance for which Luther contended against Zwingli, and
which Calvin retained, though in a different scientific form, and in a sense
rightly confined to all believers.) 3. A communion of believers with one
another as members of the same mystical body of Christ."

This, then, is Schaff's method of carrying out the proposition to unite the
Lutheran and the Reformed Churches, viz., by accepting " the true Zwinglian
view," and adding to it " the Calvinistic view," and then calling it " the
substance of the Lutheran view." That Lutheranism loses everything is too
obvious to need pointing out—and yet Dr. Schaff can go on in the same
breath and say: " The Eucharistic controversies are among the most unrefreshing and apparently fruitless in Church history. Theologians will have
much to answer for at the Judgment Day for having perverted the sacred
feast of divine love into the apple of discord. No wonder that Melanchthon's
last wish and prayer was to be delivered from the *rabies theologorum*. . . .
Fortunately, even now Christians of different denominations and holding different opinions can unite around the table of their common Lord and Saviour."

Surely, one who thus sharply condemns the Lutherans, as answerable at the
Judgment Day, for having persisted in unimportant doctrinal differences would
be prepared to yield all for the sake of a general concord. And yet, when
proposing such a concord, he preserves his own doctrine (" reconciliation by
the Melanchthonian-Calvinistic theory "), and sacrifices the Lutheran doctrine,
and calls the result union.

That Schaff, in his Symbolical work, expresses an *animus* against the
Lutheran Church is to be seen in his account of the meeting of Luther and
Zwingli at Marburg. He says, " Zwingli proposed, with tears, peace and union,
notwithstanding this difference [in the Eucharist], but Luther refused the hand
of Christian fellowship, because he made doctrinal agreement the boundary-
line of brotherhood." (*Creeds*, p. 362.) He fails to add that Zwingli's tears
[for even according to Dr. Schaff, Zwingli was no emotionalist] were not
tears respecting the Lord's Supper, but respecting the failure of a political
alliance which was at the bottom of this proposed compromise; and that the
doctrinal peace that would have ensued, would have been somewhat of the
nature between that proposed by the traditional lion to the lamb.

But the *animus* of Dr. Schaff as a unionist toward the Lutheran Church
comes out most clearly, not in speaking of the Lutheran Confessions, but
at the point where he has passed on to a consideration of the Reformed

and more worthy of Christ's own Church, than the world
has elsewhere possessed. All the parts in this whole exhibit
the same form of doctrine, and " he who candidly adopts the
Augsburg Confession will not hesitate to adopt those with

Confessions, and where he describes the historical origin of the names of the
Lutheran and the Reformed. Here he says that the followers of Luther,
" forget St. Paul's warning against sectarian names. They gradually appropriated the term, Lutheran or Evangelical Lutheran, as the official title of
the Church since about 1585, under the influence of Jacob Andreae, the chief
author of the Formula of Concord." The whole passage is instructive, and
we therefore give it as follows:
" We take the term *Reformed* here in its catholic and historical sense for
all those Churches which were founded by Zwingli and Calvin and their
fellow-reformers in the sixteenth century on the Continent and in England
and Scotland, and which agreed with the Lutheran Church in opposition to
the Roman Catholic, but differed from it in the doctrine of the real presence,
afterward also in the doctrine of predestination. By their opponents they
were first called in derision *Zwinglians* and *Calvinists*, also *Sacramentarians*
or *Sacrament-schwärmer* (by Luther and in the Formula of Concord), and in
France *Huguenots*. But they justly repudiated all such sectarian names,
and used instead the designations *Christian* or *Evangelical*, or *Reformed*, or
Evangelical Reformed or *Reformed Catholic*. The term *Reformed* assumed
the ascendency in Switzerland, France, and elsewhere. Beza, *e. g.*, uses it
constantly. Queen Elizabeth, in sundry letters to the Protestant courts of
Germany in 1577, speaks throughout of *ecclesiæ reformatæ*, and once calls
the non-Lutheran Churches *ecclesiæ reformatiores*, *more Reformed*, implying
that the Lutheran is Reformed also.
" The Lutherans, before the last quarter of the sixteenth century, called
themselves likewise *Christian* and *Evangelical*, sometimes *Reformed*, and
since 1530 the *Church or Churches of the Augsburg Confession*, or *Verwandte
der Augsburgischen Confession*. For a long time they disowned the terms
Lutheranus, Luthericus, Lutheranismus, which were first used by Dr. Eck,
Cochlaeus, Erasmus, and other Romanists with the view to stigmatize their
religion as a recent innovation and human invention. (A Papist once asked
a Lutheran, ' Where was your Church before Luther?' The Lutheran answered by asking another question, ' Where was your face this morning before it was washed?'). Eramus speaks of *Lutherana tragedia, negotium
Lutheranum, factio Lutherana*. Hence the Lutheran symbols never use the
term *Lutheran*, except once, and then by way of complaint that the ' dear,
holy Gospel should be called *Lutheran*.' Luther himself complained of this
use of his name; nevertheless he had no objection that it should be duly
honored in connection with the Word of God, and thought that his followers
need not be ashamed of him. They thought so, too; and, forgetting St. Paul's
warning against sectarian names, they gradually themselves appropriated the
term *Lutheran*, or *Evangelical Lutheran*, as the official title of their Church,
since about 1585, under the influence of Jacob Andreae, the chief author of
the Formula of Concord, and Aegidius Hunnius, and in connection with the
faith in Luther as a special messenger of God for the restoration of Christianity
in its doctrinal purity. See the proof in the little book of Dr. Heinrich Heppe,
*Ursprung und Geschichte der Bezeichnungen ' reformirte ' und ' lutherische '
Kirche*, Gotha, 1859, pp. 28, 35, 55.
" The negative term *Protestant* was used after 1529 for both Confessions
by friend and foe, and is so used to this day; but it must be explained from
the historical occasion which gave rise to it, and be connected with the
positive faith in the Word of God, on the ground of which the evangelical
members of the Diet of Spires protested against the decision of the papal
majority, as an encroachment on the rights of conscience and an enforcement
of the traditions of men."
It seems that Dr. Schaff, with his magnificent vocabulary, has reserved

which it is indissolubly connected. They constitute a complete whole." [5]

But the Seventeenth-Century Dogmatik of the Church did not flow directly and solely from the Book of Concord. The fountain-head of Lutheran Confessionalism, beginning in 1517 with the Doctrines of justification, repentance, and faith, in the Ninety-five Theses, ran on into a summary of Lutheran doctrine in the *Loci,* an application of them in the Catechism, a defense against Roman extremes in the Augsburg Confession and the Schmalkald Articles, and a defense against Protestant extremes in the Formula of Concord. Then came the further extension and development of Melanchthon's *Loci* into complete dogmatic system.

SUMMARY OF THE LUTHERAN DOGMATIK.

Martin Chemnitz was the prince of Melanchthonian theologians, who so thoroughly apprehended the Confessional substance of Luther, in his *Loci,* 1591. He was followed by Hutter in his *Compendium,* 1610, and in his *Loci.*[6] His contemporary was the mild and devout Gerhard, the standard dogmatician of the Lutheran Church, with his *Loci,* 1637. Calovius, more elaborate, followed in his *Systema Locorum Theologicorum* (1655-77). One century after the Book of Concord came Quenstedt[7] (d. 1685), and Baier,[8] 1686;

---

the use of the word 'sectarian' for the Lutheran Church, and, in particular, in connection with the author of that symbol which is the Church's most harmonious and final expression. Not in describing anabaptists, puritans, radicals and church parties of the wildest sort, does he, so far as we see, characterize them as 'sectarian.' It is the great balance wheel of the Reformation (of which the Augsburg Confession is the hub), that in Dr. Schaff's thought and mind is connected with the 'sectarian' term Lutheran, which was used by way of self-preservation against the approaches toward the Reformed faith which are historically involved in the term Melanchthonian.

[5] These are the words of Charles F. Schaeffer.—*Ev. Rev.,* I, p. 476. v. also I, p. 473.

[6] Hutter's *Loci Communes Theologici* is an extensive commentary on Melanchthon's *Loci. His Compendium Theologiæ* consists of definitions from the Book of Concord, supplemented by passages from the older dogmaticians. After the literature apologetic of the Book of Concord it is the first link that connects with the Concordia rather than with the *Loci.*

[7] Quenstedt, *Theologia Didacticopolemica.*

[8] Baier, *Compendium Theologiæ Positivæ.*

57

and the development closed half a century later with Hollazius,[9] 1750.

Schmid, who aroused a modern interest in these giant builders of living Lutheran principle, and who awakened the American confessional development through the younger Krauth and Schmucker just prior to the influence of the German Lutheran Immigration in the middle of the Nineteenth Century, happily describes the course of this Old Dogmatik as follows:—

"Melanchthon, who stands first in the series of Lutheran theologians, in the first editions of his *Loci*, *discusses only what is peculiar to the doctrine of the Lutheran Church*, and even in the following editions he treats everything that does not fall under this head, briefly and incompletely. His most celebrated commentator, Chemnitz, already aims at more fulness of systematic arrangement; the articles on God and the Trinity, etc., are already further developed; he employs with more freedom than Melanchthon the works of the scholastics, especially of John Damascenus. In Gerhard, finally, this prejudice, which, for other reasons sufficiently known, was cherished against the scholastics, was so far overcome that, in the articles that had remained unaffected by the errors of the Papacy, the theological discussions of the scholastics were laid under contribution; the whole representation of the doctrine of God, his attributes and essence, of the Trinity, of Angels, of the Person of Christ, etc., was based upon the scholastic Theology.

"But still Gerhard did not carry out this method with uniformity, nor did he thoroughly arrange his materials; some subjects are only hastily sketched, as that of the Work of Christ, or he has merely collected the raw material, as in the subject of Angels. The following theologians fill up these gaps, and introduce greater uniformity in the mode of treatment. Gerhard still arranges the whole in *Loci*, and does not allow himself to reduce it to a system. Calovius first attempted this, by introducing the so-called analytic method, which was subsequently employed by all the theologians, down to Hollazius. These theologians, therefore, first reduced Theology to a system. When these later theologians are accused of having been so much infected with the scholastic fondness for systematizing, as to give to Theology a form too scholastic, I am not prepared altogether to deny the charge."[10]

This development of Evangelical Dogmatik is unparalleled in any part of Protestantism or in Rome. But it is extra-confessional. It is the infusion of the substance of the

---

[9] Hollazius, *Examen Theologiæ Acroamaticæ.*

[10] Schmid, *Doctrinal Theology,* tr. by Hay and Jacobs, p. 9.

Book of Concord and the appropriation of so much of the
old Roman material of the scholastic doctors as could flow
through Evangelical channels, in the form and under the
principle of Melanchthon's *Loci.* [11] That in ultra-orthodoxy
it developed into extreme hardness of form, and in ultra-
pietism into an extreme softness of substance, is but a testimony to its genuineness under the usual law of extremes.
Later centuries, while they have contributed their critical,
philosophical, historical, vital and practical advances, have
not gone beyond the confessional substance of these works,
except by way of contrast in heretical ideas and errors.   The
Truth of God, the same yesterday, to-day and forever, is the
Word of Christ.   It is not enlarged under the influence of
human thought.   It is not an open field, with wide realms
unexplored, as we find to be the case in nature, in philosophy, in biology, and in science.   And the attempt to further
expand and humanize the old Evangelical Catholic Faith of
the œcumenical symbols and the later Confessions of the
Book of Concord led in the further and less objective Protestant development of following centuries to individualism
and degeneracy.   Schmid, in describing the dogmatics of the
latter part of the Seventeenth and the whole of the Eighteenth Century is correct in saying that " without at all discussing the question whether, and in how far, Pietism departed from the principles of Lutheranism, it is perfectly
evident that along with it there came a period of doctrinal
uncertainty, in which great mistrust was displayed in regard
to the whole previous development, both as to form and substance."   The rigid form, the disputatious method, the exaltation of an orthodox intellectualism, the stress on a right
belief rather than on the salvation which is its substance,
these are not the result of the Book of Concord and the
Gospel therein confessed, but they are remnants of the old

---

[11] Not only was the *Loci* the *beginning* of the Lutheran dogmatic system,
but it furnished the lines along which the doctrinal development of Lutheranism unfolded first into severe Orthodoxy in the Seventeenth, and then into
Illumination in the Eighteenth Century.

Roman scholasticism, carried down by the Præceptor Germaniae into every branch of learning, and departing more and more from the original intention as the real substance of the Gospel died away.

" The orthodox Dogmatik of the Seventeenth Century is a majestic resultant of Faith—the most painstaking and most acute intellectual work in the history of ecclesiastical Christianity. In the sum of its services, it is deeper than the theology of the Church Fathers, more true than that of the Scholastics, more scientific and candid than that of the Roman Church. It is unexampled in its deep, fundamental and critical illumination of the results of the Christian Centuries. The whole spirit of the modern world and of science poured itself out against the foundations of this Protestant system of Faith, because, in the immense safety and security of its upbuilding, it allowed all blows to penetrate to the vital parts; and dispensed with the support of the Law and the Hierarchy." [12]

The censors of this Dogmatik to-day are its old enemies, Rome, Radicalism and Rationalism; and the newer thinkers who have freed themselves from the trammels of Calvinism and Puritanism,[13] all writers who are critics rather than believers, and whose approach is by sight rather than by faith, with all liberalists and unionists. The critics include the reactionary world and the world of advanced thought. Between these two extremes stands the Rock of Confessionalism, swept by the tides on both sides. But the critical force of these more free and flowing liberal tides is not always just. If it be directed against the *systematization* of theology as

---

[12] Condensed from Gasz, *Geschichte der prot. Dogm.*, I, p. 6.

[13] " For Roman Catholic scholasticism and for Calvin there is an absolute norm by which all actions can be truly and thoroughly tested, and Church and State must apply the tests. Even opinions and doctrines held by the individual are thus subject to an infallible review. It was therefore no hasty or ill-considered action for Calvin to hand Servetus over to the State for proper punishment. Calvin would have been false to his fundamental convictions had he acted otherwise. Rome only was wrong in shedding the blood of the martyrs because Rome was not a true Church. Given a true Church and her duty was to insist that the State protect pure doctrine."— *Hibbert Journal.*

such, we need only point to modern writers who have worked
their theology into a dogmatic system more detailed, more
speculative and more elaborate than the very moderately
sized Formula of Concord. Among the more prominent of
these in the Lutheran Church are Thomasius, Philippi, Mar-
tensen, Luthardt, and Valentine. Among the American
denominations, it will suffice to recall Hodge, of Prince-
ton; Harris, of Yale; Clarke, of Colgate; Emanuel Gerhard's Institutes of the Christian Religion,—to say nothing of such modern German writers as Schweitzer, Pfleiderer,
Lipsius, Ritschl, Kaftan, and Herrmann.

If objection be taken to the *scholastic form* of treatment,
we must again recall the fact that this is derived from
old methods of the Church; that it represents Aristotle as
simplified by Melanchthon, as opposed to Bacon in modern
thought; and that much of its authoritativeness is due to
the assurance of its faith, in which much of the theology
to-day is absolutely lacking. It would be quite possible to
conceive of a Lutheran Theology identical in substance with
that of the Sixteenth Century, but inductive, or Baconian,
in form. The genetic method is modern.

It is well known that Schmid of Erlangen, already quoted
a few pages earlier, who arranged Schmid's Dogmatik drawn
from the Lutheran dogmaticians of the Sixteenth Century,
did not commit himself personally to the teachings of his
work. Yet he emphatically repudiates the charge made
by Heppe against the classic Lutheran dogmaticians.[14]

---

[14] " I do not at all agree with Heppe's idea of an early Protestant, *i. e.*,
Melanchthonian system of doctrine, and of another system (that of the
Formula of Concord) diametrically opposed to this ; nor with his idea of an
universal prevalence of this Melanchthonian system until the time of the
Formula of Concord. I agree, on the other hand, with the most widely entertained opinion, that there was a time in Melanchthon's history when he did
not in all respects remain true to Luther's system of doctrine, and, therefore,
the later theologians, especially Hutter, undertook to vindicate, in opposition
to Melanchthon, this doctrinal system of Luther, which had, it must be admitted, been more clearly developed in the consciousness of the Church through
the controversies that preceded the Formula of Concord. There is, to be
sure, a real antagonism in certain topics, but it is not an antagonism that
runs through all the topics, and renders a sharp distinction necessary between
the early Protestant theology and that of a later time. Hence I was at liberty,
yes, it was my duty, to lay at the foundation the Melanchthonian system of
doctrine. . .

He says that their method has the advantage " of more accurately defining the meaning of the single doctrine and of
rendering it more difficult for heresy to screen itself." He
believes that we ought not to consider it a task " to search
for the excellent kernel within the unsightly shell." He
then goes on to declare that scholasticism is rooted not in the
later, but in the earlier, Lutheran theology. " When, however," says he, " the charge of scholasticism is brought, as
is sometimes the case, against the contents and form of the
doctrines themselves, and made to refer to the dialectic development which some particular doctrines received at their
hands, we reply, this is a charge which does not lie against
the later theologians alone, nay, not even with any peculiar
force against them. This is, on the other hand, the method
which the theological writers of our Church adopted from the
very first, and which they derived from the treatment which
the doctrine of the Trinity, *e. g.,* experienced already in the
second period."

THE REACTION IN CALIXTUS.

The Reaction from Orthodoxy, referred to at the beginning
of this chapter, came with Calixtus. From the old dominion
of the Church, men were now passing through the Confessional Principle, to syncretism, liberalism, and rationalism.
With the triumph of rationalism over pietism, and humanism
over both, was ushered in the modern Protestantism, subject
to no authority whatsoever.

Pietism must be regarded not only as a reaction against
extreme orthodox intellectualism; but in its better and original forms as the earnest antagonist of liberalism and rationalism. Dr. Krauth says: " When Spener, Francke, and the
original Pietistic school sought to develop the spiritual life
of the Church, they did it by enforcing the doctrines of the

" This, it is true, merely explains, and does not vindicate, my method of
treating Doctrinal Theology. To do this I should have to write another
History of Protestantism as over against that of Mr. Heppe. Here it may
suffice for me to say, that my work is based upon a totally different conception of the development of Lutheran Theology from that of this writer."—
Schmid, *Doctrinal Theology,* Preface to the Fifth Edition.

Even the rationalistic Karl Hase repudiates the charge of an un-Lutheran
Scholasticism in the Old Dogmaticians.

Church in their living power. They accomplished their work by holding more firmly and exhibiting more completely in all their aspects the doctrines of the Reformation, confessed at Augsburg. The position of them all was that the doctrines of our Church are the doctrines of God's Word, that no changes were needed, or could be allowed in them; that in doctrine her Reformation was complete, and that her sole need was by sound discipline to maintain, and by holy activity to exhibit, practically, her pure faith. These men of God and the great theologians they influenced, and the noble missionaries they sent forth, held the doctrines of the Church firmly. They wrought those great works, the praises of which are in all Christendom, through these very doctrines. They did not mince them, nor draw subtle distinctions by which to evade or practically ignore them, but, alike upon the most severely controverted, as upon the more generally recognized, doctrines of our Church, they were thoroughly Lutheran. They held the Sacramental doctrines of our Church tenaciously, and defended the faith of the Church in regard to Baptism and the Lord's Supper, as they did all her other doctrines." [15]

The period of degeneracy is thus summarized by Weidner: " At the beginning of the Eighteenth Century, there was a tendency both in the Lutheran and Reformed Churches to a greater mildness, readily degenerating into laxity. The Lutheran Church was influenced by Pietism, and by the philosophic systems of Descartes, Leibnitz, and Wolff, while the Armenian tendency gained ground in the Calvinistic churches. Among the great Lutheran divines of the Eighteenth Century may be mentioned *Buddeus* (d. 1729), *Pfaff* (d. 1760) and *S. J. Baumgarten* (d. 1757). The influence of Rationalism shows itself in *Semler* (d. 1791), and the later divines of this century. The influence of *Kant* (d. 1804) was very favorable to Rationalism. The orthodox system rather on the side of formal supernaturalism than in

---

[15] *Con. Ref.*, p. 196.

its own churchly strength, was defended by *Storr* (d. 1805) and *Reinhard* (d. 1812).[16] . . .

The men who found the Confessions constrictive, and who lived on the theory that men could be Lutherans and ignore the doctrines of the Church or defend them with a reservedness practically equivalent to a betrayal, were the men who harbored unbelief as to the saving merits of their Lord's work in their hearts. Semler, Bahrdt, Gabler, Wegschneider and other Rationalists, were influenced by the all-penetrative and overwhelming spirit of the time. They were the men who, putting the Confessions aside, pretended to hold the Word of God, but corrupted its sense. [18]

"Then followed, toward the close of the Eighteenth Century, the far more radical reaction of Rationalism, which broke down, stone by stone, the venerable building of Lutheran orthodoxy, and the whole traditional system of Christian doctrine." [19]

THE DROP INTO MODERN INDIVIDUALISM.

The rule of the Church had been rejected already in the Reformation. *The Rule of Faith* had now also disappeared in the Illumination. Every man built truth as he

---

[16] *Encyclopedia: Systematic Theology,* pp. 98-99.

[17] So completely does the Formula of Concord exhibit the pure Lutheran faith, and so adequately does it express the doctrines of the Gospel, that, as the whole later history of the church demonstrates, it was invariably found that those who practically rejected the Formula of Concord after the days of Semler, also rejected the whole orthodox system of doctrine contained in the Lutheran symbols which in point of time preceded it. It would be unphilosophic and fruitless to deny the truth of the doctrines of the last of the four Gospels, and yet profess to believe those of the preceding three, since all contain precisely the same Gospel, while the new matter in St. John's Gospel is only a fuller exhibition of the spirit which alike pervades all; and it would be as unphilosophic and fruitless to reject, on doctrinal grounds, which we have here no room to discuss, the last of the Lutheran symbolical books, and yet adopt one or more of those which preceded it, since the last, the Formula of Concord contains precisely the same doctrines which they set forth, and is only a fuller exhibition of the divine spirit which breathes in them.—C. F. Schaeffer, *Ev. Rev.* V. 203-204.

[18] Yet they were not one whit worse than the Dean of the Episcopal Divinity School at Cambridge, Mass., who in 1908 said that the problem in present preaching is to tell the truth concerning the Scripture without affrighting the grandmothers of the Church.

[19] Schaff, *Creeds of Christendom,* I, p. 353.

thought it right in his own eyes: *e. g.,* Schleiermacher. The objective strength of the Gospel was gone. Each thinker was free to think out truth as he saw it. And the truth found was altogether outside the revelation of Christ. The system-makers of the mediæval church became the philosophers of the modern schools. They began with an analysis of consciousness in Descartes; with a criticism of the relation of man's own faculties to reality and truth in Kant, with the perfect mechanical orders of Creation in Leibnitz, with the moral nature in Fichte, with the laws of physical nature in Schelling, with the principle of all nature and all history in Hegel, with the application of human Reason to the Scripture—the New Testament in Baur, and its application to Dogma, with not only the Confession but the objective truth back of it lost,—in Ritschl. Thus the birds of thought had darted out of the Scriptural net, and, exulting in their freedom, were flying in all four quarters of the sky.

But the power of the Gospel was not gone. There was a reaction to the old Rule of Faith—in part in accord with the old Confession of the Faith, and in part with the new freedom from the Confessions of the Church. In the second instance the Scripture became the modern " Bible," an individual source of authority, greater or less; and individual systems of dogmatics, speculative, ecclesiastical, and even Confessional, arose once again. In the first instance, there was a return not only to the authority of the Word, but also to the Confessions of the Church.[19a] As to the Dogmatik of the later Nineteenth and the Twentieth Centuries, and the systems elaborated by individual writers under the influence of some philosophic or historical principle (in which we include not only the older Hegelian, but also the modern Ritschlian development to Harnack and those after him), it is not pretended that they represent a Church standard,

---

[19a] *E. g.,* in Sartorius (d. 1859), Vilmar (d. 1868), Thomasius (d. 1875), Philippi (d. 1882), with Luthardt and Frank.

or Confessional principle. They are a personal contemporary apprehension, apart from church or historical necessity, of the divine system, as modern insight and education conceive it. While they do influence individuals in the Church, and ultimately reach and influence the Church doctrine; as they rise and flourish, and are superseded and fade away, they have no effect on the Church's objective Confession of the truth.

Yet the Lutheran Church, guided by her Confessional Principle, has not been able to undergo a free and untrammeled development on her basis. In some countries the Confession was not adopted heart and soul, and was not witnessed to and taught in the preaching of the Word. In many of the countries it was not the pure Faith for the Faith's sake, but the Confession was a question of the government determined by the government, or a question of advantages to be gained by or through the Faith. In nearly all the countries, the training up in the Faith was not wrought out by the Faith apart from the secular arm; and in some countries we still have the anomalous spectacle of the secular arm educating, training and appointing the preachers and teachers for the spiritual work. To this must be added not merely a complete freedom from the Confession, but an avoidance of it, for prudential reasons, in the higher education; with a mechanical compulsion in lower spiritual education, in the bringing up of generation after generation, in which the supreme and decisive fact is not a good confession, but conformity to tradition, or other secondary causes. Thus the Church of the Reformation, though on a Confessional basis, has brought forth motley hordes of individual Evangelical and Rationalistic Protestants, bearing the name of the great Reformer, but not convinced of and confessing the Word on which he staked his all.

THE SITUATION IN AMERICA.

Thus, too, America while she was spared the mixed development issuing from a combined secular and spiritual control, and while she was blessed in having her earliest foundations laid on the complete Confessional basis, and in the spirit of pietism, thus escaping many of the suffocating problems of the older situation, has nevertheless mingled in with her own faith the ideas of surrounding beliefs, and absorbed mongrel elements from current Protestant sources; and in a preference for and sympathy with the common unconfessional Christianity of the day, has not been either convinced of nor borne bold and unfailing witness to the Faith which alone is the justification of her being, and in which alone she can live without fear of absorption. But Providence so ordained that the Lutheranism that came to America, and that survived, was not that of a State Church, but of the free; and that the Faith brought here as a basis was that of the Book of Concord.

Rationalism, unionism and nativism, both European and American, have been the cause of the bulk of the trouble in the Lutheran Church in America. Perhaps the most insidious and treacherous of these ostensible friends has been unionism. It was the working of an imperceptible unionism that gradually reduced to nothing the result of the Swedish work in America, and lost to us all the churches on the Delaware. Muhlenberg, as we have seen, had not set his foot on the shores of Pennsylvania for twenty-four hours before he found himself in the conflict of his life against a gigantic plan of unionism to absorb the whole Lutheran Church in Pennsylvania. His fidelity prevented such absorption.

At his death, it is sad to note the tragic inroads made upon the Church in America by these three causes, inroads from which the Church did not recover even to the third and fourth generation; but which at last have given way, to some extent, before the power of the unchanging Confessional **Principle**.

DOGMATIC SYSTEM AND THE CONFESSION.

We are not bound by the form or the substance of the Old Dogmaticians, except in so far as they are of the truth and the truth binds us. But the truth does not bind the believer: it makes him free. The dogmaticians are voluntary individual testimonies, elaborated in the form of science, valid for those who gave them forth and for those who accept them. They are not the utterances of the Church; howsoever fully they may reflect and explain the Confessions of the Church.

The Confessions do not constrict the personal utterance of the Christian who holds fast to them. None is more free than he. [20] He writes out of the assurance of faith, which is freedom. The acceptance of the Confessions does not hinder each age and each individual from gaining its own apprehension afresh, and fitting its own point of view, of the revealed Word of God. The more such adjustments of the Christian consciousness to the Gospel the better. But they are not to be adjustments of the Gospel to the individual consciousness. They are not to run alongside the Confessions or against them. They are not to start from a speculative centre or from some truth in Scripture outside the clear teachings of God's Word, and then absorb so much of the Gospel as fits in with the theory.

And above all, Dogmatik and its spirit is not to take the

---

[20] The Church is called upon not to enforce blind submission to what it has already attained, but to use the clear truth as an instrument of appeal to consciences, and to maintain its authority by persuasion, and not by external force of any kind. "The Word which has created the heavens and the earth must do the work, or nothing in the universe can do it. I will preach, I will talk, I will write; but never will I force any one by violence" (Luther, Er. ed., 28: 219). "This is the difference between the two forms of government: The godly win men by means of the Word; the wicked force **to a** prescribed course by means of the sword" (Ib., 12: 383). "*Unser Herr* **Gott** *thut nicht Grosses mit Gewalt*" (Ib., 57 : 32).—Jacobs, *Summary Christian Faith,* p 409.

place of Confession and its spirit. After all Dogmatik is only a use of the truth to satisfy or to instruct the intellectual consciousness, whereas Confession is that use of the truth which Christ expects of us. Dogmatik is the explanation of my own mind, or of what I think to be the mind of the Church. Confession is the affirmation, the testimony of that which Christ has given His Church to proclaim, and for which it exists. The main need in the Church, in its literature, its institutions and its teachings is not the satisfaction of the intellectual consciousness, but the Confession of the Gospel.

The Church needs Confessors first, foremost and always. Christ is the truth, and Christ is all and in all. Dogmaticians, critics, scientists, philosophers, free, fearless, and in the position of the latest outlook in thought and knowledge are needed by the Church in every age, but they must not take the place, nor fail to respect the place which belongs only to the Confessional Principle. They are individual, and are in addition to, not instead of the Church's witness. The Church's official work is that of testimony, and in her institutions, writings, and pulpits,[21] in all her teachings, she can substitute no other principle for this. A scientific theology, a critical theology, a Biblical theology, a historical theology, an apologetic theology, a dogmatic theology, a practical theology are each and all necessary and helpful to the Church, but only as they centre in a Confessional Theology.

"Any man, who will read thoughtfully the history of Rationalism in Europe, and of the Unionism which is even

---

[21] And indeed, when the minister sets himself above the congregation as a teaching regent, though he would anxiously appear as a *liberal*, under the standard of freedom of speech ; he yet arrogantly degrades his people, essentially entrenches on their liberty of conscience, and whilst he refuses to bind himself to their confession, he popishly wishes to keep them bound to his office. The absolution of ministers from obligation to the common confession of the church, leads either to an entire dissolution of the confessional unity of the church at large, and especially of the individual congregations, or to a ministerial despotism which appears wherever the congregation and the church are made dependent on the ministry, when the ministry at the same time refuses to be dependent on the general consciousness and confession of the church and congregation, and seeks to rule with unlimited freedom.— Seiss, *Ev. Rev.* IV, 16.

now too often its stronghold, will not wonder at the earnestness of true Lutheranism in maintaining a pure confession. He will have no difficulty in comprehending its indisposition to tolerate indifferentism, and heresy, under the guise of union." Even Belial himself, to use the expressive phrase of Dr. Krauth after the habit of Luther, " has been allowed to take shelter under the hem of the garment of Christ."

A " wide-open " confession has filled the American Protestant Churches, Seminaries, Universities and schools of learning with heresy to-day. Congregationalism, Presbyterianism, Episcopalianism, and even Methodism glide down in faith toward the valley of Unitarianism. Modern preaching and teaching does not draw the confessional line, even at this side of the Cross of Christ. It is now almost regarded as a symptom of fossilization to be true to one's confessional standard, and there is a sting in being termed orthodox.

The critical spirit has gone beyond gnawing away merely the *Confessions:* it has demanded that the attitude of the Christian to the authority of *Scripture* itself be "wide-open."

We find here in America, within a generation after Dr. Krauth's death, the beginning of what Dr. Krauth, in his day, recorded with horror of Germany: "The Bible was flung after the Confession, and men were allowed to be anything they pleased to be. The less Lutheran they were in the old sense of the word, the more were they Lutheran in the new sense. They not only insisted on being called Lutherans, but insisted they were the only genuine Lutherans. Had not Luther disenthralled the human mind? Was not the Reformation simply an assertion of the powers of human reason? Would not Luther, if he had only been so happy as to have lived to read their writings, certainly have been brought over to the fullest liberty? Who could doubt it?"

CHAPTER XXXVIII.

THE BOOK OF CONCORD AND HISTORICAL LUTHERANISM IN AMERICA.

Luther and the Discovery of America Contemporary—Was this Providential?—
The Lutheran Church Coming to America—It came on the Basis of the Unaltered Augsburg Confession and the Book of Concord—The Swedes on the
Delaware—Justus Falckner—The Palatine Immigration with the Savoy Constitution—John Casper Stoever—Henry Melchior Muhlenberg—The Book of Concord the Foundation of all Muhlenberg's Churches—The Ministerium of Pennsylvania—The Words of Melanchthon.

DOES God order the world in Providence? Was the
Protestant Evangelical Lutheran Church—the Church
of the Reformation—included in His ordering? Is it a
chance that Luther and the New World were contemporaries,
that the one was born within the decade in which the other
was discovered? First came Luther, in 1483, and, on his
heels, in 1492, America. A German in every fiber of his being, was it the counsel of God that he should be chiefly for the
Germans, and that his work should abide within the boundary
of the Fatherland? The great Englishman, Thomas Carlyle, is not of that opinion. "There was born here," says
Carlyle, "a Mighty Man, whose light was to flame as the
beacon over long centuries of the world; the whole world and
its history was waiting for this man.[1] . . . What were all Emperors, Popes, and Potentates in comparison?"[2]

Is it not the very hand of God that set the two rising auspi-
cious stars of modern life, the newly discovered Gospel and

---

[1] Carlyle is cited as an Englishman and a Protestant on the Reformed side.
[2] Thomas Carlyle, *Lecture on Luther*, May 15th, 1840.

the newly discovered World, Luther and America, in conjunction? Born and reared in the shadow of the Holy Roman Church and Empire, in the heart of the old World, the Church of the pure Gospel, of Word and Sacrament, was intended by God to be transplanted from the old battlefields of Church and State, for untrammeled development—Catholic, of many races, and polyglot, in many tongues,—to shores free from the alliance of the secular and the spiritual arm.

Some four decades after Luther's birth, the new plant of the Gospel bloomed and ripened into the historical Augustana. Four decades later it bore still richer and more perfect fruit in the Formula of Concord. Four decades after the publication of the Formula of Concord, God wafted the first seed of this new Catholic Evangelical Conservative faith to the shores of America. It perished amid the snows and the ice of the north.

After two more decades, new seeds were borne hither, some to the Island of Manhattan, and others to the shores of the Delaware, and a chain of churches arose along that river and its tributary. Four decades later still, shortly after the arrival of William Penn, the first services of the Protestantism that is Catholic—of Lutheranism—were held here in the English tongue, that is, in the language that was destined to become the Catholic language of the New World.

Four decades later still, the great German Protestant immigrations reached this country, and with them the first organizer of Lutheran Churches in Pennsylvania. In several decades more came the general organizer and patriarch of the Church, under the direction of Halle, who established sound doctrine and true piety, and whose work, seeking early touch and union with the earlier Swedish Church, issued in the first general Church body, Lutheran in doctrine and American in principle, in the New World.

Forty years after the organization of this first Ministerium of North America, which centred in the general territory of Pennsylvania, came the establishment of a second general body in New York State; and four decades later still came the first English general body. And as the first seeds of the new faith in 1517, and its first Confession in 1530, did not complete the development of the pure Lutheran Faith, so, neither did the first seeds of congregations in the Seventeenth Century, or of the general bodies in the Eighteenth and Nineteenth Centuries, complete the plan of God with reference to this continent. Wonderful immigration into the heart of our land, and four decades of testing, in attempting to take over the faith of the fathers, unaltered and unadulterated, into the tongue of the children, brings us to the condition of the Church within the memory of many still living.

It is the object of this chapter to show that the transplantation of Lutheranism from the Old World to North America was on the basis of the Book of Concord and the Unaltered Augsburg Confession.

The services held on Hudson's Bay in 1619 were unfruitful, but those held on the Delaware from 1638 on, together with those held in 1657, and earlier, in New York, were on the basis of the Unaltered Augsburg Confession. The first English Lutheran services in America, in 1684, were held by a minister whose copy of the Augsburg Confession is still extant, and it is the Unaltered Augsburg Confession. The Lutheran ministers in the Seventeenth Century and in the Eighteenth Century were ministers set to preach the doctrine of the Unaltered Augsburg Confession; and wherever John Casper Stoever or Henry Melchior Muhlenberg preached, their teaching and their work were founded on the Unaltered Confession. Justus Falckner, the first faithful Protestant pastor, so far as we know, of any denomination to be ordained in America, a German, ordained in a Swedish Church, in order to become the pastor of a Dutch Congregation, adhered faithfully to the anti-Calvinistic basis of the Unaltered Augsburg Confession.

Let us examine these striking facts somewhat more in

58

detail, from the beginning onward, and see if they be well founded.

The Constitution of the congregation at Amsterdam, framed within ten years of the publication of the Book of Concord, adopted as early as 1597 (and which, with and through that of St. Mary's of Savoy in London, adopted in 1695) *formed the basis of the Constitution of our American congregations,* in its First Part and First Article, stipulates as follows:—

" The pastors of this congregation shall regulate and determine all their teaching and preaching by the rule of the divine Word, the biblical, prophetical and apostolical writings, and according to our Symbolical Books to wit, the Unaltered Augsburg Confession delivered to Charles V. Anno 30, the Apology, the Smalkald Articles, the Formula of Concord, together with both Catechisms of Luther throughout, and shall not teach or preach anything contrary to the same, be it privately or publicly, nor shall they introduce or use new phrases (forms of statement) which are at variance with the same, or contradict them. In like manner in all points in dispute between us and others, they shall be guided and governed by the aforesaid Scriptures and also the aforesaid Symbolical Books, and shall decide and judge them by these alone, and shall plainly declare the foundation and understanding thereof to the congregation. *

Fifteen years after the completion of the Book of Concord, the States of Sweden subscribed the Unaltered Augsburg Confession.⁴ This was in 1593, one year before Gustavus Adolphus was born. Six years after the death of the mili-

---

³ *Luth. Ch. Rev.,* VI, p. 199.

⁴ In 1647 the Reichstag at Stockholm acknowledged the Formula; in 1663 a decree of the Swedish Church was to the same effect; and in 1686 the Council of Upsala bound the Swedish Church as follows: " In our kingdom and in the lands belonging thereto, all shall confess only and alone the Christian doctrine and faith, which is founded upon the Prophetical and Apostolical Scriptures of the Old and New Testaments, and is comprised in the three chief symbols, the Apostles', the Nicene, and the Athanasian, as well as in ·the Unaltered Augsburg Confession, composed in the year 1530, received in 1593 in the Council of Upsala, and explained in the entire so-called ' Book of Concord.' "

tary hero of Protestantism on the battlefield at Lützen, Gustavus' prime minister Oxenstiern sent to our shores the first colony of Swedes, in order to carry out the favorite plan of Gustavus, which he advocated on German soil only a few days before his death. One great object of Gustavus in his colonization project was to plant the Christian religion among the heathen; and the missionary idea was always prominent in the spirit and in the instructions of the line of Lutheran pastors that came from Sweden to the first settlements on the Delaware. The first services held in these primeval forests, just sixty years after the adoption of the Book of Concord, were on the basis of its full Lutheran Confession. When Governor John Printz came over in 1643, he had instructions to see that divine service be zealously conducted according to the Unaltered Augsburg Confession, but that members of the Reformed religion be allowed religious freedom; that the youth be instructed and trained in the fear of the Lord, and that Christianity be spread among the Indians. His minister, Campanius, diligently carried out these instructions, even to the holding of the daily Lutheran Matin and Vesper services and to the translating of Luther's Small Catechism into the language of the American Indian.

In New Netherlands the authorities had received instructions "to allure the Lutherans to the Dutch Churches and to matriculate them in the Public Reformed Religion." In 1640 a law was passed, prohibiting any other religion except the Reformed, which Stuyvesant 'in the name of God and the Dutch West India Company' attempted to carry out in 1647. But in 1649, on October 8th, a petition reached Amsterdam from the members of the "Church of the Unaltered Augsburg Confession in the New Netherlands." In 1656 the congregation appealed from Stuyvesant as follows, "We, the united members of the Unaltered Augsburg Confession, here in the New Netherlands, have been obedient to your Honors' prohibitions," etc. The West India Company concluded "that the doctrine of the Unaltered Augsburg Confession might be tolerated in the West Indies and the New Netherland." But when the Lutheran minister, Goetwasser, arrived, the Reformed ministers demanded his return to Holland. In 1664 Governor Nichols granted the Lutherans permission to send for ministers and to "freely and publiquely exercise divine worship according to their consciences." [5] We see here how the first beginnings of the Lutheran Church in New York City were founded on the Unaltered Augsburg Confession, and that its very existence was involved in a life and death struggle in which the Reformed Protestantism of that day was determined not to tolerate 'it.

Thus were the earliest Lutheran settlements in America planted upon the foundation of the Unaltered Augsburg Confession and the other Symbolical Books. Half a century later when the permanent memorials of this earliest Lutheranism, the Old Swedes Church in Wilmington and the Gloria Dei in Philadelphia were erected, clad in robe and surplice, three Swedish clergymen arrived from Sweden, and held their first service " according to the *true doctrines* contained in the Augsburg Confession of Faith."

When, three or four years later, another pastor was brought over, the Archbishop addressed a letter of the date of July 18th, 1701, to the congregation, making it their pastor's duty to " teach God's Word purely according to the prophetic and Apostolic Scriptures (the language of the Formula), and as it is briefly comprehended in the recognized chief symbols of the Lutheran Church and its other Symbolical Books." The decree of Upsala of 1593, followed by decrees of 1647, 1663, and 1686, had formally placed the Swedish Church upon the Book of Concord. There can be no doubt at all, then, as to the Confessional nature of this earliest Lutheranism that was planted on the shores of our American World.

Justus Falckner, the first Protestant minister to be ordained in America, and pastor of the Lutheran congregation

---

[5] *History of the Lutheran Church in Pennsylvania*, (Schmauk) I, pp. 19-21.

at New York and Albany from 1703 on, whose "Grondlycke onderricht" is the first Lutheran text-book published[6] in America, and is referred to by Valentine Löscher as a "Compendium Doctrinae Anti-Calvinianum," declares that the contents of the book are to be taken in strict conformity with the teachings, Confession and Faith of the Lutheran Church to which his grandparents belonged.

The immigration that came into New York and Pennsylvania a few years later, with Joshua Kocherthal at its head, brought with it St. Mary's, London, Kirchen-Ordnung of "The Unaltered Augsburg Confession," whose first and second articles are a reproduction of the phraseology of the Formula of Concord and whose second article declares that "the pastors shall completely and thoroughly ("gänzlich und durchgehends, nichts aber wider dieselbe") teach and confess according to our ' Symbolical Books,' namely, The Unaltered Augsburg Confession delivered to Emperor Charles in 1530 [to doubly insure the Invariata]; the Apology, the Schmalkald Articles, and the Formula of Concord, together with both Catechisms of Luther." This is the solid doctrinal foundation on which the German Palatine immigration of the early part of the Eighteenth Century into New York and Pennsylvania was founded.

When, nearly a quarter of a century later, John Casper Stoever arrived in the wilds of Pennsylvania and organized the first German congregations, and, as "the Evangelical Lutheran Pfarrherr," gathered congregations in all the early settlements, he planted them, one and all, upon the Unaltered Augsburg Confession. Stoever was a stern Lutheran of the most uncompromising kind, and the churches founded by him in Eastern Pennsylvania were on the basis of a Lutheranism of the stricter sort. In a certain sense, the Lutheranism of this land founded upon the Unaltered Augsburg Confession is a more straight and uncompromising Lutheranism even than that founded upon the designation

---

[6] By William Bradford, New York, 1708.

of all the Symbols of the Church. For the foundation of the Unaltered Augsburg Confession was a polemic antithesis to every sort and kind of Melanchthonianism whatsoever, whereas the Lutheranism of the Formula of Concord and of the Book of Concord was simply the latter's harmonic antithesis.

This fact, with the need of a short term for common use, explains the historical significance of the early usage of the phrase "Augsburg Confession" in our Church in America. C. F. Schaeffer, in his report to the Ministerium of Pennsylvania in 1853,[1] after referring to the preface of Thomasius' work on the Confessional Principle of the Evangelical Lutheran Church, declares "that the Formula of Concord is as completely a part of the Confession of the Church, as the Augsburg Confession itself, or any other symbol is part of it." He then continues:—

"The prominence which, in the church in the United States, has often been given to the Augsburg Confession, and the frequent omission of the names of the succeeding Symbolical Books, might produce the erroneous impression that the former possessed a higher rank or greater authority in that part of the church which is found in America, than the latter, unless, in addition to the explanations which have already been given above, respecting the origin of the historical name of the "church of the Augsburg Confession," the following facts are also properly appreciated; they clearly establish this principle: *That the Augsburg Confession is the representative of the whole body of the Symbolical Books, so that, under ordinary circumstances, those who formerly named it alone, nevertheless understood it to imply and include the other confessional writings with which it is inseparably connected.*" Not only the illustrations given by Dr. Schaeffer, but all others show that the Lutheran Church founded in Pennsylvania, New York, New Jersey, North Carolina and Georgia was founded upon the complete Lutheran principle, and that the Augsburg Confession never excluded or reduced

[1] *Ev. Rev.*, V, p. 205, 206.

the remaining symbols, but represented them; until we reach the later stage of Rationalism.

The congregations planted upon the Stoever foundation include those in Lancaster and Lancaster County, York and York County, Dauphin County, Lebanon County, Berks County and, to some extent, Chester, Montgomery and Philadelphia Counties, Pennsylvania. These foundations are all on Lutheranism of the strictest sort.

As soon as Muhlenberg landed in Philadelphia in 1742, he found there the beginning of a wide interdenominational union movement which had taken possession of the congregation to which he had been called. Its head was the " Evangelical Lutheran Inspector and Pastor at Philadelphia," who adhered to " Luther's evangelical doctrines as contained in the Holy Scriptures *and the Augsburg Confession*," [8] and who " showed his earnestness by publishing an edition of *Luther's Small Catechism*." [9] So nearly had this adherent of the Augsburg Confession gained control of embryonic Lutheranism in Pennsylvania, that the historian Acrelius (p. 248) says, " When Muhlenberg came to the country, Count Zinzendorf was in a fair way to bring under him the whole German population."

Muhlenberg at once proceeded to (what he supposed was) a private conference with this liberal Lutheran of the Augsburg Confession, but " he found himself confronted by all the formalties of a trial." [10] And even after he, at a regular Lutheran Service, had exhibited his credentials, including his call and ordination certificate, and the papers from Providence and New Hanover, and had obtained the acknowledgment of his call from the officers of the Philadelphia congregation, Zinzendorf would not surrender the church record until the courts compelled him to do so.

Such was the ominous conflict, between a professed ad-

---

[8] *Life of Zinzendorf,* p. 42.
[9] Jacobs, *Hist. of The Luth. Ch.,* p. 203.
[10] *Ib.,* p. 218.

herent of the Augsburg Confession and the confessor of the complete Lutheran faith, with which the larger ecclesiastical history of the Lutheran Church in this country opened. For Muhlenberg was a minister " according to the call and rule given in the writings of the prophets and apostles, the sum of which is contained in the three symbols—the Apostles', Nicene, and Athanasian—in the Augsburg Confession, A. D. 1530, laid before Emperor Charles V. in the Apology of the same, in Dr. Luther's Large and Small Catechisms, in the articles subscribed in the Smalcald Convention and in the Formula of Concord, written A. D. 1576, on controverted points of doctrine." [11]

On Muhlenberg's way to America, derogatory reports concerning his Pietism had preceded him to the city of Hanover, where, however, he was invited by the president of the Consistory to preach, after which a member of the Consistory, who had remonstrated against his preaching, a jurist, said that the sermon " had been in agreement with the Formula of Concord."

Thus Muhlenberg's arrival in 1742, brought to America

---

[11] Muhlenberg's *Ordination Certificate, v. Luth. Ch. Rev.* VII, p. 28, Article on *" Conservatism of Henry Melchior Muhlenberg."*

It will be noticed that the very language of the confessional basis of this Certificate of Ordination is, with two exceptions, a condensation of the substance of the introduction to the Epitome of the *Formula of Concord.* (For the phrase *" the Augsburg Confession, A. D. 1530 laid before the Emperor Charles V."* compare Preface to the *Book of Concord,* Jacobs ed., p. 14.)

The Certificate is of the date of 1739, and declares, on the part of the Leipzig Theological Faculty, that "we examined him with care and convinced ourselves that he received and took hold of the sum and substance of the Christian doctrines in a proper manner, reverently and firmly adopted that purity of the Gospel which our Church professes with one voice and spirit in harmony with the Catholic Church of Christ, and that he abhors all fanatical opinions of older and of more recent date, such as the errors of the Papists, Anabaptists, Sacramentarians [Reformed], which the judgment of the Catholic Church of Christ had condemned. He also promises that *in matters of doctrine he would prove himself firm* and constant."

Following the enumeration of the Symbolical Books, the Certificate says, " He solemnly promised that he would propose to his hearers what would be conformed and consentient to these writings, and that *he would never depart from the sense* which they give. And this sacred consense we intend, with the help of God, *faithfully to defend* in all our churches, and *never to adopt* any documents *conflicting with these doctrines.* . . . We further admonish the said Henry Melchior Mühlenberger and the congregation entrusted to his care that they *retain the purity* of the heavenly doctrine. . . We also admonish them that they remember the divine prospect to live in accord and *union with other churches* of the same sound *faith."*

anew the basis of the Book of Concord. When he built the old Augustus Church at Trappe, two years later, he placed it upon the foundation of the Unaltered Augsburg Confession. "I publicly state, you know for what objects this Augustus Church and schoolhouse were founded, built and designated forever in the writings of the cornerstone and in other instruments, and to secure that object you and your successors should strive, namely, that our holy Evangelical doctrine according to the apostles and prophets and the Unaltered Augsburg Confession, together with the Holy Sacraments, *be continued to the latest posterity.*" [12]

When the next minister, Brunnholtz, came in 1745, his call was " to teach the Word of God in public and in private, pure and incorrupt, according to the rule and guidance of the Holy Scriptures, and also of the Symbolical Books of the Evangelical Lutheran Church." His ordination pledge had been: " To be faithful to the Word of God even as the same is set forth in the three chief Symbols, and also specifically in the Symbolical Books of the true Lutheran Church, to wit, the Unaltered Augsburg Confession, its Apology, the Smalcald Articles, the two catechisms of Luther, and the special Formula of Concord, all drawn with great diligence out of the Holy Scriptures, and that I shall, not only for myself, by the help of God, abide steadfast in the same until I die, but also labor with the utmost diligence to build up the congregations which God may commit to my care, according to this rule."

In this same year the church at Germantown was completed, bearing the inscription " Augustanae confessioni haud variatae ejusque oeconomiae."

When, in 1748, Muhlenberg elaborated an 'agende' for the Church in this land, it was on the basis of the strict Savoy Kirchen Ordnung already mentioned. When in 1748 his first large church, old St. Michael's, in Philadelphia, was conse-

---

[12] *Hallische Nachrichten,* p. 1139.

crated, at the organization of the Ministerium of Pennsylvania, public attention was called to the fact " that the foundation stones of this Church were laid with the intention that in it the Evangelical Lutheran doctrine should be taught according to the foundation of the prophets and apostles and the Unaltered Augsburg Confession and all the other Symbolical Books." " Then the whole Church and its parts, the pulpit, the Baptismal font and altar were again consecrated to the use of the one saving Word and the Holy Sacraments, according to our Symbolical Books." [13]

At the first meeting of the Ministerium of Pennsylvania, the first candidate for ordination was examined by Brunnholtz, Handschuh, and Hartwig, and was asked, "whether our Evangelical Lutheran is the only saving and justifying faith, and upon what Scriptural foundations it rests." The answer among other things contained the following: "Yea and Amen, 1, because it teaches the Word of God in its truth and purity; 2, because we, as the children of God lead holy lives in accordance with it. If we examine our Symbolical Books, which contain the principles of our doctrine on religion, we will find that they *are taken from* the Word of God and *substantiated by* the Word of God." Before the Ordination Kurtz signed the following pledge, " To teach nothing else publicly or privately in my congregation except what accords with the Word of God and the Symbolical Books of the Evangelical Lutheran Church and to this end diligently to study the same."

In 1750 Muhlenberg and Brunnholtz inserted in the constitution of the Augustus Congregation at the Trappe, the earliest written constitution of these men, " that in the Augustus Church and school, the Evangelical doctrine, according to the foundation of the Apostles and Prophets and our Symbolical Books, be perpetuated to our descendants."

In 1760, at the Ministerium of Lancaster, Paul Bryzelius applied for admission to the Ministerium, and made the

---

[13] Muhlenberg's Report, 1748, *Hallische Nachrichten, M.* and *S.* pp. 392-393.

declaration that "I herewith promise to conform in all my sermons, public and private instruction and in the administration of the Holy Sacraments, to our Symbolical Books."

When, in 1761, Lucas Raus made charges against Muhlenberg, Muhlenberg not only declares that Raus himself did not accept "the Word of God and our Symbolical Books, though, in his pledge given before his ordination, he had, with mouth, hand, and seal, solemnly promised that he would do so;" but he says, "I herewith challenge Satan and all his servile lying spirits to prove against me the least point that would be repugnant to the teachings of the Apostles and Prophets and our Symbolical Books."

When, in 1769, the dedication of the great Zion Church in Philadelphia, during the meeting of the Ministerium there, took place, Muhlenberg said: "Hereby it is dedicated to the Triune God, Father, Son and Holy Spirit! for the use of the German Evangelical Lutheran congregation, which confesses the one Evangelical doctrine upon the foundation of the apostles and prophets, the two Holy Sacraments by Christ, according to the Unaltered Augsburg Confession and other Symbolical Books."

In the Certificate of Ordination given by the Ministerium of Pennsylvania to J. Christian Lepsius in 1774 and preserved by Muhlenberg, we find the doctrine based upon "the Three Symbols, the Unaltered Augsburg Confession, and its Apology, the Small and Large Catechisms of Luther, and the other Symbolical Books;" and the pledge of Rev. Lepsius is to bind himself to teach the doctrine "agreeable to and with the Unaltered Augsburg Confession and the rest of the Symbolical Books of the Evangelical Church."

In 1783 the Ministerium of Pennsylvania required of Mr. Hinkel, prior to permitting him preach, that he show a regular call, and that he agree, "to preach the Word of God in its purity according to Law and Gospel, as it is explained in its chief points in the Augsburg Confession and the other Symbolical Books."

And when, finally, in 1781, Muhlenberg prepared, and the "Evangelical Lutheran Ministerium in North America" adopted, its constitution, that instrument declares: "Every minister professes that he holds the Word of God and our Symbolical Books in doctrine and life . . . Every minister uses the Liturgy which has been introduced."

As for the English Lutheran Church, when in 1795, Dr. Kunze, our first English Theological Professor,[14] appended his "Account of the Lutheran Church" to the first edition of his English Lutheran Hymn Book, he described the confessional basis of the Church as follows: "The Symbolical Books of the Lutheran Church are 1. The Augsburg Confession; 2. The Apology or defence of it; 3. The Smalcaldean Articles; 4. The larger, 5. The smaller Catechism of Luther; 6. The Formula of Concord."[15]

We see thus, how thoroughly and carefully the original foundations of the Lutheran Church in North America were laid with reference to an avoidance of Melanchthonian errors, and upon the full and complete Confessional principle of the Church as expressed in its Unaltered Augsburg Confession

---

[14] Dr. Kunze was the father of English Lutheranism in America. He was not only the foe of German Rationalism, but he foresaw the process of Anglicization that must take place in our country, and attempted to prepare for it. He was Professor in the University of Pennsylvania, and in Columbia, then King's College, New York. He was the first Lutheran pastor who made provision for regular English services; he translated Luther's Catechism into English; in 1795 he published the first English Lutheran Hymn-book; and he educated the first English Lutheran pastors in America. He attempted to begin the first Lutheran Theological Seminary in this country, but was unsuccessful because of the Revolutionary War.

Dr. Kunze's own ordination vow was no exception to the rule, but as was the case with all the other's, included the Formula of Concord:

"I will not only for myself abide by the pure and unadulterated Word of God, as explained and set forth in the three Ecumenical Creeds, and especially in the Unaltered Augsburg Confession, the Apology, the Smalcald Articles, the two Catechisms of Luther and the Form of Concord, but that I will also faithfully and conscientiously teach the congregations committed to me by God in accordance with these Confessions."—Nicum, The Doctrinal Development of the New York Ministerium, *Luth. Ch. Rev.,* VI, p. 73.

[15] As our work is written in devotion to the true Lutheran Faith, and not in the interests of any Church Body, the story of the Book of Concord and its relation to the Church in America is brought to an end here. It might readily be continued from this point to the present, should such a narrative become desirable or necessary. We will, however, mention the fact that the Liturgy of the Ministerium of Pennsylvania of 1818 directs that churches be consecrated on the "Unaltered Augsburg Confession."

and the other Symbolical Books; and how the favorable influence of the Formula of Concord entered into the constitutional structure of our early congregational life.[16]

We do not see how the historic Lutheran Church in America, in whatever ecclesiastical connection it may be found, could be asked to set aside the Formula of Concord as her Confession. But if such request should be made, Melanchthon has given the reply thereto. He says, *"We cannot abandon* truth that is manifest and *necessary to the Church.* Wherefore we believe that troubles and dangers for the glory of Christ and the good of the Church should be endured. . . . For it is undeniable that many topics of Christian doctrine, whose existence in the Church is of the greatest moment, have been brought to view by our theologians, and explained."* [17]

---

[16] The brief statement given here by no means exhausts the subject under discussion; and the writer has for years been gathering material for a full presentation of the evidence on this important subject which, at some day, he hopes to be able to commit to print in final form.

The confessional foundations in Georgia and in North Carolina were on the same basis.

[17] *Apology,* 76.

CHAPTER XXXIX.

THE CONFESSIONAL PRINCIPLE OF THE BOOK OF CONCORD AND AMERICAN PROTESTANTISM.

Sources of Spiritual Authority—The Relation of Spiritual Forces—The Confessional Principle a Balance—The Confessional Principle and Liberality—Is the Confessional Principle of the Book of Concord Accepted in all Parts of the Lutheran Church?—Is the Confessional Principle of the Unaltered Augsburg Confession that of the Book of Concord?—What an ex animo Confession of the Unaltered Augsburg Confession Involves.

SOURCES OF SPIRITUAL AUTHORITY.

OF the four imaginable sources of spiritual authority, some thinkers, institutions, denominations and sects accept, if they do not officially confess, Reason, that is Nature apprehended by the mind as Law, as the ultimate arbiter. The truths of history, among which all documentary sources, including Scripture, are reckoned; and the powers of tradition, among which all organic sources, including the Church, are placed, will give way, in ultimate decision, to that existing order of Law and life and thought in which we find ourselves, which we call Nature, and whose principles are discovered and applied by Reason.

The material with which these Christians, if we may call them such, build out their conviction, faith and testimony is Scripture and the experience of history and the Church, but the plumb-line with which they test the material is Reason.

In the sphere of Faith, Reason is always our most sub-

874

tle and most persistent foe. Reason is part of man's inborn nature. Faith is the gift of God, which in many Christians has not succeeded in entirely transforming the reason. The greater the part that reason has been accustomed to play in the ordering of our Faith, and in the building of our theological views, the greater its influence becomes with us as a habit. Its ways are ways that grow. It is a good servant, but a bad master. Its only effectual check in the Church is the Confessional Principle.

In the American Churches Reason has enlarged its power —especially in many of the evangelical denominations—by an unconscious and unperceived growth. The newer literature and schools, the "historical method" (which is the application of the Order of Nature to Faith and to its documents and organisms), the influence of an undenominational and an unevangelical Christianty, has imperceptibly wrought changes in the conviction and the daily confession of American Christianity. A century and a half ago rationalism was outside the American Church. A century ago it was within the Church in open Socinian forms. To-day it is within the Church and in Sunday-school and the undenominational associations of Protestantism more subtly in evangelical forms.

A second source of spiritual authority which many confess as supreme is the Visible Church. This is the real position of Rome, also of all those Protestants—though they be Lutherans,—who look to their Church more than they do to their Faith, or who, at least, are intensely devoted in conviction and confession rather to the organism of which they are members than to the principle for which the organism should stand. Those who confess their allegiance to what the Church says and does, as practically final, even if they imagine themselves to be adherents of the most liberal Protestantism, are standing on the ground of Rome. The Papacy they obey is the uncrowned and shifting one of the Organization they venerate. In this they are at one with the

Modernists in the Roman world, who would not overthrow the Church as the supreme source of authority, but only its dogmatic content, and who introduce the new (and shifting) Weltanschauung of the age, as being a subsidiary and obedient servant of the Church.

A third source of authority in American Protestantism is composite. Scripture joined with common sense, the Word of God interpreted by the intellectual results of the day, such sifted teachings of Scripture as commend themselves to the best thought of the time, or as approve themselves to the most sober results of investigation, are accepted as the source of religious authority. This is the position, as to the source of authority, of the majority of the American Protestant Churches—more or less—as they are more or less Evangelical.

To the confessors of a composite source of spiritual authority belong also those who add the Church to Scripture and to Reason, as a co-equal principle.

A fourth source of authority is found by other American Churches in Scripture alone. And of these there are some who emphasize Scripture as a Book—the Holy Bible, an authority prescriptive, legal, to be confessed, accepted and obeyed for what it is in itself, and to be sundered from the organism in which it has always been found.

Others, and to these the Book of Concord, through its Formula, belongs, accept Scripture as the only rule of faith and life, not because it is the end in itself, but because Christ is there: it is the Word of God bringing salvation, a Word springing up from and given to not merely individuals, but given to the Church of Christ. The Book of Concord confesses Scripture—which is the Word of God— which is the Gospel of Christ—which is the Law and the Gospel—and which is testified to in the great Confessions that have been pressed out of the tribulation of believing witnesses in history; as the fruit of the action of the Holy Spirit through the Word upon the hearts of believers.

Thus, with the Book of Concord, "we believe, teach and confess" the truth in the Word, which is Christ; and the truth in the Church's Confession, of which we are convinced that it is the reflex and effect of Christ in the long and unbroken line of believers who constitute His communion and flock. This Confessional Principle, though it may separate us from contemporaries of the present moment who do not find the whole Christ or the sure Word of Christ in the Scripture, connects us with the glorious company of the Apostles, the goodly fellowship of the Prophets, the noble army of martyrs, and the unbroken line of true confessors in all ages of the holy Church throughout the world, who under whatsoever name, or in whatsoever communion, received in good and honest hearts the true faith once delivered to the saints; and constitute the one, holy Catholic Christian Church, which confesses the "one Lord, one Faith, one Baptism, one God and Father of all, Who is above all, and through all, and in us all."

THE RELATION OF SPIRITUAL FORCES.

Of the various possible spiritual forces described in the preceding pages, Reason and the Scripture may be termed centrifugal forces, *i. e.,* their reaction has proven to be varied, and, under Protestant influences, individualizing. On the other hand, the Church and the Confessions are centripetal forces, *i. e.,* their action has proven to be of a uniting and crystallizing character. We, as Lutherans, reject one centrifugal force, Reason, and surely we would not set our faith and hope on the first centripetal force mentioned, viz., the Church, as a centre of authority.

When the Confessions are disparaged, as the Church's witness to Scripture, there is no centripetal force remaining, except the ecclesiastical motive. The result is that many Protestants, thus bereft of a uniting Confessional power, must resort to the Church, the ecclesiastical idea and fact,

59

the common name and the common external bonds of a denomination, to keep them together.

As Lutherans, our only rule of authority is the Scripture, which, although, in its historical form, it be centrifugal, nevertheless becomes centripetal in its Confessional form. Rome, with a visible centre of authority in the Church and in the vicar of Christ on earth, does not need a Confessional centre. But the only spinal column that will organize and keep the Protestant Church of the future together, is *a common principle from Scripture* which has become *the common principle of the Church.* Therefore also the Church of the Conservative Reformation lays stress upon the Confessions.

A sound and conservative Confessional Lutheranism seeks to maintain the balance between the centripetal and centrifugal forces, which draw the mind of the Protestant believer in contrary directions. The Confessional Principle of the Book of Concord releases him from the Church as a source of authority, thus preserving Christian liberty; and does not allow Reason to become a source of authority, thus preserving Christian Faith. Our Confessional Principle accepts the Scripture as the only rule of Faith, and thus preserves Christ; and accepts the Confessions as the reflex of Scripture, in the testimony of which his own heart joins, and thus preserves the Church.

THE CONFESSIONAL PRINCIPLE A BALANCE.

The Confessional Principle, into which Scripture and individual conviction or assent enter as elements, which meet together in the Confession, thus becomes the balance between rationalism on the one hand and ecclesiasticism on the other; between lawless individualism on the one hand, and tyrannical external authority on the other; between unprincipled indifferentism on the one hand and intolerant bigotry on the other.

Pure Protestantism, which acknowledges no authority but Reason, or Reason and Scripture, will not hold men together in an abiding union in a visible Church.[1] Indifferent Protestantism, which reduces faith to opinions, and exalts unity, fraternity and fellowship to a rule, will unite and maintain the shell of Christianity without its substance. Federated Protestantism, which finds its authority on a common but not clearly-determined Scripture ground, with common but partial and not clearly-determined recognition of individualities in faith; seeks its purpose in furthering the work of the visible church; and its sphere of organization in a temporary union for mutual benefit, looking to something better, and thus draws its rule in part from Confession and in part from the Church.

But Confessional Protestantism, taking its authority from the Word of God alone, as reflected in the testimony, and not in the organization, of the Church; recognizing the priority of conscience, and not of practical plans, is the only unity that stands squarely on principle and conviction of the truth and yet refrains from tyranny of organization.

THE CONFESSIONAL PRINCIPLE AND LIBERALITY.

Confessional Protestantism will not yield principle to expediency. It will not extend hands as brethren at Marburg, in view of political considerations, and continue in doctrinal difference, private dislike, and in innuendo and the petty spirit of proselytism. It will be tolerant to men, but not to ambiguous measures. It will tolerate hostile convictions, but not falsehood. It will respect and love its friend and foe, but not compromise with either. It will be tolerant and

---

[1] " In vain Protestants seek to make their churches as solid as the Roman. Their basal cause of existence is fatal to unity. Acting in the direction of its origin, the force of Protestantism tends ever to disintegrate; to perfect its spirit it must destroy its organization; while the Catholic Church naturally moves onward in increasing centralization. Which of the two systems is better for the world, the reader may judge for himself, but there can be no two opinions as to which is better for itself."—Frank Crane in *Open Court,* July, 1906. This writer does not take Confessional Protestantism into account.

patient as Luther was, but not disingenuous as Melanchthon at times appeared to be.[2]

The Confessional principle of the Book of Concord is a liberal principle, but its liberality is of a far-seeing, just and thorough order. It is not the liberality of a weak, emotional and unprincipled charity, which is capable of caressing an ecclesiastical neighbor on the cheek one moment, and of criticizing or condemning him at another. It is not the liberality of a man who gladly yields to others that which is outworn in his own eye. The Church with the Confessional principle of the Book of Concord treasures what the Lord has commanded and taught, as not her own, and as not hers to barter away.

She is not of that nature which squanders charity on others, and is faithless to her own home and children. What she has, as conscience tells her, direct from her Lord, she prizes and defends, and will not allow to be hid under a bushel, even at the risk of incurring the scorn or the displeasure of others who consider it wrong in her to maintain and defend a peculiar treasure.

As to others, she gives them liberty and love, and heartily shares with them all the treasure she possesses which they will really accept and not despise. But when they seek to invade her sanctum, and to say that what is therein is of small account, that it should be removed, and that the door should be thrown open to a common life, she feels that a neighbor or relative, who calls himself a brother but is so with reservations, has trespassed on a genuine and well-meaning good-will, and has presumed on an intimacy or communion which he is not in a position and does not deserve to share. Yet she abates no love to the children of the Lord, from the rising to the setting of the sun, though they do not

---

[2] Compare his letter to Camerarius (" *Dissimulate* "). Cp. also the declaration of Schaff in his *Creeds*:—" The conduct of Melanchthon weakened his authority and influence, which had been rising higher and higher before and after Luther's death, especially in the University of Wittenberg. Before this unfortunate controversy, he was universally regarded as the theological head of the evangelical Church in Germany, but now a large number of Lutherans began to look upon him with distrust."

agree with her, and though their failure to prize the peculiar truth which is her treasure grieves her greatly.

She needs hardly to say how heartily she acknowledges that in the Evangelical Churches, in their ministry and people, there are noble exemplifications of Christian grace,[*] and that she freely admits that, "as Channing, though a Unitarian, was more lovely morally than many a Trinitarian, so, much more, may some particular Christians, who are in error on the matter of the Sacraments, far surpass in Christian grace some individuals who belong to a Church whose sacramental faith is pure. Some men are on the level of their systems, some rise above them, some fall below them. A human body, in which one lobe of the lungs is gone, may not only live, but be healthy; another may be sickly and die, in which the lungs are perfect. Nevertheless, the complete lungs are an essential part of a perfect human body. We still truly call a man a man, though he may have lost arms and legs; we still call a hand a hand, though it may have lost a finger, or be distorted. While, therefore, we freely call systems and men Christian, though they lack a sound sacramental doctrine, we none the less consider that doctrine essential to a complete Christian system, and to the perfect faith of a Christian man. The man who has lost an arm, we love none the less. If he has lost it by carelessness, we pity his misfortune, yet we do not hold him free from censure. But when he insists, that, to have two arms, is a blemish, and proposes to cut off one of ours, then we resist him."

This insistence of his may be gentle and lovely at the start. He asks to share our communion, and denies part of our Confession. For personal convenience or opinion's sake, he is willing to have our church live with a spot of falseness in her bosom. He asks only to be undisturbed in his private opinions. But as these private opinions take root in other hearts and grow, he assumes for them an equal right with

---

[*] Krauth.

the Confessional principle. It is regarded as bigotry to assert any superior right for the doctrine of the Confession. To make a resistance against the growing supremacy of his tolerated opinions is said to be un-Christian. "Truth started with tolerating: it comes to be merely tolerated. Error claims a preference for its judgments on all disputed points."

IS THE CONFESSIONAL PRINCIPLE OF THE BOOK OF CONCORD ACCEPTED IN ALL PARTS OF THE LUTHERAN CHURCH?

The great American writer on the Credal Principle in Christianity, Schaff, declares that it is not. He tells us that " The Formula of Concord *is disowned* by the Melanchthonian and Unionistic schools in the Lutheran Church." [*] There is no question that Philippists and Gnesio-Lutherans still constitute portions of the Lutheran Church. And we are not of those who would disown their historical right, traced from the Reformation period, to existence. Whether they exalt the Lutheran Church as a Church, or their own doctrine as a doctrine, or, as Schaff declares, " disown " the Confessional principle of the Formula of Concord, why should they not be left to their patrimony, and be allowed the historical right to bear the name of the great Reformer, to whose doctrines they bear the relation of Melanchthon and his principle. Why should not the Melanchthonian Lutheranism in Germany take advantage of the opportunities of the "Union," and in America be respected as exemplifying an historical European fact, one different from the Confessional Principle of the Book of Concord on which the Lutheran Church in America was founded, and which they do not all, as Schaff says, in putting the case too strongly even for his day, "disown." There are also Melanchthonians who, like Chemnitz and Chytraeus, have come to see the real heart of the Lutheran faith, and, personally, to accept the Book

---

[*] *Creeds of Christendom*, I, p. 322.

of Concord. These good Lutherans, however, cling to a less specific confession, feeling that they ought make their principle tell, as leaven in the loaf of a common American Reformed Protestantism. The old cloth is Puritanic, and the little patch of Lutheranism sewed on with so much sacrifice, will enlarge the rent rather than make seamless the garment. What respect did the founder of the Evangelical Alliance, whose fellowship in language and religion with Evangelical Protestants was boundless, have for the fraternal Melanchthonian Lutherans? Not enough to prevent him from speaking as follows:—

" Outside of Germany the Lutheran Church is stunted in its normal growth, or undergoes, with the change of language and nationality, an ecclesiastical transformation. This is the case with the great majority of Anglicized and Americanized Lutherans, who adopt Reformed views on the Sacraments, the observance of Sunday, Church Discipline, and other points." [5]

Thus did this venerable apostle of unionism in two continents show the kind of fraternal spirit and brotherly love which the Reformed principle possesses even for those under the Augsburg Confession who were most willing to extend the hand of fellowship at the Nineteenth Century Marburg colloquies. He regarded them as having no substantiality, and as only forming "the connecting link" [6] between the Lutheran Confession and the Reformed. Can we expect more of the Puritan, or the Anglican stock whose principle of fellowship practically proves to be that of the lion and the lamb—the hungry lion, to whom, as Schaff predicts, fellowship means the possibility of absorption.

But the right of the Variata is really historical. It represents and can stand for as much as is justified in its own past. It cannot represent that which has been unchanging and is genuine. Confessions cannot be altered or improved after they have become the basis of action, even with the consent of all the authors or signers.

---

[5] *Creeds of Christendom,* I, p. 213.

[6] *Ib.,* p. 214.

Neither the Declaration of Independence, nor the Ninety-five Thesis of Luther, nor an old standard hymn, nor any historic document of import and standing may be "altered and improved" by subsequent generations into whose hands it may fall.

Even the author himself, when he once has given over a confession to the church, and the church has accepted it as her own, has merged and given over his own private property rights, to the larger body in whose interests it has been composed, and to whom it now belongs. Both the interests of the public body, which accepts the confession as expressing that which is most precious to itself, and also the interests of historical accuracy prevent any private tampering of an author with his own former workmanship. One cannot add new clauses, or take away old ones, privately, from a mortgage, however desirable that may be, when once it is of record.

THE CONFESSIONAL PRINCIPLE OF THE UNALTERED AUGSBURG CONFESSION IS THAT OF THE BOOK OF CONCORD.

Historical and territorial causes led some parts of the Lutheran Church in Europe to characterize themselves as the Church of the Unaltered Augsburg Confession. The Confessional Principle of the Unaltered Augsburg Confession is identical with that of the Book of Concord, except that it is more positive, more determinedly and extremely Lutheran, and less mild and expanded, than the principle of the Book of Concord.

The Formula of Concord takes pains to identify its confessional principle with that of the Unaltered Augsburg Confession. The subjects treated in the Formula [7] are only those treated in the Augsburg Confession, and are less in number. The very Title of the Formula is, " solid, plain and clear

---

[7] Except the *Descensus.*

repetition and *declaration* of certain *articles of the Augsburg Confession."* The Preface to the Book of Concord declares that "the doctrine comprised in it" (the Augsburg Confession), "they have constantly judged to be the only and perpetual consensus of the truly believing Church." The Preface declares it to be "that godly confession, which was built upon solid testimonies of truth unmoved and expressed in the Word of God." They say: "It has never been our intention to defend any new dogma, but . . . to constantly support and retain the truth which we professed at Augsburg in the year 1530." They call the Book of Concord "a repetition of our Christian faith and Confession." They say: "We emphatically testify that we wish to embrace the first Augsburg Confession alone." They declare again: "It has always been our intention that in our lands, schools and churches no other doctrine be proclaimed and accurately set forth than that which is founded upon the Word of God, as contained in the Augsburg Confession and the Apology." They say again: "We mean that doctrine which . . . is contained in the Augsburg Confession 1530. . . . We have determined not to depart even a finger's breadth from the things or from the phrases." The Formula itself declares: "From our inmost hearts we herewith once again confess this Christian Augsburg Confession, which is so thoroughly grounded in God's Word. We abide by the simple, clear and plain meaning of the same." Still again they say: "We intend, by the grace of the Almighty to faithfully abide until our end by this Christian Confession." Further they declare: "It is our purpose neither in this nor in any other writing to compose another or new Confession."

Once again they say, "We confessionally accept the first unaltered Augsburg Confession (not because it was composed by our theologians, but because it has been derived from God's Word, and is founded firmly and well therein), precisely in the form in which it was committed to writing in

the year 1530." [8] Finally, they say, " No one who is true
to the Augsburg Confession will complain of these writings,
but will cheerfully accept and tolerate them as witnesses of
the truth." [9] The other writings referred to as witnesses of
the truth are the remaining symbols between the Augsburg
Confession and the Formula of Concord.

Words could not more clearly, more earnestly or more
emphatically declare the identity of the Confessional principle of the Book of Concord with that of the Augsburg Confession, and an examination of the bulky Church Orders and
Bodies of Doctrine out of whose confusion the Formula of
Concord was written could not more clearly testify to the
wisdom of completing the Unaltered Augsburg Confession
of 1530 by the brief repetition and declaration of the Formula.

" The whole struggle, commencing with Luther's publication of the ninety-five theses in 1517, and terminating with
the publication of the Book of Concord in 1580, was the most
remarkable which the world has beheld since the age of the
Apostles. We cannot assign its termination to an earlier date
than the one when the church came forth from the struggle
as a victor, bearing as the reward of its fidelity to its great
Head the Holy Scriptures set forth in their purity and integrity and shielded from misinterpretation by the holy
Confession comprised in the symbols of the church.

" It would, therefore, be equivalent to an attempt to put
asunder what God has joined together, if the church, at the
present day, forgetful alike of the history of its origin in its
present form, and of its obligations to the cause of divine
truth, would make a discrimination between the several symbols, and not rather receive them all as parts essentially necessary to its confession as an entire confession. This is the
view entertained not only by our older theologians, but also
by those of the last and present century. It is well known

---

[8] *Book of Concord*, p. 536.
[9] *Ib.*, p. 538.

that in the doctrinal writings of all the eminent divines of
the church, arranged as they are in various classes, characterized by various degrees of orthodoxy and various systems of
philosophy, the evidence is found that, amid all the conflicting opinions which they entertain, when they find occasion
to refer to any point as either adopted or rejected by the Ev.
Luth. Church, they quote indiscriminately from one or all
of the symbols of which mention has been made above, and
which, as an aggregate, constitute The Book of Concord.
The evidence is accessible to all, and is so little liable to
contradiction, that it needs no introduction in this place.
Still, among the innumerable illustrations of this fact, a single sentence may be quoted from the preface ('Vorwort') of
a small work of Prof. Thomasius, which he published a few
years ago (November, 1848), and which we mention in preference to others, simply because he had introduced into its
title, namely, 'das Bekenntnis der evangelisch-lutherischen
Kirche in der Konsequenz seines Prinzips,' the same phrase
of which this report is treating. His words are: 'I was
led to give attention specially to the relation in which the
Formula of Concord stands to the Augsburg Confession, because it is this point against which, at present, opposition to
the confession is specially directed, and in reference to which
it is most frequently necessary to explain and remove misunderstandings.' When he here speaks of the 'confession
of the church,' he assumes as a fact, which no theologian
would, without grave reasons, question in the present age;
that the Formula of Concord is as completely a part of the
confession of the church, as the Augsburg Confession itself,
or any other symbol is a part of it. Indeed, no theological
work of which we have any knowledge, is understood to have
been published by any modern German theologian, which
cordially acknowledges the doctrines of the Augsburg Confession, and yet rejects the succeeding symbols as capable of
being separated from the former without violence and historical unfairness.

" The prominence which, in the church in the United States, has often been given to the Augsburg Confession, and the frequent omission of the names of the succeeding Symbolical Books, might produce the erroneous impression that the former possessed a higher rank or greater authority in that part of the church which is found in America, than the latter, unless, in addition to the explanations which have already been given above, respecting the origin of the historical name of the ' church of the Augsburg Confession,' the following facts are also properly appreciated; they clearly establish this principle: *That the Augsburg Confession is the representative of the whole body of the Symbolical Books, so that, under ordinary circumstances, those who formerly named it alone, nevertheless understood it to imply and include the other confessional writings with which it is inseparably connected.*" [10]

WHAT AN EX ANIMO CONFESSION OF THE UNALTERED AUGSBURG CONFESSION INVOLVES.

From the identity of the Confessional principle of the Lutheran Church, as found in the earlier root and the later fruit of the Reformation consciousness, it follows that those who, like the authors of the Formula of Concord, "most heartily confess the Augsburg Confession of 1530 " will also, if candid and consistent, with equal heartiness confess the principle of the Book of Concord; and *vice versa.* Such a hearty, or ex animo, confession of the Unaltered Augsburg Confession involves, on the part of a Lutheran Church body, the actual teaching of the same doctrine, on points set forth in the Confession, in all the churches of that body. This is emphasized, not only in the Formula of Concord, by the oft-repeated "we believe, teach, and confess;" but also in the Augsburg Confession itself, which declares:—

" Our Churches, with common consent, do teach" (Art. I) ;

"they teach;" (Art. II) ; " they teach;" (Art. III) ; " they teach " (Art. IV) ; " they teach " (Art. VI) ; " they teach " (Art. VII) ; " they teach " (Art. IX) ; " they teach " (Art. X) ; " they teach " (Art. XI) ; " they teach " (Art. XII) ; " they teach " (Art. XIII) ; " they teach " (Art. XIV) ; " they teach " (Art. XV) ; " they teach " (Art. XVI) ; " they teach " (Art. XVII) ; " they teach " (Art. XVIII) ; " they teach " (Art. XIX) ; " they teach " (Art. XXI).

The actual and unanimous teaching of the doctrine set forth in this Confession is therefore necessary on the part of those who subscribe it; and a hearty and enthusiastic unanimous teaching is necessary on the part of those who subscribe to it *ex animo*.

The fact as to whether a body makes an *ex animo* subscription to any set of principles and doctrines or not, may be tested in two ways: first, by the official declaration of the body; second, by the official teaching acts of those set to represent it.

If a synod subscribes *ex animo* to certain principles, it thereby becomes their defender, and will so unmistakably let this fact be known in its fundamental, *i. e.,* its constitutional writings, that the whole world, especially its own members and the members of all other denominations, can make no mistake on that fact.

But, in the second place, the official teaching-acts of its teachers, whether professors, writers, pastors, catechists, delegates, must truly correspond with the principle which the body who sends them forth subscribes *ex animo*. While it is quite true that a body is to be judged solely by its official utterances; yet the fidelity and loyalty of a body to its official utterances must be tested by the utterances of its teaching officials, whether pastors, professors or writers—not by what they say in their own personal capacity, but by what they say in their pulpits, their text-books, their public statements on behalf of the body which they profess to represent, and especially by what they say and do as representatives of the Lutheran Church before Christian faiths, and other Christians.

If the body's subscription to principles is perfect, but the teaching of the teachers is different; the case is like that of a bank whose business principles are entirely correct, but several of whose officers, in contrast with the principles of the bank and in disloyalty to them, carry on their share of the business on questionable financial principles. No matter how often the bank may point to its faith and charter, and how prominently it may hang its good rules on the wall, and how unimpeachable its president and directors may be; if it permits the questionable to continue in official acts contrary to the rules and principles, on the plea that it cannot interfere with the personal liberty of its employees, then depositors and outside banking firms cannot be blamed if they withdraw their deposits and close out their accounts in that institution.

The real question is not what do you subscribe, but what do you believe and publicly teach, and what are you transmitting to those who come after ? If it is the complete Lutheran faith and practice, the name and number of the standards is less important. If it is not, the burden of proof rests upon you to show that your more incomplete standard does not indicate an incomplete Lutheran faith. The Augsburg Confession was not intended to be an explicit, adequate, and final statement of the Lutheran faith. It closes as follows: " *Only those things have been recounted,* whereof we thought that it was necessary to speak. . . If anything further be desired, we are ready, God willing, to present *ampler information according to the Scriptures.*" The later Confessions present this "ampler information according to the Scriptures," which the Augsburg Confession itself promised, and without which it is incomplete.

CHAPTER XL.

THE CONFESSIONAL PRINCIPLE OF THE BOOK OF CONCORD AND CHRISTIAN COOPERATION.

Luther and Melanchthon on Federation—Federation To-day—The Sphere of the Church in Civil Reform—The Dangers in Cooperation—The Lutheran not a Narrow-minded Church—The True Position of the Confessional Principle in Cooperation—The Attitude of the Confessional Principle toward Those Without—The Principle of Fellowship—The Union Recognized by the Confessional Principle.

LUTHER AND MELANCHTHON ON FEDERATION.

LUTHER and Melanchthon were against Confederation of any kind,—internal, as a brotherhood of Churches; or external, in civil and religious government. But Melanchthon, to whom the Roman idea of visible unity always appealed, would have sacrificed much for the sake of remaining in the historic unity of Rome; and, when that was impossible, for the sake of preventing Protestantism from splitting up into external divisions. Although Luther was less fanatical and better balanced than any of the sectarian and more radical Reformers, he was convinced that his work and duty as a Christian pastor and Professor was to testify to the truth —the whole truth—and become a martyr, if need be, the same as an apostle in New Testament days. The perilous or unpleasant consequences of the truth for the Church or for the generation in which he lived, did not concern him. That was God's affair, not his. God was able to take care of the world and of the Church. Man's affair was to stand for the Gospel of the Lord Jesus Christ.

Luther did not seem to feel that any combination of forces, in our modern sense of the term, was important to the Church. He relied solely, like the Lord Jesus Christ, upon the power of the Word. Yet the activities of Philip of Hesse, both at Augsburg and later in the Schmalkald League, with the checks placed upon them, appear to have been part of the plan of Providence. No human mind can say whether, if witness alone had been relied upon, even unto martyrdom; or if the issue between Protestantism and Romanism had been brought to an immediate and final head in the Sixteenth instead of in the Seventeenth Century, the result would have been better or worse for the Truth. Not only is Luther—but Melanchthon likewise—always with the Church, to complicate the application of the pure Confessional Principle. Of one fact we may be sure, and that is that the scenes which occurred between 1530 and 1580 were our examples.[1]

There is something fascinating in a united attack of the whole visible Church of God upon the strongholds of sin. The advance under one banner, the use of one watchword, the presentation of a solid front toward the wickedness of the world, the substitution for a loose and inconsistent organization, of one that is close, unbroken, consistent and faultless; the enthusiastic crusade under an idea, instead of patient and ineffective toil under wretched fact; the resolving of the narrower Church into the broader Kingdom of God; the great possibilities of accomplishing great work together; the sense of being in a large enterprise, of one that above all things is making progress, of one that has the mighty majority with it and is already bearing the legends of success and victory on its banner; the one concerning which the world—both friend and foe—is obliged to take respectful notice; the life with men of breadth where the whole atmosphere is free, where there is room for plenty of work and plenty of difference in personal opinion; where a

---

[1] I Cor. 10 : 11-12.

distinction is made between a few great fundamentals of Christianity and such minor matters as can be set aside,—these are the characteristics of a confederate Christianity which persuade many that convictions are not as important as work to be done; that the Faith and the Truth on their sharper sides, even if revealed and pressed on us in the Word of God, may be sacrificed—at least in some details—for the sake of a larger movement, which in some way will result in a final unity in the Truth and in its success and will justify the temporary relaxing of our conviction and the overlooking of minor matters in the Faith.

But Luther never yielded to this view. He said of the doctrine (which is not ours, but God's) : " We can remit not even a jot, nor can we permit either abatement or addition. It must be, as it were, a continuous and round golden circle. . . . If they believed the Word to be the Word of God, they would know that one Word of God is all His words, and all His words are one; likewise, one article is all articles, and all articles are one." [2] " Luther," says Köstlin, [3] " has evidently no other idea than that every congregation, or church, which desires to be faithful to its duty must publicly and decidedly confess all the truth which we have found him presenting in his doctrinal writings or defending against its assailments; and that they must do this in view of the thoroughly Scriptural character of the positions thus maintained and their intimate connection with the central point of Christian doctrine. He evidently regarded it as his unquestionable calling to labor with all his power to induce the Church, with whose guidance he was in part entrusted, to make such full and open confession." . . .

" In the confession which he was then called upon to prepare for the Church, *i. e.,* the Schmalkald Articles, he endeavored, without any regard whatever for such [*i. e.,* for those persons to whom he had shown consideration, but who were not in

---

[2] *Theology of Luther,* trans. by Hay, Vol. II, p. 273.

[3] *Ib.,* p. 272.

full accord with so important a doctrine as that of the Lord's Supper], to confess the full round truth. Such then is the position of Luther, as indicated by his own writings, upon the question of the distinction between fundamental and non-fundamental doctrines " [3a] to us Lutherans of the Twentieth Century.

FEDERATION TO-DAY.

Federation to-day is a conclusion from two premises, in which many important points are implicit, rather than explicit, and much is taken for granted. If the Confessional Principle, in all its bearings, were acknowledged explicitly in advance, by a Federation of Evangelical Churches founded upon the orthodox doctrine of the Atonement and Redemption of Christ, with a recognition of the deep gulf that divides our Faith and non-conservative Protestantism; and if it were not premised, as it always is, that the Lutheran Church is one of " some thirty orthodox Protestant denominations who are fully at one in the essentials and differ only in some doctrinal peculiarities or in gifts of administration," [4] it might be possible to enter into cooperation for definite acts along certain well-defined lines. But it is a question whether cooperation of this character, as it could practically be given, would be of value to the Christian Faith, or to our country; or whether it, surrounded and hedged in by conditions, would be appreciated by the other parts of federated Protestantism. In order to uphold the Evangelical Confessional Principle without cloud or compromise, it would be necessary for non-Lutherans to understand and to grant that the Lutheran Church though the mother Protestant church, is catholic, retaining the supremacy of Scripture, and the continuity of history in doctrine, worship, discipline and the like, but purging away Roman error; and that it differs from the other Protestant bodies of the

---

[3a] *Ib.,* p. 273.

[4] This is substantially the language, often repeated, of the Secretary of the Federation of Protestant Churches, at its meeting in 1908.

Reformation, commonly called the Reformed bodies of Protestants, and from all more recently arising sects, in its apprehension of almost every point of doctrine.[5] It, further, would be necessary to permit the Lutheran Church to lodge its protest or record its objection of conscience, to every word and deed of the Federation which indicated Confessional difference from itself.

It differs from these other Protestants in the doctrines of the Word, the Scripture, the Church, the Sacraments, the Means of Grace, the Ministry, the operations of the Holy Ghost, the freedom of the will (synergism), often on the nature of justification, good works, the Church and State in Moral Reforms, and on the Person of Christ.

These differences appear in all attempts at practical action. The Lutheran Church does not believe that it is showing its zeal in the cause of the Lord or is actively ushering in the Kingdom of God by using its power as an organization to establish divorce laws, race-track legislation, Sunday, or, still worse—*Sabbath* laws, labor legislation, Temperance Reform, and by rooting out civic corruption and immorality. It declares that the Church externalizes itself and falls short of its great regenerative mission when it fastens its eye on temporal reform, wrought chiefly by the arm of law in the State, rather than by addressing the powerful Word of God to the consciences of its members.

THE SPHERE OF THE CHURCH IN CIVIL REFORM.

It by no means agrees with the Reformed Protestantism of the American Protestant Federation, as to the task of practical reform assumed by that body. It does not agree in enforcing such reform with stringency upon the civil government, and in finding its justification thereunto either in positive Biblical ordinances, or in the name of humanity. This is admitted by Seeberg.[6] Neither can the Lutheran

---

[5] *Schaff* says we are united on all essentials and differ only in the Sacraments.

[6] *Cp. History of Doctrines*, II, p. 415.

Church enter into relations or covenants with the civil authority which would involve an attitude, if not a subordination of the State to the ordinances of the Church.

The Lutheran Church cannot enter into reforms on the Calvinistic principle. Obedience to the sovereign will of God is not the content of Christian life and the State and Society at large are not agencies for the enforcement of divine law. The Calvinistic or Reformed attitude of the Church toward the State, with all its magnificence of holy zeal, is that of Augustine and the Middle Ages. The Confessional principle of Lutheranism does not attempt to reform the State or the world by the application of law.[1]

To enter the civic field and secure the amelioration of social or spiritual conditions by legislation is not the work of the Church. This is in the sphere of the State and belongs to Christian citizens in their organized capacity in practical politics. It is not the work of the ministry, a spiritual office, which must not be used to the gain of even worthy earthly ends. The Federation's conception involves ultimate entanglement of Church and State.[8]

---

[1] "The God of Calvin is the omnipotent Will, ruling throughout the world; the God of Luther is the omnipotent energy of Love manifest in Christ. In the one case, we have acts of compulsion even in the heart, subjection, law, service; in the other, inward conquest by the power of love, free self-surrender, filial love without compulsion. The one does not necessarily exclude the other; but the tone and emphasis give rise to the differences which undeniably exist. From the practical energy of the Reformed ideals—with which praxis has not always been able to keep pace—the Lutheran church may learn a valuable lesson. But when, in any age of evangelical Christianity, faith grows dim, and love grows cold, and it seems as though the gospel were no longer sufficient to satisfy the advanced spirit of the 'modern world' then will deliverance be found, not in the views of Calvin, but in return to the gospel and the faith of Luther. Evangelical Christianity has yet much to learn from her Luther.

"I cannot therefore agree with K. Müller (*Symbolik*, 540), who regards it as 'certain' that in the evangelical church of the future 'the spirit of the general Evangelical Reformed Church will be in the ascendancy,' since Luther's contributions to the Church 'were substantially already adopted in the sixteenth century.' Müller has moreover acknowledged that in a certain sense the Reformed Church stands nearer to Roman Catholicism than does the Lutheran (p. 387a)."—Seeberg, *History of Doctrines*, pp. 416-417.

[8] The Lutheran Church, in a Federation, would be obliged to object to prayer that God "send down the Holy Ghost of a Christian Spirit among us," that we may "hear the rushing of the wind among us as the disciples did at Pentecost." It would have to object to a Sacrament "in which Baptists, Presbyterians, and Congregationalists participated and received the whole blessing, since they had the symbols upon the altar and the Holy Ghost in their hearts;" it would have to object to a definition of Lutheranism as "a series of Church bodies who hold more or less to the Reformed doc-

That such a conception of the Church is diverting it from its original purpose is discerned by the spiritual minded soul, even though it be outside of the Evangelical Faith. Thus one not rooted and grounded in the Gospel of Christ, but a Unitarian,[8a] writes:—

"The Church is tempted to abandon its real mission in the world. It is in danger of being misled by specious programs of agitators and of transforming itself into a civic forum, a therapeutic hospital, a dispensary of charities, an institution for visible social betterment. The church stands as the specific antidote of materialism, safeguards the reverences of life, cares for the moral visions of the soul and pronounces every god-ward aspiration of heart and mind as the noblest expressions of manhood and womanhood. Its legitimate work is not to supply new social furniture, but to make men righteously efficient, and then to trust them to go out with wisdom and consecration to improve in their own way the social conditions of life."

THE DANGERS IN COOPERATION.

We believe that the reader will conclude with us that our continuous alliance or connection with an American Protestant Federation is out of the question. In such an environment the Lutheran Church will find herself in a situation in which she will be unable to preserve either her Confessional principle or to conserve her practical interests. It is a fact that all the Protestant churches in America, save our own, are *Reformed* in descent, and that they together, by nature, breathe out a Reformed spirit. Therefore, when radical measures are adopted by a general organization to which they

---

trines of the Reformation, some more, some less." It would have to object, too, to the statement, as understood by the Federation that " the Church of Christ and the nation are vitally related each to the other;" that " the Church of Christ should make itself felt in American political diplomacy; and should organize into a power which can be applied to politics for spiritual ends." For, thus, evil in the State will be fought with the weapons or by the methods of Rome, and we have the spectacle of a Protestant externalization reared to checkmate the efforts of the Roman and corrupt secular influences in legislation.

[8a] *J. C. Jaynes.*

all belong, even though these measures are not approved in any instance by some part of them, they do no violence to their fundamental Reformed principle. The plan may be most vigorously disputed and denounced, but if it be carried by a majority, there is no serious and deep-seated principle injured in living under it.

But the Lutheran Church is the conservative Protestant Church of this country. She is the Church that holds on to the good of history, as well as of Scripture, and that cannot take into her bosom any form of radicalism. Therefore Lutheranism is capable of being injured indirectly at almost every point, in a common attempt at organization or action among American Protestants; and its fundamental principle in any such gathering is nearly always strained by some radical action.

For every Federation or cooperation is no more conservative than its weakest point. No one knows, in connection with any such an organization (whether it be in a general plan of action proposed, whether it be in a deliverance, perhaps highly applauded, on the floor; whether it be in the arrangement of a mere local council), where, along the line, the most un-Lutheran statements, practices, proposals, will break out; or, at least, ooze out. In a union of this kind, where we are the one branch of a different family (and, in conventions and ecclesiastical diplomacy particularly, the remaining branches cleave together in spirit, expression and action), if true to ourselves, Lutherans must be under the appearance of putting their own views on a higher plane of importance than those of all others. Nearly every sound Lutheran who has been on the floor in a general body of Protestants and tried to be consistent there, would, we suppose, at some moment recall some such feeling and experience.

There is a reason for all this. The Lutheran church cannot go very far with the Reformed churches without finding something in the atmosphere, or even in the pathway, that is prejudicial to her principles, or that becomes a strain on them. Is there any Lutheran who really in his heart believes that the Puritans, the Church of England men, and the sectarians of the East and West, will go *with him,* and will follow *his way* in such a Federation? If they will not, then he must either go their way, or both must choose a new way,—neither of which things can happen and he remain true to his Lutheran faith.

NOT A NARROW-MINDED CHURCH.

This is not narrowness—it is a historical fact. We have not invented the fact—it has thrust itself upon us; and if there be any criticism of narrowness against us, it must not be with reference to the fact, but with reference to our recognition of it. The Lutheran Church is not a narrow-minded Church. She is above and beyond all, a church that stands for clear fact, rather than for pure logic on the one hand, or for mixed sentiment on the other. The Lutheran Church can co-operate in many matters, but not on general sentiment, and only and always where definite limits are set. She is not a diplomatic church; and, because she does violence to her open-minded nature in ecclesiastical diplomacy, she is nearly always worsted when she engages in it.

We believe the Federation of Churches will do good to Reformed Protestantism. It will draw together those who belong together. It should persuade those who are united on every essential doctrine, and divided by nothing but sectarian or denominational particularity, to give up the latter, and become one mighty American religious brotherhood. We believe, too, that it will help the Lutheran Church. Those Lutherans who prize the aims of a Federation which is essentially a Reformed Protestant body in objects and methods, above the object, teaching and method of the Lutheran Church, will be kept busy in vain in refining the Reformed oil out of a Reformed mass; or will find that the Lutheran oil is being simply absorbed in the Reformed mass.

Let us sum up the reasons why the Confessional Lutheran Church stands firm against amalgamation, alliance, or federation. First of all, she is not on a common foundation with all other Protestant Evangelical denominations. This has been made to appear sufficiently. In the second place, she has had large experience in all these proposals, and has rejected them generations ago. Her very birth, her youth, and the crises of her manhood were involved in this very question. It was the great question that arose, with the birth of Protestantism, at the Diet of Spires. It was the question at the Marburg Colloquy. It was the question urged tenaciously by Philip of Hesse at Augsburg. The Augsburg Confession excluded the Reformed Principle. It was the question for whose successful solution Bucer lived in vain. It was the question of the Variata of 1540. It was the question of the extreme Philippists and Crypto-Calvinists. It was the question of the princes at the Frankfort Recess. It was the question of the Electors at the Convention at Naumburg. It was the question that split and disintegrated the Church, until it was settled, gently but firmly, in the best spirit of Luther and the best spirit of Melanchthon, in the Concordia of 1580.

THE TRUE POSITION OF THE CONFESSIONAL PRINCIPLE IN COOPERATION.

The true position of the Lutheran Church in the midst of bland Romanism and active Protestantism, is firmness without unfriendliness; love without laxity. She should strive for all movements whose aim is unity, up to the point where it becomes evident that unity does not exist. She should shun all movements whose aim is union, that is, the cover or bond of unity thrown over diversity of principle.

Wherever there is common ground, there is possibility of cooperation. But no cooperation is possible whose practical or ultimate effect is to slight or ignore even the least central and most insignificant outpost of Lutheran principle. For the truth is organic, and it is the duty of the body to stand by, and not to sacrifice, even its smallest and most remote

member—its little finger, which is faithful in the discharge
of duty. The principle formulated in the sphere of love by
our Saviour, applies here in the sphere of faith: "Inasmuch as ye have not done it unto the least of these, ye have
not done it unto me."—"He that is faithful in little will be
faithful in much." This organic nature of the faith is the
key that solves the relations of fundamental and non-fundamental, and that has practically been used by the Formula of
Concord to determine the principle of the adiaphora.

Common ground is either neutral ground or a spot at
which the inner unity of the communion of saints flashes out
into visibility. It is not union ground. There never was a
union of Christendom in the sense usually referred to, unless the mediæval union of external rule under the papacy be
meant thereby, and, we do not believe there will ever be a
permanent earthly re-union of Christendom. The antithesis
will ever be operative. But there is at this time a unity of
all Christians, the unity of Christ Himself, and it constitutes
the communion of saints. This unity should more and more
be realized and made visible, but it must start from within
outward; and outer organization must honestly express, and
not cover up, the inner condition of truth and principle. It
is the mistake of our age, for any spiritual religion whose
strength is in Faith and communion with God, to lay all
stress upon an external organization and a surface appearance
of unity. It is a still greater mistake to degenerate distinctive faiths into a low minimum of common faith, or to
attempt a union of the common minimum with a tenacious
but individual preservation of what is distinctive.

If Protestantism were to combine, by way of elimination,
or of absorption of peculiar principle, it would be the beginning of the end of Faith. The genus without the species
is an abstraction. When you broaden a stream by sacrificing
its positive life-currents, you gain a marshland and not a
mighty river. It is dangerous to unite in parallel action,
without parallel and common conviction—for the thin par-

titions of custom or half-dead conviction will soon wear away, and there will be formless coalescence. The only safe combination is by common conviction.

THE ATTITUDE OF THE CONFESSIONAL PRINCIPLE TOWARD THOSE WITHOUT THE LUTHERAN CHURCH.

The Lutheran Church bears an open and loving and helpful, not a closed attitude toward those without, *i. e.,* toward those seeking the truth, or those upholding honest convictions in the fear of God and with uncorrupt will. It is the nature of our Church to be patient, suffering all things, having pleasure in approval rather than condemnation; in concord rather than in discord. The first of our Confessions—that of Augsburg,—and the last—the Form of Concord—in substance and in tone, and our own history, are set in evidence on that point. We are willing and anxious to co-operate for the saving of souls and the upbuilding of Christ's kingdom with all of God's children wheresoever they be found.

Yet we are prevented from co-operating if thereby an injury is done to our conscience; or if we thereby compromise an iota of our prized and precious Faith, for which we have been called into existence; a treasure which is blood-bought, and above all price; and for which thousands of confessors have laid down home, friends, worldly success and life.

This treasure is the pure doctrine of salvation. With those to whom the purity of the Faith, the truth as it is in Christ Jesus, means much, we will walk up to the point where both conclude we must part. But with those to whom the purity of the Faith means little, or less than all; less than friendship, blood, practical success, the spirit of the age, and similar considerations, we are always in danger. Our chief treasure they do not so highly regard, and we cannot entrust it to them with the feeling that it is safe. They place other things on a par with this treasure, or above it, and this is a case where no man can have two masters:

for either he will hate the one, and love the other; or else he will hold to the one, and despise the other.

Since then we believe we exist for the pure Gospel principle, and all other things are subordinate, not even our best friends outside (and still less our enemies) can ask us to commit ourselves to association with any people, plan, teachings, or temperament which would derogate from our doctrine; or which would convey the impression to the wayfaring man that we have loosened our hold and relaxed our standard of the truth.[*]

If this be true, we are in a position to lay a rule for cooperation on the part of the Church, viz., the Church can cooperate in all matters in which it can openly apply its principles or Confession as a basis; and only in these. The Church must not ignore the issues of the day, or excuse herself from this responsibility, because she differs from a common Protestantism as to the end or the means; but she must bear her share of the public burden in some measure, and must find a way to do it.

And this temper of the sympathetic mind but the strong grasp and honest heart, the temper which is true at once to faith and to charity, is the only one of service in dealing with the most difficult problem of modern Protestantism, and of a common Christianity—a problem, be it remembered, which we did not create and which God Himself will have a hand in solving.

---

[*] Wherever we can work with a common Christianity, or with a common Lutheranism, with the assurance that no harm, immediate or remote, will come to our one great purpose of testimony to the truth, or to our integrity of conscience, we are ready to do so with joy; but wherever we are in doubt as to such a happy issue,—and we must be our own judges,—it is right and reasonable for us to decline to run any risk of exposing our highest good to danger, for the sake of attaining a lower and less important good; and no one in his fair and honest heart can blame us for failing to join in such a common movement.

We do attach the greatest importance to every Word of God; but we do not attach the greatest importance, except as a matter of high ideal, effective work, and wise expediency, to unity of ecclesiastical organization. Our unwillingness to cooperate with others, if it be an honest and conscientious thing, is not to be taken as a sign of dead orthodoxy, but as a sign of a living faith; it is not to be regarded as an evidence of a narrow outlook, but as a willingness to stand by one's convictions; it is not to be branded as a love of denomination or of Church above Christ, but is to be respected as an unswerving loyalty to Christ and His truth as we see it.

Since we may not rush into either extreme, but are obliged to see good wherever it may be found, and to see evil wherever it may be found; and since we cannot join in free and broad laxity on the one hand, nor resort to wholesale condemnation on the other, we must expect criticism and dissatisfaction with us from both sides, and must be satisfied patiently to bear the scorn that comes to those who try to be loving as well as just.

THE PRINCIPLE OF FELLOWSHIP.

Fellowship is a far more intimate thing than cooperation. Cooperation is a combined support in prosecution of a business plan; but fellowship is a life together. Cooperation is a limited association for definite ends; but fellowship is an unlimited association in spiritual life. Fellowship throws open all the doors, unlocks all the strong boxes, and bids the other one abide in our soul and heart.

Modern Christianity greatly abuses the principle of fellowship; and, in so far, destroys both its value and its sacredness. On the grounds of a broad humanity, it would admit to the heart of the Church even those who despise the precious merits of the Head of the Church. On the ground of a Christian brotherhood, it will admit to its fellowship those with whom it will not cooperate. The less one prizes the realities of love, the more publicly can fellowship be offered. True fellowship is with those with whom we are one in the life of the truth or fact on the basis of which the fellowship is enjoyed.

We believe that the feeling against Lutherans who do not participate in the Sacrament with all Christians, rests upon a misconception. Properly understood, we do not see how anyone who respects our belief would have us do otherwise. The Sacrament to us, it need scarcely be said, is not a sacred rite, but a solemn reality, in which we receive the body and blood of Christ. Therein, and in nothing else, lies its value to us. God's substantial pledge to us of salvation, a *divine* act, must not suffer evaluation with our acquiescence and consent.

It is not, to us, a mere mark of fellowship between Christians. It is, in truth, not a mark of fellowship at all, except in its unity. The only fellowship it expresses is between Christ and my soul, and not even that primarily. Primarily the Sacrament is the gift to me of my Saviour's body and blood for the forgiveness of my sin. It is the most sacred mystery and most holy reality of my faith. It is of the nature of miracle. It is the mystery of Sacrament. It is the "holy of holies" in my religion and worship, and means to me the eating unto life or the eating unto death.

My friends cannot claim to share all the most holy and most solemn acts of my soul. Marriage is not so holy as a sacrament, yet marriage separates me with another in its mystery from all the world; and my friends do not take it amiss if I fail to ask them to share in that holy communion. My membership in an ancestral society, in a guild peculiar to my vocation, in a discipline for the restoration of my bodily health, separates me from all except such as I am,— those who feel the need of what I need, those who wish to receive what I wish to receive. Do others think hard of me because I excuse myself from their fellowship, and go my way toward what I know I need?

If my convictions are with the historic democratic political party, but my sons and brothers and all my relatives are of the stalwart republican type, do they think any the less of me because on election day I separate myself from them, and vote in accordance with my convictions? Is the matter of family fellowship and manifestation to others that our family is in a unity, regarded as of more import than the exercise of my convictions at the polls? Do I insult and fail to show toleration and respect to the position of my relatives because I go my own way to vote?

Is *the Lord's Supper* the place to display *my* toleration, my Christian sympathy, or my fellowship with another Christian, when that is the very point in which most of all we differ; and in which the difference means for me everything—means for me, the reception of my Saviour's atonement? Is this the point to be selected for the display of Christian union, when in fact it is the very point in which Christian union does not exist?

If I will not take the sacrament myself without having been absolved at the special service held for that purpose, in the fear of being unworthy and held guilty of the body and blood of the Lord, am I kind to my neighbor, and kind to my Lord, in asking the former to come to the sacrament without such worthiness as I feel to be necessary, for safety's sake, in my own case? Am I willing to place him in the way of risk which I am not willing and dare not assume myself? Am I kind to him, and just to him, and to the Lord, in asking him to a participation as thus offered?

Our Saviour said nothing of the Sacrament as the mark of union between Christians. He said it is the forgiveness of my sins in His blood given for, and to us, and is the commemoration of Himself. The Apostle Paul declares we are one body in the communion, but—in *the* "communion of the blood of Christ," and in *the* "communion of the body of Christ." That is the communion which we Lutherans celebrate in the sacrament; and will those who believe that this is not the essence of the sacrament, desire to partake of it with us? Or, shall we desire to partake of it with them?

If they should, they are giving up nothing except respect for our convictions; and they are willing that we should be placed in the position of seeming to give up all that is most precious to us. If we should desire to participate with them in their sacrament, we are willing—in order to celebrate the mystery with them—to seem to be robbing it of the chief significance with which, in our conviction, it has been invested by our Lord.

Let us show our belief in the character of our friend and our participation in such brotherhood as can exist in Christ,

in a more practical way. Let us trust his word. Let us
praise his faith where we can. Let us demonstrate our
entire absence of jealousy of him. Let us not only tolerate
his church in our midst, but encourage him to worship in
accordance with his convictions. Let us convince him that
we believe he values his convictions; and that, though we
are not in unison with him in our principles, yet we do not
thereby set up ourselves as better Christians than he is. Let
us be humble in his presence and in the sphere of love show
him the respect and depth of an everlasting love. If we are
faithful to our unity with our Lord, and our brethren in
blood are faithful to their unity in the Lord, the Lord will
take care of the proper adjustment of our unity to each
other.

THE UNION RECOGNIZED BY THE CONFESSIONAL PRINCIPLE OF THE BOOK OF CONCORD.

Our union is in the grace of God, which has chosen us in
Christ. It is in the blood of Christ, which has been shed
for us, and has delivered us from sin. It is in the Holy
Spirit, Who has entered our heart, through the Word of
Christ, and made us one.

It is in our faith, by which we apprehend, and rest in, the
merit of Christ. It is in the communion of Christ's body,
of which we have become a part. It is in the very body and
blood of Christ, which is given an entrance into each of us,
for the remission of sin and the renewal of life.

Our union, the real union of Christ's Church with itself,
and of the various units with each other, is an inner one,
is mediated through Christ, and is not marked outwardly,
according to our Augsburg Confession, except by agreement
touching the doctrine of the Gospel. This doctrine of the
Gospel, which is the voice of Christ, should so influence every
member of His body, that they all speak the same thing, and
are perfectly joined together in the same mind and in the
same judgment.

This "speaking the same thing" is the Church's Confession. It is the result of the Church's unity, and not the cause of it. It is not the judge, or arbiter, or determinant of the Church's unity, but only the witness, the explanation and the proof of that union.

In actual fact, whatever be the reason, it is found that the Confession differs among Christians; and this brings difference in outward organization. Difference of Confession, which implies an acknowledgment of error somewhere, is the one valid ground for difference in organization.

Our Lutheran difference in Confession, in contrast with Rome, is that the unity of the Church is a unity in doctrine and faith and in the sacraments, and not in any external person or thing. Our Lutheran difference in Confession, in contrast with the Protestantism around us, is that the unity of the Church is a real invisible unity of the body with the Head, through Word and Sacrament; and not a dependency of each individual unit mediated directly, nor an outward and voluntary banding together of units into organization under some indefinite influence of the Holy Spirit.

Our unity has been established from all eternity by God the Father. It is rooted in Christ. It is mediated through Word and Sacrament. It connects all ages of the world and all true believers in every clime. It is not Lutheranism, nor any such outward *ism* or body. We are sure that the Lutheran faith is the perfect apprehension of that eternal unity, and corresponds with its revelation in Scripture; and we know by our faith that the Lutheran Confession is its most perfect expression.

If we Lutherans would witness to the Faith in its purity,—and to this we are driven, if we are true believers,—we must witness through the form of the Lutheran Confession.

The unimportant parts of the doctrine become important in our witness, where they are attacked; because they, even though unimportant, come to stand for the intrinsic value and the integrity of the whole.

The expressions of the inner unity in visible form, other than the truth or Confession, *e. g.,* in name, in ecclesiastical constitution and government, and in united action in the name of Christ—though these seem vital to us at our short range of vision—are of infinitely less importance than our adherence to the real inner unity in the body of Christ, as apprehended by a pure faith and as expressed **by a** pure principle.

For in these latter alone lie the salvation and hope of the kingdom of God even upon earth. They are the realities. They will determine the future. They will save the world.

The world will never be saved by "a union of human effort." Our united outward actions, no matter how well meant, or how well organized, or how imposing and demonstrative, or how accordant, are a vain thing, if they are not rooted in the inner unity in Christ; and are pernicious, if they are not in accord with our expressed consciousness of that inner unity in the faith. That expressed consciousness is our Confession.

61

CHAPTER XLI.

THE CONFESSIONAL PRINCIPLE OF THE BOOK OF CONCORD AND THE BROTHERHOOD OF THE CHRISTIAN CHURCH.

The Confessional Principle of the Book of Concord and Christian Love and Charity —The Question of Tolerance—The Question of the Manifestation of the Church's Essential Unity—The Question of the Majority in Religion—The Question of a Visible Unity in Protestantism—The Attitude of Lutherans Toward the Confessional Principle Revealed in their Attitude Toward Denominational Protestantism.

THE QUESTION OF CONSCIENCE, CONFESSIONAL PRINCIPLE, AND CHARITY.

EVERY Church that has a conscience, like every man in business life who has a conscience, will be obliged at some point and at some time to take its stand on principle. To remain firm in principle, and appear gracious and true in love, is not easy, even where all the elements of Christian love are really present. Where selfishness, partisanship and other considerations abound, the situation becomes even more difficult. Every Church Body that is honestly trying to be firm in principle and gracious in love may expect to be misrepresented by those in whose pathway its principle is an unpleasant obstacle.

When deep conviction on the one side, and the lack of it on another, is revealed between those who love, it is possible, in the things of earth, to put the rock of offense out of sight, and sod it over into a beautiful and inviting lawn.

910

But if such convictions concern fundamental facts of character, or precious principles which God Himself has revealed for man's salvation, if they concern the Person of our blessed Lord, the communication of His strength in Word and sacrament, the preservation of His Church from the bondage of Pelagian or humanistic error, the evaluation of means that He has given to us in the application of the sacrifice which He has made, a difference in Confessional conviction cannot be put out of sight. It is not a barrier artificially set up, but a deep and narrow gulf which really divides.

The Christian world to-day no longer sets such lofty value on principle. The great idea of the age is that Christians should, as the world states it, " get together." Every conviction that stands in the way of a cultivation, a manifestation, or a realization of brotherhood between those whose convictions would oblige them to differ, as Melanchthon and Luther did from Zwingli and Bucer at Marburg, can look to no other fate, no matter how wide its charity and how honorably its love flow out toward its neighbor, than to be regarded as narrow in outlook, sectarian in faith, bigoted in spirit, and intolerant in action.

THE QUESTION OF TOLERANCE.

There is no subject more difficult to treat confessionally than that of tolerance. The earnestness of men in their faith, according to the nature of the old Adam, varies inversely with their willingness to endure men of another faith. Conversely, the laxity of men in their religious convictions varies directly as their temperament to be broad of vision, gracious in communication, and sympathetic in feeling toward those of another party. Hence a celebrated English writer has told us that "The responsibility of tolerance lies with those who have the wider vision;" and a celebrated French writer, whose humanity may be estimated at its maximum, and his spirituality at its minimum, has declared that "Tolerance is the best religion;" while a classic essayist in the sphere of social order has observed that "Tolerance is the only real test of civilization."

Archbishop Whately, with some insight once remarked that "Tolerance is rather a matter of temper than of principle," but he felt himself constrained to admit—an admission which is the opposite of what is usually expected—that " As far as principles are concerned, certainly the latitudinarian is the more likely to be intolerant, and a sincerely conscientious man tolerant." It requires the very highest degree of Christian conviction, Christian sympathy, and Christian tactfulness to be both firm and tolerant. Mere tolerance in itself, as already has been intimated, is not a mark of religion at all, but of civilization; Isidor van Cleff was not entirely in the wrong when he pointed out that "Tolerance does not mark the progress of a religion. It is the fatal sign of its decline." Thomas Carlyle takes the same view, in touching on this very point in his discussion of Martin Luther and John Knox. He says: " We blame Knox for his intolerance." " Well, surely, it is good that each of us be tolerant as possible. Tolerance is to be noble, measured, just in its very wrath, when it can tolerate no longer. But we are not altogether here to tolerate! We are here to resist and vanquish withal. We do not ' tolerate ' iniquities when they fasten on us; we say to them, ' Thou art false.' We are here to extinguish Falsehoods in some wise way! I will not quarrel so much with the way; the doing of the thing is our great concern. Order is *Truth*,—each thing standing on the basis that belongs to it. Smooth Falsehood is not Order. Order and Falsehood cannot subsist together." In speaking of Luther before the Diet at Worms, Carlyle pictures him as respectful, wise, honest,—submissive to whatsoever could claim submission, " not submissive to any more than that."

"Great wars and contentions and disunion followed out of this Reformation; which last down to our day, and are yet far from ended. Great crimination has been made about these. But after all, what has Luther or his cause to do with that? Luther and his Protestantism is not responsible for wars. Luther answered Falsehood with No! not counting the costs. Union, organization, far nobler than any Popedom, is coming to the world; but on Fact alone, not on Semblance will it be able to come and to stand. With union grounded on falsehood we will not have anything to do. A brutal lethargy is peaceable, the noisome grave is peaceable. We hope for a living peace, not a dead one!

"I will add now that the controversy did not get to fighting so long as Luther was living. How seldom do we find a man who has stirred up some vast commotion, who does not himself perish, swept away in it! Such is the usual course of revolutionists. Luther held it peaceable, continued firm at the centre of it. A man to do this must have the gift to discern where the heart of the matter lies and to plant himself on that as a strong true man. Luther's clear deep force of judgment, of silence, of tolerance and moderation, are very notable.

"Tolerance, I say; a very genuine kind of tolerance. A complaint comes to him that such and such a Reformed preacher 'will not preach without a cassock.' Well, answers Luther, what harm will a cassock do the man? 'Let him have a cassock to preach in; let him have three cassocks if he find benefit in them!' His conduct in the matter of Karlstadt's wild image-breaking; of the Anabaptists; of the Peasants' War, shows a noble strength, very different from spasmodic violence. With sure prompt insight he discriminates what is what: a strong just man, he speaks forth what is the wise course, and all men follow him in that."

For humanity Luther had tolerance, but not for men of impure motives. For heretics he had tolerance, but not for politicians. For the Emperor Charles V., who was arrayed against him, he had tolerance, but not for "the wolves with whom he was surrounded." Luther had no tolerance for dishonesty or corruption. For men who were willing to conceal, or abate from their principles in order to unity, he had nothing but contempt.

He did not see the importance or necessity of union or federation in the forces of the Kingdom of God. The strategic marshaling of the earthly forces of the Church were of no account to him. The power with which he shook the world was not union, but Confession; while the lack of power in which Melanchthon failed to impress the world was not Confession, but the attempt at union. When he believed in the integrity of the Pope, of Zwingli, of Bucer, of Melanchthon, Luther was patient and tolerant; but when his eye was opened to the corruption of the Papacy, his outbursts of indignation were tremendous. Luther, by his outspoken sincerity, has gained the reputation for intolerance, while the Pope who was more intolerant of Luther than Luther was of him, is able to pose in history in the attitude of cultured tolerance.

The Question of the Brotherhood of the Christian Church and the Manifestation of its Essential Unity.

The judgment as to the Christian Church is almost universal, that it is her duty to be more than tolerant toward ecclesiastical organizations whose doctrine she may not approve. The great duty of the Christian Church, in the eyes of the world, is to express the Essential Unity in which all its separate organizations must, in their view, be grounded, and to emphasize the Brotherhood which they constitute. From our point of view, this identification of the visible ecclesiastical organizations now claiming to be the visible Church of Christ on earth, or parts thereof, is neither necessary, possible, nor desirable.

It is not the organization, but the principle, which expresses the unity. To insist on the visibility of the unity, and to emphasize the visible unity of Christianity as the goal of Christian endeavor, is to fall once again into the ancient and destructive error of Rome. The Kingdom of God cometh not with observation. The visualization of the Church means its externalization. To emphasize the idea of the visible Church, and the importance of its earthly union, is one of the colossal short-sighted mistakes of this age. The only unity of the Church that is vital is the unity of the Faith, and the oneness of the objects of that Faith.

We do not establish this unity. *It is* already, and has *ever* existed. It does not depend upon the coming together of the visible denominations on earth that call themselves the Church of Christ. The way in which the visible Churches are to realize and represent the invisible and original spiritual unity is for each of them to approximate and reproduce it in completeness. To approximate other visible Churches, which are themselves inferior to the original, and only imperfect images of it, is a great mistake.

This mistake is productive of three evil results. First, we get on earth a composite picture or imitation of the original (in which extent and quantity count for more than quality) instead of a vital reproduction of the original unity.

Second, we lay undue emphasis, in line with the Roman Church, on the visibility of the Kingdom of God, at the expense of the inner conviction of the individual conscience, and of the absolute supremacy, in the Kingdom of God, of Testimony to the Truth, by the Scriptural activity of Confession of Faith. This was the exact force of the point of our Saviour against Pontius Pilate, when Pilate, with the visible grandeur of imperial Rome back of him, scoffed at the supremacy of purely spiritual power, manifest through Testimony, and exclaimed, " What is Truth ? " Jesus had told him, "My Kingdom is not of this world: if my Kingdom were of this world, then would my servants fight." Pilate asked Him, "Are you really King ?" Jesus answered, "Thou sayest that I am a King. To this end was I born, and for this cause came I into the world, that I should *bear witness* unto the Truth. Every one that is of the Truth, heareth my voice." The Kingship of Christ, and the Kingdom of God, according to these words, are not of the order of earthly organization, but are a Kingship and a Kingdom of *Truth*, which is established simply and solely by the power of " Witness," or " Confession."

The third mistake in the attempt to represent the Kingdom of God by drawing the Churches together into an earthly brotherhood is, that, in so far as the undertaking proves to be a success, it will also prove to be the setting up of an ecclesiastical rule by a majority, as the major centripetal force; and will thus, for the sake of an aggregate of earthly power residing in a majority, override the supremacy of the Confessional force of the Truth as it resides in the real but small group of consciences that believe and confess alike; and will therefore be in danger of sacrificing the Truth and our apprehension of it, the Faith, which is the power of the Church, for the sake of a visible demonstration of a unity which does not exist in conscience and in the Confessional principle of the Truth.

THE QUESTION OF MAJORITY IN RELIGION.

Thus we come to a new Romanism in the Protestant World, in which decisions in the sphere of faith, instead of being made by those in spiritual unity, will, for the sake of the additional power which the weight of numbers confers, and of a combined action in external unity, be determined by the new American religious papacy, whose name is *The Majority*.

Questions of Truth, Right, Faith, and spiritual action in the Church of Christ cannot be settled by the external and legal method of vote, but must be determined by the vital and voluntary method of Confession.

THE DREAM OF A VISIBLE CHURCH.

The fundamental unity of the whole Christ in Christianity will not be exhibited in visible organic form. The Greek and the Roman establishments will not exhibit it except on terms to which the Protestant cannot in conscience accede; and if all Protestants in the world were to combine into organic fraternity, they could exhibit the fundamental unity of Christianity only as a part, and not as a whole. If we exclude the ecclesiastical frame of authority from this attempted unity, we still find the rationalistic frame among us as Protestants. If we exclude the rationalistic frame of authority, Lutheranism is still confronted with fundamental divergencies in Protestantism,—as to the great principles of the Word and Sacraments, as to the Person of Christ, as to justification by faith alone and not by works (Synergism, Salvation by Law), as to the nature of the Church, as to the separation of civil affairs from the things of God,—on which we cannot unite, and as to which we cannot—without the most thorough understanding and respect for each minor part— work in common, without being bound in conscience.

The stand thus taken by Confessional Lutheranism is a stand for conscience. It is not a stand for legal Confessionalism, but a stand for the gospel Confession.

THE QUESTION OF A VISIBLE UNITY OF PROTESTANTISM.

The Saviour nowhere emphasizes the fundamental unity of Protestant Christianity. He points to an ultimate unity, and he prays that it may be realized: "That they may all be one;" but He does not justify its manifestation where it does not exist.

And He does not say "That they may all be one." He says, "That they may all be one; *as thou, Father, art in me, and I in thee,* that they also may be *one in us.*" He emphasizes the absolute unity. The point is not a mere relative or approximate unity, an occasional interchange of courtesy, but an inner union of substance and nature. He takes further pains to show what kind of oneness He refers to. He prays, "that they may be *made perfect* in one." And He shows us the only source of that oneness. " Sanctify them *through thy truth. Thy word* is truth. Neither pray I for these alone, but for them also which shall *believe on me through thy word."*

The source of this unity is the Word. Its character is a unity of faith on the basis of the Word. It is not a unity based on "the amenities of religious people toward each other." It is not a unity which says, " It is of no concern what you believe, we all are one;" but it is a unity that says, "We are all one, for we all have the one faith, the one baptism, the one God and Father of all." All true believers do have one Faith. But are all faiths one?

It is not true that all Christians are one; but it is true that there is a true unity in the Faith. For this, it is our duty to make every sacrifice. You say, " Let us *forget* our differences, and be *neighborly."* We say, "Let us *resolve* our differences, and be one." The denominations *cannot* " all be one," *unless* they give up that which they have no intention of giving up. It is impossible for parts of the visible church to reproduce the inner and essential unity of the invisible Church, and still intend to continue a divided denominational life. If a man and a woman claim they are in unity with each other, it is not for them to be satisfied " with an occasional interchange of courtesies," or with semi-annual meals of friendship in social union; but one of them must make up her mind to give up her name, and both must give up all else and realize their life in a common home.

The unity that Christ asks is not a unity of occasional courtesy, or merely a unity of name, or a unity of diplomatic poise of separate forces; but He wants a unity of conviction, a unity of teaching, a unity of principle, a unity of doctrine. We are to be *one in the faith.*

An occasional interchange of courtesies, a sending of one man into the pulpit of another denomination to preach one sermon, who comes back unchanged and continues to preach as he did before in his own pulpit, an authorization of a member in one denomination to commune occasionally in a denomination of different faith, not only fails to show the inner unity which Christ desires; but deceives the people *as to the nature of the unity that Christ desires.* That is the kind of union which rests on nothing; is responsible for nothing; and accomplishes nothing; but simply makes people " feel good! " They delude themselves in a unity that has ignored, not cleansed, its falsehoods; that has forgotten, not resolved, its differences.

Their union has no intention of becoming even a thorough-going external union; much less does it touch the inner hurt. It says: " The bones are broken: it is too painful to set them: let us bind and mollify the skin, that the world may behold that we are one."

We say, The Christian Church is the one important organism in the world. Its bones are its principles, its doctrines, its truth. With the advent of the New Theology into American Christianity, the broken bones are numerous. They include the following principles: the Scriptures, the Word of God, the Trinity, Original Sin, the Person of Christ, the Offices of Christ, the Work and Merits of Christ, Justification, Sanctification, the Means of Grace, the Sacraments, Judgment and Eternal Life.

With these broken principles, American Protestantism is a very weak man, as a Christian unity, and the device, Alliance, Association, Federation is an elastic silk band, tied with a beautiful white ribbon, to hold the members in unity, " that they may all be one."

To set the bones right, at any cost, to prevent a false union, to break up every pseudo process, to keep up the pain until the original lines of juncture are recovered, to be satisfied with nothing temporary, is it not harshness and narrow-mindedness on the physician's part? But is he not right? Is he a " mere bigot " because, in lack of sweet and proper comity, he refuses to postpone the pain of a proper operation, appreciates the importance of doing things right, and will not sew up the skin neatly and say, " Your bones are one."

Is the invisible Church of Christ less important than the human body? Can its broken bones be united by occasional bands of interdenominational courtesy? May the Children of the Lord say: Let us forget the broken bones, and bring the body together? Is it scientific or practical to attempt to unite a broken Christendom, except by starting at the original lines of fracture? Is not all sincere Christendom foolish to suppose that the breaks are merely a matter of temperamental feeling in the patient, and that the unity can be *knit together* by applying an occasional bandage, but leaving the bones still *fractured?* The unity for which the Saviour prayed was not one of name or feeling or work, but one of nature and principle: *"as We are One."*

It is not a divided Christendom, but a partisan Christianity, which is the disgrace of the Christian religion. It is not staunchness in type of Faith, but selfishness in an aggressive competition, that undermines the cause of Christ in both home and foreign fields. It is not those who are satisfied with their Faith, and labor and live purely and peaceably under its conviction, who are the mischief-makers of Christendom. To reunite Christendom with divided Faiths is to empty the union of everything but its name. To reunite Christendom by sacrificing Faith is to sacrifice what is most precious in Christendom. To reunite Christendom by uniting or growing into one Faith, and heartily confessing the same, is a consummation devoutly to be wished. It is the only kind of union the Saviour prayed for: "That ye may all be one, *as* the Father and I are one." This is a unity from conviction, and one which will never be manufactured in convention by compromise, concession, and diplomatic arrangement.

We teach in glaring contrast with many of the American denominations about us, that the one important and supreme thing in a church is the saving Faith. We believe that the true and ultimate church is the church of the pure Faith. "No particular church has, on its own showing, a right to existence, except as it believes itself to be the most perfect form of Christianity, the form which of right should and will be universal. That communion which does not believe in the certainty of the ultimate acceptance of its principles in the whole world has not the heart of a true church. That which claims to be Catholic *de facto* claims to be universal *de jure.*" [1]

THE ATTITUDE OF LUTHERANS TOWARD DENOMINATIONAL PROTESTANTISM.

The different values placed upon the Confessional principle in the Lutheran Church of America come to light most clearly in connection with her varied attitude toward other Protestants, and particularly toward other Evangelical bodies. These relations, especially in later days, are looked to in view of a possibility of the future solution of the divisions of Protestantism; and the solution proposed has been of three possible kinds, first, alliance leading to amalgamation; second, federation leading to centralization; third, co-operation with an emphatic recognition of Confessional differences, and with a frank recognition and acceptance on each side of the limits of co-operation. These solutions have already been treated.

The first two classes of relationship, viz., amalgamation and federation, proceed upon the assumption that essential unity already exists in the Protestant Faith,—and that an essential oneness underlies all the Protestant denominations. It is assumed, that there is little difference in fundamentals between those who hold different denominational tenets, and that the distinctive tenets to be preserved are denominational peculiarities. In any event whether the denominational individuality is, or is not, worth saving, there is at least a

---

[1] *C. P. Krauth.*

common Protestant foundation beneath all the Evangelical denominations.

The great motto for those whose faith rests on this basis is, *in necessariis unitas, in dubiis libertas, in omnibus caritas.* The first clause of this saying is sound, and its last clause is equally commendable. But a great fallacy lies concealed in its middle clause. To confine liberty to merely doubtful things is giving it a very narrow berth indeed. There must be liberty, and deep conviction arrived at and held in Scriptural liberty, in *necessary* things. This is absolutely essential for the existence and for the maintenance of the truth. And there must also be liberty in the exercise of charity, that is, it must spring from the free will and intent of the heart.

But as the motto is generally used, the central clause becomes a catch-all into which to consign all principles and doctrines that are likely to give trouble. This becomes the significant feature of the whole motto and is promotive of doctrinal indifferentism. It is not true that our faith is divided into necessary things and doubtful things. It may be divided into necessary things and unnecessary things, or adiaphora. But a man may hold doubts on every one of the most important of all the articles of faith. The second clause of this motto will undermine the first. There should be conviction on all points on which it is possible to reach it; and faith, in liberty, should stretch its wing over other points. The last clause is admirable. As Dr. Schaff says, " Honest and earnest controversy promotes true and lasting union. Polemics looks to irenics—the aim of war is peace."

CHAPTER XLII.

THE CONFESSIONAL PRINCIPLE OF THE BOOK OF CONCORD AND THE FUTURE OF THE CHURCH IN AMERICA.

The Field of the Confessional Principle in America—It is to leaven all Relations—The three separated spheres of Faith, Love, and Law, and the three separate institutions of Church, Home and State, not properly Distinguished by Radical and Reformed Protestantism—The Lutheran Solution of Religious Problems in America—Reformed Results—Lutheran Results—The Confessional Principle not a Hindrance to the Future Church—Will Broaden the Church—Recapitulation of the Argument of this book—Conclusion.

HERE in America the Confessional Principle of the Book of Concord will find a free field for baptizing and teaching the nations, for its own implantation, and for the guidance and control of the whole Christian life. In this land the State has as yet laid no hand on the Church or on the Home, except that there is a growing tendency on its part to the assumption of the right of an exclusive hold on all public higher and lower education.

And the door is open to the Church to enter with its full strength and in its own way to prosecute the work of the kingdom of God. Our Confessional principle can labor for righteousness, peace, and joy in the Holy Ghost, without let or hindrance. The power of the Confessional principle must and should penetrate and leaven all relations, spiritual, social, ecclesiastical, civil, national, municipal, educational, commercial, and physical. The principle of Christianity, with

923

its laws of family, personal, and brotherly relations, includes in its scope the whole of human life, and our Confession fully realizes this fact.

Christ is a universal principle, and nothing in the spiritual or social order can escape accountability to Him. Our Christianity provides a life complete in all its aspects and relations. It is itself the life that is most full and whole. To live it here on earth is life eternal. The Sermon on the Mount, which deals no less with the social than with the more spiritual and religious relations of men in the Church of God, shows us that the Church has universal obligations, and has to do with the ideals, the hopes, and the laws of human society, in so far as these present themselves in personal and spiritual form.

Christ has set up not merely a spiritual, but a social claim upon the individual, as a member in particular of His Body, and it is a necessary part of the Christian's life to see that Christian standards are upheld and are extended, in their true application to economic, industrial, and political forms, whether in neighborhoods, states or in nations.

For Christians, from the pastor, as primus inter pares, down to the humblest member, to hold themselves aloof from the actual and real life of men and nations, and, for fear of committing or entangling themselves, not to engage in the political, social, industrial or economic problems of the day, is a sectarian, and not a Lutheran principle, as not only the sixteenth article of the Augsburg Confession proves, but also the twelfth chapter of the Formula of Concord.

If we believe that all true progress along spiritual and moral lines in modern civilization is the result of Christian ideals worked out into practice, the Christian conscience needs to be as active to-day against great sins and moral infection, and the word and act of the Christian need to be as strong and decided in behalf of the law of God, as they ever were in the heroic ages of the past. The Church, too, as the body of Christ, needs to keep herself clear from the apparent or passive acceptance of a controlling order of society, which, while it may be willing to minister to ecclesiastical comfort, in its own pathway does violence to the laws and the purpose of the kingdom of our God.

The distinction so plausibly made in the ethical life of many Christians, between religion and business, between politics and Christianity, between society and the Church, has no foundation in the Lutheran Confession. To the Lutheran there is no such possibility as the separation between the spiritual, moral and confessional principles of the Church on the one side, and the principles of earthly life on the other. There is no deed or aspiration of our life as Christians, whether private or public, into which the full content of our Christian Confession does not enter as the determinative factor. Our institutional, social, corporate, or other organized power in this world, our influence on society, the application of our activities to the affairs of the day, are to be determined solely by our ultimate spiritual, that is our confessional principle. We are to work and to work together in the real and actual things of life, under the Confession which we maintain as members of the Church of Christ.

Yet this is not to say that the Church is to be organized into a solid body for moral interests or for the execution of such higher social, political, philanthropic, or economic theory as would seem to be a great improvement on existing institutions. The Church is not here to work out, in a corporate or organized capacity, the great political, industrial, social, and moral problems that face men and society at every turn. It is surprising that the advanced religious thinkers of this age, conscious in other lines of the necessity of a strict application of the modern doctrine of differentiation of function to the forms of a complex civilization, do not see the importance of its application in the religious sphere. It is amazing to note how passively they permit the functions of the State and the Home in the warfare for righteousness, to decline to a rudimentary stage,

62

and how actively they throw all the duties of public life, reform and training upon the Church.[1]

To make use of the social and corporate power of the Church as a public lever to apply to the reform of abuses, and the uplifting of social institutions, leads straight to Rome. The visible unity of God's people on earth, maintained and applied politically and diplomatically, and in an organized and corporate way, for the uplifting of society, the attempt to assemble the whole Family of God as a visible and organized community, into one movement, cannot but shatter many principles, among which are liberty of conscience, the essential spirituality of religious faith, and the invisible and eternal order of the kingdom of God. There is a way in which the Confessional Principle of Lutheranism is fundamentally contributory to the upbuilding of the social and moral life of the nation, but it is not a way humanly planned and devised; it is the old, the substantial, the solid way pointed out by the Word of God itself.

The great confusion in American religious life and effort, under the control of Reformed Protestant ideas, in which the Lutheran Confessional principle seems decidedly out of joint with the times, has been the failure to distinguish clearly between the spheres of the three divine institutions, the Church, the Home and the State, and their intrinsic activities.

Hence the degeneracy of the Home and the corruption of the State in this age roll in *upon the Church,* and, under the Reformed principle, demand to be lifted away mechanically and immediately, instead of being resolved spiritually and gradually under the transforming and upbuilding power of the Law and the Gospel in the conscience and the heart in accord with God's unfailing processes of vital growth.   Re-

----

[1] The explanation of this situation is to be found in the disproportionate estimate of the value of the things of our earthly life here and now, in comparison with the things of eternal life.   The life of God seems to be almost absorbed and fulfilled in the religion of the day in the life toward our neighbor.

form by overthrow, the radical principle, can organize for destructive triumph, but *vital unity* is required for the natural growth of constructive and permanent triumph.

The Lutheran Confession has a solution for our American social problems, and a sphere for the constructive activities of the Christian spirit. This solution, which is not of the order of a galvanic spasm induced to regulate or restore virtue falling into ruins in the land, is as deep and thoroughgoing, as conservative and real as its own nature. It is not dependent upon great conventions and grand effects representing—nominally—so many millions of people, but it can be begun wherever two or three persons are gathered together as a congregation in the name of Jesus, who, instead of sending on a delegation to influence the Senate and Representatives at Washington, set themselves humbly at work to transform their own patch of wilderness, until it shall bloom and blossom as the rose.

The very first step in this work under the Confessional Principle is a clear and abiding distinction between the three great divine institutions, the Home, the State, and the Church. This involves also the distinction between the objects, the powers and the methods of each institution.

The work of the Church is in the sphere of faith; the work of the Home is in the sphere of love; the work of the State is in the sphere of law.

The object of the Church is the upbuilding of the spirit; the object of the Home is the upbuilding of the man in himself and in his relation to society; and the object of the State is the upholding of liberty, equity, stability of organic and individual equilibrium, protection of property and life, public justice. The real power in the Church is Spiritual Regeneration; the power in the Home and Society is intelligent conjoint development in Love; the power of the State is intelligent preventive, education, and incitation by Law. Except as a matter of public justice or public order, the State as such possesses neither the power nor the right to advance personal righteousness, nor to fix the ethical goal of personality.

The mode of the Church is Spiritual; the mode of the Home is Social and Civil; the mode of the State is Civil and Political.

The principle of the Church is Confessional, by witness to the truth; the principle of the Home is Constructive, by deeds issuing into character and into social result; the principle of the State is Regulative, by equitable and inflexible adjustment of physical, social, and political conditions.

In the Church, the distinctive emphasis is on faith, with love and action included. In the Home, the distinctive emphasis is on love, with faith and reliable action included. In the State—as civil or as Society—the distinctive emphasis is on reliable action with faith and love included. In the State—as political—the distinctive emphasis is on Law, with faith in the natural form of dependence on the invisible source of Truth and Righteousness, and Love in the social form of equal rights for the weakest and the strong.

The State has no right to compel us to love, and the Church has no right to compel us to act. The Home, in its wider sense, as the center of our personal and unorganized life, as the place from which radiate forth our work, our recreation, and our social contacts, has the right to train and to urge us both as to the inner love and the outer act. In the Home center all educational, all intellectual, and reading agencies. Above it hover all personal and social ideals. It receives strength and inspiration from the Church, it gives strength and quality, quality moral and physical, to the State. The work of the Home or Family cannot be done successfully by either the Church or the State. An institutional Church is a poor substitute, in its offer of work, of recreation and rest, of social relationships, for the Home. A socialized State, with its offer of concern for the maintenance and the welfare of the individual, will never become a practical sub-

stitute for the Home. The most difficult work of the Church
in our stage of civilization is not co-operation or control in the
State; neither is it the finding of devices or the offering of
itself as a substitute for the weaknesses of the Home; but it
is the planting and protection of the Christian Home as over
against the encroachments of sin, society, civilization, commercial and corporate life, and against false socialistic ideas
of Church and State.

The inner mission work is an emergency, and is always
most necessary; but it is not to be compared in importance
and power with the regularly ordained work of the Church.
A home is worth more than a settlement, more than
an orphan asylum, more than a hospital. The hope of our
country lies in the maintenance of its homes, and a great
hope for our Church is to be found in the fact that its
membership values the Home as a spiritual and a divine
institution. The breakup of the Home under the influence of modern commercialism, and the influx of a lighter
and more mobile civilization, is a symptom of social disintegration not less serious in its way than extreme lawlessness
cropping out in large centers of population are symptoms of
political anarchy.

The work of the Church is the work of testimony. It is
not mere words. It is the faithful application of the Law and
the Gospel to the soul and the conscience. Its work is spiritual, and therefore all the more powerful. It deals not in
ideas, or in plans, but in the destroying and saving Truth of
God.

Witness is the greatest of realities, and therefore the
greatest of powers. It knows no distinctions of earthly position. It may involve but does not seek martyrdom. It is
objective, and fearlessly separates the false from the true. It
is the light shining into the darkness. It condemns corruption by its word; and, in its own sphere, which is the congregation, by its deed, by discipline. Yet it condemns not
for the sake of the Law, or of meting out deserts and justice,

59

but for the sake of the Gospel. And this fact, that the Church does not bear the sword, but only the truth in love, holds in it a problem not yet fully solved by any ecclesiastical polity on earth.

The Confessional Principle of the Book of Concord has many lessons to teach the religious life of America, and its Church should begin, in this teaching, in accordance with its own spirit, with itself, and in its own congregations.

The first of these truths is that the Church can save the world best by attempting to be what it is in its own nature, rather than by allowing its own sphere and power to degenerate, and by reaching out for power and for work into spheres set by God for other agencies. The Church should put the Home and the State upon their feet by filling the hearts of faith with the wisdom and invincible power of God, but should not encroach upon the sphere of Home and the State by reaching in and assuming under its own name, either the work or the methods of either.

The Church is the voice of God in Christ, and not the voice of Society or Law. Its appeal is to the greatest of all fountains of strength, the conscience and the heart; but it should not rob the manhood and automatize the citizenship of its members by directing the act.

The Church deals in principles and not in measures, and however threateningly the floodtide of iniquity rolls up, it should abide by the use of its own spiritual means, which, if less spectacular, are more powerful in the final result, and do not vitiate and debase the inner fibre of the Church or State. The new covenant is not a theocracy. Apparent greatness of need, or seeming certainty of success, should not tempt the Church to the use of methods foreign to her nature.

If the Church would keep the world from the adoption of the pernicious principle that success is the best justification of any project, it should not itself act on the principle that the end justifies the means.

The Protestant Church in America under the Reformed Principle is a spectacle. Instead of meeting the corrupt politician and dealing with him singly on its own ground the Churches institute a union Reform movement and organize a campaign to meet him on his own ground. Instead of applying the Law of God, which is the invincible truth, in the fearless power of faith, in its own congregation where it has rights, it goes out to apply the Law of the State at the ballot box and in the Court where it has no right.

The Church, instead of faithfully applying the Word and Sacrament as Christ commanded, periodically confesses itself a failure in training the youth and the life of the land, and puts itself under the direction of lay evangelists experienced in *business* methods of reaching the soul; and gives itself over to the laymen's church, where worship, education, and recreation, are combined into a unity, and where the soul will be saved by the salvation of the mind and the body!

The Church, instead of establishing the Home in the power of its own strength and life with the daily presence there of the Word of God, acquiesces without continued witness against the destruction of the Home by the modern corporation in business, and while the ministry goes on marrying men and women, not as pastors, but as officials recognized by the State, the Church cries out to the State to save the institutions of Matrimony and the Home by the passage of more stringent laws of divorce!

The Church, without teaching the Home that the primary duty of Education lies with it, and the secondary but equally justified rights of Education lie with Church and State, passively gives over all primary Education to the State, fails to teach the Home as to its rights and duties, and, falling behind the secular pedagogues in a realization that Education is a slow process of gradual and toilsome growth, commits its serious responsibilities of teaching to an untrained lay institution, which, to succeed, must be largely social rather than spiritual, must reduce instruction in the

Word of God to a minimum, and ignore instruction in the Catechism, that is the training of the child of God into the habitude of a truly spiritual life in the Law and the Gospel.

What a field for the exercise of the Confessional Principle of the Lutheran Church! That Faith, not works; spirit, not laws; testimony, not ideas, is the victory that overcometh the world. That Faith grows by the Word of God, Law and Gospel, visible and audible; that the sphere of the Church is the sphere of Faith, which sacrifices even life for the Truth. That Faith goes out and builds Homes where love sacrifices business interests to the growth of Faith and Love into character and deed. That Faith and Love go out into the civil and political relations of life and purify and uplift every part of the world and society by *the personal relations* they enter into in business, society and politics, and by the abstract relations they enter into and undertake in corporate, representative, elective, executive, legislative and judicial functions, in which the truth and righteousness of the testimony in the sphere of faith, the kindliness in the sphere of love, and the energy and effectiveness in the sphere of action, combine to the complete and ultimate unification of life in Christ. What congregations, what homes, what institutions, what business principles, what a quality of men, what citizens, what schools, what children, what liberty, what virtue, what independence, what justice, what charity, what a patriotism the Confessional Principle of the Book of Concord will build, by faith alone, without compromise, and the unity of those in this Principle will not be federate, but final: "One, as the Father and the Son are One."

THE CONFESSIONAL PRINCIPLE A STRENGTH TO THE CHURCH.

Bodies weak in backbone and lacking in native strength, feel the need of support, and throw out their arms toward stronger entities. Bodies strong in their own nature will not need alliance without. The Church true to the Confes-

sional Principle of the Book of Concord, will be strong in
her own kind of spiritual life. The reality of eternal life
is growing within her. She will not need to ask or seek
power from without. It will not be a help to her to unite
in fellowship with others "who insist on partaking of the
same dish with us, and yet always put in the seasoning to
suit themselves." [2]

Our Church possesses the most positive and distinct of
Protestant Faiths. She is not made up of a common Christianity with a number of doctrinal peculiarities added on, but
is woven of one fiber and without seam from centre to circumference.

Her life is sharply limited by her Confession. She stands
in clear antagonism toward those who make Church government the mark of a pure Church, as well as toward those who
are indifferent to quality of Faith except on some such point
of method as "immersion" or "conversion." She is not
an Anglican Church, or a New England Church, or a German Church, or a Church organized by some pious man,
but she is a Scriptural Church of an unalterable Confession.
Forms, ceremonies, governments, racial heredity and denominational name count for little. Our Faith counts for everything. Our Confessions are not a dead letter, or antiquated
in parts, but they are operative in all points, and are charging and holding up our modern and latest life. We have no
intention of setting them aside. The intellect and the piety
of our church accept them. Among these, there is no longing
for a revision. They are not a mill-stone about our necks,
but a banner above our heads. [2] The colors of the Lutheran
Faith will not be struck until the last man is down.

There will be no compromise or yielding up of Faith, to
furnish a working basis for union. Yet we trust that on
every point and in every attitude which does not involve
such a compromise of Faith, our Church will learn to show
a breadth of vision, a patience under provocation and a

---

[2] Cp. M. H. Richards.

charity in demeanor which will be worthy of Christianity and of the Church herself. For she is not a narrow church. A great non-Lutheran scholar bears the following testimony to this fact: " I am not able to locate the Lutheran Church among any of the one-sided developments of the religious life; because she combines all the elements which are presented elsewhere in isolation and antagonism; they are united in her."

THE LUTHERAN CHURCH A BROAD CHURCH.

The Confessional Church is a broad Church, not a narrow Church. She does not suggest the necessity of anything but the real essence, as the basis of unity. The agreement which is needed is agreement in the Word and the Sacrament. Outward matters, such as government, ecclesiastical constitution, hereditary history, different ceremonies and customs in the Church, differences of language, thought, taste, ritual, or anything external or incidental whatever, are not a sufficient basis for separation. She is ready to sacrifice all except that which her Lord teaches and commands her, the sacrifice of which would be unfaithfulness to Him. This is a broad basis. It throws all prejudices, customs, circumstantialities, and all earthly ecclesiastical things whatsoever overboard, and leaves only the difference, where there is a difference, of conscience. It acknowledges true faith wherever found, and though it be outside her own communion.

The Lutheran Confession is not a live dog, who snaps and snarls and interferes in the pathway of his master, to be called off, cursed, condemned or apologized for, when he leaps on the benevolent and progressive Ahab whom we have invited to walk in our garden; nor a dead lion, whose glory is of a bygone age, whose usefulness is chiefly in his carcass, whither honey has been brought by golden-winged insects from lovelier zones of life and sweetness; and whose bones should be mounted and placed in an historical museum at the disposal of the student of comparative religious archæology.

But our Confession is the Word of God beating in the heart of those who have lived and died for the Truth.

If the Church of the living God is to stand on principles of pure gold and not on toes of iron and clay, as sincere and clear as the Word of her Lord, and as true and free from compromise, as was He, in all her words and deeds; if it was not justifiable for her to bend toward Judaism or toward Gnosticism in the first century; nor to reconcile Arianism and Athanasianism into Semi-Arianism in the Fourth Century; nor to lean to Nestorianism or Eutychianism in the Fifth Century; nor to unite Pelagianism and Augustinianism on the platform of Semi-Pelagianism in the Fifth Century; nor to mingle Romanism and Lutheranism in the Augsburg Confession of the Sixteenth Century; nor to combine Predestinarianism and Arminianism in the Seventeenth Century; nor to commingle Rationalism and Pietism in the Eighteenth Century; nor possible to assimilate a live Confessionalism with a fervid Emotionalism in the Nineteenth Century, it also is never possible to coalesce the truth as it is in Christ Jesus with the humanism of Zwingli, or the mediæval spiritualism of Calvin.

If Melanchthon was right in compromise, Lutheranism should compromise to-day for unity's sake, and give up her

---

[3] Melanchthon's mind was in motion, but was brought to steady anchor for a time, at the fateful moment of the Church's Confessional birth. " It was a matter of divine Providence holding control over our Confession, that it was made at a time in which Melanchthon was just as far from the deterministic thoughts of the beginning of his career, as he was from the synergistic ideas of his later years."—Die Augsburgische Konfession in ihrer Bedeutung für das kirchliche Leben der Gegenwart, p. 14.

Of the action of Providence in *all* our Confessions, Mueller says, "We do not hesitate to express the conviction that divine Providence has been active in the composition of the Confessions, so that they have come into being, with prayer to God Almighty to his honor and praise, through the especial grace of the Holy Spirit (Book of Concord, p. 9) (Compare Walch's Introduction to the religious Controversies in the Lutheran Church, Part II, p. 141ff.)" Mueller's Introduction, p. 27-28.

That Melanchthon was not the representative of an ideal Lutheranism is proven by his words to Campeggius:

" We hold no doctrine different from the Roman Church. For no other reason do we bear much odium in Germany than because we with the greatest constancy defend the doctrines of the Roman Church. Such fidelity to Christ and to the Roman Church we will, please God, show to the last breath."—*C. R. II.* 168 *sq.*

being for a common synergistic Protestantism; but if **Me-**lanchthon was wrong in compromise, Lutheranism should to-day embrace the Lutheranism that is real and hearty, that accepts not only the foundation but the roof-tree of her confessional structure. She should clothe herself in her own garments, not put together in theological patchwork, but woven throughout without seam.

THE CONCLUSION.

The reader has come with us a long way. Beginning with the New Testament, we have traced the Confessional Principle of Christianity through the winding course of history. Beginning with the Reformation, we have traced the Confessional Principle of the Conservative Evangelical Faith from its first fountain-head to its last testimony in the Formula of Concord, and have attempted to make such applications as might seem serviceable to present conditions.

We have emphasized the fact that the Word of God is the only rule of Faith and life, by which our reason and all the regulative conceptions of our age, its speculative thoughts and ideas, its customs, progress, and standards, its teachings, traditions and usages, its suggestions, methods and plans, are being tested. We have emphasized an open and unambiguous Confession of God's complete Word, and of Christ in it, as the Church's first duty, her loftiest privilege, her chief joy, and the leading source of her strength.

We have declared our assurance that the Church is strong as she is strong within, strong in conviction and Confession of the Principle and the Person on which she was founded; and that she will be preserved and saved by her Faith (sola), whose reality comes to manifestation in Confession.

We have urged, as we believe, with Christ, with Paul, with Luther, with the Augsburg Confession, with the Formula of Concord, that the chief practical thing in Christianity is not organization, or union, or tradition, or usages, but testimony. Fidelity in the Confessional Principle is what establishes and maintains the Church of Christ, and adds the increase that is permanent.

What has been presented up to this point is, it is hoped, historical in method and result. But the Principle that lies beneath the presentation, if it be of value, is above history. It is the Truth. We believe, teach, and confess the Gospel of Jesus Christ, which is the same yesterday, to-day, and forever. Time can never cause it to decay, and progress can never bring it to change. As a fact in history, and as a Body of Principles, it is complete in the past, and was revealed in the fulness of time. In its application to the human race, and in its unfolding to ultimate triumph, it belongs to the future.

It has been obliged to meet and has been able to vanquish the errors and half-truths of every age, which have always and from the very beginning in the New Testament arrayed themselves against it.

The Gospel has lived, and been active, and brought conviction to the mind, and salvation to the soul, by the power in its faithful Witness. This witness has been of the single congregation, through the ministration of the Word and Sacraments, and through the lives of its members; it has also been of the whole Church through the precious declarations of faith and solemn testimony to the truth uttered by the believing hearts faithful in time of severe trial and great peril.

The first and simplest summary of the faith, testifying to the pure Gospel, is the Apostles' Creed, which, with the Nicene Creed and the Athanasian Creed, are the "brief, plain Confessions" of the Church to the facts of the Gospel, which we also believe and teach, and confess as binding upon us, and reject all principles and teachings that are contrary to these Confessions.

The Witness of these confessions, as the substance of

Scripture, saved the Church from heathenism; but when the Church itself became overladen with heathen and human elements, the Witness of the Augsburg Confession, in the face of Rome, saved the Gospel. We believe, teach and confess the principles of the Gospel, as they are found in this Witness at Augsburg, together with its Apology, and the articles composed at Schmalkald, and with the two outlines of the Gospel composed by Luther, called the Small and Large Catechisms, which constitute the Bible of the laity.

When, after the recovery of the Evangelical principle at Augsburg, the new standpoint had developed in its weakness and strength, and the errors of Protestantism had had time to spring up during the Reformation age as the errors of Romanism sprang up in the Middle Age; there came the further and final witness to the truth, which connected the Apostolic and Catholic witness of old to the evangelical witness of Protestantism, and which at the same time disassociated the evil developments of the spirit of freedom from those that are truly evangelical. The confessional substance of the final confession is the same as that of the first confession of the Church.

From our inmost hearts, therefore, we once again confess the ancient creeds, the Christian Augsburg Confession so thoroughly grounded in God's Word, and the Formula of Concord, as the sum and substance of Gospel truth, and as the essence of the faith, doctrine and confession of us all, for which we will answer, at the last day, before the just Judge, our Lord Jesus Christ.

The Confession of the Gospel, which is God's Word assimilated and pulsating in the Church and condensed into public standards, which constitute the common principles of its faith, and the common framework of its doctrine, which is the common mark of our membership and the common flag of our loyalty, is the Christian's greatest and most precious privilege.

Such Confession does not constrict individual investigation, bind individual consciences and suppress individual liberty, but gives each of these human prerogatives a worthy ideal and goal. Such Confession draws the line between truth and error, in our day, just as the Saviour and the Apostles drew the line in their day.

This mighty Witness of the Christian Church to the fundamental facts that control its origin and purpose, is not put together by agreement of its members, and is not of the essence of contract, but is the Church's continuous and connected testimony to the substantial unities of salvation and everlasting life in Christ.

These Confessions have the right to claim cheerful and hearty loyalty from those who profess to teach their principles, and who accept office on their foundations.

They connect us directly with the Apostolic Witness in Scripture and with that of the Church in all ages. They point the pathway to the future, as they have been the highway of safety in the past, amid the winds and waves of doctrine and the shifting changes of philosophic thought. This Witness of the Evangelical Church is found most fully in the Formula of Concord.

"Here the Church, in the maturity of its powers, examines and judges itself. It subjects its conceptions of the faith to rigid analysis and discriminating criticism, and frames and fixes the terminology of theological definitions, which under its decisions lose the ambiguity that at many points had caused confusion and controversy. In it, the positive and negative elements are most carefully balanced. The predominant characteristics of the Formula are its scientific exactness and the judicial poise with which it keeps the golden mean between the extremes on both sides, which it states at the beginning of the discussion of every topic." [*]

This Confessional Witness of the Book of Concord is the Faith historically established in the early Swedish, Dutch and German immigration to America. It was the Confession of Campanius, Falckner, Kocherthal and Berkemeier,

---

Jacobs, *Summary of Christian Faith,* p. 452.

Stoever, Bolzius, and Muhlenberg. It is the Confession which alone will give to the Lutheran Church the vitality of its own nature, and the strength that need not be drawn from foreign sources. The greatest dangers through which the Lutheran Church has passed in America are those connected with the undervaluation and abatement of this Principle. We do not believe, with the broad-visioned and fraternally-minded founder of the Evangelical Alliance, that the Lutheran Church in America will ultimately be absorbed in the Reformed Principle; but it is our belief that what has prevented this from being more fully the case up to the present, despite the enormous defections in every generation, has been the Confessional Principle of the Unaltered Augsburg Confession and the Book of Concord; and that this Principle is the bulwark of the Church for the future.

We regard the Lutheran name, the Lutheran history, the Lutheran blood and Lutheran customs as a weak defence against the tides of Puritan, Reformed, and Humanitarian religion whose waves are moving toward conquest, as they ever have been in this American land. The one strength, the sling of David, which the Lutheran Church possesses, is her Faith, her conviction, her testimony.

Our Confessions are not our idols. Historically, they are not any more to us than the name, the land, the people from which they sprang. But their Principle is the very Word of God. While they are not to be worshipped any more than the flag of our country is to be worshipped, they are to be treasured and valued, as the flag is, for what of Truth and power and salvation they represent: not merely Truth and power potent in a historical past, but as a dynamic factor in the present and as a tried and sure standard for the future.

Shall we Lutherans in this American World of the Twentieth Century, where we are free to work out the spirit of the Church of the pure Word and Sacraments, repeat the internal strife and the mistakes of the Lutherans of the Sixteenth Century? Shall we use up our strength in placating and compromising with a non-Lutheran Christianity and be torn asunder into insignificant pieces, rather than live out our own principles and become their most perfect exemplification?

Shall we allow the old and time-worn standards to lie unknown, moth-eaten and covered over with dust; or, when they are brought forth, instead of unfurling them at the head of our columns, shall we give them a quasi-recognition—nay, stand by and see our own children disown them, spit upon them, and trample them in the dust?

Shall this be done! Shall we permit this to be done! in the name of Christian unity! and by a latitudinarianism that is our own heritage, which rises ever anew from the embers of the past to find such veiled support and strength in the citadel of Zion that Confessionalism is told to whisper low in Jerusalem lest she be heard on the streets of Gath.

With the Word of God and a continuous line of testimony behind us, let us lift up our great banner and press forward into the future. What a loss to the Christian Church to go back to Christ and reject the intervening experience mediated by Providence through the Holy Ghost in the contact of the Word with many generations. What a loss to the Lutheran Church to go back to the Augsburg Confession and ignore the Formula of Concord. What an unhistorical sense to select a single point, though it be our greatest, and allow the change of every wind and tide to move and make sport of our faith since then. Those who accept the prophets and ignore the patriarchs of the Old Testament as mythical; those who accept the Gospels and ignore the Epistles as private comments on the doctrine of Christ, do scant justice to the testimony of God's Word.

The Confessional question of our Church was the Confessional question of the early Christian Church: Are we to be limited to one Creed, viz., the Apostolic, and to one Confession, viz., the Augsburg Confession; or Shall we accept the further Creeds that fulfil and summarize the original principle in further development? Is the Confessional

63

principle of the Evangelical Church, as Lutheranism compre-hends it, one continuous and connecting line of development from the Scripture to the present day; or is it a certain spot in that line?

Is the Lutheran Church in America to accept her own com-plete historical foundation, and to come to her own on that basis, or is she to surrender portions of that basis in the hope of coming to Protestantism's own, on a not as yet fully determinate basis? The Word of God itself should decide. The whole Reformation period was a providential era, in which the faith first brought to the surface in the Augsburg Confession was wrought out through Providence in the history and experience of the Church, and reached complete expression in the Book of Concord.

The Evangelical principle will never die. The Confession of the Book of Concord must not, shall not be disowned in America by the children of the fathers in whose faith and churches it was maintained. It is useless to expect continued renewals of immigration from the Fatherland or other foreign shores. These sources of our strength are well-nigh spent, and if the Church shall not have established itself in her own Evangelical Faith of the living Gospel, in the life and lan-guage and blood of the generations that are to come, her children will walk, as did Israel of old, in the ways of sur-rounding nations. Her priests will sit at her altars desolate, and her prophets will mourn and weep in vain.

Yet even then, our eye shall not be filled with sorrow. For we are sure that the Word of the Lord will prevail. We look for a city which hath foundations. We look unto Jesus, the author and finisher of our faith. We hold fast the Confession of our faith without wavering, for we are not come in it unto an earthly Zion, but we are come to the Heav-enly Jerusalem and unto the city of the living God, and to His Son our Lord Jesus Christ, in Whom we trusted, after we heard His Word of Truth, the Gospel of our Salvation.

We are come to the strength and glory of the kingdom of Heaven, with its soaring and radiant pinnacles of divine promise, and its silent sweeps of measureless mystery, bridged, from crystal sphere and lofty cloud beyond, to bruised heart and lowly earth beneath, only by the unerring footprint of the Son of Man, Who shall appear in His glory, and purge away the darkness of doubt, the vagueness of error, and the blackness of heresy, and Who shall, in the truth of His own Person, illumine and order and animate the city of the living God, and its united society. We are come to the King and the Kingdom of the Truth, the pure realm in which God's power prevails in the inward parts, and the bright Word, spiritually discerned, shines as the sun, credible in its own clearness, to the believing heart; and brings the mind to utterance, for very joy at the strength of the King in His beauty, Who is the head of the Church; and of and through Whom only, of all truths in Heaven and earth, by the certainty of faith, our Confession is sure.

"Die Losung unsrer Kirche in diesem Kampfe kann nur sein: Halte was du hast, auf dass dir Niemand deine Krone raube, Unsre Krone ist unser Bekenntniss."

INDEX

NOTE—For names of authors and titles of works see the BIBLIOGRAPHY
in TABLE OF CONTENTS.